The Blackwell Encyclopedic Dictionary of Business Ethics

About the Editors

Cary L. Cooper is Professor of Organizational Psychology at the Manchester School of Management (UMIST), UK. He has also been appointed Pro-Vice-Chancellor at the University of Manchester Institute of Science and Technology (UMIST). He is the author of over 80 books, has written over 250 scholarly articles and is editor of the *Journal of Organizational Behavior*. He is also the Founding President of the British Academy of Management.

Chris Argyris is James B. Conant Professor of Education and Organizational Behavior at the Graduate School of Business, Harvard University. He has written many books and received numerous awards, including the Irwin Award by the Academy of Management for lifetime contributions to the disciplines of management. Recently, the Chris Argyris Chair in Social Psychology of Organizations has been established at Yale University.

About the Volume Editors

Patricia H. Werhane is the Ruffin Professor of Business Ethics in the Darden Graduate School of Business Administration at the University of Virginia. She is Editor-in-Chief of *Business Ethics Quarterly*, and on the editorial boards of *American Philosophical Quarterly*, *Journal of Value Inquiry*, and *Journal of Business Ethics*.

R. Edward Freeman is the Elis and Signe Olsson Professor of Business Administration and Director of the Olsson Center for Applied Ethics at the Darden Graduate School of Business Administration, University of Virginia. His areas of research are business ethics, business strategy, and organizational studies.

The Blackwell Encyclopedic Dictionary of Business Ethics

Edited by Patricia H. Werhane
and R. Edward Freeman

Darden Graduate School of Business Administration,

University of Virginia

BLACKWELL
Business

Copyright© Blackwell Publishers Ltd, 1997
Editorial Organization© Patricia H. Werhane and R. Edward Freeman, 1997

First published 1997

First published in the US 1997

2 4 6 8 10 9 7 5 3 1

Blackwell Publishers Inc.
238 Main Street
Cambridge, Massachusetts 02142, USA

Blackwell Publishers Ltd
108 Cowley Road
Oxford OX4 1JF
UK

Library of Congress Cataloging-in-Publication Data

The Blackwell encyclopedic dictionary of business ethics /
edited by Patricia H. Werhane and R. Freeman.
      p.   cm. – (Encyclopedia of management)
Includes bibliographical references and index.
ISBN 1-55786-942-1 (alk. paper)
      1. Business ethics–Dictionaries.   I. Werhane, Patricia Hogue,
      II. Freeman, R. Edward, 1951–   III. Series.
HF5387.B55   1997
174′.4′03—dc20   96-46007
                                                                              CIP

British Library Cataloguing in Publication Data
CIP catalogue record for this book is available from the British Library.

ISBN 1557869421

Typeset in 9½ on 11pt Ehrhardt by Page Brothers, Norwich
Printed in Great Britain by T. J. Press (Padstow) Ltd

This book is printed on acid-free paper

Contents

—— Preface ——

The Blackwell Encyclopedic Dictionary of Business Ethics is a labor of love undertaken by the over 250 contributors to the volume. When we began this project we did not realize that it would entail asking almost 300 friends, colleagues, acquaintances and strangers to freely and willingly write entries for this book. The result is amazing. Each entry to this volume was written voluntarily and without complaint by philosophers, theologians, social scientists, professors of management, and practitioners. A few contributors even volunteered to write second, third, even fourth pieces, should we need them. Such participation was astonishing to the editors and cannot be underestimated. This volume is dedicated to its authors.

The idea of an eleven volume *Encyclopedia of Management* that would include a dictionary of business ethics was the brainstorm of the two senior editors, Cary L. Cooper and Chris Argyris. For us it was a positive indication that business ethics had become part of mainstream management, management teaching and research, and management practice. *The Encyclopedic Dictionary of Business Ethics* will also be listed in Blackwell's philosophy catalog, indicating that perhaps applied ethics will now become part of mainstream philosophy as well. This inclusion reflects on the foresight of Tim Goodfellow and other Blackwell editors, and is a compliment to our contributors, many of whom are academic philosophers or professors of religious studies.

There are a number of other people who deserve special mention for making this book possible. The premier encyclopedia in the field is Larry and Charlotte Becker's monumental work, the *Encyclopedia of Ethics*. In that work, the Beckers set out exemplary criteria for all encyclopedias of its kind. In addition, because their work is on *ethics* we learned a great deal from their topic headings, and indeed, we asked some of the same authors to write on the same or similar topics. Surprisingly, in the interests of advancing *applied* ethics, most of these authors changed their Becker entry to be more appropriate for business ethics. This was good news for our volume, but it also meant that Charlotte Becker and our assistant, Kristi Severance, spent many hours comparing entries to make sure we did not violate any copyright agreements with Garland Publishing, the publisher of the *Encyclopedia of Ethics*. Charlotte's generosity, hard work, and good sense of humor alleviated much of the tedium of this task. Our deepest, heartfelt gratitude to Charlotte and Larry Becker.

Each entry in the volume before you was read and edited by Henry W. Tulloch, a retired executive and Senior Fellow at the Olsson Center for Applied Ethics at the Darden School. Without his tireless efforts, there would be no dictionary. Tara Radin, now a graduate student at Darden, ably assisted the launching of the project. Her successor, Maura Mahoney spent the greater part of a year working full-time to continue the organization, correspondence, and production of the volume. Susan Crandell organized the biographies. During the past year Kristi Severance has continued Maura's fine work. Without Maura and Kristi there would be only chaos, as those of you personally acquainted with the editors will verify. Karen Musselman, the administrator of the Olsson Center at Darden, has assisted all of us in a myriad of ways throughout this project. To all of these people, each of whom has made invaluable contributions, and there are others we have neglected to mention, we give our deepest thanks.

The Darden School of the University of Virginia has been most supportive of our work on this project in every way. A number of faculty contributed entries, and the administration provided encouragement, space, equipment, and release time as well as financial resources. Additional financial assistance for the volume was provided by the Olsson Center for Applied Ethics, the Ruffin Foundation, and the Batten Center for Entrepreneurial Leadership.

The shortcomings of the book are, unfortunately, the sole responsibility of its editors.

Patricia H. Werhane
R. Edward Freeman

EDITORIAL STAFF

Henry W. Tulloch, *Assistant Editor*

Assistants to the Editors:
Kristi Severance
Maura Mahoney
Tara J. Radin

The editors gratefully acknowledge Lawrence C. Becker and Charlotte B. Becker (eds) *Encyclopedia of Ethics*, New York: Garland Publishing, 1992, for permission to reprint substantial portions of: Freedom and Determinism (published here as FREE WILL); HOBBES, THOMAS; Justice, circumstances of (published here as JUSTICE); PORNOGRAPHY; RIGHTS; SUPEREROGATION; WORK.

The reader is also directed to the following entries in the *Encyclopedia of Ehtics*: Acts and Omissions; Altruism; Authenticity; Autonomy of Ethics; Bentham, Jeremy; Business Ethics; Coercion; Computers; Envy; Guilt and Shame, Harm and Offense; Interests and Needs; Kantian ethics; Liberalism; Liberty, economic; Locke, John; Mill, John Stuart; Moral Dilemmas; Partiality; Practical Reason[ing]; Promises; Reciprocity; Responsibility; Self-deception; Smith, Adam; Spencer, Herbert; Technology; Universalizability; Utilitarianism.

List of Contributors

E. M. Adams is Kenan Professor of Philosophy Emeritus, University of North Carolina, Chapel Hill. His works include *Ethical Naturalism and the Modern Mind*; and *The Metaphysics of Self and World*.

Raj Aggarwal holds the Mellen Chair in Finance at John Carroll University. Previously he has taught at Harvard, Michigan, South Carolina, and Hawaii. He is the author of twelve books and over fifty scholarly papers, serves on the editorial boards of journals such as the *Journal of Economics and Business, Financial Review, Journal of International Business Studies*, and is the editor of *Financial Practice and Education*.

William Aiken is Professor of Philosophy at Chatham College. He is co-editor of *World Hunger and Moral Obligation*.

Dean E. Allmon is Associate Professor of Marketing at the University of West Florida. In addition to teaching business ethics, he has published a number of works in the *Journal of Business Ethics*. Professor Allmon is one of the leading academics in voice stress analysis.

Robert Almeder is Professor of Philosophy at Georgia State University.

Kenneth D. Alpern Associate Professor of Philosophy, DePaul University, specializes in ethics: theoretical, historical, and applied. His most recent work is on Aristotelian ethics and on the concepts of trust and forgiveness.

Sita C. Amba-Rao is Professor of Management in the Division of Business and Economics at Indiana University at Kokomo. Professor Amba-Rao's recent research interests include issues in human resources and small business management. He is currently involved in research on comparative human resources management with reference to India.

Lyn Suzanne Amine is Professor of Marketing and International Business at St. Louis University. Her research interests are in the fields of international marketing, exporting, and cross-cultural analysis. Professor Amine has over fifty publications ranging from reference journal articles to book chapters, conference proceedings, and case studies.

Mary Beth Armstrong is a professor of accounting at California Polytechnic State University. She is the author of one text and numerous articles relating to ethics in accounting, and has served on ethics-related committees for the American Institute of CPAs, the California Society of CPAs, and the American Accounting Association.

Robert L. Arrington is Professor of Philosophy and Interim Dean of the College of Arts and Sciences at Georgia State University. His areas of specialization include ethics and the philosophy of Wittgenstein. He is author of *Rationalism, Realism and Relativism: Perspectives in Contemporary Moral Epistemology*, and co-editor of Wittgenstein's *Philosophical Investigations*.

Robert B. Ashmore is a professor of Philosophy and Director of the Center for Ethics Studies at Marquette University. He is author of *Building a Moral System* and co-editor of *Ethics Across the Curriculum* and *Teaching Ethics: An Interdisciplinary Approach*.

Sidney Axinn is Professor Emeritus of Philosophy at Temple University.

Joseph L. Badaracco, Jr. is Professor of Business Administration at the Harvard Business School.

Marcia Baron is Professor of Philosophy at the University of Illinois at Champaign-Urbana. Her publications include *The Moral Status of Loyalty*, "Impartiality and Friendship," and *Kantian Ethics Almost Without Apology*.

Julia J. Bartkowiak presently teaches Philosophy at Clarion University of Pennsylvania and has publications in the areas of business ethics, media ethics, and ethical theory.

Kaushik Basu is Professor of Economics at Cornell University.

Tom L. Beauchamp is Professor of Philosophy and Senior Research Scholar at the Kennedy Institute, George Washington University. He is currently Series Editor of *The Foundations of Philosophy Series*, and General Editor, with David Fate Norton and M.A. Stewart, of *The Critical Edition of the works of David Hume*.

Alan Beckenstein is Professor of Business Administration at the Darden Graduate School of Business at the University of Virginia.

Lawrence Becker is Professor of Philosophy at the College of William and Mary and editor of the *Encyclopedia of Ethics*.

Daniel A. Bell was the Laurence S. Rockefeller visiting Fellow at Princeton University's Center for Human Values as well as a Canada SSHRC Research Fellow. He currently teaches at the University of Hong Kong. Professor Bell is the author of *Cummunitarianism and Its Critics* and co-author of the book *Towards Illiberal Democracy in Pacific Asia*.

Rosalyn Berne formerly taught at the Darden Graduate School of Business at the University of Virginia and now serves as Head of School at the Tandem School in Charlottesville, Virginia.

Melissa H. Birch is Associate Professor of Business Administration at the Darden Graduate School of Business, University of Virginia.

Thomas H. Birins is Associate Professor in the School of Journalism and Communication at the University of Oregon.

Lawrence A. Blum is Professor of Philosophy at the University of Massachusetts at Boston. He is the authort of *Friendship, Altruism, and Morality* and *Moral Perception and Particularity*, and co-author (with V. Seidler) of *A Truer Liberty: Simone Weil and Marxism*.

John R. Boatright is the Raymond C. Baumhart, S.J., Professor of Business Ethics in the School of Business Administration at Loyola University Chicago. He is the author of the textbook *Ethics and the Conduct of Business* and the casebook *Cases in Ethics and the Conduct of Business*.

Norman E. Bowie is Professor of Philosophy and the Elmer L. Andersen Chair in Corporate Responsibility at the Curtis L. Carson School of Management at the University of Minnesota. He is the author of *Ethical Theory and Business* (with T. Beauchamp) and *Business Ethics* (with R. Duska), among other books.

F. Neil Brady is Professor of Public Administration at the Marriot School of Management at Brigham Young University.

David Braybrooke is Professor of Philosophy and Politics at Dalhousie University. Besides articles and books on a variety of other philosophical topics, he has published a number of articles on decision-making in business and politics; a book on British efforts to cope with the growth of traffic congestion; and a book, co-authored with C.E. Lindblom, on policy evaluation as a social process *A Strategy of Decision*.

George G. Brenkert is Professor of Philosophy and Department Head at the University of Tennessee, Knoxville. He specializes in the areas of business ethics, social and political philosophy, and ethics. His most recent book is *Political Freedom*.

Steven Brenner is Sponsored Professor of Business Administration at Portland State University. He teaches courses in business and society, business and environment, and business ethics. He has publications in several professional journals including *Harvard Business Review* and *Journal of Business Ethics*. He is a member of the Academy of Management and the International Society for Busiess and Society.

Susan E. Brodt is Assistant Professor of Business Administration at Duke University's Fuqua School of Business. Her research focuses on cognitive and social-psychological barriers to effective management, including impediments to rational decision behavior and negotiated conflict resolution. Professor Brodt's research has been published in academic journals such as *Organiza-*

tional Behavior and Human Decision Processes, Human Resource Management Review, and the Journal of Personality and Social Psychology.

Richard Bronaugh is Professor of Philosophy and Professor of Law at the University of Western Ontario. He is co-founder and co-editor of the Canadian Journal of Law and Jurisprudence.

Robert Bruner is Robert F. Vandell Research Professor of Business Administration at the Darden Graduate School of Business Administration, University of Virginia. His primary areas of research and course development include corporate restructurings, mergers and acquisitions, and capital investment. Recent publications include Case Studies in Finance: Managing for Corporate Value Creation, 2nd edn.

Allen Buchanan is Grainger Professor of Business Ethics, Professor of Philosophy, and Affiliate Professor of Medical Ethics at the University of Wisconsin-Madison. He is the author of numerous articles in ethics, business ethics, bioethics, and political philosophy, and of the following books; Marx and Justice, Ethics, Efficiency, and the Market, Deciding for Others (with Dan. E. Brock), and Secession: The Morality of Political Divorce.

Rogene A. Buchholz is the Legendre-Soule Professor of Business Ethics at Loyola University of New Orleans. Articles by Professor Buchholz have appeared in Human Relations, Journal of Management Studies, Personnel Psychology, Journal of Applied Psychology, Industrial and Labor Relations Review, Harvard Business Review, and Journal of Business Ethics.

Ronald J. Burke is Professor of Organizational Behavior, Faculty of Administrative Studies, York University. His research interests include occupational and life stress and coping, work and family, career development in organizations, and workforce diversity.

Martin Calkins SJ is a graduate student at the Darden Graduate School of Business Administration at the University of Virginia, where he is pursuing a Ph.D. in business ethics. He is a graduate of the Thunderbird School.

Joan C. Callahan is Professor of Philosophy at the University of Kentucky. She is author or editor of Ethical Issues in Professional Life, Preventing Birth: Contemporary Methods and Re-

lated Moral Controversies (with James W. Knight), Menopause: A Midlife Passage, and Reproduction, Ethics and the Law: Feminist Perspectives.

Archie B. Carroll is Professor of Management and holder of the Scherer Chair of Management and Corporate Public Affairs at the University of Georgia. Professor Carroll is the author of Business and Society: Ethics and Stakeholder Management, as well as dozens of articles on social responsibility and business ethics.

Thomas Carson is Professor of Philosophy at Loyola University Chicago. He is the author of The Status of Morality, and numerous papers on ethical theory and business ethics.

Jack Casey is a retired partner of Scudder, Stevens and Clark and a Visiting Fellow at Bentley College.

Bary Castro has taught at Grand Valley State University since 1973. His work has appeared in The American Economic Review, Journal of Political Economy, Harvard Educational Review, Journal of Business Ethics, Business Ethics Quarterly and other scholarly journals. He has recently published an anthology, Business and Society: A Reader in History, Sociology, and Ethics.

Gerald F. Cavanagh SJ holds the Charles T. Fisher III Chair of Business Ethics and was Provost at the University of Detroit Mercy. Professor Cavanagh, a Jesuit Priest, has authored numerous articles and five books, including American Business Values.

Susan Chaplinsky is Associate Professor of Business Administration at the Darden Graduate School of Business Administration, University of Virginia. Her research interests include security issuance, corporate finance, corporate control, and employee stock ownership plans.

Joanne B. Ciulla holds the Coston Family Chair in Leadership and Ethics at the Jepson School of Leadership Studies at the University of Richmond. Her latest book Honest Work is forthcoming in 1997.

Max B.E. Clarkson is a member of the faculty of Management at The Clarkson Center for Business Ethics at the University of Toronto.

James G. Clawson is Associate Professor of Business Administration at the Darden Graduate School of Business at the University of Virginia. His research focuses on leadership, career management, management development and mentoring. He has written two books on career and management, *Self-Assessment and Career Development* (3rd edn), and *An MBA's Guide to Self-Assessment and Career Development*.

Peggy A. Cloninger is a graduate student in the Ph.D. program at Georgia State University's college of Business Administration. She specializes in strategic management, and her research activities focus on international business and social issues in management. Her current research integrates environmental issues in management with international public-policy concerns and conflicts.

Dana Clyman is Assistant Professor of Business Administration at the Darden Graduate School of Business Administration, University of Virginia. He has published in several academic and professional journals. His research interests include negotiations, international arbitrage, and risk and rationality. He has worked extensively in the computer and financial services industries and he serves on the board of directors of the FINEX, the financial instruments subsidiary of the New York Cotton Exchange.

Philip L. Cochran is Associate Professor of Business Administration at the Smeal College of Business Administration at Penn State University. Professor Cochran is the author of articles on corporate social performance, issues in management, crisis management, and business ethics. He was the first President of the International Association for Business and Society and currently serves on the editorial boards of several journals.

Betty Smith Coffey is Assistant Professor of Management at the Walker College of Business, Appalachian State University. Her background is in strategic management and her current research focuses on corporate philanthropy, corporate governance, and healthcare–management strategic issues.

Deborah Vidaver Cohen is Assistant Professor of Management at Florida International University. Her publications include articles on creating and maintaining ethical work climates, developing corporate ethics programs, the impact of socio-legal changes on managerial strategy, and the implications of organizational power structures for ethical conduct in the workplace.

Jeffrey Cohen is a Professor at the Carroll School of Management at Boston College.

Denis Collins is a faculty member at the School of Business, University of Wisconsin-Madison. He has published numerous articles and books in the areas of business ethics, business and society, social philosophy, participatory management, and gain-sharing.

Robert Conroy is Associate Professor of Business Administration at the Darden Graduate School of Business at the University of Virginia.

Lorri Cooper is a doctoral candidate at the Curry School of Education at the University of Virginia. She has served as a consultant on several projects involving the Darden Graduate School of Business at the University of Virginia.

J. Angelo Corlett is Assistant Professor of Management at Georgia State University. He is the author of *Analyzing Social Knowledge* (forthcoming) and editor of and contributor to *Equality and Liberty: Analyzing Rawls and Nozick*. Professor Corlett has also published several articles on collective rights, responsibility, and punishment.

Maria Cecilia Coutinho de Arruda is Associate Professor in the Marketing Department in the Business School of Sao Paulo, Brazil.

Suzanne Cunningham is Associate Professor of Philosophy at Loyola University of Chicago. Her areas of research and publication include early twentieth-century philosophy with special emphasis on its relation to Darwin's theory of evolution and recent philosophy of mind. She recently published *Philosophy and the Darwinian Legacy*.

Kendall D'Andrade is Assistant Professor and Chair of the Department of Philosophy at Shawnee State University. His work on applied ethics and public policy has resulted in "Bribery" and "Should You Take Stock in America?"

John R. Danley is Professor of Philosophy in the School of Humanities at Southern Illinois University at Edwardsville.

John Darley is Professor of Psychology at Princeton University.

Sharon Davie is Lecturer in Business Administration at the Darden Graduate School of Business Administration, University of Virginia, and Director of the University of Virginia's Women's Studies Center. Her speciality is in managing the challenges of diversity.

Michael Davis is a Senior Research Associate, Center for the Study of Ethics in the Professions, Illinois Institute of Technology. He has published more than 80 articles and chapters, authored one book, *To Make the Punishment Fit the Crime*, and co-edited two others, *Ethics and the Legal Professions*, and *AIDS: Crisis in Professional Ethics*.

Peter Dean is Associate Professor of Human Resource Development at The University of Tennessee, where he teaches business ethics, organizational change, and managerial communications. He is the author of numerous articles on applying ethics in the workplace and has written extensively on how to improve performance, highlighted by *Performance Engineering at Work*.

Michael Deck has served as executive director of the Clarkson Center for Business Ethics, Faculty of Management, at the University of Toronto.

J. Gregory Dees is Associate Professor in the Graduate School of Business Administration, Harvard University and author of many articles on agency theory and bargaining and negotiation.

Richard T. De George is University Distinguished Professor and Director of the International Center for Ethics in Business at the University of Kansas. His publications include *Business Ethics* and *Competing with Integrity in International Business*.

John Deigh is Professor of Philosophy at Northwestern University.

John W. Deinhart is Professor of Philosophy at St. Cloud State University. He has written and spoken on ethical issues in medicine, psychology, and business. He is author of *A Cognitive Approach to the Ethics of Counseling Psychology* and *Individuals, Organizations, and Markets: Integrating Ethics into Business and Society*.

Robbin Derry is Associate Director of Ethics in the Department of Legal Studies at the Wharton School at the University of Pennsylvania.

Joseph Des Jardins is Professor of Philosophy at Saint John's University.

Paul de Vries is Dean of the Seminary of the East, New York City. He held the Endowed Chair in Ethics and the Marketplace at King's College,

and he was founder and first director of the Center for Applied Christian Ethics at Wheaton College. He has written extensively in business ethics, including *The Taming of the Shrewd*, an introduction to "smart ethics".

John Dobson is Associate Professor of Finance at California's Polytechnic State University. His primary research interests are agency theory and financial ethics. He is currently writing a book that combines these two fields of strategies.

Thomas Donaldson is the Mark O. Winkelman Professor of Business Ethics at The Wharton School, University of Pennsylvania. He is the author of several books, including *The Ethics of International Business*.

Karen Dowd is practice leader and senior consultant with Brecker and Merryman in New York. Her research interests include career management and recruitment and candidate selection.

Thomas W. Dunfee is the Kolodny Professor of Social Responsibility at the Wharton School of the University of Pennsylvania. Author of numerous textbooks, he now teaches courses on business ethics and commercial law. His current research interests focus on social contract theory and business ethics and on developing ethical standards for business transactions.

Craig Dunn is Assistant Professor of Management at San Diego State University.

Ronald Duska is The Charles Lamont Post Chair of Ethics and the Professions at American College. He is the author of numerous articles and books, including *Ethics and Corporate Responsibility: Theory, Cases and Dilemmas*.

Kenneth M. Eades is Associate Professor of Business Administration at the Darden Graduate School of Business at the University of Virginia. His research interests include dividend policy, corporate finance, mergers and acquisitions, and convertible securities. Recently he received the First Wachovia Award for Excellence in Research for his empirical study of convertible security pricing.

Mark Eaker is Professor of Business Administration at the Darden Graduate School of Business Administration, University of Virginia. His research interests include international finance, capital markets, and risk management.

Deni Elliott is Mansfield Professor of Ethics in Public Affairs at the University of Montana, and Senior Fellow at the Ethics Institute, Dartmouth College.

Dawn R. Elm is Associate Professor in the Department of Management at the University of St. Thomas, Division of Business.

Robin Ely is Associate Professor at the John F. Kennedy School of Government, Harvard University.

Kenneth G. Elzinga is Professor of Economics at the University of Virginia. His research interests include the economics of antitrust enforcement and the relationship between religion and economics. Under the pen name of Marshall Jevons, he writes murder mysteries in which the professor-hero uses economic analysis to determine whodunit.

Georges Enderle is the Arthur F. and Mary J. O'Neil Professor of International Business Ethics at the University of Notre Dame. He is author, editor, and co-editor of eight books, co-founder of the European Business Ethics Network, and member of the Board of Advisors to several academic journals. His research interests focus on understanding the ethical challenges of international business for corporate decision-making.

Amitai Etzioni is the University Professor at the George Washington University. He is the author of many books, most recently *The Moral Dimension*, which introduces the socio–economic paradigm. He is also editor of *The Responsive Community*, a new journal which explores the balance between individual rights and community responsibilities. He serves as founding Director of the Center for Policy Research.

Paul W. Farris is Landmark Communications Professor of Business Administration at the Darden Graduate School for Business, University of Virginia. Course responsibilities include Marketing Strategy and Marketing Management. He has published several articles in the marketing literature and general management journals such as the *Harvard Business Review* and *Sloan Management Review*.

Joel Feinberg is Professor of Philosophy at the University of Arizona, Tucson. He is the author of many books, including *Moral Concepts*.

Stephen P. Feldman is Associate Professor of Management Policy, Weatherhead School of Management, Case Western Reserve University. Professor Feldman teaches management and ethics to MBA, master's in nonprofit management, and undergraduate students. His research interests include the cultural and ethical aspects of organizations and management.

Paul Fiorelli is Professor of Legal Studies at the College of Business Administration, Xavier University.

John M. Fischer is Professor of Philosophy at the University of California, Riverside. He has edited five books and has authored *The Metaphysics of Free Will*.

Richard E. Flathman is the George Armstrong Kelly Memorial Professor of Political Science at The John Hopkins University. He has published numerous books concerning liberal theory, including *The Philosophy and Politics of Freedom, Towards a Liberalism, Willful Liberalism*, and *Thomas Hobbes: Skepticism, Individuality, and Chastened Politics*.

John Fleming is Professor Emeritus at University of Southern California.

Thomas R. Flynn is Samuel Candler Dobbs Professor of Philosophy at Emory University. He has published over fifty essays, chiefly in contemporary Continental philosophy. Professor Flynn is co-editor (with Dalia Judovitz) of *Dialectic and Narrative* and is the author of *Sartre and Marxist Existentialism: The Test Case of Collective Responsibility*. He is currently writing a two-volume study of Sartre, Foucault, and reason in history.

Timothy L. Fort is Assistant Professor of Business Ethics/Business Law at the University of Michigan. He is author of two books and several articles in law reviews and business ethics journals.

Leslie Francis is Professor of Philosophy and Law at the University of Utah.

Robert Frank is the Goldwin Smith Professor of Economics, Ethics, and Public Policy, Cornell University. He is author of *Passions within Reason*.

Robert E. Frederick is Professor of Philosophy at Bentley College.

William C. Frederick is Professor of Management Emeritus at the Joseph M. Katz Graduate School of Business, University of Pittsburgh. He is author of *Values, Nature and Culture in the American Corporation*.

James R. Freeland is the Sponsors Professor of Business Administration and the Associate Dean for Faculty at the Darden Graduate School of Business at the University of Virginia. He is the author of numerous technical and managerial papers in operations management and management science.

R. Edward Freeman is Elis and Signe Olsson Professor of Business Administration and Director of the Olsson Center for Applied Ethics at the Darden School of Business Administration, University of Virginia and Professor of Religious Studies. His books include: *Strategic Management: A Stakeholder Approach*, *Ethics and Agency Theory* (with N. Bowie); *Business Ethics: The State of the Art*, and *Corporate Strategy and the Search for Ethics* (with D. Gilbert, Jr.).

Peter A. French is the Marie E. and Leslie Cole Chair of Ethics and Professor of Philosophy at the University of South Florida. He is the author of sixteen books including *Corporate Ethics, Responsibility Matters, Corporations in the Moral Community, Spectrum of Responsibility*, and *The Scope of Morality*. Professor French is the editor of *Journal of Social Philosophy* and Senior Editor of *Midwest Studies in Philosophy*.

R. G. Frey is Professor of Philosophy at Bowling Green State University. He is author of several books, including *Interests and Rights*; *Rights, Killing and Suffering*; and *Joseph Butler*.

Marilyn Friedman is Associate Professor of Philosophy at Washington University in St Louis. She is the author of numerous articles in ethics, social philosophy, and feminist theory. Her books include *What Are Friends For? Feminist Perspectives on Relationships and Moral Theory*, *Political Correctness: For and Against*, *Feminism and Communism*, and *Mind and Moral: Essays on Ethics and Cognitive Science*.

David Fritzsche is a professor of business administration at Pennsylvania State University, Great Valley. He has studied domestic and international ethical practices and has written on business ethics for several management and marketing journals. Professor Fritzsche is the author of a forthcoming book on business ethics from a global, managerial perspective.

James C. Gaa is Professor and Chair of the Department of Accounting and Management Information Systems and Adjunct Professor of Philosophy at the University of Alberta. His research focuses on accounting, including self-regulation, public policy making, auditor independence, and the psychology of moral judgment.

Christopher Gale is Professor of Business Administration at the Darden Graduate School of Business Administration at the University of Virginia.

Harry J. Gensler is Professor of Philosophy at the University of Scranton. His publications include *Logic* and *Symbolic Logic*. Professor Gensler is currently working on books on *Formal Ethics and the Golden Rule* and *Kantian Moral Reasoning*.

Bernard Gert is Eunice and Julian Cohen Professor for the Study of Ethics and Human Values at Dartmouth College and Adjunct Professor of Psychiatry at Dartmouth Medical School. He has received NEH, NSF, and Fulbright awards, and was Principal Investigator on an NIH grant. He is the author of *Morality*, co-author of *Philosophy in Medicine*, and editor of *Man and Citizen*, by Thomas Hobbes.

Alan Gewirth is Professor of Philosophy at the University of Chicago and the author of a number of books on ethics and human rights, including *Reason and Morality*.

Daniel R. Gilbert, Jr. is Associate Professor of Management at Bucknell University. His teaching and scholarly project is to salvage corporate strategy by reinterpreting the concept as an exercise in the humanities. He is the author of *Ethics Through Corporate Strategy*

A. R. Gini is Associate Professor of Philosophy and Adjunct Professor in the Institute of Industrial Relations at Loyola University, Chicago. He is also the Managing Editor of *Business Ethics Quarterly*. His published works include *Philosophical Issues in Human Rights* (with Werhane and Ozar), *It Comes With the Territory: An Inquiry into the Nature of Work* (with Sullivan), *Case Studies in Business Ethics* (with Donaldson), and *Heigh-Ho! Heigh-Ho!: Quotes About Work* (with Sullivan).

James R. Glenn, Jr. is Professor of Management in the College of Business at San Francisco State University. His research focus is on the ethical dimensions of decisions made in business, professional, and medical organizations. His writing on decision-making, research, and teaching business ethics has appeared in several periodicals and books. He is currently revising *Ethics in Decision Making*.

Alan H. Goldman is Professor of Philosophy at the University of Miami. He is author of *The Moral Foundations of Professional Ethics*.

Leon J. Goldstein is Professor of Philosophy at the State University of New York at Binghamton, and editor of *International Studies in Philosophy*. He is author, with Lucy S. Dawidowicz, of *Politics in a Pluralistic Democracy*, and of *Historical Knowing*. A volume collecting his papers on philosophy of history is in preparation, and he is writing a book on open concepts and conceptual tension.

Kenneth E. Goodpaster holds the David and Barbara Koch Endowed Chair in Business Ethics at the University of St. Thomas. At St. Thomas, he teaches in undergraduate, MBA, and executive educational programs including an affiliation between St. Thomas and the Aspen Institute.

James Grant is Professor of Marketing at the University of South Alabama. In addition to teaching real estate, he is active in business consulting, training, and market research.

Joseph Grcic is Professor of Philosophy at Indiana State University. He has published *Moral Choices* and co-edited *Perspectives in the Family*. Articles written by Professor Grcic have also appeared in *Kant-Studien*, *Journal of Value Inquiry*, and *Journal of Social Philosophy*.

Mitchell Green is Assistant Professor of Philosophy at the University of Virginia.

Ronald M. Green is the John Phillips Professor of Religion in the Department of Religion, Dartmouth College and Director of Dartmouth's Ethics Institute. He has taught business ethics at Dartmouth's Amos Tuck School of Business Administration. Professor Green consults for many business corporations and is the author of five books, the most recent of which is *The Ethical Manager*.

Frank Griggs is Professor at the Siedman School of Finance at Grand Valley State University.

Barbara Gutek is Professor of Organizational Behavior at the University of Arizona.

Jean Hampton was Professor of Philosophy at the University of Arizona, Tucson and author of *Hobbes and the Social Contract Tradition*.

Kenneth Hanly is Professor of Philosophy at Brandon University, Manitoba.

Kirk O. Hanson is Senior Lecturer in Business Administration at Stanford University Graduate School of Business.

Russell Hardin is Professor of Philosophy, Public Studies and Political Science at New York University. He is the author of *Morality within the Limits of Reason*

R.M. Hare recently served as Professor of Graduate Studies at the University of Florida. Prior to his work in the US, Professor Hare taught as the White's Professor of Moral Philosophy and Fellow of Corpus Christi College, Oxford for many years. His principal books include *The Language of Morals*, *Freedom and Reason*, and *Moral Thinking*.

Robert S. Harris is C. Stewart Sheppard Professor of Business Administration at the Darden School, University of Virginia. Author of a number of articles and books focusing on corporate finance issues, he has been consultant to many corporations and government agencies. His current research focuses on shareholder welfare implications of both US and foreign takeovers.

David K. Hart is the J. Fish Smith Professor of Free Enterprise Studies at Brigham Young University.

Edwin Hartman is Professor in the Faculty of Management and the Department of Philosophy at Rutgers University. He is author of *Substance, Body, and Soul: Aristotelian Investigations*, *Conceptual Foundations of Organizational Theory*, and *Organizational Ethics and the Good Life*.

Brian Harvey is the Co-Operative Bank Professor of Corporate Responsibility, Manchester Business School, Manchester University, United Kingdom.

Sterling Harwood is Assistant Professor of Philosophy at San Jose University. He authored *Judical Activism* and has published numerous essays. He has edited *Business As Ethical & Business as Usual* and co-edited *Controversies in Criminal Law* and *Crime and Punishment: Philosophical Explorations*.

Mark Haskins is Professor of Business Administration at the Darden Graduate School of Business at the University of Virginia.

John Hasnas is Assistant Professor of Business Ethics at the Georgetown University School of Business. His areas of expertise include business ethics, jurisprudence, criminal and commercial law, and bioethics.

John Haughey is Professor of Religious Ethics at Loyola University of Chicago's Theology Department. He is the author and/or editor of seven books, the last two of which are: *Converting Nine to Five: Towards a Spirituality of Work* and *The Holy Use of Money: Personal Finances in the Light of Christian Faith*.

Marian V. Heacock is a Professor of Management in the Graduate School of Management and School of Business at the University of Alabama in Birmingham. Her primary interests are business ethics and the social, ethical, and legal environment of business. She is the President and co-founder of the International Center for Ethics in Business, the Professions, and Public Service.

Virginia Held is Professor of Philosophy at the Graduate School and University Center of the City University of New York. She is the author of *Rights and Goods: Justifying Social Action* and *Feminist Morality: Transforming Culture, Society, and Politics*.

Stewart Herman is Professor of Religion at Concordia College Moorehead, MN.

Larry Hickman is Professor of Philosophy at the Center for Dewey Studies at Southern Illinois University.

W. Michael Hoffman is Professor of Philosophy and former chair of the Department at Bentley College. He has authored or edited thirteen books, including *Business Ethics: Readings and Cases in Corporate Morality*, and has published over forty articles. Professor Hoffman is also the founding director of the Center for Business Ethics at Bentley College.

Rachelle Hollander is Program Director for Ethics and Values Studies at the National Science Foundation.

Barry Penn Hollar is Professor of Religion at Shenandoah University.

Alec Horniman is Professor of Business Administration at the Darden Graduate School of Business Administration at the University of Virginia.

LaRue Hosmer is Professor Emeritus of Corporate Strategy and Managerial Ethics at the University of Michigan School of Business Administration.

Richard T. Hull is Associate Professor of Philosophy at the State University of New York at Buffalo. He is the past president of the American Society for Value Inquiry and is the editor of *Ethical Issues in the New Reproductive Technologies* and *A Quarter Century of Value Inquiry: Presidential Addresses of the American Society of Value Inquiry*.

Lester Hunt is Professor of Philosophy at the University of Wisconsin, Madison.

David Ingram is Professor of Philosophy at Loyola University of Chicago. His major publications include *Habermas and the Dialectic of Reason*, *Critical Theory and Philosophy*, *Reason, History and Politics: The Communitarian Grounds of Legitimization in the Modern Age*, and *Critical Theory: The Essential Readings* (with Julia Simon-Ingram).

Lynn Isabella is Associate Professor of Business Administration at the Darden Graduate School of Business at the University of Virginia. She has written extensively on organizational behavior.

Dove Izraeli is Professor of Marketing and Business Ethics in the Faculty of Management, Tel-Aviv University. He has published ten books and numerous professional articles. Professor Izraeli is founder and chair of the Israeli Network for Social Responsibility and a founding member of the International Society for Ethics in the Public Service.

Robert Jackall is Willmott Family Professor of Sociology and Social Thought at Williams College. He is the author of *Moral Mazes*.

Kevin T. Jackson is Director of the Center for Ethics in Global Business and a member of the business faculty at Fordham University. Professor

Jackson has published numerous articles on business ethics and is the author of the book *Charting Global Responsibilities: Legal Philosophy and Human Rights.*

Gene G. James is Professor of Philosophy at the University of Memphis. He is past President of the American Society for Value Inquiry, and is author of several texts and anthologies, and a number of articles on ethics, social and political philosophy, and philosophy of religion.

Deborah G. Johnson is Professor of Philosophy in the Department of Science and Technology Studies of Rensselear Polytechnic Institute. Her latest book is an anthology of readings, co-edited with Helen Nissenbaum, entitled *Computers, Ethics, and Social Values.*

Peter T. Johnson has been the CEO of TJ International, a publicly traded company in light manufacturing. He was the Administrator of the Bonneville Power Administration and has served the National Academy of Sciences as a member of committees dealing with nuclear power and energy strategy.

Robin D. Johnson is Assistant Professor of Business Administration at the Darden Graduate School of Business Administration at the University of Virginia. She spent 10 years as an international finance professional before starting her academic career. Her research examines practices and policies that move the social equity agenda forward, such as work-family, diversity, and empowered work teams.

Donald Jones is Professor of Religion at Drew University.

Thomas M. Jones is Professor of Management and Organization at the University of Washington in Seattle. His research interests include business ethics, corporate governance, and business and society paradigms. Professor Jones also serves on the Editorial Board of the *Academy of Management Review.*

Albert R. Jonsen is Professor of Ethics in Medicine, School of Medicine, University of Washington. He is a member of the Institute of Medicine and served on two Presidential Commissions on bioethics. He is author of *The New Medicine and the Old Ethics* and co-author of *The Abuse of Casuistry* and *Clinical Ethics.*

Judith Brown Kamm is Associate Director of the Center for Business Ethics at Bentley College. She is Professor of Management and has co-chaired several international conferences. In addition to co-editing *Emerging Global Business Ethics,* her articles have appeared in *Entrepreneurship Theory and Practice, Journal of Business Ethics, Ethikos,* and *Human Relations.* Her consulting activities include business ethics training and team-building seminars.

Michael Keeley is Professor of Management at Loyola University Chicago. He is the author of *A Social-Contract Theory of Organization,* as well as related articles in many management and philosophical journals.

Jonathan King is Associate Professor of Management at Oregon State University's College of Business. His primary research interests are in systems thinking and moral philosophy.

Kenneth Kipnis is Professor of Philosophy at the University of Hawaii-Manoa. He is the author of a number of books, including *Economic Justice: Private Rights and Public Responsibilities.*

George Klosko is Professor of Government and Foreign Affairs at the University of Virginia. He is the author of *The Development of Plato's Political Theory, The Principle of Fairness and Political Obligation,* and several articles in the history of political theory and contemporary political philosophy.

Daryl Koehn is Associate Professor of Philosophy at DePaul University in Chicago. She teaches graduate and undergraduate courses in ethics and political theory and is the author of *The Ground of Professional Ethics.* Professor Koehn consults regularly with universities and corporations on the devising and implementing of programs in ethical training.

James Kouzes is CEO of the Tom Peters Group/Learning Systems.

James Kuhn is the Courtney C. Brown Professor of Management and Organization at Columbia University Graduate School of Business.

Nancy Kurland is Assistant Professor of Management and Organization in the School of Business Administration at the University of Southern California in Los Angeles. Her research interests in business ethics examine incentives, trust and accountability, and telecommuting.

Safro Kwame is a native of Ghana and currently Assistant Professor of Philosophy at Lincoln University in Pennsylvania. His current areas of research include African Philosophy, ethics, comparative philosophy, and the philosophy of mind.

Gene R. Laczniak is the Sanders Professor of Marketing at Marquette University in Milwaukee. He has published numerous articles on both marketing strategy and marketing ethics, his most recent entitled *Ethical Marketing Decisions.*

John Ladd is Professor of Philosophy at Brown University. He is a member of numerous societies and associations, among them the American Philosophical Association and the New York Academy of Sciences. He authored *The Structure of a Moral Code* and *Ethical Issues Relating to Life and Death.*

C. Jay Lambe is a graduate student working on a PhD in management at the Darden Graduate School of Business Administration at the University of Virginia.

Robert Landel is Associate Dean for MBA Education and the Henry E. McWane Professor of Business Administration at the Darden Graduate School of Business Administration at the University of Virginia.

Bruce M. Landesman is Associate Professor of Philosophy at the University of Utah. His research interests include ethics, political and social philosophy, professional ethics, Marxism, aesthetics, and morality and nuclear weapons. Professor Landesman has also authored numerous articles on these areas, appearing in journals such as *Ethics, Journal of Chinese Philosophy, Canadian Philosophical Reviews, and National Forum.*

William Langenfus is Assistant Professor of Philosophy at John Carroll University.

Andrea Larson is Assistant Professor at the Darden Graduate School of Business Administration at the University of Virginia, where she teaches entrepreneurship. Her publications have appeared in the *Journal of Business Venturing, Entrepreneurship Theory and Practice*, and *Administrative Science Quarterly.*

William S. Laufer is Associate Professor of Legal Studies at the Wharton School, University of Pennsylvania.

Lawrence G. Lavengood is Professor Emeritus of Business History at the Kellogg Graduate School of Management, Northwestern University.

Anne Lawrence is Associate Professor in the Department of Organization and Management at San Jose State University.

Sander Lee is Professor of Philosophy at Keene State College. He has published extensively on a variety of issues and is currently at work on a book exploring philosophical themes in the films of Woody Allen. He also served as president of a number of scholarly societies and he is a consulting editor for various journals.

Jeff Lenn is Professor of Management at George Washington University.

Jeanne M. Liedtka is Associate Professor of Business Administration at the Darden Graduate School of Business Administration at the University of Virginia. She teaches in the area of both strategy and ethics and her current research interests are in two areas: the teaching of strategic thinking and exploring the linkages between business values and sources of competitive advantage.

J. Ralph Lindgren is the Clara H. Stewardson Professor of Philosophy at Lehigh University. His works on Adam Smith include an edition *The Early Writings of Adam Smith*; a monograph *The Social Philosophy of Adam Smith*; and a number of essays. The latest essay, "Adam Smith's Treatment of Criminal Law" appears in *Adam Smith and the Philosophy of Law and Economics*, Mallow and Evensky (eds).

John F. Lobuts Jr. is Professor of Management Science and has taught with the Behavioral Science Faculty at George Washington University. He has published and delivered papers internationally and serves as an Associate Editor for Simulation & Gaming: An International Journal.

George Cabot Lodge is the Jaime and Josefinea Chua Tiampo Professor of Business Administration at Harvard University Graduate School and author of *The New American Ideology.*

Neil Luebke is Professor of Philosophy at Oklahoma State University.

Henk van Luijk is Professor of Ethics and Business Ethics at Nijenrode University, The Netherlands Business School, and at the University of Groningen, The Netherlands. He is chairman of EBEN, the European Business Ethics Network, and a member of the Editorial Board of *Business Ethics, A European Review*. He has published three books and over sixty articles, many of them in Dutch, in scholarly and professional journals.

David Lyons is Professor of Law at Boston University.

Thomas MacAvoy is Paul M. Hammaker Professor of Business Administration at the Darden Graduate School of Business Administration, University of Virginia. His areas of interest include innovation and strategic management. He has served as President and CEO and Vice-Chairman of the Board of Corning, Inc., and was Director of Quaker Oats, Chubb Corporation, and Lubrizol Corporation.

Michael Maccoby is Director of the Project on Technology, Work, and Character in Washington, DC. He is author of *The Gamesman*, *The Leader*, *Why Work*, *Sweden at the Edge*, and with Erich Fromm, *Social Character in a Mexican Village*. Dr. Maccoby has been consultant on participatory management to AT&T, Volvo, ABB, and several other organizations.

Tibor Machan is Professor of Philosophy at Auburn University, Alabama. He has written several books, including *Individuals and Their Rights, Capitalism and Individualism*, and *Private Rights, Public Illusions*. He also co-edited, with Kenneth Lucey, *Recent Work in Philosophy* and, with Bruce Johnson, *Rights and Regulations*.

Eric Mack is Professor of Philosophy and a Member of the Faculty of the Murphy Institute of Political Economy at Tulane University. He has published numerous articles in scholarly journals and anthologies on topics of moral, political, and legal philosophy.

Tara Madden is an MBA student at Iona College, Hagan School of Business. She is editorial assistant for two international journals: *International Journal of Value-Based Management* and *Cross-Cultural Management: An International Journal*.

Peter Madsen is executive director of the Center for the Advancement of Applied Ethics at Carnegie Mellon University where he conducts training for a number of Fortune 500 firms. He is co-editor of *Essentials of Business Ethics* and executive producer of the telecourse "Ethical Issues in Professional Life" and the video series "Diversity Dilemmas".

Wes Magat is a professor at the Fuqua School of Business at Duke University.

Thomas Magnell is Associate Professor and Chair of the Department of Philosophy at Drew University. He has written numerous papers, many of them regarding ethics and, more broadly, matters of value, including "Evaluations as Assessments, Parts I & II." Professor Magnell has also been President of the International Society for Value Inquiry, President of the Conference of Philosophical Societies, and Associate Editor of *The Journal of Value Inquiry*.

Jack Mahoney is Dixons Professor of Business Ethics and Social Responsibility at London Business School. He is author of *Teaching Business Ethics in the UK, Europe and the USA: A Comparative Study*, and founding editor of *Business Ethics: A European Review*.

John Marshall is Associate Professor of Philosophy at the University of Virginia. His areas of speciality include ethics and history of modern ethics, especially Kant, Hume, Mill and Descartes. Professor Marshall recently published "Why Rational Egoism is Inconsistent," and "The Syntheticity of Categorical Imperative."

Deryl W. Martin is Associate Professor of Finance at Tennessee Technological University. His primary research interests include investments, corporate finance, market efficiency, and business ethics. Professor Martin also serves on the editorial review board of the *Journal of Business Ethics*.

Mike W. Martin is Professor of Philosophy at Chapman University. He is author of about 50 publications including 5 books: *Ethics in Engineering* (with Roland Schinzinger), *Self-Deception and Self-Understanding* (ed.), *Self-Deception and Morality, Everyday Morality*, and *Virtuous Giving: Philanthropy, Voluntary Service and Caring*.

Marilynn Cash Mathews is President of International Consulting and Executive Development.

Larry M. May is Professor of Philosophy at Washington University in St. Louis. He is the author of *The Socially Responsive Self: Social Theory and Professional Ethics*.

Donald O. Mayer is Associate Professor of Management at the School of Business Administration, Oakland University, where he teaches law and ethics. He also serves as an adjunct professor at the University of Michigan's School of Business Administration. Professor Mayer's main interest in business ethics relates to ethical norms for multinational corporations and nation-states.

John McCall is Associate Professor in the Department of Philosophy at Saint Joseph's University in Philadelphia. He has published on the topics of welfare reform, employee participation, strict liability, employee rights and is co-editor, with Joseph DesJardins, of *Contemporary Issues in Business Ethics*.

Bruce McCandless III, a graduate of the University of Texas School of Law, practiced securities law with Brown & Wood before becoming a freelance writer. He has written for U.P.I. and for the *Asian Wall Street Journal, Texas Observer*, and other publications.

Dennis McCann is Professor of Religious Studies at DePaul University. He has written extensively on liberation theology.

Deidre McCloskey is John F. Murray Professor of Economics and Professor of History at the University of Iowa. She writes on British history and the rhetoric of economics. Among her books are, *Knowledge and Persuasion in Economics, If You're So Smart: The Narrative of Economic Expertise*, and *The Rhetoric of Economics*.

Ann L. McGill is Associate Professor of Marketing at the J. L. Kellogg Graduate School of Management, Northwestern University. She is particularly interested in the causal explanations consumers and managers may provide for changes in price or market share. Her articles have appeared in *Journal of Personality and Social Psychology, Journal of Consumer Research*, and *Organizational Behavior and Human Decision Processes*.

Christopher McMahon is Professor of Philosophy at the University of California, Santa Barbara and author of *Authority and Democracy*.

Thomas F. McMahon, C.S.V., is Professor of Management at Loyola University Chicago. His background includes a doctorate in Moral Theology from St. Thomas Aquinas University. He is the author of over fifty publications, primarily in business ethics and social responsibility of business.

Charles Meiburg is a professor of Business Administration at the Darden Graduate School of Business Administration at the University of Virginia.

Alfred Mele is Professor of Philosophy at Davidson College.

David Messick is Kaplan Professor of Business Ethics at the Kellogg Graduate School of Management at Northwestern University. He is the editor of the journal *Social Justice Research* and the author of numerous articles and books.

Diana Tietjen Meyers is Professor of Philosophy at the University of Connecticut. She is author of *Inalienable Rights: A Defense, Self, Society, and Personal Choice*, and *Subjectivity: Psychoanalytic Feminism and Moral Philosophy*. She has also co-edited a number of collections, including *Women and Moral Theory* and *Kindred Matters: Rethinking the Philosophy of the Family*. Her current work concerns emotion, figuration, and moral perception.

Alex C. Michalos is Professor in the Faculty of Management and Administration at the University of Northern British Columbia. He is also a Fellow of the Royal Society of Canada and is recognized as an internationally known scholar in the field of social indicators and quality of life measurement. His most notable piece of work is entitled *North American Social Report: A Comparative Study of the Quality of Life in Canada and the USA from 1964 to 1974*.

Barry Mitnick is Professor in the Katz Graduate School of Business at the University of Pittsburgh. He has published extensively on agency theory.

Dennis Moberg is Professor of Management at Santa Clara University.

Richard D. Mohr is Professor of Philosophy at the University of Illinois, Champaign-Urbana. He is the author of *Gays/Justice: A Study of Ethics, Society and Law, Gay Ideas: Outing and Other Controversies*, and *A More Perfect Union: Why Straight America Must Stand Up For Gay Rights*.

Jennifer Mills Moore is Assistant Professor of Law at the University of Wisconsin. She served as Research Associate of the Center for Business Ethics and taught in the Philosophy Departments at Bentley College and the University of Delaware before joining the faculty at the University of Wisconsin. She has published and/or edited numerous articles in the field of business ethics.

Christopher W. Morris is Professor of Philosophy at Bowling Green State University. He is a Senior Research Fellow at the Social Philosophy and Policy Center at Bowling Green and is Research Associate, CREA, at the Ecole Polytechnique in Paris. Professor Morris has edited several anthologies on liability, terrorism, value theory, and contemporary contractarianism, and has written numerous papers on topics in moral and political philosophy and applied ethics.

Kevin W. Mossholder is Professor in the Department of Management at Louisiana State University.

Patrick E. Murphy is Professor and Chair of the Department of Marketing at the University of Notre Dame. He recently spent a year as a Fulbright Scholar at University College, Cork, in Ireland. Professor Murphy has written two books and a number of articles on the topic of business and marketing ethics.

Jan Narveson is Professor of Philosophy at the University of Waterloo (Canada) and is author of more than a hundred papers in philosophical periodicals and anthologies, and of *Morality and Utility*, *The Libertarian Idea*, and *Moral Matters*. He is also editor of *Moral Issues* and co-author (with Marilyn Friedman) of *Political Correctness*.

Samuel M. Natale is Director for Research and Funding for the Oxford University Center for the Study of Values in Education and Business, Department of Educational Studies, Oxford, England. Concurrently he is Professor of Studies in Corporate Values, Hagan School of Business, Iona College. He is also editor of two international journals: *The International Journal of Value-Based Management* and *Cross-Cultural Management*.

Lisa Newton is Professor of Philosophy, Director of the Program of Applied Ethics, and Director of the Program in Environmental Studies at Fairfield University. Her most recent projects have been the preparation of the companion volumes and course work for the *Ethics in America* television series. She has authored more than 50 articles for professional journals, primarily in political philosophy, environmental ethics, business, and professional ethics.

James W. Nickel is Professor of Philosophy at the University of Colorado, Boulder. He is the author of *Making Sense of Human Rights*.

Kai Nielsen is Emeritus Professor of Philosophy at the University of Calgary and past President of the Canadian Philosophical Association. He also serves as an editor of the *Canadian Journal of Philosophy* and is a member of the Royal Society of Canada. His books include *Equality and Liberty: A Defense of Radical Egalitarianism* and *After the Demise of the Tradition: Rorty, Critical Theory and the Fate of Philosophy*.

Richard P. Nielsen is an Associate Professor in the Organization Studies Department of the Wallace E. Carroll School of Management, Boston College. He is the author of *The Politics of Ethics*.

William G. O'Neill is a member of the Philosophy Department at Iona College. A Woodrow Wilson Fellow, he held a Carnegie Institute grant in Philosophy of Science and also faculty study grants to India and East Africa. He teaches business and health-care ethics, moral theory, and philosophy of knowledge. His other interests include philosophy of science, logic, and philosophical analysis of practical virtue and conscience.

Daniel Ortiz is Professor of Law and Harrison Foundation Research Professor at the University of Virginia. Before teaching, Professor Ortiz worked as a judicial clerk to Judge Stephen Breyer on the United States Court of Appeals in Boston and to Justice Lewis F. Powell, Jr., on the United States Supreme Court.

Daniel T. Ostas has been a practicing attorney since 1980 and currently serves as Associate Professor at the University of Maryland, College Park. He teaches business law and business ethics. Author of more than twenty scholarly law and business publications, his research focuses on the relationships between law, economics, and ethics.

David Ozar is Professor and Co-Director of Graduate Programs in Health Care Ethics, Adjunct Professor in Medical Humanities at the Loyola Stritch School of Medicine, and Director of the Center for Ethics Across the University, Loyola University Chicago.

Lynn Sharp Paine is Associate Professor of Management at Harvard University Graduate School of Business Administration.

Laurie Pant is Professor in the School of Management at Suffolk University.

Tom Peters is the author of *In Search of Excellence* and a well-known lecturer and writer.

Michael J. Phillips is Professor of Business Law at Indiana University's School of Business. He has authored over 40 journal articles, eight of which received awards from the Academy of Legal Studies in Business. He also has served as editor-in-chief of the *American Business Law Journal*, and has twice chaired his academic department.

Robert A. Phillips is a graduate student at the Darden Graduate Business School at the University of Virginia, where he is pursuing his Ph.D. in Business Ethics.

Deborah Poff is Acting Vice President of the University of Northern British Columbia. She is author of numerous articles on ethics, violence, sexuality, feminism, global economic development, and justice issues. She is also the editor of the *Journal of Business Ethics* and co-editor of *Business Ethics in Canada*.

Lawrence A. Ponemon holds the Anderson Chair of Accounting at Bentley College.

Barry Posner is Associate Professor in the Leavy School of Business Administration at Santa Clara University.

Frederick R. Post is Associate Professor of Law and Management at the University of Toledo, College of Business Administration.

Gerald J. Postema is Professor in and Chair of the Philosophy Department at the University of North Carolina at Chapel Hill.

Patrick Primeaux is an Associate Professor in the Theology and Religious Studies Department at St John's University.

Michael H. Prosser, Professor of Rhetoric and Communications Studies at the University of Virginia since 1972, has been on academic leave from 1994 to 1996 as the Kern Professor in Communications at the Rochester Institute of Technology. Professor Prosser is editor or author of seven books, including *The Cultural Dialogue*.

Tara Radin is a graduate student at the Darden Graduate School of Business at the University of Virginia, where she is pursuing her Ph.D. in Business Ethics.

Robert J. Rafalko is currently the coordinator of the Corporate Ethics Program at Webster University in St. Louis and teaches business ethics on site at McDonnel Douglas Corporation. Professor Rafalko is the author of a textbook in logic published by Wadsworth, Inc.

Ralph Raico is Professor of History at the New York State University College, Buffalo.

George D. Randels. was the 1994–5 Cousins Fellow in Business Ethics at Emory University's Center for Ethics in Public Policy and the Professions. He is currently Assistant Professor of Religious Studies at the University of the Pacific.

David M. Rasmussen is Professor of Philosophy at Boston College and Editor-in-Chief of *Philosophy and Social Criticism*. His most recent books include *Reading Habermas* and *Universalism vs. Communitarianism: Contemporary Debates in Ethics*.

Diane Raymond is Professor of Philosophy at Simmons College.

David Reibstein is Professor at The Wharton School, University of Pennsylvania.

Donald P. Robin is Professor of Marketing at the University of Southern Mississippi. He has authored three books, two on business ethics (co-authored with Eric Reidenbach), and a basic marketing text. In addition, he has numerous articles in journals such as *Journal of Marketing*, *The Accounting Review*, *Journal of Business Research*, *Business Ethics Quarterly*, and *Journal of Business Ethics*.

Joanne W. Rockness is Cameron Professor of Accounting at the Cameron School of Business Administration, University of North Carolina at Wilmington. She conducts many programs on ethics liability, and ethics education for corporations, non-profit organizations, and accounting professors. Professor Rockness has published numerous articles on ethics, ethics education, social responsibility, and accountant's liability.

Julie A. Roin is the Class of 1963 Research Professor of Law at the University of Virginia School of Law. Her research interest is federal income taxation. Her work experience includes clerking for Judge Patricia M. Wald of the US Court of Appeals for the DC Circuit and work for Caplin & Drysdale, Ltd., a Washington, DC law firm specializing in tax matters.

Sandra Rosenthal is Professor of Philosophy at Loyola University New Orleans. She is the author (with R. Buchholz) of *Rethinking Business Ethics*.

Br. Leo V. Ryan, C.S.V., is Professor of Management at DePaul University. He is the former president of the Society of Business Ethics.

Abdulaziz Sachedina is Professor of Religious Studies at the University of Virginia.

Robert Sack is Professor of Business Administration at the Darden Graduate School of Business Administration, University of Virginia. He has published widely in the areas of ethical responsibilities of accountants. Other research interests include business management for scientists and engineers and managing critical resources. He has co-edited *Accounting Horizons*.

Mark Sagoff is Director of the Institute for Philosophy and Public Policy at the University of Maryland. He has taught at Princeton, the University of Pennsylvania, the University of Wisconsin (Madison), and Cornell. He has published extensively in journals of philosophy, law, and Public Policy. His most notable work is entitled *The Economy of the Earth: Philosophy, Law and the Environment*.

Steven R. Salbu is Associate Professor of Legal and Ethical Environment of Business at the University of Texas at Austin.

Eugene Schlossberger is Associate Professor of Philosophy at Purdue University Calumet. He is author of *Moral Responsibility and Persons* and *The Ethical Engineer*, as well as numerous articles in such journals as *Business Ethics Quarterly, Mind, Analysis*, and *Science and Engineering Ethics*.

Mark D. Schneider is Senior Lecturer in Philosophy at Loyola University Chicago, and Assistant Managing Editor of *Business Ethics Quarterly: The Journal of the Society for Business Ethics*. His published works include both cases and essays in business ethics.

Howard S. Schwartz is Professor in the School of Business Administration at Oakland University. His background is philosophy and organizational behavior.

Maureen Scully is Assistant Professor of Management at the Massachusetts Institute of Technology, Sloan School of Management.

S. Prakash Sethi is the Associate Director of the Center for Management Development and Organizational Research, Baruch College, The City University of New York. He is the author of *Multinational Corporations and the impact of Public Advocacy on Corporate Strategy: Nestle and the Infant Formula Controversy*.

Debra L. Shapiro is Professor of Management at the Kenan-Flagler Business School at the University of North Carolina at Chapel Hill.

David Sharap is at the University of Western Ontario.

William Shaw is Woodson Centennial Professor in Business at the University of Texas at Austin. He has published legal environmental texts, articles on law and ethics, and is the articles editor of the *American Business Law Journal*.

William H. Shaw is Professor of Philosophy and Chair of the Philosophy Department at San Jose State University. Among other writings, he is author of *Business Ethics* (2nd edn), and, with Vincent Barry, *Moral Issues in Business*.

Jon Shepard is Pamplin Professor of Management and Head of the Department of Management at Virginia Tech. Prominent among his current research interests are ethical climates in organizations and organizational accountability.

Kristin Shrader-Frechette is Distinguished Research Professor in the Environmental Sciences and Policy Program and the Department of Philosophy at the University of South Florida. She is the author of numerous articles which have appeared in journals such as *Ethics, Environmental Ethics, Science, BioScience*, and *Philosophy of Science*.

Paul Shrivastava is Professor of Management at Bucknell University. He is the author of *Bhopal: Anatomy of a Crisis*.

William Sihler is Ronald Edward Trzcinski Professor of Business Administration at the Darden Graduate School of Business Administration, University of Virginia. He is author of *Cases in Applied Financial Management, Financial Service Organizations: Cases in Strategic Manpower* and *The Troubled Money Business*.

A. John Simmons is Professor of Philosophy at the University of Virginia. He is an editor of the journal *Philosophy and Public Affairs* and the author of *Moral Principles and Political Obligations*, *The Lockean Theory of Rights*, and *On the Edge of Anarchy*.

Alan E. Singer is Professor in the Department of Management at the University of Canterbury. He worked in the UK private sector before taking up academic positions in New Zealand and has published widely on the subject of business ethics. He serves on the editorial boards of the *Journal of Business Ethics, Human Systems Management*.

Ming S. Singer is Professor of Psychology at the University of Canterbury. She is the author of *Diversity-based Hiring* and has published extensively in academic journals on topics related to organizational and personal issues.

Walter Sinnott-Armstrong is Professor of Philosophy at Dartmouth College. He is the author of numerous articles and books, including *Modality, Morality and Belief*.

Michael W. Small is Senior Lecturer in Management at the Curtin Business School, Curtin University of Technology (Australia). In addition to a professional interest in the areas of general management, organizational theory, and organizational behavior, his current research interests are now being focused on the areas of business ethics and social responsibility.

Patricia Smith is Professor of Philosophy at the University of Kentucky. She has published extensively on legal philosophy and on feminism.

Jack Snapper is a member of the faculty at the Lewis College of Liberal Arts, Illinois Institute of Technology.

Milton Snoeyenbos is Professor of Philosophy at Georgia State University. He is co-editor of *Business Ethics*.

Robert C. Solomon is Quincy Lee Centennial Professor of Philosophy and Business at the University of Texas at Austin. He is the author of *Above the Bottom Line*, *Ethics and Excellence*, and *New World of Business*. He is also the author of *The Passions, In the Spirit of Hegel*, and *A Passion for Justice*, among others.

Robert Spekman is a professor of Business Administration at the Darden Graduate School of Business Administration, University of Virginia.

His research interests include managing critical resources, marketing planning, developing managerial excellence, and buyer–seller relationships. He has published numerous articles on these areas in scholarly journals such as *Journal of Business Research, European Journal of Marketing*, and *Strategic Management Journal*.

Roger D. Staton is Professor of Business Law at the Miami University School of Business Administration. Over the past twenty years he has actively practiced as a trial attorney in both state and federal courts and has published numerous articles on copyright and other civil litigation issues.

Paul Steidlmeier is Associate Professor of Strategic Management in the School of Management of Binghamton University. He is a specialist in international economic development strategy and in business and society relations. He has concentrated upon intellectual property issues in China and developing countries and is the author of several articles and books on business social policy, including *People and Profits: The Ethics of Capitalism*.

Carroll Stephens is Assistant Professor of Management at Virginia Tech. Her research focuses on critical theories of organization, and ethical analysis of business.

John Stieber is Professor at the Cox School of Business at Southern Methodist University.

John R. Swanda, Jr. is Professor of Management and Dean of the School of Business and Economics at Indiana University South Bend.

Robert Sweet is a member of the faculty of Clark State Community College. His research interests are in the areas of applied ethics and philosophy of mind. He is the author of *Marx, Morality, and the Virtue of Beneficence*.

Iwao Taka was the Donald L. Fisher/Peter V. Smith Visiting Scholar in Ethics at the Wharton School, University of Pennsylvania, and is Assistant Professor in the International School of Economics and Business Administration at Reitaku University in Japan. His current research interests include ethical decision-making, ethical aspects of leadership, and ethical issues in the Japanese business community.

Meir Tamari is Director of the Center for Business Ethics at the College of Technology, Jerusalem, Israel.

Jesse Taylor is Associate Professor of Philosophy at Appalachian State University.

Lawrence S. Temkin is Professor of Philosophy at Rice University. Author of *Inequality* and several articles in the areas of ethics and political philosophy, his honors include the Harvard Program for Ethics in the Professions, National Humanities Center, and Andrew Mellon and Danforth Fellowships.

Kathryn Theus is Associate Professor of Philosophy at the University of Southern Mississippi.

Lawrence Thomas is Professor of Philosophy and Political Science Affiliate at Syracuse University. He is the author of *Living Morally: A Psychology of Moral Character* and other works in moral and social philosophy, including the Holocaust.

Tom Thomas is Professor of Management at the University of Washington School of Business.

Barbara Ley Toffler is a founding partner in Resources for Responsible Management, a Boston-based firm that consults to both private and public sector organizations in a broad range of areas related to responsible business practices and public/private sector collaboration for problem-solving issues of public interest. Her books include *Tough Choices: Managers Talk Ethics*, released in paperback as *Managers Talk Ethics: Making Tough Choices in a Competitive Business World*.

Rosemarie Tong is Thatcher Professor in Medical Ethics and Philosophy at Davidson College. Her professional interests are focused on bioethics, clinical ethics, feminist philosophy, and the philosophy of law. Her major publications include *Women, Sex and the Law*, *Feminist Thought: A Comprehensive Introduction*, and *Controlling Our Reproductive Destiny*.

Linda Klebe Trevino is Associate Professor of Organizational Behavior at the Smeal College of Business Administration, The Pennsylvania State University. She is widely published in the areas of organizational justice and the management of ethical conduct in organizations.

Jane Uebelhoer is Professor of Management at Marymount University School of Business Administration.

Cutler Umbach received a Ph.D. from Northwestern University and has taught at the College of Idaho. His business experience includes being CEO of a construction supply company and having broad experience in the clothing and food industries.

Doug Den Uyl is Professor of Philosophy at Bellarmine College. He is the author of the *New Crusaders: The Corporate Social Responsibility Debate*.

Donald VanDeVeer is Professor of Philosophy at North Carolina State University. He has published various articles on coercion, informed consent, moral autonomy, and the treatment of non-human animals. He is author of *Paternalistic Intervention: The Moral Bounds of Benevolence* and has co-edited the volumes *And Justice For All*, *AIDS: Ethics and Public Policy*, *Health Care Ethics*, and *People, Penguins and Plastic Trees*.

Manuel Velasquez is the Charles J. Dirken Professor of Business Ethics at Santa Clara University. He is a member of the American Philosophical Association and the Academy of Management and is author of *Business Ethics*. He is also co-editor of *Ethical Theory* (with Cynthia Rostankowski), and author of *Philosophy: A Text With Readings*.

David Vogel is Professor of Business and Public Policy at the Haas School of Business at the University of California at Berkeley. His books include *Ethics and Profits* (with Leonard Silk), *Ethics in the Education of Business Managers* (with Charles Powers), and *Fluctuating Fortunes: The Political Power of Business in America*. Since 1982, he has been editor of the *California Management Review* and also serves on the editorial board of the *Journal of Business Ethics*.

Clarence C. Walton has been a Dean at Duquesne University and Columbia University, and is the former President of The Catholic University of America. He has held the Philip Young Chair in Business at Columbia and the Lamont Post Distinguished Professor of Ethics at the American College in Bryn Mawr, Pennsylvania. Author, editor, and teacher, Professor Walton has also authored or edited fifteen books and approximately fifty articles.

Douglas N. Walton is Professor of Philosophy at the University of Winnipeg (Canada) and is the author of many works on informal logic and ethics, including *Slippery Slope Arguments*. Professor

Walton was a Fellow of the Netherlands Institute for Advanced Study in the Humanities and Social Sciences from 1987–8 and 1989–90.

Steven L. Wartick is Professor of Management and Policy at the University of Missouri. He is the author/co-author of several articles on corporate social performance issues, management, and business/government relations. Professor Wartick is Associate Editor of *Business and Society*, and currently serves as the Chair Elect for the SIM Division of the Academy of Management and Vice President for the International Association for Business and Society.

Mark H. Waymack is Associate Professor of Philosophy at Loyola University Chicago. His research interests include 18th-century philosophy and health care ethics.

F. Stanford Wayne has been an educator for almost twenty years and provides instruction primarily in management, communication, and education courses; he has published extensively in these areas. He is a member/officer of several professional organizations at the state, regional, and national levels. He provides seminars and training to business individuals to help them improve their communication/management skills.

Gary R. Weaver is Assistant Professor of Management at the University of Delaware. His research and writing ranges over formal corporate ethics activities, cross-national issues of ethics management, and meta-theoretical issues in organizational theory.

Jack Weber is Associate Professor of Business Administration at the Darden Graduate School of Business Administration, University of Virginia. He has authored several articles and books on leadership in business, including *Managerial Literacy: What Today's Manager's Must Know to Succeed* (with Gary Shaw), and *General Managers in Action*.

James Weber is currently an Associate Professor and Director of the Board Center for Leadership in Ethics at Duquesne University. He has published articles on managerial values and moral reasoning and the teaching of business ethics in *Journal of Business Ethics, Business Ethics Quarterly, International Journal of Value Based Management, Human Relations*, and *Organization Science*.

Leonard J. Weber is Director of the Ethics Institute of the University of Detroit Mercy in Detroit, Michigan. He has published two books and more than thirty articles on ethics.

Vivian Weil is Director of the Center for the Study of Ethics in the Professions at the Illinois Institute of Technology. She has published extensively on ethics and engineering.

Paul Weirich is Professor of Philosophy at the University of Missouri Columbia.

Carl Wellman is Lewin Distinguished Professor in the Humanities at Washington University in Saint Louis. After publishing two books on the epistemology of ethics, he turned to the general theory of rights, with applications to welfare programs and medical practice. His most recent books are *Welfare Rights, A Theory of Rights*, and *Real Rights*.

Patricia H. Werhane is the Ruffin Professor of Business Ethics at the Darden Graduate School of Business Administration at the University of Virginia. Her works include *Ethical Issues in Business*, edited with Tom Donaldson and *Adam Smith and His Legacy for Modern Capitalism*. She is Editor-in-Chief of *Business Ethics Quarterly* and on the editorial board of the *Journal of Business Ethics*, among others.

Alan Wertheimer is McCullough Professor of Political Science at the University of Vermont. He is the author of *Coercion* and articles in political philosophy and philosophy of law. He is currently working on a book on exploitation.

Henry R. West is Professor of Philosophy at Macalester College. He is author of "Utilitarianism" (*Encyclopedia Britannica*) and various other works on Mill's utilitarianism.

Laura Westra is Associate Professor of Philosophy at the University of Windsor, and the Secretary of the International Society for Environmental Ethics. Her publications include: *An Environmental Proposal for Ethics: The Principle of Integrity, Freedom in Politics*, and about forty articles in *Environmental Ethics, Environmental Values, The Journal of Agricultural Ethics*, and *Global Bioethics*.

Andrew C. Wicks is Assistant Professor of Business Ethics in the Management and Organization Department at the University of Washington School of Business. He studied both bioethics and business ethics as part of his doctoral program in Religious Ethics at the University of Virginia and has been involved in research programs spanning both fields.

Victoria S. Wike is Professor of Philosophy at Loyola University Chicago. She specializes in Kantian ethics and also teaches courses on health-care ethics. Her recent publications include *Kant on the Happiness in Ethics* and articles in *Journal of Value Inquiry* and *Philosophy Research Archives*.

James B. Wilbur is Professor Emeritus at the State University of New York at Buffalo.

Paul G. Wilhelm is Assistant Professor of Management in the Department of Marketing and Management at the University of Texas at El Paso.

Oliver F. Williams is Associate Professor and Co-Director of the Notre Dame Center for Ethics and Religious Values in Business at the University of Notre Dame. He is the author of *Is the Good Corporation Dead?: Social Responsibility in a Global Economy*.

Donna Wood is Professor in the Katz School of Management at the University of Pittsburgh. Professor Wood also serves as the Editor-in-Chief of *Business and Society*.

Thomas Wren is Professor of Philosophy at Loyola University Chicago. He is the author of *Caring about Morality* and *The Moral Self*.

Shaker A. Zahra is Professor of Strategic Management at Georgia State University.

Michael J. Zimmerman is Professor of Philo-sophy at the University of North Carolina at Greensboro. He is the author of several books and articles on ethics, including *The Concept of Moral Obligation*.

A

accounting ethics The ethical issues and problems of the accounting professions involve two related difficulties. One is that, depending on whether and how it is disclosed to interested parties, accounting information may have the characteristics of a private good or of a public good. The other is that accounting information is normally asymmetrically distributed among individuals and groups who have a stake in the organization, and therefore a stake in the information production process. Consistent with the adage that "knowledge is power," information asymmetries generate significant ethical problems. For example, corporate insiders may engage in INSIDER TRADING in the capital market to their own advantage.

The accounting profession contains three main branches: managerial accounting, external financial accounting and reporting, and public accounting. Although accountants perform a great variety of managerial tasks, the activities that define accountancy focus on recording, analysis, and reporting of financial information about the affairs of individuals and organizations. Accountants may be members of any of a number of professional associations, which control admission into the professional ranks and define the norms of competence and conduct governing their actions. With few exceptions, public accountants who perform audits of financial statements must be licensed by an agency of the jurisdiction in which they practice.

Ethical Issues in Accounting

Although a small amount of work (e.g., Carey, 1946; Mautz & Sharaf, 1961) dates from an earlier period, the ethics of the accounting profession has emerged as a scholarly field only in the last few years. Theories of the ethics of the accounting profession and even an adequate understanding of the issues are at an early stage of development. A primary reason for this is that, although the accounting profession is closely linked with the administration of organizations and the conduct of business activity, few attempts have been made to link it explicitly to the older and better established field of business ethics. For example, many of the ethical issues that arise in public accounting are not professional problems *per se*; rather, they result from the way public accounting firms are organized and managed.

The issue of whose interests should be served by accountants pervades all parts of the profession (*see* ROLES AND ROLE MORALITY; PROFESSIONAL ETHICS). The scope of services issue (discussed below) is essentially the question of whether public accountants are able successfully to act in the interest of the readers of audited financial statements when they are also acting in the interest of their client in other areas. Financial accountants regularly face the problem of being expected to act in the interest of their employers by controlling the content of financial statements (and thereby perpetuating an information asymmetry), and also to provide information to the readers of these statements. In managerial accounting, the content and flow of information (e.g., budgets and expected levels of performance) from superiors to subordinates can be used to manipulate the latter's behavior. In addition, accountants place a high value on the confidentiality of information about their employer or client, but often possess information about misdeeds that might, on ethical grounds, merit unauthorized disclosure (i.e., WHISTLEBLOWING).

Ethical Issues in Managerial Accounting

Managerial accountants, that is, corporate financial officers, produce a large variety of financial and non-financial information for use within organizations of all kinds, including accumulating information about the cost of producing goods and services, budgets, forecasts, non-routine cost analyses, transfer prices, and the measurement of economic performance. In addition to working with the accounting information system, management accountants may perform many of the general management functions in such organizations.

Managerial accounting developed around the end of the nineteenth century with the ascendancy of the scientific management movement, which magnified the need for detailed financial information and sophisticated analyses of cost of production. (*see* TAYLOR, FREDERICK W.).

Most of the basic techniques of managerial accounting were developed by about 1925; recent developments in the managerial accounting profession have caused the professional associations of managerial accountants to promote the idea that the primary role of managerial accountants is management, rather than accounting *per se*.

The ethics of managerial accounting has almost completely escaped serious attention by either scholars or practicing accountants. This may be an implicit recognition that most of the ethical issues of managerial accounting are essentially business ethics issues, where the role of managerial accountants is to design information systems and provide information to aid the management of organizations. The key ethical factor for managerial accounting is that many uses of accounting information involve the manipulation of people to perform in ways the organization prefers, but which are not necessarily in the interest of the individual being manipulated (*see* BLUFFING AND DECEPTION).

Managerial accountants are subject to the codes of professional conduct of the professional organizations of which they are members. As the codes apply to managerial accountants, their provisions are generally non-restrictive and they do not provide for significant enforcement powers. The provisions applying to managerial

accountants focus on avoiding conflict of interest and maintaining confidentiality. They are silent on many issues, including (surprisingly, in view of accountants' close involvement with confidential information) whistleblowing. More generally, the codes do not deal with the common problem of conflict between the requirement to follow the instructions of superiors and professional values or standards which may conflict with those instructions.

Ethical Issues in Financial Accounting and Reporting

Many accountants employed by organizations also engage in financial accounting and reporting, which focuses on the preparation of general-purpose financial statements (e.g., the financial statements found in the annual reports of corporations), primarily for use by parties who are external to the organization (*see also* FINANCIAL REPORTING).

A basic ethical principle governing financial accounting is that readers of financial statements should be provided with "full and fair disclosure" of all the important and relevant aspects of the organization's activities and financial position. However, as AGENCY THEORY suggests, managers have powerful economic incentives to disclose only that information to outsiders which gives the organization and/or its management a strategic advantage. The ethical dimension of this situation does not seem to have received serious attention. For example, financial accountants frequently engage in "income smoothing," i.e., manipulation of the calculation of an organization's income for strategic reasons. Many practicing accountants believe that some techniques for smoothing income are more ethically acceptable than others, even though the result may be equally deceptive. (Financial accountants are rarely punished by professional associations for misrepresentation of corporate financial statements.)

Ethical Issues in Public Accounting

Public accounting firms are usually identified with the audit or independent examination of external financial statements of their clients. However, more than half of the revenues (and even more of the profits) of most public accounting firms come from income tax planning and preparation, and a wide range of other management advisory services for their clients. Although ethical issues exist in managerial accounting and non-audit aspects of public accounting, the bulk of work on accounting ethics has focused on the role of public accountants in the relationship between management and owners of business enterprises.

Auditing. Auditing is regarded by many as the essence of public accounting for a number of reasons, including the fact that it is the only activity for which accountants are exclusively granted licenses to practice by government agencies. In addition, from society's point of view, there is a clear public interest in auditing, in view of its role in capital markets and the fact that the right to perform audits is a legally recognized monopoly. In this regard, a quid pro quo exists between members of the profession and the rest of society.

The role of auditors is quite different from that of other professionals. According to virtually all statements of professional ethics, professionals are supposed to have an overriding responsibility to act in the public interest, in exchange for the benefits they obtain through the right to organize (Gaa, 1991). For most professions (such as law, medicine, and engineering, as well as the non-audit services provided by public accountants), the public interest is supposed to be served by acting (within limits) in the interest of the client, i.e., the party paying for the services. While this is also the case for non-audit services provided by public accountants, for auditing it may mean acting against the client's interest.

It is generally agreed that auditors owe a FIDUCIARY DUTY to the non-management owners and other external stakeholders of the organizations they audit. The exact nature of that duty has, however, been a source of continual controversy (accompanied by lawsuits alleging professional negligence) since the 1880s. This is the so-called "expectations gap" between the profession's and the public's opinion about the ethical (and legal) duties of auditors, specifically the extent to which auditors are responsible for detecting fraud and other illegal and unethical acts by their clients. Generally, auditors have taken a narrow view, limiting the scope of both their examina-

tions and their legal liability, while the general public, courts, and government agencies have regularly taken a broader view.

Closely related to the expectations gap, the nature of the AUDITOR–CLIENT RELATIONSHIP has been problematic. Since the interests of their clients and of the external stakeholders are generally in conflict, auditors must make judgments that leave one of these groups better off and others worse off. Furthermore, auditors themselves have their own economic interest, which may conflict with one or more of these stakeholder groups. According to the concept of auditor independence, auditors are supposed to be able to provide objective and unbiased opinions of their clients' financial statements, and are not supposed to subordinate their judgment to their client's interests. The difficulty is that auditors and their clients inevitably develop a close economic and personal relationship that threatens this independence. The essence of this problem is CONFLICT OF INTEREST, in which there is some likelihood that the auditor will act in the client's interest at the expense of the external stakeholders to whom their auditor's report is addressed. (Gaa, 1994)

The chance that auditors may fail to act in accordance with their duty to external stakeholders has increased in recent years because of increased competition in the market for public accounting services. Although one of the primary rationales for organizing as a profession is to restrict competition and thus enable its members to earn economic rents, it is also true that competitive forces may pressure professionals either to cut costs and do substandard work or to violate the independence principle. Increasingly, auditors must provide fixed-price bids for audits, and may engage in "low-balling" (i.e., bidding below the cost of providing the service, in the hope of recovering the lost profit through subsequent audits or the provision of non-audit services).

Non-audit services. Both income tax consulting and management advisory services are essentially conventional business consulting. As such, the public accountant *qua* business consultant faces the same kinds of ethical problems as other business consultants (*see* ETHICS OF CONSULTING). However, some commentators believe that providing such services is incompatible with the independence required for the audit function.

The question is: what is the appropriate scope of services which a public accounting firm may provide for a client, while still remaining independent while performing audits (Mautz and Sharaf, 1961; Briloff, 1990)? In addition, fee arrangements common in business consulting may be incompatible with auditor independence.

Regulation of Financial Accounting and Auditing

Financial accounting and auditing are highly regulated, both by professional associations and by public- and private-sector regulatory agencies. In addition to a CODE OF ETHICS, financial accountants and auditors must act in accordance with a number of auditing standards, accounting principles, and a whole host of disclosure regulations (*see also* PROFESSIONAL CODES). These standards of behavior are promulgated by a large variety of professional associations, and private-sector and public-sector agencies. The professed primary purpose of these agencies and regulations is to protect external stakeholders from the self-interested behavior of management (*see* PROFESSIONAL ETHICS). Extensive regulation (by both government and the profession) in North America dates back to the CORPORATE GOVERNANCE debates in the early 1930s in the US, with passage of the Securities Acts of 1933 and 1934 (*see* BERLE, ADOLF; MEANS, G. C.).

A major amount of attention has been paid by both scholars and practitioners to the process of setting financial accounting and reporting standards. The primary issue is how a standard-setting agency (such as the Financial Accounting Standards Board in the US) should fulfill its responsibilities to stakeholders. Discussions of stakeholders have been generally limited to individuals and groups which have a direct connection to business activities, such as actual and potential investors and creditors, suppliers, customers, employees, regulators, and the business press. Two problems have been addressed. The standard problem of stakeholder theory, i.e., how to rank the claims of the various stakeholders, has received only minor attention. Focusing on the conflicting interests of management and groups of financial statement users, Gaa (1988) provided theoretical foundations for the "user primacy" principle based on SOCIAL CONTRACT THEORY. Although it is clear that other stakeholder groups are affected by accounting and auditing standards, the role of their interests has not been explored. The other ethical problem is the identification of principles underlying standard setters' choices among alternative regulations. Various approaches have been offered, including rights theory (Gaa, 1988), duty theory (Ruland, 1984), justice theory (Williams, 1987), and a version of utilitarianism (Zeff, 1978).

Critical Approaches to Accounting

In the last fifteen years, a literature has appeared which seeks to explain accounting as a social institution. Two primary streams have developed. One employs various continental and postmodern theories, e.g., deconstructionism (Arrington and Francis, 1989).

The other stream is based on political theory. It focuses on several basic ideas, including a collective, rather than individual, approach to ethical issues; and the concepts that accounting is part of a power structure, and plays an active role in the success of corporations; that accountants are therefore not passive or neutral, but are partisans in a struggle for economic power; and that the accounting profession is regulated for the benefit of its members. In addition, many advocates of this point of view believe that more conventional approaches to accounting ethics serve to perpetuate the traditional understanding of accounting as a purely technical and neutral activity by providing rationalizations for the status quo. Examples of this literature include Cooper and Sherer (1984) and Tinker (1984).

See also **ethical issues in information; information, right to**

Bibliography

Arrington, E. & Francis, J. R. (1989). Letting the chat out of the bag: Deconstruction, privilege and accounting research. *Accounting, Organizations, and Society*, **15**, 1–28.

Briloff, A. (1990). Accountancy and society: A covenant desecrated. *Critical Perspectives on Accounting*, **1**, 5–30.

Carey, J. L. (1946). *Professional Ethics of Certified Public Accountants*. New York: American Institute of Accountants.

Commission on Auditors' Responsibilities. (1978). *Report, Conclusions, and Recommendations*. New York: Commission on Auditors' Responsibilities (American Institute of Certified Public Accountants).

Cooper, D. & Sherer, M. J. (1984). The value of corporate accounting reports: Arguments for a political economy of accounting. *Accounting, Organizations, and Society*, 9, 207–32.

Financial Accounting Standards Board. (1978). Statement of financial accounting concepts no. 1: Objectives of financial reporting by business enterprises. Stamford, Conn: FASB.

Gaa, J. C. (1988). Methodological foundations of standard settings for corporate financial report. *Studies in Accounting Research*, 28, Orlando, Fla: American Accounting Association.

Gaa, J. C. (1990). A game-theoretic analysis of professional rights and responsibilities. *Journal of Business Ethics*, 9 (1), 37–47.

Gaa, J. C. (1991). The expectations game: Regulation of auditors by government and the profession. *Critical Perspectives on Accounting*, 2, 83–107.

Gaa, J. C. (1993). The auditor's role: The philosophy and psychology of independence and objectivity. In R. Srivastava (ed.), , *Proceedings of the 1992 Deloitte and Touche/University of Kansas Symposium on Auditing Problems*. Lawrence, Kan: University of Kansas Press. 7–43.

Gaa, J. C. (1994). *The Ethical Foundations of Public Accounting*, Research Study no. 22. Vancouver, BC: CGA-Canada Research Foundation.

Lowe, H. J. (1987). Ethics in our 100-year history. *Journal of Accountancy*, 163, 78–87.

Mautz, R. K. & Sharaf, H. A. (1961). *The Philosophy of Auditing*. Sarasota, Fla: American Accounting Association.

Macdonald, W. A., chairman. (1988). Report of the Commission to Study the Public's Expectations of Audits. Toronto: Canadian Institute of Chartered Accountants.

Noreen, E. (1988). The economics of ethics: A new perspective on agency theory. *Accounting, Organizations and Society*, 13, 359–69.

Petitioner v. *Arthur Young & Company et al* No. 82-687. March 21, 1984. US Supreme Court Opinions, October Term, 1983. Reprinted in *The United States Law Week*, 52, (36) March 20, 1984.

Previts, G. J. (1985). *The Scope of CPA Services*. New York: Wiley.

Ruland, R. G. (1984). Duty, obligation, and responsibility in accounting policy making. *Journal of Accounting and Public Policy*, 3, 223–37.

Tinker, T. (1984). Theories of the state and the state of accounting: Economic reductionism and political voluntarism in accounting regulation theory. *Journal of Accounting and Public Policy*, 3, 55–74.

Treadway Commission (National Commission on Fraudulent Financial Reporting). (1987). Fraud commission issues final report. *Journal of Accountancy*, 164 (5), 39–48.

Williams, P. F. (1987). The legitimate concern with fairness. *Accounting, Organizations and Society*, 12, 169–89.

Zeff, S. (1978). The rise of economic consequences. *The Journal of Accountancy*, 158 , (6) 56–63.

JAMES C. GAA

accounting liability   *see* LIABILITY IN ACCOUNTING

acid rain   The term used to refer to pollution caused by higher than normal acidity in rain, fog, snow, and the like. Acid rain is created, at least in part, by burning coal and other fossil fuels. Carried by prevailing winds, emitted acids rain down on various regions. Oil, natural gas, and coal combustion in utility power plants and some industrial plants has been cited in many studies as the leading cause of lake acidification and fish kills in the north-eastern United States and south-eastern Canada. It may also adversely affect forest ecosystems, farmlands, groundwater, exposed surfaces of buildings, and human health. However, even the basic facts about acid rain remain disputed.

In the United States, many focus their attention on midwestern coal mines with a particularly high sulfur content. However, existing environmental regulations controlling the use of high sulfur coal have already had a severely negative impact on the region's economy; miners fear for their jobs and unemployment in these regions is high and increasing. Costs for public utilities are substantially higher, some coal-burning utilities operate on the margin of profitability, and many small industrial coal users may not survive.

Assessing responsibility for the problem is difficult. Tracking the atmospheric routes of acid rain from sources to destination is itself problematic. Some reports have even questioned whether coal-produced pollutants are as significant as local automobile and oil-burner emissions.

In November 1990, amendments to the Clean Air Act became law in the United States, creating a nationwide utility emissions cap on sulfur dioxide emissions of 8.9 million tons a year by the year 2000. After 2000 emissions must be kept at this level. The likely effects of this policy are disputed.

Bibliography

Mohnen, V. A. (1988). The challenge of acid rain. *Scientific American,* Aug.
White, J. C. (Ed.) (1987). *Acid Rain: The Relationship between Sources and Receptors.* New York: Elsevier.

TOM BEAUCHAMP

advertising, consumer prices and   *see* CONSUMER PRICES AND ADVERTISING

advertising ethics   the systematic study of how moral standards are applied to advertising decisions, behaviors, and institutions. It is a subset of business and marketing ethics (*see* MARKETING, ETHICS OF). It should be noted that many of the practices that critics of advertising consider to be "unethical" may also be violations of the law. Thus, the discussion which follows mentions some advertising practices that are outright transgressions of the law (e.g., deceptive advertising). But also discussed are actions that are legal but are nevertheless called into question because they arguably lack the degree of moral propriety that society would like to see advertising uphold. For instance, advertising practices which are perfectly legal but still raise ethical questions involve situations such as ads for target pistols in teen magazines, featuring bevies of bikini-clad women in beer commercials, and health claims for products that are not especially healthy.

The Nature and Scope of Advertising

Given the economic importance of advertising as well as its social visibility, it is not surprising that advertising comes under great public scrutiny. Critics have often complained about the lack of ethical evaluations of certain business practices (e.g., security trading by insiders), but there has been no shortage of attention devoted to advertising ethics and the social questions that it raises. One recent survey of the literature, using the ABI/Inform database, found 127 articles published on the topic of advertising ethics between 1987 and 1993 (Hyman et al., 1994). No doubt, part of the attention garnered by advertising is due to the fact that it is such a significant economic force in society. Over $148 billion was spent on advertising in the US in 1994. The cost of running a single 30 second commercial on US TV for the 1995 Super Bowl was over $1 million. Recognizing that advertising is *by definition* a one-sided, persuasive communication using the mass media and intending to advocate a sponsor's product or service, it should not be startling that much advertising fails to tell a fully informative story about the products that it endorses. In other words, a big part of the ethical concern about advertising stems from the fact that by its nature it is propaganda about the products and services that are available for sale. Some of this intentionally persuasive information may be valuable to potential buyers, while other parts may be misleading.

Macro- and Micro-Criticisms of Advertising

The ethical criticisms of advertising can be categorized as *macro* or *micro*. Macro-criticisms of advertising generally deal with the negative impact of advertising upon society. For example, could the $148 billion allocated to advertising be more usefully spent attempting to achieve other economic goals? Does advertising help foster a culture of materialism? Micro-ethical criticisms of advertising focus on the propriety of specific advertising practices. For example, should cartoon characters be allowed to pitch products on programs targeted for children? (*See also* ADVERTISING TO CHILDREN). Should ads for contraceptives be shown on network TV? Should subliminal messages be permitted? (*See also* SUBLIMINAL ADVERTISING).

Historically, the macro-debate about advertising ethics has a long tradition. For instance in 1907, one critic of advertising wrote, "On the moral side, it [advertising] is thoroughly false and harmful. It breeds vulgarity, hypnotizes the imagination and the will, fosters covetousness, envy, hatred, and underhand competition" (Logan, 1907).

Some of the macro-ethical problems of the advertising industry might be summarized along the following lines. First, there is the contention that such persuasion violates people's inherent rights. The issue here is that so much advertising is persuasively one-sided that it violates the principle of FAIRNESS by depriving consumers of unbiased input with which to make an informed buying decision. Second, there is the charge that advertising encourages certain human addictions. The focus here would be upon the societal appropriateness of *any* advertising campaigns for controversial products such as cigarettes, tobacco, pornography, and firearms. Third, there is the fact that the motivation behind advertising involves trying to make money, not to foster the truth. The question here is the extent to which a certain proportion of advertising will always be inherently misleading because it nurtures false implications or associates product usage with a lifestyle or social image that may have little to do with the product. For example, can drinkers of Old Milwaukee beer really expect to find themselves in a situation where "it doesn't get any better than this"? Fourth, there is the belief that advertising frequently degenerates into vulgarization. For example, the exploitation of women in advertising as well as the use of fear appeals (e.g., you will be socially ostracized without fresh breath gum) would be representative of this criticism. The use of ads which parody great books and famous quotations, as well as notable art, architecture, or people is a further illustration of this critique.

The most common response to many macro-criticisms of the advertising industry is that advertising is little more than a mirror of the current character of society (Pollay, 1986). The argument goes as follows: as a "looking glass" that reflects the attitudes of society, one should expect that sometimes advertising is deceptive just as other forms of communication might be deceptive or misleading. And, sometimes advertising will be in "bad taste" just as some art or movies or political speeches might prove to be in poor taste. These defenders of advertising would further contend that the vast majority of advertising provides useful information which allows consumers to glean important facts and thereby enhances the efficiency of product choice (Levitt, 1970). Therefore, despite the

use of inherently persuasive techniques, having corporation-sponsored information about the products and services available in a complex, consumption-driven economy provides more benefits than dysfunctions. Such pragmatic and utilitarian analysis is commonly employed by defenders of advertising (*see* UTILITARIANISM).

Consider the following as a "case in point" concerning the utilitarian trade-off inherent in advertising. Recent analysis of six decades of research dealing with consumer perceptions of advertising concludes that the typical consumer finds most advertising definitely informative and the best means of learning what is available on the market (Calfee & Ringold, 1994). However, the study also suggests that, consistent over time, approximately 70 percent of consumers believe that advertising is often untruthful and may persuade people to buy things they do not want. But, on balance, the valuable information provided by advertising is worth the deficiencies caused by its inherent persuasiveness (Calfee & Ringold, 1994).

With regard to the micro-objections to advertising, the list of criticisms is long. A recent survey of advertising practitioners shows that the current area of advertising practice generating the highest level of ethical concern is the continued use of deceptive advertising. Other concerns in the "top five" involve exploitative advertising to children, ads for tobacco and alcoholic beverages, the increased use of negative political ads, and stereotyping in advertising (Hyman et al., 1994). While granting the problematic nature of many of these specific practices, defenders of advertising are quite adamant in their view that most advertising is not only ethical but helpful. Though beyond the scope of this entry, philosophers such as Arrington (1982) have provided tightly argued analyses suggesting that the vast majority of advertising is neither manipulative nor deceptive because it generally does not violate the various criteria which constitute consumer autonomy.

Regulation of Advertising Practices

In theory at least, the consumer is protected from many questionable advertising practices via government regulation as well as the self-regulation provided by the advertising industry. In the USA, industry regulation is provided by the National Advertising Division (NAD) of the Better Business Bureau. This group, established in 1971, investigates almost 200 cases of unfairness in advertising annually. Many of the questionable ads brought to the NAD are identified by fellow competitors, which would seem to indicate that advertisers are guardians of their own honesty. Most of the disputes brought at this level (approximately 98 percent) are resolved, but for those cases still at question, the National Advertising Review Board (NARB) becomes a court of appeal. The NARB is staffed by members of the advertising profession as well as informed persons from the general public. Given that this control process is an industry-wide effort to maintain the integrity of advertising, endorsed and adjudicated by the industry itself, there is great pressure upon advertisers to abide by the findings of the NAD/NARB. Still, there might be advertising practices that would require a stronger form of intervention which can only be provided by the force of government regulation.

The linchpin of government oversight of advertising in the US is provided by the Federal Trade Commission (FTC). The commission was established in 1914. It has jurisdiction to police all forms of false and deceptive trade practices, including advertising (*see* MARKETING, ANTI-COMPETITIVE PRACTICES IN). The FTC has gone through relative periods of activity and inactivity, depending upon the political climate of the country. In part, the level of regulatory fervor is due to the zeal of the commissioners who control the FTC and who are political appointees. Nonetheless, at all times the FTC protects the public from the most egregious forms of deceptive advertising. The FTC is assisted by various other government agencies, such as the Food and Drug Administration (FDA) which, as its name implies, has jurisdiction over the advertising of food and drug products. For example, the recent regulatory changes requiring improved nutritional labeling and disclosure were the result of cooperation between the FDA and the FTC. Still another government agency important in the oversight of advertising is the Bureau of Alcohol, Tobacco, and Firearms (BATF) a division of the US Department of Treasury. It regulates all aspects of the sale of products for which the division is named.

The Credibility of Advertising

While many feel the combination of industry self-regulation and the Federal Trade Commission provides an appropriate safety net against deceptive advertising, regulatory efforts are not without their critics, some of whom believe that much unethical advertising remains. For example, Preston (1994), in a comprehensive analysis contends that advertisers, by providing only partial truth (i.e., one-sided argumentation) about their products and services, contribute to the "diminishment of the truth". Why? Partial truth is a form of falsity that harms many consumers who cannot be expected to gather sufficient buying information without reliance upon advertising claims. Preston proposes a reinvention of advertising regulation via the "reliance rule" which would require that the only product claims allowed would be those that advertisers advocate as being important enough for consumers to make buying decisions on. In other words, advertisers would be limited to making claims about product attributes which embody distinct reasons for purchasing a particular product. Thus claims such as "Pontiac is excitement" would have no standing because it is an unprovable "puff". Whereas a claim such as, "This model Pontiac will provide 30 miles per gallon" would be permitted – assuming the mpg figure can be substantiated.

The Ethics of the Advertising Industry

Another set of issues to be addressed has to do with the set of actors that orchestrate modern advertising. Major players in the advertising industry are *sponsors* of advertising (e.g., corporations), *advertising agencies* (the makers of ad campaigns), and the *media* which carries advertising messages. The complexity of relationships among these three groups often creates ethical conflicts. For example, the media is dependent for much of its operating revenues upon the advertising dollars that underwrite its programming. Thus, the ethical question is often raised about the extent to which advertising is able to shape media programming – especially its influence over news media content that is critical of an advertising sponsor. Similarly, advertising agencies are often financially rewarded based on the amount of media time that they buy rather than the quality of the advertising they produce. Thus, there can be inherent pressures on ad agencies to push for more advertising rather than searching for the optimal ad campaign that best serves the sponsoring company.

To understand how ethical issues are addressed by advertisers, some questions must be asked about the values inherent in the advertising community. What do advertising people consider to be unethical? What is the prevailing professional ethic of advertising? Some of the substance of this ethic can be ascertained by looking at the codes of ethics which have been promulgated by the American Association of Advertising Agencies (4As) and the American Advertising Federation (AAF) (see PROFESSIONAL CODES). Both codes contain the following provisions:

- There are prohibitions against false and misleading statements.

- Testimonials that do not reflect the real opinion of individuals involved are forbidden.

- Price claims that are misleading are not allowed.

- Statements or pictures offensive to the public decency are to be avoided.

- Unsubstantiated performance claims are never to be used.

Such admonitions serve as absolutes in guiding advertising practice. In effect, they become the lowest common denominator in shaping the professional ethic of advertising practitioners. One major disadvantage of the approach used by the 4As and the AAF in their codes is that their prohibitions are formulated in terms of "negative" absolutes – in other words, practices that formulators of advertising should *not* engage in. These negative absolutes have value because they suggest (for example) that to be ethical, advertisers should not lie to customers, should not steal competitor ideas for their own campaigns, should not cheat the media, etc. However, some observers of the advertising industry have suggested that "positive" absolutes, which stress the meritorious duties advertisers ought to engage in, provide a more inspirational avenue for shaping advertising

practice. An example of a positive meritorious duty would be the "principle of fairness." Applied to advertising, it might be stated as follows: "Advertisers must take fairness into consideration in their dealings with consumers, clients, suppliers, vendors, the media, employees, and agency management." And taking this meritorious duty a step further and linking it with elements of Kant's well-known categorical imperative, one could further add that "advertising should never treat its audience or spokespersons as mere means." An illustration of a TV ad campaign to which the above principle might be applied is the controversial Swedish bikini team commercial which was used by Heilemann Brewing Company to promote one of its brands of beer. In this situation, one could apply the principle and contend that while the use of such blatant sex appeals constituted a memorable television commercial, the salacious portrayal of women featured in the ad was an inappropriate means for seeking economic success.

The difficulty of all moral imperatives such as the fairness principle is that they are often difficult to apply to specific situations. For example, the vast majority of advertising practitioners would agree with the guideline that testimonial ads should not use celebrity spokespeople to endorse products which the spokespeople have never used. Suppose, however, a company hires a well-known actor who has never previously used a particular product but upon signing his endorsement contract, honestly concludes that the product is a superior one. Is this a misleading use of testimonials? The case is debatable.

Conclusion

In the end, many advertising practitioners fall back to a pragmatic defense of the current system of advertising. They argue from a consequentialist point of view that "if you don't like the advertising, consumers won't buy the product and the ad sponsors will be punished at the cash register."

In summary, advertising contributes much informational value to consumers. The most obvious forms of deception and unfairness in US advertising are mitigated by industry self-regulation, governmental controls, and the inherent professional ethic of the ad industry. But because advertising is undertaken for the primary purpose of selling specific products and services, it undoubtedly will continue to generate much ethical controversy because it is fundamentally an exercise in commercial persuasion.

Bibliography

Arrington, R. L. (1982). Advertising and behavior control. *Journal of Business Ethics,* **1,** 3–12.

Calfee, J. E. & Ringold, D. J. (1994). The 70% majority: Enduring consumer beliefs about advertising. *Journal of Public Policy and Marketing,* **13,** 228–38.

Hyman, M. R., Tansey, R. & Clark, J. W. (1994). Research on advertising ethics: Past, present, and future. *Journal of Advertising,* **23,** 5–15.

Laczniak, G. R. & Caywood, C. L. (1987). The case for and against televised political advertising: Implications for research and public policy. *Journal of Public Policy and Marketing,* **6,** 16–32.

Levitt, T. (1970). The morality (?) of advertising. *Harvard Business Review,* **48,** 84–92.

Logan, J. D. (1907). Social evolution and advertising. *Canadian Magazine,* **28,** 333.

Pollay, R. W. (1986). The distorted mirror: Reflections on the unintended consequences of advertising. *Journal of Marketing,* **50,** 18–36.

Preston, I. L. (1994). *The Tangled Web They Weave: Truth, Falsity, and Advertisers.* Madison, Wis: University of Wisconsin Press.

Rotzoll, K. & Haefner, J. (1990). *Advertising in Contemporary Society.* Cincinnati, Ohio: South-Western.

GENE R. LACZNIAK

advertising to children, ethics of   It has been estimated that children between the ages of 4 and 12 spent over $6 billion in the United States in 1989, and that expenditures in major media directed explicitly to children might be as high as $750 million (McNeal, 1992). In addition, many other channels are used to reach children, including in-store merchandising, in-class TV shows and school hall billboards (Consumer Reports, 1995), 30- to 60-minute TV cartoon shows based on commercially available toy personalities, product placements in the movies, product packaging ads ostensibly directed to parents, "kids clubs," all of which mean that the actual expenditures are much higher.

The historical criticisms of advertising – even when the claims are factually correct – have included a putative ability to manipulate persons to buy products "they don't need," a tendency to materialism in society, and a development of "false values" (Drumwright, 1993). False and grossly misleading advertising is universally condemned, and while "puffery" – partial truths and/or exaggerated suggestions and tone – is accepted, it is said to develop cynicism toward the practice and worth of advertising in particular and to market economies in general. The ethical issues surrounding advertising are magnified when children become the target. In a survey of 124 *Journal of Advertising* reviewers and a random sample of American Academy of Advertising members, respondents ranked "advertising to children" (after "use of deception in ads") as the second most important topic for the study of advertising ethics (Hyman et al., 1994).

Most societies hold children in special regard: the mistreatment of children is seen as more odious than that of adults, and their protection is given high priority. The major concerns with respect to children's advertising center on a child's relative inexperience with money and shopping, and therefore with his/her poorly developed sense of critical judgment. Children have, fundamentally, an undeveloped sense of "self" – and so critics view advertising as engendering a false sense of needs, a short-term horizon for satisfaction and a taste for banal or even harmful products. In this view, the child is seen as an easier prey, a dupe to the lure of slickly packaged advertising claims, and is exhorted to put pressure on mom or dad to "make me happy." Studies have shown that children "lack the conceptual wherewithal to research and deliberate about the relative merits of alternative expenditures in light of their economic resources" (Paine, 1992). In the extreme, there is the concern that children are "trained" to be materialistic and will become cynical about society through what critics feel will be inevitably unfulfilled product expectation.

The increasing use of television advertising to children led to consumer pressure for more US government regulation starting in the late 1960s. After continued pressure from parents, The Children's Television Act of 1990 was passed, which limits advertising to 10.5 minutes per hour of weekend shows and to 12 minutes per weekday hour, and which requires television stations to document how they have served the "education needs" of children as part of their license renewal review (Drumwright, 1993).

Bibliography

Drumwright, M. E. (1993). Ethical issues in advertising and sales promotion. In N. Craig Smith & J. A. Quelch (eds), *Ethics in Marketing*. Homewood: Irwin.

Hyman, M. R., Tansey, R. & Clark, J. W. (1994). Research on advertising ethics: Past, present, and future. *Journal of Advertising* (Special Issue on Ethics in Advertising),**23** (3), 5–15.

McNeal, J. U. (1991). *A Bibliography of Research and Writings on Marketing and Advertising to Children*. New York: Lexington Books.

McNeal, J. U. (1992). *Kids as Customers, A Handbook of Marketing to Children*. New York: Lexington Books.

Paine, L. S. (1993). Children as consumers: The ethics of children's television advertising. In N. Craig Smith & J. A. Quelch (eds), *Ethics in Marketing*. Homewood: Irwin.

Selling to school kids. *Consumer Reports,* May 1995, 327–9.

CHRISTOPHER GALE

affirmative action programs   are efforts to increase the representation, in certain positions of organizations, of groups that have not traditionally been part of such organizations or have not held such positions. These efforts are especially to be found in cases where the groups in question have traditionally been discriminated against for such positions, or actively discouraged from applying for them. Affirmative action includes attempts to recruit men as nurses and women as engineers; attempts to recruit African American students at Amherst College and white students at Howard University. Affirmative action can occur on a national level: since women, Hispanics, and African Americans have traditionally not attained positions of high rank in business or in government, all efforts to place persons of that description in such positions count as affirmative action. More familiarly, it occurs on a local level: for historical reasons, Jews and African Americans may be in short supply at some universities, and Hispanics and Asians lacking in some occupations, in which cases it would be an effort of "affirmative action" to find members of just those groups to become part of just those institutions.

Affirmative action is justified primarily by an appeal to justice, and derives from a national commitment to equality of opportunity to participate in all occupations and all educational programs. On its usual rationale, it is argued that all groups of people are fundamentally equal in distribution of talents; therefore, if we find one group participating in some occupation or profession in percentages well below that found in the population (especially the local population), it's probably because the members of that group have been discriminated against in the past. Because of that history, it is no longer sufficient just to open the doors and say that from now on one will honor the principles of equal opportunity, for the members of the disfavored group have given up looking to enter by those doors. Therefore, it is argued that one must seek out and find qualified members and actively work to incorporate them in professions and enterprises. This effort is demanded by the duty of COMPENSATORY JUSTICE to make up for past wrongs.

Affirmative action can also be justified by utilitarian considerations, since a richer social environment is better than a poorer one, and persons of many groups and backgrounds make for a more interesting organization (*see* UTILITARIANISM). It is also good for students and managers to get used to having African Americans and women in the roles of authority from which they had been excluded, since it will be more difficult for them to work productively with supervisors whose legitimacy they doubt on grounds of group membership. Multinational corporations often seek a diversified workforce to represent the diverse nations in which they carry on their operations (*see* MULTINATIONALS).

If the duty to engage in affirmative action spills over into "reverse discrimination," i.e., a requirement that *only* a person of the previously disfavored group may be accepted or hired, then a serious injustice occurs unless all advertising for that position make the exclusion clear. It cannot be fair to advertise a job as open to all on the basis of equal opportunity, while privately intending to examine the credentials of only certain groups.

Bibliography

Cahn, S. M. (ed.), (1995). *The Affirmative Action Debate*. London and New York: Routledge.

Gold, S. J. (ed.), (1993). *Moral Controversies: Race, Class and Gender in Applied Ethics*. Belmont, Calif: Wadsworth.

Gross, B. R. (ed.), (1977). *Reverse Discrimination*. Buffalo, NY: Prometheus Books.

LISA H. NEWTON

Africa, business ethics in *see* BUSINESS ETHICS IN SOUTH AFRICA

agency theory   The theory of agency, an approach that has seen many applications across the social sciences and the disciplines of management, seeks to understand the problems created when one party is acting for another. Agents typically face a variety of problems when acting for their principals, and principals face many problems in ensuring that the actions of their agents realize the principal's preferences. Thus agency, and the agency theory constructed to provide understanding of agency behaviors, shows two faces: the activities and problems of identifying and providing services of "acting for" (the agent side), and the activities and problems of guiding and correcting agent actions (the principal side).

One of the key observations in agency theory is that all action has real or perceived costs, so that the corrections necessary to improve the quality of agent and principal actions in their relationship all have costs. As a result, it may not pay the agent, the principal, or third parties to invest in correction of this behavior where the gains from correction do not exceed the costs of performing the correction. A similar reasoning applies to the identification and specification of actions to be taken by the agent; it may not pay to find out exactly what the principal wants, nor to tell the agent that. In addition, a host of factors can produce specification and correction attempts that occur imperfectly; they may even fail to occur at all. Such factors include errors in

perception, inadequacies in detection and/or in performance skills, failures in communication, conflicts of interest and/or risk preference, variations in information possession, emergent processes from system or network behavior, and problematic institutional structures. Deviant behaviors may even be institutionalized and socially protected. Kenneth Arrow terms the critical problems of agency "hidden information" (adverse selection) and "hidden action" (moral hazard) problems (Arrow, in Pratt and Zeckhauser, 1985); these terms may not, however, capture the full range of factors at work (*see* MORAL HAZARD). Indeed, the careful identification of the sources of problems in agency is still a current area of research.

The logic of agency therefore predicts that deviant behaviors can persist, and be tolerated. Indeed, "perfect agency" rarely occurs, and agency theory itself becomes a study in the production, the persistence, and the amelioration of failures in service and in control.

Because agency typically occurs not only in dyads but also in organizational and higher-level systems, the complexity of agency problems, as well as of their remediation, can multiply. Agency theory seeks to build theoretical explanations of behavior within such dyadic relationships, as well as within the complex networks in which they are embedded. To date relatively little agency theory has examined organizational systems, networks, and extended emergent structures composed of agency relations; there is indeed work in this area, but most study has been directed at more accessible problems within dyads, simple multiple agent/multiple principal conditions, and relatively simple supervisory or hierarchical structures. Agency relations can be viewed as building blocks of more complex settings, however, and so future work may tackle such contexts.

Though it is most closely associated with the modeling of firm behavior by financial economists and accountants, agency theory in fact is not, nor has it ever been, limited to theoretical contexts constrained by particular assumptions embedded in economic theory, nor to the modeling of the corporation alone. Its potential lies in its status as a general social theory of relationships of "acting for" or control in complex systems. The trend in work in agency is to introduce ever more descriptive analysis, with better grounding in the descriptive details of organizational life.

Despite this, references in the literature to "agency theory" often assume that agency theory is a narrow approach rooted in economics. As such it is assumed to make relatively simple or incomplete assumptions about human motivation (either self-interest or utility maximization) and to model organizations in terms of decision structures, assignments, and processes, thereby greatly simplifying institutional features. A great deal of criticism has been directed at the agency approach as a result, but at least some of that criticism really applies only to a particular modeling subset of work in agency.

In fact, work in agency theory extends considerably beyond the economics paradigm and includes attention to a variety of normative, institutional, cognitive, social, and systemic factors. In addition, agency theory should not be viewed as a theory of the firm alone, which is merely one application of it. Agency is a general approach to the study of a common social relation, that of "acting for."

The intellectual ancestors of agency theory go back at least to the 1930s, with Ronald Coase's work on the firm and Chester Barnard's classic work on the functions of the executive. There are forebears as well in sociology in some of the classic works of Mead and Simmel.

In economics, the stream passes through the series of studies in the divergence of owner and manager interests and behavior (from scholars such as BERLE and MEANS through Papandreou, Penrose, Marris, and Baumol to Williamson's theory of managerial discretion; see also work on agency and the firm by Harvey Leibenstein). Marshak and Radner's work on the theory of teams and Spence and Zeckhauser's work on risk and insurance highlighted the effects of differing information states and risk preferences. Oliver Williamson's transaction-costs approach applied a costs model to the study of exchange and its internalization in organization that has a cousin in agency's use of costs of correction in its modeling of control. Alchian and Demsetz explained the emergence of organization based on the need to monitor individual contributions in situations of joint production; it is often seen as one of the

foundational works in an agency theory of the firm. In several works, Arrow observed the importance of considering non-economic factors in relations in which one party acts for another. Several other early papers used agency concepts in an economics context, though they did not appear to see or propose agency as a coherent and general theoretical approach; these included works by Victor Goldberg and Barry Weingast.

In political science, Herbert Simon's work on administrative behavior and on the employment relation (see also the later related work on this in economics by Williamson, Wachter, and Harris), March and Simon's inducements-contributions model, and Clark and Wilson's incentive systems theory constructed a stream out of Barnard that flows directly into modern institutional agency theory. Those who view agency as a creature of economics often miss these critical theoretical ties. In addition, work in sociology on exchange theory by such scholars as George Homans, Peter Blau, Richard Emerson, Bo Anderson, Karen Cook, and Peter Marsden should be seen as theoretical development cognate to that in agency and in the transaction-costs literature in economics.

The first explicit proposals that a systematic theory of agency would be valuable and ought to be constructed, and the first works explicitly beginning such construction, apparently came from Stephen Ross (1973) and Barry Mitnick (1973, 1975), independently. Ross's work was anchored in financial economics; Mitnick's was more generally based in social science, including political science and sociology. Each reflected the tools then currrent in their disciplines. Ross was the first to clearly identify and worry about the resolution of "agency problems" and to try to derive formal conclusions about the nature of successful incentive contracts in agency; Mitnick's work was the first to lay out a broad framework structuring agency theory and to actually develop a series of small theoretical applications of agency, such as the consequences of agents bargaining with each other. Ross's work may be seen as the explicit start of the "economic" theory of agency; Mitnick's, of what may be termed the "institutional" theory of agency.

The work that has probably had the biggest impact on agency studies is the already classic piece by Jensen and Meckling (1976), which provided an explicit agency theory of the firm as a "nexus of contracts" (*see* CONTRACTS AND CONTRACTING). Subsequent work by Eugene Fama and Jensen identified the decision process in firms as central, and argued that study of the assignment of rights to "decision management" and "decision control" could explain many features of firm behavior. The contexts of this work usually concern the economic theory of the firm, not necessarily a general theory of agency relations in social behavior.

At present there is no unified, coherent "theory of agency." Depending on the research tradition in which the particular work in agency has been developed, different explicit logics, based in different social science literatures, such as economics or sociology, and sometimes displaying divergent approaches even within disciplines, are used to construct explanations. This produces the appearance of streams of work, each stream tending to operate within its own assumptional world. This is true even within the economics area, where agency work divides into formal mathematical modeling and modeling based in a more descriptive theory of the firm. The accounting literature also features behavioral/descriptive theoretic works in such areas as auditing relationships, ethical issues (see Noreen, 1988), and contract design (including such public sector application areas as contracting out and municipal bond decisions). The formal work in economics, finance, and accounting features proofs of theorems based in assumptions about such characteristics of the agency situation as the preferences (including risk) of the agent and principal, the contract between them and its incentive structure, the sequencing of action in the relation, and conditions of information held by the parties about each other and the state of the environment.

In contrast, some of the work in management, sociology, and political science has explored agency using variables and perspectives that are of more traditional interest within those fields. For example, there is work in agency now examining the role of trust and of sociological norms (e.g., Mitnick, 1973, 1975, on norms in agency; Shapiro, 1987, on trust; there is work by Mitnick and by the sociologist Arthur Stinchcombe on what they call the "fiduciary norm") (*see* FIDUCIARY DUTY; FIDUCIARY RESPONSI-

BILITY). The study of control has been linked to older traditions in those fields, as well as to newer networks approaches, by such scholars as Robert Eccles, Kathleen Eisenhardt (1989), and Harrison White. Agency analysis has been applied to such older topics for study as political corruption and bureaucratic behavior by such scholars as Edward Banfield, Gary Miller, Barry Mitnick, Terry Moe (1984), and Susan Rose-Ackerman. In addition, agency has been used to study corporate political activity (e.g., Mitnick, 1993). There are quite a number of applications of agency to government regulation, for example, by Mitnick, Barry Weingast, Pablo Spiller, and Jeffrey Cohen. In management, scholars have used (or modified) agency approaches to explore such topics as behavior in boards of directors (e.g., work by Barry Baysinger, by Gerald Davis, and by Edward Zajac), organizational control (e.g., work by Donaldson and Davis, by Kathleen Eisenhardt, by Huseyin Leblebici, by Benjamin Oviatt, and by James Walsh), bargaining (e.g., work by Lax and Sebenius), and compensation practices (e.g., work by Luis Gomez-Mejia, by Henry Tosi, and by Conlon and Parks) (*see* CORPORATE GOVERNANCE; NEGOTIATION AND BARGAINING). Agency has also seen some attention in the marketing literature. The appearance of each body of work more nearly resembles the kinds of theory construction and hypothesis testing practiced in these disciplines.

In an important stream of work, Lex Donaldson and James Davis (see, e.g., 1994) demonstrate via their "theory of stewardship" how theory development on the firm can escape or modify the constraints of the economics model. Indeed, given our view of the duality of agency, the economic theory of agency seems biased toward the analysis of corrections; it is a theory of control (or of who gets control, such as decision rights). But agency has two sides: control and service. There is no reason why a viable theory of the firm cannot be constructed taking the service side as primary (e.g., other things equal, managers seek performance; correction is then taken as a secondary, marginal activity). Of course, the most descriptive theory of the firm may take a contingent approach that simply uses the conceptual tools of both service and control to understand the production of behavior in and around the firm.

It is probably true that the scholars using agency theory have tended to rely on the sources for that theory with which they are most familiar. Because most scholars have assumed that agency originated in economics they have tended to use the major works there, such as Jensen and Meckling (1976), and adapted its features to the study at hand. This tends to lead to more limited kinds of analysis as assumptions more appropriate to the economics paradigm are imported into settings for which social science has additional tools available.

It is important to be aware of the differences between agency theory and the law of agency. In the law of agency it is presumed that the agent is acting under the orders of the principal; the law itself acts, of course, as a normative guide to behavior and to the resolution of disputes regarding appropriate action in agency roles (see the *Restatement of Agency, 2d*). Agency theory is just that, a group of descriptive theoretical approaches that seek to provide understanding of a broad class of social behaviors; agents need not be presumed to be under explicit direction and hence possessing particular obligations. The law of agency does, however, provide rich materials for exploration via agency theory, and contributes central insights that can expand the quality and domain of agency theory (the first such use of the law of agency was by Mitnick, 1973, but there has been a scattering of work by such scholars as Robert Clark, Frank Easterbrook, and Daniel Fischel, and in a number of law reviews). The same may be said of the related bodies of law and legal analysis in contracts and trusts; of particular interest is work on "relational contracting" by Ian Macneil.

Applications of concepts relevant to agency are found in numerous places in the business ethics literature, but, with the exception of the volume edited by Bowie and Freeman (1992) and some scattered work elsewhere (see, e.g., Noreen, 1988, and work in accounting by Wanda Wallace), most applications in business ethics use materials based in the law of agency (e.g., the concept of fiduciary duty) and in moral philosophy (e.g., the obligations of the moral agent) (*see* MORAL AGENCY; CORPORATE MORAL AGENCY). Agency as a descriptive theory of service and control ought to be capable of providing increased understanding of the dilemmas produced in the pervasive agency relations of business.

Bibliography

Donaldson, L. & Davis, J. (1994). Boards and company performance: Research challenges the conventional wisdom. *Corporate Governance: An International Review*, **2**, 151–60.

Eisenhardt, K. M. (1989). Agency theory: An assessment and review. *Academy of Management Review*, **14**, 57–74.

Jensen, M. C. & Meckling, W. H. (1976). Theory of the firm: Managerial behavior, agency costs and ownership structure. *Journal of Financial Economics*, **3**, 305–60.

Mitnick, B. M. (1973). Fiduciary responsibility and public policy: The theory of agency and some consequences. *Proceedings of the 1973 Annual Meeting of the American Political Science Association*, New Orleans, La., 69, Ann Arbor, Mich.: UMI.

Mitnick, B. M. (1975). The theory of agency: The policing "paradox" and regulatory behavior. *Public Choice*, **24** (winter), 27–42.

Mitnick, B. M. (1992). The theory of agency and organizational analysis. In N. Bowie and R. E. Freeman (eds), *Ethics and Agency Theory*. New York: Oxford University Press, 75–96.

Mitnick, B. M. (ed.), (1993). *Corporate Political Agency: The Construction of Competition in Public Affairs*. Newbury Park, Calif.: Sage Publications.

Moe, T. M. (1984). The new economics of organization. *American Journal of Political Science*, **28**, 739–77.

Noreen, E. (1988). The economics of ethics: A new perspective on agency theory. *Accounting, Organizations and Society*, **13**, 359–69.

Pratt, J. W. & Zeckhauser, R. (eds), (1985). *Principals and Agents: The Structure of Business*. Boston: Harvard Business School Press.

Ross, S. A. (1973). The economic theory of agency: The principal's problem. *American Economic Review*, **62**, 134–9.

Shapiro, S. P. (1987). The social control of impersonal trust. *American Journal of Sociology*, **93**, 623–58.

BARRY M. MITNICK

agriculture, ethics of   Agriculture ethics is the field of study concerned with normative assumptions, value conflicts, and ethical controversies surrounding the production and distribution of food and fiber. Like most other sub-fields of applied ethics, it arose in the last two decades as is indicated by the year of the initial publication of its two primary professional journals, *Agriculture and Human Values* (1984) and *Journal of Agriculture and Environmental Ethics* (1988), and by the publication in 1991 of its first comprehensive teaching anthology, *Ethics and Agriculture* (Blatz). However, the social, ethical, and value issues surrounding agriculture have long been debated. Agriculture plays a distinctive role in the life of our species. Its origin parallels the rise of human civilization some ten thousand years ago, and no doubt played a substantial role in that rise. For most people who have lived since then, agriculture has provided not only the sustenance necessary for life itself, but a way of life as well. Only recently and only in some parts of the world has it become predominantly an industrialized business enterprise. Adequate food has always been crucially linked to human survival, well-being, and thriving. So, too, has the production and distribution of food. It is of ever-increasing importance to human beings whose nearly six billion numbers will increase to over ten billion in the next century. With one billion people currently undernourished, human well-being will increasingly depend upon the production and distribution of a sufficient quantity and quality of agriculture products. Thus, unlike some other activities, agriculture is essential for human survival.

Although the ethical issues surrounding agriculture are numerous, complex, and overlapping, they can be described in four basic types.

Production

First, are ethical concerns surrounding production. For instance, assuming the responsibility not to harm consumers, there are ethical issues involving product quality and safety, such as the safety of pesticide residue on fruits and vegetables and chemical additives in animal products, including those created by biotechnological methods. Assuming the responsibility not to endanger workers, there are ethical issues involving the health, safety, and fair treatment of farm workers, especially seasonal workers who traditionally have not been protected by government labor laws. Assuming the responsibility to treat animals in a morally acceptable manner, there is much controversy over intensive "factory farming," especially of poultry. Assuming there is value in preserving rural culture and communities with owner-operator farms, there is concern over the acceptability of the social consequences of the increasing trend toward concentration, vastness of scale, corporate contract farming, and vertical integration. Of course, each of these initial moral assumptions requires defense.

The Environment

Second, there are ethical issues involving environmental impact and use of natural resources. For instance: the conservation, protection, and just distribution of ground and surface water; the consequences of cultivation involving intensive chemical fertilizers and poisons, and their uses, on the soil's long-term fertility, regional ecosystems, beneficial insects and birds, and other wild species of flora and fauna; the protection of fragile semi-arable land from destructive agriculture or ranching practices; the necessity of preserving the genetic diversity of wild-land races and locally adapted cultivars to guard against disastrous crop failures and to ensure a sufficient gene pool for future generations. These controversies raise moral questions about our obligations to future generations, about our responsibility to preserve and protect other species and biodiversity, and about our role in enhancing ecosystem integrity and health. They also raise questions of the scope and strength of property rights and rights to water use.

The Role of the Public

Third, there are controversies surrounding the public's role in agriculture. What should be the primary goals and objectives of a government's agricultural policy, regulation, research, and extension services? Should it be to ensure national food security, to protect rural communities and the family farm, to insure high quality and low consumer prices, to control land use and regulate practices to enhance long-term sustainable methods, to enhance competition and market efficiency, to restrict urban growth on arable land? Involved here are moral controversies involving both property rights, group rights, and human rights; the identification and weight of the common good within a representative system; the time frame for calculating public social utility; and issues of distributive justice, social equity, and fairness.

International Issues

Fourth are moral issues involving international development of agriculture. There are controversies which arise over the moral appropriateness of using food as a "weapon" to manipulate other governments. Also of concern are protectionistic policies which severely disadvantage other nations, for example, price supports for some commodities such as sugar, or the subsidized dumping of surplus grain that can undercut the recipient's indigenous agriculture and create a dependency on imports. There is a concern over aggressive marketing of agricultural chemicals overseas that are banned from use in this country. Finally, are the concerns over the moral acceptability of social, political, environmental, cultural, and economic consequences of the exportation of agricultural technologies that are energy and chemical intensive, such as the 1970s Green Revolution and the present "gene revolution." Involved here are the basis, nature, and extent of our moral responsibility to distant peoples; is it just to refrain from directly harming or wronging them, or does it also involve furthering their prospects or even enhancing their welfare? Do all humans have a moral right to adequate food and clothing, and, if so, who is obligated to satisfy these rights? What are the proper roles, if any, of individuals, governments, agribusiness corporations, and international agencies in promoting a just international economic order that would grant all people access to affordable food sufficient to meet their basic needs?

There are many fundamental ethical questions raised by the rapidly changing enterprise of agriculture and its increasingly global standardization that are of yet unanswered. As agriculture ethics matures as a discipline and as dialogue between the various interested and affected sectors and actors increases, hopefully there will emerge more clarity and agreement on some of these important issues.

Bibliography

Blatz, C. V. (ed.). (1991). *Ethics and Agriculture: An Anthology on Current Issues in World Contexts.* Moscow, Idaho: University of Idaho Press.

Busch, L. & Lacy, W. B. (eds). (1984). *Food Security in the United States.* Boulder, Colo.: Westview Press.

Dahlberg, K. A. (ed.). (1986). *New Directions for Agriculture and Agricultural Research.* Totowa, NJ: Rowman and Allanheld.

Dreze, J. & Sen, A. (1989). *Hunger and Public Action.* Oxford: Clarendon Press.

Gendel, S. M., et al. (eds). (1990). *Agricultural Bioethics: Implications of Agricultural Biotechnology.* Ames, Iowa: Iowa State University Press.

Haynes, R. & Lanier, R. (eds). (1984). *Agriculture, Change and Human Values: Proceedings of a Multidisciplinary Conference.* Gainesville, Fla.: The Humanities and Culture Program of the University of Florida.

Thompson, P. B., et al. (eds). (1994). *Ethics, Public Policy, and Agriculture.* New York: Macmillan.

WILLIAM AIKEN

AIDS an acronym for Acquired Immunodeficiency Syndrome. AIDS is generally, although not universally, thought to be associated with the presence of HIV, the Human Immunodeficiency Virus. Evidence suggests that HIV is spread through transmission of bodily fluids typically associated with intimate sexual contact and/or intravenous drug use. HIV is fragile once outside the body, and is therefore not transmittable through casual contact. The United States Centers for Disease Control (CDC) currently estimates over 40 million persons worldwide are infected with HIV; in the United States alone estimates place the infection rate at one in every 250 persons, or approximately one million individuals. All these persons cannot appropriately be said to have AIDS; however, the CDC's technical descriptor of AIDS has to do with either the presence of an opportunistic infection associated with the HIV, and/or a diminution of the body's CD4 (T-lymphocyte or T-cell) count to below 200 per cubic millimeter of blood.

Within the United States the 25 to 44 age group has the largest number of reported AIDS cases; however, the fastest-growing category for infection with HIV consists of women in their teens. The current wisdom is that AIDS is treatable but not curable. With proper treatment, it is not unusual for individuals to live 10 years or longer from time of initial diagnosis with HIV to eventual death, with the average longevity following onset of AIDS symptoms being 24 months.

Such is the current state of our knowledge of AIDS. Nearly two-thirds of large businesses (more than 2,500 employees) and one in ten small businesses (fewer than 500 employees) report having had an employee with either HIV or AIDS in their employ, making this a workplace issue. Links between HIV infection and such social "baggage" as homosexuality and drug abuse make this a volatile issue for those formulating corporate policy. From the view of KANTIAN ETHICS, or deontology, there is a potential clash of rights between the HIV+ worker and the HIV– co-workers (*see* RIGHTS). The concern on the part of some individuals is that the ease of transmitability of HIV has been grossly understated. One study of corporate and public-service employees found that "30 percent of the respondents expressed skepticism about the accuracy of public information" related to AIDS, with nearly one in four stating they would be "afraid of getting AIDS from working near PWAs [Persons with AIDS]" (Barr et al., 1992, p. 226). Such individuals typically advocate disclosure of co-workers' HIV status. Conversely, those infected with HIV are concerned with the variety of discriminatory practices, including erosion of the right to PRIVACY, revocation of health benefits or escalation of the cost of such benefits, shunning by co-workers, and even termination of employment, which often accompany making a positive diagnosis with HIV a matter of public record (*see* HEALTH-CARE ETHICS AND BUSINESS ETHICS). Additionally, the right of the AIDS sufferer to his or her work must be considered against the backdrop of the right of the employer to exercise the doctrine of employment at will (*see* RIGHT TO WORK; EMPLOYMENT AT WILL). This particular conflict is compounded by the Americans with Disabilities Act (ADA), which most commentators believe is, in part, intended to treat workers with AIDS as a disabled class subject to the protections contained in this legislation.

The issue of resolving rights conflicts with respect to persons with AIDS in the workplace is necessarily complicated by consideration of RISK tolerance. Few, if any, rights are absolute; therefore, the challenge for the deontologist is to

decide which among a competing set of rights is most foundational. This determination is in some sense dependent upon the probability, or risk, of alternative realizable policies. Neither the view that the rights of the AIDS sufferer must be protected at all cost, nor the view that the rights of co-workers are inviolate, seems correct. However, the suggestion that determination of a "rights hierarchy," and thereby of one policy versus another, is dependent upon risk assessment necessarily moves the argument toward consideration of the utilitarian consequences of alternative policies.

UTILITARIANISM requires that we consider the consequences of including or excluding AIDS sufferers from the workplace, with an eye toward bringing about the "greatest good for the greatest number." Those familiar with the debate over whether HIV+ medical providers should be compelled to disclose their HIV status to patients have seen this particular issue evolve from one in which rights were of central importance to concern over the impact of mandatory disclosure policies on the health-care profession in general and ultimately the welfare of society at large. The presupposition of utilitarian argumentation is that relevant benefits and costs can be both identified and quantified. While utilitarians are well versed in dealing with such complexities, when it comes to workplace AIDS transmitability, the issue is so emotive as to make consensual policy formulation a virtual impossibility. What is known is that the well-being of the AIDS sufferer is to a great extent a function of AIDS policy. Research into the longevity of HIV+ individuals indicates that a supportive community leads to life extension (*see* COMMUNITARIANISM). One of the drawbacks of traditional utilitarianism, however, is its compatibility with injustices: in seeking to promote the greatest good for the greatest number, the interests of the non-majority are rather easily overridden. For the HIV+ minority, the consequences of restrictive workplace AIDS policy might well be the foreshortening of their very lives.

At least one writer suggests Kantian and utilitarian ethics can be meaningfully combined. Brady suggests we should make "exceptions to rules when so doing recognizes or promotes the affiliation and connectedness of persons" (1990, pp. 144–5). With this understanding, should

HIV+ individuals be offered organizational membership in spite of a general rule affording all employees a safe working environment? Consistent with designation of HIV infection as a disability under the ADA, Brady's principle implies that the objective of affiliation should override more general workplace safeguards. In effect this principle injects classical utilitarianism with justice considerations (*see* JUSTICE). The objective is to have the manager approach the drafting of workplace AIDS policy with specific reference to the idiosyncrasies of each specific work environment.

Consideration of the personal – and relational – implications of AIDS policy formulation and implementation suggests we consider the ETHICS OF CARE. The topic of AIDS in the workplace needs to be a matter of conversations about how we as human beings live, and more particularly how we live in a caring relationship with one another. Such caring conversation is hindered by language which creates unnecessary – or even inflammatory – distinctions. As Sedgwick has noted, "many of the major nodes of thought and knowledge in twentieth-century western culture as a whole are structured – indeed, fractured – by a chronic, now endemic crisis of homo- heterosexual definition, indicatively male, dating from the end of the nineteenth century" (1990, p. 1) (*see* POST-MODERNISM AND BUSINESS ETHICS). This is nowhere more true than in conversations about the appropriate policy response to persons in the workplace who happen to have been infected by HIV. Jonsen offers perhaps the best closing to this discussion of policy alternatives relating to AIDS in the workplace: "In all epidemics, fear stimulates isolation and responsibility requires inclusion . . . [t]his might even be called the moral law of epidemics" (1991, p. 660).

See also **Gay rights**

Bibliography

Barr, J. K., Waring, J. M. & Warshaw, L. J. (1992). Knowledge and attitudes about AIDS among corporate and public service employees. *American Journal of Public Health*, 82 (2), 225–8.

Brady, F. N. (1990). *Ethical Managing: Rules and Results*. New York: Macmillan.

Cohen, E. D. & Davis, M. (eds), (1994). *AIDS: Crisis in Professional Ethics*. Philadelphia: Temple University Press.

Deka, D. (1994). AIDS in the workplace. Graduate thesis, College of Business Administration, San Diego State University.

Feldblum, C. R. (1991). The Americans with Disabilities Act: Definition of disability. *The Labor Lawyer*, 11, 11–26.

Gilbert, D. R. & Freeman, R. E. (1994). AIDS in the workplace: A critique from lesbian/gay theory. Presentation within Social Issues in Management Division. *Academy of Management Annual Meeting*.

Heacock, M. V. & Orvis, G. P. (1990). AIDS in the workplace: Public and corporate policy. *Harvard Journal of Law & Public Policy*, 13 (2), 689–713.

Jonsen, A. R. (1991). Is individual responsibility a sufficient basis for public confidence? *Archives of Internal Medicine*, 151, 660–2.

Sedgwick, E. K. (1990). *Epistemology of the Closet*. Berkeley: University of California Press.

Stone, R. A. (1994). AIDS in the workplace: An executive update. *The Academy of Management Executive*, 8 (3), 52–61.

CRAIG P. DUNN

altruism and benevolence   a concern for the well-being of persons other than oneself. (Both contrast with "beneficence," which refers to actions that promote the welfare of others, independent of the motive behind them.) This concern cannot, however, be in service of one's own interest, as when we help out another with the expectation that our doing so will result in greater benefit to ourselves. The concern must be directed toward the other *for her own sake*. Otherwise it is not altruism or benevolence. Altruism concerns not merely the results of action, but the agent's *motivation* to engage in such action.

Concern for others for their own sake does not necessitate actual self-sacrifice, or, more moderately, a loss of personal well-being. The view that it does may stem from the false belief that every situation presents us with a choice between fostering our own good and fostering the good of others. Bishop Joseph Butler (1692–1752) gave the classic arguments showing that action on behalf of others need involve no loss to the self.

Beyond this, to say that someone is "altruistic" does seem to carry the implication that the person neglects her own well-being in favor of others'. (The same implication is not carried by "benevolence", however.) Yet we need to retain a term for a concern for the good of others *without* the further implication of self-sacrifice or self-neglect.

However, when altruism *does* involve great personal risk or sacrifice it is generally thought to be more admirable than altruism with minimal risk. Thus rescuers of Jews during the Nazi era – a group extensively studied as exemplars of heroic altruism – exhibited the highest moral virtue. Nevertheless, self-sacrifice is not a virtue in its own right. It must be in the service of a great good, or at least a good greater than the loss to the agent (as in the rescuers' case). Otherwise it might just be foolish. And even self-denying altruism is not always admirable or advisable. Some persons may give too much of themselves, even to promote a great good for others. Feminists have claimed that women have been victims of just such a debilitating self-denying ideology. Still, by and large, appropriate self-sacrificing altruism is good and admirable.

Altruism and self-interest need not be opposed; they may be mutually enhancing. Often those with the most secure sense of self and self-worth are also very altruistic persons. Their self-confidence allows them to respond to the plight of others without a debilitating self-absorption. They are happy people who derive satisfaction from their altruistic activities, though these may involve a sacrifice of comfort, convenience, and missed pleasures. Some take this truth a step further and argue that the *most* fulfilled and flourishing individuals are those whose lives involve a substantial degree of altruism. They claim that persons who are non-altruistic, whose lives are devoted to the pursuit of self-oriented satisfaction are, paradoxically, less likely to achieve such self-satisfaction.

Yet if altruism is satisfying to the self, is it still really altruism? More generally, many question whether altruism actually exists. Psychological egoism is the view that behind all beneficent action lies a pursuit of self-benefit, whether conscious or unconscious. It is true that the most apparently altruistic actions may be egoistically driven. If my beneficent pursuits are in the service of an image of myself as an altruistic person, because I think that will make me happy, then I am not altruistic (*see* EGOISM, PSYCHOLOGICAL EGOISM AND ETHICAL EGOISM).

However, being *aware* of the satisfaction one derives from altruistic pursuits is not the same as being *motivated* by that satisfaction. In fact it is impossible to gain altruistic satisfaction by deliberately aiming at it; for then it will not involve a true regard for the other for her own sake. The satisfaction derived will not be altruistic but egoistic.

Since altruism is a matter of motivation, it cannot guarantee that the results of altruistic action will actually be beneficial, even if that is the agent's intent. An altruistic person may be mistaken as to the interests of the party she wishes to help; her action may thus fail to benefit. Yet since an altruistic person does wish for the good of the other, she should also be concerned about understanding what that good is, and open to revising her view of that good in light of new information. Thus, an ideally altruistic person will be concerned not only for the other's good, but to figure out what that good is. Nevertheless, it would be misleading to deprive the term "altruism" of application when the agent seeks the good of the other for its own sake but is non-culpably mistaken about the nature of that good.

Motivations are sometimes difficult to discern. And so some say, "Why should we care what the agent's motive is, as long as she gets results, that is, as long as others are benefited? We should arrange out political and social institutions so that self-interested motives will produce beneficent results and we will not need to rely on people acting altruistically." It can be doubted whether such a social order is possible; political, social, and even economic life depends in all sorts of ways on people not pursuing their own self-interest to the utmost, but rather taking some account of the interests of others (see Mansbridge, 1990). Beyond this, we do in fact take a moral interest in people's motivations and character. We admire the benevolent and altruistic person but not the selfish, opportunistic person, even if we are relieved when the latter's actions happen to produce beneficial results.

See also **ethics of care; feminist ethics; supererogation**

Bibliography

Baron, L., Blum, L., Krebs, D., Oliner, P., Oliner, S. & Smolenska, M. Z. (1992). *Embracing the Other: Philosophical, Psychological, and Historical Perspectives on Altruism.* New York: New York Univesity Press.

Blum, L. (1980). *Friendship, Altruism, and Morality.* London: Routledge and Kegan Paul.

Butler, J. (1983 [1726]). *Five Sermons Preached at the Rolls Chapel.* Indianapolis, Ind.: Hackett.

Mansbridge, J. (1990). *Beyond Self-Interest.* Chicago: University of Chicago Press.

Social Philosophy and Policy, **10** (1), winter 1993.

Thomas, L. (1989). *Living Morally: A Psychology of Moral Character.* Philadelphia: Temple University Press.

LAWRENCE A. BLUM

anti-competitive practices in marketing marketing practices that reduce or discourage competition, typically thought of in terms of antitrust violations. Antitrust: of, relating to, or being legislation against or opposition to trusts or combinations; consisting of laws to protect trade and commerce from unlawful restraints and monopolies or unfair business practices (*Webster's College Dictionary*, 1993).

Under certain conditions, examples of anti-competitive practices in marketing, which are considered violations of US antitrust law, include the following: conspiring to monopolize a market by using a size advantage to underprice competitors and drive them from the market (predatory pricing), offering larger business customers lower prices than smaller business customers with whom they compete (discriminatory pricing), and conspiring to monopolize a market through mergers or collusion with competitors.

Perhaps the best way to understand the rationale behind antitrust legislation, and why it has evolved as it has, is to place these events in a historical perspective. Essentially, the industrial revolution, and its expanding scope in the late 1800s, led to the initiation of antitrust legislation in the US. As technology expanded and developed, the size and power of certain companies grew tremendously, which led to heightened social and political concern about large business enterprises. The general consensus was that the market power of these large industries (e.g., steel, oil, railroads) discouraged competition. As a result, the period of 1861 to 1901, often called the age of "Robber Barons," was accompanied by populist movements that contended that big business was endangering the livelihoods of small, independent businessmen and farmers. These movements led to the first major federal regulatory antitrust enactment, the Sherman Anti-trust Act of 1890.

The Act regulated the form and size of organizations and expressly prohibited monopolies. In a monopoly a firm has sole, or nearly sole, control of a certain market. Section 1 of the Act forbids entering into a contract, combination, or conspiracy in restraint of trade. Section 2 of the Sherman Act prohibits monopolizing or attempting to monopolize trade, including acts such as predatory pricing. Perhaps the most famous example of alleged predatory pricing involved Standard Oil Company of New Jersey. In evidence presented before the Supreme Court, the government demonstrated that Standard Oil would sharply reduce prices in local markets where competition existed, while holding prices at a much higher level in other markets, with the objective of persuading competitors to merge.

Although the Sherman Act discouraged monopolistic practices, it was only effective against a few obvious monopoly consolidations. In order to more specifically attack the methods by which firms developed monopoly power, the federal government passed the Clayton Act and the Federal Trade Commission Act in 1914. The Clayton Act provisions are an effort to deny firms the ability to develop monopolies through mergers or collusion with other firms. Specifically, Section 7 of the Act prohibits stock acquisitions by any corporation "where the effect of such an acquisition may be to substantially lessen competition . . . or to restrain such commerce in any section or community, or tend to create a monopoly of any line of commerce." Section 3 prohibits entering into exclusive dealing and tying contracts in order to develop monopoly power. The Federal Trade Commission Act created the Federal Trade Commission (FTC) to police anti-competitive conduct.

Two later Acts amended the Clayton Act, addressing what some considered "loopholes" in the existing legislation. In 1936, the federal government initiated the Robinson-Patman Act to address the issue of discriminatory pricing by amending Section 2 of the Clayton Act. Provisionally, discriminatory pricing is selling or purchasing different units of the same product at price differentials not directly attributable to differences in the cost of supply. Pressure for this enhancement to the Clayton Act came from relatively small wholesalers and retailers who competed against A&P and other emerging retail chain organizations. These businesses complained that the favorable pricing received by larger competitors created an advantage that was competition-threatening. The argument was that these larger companies could establish prices that were profitable for them, but unprofitable for the smaller firms that must pay more for inputs, and thus could eliminate competition. In agreement with this logic, the Robinson-Patman provision prohibits price discrimination among business purchasers to an extent that cannot be justified by a difference in cost or as a good-faith attempt to meet the price of a competitor. Addressing another omission, the 1950 Celler-Kefauver Act amended Section 7 of the Clayton Act. This amendment made asset acquisitions of competitors that substantially lessen competition illegal. Proponents of this amendment successfully pointed to anti-competitive acquisitions, such as those made by Standard Oil when it bought competing oil refineries, not by buying the stock of the target firm, but by purchasing its assets.

Given the past development of antitrust laws and the legacy that remains, what does the future hold for antitrust? As it has in the past, antitrust legislation will continue to evolve as it is presented with new challenges. A major difference, though, is that some existing legislation may be rolled back, or at least softened, particularly in the area of mergers and interfirm collusion. Several phenomena seem to be responsible for this retreat. Based on a trend that started with the emergence of strong Japanese competition and the Reagan presidency, it appears that the American public and the government view a lessening of these antitrust provisions, and regulation as a whole,

as vital to the international competitiveness of the US. Recent consortia of high-technology firms engaged in research to improve US global competitiveness attest to a shift in the interpretation of antitrust behavior. In addition, the increasingly dynamic nature of technology often ensures that no one firm will have long-lived market dominance. Thus, given the increasingly tenuous position of market leaders, there is naturally less concern about monopolistic practices. And, some have questioned the efficacy of the Robinson-Patman Act. The argument here is that a too literal interpretation of the Act protects inefficient firms and, therefore, does not promote free-market competition. As always, though, future legislation will be dependent upon the prevailing political climate.

See also advertising ethics; ethics of marketing

Bibliography

Caves, R. (1982). *American Industry: Structure, Conduct, Performance.* Englewood Cliffs, NJ: Prentice-Hall.

Stern, L. W. & Eovaldi, T. L. (1984). *Legal Aspects of Marketing Strategy: Antitrust and Consumer Protection Issues.* Englewood Cliffs, NJ: Prentice-Hall.

Stern, L. W. & Grabner, J. R., Jr. (1970). *Competition in the Marketplace.* Atlanta: Scott, Foresman.

The Wall Street Journal, (1995). Land of the giants. May 5, p. A12.

Werner, R. O. (1989). *Legal and Economic Regulation in Marketing.* New York: Quorum Books.

C. JAY LAMBE and ROBERT E. SPEKMAN

applied ethics   Although applied (or "practical") ethics borrows insights from theories of moral axiology (i.e., theories of the morally good and evil), theories of moral obligation (i.e., theories regarding what is morally permissible, morally required, and morally impermissible), and from metaethics (i.e., theories regarding the meaning of moral terms, the nature of moral discourse, and the justification of moral claims), the task in engaging in practical ethics is not simply to work out applications of existing ethical theories. It is, rather, to attempt to find acceptable resolutions of moral problems of present and practical urgency. This involves much more than merely doing some sort of philosophical technology where high-level theory is simply brought over to practice. When done well, questions addressed within practical ethics continually raise important theoretical and methodological questions for general theories of moral good and moral right, and for metaethics. For example, attempting to answer questions pertaining to choosing and changing jobs raises a number of significant questions about what it means for any choice to be rational and genuinely voluntary. Similarly, questions in professional ethics regarding the distribution of certain goods and services raise deep questions regarding basic human goods and the possibility of maximizing the potential of characteristically human lives. In raising and addressing these questions, theorists working in practical ethics are inseparable from theorists working in more familiar areas of ethics. What is true, however, is that engaging in practical ethics is in some important ways quite different from attempting to construct a full and general moral theory. Specifically, there are differences in the content of the questions asked, and differences in focus, goals, and method.

Goals

The differences in content and focus in moral theory and practical ethics provide some clues as to how goals in engaging in these projects might differ. A legitimate goal in studying and engaging in moral theory construction might consist in acquainting oneself with one branch of the history of philosophy or one branch of systematic philosophy as a matter of purely intellectual interest, much as an academic approach to religious studies might focus on understanding certain religious traditions as a way of deepening one's appreciation of a culture's heritage. That is, a study of moral theory need not concern itself with resolving any real-life moral dilemmas, any more than studying a religious tradition need concern itself with resolving any theological dilemmas. Genuine engagement in practical ethics, on the other hand, disallows neutrality on the goal of attempting to resolve some morally dilemmic issues, since practical ethics takes the resolution of such issues as its proximate concern. This concern issues in several projects to be pursued in engaging in practical ethics.

1. *Recognizing moral issues.* A first step in practical ethics is developing skill in recognizing moral issues. Issues that have a moral content are those that involve the rights and/or welfare of persons (and/or other sentient beings), the character of the acting agent, the flourishing of relationships and communities, and/or special obligations that attach to special roles. Being able to recognize such issues where they often go unnoticed is crucial. In business ethics, seeing that some rather standard behaviors are unjustifiably manipulative or even coercive is to be aware of morally crucial dimensions of conventional, unreflective action or practice. An important first project in engaging in practical ethics, then, is a kind of consciousness raising that enlivens one to the moral complexity of the world in a number of domains.

2. *Developing the moral imagination.* Closely connected to the task of developing skill in recognizing moral issues is the task of developing the moral imagination. As elementary as it may seem, we are often unaware that our attitudes toward (or indifference to) what is morally acceptable issue in actions or failures to act that can have serious effects on the rights and well-being of other individuals as well as the various communities to which we belong. Thus, for example, people who are not enlivened to the fact that certain public policies or institutional policies are oppressive to women or members of certain minorities or persons generally, may support those policies or miss opportunities to oppose those policies. Such enlivening often requires nurturing the capacity to imagine what it feels like to be a person directly affected by a certain practice or policy. To genuinely understand, say, the vulnerability of workers in sweat shops, one must be able imaginatively to assume the place of the worker, who may be desperate for work, bored, confused by complex machinery and terminology, feeling displaced, and affected by any number of the other daunting features of work. Similarly, being able to imagine what it is like to be an elderly person on a fixed income might lead one to see how problematic it is that pharmaceutical companies spend more money on marketing than on research and development, and that those marketing costs get carried over to one of the most vulnerable segments of the community–the elderly who are ill. Devel-

oping moral imagination is closely related to the skill of recognizing moral problems, since in using a well-developed moral imagination, we often see moral issues where we had not noticed them before.

3. *Sharpening analytical/critical skills.* At least two more tasks of practical ethics are connected to issues of moral relativism (*see* RELATIVISM, CULTURAL AND MORAL). Many of us are extremely reluctant to call *any* action (or practice) morally wrong. To be sure, calling another person's action morally wrong does amount to a strong and important claim. And establishing exact criteria for moral rightness and wrongness has eluded philosophers for centuries. Aware of the hazards of moral evaluation, we often do not want to "pass judgment" – we want to be careful about condemning the actions of other persons, the practices of other societies, and practices in earlier stages of our own society. We want to be tolerant of differences, and this is a good thing. But when "tolerance" becomes so extreme that we are left morally resourceless, the virtue of tolerance swells into its excess and everything becomes permissible.

One of the goals of thoughtful engagement in applied ethics is to help reveal that even though moral questions are difficult, we can go a long way before we need to say, "Well, we just disagree on our fundamental moral commitments." By honing analytical skills, we can come to see that we share a large common moral ground that can be defended on the basis of reasonable moral principles, and that ground can provide us with reasons for ruling out certain kinds of actions and practices as morally unacceptable. This is not to suggest, of course, that all morally aware, imaginative, and reasonable persons will always agree on how morally dilemmic cases and issues are to be decided. But it is to suggest that careful reflection on what might initially seem to be an utterly unresolvable case or issue will often at least reveal that some potential resolutions are not consistent with moral principles to which disputants are committed, or that what was initially thought to be a case or issue requiring some substantive resolution might be given a procedural resolution. For example, in some cases careful reflection might reveal that the question to be resolved is not what should be done, but rather who should decide what should be done. Thus, sharpening analytical skills can help to rule out certain potential resolutions that might initially seem acceptable, and can help with the engendering and consideration of potential resolutions that were not initially apparent.

4. *Sorting out disagreements.* Hard moral questions are hard because they tend to leave residues of disagreement among even the most sensitive and astute moral agents. No matter how refined one's analytical skills become, such residues will tend to remain. It is here that tolerance in ethics has its proper place. Among the chief tasks in practical ethics is the twofold task of learning not only to put *oneself* in the position of others, but learning to put oneself in the position of *others*. That is, part of the task is to realize that there are legitimately differing ways of ordering values and that some differences in value judgment are inevitable and acceptable. In many cases, decisions to be made will need to be made collectively; and an important part of careful reflection in practical ethics is to encourage others to express their moral misgivings about proposed resolutions to morally dilemmic cases and issues, to sort out disagreements that are morally reasonable from those that are not, and to work toward acceptable moral closure despite some residual disagreement. Indeed, often decisions will need to be made despite serious and morally responsible disagreements.

5. *Affecting decisions and behavior.* If applied ethics is worth doing and worth doing well, it is precisely because doing applied ethics holds out promise of affecting individual behavior, public policy, corporate practices, and so on, in a morally positive way. Indeed, the main difference between studying ethical theory and engaging in practical ethics lies in the practical ethics goal of contributing directly and immediately to behavior and policy creation that is reflective, well-reasoned, intellectually responsible, and morally sensitive.

Implementation: Closure and Process

If we accept the goals sketched above as proper to applied ethics, what kinds of problems might be expected in pursuing them, and what might be some strategies for avoiding these problems?

One problem has already been mentioned – the problem of hasty relativism. Given the pluralism of our society, the desire to be tolerant, and the very real problems that intrapersonal and intrasocietal disagreements about morality raise, temptation to retreat into a relativism or subjectivism where everything is permitted, or a simple pragmatism – that is, a view that morality is one thing, getting through life is another – is pervasive. But such retreats make moral reflection irrelevant, since they are really failures to attempt to come to satisfactory moral closure in the face of moral pluralism and moral complications. A theory of retreat from morality cannot possibly serve as an adequate moral theory. But tolerance and taking pluralism seriously are certainly consistent with responsible moral reflection which works toward moral closure. "Closure" is the resolution of a moral dilemma or debate, a resolution that is supported by the best reasons available and recognized by the disputants as a morally responsible solution that takes seriously the positions of those who may still disagree. That is, when there is serious moral disagreement, the task is to search for a decision that everyone involved can "live with," even though not everyone might agree that the solution is ideal. When coming to closure is difficult, the reasons for failure to come to closure can be explored. Is the remaining disagreement one that can be well defended? If not, why not? If so, can anyone offer a solution that avoids the problem(s) giving rise to the disagreement? If not, given that a decision must be made, what can be done or decided to ensure that the least morally problematic decision is made? Pressing for closure by asking such questions can help disputants to discover the moral ground that they share and can lead to considerable confidence in decisions made after responding to such questions.

In the moral realm, we often labor under conditions of uncertainty. This is the case whether we are trying to make a hard moral decision alone or with others. Because of the intrinsic uncertainty that moral dilemmas involve, often the best that can be done is following a decision procedure that is careful to take into account the morally relevant considerations that support deciding a case or issue in various ways. Although we may never enjoy complete certainty about the content of our decisions in morally hard cases, we can enjoy confidence in the procedures we use to make such decisions. One helpful procedure involves the following steps.

1. *Set out the various possible resolutions of the case.* Be sure to tax your imagination. The case may admit of more alternatives than are initially obvious.

2. *Set out the facts relevant to supporting each resolution you have identified.* Generate as complete a set of lists as possible of the facts (known, possible, probable) that might be used to support each of the options you have identified on how the case might be resolved. Relevant facts might include: someone will be or is likely to be harmed (physically, emotionally, financially, in reputation, etc.) if a certain resolution is chosen; limited resources expended in one way could be expended in another way, meeting some (other) pressing need; some decision will interfere with the liberty of an individual; a proposed resolution involves coercion, deception, manipulation, breach of trust, keeping a promise, breaking a promise, exploitation, unequal treatment, and so on.

3. *Set out the moral principles that underpin the selection of the facts on your lists.* That is, each fact that you identify as supportive of a possible resolution will be relevant because of some underlying moral principle. Articulate these principles clearly. Relevant principles might include: Prevent harm; Do good; Be fair; Be loyal; Keep your promises; Do not inflict harm on other persons/sentient beings; Maintain integrity; Be candid; Live up to the requirements of your office or role; It is permissible to protect one's own interests; Respect the liberty/autonomy of persons; Contribute to the flourishing of relationships within this community or that one; and so on. Combining these principles with the relevant facts you have selected provides moral arguments for the possible resolutions you have identified.

So, for example, an argument from your lists for some option (call it "Option A") might look like this:

Premise 1, Principle: Keep promises.
Premise 2, Fact: Doing X, which will be done if Option A is selected, involves keeping a promise.
Conclusion: Choose Option A.

4. *Reflect on the options you have identified on your lists.* Ask yourself (again) if you have included all potentially acceptable options; and if your lists of facts, and the principles that lead you to select those facts as supportive of the options you've identified, include all the plausible arguments for each of the alternatives you have identified. Are the lists of facts and principles supporting the view you are inclined to take, longer than your other lists? If so, be sure that you have been as thorough as possible in laying out the facts and principles supportive of the resolutions that differ from the one you are inclined to favor.

5. *Make and articulate your decision.* After careful consideration of the options you have identified and the arguments supporting each of those options that you have identified, select the option you think is the one that should be chosen.

6. *Justify your decision.* Set out your positive reasons for the decision you have made. This will take you back to your lists. Make explicit which considerations on your lists of facts and principles you found the most compelling.

7. *Anticipate and respond to the most serious potential objection to your decision.* Go back to the lists supporting the option(s) other than the one you have chosen. Use these lists to help you clarify what you take to be the strongest potential objection to your position or to your positive argument for your decision. What is your reply to that objection? Given your reply, is it reasonable to believe that a proponent of that objection could be brought to see the preferability of the resolution you support?

8. *Clarify the costs or downside of your decision.* Go back to your lists a final time and use them to help you articulate what you take to be the most morally significant cost(s) of your decision. (This may be related to what you take to be the strongest potential objection to your decision.)

A procedure incorporating such steps goes a long way toward fulfilling the goals that are suggested here as proper to engagement in practical ethics, which is direct engagement with the hard moral questions that inevitably challenge us all in the lived world of moral responsibility.

Bibliography

This article has been adapted from Callahan (1990), with permission.

Bayles, M. (1989). *Professional ethics,* 2nd edn, Belmont, Calif.: Wadsworth.

Callahan, D. (1980). Goals in the teaching of ethics. In D. Callahan & S. Bok (eds), *Ethics Teaching in Higher Education.* New York: Plenum, 61–80.

Callahan, J. (1990). From the "applied" to the practical: Teaching ethics for use. *American Philosophical Association Newsletter on Teaching Philosophy,* **90** (1), 29–34.

Callahan, J. (ed.), . (1988). *Ethical Issues in Professional Life.* New York: Oxford University Press.

Caplan, A. (1980). Ethical engineers need not apply: The state of applied ethics today. *Science, Technology, and Human Values,* **6** (33), 24–32.

Gorovitz, S. (1985). *Doctors Dilemmas: Moral Conflict and Medical Care.* New York: Oxford University Press.

Klinefelter, D. S. (1990). How is applied philosophy to be applied? *Journal of Social Philosophy,* **21** (1), 16–26.

Midgley, M. (1990). Homunculus trouble, or, What is applied philosophy? *Journal of Social Philosophy,* **20** (1), 5–15.

Singer, P. (1986). *Applied Ethics.* New York: Oxford University Press.

Joan C. Callahan

Arendt, Hannah a respected and controversial philosopher and political theorist who died in 1975. Her most noted work was *Eichmann in Jerusalem: A Report On The Banality of Evil* (1964). Originally commissioned by and published in *The New Yorker,* it was later expanded into book form. Arendt's analysis of Eichmann as a person and of his organizational situation, while an extreme case, can be an important aid in helping us understand a type of unthinking, "in-the-box" facilitation of unethical organization behavior.

From Arendt we learn that Eichmann was an upper-middle-level manager in a Nazi institution engaged in, as Arendt phrased it, the "administrative massacre" of millions of people. Eichmann did not participate in making policy decisions. Eichmann never belonged to the higher Party circles. He managed in an organizational environment where obeying authority was valued, expected, and required.

According to Arendt, Eichmann believed that he was practicing the virtue of obedience when he was aiding his organization. He obeyed orders without thinking about ethical implications. Arendt (1964, p. 247) explained what she thinks Eichmann thought. "His guilt came from his obedience, and obedience is praised as a virtue. His virtue had been abused by the Nazi leaders. But he was not one of the ruling clique, he was a victim, and only the leaders deserved punishment."

Arendt concludes her analysis of Eichmann and his organizational situation with the judgment that Eichmann was guilty, but instead of being an insane or monstrously evil person, Eichmann was, perhaps more horribly, well within the range of sanity and normality – he was neither abnormal nor a monster. Eichmann was a "thoughtless" and "banal" man who did not think about what was right or wrong about his role as a manager in an organization that harmed people. He did not try to distinguish right from wrong in his organizational context. He did not think about what he was doing and cooperating with. For Eichmann, his job was not to think about the ethics of organization policies or decisions made by higher authority. His thinking was more narrowly directed toward efficient implementation of policy decisions. Eichmann was capable of being both a good technical manager and unthinking about the unethical role he was playing in efficiently implementing unethical policies.

Despite the extreme evil his organization committed, Eichmann as a model, as well as the individual person Eichmann as a thoughtless man, brings into serious question the validity of assuming that all managers and employees naturally think about what is right or wrong in organizational contexts where efficient implementation and obeying orders are at a high premium.

Arendt's politics of organizational ethics integrates two key concepts: the importance of the habit of independent thinking and judgment that is capable of challenging habitual, routinized "in-the-box" frameworks that do not include the ethical; and the need to act civically, i.e. as a citizen, with others in organizational and bureaucratic contexts.

Arendt (1978, pp. 3, 5) explains her action philosophy as related to the Eichmann phenomenon. "The immediate impulse came from my attending the Eichmann trial in Jerusalem. In my report of it I spoke of the banality of evil. Behind that phrase, I held no thesis or doctrine, although I was dimly aware of the fact that it went counter to our tradition of thought – literary, theological, or philosophic – about the phenomenon of evil . . . Absence of thought is not stupidity; it can be found in highly intelligent people and a wicked heart is not its cause; it is probably the other way round, that wickedness may be caused by absence of thought."

Arendt further observed that such narrow, routinized, "in-the-box" thoughtlessness that does not include ethical dimensions is encouraged by authoritarian systems. In such authoritarian environments, it is often necessary to act civically with others, i.e., as a citizen of an organization, to resist unethical behavior.

Arendt's concerns were to be both with oneself, to which the activity of thinking corresponds, and to be together with others, from which flows action. She was concerned with relationships: between independent, out-of-the-box thinking and acting; and, between critical philosophy and politics. Arendt made a distinction between a "good person" and a "good citizen," between a moral stance and a political action. This distinction was important because in order for action and learning to be effective in organizational contexts, it frequently has to come from people acting and learning together.

Arendt argued that this acting and learning with others was crucial for several key reasons. One reason revolved around the idea of a public space. That is, people need to be able to have a space to interact with others in order to discuss and persuade each other on important issues. People need to act and learn with others so as not to be atomized and isolated from the organization they are trying to serve. Otherwise, there is a strong tendency to be concerned only with narrow, private security and private interests. This not only makes people ineffective as citizens but also makes them more susceptible to explicit and implicit coercion, narrow in-the-box thinking, unethical ideologies, and unethical behaviors. The act of working and learning with others helps establish a place in the organization, a political space which makes opinions significant and action effective.

Arendt also understood that organizational civil liberties could be important as encouragement and protection for responsible organizational citizenship. Arendt (Young-Bruehl, 1982, p. 206) explains, "All other differences between the institutions of democratic and totalitarian countries can be shown to be secondary and side issues. This is not a conflict between socialism and capitalism, or state-capitalism and free enterprise, or a class-ridden and classless society. It is a conflict between . . . civil liberties and the . . . abolition of civil liberties."

This is a key problem with many organizations. There can be few and no protected civil liberties within organizations. When there is no or little protected civic space available, this can make it very difficult to act and learn civically with others.

Bibliography

Arendt, H. (1958). *The Human Condition.* Chicago: University of Chicago Press.

Arendt, H. (1964).. *Eichmann in Jerusalem: A Report on the Banality of Evil.* New York: Schocken.

Arendt, H. (1978). *The Life of the Mind,* (ed.), M. McCarthy. New York: Harcourt Brace Jovanovich.

Nielsen, R. P. (l984). Arendt's action philosophy and the manager as Eichmann, Richard III, Faust, or Institution Citizen. *California Management Review,* 26 (3), 191–201.

Nielsen, R. P. (1993). Organization ethics from a perspective of praxis. *Business Ethics Quarterly,* 3 (2), 131–51.

Young-Bruehl, E. (1982). *Hannah Arendt: For Love of the World.* New Haven: Yale University Press.

RICHARD P. NIELSEN

Aristotle Aristotle of Stagira (384–322 BC) is regarded by many as the greatest of the Western philosophers. His metaphysical and ethical works, based on the sophisticated elaboration of common sense, in contrast to those of his great teacher Plato, continue to engage philosophers and others.

Aristotle's works show no great respect for business. For example, he claims in his *Politics* that the money-lender charging interest is doing something unnatural and therefore wrong, as is the middleman, who is acquisitive at others' expense.

Yet we can adapt Aristotle's views on ethics, found primarily in the *Nicomachean Ethics*, to business and find many of them attractive. Aristotle claims that the life of the citizen in a good city is the good life in the truest sense, and suggests that the individual is defined by community-related attachments and emotions. An Aristotelian of our time would find support in COMMUNITARIANISM for that claim, and for an account of JUSTICE as what creates and maintains happiness for a community. The Aristotelian who regards the organization as the paradigm case of the community would hold that the good organization is populated by free people who have purposes and much else in common, and are united by friendship and justice. These we may recognize as components of a strong ORGANIZATIONAL CULTURE.

Aristotle argues that right action is naturally compatible with the agent's happiness. Unlike many economists and others, he does not presuppose psychological egoism; on the contrary, he claims that natural happiness lies in just and friendly association with others in a good community (*see* EGOISM, PSYCHOLOGICAL EGOISM AND ETHICAL EGOISM). One's CHARACTER is revealed by the sort of thing that pleases one; for the good person, therefore, it is a pleasure to be virtuous.

As one might expect from Aristotle's account of virtue, his views do not comfortably accommodate UTILITARIANISM (*see also* VIRTUE ETHICS). Aristotle does not accept the commensurability of all goods, and rejects the identification of happiness with the fulfillment of desire.

Aristotle focuses on the virtuous person rather than on MORAL RULES. He argues that we can properly apply principles to specific situations only by means of the sort of "perception" that practical wisdom imparts to the virtuous. A good person has the kind of familiarity with morally significant situations that right action requires; and his or her emotions are allied with reason. It follows that moral education is not aimed merely at the intellect. It follows too that Aristotle would not agree that business ethics is just a matter of applying ethical principles to business situations.

We cannot be as confident as was Aristotle about what is natural and what is not, or even about what is essential and what is accidental. He does not consider that different social conditions might make different virtues appropriate, or that different communities might reasonably sponsor different virtues, as our own society encourages BOURGEOIS VIRTUE. In spite of the rigid and parochial aspects of his thought, we can learn a great deal from Aristotle.

Bibliography

Aristotle. (1985). *Nicomachean Ethics,* trans. Terence Irwin. Indianapolis: Hackett. (Includes glossary of key terms).

Everson, S. (Ed.). (1988). *Aristotle: The "Politics".* New York: Cambridge. (Translation and commentary).

Finley, M. I. (1977). Aristotle and economic analysis. In J. Barnes, M. Schofield, & R. Sorabji (eds), *Articles on Aristotle II: Ethics and Politics.* London: Duckworth, 140–58.

Solomon, R. C. (1992). *Ethics and Excellence: Cooperation and Integrity in Business.* New York: Oxford. (Considers business ethics from an Aristotelian point of view).

EDWIN M. HARTMAN

auditor–client relationships Auditors examine the financial statements of publicly held companies and give their expert opinion concerning the "fairness" of those statements, or whether or not they adhere to "generally accepted accounting principles." Auditors' relationships with their clients must be based on the professional attributes of independence, integrity, and objectivity if the auditors' opinions on their clients' financial statements are to be credible. The auditors' opinion is intended to add credibility to published financial statements, and hence to contribute to the optimal allocation of scarce financial resources in a market economy. But the credibility of the opinion itself rests on the auditors' independence, integrity, and objectivity.

Ethical responsibilities are often related to one's *function.* Auditors have simultaneous, and sometimes competing functions: They serve the public interest (attest function) while simultaneously serving the corporate clients who hire them, fire them, and pay their fees. Thus, balancing auditors' conflicting responsibilities may be likened to walking a moral tightrope.

Three main forces (among others) help to balance the auditors' responsibility toward the public interest, while three other factors (among others) tip it toward the clients' interests:

Toward the Public Interest

1. Professional/firm culture that emphasizes professional attributes (concern for public interest, independence, integrity, objectivity).
2. Generally accepted accounting principles and generally accepted auditing standards.
3. The threat of litigation.

Toward Clients' Interests

1. The fact that clients hire and fire auditors and pay their fees.
2. Non-attestation work for audit clients.
3. Confidentiality rules.

The need for appropriate professional/firm culture is fundamental, since so many individuals look to colleagues to help them discern right from wrong. Accounting principles and auditing standards serve as a threshold, defining minimum corporate disclosures and audit work required. And litigation against auditors has become a very real threat, not only to an adequate livelihood, but to the existence of the firms themselves.

The fact that clients hire auditors, negotiate fees, and may fire them at will creates a mutuality of interests that is difficult, but certainly not impossible, for auditors to rise above. However, the more significant the client is, the more difficult the task becomes.

Consulting and tax work for audit clients have expanded rapidly in recent years. Such work may impair independence in fact, because auditors may end up auditing their own work, or the sheer size of consulting engagements may create a mutuality of interests, or the pressure on audit staff to sell additional services may chip away at their integrity or objectivity. To date, empirical evidence has not supported the wide-spread existence of any of the factors just described. However, independence in appearance, for the profession as a whole, may be affected by the continued growth in non-attest services for audit clients. (For further discussion see Armstrong, 1993.)

Confidentiality rules prohibit auditors from revealing information about their clients beyond that required by generally accepted accounting principles or auditing standards. The public interest, however, may not be well served when certain confidences are not revealed (see Ruland & Lindblom, 1992 and Armstrong, 1994).

Bibliography

Armstrong, M. B. (1993). *Ethics and Professionalism for CPAs*. Cincinnati, Ohio: South-Western.

Armstrong, M. B. (1994). Confidentiality: A comparison across the professions of medicine, engineering, and accounting. *Professional Ethics: A Multidisciplinary Journal*, 3 (1), 71–88.

Ruland, R. G. & Lindblom, C. K. (1992). Ethics and disclosure: An analysis of conflicting duties. *Critical Perspectives on Accounting*, 3, 259–72.

MARY BETH ARMSTRONG

auditing, ethical issues in   *see* ETHICAL ISSUES IN AUDITING

Australia, business ethics in   *see* BUSINESS ETHICS IN AUSTRALIA

authenticity   "Being true to one's self, to one's situation" (Taylor, 1991) where "situation" denotes concrete condition and "condition" replaces "human nature" as our common moral bond. Our condition includes being born, belonging to a particular race, linguistic community, and the like, and dying; in sum, being finite. It does not include a pregiven "self" to be realized or to which one must be true; that would be inauthentic flight from the human condition. The authentic subject is the ongoing result of creative choosing. The authentic person owns his or her situation as non-transferable and radically free. The basis of this existential freedom is our conscious surpassing of the givens of our situation. Authenticity also refers to being worthy of trust.

Sartre's classic definition, "authenticity . . . consists in having a true and lucid consciousness of the situation, in assuming the responsibilities and risks that it involves, in accepting it in pride or humiliation, sometimes in horror and hate" (Sartre, 1948, p. 90), seemed to yield an ethical style more than a content. He corrected this impression in his posthumously published *Notebooks for an Ethics* by lengthy discussions of such concepts as good faith, generosity, positive reciprocity, and gift-appeal as a model for authentic interpersonal relations.

See also **free will; responsibility; self-deception; situation ethics; truthtelling**

Bibliography

Martin, M. (1986). *Self-Deception and Morality*. Lawrence, Kan.: University of Kansas Press.

Sartre, J.-P. (1948 [1946]). *Anti-Semite and Jew*, trans. G. J. Becker. New York: Schocken Books.

Sartre, J.-P. (1956 [1943]). *Being and Nothingness*, trans. H. E. Barnes. New York: Philosophical Library.

Sartre, J.-P. (1992 [1983]). *Notebooks for an Ethics*, trans. D. Pellauer. Chicago: University of Chicago Press.

Taylor, C. (1991). *The Ethics of Authenticity*. Cambridge, Mass.: Harvard University Press.

THOMAS R. FLYNN

authority   is the right or power of *X* (the bearer of authority), by giving some command or making some statement in or with respect to some domain, to produce an appropriate reaction in *Y* (the subject of authority). An authority may be a person, a text (such as the Bible), or a set of rules or laws. The power the person or text wields is sometimes called that person's or that text's authority.

Authority is either executive or epistemic (corresponding to the distinction between someone being *in* authority and someone being *an* authority on a topic). Executive authority results in *Y*'s doing or being required to do some action *A* because commanded by *X*. Whether authority is always legitimate or whether it is proper to speak of illegitimate authority is debated. Authority that is exercised in fact is called *de facto*. Authority that reflects laws or prescriptions of what should be is called *de jure*.

For purposes of business ethics, two aspects of executive authority are relevant: political authority and operative authority, especially entrepreneurial authority. Business is subject to political authority and is widely acknowledged as having an ethical as well as a legal obligation to obey morally justifiable laws. Operative authority consists in the authority a bearer of authority has as a result of being delegated such authority by those subject to it. Thus a corporation may be formed and those involved in its formation agree on rules by which they will choose officers and to whom they will delegate the right and power to make decisions, set policies, and give commands within the domain of the business. Entrepreneurial authority is a type of operative authority in which someone or some group establishes a firm, and others who choose to join the firm as shareholders or employees do so on terms set by the entrepreneurs to which others agree.

Whether there is any justifiable executive authority in ethics, and so in business ethics in the sense that actions become right or wrong in themselves because commanded, is debated. The Divine Command theory grants this right or power to God. Others argue that even God says what is wrong, such as killing innocent human beings, because it is wrong for good reasons and not as a result of his arbitrary decision. Whether there are epistemic authorities in ethics who have knowledge of right and wrong and who are comparable to experts in other fields, such that their saying so is reasonable justification for believing an action right or wrong, is also disputed. Nonetheless, there are clearly exemplary moral authorities, such as Christ and Gandhi, who by their example are taken by others as models of ethical behavior. Those who emphasize virtue-ethics have been especially active in seeking to present the story or lives of individuals who might serve as exemplary moral authorities in the realm of business.

Bibliography

De George, R. T. (1985). *The Nature and Limits of Authority*. Lawrence: University Press of Kansas.

Flathman, R. E. (1980). *The Practice of Political Authority: Authority and the Authoritative*. Chicago: University of Chicago Press.

Friedrich, C. J. (ed.) (1958). *Authority*. Cambridge, Mass: Harvard University Press; reissued, Greenwood, 1981.

Peters, R. S., Winch, P., & Duncan-Jones, A. (1967). Symposium: Authority. *Proceedings of the Aristotelian Society*, supplementary volume 32.

RICHARD T. DE GEORGE

autonomy (self rule): became an issue in moral theory with the rise of modern liberal individualism and the scientific view of the world as devoid of inherent ends and normative laws. The issue was not only how one could be free and subject to political authority, but, more fundamentally, how one could be free and subject to moral obligation. THOMAS HOBBES (1588–1679) grounded moral as well as political obligation in a social contract concurred in by individuals on the basis of self-interest. David Hume (1711–76) and utilitarians followed Hobbes in regarding reason as the servant of desires (*see* UTILITARIANISM). Kant (1724–1804), taking a lead from Rousseau (1712–78), who claimed that one is politically free only if one is subject to only one's own legislation, understood moral autonomy negatively as not being governed by desires nor subject to any moral law imposed on one from an external source, and positively as having a will that is subject to only the requirement of reason that its maxims be such that they could be universal laws (*see* KANTIAN ETHICS). JOHN RAWLS, melding Hobbes and Kant, holds that individuals are, in effect, autonomous, if the principles under which they live are such that rational and free individuals would adopt them, if they were blind to their own interests and circumstances (*see also* INDIVIDUALISM; LIBERALISM; SOCIAL CONTRACT THEORY).

One line of development from Kant threatens individualism. Hegel (1770–1831) identified an individual's real self with the universal Reason that, according to his objective idealism, generates the cosmos and is expressed in a rational society. Thus individuals are said to be most fully themselves and most fully free when they are submissive to their historically evolved society. Their larger self (cosmic Reason) is the author of the social order According to Hegel, some contemporary conservatives (F. A. HAYEK) and communitarians (ALASDAIR MACINTYRE, Robert Bellah, and Amitai Etzioni) are Hegelian in spirit but without Hegel's metaphysical theory of the self (*see* COMMUNITARIANISM). They agree that an historically evolved system of institutions and social practices under the rational constraint of coherence is the basis of morality and that individuals ought to conform to it, but they do not claim that individuals in conforming to established ways are only complying with their own legislation.

Another line of development from Kant leads to subjectivistic individualism and threatens the social order. Some moral philosophers, notably Sartre (1905–80) and R. M. Hare, hold that moral agents are autonomous insofar as they choose their own principles by which to live without any constraint on their will other than the requirement of reason that they judge others by the same principles. So there is nothing to assure a basic moral consensus, a necessary condition for a social order.

Realistic humanism (see Adams, 1991) offers a way of reconciling the autonomy of the individual, basic moral consensus, and a form of communitarianism on the basis of moral realism and a governing self-concept that embraces one's inherent normative constitution as a rational agent and one's several social identities and enduring relationships with their inherent responsibilities.

See also **liberal–communitarian debate, the**

Bibliography

Adams, E. M. (1991). *The Metaphysics of Self and World*. Philadelphia: Temple University Press, chs 6 and 7.

Bellah, R. N., et al. (1991). *The Good Society*. New York: Alfred A. Knopf.

Dworkin, G. (1988). *The Theory and Practice of Autonomy*. Cambridge: Cambridge University Press.

Etzioni, A. (1993). *The Spirit of Community*. New York: Crown Publishers.

Feinberg, J. (1980). *Rights, Justice, and the Bounds of Liberty*. Princeton: Princeton University Press.

Hare, R. M. (1963). *Freedom and Reason*. Oxford: Clarendon Press.

Haworth, L. (1986). *Autonomy: An Essay in Philosophical Psychology and Ethics*. New Haven: Yale University Press.

Hayek, F. A. (1976). *Law, Legislation and Liberty*, vol. 2 of *The Mirage of Social Justice*. London: Routledge & Kegan Paul.

Hegel, G. W. F. (1942 [1821]). *Hegel's Philosophy of Right*, trans. T. M. Knox. Oxford: Oxford University Press.

Hill, T. E., Jr. (1991). *Autonomy and Self-Respect*. Cambridge: Cambridge University Press.

Hobbes, T. (1968 [1651]). *Leviathan*, (ed.), C. B. Macpherson. Harmondsworth, England: Penguin.

Hume, D. (1978 [1748, 1751]). *Enquiries*, (eds), L. A. Shelby-Biggie & P. N. Nidditch. Oxford: Clarendon Press.

Kant, I. (1964 [1785]). *Groundwork of the Metaphysics of Morals*, trans. H. J. Paton. New York: Harper and Row.

MacIntyre, A. (1981). *After Virtue*. Notre Dame, Ind.: University of Notre Dame Press.

Rawls, J. (1971). *A Theory of Justice*. Cambridge, Mass.: Harvard University Press.

Sartre, J.-P. (1948). *Existentialism and Humanism*, trans. P. Mariet. London: Methuen.

Taylor, C. (1975). *Hegel*. Cambridge: Cambridge University Press.

E. M. ADAMS

B

banking The fundamental activities of banks are borrowing and lending money. A bank borrows from its "depositors" and lends to its loan customers. "Deposits" to a checking or savings account are not "on deposit" in safe-keeping. They have gone into the bank's coffers the way a shopper's cash goes into a super-market's till at the check-out counter. That cash has become the bank's (or the supermarket's) property to use in its own interest. Depositors, moreover, are likely to be borrowers as well as lenders, if only through overdraft and credit-card accounts.

Over the years, several types of "bank" – including credit unions, trust companies and savings institutions – have sprung up to provide specialized banking services. The crown jewel of the American banking system, however, is the nation's network of over 10,000 commercial banks with its remarkably successful system of internal self-regulation and oversight by the Federal Reserve System (the US "central bank"), the Federal Deposit Insurance Corpora-tion, the Comptroller of the Currency, and state banking superintendents. It is banks and regulators who, together, take on responsibility for the short-term liquidity and long-term solvency of the banking system.

A powerful parallel banking system is also in place. When the Glass-Steagall Act of 1933 banned commercial banks from securities underwriting, the two industries went their separate ways. Since that time, investment banking has been conducted by such broker dealers as elect to be in the underwriting business. (Those who invest their own capital in a deal are considered "merchant bankers.") A typical bank loan differs considerably in form and regulatory supervision from the creation and sale of a borrower's commercial paper by an investment bank. In practice the results for the borrower can be very similar.

Insights from Ethics

In both commercial and investment banking, ethics plays an important role in safeguarding consumer interests and confidence. Commercial banks rely on compliance training, internal rules, regulatory oversight, the fiduciary ethos embedded in the bank's own trust department, and reinforcement from outside professional groups to maintain ethical standards. The Code of Conduct of The Robert Morris Associates, the national association of commercial loan officers, is a particularly important daily affir-mation of the ethical duties of its members to:

- Ensure that personal interests do not conflict with duties owed to the bank and customers.

- Support good internal governance by full and fair internal disclosure.

- Honor the confidentiality of privileged and proprietary information.

- Help the bank act fairly and in good faith toward customers, while protecting legitimate interests of the bank.

- Provide services on the basis of rational business criteria rather than inappropriate factors such as race, gender, or religion.

- Uphold the standards, policies, and goals of the bank and protect its interests, challenging within the bank any values or policies that are inconsistent with the Code.

Nevertheless, there are always temptations to "take care of number one," especially if this sort of behavior seems to be encouraged by management. Incentive bonuses tied to the number and value of loans sold by an employee can, for example, blind him to concerns about the debt load and resources of the borrower. Bankers need to be able to spot such conflicts and do something about them, perhaps (in this case) by modifying the bonus plan explicitly to reward employee maintenance of satisfactory long-term customer relationships. To catch such an issue in the first place requires a clear sense of corporate business ethics.

The Change from Relationship Banking to Price Banking

In their efforts to maintain a healthy banking industry, banking regulators have at various times set minimum capital reserves, prohibited banks from investing in equities, designated maximum-allowable interest rates payable on deposits, enforced the Glass-Steagall ban on interstate banking, and denied banks the right to enter the insurance and brokerage businesses. They have, however, permitted banks to act as transfer agents for corporate securities, as servicing agents for real estate mortgages, and as managers of personal and corporate retire-ment trusts. These businesses have seemed a good fit for the banks and, in practice, enriched the codes of conduct and oversight for the bank as a whole. Still, they were not the big revenue generators that the American banking industry felt it needed as the financial world began to move.

By the mid-1970s, foreign "universal" banks (with both investment and commercial banking services under one roof), global investment banks, and domestic money-market mutual funds had all begun to poke at traditional US bank markets. To meet the new competition, banks pressed for changes in regulations, for a "level playing field." They were granted the ability to pay flexible interest rates on deposits, allowed to engage in interstate banking, and given opportunities to participate in the mutual fund business so long as an independent broker was in the picture. Despite its willingness to allow these new freedoms, the federal govern-ment's ban on investment banking held firm.

The largest banks sought to cope by exercis-ing very aggressively what powers they did have. Loan relationships were dismantled, with banks selling loans after they were negotiated

and keeping the origination fees. Some banks expanded securities trading for their own account (forgetting how much money can be lost trading even in sound credits like US Treasury obligations). Others made bigger bets on loans to borrowers with lower credit ratings. And a few took on the investment bankers of the world by flexing their overseas investment-banking muscle, developing "innovative invest-ment instruments" (also known as "derivatives") and risking takeover bridge loans.

Then, in 1987, by a 3 to 2 vote, the Board of the Federal Reserve authorized three bank holding-company applicants (Citicorp, J. P. Morgan & Co. Incorporated, and Bankers Trust New York Corporation) to engage in activities their banks were banned from: dealing (buying and selling as principal in the secondary market) and underwriting (through a separate broker affiliate) municipal bonds (including revenue bonds), mortgage-related securities, credit card receivables, and commercial paper, on condition that the broker affiliate's revenues did not exceed 5 percent of the bank's total revenues. Soon, the Board increased permissible revenues to 10 percent, added asset-backed securities, futures, options, and foreign exchange to the dealing list, and, in 1992 allowed bank complexes to offer full-service securities brokerage.

The Challenge for Ethics

As a discipline focusing on the rights of others, ethics is especially important to the financial industry, where so many products and transactions are subtle and complex, the product is money, time is often tight, and a premium is placed on innovation. Decision-makers with ethics training can anticipate persons potentially at risk of harm who might be invisible to another person:

- employees of target companies whose jobs are needlessly put at risk in leveraged buyouts;

- customers who rely on brand-name products because of the quality achieved by prior owners;

- brokerage employees entitled to a workplace that is not morally corrosive;

America's taxpayers, who may have to underwrite losses of pension funds or bank-deposit insurance or the capital of risk-taking municipalities;

optimistic, trusting widow-and-orphan type investors who can be enticed into risky investments.

When ethics is on the agenda, such interests will be noticed and can be addressed. Without such a vision, the analysis and the effects of a decision may be fatally flawed.

Other challenges include the following: In weighing the regulatory risks of expanding bank powers against the competitive risks of restricting them, the Federal Reserve Board focused first and foremost on the safety of shareholder capital, considering how the conflicts inherent in the bank's lending to corporate customers of a bank-affiliated broker-dealer might be fairly managed and what would constitute adequate disclosure in this regard to customers. The Board also studied the effectiveness of a "fire wall" to separate conflicting interests within the bank complex. As part of the solution, the SECURITIES AND EXCHANGE COMMISSION has become the regulator of the brokering activities of the bank, providing eyes trained to catch subtle predatory trading practices.

Each of these new ventures and products has its own ethos, risks, professional demands, and regulatory nets which must be understood and maintained in their own environment as they are integrated into the life of the complex as a whole. Even as the banks work to integrate these new business opportunities, regulators seem increasingly willing to rely on market forces of supply and demand not only to price products, but potentially to determine which banks will fail, which survive, and how. Self-regulation, therefore, is becoming both more complicated and more important. In order for the system to work, banking executives must involve themselves in the development of workable and fair standards of practice and pledge themselves to applying a common ethic appropriately to the bank's various business enterprises. At the least this ethic should reward employee candor and

encourage all bank personnel to treat each other and the bank's shareholders, managers, customers and competitors, with honesty and respect.

JOHN L. CASEY and
BRUCE MCCANDLESS III

bankruptcy, ethical issues in   *see* ETHICAL ISSUES IN BANKRUPTCY

Barnard, Chester   Chester Barnard's ideas on management ethics presented in his classic book on management theory, *The Functions of the Executive* (1938), are formulated in terms of "executive responsibility." Barnard splits the individual into two personalities: "organization personality" and "individual personality" (p. 88). The "individual personality" is utilitarian and makes decisions according to a cost–benefit calculus. This is the autonomous individual decision-maker from economic theory (*see* UTILITARIANISM).

The individual assumes an "organization personality" when he or she views organization purpose, not from his or her own personal interest, but from the view of the cooperative process as a whole. This idea is central to Barnard's understanding of management ethics. The executive, to be ethical, must take on an "organization personality." He or she must make decisions that are in the interests of the organization as a whole. This is why Barnard defines "loyalty" as the "most important single contribution required of the executive" (1938, p. 220).

Formulating executive responsibility in this way presents two problems. First, how does the executive know what common purpose to apply to the organization as a whole? Barnard finesses this problem by assuming that the "subjective" individual commits to the "objective purpose" of the organization (1938, p. 89). "Objective purpose" is one of Barnard's myths, because deciding what should be the purpose of an organization has both subjective and political aspects. Whether one or several individuals decide what the purpose should be, subjectivity is not removable from the process. For example, should I dedicate my organization to average profits and job security or maximum short-term profits and no job security? There is no purely objective way to make this decision. One must choose what one values most. Barnard conceals the subjective aspect of these choices in his assumption of objective purpose.

Objective purpose is part of Barnard's belief that organizations are ends in themselves. In the words of William G. Scott (1992), Barnard believed "organizational decisions were driven by an enterprise's needs, not by the needs of the people in it" (p. 142). It can be seen, then, that Barnard reifies the idea of organization into a self-defined or "formal" organization. This allows him to avoid the primarily political nature of formulating a common purpose by assuming the organization has its own purpose. Hence, Barnard's concept of executive responsibility has a bias built into it, because the assumption of objective purpose legitimizes the established power-holders.

Second, by defining executive responsibility in terms of organization purpose, Barnard's management ethics is silent about the relations between organizations. If the executive is responsible only to his or her organization, then there is no ethical regulation of how the executive treats competitors, communities, or anybody outside the organization. What tends to happen in this situation and indeed what has happened this century is that each organization pursues its own interests only within the constraints of the law and more than a small number of times even the law is not respected. As Durkheim (1957) noted, the law will be a weak and ineffectual institution in a society whose members do not have a strong commitment to the ultimate beliefs of the society as a whole.

Barnard, on the contrary, attempts to justify formal organizations as the central institutions of society. In fact, he defines society as an "indefinite, nebulous, and undirected system" (1938, p. 79). He thinks society has an influence on individuals and organizations, but this influence is not organized. In an "indefinite" society, Barnard concludes that individuals develop "several private moral codes," corresponding to all the different associations they join (p. 262). Barnard assumes there is no overall organization of society to provide priorities among different moral codes. This assumption is a result of the misleading concept of culture Barnard utilizes in his work. In contrast, Mead (1934), for example, insists that societies represent an "organized pattern of experience" (p. 222).

But Barnard's assumption of societal disorganization is not altogether wrong. To the extent his concepts of "several private moral codes" and an "indefinite" society are accurate, they describe the cultural and moral fragmentation of modern society. This demonstrates the ahistorical nature of Barnard's work. Instead of recognizing the ahistorical problem of cultural and moral fragmentation, he defines society as a fragmented entity. This opens the way for him to recommend formal organizations and the executives who control them as, in Scott's (1992) words, the new "guardians of the managerial state." This is the underlying political purpose in Barnard's theoretical effort.

Barnard's political purpose is based on his faith that executives, dominated by the "organization personality," are able to provide moral leadership to organize a morally complex and diverse organizational situation. Ultimately, however, in situations of conflict between different codes, Barnard leaves the executive to his or her own "personal codes" (1938, p. 281). This is why Barnard stresses "moral creativeness" as the highest level of executive responsibility (p. 279). Hence, the bottom line is that morality originates with the individual. This is a key point because this extreme individualism shows Barnard's management ethics has practically no social base.

This presents Barnard's management ethics with a major problem. In a morally fragmented society, where there is no moral consensus, from where does the executive get his moral codes and why are they legitimate? Barnard does not answer these questions. Barnard's concept of executive responsibility, like his concept of organization purpose, assumes moral legitimacy, but never demonstrates it. Thus, falling short of a management ethics, Barnard's work can be seen as an ideological justification of executive control.

See also **managerial ethics and the ethical role of the manager**

Bibliography

Barnard, C. I. (1938). *The Functions of the Executive.* Cambridge, Mass.: Harvard University Press.

Durkheim, E. (1957). *Professional Ethics and Civic Morals*. New York: Routledge.

Mead, G. H. (1934). *Mind, Self, and Society*. Chicago: University of Chicago Press.

Scott, W. G. (1992). *Chester I. Barnard and the Guardians of the Managerial State*. Lawrence, Kan.: University Press of Kansas.

Weber, M. (1946). *From Max Weber: Essays in Sociology*. London: Routledge and Keagan Paul.

STEVEN P. FELDMAN

Baumhart, Rev. Raymond C., SJ Father Raymond Baumhart, SJ, is perhaps best known to students and scholars of business ethics for his ground breaking empirical research that helped to define the field. His career is far more expansive: he is also known for his teaching, scholarship, university administration (including 23 distinguished years as President of Loyola University of Chicago), church and civic leadership.

While a Doctoral Candidate at Harvard Business School, Baumhart published the first findings of his definitive empirical research on the thoughts of business executives about ethics in business. His article "How Ethical Are Businessmen?" appeared in the *Harvard Business Review* in 1961. The questionnaire, a six-page, 29-question form "was mailed to a systematic sample of 5,000 subscribers to the *Harvard Business Review*" (1968, p. 5). 1,700 forms were returned, 1,531 were tabulated for the article (1961, p. 8).

The questionnaire employed several different approaches to establish the respondents' assessment of ethical problems and attitudes in business. Respondents were asked to indicate their level of agreement with statements about business practice. They were given cases or vignettes and asked either what they would do or what other business executives would likely do. They were asked to evaluate codes of ethics and what clergymen have to offer businessmen.

In 1968 Baumhart published *An Honest Profit: What Businessmen Say About Ethics in Business*. In this book he reports not only the questionnaire results but is able to provide rich interpretation of the data that he drew from 100 "focused interviews" with a "quota sample" of businessmen which he completed in 1962 (1968, p. 7).

A wide variety of partial replications of the Baumhart study have been published over the years: Baumhart (1968) reported a study that administered part of his questionnaire to 156 students at Dartmouth, Boston College, and Loyola University; Greyser (1962) used a few of the questions in a study of business managers which focused on advertising; Fulmer (1967) administered part of the questionnaire to 1,158 graduate business students; McHale (1970) studied 373 students at Loyola University of Chicago's Rome Center; Purcell (1977) looked at Dartmouth students' responses while in school in 1961 and then 10 years later; Glenn (1988, 1992, 1993) collected data from undergraduate and graduate business students from 1975 to 1985 at five institutions (N = 1,274) and then in a national replication at 18 business schools (N = 1,668); in 1976 Brenner and Molander (1977) replicated part of the study with 1,227 *Harvard Business Review* readers; Monappa (1977) replicated the study with Indian Managers; Becker and Fritzsche (1987) used some of his questions in their cross-cultural study of managers (N = 226); and most recently in Japan, Chiaki Nakano, at Reitaku University, is using some of Baumhart's questions in his research.

The significance of the empirical research Baumhart produced has been acknowledged by a variety of scholars: Preston (1986) in his review of social issues and public policy in business speaks of "the classic study by Baumhart" (p. 29). Cavanagh and Fritzsche (1985) in their review of business ethics research note that Baumhart's work is "the most quoted and the most replicated empirical study of business ethics" (p. 284). And its importance continues to be recognized in texts for courses in Business, Government, and Society (Carroll, 1993, p. 85; Steiner & Steiner, 1994, p. 185).

Bibliography

Baumhart, R. C. (1961). How ethical are businessmen? *Harvard Business Review*, **39** (4), 6–19, 156–76.

Baumhart, R. C. (1968). *An Honest Profit: What Businessmen Say About Ethics in Business*. New York: Holt, Rinehart, & Winston. (Also published in paperback version as *Ethics in Business*.)

Baumhart, R. C. with Garrett, T. M., Purcell, T. V. & Roets, P. (1968). *Cases in Business Ethics.* New York: Appleton-Century-Crofts.

Becker, H. & Fritzsche, D. J. (1987). Business ethics: A cross-cultural comparison of manager's attitudes. *Journal of Business Ethics,* **6,** 289–95.

Brenner, S. N. & Molander, E. A. (1977). Is the ethics of business changing? *Harvard Business Review,* **57 (1),** 57–71.

Carroll, A. B. (1993). *Business and Society: Ethics and Stakeholder Management,* 2nd edn. Cincinnati, Ohio: South-Western Publishing Co.

Cavanagh, G. F. & Fritzsche, D. J. (1985). Using vignettes in business ethics research. In Preston, L. E. (ed.), *Research in Corporate Social Performance and Policy.* Greenwich, Conn.: JAI Press, 279–93.

Fulmer, R. M. (1967). An investigation into the ethical standards of graduating M.B.A.s. Working paper no. 67-68-1, Tallahassee, Fla.: Florida State University School of Business.

Glenn, J. R., Jr. (1988). Business curriculum and ethics: Student attitudes and behavior. *Business and Professional Ethics Journal,* **7 (3&4),** 167–85.

Glenn, J. R., Jr. (1992). Can a business and society course affect the ethical judgment of future managers? *Journal of Business Ethics,* **11 (3)** 217–23.

Glenn, J. R., Jr. & Van Loo, M. F. (1993). Business students' and practitioners' ethical decisions over time. *Journal of Business Ethics,* **12 (11),** 835–47.

Greyser, S. A. (1962). Businessmen re advertising: "Yes, But . . . ". *Harvard Business Review,* **40 (3),** 20–30.

McHale, J. P. (1970). An evaluation of collegians' ethics and the implications of this evaluation for personnel selection by business firms. Unpublished M.A. thesis, Chicago: Loyola University Institute of Industrial Relations.

Monappa, A. (1977). *Ethical Attitudes of Indian Managers.* New Delhi: All India Management Association.

Nakano, Chiaki. (1996). A survey study on Japanese managers' views of business ethics. *Journal of Business Ethics,* forthcoming.

Preston, L. E. (1986). Social issues and public policy in business and management: Retrospect and prospect. College Park, Md.: Center for Business and Public Policy.

Purcell, T. V. (1977). Do courses in business ethics pay off? *California Management Review,* **19 (4),** 50–8.

Steiner, G. A. & Steiner, J. F. (1994). *Business, Government, and Society,* 7th edn, New York: McGraw-Hill.

JAMES R. GLENN, JR.

Bentham, Jeremy Bentham (1748–1832) gave UTILITARIANISM its name and its first articulate secular defense. Born to a prosperous London lawyer in 1748, he trained for the bar, but decided early to devote his life "to rear[ing] the fabric of felicity by the hands of reason and of law" through radical reform of English law, society, and politics. When he died in 1832, the influence of his "science of legislation" had spread to Europe and most of Latin America. John Stuart Mill, Bentham's godson and protégé, molded utilitarianism into one of the most influential moral and political theories of the nineteenth and twentieth centuries.

Bentham grounded his reform project on the "principle of utility," which requires that we always act to produce the greatest overall happiness. Critics argue that utilitarianism endorses cold-blooded calculation and an abstract and impoverished conception of human happiness. Also, Bentham's dismissal of natural rights as "nonsense on stilts" led critics to portray his theory as morally blind. However, its motivation was more humane and morally sensitive than his critics allow. Bentham believed that the principle of utility issued two complementary directives: "the greatest happiness principle" and "the happiness enumeration principle." The former sets the focus for utilitarian deliberation; it requires that we seek to maximize the happiness of *each* sentient being. The latter principle requires that we seek "the greatest happiness of the greatest number" when we can promote one person's happiness only at the expense of another's. Philosophers dispute whether the result is coherent, but it is clear that Bentham's principle rested on the conviction that the most fundamental moral concern is a benevolent regard for the concrete well-being of each individual human being.

Bentham thought it is always rational for one to pursue one's own happiness, but the utilitarian principle demands that we promote the happiness of *any* and every human being. To show that this demand is also rational, he argued that moral judgments are rational and public and so are valid only if they can be justified in terms of reasons accessible to others. Thus, to justify demands we make on others we must express them in terms of happiness viewed impartially. This forces us to regard the happiness of each person as equally morally important. ("Each is to count for one and no one for more than one," as Mill put it later.) Thus, at its core, Bentham's utilitarianism is humane and egalitarian. This may explain in part its continued appeal over the past two centuries.

Bentham's hedonistic view of human motivation influenced his account of the aim and structure of social morality. All human action, he believed, is caused by the agent's attraction to pleasure and aversion to pain. He often confused this with the view that all human action is directed to promotion of the agent's own pleasure (psychological egoism). Yet, he also recognized that people often act from good (or ill) will towards others, which puts his commitment to psychological egoism in doubt. There is no doubt, however, that he advocated *strategic egoism*. Since we are more likely to be moved by self-interest than by any other motive, he argued, officials and moral teachers must build incentives into social norms to ensure that "duty" and "interest" coincide. Thus Bentham viewed social morality as an informal kind of law designed to provide individuals with motives sufficient to ensure compliance with the utilitarian principle.

See also **egoism, psychological egoism and ethical egoism**

Bibliography

Bentham, Jeremy. (1968–). *Collected Works of Jeremy Bentham*, eds J. H. Burns, J. R. Dinwiddy, & F. Rosen. London: Athlone Press; Oxford: Oxford University Press [In progress; definitive editions of work previously published and unpublished.]

Bentham, Jeremy. (1970). *An Introduction to the Principles of Morals and Legislation [1789]*, (eds), J. H. Burns & H. L. A. Hart. London: Athlone Press.

Dinwiddy, John. (1989). *Bentham*. Oxford: Oxford University Press.

Harrison, Ross. (1983). *Bentham*. London: Routledge & Kegan Paul.

Postema, Gerald J. (1986, rev. edn 1989). *Bentham and the Common Law Tradition*. Oxford: Clarendon Press.

GERALD J. POSTEMA

Berle, Adolf A.   (1895–1971): Brilliant product of Harvard's College and Law School, Adolf Berle was superbly prepared when called to serve in President Roosevelt's brain trust and, later, in high positions at the State Department and in other diplomacy-related assignments. He is best remembered by business scholars, however, for his seminal studies on the contemporary corporation. With Columbia colleague Gardiner Means, Berle published in 1932 *The Modern Corporation and Private Property*, an incisive analysis of how ownership and control had become disconnected. Such separation left stockholders with only "derivative rights," that is, rights simply to retain or sell their holdings.

Berle sounded the alarm against the concentrated power of the new professionally educated managerial elites whose influence was felt by the entire society. He looked for countervailing forces. Since investment bankers, traditionally the disciplining agents, had lost ground as corporations generated their own investment-capital needs out of earnings, the only two remaining restraints were federal regulation and "people's capitalism," by which he meant the diffusion of stockholding among the general public. Aware of their inadequacies, Berle nevertheless felt that corporate capitalism was the most productive system in the world and emphasized this point in his 1954 study, *The 20th Century Capitalist Revolution*.

Despite sharp criticisms, Berle consistently maintained that managements would be driven by public opinion to balance the interests of various claimants through a social covenant where private cupidity had no place: maximizing short-term profits is subordinate to other goals, such as adequate dividends to stockholders, good wages for labor, and fair prices to consumers.

Anticipating the growth of Big Labor and Big Government as additional constraints on large corporations, Berle published in 1963 *The American Economic Republic*, wherein he outlined the need for a fourth player in the economic game, namely, the stockholders themselves. Absent their voice, the triad of Big Business, Big Labor, and Big Government might develop mutual interests that would frustrate the legitimate claims of stockholders and consumers.

Berle raised questions that business ethicists still confront. If corporations are guided by "tiny self-perpetuating oligarchies" whose major restraints are the consciences of those who compose them, the *virtue ethic* becomes important. But is conscience enough – or should corporations be required to include on their boards representatives of workers, consumers, and governments? (Berle himself disliked this idea.) Are pension-fund managers the new police? What is the meaning of corporate social responsibilities? If the manager's conscience is King, should business schools require ethics courses? What are the appropriate relationships between boards and managers?

See also **Means, Gardiner Coit; virtue ethics**

Bibliography

Berle, A. A. (1954). *The 20th Century Capitalist Revolution*. New York: Harcourt, Brace and World.
Berle, A. A. (1959). *Power without Property*. New York: Harcourt, Brace and World.
Berle, A. A. (1963). *The American Economic Republic*. New York: Harcourt, Brace and World.
Berle, A. A. (1970). *Power*. New York: Harcourt, Brace and World.
Berle, A. A. & Means, G. (1933). *The Modern Corporation and Private Property*. New York: Macmillan Company.

CLARENCE C. WALTON

biodiversity The word biodiversity refers to the manner in which life has evolved to produce a wide diversity of species filling an extraordinary range of environments. From Antarctica where fish live in water so cold that it turns the blood of warm blooded creatures to ice, to boiling springs and volcanic vents in the deep ocean where unique strains of bacteria live, life has flourished on this planet. Because life is so widely distributed, whenever some local disaster or change of climate occurs, the affected area is usually quickly repopulated by species from other areas. If life were not so diverse, it is unlikely that it would have successfully evolved to its present state. Nevertheless, life is still vulnerable because of the fragile, interconnected nature of ecosystems. If one species becomes extinct, others usually increase to take over its roles in maintaining the ecosystem. But some

species, known as keystone species, play such important roles in their ecosystems that if they decline the entire ecosystem undergoes radical change or total collapse. The fewer the types of organisms in the ecosystem, the more likely this is to occur. Biodiversity, therefore, serves an indispensable role, not only as a reserve to repopulate depleted areas, but in the maintenance of ecosystems. Keystone species are not necessarily large, easily identified organisms, but include tiny, obscure micro-organisms. A handful of soil from most places on earth will contain numerous micro-organisms, fungi, and insects essential to the ecosystems of which they are a part. If insects were to die off, most flowering plants would become extinct, and many other species, including *homo sapiens*, would quickly follow. Other inconspicuous species play an equally essential role in the maintenance of marine ecosystems.

Biodiversity is currently declining at a rapid rate. The primary cause of the decline is massive human population growth that has brought about habitat destruction, pollution, and hunting of species to extinction. Other causes include introduction of foreign species into new habitats, bringing diseases and crowding out or killing native species. If global warming brings about a temperature increase of only one or two degrees, it will produce climatic changes and flooding that will result in the extinction of many species, especially arctic species and species living along coasts.

Tropical rain forests, which are estimated to contain more than half of all species, are especially at risk because they are situated in countries with large populations whose need for jobs and resources is bringing about destruction of the forests by slash-and-burn agriculture, ranching, and logging. Despite their great fertility, tropical rain forests are among the most fragile of all ecosystems. Most grow in acidic soil from which nutrients are quickly lost when the forests are cut, so that within two or three years, artificial fertilizers are required to grow crops. Over half of all rain forest has already been cut, and at the present rate of destruction, only one fourth of the original growth will remain in 30 years. Unless population growth can be curbed, and alternative employment found for people of tropical countries, it seems unlikely that further destruction can be prevented. Since rain forests contain species of plants and animals that have great potential as sources of food, medicine, and other products, one hope is to increase the quantity of products that can be extracted from the forests without destroying them. Ecotourism is another way to increase income from the forests. However, it is unlikely that these sources of revenue will be sufficient to prevent the destruction of the forests. Unless governments declare them natural preserves, the destruction will continue. But, because third world countries lack the money to police them, the biodiversity of existing preserves is by no means secure. Thus, only international assistance can save the rain forests. It is important that they be preserved as intact as possible, for the larger the area, the greater the biodiversity. Indeed, many existing preserves need to be expanded because the area set aside is too small to provide sufficient territory for many of the species they contain to survive. Smaller preserves need to be created within already settled areas. Additional zoos, botanical gardens, seed banks, etc., need to be created. Also coral reefs, which contain the heaviest concentrations of marine biodiversity, need to be more vigorously protected, and aquaculture expanded as an alternative to fishing.

Since most people are ignorant of the importance of biodiversity in maintaining ecosystems, and are often motivated by immediate financial gain, attempts to expand natural preserves are likely to meet even stronger resistance than in the past. If the loggers of the Pacific Northwest are unable to understand the importance of preserving the spotted owl, they are even less likely to understand the necessity of preserving still more obscure species. Like most of the world's population, they believe that it will not make any difference if species continue to vanish from the earth. They foolishly think that the remainder of life will continue as before. The problem of how to save the world's biodiversity is thus, in part, one of education. In attempting to educate the public about environmental issues, environmentalists need to shift their focus from preserving individual species to preserving ecosystems. The spotted owl is only one of many species that will be extinguished if the Pacific Northwest forests are cut, among them the western

yew, source of a promising anti-cancer agent. The world's biodiversity should be preserved, if for no other reason, until scientists have had sufficient time to assess its economic worth, which will no doubt greatly increase with the further development of genetic engineering. But, economic analysis is an inadequate tool for measuring the full value of biodiversity, which is essential for the continuation of life on earth. It is perhaps too much to hope that humankind in general might develop a sense of respect for other species as having intrinsic worth, but perhaps they can be brought to see that the more we preserve biodiversity the more secure our own future will be.

Bibliography

Myers, N. (1988). *Biodiversity.* Washington, DC: National Academy of Science Press.
Pierce, C. & VanDeVeer, D. (eds),. (1994). *Environmental Ethics and Policy Book: Philosophy, Ecology, Economics.* Belmont, Calif.: Wadsworth Publishing.
Wilson, E. O. (1992). *The Diversity of Life.* New York: W. W. Norton.

GENE G. JAMES

bluffing and deception Deception can be defined as causing someone to have false beliefs (or intentionally causing someone to have false beliefs). To bluff in a negotiation is to attempt to deceive the other party about one's intentions or negotiating position. Another kind of deception that is common in both negotiations and sales is deception about the features of the good or service being sold.

Bluffing

It is generally contrary to one's own self-interest to reveal one's intentions while negotiating. A seller who is negotiating with a potential customer usually has a minimum price below which she is unwilling to sell. Generally, it would be contrary to her own self-interest for her to reveal her minimum price, for, if she does, the buyer will be unwilling to offer anything more than that minimum. It can be to one's advantage to make false claims about one's negotiating position, e.g., a seller stating a minimum acceptable price that is higher than her actual minimum or a buyer misstating the maximum price she is willing to pay. Such claims can enable one to reach a more favorable settlement than one would have otherwise obtained. But, if (as in most cases) the parties to the negotiation don't know the negotiating position of the other party, misstating one's intentions in this way risks losing an opportunity to reach a mutually acceptable agreement. (One might state a position unacceptable to the other party when, in fact, one's actual position is acceptable to him.)

Is it morally wrong for negotiators to make deliberate false claims about their intentions or negotiating positions? For example, would it be wrong for me to tell you that $90,000 is absolutely the lowest price that I will accept for my house, when I know that I would be willing to accept as little as $80,000? Such statements count as lies according to most dictionary definitions of lying; they are intentional false statements that are intended to deceive others. However, Carr argues that such statements are not lies since people do not expect to be told the truth about such matters in negotiations. On Carr's account, nothing said by a notoriously dishonest person could constitute a lie, because others do not expect her to speak truthfully. (See Carson 1993 for a detailed discussion of the question of whether bluffing constitutes lying.)

According to Carr, it is morally permissible for people to misstate their intentions in negotiations, because "it is normal business practice" and is "within the accepted rules of the business game." Carr claims that actions which conform to normal and generally accepted business practices are *ipso facto* morally permissible. This principle seems highly implausible in light of reflection on such things as slavery and child labor, which were once normal and "generally accepted" business practices. Carson, Wokutch, and Murrmann (1982) argue that the morality of misstating one's negotiating position depends on the actions of the other parties to the negotiation: there is a strong presumption against misstating one's negotiating position if the other party is not misstating her position, but little presumption against doing this if the other person is misstating her position. Carson (1993) develops a "generalized principle of self-defense." This principle implies that the moral presumption

against lying and deception does not hold when one is dealing with people who are, themselves, engaged in lying and deception and thereby harming one.

Deception about the Nature of the Products being Sold

In negotiations sellers often provide prospective buyers information about the goods or services being sold. What are the obligations of sellers in such cases? This question is central to ethics of sales. We need to distinguish between deception, lying, withholding information, and concealing information. Roughly, deception is causing someone to have false beliefs. Lying arguably requires the intent to deceive others, but lies that don't succeed in causing others to have false beliefs are not instances of deception. A further difference between lying and deception is that, while all lies are false statements, deceiving someone needn't involve making false statements; true statements can be deceptive and some forms of deception don't involve making any statements. Withholding information does not constitute deception. It is not a case of *causing* someone to have false beliefs; it is merely a case of failing to correct false beliefs or incomplete information. On the other hand, actively concealing information usually constitutes deception. Both negotiators and salespeople make factual representations about goods and services they are selling. Deceptive statements about what is being sold (whether or not they are lies) raise serious ethical questions. There is, on the face of it, a strong· moral presumption against such statements due to the harm they are likely to cause potential buyers.

Discussions of the ethics of sales often focus on the ethics of withholding information. The legal doctrine of *caveat emptor* ("buyer beware") says that sellers are not obligated to inform prospective buyers about the properties of the goods they sell. Buyers, themselves, are responsible for determining the quality of the goods they purchase. *Caveat emptor* permits sellers to withhold information about the things they sell, but it doesn't permit lying or (active) deception about such matters. Many take this legal principle to be an acceptable moral principle and hold that sellers have no moral duty to provide buyers with information about the goods they are selling. David Holley argues that *caveat emptor* is no longer an acceptable standard. Given the complexity of many modern goods, it is impossible for most people to judge their quality with any accuracy. Holley claims that salespeople are obligated to reveal all information they would want to know if they were considering buying the product. This seems too strong; it implies that a sales clerk in a store is obligated to inform customers if he knows that the product they are looking at can be purchased at a lower price elsewhere.

See also **advertising ethics; ethics of marketing; negotiation and bargaining; ethical issues in real estate sales; truthtelling**

Bibliography

Carr, A. (1968). Is business bluffing ethical? *Harvard Business Review,* **46,** 143–53.
Carson, T. (1993). Second thoughts about bluffing. *Business Ethics Quarterly,* **3,** 317–41.
Carson, T., Wokutch, R., & Murrmann, K. (1982). Bluffing in labor negotiations: Legal and ethical issues. *Journal of Business Ethics* **1,** 13–22.
Dees, J. & Crampton, P. (1991). Shrewd bargaining on the moral frontier: Towards a theory of morality in practice. *Business Ethics Quarterly,* **1,** 135–67.
Ebejer, J. & Morden, M. (1988). Paternalism in the marketplace: Should a salesman be his buyer's keeper? *Journal of Business Ethics,* **7,** 337–9. (This paper criticizes both *caveat emptor* and Holley's views.)
Holley, D. (1986). A moral evaluation of sales practices. *Business and Professional Ethics Journal,* **5,** 3–22.
Kavka, G. (1983). When two "wrongs" make a right: An essay in business ethics. *Journal of Business Ethics,* **2,** 61–6.

THOMAS L. CARSON

boundaries of the moral community Who or what is a moral agent, capable of acting ethically, and to whom (or what) does a moral agent owe some degree of consideration? Reasonable people have differed over whether corporations, states, or nations are moral agents in the same sense that individuals are. People have also differed over whether moral agents should include non-human entities – such as ants, aardvarks, or aliens from outer space – in their moral deliberations. (For example, are there ethical problems in killing ants at a picnic, in driving aardvarks to extinction, or assuming that the alien is hostile and must, if possible, be destroyed?) The boundaries of the moral community are thus not firmly fixed, and will vary depending on who are properly considered as moral agents and what kinds of entities are entitled to moral consideration.

Some have argued that a corporation, being a legal entity rather than a "natural" one, cannot have the same kind of moral will, nor the same kind of ethical accountability, as an individual person. Still others (Friedman, 1970) would argue that, even if a corporation can be ethically accountable, its ethical obligations are limited to the corporation's shareholders; any considerations given to customers, suppliers, employees, or the community would only exist because it is profitable for the corporation to do so (*see* FRIEDMAN, MILTON). That view is disputed by many ethicists, who argue that a corporation's stockholders are not its only stakeholders (Goodpaster, 1991) (*see* STAKEHOLDER THEORY).

Nations and states are significantly different from individuals or corporations, yet individual people (and various political institutions) tend to make judgments about them. In the twentieth century, moral judgments have been made and followed with reference to Nazi Germany, the Stalinist Soviet Union, and apartheid South Africa, among others. More recently, international trade has been tied by some nations (somewhat sporadically) to progress in human rights, and some nations refuse to allow the importation of products made by prison labor.

Aside from questions of who may be moral agents, there are boundary questions of who should be included in any moral/ethical calculation. UTILITARIANISM's touchstone, "the greatest good for the greatest number," or "the greatest pleasure for the greatest number," does not identify *whose* good or pleasure is to be counted in any ethical calculus. The effects of any decision on ants, amoebas, or antelopes are presumably not counted unless those effects, in turn, affect human interests. (This is an anthropocentric view of the boundaries of the moral community, rather than an eco-centric or bio-centric view.) (*See* ENVIRONMENT AND ENVIRONMENTAL ETHICS). For Kantian deontology, universalizing presumably involves considering categorical imperatives for human (rather than non-human) action (*see* UNIVERSALIZABILITY). For a libertarian philosophy, freedom of human beings from coercion by other human beings is a central concept. In the libertarian view, humans exerting control or coercion over non-human entities such as aardvarks or antelopes does not raise moral concerns (*see* LIBERTARIANISM).

Thus, expanding moral boundaries to include non-humans in a moral calculus departs from traditional approaches to ethics. The work of Peter Singer, Arne Naess, and others who argue for a shift from homo-centric to bio-centric or eco-centric ethics would expand our moral boundaries beyond human-centered interests. The passage of the Endangered Species Act and the Marine Mammal Protection Act in the United States is, by some accounts, some evidence of the law's willingness to move toward a less homo-centric ethic. R. F. Nash has suggested that the inclusion of animals' rights in public policies may be a further extension of a liberating process that began centuries ago, when men with property wrested rights from the king, and gradually certain rights were extended to slaves, women, and children.

As children, our moral universe is arguably limited to ourselves. As we age, and comprehend the existence and needs of others, our moral universe expands. The needs and desires of family, friends, and others are more likely to be part of our ethical deliberations. Lawrence Kohlberg believed that moral development required an individual to move beyond personal reward or punishment to consider the greatest good, or to adopt a decision which could be universalized. Gilligan's work is often interpreted as suggesting that an ethic of caring that put family and friends before unknown others was defensible yet different from Kohlberg's approach.

"Boundaries for the moral community" thus involves basic issues for business ethics: 1) Are corporations and nations moral agents in the same sense that human individuals are? If not, what are the relevant differences? 2) Are non-humans to be considered at all in ethical decisions? If so, what level of consideration is appropriate? 3) To what extent should any moral agent take into moral account the interests of anyone or anything not closely connected with themselves?

Answers to such questions vary widely. For global politics, many have historically advocated national self-interest as the supreme organizing principle. Some individuals operate from a purely egoistic framework, or put self and family before and above all others. In more communitarian societies, obligations extend to larger groups of people (*see* COMMUNITARIANISM). Some ethicists believe that a business organization's most ethical decision will sometimes involve some sacrifice to the business (including employees and shareholders) or to the decision-maker personally. Some others have concluded that for business ethicists to seriously advise such sacrifices can only ensure that ethics is not taken seriously by those who do business.

Bibliography

Evan, W. M. & Freeman, R. E. (1988). A stakeholder theory of the modern corporation: Kantian capitalism. In T. Beauchamp and N. Bowie (eds), *Ethical Theory and Business*, 3rd edn. Englewood Cliffs, NJ: Prentice-Hall, 97–105.

Friedman, M. (1970). The social responsibility of business is to increase its profits. *New York Times Magazine*, Sept. 13, 32–3, 122–6.

Goodpaster, K. E. (1991). Business ethics and stakeholder analysis. *Business Ethics Quarterly*, 1, 53–73.

Lickona, T. (ed.), . (1976). *Moral Development and Behavior: Theory, Research, and Social Issues*. New York: Holt, Rinehart, and Winston, 31–53. (Reviewing literature in support of and critical of Kohlberg's work.)

Nash, R. F. (1989). *The Rights of Nature: A History of Environmental Ethics*. Madison, Wis.: The University of Wisconsin Press.

DON MAYER

bourgeois virtue   The moral excellence of businesspeople, such as responsibility, honesty, prudence, and enterprise. The bourgeois virtues are contrasted with aristocratic virtues such as courage and magnanimity, or with peasant virtues such as faith and solidarity. Since the middle of the nineteenth century most philosophers and novelists have rejected bourgeois virtue, seeing it as a contradiction in terms, a disguise for the vice of greed. The "ethics of the virtues", an approach as old as ARISTOTLE but revived since the 1970s, suggests another view: that any practice develops a set of virtues, and that a practice as widespread as business is unlikely to thrive without them. Bourgeois virtue reinvents an eighteenth-century project, especially in Scotland, of developing a vocabulary of virtue for a commercial society.

The bourgeois virtues apparent in business practice might include enterprise, adaptability, imagination, optimism, integrity, prudence, thrift, trustworthiness, humor, affection, self-possession, consideration, responsibility, solicitude, decorum, patience, toleration, affability, peaceability, civility, neighborliness, obligingness, reputability, dependability, and impartiality. The point of calling such virtues "bourgeois" is to contrast them with non-business virtues, such as (physical) courage or (spiritual) love. Bourgeois virtues are the townsperson's virtues, as distinct from those of a military camp for the aristocracy or a commons for the peasantry. Sometimes the distinction between bourgeois and other virtues is mere verbal shading. An aristocrat has wit, a peasant or worker jocularity. A businessperson must have humor. But the contrast can be more than shading. Physical courage, shown by aristocrats in war and sport, resembles bourgeois enterprise. But to make the two into one virtue is to encourage warfare in business, which has led sometimes to shooting wars bad for business. Trustworthiness is a business virtue, paralleled in some ideals of a peasant or working-class community by a loving solidarity. But solidarity has socialist outcomes, also bad for business.

The usual vocabulary of the virtues, persisting to the present, tells only of a world of heroes or laborers. Our moral talk overlooks the growing world of management, negotiation, leadership, persuasion, and other business. The eighteenth century began to construct an ethical vocabulary for merchants, especially in Scotland, and most especially in the writings and teaching of ADAM SMITH. As Michael Novak put it recently, "Smith saw his own life's work as moral teaching for the 'new class' of his era." In a dedication to the memory of Mr William Crauford, a merchant of Glasgow, Smith praised his "exact frugality, . . . downright probity and plainness of manners so suitable to his profession. . . . unalterable cheerfulness of temper . . . the most manly

and the most vigorous activity in a vast variety of business" (Smith, 1756, in *Essays*, p. 262). Smith's *The Theory of Moral Sentiments* (1759, 2nd edn 1790) is often neglected in favor of *The Wealth of Nations*, but both of the books published in Smith's lifetime exposit a bourgeois virtue. Many eighteenth-century people admired commerce, as distinct from the violence of aristocrats and the piety of peasants. As Doctor Johnson put it, "There are few ways in which a man can be more innocently employed than in getting money." The eighteenth-century admiration for commerce was overwhelmed in the middle of the next century by anti-business sentiments on the left and right, what George Bernard Shaw called "the great conversion" and what others have called "the treason of the clerks."

The oldest argument in favor of bourgeois virtue is that it is good for business. A roofer in a small town who installs a bad roof will not be in business long. The pressures of entry and exit force the bourgeoisie to exhibit virtue. The trouble with such an argument is that pressure is the absence of ethics. A businessperson induced by prospective profits or forced by potential loss to speak honestly to her customers is not behaving out of ethical motives. The reply would be that it does not matter why she is virtuous: anyway, she is. And the rejoinder would be that as soon as the balance of advantage turns to lying, she will.

A deeper argument is that bourgeois life is good for ethics. This is what European novelists and philosophers have denied since the middle of the nineteenth century. In Flaubert's *Madame Bovary* (1857) or Sinclair Lewis's *Babbit* (1922) the only way to be a good bourgeois is to stop being one. It has become conventional wisdom that the market eats away at virtue, and at society and the environment as well. As someone put it recently, "the expansion of the exchange system by the conversion of what is outside it into its terms . . . is a kind of steam shovel chewing away at the natural and social world."

The new research in bourgeois virtue mistrusts such conventional views, and wishes to return to the eighteenth-century project of recognizing our bourgeois character. The economist Albert Hirschman (who himself speaks of "bourgeois virtues") has recounted the career from Montesquieu to *Marx* of the phrase "*doux commerce*," quoting for instance the Scottish historians William Robertson in 1769: sweet commerce "tends to wear off those prejudices which maintain distinctions and animosity between nations. It softens and polishes the manners of men."

See also **virtue ethics**

Bibliography

Hirschman, A. (1977). *The Passions and the Interests: Political Arguments for Capitalism before its Triumph*. Princeton: Princeton University Press.

McCloskey, D. N. (1994). Bourgeois virtue. *American Scholar*, **63** (2), 177–91.

Novak, M. (1990). *This Hemisphere of Liberty*. Washington, DC: American Enterprise Institute.

Smith, A. (1980 [1790]). *Essays on Philosophical Subjects*. Glasgow edn of *the Works and Correspondence of Adam Smith*, (eds) W. P. D. Wrightman & J. C. Bric. Oxford: Oxford University Press; Indianapolis, Ind.: Liberty Classics.

DEIDRE N. McCLOSKEY

bribery   I hand you some money, you deliver a good or service; have I bribed you? have you extorted money from me, or is this a simple exchange, and thus presumably legal as well as morally acceptable? If we insist that this simple description "captures the essence of the act" then bribery becomes just another way of doing business, with extortion merely the report of the payer's unhappiness over the cost. To retain our moral intuitions that bribery and extortion are morally objectionable, we will need to accept some limits on freedom of exchange.

Two examples (treating blackmail as one species of extortion): the person who pays the blackmail prefers to pay rather than risk the threatened exposure. That that person would prefer a third alternative, neither paying nor being exposed, is not enough to show that blackmailing is wrong; compared to either having my electricity turned off or paying the current rates, I would much prefer to have my electric service for a penny a day, but that alone does not show that the utility has acted improperly in setting its rates. Bribes are even more willingly given and received, with both parties feeling they have benefited; I may be

happy to slip you $10,000 if you will commit your company to a $10 million purchase from mine. And we both claim to benefit from the transaction. Just as with extortion, one obvious objection condemns too much; while my competitors disapprove of my action, they might object to any act which resulted in the sale not going to them.

If there were only two parties to the bribe, the one who gives it and the one who takes it, then it's hard to find anything to object to. So let's bring in a third party, the person or entity that the bribe-taker has a prior obligation to. For the purchasing agent, that's the company in whose name he's making the purchase. To see that this role of representing another, acting for that other, is essential, try imagining how you could bribe someone to spend her own money buying from you. An offer of cash is simply an offer of a lower price, which is perfectly reasonable market behavior. The "bribe" doesn't buy you anything just because all the costs and all the benefits go to the same person; quite the opposite of the purchasing agent's situation where the costs and some benefits go to the company while some other benefits, the bribe especially, go to the person authorizing the purchase. Here is a definition that exposes what is wrong with the practice: bribery is persuading the bribe-taker to act as the bribe-giver's agent while pretending to continue acting as another's agent. That third being can be a person, a corporation, another more or less organized body, even an ideal. What is vital is that the bribe-taker has accepted an obligation to act in the interests of that third being, which is part of the reason the bribe-taker was given the power to act for the other, committing its resources and generally acting in the name of that other.

From this definition, it follows that bribes can only be given for services, in fact for the specific service of acting as my agent, not the agent of the person to whom you have a prior and continuing obligation. But that doesn't help much, since acting as my agent may mean delivering another's good to me, as when I bribe you to let me into the vault you are supposed to be guarding. The legality or illegality of what one is paid to do is irrelevant to deciding whether the payment is a bribe. Murder for hire requires a payment, but the murderer is not acting as if he were another's agent while covertly acting as mine when committing the murder. And the purchasing agent may have the authority to conclude a perfectly proper purchase, even believe that in this case the order he is bribed to place also happens to be in the company's best interest, yet still be taking a bribe because he is surrendering his independence of judgment, or at least action, by agreeing to act as the bribe-giver wishes.

The real interest in bribery as a topic in business ethics comes from claims that certain payments should not be counted as bribes, or that, even though they are bribes, they are still acceptable, generally as the lesser of two evils.

"Grease" and "tips" are two ways to characterize small payments which are an expected, though not quite legally required, part of the implicit contract for a service. Insofar as they are both small, as measured by the receiver, and part of the normal course of doing business, this type of payment does not change the receiver's loyalties; only their absence does, and then to the non-giver's cost. So if there is anything wrong with these payments, it is that they are extorted. But that claim fails when the payments are seen by all to be part of an implicit contract, one based on common industry practice. However, even industry practice changes. Where those with influence over large purchases could once expect expensive gifts at Christmas and other "tokens" throughout the year, many companies now place a ceiling on the value of what their employees can accept, usually around $50. Such a policy recognizes that even the hope for continuing gifts may have some influence on the receiver's decisions, and thus compromise her independence from the suppliers. Then they would be non-specific bribes, bribes to create "good will," which it was hoped would result in favorable actions at some point, although no specific action would be mentioned, or implied.

Some have extended this model to very large payments ($1–10 million), often to very high officials in other countries, a type of payment specifically outlawed by the FOREIGN CORRUPT PRACTICES ACT of 1977. This extension only works if amounts do not matter, a highly questionable claim, and if the practice of receiving these payments is acceptable in at least the receiver's own country. But the second

claim is clearly false; every public exposure of acceptance brought disgrace, virtually always with at least the loss of office.

Initially more promising was the view that these bribes were necessary for consideration of a proposal. If in fact the purchasing agent evaluated only those proposals accompanied by bribes but evaluated them without regard to the amount of the bribe or any expectation of future bribes, then such payments are extorted. We may wonder whether anyone can ignore even the hope for a continuing supply of side payments in evaluating competing proposals; thus such an official might award an occasional contract just to keep that supplier competing in his market, and paying the "fees for consideration." If the payments have some effect on the recipient, even one he is unaware of, then they function to affect his actions and his reasons for choosing, and so are bribes. Then the company, and its representative, are offering bribes. But even if they could show that making the payments was simply bowing to extortion, they are not off the hook. Since both bribery and extortion are wrong, what is the extortion payer doing to resist the extortion? What is she doing to combat the practice? If the answer is nothing, then she seems satisfied with the current arrangement, in which case the payments look a lot like bribes *and* extortions.

Since bribery is undermining the agreement to act in another's interest, in situations where it is appropriate for the agent not to act in the principal's interest, there bribery will at least seem less offensive. What if you bribed me to give evidence about my company's dumping hazardous wastes in the river? Ideally I should simply act in the public interest; but if I need a little extra persuading, your offer is at least a lot more defensible than the standard examples of bribery. Many things besides money will influence a person's choices: love, friendship, another's support of a cause or program one values highly. So unless a person is prepared to commit himself solely to the corporation, or other principal, there will always be some limits to his faithful service. The most that the principal can expect is that both parties understand in advance approximately what those limits are.

Bibliography

Alpern, K. (1985). Moral dimensions of the Foreign Corrupt Practices Act. In Werhane & D'Andrade (eds), (1985).

Calero, T. (1985). Business and the Foreign Corrupt Practices Act. In Werhane & D'Andrade (eds), (1985).

D'Andrade, K. (1985). Bribery. *Journal of Business Ethics*, **4**, (Aug.), 239–48.

Danley, J. R. (1983). Toward a theory of bribery. *Business and Professional Ethics Journal*, **2** (3), 19–39.

Pastin, M. & Hooker, M. (1985). Ethics and the Foreign Corrupt Practices Act. In Werhane & D'Andrade (eds), (1985).

Philips, M. (1984). Bribery. *Ethics*, **94**, (July), 621–36.

Werhane, P. & D'Andrade, K. (eds),. (1985). *Profit and Responsibility: Issues in Business and Professional Ethics*. Lewiston, NY: Edwin Mellen Press.

KENDALL D'ANDRADE

business and society   Business and Society has two meanings. (1) It refers to the relationships that business firms have with society's institutions and nature's ecosystems. (2) The term also refers to the field of management study that describes, analyzes, and evaluates these complex societal and ecological linkages.

Business and Society Relationships

Business, while recognized as an economic activity, is strongly affected by the surrounding social and ecological environment. A society's legal system, its politics and government regulations, community attitudes and public opinion, concepts of morality and ethics, and the forces of social change including science, technology, and rivalry among nations, can exert both negative and positive influences upon a business firm's costs, prices, and profits. Global business firms particularly must learn to deal effectively with demographic diversity, religious and ethnic movements, and public concerns about ecological impacts of business operations.

Business exerts a reciprocal influence upon society through its economic decisions and policies, such as providing jobs, creating income, producing goods and services, and investing capital in plant, equipment, and new product development. These beneficial economic impacts are frequently accompanied by negative social impacts, such as environmental pollution, hazardous working conditions, unsafe or unreliable consumer products, various forms of discriminatory practices, illegal and unethical actions, and excessive political influence on a society's political and governmental systems. A positive social influence may be felt when business firms provide social services not otherwise available, such as health care and retirement plans for employees; when they design and build attractive and environmentally sensitive plants and offices, or lend executives to local governments or nonprofit institutions, or support local community initiatives through philanthropic contributions to educational, cultural, and charitable organizations.

Quite clearly, in these and other ways, business and society influence one another, sometimes negatively and sometimes with positive results for both (Paul, 1987; Sethi and Falbe, 1987).

Business and Society as a Field of Management Study

In the United States, the two central questions that led to the formation of a new field of management study, variously called "Business and Society," "Business and Its Environment," and "Social Issues in Management," were rooted in the reciprocal ties that bind business and society to one another. The questions were: (1) Should a business firm deliberately and voluntarily try to promote social goals and purposes other than those involved in the pursuit of profits? (2) If so, what criteria should determine the content, scope, and limits of business's social responsibilities?

Two schools of thought developed. One asserted that corporations should voluntarily act in socially responsible ways, even if doing so lowered profits. Howard Bowen's 1953 book, *Social Responsibilities of the Businessman*, was the first comprehensive statement of this doctrine. Earlier in the century, however, a few corporate leaders had acknowledged the need for business firms to look beyond profit goals by accepting a measure of social responsibility for their actions (Heald, 1970). The Committee for Economic Development (1971) affirmed this position by proposing a social contract between business and society that broadened business's social responsibilities.

Others (Friedman, 1970) opposed these views, saying that business makes its main contribution to society by producing goods and services at a profit under competitive market conditions. Nothing should be allowed to interfere with this economic function, as long as business operations are conducted legally and ethically. Voluntarily seeking social goals would be economically diversionary, would penalize socially responsible firms by imposing extra costs not experienced by their less responsible competitors, would substitute private corporate judgments for public policy, and would reintroduce a corporate paternalism hostile to free choice. A related view (Chamberlain, 1973) expressed doubt that even the most well-intentioned social initiatives undertaken by corporations could have a significant impact due to their interference with deeply ingrained profit motives, economic growth, and the public's preference for high levels of consumer goods and services.

This basic philosophical argument was gradually replaced by three further theoretical developments, each of which became a conceptual pillar of this new field of study. Some scholars (Preston & Post, 1975; Buchholz, 1992) argue that corporate social performance is best monitored through the instruments of public policy and government regulatory agencies such as the Environmental Protection Agency, the Consumer Product Safety Commission, the Equal Employment Opportunity Commission, the Occupational Safety and Health Commission, etc. Companies could take their cues for publicly desired social actions by adhering to the nation's laws, public policies, and government regulations, rather than relying on the social conscience of the firm's executive managers.

Other scholars (Freeman, 1984) believe that corporations can best attain their overall strategic objectives, both economic and social, by responding positively to stakeholder demands, thus substituting CORPORATE SOCIAL PERFORMANCE for the more philosophical principle of SOCIAL RESPONSIBILITY (Ackerman, 1975; Frederick, 1994; Miles, 1987). A closely related view is that specific social issues affecting a given company can be identified, tracked, and managed to the firm's advantage (Wartick & Cochran, 1985). Theories incorpor-

ating the public policy/stakeholder responsiveness/issues management approaches had become the field's dominant conceptual paradigm by the early 1990s.

During the 1980s, BUSINESS ETHICS also became a significant component of Business and Society studies. Introduced into the field by business ethics philosophers, it represents an effort to apply moral principles to ethical issues that arise in the workplace (Beauchamp and Bowie, 1988; Donaldson, 1989).

To summarize, the Business and Society field of management study attempts to clarify business's multiform relations with society and thereby to improve the ability of firms to plan and manage their interactions with this broad social and ecological environment. Because economic, social, political, ecological, and ethical interests are affected by these linkages, many of the questions studied are controversial and ultimately philosophical in nature, while nevertheless bearing on the effective management of the firm (Preston, 1986; Wood, 1991).

In the United States, four professional academic organizations promote Business and Society teaching and research: the Social Issues in Management division of the Academy of Management, founded in 1971; the Society for Business Ethics, founded in 1978; the Society for the Advancement of Socio-Economics, founded in 1989; and the International Association for Business and Society, founded in 1989–90.

See also **economics and ethics; managerial values; Friedman, Milton; investment ethics; social responsibility; socio-economics; stakeholder theory**

Bibliography

Ackerman, R. W. (1975). *The Social Challenge to Business.* Cambridge, Mass: Harvard University Press.

Beauchamp, T. & Bowie, N. E. (1988). *Ethical Theory and Business,* 3rd edn, Englewood Cliffs, NJ: Prentice-Hall.

Bowen, H. R. (1953). *Social Responsibilities of the Businessman.* New York: Harper.

Buchholz, R. A. (1992). *Business Environment and Public Policy: Implications for Management and Strategy,* 4th edn, Englewood Cliffs, NJ: Prentice-Hall.

Chamberlain, N. W. (1973). *The Limits of Corporate Responsibility.* New York: Free Press.

Committee for Economic Development. (1971). *Social Responsibilities of Business Corporations.* New York: Committee for Economic Development.

Donaldson, T. (1989). *The Ethics of International Business.* New York: Oxford University Press.

Frederick, W. C. (1994). From CSR$_1$ to CSR$_2$: The maturing of Business and Society thought. *Business and Society,* 33, 150–64.

Freeman, R. E. (1984). *Strategic Management: A Stakeholder Approach.* Boston: Pitman.

Friedman, M. (1970). The social responsibility of business is to increase its profits. *New York Times Magazine,* 13 Sept.,122–6.

Heald, M. (1970). *The Social Responsibilities of Business: Company and Community, 1900–1960.* Cleveland, Ohio: Case-Western Reserve Press.

Miles, R. H. (1987). *Managing the Corporate Social Environment: A Grounded Theory.* Englewood Cliffs, NJ: Prentice-Hall.

Paul, K. (ed.), ,. (1987). *Business Environment and Business Ethics: The Social, Moral, and Political Dimensions of Management.* Cambridge, Mass: Ballinger.

Preston, L. E. (1986). Social issues in management: An evolutionary perspective. In D. A. Wren & J. A. Pearce (eds), *Papers Dedicated to the Development of Modern Management.* Ada, Ohio: Academy of Management.

Preston, L. E. & Post, J. E. (1975). *Private Management and Public Policy: The Principle of Public Responsibility.* Englewood Cliffs, NJ: Prentice-Hall.

Sethi, S. P. & Falbe, C. M. (eds),. (1987). *Business and Society: Dimensions of Conflict and Cooperation.* Lexington, Mass: Lexington Books.

Wartick, S. L. & Cochran, P. (1985). The evolution of the corporate social performance model. *Academy of Management Review,* 10, 758–69.

Wood, D. J. (1991). Corporate social responsiveness revisited. *Academy of Management Review,* 16, 691–718.

WILLIAM C. FREDERICK

business associations for social responsibility

The Business Roundtable

The Business Roundtable, founded in 1972, is an association of business executives who examine public issues that affect the economy and develop positions "which seek to reflect sound economic and social principles." It was established to encourage business executives at the largest American companies to take an increased role in continuing debates about public policy and was originally conceived to provide a supplementary voice to those of the US Chamber of Commerce and the National Association of Manufacturers, two of the primary business lobbies at the time. The membership has generally been limited to chief executive officers of the approximately 200 largest US companies and is by invitation only. The Roundtable operates from its offices in Washington, DC. Most of the Roundtable's work is done through committees chaired by member CEOs.

During the 1970s, the executives at some very large companies believed they needed a political voice of their own, independent of the US Chamber of Commerce, which was dominated by smaller businesses, and the National Association of Manufacturers, whose membership was primarily medium-sized manufacturers. Some of the founders hoped the Roundtable would take political positions which reflected a longer-term perspective on the relationship between business and government, would be less likely to oppose all business regulation and taxation, and would seek instead to influence the shape of regulatory and tax policy through cooperation with government. In the 1970s and 1980s, the Roundtable broke ranks several times with the other major business lobbies on tax and regulatory matters.

In the 1990s the Roundtable's priorities have included education and the federal budget. A ten-year commitment to education reform was launched in 1989 and has promoted comprehensive educational reform strategies in all 50 states. The Roundtable members have worked with governors, state-school chiefs and other businesses and educational organizations to promote performance-based standards. Other active task forces include construction cost containment; corporate governance; environment; government regulation; health; welfare and retirement income; human resources; international trade and investment; taxation; and tort policy. (The Business Roundtable, 1615 L Street, NW, Suite 1100, Washington, DC 20036. Tel: 202-872-1260.)

The Business Enterprise Trust

The Business Enterprise Trust is a national nonprofit organization established in 1989 to honor "acts of courage, integrity and social vision in business." In 1995, *US News and World Report* describes its annual awards as the nation's most prestigious business responsibility recognition. The Trust conducts an annual nomination and selection process, presents its awards at a ceremony in New York, and produces case studies and short video documentaries on the award recipients for use in business schools and other educational programs.

The five annual recipients of the Business Enterprise Awards are honored for programs or management innovations that combine sound management and social vision. Among the recipients have been Louis Krouse, an entrepreneur; Gail Mayville, the environmental manager of Ben & Jerry's Homemade; Merck & Co.; Hanna Andersson CEO Gun Denhart; Prudential Insurance Company of America; Daka International; construction executive Julia Stasch; Fel-Pro Inc.; photo agency president Barbara Roberts; and Starbucks Coffee CEO Howard Schultz. Prudential was honored in 1992 for promoting the concept of "living needs benefits," a provision in many life insurance policies that now permits claiming the insurance when one is suffering from AIDS or other terminal illness. Merck received its award in 1991 for developing and distributing the drug Mectizan to Third Wold victims of "river blindness." The four recipients of the Trust's lifetime achievement award have been developer James W. Rouse, Cummins Engine leader J. Irwin Miller, former CBS president Frank Stanton, and Xerox Corporation.

The Trust was conceived and founded by television writer-producer Norman Lear, creator of *All in the Family* and other comedies which focused on social issues. The Trust's mission states: "Private enterprise . . . exercises a profound influence on American life and culture . . . it is increasingly important to explore how business can contribute to both economic and social progress." Founder Norman Lear believes business executives must struggle daily with the "inevitable tension between business and social objectives." (The Business Enterprise Trust, 204 Junipero Serra Blvd., Stanford, CA 94305. Tel: 415-321-5774.)

Business for Social Responsibility

Business for Social Responsibility (BSR) is a national business lobby and educational organization established in 1993 to be "the new voice of American businesses." BSR was created by leaders of several self-proclaimed "socially responsible businesses," including Ben & Jerry's Homemade Inc., The Body Shop, Reebock, Starbucks Coffee, Stride-Rite Shoes, Stonyfield Farm Yogurt, and others. By mid-1995 BSR had 800 corporate and individual members, including several large mainstream companies.

BSR's mission is to create a network of like-minded businesses to influence each other and the broader business culture. BSR sponsored the preparation and publication of *Beyond the Bottom Line: Putting Social Responsibility to Work for Your Business and the World*, by Joel Makower (published by Simon & Schuster). BSR also sponsors an Education Fund which prepares reserach and case studies on social resposibility. (Business for Social Responsibility, 1683 Folsom St., San Francisco, CA 94103. Tel: 415-865-2500.)

KIRK HANSON

business ethics The study of ethics is the study of human action and its moral adequacy. Business ethics, then, is the study of business action – individual or corporate – with special attention to its moral adequacy. Business persons confront ethical issues, whatever their position in the corporate structure and whatever the size and complexity of the organization. Sometimes responsible judgment and action are clear, but not always. Consider the problems surrounding whistleblowing and loyalty, sexual harrassment in the workplace, intellectual property, the limits of product safety, and ethical differences across cultural borders. What managers often need is an orderly way to think through the moral implications of a policy decision – a perspective and a language for appraising the alternatives available from an ethical point of view. For many, this is the most operational definition of business ethics.

The field of business ethics is at least as old as commerce itself, but in the modern period we can date it from the industrial revolution. Individuals, corporate forms of organization, and even capitalism as a socio-economic system have come under moral scrutiny from proponents and critics alike. In the second half of the twentieth century, there has been a renaissance of interest in the subject, spurred by events and by disciplinary realignments. The events included political and social movements for civil rights, women's equality, and environmental awareness. Also deserving of mention in relation to ethical reflection in the US are Watergate, the Wall Street Insider Trading scandal, the Savings & Loan crisis, and the collapse of the Soviet Union. In terms of disciplinary focus, business education has expanded beyond psychology and the social sciences in search of a more humanistic outlook, so that recent efforts in the field are philosophical, theological, and literary.

The modern corporation is a microcosm of the community in which it operates and also a macrocosm of the individual citizen living and working in that wider community. Insofar as the corporation resembles the wider community, issues arise that are similar to those in classical political philosophy: the legitimacy of authority; the rights and responsibilities associated with entry, exit, membership, promotion, and succession; civil liberties; moral climate. Insofar as the corporation resembles an individual person in the community, issues arise that are similar to those in classical moral philosophy: responsibility, integrity, conscience, virtue; duties to avoid harm and injustice; respect for the law; provision for the needs of the least advantaged. There are differences in each realm, of course, since the respective analogies are imperfect, but the similarities are strong enough to help organize the normative issues that present themselves to business management (*see* MORAL STATUS OF CORPORATIONS).

Modes of Ethical Inquiry

It has often been observed that ethical inquiry can take three forms: descriptive, normative, and analytical. Descriptive ethics is not, strictly speaking, philosophical. It is better classified among the social sciences, since it is aimed at empirically neutral descriptions of the values of individuals and groups. To say, for example, that a business executive or an organization disapproves of workplace discrimination or approves of bribery is to make a descriptive ethical observation, one that can presumably be supported or refuted by pointing to factual evidence.

Normative ethics, by contrast, is not aimed at neutral factual claims, but at judgments of right and wrong, good and bad, virtue and vice. To say that a business executive or an organization disapproves of workplace discrimination or approves of bribery and is right or wrong in doing so is to add a normative ethical claim to a descriptive one. If it is to be supported or refuted, of course, some criteria of "rightness" or "wrongness" must be provided.

Analytical ethics (sometimes called metaethics) is neither a matter of describing moral values nor advancing criteria for right and wrong. Instead, it steps back from both of these activities in order to pose questions about the meaning and objectivity of ethical judgments. At this remove, the aim is to explore differences among scientific, religious, and ethical outlooks; the relation of law to morality; the implications of cultural differences for ethical judgment, and so forth.

The Dynamics of Normative Ethics

Within normative ethics, there are two interacting levels of reasoning that need to be distinguished. First, and most familiar, is reasoning from moral common sense. In our personal lives and in our professional lives, most of us operate with a more or less well-defined set of ethical convictions, principles, or rules of thumb that guide decision-making. Seldom are such values or rules spelled out explicitly in a list, but if they were, the list would probably include such items as:

- Avoid harming others

- Respect others' rights (Be fair, just)

- Do not lie or cheat (Be honest)

- Keep promises and contracts (Be faithful)

- Obey the law

Such a repertoire of common-sense moral judgments is often sufficient. It functions as an informal checklist that we are prepared to live by both for the sake of others and for our own inner well-being. In the context of business behavior, the toleration of toxic workplace conditions, racial discrimination, and false advertising are as clearly contrary to moral common sense as honoring agreements with suppliers and obeying tax laws are in accord with it.

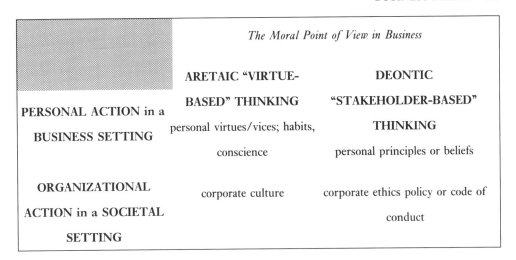

The Moral Point of View in Business

	ARETAIC "VIRTUE-BASED" THINKING	DEONTIC "STAKEHOLDER-BASED" THINKING
PERSONAL ACTION in a BUSINESS SETTING	personal virtues/vices; habits, conscience	personal principles or beliefs
ORGANIZATIONAL ACTION in a SOCIETAL SETTING	corporate culture	corporate ethics policy or code of conduct

Figure 1 Two units of analysis and two aspects of action

Unfortunately, problems arise with common sense both hypothetically and in practice. And when they do, we seem forced into another kind of normative thinking. The problems come from two main sources: (1) internal conflicts or unclarities about items on personal or corporate checklists, and (2) external conflicts in which others' lists (persons or corporations) differ, e.g., are longer, shorter, or display alternative priorities. How can we keep this promise to that supplier while avoiding risk to those customers? What does it mean to be fair to employees? When, if ever, does "affirmative action" become "reverse discrimination"? If competitors don't value honesty, why should we? Such questions drive us beyond moral common sense to what is called critical thinking. Here the search is for principles or criteria that will justify the inclusion or exclusion of common-sense norms, clarify them, and help resolve conflicts among them. It is the dynamic interaction between moral common sense and our attempts at critical thinking that lead to what some call "reflective equilibrium" (Rawls, 1971, p. 20ff).

Aspects of the Moral Point of View

The history of ethics reveals a widely shared conviction that ethics can and should be rooted in what has been termed the moral point of view. For many, the moral point of view is understood in religious terms, a perspective that reflects God's will for humanity. For others, it is

understood in secular terms and is not dependent for its authority on religious faith. But setting aside differences about its ultimate source, there is significant consensus regarding its general character. The moral point of view is a mental and emotional standpoint from which all persons are seen as having a special dignity or worth, from which the Golden Rule gets its force, from which words like "ought," "duty," and "virtue" derive their meaning. It is our principal guide for action. Two basic features of action deserve special notice. Any action or decision has:

(i) an aretaic aspect, highlighting the expressive nature of our choices. When a person acts, she or he is revealing and reinforcing certain traits or "habits of the heart" which are called virtues (and vices). The same may be true of groups of persons in organizations. Sometimes we refer in the latter cases to the culture or mindset or value system of the organization. The key to the aretaic aspect of action is its attention to actions as manifestations of an inner outlook, character, set of values or priorities. Four classical virtues that have often been the focus of ethical analysis and reflection in the past are: prudence, justice, temperance, and courage. Others include honesty, compassion, fidelity (to promises), and dedication

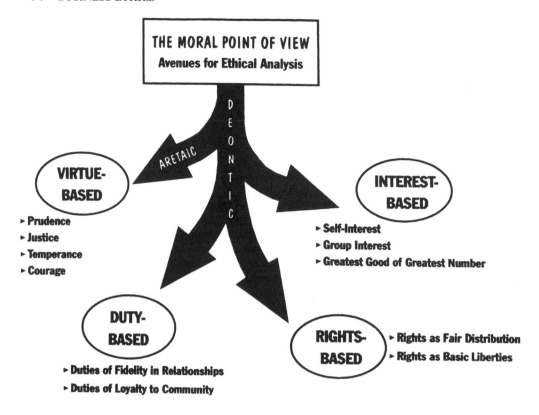

Figure 2 The moral point of view and four avenues of ethical analysis.

to community (the common good). Vices of individuals or groups include greed, cruelty, indifference, and cowardice.

(ii) a deontic aspect, highlighting the effective nature of our choices – the way in which our actions influence our relationships with others and change the world around us. Actions have stakeholders and consequences when viewed from this perspective; they are transactions that affect the freedom and well-being of others (*see* STAKEHOLDER THEORY). The deontic aspect of actions relates to their effects on the world, in particular, their effects on living creatures whose interests or rights might be at stake. Management and the board are bound legally and ethically to a fiduciary role in relation to the shareholders of the enterprise, but they must also be attentive to other stakeholders. This kind of extended moral awareness, despite the ambitions of some of the great thinkers of the past, is no

more reducible to a mechanical decision procedure than is balanced judgment in education, art, politics, or even sports. Ethics need not be unscientific, but it is not a science. It may be more akin to staying healthy. Acknowledging our limitations regarding knowledge and certainty in ethics is not the same as embracing the motto "There's no disputing tastes." Sometimes stakeholder interests and rights, as well as the needs of the wider community are in tension with one another, making ethical judgment very difficult for individuals and for managers of organizations.

This "bifocal" perspective on action (expressive and effective) signals a duality in what we referred to as the moral point of view. Through one set of lenses, moral judgment concentrates on the expressive meaning of actions and policies – what they reveal about those who initiate them. Through another set of lenses, the focus shifts to the effective or transactional significance of what we do. If our inquiry concentrates on an individual's or an organization's habits or culture (content, genesis, need for maintenance or change, etc.) it is aretaic. If the focus is on the interests and rights of stakeholders of personal or corporate decisions, it is deontic.

While a comprehensive review of the many ways in which philosophers, past and present, have organized critical thinking is not possible here, we can sketch several of the more important normative views that have been proposed. These views provide avenues for ethical analysis in the sense that discussions of cases or pending decisions often can be illuminated (and even resolved) by one or more of them. Three of these avenues fall under the heading of "Stakeholder-based" thinking (Figure 1), while the fourth maps onto "Virtue-Based" thinking. (See Figure 2.)

Stakeholder-based Thinking

Stakeholder thinking is the most highly developed approach to ethical analysis, and displays three distinctive "logics" or avenues – interest-based, rights-based, and duty-based.

Interest-based Avenues. One of the more influential avenues of ethical analysis, at least in the modern period, is what we can call interest-based. The fundamental idea behind interest-based analysis is that the moral assessment of actions and policies depends solely on consequences, and that the only consequences that really matter are the interests of the parties affected (usually human beings). On this view, ethics is all about harms and benefits to identifiable parties. Moral common sense is thus disciplined by a single dominant objective: maximizing net expectable utility (happiness, satisfaction, well-being, pleasure). Critical thinking, on this view, amounts to testing our ethical instincts and rules of thumb against the yardstick of social costs and benefits.

There is variation among interest-based analysts, depending on the relevant beneficiary class. For some (called egoists) the class is the actor alone – the short- and long-term interests of the self. For others, it is some favored group – Greeks or Englishmen or Americans – where others are either ignored or discounted in the ethical calculation of interests (*see* EGOISM). The most common variation (called UTILITAR-

IANISM) enlarges the universe of moral consideration to include all human beings, if not all sentient (feeling) beings. In business management, interest-based reasoning often manifests itself as a commitment to the social value of market forces, competitive decision-making, and (sometimes) regulation in the public interest. Problems and questions regarding interest-based avenues of ethical analysis are several: How does one measure utility or interest satisfaction? For whom does one measure it (self, group, humankind, beyond)? What about the tyranny of the majority in the calculation? (*see* STAKEHOLDER PARADOX).

Rights-based Avenues. A second influential avenue is rights-based analysis. Its central idea is that moral common sense is to be governed not by interest satisfaction, but by rights protection. And the relevant rights are of two broad kinds: rights to fair distribution of opportunities and wealth (contractarianism), and rights to basic freedoms or liberties (LIBERTARIANISM) (*see* COMMUNITARIANISM). Fair distribution is often explained as a condition that obtains when all individuals are accorded equal respect and equal voice in social arrangements. Basic liberties are often explained in terms of individuals' opportunities for self-development, property, work's rewards, and freedoms including religion and speech.

In management practice, rights-based reasoning is evident in concerns about stakeholder rights (consumers, employees, suppliers) as well as STOCKHOLDER (property) rights. Questions regarding this avenue include: Is there not a trade-off between equality and liberty when it comes to rights? Does rights-based thinking lead to tyrannies of minorities that are as bad as tyrannies of majorities? Is this avenue too focused on individuals and their entitlements with insufficient attention to larger communities and the responsibilities of individuals to such larger wholes?

Duty-based Avenues. The third avenue of ethical analysis is duty-based. While this avenue is perhaps the least unified and well-defined, its governing ethical idea is duty or responsibility not so much to other individuals as to communities of individuals. In the duty-based outlook, critical thinking turns ultimately on individuals conforming to the legitimate norms of a healthy community. According to the duty-based thinker, ethics is not finally about interests and rights, since those are too individualistic. Ethics is about playing one's role in a larger enterprise – a set of relationships (like the family) or a community (communitarianism). The best summary of this line of thinking was echoed in John F. Kennedy's inaugural speech: "Ask not what America can do for you, ask what you can do for America."

In practice, duty-based thinking underlies appeals to principles of fiduciary obligation, public trust, and corporate community involvement (*see* FIDUCIARY DUTY; FIDUCIARY RESPONSIBILITY). Problems and questions regarding this avenue include the fear that INDIVIDUALISM might get swallowed up in a kind of collectivism (under the communitarian banner) and that priorities among conflicting duties are hard to set.

Virtue-based Thinking

Virtue-based thinking lies on the expressive side of the distinction made earlier between deontic and aretaic outlooks on human action. The focus of virtue-based thinking is on developing habits of the heart, character traits, and acting on them. Actions and policies are subjected to ethical scrutiny not on the basis of their effects or their consequences (for individuals or for communities), but on the basis of their genesis – the degree to which they flow from or reinforce a virtue or positive trait of character. *Newsweek* magazine devoted its June 13, 1994 issue to the theme of virtue-based ethics in American culture. In an article entitled "What is Virtue?", Kenneth L. Woodward observed that "[T]he cultivation of virtue makes individuals happy, wise, courageous, competent. The result is a good person, a responsible citizen and parent, a trusted leader, possibly even a saint. Without virtuous people, according to this tradition, society cannot function well. And without a virtuous society, individuals cannot realize either their own or the common good" (pp. 38–9).

There is an emphasis in virtue-based analysis on cultivating the traits and habits that give rise to actions and policies, on the belief that too often "the right thing to do" cannot be identified or described in advance using one of the other avenues. The most traditional short list of basic (or "cardinal") virtues includes

prudence, temperance, courage, and justice. Some of the most popular management books in recent years have suggested virtue-based thinking in their titles: *The Art of Japanese Management* (Pascale and Athos, 1981), *In Search of Excellence* (Peters and Waterman, 1982), *The Seven Habits of Highly Effective People* (Covey, 1989). In the wider philosophical and cultural literature, *After Virtue* (MACINTYRE, 1981), and *A Book of Virtues* (W. Bennett, 1993), have extended the rediscovery of virtue-based thinking.

In management contexts, the language of virtue is frequently encountered in executive hiring situations as well as in management development training. Another management context that may prove to be more amenable to virtue-based thinking than to stakeholder-based thinking is environmental awareness. Often debates over the impacts of business behavior on the environment have focused on the economic inclusion of "special" stakeholders (like future generations or animals or living creatures generally). While this approach is, logically speaking, an option, it may be less practically compelling than an approach which interprets management ethics in this arena, alongside community involvement, as a virtue akin to temperance.

Questions associated with virtue-based thinking include: How are we to understand the central virtues and their relative priorities in a secular world that does not appear to agree on such matters? Are there timeless character traits that are not so culture-bound that we can recommend them to anyone, particularly those in leadership roles? And can virtue(s) be taught?

Each of the four avenues (Figure 2) represents a concentration of critical thinking in ethical matters from which specific ethical challenges might be addressed, if not resolved. All have in common a sustained effort to give practical voice to the moral point of view in business life.

Bibliography

Beauchamp, T., & Bowie, N. (eds). (1993). *Ethical Theory and Business*, 4th edn. Englewood Cliffs, NJ: Prentice-Hall.
De George, R. T. (1993). *Competing with Integrity in International Business*, New York: Oxford University Press.

Donaldson, T. (1989). *The Ethics of International Business,* New York: Oxford University Press.

Donaldson, T. & Werhane, P. H. (1993). *Ethical Issues in Business: A Philosophical Approach,* 4th edn. Englewood Cliffs, NJ: Prentice-Hall.

Freeman, R. E., and Gilbert, D. R. (1988). *Corporate Strategy and the Search for Ethics,* Englewood Cliffs, NJ: Prentice-Hall.

Matthews, J., Goodpaster, K. & Nash, L. (eds) (1991). *Policies and Persons: A Casebook in Business Ethics,* 2nd edn. New York: McGraw-Hill.

Novak, M. (1993). *The Catholic Ethic and the Spirit of Capitalism,* New York: Free Press.

Rawls, J. (1971). *A Theory of Justice,* Cambridge, Mass.: Harvard University Press.

Regan, T. (1984). *Just Business: New Introductory Essays in Business Ethics,* New York: Random House.

Stone, C. (1975). *Where the Law Ends: The Social Control of Corporate Behavior,* New York: Harper & Row.

Velasquez, M. (1992). *Business Ethics: Concepts and Cases,* 3rd edn Englewood Cliffs, NJ: Prentice-Hall.

Walton, C. (1988). *The Moral Manager,* Cambridge, Mass: Ballinger.

Werhane, P. (1991). *Adam Smith and His Legacy for Modern Capitalism,* New York: Oxford University Press.

KENNETH E. GOODPASTER

business ethics, history of   *see* HISTORY OF BUSINESS ETHICS

business ethics and Hinduism   India, and Hinduism – the dominant religion of a majority of its people – meets both the criteria of a strong culture and a history of highly developed civilization, and a deeply felt sense of morality based on religious tenets. Therefore, while on the surface India's people in general, and its businesspeople in particular, may appear to be highly rational in their business and economic activities, and may even seem to make similar decisions which would be made by business-people in industrially-advanced and morally Judeo-Christian societies of the West; it would be extremely misleading to conclude that the two societies are similar at least to the extent of decision-making in the economic arena either at the macro or micro levels. For the thought process and the underlying set of moral values in the two systems is quite dissimilar. For the same reason, two apparently inconsistent decisions, from the Western point of view, would appear quite consistent in the Indian framework because they conformed to a common set of underlying moral rationale.

Basic Tenets of Hinduism

Hinduism, as it is practiced today, has evolved over a period of 3,000 years. In the process, it assimilated a variety of religions and moral beliefs, as successive waves of invaders from the North, East, and West occupied her land and eventually became part of the landscape. This is why Hinduism can accommodate a wide variety of behaviors and moral rationales which on the surface may appear to be internally inconsistent.

Notwithstanding the bewildering varieties of religious rituals, multitudes of gods, sects, cults, and holy persons of all ilks and persuasions, most scholars of Hindu religion recognize that doctrines of *samsara, karma,* and *moksha* lie at the core of Hindu philosophy (Milner, 1993). The description of the basic tenets of Hindu philosophy, in the present instance, is of necessity selectively confined to those concepts that are of particular relevance to the economic arena. *Samsara* pertains to the rebirth or the transmigration of self and has great impact on the mode of thinking and way of life of people of the Hindu faith. *Karma* denotes fate or manifest destiny in common parlance. It literally means "actions" or "deeds". The *law of karma* operates like a causation, whereby the life of the individual self is determined by its actions – the present life is the result of actions in the past life, and actions in the present life will determine the pattern for future lives. *Moksha* (*Nirvana*) refers to the liberation from the constant cycle of birth-death-birth-death to becoming part of ultimate infinite universe, i.e., union with God (Uppal, 1977, pp. 122–35).

The other concepts of Hindu religion are important in terms of their impact on the economic life and business conduct of the Indian people. These are: (a) *Dharma* – the notion of one's duty and obligation to others and to oneself, and the practice of virtue, in the discharge of life's day-to-day functions; (b)

Artha – the acquisition of wealth for use; and (c) *Kama* – the enjoyments of the pleasures of life (Anand, 1963, pp. 18–24).

The Hindu notions of Heaven and Hell are quite different than those prevailing in other religions, notably Christianity and Islam. There is no rainbow or pleasure dome at the end of the current life's journey. All actions – good and bad – are rewarded and punished in one incarnation or another; it is the soul that is everlasting, and it is the soul that seeks liberation from being trapped in the constant cycle of earthly forms. One's station in life is largely predetermined by one's actions in previous lives. *Karma* operates like an iron law of inescapable retribution. The notion acts both as a coping mechanism where life's injustices and miseries, as well as possession and enjoyment of worldly goods, are accepted as part of one's fate. It provides a rational justification. It propels people toward good deeds because they determine one's fate in the next life, and finally, it puts brakes on one's unbridled self-interest for fear of retribution of bad deeds. The concept of *Dharma* adds another dimension to *Karma* in that it defines one's duties and obligations to others, i.e., social hierarchy of kinship, and also, suggests means for choosing among different moral values and alternative courses of action. *Dharma* are a set of moral guidelines for an individual to follow in everyday life in various spiritual aspects. Some important virtues stressed are truth, non-violence, sacrifice, purity, and renunciation or detachment. Great emphasis is placed on detachment from all associations with the material world (Uppal, 1977, pp. 126–9).

Artha (wealth) and *Kama* (enjoyment of life) are treated as important values that must be actively sought. They provide the vigor of the Indian entrepreneur, and the relative absence of guilt that accompanies enjoyment of life's munificence. Wealth and enjoyment of life, however, have to have a purpose, i.e., of reaching toward liberation of soul or *Nirvana*. *Artha* guides all acquisition and use of material means for sustaining life. The two Holy books, *Mahabharata* and *Panchatantra*, illustrate Hindu philosophy toward material means and their enjoyment. "What is here regarded as *Dharma* depends entirely upon wealth (*Artha*). One who robs another of wealth robs him of his

Dharma as well. Poverty is a state of sinfulness. All kinds of meritorious acts flow from the possession of great wealth, as from wealth spring all religious acts, all pleasures and heaven itself. . . . He that has no wealth has neither this world nor the next. . . . Poverty is a curse worse than death. Virtue without wealth is of no consequence. The lack of money is the root of all evil. But material wealth is to be sought in ways consistent with the requirements of detachment or renunciation required under *Dharma* as explained above. *Kama* is the enjoyment of the appropriate objects of the five senses of hearing, feeling, seeing, tasting, and smelling, assisted by mind together with the soul" (Uppal, 1977, p. 129; Koller, 1970, pp. 42–3).

The importance of "actions" raises some important questions for the sake of achieving "real-self" or *Atman*. (1) Should we cease to perform actions, or in other words, is renunciation from all worldly activities the answer? (2) Is there any ordering of good actions versus bad actions? (3) Can an individual be guided to perform good "actions"? The answer to the first is found in the sacred book, the *Bhagavad Gita*. It is maintained that action is necessary, "for no one can remain even for a moment without doing work; every one is made to act helplessly by the impulses born of nature." The crucial thing is to engage in worldly activities without becoming attached to them. "To action alone hast thou a right and never at all to its fruits; let not the fruits of action be thy motive; neither let there be any attachment to inaction. Therefore, without attachment, perform always the work that has to be done, for man attains to the highest by doing work without attachment" (Radhakrishnan, 1948, pp. 119–38; Uppal, 1977, p. 128; Weber, 1958, p. 4).

Hinduism and Contemporary (Western) Business Practices and Ethical Norms

In a perfect world, Hindu religion and its followers would provide an ideal combination of attributes that are conducive to business development in general and business conduct in a highly ethical manner in particular. *Dharma* would indicate a heightened sense of duty and self-responsibility which could be counted upon as a basic value promoting people to: meet their obligations; operate in a highly principled manner; and pursue the acquisition of wealth in a virtuous, i.e., fair manner. *Karma* would suggest an acceptance of one's position in life; encourage one to regard work as seen as a moral duty; and suggest that excellence be pursued for its own sake and not necessarily as a means to bigger financial rewards or higher status.

Wealth creation and enjoyment of means of life (*Artha* and *Kama*) are seen as having divine approval and should be enjoyed without any guilt or fear of opprobrium. In business conduct, especially dealing with Western types of businesses, the two concepts would imply a greater scope of cooperation and trust under conditions where the local partners visualize their gains in terms of *wealth accumulation* and *control of productive assets* rather than being doled out as mere rewards, no matter how munificent.

While there may be a common agreement as to the principles of *Dharma* and *Karma*, *Artha* and *Kama*, their interpretation takes place with a far wider latitude than is prevalent in Western work. Even more important, the degree to which different individuals would emphasize one value over the other under the Hindu philosophy is based to a greater extent on intuitive, or spiritually felt, emotions. Thus one might find an Indian less compromising on a vaguely defined "principle" than otherwise reasonable people would consider plausible. It is not uncommon for Indians to take offense, and act almost irrationally, when they feel that a principle is at stake, or that the person has not acted in a morally responsible manner consistent with his status in life and in accordance with his stature in the social and transactional context of a given situation. Similarly, a devotion to work and separation of work from reward would make many an Indian work and excel to the extent that they might be perceived, from the point of view of a "non-Indian" socio-economic framework, to be undermining a common level of expectations and skewing the relationship between supply and demand for services. Thus contracts are likely to be honored; a full day's wage buys more than a full day's work; and business is conducted in a highly ethical manner. Consequently, norms of business conduct and behavior appear – at least to the uninitiated – to be inconsistent and illogical

because they seem to be applied in different situations in such a manner that their rationale is not easily explained.

The other negative side-effects of Hindu philosophy are inherent in their very nature. *Karma* creates a sense of fatalism and pessimism and thus contributes to risk avoidance. It also rationalizes the inequities of a caste system which allows for exploitation of the less fortunate as a matter of divine right and the sufferers' inherent misfortune. While in times past the caste system was somewhat akin to a craft guild, with flexibility created for expertise, work specialization, and productivity gains, it also created a social order which was acceptable to the feudal system of political governance. Over time, it has become rigid and ossified, and inimical to individual growth. At the state level, it has created an ever-increasing class of "suffering minorities" seeking to codify social entitlement for an indefinite period (Dehejia & Dehejia, 1993; Milner, 1993; Mishra, 1962; Uppal, 1977).

In the business context, it is not unusual for the high-caste Hindus to exploit those of lower caste status with relative lack of guilt or remorse. The classification also extends to social relationships. Thus, while modern businesses may easily integrate the workplace, the real integration is sometimes not easily achieved. At the social levels, groups do not seek integration or even intermingling. Where economic stakes are high, each caste group is likely to create all types of subterfuges to favor their own caste, group, etc. to the detriment of others. This phenomenon is all too apparent in any socio-political and economic arrangement involving power-sharing or allocation of economic entitlement – for example, jobs. Only the truly uninitiated are oblivious to the subtle machinations of the individuals and groups as they vie for power and influence.

Detachment of work from its reward has a number of implications for business behavior. Since work is revered for its own sake, there is often a tendency to disregard its adverse effects. Thus poor work conditions, low pay, and other inequities may be condoned by the social system as the lot of the poor, the nature of work itself, and not the responsibility of the owner. Where responsibility is assumed, it is deemed to be a matter of conscience or good business practice rather than a moral imperative. Poor are poor because it is their fate. The rich have been chosen by the gods to accumulate wealth and do good deeds for their ultimate salvation – as it is their wont to do. One should not be surprised to find echoes of robber barons and the era of exploitative capitalism in America where workers were ruthlessly suppressed so that capitalists could maximize surplus value and build bigger monuments to the glory of God and supremacy of Western civilization. The Taj Mahal and other monuments may inspire awe for their grand design and superb execution, but they also tell a story of untold suffering on the part of millions of craftsmen who worked and died in literal bondage to their feudal Lords to glorify the latter's conquests and appeasement of gods.

Another stark example of differences between Western and Hindu notions of good works and the bearing of *Karma* shows up in the domain of charitable activities. Wealthy Hindu businesspeople would more likely spend a far bigger portion of their fortunes in building temples for their favorite gods to seek favors for the next life, rather than devote resources to helping the poor and building social institutions to help the poor. Socially responsible corporate behavior on the part of indigenous Indian businesses is primarily in the form of acts of charity on holy days rather than treating the poor and disadvantaged as stakeholders deserving of help and entitled to dignity. Indian businesses, except for the Parsees (members of the Zoroastrian religious sect in India descended from Persians) are less prone to acts of civic philanthropy unless they have a religious tint.

The sense of duty or *Dharma* manifests itself in a variety of ways in business conduct. At one level, it is the concept of devotion to principle defined as one's primary obligation to one's values and social, i.e., group or kinship responsibilities. A principle, for its sake, is quite important and propelled many a Hindu to make extreme sacrifices because to do otherwise would be a violation of his *Dharma*, a divine sin, and, therefore, morally repugnant. From the Western perspective, a person acting under the belief of his *Dharma* is more likely to act irrationally, and is likely to make compromises to achieve a "win win" solution. Thus an understanding of *Dharma* and its situational and personal context is very important in

determining the applicable norms of social behavior in a particular situation and given the particular set of people involved.

Dharma is also a fluid concept and is situation and person specific. Thus *Dharma* in one case may justify fighting and even killing one's own kin, while in another case, *Dharma* may justify fighting and even killing another person to protect one's own kin. The Western mind, not attuned to Indian thought processes and often applying a Western sense of cost/benefit rational analysis, could easily violate an Indian's concept of *Dharma* and principle and thereby provoke a major confrontation. By the same token, *Dharma* may force a person to act in ways which might violate the Western sense of social or commercial contact, although the Indian mind would feel absolved of responsibility because it was his duty to do so.

Hinduism also manifests itself in contradictory behavior of tolerance/intolerance when dealing with people of other cultures and religions. Although, Hindu religion is extremely tolerant of other religions and people's right to worship their own gods, this tolerance does not extend to according them the same privileges and rights as one accords to one's own in social or commercial dealings. One has a lesser duty or *Dharma* to treat a business transaction or a person from another religion/community fairly when this treatment is likely to impair benefits or advantages to one's own self or one's kin. While such a behavior may manifest itself just as easily in Western societies in terms of race or color bias, the system in India is likely to be more egregiously tolerant of discriminating behavior.

Artha and *Kama*, i.e., acquisition of wealth and the means of its enjoyment have positive influence on business behavior in that they favor savings and consumption, thus contributing to economic growth. They also manifest themselves often in conspicuous consumption and wealth hoarding in non-productive assets. In part, these actions also arise out of a desire to avoid paying confiscatory taxes to a national government – a concept that is not central to the Hindu culture. Historically, the state has been seen primarily as the King's domain known for its extortion of other people's labor rather than protection of its subjects. Thus while India has all the trappings of a modern democracy, its foundations are still based on bribe and corruption, the coin of the realm of a feudal mind-set. The corruption and buying of elections are endemic to India's democratic system. The bureaucracy's indifference to the plight of the masses is pervasive. Like most other developing countries of Asia and Latin America nothing moves without paying a bribe, and this includes virtually all levels of government.

Summary and Conclusions

Hinduism as a religion exerts a strong influence on its followers. It accommodates a wide variety of behaviors and is quite flexible in applying various religious tenets to real-life situations. At the same time, it is highly spiritualistic, and seeks virtuous behavior and adherence to principle and social obligation. It creates conditions that rationalize the sanctity of work even when work is unpalatable and unrewarding. The accumulation of wealth and enjoyment of the means of life are stripped of their guilt connotations and Hindus are encouraged to pursue such activities provided they are undertaken within the framework of one's *Dharma*. The system provides a built-in mode for coping with adversity. However, when carried to extremes, it engenders pessimism, risk avoidance, and a rationale for exploitation by the haves of the have-nots.

Bibliography

Anand, M. R. (1963). *Is There A Contemporary Indian Civilization? Bombay: Asia Publishing House.*

Dehejia, R. H. & Dehejia, V. H. (1993). Religion and economic activity in India: An historical perspective. *American Journal of Economics and Sociology*, 52, 145-54.

Kapp, W. P. (1963). *Hindu Culture, Economic Development and Economic Planning in India.* New York: Asia Publishing House.

Koller, J. (1970). *Oriental Philosophies.* New York: Scribner.

Radhakrishnan, S. (ed.). (1948). *The Bhagavad Gita.* London: Allen & Unwin.

Milner, Murray Jr.,. (1993). Hindu eschatology and the Indian caste system: An example of structural reversal. *The Journal of Asian Studies*, 52 (2), 298-319.

Mishra, Vikas. (1962). *Hinduism and Economic Growth.* Bombay: Oxford University Press.

Uppal, J. S. (1977). *Economic Development in South Asia.* New York: St. Martin's Press.

Weber, M. (1946). The social psychology of the world religions. *From Max Weber,* (eds), Hans Gerth & C. Wright Mills. New York: Oxford University Press.

Weber, M. (1958). *The Protestant Ethic and the Spirit of Capitalism.* New York: Free Press.

Welty, P. T. (1973). *The Asians: Their Heritage and Their Destiny.* Philadelphia: Lippincott.

S. PRAKASH SETHI and PAUL STEIDLMEIER

business ethics and Islam   Islam (meaning "submission" to divine will) was originally proclaimed in Mecca, the most important trading center of western and central Arabia in about 610CE. As a result, Meccans played a dominant role in the creation of a culture that nurtured the cultivation and development of a socio-economic system based on Islamic justice.

Sources of the Shari'ah Regulating Business Proceedings

By the middle of eighth century Islamic jurisprudence laid down a legal theory to allow a judge or a mufti to find out in all circumstances what is the legal-moral action. The two fundamental sources for deriving authoritative guidance were the Qur'an, the basic scripture of Islam, and, the Traditions (*sunna*), the normative directives deduced from the Prophet Muhammad's own actions. Duties and right actions that were not mentioned in these two sources were to be determined by the exercise of independent personal judgment of lawyers. The underlying principle in deciding such cases was proportionality based on determining benefit as compared to harm to the well-being of the community. Judgments of public interest (*maslahah*), convenience, or similar considerations were usually issued by legal scholars and other administrative officials exercising judicial powers. Although the system allowed the latitude to cope with changing conditions of the community, the dominating attitude among lawyers was the fear of arbitrariness in the decisions of those who held power.

Islam requires a good public order in which spiritual interests are organically related to individual material well-being. Hence the law of the marketplace is almost equally a public concern with the regulations connected with acts of worship in the mosque. Whereas the ritual acts, whether performed publicly in a group or privately, are the homage humankind paid to God, commercial engagements are closely tied to the notions of interpersonal justice. The main concern of the Islamic public order is not so much collective interests as individual justice that has to be protected outside of close friendship and family ties. It is expected that most human relations would tend to take the form of contract relations rather than be determined in advance by social status. Many provisions in the Islamic law attempt to back those who are weak in one way or another against the strong taking great advantage of them. On the whole, faith in Islam constitutes ten parts of which only one part is related to God–human relationship and claims the status of a common universal obligation. The other nine parts are related to human–human relationship determined by contractual responsibilities and specific social and cultural experience. Islamic ethics, mediated through God's will, is an integral part of Islamic law – the Shari'ah. The Shari'ah determines the specifics of a system in which judgments of public interest and equity are causally related to the overall prosperity of the community in this and the next life. The end of humanity is happiness, and this results from the rewards of God on the Day of Judgment.

Market Ethics in the Islamic Legal-ethical Formulations

Muslim juridical writings give detailed rulings related to acquisition and disposal of private and business property and purchase and sale of merchandise. The underlying principle operative in the market law is the autonomy of the individual to own productive resources to further her/his economic interest within a COMMUNITARIAN ethic requiring one to take the competing interests of the community at large as morally binding. Therefore, any individual business undertaking that causes harm to the moral and spiritual fabric of the society is to be condemned and prohibited. The principle that operates to protect the consumer is non-maleficence which requires that resource-owners not seek to cause harm to buyers by false evaluation and other means of raising sales. Hence, deceptive advertising is regarded as morally wrong and legally punish-

able. The principle of common good requires that free mutual consent of the buyer and the seller be regarded as a necessary condition for any business transaction. The Qur'an provides the grounds for the ruling: "O believers, consume not your goods between you in vanity, except there be trading, by your agreeing together" (4:29). Individual freedom in negotiating business transactions is recognized in the directive given by the Prophet: "Leave people alone for God provides them sustenance through each other." Thus freedom of enterprise leaves the conduct of a large part of the production and distribution of goods and services to individuals or voluntarily constituted groups. However, even this otherwise absolute freedom is regulated by the legal principle of public interest which requires that the good of its commission, when compared to the harm, should be predominant.

The market mechanism is an integral part of the Islamic economic system because the institution of private property depends on it for its operation. It also allows the consumers to express their desires for the production of goods of their liking by their willingness to pay the price. However, the profit motive, while essential for the operation of free enterprise, if not controlled, could become a source of individual self-interest and violate Islamic goals of social and economic justice and equitable distribution of income and wealth. According to Muslim jurists:

> Buying and selling are permitted by the law in order for the people to benefit mutually. There is no doubt that this can also be a cause of injustice, because both buyer and seller desire more profit and the Lawgiver has neither prohibited profit nor has he set limits to it. He has, however, prohibited fraud and cheating and ascribing to a commodity attributes that it does not possess. (al-Jaziri, *Kitab al-fiqh 'ala al-madhahib al-aba'a* (Cairo, 1965), vol. 2, pp. 283–4)

Another aspect of Islamic concern for fairness in business dealings is reflected in its prohibition of business transactions that call for taking interest (covering money payment for money). Islamic lawyers are working out ways of carrying out more business-like proceedings, without setting aside the more idealistic provisions of the Shari'ah as basic norms. The ruling they provided was to stop Muslims from profiting from someone in distress and in need of a loan, while making it legitimate for two businessmen to profit by the consequences of a present deal if they also agreed to share their profits in a complementary future deal. Such rulings were casuistically made and were regarded as "tricks" (*hiyal*) to safeguard the spirit of the basic norm of justice and fairness. Like any casuistry the legal "tricks" were open to abuse and in practice they amounted to exploitation of legal rules to benefit wealthy businessmen.

With technicalization of the Muslim world, international trade regulations have replaced or even ignored classical juristic rulings of the pre-modern Islamic law of transactions: Today contemporary issues are part of the ongoing debate in the areas of corporate social responsibility, advertising, conflict of interest and conflict of obligation, and environmental responsibility from an Islamic perspective.

Bibliography

Ahmad, Khursheed. (ed.) (1980). *Studies in Islamic Economics*. Leicester, UK: The Islamic Foundation.

Sadr, Ayatullah Baqir al- (1982). *Islam and Schools of Economics*. Karachi: Islamic Seminary.

Siddiqi, M. N. (1981). *Muslim Economic Thinking: A Survey of Contemporary Literature*. Leicester, UK: The Islamic Foundation.

Taleqani, S. M. (1983). *Islam and Ownership*, trans. A. Jabbari and F. Rajaee. Lexington, Ill.: Mazda Publishers.

ABDULAZIZ SACHEDINA

business ethics and Judaism

Divine Source of Wealth

There is no anti-business bias in Judaism since economic wants, like all other human needs, are satisfied through human endeavor in normal non-miraculous ways. The drive for economic wealth is morally legitimate and an essential prerequisite of the Divine blueprint for the existence and welfare of the world. However, the selfsame drive can result in widespread injustice and pervasive economic immorality. Greed is the most powerful of all human drives. "The less one has, the more one wants, the more one has, the more one wants." The Talmudic Sages contrasted this with sex where "the more one has the more one wants, the less one has the less one wants." This insatiable need is enhanced by man's perpetual fear of economic uncertainty, which leads to a search for the protection of wealth against the risks involved in the market and in the human condition. Sometimes, this is achieved through legitimate means but it is often the real mainspring for business immorality.

The tension between necessary economic activity and the potential for immorality inherent in wealth creation, is adjudicated by the acknowledgment of the divine source of all wealth and the assurance of divine providence. Faith in God as the provider of all human needs obviates recourse to dishonesty as a protection against uncertainty, yet permits entrepreneurial risk-taking. The divine source of wealth mandates that it not be earned through immoral or unjust ways, so that greed is channeled into morality. Rejecting the idea that luck, hard work, or ability are the real sources of economic success, in favour of the divine source, makes the marketplace a potential vehicle for achieving sanctity. The course book of Jewish commercial, civil, and criminal law was named the *Book of Salvation*.

Real moral dilemmas exist only in those areas where actions do not give rise to legal claims or punishment, but are nevertheless unethical. In others, they are simply criminal alternatives. The solution of such dilemmas is guided by two concepts; "the stumbling block in the path of the blind" and "clean before man and God."

The biblical injunction against putting a stumbling block in the path of the blind is rabbinically understood to refer either to concealing conflicts of interest or to providing goods or services that can be morally or physically detrimental to the buyer. This applies even where the buyer knowingly accepts the goods, or where the trade is within the limits of the law. Advertising and sale of cigarettes and drugs, the arms trade not concerned with self-defense, and pornography have been cited as such a stumbling block.

Another aspect of business activity covered by the biblical injunction, includes the provision of advice which is detrimental to the other party since it conceals conflicts of interest or may entangle them in situations from which they may not be able to escape.

There often exist situations in the market, in which the injured party for technical reasons or for shortcomings in the law, cannot claim for damages suffered or losses incurred. Nevertheless, Judaism insists that one who considers himself a God-fearing person should refrain from initiating such acts or pay for their results, even if not legally liable. Certain types of nuclear damages, for example, may only affect health and environment in many years to come, so that perhaps the perpetrator may not have any obligations, yet it is forbidden to deliberately cause such damage. Furthermore, one is not allowed to cause damage to another's property or health, even while accepting the financial liability for such acts. This could occur when the cost of preventing such damage is greater than the compensation paid for the damages.

It is pertinent to mention that most economic crimes are committed in secret and are a rejection of God's ability to see and punish all. This is exemplified by biblical commentary on the laws of just weights and measures. The requirement therefore to be clean before God is a major bulwark against economic immorality.

Above all, the spiritual damage to the perpetrator of unethical acts is of greater concern in Judaism, than rectifying the financial damage suffered by the victim.

"Mine and Yours"

Although private property is protected against damage and fraud, by a ramified network of legislation and education, there is no concept of unlimited private ownership. The wealth provided by God creates not only a vertical relationship between man and God, but also a horizontal one between man and man, so that there is a large human family, linked by their common Creator. Primarily, this wealth is for the satisfaction of the needs and wants of the owner; to presume otherwise is to defy human nature, and therefore not viable. At the same time, it is also meant to be used to provide for the poor and the inefficient – the old, the weak, and even the lazy or addicted. This provision is balanced between the voluntary sharing of wealth through philanthropy, Tzedakah (char-

ity), and the compulsory participation, Tzedek (justice), through public taxation and macroeconomic policies, in the funding of these needs.

However, none of this is really possible unless there is an ideological and legislated framework for limitations on private ownership. Satisfaction of the social needs requires a willingness on the part of the possessors of wealth, to relinquish some of their legal rights, not only for the needy but also simply for the benefit of others.

So lifnim mishurat hadin – beyond the letter of the law – is the mark of Judaism's role models. Hereby demands on debtors or workers, while legal, may be waived. The right of first refusal is granted to neighbors in the sale of real estate or to existing stockholders in corporate restructuring. Trespassing is permissible if no damage is done to the property of others. All this in fulfillment of the dictum that "one should walk in righteous ways," doing favours with one's wealth. The non-interest loan is presented by Judaism, not as a denial of the legitimate role of capital, but rather as an act of charity.

Despite this network of voluntary and legislated charity, limitations are placed on the transfer of wealth. One is not required to beggar oneself nor is taxation allowed to be confiscatory, in order to provide for others. Corporations therefore have no obligation to employ redundant workers other than their legal or contracted obligations, beyond the capacity of the shareholders to provide charity.

The use of wealth partially for the satisfaction of social needs is an obligation on the possessor not an entitlement of the recipient. So the mark of a pious person, "what's mine is yours and what's yours is yours" is not synonymous with the mark of an ignoramus – "what's mine is yours and what's yours is mine."

The Rights and Obligations of Society

Beyond providing a moral basis for taxation, Judaism insists on an equitable macroeconomic policy. Price control, actively promoting competition except where it is harmful to society, and symmetrically protecting property rights and actively ensuring truth in trading, are an inherent role for the courts and for the elected representatives of society. Non-Jews, Noachides, are obligated as are Jews to establish a legal system that will prevent economic immorality and promote social justice.

In pursuit of justice, society acquires, as it were, a property right in the wealth of others in order to fulfill its obligations. Otherwise human nature being what it is and the persistent lust for wealth would limit the mutual assistance. At the same time provisions need to be made to prevent the emergence of a soulless bureaucracy or corruption or the confiscation of private wealth. The divine insistence on using part of that wealth for the needs of others makes it holy money that must neither be wasted nor abused. Since the power of the state is far greater than that of the individual, additional limitations are placed on society's rights, beyond those placed on the individual. These require full accountability, protection against abuse of power, and the avoidance of even seemingly unethical behaviour.

It should be pointed out that there is no "corporate veil" in Judaism that permits the individual to escape the social and moral obligations accompanying wealth.

Economics of Enough

Efficiency in wealth creation and equity in distribution are essential but not sufficient for the sanctification of humanity, which is the ultimate purpose of Judaism. The wide-ranging Jewish framework for business morality cannot be sustained unless it rests on the assumption of "enough." Despite the manifold difficulties of defining this "enough," it stands in direct contradiction to the free-market philosophy of "more is always better than less."

The time available for business activity is limited by the Sabbath, Festivals, Sabbatical and Jubilee years, but even more so by the obligation to study Torah, the revealed Law of God. Every Jew, irrespective of age, social status, wealth or intellect, has this obligation that is unlimited. This leads both to a brake on the accumulation of wealth and to a constant exposure to the ethical obligations and limitations involved in that wealth.

Furthermore, this religious milieu contributes to an ingrained modesty in consumption. This modesty substantially dampens the individual's demand for a spiraling standard of living, and to a reduced pressure to find immoral ways

to satisfy it. The same modesty offers protection against the economic, social, and spiritual ills accompanying the clamor for instant gratification and for an unlimited consumer society. Naturally, this will be reflected in business behavior regarding advertising, planned obsolescence, and marketing.

The "economics of enough" must not be confused with poverty or utopianism. Judaism sees no spiritual value in poverty nor is it a way to achieve spiritual redemption. It is not trivial to point out that the founding fathers of Judaism were all wealthy men and that the divine blessings granted to man for obeying His commandments are all material ones. What is involved is the ability to say as the Patriarch Jacob does, "I have all I need."

Although this is reflected in all the ramified legal and educational aspects of Jewish economic life, nowhere is it more pronounced than in regard to ecology and the environment. A balance is needed between the legitimate use of resources for the creation of wealth and the regulation of methods that disturb or damage the property, health and aesthetic pleasure of others; these include waste and wanton destruction of the animal, plant, and aquatic worlds. Man may not dissipate or destroy even that which is legitimately his own.

As the custodian of natural resources man needs to husband them for the use of future generations. Since natural resources are limited, this means that society needs to limit its economic development in order to provide protection against environmental damage, both at the individual and at the macroeconomic levels. This involves zoning laws, technical methods of controlling pollution or aesthetic damage, and preventing waste of limited fossil or other fuels. Society is also granted the right of eminent domain. Urban policy based on the biblical laws of the Levitical cities, requires small units surrounded by green belts, which may not be reduced even with the agreement of the citizens. Expansion would require the establishment of new units in contrast to the modern urban sprawl, with its resultant social and physical decay.

The Rabbis saw in the eternal search for more, the cause of the biblical Flood that destroyed the world. The generations that preceeded the Flood became concerned that with the growth in population and economic development, there would be insufficient natural resources for material, aesthetic, and economic needs. Not only would this lead to strife and even scarce economic good but also to a degeneration of all species and the quality of life. So they instituted strict birth control and the search for non-procreative sexual lifestyles. When this was insufficient, they began to steal, rob, and kill each other, which ultimately led to the Flood.

Bibliography

Tamari, M. (1990). Ethical issues in bankruptcy: A Jewish perspective. *Journal of Business Ethics*, **9**, 785–9.

MEIR TAMARI

business ethics in Africa   Business ethics in Africa may be said to be the theory, practice, and/or critique of financial and economic transactions with or among Africans, from a moral point of view. It concerns the rightness or wrongness of doing business with Africans or in Africa. "Doing business with Africans" should be interpreted broadly to include individuals and groups of Africans as well as African countries and governments.

The Geography and Economy of Africa

It is important to note that Africa is not a country but a huge continent – the second largest in the world – with over 1,000 distinct languages and over 11 million square miles. Consequently, statements about business practices in Africa are, at best, generalizations and, at worst, hasty or inaccurate.

Most countries in Africa have what may be termed developing or low- to middle-income economies. According to World Development Indicators of the World Bank, most of the low-income countries, which are those with a 1992 per capita GNP of $675 or less, are African countries; and developing countries invest approximately $200 billion in new infrastructure each year. Infrastructure development includes power and water supplies, building and maintaining dams, roads, railways, and ports, as well as dealing with inefficiency and waste in investment and delivery services, and respond-

ing effectively to user demand. Herein lies the opportunities for both doing business with Africans or in Africa as well as opportunities for dealing with ethical and unethical business practices.

Further, since most African countries are agricultural and dependent on the production and exportation of cash crops which are subject to falling demands and falling prices, many countries in Africa can neither produce nor export enough to meet national demand. The opportunities for unethical business practices in Africa are, thus, enormous. It is easy for government and private individuals, whether African or foreign, to practice profiteering, bribery, or favoritism; resulting in starvation, death, and social and political turmoil in these multi-ethnic societies that recently gained their independence from Western colonialism.

Ethical Principles

The opportunities for business and abuse of political and economic power in Africa raise several questions in business ethics. The first concerns the social responsibility of business persons and organizations. It is apparent that Africa provides some consideration for businesses to be concerned with morality, apart from making and maximizing profits. Secondly, it raises the question as to whether consequences, especially for a society as a whole, determine the rightness or wrongness of business and other kinds of human conduct. Thirdly, since there is a widespread belief that Africans and their beliefs tend to be religious, the question arises as to whether African principles of ethics and, hence, business are religious or divine commands that are independent of the consequences for the society. Fourthly, the question as to whether ethics is discovered or invented would seem to have a bearing here.

Contrary to popular opinion, there is very little evidence in traditional African beliefs to suggest that morality in the African tradition is dependent on religion. In the first place, unlike Christianity and Islam which originated in the Middle East, most traditional African religions are not revealed religions. Most of them have no temples, special days of worship, or messiahs to whom God gave divine commandments or criteria. Secondly, the rural, communal, and extended-family nature of these societies – in which nature, people, departed ancestors, and so-called spirits live in close cause-and-effect relationships without sharp ontological divisions – make the consequences for the community the primary determinant of good conduct. As the Akans of West Africa put it, it is people who matter (*Onipa ne asem*) not money (*sika*), clothes (*ntama*), or anything else and none but people respond when one calls out for help.

The humanicentric conception of traditional African ethics is borne out by critical rather than descriptive accounts of several traditional African beliefs; but it still does not settle the issue of whether African criteria of morality tend to be based on consequences or something other than consequences. There is little doubt that egoism or a business practice that is motivated by extreme forms of capitalism and personal gain rather than societal gain is usually frowned upon in many African societies. Further, it has been suggested that the divine command theory is, strictly speaking, not descriptive of African morality. But egoism is not the only theory which bases morality on consequences, and the divine command theory is not the only non-consequential theory there is. It still leaves open the possibility that some form of non-pleasure-centered utilitarianism, which does not encourage the sex and drug culture criticized by many Africans, is consistent with African morality. But so is a Kantian interpretation of African morality which bases morality not primarily on the consequences but respect for humanity.

It is arguable, however, that the choice between consequences and non-consequences is a false but popular dilemma in Western moral philosophy. After all, it would seem that even when one has decided on consequences as the criterion for determining whether something is right or wrong, one needs to use something other than consequences to determine which type of consequences will count. If this account and thinking is correct, then while the ultimate criterion of morality and thus business ethics could be something other than consequences, it is the consequences that will determine whether the criterion has been achieved.

In any case, whether conceived in terms of consequences or something else, in the end it would seem that the African values used to evaluate foreign and indigenous businesses tend to emphasize communalism (not necessarily communism), respect for age and human life, and the subordination of monetary concerns and interests to those of human welfare.

Bibliography

Kwame, S. (1983). Doin' business in an African country: Business ethics and capitalism in a poor country. *Journal of Business Ethics*, **2**, 236–68.

Oruka, O. (ed.), . (1991). *Sage Philosophy: Indigenous Thinkers and Modern Debate on African Philosophy*. Nairobi, Kenya: African Centre for Technology Studies (ACTS) Press.

Wiredu, K. (1991). Morality and religion in Akan thought. In N. R. Allen Jr. (ed.), , *African-American Humanism: An Anthology*. Buffalo, New York: Prometheus Books.

World Bank. (1994). *World Development Report 1994: Infrastructure for Development*. New York: Oxford University Press.

SAFRO KWAME

business ethics in Australia   "Business Ethics" as an academic discipline is a relatively new phenomenon in Australia. The title has appeared in university handbooks in recent times, and then only grudgingly. However, during the last ten years or so (1980s–1994) a lot of questionable activity occurred in Australia in the areas of commerce and public-sector management. This activity prompted responsible citizens (and there are quite a few) to realize that dramatic changes were necessary in the way business affairs were transacted and public administration managed. Hitherto, "business ethics", i.e. the subject studied at tertiary level by business and commerce students, had been given fleeting lip service in most Australian business schools and faculties. The subject was possibly referred to in business policy or marketing classes or perhaps not at all. Business ethics, that intangible product upon which honest business deals depend so much, was, and still is in some quarters, virtually non-existent in many parts of business Australia. This criticism could of course be leveled at other countries in addition to Australia, for there does appear to be a trend towards unethical business practice which is worldwide. For more detail see Small (1993, 1994) and Pech and Small (1994).

With the wisdom of hindsight, the reason in part for this state of affairs in Australia is now somewhat easier to explain. During the period of the late sixties to the early seventies Australia experienced a mineral/mining boom. This period produced instant millionaires, and people who had never played the stockmarket made fortunes almost overnight (some even gave up tenured positions, bought themselves a luxurious lifestyle, and retired early). In addition, with the steady increase in population, there was a strong demand for land and property development in all the major capital cities, and the entrepreneur or developer who had the ability or foresight to sense a potential profitable opportunity stood to make large financial gains. Some of these entrepreneurs and developers were new arrivals in Australia, and although many lacked formal training in financial management they were still prepared to become involved in risky business ventures. In brief, land and property development schemes, TV stations, and shopping centers were amongst the business ventures commenced and carried over into the eighties. To sum up this period, a few people made a lot of money in a very short space of time. This trend continued at a frenetic pace into the eighties. More people wanted to make their fortunes and it all seemed so very easy.

However, the fallout associated with the stockmarket crash of 1987, which produced numerous examples of sloppy accounting practices, also highlighted very questionable business ethical standards in many of the business and corporate deals. It also became very obvious that the same entrepreneurs kept appearing in some of the more outrageous deals. In some cases, an absence of personal ethical standards was also revealed. The time was thus right for the introduction of "Business Ethics and Social Responsibility" courses across the Australian academic scene, and while some people welcomed this move, there was also resistance. Australia's population is only 18 million (approximately) compared with the United States' 248.8 million, and California which alone has 28.8 million. Therefore, when misdemeanors involving business or public sector ethics did occur in Australia, it was quite easy

for the details concerning these occurrences to be circulated among the business communities very quickly.

To illustrate, there are six Australian states, plus the Northern Territory. (The Northern Territory University, incidentally, has been very proactive in this area by introducing a "Business Ethics" stream for senior police in its recently developed (1994) Master of International Management.) All the Australian state governments had received unwelcome publicity concerning improper or unethical conduct and illegal conduct on the part of some of their politicians, public servants, and senior police officers. Royal Commissions or Commissions of Inquiry into alleged corruption were held in five Australian states, viz. Queensland, Victoria, Tasmania, Western Australia, and South Australia. In Western Australia, a situation had developed in the eighties with the Labor government of the day becoming closely involved with a number of entrepreneurs now known to be of dubious character. This period was referred to colloquially as "Western Australia, Inc.", or "WA, Inc." Some of the more highly publicized events in this era included the jailing of a former Labor Premier and one of his ministers, the exodus of former advisers to places such as Vietnam, Poland, and Hong Kong, and the eventual toppling of a government. The period also featured reports in the media of used bank notes being stuffed into a brown leather satchel, confidential government files going missing, documents ending up in the shredder, bribes and "bagmen", huge political donations, and money going missing. In Queensland ("the deep North"), the Fitzgerald Commission (1988) brought down a number of findings about corruption in Queensland. As a result of this inquiry the Criminal Justice Commission (the CJC) was set up to implement the reforms proposed by the Fitzgerald Commission. In New South Wales, the state government established the Independent Commission Against Corruption (ICAC). This Commission targeted ministers, including the state's Liberal Premier, who was required to resign from his position. When these stories broke, and even long before they made the headlines, the intimate details of most business scandals were usually known throughout Australia almost immediately.

Two factors may help to explain the success of the people who were engaged for so long in illegal and unethical business practice. One may be termed "a culture of indifference." This requires an understanding of the basic Australian ethos or culture. Many people were, and some still are, indifferent to the stories circulating about malpractice in business and government circles, and even when the Royal Commissions were hearing submissions, the media reports were largely ignored. In recent days, a former senator who has just published his memoirs, stated that lying was quite a normal practice amongst politicians, and so far few people have taken exception to this statement. A second factor, and one which is really more serious, is the failure of the Australian judicial system to freeze assets of persons charged with serious or complex fraud. There are endless stories of persons charged with serious business fraud and similar offences who are still living in luxury overseas, have assets invested overseas, or who have off-loaded their wealth to members of their immediate families. Comments have been made that the Commonwealth Attorney-General should appoint an adminstrative body which would prevent financial assets being concealed in this way, and that Australian judges should be more. *au fait* with international business practice, particularly the way monies can be moved around the globe almost instantly.

The Current Status of "Business Ethics"

"Business Ethics," i.e. the subject for academic study, is not yet totally acceptable in all academic circles, but it is seen as a "growth industry," and with government funding for universities directly tied to student enrollment numbers, viable courses such as "Business Ethics" which attract student enrollment acquire new significance. Practically all 36 Australian universities now include a "Business Ethics/Social Responsibility" section or course in their business/commerce degree programs. In the majority of cases, these courses are normally located in a school or department of management or marketing with the teaching staff located in management or marketing departments. However, there are exceptions to this; some teaching staff are philosophers who have an interest in business matters. In addition,

the point must be emphasized that in most cases "Business Ethics" is normally offered as an elective or optional subject, and is not yet a core unit in MBA programs. Resistance to listing "Business Ethics" as a required unit in MBA programs is still noticeable, for if "Business Ethics" is adopted (or so the argument goes), then some other unit must be dropped.

From observation and discussion with colleagues in the field, it seems that the majority of business ethics courses in Australia are based on the well-known texts published in the United States, and supplemented by journals originating in the United Kingdom, Canada, and the United States. From an epistemological standpoint, problems are likely to be experienced in introducing a subject such as "Business Ethics." The "average" Australian business/commerce student would have had minimal exposure to a liberal arts or a philosophy-oriented curriculum. Most students would be pragmatic and job oriented in their approach to study programs, and while subjects such as Accounting, Business Policy, Finance, Marketing, Strategic Management etc., present little problem, apart from the normal-to-be-expected student concerns, "Business Ethics" does present real concerns for some students. For example, comments from students about studying "Business Ethics" highlighted difficulties which some of them encountered in studying a subject which was essentially abstract, and based on argumentation and reasoned justification of a particular philosophical standpoint. Nevertheless, progress is being made and "Business Ethics" is gradually becoming more firmly established as a bona fide and accepted academic subject. Research and publication of research is becoming more evident in the well-known journals. To illustrate this point, there is the three-phase "Australian Business Ethics Project" directed by Milton-Smith (1994). This research project is currently ongoing with Parts 1 and 2 completed. In addition, there was a visit to Australia in July/August 1994 by the eminent scholar in the field, the very distinguished Richard De George, whose lecture series did much to raise the profile, visibility, and credibility of the subject in a very brief period of time.

Bibliography

Fitzgerald, G. E. (chairman). (1989). *Report of a Commission of Inquiry Pursuant to Orders in Council.* (The Fitzgerald Inquiry Report). Brisbane, Australia.

Milton-Smith, J. (1994). *The Australian Business Ethics Project,* Parts 1–3. (An ongoing three-phase project, Part 3 to be completed.) Bentley, Western Australia: Curtin Business School.

Pech, R. J. & Small, M. W. (1994). Management, white-collar crime and the practising manager: who should be most concerned? *The Practising Manager, Australian Journal of Applied Management Issues,* 14, (2).

Report of the Royal Commission into Commercial Activities of Government and Other Matters, Part I, vols. 1–6, Western Australia, 1992.

Small, M. W. (1993). Ethics in business and administration: An international and historical perspective. *Journal of Business Ethics,* 12, 125–32.

Small, M. W. (1995). Business ethics and commercial morality: Report of the Royal Commission into Commercial Activities. *Journal of Business Ethics,* 14, (8), 613–28.

Small, M. W. (ed.), . (1995). *Journal of Business Ethics,* 14, (7). A special double issue, comprising eleven articles by authors with experience in Australasia titled *Research on Business and Public Sector Ethics: An Australian Perspective.*

MICHAEL W. SMALL

business ethics in Canada   Some might argue that it is unnecessary to specify a particular nation state when speaking about business ethics. Since all human action has moral consequences and ethical theories about assessing the morality of human action, surely business ethics can be discussed in universal rather than country-specific terms.

While it is true that the particular activities of any business in any country can be discussed by appeal to general mainstream ethical theories (e.g., utilitarianism or deontology), individual characteristics are important. The specific ethical issues of relevance to a given country have a great deal to do with its political and legal history, its religious history, its economic status, its natural resources, its industrial base, and its relationship to other nation states.

For Canada, two key relationships have conditioned the development of both law and the evolution and context in which business and ethics converge. Canada was a British colony and is, consequently, a member of the Commonwealth nations. Consequently, the Canadian government is a parliamentary government and Canada has had closer ties with other Commonwealth countries than geography alone would make evident. Secondly, Canada shares a boundary with the United States, its largest trading partner, a neighbor with ten times its population.

Canada's historic relationship with Great Britain is partly evidenced by its recent constitutional autonomy. Canada's Charter of Rights and Freedoms was "repatriated" or came into constitutional legal existence in 1982. With the exception of the Quebec provincial judicial system, Canada's legal history is grounded in British common law. Canada has not had the litigious history of its American neighbor and Canadian victims of ethical wrongdoing by corporations have not sought class-action suits to rectify the wrong even when evidence of the wrongdoing has been significant and well documented (e.g., compare the series of lawsuits against US asbestos companies with the virtual lack of suits by Canadian victims of the asbestos industry).

It is perhaps not surprising that cultural and economic autonomy are common themes in Canadian business ethics. Canadians have one state-subsidized radio and television network (the Canadian Broadcasting Corporation) and a partially subsidized film industry, the National Film Board. Over the past decade, these cultural industries have received significant budget cuts and cultural nationalists debate the seriousness of this. Most Canadians watch American television, read American magazines, and go to American films for entertainment. The extent to which Canada as a nation state has a different cultural and national identity distinct from the United States and whether, in fact, state-subsidized initiatives should bolster such differences is an ongoing and familiar debate within the country.

As a sparsely populated, traditionally resource-based economy, Canada has had a high quality of life with state-subsidized education (including post-secondary education) and universal healthcare. With a national debt growing at the rate of $1,000 per minute, the pressures of globalization, trade liberalization, and deregulation are also common themes in articles and books on business ethics in Canada. The critics of the North American Free Trade Agreement (NAFTA) in Canada focused primarily on two issues. Would NAFTA increase unemployment in Canada by shipping low-paying jobs to a poorer nation state (i.e. Mexico), where lower wages and less stringent worker and environmental protection laws are the norm? Secondly, even if the quality of Canadian life were advanced through NAFTA, would it be ethical to benefit by shipping the worst jobs to a third world country?

The environment and sustainability are also critical issues in a country built on resource-extraction. The successive Canadian governments over the past decade have stressed the need for the diversification of the Canadian economy from primary resource-extraction and emphasized the importance of increasing global competitiveness through value-added industries.

Canadian business ethics is not, however, solely idiosyncratic and concerned only with issues circumscribed by Canadian boundaries. *The Corporate Ethics Monitor*, the bi-monthly newsletter of EthicScan Canada Ltd (a private company), regularly features Canadian companies' ratings on a series of ethical indicators including: code of ethics; community relations; employment of women (at all levels of the corporation); charitable donations; extended maternity leave; corporate-sponsored daycare; environmental performance; international relations; labour relations; health and safety; military and nuclear involvement.

Canadian concern with the impact of globalization of the economy on national and international ethics and law is shared internationally with other industrialized and developing nations. Employment equity (Canada's term for affirmative action); First Nations' land claims over privately owned land and crown land; criminal wrongdoing; taxation of businesses; corporate donations to political parties; the online civilization and regulation are all ethical business issues Canadians share with the world.

Recently, Canadian business ethics has joined the world of cyber-net with the growth of a number of internet think-tanks on business ethics. The Canadian Business and Professional Ethics Network (cbpenet) links the majority of academics working on business ethics in Canada. SUSNET links ethicists concerned with sustainability, justice, and global economic development, while members of ESAC-L (the network of the Environmental Studies Association of Canada) discuss environmental issues and problems. These networks also connect Canadian ethicists with a number of US and international internet lists.

While Canadian history makes the discussion of business ethics somewhat culture-specific, the Canadian future may include the erosion of such specificities through free-trade agreements, information highways, and a globalized economy which diminish the importance of national boundaries and the strength of autonomous nation states. If this does prove to be the case, business ethics and international standards and the monitoring of those standards will supersede and transform current political boundaries and political realities.

Bibliography

Bienefeld, J. P. (1992). Financial deregulation: Disarming the nation state. *Studies in Political Economy*, 37, 31–58.

Brooks, L. (ed.). *The Corporate Ethics Monitor*, published six times per year by EthicScan Canada Ltd, Box 54034, Toronto, Ontario, M6A 3B7.

Cragg, W. (1992). *Contemporary Moral Issues* Toronto: McGraw-Hill Ryerson.

Michalos, A. (1995). *A Pragmatic Approach to Business Ethics*. Thousand Oaks, Calif: Sage.

Poff, D. (1994). Reconciling the irreconcilable: The global economy and the environment. In T. Schrecker & J. Dalgleish (eds), *Growth, Trade and Environmental Values*. London, Ont: Westminster Institute for Ethics and Human Values.

Poff, D. & Waluchow, W. (eds),. (1991). *Business Ethics in Canada*. Scarborough, Ont: Prentice-Hall.

Schrecker, T. & Dalgleish, J. (eds),. (1994). *Growth, Trade and Environmental Values*. London, Ont: Westminster Institute for Ethics and Human Values.

Snider, L. (1993). *Bad Business: Corporate Crime in Canada*. Toronto: Nelson.

Swift, J. & Tomlinson, B. (eds),. (1991). *Conflicts of Interest: Canada and the Third World*. Toronto: Between the Lines.

DEBORAH C. POFF

business ethics in China Business ethics in China rest upon a rich and diverse cultural moral heritage that emphasizes personal virtue (*de*) and justice (*zheng yi*), which manifest a right ordering of personal relationships in social organization and institutions. The most prominent forebears of this tradition are Confucian, Daoist, and Legalist schools of thought, as well as a very strong influence derived from Buddhism. In modern times, Western Enlightenment philosophies of business and society have come to exert increasing influence on Chinese approaches to business ethics, as China has been caught up in social processes of modernization (*see* LOCKE, JOHN; MILL, JOHN STUART; MARX, KARL).

Contemporary discussions of business ethics in China reflect very traditional moral issues: the corruption of officials, conflicts of interest, selfishness, and every type of power abuse and opportunism that forsakes the social virtue of benevolent humanity (*ren*). At the same time Chinese moral thinkers are also trying to come to terms with the moral virtues of Western economic theory and political ideals: individual liberty and rights, the moral rightness of public-policy choices, distributive justice.

Traditional Chinese approaches to ethics, in general, are communitarian and emphasize a path or a way to follow (*dao*) to achieve moral integrity (*see* COMMUNITARIANISM). The elements of this fundamental doctrine were spelled out by various schools of thought in terms of the inner logic or truth of human relatedness (*lwun li*) as expressed in fundamental moral principles. This pathway of ethical behavior gave expression to concrete criteria of virtues and moral character (*dao de*).

The underlying Chinese ethical traditions provide a moral compass for contemporary discussion of business practices. The central category of analysis is the quality of relationships (*guanxi*). Normatively, the virtue of *ren* expresses complex notions of benevolence, kindheartedness and humanity, that form the basis of the notions of virtue and justice in both personal conduct and social institutions. Regarding prescriptive ethics, proper conduct (*li*) provides a map of routinely expected ethical patterns of behavior. Chinese social philosophy of relationships embodies both the respect one person owes another in terms of face (*myan dz*)

as well as obligations of mutual rights and duties (*ren yi dao de*), which bind people together.

On the prescriptive level, there is a very important ethical difference between the morally and socially acceptable standards of conduct (*li*), which are thought of culturally as the religious and social standards of proper personal conduct necessary to moral order in society, and law (*fa*). The Confucian concept of *li* is motivated by good character and personal virtue and suggests that positive moral laws and codes are unwarranted, because acting contrary to *li* would result in interpersonal and social sanctions with far graver consequences than any embodied in a penal code. The legalistic concept of *fa*, or law, is something of a necessary evil, that is needed to ensure a moral society when virtue fails. In theory, law is reserved only for those so low on the moral stratum that they have forsaken the ethics of right relationships. Moral teaching, therefore, tends to exalt virtue and downplay codified law.

It would be naive to believe that the traditional emphasis on unwritten, accepted norms governing behavior in society are now forgotten in this era of economic reform in China. At the same time, traditional Chinese ethics is clearly not individualist nor simply utilitarian in the Western usages of the terms, such that business ethics in China is in the midst of dynamic transitions.

Bibliography

Fairbank, J. K. (1987). *The Great Chinese Revolution, 1800–1985.* New York: Harper and Row.

Latourette, K. S. (1971). *The Chinese: Their History and Culture,* 4th edn, New York: Macmillan.

Menthe, B. de (1990). *Chinese Etiquette and Ethics in Business.* Lincolnwood, Ill: NTC Business Books.

PAUL STEIDLMEIER

business ethics in developing countries Study of values and standards of behavior in the economically developing and emerging countries; including the gamut of global ethical issues: Business relationships in society, business–government collaboration, ethical issues in a free market, universal standards versus country-specific norms, intercultural ethics comparisons and views from developing countries, corporate and transnational codes of ethics, various stakeholder issues, and ethics education.

Significance

Attention has been drawn to the developing countries in the past two decades because of the growth in global competition and worldwide multinational corporations (MNCs) (*see also* MULTINATIONALS). MNC operations under varied business conditions are having an impact on economic and social outcomes. The laws, economic system (free market or government controlled), level of economic development, and acceptable moral standards, all would determine business practices. When these differ from the home-country situation dilemmas arise which have to be resolved. Should country-specific norms and practices be respected, or should they be superseded by some universal principles and standards of behavior? And, do MNCs have any special obligation in developing countries?

A recent development is the worldwide shift of command or centrally controlled economies to a free-market system, with its implications for BUSINESS AND SOCIETY. Discussions at international and national levels led to conclusions that a command economy fails in its goal of efficient production of goods and fair distribution of the benefits among the stakeholders of society. For example, in a national conference on business ethics conducted in India in 1992, the participants agreed that strong state control led to a stagnation in the economy and a decline in values in government and business, thereby compromising the very purpose of the economic system (Mathias, 1994). While abuse of the new freedom can bring ethical challenges, the dangers are less. The participants cautioned, however, that environmental neglect and over-consumerism can be equally dysfunctional.

Other Key Concepts

Corporate social responsibility (CSR) and business ethics are sometimes used interchangeably. However, business ethics refers to morality as it affects stakeholders and includes the basis for attitudes and actions. The domain of CSR is the extent of involvement and obligation of business towards society. Explanations range from obligation to stockholder interests and legal compliance, recognition, and accommodation of the concerns of other stakeholders, to commitment to societal goals in addition to the firm's economic goals (*see also* STAKEHOLDER THEORY; CORPORATE SOCIAL PERFORMANCE). The last notion takes a systemic view of mutual obligations. Extending this to the global context, the major stakeholder is the host government where the relationship is governed by mutually acceptable rules regarding the fair distribution of costs and benefits. More generally, one can argue that the responsibility of the corporations is to satisfy the socioeconomic needs of the host country while making profits. However, the concepts of CSR and business ethics in developing countries are evolving and there is no unified view.

Framework for Analysis

Applying ethical principles across countries is complicated due to cultural or economic differences. In the international arena, the predominant principles are: universal rights and cultural relativism. Universal fundamental rights, such as rights to subsistence and anti-discrimination, must be observed by businesses in all countries. Similarly, some scholars justify "transcultural corporate ethics" (Frederick, 1991, p. 165). A number of international initiatives in regulating multinational corporate activities and governments exist at different levels, including the levels of firms/industries, countries, business and government, and world organizations. While international codes are not legally enforceable, social, moral, and political influences have significant impact on corporate behavior in some areas, such as technical clarification, information sharing, and safety. Other areas are subject to controversy and conflicting interests and viewpoints, hence fail to obtain consensus or enforcement. Thus, the long-standing proposal, "UN Code of Conduct for Transnational Corporations," is not yet approved in view of its comprehensive and diverse provisions. Nevertheless, continuing discussions and information sharing are promoting understanding and consensus, reflecting an evolutionary process.

In contrast, "cultural relativism" implies that social norms are culture specific (*see also* RELATIVISM, CULTURAL AND MORAL). In this view, corporations should follow the host country's practices when they differ from those of the home country. Imposing one's own laws and practices, for instance the FOREIGN CORRUPT PRACTICES ACT of the US prohibiting gifts or other payments beyond certain limits, on this account, is suggestive of ethnocentric superiority. Other explanations include variations of the contingency approach to decision-making, where the one best method involving "right and wrong" is substituted by considering legitimate alternatives. For example, Donaldson's (1993) "extant social contract" calls for respecting the existing understanding regarding moral behavior in a business culture, considering the local ethical context; for instance, behavior based on personal relationships in business. Yet, this does not nullify the universally applicable norms. On the contrary, this approach calls for a reconciliation between a universal code of conduct and cultural tradition avoiding either of the extremes – an optimizing rather than a maximizing goal, and based on "bounded rationality."

Two other concepts are relevant. According to the principle of "adoptive stakeholders," corporations have a special responsibility in the developing host countries, because of stakeholder disadvantages. For example, there may be a lack of consensus on social expectations, inability of consumers to make informed choices, and regulatory inadequacies. Consequently, stakeholder interests were represented by external interest groups, as in the case of the Nestlé boycott against indiscriminate sale of infant formula in many developing countries, and these activists became surrogates or "adoptive stakeholders" (Tavis, 1988). Extending this to MNCs, Tavis argues that the local subsidiary represents the multinational corporation in adopting stakeholders. Due to its central position, the subsidiary could ensure that its constituents' needs are represented to corporate headquarters, and inform government policy in the host country. Similarly, surveys of developing countries will aid in identifying relevant social needs. The extent of corporate involvement, of course, varies with the level of public sophistication in different countries. However, others oppose social activism on the part of MNCs, beyond business necessity or enlightened (long-term) self-interest (Werhane, 1994; Sternberg, 1994). A similar advocacy role, that of a trustee, for corporations, reflecting communal interests, is posited by religious activism, for example liberation theology (Sethi and Steidlmeier, 1990) (see also FIDUCIARY RESPONSIBILITY; LIBERATION THEOLOGY AND BUSINESS ETHICS). The second concept is "social partnership" (Frederick, Davis, and Post, 1988), wherein the business group consisting of MNCs and domestic businesses would collaborate with government in establishing standards and regulations, for example, on safety or foreign-investment issues.

Institutional and Professional Roles

Governments of developing countries will need to undertake legal and administrative reforms with the change in the political-economic system, and corporations will have to consider internal systemic change (Amba-Rao, 1993) (see also STRATEGY AND ETHICS). The role of professionals, such as those in marketing and environment, is crucial in recognizing ethical contexts in economies that are undergoing major changes (see also PROFESSIONAL ETHICS). Initiatives of government, education and business in meeting these challenges will be the subjects of further scrutiny and study.

See also **organizational culture; social responsibility**

Bibliography

Amba-Rao, S. C. (1993). Multinational corporate social responsibility, ethics, interactions and third world governments: An agenda for the 1990s. *Journal of Business Ethics, 12*, 75–94.

Donaldson, T. (1989). *The Ethics of International Business.* New York: Oxford University Press.

Donaldson, T. (1993). International principles of business ethics. *Fairfield Business Review,* spring 1993, 19–23.

Frederick, W. C. (1991). The moral authority of transnational corporate codes. *Journal of Business Ethics, 10*, 165–78.

Frederick, W. C., Davis, K. & Post, J. E. (1988). *Business and Society,* 6th edn, New York: McGraw-Hill.

Freeman, R. E. & Gilbert, D. R., Jr. (1988). *Corporate Strategy and the Search for Ethics.* Englewood Cliffs, NJ: Prentice-Hall.

Hoffman, W. M., Kamm, J. B., Frederick, R. E. & Petry, E. S., Jr. (eds),. (1994). *Emerging Global Business Ethics.* Westport, Conn: Quorum Books.

Mathias, T. A. (ed.). (1994). *Corporate Ethics*. New Delhi: Allied Publishers.

Sethi, S. P. & Steidlmeier, P. (1990). A new paradigm of the business/society relationship in the third world: The challenge of liberation theology. In W. C. Frederick & L. E. Preston (eds), *Research Issues and Empirical Studies*. Greenwich, Conn: Jai Press, 279–93.

Sternberg, E. (1994). Relativism rejected: The possibility of transnational business ethics. In W. M. Hoffman et al. (eds), *Emerging Global Business Ethics*. Westport, Conn: Quorum Books, 143–50.

Tavis, L. A. (ed.). (1988). *Multinational Managers and Host Government Interactions*. Notre Dame, Ind: University of Notre Dame Press.

Tavis, L. A. (1994). Bifurcated development and multinational corporate responsibility. In W. M. Hoffman et al. (eds), *Emerging Global Business Ethics*. Westport, Conn: Quorum Books, 255–74.

Werhane, P. H. (1994). The moral responsibility of multinational corporations to be socially responsible. In W. M. Hoffman et al. (eds), *Emerging Global Business Ethics*. Westport, Conn: Quorum Books, 136–42.

SITA C. AMBA-RAO

business ethics in Europe   In Europe, business ethics appeared on the scene from the mid-1980s onward, both as an academic discipline, taught at universities and business schools, and as a phenomenon within business circles. Signs of an academic maturation can be found in the number of professorships, in publications of books and journals, in courses at academic institutions, and in professional and scholarly associations. In 1984 the first European chair in Business Ethics was founded at Nijenrode University, The Netherlands Business School. Ten years later the number of chairs amounts to 15, including the prestigious Dixons Chair for Business Ethics and Corporate Responsibility at the London Business School. Courses in business ethics are taught in many universities and business schools all over Europe. Numerous books and articles in the field have been published in various European languages. In 1992 a quarterly, *Business Ethics: A European Review* was started; in 1995 a bilingual journal in French and English, was launched; and in 1994 a collection of essays appeared under the telling title: *Business Ethics: A European Approach*. All this indicates that business ethics in Europe is not only taking shape, but is taking a specific European shape, compared to its counterpart in the United States.

Worth mentioning also in this respect is EBEN, the European Business Ethics Network. Founded in 1987 as the outcome of the First European Conference on Business Ethics, EBEN in its first seven years has grown to over 500 members from both academia and the business world. The aim of the network is to foster the moral quality of decision-making processes in business, and to serve as a clearing house for exchange of experiences and for joint initiatives. What makes it specifically European is the emphasis on discussion and cooperation, involving academics, business representatives, governmental agencies and the professions alike. It is not accidental that in the first major European volume on business ethics, Steinmann and Löhr's *Unternehmensethik*, a central place is given to *Diskursethik*, or "communicative ethics."

There are clear similarities between business ethics in the United States and in Europe. Both branches pay due attention to the description and analysis of single cases. In fact, this is the field in which commonly most of the available moral energy is invested. Cases in environmental management, personnel management, product quality, marketing practices, financial constructions, accounting techniques, proprietary knowledge, and business transactions abroad get the attention they deserve on both sides of the Atlantic. The same applies to corporate culture, the moral climate in the company, and the development of ethics codes. During the eighties, corporate Europe lagged behind the US in elaborating ethics codes, but in the nineties this is gradually being eliminated. Codes are more and more accepted in Europe as a means to straighten the moral backbone of an organisation and to keep fraudulent and criminal or semi-criminal influences outside its precincts.

There are also striking dissimilarities between Europe and the US in the topics studied and in the ways moral problems in business are handled. With regard to the topics studied it is revealing to compare the content of White's comprehensive anthology *Business Ethics: A Philosophical Reader* with the German *Lexikon der Wirtschaftsethik* (Lexicon of Business Ethics). The American *Reader* presents valuable studies on specific moral dilemmas that can arise between various interest groups and individuals in business, such as insider trading, sexual harassment, environmental responsibility, and privacy protection in the workplace. Some of these topics are treated in the German lexicon as well, but by far not all. Ample attention is given instead to topics like the ethical aspects of privatization, the moral foundation of co-determination rights of employees, the ethics of investment policies, and the moral proprieties of a market economy. In short, the German lexicon of business ethics encompasses many items that could also be covered under the heading of social and political philosophy and economic ethics. And in this respect the lexicon represents business ethics in Europe as a whole. This is not just a question of definition, European scholars obviously being more willing to use a broad definition of the field. Behind the difference in definition lies a deeper difference with regard to the prevalent conception of ethics. In the European context, ethics is not confined to the responsibility of the individual in distinct situations of conflict, but comprises as well a collective responsibility for the shaping of what is called, in German political terms, the *Soziale Marktwirtschaft*, a social market economy, in which the opportunities given in a free-market system are combined with the acceptance of a share in the fostering of the common good by corporations, governmental agencies, trade unions, and professional and other interest groups alike.

There are legal as well as political and cultural reasons why European business ethics is partly developing along its own lines. The legal reasons have to do with a fundamental difference in the legal systems. Citizens in the US, as in the United Kingdom, are accustomed to the *common law* system of British descent, with its extensive reliance on judge-made laws, whereas social arrangements in European countries are mainly based upon the *civil law* system stemming from the Roman and the Napoleonic Empires, which places great trust in governmental officials and government-made provisions. These different legal systems pervade the way in which ethical conflicts are tackled. A moral culture based on common law generates

winners and losers, whereas a culture based on civil law aims at balanced agreements. Ethical conflicts in business in Europe are less spectacular than on the other side of the Atlantic, not because European business people are less passionate or more ethical, but because they invest their ethical energy in settlements rather than in moral victories. Political and cultural reasons corroborate this picture. European political history is marked by a system of proportional representation and the accompanying necessity of frequent governmental coalitions. A give-and-take on the basis of a predefined common interest that is normal in political life has found its way also into corporate relations. European employers and employees meet each other at the negotiation table more often than in court or in the street on the barricades. Many issues that, in the US, are the subject of vehement ethical discussions and subsequent lawsuits, in Europe find their way to negotiated agreements between employers and trade unions, often with governmental agencies as supporting third parties, and eventually as law-giving institution.

The insight is that, in the domain of business relations, ethics cannot be confined to personal values and individual attitudes, nor to the analysis of single cases, or to the designing of codes and guidelines, important as all this undoubtedly is. Ethics in business, in its European variety, is as much about the moral solidity of the economic system we are able to establish. It is about the freedom of action we create for all market participants, not just for a few. And it is about the collective attention given to the unfortunate, an attention that is sedimented in welfare arrangements as the outcome of a long process of political as well as moral agreements. All these features taken together entitle us to speak of a plainly *European* version of ethics in business.

Bibliography

Enderle, G., Homann, K., Honecker, M., Kerber, W., & Steinmann, H. (eds) (1993). *Lexikon der Wirtschaftsethik*, Freiburg: Herder.

Harvey, B. (ed.) (1994). *Business Ethics: A European Approach*. Prentice-Hall.

Harvey, B., van Luijk H. & Steinmann, H. (1994). *European Casebook on Business Ethics*. New York: Prentice-Hall.

Steinmann, H. & Löhr, A. (eds) (1989). *Unterneh-mensethik*. Stuttgart: Verlag Poeschel.
White, T. I. (ed.) (1993). *Business Ethics: A Philosophical Reader*. New York: Macmillan.

HENK VAN LUIJK

business ethics in Great Britain   British interest in business ethics has been growing steadily in recent years, partly influenced by developments in the United States, but mainly in response to various scandals affecting British companies and also to increasing social expectations of business within British society. Three major areas of activity can be identified: educational institutions, business ethics centers, and the business world itself.

British Educational Institutions

Courses in business ethics are becoming regular options in many business schools and departments throughout Britain, frequently on the initiative of interested faculty members whose primary discipline is in some other field of study. There is clear American influence in the topics dealt with and in the literature referred to, but there are also increasing indications of native British developments in the structure of programs and in the production of original literature and case studies. As yet there is very little scope for specialized graduate and doctoral study in the field, and the recent introduction jointly by the University of Leeds and Leeds Metropolitan University of a master's degree in Business Policy and Ethics is therefore to be welcomed. Institutional (and business) recognition of the subject is also evident in the establishing in 1993 at London Business School of the Dixons Chair of Business Ethics and Social Responsibility, as the first British professorial post exclusively devoted to the subject.

Centers of Activity

A number of centers concerned with business ethics have also contributed to advancing the subject in Britain. The first academic research center was founded in 1987 at King's College, University of London, and transferred its personnel and activities in 1993 to London Business School, while some other Universities have developed centers of applied ethics whose program often includes business and economic ethics. Religious institutions have also played a significant part in developing resource centers for business people, beginning with the Institute of Business Ethics (IBE, London 1987), as an interfaith offshoot of the Christian Association of Business Executives. Anglican initiatives include the program Faith in Business, organized by the Ridley Hall Foundation, Cambridge (1989). The culmination of British religious interest to date is the founding in London in 1994 of a Jewish Institute for Business Ethics. Bridging the area between private and public sectors is the Cambridge Centre for Business and Public Sector Ethics (1990).

British Businesses

Finally, but most importantly, there is in Britain a growing awareness of the subject among business people themselves, as shown in the increased media attention, the activities of various interest and pressure groups and response to them, growing interest in ethical investment groups and trusts, collaboration by various companies in ethics research projects, and an increasing number of conferences and seminars on the subject.

Concern on the part of British business for the ethical quality of its conduct goes back at least as far as the 1973 Report of the Confederation of British Industry (CBI) on. *The Responsibilities of the British Public Company*. Most recently continued – and increased – concern has found expression in a number of major statements emanating from other national business bodies and organizations. The Institute of Management, which represents 70,000 individuals and 800 companies, recently (1992–3) produced a new *Code of Conduct and Guides to Professional Management Practice*. The Royal Society of Arts has conducted a major enquiry sponsored by business, entitled *Tomorrow's Company*, whose Inquiry Report (1995) stresses the need, if British business is to achieve sustainable success, for it to adopt an "inclusive approach" to take account consciously of all its stakeholders. Britain's Institute of Directors has produced for its 48,000 individual members a Consultative Paper (1994) on *Enterprise with Integrity*, reflecting the Institute's motto, which rejects the stakeholder approach to business yet emphasizes and explores the need for integrity as essential to the contractual relationships required for success in the market economy.

The most visible and popular expression of ethical concern within British business is the existence of various types of codes of conduct. Professional associations ranging from accountancy to real estate are engaged in producing or updating a code of conduct for their members. A recent survey by the IBE (1993) of 500 major UK companies found that 33 percent now possessed or were preparing a corporate code of business ethics. On a wider scale, 1994 saw the promulgation in London of *A Code of Ethics on International Business for Christians, Muslims and Jews*, a joint declaration resulting from five years of consultation among representatives of those three monotheistic faiths.

The British Agenda

British concern for ethical business encompasses all the standard topics of interest to be found in the literature. In addition, financial issues have occupied most business and public interest in Britain in recent years, which led to a national enquiry and the 1992 *Report of the Committee on The Financial Aspects of Corporate Governance*. Primarily concerned with standards of corporate financial reporting and accountability, the "Cadbury" Report (named after its chairman, Sir Adrian Cadbury) also drew attention to three desired developments whose adoption would not only improve the financial accountability of UK corporations, but could also enhance their ethical profile and performance: a Code of Best Practice, based on principles of openness, integrity, and accountability for the boards of all listed companies registered in the UK; closer attention to the number, appointment, and independence of non-executive directors, including their responsibility for standards of conduct; and the drawing up for all a company's employees of a code of ethics to be published both internally and externally. What is of most relevance in the Cadbury Report from the point of view of business ethics is its stated overall aim of enabling a company's shareholders to exercise their responsibilities as its owners. Perhaps the greatest priority for British business ethics today is to impress upon investors, including institutional investors, that they share in the ethical responsibility for the policies, procedures, and practices of those companies of which they also share the ownership.

Bibliography

Adams, R. A. et al. (1990). *Changing Corporate Values: A guide to social and environmental policy and practice in Britain's top companies*. London: Kogan Page.

Business Ethics. A European Review. (quarterly; published by Blackwell, Oxford).

Cannon, T. (1992). *Corporate Responsibility*. London: Pitman.

Goyder, G. *The Just Enterprise: A Blueprint for the Responsible Company*. London: André Deutsch, 1987; republished Adamantine Press, 1993.

Mahoney, J. (1990). *Teaching Business Ethics in the UK, Europe and the USA: A Comparative Study*. London: Athlone.

Sorell, T. & Hendry, J. (1994). *Business Ethics*. Oxford: Butterworth Heinemann.

JACK MAHONEY

business ethics in Israel In Israel's business world and academia there is little awareness of Business Ethics as a specific field of inquiry and activity. Few businesses have either a formalized code of ethics or a specialized organizational function to deal with issues of social responsibility. Furthermore, the need for such measures to promote business ethics is not an issue with any priority on the public agenda. This is not to say that Israeli business practice is unethical. On the contrary, studies of ethical attitudes and behaviors among business professionals reveal that Israelis have relatively high ethical standards (Izraeli, 1988; Izraeli & Glass, 1994). These are infused with the ideals and standards of over 3,000 years of the Jewish tradition of law and ethics re-enforced with turn-of-the-century socialist ideals of a free and just society that imbued the founders of modern Israel (Eisenstadt, 1985) (*see* BUSINESS ETHICS AND JUDAISM).

Compared to other Western democracies, Israel has a more centralized, state-regulated economy, with a high level of government control and intervention in many aspects of economic life. Most of Israel's capital comes from abroad and is funnelled through government bodies. Centralized control of resources was functional for massive immigrant absorption and military defense. However, the widespread dependence of business on government and the close ties that developed among the economic, political, and administrative elites became a major source of corruption. The dominant political parties used their control over access to economic opportunity and jobs as a political resource to secure their own power and political patronage in the government and trade-union controlled economic enterprises was common, if not the norm (Aharoni, 1991). In response to competitive pressures from a global economy, Israel's economy is moving toward greater liberalization and privatization. At the same time an increasing number of private firms have gone public. However, the new consciousness prevalent in the West concerning business's responsibility toward stakeholders and the environment is still in an embryonic stage.

Stakeholders

Israeli businesspeople have a narrow and limited conception of who the stakeholders are in their companies. An illustrative example is an advertisement by an Israeli business daily of a publication listing the approximately 500 corporations trading on the Tel Aviv stock exchange and "the stakeholders" – referring to those who own 5 percent or more of the corporate shares. The implication is that other people – workers, suppliers, consumers, the public at large – have no stake in the firms. This failure to recognize all people affected by the actions of business firms as stakeholders is quite remarkable considering that only a few months prior a sizeable portion of the population lost a large proportion of their investments following a major stockmarket crash precipitated by insider information and manipulation of the market. The business community's incognizance of the existence of wider circles of stakeholders and its indifference to them maligns the quality of life in Israel and is detrimental to Israel's standing in the global business market.

Ecology

Environmental protection is another issue that to date has failed to involve the business community who continue to be major offenders. There is growing awareness among the Israeli public of the protracted decrease in environmental quality, reflected in, for example, the increase in pollution and noise levels (Gabai, 1994). The contribution of business to environmental pollution, however, has not been given sufficient public attention.

Most of the initiative in this respect has come from government, which in 1973 established the Environmental Protection Service. Subsequent governments have set up specialist units for the study, protection, and fostering of the ecology which, in 1988, were transferred to the newly established Ministry of the Environment. Numerous citizen groups have organized around ecology issues and within the domain of social responsibility the ecology lobby is probably the strongest.

Combating Corruption

The Knesset (Israeli parliament) has been the prime mover in passing legislation and creating institutions and specialized agencies for coping with corruption and regulating the ethical behavior of the business community. These include the State Comptroller's Office, the Ombudsman's Office, special police units for "white-collar crime", and the requirement of internal auditors for all government offices and public companies. The courts and especially the Supreme Court have played a very significant role in defining the boundaries and reaffirming the norms of ethical behavior.

The media, with its strong tradition of investigative reporting, plays a central role in exposing business scandals and supporting individual citizens harmed by business or establishment corruption. In addition there are dozens of citizen action groups active on a wide variety of issues. In many cases, however, their dependence on government for funds has undermined their effectiveness as watchdogs on government and business.

Emerging Trends

Recent developments include an emerging awareness of the need to pay special attention to Business Ethics. Israeli academics, influenced by developments in American academia, have introduced social responsibility in business and management as a field of teaching and research in all business schools in Israel's universities, and the first generation of graduates are beginning to have an impact on the field of practice. A number of pioneering business firms have sought consultation for introducing socially responsible policies that reflect a new understanding of the stakeholder concept. Some, especially subsidiaries of American multinationals and Headquarters of Israeli multinationals, have adopted official codes of ethics. Progress towards peace and Israel's growing integration into the global economy are factors encouraging the continued liberalization of Israel's economy and the awareness of the need to promote business ethics.

Bibliography

Aharoni, Y. (1991). *The Israeli Economy: Dreams and Reality.* London/New York: Routledge.
Eisenstadt, S. N. (1985). *The Transformation of Israeli Society.* Boulder, Colo: Westview Press.
Gabai, S. (1994). *The Environment in Israel.* State of Israel, Ministry of the Environment.
Izraeli, D. (1988). Ethical beliefs and behavior among managers: A cross cultural perspective. *Journal of Business Ethics,* 7, 263–71.
Izraeli, D. & Glass, D. (1994). The changing ethical beliefs and behavior of Israeli managers. In U. Berlinski, A. Friedberg, & S. B. Werner (eds), *Corruption in a Changing World: Comparisons, Theories and Controlling Strategies.* Jerusalem: Chen Press, 448–58.

DOVE IZRAELI

business ethics in Japan In Japan, ethics is bound up with a religious dimension (two normative environments) and a social dimension (framework of concentric circles). The normative environments, influenced by Confucianism, Buddhism, and other traditional and modern Japanese religions, emphasize that not only individuals but also groups have their own spirit (numen) which is connected to the ultimate reality. The framework of concentric circles lets moral agents apply different ethical rules to the

circles. The dynamics of these religious and social dimensions lead to a different view of both individuals and corporations from that dominant in the West.

The Religious Dimension – Two Normative Environments

The religious dimension supplies a variety of concrete norms of behavior to the Japanese in relation to the ultimate reality that may be called the "normative environment." There are mainly *two* influential normative environments in Japan: the "transcendental normative environment" and the "group normative environment."

1. Transcendental normative environment. In the transcendental environment, everyone has an equal personal numen (soul, spirit). This idea has been philosophically strengthened by Confucianism and Buddhism. In the case of neo-Confucianism, people are assumed to have a microcosm within themselves, and are considered condensed expressions of the universe (macrocosm). Their inner universe is expected to be able to connect with the outer universe.

In the case of Buddhism, every living creature has an equal Buddhahood, a Buddhahood which is similar with the idea of numen and microcosm. Buddhism has long taught, "Although there are differences among living creatures, there is no difference among human beings. What makes human beings different is only their name."

In addition, however, under the transcendental normative environment, not only individuals but also jobs, positions, organizations, rituals, and other events and things incorporate their own "numina." These numina are also expected to be associated with the numen of the universe.

Deities of Shintoism, Buddhism, and the Japanese new religions, which have long been considered objects of worship, are often called the "great life force of the universe." In this respect, the life force can be sacred and religious. On the other hand, many Japanese people have unconsciously accepted this way of thinking without belonging to any specific religious sect. In this case, it is rather secular, non-religious, and atheistic. Whether it is holy or secular, the significant feature of Japan is that this transcendental normative environment has been shared by Japanese people.

Inasmuch as Japanese people live in such a normative environment, the meaning of work for them becomes unique. Work is understood to be a self-expression of the great life force. Work is believed to have its own numen so that work is one of the ways to reach something beyond the secular world. Accordingly, Japanese people unconsciously and sometimes consciously try to unify themselves with the great life force by concentrating on their own work.

Whereas Western managers place priority on innovation, Japanese managers and workers put emphasis on *Kaizen* (continuous improvement of products, of ways to work, and of decision-making processes). While innovation can be done intermittently, *Kaizen* can be carried on continuously by almost every person.

In this way, the transcendental environment has supplied many hard workers to the Japanese labor market, providing an ethical basis for "diligence." Nonetheless, it has not created extremely individualistic people who pursue only their own short-term interests. Because they have hoped for job security and life security in the secular world, they have subjectively tried to coordinate their behavior so as to keep harmonious relations with others in the group. Within this subjective coordination, and having the long-term perspective in mind, they pursue their own purposes.

2. Group normative environment. The second or group normative environment necessarily derives from this transcendental normative environment, insofar as the latter gives special *raison d'être* not only to individuals and their work, but also to their groups. As a result of the transcendental environment, every group holds its own numen. The group acquires this *raison d'être*, as long as it guarantees the life of its members and helps them fulfill their potentials.

But once a group acquires its *raison d'être*, it insists upon its survival. An environment in which norms regarding the existence and prosperity of the group appear and affect its members is called the "group normative environment," and the set of the norms in this environment is called "group logic." Groupism

and a group-oriented propensity, which have often been pointed out as Japanese characteristics, stem from this group normative environment.

Japanese often face an ethical dilemma arising from the fact that they live simultaneously in the two different influential normative environments. In the transcendental environment, groups and individuals are regarded as equal numina and equal expressions of the great life force. In the group environment, however, a group (and its representatives) is considered to be superior to its ordinary members, mainly because the members are not related to the force in the same way. The only way for members to connect with the life force is through the activities of their group.

Social Dimension – Ethics of Concentric Circles

Due to human-bounded cognitive rationality or cultural heritage, Japanese moral agents, whether individuals or corporations, tend to conceptualize the social environment in a centrifugal order similar to water ripples. Although there are many individuals, groups, and organizations which taken together constitute the overall social environment, the Japanese are likely to categorize them into four concentric circles: family, fellows, Japan, and the world. On the basis of this way of thinking, Japanese people and organizations are likely to attribute different ethics or moral practices to each circle.

The concentric circles of corporations.
(1) First, corporations have a quasi-family circle. Of course, though corporations do not have any blood relationships, they might still have closely related business partners. For example, parent, sister, or affiliated companies can be those partners. "Vertical *keiretsu*" (vertically integrated industrial groups like Toyota, Hitachi, or Matsushita groups) might be a typical example of the quasi-family circle. In this circle we find something similar to the parent–child relationship.

The main corporate members (about 20 to 30 companies in each group) of "horizontal *keiretsu*" (industrial groups such as Mitsubishi, Mitsui, Sumitomo, Dai Ichi Kangyo, Fuyo, and Sanwa groups) might be viewed as quasi-family members. Nonetheless, most of the cross-shareholding corporations in the horizontal *keiretsu* should be placed in the second circle, because their relations are less intimate than commonly understood.

(2) In the fellow circle, each corporation has its own main bank, fellow traders, distant affiliated firms, employees, steady customers, and the like. If the corporation or its executives belong to some outside associations like *Nihon Jidousha Kogyo Kai* (Japanese Auto Manufacturers Association), *Doyukai* (Japan Association of Corporate Executives), *Keidanren* (Japan Federation of Economic Organizations), etc., the other members of such outside associations might constitute part of its fellow circle. And if the corporation is influential enough to affect Japanese politics or administration, the Japanese governmental agencies or ministries and political parties might constitute part of its fellow circle.

Recognition within the fellow circle requires that there must be a balance between benefits and debts in the long run. On account of this, if a corporation does not offer enough benefits to counterbalance its debts to others in this circle, the corporation will be expelled from the circle, being criticized for neither understanding nor appreciating the benefits given it by others. On the other hand, if the corporation can successfully balance benefits and debts or keep in the black, it will preferentially receive many favorable opportunities from other companies or interest groups. For these reasons, every corporation worries about the balance sheet of benefits and debts in the fellow circle.

(3) In the Japan circle, the fellow-circle ethics is substantially replaced by "the principle of free competition." Competitors, unrelated corporations, ordinary stockholders, consumers, (for ordinary corporations, the Japanese government constitutes part of this circle), and so forth, all fall within this circle. Yet almost all corporations in this circle know well that the long-term reciprocal ethics is extremely important in constructing and maintaining their business relations because of their similar cultural background. This point makes the third circle different from the world circle.

(4) In the world circle, corporations positively follow "the principle of free competition," subject to the judicial system, with less worrying about their traditional reputations. The behavioral imperatives for corporations turn out to be producing or supplying high-quality and low-price products, dominating much more market share and using the law to resolve serious contractual problems.

Dynamics of the concentric circles. Now that I have roughly described the static relations among the concentric circles of corporations, I need to show the dynamic relations among these circles, that is to say, how they are interrelated. Generally speaking the relations are similar to those of "operation base and battlefield."

For example, when the second circle of an individual is recognized as a battlefield, the first circle takes on the role of operation base. When there is severe competition among the members of the second circle, individuals look for peace of mind from their first circle. I cannot show the same picture in relations between the first and second circles of corporations as clearly as in those of individuals, due to the fact that a corporation does not have similar feelings toward its quasi-family members as does an individual.

But when it comes to Japan as a whole, I can draw almost the same picture between the first/second and third circles of corporations as in those of individuals. At this level, while Japan is viewed as a battlefield, an individual person or an individual corporation expects that both the first and second circles of each of them will serve the role of an operation base. These multilayered inner circles can be called "multiple operation bases." When the fourth is understood as a battlefield, however, this third circle also turns into one of the multiple operation bases (conversely, I can postulate the existence of "the multiple battlefields").

Japanese Perspective on American Business Ethics Issues

1. Job discrimination and the transcendental logic. In the transcendental normative environment, whatever job people take, they are believed to reach the same goal or the same level of human development. Because of this logic, Japanese are unlikely to evaluate others in terms of their "job" (specialty). They would rather evaluate one another in terms of their "attitudes" toward work.

It is not important for Japanese to maintain the principle of the division of labor. Of importance is the process and the result of work. If people cannot attain goals in the existing framework of the division of labor, they are likely to try other alternatives which have not been clearly defined in the existing framework. This kind of positive attitude toward work is highly appreciated in Japan.

2. Employees' interest and the group logic. Second, in the group normative environment, the group is believed to hold its own numen and expected to guarantee the members' life. A corporation is thought to exist for its employees rather than for its shareholders.

Even in Japan, shareholders are legal owners of a company so that the shareholders might use their legal power to change the company in a favorable way for themselves. Therefore, many Japanese corporations have invented a legitimate way to exclude the legal rights of shareholders, i.e., "cross-shareholding." This is the practice in which a corporation allows trusted companies to hold its own shares, and in return the corporation holds their shares. By holding shares of one another and refraining from appealing to the shareholders' rights, they make it possible to manage the companies for the sake of the employees. Because this cross-shareholding is based on mutual acceptance, any attempts to break this corporate consortium from the outside, whether Japanese or foreigners, are often stymied by the consortium of the member corporations.

In Japan, when executives face serious difficulties, they first reduce their own benefits, then dividends and other costs and, after that, employees' salary or wage. If the situation is extremely hard to overcome with these measures, they sell assets and only as a last resort do they lay off workers. Even in this case the executives often find and offer new job opportunities for those who are laid off, taking care of their family's life.

3. Claims against the Japanese market and the concentric circles' ethics. Because the framework of concentric circles, especially of the ethics of the fellow circle, foreign corporations often face difficulties entering the Japanese market.

Although Japanese admit that the market is very hard to enter, a majority of them believe that it is still possible to accomplish entry.

Even if the Japanese market has many business-related practices such as semi-annual gifts, entertainment, cross-shareholding, a "triangular relationship" among businesses, bureaucracy, and the Liberal Democratic Party, the long-term relationship is formed mainly through a series of business transactions.

That is to say, the most important factor in doing business is whether suppliers can respond to the assemblers' requests for quality, cost, and the date of delivery, and the like, or how producers can respond to the retailer's or wholesaler's expectations.

Foreign corporations might claim that because they are located outside Japan, they cannot enter even the Japan circle. On this claim, the Japanese business community is likely to insist that if they understand the "long-term reciprocal ethics," they can enter the Japan circle; and what is more, might be fellows of influential Japanese corporations. As I have described, what makes the Japan circle different from the world circle is that people in the Japan circle know well the importance of this ethics. In fact, foreign corporations successfully enjoying the Japanese market include IBM, Johnson & Johnson, McDonald's, Apple, and General Mills, which have well understood this ethics.

In this respect, realistically, the Japanese community interprets criticism by the American counterpart of the Japanese market as unfair and unethical. To put it differently, Japanese believe that if foreign corporations understand the long-term ethics, they will easily be real members of the Japanese business commnity.

Ethical issues of the Japanese Business Community

I have shown how Japanese corporations conceive the American business society and its business-related practices from the viewpoint of the two normative environments and the concentric circles. Yet this does not mean that the Japanese business community has no ethical problems. On the contrary, there are many issues it has to solve.

In order to reveal some of the issues, I shall confine my interest to the concept of "fairness." When it comes to "fairness," I hypothetically interpret it as "openness, " since "fairness" generally implies "treating every agent equally according to the same rule," or "opening the market or organizations for every agent who is willing to follow the same rule" On the basis of this simplified definition, I will cover two levels of ethical issues: "opening Japanese organizations" and "opening the Japanese market" (*see* FAIRNESS).

Moreover, I will identify three ethical "prime values," which I will use to discuss the issues and possible solutions. By "prime values" I mean the core concepts of the transcendental logic, group logic, and fellow circle's ethics.

1. Discrimination and the transcendental logic. The prime value here is that "everybody has an equal microcosm." Whether men or women, Japanese or foreigners, hard workers or non-hard workers, everybody has to be treated equally as a person. When we observe the organizational phenomena from the viewpoint of this value, there are two discriminatory issues.

First, the transcendental logic has worked favorably only for male society. That is, in this normative environment, Japanese women have been expected to actualize their potentials through their household tasks. Those tasks have been regarded as their path toward the goal. Of course, insofar as women voluntarily agree with this thinking, there seems to be no ethical problem. And in fact, a majority of women have accepted this way of living to date. Nonetheless, now that an increasing number of women work at companies and hope to get beyond such chores as making tea to more challenging jobs, the Japanese corporations have no longer been allowed to treat women unequally.

Second, the transcendental normative logic itself has often been used to accuse certain workers of laziness. As far as a worker voluntarily strives to fulfill his or her own potential according to the transcendental logic, this presents no ethical problems. Nevertheless, once a person begins to apply the logic to others and evaluate them in terms of their performance, the transcendental logic easily becomes the basis for severe accusations against certain workers.

If the person does not follow this teaching, thereby refusing overtime or transfers, he will jeopardize his promotion and be alienated from his colleagues and bosses, since he is not regarded as a praiseworthy diligent worker. Even if he is making efforts to fulfill his potential in work-unrelated fields, he is not highly appreciated simply because what he is doing is not related to the company's work.

2. Employees' dependency and the group logic. In the group normative environment, groups are regarded as having a higher status than their individual members. Because the members are inclined to take this hierarchical order for granted, they come to be dependent on the groups. This dependency of the agents, whether of individuals or groups, brings the following two problems into the Japanese business community. Because of the dependent trait, (1) the individual members of the group refrain from expressing their opinions about ethical issues, and (2) they tend to obey the organizational orders, even if they disagree with them. The first tendency is related to decision-making, while the second affects policy-implementation.

When we look at the two tendencies mentioned above from the viewpoint of this prime value, they will be translated into the following two ethical issues: (1) Japanese corporations are likely to exclude the employees' participation in ethical decision-making, and (2) in some cases, they might not guarantee the employees' right to life.

The first issue is that the dependent trait ends up excluding different opinions or ideas. *A fortiori*, in exchange for job security, the rank and file rarely raise questions about the decisions made by management, even if the decisions are against their sense of righteousness. In this respect, the rank and file are likely to take no ethical responsibility for the decisions.

Because both authority and responsibility of the individuals are not clearly defined in the Japanese organizations, the individual employees do not regard involvement in wrongdoing as their own responsibility, but rather as the responsibility of the middle management. Even in middle management, however, it is not clear who will take responsibility for wrongdoing.

The top management quite often does not know exactly what the employees or middle management are doing in daily business.

Second, the dependent trait is inclined to force individual members to devote their time and energy to work. The dependency might encourage the individual employees to behave ethically, if the higher groups such as *Doyukai*, *Keidanren*, or the board of directors seriously proclaim the necessity of business ethics. If a member pursues his own interest in the company, this behavior often hurts the interststs of other members. In this case, the other memers exert social pressures on the member to comply with the group's aggregate interest. For this reason, in the end, in the group normative environment the member is likely to give up his own interest and obey the group orders.

One of the typical examples which show this tendency of members to waive their basic rights is *karoshi* (death caused by overwork). In 1991, the Japanese Labor Ministry awarded 33 claims for *karoshi*. Since it is very hard to prove a direct and quantifiable link between overwork and death, this number is not large enough to clarify the actual working condition, but is certainly large enough to show that there is a possibility of turning the group logic into unconditional obedience.

This corporate climate not only jeopardizes the employee's right to life, but also hampers the healthy human development of the individual members. Because of this, the Japanese business community has to alter this group-centered climate into a democratic ground on which the individuals can express their opinions more frankly than before.

Exclusiveness of the concentric circles. The Japanese conceptualization of the social environment in a centrifugal framework is closely connected with Confucianism (the differential principle): it allows people to treat others in proportion to the intimacy of their relationships. If I look at opening the Japanese market from the viewpoint of this prime value, there appear to be at least the following two issues. (1) The Japanese business community has to make an effort to help foreigners understand the concept of long-term reciprocal ethics. This effort will bring moral agents of the world circle into the Japan circle. (2) The Japanese community has to give business opportunities to as many newcomers as possible. This effort will bring the newcomers into the fellow circles.

The first issue is how to transfer foreign corporations from the world circle to the Japan circle. Takashi Ishihara (1989) recommends that Japanese corporations follow the spirit of "fairness." This "fairness" implies that they treat foreign companies the same as they treat other Japanese firms. To put it differently, the concept of "fairness" encourages the Japanese corporations to apply the same ethical standard to all companies.

Although this is a very important point of "fairness," there is a more crucial problem involved in opening the market, which is how to let newcomers know what the rules are and how the Japanese business community applies the rules. As mentioned before, for the purpose of constructing and maintaining business relationships with a Japanese company (a core company), a foreign firm has to be a fellow of the company. In this fellow circle, every fellow makes efforts to balance benefits and debts with the core company in material and spiritual terms in the long run, since making a long-term balance is the most important ethic. Yet balancing them is too complicated for the foreign corporation to attain, as long as benefits and debts are rather subjective concepts.

But even if they can enter the Japan circle successfully, there still remains another problem. That is how those foreigners, which have been in the Japan circle already, enter fellow circles of influential Japanese corporations. This is related to the second issues of opening the Japanese market.

Even when foreign companies understand and adopt long-term reciprocal ethics, they might not be able to enter those fellow circles, if they rarely have the chance to show their competitive products or services to the influential corporations. On account of this, as an ethical responsibility, the Japanese corporations should have "access channels" through which every newcomer can approach equally.

I conclude that: (1) From the transcendental prime value, the Japanese business community has to change its discriminatory organizational climate. (2) From the group prime value, it has to alter the group-centered climate into a democratic ground. (3) From the prime value of the concentric circles' ethics, it has to have access channels open to every newcomer.

These ethical suggestions might hurt the efficiency or competitiveness of Japanese corporations. Because of this, I have to discuss them in relation to those economic factors, too. What is more, in order to proceed in the direction of the suggestions, each corporation will have to establish its own concrete code of business ethics.

Bibliography

Benedict, R. (1946). *The Chrysanthemum and the Sword: Patterns of Japanese Culture*, New York: Meridian.

Egami, N. (1989). *Nihon Minzoku to Nihon Bunka*, (Japaanese People and Culture). Tokyo: Yamakawa Shuppansha.

Imai, K. and Komiya, R. (1989). *Nihon no Kigyo*, (Japanese Corporations) Tokyo: Tokyo University Press, 131-58.

Ishihara, T. (1989). *Keizai Doyukai*, (Annual Report of Japan Association of Corporate Executives).

Japanese Fair Trade Commission. (1991). *Annual Report of the Japanese Fair Trade Commission: White Paper of Antimonopoly*, Tokyo: JFTC, 88-92.

Kyogoku, J. and Kyogoku, J. (1983). *Nihon no Seiji*, (Politics of Japan) Tokyo: Tokyo University Press.

Upham, F. K. (1987). *Law and Social Change in Postwar Japan*, Harvard University Press, 14-16.

Upham, F. K. (1987). *Law and Social Change in Postwar Japan*. Boston: Harvard University Press.

Yamamoto, S. (1979). *Nihon Shihonshugi no Seishin*, (The Spirit of Japanese Capitalism) Tokyo: Kobunsha, 118-41.

IWAO TAKA

business ethics in New Zealand Since the environment and conduct of New Zealand business has become increasingly internationalized, business ethics "in" this island nation of 3.4 million people is now only partially defined by national geography and identity. Accordingly, the main focus of this entry will be upon the more *distinctive* features of the local culture, institutions, and *zeitgeist*.

There is, in New Zealand, a national culture that strongly values practicality, while it respects individuality. This is reflected in commerce in general, but especially in the high regard for engineering, construction, and agriculture. In almost all fields, there is a keen monitoring of overseas developments, coupled with a real willingness to experiment. Yet, at the same time, there remains some ambivalence towards overseas competition, a tendency to look inwards for solutions to local problems, with an orientation towards cooperative problem-solving in groups.

Many people in New Zealand derive a special sense of enlightenment and spiritual replenishment from the land itself, with the surrounding oceans. Concern for the environment is now manifest in the Resource Management Act, which creates individual and collective liabilities for pollution, while requiring decisions about resource use to be framed as problems of constrained optimization. This sense of the land is, in turn, related to the continuing vitality of an indigenous *Maori* culture. Maori business has some separate institutional arrangements that successfully coexist with and operate alongside the mainstream. Moreover, a number of synergies appear to exist between the ethos of Maori business and the more economically rational practices of the mainstream.

These synergies may be found in areas such as consensual decision-making, commitments to shared ideals, and the guardianship of natural resources. The latter, in particular, now sees a happy coincidence of imperatives flowing from ecological and strategic concerns. Both the tourism industry and the cooperative management of exports demand maintenance of the clean and green national image that yields positive country-of-origin effects for a great many *Kiwi* products and services.

In other areas of business ethics there has been much less convergence between cultural ideals and practical reality. The concept of a "fair go" is important for the people of New Zealand, yet it has increasingly become subordinated to an ideology of the market in all spheres of life. This ideology has itself been heavily marketed by powerful coalitions, ostensibly and arguably for collective benefit. For example, Equal Employment Opportunity (EEO) legislation, aimed at directly improving the lot of women, Maori and Pacific Islanders, quickly became a political football, with the right wing insisting that the market provides equitable outcomes. Thus, concepts of fairness from the centre left, such as that conceived by Rawls or Kant, are not currently in vogue.

Together with the ethos of the "fair go" comes a corresponding dislike of privilege; yet, paradoxically, the families and associates of the early (ca. 1850) European settlers continue even now to play a disproportionate role in the management, ownership, and control of the larger New Zealand businesses (still small by world standards). Moreover, in Maori business, there is some similar tension between positions based upon lineage versus levels of management expertise. Of course, New Zealand is by no means unique among former UK colonies in this regard, nor in its time-honored tendency to indulge in a "fair" share of restrictive and collusive business practices.

There is another characteristic of Kiwi ethos of relevance to business ethics, that of "she'll be right" (i.e., all will be well). This folksy sentiment may well have been one factor (amongst others) in some of the more blatant recent lapses of business and professional ethics. Examples include the disappearance of all of a client's funds in the course of a routine domestic property transaction, as well as notable incidences of audited accounts showing profit, for important companies about to enter receivership. Nonetheless, there has been considerable willingness to experiment with institutional arrangements. Recently there have been strong moves to clarify directors' responsibilities, strengthen supervisory agencies, and create a heightened sense of collegiality amongst various industry bodies. In addition, the serious fraud office in New Zealand is now valiantly and quite successfully striving to prosecute various forms of corporate crime. Despite this, there remains some unease about general standards of business and professional integrity.

A final distinctive element concerns ethics in sports. As in the UK, the links between business and sports have been greatly strengthened, in recent times, with a rapid transition towards professionalism. All the generally accepted limitations of market-based societies have become writ large in this arena, including (i) the distinction between entertainment and actual sporting achievement, (ii) sponsorship funds directed at sports that have more TV appeal, (iii) limitation of access for those who cannot pay, and (iv) controversies about promotions involving liquor and tobacco. Legal battles continue, particularly in the latter arena. Conflicts have also arisen between institutionalized sports practices and commercial principles. For example, a bylaw of the NZRL (rugby league) was recently found to be an "unreasonable restraint of *trade*".

There are many features of business ethics "in" New Zealand, that reflect similar developments elsewhere. Most notably, the *zeitgeist* has been influenced by Thatcherism, with a marked transition away from welfare statism. Income tax and national debt has been reduced, with commensurate reductions in public and welfare expenditure. Many former government departments have been restructured as SOEs (State Owned Enterprises), charged with being as profitable as the private sector but also with "endeavoring to accommodate or encourage community interests". Yet, many of the new SOE managers were then recruited from the private sector.

The resulting rise of a hoped-for "enterprise culture" has not been uniformly pretty to observe. For example, when the 1980s wave of corporate acquisitions crashed on these particular shores, the debris revealed a quite astonishing level of criminal activity. Quite a number of "enterprising" corporate high flyers of that decade have since been convicted. There have also been changes to the takeover code, aimed at protecting minority (ownership) interests. In the push to improve business ethics, many have settled upon a mission of customer service (TQM, or "total quality management") coupled with "satisfactory" rates of return. In addition, there is a growing responsiveness to social issues, as required by law (e.g., EEO) or to accommodate pressure groups.

These developments have now brought New Zealand to the point where it must once again face the central question of business ethics: direct involvement in improving social conditions. Several New Zealand companies have set recent precedents here, by establishing charitable trusts, by funding local school science labs, or by recruiting from the long-term unemployed. At the time of writing New Zealand is indeed at a crossroads. This small island nation could settle upon a market-based society that inevitably breeds a degree of disparity and resentment, or else risk reverting to a form of welfare statism . . . or, alternatively, go beyond the traditional logic of the market to a society comprised of multiple *welfare-entities* in which all players engage in authentic attempts to serve others, at least partly according to their needs. This third choice could indeed be a most noteworthy experiment.

Bibliography

Alam, K. F. (1993). Ethics in New Zealand organisations. *Journal of Business Ethics*, **12**, (6), 433–40.

Brennan, M., Ennis, M. & Esslemont, D. (1992). The ethical standards of New Zealand business managers. *New Zealand Journal of Business*, **14**, 100–24.

Deeks, J. & Enderwick, P. (1994). *Business and New Zealand Society*. Auckland: Longman Paul.

The Press. (1994). Editorial on New Zealand Culture. Sept. 10, Christchurch.

Reid, B. (1994). New Zealand seeks the middle ground. *Time International*, March 14, 40–5.

Singer, A. E. (1994). Doing strategy as doing good: The new pragmatism. *New Zealand Strategic Management*, **1**, 44–51.

ALAN E. SINGER

business ethics in Russia most accurately could be described by the ancient maxim, *caveat emptor* (buyer beware). Virtually all domestic business transactions are legally unregulated and self-policing. To appreciate the condition of its ethos, one must understand that the simplest concepts we often take for granted in other cultures are relatively new to the former Soviet Union. For example, though perhaps initially inconceivable, the notions of property rights, ownership, freedom of contract, profit, and even the idea of a market itself are new ideas in modern Russian society (*see* PROPERTY, RIGHTS TO; FREEDOM OF CONTRACT; PROFIT, PROFITS). With the apparent collapse of the Commonwealth of Independent States and the troubles inherent in the present government, by necessity the Russian people are embracing capitalism to provide daily needs. With neither a legal basis to enforce sanctions nor even a history of contract law, the Russian people are groping with the ethics of unbridled commerce.

As Kolosov, Martin and Peterson (1993) detail, it became legal in January of 1991 for private Russian concerns to broker the buying and selling of almost any commodity. With the attendant and requisite expansion of what constitutes private property, several businesses developed for the purpose of providing a forum (i.e., a market) for the unfettered buying, selling, and trading of such property. Due primarily to lack of accurate and reliable information concerning supply, demand, and ownership encumbrances, however, the agreements to trade goods on these "exchanges" are not guaranteed by market owners unlike more developed markets in Western and other cultures. With no legal structure to enforce contract compliance, all Russian business transactions essentially occur in a legal vacuum where self-interest and determined personal (microeconomic) and societal (macroeconomic) outcomes (see Martin & Peterson, 1991, and Werhane, 1989). Thus, the nature of these markets is consistent with the notion of *caveat emptor* in its strictest sense.

The state of business ethics in Russia is continuing to evolve. Despite the potential repercussions of its unregulated environment, new Russian businesses are being created exponentially and existing companies are thriving. Gradually, these new enterprises are becoming the provider of the bulk of life's basic goods for the Russian people as they grapple with the ethics of their new-found freedom. It is perhaps most important to note that although the notion of private property is again new to their culture, Russian businessmen and women apparently realize that behaving in an ethical fashion – fulfilling contractual obligations – is in their long-run self-interest. Absent a prolonged armed conflict between centrist Russian and its outlying regions, the current trend of high growth in commerce, income, and ethical development should continue into the next century.

Bibliography

De George, R. T. (1993). *Competing with Integrity in International Business*. New York: Oxford University Press.

Filatov, A. (1994). Unethical behavior in post-communist Russia: Origins and trends. *Business Ethics Quarterly*, **4**, 11–15.

Kolosov, M. A., Martin, D. W. & Peterson, J. H. (1993). Ethics and behavior on the Russian commodity exchange. *Journal of Business Ethics,* 12, 741-4.

Martin, D. W. & Peterson, J. H. (1991). Insider trading revisited. *Journal of Business Ethics,* 10, 57-61.

Werhane, P. H. (1989). The ethics of insider trading. *Journal of Business Ethics,* 8, 841-5.

DERYL W. MARTIN

business ethics in South Africa   Are multi-national corporations ever morally required to terminate all business transactions in a host country? That question was the subject of intense debate throughout the 1980s over the issue of the ethics of investing in an apartheid South Africa, and much may be learned from that situation for dealing with future human rights violations. Apartheid literally means "separate development" and was a system of oppression based on skin color. Over 300 racial laws in South Africa denied blacks many of the rights most take for granted – the right to vote, to move freely in their own country, to attend the better white schools, and to have the opportunity for decent housing.

Finally, in April 1994, statutory apartheid was completely ended when, in a move almost as dramatic as the fall of the Berlin Wall, South Africa had its first national election where all – blacks *and* whites – could vote. This vote was the culmination of several years of intense negotiation among all the major groups in the country, and was in the face of strong internal pressure from the community of nations. The issue in contention is what sort of response was morally required by a multinational business with operations in South Africa during the apartheid regime. Must a company terminate all business transactions, or could a moral argument be made that the companies should remain in the country, assist the blacks in their struggle, and prepare the way for a strong economy in the post-apartheid South Africa? (*See* INVESTMENT ETHICS).

History of International Involvement

Concern about racist policies in South Africa on the part of US groups dates back to 1912 when the National Association for the Advancement of Colored People (NAACP) provided assistance to what later became the African National Congress (ANC) of South Africa. It was not until the mid-sixties, however, that college students, civil rights leaders, and church groups began to devise strategies in response to the evil of apartheid. In 1973 a major offensive was launched by church groups against bank loans to the Republic of South Africa (RSA). Although the campaign did not have a significant effect on the loan policy of the banks, it did give much visibility to the apartheid problem.

In 1971 the first shareholder resolution on South Africa, calling for the termination of the operations of General Motors in RSA, was presented by the Episcopal church. At that time, church officials candidly stated that their goal was not to have GM leave South Africa but, rather, to pressure the company to use its power to help change the RSA government policy on the races and to better the lot of blacks at home and in the workplace. Until the mid-1980s this was the strategy of most US groups opposing apartheid, even though their official positions often advocated toal withdrawal of US firms. Since 1971 there have been over five hundred shareholder resolutions on South Africa, targeted at dozens of US companies.

Until the mid-1980s most US businesses with operations in South Africa responded to the churches' call to help solve the racial problem in South Africa by adopting the code of conduct developed by the Reverend Leon H. Sullivan. Sullivan, an early civil rights leader and, for many years, a leading black pastor in Philadelphia and a member of the board of directors of the General Motors Corporation, called twelve major US companies together in 1977 and formulated a code of conduct that has come to be known as the Statement of Principles Program. If US companies were in South Africa, they must pursue policies outlined in seven principles. Among other things, these principles required desegregating all facilities, equal pay for equal work, training programs for blacks at all levels, AFFIRMATIVE ACTION for blacks in management and supervisory positions, projects designed to improve the quality of life for blacks outside the workplace, and actions calculated to eliminate all apartheid laws.

Similarly, codes were enacted for Canadian firms and those in Common Market nations (*see* CODES OF ETHICS).

Each year, until the program ceased operation in 1994, the companies in the Statement of Principles Program were audited by Arthur D. Little, Inc., as part of the requirements. A typical report notes that the annual expense for programs designed to eliminate apartheid averaged about US$500,000 a company. Some of these dollars went to assist in black educational endeavors, but many went to activities that most South Africans considered too risky because they directly challenged the status quo and advanced social change. For example, some companies directly challenged white merchants in Johannesburg by assisting blacks in doing business in the downtown areas. Several companies used their resources to secure the freedom of union leaders who were detained by the police, and many companies purchased homes in white areas for their black employees, thus challenging and eroding one of the pillars of apartheid.

Because of the growing impatience that the evil system of apartheid continued to produce, in 1985 a broad coalition of black activists, church groups, and political leaders in the United States rallied around the call for complete disinvestment and economic sanctions. In October 1986, overriding President Reagan's veto, Congress passed the Comprehensive Anti-Apartheid Act of 1986. While the bill did not mandate the US firms to leave South Africa, it did ban new US loans and investments, curtailed direct air links between the United States and South Africa, and prohibited a number of imports.

In June 1987, carrying out a promise he made two years earlier, the Reverend Leon Sullivan called for all US companies to withdraw from South Africa by March 1988. While he acknowledged that the Principles has been "a tremendous force for change," he stated that much remained to be done and that more pressure was needed to force the RSA government to the negotiating table. In 1986, 50 US companies left South Africa. Between 1986 and 1989 over 90 more companies withdrew. By 1994, with apartheid ended, there were about 60 major US companies still in South Africa, having endured intense pressure. The reasons for the company departures were well summarized in a March 20, 1987, *Wall Street Journal* story on the Xerox disinvestment. Quoting Xerox chairman David T. Kearns, the *Journal* wrote:

> Mr Kearns said he still feels staying put is best for South Africa's 23 million blacks. But he now says leaving is what is best for Xerox. "It was clear things were continuing to deteriorate on all fronts," he said. The nation's economy and social climate were worsening; pro-disinvestment groups' criticism was rising; and Xerox was beginning to lose sales in the US to local governments that were banning contracts with companies doing business there

Learning for the Future

There is no question that the pressure for complete disinvestment from South Africa was increasingly intense in the late 1980s. To glean some insight for dealing with future cases of human rights violations by nation-states, it may be helpful to review the logic of the arguments concerning disinvestment. After surveying the many ethical arguments made for and against investments in South Africa, Williams (1986) claimed that three main approaches emerged: (1) the "clean-hands" approach; (2) the "solidarity-with-victims" or prophetic approach; and (3) the "stewardship" approach. Each style has a unique, dominant concern. Advocates of the clean-hands approach were mainly concerned to avoid complicity in the evil of apartheid. Followers of the prophetic style emphasized the crucial need to identify with the oppressed of South Africa in a clear and dramatic manner, while followers of the stewardship approach sought to determine the best way to use corporate and government power to advance the welfare of black south Africans. Often those arguing in the clean-hands and prophetic modes were strong advocates of disinvestment, while the followers of the stewardship ethic were about evenly divided, some arguing for continuing presence and others arguing for "full" or some lesser level of disinvestment.

Using the clean-hands approach, Donaldson (1989) makes a strong argument that full disinvestment was required since there was a systematic violation of the most basic human rights. Citing Dworkin (1978), he notes that consequential goals (the stewardship approach) are ordinarily "trumped" by rights considerations unless "extraordinary moral horrors could be expected to ensue from their exercise (*see* CONSEQUENTIALISM). Developing a "condition of business principle," Donaldson also states that "transactions are impermissible unless those transactions serve to discourage the violation of rights and either harm A or, at a minimum, fail to benefit A, in consequence of A's rights violating activity" (1989, p. 133). Since he finds neither of these conditions present, he judges that doing business with an apartheid South Africa was wrong. Most advocates of full disinvestment, however, were using a stewardship approach.

In the context of the late 1980s, it seems that the first judgment most were making was whether the glass was half empty or half full, that is, was the apartheid regime determined to hold on with no possibility of negotiating a future, or was it on the way out, simply trying to renegotiate the best deal possible for the minority whites? Thus, many powerful groups argued, with the half-empty assumption, that the only moral course was for all foreign firms to withdraw from South Africa. This would weaken the economy and hasten the end of apartheid as the white leaders would yield in the face of economic disaster.

Others, however, with the half-full assumption, argued that the moral course was for the companies to remain in South Africa, provided they took measures to assist the blacks in their struggle and to prepare the way for job creation and investment in the new South Africa. With the half-full assumption, Donaldson's "extraordinary moral horror" was a new black government trying to lead a country with over 40 percent unemployment and little prospect for new investment because all foreign firms and capital had been forced out. Those arguing this position, while not denying the great achievement of attaining political rights, continued to look forward during the struggle to the day when overcoming *economic* apartheid would be the challenge. That challenge, which is the current one, requires a well-developed infrastructure and a critical mass of multinationals to attract new investment and job creation as well

as a renewed emphasis on affirmative action. Should the quest to attain economic rights fail in South Africa, there is little hope for a democratic future and little hope for a land of peace and justice.

At present, South Africa, under its new state president, Nelson Mandela, is leading a vigorous campaign for new investment and doing reasonably well in attracting new firms and capital. What would have happened if all foreign firms and capital had fled? (Most non-US firms remained in RSA, along with some 60 major US multinationals.) Since total disinvestment never happened, one can only speculate, but this speculation may be most helpful in guiding policy in other situations, such as that of the human rights struggle in China. More research on those issues could prove crucial for future policy. It seems clear that in the South African experience, there was value in the international pressure provided by strategic sanctions, that is, carefully crafted sanctions designed to reach specific groups and a limited objective (for example, the cultural and sports sanctions, the denial of landing rights for RSA airplanes, and the curtailing of loans from international banks). For many, it is not clear that total disinvestment by multinational businesses was the morally right position. As it turned out, the plurality of apparently conflicting strategies yielded the result sought by all. Perhaps there is a lesson here.

Bibliography

Donaldson, T. (1989). *The Ethics of International Business.* New York: Oxford University Press.
Dworkin, R. (1978). *Taking Rights Seriously.* Cambridge, Mass: Harvard University Press.
Hufbauer, C. & Schott, J. (1983). *Economic Sanctions in Support of Foreign Policy Goals.* Washington, DC: Institute for International Economics.
Sethi, S. P. (1993). Operational modes for multinational corporations in post-apartheid South Africa. *Journal of Business Ethics,* 12, 1–12.
Sullivan, L. (1983). Agents for change: The mobilization of multinational companies in South Africa. *Law and Policy in International Business,* 15, 427–44.
Voorhes, M. (1944). *Challenges and Opportunities for Business in Post-Apartheid South Africa.* Washington, DC: Investor Responsibility Research Center, Inc.

Williams, O. (1986). *The Apartheid Crisis.* San Francisco: Harper and Row.

OLIVER F. WILLIAMS

business ethics in South America   Constitutes the study of what is right or wrong, good or bad, in the human conduct in the business context in South American countries (SACs). Most SACs have gone through deep political and economic changes since 1960. The influences of different ideologies and governmental actions, together with the developing FREE ENTERPRISE system made the organizations become aware of their SOCIAL RESPONSIBILITY.

The MULTINATIONALS, or multinational corporations (MNCs), started opening overseas subsidiaries in most SACs, which contributed a great deal of emphasis to business ethics practice. By offering better wages, they oriented their internal politics toward social justice (*see* JUSTICE, CIRCUMSTANCES OF). By improving manufacturing processes and QUALITY control, the society began to find new, better, and healthier products in the market. By correctly paying their taxes, these companies brought significant increase of government income. To face the MNC competition, national companies had to review their ethical standards. They began to deal more carefully with issues like training, health and life insurance, codes of ethics, innovations in manufacturing processes, products, and working conditions.

In order to guarantee high levels of ethical performance, it was necessary to create laws, agreements, business and professional associations, and voluntary technical norms. As an example, the Associacao Brasileira de Fabricantes de Brinquedos (ABRINQ), a strong association of over 300 toy manufacturers in Brazil, prepared a voluntary technical norm, to avoid the production of all dangerous features in any toy. The government supported the initiative, making this norm mandatory to all toy manufacturing companies.

Rich in natural resources, SACs have been attractive to international investors, mainly large corporations. Nevertheless, the economic growth in SACs has been extremely unequal. The new flow of wealth has protected elites, who prospered by working for the government and became even wealthier after acquiring auctioned assets. The new jobs have tended to be temporary, low paid, and concentrated in specific economic sectors. Although managing PRIVATIZATION changes became a highly profitable activity, many middle- and lower-class workers lost their jobs, in order to make the companies more competitive.

Another ethics problem that arose with these trends in SACs was the concentration of investments mostly in large cities, while distant regions struggled to survive, without many chances of receiving new investments in the short term. Even in urban areas, many South American citizens live in slums, with little or no access to running water, electricity, drain systems, adequate housing, education, and health. Chile, Argentina, Bolivia, Peru, and Brazil established governmental programs to reduce the social price of warming up the economic development in the 1980s, but poverty is still an important issue in the business ethics arena: over 30 percent of SACs' populations live in real poverty, according to the Economic Commission for Latin America (CEPAL), a regional sector of the United Nations located in Santiago, Chile.

The unfair income distribution as a consequence of the materialism generated by inflation, allowed corruption to increase significantly. If one considers money alone as a value criterion of a society, corruption occurred among all social classes in most SACs (Appy, 1992, p. 50). The inflationary culture led citizens to lack of responsibility, unconcern about productivity, devaluation of professional work, and seeking for easy ways of earning money (*see* PROFIT AND THE PROFIT MOTIVE).

Business people have encountered difficulties in trying to recuperate ethical practices in their relationship with government agents, clients, suppliers, and stakeholders. BRIBERY, percentages, gifts, and other "payments" have become usual or mandatory in many sectors, and real MORAL dilemmas appeared concerning managerial ethics and the ethical role of the manager.

Illiteracy and low levels of education in SACs also lead to the settlement of unethical practices. Even though Roman Catholicism is the most important religion in SACs, many people have lost their feeling of right or wrong. A complete revolution in habits seems to be necessary, in order to recover the consciousness of citizens. Some business executives are already playing an important role in this effort, by avoiding any kind of corruption, paying their bills on time, protecting the environment and environmental ethics, having the courage to be honest. Recognized as third world countries, SACs faced increasing competition in world markets, which induced industrialized nations to cluster together in regional economic blocks: the European Community (EC), the North American Free Trade Agreement (NAFTA), and some alliances among Japan and its East Asian neighbors. According to principles of INTERNATIONAL BUSINESS ETHICS, SACs felt the need to face both fair and unfair competition (*see* ETHICS OF COMPETITION). Argentina, Brazil, Paraguay, and Uruguay created the Common Market of South America (MERCOSUR) in March 1991, attempting to integrate their economies and defend themselves from discriminatory tariffs from other countries (Manzetti, 1994).

Business ethics have become an imperative in South America, at either the micro or macro level. Companies, universities, and governmental agencies are starting to successfully implement ethical systems, based on solid and moral VALUES.

See also **Foreign Corrupt Practices Act; ethics of marketing; organization ethics; religion and business ethics; social cost–benefits; socio-economics; work and family**

Bibliography

Appy, R. E. (1992). Etica empresarial e inflacão. In N. G. Teixeira (ed.), *A Etica no Mundo da Empresa*, São Paulo: Pioneira, 47–55.

Manzetti, L. (1994). The political economy of MERCOSUR. *Journal of Interamerican Studies and World Affairs*, 3, (4), 101–41.

Newton, L. & Ford, M. M. (1992). *Taking Sides: Clashing Views on Controversial Issues in Business Ethics and Society*, 2nd edn, Guilford, Conn.: the Dusking Publishing Group.

MARIA CECILIA COUTINHO DE ARRUDA

business ethics periodicals The topic of "business ethics" appears in print in a wide variety of forms: 1) books (authored and edited); 2) general readership newspapers; and 3) a vast array of periodicals and professional publications that can be categorized in many different ways. What follows is one attempt to organize this last group of publications.

I. Academic Journals with Business Ethics as a Primary Focus

Journals addressed primarily to scholars and utilizing peer reviewing:

Business Ethics: A European Review, 1992–, quarterly.

Business Ethics Quarterly, 1991–, quarterly (Society for Business Ethics).

Business & Professional Ethics Journal, 1981–, occasionally.

Business & Society, 1960– (Roosevelt University); 1992–, quarterly (International Association for Business and Society).

Employee Responsibility and Rights Journal, 1988–, quarterly (The Council on Employee Responsibilities and Rights).

International Journal of Value-Based Management, 1988–, three issues per volume.

Journal of Business Ethics, 1982–, monthly.

II. Periodicals with Business Ethics as a Major Focus

Magazines and journals that advocate good business and professional ethics, that address the business and professional community, and that do not utilize academic peer reviewing:

Business Ethics, 1986–, bimonthly.

Business and Society Review, 1972–, quarterly.

Corporate Conduct Quarterly, 1991–, quarterly.

Ethics: Easier Said Than Done, 1989–, quarterly (The Josephson Institute of Ethics).

Ethikos, 1987, bimonthly.

III. Professional Publications that Include Articles on Business Ethics

Many utilize academic or professional peer review, but not all. Most are addressed to identifiable academic or professional or business constituencies. All included have published three or more articles on business ethics in the last seven years.

The Academy of Management Executive

The Academy of Management Journal

The Academy of Management Review
Across the Board
American Business Law Journal
Australian Accountant
Business
Business and Economic Review
Business Forum
Business Horizons
Business Insights
California Magazine
California Management Review
Canadian Business Review
Common Boundary
Co-op American Quarterly
The Executive
Executive Excellence
Harvard Business Review
Humanomics
Internal Auditor
International Management
Journal of Accountancy
The Journal of Blacks in Higher Education
Journal of International Business Studies
Journal of Management Development
The Journal of Socio-Economics
Leadership and Organization Development Journal
Management Accounting
Management Decisions
Management Review
Marketing
Public Affairs Quarterly
SAM Advanced Management Journal
Security Management
Sloan Management Review
Social Justice Research
Vital Speeches
Working Women

(Running a computer search on ABI/Inform for articles on "business ethics": between January 1987 and July 1994 there were 978 citations. In all, 137 different journals were cited. Only 29 journals had more than two articles during this seven-year time period. Only six had more than five articles. While ABI/Inform is generally regarded as the most extensive business journal data base, for whatever reason(s), there are journals that regularly address business ethics that are not included in this data base.)

IV. Business Publications that Include Coverage of Business Ethics

A sampler of publications addressing broad business readership (stories may appear with or without attribution of authorship):

Business Week
Computerworld
The Economist
Fortune
Inc.
Industry Week

V. Newsletters Focusing on Business Ethics

Newsletters produced by individuals, ethics centers and institutes, professional associations, and consulting firms:

Benchmarks, 1994–, monthly (Minnesota Association for Applied Corporate Ethics).

Business Ethics Resource, 1987–, quarterly.

Business & Society, 1968–74, biweekly.

Business & Society Briefings, 1992– (The Conference Board).

C B E News, 1992–, biannual (Center for Business Ethics).

Center For Ethics Studies Newsletter (Center for Business Ethics Studies).

The Corporate Examiner (Interfaith Center on Corporate Responsibility).

Ethical Management, monthly.

Ethically Speaking (The Association for Practical & Professional Ethics).

Ethics & Policy, 1974–, quarterly (Center for Ethics & Social Policy).

Ethics in Action, bimonthly (The Josephson Institute of Ethics).

Ethics Journal, 1991– (Ethics Resource Center).

The Executive Citizen, 1992–, quarterly.

Executives Alert (National Center for Policy Analysis).

Managing Ethics (Lincoln Center for Ethics).

The New Leader.

On Achieving Excellence.

Research Report of the Council on Economic Priorities.

VI. Newsletters Focusing on the Business of Ethical Investing

Published by individuals and organizations advising or evaluating the ethical performance of businesses for potential or current investors.
Clean Yield
Franklin Research's Insight
Good Money
The Greenmoney Journal
Investing for a Better World

JAMES R. GLENN, JR.

business ethics research centers Generally not-for-profit organizations funded by the college or university of which they are a part, or by government grants, such as grants from the National Endowment for the Humanities. Alternatively, corporate and individual donors may support them. It is most common for centers to be supported by a combination of these sources.

As the field of business ethics has grown since the mid-1970s, centers have been established to stimulate, support, conduct, and disseminate research related to business ethics and corporate social responsibility. Business ethics research centers are typically small. Many are housed within colleges or universities. They may consist of a full-time director, several part-time faculty who also teach in their discipline-based departments, and full- and part-time support staff. Among the oldest such centers are the Olsson Center for Applied Ethics at the Darden Graduate School of Business, University of Virginia, which was established in 1969, and the Center for Business Ethics at Bentley College in Waltham, Massachusetts, which was founded in 1976.

There are also a few independent centers that conduct research in addition to or as part of their other functions, such as management consulting and education. The Ethics Resource Center in Washington, DC, and The Business Enterprise Trust are examples of this type of center.

Most centers are located in the United States, although the number of centers in other countries is increasing. Examples of non-US centers include The Institute for the Study of Business Values at the University of Hong Kong and Westminster Institute for Ethics and Human Values in London.

Although some research centers may be entirely dedicated to conducting and collecting research (The Hastings Center in New York), most have multiple functions, such as preparing teaching materials, conducting conferences and seminars, providing speakers and scholars for media interviews, and acting as a repository for books, journals, newsletters, videos, and corporate ethics materials. Centers differ in the extent to which they specialize in studying ethics in business, in contrast to professions such as law, medicine, and education. Harvard University's Program in Ethics and Professions at the Kennedy School of Government is an example of the latter type of center.

Centers oriented solely toward business may be general (the Center for Corporate Community Relations at Boston College, the Center for Business Ethics Studies at Marquette University, and the Center for Ethics and Corporate Policy at Loyola Chicago) or specialized (The Marion W. Isbell Endowment for Hospitality Ethics at Northern Arizona University's School of Hotel Management and Center for the Study of Ethics and Behavior in Accounting at State University of New York at Binghamton).

Some business ethics centers focus on empirical research to describe, explain, and evaluate companies' practices, using qualitative methods such as case studies and/or quantitative methods based on large-sample survey research. Studies are also conducted using secondary sources such as media coverage, corporate publications, and directories. Other centers also perform theoretical work that is usually grounded in the discipline of philosophy.

JUDITH BROWN KAMM, DBA

business ethics societies *see* SOCIETIES OF BUSINESS ETHICS

C

Canada, business ethics in *see* BUSINESS
ETHICS IN CANADA

care, ethics of *see* ETHICS OF CARE

caring organization A caring organization is
one whose values and practices are consistent
with, and supportive of, an ethic of care. An
ethic of care focuses on the self as connected to
others, with an emphasis on the care-giver's
responsibility to the "other" to maintain that
connection (Gilligan, 1982). It is often compared
with the stereotypically masculine ethic of
justice, with its focus on defining the self as
separate and its use of rights to protect
boundaries between the self and other. Gilligan's
metaphor of the web to represent feminine
thinking has been juxtaposed against the use of
hierarchy to represent masculine thinking
(White, 1992).

A decade of writing in feminist morality has
focused on the concept of an ethic of care. In
examining the relevance of an ethic of care for
business practice, the question has been raised,
can organizations care? In other words, is it
possible to take this essentially individual-level
theory and extend it to the level of an
organization, without subverting it in the
process?

Central to the question of whether organizations can care is Noddings' (1984) distinction
between "caring for" and "caring about."
Ethical caring, she argues, only applies to
those *persons* that we care *for*. She uses the
term, "aesthetical caring" for objects and things
that we care *about*. She is concerned about the
extent to which our caring for things subverts
our caring for people, by encouraging us to use
them instrumentally to achieve other ends.
Similarly, if it is people that we care *about*,
versus *for*, she views this as representing only a
"verbal commitment to the possibility of care"
(1984, p. 18). We cannot, she argues, care "for"
those who are beyond our reach. Caring
represents a personal investment that must
always remain at the level of "I"; caring at the
more abstract level of "We" is an illusion. This
quality of particularity is essential. Without
particularity the caring connection is lost and we
must re-label the new process: no longer
"caring," it becomes "problem-solving," in
Noddings' terminology.

But, what does it mean, within the literature
on feminist moral theory, to "care for" this
particular other? Noddings remains vague on
this point, alluding to an "inclination" towards
them. Along with other scholars (Held, 1993;
Ruddick, 1989), Noddings has used the relationship between a mother and her child to
illustrate, at its deepest level, her notion of what
it means to care. Thus, the essence of caring
becomes a focus on acceptance of the other,
both in his or her current state, *and* as one
capable of growth. Nurturing the development
of the one cared-for becomes the critical activity
in caring relationships. To say that I care about
my customers, then, would be to place them and
the potential that they represent at the center of
my attention, and to work with them to realize
that potential. In addition, caring always
involves "feeling with" – receiving the other,
rather than projecting one's own view onto the
other. Thus, the development process evolves
out of the aspirations and capabilities of the
cared-for, rather than being driven by the needs
and goals of the care-giver.

Thus, Noddings would maintain that, in order for an organization to "care," such caring would need to be:

1. focused entirely on *persons*, not "quality" or "profits," for example;
2. an *end* in and of itself, and not merely a means toward achieving quality, profits, etc.;
3. developmentally focused at a personal level, in that it involves particular individuals engrossed, at a subjective level, in nurturing the development of other particular individuals.

Does, then, an assembly of appropriately caring individuals constitute a "caring" organization? Considerable precedent exists, of course, for such anthropomorphizing – we speak of organizations that have values, that learn, that reward. Yet, it would certainly be possible for a subgroup of caring individuals to exist within an organization that worked to subvert their efforts. Thus, we would argue that a caring organization, in addition to being comprised of individuals who met the conditions, would need to actively support their efforts.

In fact, some authors have argued that individual caring is only sustainable, in the long term, within caring systems (Kahn, 1993): "To be cared for is essential for the capacity to be caring" (Gaylin, 1976). Caring, though a particular relationship between individuals, is situated within the context of a community and derives its focus from the needs of that community. We care, not because we are inherently "good," Noddings asserts, but because it is self-serving for the group, as a whole, to care for each other; care is self-reinforcing within that context. Thus, both because it derives its meaning within the context of community, and because of the personal investment required to care, organizations that support individual caring, that create self-reinforcing systems of caring, are not only possible – they are essential if caring is to persist at all.

At this point, however, given Noddings' concerns about instrumentality, we must raise the question, can *business* organizations care? The question of instrumentality and the profit motive is a thorny one. At one level, we might read Noddings as asserting that positive out-comes for anyone other than the cared-for could never be allowed to provide the incentive to care, but must be viewed as mere by-products. Yet, she acknowledges that, at the community level, an ethic of care is clearly self-serving. We might deduce, then, that caring which both honors the growth and development of the particular individual, *and* perpetuates the health of a vibrant caring community (which, in turn, fosters more growth of particular individuals) is not instrumental. Thus, the instrumentality caveat would be breached only by the subordination of the particular other cared-for to the interests of the abstract cared-about.

Other concerns raised in the literature relate to questions about the utility of using the mother/child dyad, so prevalent in feminist moral writings, as a model for non-familial relationships and issues around freedom and fairness that a more rights-focused perspective offers. The "mothering" image of caring that is so powerful also raises significant concerns. One of these relates to the issue of power. Is the power differential between parent and child one that we want to embrace as a model for relationships at work? What are the risks of replacing patriarchy with matriarchy? Few, asserts Held (1993), in proposing her "post-patriarchal" model. Disparity in power is a given in our society and cannot be avoided. Yet, traditional notions of power are useless in the mothering context. Mothers, she argues, do not "wield" power. Instead, "the power of a mothering person is to empower others – to foster transformational growth" through *influence* (1993, p. 209).

Ferguson (1984) believes otherwise, asserting that both the presence of inequality and the "natural love" inherent in mothering make it unsuitable for generalization outside the bounds of the family. Instead, she offers the model of citizenship, and uses the town meeting with its decentralization, public decision-making, and openness to conflicting views as a guide for care-based organizations. Her view is strikingly similar to that contained in Charles Handy's recent (1994) call for "federated structures," which contain local and separate activities served by a common center. Such structures, he believes, led by the center and managed by the parts, "combine the benefits of scale and autonomy, while retaining a sense of meaning that connects people to purpose" (1994, p. 110).

But how are concerns related to fairness and equality addressed within a care-based ethic? Again, Held (1993) argues that our definitions need reframing. Equality no longer corresponds with equal rights or equal treatment; rather, it requires that we view each member as worthy of equal respect and consideration, and respond to the unique needs they bring with them. In a similar vein, Ferguson (1984, p.31) asserts that freedom is essential. But rather than viewing freedom as "an arena of privacy surrounding each individual, [where] community is a secondary arrangement among already autonomous beings; freedom must be located in relations among others . . . caring for others by caring for their freedom."

Thus, the issues of freedom, fairness, and power can be reconciled within the framework of a care-based organization. Gilligan, in fact, believes that rights are an essential, though not dominant, component of caring. Without rights, "the injunction to care is paralyzing, rights allow us to appropriately value self-interest . . . to act responsively towards self *and* others and thus to sustain connection" (1982, p. 149).

Bibliography

Belensky, M., Clinchy, G., Goldberger, N. & Tarule, J. (1986). *Women's Ways of Knowing*. New York: Basic Books.

Ferguson, K. (1984). *The Feminist Case Against Bureaucracy*. Philadelphia: Temple University Press.

Gaylin, W. (1976). *Caring*. New York: Knopf.

Gilligan, C. (1982). *In a Different Voice*. Cambridge, Mass.: Harvard University Press.

Handy, C. (1994). *The Age of Paradox*. Boston: Harvard Business School Press.

Held, V. (1993). *Feminist Morality*. Chicago: University of Chicago Press.

Kahn, W. (1990). Psychological conditions of personal engagement and disengagement at work. *Academy of Management Journal*, 33, (4), 692–724.

Kahn, W. (1993). Caring for the caregivers: Patterns of organizational caregiving. *Administrative Science Quarterly*, 38, 539–63.

Lyons, N. (1983). Two perspectives: On self, relationships, and morality. *Harvard Educational Review*, 53, (2), 125–45.

Noddings, N. (1984). *Caring: A Feminine Approach to Ethics and Moral Education*. Berkeley: University of California Press.

Ruddick, S. (1989). *Maternal Thinking*. Boston: Beacon Press.

White, T. (1992). Business, ethics, and Carol Gilligan's "two voices". *Business Ethics Quarterly*, 2, (1), 51–9.

JEANNE LIEDTKA

case method   The use of descriptions of situations, called "cases," as a basis for discussion in teaching. Cases, which may be oral or written, actual or invented, provide students with a common set of data that they can read, analyze, and discuss. The Harvard Business School borrowed the technique from the medical and legal educational processes to become, in 1919, the first champion of the use of written, actual cases in business education. Two other schools, the Darden Graduate School of Business at the University of Virginia and the University of Western Ontario in Canada, later also became primarily case-oriented schools. Many other schools use cases to varying degrees and in various ways. Written cases vary in length from one to almost 100 pages; the usual length is between 15 and 25 pages.

Case method is used to refer to a wide range of case-based instructional methodology, most clearly seen in the proportion of teacher to student talk. The "classical" Harvard method intended to provide intelligent, experienced students with actual, current descriptions of difficult business problems and let the students, at their own pace and level of insight, debate the different aspects of the problems with their peers. This was a "student-centered" approach in that the discussion relied heavily on the experience, analysis, contributions, and insight of the students. Some Harvard professors occasionally said nothing during a class. This approach relied on a four-step learning process: careful, pre-class individual preparation, continued analysis in small study groups, large, full class debate, and post-class personal distillation of general principles.

At the other end of the scale, cases are often used by instructors elsewhere as illustrations of lectured, theoretical points. This "instructor-based" use of cases proceeds at the pace and level of insight comfortable to the professor such that students might never speak. Here, what is to be learned is determined by the instructor rather than the student.

Case advocates argue that the classical case method is more effective because it begins where students are, proceeds at their pace on pragmatic rather than theoretical problems, and infuses energy into the learning process, hence accelerating the development of business judgment. Dissidents argue that cases are single examples missing the generalizable lessons of larger sample pools, that the classical case approach ignores the input of more experienced instructors, and that case classes are easily manipulated by case instructors in case selection and presentation.

Current, decision-based cases and skilled instructors are the lifeblood of the case method. Finding, researching, and writing good cases is a mixture of science and art that is time-consuming and expensive, often requiring a month or more of a researcher's time. Good cases present rich data surrounding an important decision to be made in such a way that many avenues could be argued reasonably. Case courses are built by the selection of cases that present a sequential series of decisions that follow the design intentions of the instructor.

Bibliography

Christensen, C. R. (1987). *Teaching and the Case Method*. Boston: Harvard Division of Research.

Clawson, J. G. & Frey, S. C., Jr. (1986). Mapping case pedagogy. *Organizational Behavior Teaching Review*, now titled *Journal of Management Education*, 11 (1), 1.

Dooley, A. R. & Skinner, W. (1977). Casing case method methods. *Academy of Management Review*, 2 (2).

Gragg, C. I. (1940). Because wisdom can't be told. *Harvard Alumni Bulletin*. Boston: Harvard University.

JAMES G. CLAWSON

casuistry a word coined, and almost always used, with a pejorative intent: it refers to the ability of clever and devious persons to argue, under the cover of specious moral reasons, for the rightness of their own case. Historically, this negative meaning arose out of theological disputes of the seventeenth century. At that time, Roman Catholic theologians commonly presented "cases of conscience," short analyses of a wide variety of moral dilemmas, to educate believers about their moral duties and to help confessors judge the seriousness of sins and faults revealed to them in confession. Although this study had been common since the late Middle Ages, it aroused vigorous opposition from the Protestant Reformers and, in particular, from rigorist French Catholics, called Jansenists, in the mid-1660s. One of those, the brilliant mathematician Blaise Pascal, attacked the professors of cases of conscience, accusing them of a lax and self-serving interpretation of the laws of God and the Church. His attack, *The Provincial Letters*, was a literary success and tarnished the reputation of "cases of conscience." The word "casuistry" itself was coined in a similarly sarcastic vein by the English poet Alexander Pope in 1702. Since that time it is applied almost exclusively to a moral argument that is seen as overly complex, devious, and self-justifying. A patently obvious example: the general said that Vietnam villages had to be destroyed in order to save them.

This pejorative meaning, however, hides an important feature of moral reasoning and a respectable method for analyzing it. The important feature of moral reasoning arises from the fact that moral dilemmas are posed in particular cases. The conflict of moral principles appears in a set of unique circumstances. The circumstances and their relationship to the principles must be understood as precisely as possible in order to reach a judgment. An appreciation of this fact gave rise to the method of "cases of conscience." That method, in essence, called for a careful examination of the proposed case and a comparison of the case to other cases in which similar problems appeared. Such comparison would often show why a change of circumstances rendered one case a more, or less, serious matter than the other. Careful methods were developed to analyze the relevant features of cases and to draw appropriate comparisons. The authors of these cases of conscience carried on incessant critique of each other's work, attempting to show inconsistencies in argument or offering stronger reasons to support conclusions. This constant dialogue about cases kept the classical casuists honest, although there were exaggerated practitioners of the art. The value of the method was that it made persons sensitive to the special features of cases and refined their moral judgment about them.

This method contrasts with the broad, abstract study of morality that appears in the standard academic disciplines that deal with morality, moral philosophy, and theological ethics. These disciplines usually devise comprehensive theories of morality. In recent times the moral disciplines have neglected case analysis. However, the interest in the ethics of medicine and health care that emerged in the 1970s under the title "bioethics" drew attention to the need for close case analysis: cases are the stuff of medicine. Thus, casuistry, as a method for ethical analysis, was rediscovered.

Other areas of ethical concern, such as business, journalism, politics, and media find the case approach congenial. It allows practitioners in the field to work with materials familiar to them and brings the moral issues close to the practical realities of their activities. It is interesting to note that in one of the earliest case discussions in an ethical treatise, the Roman philosopher Cicero offers two cases about business ethics, one in which a seller of property wonders how truthful he must be about the condition of the house, the other in which a merchant wonders how to set a fair price for grain in a famine (*On Duties* III, 13–15). In both cases, the considerations offered by the ancient philosopher are relevant to modern business.

The CASE METHOD is familiar to all students of business and finance, since it was introduced at the Harvard Business School as a basic teaching technique in the 1920s. The Business School adopted the method from the Harvard Law and Medical Schools, which had initiated this technique in the late 1890s. When used as a teaching technique, it can stimulate vivid discussion and creative solutions to problems. However, in business, law, and medicine, the ethical dimensions are seldom factored into the cases. The contemporary interest in ethics in these fields may encourage a more sophisticated attempt to create a casuistry. This requires not only the presentation of the facts of the case in a realistic way, but the invention of a method of interpreting ethical values in the setting of those facts.

This method must include statements of the goals and essential elements of the enterprise, in addition to its place within the wider society. These features are associated with the range of moral values and principles that naturally come to mind when the enterprise is considered. Thus, in medicine the doctor's duty to benefit the patient and the autonomy of the patient's choice; in diplomacy, the responsibility of furthering the interest of the nation and fidelity to agreements; in business, the legitimacy of profit and the value of honesty. Even in the abstract, these values and principles are somewhat in opposition and, in the concreteness of the case, may come into conflict. Thus a casuistry for each enterprise will work at the intersection of the general features and values of the enterprise and the particular circumstances of the case. The results of this analysis will sometimes show that there is no conflict, but more often suggest ways of minimizing or eliminating conflict. In some cases, it will reveal the stark choice, unavoidable by the responsible person, between good and evil, right and wrong.

Bibliography

Cicero, Marcus Tullius. (1975). *On Duties*. The Loeb Classical Library. Cambridge, Mass.: Harvard University Press.

Jonsen, A. & Toulmin, S. (1987). *The Abuse of Casuistry: A History of Moral Reasoning*. Berkeley and Los Angeles: University of California Press.

McNair, M. (ed.). (1954). *The Case Method at Harvard Business School*. New York: McGraw-Hill.

Pascal, Blaise. (1967). *The Provincial Letters*, trans. A. Krailsheimer. London: Penguin Books.

ALBERT R. JONSEN

Catholic social teaching The view that capitalism considered in isolation from a context of a humane community seems inevitably to shape people into greedy and insensitive human beings.

While there has always been some reflection on the social and political implications of biblical teaching, within the last one hundred years there has developed a body of official Catholic church teaching on social ethics known as Catholic Social Teaching. The insight of

Church teaching accepts the market economy but with a key qualification that the state intervene where essential to promote and protect human dignity. Most official church teachings are promulgated as pastoral letters of a national conference of bishops or as encyclicals, pastoral letters issued by the Pope as the chief shepherd of the church. An encyclical's title is taken from the first two words in the Latin edition.

At their best, church statements that reflect on and offer guidance to capitalist economies are attempts to be a moral force, ensuring that an acquisitive economy does not degenerate into an acquisitive society. For example, Pope Leo XIII in *Rerun Novarum* (1891), put the church squarely on the side of the workers in the struggle for recognition of labor unions. Monsignor John A. Ryan was most influential in Catholic circles, writing *A Living Wage* (1906) and *Distributive Justice* (1916). Ryan drafted a crucial document of the National Catholic Welfare Conference (the predecessor of the United States Catholic Conference), issued in 1919 by the US bishops and often cited as the forerunner of some of Franklin Roosevelt's New Deal policies. Titled *Social Reconstruction: A General Review of the Problems and Survey of Remedies*, Ryan's document offered a moral perspective on the economy and made suggestions for such reforms as minimum-wage laws, child-labor laws, the right of labor to organize, and unemployment and health insurance. For the most part, Ryan's suggestions have become public policy in the United States.

In 1931 Pope Pius XI issued *Quadragesimo Anno*. While its proposed alternative model of society is of dubious value today, the role of the church as an agent of change in the sociopolitical order was clearly established. Three principles enunciated in the document have been dominant in all subsequent Catholic social theory: the need to protect the dignity of the person; the concern that organizations be no larger than necessary – subsidiarity; and the focus on the necessity for mediating structures (family, professional associations, church, etc.) between the person and the state.

Quadragesimo Anno outlined a vision of society and its relationship to the state, which has continued to develop in Catholic social thought. Society is composed of all the various groupings that people find necessary or helpful – families, churches, unions, professional associations, business corporations, social clubs, neighborhood associations, and so on. The role of the state is to be *in the service* of society, that is, its role is primarily to facilitate the cooperation and well-being of all these groupings or "mediating structures" as they are often called today. The encyclical uses the verbs *direct*, *watch*, *urge*, and *restrain* "as occasion requires and necessity demands" when describing the role of the state (para. 80). The 1961 encyclical of Pope John XXIII, *Mater et Magistra*, employs similar terms: the role of the state is to "encourage, stimulate, regulate, supplement and complement" (para. 53).

Catholic social thought is ever vigilant against collectivist tendencies which tend to obliterate legitimate mediating structures. This defense of personal rights is clearly evident in the 1981 encyclical, *Laborem Exercens*, in which Pope John Paul II vigorously defends the solidarity of workers and their right to come together in organizations to defend common interests. Eschewing the model of interest-group pluralism which tends to view the world exclusively through the prism of one set of interests, Catholic social thought repeatedly returns to the notion of the common good as the appropriate context in which to consider one's own interests. John Paul II emphasizes this point in *Laborem Exercens*.

Assuming that human nature is flawed, one of the roles of the state, according to this religious perspective, is to facilitate the growth of desirable character traits and mute those that are less noble. Yet there is a confidence in the goodness, the cooperative dimension of the person, so that the social constraints of the state are designed to enhance human freedom and curtail selfishness for the common good.

This confidence in the fundamental goodness of the person underlies the church's basic strategy of appealing to the consciences of those who control wealth and power, to bring about basic changes in society that are designed to alleviate the plight of the poor. Pope Paul VI in *Populorum Progressio* (Development of Peoples) argues for a new international economic order but he appeals for strategies of negotiation and consensus rather than any violent means.

The 1991 encyclical *Centesimus Annus* of Pope John Paul II is perhaps the most forthright defense of the wealth-creating capacity of a market economy but it too stresses a modest role for government intervention to ensure a humane community. A major theme of the criticism of capitalism by the church is summed up well by John Paul II, in speaking of alienation. He notes that the Marxist analysis of alienation is false, but there is a type of alienation in our life today. The point is that it is quite possible for people in a market economy to lose touch with any real meaning or value in life (para. 4). One of the ways this happens is called "consumerism," an easily misunderstood term. Consumerism, as a pejorative term, is certainly not referring to the consumption of material goods, which is, after all, required for a market economy to function and for people to have employment. Consumerism refers to that aberration where people are led to believe that happiness and self-fulfillment are found solely in acquiring material goods. The values of friendship, music, and beauty, for example, come to pale in importance and, because basic, non-materialistic needs are not met, there is alienation. Consumer advocates in the United States have long been critical of certain kinds of advertising because of their adverse cultural and social effects similar to those described above. Seeking ways to strengthen the influence of the family, the schools, and the church is the challenge put forward. Some disciples of ADAM SMITH believed in God's providence working to ensure the common good, a self-regulating economy. Catholic social teaching says, in effect, that we must make God's work our own.

Bibliography

Byers, D. M. (1985). *Justice in the Marketplace: Collected Statements of the Vatican and the US Catholic Bishops on Economic Policy, 1891–1984*. Washington, DC: United States Catholic Conference, Inc.. (The periodical *Origins* prints all encyclicals and pastoral letters).

Curran, C. E. (1985). *Directions in Catholic Social Ethics*. Notre Dame, Ind.: University of Notre Dame Press.

Houck, J. W. & Williams, O. F. (eds). (1983). *Co-Creation and Capitalism: John Paul II's Laborem Exercens*. Washington, DC: University Press of America.

Houck, J. W. & Williams, O. F. (eds) (1984). *Catholic Social Teaching and the US Economy: Working Papers for a Bishops' Pastoral*. Washington, DC: University Press of America.

Ryan, J. A. (1942). *Distributive Justice*. New York: Macmillan.

Williams, O. (1993). Catholic social teaching: A communitarian democratic capitalism for the new world order. *Journal of Business Ethics*, **12**, 919–32.

Williams, O. F. & Houck, J. W. (eds) (1991). *The Making of an Economic Vision*. Washington, DC: University Press of America.

Williams, O. F. & Houck, J. W. (eds) (1993). *Catholic Social Thought and the New World Order*. Notre Dame, Ind.: University of Notre Dame Press.

OLIVER F. WILLIAMS

causal background In causal reasoning, the comparison case against which people judge an occurrence.

Recent research in psychology suggests that in devising an explanation for an occurrence, people compare the occurrence – called the "target episode" – to some contrasting case in which the event did not occur. This contrasting case is the "causal background." The factor selected as the basis of the causal explanation is a distinguishing feature between the target episode and the contrasting causal background (McGill, 1989 and 1990; see also Einhorn & Hogarth, 1986; Hastie, 1984; Hilton & Slugoski, 1986; Hart & Honoré, 1959; and Mackie, 1974). For example, in devising an explanation for a train derailment, people might compare the accident (the target episode) to an earlier time when the train was moving along fine (the contrasting causal background). In this comparison, the to-be-explained event is the *change* in the performance of the train (Hastie, 1984), and some distinguishing feature between the time when the accident occurred and when it did not occur, for example, the engineer speeding around a bend, might be a plausible explanation for the occurrence.

Central to this view of causal reasoning is the contention that the same target episode may be compared to different causal backgrounds. For example, one might compare the train that derailed (i.e., the same target episode) to another train that also went speeding around the bend but which did not derail (a competing causal background). In this comparison, the to-be-explained event is the *difference* in the performance of the two trains under similar conditions. Speeding around the bend lacks explanatory relevance in this case because this feature is common to the target episode and the contrasting causal background. Instead, distinctive features of the train that derailed, such as the amount of weight it was carrying, or the experience of its engineer, are relevant. Thus, people may provide different explanations for an occurrence depending on the causal background adopted.

Kahneman and Miller's (1986) norm theory describes the process by which people adopt one causal background versus another. This theory holds that people use characteristics of the target episode as a basis for constructing the comparison case. The comparison case shares some features with the target, while it differs on other features. The key ideas behind this characterization are "that the mental representation of a state of affairs can be modified in many ways, that some modifications are much more natural than others, and that some attributes are particularly resistant to change" (1986, pp. 142–3). The unchanged (shared) features between the target and the comparison case are referred to as the *immutable* features of the episode, and the features that differ as the *mutable* features. Hence, the rules that govern mutability guide the construction of the causal background.

While a general theory of mutability is lacking in the literature, studies suggest a list of features that vary in degree of mutability. For example, studies suggest that the genders male and female differ in perceived mutability, with the gender male perceived to be less mutable than the gender female (McGill, 1993). Hence, in imagining alternatives to events, people may imagine female actors to have been men more frequently than they imagine male actors to have been women, and so be more likely to attribute a problem to the presence of women than men.

Other factors identified in the literature as differing in perceived mutability include temporal order (Miller & Gunasegaram, 1990), whether the event is exceptional or routine, (Kahneman & Tversky, 1982), and prominence of an actor in a story (Lerner & Miller, 1978). Specifically, people appear to perceive later events in a sequence to be more mutable than

earlier events, exceptional events more mutable than routine events, and focal actors in a story more mutable than background actors. Responsibility judgments may follow these lines of feature mutability. For example, people may blame recent events, such as hiring of new employees, changes in policy, or shifts in environmental conditions, more than earlier events for negative outcomes. Further, people may blame exceptional actions more than routine actions.

Focus on the recent and the exceptional may prevent people from identifying the persistent, central, and enduring causes of events. Kahneman and Miller note the perverse effect of evaluating alternatives relative to constructed norms, suggesting that "judgments of a stimulus evaluated in isolation will tend to be dominated by features that are not the most central" (1986, p. 141). Thus, people may explain negative social events such as rape in terms of small details associated with specific incidents – e.g., the woman's decision to walk a different way home from work – and not in terms of enduring societal characteristics that make rape frequent and familiar. Only by comparing societies in which rape is common with those, perhaps imagined, in which rape is rare, is one likely to identify those "routine" factors that produce such tragedies. Unfortunately, research on feature mutability and its role in constructing alternatives suggests that such broad comparisons are less likely than those involving small details.

Similarly, causal explanations and responsibility judgments for accidents, incidents of product failure, employee illness, and other negative events associated with conducting business may be explained more frequently by reference to recent and exceptional events leading up to the occurrence than by consideration of the stable and familiar practices of the firm. These familiar practices may, however, be precisely those that enable negative events to repeat; and separate instances each with their own distinctive and potentially distracting details may share the same underlying cause. The types of comparisons needed to identify such causes may seem, however, extreme or even unrealistic because they involve constructing alternatives around the less mutable features of an event.

Finally, the finding that focal actors are perceived to be more mutable than background actors raises the concern that causal explanations and, hence, responsibility judgments may vary depending on how the event is framed. Specifically, changing the story so that different actors are in the foreground may shift perceptions of who caused the event and who is to blame (Lerner & Miller, 1978). More generally, background effects in causal judgment imply that blame and responsibility for events may be easily deflected simply by suggesting other plausible comparison cases against which to view the event.

Bibliography

Einhorn, H. J. & Hogarth, R. M. (1986). Judging probable cause. *Psychological Bulletin*, **99**, 3–19.

Hart, H. L. A. & Honoré, A. M. (1959). *Causation in the Law*. London: Oxford University Press.

Hastie, R. (1984). Causes and effects of causal attribution. *Journal of Personality and Social Psychology*, **46**, 44–56.

Hilton, D. J. & Slugoski, B. R. (1986). Knowledge-based causal attribution: The abnormal conditions focus model. *Psychological Review*, **93**, 75–88.

Kahneman, D. & Miller, D. T. (1986). Norm theory: Comparing reality to its alternatives. *Psychological Review*, **93**, 136–53.

Kahneman, D. & Tversky, A. (1982). The simulation heuristic. In D. Kahneman, P. Slovic, & A. Tversky (eds), *Judgment Under Uncertainty: Heuristics and Biases*. New York: Cambridge University Press, 201–8.

Lerner, M. J. & Miller, D. T. (1978). Just world research and the attribution process: Looking back and ahead. *Psychological Bulletin*, **85**, 1030–51.

Mackie, J. L. (1974). *The Cement of the Universe: A Study of Causation*. Oxford: Clarendon Press.

McGill, A. L. (1989). Context effects in judgments of causation. *Journal of Personality and Social Psychology*, **57**, 189–200.

McGill, A. L. (1990). Conjunctive explanations: The effect of comparison of the target episode to a contrasting background instance. *Social Cognition*, **8**, 362–82.

McGill, A. L. (1993). Selection of a causal background: Role of expectation versus feature mutability. *Journal of Personality and Social Psychology*, **64**, 701–7.

Miller, D. T. & Gunasegaram, S. (1990). Temporal order and the perceived mutability of events: Implications for blame assignment. *Journal of Personality and Social Psychology*, **61**, 5–12.

ANN L. McGILL

change   A necessary and natural condition affecting both individuals and organizations. Change is always a dynamic process with both positive and negative outcomes depending upon consequences, real and/or perceived. Consequently some changes are resisted while other changes are embraced. Change is often experienced as difficult, destructive, and threatening. The phrase "people are resistant to change" is repeated so often it is believed by many people to be true.

Change can be defined in different ways to include *types, stages, objects,* and *consequences.* The types of change can be defined as *transactional, transitional,* and *transformational.* Each of these types includes a unique set of moral and ethical issues. Transactional change 1) refers to changes in behaviors that typically reflect a minimal personal investment. Examples are: learning additional skills, changing behaviors that have little time and energy invested in them, and/or deleting behaviors that have had a short habit life. Transactional changes are behavioral exchanges between people or between people and objects that create, or result in, minimal loss or discomfort. Transactional changes typically are associated with the fewest, hence least, moral costs. Since the term "transactional" implies operating at the boundary or point of interface, transactional change reflects a minimal investment in belief, assumption, and value.

Transitional changes are those that affect people's beliefs and assumptions and consequently imply a greater threat and potential loss. This threat–loss consequence creates significant ethical implications for the individual or group experiencing the change. Transitional changes result from such actions as downsizing (often referred to as "rightsizing," perhaps in an attempt to relieve guilt), merging, divesting, promoting, demoting, and transferring. As is evident by the descriptors, these transitional changes create individual and organizational outcomes that directly affect people's *beliefs, values,* and, for some, even *basic assumptions.*

Degree of change	Focus of change	Degree of personal, psychological, and moral investment in change	Ethical/moral implications of change
Transactional	Behavior	Minimal	Minimal
Transitional	Behavior and beliefs	Moderate	Moderate
Transformational	Behavior and beliefs; assumption and mindset	Significant	Significant

Figure 1   Types and implications of change

Issues of rights, duties, entitlements, and obligations are quite often at the forefront of these types of changes. Personal versus corporate responsibilities are often placed in conflict by transitional changes, issues of loyalty and trust are often found at the center of these changes. Despite the ethical implications of transitional change, these implications are often left unexamined and excluded.

Transformational change is a term that is often inappropriately used to refer to too many actions. A true transformational change, like a true paradigm shift, *significantly alters* the *mindset* and *action set* of the person or persons at stake. At the individual level a transformational change would be the outcome of prolonged and successful therapy or a spiritual experience leading to a "born again state." At an organizational level transformational change would find the members of the organization thinking and acting in profoundly different ways. The "profoundly different" ways issue reduces the number of real transformational changes that actually take place. Examples that come close to transformational change would be Motorola Corporation in terms of quality and speed (6-year journey), Milliken in terms of quality (15-year journey), and 3M Corporation in terms of innovation (11-year journey). These changes not only required a long time, but they changed the fundamental business processes of these organizations. The consequences associated with transformational change create ethical issues that are significant and far reaching. For example, do an organization's leaders have a right to ask people to change in fundamental

ways? If so, what are the time requirements and support obligations that are necessary? What obligations, if any, are owed to those people who are slow to change or incapable of change? Is it morally wrong not to demand transformational change, if extinction is the only alternative? These and other questions dot the transformational change landscape.

The magnitude of change reflected in these three types (transactional, transitional, and transformational) implies an increasing and challenging set of ethical issues, especially in terms of their complexity and consequences (see Figure 1). Change at each level brings with it a set of ethical/moral issues. This dimension is usually either ignored or seriously underappreciated.

Change can also be defined in terms of *direction or vector, domain,* and *stages. Proactive* change refers to those changes created by one or more persons that are in turn likely to have an impact on others. Innovation, new ideas, major initiatives, and various forms of creative endeavor are examples of focus. Proactive change requires a series of stages which include: 1) uninformed optimism, 2) uninformed permission, 3) informed doubt, 4) informed hope, and 5) achievement and accomplishment (see Figure 2). Anyone who has created, invented, or introduced a *transitional* or *transformational change* will recognize these stages. It is important to note that there is a set of related ethical issues relevant to each stage which in turn influences their outcomes.

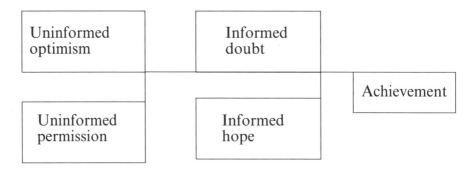

Figure 2   Stages of proactive change

Reactive change (see Figure 3), on the other hand, defines how people deal with rather than initiate change. The stages of reactive change include 1) denial, 2) anger, 3) bargaining, 4) depression, and 5) integration. Examples of reactive change include death of loved one, loss of major bodily function, loss of job, or major lifestyle shift. As in the case of proactive change each stage in the process has a related set of ethical issues. When the reactive change is transitional or transformational in nature, the personal and organizational consequences are increased.

The change dynamics always involve *objects* of change. These objects include individuals, groups, organizations, and larger systems to include nation states. As change alters its object of focus from the individual to the nation state, issues of rights, entitlement, equities, duties, and obligations increase in complexity and consequences. Despite the increase, the ethical issues are seldom, if ever, at the forefront of the change process.

Just as there are objects of change, there is a "currency" of change and trust in that currency. It is difficult if not impossible for people to change if trust is weak or nonexistent. Trust is typically the derivative of many experiences of TRUTHTELLING, promise-keeping, treating people fairly and with respect (*see also* PROMISES, PROMISING). If one or more of these experiences is missing, or minimal in nature, the trust necessary to support change is often insufficient, and the change process is experienced as negative and dysfunctional.

As trust is the currency of change, information provides the *stimulus* of the change process. Therefore integrity and consistency of the

Figure 3   Stages of reactive change

information is central to the initiation and sustainability of any change process. Without significant and accurate information, individuals, groups, and communities are unlikely to change very much. Yet, if people do not continue to change throughout their lives they fail to achieve their potential. Consequently the challenges of lifelong learning and personal growth become not only dynamic change issues, but also significant ethical issues. If people do not continue to learn and grow over their lifetime they lose their effectiveness and ability to add value to society.

Who bears the responsibility to ensure that these learning, adapting processes occur? Does it reside in the individual or society? Where do the duties, obligations, and rights for this necessary process reside? These are but a few of the critical issues of dynamic change (or lifelong learning and growth) that are so vital to our society and are fast becoming a central focus on the change stage.

The ethical issues of change are frequently left unexamined, and for this reason the possible richness of the change process is diminished. The opportunities to integrate ethical theory and change theory and practice are numerous and begging for investigation.

Bibliography

Bridge, W. (1988). *Surviving Corporate Transition: Rational Management in a World of Mergers, Layoffs, Start-ups, Takeovers, Divestitures, Deregulation, and New Technologies.* New York: Doubleday.

Gould, R. (1978). *Transformations: Growth and Change in Adult Life.* New York: Simon and Schuster.

Kubler-Ross, E. (1975). *Death: The Final Stage of Growth.* Englewood Cliffs, NJ: Prentice-Hall.

Kubler-Ross, E. (1981). *Living With Death and Dying.* New York: Macmillan.

Wheelis, A. (1973). *How People Change.* New York: Harper & Row.

ALEC HORNIMAN

character Character is revealed in a person's typical behavior in important matters, including moral ones. Your character may be good or bad according to whether you are virtuous or vicious, and strong or weak according to whether you can be relied on to act on your VALUES even under pressure. Ethicists and psychologists, particularly personality theorists, study character and the causal and conceptual links among traits.

To identify your self with your character is misleading in this sense: a significant character change would not by itself mean that you have ceased to exist and have been replaced by someone else. Yet an extreme change in character may justify saying, meaningfully but with some exaggeration, that Jones is a different man, or not the man I married. Strong character does have to do with consistency of thought, value, and action over time. One who is consistent in this way, especially one who acts according to the values one espouses, is a person of INTEGRITY.

ARISTOTLE famously claims that ethics is primarily about the virtues of character rather than about principles, though he grants principles a role in ethics. His view is no longer quaint: in recent years the notions of virtue and character have gained respectability among business ethicists.

This is not to say that character and virtue have obviated principles. We cannot assume that any single sort of ethical theory will address all issues equally well, but principle-based theories seem particularly ill-suited to certain practical moral issues with which managers and others must often deal. Faced with a moral problem that requires action, a manager will likely find that (for example) KANTIAN ETHICS and UTILITARIANISM yield no determinate results, but instead create subsidiary arguments about the right sort of preference, or the precise maxim of the act in question. If those arguments could be settled, there would be a further one about which of the general approaches is right. If that problem could be solved, moreover, there would still be the practical issue of whether people will actually do the right thing, as those of good character do. Depending in part on the nature, size, and environment of an organization, a manager may be able to bring about morally good behavior most effectively by populating the organization with employees of good and strong character rather than by enforcing MORAL RULES.

If the virtues of character were simply dispositions to act according to certain principles, then virtue and character ethics would not differ from principle-based ethics; but virtue and character ethicists deny that there are algorithms linking virtues to action-guiding principles. On the contrary, a person of good character does not merely act according to principles, but in cases in which principles give little guidance is sensitive to all significant aspects of the situation, including possible indirect and long-term consequences. This practical wisdom resembles the ability of a consistently successful businessperson to assess opportunities and act effectively; it is not a matter of simply knowing textbook rules, important as these may be.

A person of good and strong character is one whose interests are such that being moral makes him or her happy and fulfilled. For such a person the question, Why is it in my best interests to be moral? can hardly arise. A life anchored by a set of clear and coherent values will likely be preferable to one in which HAPPINESS is based on ephemera. But couldn't a bad person of strong character be equally well off? Probably not: such people arouse opposition and lose the benefits of cooperation.

A person of bad character is capable of good acts where these serve that person's interests or fit enforced norms comfortably, much as a person who lacks knowledge may make true statements. But just as education is a matter of imparting actual knowledge, so training in morality should build good character. Acting morally need not be painful – for the person of good character it is not – but it cannot be based on self-interest alone.

To understand how your virtues are related and why you have them requires understanding your character, of which virtues are its iceberg's tip. Teachers, parents, and managers who would affect character must consider psychological relations, which are not relations merely among virtues. Here is another reason why a character is not simply a disposition to act in a certain way: a character trait has no less ontological status than does a psychological state, which is not a mere disposition. A description of a character trait may explain a whole set of virtues. In fact, a particular trait (firmness, for example) may be the psychological basis of both a virtue (courage) and a vice (obstinacy), especially in one who is not perfectly rational.

A pervasive ORGANIZATIONAL CULTURE can make people of weak character act against their values, though it may occasionally support good character. There is no obligation for managers to improve their employees' character, but they should maintain an organization in which good character does not put one at a disadvantage.

Can character be taught, by BUSINESS ETHICS professors or anyone else? If, as Aristotle claims, habituation creates character, there is a problem: how can character be related to the rationality definitive of humans, whereby the agent controls ephemeral desires in aid of an appropriate long-term conception of happiness? If building character is just a matter of forming habits, then moral education should proceed not by appeals to the intellect but by positive and negative reinforcement, and business ethics courses taught in the usual way are a waste of time, and too late.

Yet a business ethics course may indeed help build character. The case study method, or CASE METHOD, can assist students in developing practical wisdom, including the sensitivity to details, consequences, and nuances that we attribute to a person of character. Insofar as it deals with issues of character, moreover, a course in business ethics can show the moral importance of corporate culture and of a human resources policy that takes character into account.

Bibliography

Aristotle. (1985). *Nicomachean Ethics,* trans. T. Irwin. Indianapolis: Hackett. (Includes a glossary of key terms.)

French, P., Uehling, T. & Wettstein, H. (eds). (1988). *Ethical Theory: Character and Virtue,* Midwest Studies in Philosophy 13. Minneapolis: University of Minnesota. (Includes several essays on character.)

Hartman, E. M. (1996). *Organizational Ethics and the Good Life.* New York: Oxford University Press.

Kupperman, J. (1991). *Character.* New York: Oxford University Press.

Schoeman, F. (ed.), . (1987). *Responsibility, Character, and the Emotions.* New York: Cambridge University Press. (Includes several essays on character.)

Solomon, R. C. (1992). *Ethics and Excellence: Cooperation and Integrity in Business.* New York: Oxford University Press. (An important analysis of business ethics from an Aristotelian point of view).

EDWIN M. HARTMAN

China, business ethics in *see* BUSINESS ETHICS IN CHINA

churning Three definitions of "churning" are presented here, and their advantages and disadvantages are discussed.

Definition 1: Churning is trading in a customer's account that is excessive in view of the account's character (i.e., the investor's objectives). To remove the vagueness in this commonly employed definition, it has been argued that we should use a numerical criterion, e.g., courts often use the "6 rule," which regards a turnover ratio of more than 6 times per year as marking off excessive trading.

The advantage of the 6 rule, or any numerical criterion, is that judges as well as brokers know exactly when churning has occurred. However, trading patterns exceeding the 6 limit may be clearly ethical. A trader using a reliable market timing indicator may maximize an account's value by a turnover ratio of, say, 11, and in a highly volatile market a high ratio may be rational and ethical. Furthermore, for any plausible numerical value proposed to mark off "excessive," some trading patterns with less than that value will still count as churning. A broker who had a market-beating increase in a client's account with no turnover over a 50-week period might churn it up to the 6 limit in the last two weeks merely to generate commissions.

Excessive trading is necessary for churning, but we will have to leave "excessive" vague. That is acceptable, as long as there are some clear cases of excessive trading. But excessive trading is not sufficient for churning. There is nothing wrong *per se* with an account that is turned over rapidly in which big profits are realized.

Definition 2: Churning is trading in a customer's account that is excessive in view of the account's character, and in which that broker's intent is primarily to act in his own interest to generate commissions. Although more commonsensical than the first definition, the problem with this commonly employed legal definition is that most brokers are motivated primarily by commissions. But nothing is wrong with that if their self-interest is enlightened, i.e., they realize that they will not succeed in their primary aim of generating commissions unless their choices also benefit their clients significantly. A broker who satisfies both necessary conditions of definition 2, but who benefits his client significantly, has not acted unethically.

Definition 3: Churning is trading in a customer's account that is excessive in view of the account's character, and in which the broker's intent is to act in his own interest to generate commissions and against his customer's interests. This definition squares with our intuition that the enlightened egoist broker who actually increases his customer's wealth while also acting in his own interest is not necessarily acting unethically. He may not have acted against his client's interests. Furthermore, a broker who trades excessively in an account which suffers serious losses has not necessarily churned it; he may have acted in good faith, with no intent of acting against his client's interest. The difficulty here is that except in rare cases (e.g. a pattern of excessive trading which contains some cross-trades) it will be very difficult to establish that a broker's intent was to act against his clients' interest independent of excessive trading.

Bibliography

Almeder, R. & Snoeyenbos, M. (1988). Churning: Ethical and legal issues. *Business and Professional Ethics Journal*, 6, 22–31.

Heacock, M., Hill, K. & Anderson, S. (1988). Churning: An ethical issue in finance. *Business and Professional Ethics Journal*, 6, 11–21.

MILTON H. SNOEYENBOS

classical and managerial business ideologies An ideology can be understood as a system of ideas (beliefs, values, principles) held in common by members of a collectivity (Rejai, 1973, p. 556). In the case of the business community, these are highly systematized around a few important values, formulated fairly explicitly over a wide range of objects, and authoritative for members (Shils, 1968, p. 66). Although by their very nature ideologies tend toward oversimplification and distortion, they are not merely useful but necessary, providing cognitive, normative, and emotive orientation to members of a collectivity without which experience would be confusing and actions devoid of meaning or value. Normatively, ideologies play a special role in legitimizing authority, the central institutions, social status rankings, and distributions of particular benefits and burdens within society.

The publication of *The American Business Creed* (Sutton et al., 1956) brought scholarly credibility to the belief, already widely held, that within the American business community there exist two relatively distinct orientations known as the "classical" and "managerial" business ideologies.

For the business community, the key issues, for example, will concern the legitimacy of the market, the business firm and its managers, and the government. Simply put, the ideologies of the American business community must address the *descriptive* question of the role that business (and/or the large modern corporation) *does* play in a free society, and the *normative* question of the role that business (and/or the large modern corporation) *should* play in a free society. The flip side of either is the role that government *does* or *should* play (Danley, 1994).

Stated briefly, the classical business ideology claims that the legitimate role of business is primarily economic, to compete vigorously within the constraints of a free market, that management's primary or sole responsibility is to stockholders to profit maximize, and that the function of government should be to remain minimal, leaving the market alone. Within the managerial business ideology, the large modern corporation is claimed to have a special role in society. Corporations and their managers have a responsibility, it is claimed, to do other than profit maximize, and to be socially responsible and responsive, to function as good citizens, not as selfish private agents. The legitimate role of government is also broader, working with business to solve problems that the market, by itself, cannot or does not address.

Because these two ideologies share a number of significant features, Sutton describes them as different variations of the same American creed. Although Sutton does not explicitly make the claim, it is very likely that the common creed is the tradition of political philosophy known as LIBERALISM (Gray, 1986). In this tradition, a dominant one in the US, individual liberty is a hallowed fundamental value. The burden of proof is upon anyone who would seek to interfere in an individual's right to do with her own person, property, possession, etc., as she wishes. Hence, liberalism supports protections from unwarranted government interference. The commitment to freedom also entails that economic freedom within the market will be valued highly.

Within this tradition, however, there is room for significant disagreement. Thus, classical liberals lean more heavily toward individual liberty and belief in an unfettered free market with minimal government, while revisionist liberals are more sympathetic to a more than minimal government which plays an important role in the market. Classical liberals would today be described as conservatives, provided that one understands that classical liberals are opposed to the attempt to use government to impose moral or social values on anyone. For classical liberals, government should be restricted to preventing one individual from harming another (*see* NOZICK, ROBERT; LOCKE, JOHN). Revisionist liberals would today be described as liberal. On this interpretation, the genuine difference between the classical business ideology and the managerial business ideology is, at bottom, a disagreement between two different versions of the common liberal creed. This creed may be widely shared across the American society as a whole.

Within the classical business ideology, "the system," that is, the system of free-market capitalism with minimal government, is central. The extraordinary economic development of the US is explained as the consequence of the efficiency of this system. From this perspective, the consumer is heralded as king, the driving force behind market changes. Business responds to these demands or is replaced by other firms more sensitive to consumer needs. As a result, long before Total Quality Management, the notion of customer service was critical in the rhetoric of the classical business ideology. Moreover, in this view there are no significant differences between the structure of the market today, as compared with that of 100 or 200 years ago, or any important difference in the structure of firms. That is, in principle, there is no relevant difference between a mom and pop corner grocery store and General Motors or Exxon. Except for the fact that the US Constitution is viewed as the embodiment of the basic principles of laissez-faire market capitalism with minimal government, and for that reason cherished, references to government are almost entirely negative. Government is characterized as wasteful, a drain on the productive energies of the private sector. Similarly, unions are viewed with suspicion, if not outright hostility, as a threat to the system.

The classical business ideology is not merely venerable but resilient. Informed by a somewhat simplistic reading of classical liberals such as Adam Smith and John Stuart Mill, and by the laissez-faire social Darwinists in the nineteenthth century, the ideology not only provided the basic framework for the opposition to the growth of the federal government during the Depression, but after the Second World War reignited a movement to prevent further growth in the powers of government, and even to turn back the clock, especially with respect to the labor movement. By the 1960s, however, many observers were diagnosing the classical business ideology moribund if not dead. The managerial business ideology, rooted in the 1920s and more explicitly formulated in the great debate over the role of government during the Depression of the 1930s, was becoming ascendant in the 1960s, and appeared to have won the day, at least among the "enlightened" business leaders. Nonetheless, beginning in the 1970s, a number of intellectual developments, especially the influence of the "Chicago school" of economics, brought renewed credibility to the classical business ideology. Milton Friedman, a well-known representative of this school, has offered one of the most widely read defenses of the position that "The Sole Responsibility of Business is to Increase Profit" from this perspective (Friedman, 1962, 1982). Politically, these ideas clearly remain powerful, as supply-siders, neoconservatives, and mainstream Republicans echo the familiar themes. In a real sense, this ideology is associated with the "Reagan revolution" of the 1980s and continues to attract a strong following today (*see* SMITH, ADAM; MILL, JOHN STUART; FRIEDMAN, MILTON).

In the managerial ideology, although still committed to the free market and protections against unwarranted government interference, "the firm" has replaced "the system" as central. Managerialists believe that in the twentieth century profound changes have altered both the basic structure of American capitalism and the nature of the corporation, changes, they believe, which demand a new look at the role that corporations and the government *do* and *should* play in society.

Disagreement between ideologies, especially these two, is not necessarily or even primarily a disagreement over different moral values or principles, but is often prompted by theoretical disputes, allegedly far removed from normative concerns. For instance, the classical business ideology incorporates classical or neoclassical economic theories which purport to establish that markets are self-regulating, and that, if left alone, markets will overcome problems. On this view, there is no need for government to interfere to ensure adequate levels of employment, investment, savings, or to provide incentives to ensure that markets will address serious social needs. Managerialists, on the other hand, while accepting the importance of leaving the market alone in principle, endorse economic theories which purport to demonstrate rigorously that the market is not entirely self-regulating, or that the market will not, if left alone, address serious social problems. On this view, market intervention is, occasionally at least, desirable. Thus, even assuming a common set of values and principles, disagreements over the role that business and government should play will arise precisely because of deep theoretical disagreements.

Indeed, the managerial ideology took clearer form in the 1930s, as many within the business community began to move toward an acceptance of Keynesian macroeconomic principles, and the idea that the government needed to encourage economic growth and employment by stimulating investment and savings through various kinds of tax incentives and credits. (Only rarely would emergency deficit spending be required.) Against that theoretical background, however, the focus of the ideology is the firm. In this regard, no book has shaped managerialism more than *The Modern Corporation and Private Property* by A. A. Berle and

Gardiner Means (Berle & Means, 1932). John Kenneth Galbraith believes that this is the most important work in economics published in the 1930s, second only to Keynes's *General Theory*, and one which has had an enduring impact not only on managerialists, but on a wide range of thinkers (*see* BERLE, ADOLF A.; MEANS, GARDINER COIT).

From this perspective, "the modern corporation" is a very different kind of business enterprise than has ever existed. Building upon Berle and Means, the managerial ideology believes that a managerial revolution has occurred in this century, the effects of which are continuing to be felt (the "thesis of managerial revolution"). Although multifaceted, one critical dimension of the revolution is the separation of control and ownership. In the modern corporation, owners no longer manage, and managers no longer own significant shares. With the growth of stock offerings, stock ownership has become widely dispersed as well. This, one can argue, frees managers from the narrow, short-term interests of stockholders, and provides managers an opportunity for wide discretion in use of company revenues (the "thesis of managerial discretion"). Whether managers actually have such discretion depends upon whether other incentives for short-term or long-term profit maximization have replaced the ones which have allegedly been lost.

Assuming, nonetheless, that management of the large modern corporation possesses fairly wide discretion, an agency problem arises. If management is no longer merely an agent of the owner(s), whose interests *will* management in fact reflect? Whose interests *should* management reflect? The former question is a descriptive one, the answer to which involves making a prediction about what will happen. The latter question is a normative or moral one, the answer to which requires appealing to normative or moral principles. If there is robust managerial discretion, a number of alternatives present themselves (*see* AGENCY THEORY).

1) Management could continue to act primarily or solely in terms of the interests of stockholders. Advocates of the classical business ideology, such as Milton Friedman, take this view, claiming that new market incentives have arisen which ensure that this is the way managers will and must act, and that this is the way managers ought to act (*see* FRIEDMAN, MILTON).

2) Or, managers could act in their own self-interest, rendering the corporation a vehicle for self-aggrandizement. While virtually no one defends the thesis that managers ought to act this way, in light of the very high levels of executive compensation (compared with similarly situated executives in other nations with which the US competes), a number of analysts have argued that this is, in fact, what has happened. Defenders of corporate takeovers in the 1980s, especially the corporate raiders, charged that managers of many corporations were doing just this, and defended TAKEOVERS as a means for bringing discipline to an entrenched, self-centered, and insensitive management.

3) Or, management could use its newly won freedom to act on behalf of broader interests, including the public good. This is the alternative which stands at the heart of the managerial business ideology, has been adopted by the field of BUSINESS AND SOCIETY, and which informs many if not most of the analyses in BUSINESS ETHICS. Two theses are generally involved.

The Descriptive Thesis of Social Responsibility claims that either society has already entered into a new age in which managers are acting on the basis of broader concerns, or that the new age is close at hand. Sutton refers to this as the "managerial version of the creation myth," and the theme is reflected in popular works of the 1950s, such as Frederick Allen's *The Big Change*, as well as more academic treatments, such as Gerald Cavanagh's *American Business Values in Transition* (1984) and George Lodge's *The New American Ideology* (1979). At least three important reasons can be offered for believing in such a change. Berle and Means believed that the corporations would move in this direction because of the increasing importance of public image, because corporations would seek to avoid unwanted government regulation which might arise from actions which were not public minded, and because management itself was becoming professionalized, bringing with it the values of public service. (Whether this is true remains, of course, subject to dispute.)

The Prescriptive Thesis of Social Responsibility claims that whether or not managers act in socially responsible ways, they *should* act that way. The concept is often attacked as vague, since proponents do not make clear the extent to which profit can or should be sacrificed for these other ends, but by emphasizing cases in which "doing the right thing" pays, this weakness is obscured. The concept of social responsibility involves two components. One is the idea of corporate philanthropy according to which corporations take over to some extent philanthropic endeavors once shouldered by wealthy individuals (often owner/managers). The other is the idea which has come to be known as the theory of modern stakeholder management, in which managers (should) identify the primary and secondary stakeholders of the corporation and make decisions taking into consideration these interests, not merely those of stockholders (*see* STAKEHOLDER THEORY).

A number of arguments are offered in defense of the thesis. Generally, it is claimed that these broader responsibilities arise by virtue of the nature of the large modern corporation. That is, because of its relative size, for instance, managers must consider the potential negative impacts of corporate decisions on stakeholders. Or, some allege that the large modern corporation is no longer a genuinely private institution but a quasi-public one, and as such, should be managed as a quasi-public one, for the public good.

While both ideologies continue to flourish, there are some who believe that in light of the intensely competitive markets which now characterize the business environment, the ideas of the managerial ideology have "gone the way of the Edsel." Critics of the classical views also remain active.

Bibliography

Berle, A. A. & Means, G. C. (1932). *The Modern Corporation and Private Property*. New York: Macmillan.

Cavanagh, G. F. (1984). *American Business Values in Transition*. Englewood Cliffs, NJ: Prentice-Hall.

Danley, J. R. (1994). *The Role of the Modern Corporation in a Free Society*. Notre Dame, Ind.: University of Notre Dame Press.

Friedman, M. (1962, 1982). *Capitalism and Freedom*. Chicago: University of Chicago Press.

Friedman, M. (1970). The social responsibility of business is to increase profit. *New York Times Magazine*, Sept. 13, 32–3, 122–6.

Gray, J. (1986). *Liberalism: Concepts in Social Thought*. Minneapolis: University of Minnesota Press.

Heald, M. (1970). *The Social Responsibilities of Business: Company and Community, 1900–1960*. Cleveland, Ohio: Case Western Reserve University Press.

Lodge, G. C. (1979). *The New American Ideology*. New York: Alfred A. Knopf.

Rejai, M. (1973). Ideology. In P. P. Wiener (ed), *Dictionary of the History of Ideas*, vol. 2. New York: Charles Scribner's Sons.

Shils, E. (1968). Ideology: The concept and function of ideology. In D. Sills (ed.), *International Encyclopedia of the Social Sciences*, vol. 7. New York: Macmillan & The Free Press.

Sutton, F. X., Harris, S. E., Kaysen, C. & Tobin, J. (1956, 1962). *The American Business Creed*. Cambridge, Mass.: Harvard University Press.

JOHN R. DANLEY

codes of ethics   (also called codes of conduct or PROFESSIONAL CODES): statements of behavioral ideals, exhortations, or prohibitions, common to a culture, religion, traditional professions, fraternal organizations, corporations, and trade associations. Codes combine philosophical statements and high ideals with admonitions to avoid specific illegal actions and to espouse certain moral principles, especially those that elevate personal behavior or improve interpersonal relationships.

Codes have been considered the primary means of institutionalizing ethics into the culture, religion, professions, learned societies, or corporations. Historically, the Code of Hammurabi contained almost 300 paragraphs of rules governing business, moral, and social life reaching back into the third millennium BC to the earlier Codes of UrNammu (ca. 2060–2043 BC), the Code of Lipit-Ishtar (ca. 1983–1733 BC), and the Code of Eshnunnia (ca. 1950 BC). These codes were compilations of customs, laws, and rules of ancient Mesopotamia, going back to Sumerian times. The UN Universal Declaration on Human Rights (1948) is our most contemporary counterpart.

Among Hebrew Laws there are two that are truly codes, containing casuistic laws and moral principles: The Book of the Covenant and the Book of Deuteronomy. The Ten Commandments represent a code of conduct taught by all Christian denominations. The Koran offers similar guidance for Muslims.

A Code of Conduct is one mark of a profession, as in the Hippocratic Oath sworn by medical doctors. Professions are characterized by both the promulgation and enforcement of their codes. For example, the legal profession can disbar lawyers for unethical conduct. Ethics is a qualifying component for the CPA examination. Fraternal organizations and learned societies have increasingly adopted codes or standards of professional conduct. The Academy of Management has adopted a Code of Ethical Conduct. Public-sector codes exist for civil servants (US Code for Federal Civil Servants), for city managers, and for public administration professionals.

De George proposes that:

> codes should be regulative; should protect the public interest and the interests of those served; should not be self-serving; should be specific and honest, and should be both policeable and policed. (1982, p. 229)

During the 1970s and 1980s, codes gained widespread acceptance in business. Codes vary according to their intended function. Codes are sometimes called Corporate Directives, Administrative Practices, Standards of Business Conduct, or a Code of Best Practice. The preface or preamble usually defines the basic philosophy of the corporation and the scope of the codes.

Scholars have examined the varied contents of corporate codes. The most comprehensive listings of contents has been published in the Hammaker, Horniman, and Rader study of *Standards of Conduct in Business* (1977, pp. 55–8). Their listing contains 17 categories of topics covered in the codes of *Fortune* 500 firms, along with specific prohibitions within each category ranging from 3 to 38 examples each.

Codes are developed to highlight company philosophy or policy, to define employee rights and obligations, and to specify environmental responsibilities. Most codes speak to the purpose, administration and authority of the code, the nature of the company, employee issues, legal requirements, and civic responsibilities (Weaver, 1993, pp. 49, 55–6) .

Surveys conducted by the Conference Board, Bentley, and Touche Ross all reveal significant numbers of corporate codes. Berenbeim (1992) reported that 83 percent of US firms have codes. In 1993 Bentley College reported that 93 percent of the responding *Fortune* 1,000 indicated codes as "the best means to achieve their goals" (Weaver, 1993, p. 46). A Touche Ross National Survey revealed their correspondents believed codes are the "most effective measure for encouraging ethical behavior" (1988, p. 3).

Attempts to develop universal business codes have been undertaken by various international governmental bodies with minimal success. Conflicts in ideology and special interests defeated the multiyear effort to introduce a UN Code of Conduct for Transnational Corporations. Some specialized UN agencies have achieved success on industry-specific issues, for example, WHO Code on Pharmaceuticals and Tobacco. The International Monetary Fund (IMF) and World Bank have codified specific industry practices between nations.

More success toward international codes appears to have been achieved in the non-governmental area. The International Chamber of Commerce (ICC) "Business Charter for Sustainable Development" or the Sullivan Principles Governing Business in South Africa are examples of non-governmental codes.

Regional efforts to develop codes for business include new European Community (EU) legislation, for example, the European Convention on Human Rights (1950), or Organization for Economic Cooperation and Development (OECD) Guidelines for Multinational Enterprises (1976).

Corporations themselves develop codes according to their geography. Caterpillar and Levi Strauss and Co. have worldwide codes of ethics; Johnson and Johnson, a worldwide credo; and McDonald's, worldwide standards of best practice. Most firms operate in the domestic market and their codes reflect prevailing domestic corporate and public concerns.

Enforcement of codes presumes promulgation, implementation, and incorporation into the system to insure compliance. Advocates and critics agree that code enforcement often fails because of inadequate communication, inconsistent implementation, and weak systems of enforcement. Compliance with the "spirit of the code" is often too general and sporadic; compliance with the "letter of the law" too legalistic and stultifying. Because codes mix ideals, rules, protocol, laws, and etiquette, enforcement often admits to varied interpretations, and suffers the risk of unequal application sometimes resulting in discrimination and injustice. Internal compliance includes supervision, ethics training, personal integration, ethics officers or ombudsmen, and review panels. External compliance involves audits, government regulation and enforcement, and the courts.

Only cooperatively developed, carefully articulated, clearly understood, widely promulgated, and sympathetically enforced codes preserve the individual conscience, promote the ethical environment, and permit the code to be efficacious – whether in the corporate or public sector.

Future codes will continue to address company authority, employee rights, and obligations, and introduce more specific stakeholder references, with increasing emphasis on accountability, self-development, globalization, the environment, and new public-interest areas. Codes must be recognized as only one aspect of a larger system of institutional efforts directed to developing and promoting an ethical environment.

Bibliography

Berenbeim, R. (1992). *Corporate Ethics Practices.* New York: The Conference Board.

De George, R. T. (1982). *Business Ethics.* New York: Macmillan.

Hammaker, P. M., Horniman, A. B. & Rader, L. T. (1977). *Standards of Conduct in Business.* Charlottesville, Va.: Olson Center for the Study of Applied Ethics.

Touche Ross. (1988). *Ethics in American Business.* Detroit: Touche Ross.

Weaver, G. R. (1993). Corporate codes of ethics: Purpose, process, and content issues. *Business and Society,* **32**, (1), 44–58.

LEO V. RYAN

coercion   is one of a family of concepts such as duress and force. It refers to one method by which one person can motivate another to do something. We typically say that A coerces B to do X when A gets B to do something by threatening to harm B or by making B worse off in case B should not do X. We also often say that coercion interferes with one's freedom or autonomy, that if B is coerced into doing X (or does X under duress), then B's action is involuntary.

Roughly speaking, there are two philosophical questions about coercion: (1) what *counts* as coercion? (2) when are individuals or the state *justified* in using coercion? The second question is, of course, a central problem of political philosophy (*see* HARM; LIBERTY; PATERNALISM; JOHN STUART MILL). This entry focuses on (1).

Understanding what counts as coercion is important for several reasons. First, we do not hold individuals responsible for actions that are the products of coercion. A coerced promise or contract is neither morally nor legally binding; a defendant is not guilty if he was coerced into performing a crime. Second, various social practices such as surrogate motherhood, sales of bodily parts, and the volunteer army, have been criticized on the grounds that poverty effectively coerces people into such an arrangement. Third, capitalist theory assumes that market transactions are free, even if they are made against a background of economic necessity. What sort of coercion invalidates an agreement or excuses wrongdoing or interferes with one's liberty? To answer these questions, we must know what counts as coercion.

Consider three examples: (1). Gunman says to Victim, "your money or your life." Victim turns over his wallet. (2). Prosecutor says to Defendant, "Plead guilty to manslaughter or I will convict you on a murder charge." Defendant pleads guilty. (3). Doctor says to Patient, "consent to amputation or you will die of gangrene." Patient consents (*see* CONSENT). We think that Victim is coerced but that Defendant and Patient are not. Are we right? Why?

One view maintains that coercion is essentially *empirical*. On this view, A coerces B because A's threat puts B under great psychic pressure or leaves B with no other rational choice. But this view has trouble explaining why

Victim is coerced but Defendant and Patient are not. A second view maintains that coercion is essentially moralized. On this view, one is coerced only when one's rights are violated, even if one has "no choice" but to agree. This view is compatible with our intuitions about the cases, but how do rights violations relate to coercion?

On the standard view, threats coerce and offers do not. *A* makes a *threat* when *B* will be *worse off* than in some relevant baseline position if *B* does not accept *A*'s proposal. *A* makes an *offer* when *B* will be *better off* than in some relevant baseline position if *B* accepts *A*'s proposal. The key to coercion is to establish *B*'s baseline. In *Coercion* (1987), I argue that a moral tenet for *B*'s baseline can explain why Gunman threatens Victim, but Prosecutor and Doctor both make offers. Only Gunman proposes to violate a right if the proposal is not accepted.

Interestingly, some coercive proposals do not actually coerce. If Gunman says to Victim, "Kill *C* or I will break your arm," Victim cannot claim to have been coerced into killing *C*. An adequate account of coercion will explain why this is so. It will also consider these questions: Are there coercive *offers*? Can one be coerced by background conditions? Are coerced actions involuntary?

Questions as to what constitutes coercion can arise within several different business contexts. Within the workplace, we may want to know when sexual harassment is coercive. If a supervisor offers an employee a promotion she would not otherwise receive if she has sexual relations with him, has she been coerced? (Note that SEXUAL HARASSMENT can be seriously wrong even when it is not coercive.) With respect to market transactions, some people have argued that one is coerced into purchasing a drug if one would die without it, or that one can be coerced into employment if one's only alternative is a life of desperation.

Bibliography

Frankfurt, H. (1973). Coercion and moral responsibility. In T. Honderich (ed), *Essays on Freedom of Action*. London: Routledge and Kegan Paul, 65–68.

Nozick, R. (1969). Coercion. In S. Morgenbesser, P. Suppes, & M. White (eds), *Philosophy, Science and Method*. New York: St. Martins, 440–72.

Pennock, J. R. & Chapman, J. (eds). (1972). *Nomos XIV: Coercion*. New York: Aldine-Atherton.

Wertheimer, A. (1987). *Coercion*. Princeton: Princeton University Press.

Wertheimer, A. (1992). Coercion. In L. C. Becker & C. B. Becker (eds), *Encyclopedia of Ethics*. New York: Garland, 172–5.

Zimmerman, D. (1981). Coercive wage offers. *Philosophy and Public Affairs*, **10**, 121–45.

ALAN WERTHEIMER

collective bargaining   Legally mandated group bargaining between an employer, or employers, and organized employees seeking to reach an agreement on wages, hours, and other working conditions. Unlike other bargaining which allows either party to freely terminate the negotiation, the process of collective bargaining is legally regulated both substantively as to work-related issues discussed and procedurally as to both timetable and process of bargaining, the purpose of which is to pressure the parties to reach a collective bargaining agreement.

The US National Labor Relations Act of 1935, usually called the Wagner Act, ensures the right of employees to form unions and to negotiate as a group with employers. Absent such legal compulsion, there would be no collective bargaining. The employer would be free to establish and change conditions of employment unilaterally at will based solely on its conceptions of fairness, attitudes toward maximizing of profit and social responsibility, and knowledge of current labor-market conditions (Taylor and Whitney, 1987). With the advent of an organized workforce, usually represented by an outside labor union, such unilateral employer action ceases and is replaced by a joint determination of employment conditions.

This unique regulated group bargaining replaces the legal right of individual freedom of contract in the workplace when employees conclude that it is a worthless right due to the inordinate imbalance of power between an individual employee and an employer. The process seeks to resolve a series of ethical issues relating to fairness, power-sharing, and profit-sharing previously left to the employer's sole discretion. While collective bargaining provides a mechanism for resolving such issues, the process generates additional ethical issues as the parties seek victory through the assertion of power while complying with the several "good faith" bargaining duties required by law.

As an adversarial process, the efforts of the parties are directed solely toward concluding an agreement most favorable to their self-interest based exclusively on their relative bargaining power (Post, 1990). Since the remedies for illegal bargaining are minimal, the parties are encouraged to manipulate and exploit each other based upon self-interest (Post, 1990). Typical unethical behaviors practiced during collective bargaining include deception, bluffing, and lying. Such practices usually produce sub-optimal agreements characterized by an undermining of the moral value of truth and honesty. This promotes distrust throughout the organization, the development of confused, divided loyalties, the ignoring of broader stakeholder interests, the frustration of efforts to encourage team and quality commitments. An over-emphasis on bargaining over extrinsic (wages, fringes, seniority) job conditions is often at the expense of higher level intrinsic (job responsibility, job content, recognition) job conditions (Post, 1990). Such behaviors are cited as part of the reason for the alleged shortcomings of American business to compete effectively in the global marketplace (Dertouzos et al., 1989; Kochan, Katz, & McKersie, 1986).

Carson, Wokutch, & Murrmann (1982) argue that to the extent there are unethical behaviors practiced in collective bargaining, they are the result of pre-existing dispositions of the bargainers. Post (1990) disagrees and asserts that the legal environment of collective bargaining dictates that the parties act unethically to win. Bowie (1985) proposes a "family model" to effectuate attitude change when bargaining. Post (1990) proposes the "collaborative collective bargaining" process as a moral approach to labor negotiations and later reports on its implementation via an in-depth case study (Post, 1994).

Bibliography

Bowie, N. (1985). Should collective bargaining and labor relations be less adversarial? *Journal of Business Ethics*, 4, 283–91.

Carson, T., Wokutch, R. & Murrmann, K. (1982). Bluffing in labor negotiations: Legal and ethical issues. *Journal of Business Ethics*, 1, 13–22.

Dertouzos, M., Lester, R., Solow, R. & the MIT Commission on Industrial Productivity (1989). *Regaining the Competitive Advantage*. Boston, Mass.: Houghton Mifflin.

Kochan, T., Katz, H. & McKersie, R. (1986). *The Transformation of American Industrial Relations*. New York: Basic Books.

Post, F. (1990). Collaborative collective bargaining: Toward an ethically defensible approach to labor negotiations. *Journal of Business Ethics*, 9, 495–508.

Post, F. (1994). Use of the collaborative collective bargaining process in labor negotiations. *The International Journal of Conflict Management*, 5, 34–61.

Taylor, B. & Whitney, F. (1987). *Labor Relations Law*. New Jersey: Prentice-Hall.

FREDERICK R. POST

collective punishment

The Nature and Function of Collective Punishment

A *collective* is any collection of persons and/or non-persons which constitute a diversified whole. Examples of collectives include random aggregates such as mobs, organized conglomerates such as corporations, coalitions, nations, and even organized or unorganized ethnic groups. *Punishment* is the attachment of legal penalties to the violation of legal rules (Rawls, 1955). It "must involve pain or other consequences normally considered unpleasant;" must be of an actual or supposed offender for her legal offense against legal rules; must be intentionally administered by humans other than the offender; and must be imposed and administered by an authority constituted by a legal system against which the offense is committed (Hart, 1968). Among the expressive functions of punishment are the communication of the community's vindictive resentment of the criminal for her offense(s), authoritative disavowal, symbolic non-acquiescence, vindication of the law, and absolving the innocent of guilt (Feinberg, 1970) (*see* CORPORATE PUNISHMENT; PUNISHMENT).

It is often believed that the subject of collective punishment focuses on whether or not, or the extent to which, certain collectives of the conglomerate sort qualify as punishable agents. Collective punishment may involve collective compensation whereby a guilty collective is forced by the state to pay a victim of that collective's negligence or intentional action to restore the victim's losses (*negligence*, according to Joel Feinberg, is the creation of an unreasonable risk of harm. A *harm*, according to Feinberg, is the setting back of another's interest) (*see* COMPENSATORY JUSTICE).

Models of Collective Punishment

There are various models of collective punishment. *Punishment collectivism* holds that it is legitimate to punish some collectives (such as organized conglomerates) because they can be legitimately held responsible for their being at least contributory causes of untoward actions, events, or states of affairs. On the other hand, *punishment individualism* denies that some collectives ought to be punished, and for one of at least three reasons. One is that such collectives cannot satisfy the conditions of collective responsibility, and hence cannot qualify as punishable agents (Corlett, 1988). Another is that, though some such collectives can *in principle* satisfy the conditions of collective responsibility (or can be restructured to do so), they typically do not satisfy collective responsibility conditions which are either requisite or sufficient for the punishment of collectives. This version of punishment individualism, it is important to note, does not logically conflict with punishment collectivism. Thirdly, one might argue, as does the methodological (punishment) individualist, that collective punishment language is reducible, without loss of cognitive *meaning*, to talk of individual punishment, and that this suggests that collective punishment language does not refer to *anything* except one's confusion about what one intends to say about individual punishment. Against this view, it has been argued that from the supposition that claims about collective punishment are reducible to those of individual punishment it hardly follows that collectives are inappropriate subject of punishment (Corlett, 1992). For if the linguistic reduction of collective punishment claims to individual punishment statements amounts to an identity relation between the two kinds of claims, then to affirm, as the methodological

individualist does, the meaningfulness of statements about individual punishment *just is* to affirm the meaningfulness of the language of collective punishment. (For a more detailed discussion of this topic as it pertains to collective responsibility, see COLLECTIVE RESPONSIBILITY.)

The Justification of Collective Punishment

If (or when) collective punishment is justified both as an institution and in its multifarious and particular instantiations (recall RAWLS's distinction between the justification of a rule, and the justification of something's falling under it, a distinction which is borrowed by Hart when he distinguishes between "Retribution in General Aim" and "Retribution in Distribution" (Rawls, 1955; Hart, 1968)), it might be justified in various ways. It might be argued that collective punishment is justified only to the extent that it provides a genuinely therapeutic service for the subject of punishment (Menninger, 1968). Whatever else punishment might involve, on this view, it must at least realize a significant therapeutic output for the collective wrongdoer. But there is also a vengeance justification of collective punishment. According to this justification, collective punishment carries out the community's sense of vengeance toward that collective wrongdoer, and that such vengeance is legitimate. On this justification, the punishment of guilty collectives is either an orderly outlet for legitimate aggressive feelings, a pleasure in knowing that a guilty collective is being punished, or the expression of emotions of vengeance which are themselves self-justifying in cases of legitimate collective responsibility and punishment (Feinberg, 1989). The moral education model of collective punishment seeks to justify such punishment on the basis of its teaching the collective offender that what it did (or failed to do) was morally wrong and should not have been done for that reason (Hampton, 1984). A utilitarian justification of collective punishment might follow the theories of justifying individuals as articulated by Jeremy Bentham, John Stuart Mill, David Hume, and John Rawls, respectively. An act-utilitarian justification of collective punishment would argue that such punishment is justified to the extent that it concerns only future consequences of the punishment in reference to its probable consequences of the state's maintenance as a means of social order, and to the extent that punishing the guilty collective would promote effectively the best societal interest (Hume, 1875; Bentham, 1946). A rule-utilitarian justification of collective punishment would recognize the importance of punishing only guilty collectives, and it would institute a rule whereby innocent collectives would be used as a mere means to the end of social utility by the *institution* of punishment (Rawls, 1955). A retributivist justification of collective punishment would argue that collective punishment can only be justified to the extent that no innocent individuals are significantly and adversely effected in the punishing of the guilty collective. Primarily, collective punishment is justified because wrongdoing on the part of the collective merits punishment of that collective, and that it is a moral obligation and right of the state to punish guilty collectives, e.g., those collectives guilty of significant wrongdoing. Secondarily, collective punishment is justified to the extent that it maximizes social utility, or, that it at least takes social utility considerations seriously (for accounts of retributive individual punishment, see Corlett, 1993; Kant, 1965; Murphy, 1970; Murphy, 1979; Murphy, 1987). This retributivist justification of collective punishment is logically compatible with punishment individualism as well as punishment collectivism (*see* BENTHAM, JEREMY; KANTIAN ETHICS; MILL, JOHN STUART; UTILITARIAN-ISM).

Collective Proportional Punishment

Both utilitarian and retributivist views of collective punishment must take seriously the notion that whatever punishment is inflicted on a collective must "fit" (or be proportional to) the wrongdoing for which that collective is liable. Proportional punishment is *not* the same as *lex talionis*: "an eye for an eye, a tooth for a tooth." For proportional punishment recognizes, as *lex talionis* does not, that some cases of wrongdoing cannot be satisfactorily punished in such an exacting way. Instead, approximate proportional punishment is the aim of fair punishment. Although there are difficulties with exactness in determining the precise punishment for the wrongdoing, the problem of proportional punishment seems to face every view of punish-

ment. It is recognized as a difficulty by both Bentham and Kant, respectively (Bentham, 1946; Kant, 1965). Proportional punishment must take into account at least the following factors of each case of collective punishment. First, the extent of the punishment must be congruent with the degree of negligence. Second, the harshness of the punishment must be according to the extent to which the collective intended the negative outcome of the wrongdoing. Third, punishment is mitigated to the extent that the collective was epistemically non-responsible concerning the probable consequences of the act or omission which amounted or led to the wrongdoing. Fourth, mitigation or excuse in relation to collective punishment is contingent on the degree to which the collective acted freely or voluntarily concerning the wrongdoing. In short, proportional punishment is contingent on the degree to which the collective agent acted as a liable agent. Perhaps there is nothing except moral intuition, a sense of fairness, and a careful examination and consideration of such "facts" of each case that can best enable decisions about collective punishment to be administered properly and justly.

While some cases of collective punishment seem relatively easy to handle with fairness, others are less simple. Take the case of the Union Carbide toxic chemical leak in Bhopal, India, the result of which was the killing and harming of thousands of persons. Or consider the Exxon Valdez disaster which forever destroyed the environment of Prince William Sound. What (proportional) punishment could possibly suffice in such cases? (It is assumed here that these corporations themselves are indeed to some extent morally and legally liable for the wrongdoings mentioned.) Perhaps these are some of the collective wrongdoings which in some way coincide with the problems of proportional punishment facing courts in cases of individuals guilty of mass unjustified homicide. There seems to be nothing which can suffice to punish such perpetrators. Thus proportional punishment is unrealizable. It would not follow, however, that the courts ought not to punish such wrongdoers as severely and fairly as humanly possible.

Methods of Collective Punishment

Perhaps the most widely discussed method of collective punishment is the proposal of adverse publicity and/or fines of corporations guilty of wrongdoing (Corlett, 1987; Corlett, 1988; Corlett, 1992; French, 1984; May, 1987). But what is rarely addressed is the possibility of the administration of seizure of collective assets and/or hard treatment. Perhaps this is at least partly because it is difficult to understand precisely *how* the state might mete out such punishments against guilty collectives. But if law is to track objectively true morality, especially in matters of punishment and responsibility, then the law must take seriously the possibility of collective punishment. This seems to suggest that hard treatment, the seizure of collective assets, etc., must be viewed as live options in at least some cases of collective wrongdoing. If collectives are moral and legal agents, then they simply must be treated as such. The implications of this point for the sentencing of guilty collectives need to be explored.

Bibliography

Bentham, J. (1946). *The Principles of Morals and Legislation.* New York: Hafner Press.

Corlett, J. A. (1987). French on corporate punishment: Some problems. *Journal of Business Ethics,* 7, 205–210.

Corlett, J. A. (1988). Corporate responsibility and punishment. *Public Affairs Quarterly,* 2, 1–16.

Corlett, J. A. (1992). Collective punishment and public policy. *Journal of Business Ethics,* 11, 207–216.

Corlett, J. A. (1993). Foundations of a Kantian theory of punishment. *The Southern Journal of Philosophy,* 31, 263–216.

Feinberg, J. (1970). *Doing and Deserving.* Princeton: Princeton University Press.

Feinberg, J. (1989). *Reason and Responsibility,* 7th (edn). Belmont, Calif.: Wadsworth Publishing Company.

French, P. (1984). *Collective and Corporate Responsibility.* New York: Columbia University Press.

Hampton, J. (1984). The moral education theory of punishment. *Philosophy and Public Affairs,* 13, 208–238.

Hart, H. L. A. (1968). *Punishment and Responsibility.* Oxford: Oxford University Press.

Hume, D. (1875). Of the immortality of the soul. In *Essays Moral, Political and Literary,* vol. 2, eds T. H. Green & T. H. Grosse. London: Longmans.

Kant, Immanuel. (1965). *The Metaphysical Elements of Justice,* trans. J. Ladd. London: Macmillan.

May, L. (1987). *The Morality of Groups.* Notre Dame: Notre Dame University Press.

Menninger, K. (1968). *The Crime of Punishment.* New York: Viking.

Murphy, J. G. (1970). *Kant: Philosophy of Right.* New York: St. Martin's.

Murphy, J. G. (1979). Kant's theory of criminal punishment. In J. G. Murphy (ed.) *Retribution, Justice and Therapy: Essays in the Philosophy of Law.* Dordrecht, the Netherlands: D. Reidel.

Murphy, J. G. (1987). Does Kant have a theory of punishment? *Columbia Law Review,* 87, 509–532.

Rawls, J. (1955). Two concepts of rules. *The Philosophical Review,* 64, 3–32.

J. ANGELO CORLETT

collective responsibility A collective is any collection of persons and/or non-persons which constitutes a diversified whole. Collectives vary in structure, from highly organized conglomerates such as large corporations, universities, and the like, to random collectives such as mobs having minimal or no organizational structure. The problem of collective responsibility concerns the possibility of such collectives being responsible agents.

But "responsibility" is an ambiguous term, having several senses. There are duty, blame, praise, causal, and liability senses of "responsibility", each of which might be construed either legally or morally (Corlett, 1992). There are also different ways in which a collective might be responsible: retrospectively, for the future, or *tout court* (Feinberg, 1988–9). In the context of moral philosophy, however, discussion has focused on the extent to which collectives of certain kinds (Corlett, 1992; French, 1984; Held, 1970; May, 1987) are (French, 1984; May, 1987) or could be (Corlett, 1992) properly deemed retrospectively and morally liable for an untoward action, event, or state of affairs. Such collective liability is discussed in contexts of racism (McGary, 1986), corporate crimes or torts (Corlett, 1988a; Corlett, 1988b; French, 1984; French, 1992; May, 1987; Wilkins, 1992), military groups (French, 1972; Wilkins, 1992), random collectives (Held, 1970; May, 1987), the law in general (Feinberg, 1970), and even in more general terms (Corlett, 1992; French, 1991; French, 1992; May, 1992; Mellema, 1988). Focus in the present article is on collective, retrospective, moral liability responsibility for wrongdoings.

There are at least two opposing views on collective moral responsibility, each founded on certain metaphysical presuppositions. *Methodological individualism* states that to attribute moral properties to collectives is to mistake what are fundamentally and irreducibly properties of individuals for collective ones. That is, language about collective moral properties is reducible to the language of individual relations. More precisely, "Social processes and events should be explained by being deduced from (a) principles governing the behavior of participating individuals, and (b) descriptions of their situations" (Watkins, 1973). This position is dubbed "strong analytic individualism," and its content is described in the following way: "everyday collectivity concepts are analyzable without remainder in terms of concepts other than collectivity concepts, in particular, in terms of the concept of an individual person, his goals, beliefs, and so on" (Gilbert, 1989). As a species of this sort of position, *Moral responsibility individualism* holds that it is unjustified to ascribe moral responsibility to collectives because statements about collective moral responsibility are reducible to those of morally responsible individual agents within the collective (Lewis, 1948). From this, it is argued, talk of collective moral responsibility is meaningless. There are pure ontological versions of individualism, but I am here concerned with its reductionist counterpart.

But just what does the moral responsibility individualist mean when she argues that collective moral responsibility statements are reducible to those of individual moral responsibility? "Reducible" seems to mean something like "linguistically reducible" or "redescribable in terms of." In other words, the moral responsibility individualist argues that all statements of collective moral responsibility are linguistically redescribable in terms of those individuals (being members of the collective) who are morally responsible for something. But what

does this mean? "Linguistic reducibility" means that collective moral responsibility statements are redescribable, without loss of cognitive meaning, in terms of individual moral responsibility statements.

Notice, however, for what the reductionist (individualist) seems to argue. She is claiming that all statements of collective moral responsibility are linguistically redescribable, without loss of cognitive meaning, to statements of individual moral responsibility. Yet for individualism to succeed it must be shown that collective moral responsibility ascriptions are *unreasonable* or *unjustified*. But from the supposition that collective moral responsibility statements are completely redescribable in terms of individual moral responsibility, it does *not* logically follow that collective moral responsibility ascriptions are unreasonable or unjustified.

The reason for this is because the successful redescription of collective moral responsibility statements provides one with an *identity* relation between the collectivist statements on the one hand, and the individualist ones on the other hand. This means that the set of collective moral responsibility statements being redescribed or "reduced" is logically equivalent to the set of individual statements which redescribe it. Given Gottlob Frege's Law of the substitutivity of co-referential terms or expressions in propositional attitude contexts ("If a declarative sentence S has the very same cognitive information content as a declarative sentence S' then S is informative ("contains an extension of our knowledge") if and only if S' is (does)" (Frege, 1984; Salmon, 1986)), equivalent expressions retain truth and are substitutable for one another in *any* propositional attitude context. Thus the belief (or proposition attitude) that "The Exxon Corporation is morally responsible (liable) for the oil spill in Prince William Sound and ought to be severely punished with impunity" is indeed reducible to and redescribable in terms of the moral responsibility and punishability of certain individuals of Exxon at the time of the disaster (perhaps in terms of Exxon's President at the time of the disaster, as well as certain members of the Board of Directors and higher-level managers who served Exxon at the time of the decisions made which "caused" the incident, etc.). But this hardly shows that *collective* responsibility ascriptions are unreasonable or unjustified. The point here is that the linguistic reducibility of collectivist statements does not affect the *elimination* of the sense or meaningfulness of such language. For if the moral responsibility individualist's reduction preserves truth (and sense), then both the collectivist *and* the individualist statements about moral responsibility share the same truth-value. It would appear, moreover, that the moral responsibility individualist is in fact committed to the very meaning of the statements she seeks to eliminate or render senseless! On what basis, then, would collective moral responsibility claims (at least some of them) be unreasonable or unjustified?

A view which affirms the meaningfulness of collective moral responsibility talk is *moral responsibility collectivism*. This position, in its various forms, is well represented (Bates, 1971; Cooper, 1968; Corlett, 1992; French, 1984; Held, 1970; May, 1987; May, 1992). But the failure of the moral responsibility individualist's reductionism to render senseless collective moral responsibility statements is insufficient reason to infer that the information content of collective moral responsibility language is meaningful. Substance must be provided for such claims. One way to attempt this is by providing conditions which, if satisfied, would make a collective morally liable for a wrongful act, event, or state of affairs.

One condition of collective moral responsibility in the context, for instance, of corporate-collective wrongdoing and harm to others, is that those officially working "for" the corporation *act intentionally* in regard to the wrongdoing (*see* INTENTIONALITY). For an agent to act intentionally, she must act according to her beliefs, wants, and desires (Goldman, 1970). To be sure, there are degrees to which agents within a collective might be said to act intentionally and liably concerning a wrongdoing. One might do so in a strong sense, such as when a higher-level manager or the Board of Directors acts or omits to act in such a way so as to become a contributory cause of the untoward event, act, or state of affairs. There is also a weak sense of intentionality, whereby those in lower-level managerial positions act or omit to act as contributory causes of the wrongdoing. Here a hierarchical notion of the power to effect corporate change is assumed.

The case for collective intentionality has been set forth, defended (French, 1984; May, 1987), and criticized (Corlett, 1988a/b) in various ways. But the way the typical corporation in the United States is organized, few individuals act intentionally. Yet a collective's acting intentionally is crucial for it's being legitimately ascribed moral liability.

It would seem, then, that collective moral liability ascriptions are justified to the extent that each and every individual member of the collective has significant power to act intentionally in relation to the specific wrongdoing in question. This might well require the restructuring of the typical US corporation, which is currently structured along the lines of a hierarchical model of organization (Hersey & Blanshard, 1977; Katz & Kahn, 1966). It might very well imply that to legitimately hold collectives liable for wrongdoings (and hence make US capitalism a morally viable economic system which can and does take corrective justice seriously), such entities must resemble something akin to a democratically organized structure. For within such a structure, collectives will be more likely to provide each and every individual with sufficient power to intentionally effect change within the organization to make collective liability ascriptions less problematic. Under such conditions, it would make much better sense to say of Exxon that it (e.g., the individuals of Exxon) is (are) liable for the oil spill which destroyed Prince William Sound.

There are at least two different ways in which a corporate structure might be democratized: representatively or directly. When a corporation is democratized in a representative manner, a corporation's top managers are elected by its employees to represent the employees on matters of institutional obligations, rights, etc. However, representative corporate democracy provides the employees with insufficient opportunities to significantly determine corporate policy which in turn affects employees' activities (McMahon, 1989). Thus directly democratic corporate structures are preferred over less direct ones insofar as the empowerment of all members of the corporation is concerned. This might mean that "some form of codetermination" of corporate policy, "in which boards of directors contain in equal numbers representatives of employees of nonemployee investors," is preferable to representative corporate democracy (McMahon, 1989).

But there is more to collective intentional agency (action or omission) than the empowerment of employees. What is also required is a *publicity condition* which would clearly state to each and every individual that he or she will be held accountable (either personally and/or as a corporate agent) for corporate wrongs to the extent that he or she was an intentional agent concerning them. Currently, no such communication is made to corporate employees in a consistent and unambiguous manner. So it is far from obvious that (in their assuming a position in a corporation) employees willingly or intentionally assume liability for some other individual's action or omission. It is important, then, that the publicity condition is satisfied for collective liability ascriptions to be plausible.

If both a restructuring of US corporations and the empowering of each and every individual within such collectives are effected, then it is less morally problematic to say of an organized, decision-making corporation that *it* can legitimately be held liable for "its" wrongs.

However, collective intentionality is not the only condition requisite for legitimate attributions of collective responsibility. For it is possible that a corporation is democratically structured for intentional action (or inaction, as the case may be), yet lacks a crucial capacity for *voluntariness* which wold render it non-responsible for an untoward event (*see also* FREE WILL).

To say that a corporation is a voluntary agent means, at the very least, that the corporation "acts freely." This means it is sufficient that a corporation have the capacity to have a higher-order volition concerning an action, event or state of affairs. In turn, this means that it would be able to "really want" to do what it does, even if it lacks the ability to do otherwise. But acting freely, if it is a condition at all, is but a sufficient condition of voluntariness and moral responsibility (Frankfurt, 1988). And some would argue that the ability to do otherwise is a necessary condition of freedom. There are higher-order compatibilists who argue that the ability to do otherwise is a necessary condition of freedom (Lehrer, 1991), and there are incompatibilists who arrive at the same conclusion (van Inwagen, 1983). In any case, it is clear that in general

voluntariness is necessary for an agent's being legitimately held morally liable for wrongdoing. And collective moral responsibility requires voluntariness which in turn requires at least either the corporate capacity to act freely or the corporate ability to do otherwise.

Not only are collective intentionality and voluntariness required for collective moral responsibility, so too is collective epistemic action. What this means is that a collective, in order to qualify as a morally liable agent concerning a certain untoward action, event or state of affairs, must have acted knowingly. *Acting knowingly* involves more than an agent's merely believing that such and such is the case in regards to a certain policy and its possible outcomes. It involves, among other things, that agent's being justified in believing certain things about a policy enacted by the agent. Moreover, it involves that agent's duty to reflect on and consider various alternative actions or policies. In short, it involves critical reflection on the part of the agent.

The answer to the question of whether or not collectives are the kinds of agents which qualify as epistemic agents which act knowingly is contingent, at least in part, on the extent to which the collective is directly democratic and solidary, and the extent to which collectives qualify as epistemic agents at all (Corlett, 1991; Corlett, 1996; Fuller, 1988; Goldman, 1992; Schmitt, 1987; Schmitt, 1994). What is clear is that the capacity to act knowingly is requisite for a collective's being legitimately ascribed moral liability.

But even if a collective acts intentionally, voluntarily, and knowingly, there are cases in which these conditions do not jointly suffice for our ascribing to it moral liability. Consider The Schmexxon Corporation, and oil conglomerate with the same strength of assets as Exxon, except that Schmexxon is directly and democratically structured, acts with intent, voluntariness, and knowledge to transport oil by way of Prince William Sound. And, just as with Exxon, a Schmexxon tanker loses thousands of gallons of crude oil into the Sound. Even though Schmexxon (unlike Exxon) takes precautions well beyond what is required by law, and above and beyond what any competing corporation has even considered taking, there was a spill. But it is discovered that the spill was caused by natural disaster of some sort (say, an earth-quake's sending the tanker crashing into a reef), not the result of human error. So even though Schmexxon acted intentionally, voluntarily, and knowingly in shipping the oil through the Sound, it is not morally liable for the oil spill, though it might be held "strictly liable" by the law for a variety of reasons.

The example of Schmexxon is intended to demonstrate that additional requirements must be satisfied by morally liable agents, namely, guilt and fault. A guilty agent must be "at fault" in doing X for that agent to be morally liable for X. So it is for corporations. Since Schmexxon cannot reasonably be held at fault for the oil spill in question (because it was caused by a natural disaster), it cannot be held morally liable for it. Again, this does not imply that Schmexxon cannot be held *legally* liable for the oil spill. For considerations of social utility might suggest that there is good reason to hold corporations in the oil-transport industry strictly (legally) liable for oil spills. In any case, collective *fault* must obtain in order for the corporation to be legitimately construed as being morally liable for the disaster.

Bibliography

Bates, S. (1971). The responsibility of "random collections". *Ethics*, **81**, 343–9.

Cooper, D. E. (1968). Collective responsibility. *Philosophy*, **43**, 258–68.

Corlett, J. A. (1988a). Corporate responsibility and punishment. *Public Affairs Quarterly*, **2**, 1–16.

Corlett, J. A. (1988b). Schefflerian ethics and corporate social responsibility. *Journal of Business Ethics*, **7**, 631–8.

Corlett, J. A. (1991). Social epistemology and social cognition. *Social Epistemology*, **5**, 135–49.

Corlett, J. A. (1992). *Moral compatibilism: Rights, Responsibility, Punishment and Compensation*. Ph.D. dissertation, University of Arizona.

Corlett, J. A. (1996). *Analyzing Social Knowledge*. Lanham, Md.: Rowman & Littlefield.

Feinberg, J. (1970). *Doing and Deserving*. Princeton: Princeton University Press.

Feinberg, J. (1988–9). "Responsibility for the future" and "responsibility *tout court*". *Philosophy Research Archives*, **14**, 73–113.

Frankfurt, H. G. (1988). *The importance of What We Care About*. Cambridge: Cambridge University Press.

Frege, G. (1984). *Collective Papers on Mathematics, Logic, and Philosophy*. ed. B. McGinnis; trans. M. Black, V. H. Dudman, P. Geatch, H. Kaal, E.-H. W. Kluge, B. McGinnis. Oxford: Blackwell.

French, P. (ed.). (1972). *Individual and Collective Responsibility*. Cambridge: Schenkman.

French, P. (1984). *Collective and Corporate Responsibility*. New York: Columbia University Press.

French, P. (ed.). (1991). *The Spectrum of Responsibility*. New York: St. Martin's.

French, P. (1992). *Responsibility Matters*. Lawrence, Kan: Kansas University Press.

Fuller, S. (1988). *Social Epistemology*. Bloomington, Ind.: Indiana University Press.

Gilbert, M. (1989). *On Social Facts*. Princeton: Princeton University Press.

Goldman, A. (1970). *A Theory of Human Action*. Princeton: Princeton University Press.

Goldman, A. (1992). *Liaisons*. Cambridge, Mass.: MIT Press.

Held, V. (1970). Can a random collection of individuals be morally responsible? *Journal of Philosophy*, **67**, 471–80.

Hersey, P. & Blanshard, K. H. (1977). *Management of Organizational Behaviour: Utilizing Human Resources*. Englewood Cliffs, NJ: Prentice-Hall.

Katz, D. & Kahn, R. L. (1966). *The Social Psychology of Organizations*. New York: John Wiley & Sons.

Lehrer, K. (1991). *Metamind*. Oxford: Oxford University Press.

Lewis, H. D. (1948). Collective responsibility. *Philosophy*, **23**, 3–18.

May, L. (1987). *The Morality of Groups*. Notre Dame: Notre Dame University Press.

May, L. (1992). *Sharing Responsibility*. Chicago: University of Chicago Press.

McGary, H. (1986). Morality and collective liability. *Journal of Value Inquiry*, **20**, 157–65.

McMahon, C. (1989). Managerial authority. *Ethics*, **100**, 33–53.

Mellema, G. (1988). *Individuals, Groups, and Shared Moral Responsibility*. New York: Peter Lang.

Salmon, N. (1986). *Frege's Puzzle*. Cambridge, Mass.: MIT Press.

Schmitt, F. (ed.). (1994). *Socialising Epistemology*. Lanham: Rowman & Littlefield.

Synthese. (1987). Issue devoted to social epistemology, guest (ed.)F. Schmitt.

van Inwagen, P. (1983). *An Essay on Free Will*. Oxford: Oxford University Press.

Watkins, J. W. N. (1973). Ideal types and historical explanation. In A. Ryan (ed.) *The Philosophy of Social Explanation*. Oxford: Oxford University Press.

Wilkins, B. (1992). *Terrorism and Collective Responsibility*. London: Routledge.

J. ANGELO CORLETT

commission A payment for the provision of a service. The sum given to an agent or broker by a principal or middleman in payment for services provided (Avneyon, 1988).

In banking and financial services, commissions may be paid to an agent, a broker, or financial institution, and are normally paid upon the consummation of a transaction (Rosenberg, 1985). In the United States, fixed-rate schedules for broker members of stock and commodity exchanges were abolished on May 1, 1975, with all commissions becoming fully negotiable (Heacock, Hill, & Anderson, 1987).

Incentive compensation in sales management is based on the actions of an individual, rather than those of an entire group (Riso, 1980).

In marketing, compensation is based on a fixed formula, related to sales activity (Bennett, 1988). Commission payments may be given as a percentage of sales revenue, or a fixed payment for sales in excess of a pre-set target (Baker, 1984).

Compensation for insurance agents and brokers allows a retention of a certain percentage of premiums produced (Davids, 1990).

For the successful sale of property or negotiation of a loan transaction, a real estate broker is paid a percentage of the sale price or mortgage amount (Allen & Wolfe, 1983). Commissions may be legally claimed even in the absence of a sale if the failure of the consummation of the sale is a defect caused by an action of the seller, the terms and conditions of such claims being governed by legal jurisdictions (Brownstone & Franck, 1981).

In 1977, the Foreign Corrupt Practices Act addressed the issue of United States owned businesses operating in other nations of the world which were making payments to foreign officials, foreign political parties or party officials, or candidates for foreign political office. While these payments had not been illegal prior to 1977, they were clearly a major ethical issue in the conduct of business behavior, as these payments were often equated to bribes. After 1977, these payments were prohibited by law, if such payments were for the purpose of securing or retaining business or directing business to any person in a foreign nation (Frederick, Post & Davis, 1992; Sturdivant, 1985).

The use of a third-party or independent agents to carry out business transactions between nations is a practice which allows for the third party to charge and collect a sales commission. The FOREIGN CORRUPT PRACTICES ACT prohibits the payment of sales commissions to these individuals if the United States owned business has reason to know that any portion of the sales commission will be passed forward to foreign officials, political parties, party officials, or candidates for political office (Frederick et al., 1992).

Bibliography

Allen, R. D. & Wolfe, T. E. (eds). (1983). *The Allen and Wolfe Illustrated Dictionary of Real Estate*. New York: John Wiley.

Avneyon, E. A. (1988). *Dictionary of Finance*. New York: Macmillan.

Baker, M. J. (ed.). (1984). *Macmillan Dictionary of Marketing and Advertising*. New York: Macmillan.

Bennett, P. D. (ed.). (1988). *Dictionary of Marketing Terms*. New York: American Marketing Association.

Brownstone, D. M. & Franck, I. M. (1981). *The VNR Real Estate Dictionary*. New York: Van Nostrand Reinhold.

Davids, L. E. (1990). *Dictionary of Insurance*, 7th edn, Savage, Md.: Littlefield, Adams.

Frederick, W. C., Post, J. E. & Davis, K. (1992). *Business and Society: Corporate Strategy, Public Policy, Ethics*, 7th edn, New York: McGraw-Hill.

Heacock, M. V., Hill, K. P. & Anderson, S. C. (1987). Churning: An ethical issue in finance. *Business & Professional Ethics Journal*, 6, 3–17.

Riso, O. (ed.), . (1980). *The Dartnell Sales Manager's Handbook*, 13th edn, Chicago: Dartnell.

Rosenberg, J. M. (1985). *Dictionary of Banking and Financial Services*, 2nd edn, New York: John Wiley.

Sturdivant, F. D. (1985). *Business and Society: A Managerial Approach*, 3rd edn, Homewood, Ill.: Irwin.

MARIAN V. HEACOCK

communitarianism A theory that contends that the individual develops and can flourish morally and politically only within the context of a community. Modern-day communitarianism began in the upper reaches of Anglo-American academia in the form of a critical reaction to JOHN RAWLS' landmark 1971 book *A Theory of Justice*. Drawing primarily upon the insights of Aristotle and Hegel, political theorists such as ALASDAIR MACINTYRE (1984), Michael Sandel (1981), and Charles Taylor (1985), disputed Rawls' assumption that the principal task of government is to secure the liberties and economic resources individuals need to lead freely chosen lives.

These critics of Rawlsian LIBERALISM identified two main problems with this approach. First, Sandel among others argued that Rawlsian liberalism rests on an overly individualistic conception of the self. Whereas Rawls argues that we have a supreme interest in shaping, pursuing, and revising our own life plans, he neglects the fact that our selves are often defined or constituted by various communal attachments (e.g., ties to the family or to a religious tradition) so close to us that they can only be set aside at great cost, if at all. Hence, politics should not be concerned solely with securing the conditions for individuals to exercise their powers of choice, as there may also be a need to sustain and promote the social attachments crucial to our sense of well-being and respect.

Second, communitarians have sought to deflate the universal pretensions of liberalism. Whereas Rawls seemed to present his theory of justice as universally true, critics argued that moral judgment will depend on the language of reasons and the interpretive framework within which agents view their world, that it makes no sense to begin the political enterprise by abstracting from the interpretive dimension of human beliefs, practices, and institutions. And whatever the philosophical appeal of liberal universalism, Michael Walzer (1983) has developed at length the additional argument that *effective* social criticism must derive from and resonate with the habits and traditions of actual people living in specific times and places.

Liberals have of course responded to these criticisms (Rawls (1993) in particular has cleaned up his theory of individualist and universalist presuppositions), but a growing number are settling on the conclusion that communitarian critics of liberalism may have been motivated not so much by philosophical concerns as by certain pressing *political* concerns, namely, the negative social and psychological effects related to the atomistic tendencies of modern liberal societies. Whatever the soundness of liberal principles, in other words, the fact remains that many communitarians seem worried by a perception that traditional liberal institutions and practices have contributed to, or at least do not seem up to the task of dealing with, such modern phenomena as alienation from the political process, unbridled greed, loneliness, urban crime, and high divorce rates. And given the seriousness of these problems in the United States, it was perhaps inevitable that a "second wave" of 1990s communitarians such as Amitai Etzioni and William Galston would turn to the more practical political terrain of emphasizing SOCIAL RESPONSIBILITY and promoting policies meant to stem the erosion of communal life in an increasingly fragmented world.

Such "political" communitarians blame both the left and the right for our current malaise. The political left is chastised not just for supporting WELFARE RIGHTS economically unsustainable in an era of slow growth and aging populations, but also for shifting power away from local communities and democratic institutions and towards centralized bureaucratic structures better equipped to administer the fair and equal distribution of benefits, thus leading to a growing sense of powerlessness and alienation from the political process. Moreover, the modern welfare state with its universalizing logic of rights and entitlements has undermined family and social ties in civil society by rendering superfluous obligations to communities, by actively discouraging private efforts to help others (e.g., union rules and strict regulations in Sweden prevent parents from participating voluntarily in the governance of the daycare centers to which they send their children), and even by providing incentives that discourage the formation of families (e.g., welfare payments are cut off in most American states if a recipient marries a working person) and encourage the break-up of families (e.g., no-fault divorce in the US is often financially rewarding for the non-custodial parent, usually the father).

LIBERTARIAN solutions favoured by the political right have contributed even more directly to the erosion of social responsibilities and valued forms of communal life, particularly in Britain and the US. Far from producing beneficial communal consequences, the "INVISIBLE HAND" of unregulated free-market capitalism undermines the family (e.g., few corporations provide enough leave to parents of newborn children), disrupts local communities (e.g., following plant closings or the shifting of corporate headquarters), and corrupts the political process (e.g., since the mid-seventies special economic interests in the US have gained more power by drawing on political action committees to fund political representatives, with the consequence that representatives dependent on PAC money for their political survival no longer represent the community at large). Moreover, the valorization of greed in the Thatcher/Reagan era justified the extension of instrumental considerations governing relationships in the marketplace into spheres previously informed by a sense of uncalculated reciprocity and civic obligation.

More specifically in the American context, communitarians such as Mary Ann Glendon (1991) indict a new version of RIGHTS discourse that has achieved dominance of late. Whereas the assertion of rights was once confined to matters of essential human interest, a strident rights rhetoric has colonized contemporary political discourse, thus leaving little room for reasoned discussion and compromise, justifying the neglect of social responsibilities without which a society could not function, and ultimately weakening all appeals to rights by devaluing the really important ones.

To remedy this imbalance between rights and responsibilities, "political" communitarians propose a moratorium on the manufacture of new rights and changes to our "habits of the heart" away from exclusive focus on personal fulfillment and towards concern with bolstering families, schools, neighborhoods, and national political life, changes to be supported and reinforced by certain public policies.

While communitarians generally emphasize that changes ought to be made in the context of basic civil and political liberties (see e.g., Etzioni, 1993, part II), critics may nonetheless worry that communitarians are embarking on a slippery slope to authoritarianism. Others may worry that marginalized groups demanding new rights, e.g., homosexual couples seeking the right to legally sanctioned marriage, will be paying the price for the excesses of others if the communitarian proposal to declare a moratorium on the minting of new rights is put into effect. Most serious from the standpoint of those generally sympathetic to communitarian aspirations, however, is the worry that some communitarian ideals may conflict if translated into practice. Etzioni, for example, argues for a whole host of pro-family measures: mothers and fathers should devote more time and energy to parenting (in view of the fact that most childcare centers do a poor job of caring for children), labour unions and employers ought to make it easier for parents to work at home, and the government should force corporations to provide six months of paid leave and another year and a half of unpaid leave. The combined effect of these "changes of heart" and public policies in all likelihood would be to make "citizens" into largely private, family-centered persons.

Yet Etzioni also argues that the American political system is corrupt to the core, concluding that only extensive involvement in public affairs by virtuous citizens can remedy the situation: "once citizens are informed, they must make it their civic duty to *organize others* locally, regionally, and nationally to act on their understanding of what it takes to clean up public life in America" (1993, p. 244). But few can afford sufficient time and energy to devote themselves fully to family life and public affairs, and favouring one ideal is most likely to erode the other. Just as liberals sometimes have to choose between ideals (e.g., freedom and equality) that come into conflict with one another if a serious effort is made to realize any one of them fully, so communitarians may have to make some hard choices between valued forms of communal life.

Bibliography

Bell, D. A. (1993). *Communitarianism and Its Critics*. Oxford: Clarendon Press.

Etzioni, A. (1993). *The Spirit of Community: Rights, Responsibilities, and the Communitarian Agenda.* New York: Crown. (Written primarily for the general public).

Galston, W. A. (1991). *Liberal Purposes: Goods, Virtues, and Diversity in the Liberal State.* Cambridge: Cambridge University Press.

Glendon, M. A. (1991). *Rights Talk: The Impoverishment of Political Discourse.* New York: Free Pres.

MacIntyre. A. (1984). *After Virtue,* 2nd edn, Notre Dame, Ind.: University of Notre Dame Press.

Rawls, J. (1971). *A Theory of Justice.* Cambridge, Mass.: Harvard University Press.

Rawls, J. (1993). *Political Liberalism.* New York: Columbia University Press.

Sandel, M. (1981). *Liberalism and the Limits of Justice.* Cambridge: Cambridge University Press.

Taylor, C. (1985). *Philosophy and the Human Sciences: Philosophical Papers, 2.* Cambridge: Cambridge University Press, esp. section II.

Walzer, M. (1983). *Spheres of Justice: A Defence of Pluralism and Equality.* Oxford: Blackwell.

DANIEL A. BELL

comparable worth is a strategy for raising wages in traditionally female job categories by making the pay of women in such jobs equal to the earnings of men in comparable male-dominated lines of work.

The implementation of comparable worth begins with a *comparable-worth study*, in which a *job evaluation* is conducted to determine the skill, effort, responsibility, and working conditions of each job category in a place of employment. These factors are assigned point values, and the resulting sums are used to rank the value of all jobs to an employer. The study then identifies wage disparities among job categories with the same or a similar number of points, and a *comparable-worth policy* is adopted that adjusts the pay of job categories so as to reduce or eliminate the wage disparities.

Comparable worth assumes that disparities in income between men and women are due to sex-segregated job categories and that women's jobs have been systematically undervalued by the market. Other remedies for sex discrimination, such as the US Equal Pay Act of 1963 and Title VII of the 1964 US Civil Rights Act, do not address the wage disparities that result from the undervaluing of work done by women. In particular, removing barriers to the entry of women into traditionally male job categories so as to reduce job segregation – a strategy known as *alignment* – does not increase the wages of women in female-dominated areas.

Supporters of comparable worth generally accept the standard economic view that the value of a job is the price of a worker's productivity in a competitive labor market. Insofar as productivity is a function of skill, effort, responsibility, and working conditions, jobs that are comparable in these respects would be paid the same in a market free of discrimination. Alternatively, the lower pay of women in comparable female-dominated job categories can be assumed to result from discrimination and not lower productivity. Thus, comparable worth is offered not as an alternative to the market but as a means of identifying and correcting the distorting effects of discrimination on an otherwise free-market economy.

Comparable worth has been adopted in the United States by some municipalities, counties, and states for public-sector employees, but it has been largely rejected on the federal level. Elsewhere in the world, Australia and Canada have adopted comparable-worth policies that apply to both the public and private sectors. US courts have ruled that the failure to pay the same wages for comparable work is not a violation of law, except in cases where the intent to discriminate can be proved. Virtually no US business firms have adopted comparable-worth policies, although the widespread use of job evaluation to set wages and the efforts of corporations to comply with discrimination law have resulted in some reduction of wage disparities between male- and female-dominated job categories.

The prevalence of sex-segregated job categories and the lower wages of women in traditionally female jobs are well-documented features of the workplace, but whether these are due to discrimination is widely disputed. Many economists argue that the wage disparities between men and women can be explained by two models of occupational choice: (1) the human capital model, which holds that women choose not to acquire the knowledge and skills and to make the sacrifices that would increase their value to employers; and (2) the model of compensating differentials, according to which women, in choosing jobs, express preferences for clean, safe working conditions and other desirable features over higher pay. Critics counter that women invest less in their own human capital and prefer certain kinds of work because of discriminatory forces in the socialization process. Women may also rationally choose to invest less in themselves if their human capital is worth less in a labor market that discriminates against them. The available evidence suggests that after controlling for the variables of human capital and compensating differentials, some wage disparities still exist as a result of discrimination.

One objection to comparable worth is that job evaluation is inherently subjective and arbitrary. Studies have revealed considerable variation in evaluators' judgments of the relevant features of jobs and the number of points assigned to them. The judgments of evaluators tend, in particular, to reflect the prevailing status and pay of jobs, thereby ratifying existing patterns of discrimination. Scientifically designed, statistically reliable methods for job evaluation are available, however. Experts in the field recommend that decisions be made by consensus among groups of people who are familiar with the jobs being evaluated. Job evaluation methods can also be validated by applying them to male-dominated job categories and comparing the predicted wages with those actually earned.

Opponents of comparable worth also argue that ignoring market forces in setting wages would produce an inefficient allocation of labor with a resultant lowering of productivity. Comparable-worth policies are apt to include complex administrative structures that would further reduce productivity by increasing the involvement of government in business. This argument is criticized, however, for ignoring the extent to which the personnel practices in both government and business do not conform to the market ideal. Employers in the public sector have long used comparable-worth studies in order to match the wages of private-sector employees. And private-sector employers already use job evaluation extensively as a rational means for setting wages for the multitude of jobs in large organizations where individual productivity is difficult to measure. Comparable worth, according to its supporters, would not be a substantial departure from the existing labor market.

Comparable worth addresses a serious problem: women are paid less than men for performing comparable work. Whether comparable worth ought to be adopted, however, depends on complex empirical and normative analyses of the causes of the wage disparities and the effectiveness and desirability of the possible solutions.

Bibliography

Aaron, H. & Lougy, C. (1986). *The Comparable Worth Controversy*. Washington, DC: The Brookings Institution.

Acker, J. (1989). *Doing Comparable Worth*. Philadelphia: Temple University Press.

England, P. (1992). *Comparable Worth: Theories and Evidence*. New York: Aldine de Gruyter.

Gold, M. E. (1983). *A Dialogue on Comparable Worth*. Ithaca, NY: ILR Press.

Hartmann, H. I. (ed.). (1985). *Comparable Worth: New Directions for Research*. Washington, DC: National Academy Press.

Remick, H. (ed.). (1984). *Comparable Worth and Wage Discrimination*. Philadelphia: Temple University Press.

Sorensen, E. (1994). *Comparable Worth: Is It a Worthy Policy?* Princeton: Princeton University Press.

Treiman, D. J. & Hartmann, H. I. (eds),. (1981). *Women, Work, and Wages: Equal Pay for Jobs of Equal Value*. Washington, DC: National Academy Press.

JOHN R. BOATRIGHT

compensatory justice The fairness that obtains when an agent adequately compensates a party whom he or she has injured for the losses that party suffered. Compensatory justice is sometimes wrongly confused with retributive justice, which is the fairness that obtains when a person is adequately punished for wrongdoing. Just compensation is limited to the losses suffered by the injured party, may imply no wrongdoing, and is focused on making the injured party whole, but just retribution may be more or less severe than the injuries inflicted on victims, always implies wrongdoing, and is focused on punishing the wrongdoer. That the two notions are distinct is recognized in contemporary torts law, which allows both "punitive damages" and "compensatory damages."

The earliest treatment of compensatory justice is Aristotle's discussion of "corrective justice" in "involuntary exchanges" such as theft, assault, or murder in *Nicomachean Ethics*, book 5. Unfortunately Aristotle's overly mathematical analysis of corrective justice conflates retributive justice and compensatory justice. Aquinas, in his thirteenth-century *Summa Theologiae*, (II-II, 61, 4), more carefully distinguishes the two notions. Later moralists discussed compensatory justice under the rubric of "just restitution."

In business ethics compensatory justice is of central importance in discussions of product liability, employer liability for employee injuries, and the justification of affirmative action. In these areas the main controversies over compensatory justice have revolved over questions of (1) how much compensation injured parties are due, (2) under what conditions compensation is due, and (3) to whom and from whom compensation is due. First: some claim that compensatory justice requires that compensation should equal the actual losses suffered by the injured party. But this claim assumes it is possible to quantify all losses, which may be incorrect. What, for example, constitutes just compensation for the loss of reputation, life, or sight, or for the infliction of pain and suffering? Second: traditional moralists have held that an agent owes compensation to an injured party when (a) the agent voluntarily performed the action that inflicted the injury, (b) the injury was caused by that action and not by the injured party's own actions, and (c) the agent's action was wrongful or negligent. But twentieth-century product liability law has stretched the notion of negligence to include also an agent's failure to exercise "due care" even when an injury is due to the injured party's own actions, and strict liability theories have imposed liability even on agents who have done all they could to protect parties from harm, and so whose actions were neither wrongful nor negligent. Third: some arguments supporting affirmative action programs claim that such programs constitute the just compensation that whites as a group owe to minorities as a group for past injuries. But this raises the question whether present-day minorities should be compensated, and whether present-day whites should pay compensation, for injuries that past generations of whites inflicted on past generations of minorities. Can mere membership in a group make a person deserving of, or liable for, compensation?

Bibliography

Chapman, J. W. (1991). *Compensatory Justice*. New York: New York University Press.

MANUEL VELASQUEZ

computers and computer technology, ethical issues in   *see* ETHICAL ISSUES IN COMPUTERS AND COMPUTER TECHNOLOGY

conflict   In the vernacular, conflict is often associated with verbal or physical fighting. It is also taken as a condition in which we find ourselves, a condition that may lead to fighting. For example, we speak of a CONFLICT OF INTEREST not as a battle between two parties but as a condition in which individuals may find themselves. In social interactions there is often conflict in the simple sense that the parties' interests are not congruent. This strategic condition is most clearly illustrated in game-theoretic representations of interaction.

Game theoretically, there are two pure categories of social interaction (pure conflict and pure coordination), and one large mixed category that combines elements of conflict and coordination. (See Exhibit 1, at the end of this entry.) The most important member of the mixed category is cooperation in the face of some conflict, as in ordinary exchange. In a two-person pure conflict, one person can do better in going from one outcome to another only if the other does worse. Pure conflict is game theoretically odd. In a pure-conflict game, Row and Column have exactly opposite rankings of the outcomes, as in Game 1. The first number in each payoff cell is Row's ranking of the outcome, from first to last or from best to worst. The second number is Column's ranking. In pure conflict, when Row does better, Column does worse. In a game of pure coordination, as in Game 2, all players have identical rankings of the outcomes. The most studied and arguably the most important of all mixed-motive games is the prisoner's dilemma, as in Game 3. In this game Row and Column would prefer to coordinate if the choice were between the upper-left and lower-right cells, but they would conflict if the choice were between the upper-right and lower-left cells. The prisoner's dilemma represents the structure of simple exchange: Each of us would prefer to have what belongs to both of us but, barring that possibility, we would prefer to exchange with each other.

Coordination interactions can commonly be resolved spontaneously or with little more than modest signaling. Cooperation in mixed-motive interactions often requires some institutional structure to prevent the element of conflict from dominating. Pure-conflict interactions are rare if we think of the full structure of interactions in which we are embedded, although they may seem prevalent if we think only of momentary aspects of interactions. For example, even in warfare there are typically strong shared interests in coordinating on keeping the conflict from being too destructive. Hence, interactions that involve occasional or even pervasive conflict are commonly mixed-motive interactions. We may all be almost cut-throat in our competition, but we still all benefit from having a structure of laws and institutions to regulate our means of competing. Coordination looms in the background of virtually all our relations, even though conflict often seems to dominate the foreground.

Bibliography

Hardin, R. (1995). *All for One: The Logic of Group Conflict*. Princeto: Princeton University Press.
Schelling, T. (1960). *The Strategy of Conflict*. Cambridge, Mass.: Harvard University Press.

Exhibit 1 Categories of social interaction

Game 1: Pure Conflict

		Column	
		I	II
Row	I	1 , 4	4 , 1
	II	3 , 2	2 , 3

Game 2: Pure Coordination

		Column	
		I	II
Row	I	1 , 1	2 , 2
	II	2 , 2	1 , 1

Game 1: Prisoner's Dilemma or Exchange

		Column	
		Yield x	Keep x
Row	Yield y	2 , 2	4 , 1
	Keep y	1 , 4	3 , 3

RUSSELL HARDIN

conflict of interest occurs if and only if a person. P is in a relationship with one or more others requiring P to exercise judgment in their behalf, and P has a (special) interest tending to interfere with the proper exercise of judgment in that relationship. The crucial terms in this definition are "relationship," "judgment," "interest," and "proper exercise of [that] judgment."

Relationship: This term is quite general, including any connection between P and another person justifying that other's reliance on P for a certain purpose. So, for example, employers typically have such a connection with their employees.

Judgment: Judgment (as used here) is the ability to make certain decisions correctly more often than would a simple clerk with a book of rules and all – and only – the same information. Some jobs, such as assembly-line worker, require little or no judgment; most, especially at the professional level, require a good deal.

Interest: An interest is any loyalty, concern, emotion, or other feature of a situation tending to make P's judgment (in that situation) less reliable than it would normally be (without rendering P incompetent). Financial influences and family connections are the most common interests discussed in this context, but love, prejudice, gratitude, and the like can also be interests.

Proper Exercise: What constitutes proper exercise of judgment is generally a question of social fact, including what people ordinarily expect, what *P* or the group *P* belongs to invite others to expect, and what various laws, professional codes, or the like require. What is proper exercise of judgment in one job may well not be in another. For example, a lawyer who resolves every reasonable doubt in favor of an employer when presenting the employer's case in court exercises professional judgment properly; an industrial chemist who does the same thing when presenting research at a conference does not.

What's wrong with conflict of interest? To have a conflict of interest is to be less reliable than one normally is (that is, to be less deserving of reliance). In this respect, the interest in question is *special*: To exercise one's judgment when one has a conflict of interest is to take an unusual risk of error. A conflict of interest is not simply a conflict within one's interests, commitments, or values. Rather, it is a conflict between some special interest and the proper exercise of competent judgment. So, for example, I do not have a conflict of interest just because I promised to work here and also promised to work somewhere else during the same period. That conflict of commitment does not threaten my judgment. I would, however, have a conflict of interest if, as director of purchasing, I had to choose among suppliers when one was my daughter. I would find it harder than a stranger to judge accurately the relative quality of her product or service. Would I be harder on her than a stranger would, easier, or just the same? Who knows?

Accountants often describe this inability to judge as someone less involved would as a loss of "objectivity"; other professions have other terms. But the underlying idea is the same: The judgment in question depends on something it does not ordinarily depend on, something it should not depend on. A conflict of interest is therefore objectionable for at least one of three reasons:

1) Insofar as *P* is unaware of the conflict, she is incompetent. We generally suppose people in positions of responsibility to know their limits, especially when these are obvious.

2) If those justifiably relying on *P* for a certain judgment do not know of *P*'s conflict of interest and *P* knows (or should know) that they do not, *P* is allowing them to believe that she is what she is not; she is, in effect, deceiving them (since their reliance on her is justified until she reveals what she knows).

3) Even if *P* informs those justifiably depending on her judgment that she has a conflict of interest, her judgment will still be less reliable than it ordinarily is. *P* therefore risks appearing less competent than usual (and perhaps less competent than someone in her position should be). Conflict of interest can be a technical problem even when no longer a moral problem (and, even as a technical problem, can harm the reputation of the profession, occupation, or individual in question).

What can be done about a conflict of interest? One can *avoid* some conflicts of interest (for example, by putting one's stocks in a blind trust or by refusing a gift); *escape* others (for example, by divesting oneself of the conflicting interest or by withdrawing from, or redefining, the relationship of dependence); or, in some cases, *disclose* the conflict to those relying on one's judgment (thereby preventing deception and allowing those relying on one to adjust their reliance accordingly). In general, disclosure does not end the conflict of interest but merely renders it less likely to be harmful.

P has a *potential* conflict of interest if and only if *P* has a conflict of interest with respect to a certain judgment, but is not yet in a situation where he must make that judgment. Potential conflicts of interest, like time bombs, may or may not go off.

P has an *actual* conflict of interest if and only if *P* has a conflict of interest with respect to a certain judgment and is in a situation where he must make that judgment.

P has a (mere) *apparent* conflict of interest if and only if *P* does not have a conflict of interest (actual or potential), but someone other than *P* would nonetheless be justified in concluding (however tentatively) that *P* does have a conflict. An apparent conflict is objectionable for the same reason that any apparent wrongdoing is objectionable. It may mislead people about their security, inviting waste of resources on unnecessary precautions. An apparent conflict is resolved by making available enough information to show that there is no actual or potential conflict.

Bibliography

Davis, M. (1992). Conflict of interest. *Business & Professional Ethics Journal*, 1, 17-28.
Davis, M. (1993). Conflict of interest revisited. *Business & Professional Ethics Journal*, 12, 21-41.
McMunigal, K. (1992). Rethinking attorney conflict of interest doctrine. *Georgetown Journal of Legal Ethics*, 5, 823-77.

MICHAEL DAVIS

conscience is inner awareness of right and wrong, good and evil. Persons said to "have a conscience" manifest three characteristics: 1) they evaluate actions, motives, and states of character to determine if these are appropriate from a moral point of view; 2) they experience feelings such as guilt or satisfaction that are consistent with moral judgments that they have made; and 3) they are disposed to act on the basis of their moral perceptions.

Historically, there has been much debate about the nature and the sources of moral awareness. Thomas Aquinas (1225–1274) argued that conscience is an act of reason in which we apply our knowledge to an individual case. This was evident, he thought, from the etymology of the word: *cum alio scientia*, or knowledge related to something. The causes of conscience are various, Aquinas held, since knowledge is formed in many ways. However, the ultimate starting-points are self-evident practical principles naturally known by all. For example, what human beings have a natural inclination to seek in order to preserve their being is apprehended as good and becomes a motive to action.

Eighteenth-century British moralists such as Shaftesbury, Hutcheson, and Hume viewed conscience as a moral sense, an inborn faculty that produced feelings of approval and repugnance. Analogous to aesthetic appreciations, these intuitions were thought of as immediate perceptions of moral qualities in concrete situations. Modern behaviorists, on the other hand, explain conscience as conditioned responses to stimuli, learned through positive and negative reinforcers that are either natural or fashioned by society.

Sigmund Freud (1856–1939) distinguished three systems in the personality: id, ego, and superego. The latter includes an ego-ideal and a conscience that originate in the child's conceptions of what its parents consider to be morally good and bad. Rewards and punishments exercised by parents and other prestige figures contribute to an internalization of external authority that guides the individual's moral judgments.

According to Aquinas, errors in judgment about moral matters are possible, especially given the fact that we must have accurate information about particulars in order to make correct assessments in individual situations. This gives rise to questions concerning whether an erroneous conscience always binds us, and whether we are ever morally at fault for obeying our erring conscience. One may argue that we must always act according to our conscience, since we are in effect judging that this is the morally right act. Otherwise, in disobeying conscience we would be doing what we perceive to be wrong and violating our own integrity. This is not to say, however, that an erroneous conscience always excuses us from moral blame for our action. If we are ignorant of circumstances that it is our responsibility to know, or if we willfully and negligently fail to inform ourselves of relevant facts, then we act badly in following our conscience. Thus, we have a twofold moral duty – to form our conscience as well as we are able, and to follow our conscience once it is formed.

It can be inferred from this that sometimes others may have a moral duty to prevent someone from following his or her conscience, for example, if that person is bent upon great harm because of an ignorant or crazed judgment. Distorted awareness can contribute to mistaken dictates of conscience, but others in society may be obliged to prevent wrongful acts that the individual misperceives to be right.

Bibliography

Aquinas, T. (1947). *Summa Theologica*. New York: Benziger Brothers. (See I, 79, 12–13; I–II, 19, 5–6.)

Ashmore, R. B. (1987). *Building a Moral System.* Englewood Cliffs, NJ: Prentice-Hall.

Broad, C. D. (1952). Conscience and conscientious action. In *Ethics and the History of Philosophy.* London: Routledge & Kegan Paul, 244–62.

Freud, S. (1962). *The Ego and the Id.* New York: W. W. Norton.

Selby-Bigge, L. A. (ed.). (1964). *British Moralists.* Indianapolis, Ind.: Bobbs-Merrill.

ROBERT B. ASHMORE

consent   An act by which one freely changes the existing structure of rights and obligations, typically by undertaking new obligations and authorizing others to act in ways that would otherwise have been impermissible for them.

Consent is a concept of central importance in moral, political, legal, and economic contexts. In typical cases, a person's consent to another's acts removes moral or legal objections to, or liability for, the performance of those acts. In medical practice, for instance, the "informed consent" of a patient to a procedure can justify the physician's actions. In law and business, the maxim *volenti non fit injuria* (the willing person is not wronged) governs a wide range of acts and transactions. And in politics, it is often supposed that it is "the consent of the governed" that justifies the use of official coercion to compel obedience to law.

Consenting is closely associated with acts like promising, contracting, entrusting, etc. Justification by appeal to consent is especially central within liberal thought. Liberalism conceives of persons as self-conscious sources of value who have rights to govern themselves (within the bounds set by the rights of others). Consent is seen as the means by which this individual moral liberty may be limited in a fashion consistent with respect for liberty.

Consent may be either express or tacit. Express consent is consent given by an explicit verbal or written undertaking or by other direct but nonverbal consensual acts (such as raising one's hand). Tacit consent is given by actions or omissions (such as inactivity or silence) that do not involve an explicit undertaking, but that nonetheless constitute the making of a morally significant choice in the context of a clear, noncoercive choice situation. Some attempted justifications by consent appeal not to actual (express or tacit) consent, but to hypothetical consent. Hypothetical consent can be ideal (what fully rational persons would consent to) or dispositional (what real persons would have consented to, had they been able). Only appeals to the latter (by which we justify, e.g., imposing medical treatment on an unconscious injured person) seem to be genuine justifications by consent. Appeals to the former are really disguised attempts to justify by showing that an arrangement is best or acceptable, independent of people's consent.

Consent of whatever form can only justify acts or arrangements given the satisfaction of a complex set of conditions for binding consent. First, there are knowledge conditions (consent must be "informed"). Second, binding consent must be intentional. Third, consent can only be given by the competent (which may exclude in various contexts apparent consent given by the insane, severely retarded, emotionally disturbed, immature, intoxicated, etc.). Fourth, binding consent must be voluntary (limiting it to cases not involving the extraction of consent by coercion, undue influence, exploitation, unfair bargaining advantage, etc.). Finally, consent only binds given acceptability of content. In most legal systems, for instance, agreements you make to commit crimes, become a slave, or allow yourself to be killed are not enforceable.

See also **authority; contracts and contracting; liberalism; Locke, John; obedience, to authority and to the law; promises, promising**

Bibliography

Beran, H. (1987). *The Consent Theory of Political Obligation.* London: Croom Helm.

Feinberg, J. (1986). *Harm to Self.* New York: Oxford University Press.

Kleinig, J. (1982). The ethics of consent. *Canadian Journal of Philosophy*, supp. vol. 8, 91–118.

Rawls, J. (1971). *A Theory of Justice.* Cambridge, Mass.: Harvard University Press.

Simmons, A. J. (1993). *On the Edge of Anarchy: Locke, Consent, and the Limits of Society.* Princeton: Princeton University Press.

A. JOHN SIMMONS

consequentialism is the claim that the moral evaluation of acts, dispositions, or any other possible object of moral assessment, is exclusively related to their contribution to an impartially good overall state of affairs. The continued appeal that such a conception of morality has for many of its adherents – even in the face of strenuous objections by critics – rests upon this fundamental idea. Somehow, it is thought, morality *must* have something essentially to do with how our acts, dispositions, etc., which affect the world and make it either a better or worse place. A consequentialist perspective inherently captures this idea and makes it the ultimate basis of morality.

This very general characterization covers a multitude of complexities, however, which call for some discussion. First of all, consequentialist theories can be differentiated, in part, by their reliance upon different conceptions of the good. The actual application of any consequentialist conception of ethics will necessarily presuppose some specified general conception of the good where this is defined independently of moral evaluation. Obviously, if the *moral* evaluation of our acts, dispositions, etc., depends on how these contribute to an impartially good state of affairs, to actually make such an evaluation, we must first have some conception of what is "good" or "valuable" that is independent of the moral evaluation itself. Otherwise, the consequentialist moral assessment could not get started – it would have nothing to work on. Because of this, consequentialist ethical theories must rely upon conceptions of value that are independent from *moral* evaluation.

There are a number of well-known candidates for this. For instance, the classical UTILITARIANISM of JEREMY BENTHAM (along with that of Henry Sidgwick) was fundamentally a combination of a consequentialist conception of moral evaluation with a hedonistic conception of the good that defines the good ultimately in terms of pleasure. JOHN STUART MILL'S form of this theory incorporates a more complicated idea of the good that cannot be reduced easily to the pure form of hedonism of the type Bentham held. Recent versions of utilitarianism have employed a conception of the good that is defined in terms of individual "preference" or "desire" satisfaction (see Griffin, 1986, chs. 1 and 2). And there are other

(non-utilitarian) consequentialist theories that employ fundamentally different conceptions of the good besides these (see Nagel, 1979, ch. 9, and Griffin, 1986, chs. 3 and 4). Hence, although all consequentialist theories are alike in maintaining that moral evaluation is strictly a matter of contribution to an impartially "good" state of affairs, they can be differentiated, in part, by the various conceptions of the good that might be incorporated within them.

A second major element underlying a consequentialist approach to moral evaluation is its conception of rationality. Consequentialist theories are regarded as embodying a certain form of practical rationality. This is where they gain their normative force – moral requirement being essentially a dictate of practical reason in its impartial or impersonal form. It is often thought that such practical rationality involves a "maximization" of the good. For this reason, consequentialist ethical theories are most often defined in terms of requiring a *maximizing* relation between the objects of moral assessment (acts, dispositions, etc.) and the production of an impartially good outcome.

However, this is not the only possible way to view this relation. It has been claimed by some that it is rational to be satisfied with a resulting state of affairs that is judged to be good enough even though it may be less than the best possible one, given the various open alternatives. It is therefore possible to develop a consequentialist ethical theory incorporating this (less demanding) "satisficing" conception of practical rationality (see Slote, 1985, ch. 3). The result would be a form of consequentialism requiring a promotion of the good that is "satisfactory." Hence, consequentialist theories can also be differentiated by whether they embody either a maximizing or satisficing conception of rationality.

Because a consequentialist approach to ethics places its exclusive emphasis on (good) outcomes, *any* factor associated with moral agents that has an influence on states of affairs can be assessed in consequentialist terms. Such factors have what might be called "consequentialist relevance." The most obvious such factor is an agent's *acts*. What actions are performed in the various circumstances in which one finds oneself can have a significant effect on states of affairs. Indeed, consequentialism has most often been defined exclusively in terms of the moral assessment of particular acts – that is, as providing a criterion of morally right action. However, there are other factors that have a clear influence on the acts that agents perform, and thus, at least have an important *indirect* consequentialist relevance. Prominent in this regard is the whole host of dispositions that provide the motivational background against which agents perform many (if not all) of their acts. Many of these dispositions have to do with how agents are deeply motivated to act or, more broadly, how to live their lives. And many of the acts that agents perform in the course of their lives depend, ultimately, on such motivational elements. A concern, therefore, for the development and maintenance of those dispositions (including deep traits of personal character) that will tend to bring about a good overall state of affairs can be regarded as a crucial part of any complete consequentialist approach to ethics.

The version of the theory that is most often discussed is a maximizing one, whose exclusive focus is the consequentialist assessment of particular acts – so-called "act-consequentialism." This is essentially defined by its criterion of right action that holds that an act is morally right if and only if that act will promote as much good – impartially considered – as any other feasible act open to the agent. In other words, the only acts of an agent that are morally permissible on this view are those that produce a maximally good outcome from an impartial or impersonal point of view, relative to the available alternatives. This conception of ethical requirement is a very demanding one. This is because of its inherently "impersonal" standpoint (that is, that the good produced must be regarded as such from the perspective of the interests of no particular agent), and its maximizing conception of practical rationality (requiring that such good be maximally produced). As a result of its impersonal character, the moral requirements that would typically be generated by this criterion of right acts are likely to be very demanding on the personal projects and interests of most human agents. In addition to this, because one can always be doing *something* (whatever it happens to be) to produce such maximally good outcomes, the theory is

pervasively demanding. Agents are literally *always* subject to such possibly sacrificial moral requirements on this view.

The most prominent objections to act-consequentialism stem, in various ways, from this extremely demanding character. First of all, it is simply un-intuitive from the perspective of ordinary common-sense morality to be pervasively under such demanding moral requirements. Ordinary moral intuitions usually allow for a rather large area of life where one is free from moral requirement, and thus able to pursue, without moral compunction, one's own personal projects and interests. Since this area of optional moral freedom is ruled out by the pervasiveness of the act-consequentialist perspective, so the argument goes, so much the worse for that approach. While this objection might seem question-begging (in favor of the common-sense, non-consequentialist, perspective), the sway of ordinary moral intuitions in this matter has tended to exert a strong influence in discussions of the viability of this theory.

A second, perhaps more influential, way in which the demanding nature of the act-consequentialist conception has been regarded as problematic has been to argue that it cannot adequately account for, or reflect, the "personal" perspective of ordinary human agents. According to this objection, ordinary human moral agents, as a matter of their very nature, are deeply motivated to act and, indeed, live their lives, from a *personal* perspective. Their own interests and projects have a significance that is disproportionate to that given to them by the impersonal perspective of the consequentialist conception. The act-consequentialist conception can be regarded as problematic in this regard in essentially two different ways. First, it can be alleged that it is *motivationally futile* to require such agents to abide by the pervasive, impersonally generated, consequentialist demands. Such requirements, it can be argued, simply cannot have a secure motivational backing given the deep personal bias of ordinary moral agents. Hence, it is claimed, act-consequentialism is ill-suited to the actual motivational capacities of ordinary moral agents and is, thus, to be rejected as a reasonable theory grounding such requirements. Second, it can be argued that even the *attempt* to live one's life according to such a moral conception can be positively destructive of this valuable element of human nature. It has been argued, for instance (notably, by Williams, 1973, esp. 108–18), that the INTEGRITY of an agent's personal projects and commitments can be fragmented by the attempt to abide by this sort of impersonal morality. One must, it seems, be willing to "step aside" from any personal commitment (e.g., career, friends, family, etc.) any time the consequentialist morality requires it. But this seems incompatible with the sort of attitude one must necessarily take to such deeply personal, significant, pursuits. If this is so, the attempt to live the pervasive consequentialist life would likely end up destroying the ability to maintain this sort of integrity and authenticity of one's own personal projects and commitments. If, as Williams and others claim, this is regarded as a loss of something inherently valuable, then this would certainly be a troubling aspect associated with the act-consequentialist approach.

A number of different responses to these objections to the alleged overly demanding nature of act-consequentialism have been offered. Four of these will be discussed here. The first involves defining the act-consequentialist criterion of right acts itself in terms of the "satisficing" conception of rationality discussed above. This, at least, would appear to generate moral requirements that may be far less sacrificial from an agent's personal perspective than the usual maximizing version. One would not be required to act in a way that leads to the *best* overall outcome, but rather, in such a way that the outcome is judged to be good enough. One problem with this is that if the criterion is not going to end up involving a basic indeterminacy regarding actual moral requirement, a determinate standard of satisfactoriness must be established. But it is not at all clear how one would go about doing this without relying, ultimately, upon an agent's own discretion. But, if this is so, the objective nature of the consequentialist theory might be jeopardized.

A second alternative has been to modify the act-consequentialist conception by reflecting, directly, the personal point of view. Samuel Scheffler (1982) has argued along such lines for the inclusion of what he calls an "agent-centered prerogative" which would make it *permissible* for agents to devote energy and attention to their own projects (including, perhaps, a personal commitment to promote the overall good) out of proportion to the strictly impersonal or impartial weighting involved in the pure consequentialist conception. The theory would still allow, however, for the incorporation of an act-consequentialist moral commitment *as part of* an agent's own framework of personal motivation. In this way, it is claimed, the theory would not place an excessive strain on the personal integrity of agents, and yet, could still incorporate much of the act-consequentialist conception of moral requirement. However, a major problem encountered here is, again, the apparent difficulty in determining when the (strict consequentialist) requirements should override the agent's own prerogative. If this cannot be answered in some non-arbitrary fashion, this "hybrid" theory is in danger of collapsing into a view which would place no real, clearly determinable, *requirements* on agents at all.

A third response to the demandingness objection to the act-consequentialist conception concedes that the criterion (in its usual maximizing form) is extremely demanding, but holds, nonetheless, that it is still a true account of moral requirement. Those who take this route usually attempt to show that the consequentialist conception maintains a basic coherence and rationality that has not been able to be equalled by rival, non-consequentialist moral perspectives (see, most notably, Kagan, 1989). Further, it is often argued that human nature is much more malleable – capable of being motivated to much more highly demanding moral requirements – than critics of the consequentialist view tend to think. This being so, such agents can, indeed, be motivated to act in accordance with the strict consequentialist conception (without unduly fragmenting their own personal integrity). Hence, this conception can continue to be regarded as plausible, and true, even in light of its extremely demanding nature. The issue here is whether this portrays a true picture of the motivational capacities of ordinary human moral agents, and whether certain non-consequentialist conceptions can better respond to it.

A final response on the part of some consequentialists attempts to redefine the whole theory in a way that simply excludes the act-consequentialist criterion of right action (at least as part of the motivational framework of agents generally). Moral assessment, on such views, is *primarily* directed at the inculcation and maintenance of general dispositions (including, perhaps, certain moral beliefs) and character traits which will best tend to promote the good. Morally right action, accordingly, is that which would be motivated by the best overall framework of such general dispositions. Because, on such views, there is no direct appeal to (or inclusion of) an act-consequentialist criterion of right action, and the moral assessment is directed exclusively at certain value-generating dispositional factors, there is far less likelihood of this moral conception generating demands that will tend to fragment an agent's personal integrity. Whether such indirect forms of consequentialism can be maintained in a coherent manner (excluding, as they do, an act-consequentialist assessment of acts) is a matter of some controversy.

Consequentialism in its (growing) variety of forms continues to be a major alternative in general ethical theory. Much of its plausibility depends upon a widely-shared (although, not universal) intuition that, somehow, consequences count in our moral assessments, and that those assessments should be grounded in an impartial practical rationality. However, the complete establishment of such a theory depends upon whether a stable and coherent form can be developed which will adequately reflect a plausible and complete view of human motivation.

Bibliography

Brink, D. (1986). Utilitarian morality and the personal point of view. *Journal of Philosophy*, 83, 417–38.

Griffin, J. (1986). *Well-Being*. Oxford: Clarendon Press.

Kagan, S. (1984). Does consequentialism demand too much? *Philosophy and Public Affairs*, 13, 239–54.

Kagan, S. (1989). *The Limits of Morality*. Oxford: Clarendon Press.

Nagel, T. (1979). *Mortal Questions*. Cambridge: Cambridge University Press.

Railton, P. (1984). Alienation, consequentialism, and the demands of morality. *Philosophy and Public Affairs*, 13, 134–71.

Scheffler, S. (1982). *The Rejection of Consequentialism*. Oxford: Clarendon Press.

Scheffler, S. (ed.). (1988). *Consequentialism and Its Critics*. Oxford: Oxford University Press.

Slote, M. (1985). *Common Sense Morality and Consequentialism*. London: Routledge & Kegan Paul.

Williams, B. (1973). A critique of utilitarianism. In J. J. C. Smart and B. Williams, *Utilitarianism: For and Against*. Cambridge: Cambridge University Press, 75–150.

Williams, B. (1985). *Ethics and the Limits of Philosophy*. London: Fontana Press.

WILLIAM L. LANGENFUS

consulting, ethics of   *see* ETHICS OF CONSULTING

consultants   External consultants offering advice to organizations on how to establish work environments in which ethical decision-making is the norm.

One end goal of business ethics consultants is to facilitate sound ethical decision-making in business and industry. Consultants combine the normative theories of ethics and research in business ethics with the methods and processes of organizational-development consulting to achieve that goal. They identify the factors in the organization that encourage and/or block ethical decision-making, help the organization gain the knowledge and skills needed to eliminate the barriers, and design systems and/or provide training that will enable ethical decision-making on the part of all employees.

Consultants influence the ethical climate of an organization by demonstrating the systemic nature of organizations and how the ethical climate in an organization impacts ethical decision-making; and by helping the organization design, develop, implement, and evaluate:

• organizational values that provide direction and consistency in decision-making,

• ethics strategies that define ethics goals and objectives and allow the organization to measure progress,

• ethics policies and procedures that describe how ethics strategies are to be implemented,

- guidelines for decision-makers who must deal with situations not addressed by ethics policies and procedures,

- measures of ethical effectiveness that determine if ethical standards are being maintained and are yielding the desired results and the degree of congruence between collective perceptions of the organization's values and individual values,

- support for ethical practices from formal and informal systems and application of ethical guidelines to all aspects of all jobs,

- ethical leadership practices that model ethical behavior expected by all employees,

- ethics training to enable employees to act on their responsibilities for the ethical effectiveness of the organization,

- evaluation of the impact of ethical practices on productivity and profitability,

- rewards for ethical behaviors and decisions that the organization wants to sustain, and

- respect for employees' personal values that will encourage their support for what they are asked to do for the organization. (Navron, 1990)

Consultant   Competencies   and   Professional Preparation

Cohen (1992) found in her interview with business managers and business ethics consultants that "business knowledge and the range of behavioral-science techniques associated with traditional organizational consultancy training were more critical to the success of an ethics consulting engagement than a deep understanding of philosophical theory. In their [the consultants] view, attempts to intervene in organizations without this expertise could be potentially destructive to the firm" (p. 157).

Professional preparation for business ethics consultants should include knowledge of:

- normative theoretical frameworks of business ethics;

- emperical research in ethics – discovery of practical approaches to ethical decision-making;

- organizational development and change processes.

Bibliography

Cohen, D. (1992). Resisting the right stuff: Barriers to business ethics consultation. *Proceedings of the Academy of Management Annual Meeting.* Las Vegas, Nevada: 155–9.
Navron, F. (1990). Personal interview, Navron Associates, Atlanta, Ga.

PETER J. DEAN

consumer prices and advertising

Two Models

Economists use two principal models to describe the effects of advertising on the prices consumers pay. In the Advertising = Market Power model, advertising is thought to change consumer tastes, establish brand loyalty, and ultimately raise profits and consumer prices while decreasing price sensitivity and competition. In the Advertising = Information model, advertising is seen as providing information to consumers, resulting in increased price sensitivity, lower prices, and reduced monopoly power.

Of course, price sensitivity, as well as brand loyalty, are created and supported by other factors, such as product quality, better packaging, favorable user experience, market position, warranty, and/or service. Also, the observation that companies with relatively higher advertising budgets also usually charge the higher prices can be confusing. Some see the higher prices of advertised products as clear-cut evidence that advertising causes consumers to pay more. The relationship between advertising and price is anything but clear-cut. When other factors, such as high quality, give marketers "something to say" in advertising, they are more apt to say it with more advertising support. Similarly, if quality helps increase prices and margins, then the evidence is confounded by the fact that when the profit on an individual item is higher, there is more incentive to advertise, as the return on investment will be proportionately greater. Unfortunately, it is easy for this "evidence" to be misinterpreted. Some critics of advertising have even gone so far as to imply that all advertising is wasteful and that consumer prices would be reduced by the percentage that advertising constitutes of sales (about 2 to 3 percent for a wide variety of products, but as much as 30 to 40 percent for some).

Advertising and Product Quality

The argument that advertising "explains" and communicates product quality to consumers is considered specious by some. They argue that advertising too often creates the impression of higher quality when no real differences exist. Advertising is often thought to raise costs, instill artificial preferences (i.e., create excessive product differentiation), and increase consumer prices. Indeed, there is little doubt that in many cases marketers attempt to justify price premiums and escape the intensity of price competition by using advertising to communicate marginal product benefits to consumers. Even without clear product differences advertising may enable some marketers to charge higher prices relative to competition. In the alcoholic beverage market, for example, without advertising, certain brands, such as "Absolut" vodka, could not charge their current prices.

Can we reconcile the idea that highly advertised brands charge higher prices than competitors with the notion that advertising is essential to competition? The answer is yes, as will be shown. Our arguments rely on the distinction between manufacturer price and retail price on the one hand, and relative price and absolute price on the other.

Manufacturer Prices, Retail Prices, Relative Prices, Absolute Prices

For our purposes, manufacturer price is the manufacturer's selling price, and, except in situations where there are intervening parties such as distributors, this price is usually the retailer's purchase price. The retailer's selling price refers to the retail price, and as used here is synonymous with consumer purchase price. Relative price is a ratio or difference between the price of one brand versus the price of another, measured either in retail or manufacturer prices. Absolute price is an average of all prices of products in a category. In the main, we believe that it is the effect of advertising on the long-term level of absolute consumer prices that

is the primary concern. On the other hand, it is the sums spent by manufacturers for advertising that are argued to increase prices. Retail advertising almost always features prices and has, to our knowledge, never been argued to increase prices.

In studies conducted to examine the effect of manufacturer advertising on prices, as one might imagine, support exists for both the "power" and the "information" models. It is relevant that, with a single exception, the studies examining manufacturer price reported that advertising decreases price sensitivity, while studies examining retail price concluded the opposite, that manufacturer advertising increases price sensitivity.

These studies are not necessarily in conflict. The reason is that advertised brands are often the subject of intense inter-store price competition. The manufacturer's price may initially be low to encourage retailers to carry a product and, when advertising creates product demand, the manufacturer may charge a higher price to the retailer. The retailer could pass on this increase to the consumer, but this does not often happen because of the retailer's desire to remain competitive with other retailers (inter-store competition). If a retailer wants to be known as the low-priced store it will be especially competitive on advertised products that are stocked by other retailers. Such low-priced, highly advertised brands are often used as traffic builders. Indeed, manufacturers sometimes fear that the extreme popularity of some advertised brands causes retailers to become unhappy with the intense retail price competition. When retailers are unhappy with the retail margins they earn on the manufacturer's product they may try to switch consumers to one that "is just as good," but on which the retailer earns a higher margin. The overall level of prices is a mix of the advertised products and the unadvertised products.

The real issue is not what one brand in a particular category costs consumers in relation to another, but what the absolute price level of the entire category would be without advertising. This is relevant because, although we often observe that advertised brands charge more, in reality it is the unadvertised brands that cost less. In other words, advertised brands set the price ceiling for unadvertised brands. These unadvertised brands may be able to "ride free" on the reputation created by the advertisers. "Just as good as . . . " is often the argument (sometimes valid, sometimes not) for buying the unadvertised brand.

Advertising may create brand differentiation, but this brand differentiation is relative to the products of other manufacturers. For retailers, advertised products are more of a commodity (less differentiated) as concerns retail price competition. Advertising can create additional value to the retailer for products that can create an image, act as traffic builders, and experience quick inventory turnover. For the retailer, a "quick nickel is as good as a slow dime." Indeed, advertising can "force" distribution, and it often results in far lower retail profits. In some extreme cases, the manufacturer's price of one product could be higher than for another, but because of the difference in retail profit margins the retail price is higher for the product with the lower manufacturer price.

Such effects depend on the manufacturer's distribution policy. With exclusive or selective distribution, intense inter-store competition is mitigated. The best competition involves comparison between brands and between retailers, that is, both intra-store and inter-store competition. Private labels and retail discounts counterweight the power of advertising to enable marketers to charge a higher retail price. Private-label products are not subject to inter-store comparison; however, they are usually priced below the highly advertised brands, and provide a price control through intra-store competition.

It is almost impossible to believe that consumers would be willing to pay more for a product whose sole distinction is that it is unadvertised, even if these products were of the same quality. This remains so in spite of the fact that the higher sales volume of advertised products often imparts substantial economies in product, distribution, or overhead costs, so that unadvertised products have higher costs. Why should you pay the manufacturer not to advertise the product?

Advertising can certainly help establish barriers to entry into a market in which it has differentiated brands, and created brand loyalty that new entrants must overcome. But whether such potential barriers cause consumers to pay more in the long term is highly questionable. The reasons are that manufacturer brand loyalty can cause retailers to compete more fiercely and that prices for advertised brands can set ceilings for unadvertised brands. In some sense, advertised brands can take credit for the low prices they forced competitors and retailers to charge. Unadvertised brands are responsible for keeping the prices of advertised brands from rising too high. Together, they help balance retail and manufacturer power, give the consumer more choices, and enhance price and quality competition at all levels of the distribution system.

Whether consumers, in general, are wise to pay the premiums that advertised brands charge is quite another question.

Bibliography

Albion, M. S. & Farris, P. W. (1980). The impact of advertising on the price of consumer products. *Journal of Marketing,* summer.

Farris, P. W. & Reibstein, D. J. (1979). How price, ad expenditures, and profits are linked. *Harvard Business Review,* Nov./Dec.

Steiner, R. . Manufacturer's promotional allowances, free riders, and vertical constraints. *Antitrust Bulletin,* **36** (2), 383–411.

PAUL W. FARRIS
DAVID J. REIBSTEIN

contemporary work values Contemporary work values are a set of principles of conduct and values including less dependence on, and hence less commitment to, the physical aspects of labor or work, less obedience and respect for authority for the sake of discipline and power, and a desire for more leisure time. These principles of conduct and values are drawn from the new focus of work tasks made available through a highly technological and bureaucratic society which is more highly intent on getting tasks completed and less dependent on hard, physical aspects of labor (Wayne, 1984).

During the late nineteenth century, many individuals began to question whether accumulating material goods alone was sufficient to motivate them to give most of their energy and time to a job. These individuals began to feel "right" about work in terms of individual choice and self-determination, rather than feeling "righteous" through work seen as the fulfillment of societal obligations.

From 1955 through the end of the 1970s, several new value clusters evolved from the traditional Protestant work ethic values and resulted in that ethic becoming less meaningful and seemingly less appropriate for individuals.

Major causes cited for a shift in values orientation were the women's movement, the popularity of developmental psychology, and the impact of television. Old values of upward mobility, materialism, and strictly defined social roles strong in the Protestant work ethic, were challenged by new values of entitlement and focus on one's self. By the end of the 1970s, individuals wanted to choose personal goals, reward for achievement, their roles within relationships, lifestyles within the greater organization of society, and to emphasize self-fulfillment and pleasure.

See also **Protestant work ethic**

Bibliography

Cherrington, D. J. (1980). *The Work Ethic: Working Values and Values that Work*. New York: ANA-COM.

Ravlin, E. C. (1988). *Stability of Work Values: Individual Differences and Relationships with Decision Making*. EDU ERIC, doc. no. ED303751.

Wayne, F. S. (1984). An instrument to measure adherence to the Protestant ethic and contemporary work values. Arizona: Ph.D. dissertation, Arizona State University.

F. STANFORD WAYNE

contingent work A classification that encompasses a variety of part-time, temporary, and contract jobs. Consequently, employees who are considered contingent workers are engaged in diverse types of work, ranging from migrant farming to college teaching. Contingent work may also be either voluntary, that is, the employee does not desire a permanent position, or involuntary, that is, the employee desires a permanent position but is unable to find one. Because of this diversity, contingent workers are defined as "those who have a loose affiliation with their employers" (Parker, 1994, p. 145). However, low wages, lack of benefits, and a non-permanent classification are common factors for most contingent workers.

During recent years, the number of contingent workers has drastically increased. Although statistics vary, an estimated one-fifth to one-third of all US workers are contingent. In fact, contingent jobs have been produced at a much higher rate than other types of jobs, and most are within the service industry (Hearing, 1990; Parker, 1994). Because of this increase in contingent hiring, it is more difficult for an employee to leave a contingent position in order to accept a permanent one. This trend in hiring is primarily the result of attempts to increase profit margins. Contingent workers, in the short term, do not cost the company as much, since they are typically hired at lower salaries and often are not eligible for benefits (*see* RESTRUCTURING). There is disagreement concerning the long-term profitability of hiring a contingent workforce (Hearing, 1990).

The practice of hiring employees in contingent positions has extensive moral consequences. A primary concern regarding contingent work is the disproportionate representation of minorities, the poor, and women. Because so many contingent employees are from these populations, the growth of contingent work may perpetuate discriminatory practices in hiring (*see* DISCRIMINATION IN EMPLOYMENT). Contingent workers are also typically hired for short periods of time. Thus, contingent work increases instability for the worker and regularly relies on federal and state resources to provide for periods of unemployment. Those contingent workers that remain with a company for an extended period of time are usually not entitled to the same pay increases that permanent employees would receive. This decrease in earnings over time will impact all aspects of that employee's life as well as the lives of their children, since contingent workers are less likely to live in neighborhoods that provide a healthy environment with a quality public school.

Additionally, most contingent work does not include healthcare, leave/vacation, or retirement benefits. This lack of medical benefits makes it difficult to acquire quality, or preventative, medical care, and a major illness for any family member could result in financial ruin. Contingent employees typically are paid only for those days they work, and the lack of retirement benefits results in insecurity during old age. All of these factors negatively affect the workers' ability to provide for themselves and their families and also result in increased social costs.

Bibliography

Bartkowiak, J. J. (1993). Trends toward part-time employment: Ethical issues. *Journal of Business Ethics*, **12**, 811–15.

Callaghan, P. & Hartman, H. (1991). *Contingent Work*. Washington, DC: Economic Policy Institute.

Hearing Before the Committtee on Labor and Human Resources (July 19, 1990). *Meeting the Challenges of a New Work Force*. United States Senate, One Hundred First Congress, Second Session.

Parker, R. E. (1994). Race, sex, class: The contingent work force in the United States. *Race, Sex and Class*, **2** (1), 145–59.

JULIA J. BARTKOWIAK

contracts and contracting   The civil wrong identified by contract law is the existence of a broken promise. However, to show that a legal obligation was transgressed, a broken promise is not enough. Indeed, so much of contract doctrine is about when a promise breaker is *not* bound, it may look as if the law has been designed for those who elude responsibilities rather than for those who keep their word. Nonetheless, contract law is rooted in an aspect of morality; *promise* by its nature is a moral concept and failing to keep one's promise is a moral wrong.

When does a promise become a legally binding contract? In common-law jurisdictions a single written promise with a red seal affixed is a contract. However, as a thing anachronistic or too often morally abused, the seal has lost legal support in over half of US states and is limited in effect elsewhere. A contract can exist even though it is not in writing, though some, e.g., for land, must be in writing to be enforced. When one puts all issues about writing to the side, what is required in essence for a contract to exist? Broadly, there are three kinds of requisite.

First of all, putative contracts are subject to various *invalidating conditions*, for example, the contractors were legal infants, a party was insane at the time of contracting, has promised a crime or sexual immorality, sought to oust the jurisdiction of the courts, or the agreement was secured by force or fraud. "On Sunday"

was once on the invalidity list, as was "wife acting without her husband's permission." In the absence of such conditions, the contract is valid so far. Next there is the basic requisite, known as *consideration*.

There is a promise to give a gift. The common law was clear that, even when there was substantial reliance by the promisee in expectation, the promisor could not be held to the promise of a gift (unless under seal) because there had been no consideration. Each who receives a promise must *during the life of the offer and in return* give something back, either as an act or a promise of one's own, for the promise received. "Consideration must extend from the promisee," as it is put, to make the other's promise legally enforceable. If promises of future action are exchanged (in what is known as a bilateral contract, as distinguished from a unilateral contract) then each party is a promisee as well as a promisor. The promise of a gift lacks this element of exchange. (To suggest that substantial reliance can serve as "consideration" makes no sense, because reliance must come, if it does, after the formation of the contract.)

In two similar situations, one person invites another to "take 48 hours to think it over – I'll wait"; or says "Okay, pay me half you owe and I'll be satisfied." These were not contractual promises at common law and could not be enforced. Many North American jurisdictions now have enacted statutes to protect those who were once told that their reliance on a "bare" promise was misplaced. While not everything, reliance is important to the law. Indeed, when no obvious reliance had been placed upon a promise, some courts have demanded that the promisee (seeking enforcement) must show that at least some opportunity was forgone as a result of having made the agreement.

It would be natural to think when courts *enforce* a contract that they compel the promised act. But that remedy is rare. Typically, the relief for a breach of contract is "damages" not "specific performance." (Too often the act is no longer available, as it were, to be done.) What these damages provide is the money equivalent of the performance (its expectation) – as if the contract had been fulfilled and then reduced to cash.

The final requisite involves what might be called *overarching* concerns. Must parties *be* in agreement to have an agreement? The logic of "offer and acceptance" (as a way of characterizing the exchange needed for contract formation) requires a subjective meeting of minds, that is, being "in agreement." Nonetheless, because confusion (and misrecollection) within communications is so common, the law tends to be objective in this area. The court may discover – as a matter of what is reasonable – "an agreement" that neither party quite imagined it had made. "Reward cases" raise another issue about the logic of offer and acceptance. Someone finds a lost child but knew nothing of the reward offered. Logic would deny her any reward unless she knew of the offer in order to accept it. If things come out otherwise in court, some overarching concern about the fair and reasonable would have been in play.

Contract is often characterized as a bastion of individualism, where, having created one's own "law" through the contract, one stands by its terms whatever (barring frustration or impossibility). Common-law courts always said they would not make people's bargains for them, outside the area of unreasonable miscommunication. Yet courts today will consider a gross imbalance of bargaining power between the parties at the time of contract formation. Mr Big may not have made a valid contract with Mr Little when the terms were, or the particular bargaining context was, "unconscionable" for Mr Big to have enjoyed. Here individualism is tempered by a standard of fair play aimed against undue influence.

A final related overarching concern involves promising away one's contractual remedies in an exemption clause written by the other side. You rent a car and declare (without a shred of truth) that you have read and understood the conditions and exclusions of the contract of bailment. The circumstantial pressure at the counter is neither undue nor fraudulent. So you jeopardize your rights, hoping that not too many devils can dance on the head of a pen. Exemption clauses as such are a fact of life, yet one may condemn some of them as morally unjust, as "unfair contract terms."

See also duty; freedom of contract; individualism; justice; negotiation and bargaining; promises, promising; unconscionability

Bibliography

Atiyah, P. (1979). *The Rise and Fall of Freedom of Contract*. Oxford: Clarendon Press. (Historical study).

Cheshire, G. C. & Fifoot, C. H. S. (1945). *The Law of Contract*, 1st edn, London: Butterworths. (Classic English text with many updated editions).

Collins, H. (1986). *The Law of Contract*. London: Weidenfeld and Nicolson. (A restatement of contract to reflect interventions designed to correct free-market injustices).

Corbin on Contracts. (1952). St. Paul: West Publishing. (US classic, with updates).

Fried, C. (1981). *Contract as Promise*. Cambridge, Mass.: Harvard University Press. (Philosophical analysis).

Waddams, S. M. (1977). *The Law of Contract*, 1st edn, Toronto: Canada Law Book. (Canadian textbook).

RICHARD BRONAUGH

copyright

1) Pursuant to authority provided under Article I, Section 8 of the United States Constitution, Congress enacted Title 17 United States Code, known as the Copyright Act. The purpose of the Copyright Act is to protect authors and artists from the unauthorized exploitation of their creations, and to provide financial incentives to the copyright holders. A 1980 amendment to Title 17, Section 106, provides protection for computer programs.

2) Under the present copyright law, protection begins immediately upon creation of the work. Individuals are given statutory protection for the life of the creator plus 50 years, and a corporation is given protection for 100 years from the date of creation or 75 years from the date of publication.

3) Copyright protection is not absolute, and the law permits some limited unauthorized use through the Fair Use Doctrine. This doctrine has been codified under Section 107 United States Code. A number of factors are recognized as providing an exemption for Fair Use under

copyright law. These factors include purpose and character of use, nature of copyrighted work, amount and substitutability of the portion used, and the effect on potential market for copyrighted works. In order to be protected under the Fair Use Doctrine, the copied portions of the work can be used for criticism, comment, news reporting, teaching (including multiple copies for classroom use), scholarship, or research. If these copied works are used for these purposes and meet tests of brevity and spontaneity, and the cumulative-effect test, the copier and user of copyrighted works without the permission of the owner will not be considered an illegal infringer.

Most legal experts would not argue against the existence of the Fair Use Doctrine. Although the Copyright Act has as its primary intent to protect authors from the unauthorized exploitation of the economic benefit of their works, there is also the important need to encourage widespread dissemination and use of the works for teaching and scholarship. The Fair Use Doctrine is an attempt to permit certain users to ethically and legally assist the dissemination of copyrighted works while generally protecting the financial incentive of the creator.

Bibliography

Basic Books, Inc. et al. v. *Kinko's Graphics Corporation in Nimmer,* Copyright, (1989). Mathew Bender, 758 F. Supp. 1522 (S.D.N.Y. 1991).

ROGER D. STATON

corporate crime   any act that is committed by a corporation that is punished by the state, regardless of whether it is punished under administrative, civil, or criminal law (Clinard and Yeager, 1980, p. 16).

While some authors have used the terms white-collar crime and corporate crime to mean the same thing, the distinction between the two types is important to note. Corporate crime is illegal activity that is undertaken on behalf of the company in order to benefit the organization (such as the manufacture and sale of unsafe products). In contrast, white-collar crime (such as embezzlement) is crime that is undertaken against the company and solely benefits an individual or individuals. Because government regulatory agencies (e.g., Environmental Protection Agency, Food and Drug Administration, Securities and Exchange Commission, etc.) are the bodies that generally deal with corporate lawbreakers, regulatory reform has been the primary means of controlling corporate wrongdoing.

While many companies and their executives are law abiding and socially responsible, the public perception has been that most large corporations and their executives are law-breakers with little or no concern for the well-being of the public. The attempt to achieve a balance among business, society, and government has produced the concept of stakeholders – all those individuals and groups who are directly affected by the actions of the corporation (*see* STAKEHOLDER THEORY). While many notable researchers have engaged in the study of corporate crime in recent years, Edwin Sutherland's systematic approach to the study of corporate crime in the late 1930s and the 1940s laid much of the substantial groundwork for researchers. Sociologist and criminologist Donald Cressey (1976) followed up on Sutherland's work, concluding that corporate criminal behavior was learned by executives just as street crime is learned by juvenile delinquents. Clinard and Yeager's (1980) oft-cited study of corporate crime provoked much of the interest from both the academic world and the popular press. Mathews' (1988) study of corporations and their codes of conduct/ethics demonstrated that codes alone did not lower or prevent incidents of corporate illegalities (*see* CODES OF ETHICS). Because executives and managers are in essence role models, they set the tone for the organization – law abiding or law breaking.

Corporate illegalities have had a peculiar position within both the legal and social worlds. The early English common-law view was that a corporation could not commit a crime because it had no mind and thus could not form intent. Further, because the corporation had no body, it could not be imprisoned. From these concepts it was concluded that a corporation could not be guilty of a crime. Therefore, tort law was often used to handle the illegal behavior of corporations and their employees, especially in areas where consumers' interests conflicted with manufacturers' interests such as in the area of products liability (*see* LIABILITY). As Friedman (1973, p. 454) suggests, "In nineteenth-century law, where there was a corporate will, there was generally a corporate way, at least eventually."

In earlier eras, because of a corporation's status as a fictional entity, corporate executives who engaged in illegal activities on behalf of a corporation generally were able to avoid prosecution. Further, the criminal justice system historically focused on lower-class or street crime. Penal sanctions were almost exclusively reserved for those in the lower income brackets – the corporate "criminal" has been regarded as highly unusual. Holding corporate officials/ actors liable for illegal acts of the corporation is an idea that is gaining acceptance in the legal world, yet is steeped in controversy. In some instances, managers and directors can be held responsible for illegal acts taken by others on behalf of the corporation – even if the managers and/or directors had no knowledge of the illegal acts (*see* CORPORATE PUNISHMENT).

The progression from *caveat emptor* to the notion of social responsibility of corporations and their executives has been the result of social change over the past century (Nader and Shugert, 1980). The evolution in tort law is particularly a reflection of the change from a *laissez-faire* economic model to one in which the government is considered a major force in effecting social change and promoting the general welfare of the public.

There have been three distinct periods in the last 100 years in the United States when the public's distrust of big business reached extremely high levels. The first period extended from the late 1800s up to World War I, when the American public became increasingly irate over abuses by the business world. As a result, the Interstate Commerce Commission was established in 1887 and the Sherman Anti-Trust Act was passed in 1890. In the first part of the new century, Upton Sinclair's treatise (1906) helped to create federal regulation of food and drugs, and other reforms followed, including the establishment of the Federal Reserve system, the passage of the Clayton Antitrust Act (1914), and the creation of the Federal Trade Commission (1914) to police business. Public displeasure subsided until the Great Depression of the 1930s, when once again distrust of big business was rampant. In this, the second era, the end result was New Deal legislation including the establishment of the new regulatory agencies such as the Federal Deposit Insurance Corporation (1933), the SECURITIES AND EXCHANGE COMMISSION (1934), and the National Labor Relations Board (1935).

Discontent with the business world did not emerge again until the 1960s, the years of the Vietnam War and the period when Ralph Nader became a nationally known consumer activist. Nader popularized the issue of corporate crime by making the issue accessible to the public. (Vilified by corporate heads and beloved by corporate critics, Nader's name is synonymous with corporate crime investigation.) This incipient stage was followed in the early seventies by the overseas payments scandals and the Watergate fiasco (*see* FOREIGN CORRUPT PRACTICES ACT). Respect for the business world plummeted. The third era, like the earlier ones, brought about the establishment of a host of new federal regulatory agencies (e.g., the Consumer Product Safety Commission (1972), Environmental Protection Agency (1970), National Highway Traffic Safety Administration (1970)) and new legislation regulating corporations. The following years of 1973 to 1980 ushered in the era of SOCIAL RESPONSIBILITY. It was during this time that corporations and their executives began to be seriously concerned with consumer calls for social responsibility. In the hope of staving off further external regulation, many corporate leaders attempted to demonstrate effective internal regulation, through gestures of social responsibility and social responsiveness such as written codes of ethics, community involvement, philanthropic endeavors, and the like.

The 1980s were generally considered a time of corporate excess and avarice. By the latter part of the decade the public perception of corporate greed resulted in greater scrutiny of corporations and their executives. By the mid-1990s, discontent with the corporate world was once again on the upswing.

Bibliography

Braithwaite, J. (1984). *Corporate Crime in the Pharmaceutical Industry*. London: Routledge & Kegan Paul.

Clinard, M. B. (1983). *Corporate Ethics and Crime: The Role of Middle Management*. Beverly Hills, Calif.: Sage.

Clinard, M. B. & Yeager, P. C. (1980). *Corporate Crime*. New York: Free Press.

Coleman, J. W. (1988). *The Criminal Elite: The Sociology of White Collar Crime*, 2nd edn, New York: St Martin's Press.

Cressey, D. R. (1976). Restraint of trade, recidivism, and delinquent neighborhoods. In J. F. Short, Jr. (ed.), , *Delinquency, Crime and Society*. Chicago: University of Chicago Press.

Cullen, F. T., Maakestad, W. J. & Cavender, G. (1987). *Corporate Crime Under Attack: The Ford Pinto Case and Beyond*. Cincinnati, Ohio: Anderson.

Friedman, L. (1973). *A History of American Law*. New York: Simon & Schuster.

Keenan, J. (forthcoming 1996). Whistle-blowing and the first level manager: Determinants of feeling obliged to blow the whistle. *Journal of Social Behavior and Personality*,

Mathews, M. C. (1988). *Strategic Intervention in Organizations: Resolving Ethical Dilemmas*. Newbury Park, Calif.: Sage.

Nader, L. & Shugert, C. (1980). *No Access to Law*. New York: Academic Press.

Nader, R. (1965/1972). *Unsafe at Any Speed*. New York: Grossman.

Shapiro, S. (1984). *Wayward Capitalists: Target of the Securities and Exchange Commission*. New Haven: Yale University Press.

Sinclair, U. (1906/1980). *The Jungle*. New York: New American Library.

Sutherland, E. H. (1949). *White Collar Crime*. New York: Holt, Rinehart, & Winston.

Westin, A. (1981). *Whistle-Blowing: Loyalty and Dissent in the Corporation*. New York: McGraw-Hill.

MARILYNN CASH MATHEWS

corporate finance, ethical issues in *see* ETHICAL ISSUES IN CORPORATE FINANCE

corporate governance   In the *broad sense* "corporate governance" is concerned with those decisions made by the senior executives of a firm and the impacts of their decisions on various stakeholder groups. Normally these executives are the officers in charge of specific functional areas (finance, marketing, etc.) and, depending on the corporate structure, could also include officers in charge of geographic areas or major product lines. In the *narrow sense* "corporate governance" refers only to the activities of the actual board of directors. In this sense the term refers to the relationship between the board and the firm.

The ethical issues in corporate governance are more subtle than in many of the other areas of firm/stakeholder relations. The reason for this is that, following a strict interpretation of neoclassical economics, it is possible to make an argument that would *favor* the "exploitation" of various stakeholder groups such as customers or employees if the shareholders would thus benefit. Many products entail a certain degree of risk to the consumer. For example, it is all but impossible to manufacture an automobile that is 100 percent safe. From a neoclassical perspective the firm should increase the safety of a product until the marginal costs of more safety equals the marginal benefits of more safety. Thus, from the neoclassical perspective the level of safety built into a product should be a function of the costs (such as bad public relations, lost sales, costs of lawsuits and regulations, and so on) and benefits (generally higher profits) to shareholders.

According to a strict reading of neoclassical economics the one and only responsibility of senior management is to the firm's shareholders. In the case of corporate governance the principal stakeholders are the shareholders. The senior management team and the board are in both theory and law the agents of the shareholders. Their goal, according to the theory, should be to maximize the utility of the shareholders.

Even from a neoconservative perspective no argument can be made that senior management should "exploit" the firm's shareholders. Miles Mace has noted that a major finding of his pathbreaking work "was that directors of large- and medium-sized companies did not do much to represent their principal constituency, the stockholders" (1986, p. vii). Whom then do they represent? In general they appear to represent the interests of senior management. Excessive executive pay, lavish perquisites, and insider trading, are all cases where senior management can and often does exploit the shareholders. Thus even if it is possible to weave an argument that would defend exploitation of customers, workers, and other stakeholders it is not possible to make such an argument with respect to shareholders.

The structure of boards of directors is a key area of study in corporate governance. In the United States, Canada, and Great Britain most corporations have boards of directors that are composed of a mix of "inside" and "outside" directors. Inside directors are corporate employees (such as the CEO, executive vice-presidents of functional areas, and general counsel who also sit on the board). Outside directors (also known as "non-executive" or "independent" directors) are individuals who are not employees of the company (such as university presidents, politicians, union leaders, representatives of institutional investors, or executives from other firms).

Historically, boards were dominated by outside directors. However, earlier in this century as professional managers began to replace founder-owners the composition of boards began to shift in the direction of more insiders. Some have argued that this could be a serious problem. An inside director is "in a very precarious position at a board meeting. Unwilling to say anything in disagreement with his boss, he usually sits quietly and waits until he is called upon to speak" (Nader, Green, & Seligman, 1976, p. 98). As a result some reformers such as Harold Williams, US Securities and Exchange Commission Chair 1977–81, suggested that boards should have only one inside director – the CEO. Others, such as retired ITT chair Harold Geneen, have suggested that boards should have no inside directors (Braiotta & Sommers, 1987, p. 10). In part as a result of this pressure there has been a trend over the last several decades away from insider-dominated boards and back toward outsider-dominated boards.

Pay differentials and executive compensation are other major issues in corporate governance. One company that is often regarded as one of the more socially responsible firms in the world, Ben and Jerry's Homemade, Inc., until recently capped the CEO's salary at seven times that of the entry-level employees. However, in the United States today the average CEO of a major firm earns more than 150 times the salary of an average employee (Monks & Minow, 1995, p. 157). This is considerably higher than the differentials in any other major industrialized country.

Ethical issues in corporate governance are a particularly interesting subset of issues encountered in the field of business ethics because of the distinctive roles of the board and senior management in the modern corporation. Theoretically, no argument can be made that would justify the "exploitation" of the firm or its stockholders by the senior management team. Nonetheless, in the "real world" there are innumerable examples of such behavior.

Bibliography

Braiotta, L. Jr. & Sommers, A. A. Jr. (1987). *The Essential Guide to Effective Corporate Board Committees*. Englewood Cliffs, NJ: Prentice-Hall.

Crystal, G. (1991). *In Search of Excess*. New York: W. W. Norton.

Cochran, P. L. & Wartick, S. L. (1988). *Corporate Governance: A Review of the Literature*. Morristown, NJ: Financial Executives Research Foundation.

Conference Directorship Practices. (1967). Joint report from National Industrial Conference Board and American Society of Corporate Secretaries (Studies in Business Policy no. 125), New York.

Demb, A. & Neubauer, F.-F. (1992). *The Corporate Board: Confronting the Paradoxes*. New York: Oxford University Press.

Lorsch, J. W., with MacIver, E. (1989). *Pawns or Potentates: The Reality of America's Corporate Boards*. Boston: Harvard Business School Press.

Mace, M. L. (1986). *Directors: Myth and Reality*. Boston: Harvard University Press.

Monks, R. A. G. & Minow, N. (1995). *Corporate Governance*. Cambridge, Mass: Blackwell Publishers.

Mueller, R. K. (1982). *Board Score: How to Judge Boardworthiness*. Lexington, Mass.: Lexington Books.

Nader, R., Green, M., & Seligman, J. (1976). *Taming the Giant Corporation*. New York: W. W. Norton.

PHILIP L. COCHRAN

corporate moral agency (or the theory of the corporation as a moral person): the theory that corporations and corporate-like entities, in and of themselves, can and do satisfy the conditions of being intentional actors and so should qualify as full-fledged subjects of moral principles and rules. It argues that corporations can be held morally responsible for what they do or fail to do. It offers an alternative to atomistic or METHODOLOGICAL INDIVIDUALISM's interpretation of the corporation. According to AGENCY THEORY, a currently popular transposed version of INDIVIDUALISM, a corporation is understood to be nothing more than a contractual nexus, a collection of self-interested humans acting either as principals or agents with respect to each other. Principals hire agents to represent their interests in various dealings. In the corporate setting, STOCKHOLDERS hire directors and managers to try to maximize the return on their investments in the corporation. The agents, agency theory assumes, only work for their principals because of what those agents expect personally to gain from the relationship. A corporation is but the financial and contractual "playing field" for a number of individual dealings, and it has no existence independent of those dealings. The "agency problem": how to create an incentive system that can align the self-interests of the agents with those of their principals – how to get managers to act in the best interests of the stockholders – dominates that conception of a corporation.

Corporate moral agency theory opposes the individualist tradition and agency theory. It argues that though corporations are artificial entities, they exist in much more than the "contemplation of law" (*Trustees of Dartmouth College* v. *Woodward* 17 US (4 Wheat.) 518 (1819)). Corporate moral agency reflects the findings of many sociologists, who, like James Coleman (Coleman, 1982 and 1990), regard corporate entities to be the dominant "players" on our social scene. It is squarely in the tradition of German law known as the Reality Theory and identified with Gierke (Gierke, 1868), which understands corporations to be sociological persons independent of being conferred legal status. But it is one thing to treat corporations as sociological/legal persons and quite another to maintain, as does corporate moral agency, that they also have the status of moral persons.

In order to qualify as a moral person, to be a moral agent, at least minimally, philosophers, as far back as ARISTOTLE, are likely to agree that an entity must be capable of genuine rational intentional (or voluntary) actions. To say that something is an intentional rational agent is to say that it motivates itself because it has reasons for doing so, and those reasons typically reflect its desires, wants, interests, goals, etc. It is rational in that it seeks to maximize its satisfaction of its interests at minimal cost. Corporate moral agency theory has the burden of providing a convincing argument that some of the things a corporation does are intended by the corporation itself. It must counter the claim that its actions, as the methodological individualist maintains, always are reducible to or a shorthand way of talking about the intentions and actions of humans who happen to comprise, say, its management or its board of directors.

Peter A. French (1979; 1984; 1995) has argued that all corporations have corporate internal decision structures (CID structures) that provide the grounds for attributing moral agency to them. He identifies two elements in CID structures: 1) an organizational flow chart that delineates stations and levels within the corporation; and 2) rules that reveal how to recognize decisions that are corporate ones and not simply personal decisions of the humans who occupy the positions identified on the flow chart. These rules are typically embedded, whether explicitly or implicitly, in statements of corporate policy. Its CID structure is an organization of personnel (agents) for the exercise of the corporation's power with respect to its ventures and interests. As such, its primary function is to draw various levels and positions within the corporation into rational decision-making, ratification, and action processes, forming a functioning intentional entity.

To get a sense of how this works, think of the CID structure of a corporation as containing two sorts of rules: organizational rules and policy/procedure rules. These rules make descriptions of events possible that would not be possible if those rules did not exist. These rules play a role similar to the role that rules play in our descriptions of sporting events. A person may toss a round ball into a hoop on a gymnasium wall, but without the rules of basketball the activity is not describable as sinking a jump shot and scoring two points. In basketball, there are also two types of rules: those that define positions, the dimensions of the court, the number of players per side, etc., and those that allow certain activities of the players and forbid others – rules that permit attempting to shoot the ball into the basket in some ways and not others, that forbid certain ways of stopping an opponent from scoring, etc.

The organizational chart of a corporation distinguishes players and clarifies their rank and the interwoven lines of accountability within the corporation. It maps the interdependent and dependent relationships, line and staff, that produce corporate decisions and actions. The organizational chart provides what might be called the grammar of corporate decision-making. The policy/procedure rules provide its logic.

Policy/procedure rules are, in effect, recognition rules (following H. L. A. Hart) because they yield conclusive and affirmative grounds for describing a decision or an act as having been made or performed for corporate reasons in the structured way. Some of the procedural rules are already embedded in the organizational chart. For example, by looking at the chart, we should be able to see that certain kinds of decisions are to be reached collectively at certain levels, but that they must be ratified at higher levels.

A corporate decision, and subsequently a corporate action, is recognized, however, not only by the method of its making, but by the policy that it reflects. Every corporation creates a general set of relatively transparent policies (as well as an image) that must inform its decisions if they are properly described as decisions of that corporation. Such policies must be clearly knowable by both its agents and those with whom it interacts. These policies are necessary for the attribution of intentionality to corporations and so for the identification of the actions of corporate agents as corporate. When an action performed by someone in the employ of a corporation is an implementation of its corporate policy, then it is proper to describe the act as done for corporate reasons or for corporate purposes and so as an action of the corporation.

Corporate moral agents appear in their full form at the level of description that CID structures make available to us. Corporate moral agency depends on the possibility of truthfully describing an event as 1) the intentional action(s) of a human or humans, *and* also as 2) the intentional action(s) of a corporation for whom that/those human(s) works. French,

following Donald Davidson, maintains that there may be a number of different layers of description of a single event at which intentional agents appear on the moral scene or, simply, intentionality and morality are not limited to only one level of description: the one where we describe events as the intentional actions of individual humans. For example, the same event might be truthfully described as the president of a company signing a document, but also as the company raising the wholesale price on one of its products. The corporate moral agency theory uses the CID structure idea as a way of justifying redescriptions of events from the individual human to the corporate intentional type.

Consider again the two descriptions of the same event: "The corporation's president signed a document" and "The corporation raised its wholesale prices." The human act and the corporate act certainly have different properties. They also have different causal ancestries, even though they are causally inseparable. The president's signing the document is not the cause of the corporation's raising its wholesale prices, nor vice versa. But if the corporation's raising wholesale prices has a certain causal effect, for example, losing its contract with a small distributor, then the president's signing the document has the same effect.

The way a corporation typically has of trying to achieve its goals, realize its interests, is through the actions of its human personnel. However, corporate goals, interests, etc. may be radically different from those of the humans who occupy positions in the corporation, even very senior positions. Corporations now may even act through computers while humans in the company are left unaware of what is actually happening.

Corporate moral agency theory maintains that corporations themselves have rational reasons for doing things because they have interests in realizing their established corporate goals regardless of the transient self-interests of directors, managers, etc. Corporations, on this account, are intentional actors, capable of being motivated to respond to ethical considerations. They should therefore be treated in ethics as full-fledged moral persons and not as fictions that disappear completely when questions of moral responsibility are raised with respect to corporate activities. Corporate moral agency does not entail that if a corporation is held morally responsible for some state of affairs, individual humans may not also be held responsible as well. Instead, it argues for a broadening of the spectrum of subjects of morality by identifying non-moral reasons why corporations should join humans within the BOUNDARIES OF THE MORAL COMMUNITY.

Bibliography

Coleman, J. . (1982). *The Asymmetric Society*. Syracuse: Syracuse University Press.
Coleman, J. (1990). *Foundations of Social Theory*. Cambridge, Mass.: Harvard University Press.
Curtler, H. (ed.). (1986). *Shame, Responsibility, and the Corporation*. New York: Haven.
Donaldson, T. (1982). *Corporations and Morality*. Englewood Cliffs, NJ: Prentice-Hall.
Drucker, P. (1946). *The Concept of the Corporation*. New York: John Day.
French, P. A. (1979). The corporation as a moral person. *American Philosophical Quarterly*, July.
French, P. A. (1984). *Collective and Corporate Responsibility*. New York: Columbia University Press.
French, P. A. (1995).Corporate Ethics. Fort Worth: Harcourt Brace.
French, P. A., Nesteruk, J. & Risser, D. (1992). *Coporations in the Moral Community*. Fort Worth: Harcourt Brace.
Gierke, O. (1868). *Das deutsche Genossenschaftrecht*. Berlin: Weidmann.
Ladd, J. (1970). Morality and the idea of rationality in formal organizations. *Monist*, **54**, 488–516.
May, L. (1987). *The Morality of Groups*. South Bend, Ind.: Notre Dame University Press.
Schrader, D. E. (1993). *The Corporation as Anomaly*. Cambridge: Cambridge University Press.

PETER A. FRENCH

corporate philanthropy   Corporate philanthropy, or corporate giving, describes the contributions of business firms to charitable causes, educational institutions, and other non-profit organizations. Corporate philanthropy encompasses monetary contributions and, increasingly, other forms of charitable donations. For example, corporations often provide employee volunteers, managerial expertise, packages of goods and services, scholarships, and technological resources for causes or organizations which they support.

Individual business leaders in the United States have long donated to charitable causes, but not until the federal government encouraged corporate philanthropy through the Revenue Act of 1935 did business firms begin to make charitable contributions. Following a court decision in 1953, *Smith* v. *Barlow*, which ensured the legitimacy of corporate giving, US companies have since routinely contributed to social causes. Tax incentives permit corporations to deduct from their taxable income the corporate giving that does not exceed 10 percent of pre-tax income. Generally, the level of corporate giving for most US companies has averaged less than 2 percent of pre-tax income over the last several decades.

Several motivations for corporate philanthropy have been offered in the literature. Critics of corporate giving have argued that firms incur unnecessary costs by giving away shareholders' resources (Friedman, 1970). In contrast, proponents contend that companies can benefit from corporate philanthropy in terms of improved public relations, increased employee productivity and morale, greater satisfaction of various stakeholders in the community, and an enhanced corporate reputation or image (e.g., Fry, Keim, & Meiners, 1982; Smith, 1994; Useem, 1988). Corporations often engage in philanthropic initiatives in anticipation of economic and non-economic outcomes.

Self-interest, or the reciprocity motive, predicts that business firms expect to benefit in return for corporate giving. Observers recognize that self-interest is "not always in opposition to the 'greatest good for the greatest number' because the giver is a member of the community that reaps the reward" (Shaw & Post, 1993, p. 750). Recently, companies have begun to link corporate philanthropy directly to the strategic objectives of the corporation. The strategic paradigm of corporate philanthropy views companies as corporate citizens. "Like citizens in the classical sense, corporate citizens cultivate a broad view of their own self-interest while instinctively searching for ways to align self-interest with the larger good" (Smith, 1994,

p. 107). Corporations link their philanthropic initiatives to the company's profit-making strategies and, at the same time, demonstrate a proactive stance on social issues.

Corporate philanthropy is not as extensively developed in most countries as in the US, but international companies are beginning to expand their philanthropic interests along global lines in response to the challenges of a rapidly changing corporate environment. Despite the negative impact of economic recessions, the consequences of tax reform, and decreased earnings potential in any given year, experts predict that business firms will continue to make substantial charitable contributions with the expectation that the well-being of both the company and the community is enhanced by corporate philanthropy.

Bibliography

Friedman, M. (1970). The social responsibility of business is to increase its profits. *New York Times Magazine*, Sept. 13, 122–6.

Fry, L. W., Keim, G. D., & Meiners, R. R. (1982). Corporate contributions: Altruistic or for profit? *Academy of Management Journal*, 25, 94–107.

Shaw, B. & Post, F. R. (1993). A moral basis for corporate philanthropy. *Journal of Business Ethics*, 12, 745–51.

Smith, C. (1994). The new corporate philanthropy. *Harvard Business Review*, May/June, 105–16.

Useem, M. (1988). Market and institutional factors on corporate contributions. *California Management Review*, winter, 77–88.

BETTY SMITH COFFEY

corporate punishment   The question of whether some form of punishment is appropriate and warranted for corporations that break the law centers around two chief issues. The first issue is the metaphysical status of the corporation: is "corporate punishment" a *meaningful* pairing of terms? – in other words, is the corporation the sort of entity that can be punished? The second issue concerns the justice and effectiveness of punishment, assuming we answer the previous questions in the affirmative.

Another way of phrasing the first issue is to ask whether the corporation is a moral agent (*see* MORAL AGENCY). Only moral agents are punishable. For example, a person who is judged criminally insane will not be punished: rather his activities will be curtailed or monitored, or he will be separated from society at large or confined and treated. This may be done to protect the person so judged, or to protect the public from that person.

One school of thought regarding the metaphysical status of the corporation is what Thomas Donaldson refers to as the Structural Restraint View (Donaldson, 1982). This point of view holds that the corporation is tightly bound to its charter and as such lacks the basic moral prerequisite of freedom to act morally or immorally. If this view is correct, then the concept of punishment is irrelevant, and we must treat the offending corporation in much the same way that we treat the criminally insane: by way of regulations and restrictions.

Another school of thought holds that corporations are best thought of as "artificial and invisible" persons. According to this view, advanced first by the philosopher Peter French, corporations are sufficiently like persons to be held morally accountable for their actions. Like persons, corporations display intentional behavior because they have in place central decision-making units such as boards of directors, which "direct" the conduct of the corporation. Thus, the problem of assigning moral responsibility to corporations vanishes because corporations are *collective* persons and all persons are morally accountable for their actions.

These considerations about the metaphysical status of the corporation are important for the application of the kinds of theories of punishment that are found in the study of ethics. Such theories conceive of justifiable punishment along grounds of retribution, rectification, rehabilitation, deterrence, and others. ARISTOTLE defines retribution as "suffering in return for one's action." He defines rectification as "taking away the gain restoring the equilibrium" for wrongs done by one and inflicted on another. Rehabilitation is the theory which holds that just punishment should show the offender the error of his ways, allowing him one day to return to society as a respectable citizen. Punishment as deterrence holds that justice is served if the nature of the punishment is so fearful that it discourages the offender or others from committing crimes.

Notice that justice as retribution seems to have little application to the punishment of corporations unless the corporation is sufficiently like a person that it can be "made to suffer" – an intentional notion that seems to have little relevance to the nature of corporations. However, the other notions of punishment – rectification, rehabilitation, and deterrence – do seem to have meaningful applications where corporate lawbreaking takes place, so we do not need to be driven to the other extreme, the Structural Restraint View. Corporations may be moral agents in the way that nation-states are conceived of as moral agents – and nations can be and are punished by way of reparations, and such punishments can set an example to that nation and others as deterrents for similar conduct in the future.

Thus, it is clear that in order to decide whether a corporation is the sort of entity that can be punished, we must decide the appropriateness of referring to this institution within a framework of a close family of moral terms: responsibility, liability, moral blame and censure, moral freedom, and agency. The fact that corporations are best defined as "liability-limiting mechanisms" makes the ascription of moral responsibility (and the assignment of punishment) especially problematic.

The second issue concerns the balance between justice and effectiveness of punishment of corporations which have broken the law. Corporations, unlike persons, cannot be incarcerated, so we are left to the recourse of imposing fines on them. Unfortunately, the levying of fines by judges on lawbreaking corporations can have unintended and unwanted effects. If the fines are truly weighty, they can easily harm innocent people. For example, a large fine imposed on a chemical corporation for illegal disposal of toxic wastes can have the unintended and undesirable effect of causing layoffs in the company, thus harming employees who had no part in the decision to dump wastes illegally and no part in the activity of illegal dumping. Such fines can also result in a company's decision to close down a less profitable plant in a small community, possibly depriving that community of its largest tax base and source of employment. Ponderous fines can also cause higher prices for the company's product, thus making the product less compe-

titive and narrowing the range of consumer choice. If the fine is very large, it may even have the effect of putting the company out of business altogether.

Because of these considerations, judges have been understandably reluctant to impose large fines on lawbreaking corporations. The US Sentencing Commission learned that between 1984 and 1987, the average federal fine imposed on corporations for violations of the law was $48,000, and 67 percent of those fines amounted to $10,000 or less. Thus, it is understandable that many corporate executives began to reason that it was often cheaper to break the law and pay the fine than it was to treat hazardous chemicals or eliminate smokestack emissions – the fines became part of the "cost of doing business."

In November of 1991, the US Sentencing Commission, after years of deliberation, issued a new set of guidelines for federal judges sentencing individuals and especially organizations convicted of breaking the law. In part, these sentencing guidelines were inspired by the success of the Defense Industry Initiatives (DII) – a voluntary agreement signed by 46 defense contractors in 1986 designed to prevent fraud and overcharging on government contracts. The DII mandated the creation of codes of conduct, designated officers of the corporation whose responsibility it was to oversee ethics of compliance, required internal reporting systems made up of telephone "hotlines" and ethics "ombudsmen" to allow reporting of legal and ethical violations without fear of retribution, and provided for compulsory ethics training for each of the company's employees and agents.

The 1991 US Sentencing Guidelines likewise mandated the creation of such an ethics compliance program but broadened the requirement to include *all* organizations, defense or otherwise, profit or nonprofit. Under the new guidelines, fines are to be assessed against lawbreaking organizations on a multiple of three to four times the cost of harm or damage done by the violating corporation. However, these fines could be reduced to less than 1 percent of that total provided that the offending organization fully and sincerely took part in the investigation of the wrongdoing (which can lead to mandatory jail sentences for individuals responsible for the crime), and provided that the company or organization had already in place a seven-step ethics and legal-compliance program similar to the one developed for the DII.

How extensive the ethics-training and compliance program must be in order to be granted leniency under these guidelines depends on three factors: the size of the organization, the ethically sensitive nature of its business, and the organization's prior history of enforcement actions taken against it.

Bibliography

Donaldson, T. (1982). *Corporations and Morality*. Englewood Cliffs, NJ: Prentice-Hall.

Ewing, A. C. (1970). *The Morality of Punishment*. Montclair, NJ: Patterson Smith.

French, P. (1979). The corporation as a moral person. *American Philosophical Quarterly*, 16, 207ff.

Rafalko, R. (1989). Corporate punishment: A proposal. *Journal of Business Ethics*, 8, 917–28.

Rafalko, R. (1994). Remaking the corporation: The 1991 US Sentencing Guidelines. *Journal of Business Ethics*, 13, 625–36.

Werhane, P. (1985). *Persons, Rights and Corporations*. Englewood Cliffs, NJ: Prentice-Hall.

ROBERT J. RAFALKO

corporate social performance (CSP) is defined as a business organization's configuration of principles of social responsibility, processes of social responsiveness, and observable outcomes as they relate to the firm's societal relationships (Wood, 1991, p. 693). CSP theory is in part a response to neoclassical economics' narrow emphasis on maximizing shareholder wealth. CSP scholars envision societies as complex webs of interconnected stakeholders, multiple cause and effect, and they see business as a social institution with both power and responsibility. CSP, then, has to do with the antecedents, processes, and outcomes of business organization operations. Although CSP is often thought of as having normative content, it need not have any particular normative content, but rather forms an intellectual framework for grasping the structure of business and society relationships. It is a theory of how corporations are held accountable to stakeholders and the societies in which they operate.

In the CSP model, three principles of corporate social responsibility – institutional legitimacy, public responsibility, and managerial discretion – define structural relationships among society, the business institution, business organizations, and people.

The principle of institutional legitimacy states that society grants legitimacy and power to business, and that the business institutions must use its power in a way that society considers responsible. General institutional expectations are made of any business organization, and organizational legitimacy is achieved and maintained by complying with these institutional expectations. Finally, individuals working in and on behalf of business organizations are obliged to abide by these general norms applying to the institution of business.

The principle of public responsibility states that business organizations are responsible for outcomes related to their primary (mission- or operations-derived) and secondary (related to, but not derived from, mission or operations) areas of societal involvement (Preston & Post, 1975). Each business organization has unique responsibilities because of the type or business it is – its size, industry, markets, product/service mix, etc. For example, some businesses pollute the air and water more than others do; some are uniquely situated to take advantage of or aid poor populations; some routinely fact ethical issues of honest disclosure and others more often face product safety issues.

The principle of managerial discretion states that managers are moral actors and are obliged to exercise all available discretion toward socially responsible outcomes. This principle of individual responsibility emphasizes that within various domains of business activities (economic, legal, ethical, charitable; Carroll, 1979), managers are not completely constrained in their choices. This principle acknowledges the creative tension between a manager's decision-making autonomy and agency relationship. Even more, it emphasizes that the support of moral choice is the fundamental responsibility of a business organization (Kang & Wood, 1995).

Processes or corporate social responsiveness, the second dimension of CSP, represent characteristic boundary-spanning behaviors of businesses. These processes, linking social responsibility principles and behavioural outcomes, include (a) environmental assessment; gathering and assessing information about the external environment, (b) stakeholder management; managing the organization's relationships with those persons, groups, and organizations that can affect or are affected by the company's operations (Freeman, 1984); and (c) issues management; tracking and developing responses to social issues that may affect the company. Responsive processes can be implemented without reference to principles of social responsibility, but the result is purely self-interested rather than society-oriented organizational behavior, thus leaving the firm subject to external control processes such as regulation.

Outcomes, finally, show that answers to the question of "to whom does organizational behavior make a difference, and what difference does it make?" In the neoclassical economic tradition, business outcomes are thought of a narrow financial measures such as profit, share value, and market share, making a difference primarily to owners. In the stakeholder view of organizations, outcomes are defined as consequences to stakeholders, including persons, organizations, and societies; for example, product safety, human rights, natural resource use, pollution, and effects on local communities.

Previous research has attempted to link corporate social and financial performance, but crude measures and the lack of adequate theory have precluded any consistent findings (Ullman, 1985). Current scholarship instead considers financial performance to be only one dimension of social performance. Current research focuses on linking CSP to theories of stakeholders, ethics, and organizations; systematizing the assumptions and theoretical implications of the CSP model; empirically testing ideas about how people perceive, interpret, and enact CSP; examining the validity of the CSP model in cross-cultural and multinational settings; and critiques of existing CSP theory.

Bibliography

Carroll, A. B. (1979). A three-dimensional model of corporate performance. *Academy of Management Review*, **4** (4), 497–505.
Freeman, R. E. (1984). *Strategic Management: A Stakeholder Approach*. Boston: Pitman.
Kang, Y.-C. & Wood, D. J. (1995). Before-profit social responsibility: Turning the economic paradigm upside down. IABS Proceedings (Vienna, Austria, June 1995 – forthcoming).
Preston, L. E. & Port, J. E. (1975). *Private Management and Public Policy: The Principle of Public Responsibility*. Englewood Cliffs, NJ: Prentice-Hall.
Ullmann, A. (1985). Data in search of a theory: A critical examination of the relationships among social performance, social disclosure, and economic performance. *Academy of Management Review*, **10**, 540–77.
Warrick, S. L. & Cochran, P. L. (1985). The evolution of the corporate social performance model. *Academy of Management Review*, **10** (4), 758–69.
Wood, D. J. (1991). Corporate social performance revisited *Academy of Management Review*, **16** (4), 691–718.

DONNA J. WOOD

corporate social responsibility   *see* SOCIAL RESPONSIBILITY

corporations and the law   This broad subject involves at least four interrelated topics.

Corporation Law and Economic Growth

The law defines a corporation as an artificial legal person created by the state. This artificial corporate person has long been able to hold and transfer property, make contracts, sue, and exercise other legal powers for conducting business. Traditionally, however, the law limited those powers. Early in the nineteenth century, so-called special charters restricted the use of the corporate form and the powers corporations could exercise; most corporations only pursued quasi-public purposes such as banking, insurance, and the operation of turnpikes, canals, and bridges; and the doctrine of *ultra vires* ensured that the charter's statement of corporate powers was strictly construed. By 1900, however, general incorporation statutes allowed widespread use of the corporate form, corporations increasingly could pursue any lawful purpose, and *ultra vires* had lost most of its teeth. These changes helped make corporations the devices through which entrepreneurial energies found expression, provided entrepreneurs the freedom and flexibility to pursue new opportunities, and thus facilitated economic growth.

American corporation law also promoted economic growth by establishing shareholder ownership of corporations. By creating the possibility of dividends and share appreciation, and by granting investors some control over the firm's operation, shareholder ownership gave owners of capital an incentive to invest in corporations. This incentive was increased by another important feature of corporation law: shareholders' limited liability for the corporate entity's obligations. In these ways, shareholder ownership of corporations has enabled businesses to amass the capital required for industrialization and economic growth.

Legal Controls over Corporations

Due partly to the legal doctrines just noted, business corporations have grown tremendously in size and power. Despite that power, they are not as accountable to the public as are the formal organs of government. In addition, corporations mainly pursue profits, and may compromise other important values in that pursuit. For such reasons, checks on corporate activities are necessary. The law provides many such checks, most of which reside outside the law of corporations.

Perhaps the most important legal check on corporate misbehavior is government regulation in all its forms, including the imposition of criminal liability on corporations and their officers and employees. But actual and potential civil liability also restrains business misconduct. In addition to these familiar controls, there have been many proposals for changing the internal governance of corporations, relatively few of which have been adopted in any aggressive form. These include giving increased power to shareholders (e.g., the ability to pass binding resolutions), requiring that certain constituencies be represented on the board of directors (e.g., environmentalists), requiring that the board have fewer inside directors or that it contain some public-interest directors, and

changing the corporation's internal management structure so that it can better correct the harms its activities generate.

Problems with Legal Controls

Despite its immense importance in checking business misbehavior, the law is an imperfect corporate control device. For example, legal controls: (1) consume money and resources; (2) provide at best an after-the-fact remedy when the relevant risks were unknown to law-makers at the time they arose; (3) often bear the marks of business influence in both their content and their enforcement; and (4) may be consciously disobeyed if penalties are too light or their imposition too improbable. Also, the law sometimes fails to deter corporate misconduct because deterrence requires rationality from the party to be deterred, and some intra-organizational phenomena make corporations behave irrationally on occasion. Examples include "groupthink" and the tendency for bad news not to get to the top. Besides suffering from all these problems, criminal sanctions pose some special difficulties of their own. Because firms often can pass on the costs fines impose, they may fall on innocent consumers, shareholders, or employees rather than the responsible managers. As for criminal sanctions targeting those managers, the diffused nature of corporate decision-making sometimes makes their identification difficult, and such people often get light penalties even when they are identified and convicted.

The proposals comprising the corporate governance agenda also have their difficulties. Due to the pecuniary orientation of most shareholders, why should greater shareholder power generate more responsible corporate behavior? The various proposals for changing the board's composition suffer from some practical problems – for example, which constituencies and how much representation for each? By allowing competing social interests representation on the board, moreover, some of these proposals may impair corporate decision-making. On the other hand, constituency directors also may be co-opted by management, especially if they lack business experience. Finally, changes in internal management structure have not been adopted to any great extent, and business's political influence may prevent their future adoption.

The Problem of Corporate Moral Personhood

The law's inadequacy as a corporate control device is one (but only one) reason for the growing interest in business ethics and corporate social responsibility. Partly underlying that interest is the perception that if corporations can be made to recognize certain ethical obligations, the law's inadequacies may prove less troubling and the need for legal controls may even decline. Any such program, however, must confront at least two basic questions. First, are corporations capable of having moral obligations and being blameworthy for failing to meet those obligations? Second, even if corporations can be morally culpable, does such responsibility "buy" society more control over corporate misconduct than the purely individual moral responsibility of corporate managers and employees? The first question, which has been extensively discussed in the business ethics literature, seems to depend critically on what corporations are. Specifically, it seems to depend on whether a corporation is a real entity distinct from the people who form it, and on whether this entity can have moral obligations. The standard answer to the second question is that purely corporate moral responsibility assumes importance in situations where the corporate entity is morally responsible but its human constituents are not. Identifying such situations, however, is a difficult matter.

See also **corporate social performance; corporate moral agency; corporate crime; corporate governance; moral status of corporations; economic efficiency; methodological individualism; corporate punishment**

Bibliography

Friedman, L. (1985). *A History of American Law*, 2nd edn, New York: Simon & Schuster.
Herman, E. (1981). *Corporate Control, Corporate Power*. Cambridge: Cambridge University Press.
Kempin, F. (1990). *Historical Introduction to Anglo-American Law*, 3rd edn, St Paul, Minn.: West Publishing Company.
Phillips, M. (1992). Corporate moral personhood and three conceptions of the corporation. *Business Ethics Quarterly*, **2**, 435–59.
Stone, C. (1975). *Where the Law Ends: The Social Control of Corporate Behavior*. New York: Harper & Row.
Werhane, P. (1985). *Persons, Rights, and Corporations*. Englewood Cliffs, NJ: Prentice-Hall.

MICHAEL J. PHILLIPS

corporations, moral status of   *see* MORAL STATUS OF CORPORATIONS

cross-cultural consumer marketing   Marketing goods and services to consumers who have a culture different from one's own and live outside one's own country. Cross-cultural consumer marketing often involves marketing simultaneously in many different cultures and environments.

Ethical problems arise when managers apply different ethical standards in their home and overseas markets. A key danger is the exploitation of vulnerable consumers abroad. "Vulnerable" describes consumers who, for various reasons, find themselves at a disadvantage relative to a business entity, not being fully able to understand, express, claim, or defend their rights as consumers. Since passage of the Consumer Bill of Rights in the US in the early 1960s, at least four basic rights have been identified: the right to safety; the right to be informed; the right to choose; and the right to be heard (i.e. to have one's interests fully and fairly considered in the formulation and administration of government policy). Children, the elderly, the poor, and the illiterate may not have the necessary cognitive ability with which to defend their rights to information, choice, and due consideration. The burden of responsibility for consumer safety would appear to fall on the sellers of goods and services and national governments and their agencies.

The US Consumer Bill of Rights is not always honored in cross-cultural marketing. Examples from the 1970s and 1980s of exploitation of vulnerable consumers in developing countries included over-the-counter sales of high-dosage contraceptives banned in developed markets; weaning food promoted using high-pressure sales tactics; continued sale of pesticides and high-tar cigarettes after their forced withdrawal from Western markets; inadequate health and safety precautions during production of asbestos; and the explosion of a chemical plant due to lax safety standards. Numerous cases of 7 cross-cultural marketing were seen in Malaysia during the early 1980s (Newman, 1980). Problems included adulterated products, use of known carcinogens, deceptive and misleading labeling, inadequate product information and warnings, phony discounts, short weights, and unlicensed practitioners. Perpetrators included both domestic and foreign companies. When queried about these practices, some foreign company managers claimed they were doing their best in a largely under-regulated market; others said it was not their responsibility to act for the government which they claimed was conniving in the exploitation of its citizens.

One might reasonably wonder why well-educated, professionally trained managers in companies with international reputations might take decisions that risk provoking public censure and harming unsuspecting consumers. Shue (1981, p. 599) tried to explain this behavior as follows:

> [It] has a great deal to do with the discounting of the welfare of people across national boundaries, especially when the boundaries also mark cultural, ethnic, or racial differences. Harm to foreigners is simply not taken as seriously.

One may argue that discounting others' welfare results from the unequal interplay of *deontological* (process) and *teleological* (outcome) evaluations during decision-making (see Hunt & Vitell, 1986). It seems more likely that it comes either from a failure to recognize the existence of an ethical choice or from a misplaced sense of LOYALTY to the company or one's superiors. Failure to identify a moral choice may be the result of a low level of *cognitive moral development*, or a lack of ethical sensitivity, or a lack of moral character (see Kohlberg, 1969; Hunt & Vitell, 1993; Williams & Murphy, 1990).

Managers may attempt to justify questionable ethical behavior overseas by invoking the following specious arguments:

1 *Moral Projection*: Organizations cannot be expected to have the same moral attributes as individuals.

2 *Level of Economic Development in Overseas Markets*: Any national government is at fault if it does not adequately protect its people. It is not a foreign company's role to stand "in loco parentis."

3 *Why Us?*: The argument here boils down to the naive question of "Why should we change when everyone else is doing it?"

4 *Conflict of Duties*: Company resources belong to the shareholders, not the managers. Shareholders should decide on any act of SOCIAL RESPONSIBILITY that will increase the company's cost of doing business in other national markets.

5 *Competence and Legitimacy*: Managers may not feel sure about what ethical decisions are within their purview or how to go about actively "doing good."

Smith (1990, pp. 56–60) summarized these arguments as four types of managerial attitude toward corporate social responsibility:

(i) *Profit maximization and social irresponsibility*: Companies may do good as a result of serving their own self-interest but may also cause harm to consumers and would not act to prevent such harm.

(ii) *Profit maximization tempered by the"moral minimum" operating through self-regulation*: This means avoiding causing harm. Most firms and managers appear to operate at this level.

(iii) *Profit as a necessary but not sufficient goal, with affirmative action extending beyond self-regulation*: This is where actively doing good starts to be an important element in company missions and managers' decisions. Companies may elect to play the role of "moral champions" (Amine, 1996).

(iv) *Profit as a necessary but not sufficient goal, with social responsibility extending beyond self-regulation and affirmative action to include the championing of political and moral causes unrelated to the corporation's activities*: An example would be Bata Shoe Company's sponsorship of the Boy Scouts in Kenya.

In order to protect vulnerable consumers from potentially harmful effects of unethical cross-cultural marketing, companies should adopt a proactive policy of information disclosure. All stakeholders should be provided with sufficient relevant information to allow them to make informed choices about buying and using products and services (*see* STAKEHOLDER THEORY). This avoids casting potentially vulnerable consumers in the role of victim. As Shue (1981, p. 599) has asked: "Why is informed consent not more appealing when it does in fact relieve a firm of the responsibility of having inflicted harm upon unsuspecting people?"

In the age of satellite news and computerized communications, managers cannot pursue unethical behavior undetected for long. Fear of discovery, if nothing else, should discourage managers from pursuing questionable actions in their cross-cultural markets. One would hope that moral championship would be considered a far preferable mode of conduct in all cross-cultural markets.

See also **business ethics in developing countries; multiculturalism; multinationals; regulation**

Bibliography

Amine, L. S. (1996). The need for moral champions in global marketing. *European Journal of Marketing*, **30 (2)**.

Hunt, S. D. & Vitell, S. J. (1986). A general theory of marketing ethics. *Journal of Macromarketing*, **6 (1)**, 5–16.

Hunt, S. D. & Vitell, S. J. (1993). The general theory of marketing ethics: A retrospective and revision. In N. C. Smith & J. A. Quelch (eds), *Ethics in Marketing*. Homewood, Ill.: Irwin, 775–801.

Kohlberg, L. (1969). Stage and sequence: The cognitive developmental approach to socialization. In D. A. Goslin (ed.), *Handbook of Socialization Theory and Research*. Chicago: Rand-McNally, 347–480.

Newman, B. (1980). Consumer protection is underdeveloped in the Third World. *Wall Street Journal*, April 8, 1/23.

Shue, H. (1981). Exporting hazards. *Ethics*, **91** (July), 579–606.

Smith, N. C. (1990). *Morality and the Market: Consumer Pressure for Corporate Accountability*. New York: Routledge.

Williams, O. F. & Murphy, P. E. (1990). The ethics of virtue: A moral theory for marketing. *Journal of Macromarketing* 10 (spring), 19–29.

LYN SUZANNE AMINE

— D —

Darwinism and ethics Darwinism is the view, arising from the work of Charles Darwin (1809–82), that all species, including human beings, have evolved through the process of natural selection. One consequence of Darwinism is that all human characteristics, mental and moral as well as physical, have an evolutionary origin. Charles Darwin devoted a portion of his *Descent of Man* (1981 [1871]) to a discussion of the evolutionary origin of the moral sense and of various of our moral VALUES. He does not offer a systematic *theory* of ethics, but tries rather to explain how morality could arise through a process of natural selection.

He specifies three necessary conditions for the development of the moral sense. The first is the fact that we have *social instincts*. These, with sympathy at their root, are the product of natural selection. Individuals concerned about the welfare of others were themselves more likely to receive help when it was needed. As a consequence, such cooperative individuals were more likely to survive and reproduce. Social instincts also made humans susceptible to concern about the approval and disapproval of the group.

A second condition for the development of a moral sense was the evolution of *mental powers*. With these, human beings were able to understand and remember the expectations of the group and to be remorseful when they failed to meet them. As mental powers increased, and language developed, the needs and expectations of the group could be expressed in greater detail, generating an increasingly refined awareness of what the group counted as acceptable behavior. More highly developed mental powers also made it possible to foresee some of the consequences of one's actions. Darwin believes that as our intellectual capacity increases, allowing us to recognize more of the consequences of our actions, the scope of our moral sense increases, so that it eventually extends to all nations and races and ultimately to non-human animals.

The third dimension in the development of the moral sense was *community* selection. On the one hand, Darwin says that natural selection must always work on variations that benefit the individual that has them. But in *Origin of Species* he also says, "In social animals it [natural selection] will adapt the structure of each individual for the benefit of the whole community; if the community profits by the selected change" (1964 [1859], p. 87). A social animal is one whose individual well-being is inextricably bound up with the well-being of its group. The social animal cannot survive or flourish without the support of its group, in the form of infant care, sharing of resources, etc. Furthermore, each individual benefits from the overall fitness of the group. The swift, alert, cooperative group is less vulnerable to attacks from other groups or to starvation than is a slow, inattentive, fragmented group. In social animals, individual and group welfare cannot easily be separated. Among the variations that strengthen the group and its individual members Darwin counts a willingness to regulate one's conduct in ways that contribute to the well-being and survival of the group. This is the moral sense.

With respect to moral values, Darwin says, "No tribe could hold together if murder, robbery, treachery, etc., were common" (1981 [1871], p. 93). Similarly, lying, selfish and contentious behavior, and the like, are forbidden, while courage, self-sacrifice, self-command, fidelity, obedience, and the like, are required from the group.

Darwin claims that in the early development of morality, the focus was entirely on the welfare of the group – not on the species and not on the individual. The "self-regarding" virtues had no place because the intellectual powers of primitive human beings could not adequately trace the long-term consequences of actions. They failed to understand that self-regarding virtues might ultimately be beneficial to the group. This recognition came in due course.

Darwin's account of the development of both the moral sense and moral values falls squarely within his account of natural selection, with an emphasis on the role played by the struggle to survive. To that extent, it is clearly a form of naturalism. On his account, the general good is to be defined not simply as HAPPINESS or pleasure (as UTILITARIANISM would say), but as "the means by which the greatest possible number of individuals can be reared in full vigour and health, with all their faculties perfect, under the conditions to which they are exposed" (1981 [1871], p. 98).

Darwin's account of the general good has sometimes been interpreted simply as "reproductive success." But such an interpretation is too narrow. He speaks of rearing individuals, not merely of reproducing them. And he notes that "Great lawgivers, the founders of beneficent religions, great philosophers and discoverers in science, aid the progress of mankind in a far higher degree by their works than by leaving a numerous progeny" (1981 [1871], p. 172). And the good to be achieved is not merely *survival*. The well-being of the members of the group also counts – raising them "in full vigour and health, with all their faculties perfect."

Some early proponents of an evolutionary account of ethics, in addition to Darwin, include HERBERT SPENCER, Leslie Stephen, and John Dewey. The opposition included T. H. Huxley, one of Darwin's staunchest supporters with respect to the biological theory of evolution. Later, Henry Sidgwick and his former students G. E. Moore and Bertrand Russell joined the attack. Moore's *Principia Ethica* became extremely influential in the efforts of early twentieth-century philosophers to disassociate ethics from evolution.

More recent efforts to reintroduce evolutionary considerations into moral theory include work by James Rachels, Robert Richards, Michael Ruse, and the sociobiological works of E. O. Wilson and Richard Dawkins.

The sociobiological account differs from classical Darwinism in that it claims that *genes*, not individuals or communities, are the unit of selection and guide behavior. As a consequence, sociobiology focuses on behaviors that contribute to the reproduction of gene pools rather than to the survival and well-being of individuals or social groups, as Darwin's account of ethics did. On the sociobiological view, with its "selfish genes," altruism appears to be problematic, particularly when it involves behavior detrimental to the organism carrying the genes (*see* ALTRUISM AND BENEVOLENCE). It is generally explained in terms of the efforts of a gene pool to reproduce *some* portion of itself (for example in close relatives), even if that portion does not reside in the individual performing the altruistic action.

Bibliography

Caplan, A. (Ed.) (1978). *The Sociobiology Debate: Readings on Ethical and Scientific Issues.* New York: Harper & Row. (Includes essays by classical sources like Darwin, Spencer, and Huxley, and recent work by Wilson, Gould, Ruse, et al).

Darwin, C. (1964 [1859]). *On the Origin of Species,* 1st edn, Cambridge, Mass.: Harvard University Press.

Darwin, C. (1981 [1871]). *The Descent of Man and Selection in Relation to Sex.* 1871 facsimile. Princeton: Princeton University Press. (See esp. ch. 3 in *Descent.*)

Dennett, D. (1995). *Darwin's Dangerous Idea.* New York: Simon & Schuster.

Moore, G. E. (1968 [1903]).. *Principia Ethica.* Cambridge: Cambridge University Press.

Paradis, J. & Williams, G. C. (1989). *Evolution and Ethics: T. H. Huxley's "Evolution and Ethics" with New Essays on Its Victorian and Sociobiological Context.* Princeton: Princeton University Press.

Rachels, J. (1990). *Created from Animals: The Moral Implications of Darwinism.* Oxford: Oxford University Press.

Ruse, M. (1986). *Taking Darwin Seriously: A Naturalistic Approach to Philosophy.* Oxford: Blackwell.

Wilson, E. O. (1978). *On Human Nature.* Cambridge, Mass.: Harvard University Press.

SUZANNE CUNNINGHAM

decision analysis It is often believed that quantitative methods are insufficient to explore fully the qualitative elements of important decisions, particularly when one is concerned with such ethical considerations as individual rights, interests of multiple stakeholders, and non-financial societal concerns. Indeed, in their now famous book, *Decisions with Multiple Objectives: Preferences and Value Tradeoffs,* Keeney and Raiffa write,

> It is almost a categorical truism that decision problems in the public domain are very complex. They almost universally involve multiple conflicting objectives, nebulous types of nonrepeatable uncertainties, costs and benefits accruing to various individuals, businesses, groups, and other organizations – some of these being nonidentifiable at the time of the decision – and effects that linger over time and reverberate throughout the whole societal superstructure. (Keeney & Raiffa, 1976, p. 12)

The fundamental objections to formal quantitative methods are 1) all models, whether qualitative or quantitative, necessarily abstract away some of the richness of particular situations, and 2) complex problems require subjective evaluations, and it is exactly these subjective evaluations that are often missed by the analysis. While it is tautologically true that "bad" models leave much to be desired, the trouble with formal analysis is not that subjective evaluations cannot be incorporated, but that too often, too few decision-makers are willing to formalize their personal preferences and subjective assessments.

Many decision-makers are concerned that formal analysis tries to quantify the "unquantifiable." But, it is at least as wrong, if not quite a bit more so, not to quantify that which can be quantifiable. While an artist may be hard pressed to provide a formula that captures her sense of the quality of her work, she is certainly able to compare any two and say which she prefers. This, of course, leads to rank orderings, and where there are rank orderings, numbers cannot be far behind. Indeed, most artists, when pressed, are able to attach a price tag to each work, thereby quantifying at least one aspect of the subjective evaluation.

This sort of quantification is not done by formula, but through the much more complex process of subjective introspection. Thus, the question becomes: Is it legitimate to work with numbers that are determined not objectively, but rather are arrived at subjectively? The answer is a resounding yes, and decision analysis provides the framework for accomplishing this task.

So what is decision analysis? It is a formal and coherent, theoretical methodology for modeling complex decisions in an uncertain world that integrates objective inputs with subjective judgments and personal preferences. It takes the point of view of an individual decision-maker contemplating alternative actions (decisions) in an uncertain environment. The approach combines systematic analysis, with various analytical techniques, to help clarify the optimum choice for that particular decision-maker given her values, preferences, and risk tolerance. "In this sense, the approach is not *descriptive*, because most people do not attempt to think systematically about hard choices under uncertainty. It is also not *normative* since it is not an idealized theory designed for the super-rational being with an all-powering intellect. It is, instead, a *prescriptive* approach designed for normally intelligent people who want to think hard and systematically about some important real problems" (Keeney & Raiffa, 1976, p. vii).

The paradigm consists of five basic steps, usually conducted sequentially and iteratively. The first step is one of *identification*. In this step, the decision-maker and other stakeholders are identified, their objectives and values are examined, and a preliminary collection of action alternatives is established (*see* STAKEHOLDER THEORY). Indeed, whole books have been written about this step, most notably, *Value-Focused Thinking* by Ralph Keeney, which explores in detail how to create and integrate the objective hierarchies of multiple stakeholders.

The second step is one of *structural analysis.* Here, the qualitative anatomy of the problem is explored. What information is available and what will become available without further intervention? What data can be collected, and what are the experiments that can be conducted to augment our understanding? Similarly, which of the decisions that must be addressed must be made immediately, and which can be deferred? Questions like these are explored in this phase of the process, and the information is arranged in an orderly and systematic fashion, often utilizing decision trees or influence diagrams to organize it.

The third step is *uncertainty analysis.* Here both objective and subjective assessments are incorporated to capture the best understanding possible of the chances of various events occurring. The techniques used to accomplish this task include analysis of prior empirical data, examination of assumptions, results of stochastic models, expert testimony (calibrated to account for any personal biases or idiosyncrasies that might affect the expert's judgment), and the subjective assessments of the decision-maker.

The fourth step is *utility and value analysis.* Here, the decision-maker formally assigns to every possible consequence, or outcome, a series of attribute values that completely describes the implications of that outcome. It is in the collection of attributes used to measure outcomes that the rights and interests of the various stakeholders are incorporated. The decision-maker then encodes her preferences for these consequences with cardinal utility numbers that not only enable ordinal rankings of consequences but encode the decision-maker's tolerance for risk. When the accomplishment of these tasks conforms to the desiderata of the theory, the result is a complete description of the problem such that expected utility becomes the appropriate criterion for determining the decision-maker's optimal action.

The final step is one of *optimization.* After the decision-maker identifies the objectives and values, structures the problem, and assigns probabilities and utilities, it is possible to calculate the optimal strategy – that is, the strategy that maximizes that decision-maker's expected utility. This strategy indicates what to do at the start of the decision tree and what choices to make at every other decision node

that can be reached along the way. Nevertheless, the analysis is not complete, because, as already noted, all models must abstract away from the full richness of the situation. Therefore, as part of the optimization analysis, one conducts what has become known as sensitivity analysis to assess the sensitivity of the model to the various assumptions underlying it. This is accomplished by testing how the model's results change with changes in those assumptions and with the inclusion of excluded factors.

So does it work in practice? Can the rights and interests of multiple stakeholders be incorporated? Can soft qualitative factors and subjective judgments be included? Can the full complexity of real-world problems be analyzed? The answer is yes, and the case is substantiated by the many successful decision-analysis applications that have been conducted over the past several decades. These applications have ranged from common business issues to large-scale public-policy debates. And while no list could begin to be complete, by way of example, the applications have included issues of public policy and disease control, medical diagnostics and treatment, technology choice, power generation and the disposal of nuclear waste, air pollution, validity of legal evidence, and a host of business and financial applications like research and development, product introduction, capital budgeting, and so on and so forth. In *Value-Focused Thinking* well over 100 examples and applications are presented and discussed, ranging broadly from such personal decisions as identifying the best job opportunity and deciding whether to have a child, to such large public-policy questions as deciding on the appropriate leadership role for NASA in space exploration and deciding what to do about the possibility of global climate change.

Bibliography

Clemen, R. T. (1991). *Making Hard Decisions: An Introduction to Decision Analysis.* Belmont, Calif.: Duxbury.

Keeney, R. L. (1992). *Value-Focused Thinking: A Path to Creative Decisionmaking.* Cambridge, Mass.: Harvard University Press.

Keeney, R. L. & Raiffa, H., with a contribution by R. F. Meyer. (1976). *Decisions with Multiple Objectives: Preferences and Value Tradeoffs.* New York: John Wiley & Sons.

Raiffa, H. (1968). *Decision Analysis: Introductory Lectures on Choices under Uncertainty*. Reading, Mass.: Addison-Wesley.

DANA R. CLYMAN

decision theory The study of decision-making. It has a descriptive side that considers how decisions are actually made, and a normative side that considers how to make decisions rationally (*see* NORMATIVE/DESCRIPTIVE). It is interdisciplinary. Disciplines contribute according to their special interests. Philosophy and management science provide normative standards for decisions. The social sciences and cognitive psychology provide descriptive accounts of decision-making. Applied mathematics and statistics treat the technical aspects of decision rules. Since descriptive and normative studies of decision-making are complementary, the disciplines collaborate. For instance, economics uses rules of rational decision-making from the normative disciplines to obtain approximate descriptions of actual decision-making. However, each discipline formulates decision principles according to its own methods. For instance, the empirical sciences favor concepts that are operationalistic, such as preference, whereas philosophy freely uses non-operationalistic concepts, such as interpersonal utility.

Philosophy classifies normative decision theory as the branch of logic covering practical reasoning (*see* PRACTICAL REASONING). Its normative nature also makes decision theory part of a theory of ethics broadly conceived to include rules for leading a good life. Decision theory also provides the foundation for certain ethical theories, for example, social contract theories of morality (*see* SOCIAL CONTRACT THEORY; RAWLS, JOHN). (Because of its special relevance to business ethics, the following account of decision theory concentrates on normative decision theory.)

History

Decision theory goes back at least as far as ARISTOTLE's treatment of practical reasoning, in particular, his analysis of the practical syllogism, an argument whose conclusion is an action to be performed rather than a proposition to be believed. Technically, decision theory, along with probability theory, developed in the seventeenth and eighteenth centuries. Interest in probability was prompted by the problem of making decisions rationally in the face of uncertainty about their consequences. Decision theory has progressed rapidly in the twentieth century. Probabilities and utilities in decision rules have come to be understood respectively as rational degrees of belief and rational degrees of desire. Measurement theory has been applied to derive probabilities and utilities so understood from preferences. Decision theory in conjunction with probability theory has generated an approach to inductive reasoning known as Bayesian statistics. And two new branches of decision theory have arisen: game theory, which treats decision problems with multiple interacting agents, and social choice theory, which treats decisions made by groups.

Individual Choice

Decision theory has three main branches: individual choice, choice in games, and social choice. The branch treating individual choice considers individuals making decisions, and directs them to maximize expected utility. This is done by computing the expected utility of each option, and selecting an option that has maximum expected utility. The expected utility of an option is obtained by considering the option's possible outcomes, divided so that they are mutually exclusive and exhaustive. Each possible outcome is assigned a probability and utility. The probability and the utility for a possible outcome are multiplied, and the products for all the possible outcomes are added. The sum of the products is the expected utility of the option. For example, the expected utility of a bet that pays \$4 if a coin toss yields heads and \$2 otherwise is $(1/2 \times 4) + (1/2 \times 2)$, or 3, provided that dollar amounts correspond to utilities. For simplicity, applications of the expected utility principle often focus on monetary consequences, but the principle itself attends to all consequences, including, for example, emotional consequences.

Choice in Games

Game theory seeks solutions to games. A game is broadly interpreted as a decision problem involving multiple agents where the outcome for an agent depends on the other agents' decisions as well as the agent's own decision. A solution is a set of decisions, one for each agent, such that each decision is rational given the set of decisions. A solution thus comprises decisions that are jointly rational as opposed to individually rational. One widely accepted proposal is that a set of decisions is a solution only if it is an equilibrium in the sense that each decision in the set maximizes expected utility for its agent given the other decisions in the set (*see* NEGOTIATION AND BARGAINING).

Social Choice

Social choice theory extends principles of individual choice to groups making decisions. One of its main results is negative. Kenneth Arrow proved that (given certain plausible criteria for the definition) it is impossible to use the preferences of the members of a group to define the preferences of the group itself. This has important implications for the theory of voting. Utilitarians avoid the problem by using interpersonal comparisons of utilities, not just individual preferences, to define group preferences (*see* RATIONAL CHOICE THEORY; UTILITARIANISM; WELFARE ECONOMICS).

Research

Research in decision theory addresses a variety of additional topics. In order to extend decision theory, it examines ways of applying decision principles to decisions made by professionals on behalf of their clients (*see* AGENCY THEORY). It also formulates decision principles for cases that do not meet the idealizations and restrictions of common decision principles. It puts aside idealizations about the cognitive powers of agents, and determines when cognitive limits provide good excuses for falling short of the standards of rationality expressed by common decision principles. It also puts aside restrictions that require beliefs and desires to be quantitative, and advances decision principles for cases where they are non-quantitative.

In order to enrich decision theory, current research advances rules for evaluating the desires and beliefs that serve as input for common decision principles, thus supplementing the account of instrumental rationality those principles provide. It also unifies the theory of individual decision-making and game theory by showing how solutions to games can be derived

from rules of individual decision-making. And it proposes new forms of utility analysis, for example, forms that break down the utility of an option according to its consequences over time, rather than according to its possible outcomes.

See also **Prisoner's Dilemma**

Bibliography

Behn, R. & Vaupel. J. (1982). *Quick Analysis for Busy Decision Makers.* New York: Basic Books. (Expected utility analysis).
Campbell, R. & Sowden, L. (eds). (1985). *Paradoxes of Rationality and Cooperation.* Vancouver: University of British Columbia Press. (Treats two important decision problems, the Prisoner's Dilemma and Newcomb's Problem).
Heap, S., Hollis, M., Lyons, B., Sugden, R., & Weale, A. (1992). *The Theory of Choice.* Oxford: Blackwell.
Kahneman, D. & Tversky, A. (1981). The framing of decisions and the psychology of choice. *Science,* **211**, 453–8. (An illustration of descriptive decision theory).
Luce, R. D. & Raiffa, H. (1957). *Games and Decisions.* New York: Wiley. (The classic introduction).
MacKay, A. (1980). *Arrow's Theorem: The Paradox of Social Choice.* New Haven: Yale University Press.
Mullen, J. & Roth, B. (1991). *Decision-Making: Its Logic and Practice.* Savage, Md.: Rowman & Littlefield.
Resnik, M. (1987). *Choices: An Introduction to Decision Theory.* Minneapolis: University of Minnesota Press.

PAUL WEIRICH

defense industry, ethical issues in the
see ETHICAL ISSUES IN THE DEFENSE INDUSTRY

dependent care Caring for children, partners, or other family members who get their main source of support from "you."

Recent studies indicate that 47 percent of all workers feel responsible for the care of their dependents, which means that nearly half of the American workforce carries obligations to ensure that the needs of their children, ill spouses or partners, or elders are met. These obligations often place a strain of financial resources, time, and thoughts directly on the care-givers and their families. In general, those workers with dependent-care concerns live with greater stress than those who do not have dependent-care responsibilities, and believe that they are not coping as well as their peers who do not share similar responsibilities outside of work. Reliable, affordable support systems for dependent care translate for most employees into a less stressed, healthier life.

In terms of pure practicality, the reduction of workplace attrition, increased productivity, greater company loyalty, and worker satisfaction could easily offset the costs associated with establishing systems within businesses to assist employees who have dependent-care responsibility. A growing number of companies are doing just that. Businesses have established and/or sponsored programs and referral services for dependent care such as on-site child and elder day care. Flexible time, leave programs, job sharing, and telecommuting are examples of other measures taken by many companies to support their employees who have dependent-care responsibilities. Employees who need the services find them to be immensely beneficial, and the company benefits from the increased level of employee commitment and well-being.

Clearly there are practical implications for a company which seeks to alleviate the financial, emotional, and time pressures of their worker's family lives. Based solely on the demographic projections of an aging population, dependent care will necessarily be an increasing matter of employer and employee concern. Also influential is the dominant social trend among younger workers away from notions of meeting work demands in spite of family life, and toward relinquishing employment mobility and success specifically for the family. In practical terms, dependent-care support programs make good business sense. The interesting question is whether there is a moral obligation for such company support, irrespective of the utilitarian one which seeks the greatest good for the greatest number.

It could be argued that child- and elder-care support, leave time, flex time, and the like should be available because they give back to the community what companies necessarily take away in conducting business. When a company knowingly hires a parent of young children or the spouse of a dependent partner, etc., is there an obligation to provide support for their dependent-care responsibilities? One response is, "No, their salary is their support." Unfortunately, only high salaries can afford the cost of reliable, high-quality care for elders, children, and the indigent. But why, it could be asked, should a company be responsible in moral terms? One response is that companies would not be able to thrive without the community which sustains them, and therefore the relationship between the business and its community is interdependent. There could be a moral problem when companies make the community a means to its own end (or the financial end of it's owners) without regard to the sacrifices made by its employees (i.e. the community) for that end. Addressing issues of employee dependent-care responsibility is a question of ethics because in part these responsibilities can be exacerbated or alleviated by workplace requirements. Dependent care is obviously a matter of practical choice based on company policy. If policy is claimed to be grounded in responsibility to the community, then the subject-matter of dependent care is also a matter of ethics.

Bibliography

Families and Work Institute, press release, "National Study of the Changing Workforce shows Strong but Changed Work Ethic: Beleaguered, Resilient Workers want Quality Work Environment, More Flexibility, More Time for Personal and Family Life." Embargoed for release Fri. Sept. 3, 1993, from Families and Work Institute, 330 7th Avenue, New York, NY 10013.

ROSALYN W. BERNE

developing countries, business ethics in *see* BUSINESS ETHICS IN DEVELOPING COUNTRIES

disclosure   In our complex society, few people would argue for complete *laissez-faire*; but in this era of individualism few will argue for complete centralized control over any significant aspect of the community's life. In the United States, the notion of full disclosure has become an accepted compromise between those two extremes. Calling on a current example, we have evidently agreed (through our elected representatives) that something needed to be done to reduce the social costs of cigarette smoking, and that it was not enough for the Surgeon General to take to the bully-pulpit. We have also evidently agreed that regulated prohibition of smoking was inappropriate because it would conflict with individual freedoms. We have however agreed that we would insist on warning labels on cigarette packs and advertisements – providing full disclosure of the risks of smoking – as the best compromise. Interestingly, that disclosure of the risks of smoking was imposed on the tobacco companies by federal regulation, but it is now being used by the companies as a defense against product-damage litigation.

In their classic text on securities regulation, Loss and Seligman quote Louis D. Brandeis as arguing for publicity as the remedy for social and industrial diseases; In *Other Peoples Money*, published in 1942, Brandeis said, "Sunlight is said to be the best of disinfectants; electric light the most efficient policeman" (Loss and Seligman, 1989, p. 173). Although that full-disclosure philosophy is central to most of the regulatory schemes in the US, different times and different areas have relied more or less on central control. Loss and Seligman also cite Justice William O. Douglas, who criticized the proposal for a disclosure-based securities law (which became the Securities Act of 1933), argued that the law would not protect the people who needed it because "They either lack the training or intelligence to assimilate [the disclosures] and find them useful, or are so concerned with a speculative profit as to consider them irrelevant" (Loss and Seligman, 1989, p. 174).

We continue to have examples of that conflict between control and disclosure. In prior years, the US Food and Drug Administration was criticized because it insisted on strict control over drug distribution, and rejected proposals to allow distribution of new drugs even if accompanied by full disclosure of the attendant risks and uncertainties. The spirit of deregulation in the 1980s – and the magnitude of the AIDs crisis – forced the FDA to adopt more flexible policies, allowing speedier clearance of drugs directed to life-threatening diseases. But a change in the time required to approve the drug does not change the approach to regulation – the regulation remains centralized and controlling. Salbu (1994) describes that approach to regulation as paternalistic and suggests that the FDA should instead adopt a contractual approach to regulating new drugs. In that way, a patient suffering from a threatening disease would be able to obtain an unproven drug by signing a "waiver of informed consent" accepting responsibility for the risks which might accompany the use of the drug.

In many commercial transactions, the terms of the contract between the buyer and seller are implied, rather than "informed," and it is the ambiguity in those implied terms which causes subsequent disputes. Enhancing the disclosure reduces the ambiguity of the terms of a transaction, and helps to establish responsibility between the parties.

In the corporate world, the announcement of large salary payments to executives created calls for controls. Villasana (1995) reported that in the early 1980s the average pay of the CEO was $624,996, which was 42 times the pay of the average factory worker. By 1990, the average executive's pay had increased to $1,214,090, which was 85 times that of the average factory worker. In response to that development, Congress amended the tax law in 1993 to deny the payor company a tax deduction for any compensation (other than from a performance-based plan) which was in excess of $1 million. As with all categorical rules, that tax provision can be circumvented in a number of ways. In 1992, the SEC adopted new proxy rules which required every publicly traded company to disclose (among other things) (1) a summary of all forms of compensation paid to their top executives; (2) a performance graph that compares the 5-year cumulative total return of the company's stock to a broad market index and a peer-group index; and (3) a report from the Compensation Committee of the Board which sets out the rationale for the compensation program followed by the company. Regarding the new SEC requirements, Robert Lear (1993) commented that the disclosures would provide a wonderful opportunity for every company to reappraise its compensation systems. He concluded, "After all, it is about time executive compensation came out of the closet.

closet. It is through compensation that a company says its executives have done a (superb, excellent, good, fair, poor) job of managing in the light of current conditions and competition. This is too important a measurement to be left to a small committee of senior directors and the CEO. It must be viewed in the open and judged fairly in the market place."

The world of accounting demonstrates an interesting ambivalence about controls and disclosures, perhaps reflecting Justice Douglas's concerns. Academic studies have demonstrated that the securities market – as a whole – processes information efficiently, regardless of the vehicle used for the dissemination of the information. That theory suggests that the market will respond exactly the same whether a company discloses the terms of a lease by which it acquired a new piece of equipment, or whether the company buys the equipment and records the purchase and the related debt. Based on that research, it can be argued that accounting rules should be flexible and allow for a wide variety of choice in the dissemination of information, or at least accountants ought not impose significant costs on society in pursuit of specific accounting rules. Regardless of that evidence, a significant superstructure has been established to formulate accounting rules for specific transactions, going far beyond simple disclosure. Confronting that policy question, Imhoff, Lipe and Wright (1993) found that the securities market in general was able to use disclosure in lieu of explicit transaction accounting, but also found that (1) the level of disclosure is important, and (2) not all users of financial information were similarly influenced by disclosure – some were only influenced by the explicit accounting. As a consequence, they suggested that regulators were faced with the task of identifying "the point on the continuum between no disclosure and full recognition [full transaction accounting] that best serves the target user group, while minimizing the cost to other constituents" (1993, p. 363).

Bibliography

Imhoff, E. A., Jr., Lipe, R., & Wright, D. W. (1993). The effects of recognition versus disclosure. *Journal of Accounting, Auditing and Finance*, 8, (4), 333–63.

Kotner, K. B. (1993). Final SEC proxy disclosure rules. *Benefits Quarterly*, second quarter, 22–30.

Lear, R. W. (1993). Read my proxy. *Chief Executive*, 87, 10.

Loss, L. & Seligman, J. (1989). *Securities Regulation*. Boston: Little Brown and Company.

Salbu, S. R. (1994). Regulation of drug treatments for HIV and AIDS: A contractarian model of access. *Yale Journal on Regulation*, 11, (2), 402–53.

Villasana, G. A. (1995). Executive compensation and RRA '93. *CPA Journal*, Feb., 3640.

ROBERT SACK

discourse ethics   asserts that moral claims must be justified on either of two grounds: that persons would accept them after rationally discussing them; and that discussion itself implies them. More precisely, discourse ethics appeals to communication as a way of (a) articulating a fair procedure for coordinating action, (b) defending the universal validity of rights and obligations associated with the moral point of view, and (c) adducing an ideal standard for use in criticizing ideology (beliefs and attitudes that arise from constrained and distorted communication) and subrational, unfair forms of democratic deliberation.

a) Philosophers have appealed to discussion as a coordination procedure for two somewhat different reasons. As a procedure for resolving CONFLICT, discussion provides a method for agreeing on rules of fair play that are neutral with respect to divisive interests. As a political procedure for determining mutually beneficial policies, it provides a method for transforming divisive interests into more convergent interests. In both instances, the principles and policies agreed on are regarded as legitimate, or morally binding, only if they advance common interests, as these have (or would have) emerged in the course of an inclusive, open, and impartial discussion. So understood, the justice of any moral and political norm is solely a function of the rationality and fairness of those discursive procedures in accordance with which it has been discussed and accepted (*see* JUSTICE, CIRCUMSTANCES OF).

While conflict resolution and determination of shared political aims are not entirely separable, they are sufficiently so as to suggest different sorts of discursive procedures. If conflict resolution depends on adducing *universal* principles of fair play that could be accepted by everyone, irrespective of differences in individual interests, the procedure called for will not be significantly different from the UNIVERSALIZABILITY procedure recommended in KANTIAN ETHICS. That means, ironically, that the procedure will not involve a real discussion, but will consist in a personal thought experiment, in which I ask myself what sorts of moral principles anyone would consent to, if he or she participated in an ideal conversation with everyone else. Imagining this conversation is like imagining the thought processes of a single impartial spectator since perfectly rational and informed participants in a spatially all-inclusive and temporally unlimited conversation would probably converge in their PRACTICAL REASONING (*see* IMPARTIAL SPECTATOR THEORIES).

Real not imaginary discourse will be required, however, if the aim is to reach agreement on less general, legally sanctioned rules of fair play. Here, the appropriate procedure will more closely resemble a real social contract than a universalizability test (*see* SOCIAL CONTRACT THEORY). In seeking consensus on the scope of basic constitutional liberties, persons might choose a procedure that prohibits them from discussing those private interests pertaining to religion and lifestyle on which they cannot – and perhaps should not – agree. This bracketing procedure functions to focus discussion on a common interest that cannot threaten our private interests, namely, our mutual desire to protect our private interests, compatible with a like protection of other persons' private interests.

A very different procedure will be required, however, if the laws and policies being discussed are intended to advance a common interest other than mutual toleration of differences. This procedure reverses the strategy deployed by the gag rule mentioned above, in that it requires discussion of private interests as a way of transforming them into non-divisive interests. In order for this transformation to be effected as non-coercively and impartially as possible, all parties affected by the outcome would have to have equal opportunities, skills, and resources to speak in the general discussion, free from the constraints of poverty, power, and prejudice.

Although the procedure of bracketing seems appropriate in certain public forums, such as in courtroom proceedings – where, for example, the admissibility of religious arguments about the personhood of fetuses might prejudice an impartial ruling on abortion rights – it is less so in others, where what is at issue are public policies aimed at advancing, say, the environmental well-being of the population as a whole. Social accountability requires that each citizen understand the OPPORTUNITY COSTS of his or her chosen lifestyle in diminishing the life prospects of other persons, citizen and non-citizen alike. By compelling us to exchange roles hypothetically with those with whom we talk, a truly inclusive and impartial dialogue expands our moral horizons and promotes solidarity; by checking our prejudices against the critical resistance of opposing viewpoints, it promotes AUTONOMY (*see* ROLES AND ROLE MORALITY).

b) Skeptics ask, Why be moral? Discourse ethics answers this question by pointing out that the only motive we have for adopting the moral point of view – that is, for dealing impartially with our own interests as these impact on the interests of others, treating others with equal respect, and ascribing the same rights and obligations to others that we ascribe to ourselves – is grounded in the communicative conditions underlying a healthy, well-integrated identity. The argument for this claim runs as follows:

Our sense of our own identity and self-worth is largely a function of the familial, vocational, and citizenship roles with which we identify. These roles, however, are social in nature. They function as stable centers of identity because other persons recognize them in us. Since the recognition and constitution of meaningful roles occurs in communicative interaction, the more rational the communication – that is, the more freely and authentically others personally communicate their recognition of us – the more unrepressed and undistorted our own sense of self.

How does this psychological motive for entering into rational communication entail moral commitment? Communicative RECIPROCITY requires that we take our fellow interlocutors seriously, as agents worthy of equal respect. If we did not – that is, if we denied them an equal chance to speak or failed to ensure their right to do so unconstrained by prejudice, ignorance, and incompetence – neither we nor they could be rationally persuaded by what was said. Moral skepticism thus stands discredited, since refusal to enter rational conversation endangers psychological integrity, but participation entails moral commitment.

c) The discourse-ethical ideal of justice might well require the democratization of all areas of public life, including the workplace. Still, the need to reach decisions in timely fashion will often favor strategic compromise and preference aggregation over consensual deliberation. Here, consensual deliberation can reduce the conflicts that make strategic compromise and preference aggregation an unmitigated expression of brute power. More importantly, discourse ethics enjoins the freedom, EQUALITY, and universal inclusion of all citizens in shaping public opinion. The high standards for fairness, freedom, and inclusion established by such an ethics can thus be used to critically assess the degree to which agenda-setting, campaign advertising, media coverage, and political debate are constrained and distorted by social and economic power.

Bibliography

Ackerman, B. (1989). Why dialogue? *Journal of Philosophy*, **86**, 5–22.

Alexy, R. (1989). *A Theory of Legal Argumentation: The Theory of Rational Discourse as Theory of Legal Justification*, trans. R. Adler & N. MacCormick. Oxford: Clarendon.

Apel, K.-O. (1980). The a priori of the communication community and the foundation of ethics. In *Toward a Transformation of Philosophy*, trans. G. Adey & D. Frisby. London: Routledge, 225–300.

Benhabib, S. & Dalmayr, F. (eds.) (1990). *The Communicative Ethics Controversy*. Cambridge, Mass.: MIT Press.

Habermas, J. (1990). *Moral Consciousness and Communicative Action*, trans. C. Lenhardt & S. Weber Nicholsen. Cambridge, Mass.: MIT Press.

Larmore, C. (1987). *Patterns of Moral Complexity*. Cambridge: Cambridge University Press.

Rehg, W. (1994). *Insight and Solidarity: A Study in the Discourse Ethics of Jürgen Habermas*. Berkeley: University of California Press.

Wellmer, A. (1991). Ethics and dialogue: Elements of moral judgment in Kant and discourse ethics. In *The Persistence of Modernity: Essays on Aesthetics, Ethics and Postmodernism*, trans. D. Midgley. Cambridge, Mass.: MIT Press, 113–231.

DAVID INGRAM

discrimination in employment   is treating some employees, job applicants, or other job applicants less favorably than others on the basis of characteristics that have little or no relationship to the person's abilities to perform a particular job. Most such behavior is unregulated. Under the traditional EMPLOYMENT AT WILL doctrine, unless bound by contract or law, an employer may make whatever employment decisions it wishes for any reason whatsoever or, indeed, for no reason at all.

The United States Constitution and various federal and state statutes abrogate the traditional "at will" rule in many respects. The Fourteenth Amendment's equal protection clause, for example, prevents public employers from intentionally discriminating on the basis of race, sex, national origin, religion, illegitimacy, or, in some cases, even citizenship absent a persuasive justification. Section 1981, a Civil War era statutory provision, prohibits racial discrimination in the making, enforcing, and performance of employment contracts by private employers.

Four modern federal statutes fill out the picture. The Age Discrimination in Employment Act prohibits both private and public employers of 20 or more employees from discriminating against workers 40 years old or older. The Rehabilitation Act and the Americans with Disabilities Act prohibit public and private employers with at least 15 employees from discriminating against the disabled. Title VII of the Civil Rights Act of 1964 prohibits public and private employers with 15 employees or more from discriminating on the basis of race, color, religion, sex, national origin, and citizenship. Of these statutes, Title VII is the most important. It provides the widest coverage and, in many respects, serves as the model for the others.

Title VII covers discrimination in all aspects of employment. It makes it unlawful for an employer to fail or refuse to hire or to discharge any individual, or otherwise to discriminate against any individual with respect to his compensation, terms, conditions, or privileges of employment, . . . [or] to limit, segregate, or classify his employees or applicants for employment in any way which would deprive or tend to deprive any individual of employment opportunities or otherwise adversely affect his status as an employee, because of such individual's race, color, religion, sex, or national origin. (Title VII, §2000e-2(a)(1)–(2))

It also prohibits labor unions and employment agencies from engaging in similar activities.

There are two primary restrictions on Title VII's reach. It covers discrimination on the basis of only a few specified characteristics and it requires that the challenged practice concern the employment relationship. Thus, Title VII does not prohibit employment discrimination on the basis of sexual orientation, although some state statutes and local ordinances do, and it does not prohibit an employer from discriminating against minority-owned vendors, although other federal and state civil rights provisions may (*see* GAY RIGHTS).

Title VII prohibits practices whose aim is to discriminate and practices pursued for other, perhaps legitimate, reasons that have a discriminatory effect. The first type of practice is called disparate treatment. To prove such intentional discrimination, the employee or applicant must show that a prohibited characteristic, such as race or sex, was a motivating factor in an employment decision adverse to her. She can prove this in many different ways. One way is to prove that she is a member of a protected class and possesses the minimal qualifications for the job, that she applied for it and was rejected, and that the employer continued to seek applications from people with the same qualifications. If she shows all that, then the employer must provide a legitimate business reason for its action, which the employee bears the burden of disproving.

The second type of practice may be challenged under a theory of disparate impact. If an employee or applicant can show that an otherwise valid practice has an adverse, disproportionate impact on individuals in a protected group, the burden of proof switches to the employer to show that the challenged practice is "job related . . . and consistent with business necessity" (Title VII, §2000e-2(k)(1)(A)(i)). If an employer fails to carry this burden, the practice is declared unlawful and liability follows. Although disparate treatment actions can challenge employment practices affecting individuals or whole groups, disparate impact actions can challenge only practices affecting groups of employees or applicants. By its nature, a disparate impact action requires statistical evidence of how a disputed employment practice affects various groups differently.

In addition, Title VII requires employers to make reasonable accommodations for employees whose religious beliefs make it difficult, if not impossible, for them to fulfill standard employment requirements. An employer must, for example, ask other employees whether they would be willing to substitute for an employee whose religion forbids her from working on a day the employer requires her services. Whether an accommodation is reasonable depends on the burden it would place on the employer and other employees. Similarly, the American with Disabilities Act requires covered employers to make reasonable accommodations for employees' and applicants' disabilities if they are otherwise qualified for a particular job. Thus, for example, an employer would have to make training materials available in large print or otherwise accessible to a sight-impaired employee who would otherwise be able to fulfill a particular job's requirements.

Strictly speaking, accommodation requirements embody a different theory of anti-discrimination than do ordinary anti-discrimination provisions. Whereas ordinary provisions prohibit an employer from taking some characteristic into account on the grounds that the characteristic should make no difference, accommodation requirements place an affirmative duty on the employer to recognize and alleviate certain differences. Accommodation provisions, in other words, require the employer to take into account characteristics that ordinary anti-discrimination provisions would insist that it be blind to.

See also **affirmative action programs; discrimination in employment; sexual harassment; racism**

Bibliography

Brest, P. (1976). Foreword: In defense of the antidiscrimination principle. *Harvard Law Review*, **90**, 1–54.

Epstein, R. (1992). *Forbidden Grounds: The Case Against Employment Discrimination Laws.* Cambridge, Mass.: Harvard University Press.

Rutherglen, G. (1987). Disparate impact under Title VII: An objective theory of discrimination. *Virginia Law Review*, **73**, 1297–345.

Sunstein, C. (1991). Why markets don't stop discrimination. *Social Philosophy and Policy*, **8**, 22–37.

Title VII of the Civil Rights Act of 1964. *United States Code*, **42**, §§2000e–2000e-17.

DANIEL R. ORTIZ

distributive justice Fairness in the allocation of societal benefits and burdens by the state and other institutions. Taxation, minimum-wage laws, welfare payments, housing subsidies, health care, and retirement benefits are common methods by which the state distributes wealth in a society.

The Concept of Distributive Justice

A liberal concept of distributive justice is provided by JOHN RAWLS. He expounds two principles of justice that people would rationally choose in an imaginary "original position" where they are unaware of their own status in society. One of these principles — dubbed the "difference principle" — gives criteria for distributive justice. It states that social and economic inequalities should be allowed only insofar as such differences will lead to the greatest advantage of all (including the least advantaged), and attach to opportunities open to everybody (*see* JUSTICE, CIRCUMSTANCES OF).

In contrast, a libertarian conception of distributive justice stresses the individual's liberty to acquire, own, and transfer holdings without the state intervention that a liberal understanding of distributive justice contemplates (*see* LIBERTARIANISM; NOZICK, ROBERT).

Corporations and Distributive Justice

The changeover from public to private ownership of business and the transition to free-enterprise market economies occurring in many parts of the world raise issues of distributive justice for corporations. The legal and ethical question arises whether a corporation purchasing a factory previously owned by a communist-style government owes workers benefits (such as pensions and retirement payments) formerly expected by the workers from the state.

With the dismantling of apartheid in South Africa, a debate erupted concerning large conglomerates built up during the former regime. It is uncertain whether distributive justice permits such conglomerates to remain intact or requires them to "unbundle" into smaller businesses that might be more amenable to egalitarian ownership and control of the sort denied under apartheid laws.

International Distributive Justice

Philosophers dispute whether, and to what extent, principles of distributive justice apply internationally. One view contends that the international arena lacks the requisite background institutions and cooperative arrangements to permit redistribution of wealth from developed countries to poor countries. Opponents contend that proper respect for distributive justice dictates that concerted efforts be made to further develop global institutional mechanisms (such as the United Nations) to this end. Even if such institutions are dissimilar to nation-states, they might lend greater warrant to the redistributive mandates of global justice.

International distributive justice may be seen as requiring fair risk distribution by multinational corporations (*see* MULTINATIONALS). The idea is that by transferring hazardous technology to less-developed countries, multinational businesses should not impose significantly higher risks by operations in host countries than would be permitted in a home country. In addition, international distributive justice encompasses the controversial question of whether corporations ought to render assistance to people deprived of basic human rights in less-developed countries with which they do business.

Executive Salaries

Executive salaries are sometimes criticized as inimical to the requirements of distributive justice. This is especially so in cases where a company's profits decline while the executive's salary increases, and those in which there is an unconscionably high ratio between the salaries of the lowest-paid employees and executives. Even if an executive's salary is lowered, his or her overall compensation may appear excessive due to bonuses and stock options. However, to the extent that such latter forms of compensation are tied to successful corporate performance from the executive's leadership, arguments that such compensation is undeserved tend to carry less weight (*see* EXECUTIVE COMPENSATION).

Bibliography

Arthur, J. & Shaw, W. (eds). (1978). *Justice and Economic Distribution.* Englewood Cliffs, NJ: Prentice-Hall.

De George, R. T. (1993). *Competing with Integrity in International Business.* New York: Oxford University Press.

Donaldson, T. (1989). *The Ethics of International Business.* New York: Oxford University Press.

Jackson, K. (1994). *Charting Global Responsibilities: Legal Philosophy and Human Rights.* Lanham, Md.: University Press of America.

Nozick, R. (1974). *Anarchy, State and Utopia.* New York: Basic Books.

Rawls, J. (1971). *A Theory of Justice.* Cambridge, Mass.: Harvard University Press.

KEVIN T. JACKSON

diversity   refers to 1) an array of characteristics of human beings which significantly mark their own and/or others' perceptions of their individual and group identities, especially characteristics of race, gender, ethnicity, age, national origin, sexual orientation, religion, physical ability, and class; and 2) the heterogeneity of a group or organization based on the inclusion of individuals of different backgrounds or experiences, especially in the areas listed above. As a positive goal for organizations, achieving diversity usually refers not only to numerical inclusion, but also to the creation of an organizational climate in which diverse individuals are able to perform optimally as individuals, in teams, and as a community of the whole.

The Concept of Diversity

Diversity as a concept involves complexity and ambiguity along several dimensions. First, the differences between individuals which are seen to constitute "diversity" vary according to the observer. Characteristics other than those listed above which are sometimes perceived to indicate the "diversity" of human beings include veteran's, educational, and marital/parental status; geographic origin; learning styles; "functional" differences (the function played by an individual within the organization, e.g., engineering, human resource management); status within an organization (managerial or nonmanagerial, for instance, or exempt or nonexempt); and corporate personnel identification, in the case of acquisitions and mergers.

The differences between individuals are myriad; usually only those we invest with cultural importance are seen as aspects of "diversity." "Cultural" here refers to that which carries with it a pattern of beliefs, perceptions, or experiences adhering to a group. Thus the opening definition indirectly suggests that the characteristics of race, gender, ethnicity, age, national origin, sexual orientation, religion, physical ability, and class may be invested with cultural importance – patterns of experiences, beliefs, self-perceptions, or perceptions by others – for members of that group.

A second complication immediately emerges: all of us occupy a number of these "categories of identity" at once. For instance, an upper-class heterosexual Hispanic woman and a white lesbian living close to the poverty line share the category of gender. But economic class, race, and sexual orientation will mark their experiences as well as gender; and the very meaning of gender – the particular way in which it is constructed for and by them – will be shaped in some way by the particular ways in which our culture constructs and invests with meaning other categories that they occupy. Companies assessing and responding to diversity issues for "women" find that diversity *among* women must be responded to as well. Xerox Corporation's attempt in the 1970s to create a monolithic "women's caucus" was unsuccessful; today women employees at Xerox have created numerous women's caucuses, some solely for minority women, some for exempt women, some for non-exempt women, among others (Sessa, 1992, p. 49). (*See* FEMINIST ETHICS; WOMEN AT WORK).

A third abiding tension in the diversity movement is the organization's – and employee/manager's – need to recognize a particular individual's complexity, even as the significance of her or his group identities and needs is recognized. If this tension is not maintained, recognizing "difference" based on group categories can come perilously close to the stereotyping that diversity programs aim to eliminate. Clearly the unique complexity of a particular individual exceeds the shaping of her or his identity by race or gender or any other category or combination of categories of experience.

Fourth, it is useful to notice the relational nature of diversity: we see a characteristic in ourselves or others as constituting "difference" when that characteristic varies from the culturally-prescribed norm. Thus in many fields of work, women add "diversity" – because men are seen as the norm in that field. In a field traditionally dominated by women, like nursing, men add "diversity" and represent "difference." As Martha Minow points out, "If difference is no longer presumed to be inherent in the 'different' person but is instead a feature of a comparison drawn between people, the relationships behind the comparisons become salient and crucial. . . . The [individual] . . . in a wheelchair becomes less 'different' when the building, designed without him in mind, is altered to permit his access" (1990, p. 12).

A final aspect of complexity in the concept of diversity can also be understood with this example. Equality in a diverse workplace may sometimes be achieved through providing different treatment for the "different" group, and sometimes through ensuring the same treatment for the different group as for those in the majority group. To ensure equal access to the workplace for the individual in a wheelchair, different accommodations for that individual are necessary. Perhaps an even clearer example is

the case of schoolchildren in the 1960s in San Francisco public schools who spoke primarily Chinese, who were falling behind in classes taught only in English. After their concerned parents were met by the school system with the argument that the children simply were being given equal treatment, the same provided by the schools for all children, their parents took the matter to court. Finally in 1974 the Supreme Court ruled that in order to ensure "equality" – equal access to education – for these children, "difference" in treatment was necessary: some affirmative plan was necessary "to rectify the language deficiency" (Minow, 1990, pp. 19–20) (*see* EQUALITY).

Perhaps more than any other aspect of diversity, this concept – that organizational equality may mean "difference" rather than "sameness" of treatment – has been a source of friction. A tension between majority rights – often couched as "individual rights" – and minority rights – often couched as "group rights" – often exists within efforts to diversify organizations (see *Regents of the Univ. of California* v. *Bakke*, which popularized the concept of "reverse discrimination": 347 US 483, 74 S. Ct. 686, 98 L.Ed. 873 (1954). This tension particularly resides around legal mandates for affirmative action. Embedded in many arguments against affirmative action is the assumption that the status quo situation is neutral and "natural," and that thus a neutral stance toward the individual who is judged "different" from the norm is indicated. Proponents of affirmative action reply that a neutral stance will simply perpetuate an inequity – not "natural" but historical – that is part of the status quo.

Roots of the Diversity Movement

The current movement in the US aimed at addressing diversity issues in organizations was immediately preceded and made possible by the Civil Rights Movement of the 1950s and 1960s, and the Women's Movement of the 1960s and 1970s. Since those two seminal social-change movements, various other group movements have emerged – for the rights of immigrants, gays, those with disabilities, Hispanics, Native Americans, Asian Americans, and others – that have also been interwoven into the fabric of what we understand to be diversity.

Legal decisions, executive orders, and regulations have paved the way for an increased attention to diversity issues in organizations. Probably the most powerful of these was *Brown* v. *Board of Education* (438 US 265, 98 S. Ct. 2733, 57 L.Ed.2d 750 (1978)), which ruled as illegal the practice of creating so-called "separate but equal" systems of racially segregated public schools.

Rulings during the 1960s which have had particular impact in the area of current diversity initiatives include Title VII, the 1964 Civil Rights Act (as amended in 1972), which prohibits employment discrimination on the basis of race, religion, gender, or national origin; Executive Order 11246 (1965), which requires employers holding federal contracts to create affirmative action plans for minorities, women, persons with disabilities, and veterans; and the Age Discrimination in Employment Act (1967). More recently came the Immigration Reform and Control Act of 1986, prohibiting discrimination by employers on the basis of national origin; the Americans with Disabilities Act of 1990; and the Civil Rights Act of 1991, which granted to individuals charging discrimination on the basis of race, color, gender, age, disability, and/or national origin the right to a jury trial, and the possibility of compensatory and punitive damages. The Civil Rights Act of 1991 also specifically provides that victims of sexual harassment, who previously could receive settlements only of back wages, can win punitive and legal damages.

Civil rights legislation and court decisions have been joined by the forces of demographic and social change in shaping the diversity movement within business. Though Friedman and DiTomaso have argued convincingly that the projections of workforce diversity in the Hudson Institute's *Workforce 2000* (Johnson & Packer, 1987) have been misunderstood and thus exaggerated, they acknowledge that several demographic forces are at work: 1) increasing numbers of white men are projected to retire from the workforce by the end of the century; 2) white women have been entering the workforce in unprecedented numbers; and 3) while the percentage of African American men and women in the workforce is fairly stable, immigration will support increased percentages of other minorities in the workplace, especially Hispanic men (Friedman & DiTomaso, 1994).

Social change, though inseparable from both legal and demographic change, has manifestations that affect business which are beyond either of these. Xerox Corporation, for instance, began a powerful commitment to affirmative action and diversity after race riots occurred in 1964 in Rochester, New York, where corporate headquarters are located; confirming that commitment were legal actions (the Civil Rights Act of 1964, Executive Order 11246, a class-action suit), a second race riot in Rochester in 1967, and the initiation of black caucus groups within Xerox (Sessa, 1992, p. 41). Another kind of revolution among women in terms of self-perception has led to vastly increased numbers of white women in the workplace (African American women already having been involved in the workplace in relatively high percentages), and more recently to increased emphasis on the quality of life in that workplace for all women, regardless of race. As Fernandez points out, "Nearly 90 percent of Fortune 500 companies have received complaints of sexual harassment, and more than one third have been sued at least once" (1993, p. 203).

Current and Developing Trends

Based on several decades of involvement with affirmative action programs and with the diversity movement, many business organizations are recognizing the continued need for both. Building the critical mass necessary to escape tokenism and combat stereotyping is a first step that is still necessary in many organizations (see Bowens et al., 1993, p. 40). What is increasingly evident is the need to diversify business organizations across strata. Least successful have been attempts to infiltrate the top levels of American management, which remain peopled almost solely with white males. Inevitably this is an increasing focus as middle management becomes more diverse by gender, race, and ethnicity, and ready to take on top leadership positions.

Five trends seem to be developing in the area of diversity in business organizations. First, diversity is seen increasingly as part of a "business strategy" – that is, something that is integrated into the strategic plan for the business, and inseparable from the goals of the organization as a whole. Effective communication between diverse employees; the ability of management to make decisions that are not distorted by stereotypes; service to customers who are increasingly diverse; responsiveness to (and good public relations with) the surrounding community; and not just competent but visionary leadership for change within both domestic and international workplace and market arenas – these are joining the traditional goals of legal mandates to foster diversity in business organizations.

Second, it has become clear that recruiting increasing numbers of employees who are "different" from the white male norm is not sufficient to create a stable and optimally functioning diverse workforce. Assimilation, a mistaken goal of some affirmative action programs, has been replaced by the goal of reshaping the organization so that it is flexible enough to meet different needs. The "norm" once aimed at through assimilation is itself shifting.

Demographics may not be destiny, as the Hudson Institute's *Workforce 2000* would have it; but demographics may provide a map which if followed will lead to a new destination. For instance, by the year 2000, 47 percent of the labor force in the US will be women (Johnson & Packer, 1987, p. 85). More than two of every three children under the age of six have mothers who are part of this labor force (Morrison, 1993, p. 57). Other studies show that three-quarters of working women are in their childbearing years (Morrison, 1993, p. 58). Some business organizations have begun to respond to this reality with maternity- and family-leave policies, childcare support, flex time, job sharing, part-time and work-at-home options, and other "family-friendly" policies. Many more will do so in the future. Again, economic reasons will drive this: turnover at Corning, for instance, has dropped 50 percent since family-friendly policies were introduced (Fernandez & Barr, 1993, p. 209).

Reshaping the organization may be the solution in other ways in the future as well. Demographic studies show a projected shortage of new entry workers who are educated or trained sufficiently to fill positions which are increasingly technical or communication-oriented in nature. The California Franchise

Tax Board, faced with such a situation in the context of mandated hiring of ethnically diverse and under-educated welfare recipients, chose to build into the company itself on-site responses to the issues facing their employees. The result was a visionary sweep of on-site programs aimed at upgrading skills at every level of the organization: FTB felt that "making the program inclusive reinforced the participative element of the organization's culture . . . [t]raining programs ranged from basic skills for operators to a Master's degree in taxation for auditors" (Barzelay & Moukheibir, 1993, p. 2). Even more impressive in their innovation were support programs for employee needs like childcare and transportation to work. The latter was a particularly egregious problem for many low-level workers; FTB worked with the Sacramento public transit system to extend light-rail service to FTB's front door.

The California Franchise Tax Board worked closely with the local school system as well, going so far as to collaboratively design courses which would ensure students having the skills to fulfill positions at FTB upon graduation. At the managerial level, Pacific Bell and other major corporations have introduced successful "grow-your-own" programs to support minority college and graduate students who then fill management positions in the companies upon graduation. This is a technique increasingly used successfully by companies which want to shape the demographic picture rather than be shaped by it.

A third trend in responding to diversity in the workplace is the recognition that issues of climate demand attention, if diverse individuals are to flourish. Approaches vary widely, from sensitivity training to skills training; increasingly it appears that a combination of the two may be most effective. A recent survey of 55 major corporations showed that more than half are conducting diversity training of some kind (Laabs, 1993). Some of the impetus here is avoidance of litigation: between 1985 and 1992, for instance, more than 7,500 sexual harassment complaints were filed with the Equal Employment Opportunity Commission (the EEOC) (Fernandez, 1993, p. 203).

A fourth trend is related to this: there is much less trepidation about support for initiatives that focus on difference than when, for instance, the first Black caucus groups formed at Xerox Corporation in 1965. But part of this trend is an increasing recognition of the complexity of difference – the diversity of diversity. At Xerox, for instance, where Hispanic and women's caucuses have joined the Black caucus groups, this diversity among caucus groups has affected the very categories that Xerox uses to monitor its Balanced Work Force goals; from the previous groupings of majority and minority male and female, the categories are shifting to reflect gender categories of specific minority groups (African Amercian, Asian American, Hispanic, and Native American).

Inevitably there has been and will be a backlash against diversity movements within business organizations. The very attention to the complexity of difference can be threatening to those who perceive that ethnic or racial or gender identity can fracture community wholeness and harmony. Partly for this reason, a last trend is to approach diversity within an organization as a reality and an opportunity for the whole. "Difference" is recognized not as residing only within the ethnicity or gender or sexual orientation or other quality of those who do not fit the putative "norm," but as part of every individual within the organization. At its best this trend becomes not a pulling back from hard issues of race or gender or other "minoritized" categories, but a deepening of an organization's commitment to genuine change.

Again, different approaches are taken here, ranging from the emphasis on skill improvement for all sectors and strata at California Franchise Tax Board to the small group dialogues promoted at Digital through their "Valuing Differences" program. What seems strongest about this trend toward exploring the diversity of the whole is related to the insights of the "learning organization" movement, as espoused by Peter Senge (1990) and others: through suspending and testing assumptions in dialogue with others, relationship may be fostered; through risking the surfacing of mental models, learning will be experienced. That experience of relationship and learning, on both the organizational and interpersonal levels, is the ultimate goal of managing diversity in business organizations.

See also **affirmative action programs; equal opportunity; gay rights; multinational marketing; multiculturalism; racism; sexual harassment; women in leadership; work and family**

Bibliography

Barzelay, M. & Moukheibir, C. (1993). *The California Franchise Tax Board: Strategies for a Changing Workforce.* Case Program, Kennedy School of Government. Cambridge, Mass.: Harvard University.

Bowens, H., Merenivitch, J., et al. (1993). Managing cultural diversity toward true multiculturalism: Some knowledge from the black perspective.In R. R. Sims & R. F. Dennehy (eds), *Diversity and Differences in Organizations: An Agenda for Answers and Questions.* Westport, Conn.: Quorum Books, 33–46.

Fernandez, J. P. & Barr, M. (1993). *The Diversity Advantage: How American Business Can Out-Perform Japanese and European Companies in the Global Marketplace.* New York: Lexington Books of Macmillan.

Friedman, J. & DiTomaso, N. (1994). What managers need to know about demographic projections. Unpublished paper, July 1994. Presented at the AACSB/GMAC Conference on New Models of Management Education, Philadelphia, 23 and 24 Sept.

Johnson, W. B. & Packer, A. H. (1987). *Workforce 2000: Work and Workers for the 21st Century.* Indianapolis, Ind.: Hudson Institute.

Laabs, J. (1993). Interest in diversity training continues to grow. *Personnel Journal,* Oct., 18–20.

Minow, M. (1990). *Making All the Difference: Inclusion, Exclusion, and American Law.* Ithaca: Cornell University Press.

Morrison, P. A. (1993). Congress and the year 2000: Peering into the demographic future. *Business Horizons,* Nov./Dec., 55–63.

Senge, P. M. (1990). *The Fifth Discipline: The Art and Practice of the Learning Organization.* New York: Doubleday.

Sessa, V. I. (1992). Managing diversity at the Xerox Corporation: Balanced workforce goals and caucus groups.In S. E. Jackson & Associates, *Diversity in the Workplace: Human Resource Initiatives.* New York: Guilford, 37–64.

SHARON L. DAVIE

Drucker, Peter F. (1909–), probably the postwar era's best-known authority on management, was born in Vienna, Austria, and was educated there and in Frankfurt, Germany. Since 1971, he has been a professor at the Claremont Graduate School in California.

Two principle themes run through Drucker's discussions of BUSINESS ETHICS. In his book *Management.*, published in 1974, he rejects two contrasting views of business ethics. One is the SOCIAL RESPONSIBILITY view, which asks, in his mind, "that business become the keeper of society's conscience and the solver of society's problems." Here and elsewhere in his writings, Drucker conceptualizes modern society as a society of special-purposes organizations, each with limited capabilities and bounded authority (Drucker, 1974, p. 315). At the same time, he rejects Milton Friedman's argument that business should confine itself exclusively to its economic task (*see* FRIEDMAN, MILTON). Drucker's position is that business executives must seek a middle ground, taking responsibility for the social impacts of their organizations, but limiting their efforts to tasks suited to their organizations' capabilities and their politically legitimate spheres of influence.

Drucker's second theme is that business ethics "is to ethics what soft porn is to the Platonic Eros" (Drucker, 1993, p. 195). Ethics is a matter of the right actions of individuals – regardless of the social role an individual may hold. He interprets contemporary business ethics as a version of CASUISTRY, which for Drucker is the long-discredited idea that leaders are exempt from the ethical obligations that bind ordinary men and women. Drucker's own view of business ethics draws partly upon a tradition of prudence that he traces to ARISTOTLE and to several ideas from the Confucian tradition. Members of organizations – businesses, hospitals, churches, or universities – are inevitably enveloped, he believes, in a web of obligations to other parties, and these fundamental relationships, and in particular the explicit and tacit rules that guide them, as well as the everyday behavior and practices they require, are the soundest guides to ethical action.

Bibliography

Drucker, P. F. (1974). *Management.* New York: Harper & Row.

Drucker, P. F. (1993). Can there be "business ethics"? In P. Drucker, *The Ecological Vision*. New Brunswick: Transaction Publishers, 195–214.

JOSEPH L. BADARACCO, JR.

drugs: abuse, advertising, testing   *see* SUBSTANCE ABUSE, DRUG TESTING, ADVERTISING SUBSTANCES

due process   a means by which one can appeal a decision in order to get an explanation of that action and/or a disinterested, objective, or fair judgment of its rightness or wrongness. In the law due process guarantees people protection from governmental action. According to the Fifth and Fourteenth Amendments of the US Constitution, every accused person has a right to a fair hearing and an impartial evaluation of his or her guilt or innocence.

There are two components of due process: procedural and substantive. Procedural due process demands that people have access to channels through which they can challenge decisions; substantive due process entails inquiry into the types of reasons that undergird decisions.

In the context of the workplace, due process is, or should be, a formal procedural right: the right of employees and employers to grievance, arbitration, or some other appeals procedure to evaluate an employer's decision in firing, promotion, or demotion, or to judge questionable activities of employees. At a minimum, it would give a person a right not to be transferred, demoted, or fired without a hearing or some other grievance procedure. Procedural due process would give employees rights to some form of grievance procedure; substantive due process would require that there be good reasons for employment decisions. Substantive due process does not preclude demotion or firing, but it questions the arbitrariness of employment decisions.

Traditionally, courts have recognized the rights of corporations in the private sector of the economy to procedural due process without requiring due process for employees within those companies. The justification put forward is that since corporations act in the public interest, they, like persons in the public areas, should be afforded the right to due process. Persons in private employment, on the other hand, are not subject to or protected by the principles that govern the public domain.

The rationale for not requiring due process in the workplace is grounded in the distinction between the "public" and the "private." This distinction falls out of a tradition in Western thinking that distinguishes between the public and private spheres of life. The public sphere contains that part of a person's life that lies within the bounds of government regulation; the private sphere contains that part that lies outside those bounds. This is essentially an appeal to the right to privacy: at home a person may do as she wishes, but in public these activities are restricted by the rights of others. By analogy, what goes on in a privately owned business or corporation lies outside the public domain of jurisdiction (Wallace, 1986, pp. 583–600).

Recently, however, there has been an increasing overlap between private enterprise and public interests such that at least one legal scholar argues that "developments in the twentieth century have significantly undermined the 'privateness' of the modern business corporations, with the result that the traditional bases for distinguishing them from public corporations have largely disappeared" (Frug, 1980, p. 1129). Yet, despite this trend, the failure to recognize employee rights including the right to due process has not been affected.

Interestingly, due process *is* guaranteed for permanent full-time workers in the public sector of the economy, that is, for workers in local, state, and national government positions. The reasoning for that is as follows. The Constitution restricts governmental actions, even when the government is acting as an employer. The Constitutional provisions that protect liberty and property rights guarantee that any alleged violation or deprivation of those rights may be challenged by some form of due process, and employment falls within the relevant category of liberty and property rights. According to recent US Supreme Court decisions, when a state worker is a permanent employee he or she has a property interest in his or her employment. Because his or her productivity contributed to the place of employ-

ment, a public worker is entitled to his or her job unless there is good reason to question that (e.g., poor work habits, habitual absences, and other abuses). Moreover, if a discharge would prevent him or her from obtaining other employment, that employee has a right to due process before being terminated.

This justification for extending due process protections to public employees is grounded in a public employee's proprietary interest in her job. If that argument makes sense, it is curious that this justification does not apply to rights of employees in the private sector as well, since the distinction between public and private employment rests on the nature of employer, not on the proprietary interests or lack thereof in one's job.

The expansion of employee protections in the private sector to what might be considered just claims to due process gives to the state and the courts more opportunity to interfere with the private economy, and thus might further skew a precarious but delicate balance between the private economic sector and public policy. But, if the distinction between public and private institutions is no longer clear cut, and the tradition of the public versus private spheres is no longer in place, it is increasingly difficult to distinguish rights of public employees from those of employees in the private sector. It is inconsistent not to recognize and extend constitutional guarantees so as to protect all citizens equally. Moreover, if due process is crucial to political relationships between the individual and the state in all areas, even in employment, why is it not central in relationships between employees and corporations, since at least some of the companies in question are as large and powerful as small nations? It is, in fact, not in keeping with our democratic tradition *not* to mandate such rights.

Bibliography

Ewing, D. (1977). *Freedom Inside the Organization*. New York: McGraw-Hill.

Frug, G. E. (1980). The city as a legal concept. *Harvard Law Review*, **93**, 1059–154.

Wallace, R. (1986). Union waiver of public employees' due process rights. *Industrial Relations Law Journal*, **8**, 583–600.

Werhane, P. (1985). *Persons, Rights, and Corporations*. Englewood Cliffs, NJ: Prentice-Hall.

Werhane, P. & Radin, T. (1995). Employment at will and due process. In T. Donaldson & P. Werhane (eds), *Ethical Issues in Business,* 4th edn. Englewood Cliffs, NJ: Prentice-Hall.

PATRICIA H. WERHANE and TARA J. RADIN

duty An obligation, that is, an action which is morally obligatory. An ethical theory which focuses on identifying a person's duties is called a duty-based theory. Hence, duty refers both to the obligatory nature of particular actions and to a way of reasoning about what is right and what is wrong in terms of what a person's obligations are.

A particular duty-based theory will lay out its own system of determining what duties a person has. Generally such theories recognize duties like the following: duties not to commit suicide, not to lie, not to kill or harm or use others as means to some other end, and duties to act justly, to make reparation, to benefit the lives of others, and to respect persons. There may be many more duties and duties that appear in a more particular form, for example, duties that are qualified, as in the duty not to kill another except in self-defense.

Duties can be classified in various ways. A duty may require that the moral agent omit some act, that is, not do something (not lie), or a duty may require that the agent commit some act, that is, do something (benefit others). A duty may be a duty to self (not to commit suicide) or it may be a duty to others (not to make false promises). Some duties may be seen as absolute or primary (preserve life) while other duties are seen as relative, capable of being overridden, or secondary (preserve confidentiality). Duties are said to be perfect if they allow no exceptions and imperfect if they allow exceptions. Some duties are said to hold universally and obligate all persons (act justly) while others hold only for those in certain professions (physicians, CEOs) or those holding certain positions (parent).

The concept of duty is also related to the concept of right. Some theorists maintain that RIGHTS or moral claims give rise to duties and so are a more fundamental way of analyzing moral situations. Whether or not rights ground duties, there is recognized to be a correlativity between rights and duties. For every right there is a corresponding duty (one's right to privacy corresponds with the duty of others not to interfere with one's privacy). But the reverse relationship does not hold. For each duty there is not always a corresponding right (one's duty to be generous does not correspond with a right on the part of specific others to expect that generosity be practiced towards them). The duties that correspond with rights are called duties of perfect obligation, while those that do not correspond with rights are duties of imperfect obligation.

Duty-based ethical theories can be characterized in three ways. First, they do not consider virtues or rights or consequences to be fundamental ways of analyzing moral situations. An ethical theory grounded on duty posits that a moral agent must carry out duties or even act for the sake of duty in order to be acting morally. A duty-based theory considers what obligates the moral agent. It is not concerned primarily with the virtuous state of the moral agent's character or the rights of individuals or groups or the ends aimed at by the action.

Second, duty-based theories are described as non-consequential or deontological (*see* CON-SEQUENTIALISM). A non-consequential theory is one in which the rightness or wrongness of an action does not depend solely on whether the action produces good or bad consequences. A consequential theory maintains that an action is right if it has good consequences and wrong if it has bad consequences. For a consequential theory, rightness is a function of goodness whereas for a non-consequential theory, rightness is independent of goodness. Hence, for a duty-based theory, rightness and wrongness are defined by whether the act follows from duty or does not.

Third, duty-based theories focus on the moral agent and his or her actions and reasons for acting. In this approach, the person who will be acting is the focus of moral consideration and not the moral claims or rights of others. It is especially to the moral agent himself or herself that a duty-based approach looks and not particularly to the moral agent in a community.

Duty-based theories may differ from one another in several ways. First, they may make different assessments of the role of consequences in their non-consequential theories. A duty-based theory may not allow consequences to play any role in identifying duties or resolving conflicts among duties. On the other hand, it may allow that consequences play a role in determining what duties a person has or in the process of prioritizing duties when a person cannot act in a way to carry out all his or her duties. Also, these theories offer different explanations of what grounds or generates duties (in other words, different accounts of where duties come from). In addition, they posit different lists of the precise duties that people have (in other words, different accounts of what a person's duties are).

Three examples of duty-based theories are: the Divine Command theory, Immanuel Kant's categorical ethic, and W. D. Ross's *prima facie* duty ethic. The Divine Command theory maintains that God's law is the source of duties. For Kant, reason or rational nature is the source of duties, and for Ross *prima facie* duties are self-evident. For the Divine Command theory, duties arise from a source (namely, God) external to or outside the moral agent. For Kant, duties arise from an internal source (reason). Ross asserts that duties arise because the acts themselves are of a certain kind and have a certain nature. Kant's categorical ethic is well-known as the best example of a pure duty-based ethic in which consequences are understood to play no role in determining duties or judging among duties (*see* KANTIAN ETHICS).

See also **Rawls, John**

Bibliography

Braybrooke, D. (1972). The firm but untidy correlativity of rights and obligations. *Canadian Journal of Philosophy*, 1, 351–63.

Frankena, W. (1963). *Ethics*. Englewood Cliffs, NJ: Prentice-Hall.

Kant, I. (1964). *Groundwork of the Metaphysic of Morals*, trans. H. J. Paton. New York: Harper and Row.

Lyons, D. (1970). The correlativity of rights and duties. *Nous*, 4, 45–55.

Prichard, H. A. (1912). Does moral philosophy rest on a mistake? *Mind*, 21, 121–52.

Rawls, J. (1971). *A Theory of Justice*. Cambridge, Mass.: Harvard University Press.

Ross, W. D. (1930). *The Right and the Good*. Oxford: Clarendon Press.

VICTORIA S. WIKE

E

economic efficiency The ethical implications of economic efficiency arise within a behavioral definition of profit maximization and focus on long-term OPPORTUNITY COST decisions about the allocation of scarce resources.

From a technical perspective, profit maximization is defined as the set of conditions where marginal revenue is equal to marginal cost (MR=MC), and the marginal-cost curve intersects the marginal-revenue curve from below. It is at that point, and only at that point, that a firm operates at a level of output that guarantees the community the maximum amount of goods and services produced from a given set of scarce resources.

From a behavioral perspective, MR=MC can be translated into producing the right kind and the right amount of goods and services consumers want at the lowest possible cost. The right kind and amount of goods and services are determined by the market, that is, supply and demand. Producing at the lowest possible cost is probably the most recognizable tenet of business behavior. Assuming consumer sovereignty (consumer wants) and low-cost market advantage (lowest possible cost), the behavior of profit maximization also recognizes that all resources used in production are scarce. Accordingly, inefficient use of any scarce resource is unethical because it yields fewer goods and services to the community of individual consumers. Efficient use of scarce resources is ethical because it yields more goods and services to the community of consumers.

Within profit maximization, economic efficiencies are tied to cost-allocation decisions. These costs are usually defined as fixed, variable, and opportunity costs. In accounting, these cost allocation decisions are defined in terms of fixed and variable costs. From this perspective, efficiency is focused on the allocation of fixed and variable costs. In economics, these cost-allocation decisions are defined in terms of fixed, variable, and opportunity costs. This difference in determining profits is crucial.

Opportunity costs are forgone goods and services that could have been produced from a given set of resources that were used to produce other goods and services. Once resources are allocated to establishing a used-car lot in an Amish community, or to producing chairs rather than automobiles, these resources are forgone. They can never be used to provide other goods and services for the community.

Rather than centering allocation decisions simply on fixed and variable costs, economic efficiency and profit maximization would situate the allocation of these costs within the wider context of opportunity costs. Internally, the focus would be on efficient use of the factors of production: capital, labor-time, land, creativity-entrepreneurship.

The costs associated with the factors of production are described as payments: the payment to capital is interest; to labor-time, wages; to land, rent; to creativity-entrepreneurship, profits. When each of the factors of production is regarded as a scarce resource, it is a matter of economic efficiency and of good ethics to pay each according to market standards, that is, the value of its marginal product. To pay either more or less is economically inefficient and unethical. It would also result in opportunity costs for the company. Paid less than the value of his/her marginal product, the employee, a scarce human resource, would leave the company. Paid more, the company's opportunity costs would result in fewer resources from which to produce the goods and services the community wants.

Externally, a firm's opportunity costs are tied to every consideration arising from the greater community in which the firm exists, from the immediacy of geographical location to philosophical, religious, legal, sociological, and cultural implications of the greater world. To choose to establish a used-car lot within an Amish community would be inefficient and unethical because the religious practices of a certain people within a certain place were not considered. Likewise, to ignore gift-exchanging in Japan would be inefficient and unethical.

From an ethical perspective, profit maximization and the efficiencies of profit maximization become the primary standard of judgment. Other implications, for example, legal, religious, philosophical, enter into judgment as opportunity-cost considerations. These considerations can and do change. The changing medical and political sentiment against smoking cigarettes would be an opportunity-cost consideration for the tobacco industry. Similarly, social and legal prohibitions against certain drugs can and do change. Profit maximization and economic efficiency, valuing the sovereignty of the individual consumer and of the individual producer, reserves judgment, in the final analysis, to the market. However, it brings all of these market interests into the equation through long-term opportunity cost considerations.

Opportunity cost decision-making does not ignore CONFLICT OF INTEREST between individual ethics and corporate ethics. Rather, it assumes a distinction between an individual's ethics and a company's ethics. As the individual's ethics could be religiously or philosophically determined, the firm's ethics should be economically determined. It is, therefore, of tremendous importance that the individual defines his/her own ethics and that the company does the same. The individual is, then, in a position to judge whether to enter into, and contribute to, a certain industry or company. The ethical mandate of the company is to profit maximize through economic efficiencies. Ethical concerns about the company's

product (the right kind of goods and services) are determined primarily by the market and individual producers and consumers.

This paradigm for business ethics focuses on economic efficiency as explained in the behavior of profit maximization and measured by opportunity costs. It is grounded in business theory and practice, uses the language of business, and relates directly to the ordinary behavior of men and women in business.

See also **profit, profits; profit and the profit motive**

Bibliography

Primeaux, P. & Stieber, J. (1994). Profit maximization: The ethical mandate of business. *Journal of Business Ethics*, 13, 287–94.

Primeaux, P. & Stieber, J. (1995). *Profit Maximization: The Ethical Mandate of Business.* San Francisco: Austin & Winfield.

Stieber, J. & Primeaux, P. (1991). Economic efficiency: A paradigm for business ethics. *Journal of Business Ethics*, 10, 335–9.

PATRICK PRIMEAUX
JOHN STIEBER

economic justice   The core problem of economic justice is straightforward: On what basis should economic goods and services be distributed? This question has long interested philosophers and other thinkers, but it gains urgency in light of the vast disparities in income and wealth we see all around us. How, for example, can it be just or fair that some eat food scrounged from garbage cans while others dine at expensive restaurants, that the top 1 percent of US households own more than the entire bottom 90 percent, or that since 1980 the compensation of the average CEO has jumped from 42 to 157 times that of a production worker?

Various principles of economic justice have been advanced. Some believe that justice requires an equal distribution of goods and resources. Others recommend that distribution correspond to individual need, effort, merit, or social contribution. Each of these principles seems plausible in some circumstances – for example, merit seems the appropriate basis for promotion, need the basis for distributing food stamps. Yet each of these common principles has its problems, and none seems to work in enough circumstances to be successfully defended as *the* principle of economic justice.

Some philosophers are content with saying that there are various principles of economic justice and that one must simply choose the one that best applies to the situation. If several principles apply, one must weigh them as best one can. Other philosophers, however, have offered more comprehensive theories of economic justice as a basis for assessing rival economic systems. Among the most influential of these theories have been UTILITARIANISM, LIBERTARIANISM, and the social-contract approach of John Rawls (*see* SOCIAL CONTRACT THEORY; RAWLS, JOHN).

Utilitarianism

Utilitarians assess actions, policies, and institutions in terms of the happiness or unhappiness they produce. Economic justice, too, is a function of what maximizes happiness. Thus, John Stuart Mill (1806–73) argued that whether more talented workers should receive greater remuneration cannot be determined by abstract principles but only by social utility. Utilitarianism ties questions of economic justice to the promotion of social well-being or happiness, and utilitarians thus favor whatever economic system will produce the most social good. But which system is that? The answer depends on the utilitarian's understanding of the relevant social, economic, and political facts and possibilities. Utilitarians in the early nineteenth century typically advocated laissez-faire capitalism, believing that unregulated markets and free competition would best promote the total social good. Today there is no consensus among utilitarians on economic matters, but they are likely to favor social welfare and a more equal distribution of income. The reason for this rests on "the declining marginal utility of money" – the idea that successive additions to one's income produce, on average, less happiness or welfare than did earlier additions. This suggests that increasing the income of those who now

earn less would do the most to boost total welfare (*see* MILL, JOHN STUART).

Libertarianism

Libertarians reject utilitarianism's concern for total social well-being and contend that justice consists in permitting each to live as he or she pleases, free from the interference of others. Libertarians place individual liberty at center stage and believe that we possess certain natural rights, including the right to property and the right not to be coerced by others, independently of any social or political institutions.

The influential libertarian Robert Nozick has argued that a state that uses taxes to redistribute income violates individual liberty by forcing people to support projects or people they have not freely chosen to support. Nozick's *entitlement theory* states that one is entitled to one's holdings (that is, goods, money, and property) as long as one has acquired them fairly, that is, without injuring others, defrauding them, or otherwise violating their rights. If you have acquired your holdings justly, you are entitled to do with them as you wish. No one else has a legitimate claim on them. Even though other people may be going hungry, justice imposes no obligation on you to help. Nozick rejects theories that require distribution to fit some pattern. His theory is historical: What matters is how people come to have what they have. If people are entitled to their possessions, then the distribution of economic holdings is just, regardless of what it happens to look like. Rival theories inevitably involve violations of liberty by forbidding "capitalist acts between consenting adults" (*see* NOZICK, ROBERT).

Rawls's Theory

Although Rawls represents his hypothetical-contract theory as an alternative to utilitarianism, he conceives of society as a cooperative venture for mutual advantage, and does not base his theory, as Nozick does, on the postulate that individuals possess certain natural rights. Rawls's strategy is to ask what principles people would choose to govern society if, hypothetically, they were to meet for this purpose in what he calls the "original position." Although in the original position people choose on the basis of self-interest, they are imagined to be behind a "veil of ignorance," not knowing their race, sex, personal talents and characteristics, or whether they are rich or poor. Rawls argues that people in the original position would not insist on absolute equality. Rather they would embrace the *difference principle*, which permits social and economic inequalities but only if they are to the greatest expected benefit of the least advantaged. Inequalities are not justified if they maximize total happiness; rather, they must make the least-well-off segment of society better off than it would otherwise have been. Rawls suggests that either a democratic socialist system or a liberal form of capitalism with sufficient welfare provisions might satisfy his principle.

Whether a theory like Rawls's can be extended internationally and whether one can talk meaningfully of global economic justice have been debated issues. Even more controversial has been COMMUNITARIANISM's critique of LIBERALISM (seen as embracing utilitarianism, libertarianism, and Rawls) and its skepticism toward abstract theories of economic justice. Communitarians insist instead on the complexity of justice and stress its intimate connection to particular practices and historically evolved conceptions of the good that characterize different communities. The debate over communitarianism and among the theories of economic justice described above lies at the heart of contemporary political and moral philosophy.

Bibliography

Arthur, A. & Shaw, W. H. (eds). (1991). *Justice and Economic Distribution*, 2nd edn, Englewood Cliffs, NJ: Prentice-Hall.

Brandt, R. B. (1992). Utilitarianism and welfare legislation. In *Morality, Utilitarianism, and Rights.* Cambridge: Cambridge University Press, 370–87.

Kymlicka, W. (1990). *Contemporary Political Philosophy*. Oxford: Oxford University Press.

Mill, J. S. (1979 [1861]). *Utilitarianism*. Indianapolis, Ind.: Hackett.

Nozick, R. (1974). *Anarchy, State, and Utopia*. New York: Basic Books.

Pogge, T. W. (1989). *Realizing Rawls*. Ithaca: Cornell University Press.

Rawls, J. (1971). *A Theory of Justice*. Cambridge, Mass.: Harvard University Press.

WILLIAM H. SHAW

economic liberty   consists in the freedom of agents to dispose, for economic purposes, of the objects or powers to which they are entitled in any way they choose as long as this disposition does not prevent other agents from enjoying a comparable discretionary control over the objects and powers to which they are entitled. Thus, economic liberty is a major subcategory of liberty understood as the freedom to depose of one's own as one chooses. As the definition of economic liberty makes clear, determining whether an agent enjoys or suffers a loss of economic liberty requires prior judgments about what entitlements that agent has.

Since there are many competing views about what entitlements people have, there are many particular conceptions of economic liberty. An advocate of everyone's joint entitlement to all economically useful objects and powers will have to hold that economic liberty is fully realized only when collective decisions determine the economic use of everything. Any individual's private economic deployment of anything will count as an infringement upon economic liberty. At the other end of the ideological spectrum, the advocate of the justice of private rights in economically useful objects and powers will hold that economic liberty is fully realized only when each individual rightholder has full discretionary control over her own. PROPERTY (subject to the limitations to which she has freely agreed).

This familiar capitalistic conception of economic liberty envisions an economic regime of extensive and robust private property in which single agents or voluntary associations coordinate the exercise of their rights through market and contractual relationships. In search of economic gains and guided by the price signals generated by competitive markets and by their special knowledge of their own skills and circumstances, agents will deploy, recombine, transform, or exchange their holdings so as maximally to meet others' demands for goods and services. Capitalist economic liberty (CEL) is compromised whenever any agent, including any governmental agent, constrains private owners in their separate or mutually agreed-to utilizations of their legitimate holdings.

Among the justifications offered by advocates of CEL are: (a) Respect for CEL is respect for people's underlying rights over themselves and their holdings; (b) CEL tends to move existing skills and resources to their most highly valued uses and to motivate the discovery of talents and resources and their development by those generally best situated to deploy them; (c) CEL's requirement that people interact on the basis of voluntary exchange, and not on the basis of force or fraud, guarantees that all interacting parties benefit from their interactions; (d) As long as individuals are not subject to force or fraud, any negative externalities they may suffer from others' transactions are likely to be counterbalanced by positive externalities; (e) The introduction of regulatory and redistributive mechanisms which contravene CEL tend increasingly to divert effort, talent, and resources from productive economic activity to the unproductive pursuit of political clout; (f) Even if large-scale economic coordination of an efficiency comparable to that achieved through CEL could be achieved through central planning or regulation, imposed coordination would require a vast and dangerous expansion of the State's coercive powers.

Thoroughgoing critics of CEL reject most or all of these contentions. They reject the model of individual rights to human and extra-human resources and may even challenge the presumption that individuals are the loci of moral claims. Such critics will reject the idea that complex and mutually beneficial economic coordination is more likely to emerge endogenously out of market and contractual processes than out of conscious political design and organization. Thoroughgoing critics will often reject the conception of voluntariness presupposed within the capitalist model of economic liberty, arguing instead that many capitalist relationships are coerced or exploitative. This charge of exploitation will often be linked to the claim that the distribution of holdings which sets the stage for capitalist transactions is itself unjust, while other critics will charge that the distributive outcome of CEL is unjust. (These last two charges suggest a program of melding CEL with some system of resource redistribution.)

Other critics of CEL raise more technical objections about, e.g., the tendency of CEL to give rise to harmful economic monopolies or to fail to promote unprofitable public goods. Many additional criticisms of CEL are essentially cultural. The central and honored place advocates of CEL propose for economic self-interest, bargaining, commerce, and profit-making is said to create a world which is mean-spirited, dehumanizing, alienating, and/or corrupting. Cultural critics from both ends of the conventional political spectrum argue that the rise of capitalist interactions and the dispositions and values they foster undermine our affective ties and capacities and thereby damage both ourselves and those who otherwise would be beneficiaries of our affections. These critics maintain that, in a social order which gives considerable scope to CEL, the perception of certain objects or activities, e.g., bodily organs, blood, sexual encounters, the bearing of babies, as commodities to be delivered if the price is right leads to the displacement or degeneration of valuable, non-market, forms of life and interaction, viz., spontaneous donations of organs and blood, loving sex, meaningful maternity. Cultural critics of CEL believe that the seductive allure of the rewards and practices of commercial society generates distorted or inauthentic preferences. Individuals can only be protected from succumbing to these damaging preferences by legal restrictions upon those rewards and practices or on people's pursuit of them – legal restrictions formulated by those with undistorted insight about people's authentic preferences.

Bibliography

Buchanan, A. (1985). *Ethics, Efficiency, and the Market.* Totowa, NJ: Rowman and Allanheld. (Especially for moral arguments against economic liberty).

Cowen, T. (ed.), (1988). *The Theory of Market Failure.* Fairfax, Va.: George Mason University Press.

Hayek F. A. (1960). *The Constitution of Liberty.* Chicago: University of Chicago Press.

Machan, T. R. (1990). *Capitalism and Individualism.* New York: St Martin's Press.

Mack, E. (1992). Economic liberty. *Encyclopedia of Ethics.* New York: Garland Publishing. (Especially describes cultural criticisms).

Murphy, J. (1981). Consent, coercion, and hard choices. *Virginia Law Review,* 67, 79–95.

Radin, M. (1987). Market-inalienability. *Harvard Law Review,* 100, 1865–1937. (A version of cultural criticism).

Siegan, B. H. (1980). *Economic Liberties and the Constitution*. Chicago: University of Chicago Press.

ERIC MACK

economics and ethics

I. Economics

"Economics" is frequently defined as the science of choice, where choice is understood to be the selection of one course of action (or policy) from among a set of options, on the basis of weighing costs and benefits. Essential to the economic conception of choice is the recognition that every choice involves costs – at the very least, the cost of the most valued forgone alternative that could have been chosen. Economics attempts to explain particular choices of individuals by applying a model of rationality. Large-scale social phenomena, such as the behavior of markets, are then explained by showing how they emerge from the interactions of large numbers of individual choices.

The model of rationality that mainstream economics employs is that of. *individual utility-maximization*. The rational individual is understood to be an agent who attempts to maximize his expected utility. In contemporary economics, utility is identified with the satisfaction of preferences.

As a *positive* (that is, explanatory and predictive) theory, economics purports to be able to account for human behavior so far as individuals act rationally (in the defined sense). However, to the extent that human beings care about being rational, to describe an action as rational is to commend it, while to characterize an action as irrational is usually taken to be a criticism. For this reason, the model of rationality with which economics operates is viewed as *normative* as well as positive. In other words, economics purports not only to explain and predict behavior (so far as it is rational), but also to guide behavior by determining how agents, including policy-makers, should act if they wish to act rationally.

II. Ethics

"Ethics" is sometimes understood to refer to a code of conduct, but in the literature of contemporary ethics generally and of business

ethics in particular it is more often understood to be a *practical activity* – a reflective and self-critical process of making decisions about which acts (or policies) are right, wrong, or permissible. As a practical activity, ethics is also understood to include the process of making judgments about the praiseworthiness or blameworthiness of particular agents. Furthermore, ethics is a *rational* practical activity at least in the sense that both in ethical theorizing and in everyday ethical discourse, *reasons* are given to support or to criticize the moral judgments individuals make.

It is therefore appropriate to request that one who advances a moral judgment be prepared to support it, and to support it with relevant considerations. Generally speaking, only certain sorts of considerations are widely recognized to be relevant in moral discourse – only certain types of reasons count as reasons to support or criticize moral judgments. Among the most important are appeals to basic and widely shared values – fairness, human welfare, and individual autonomy being among the most common. One distinctive feature of moral reasons is their *impersonal* character. If A declares that abortion is wrong, it is appropriate for B to ask "And why is it wrong?" Moreover, if A were to answer "Because it makes me ill" he would not have given the right sort of reason to support his judgment, because a statement of personal distaste does not qualify as the sort of consideration that can support a moral judgment.

Many ethical theorists have also observed that moral judgments themselves have an equally important characteristic: They are made from a point of view which purports to be impartial. Thus if a person sincerely makes a moral judgment (for example, about the rightness of a certain act) then he is understood to be committed to universalizing the judgment – that is, to judging that the same type of act, in the same circumstances, would be right if another person performed it.

III. The Apparent Conflict Between Economics and Ethics

Economics appears to recognize only one reason for acting – namely, that doing this rather than that will maximize one's expected utility. Ethics, in contrast, not only offers a variety of considerations (human welfare, individual autonomy, fairness, etc.), but also requires that individuals sometimes act contrary to their own interests. On the surface at least, then, ethics and economics advance opposing conceptions of how one ought to choose. Moreover, if the model of economic rationality is accepted as a positive theory, an account of how human beings do in fact invariably behave, it seems to rule out the possibility of ethical conduct. If all people actually do – and all they can do because of the laws of human psychology – is to seek to maximize their expected utility, then it is futile to exhort them to act ethically. To the extent that economic thinking dominates the methodology of the sorts of courses that are taught in business schools and pervades the characteristic patterns of decision-making of business people, the very idea of business ethics becomes problematic.

IV. The Theory of the Market as the Reconciliation of Ethics and Economics

Some of the most eloquent advocates of the extensive market systems of social interaction that emerged in Western Europe in the seventeenth and eighteenth centuries proposed a way of reconciling economics and ethics. DeMandeville (1714) argued that in a market system "private vices" make "public virtues": purely self-interested conduct that fits the traditional description of moral vices, if it occurs within the context of market institutions, produces public benefits. Similarly, Adam Smith (1776) extolled the market as a system that harnesses self-interested action for the common good. DeMandeville and Smith presaged the First Fundamental Theory of Welfare Economics: In a perfectly competitive market, free exchanges among individual utility maximizers will result in an equilibrium that is efficient in the Paretian sense of efficiency – there will be no redistribution of goods that will make anyone better off without making someone worse off.

According to this simple conception of the relation between ethics and economics, the realm of market exchanges is an area of human life in which ethics is not needed for the production of morally admirable results. Human welfare emerges, in the aggregate, as a fortunate by-product of amoral or even immoral behavior.

This simple view of the relationship between economics and ethics is itself subject to ethical criticism, however. One obvious difficulty, of course, is that markets in the real world are not perfectly competitive and lack other features, such as perfect information, which the ideal market of the First Fundamental Theorem possesses. Thus the justification for reliance upon market systems, and for tolerating unethical behavior within them, cannot be that market systems are necessarily efficient.

More importantly, however, a number of ethical theories, as well as much common-sense moral thinking, challenge the assumption that efficiency is a sufficient standard for evaluation. The main difficulty is that outcomes can be efficient (in the technical economic sense explained above) and yet grossly unfair. For example, a system in which a minority of masters owned everything and a majority of slaves owned nothing would be efficient in the Paretian sense if it were not possible to improve the lot of the slaves without worsening that of the masters.

The basic point can be put in a different way, without recourse to such an extreme example. Economic theory only tells us that in perfect markets efficient outcomes will emerge from free exchanges for gain, but market processes cannot be expected to correct for inequities in the initial distribution of assets which individuals bring to the market. Some individuals, through no fault of their own, simply have fewer assets to bargain with. Ethical reasoning is needed to determine whether, or under what conditions, undeserved differences in initial endowments are unjust; and if so, what means of correcting or preventing them are permissible.

A second major area in which economic thinking by itself is inadequate and in which reliance upon ethical reasoning is unavoidable is the problem of *externalities*. In all real-world markets there are externalities or "spill-over" effects, costs or benefits that arise from exchanges but that accrue to others than (or in addition to) the exchangers themselves. A familiar example is pollution. When a manufacturer and a supplier of raw materials make an exchange which allows the manufacture of a chemical, they each calculate the costs and the benefits of the exchange to themselves. However, if, as a result of the exchange, toxic fumes are discharged into the air, costs will be imposed on others and these costs will not be fully taken into account in the exchange. In some cases economics can offer suggestions as to how to "internalize external costs" (for example, by a policy in which the government issues exchangeable permits to spill certain amounts of pollution into the air), but economics cannot by itself tell us whether such a policy is fair or even whether the harm which the externality represents is important enough to require such remedies.

Two more examples will illustrate the dependence upon ethics of economics, as a discipline which purports to provide guidance for policy. First, consider the pervasive policy question of which sorts of goods or services ought to be offered for sale in markets. Should not only cars and legal services but recreational drugs, sex, or babies for adoption be marketable? Positive economics can tell us under what conditions marketing an item will contribute to efficient outcomes, but it cannot tell us whether it ought to be marketed if it is admitted that there are other considerations that are relevant besides efficiency. To assume that efficiency is the only thing that matters is to endorse a particular moral theory – namely utilitarianism – not to avoid moral theory, and economics by itself cannot tell us which moral theory to endorse.

Second, consider a basic tool of economic analysis for government bureaucracies and businesses as well: Cost–benefit analysis. Although cost–benefit analysis is often presented as if it were a value-neutral, scientific procedure for making decisions about the use of scarce resources, in fact a number of difficult ethical questions must be answered before it can be employed. The first of these, of course, is "Whose costs and benefits are to count?" The second is "Whose judgments about costs and benefits are to be used?" (For example, in deciding whether to commit public funds for abortion, do we count costs to fetuses?) A third question is a variant of a complaint noted above concerning the use of efficiency as the sole or overriding standard for evaluation: "Why should we be concerned only with maximizing the ratio of benefits to costs rather than with how costs and benefits are distributed among

people who will be affected?" (For example, if we think that one element of a just health-care system is the fair distribution of the costs of providing access to care for all, then we are denying that distribution of costs and benefits is irrelevant.) In addition, the standard ways of measuring costs and benefits are themselves subject to serious moral criticisms. For example, when cost–benefit analysts assign a value to lives they typically either equate the value of a life with total expected life-time earnings or with how much the individual would be willing to pay to avoid some specified probability of death. The former measure systematically disadvantages women and minorities who have lower expected life-time earnings, due to historical patterns of educational and employment discrimination. The latter, if taken literally, automatically assigns higher value to the lives of the wealthy, since how much an individual is willing to pay is a function of how much resources he or she has access to.

None of this is to deny, of course, that ethics does not also depend upon economics, as well. Any ethical theory in which a consideration of the consequences of actions and policies for human welfare or freedom is understood to be relevant will require some way of estimating costs and benefits. Similarly, any acceptable view of the ethically responsible use of resources will have to be concerned with efficiency to some extent.

V. The New Economics: Making Room for Ethics

One of the most striking and fruitful developments in economics in recent years has been a growing awareness that peoples' ethical commitments do in fact influence their behavior in all areas of human life, even the life of "economic man" in the market. As a consequence, economists are rethinking the very foundations of their discipline, as well as their conception of its subject matter. Instead of assuming that all behavior is self-interested and in consequence proposing far-fetched egoistic explanations of what certainly seems to be non-self-interested behavior, more and more economists are attempting to see how the standard tools of economic analysis can be adapted to model moral behavior. Thus far, four main areas of research have been especially prominent: (1) the role of moral commitments in solving or avoiding problems in the supply of public goods; (2) the function of moral commitments in fostering successful cooperation within organizations; (3) the necessity of moral commitments for the well-functioning of markets; and (4) the contribution which moral commitments make to the welfare of the individuals who have them.

(1) *Morality and public goods.* Standard economic analyses which assume that most agents act in purely self-interested ways in all circumstances predict that public goods will not be supplied or will be undersupplied if contribution to them is left voluntary. The prediction is that if he can expect to enjoy the good if it is produced through the contributions of others, each self-interested individual will refrain from contributing because he will regard his own contribution as an available cost. Unfortunately for the analysis, there are many cases in which public goods are supplied at higher levels than the analysis predicts, even without resorting to coercion to ensure contributions. Substantial voter turn-out is one example among many: If voters behaved as standard economic theory predicts no one would vote in elections in which the chance that his vote would determine the outcome are negligible, yet many people do vote in these circumstances. Once we allow the possibility that significant numbers of people may vote because they believe it is their *duty* to do so and that their sense of duty overrides or suspends a purely self-interested calculation of the expected costs and benefits of contributing to the public good of substantial voter turn-out, we have the beginnings of a more satisfactory analysis of voting behavior.

(2) *The contribution of morality to successful cooperation in organizations.* A number of empirical studies (e.g. Guth et al., 1982) have revealed the role that moral values play in fostering successful and sustained cooperation in organizations, including business firms. In particular, there is considerable evidence that commitment to moral norms concerning fairness is often crucial in avoiding or resolving conflicts between labor and management and that recognition of workers' rights to participate in decision-making can increase productivity.

(3) *The moral underpinnings of markets.* Unless most participants in market exchanges have a modicum of trust and honesty, for example, transaction costs and enforcement costs for commercial contracts would be prohibitively high. Moreover, since the efficiency of markets depends upon competitiveness, moral inhibitions against engaging in anti-competitive practices (including sabotaging one's rivals) play an important role even if they are viewed only as supplementing the fear of prosecution for violations of antitrust law. For these reasons what may be called the morality of the market is sometimes described as a public good for all who seek to benefit from markets: It is in everyone's interest that there be sufficient moral commitments among others so that markets can function well, even though from a purely self-interested point of view, being moral is a cost to the individual and he has reason to attempt to take a free ride on the moral restraint of others.

(4) *The contribution of an individual's moral commitments to his own self-interest.* The final area of economic research on ethics challenges the preceding assumption that individual self-interest only speaks in favor of encouraging moral commitments in *others*, as opposed to oneself. To take only one example that has been studied in some detail (Frank, 1988), the fact that an individual who is a potential cooperator is known to be honest can make it possible to overcome "commitment problems" that otherwise might block mutually advantageous cooperation. Commitment problems are ubiquitous in business and wherever there are principal/agent relationships with significant agency risks. An agency risk exists whenever there is a divergence between the interests of an agent to whom a principal entrusts some activity and the interests of the principal which he engaged the agent to further. Often, close monitoring of the agent's activity is not feasible or would be too costly to the principal. Under such circumstances the ability of the agent to make a credible commitment to serve the principal's interest even when not doing so would further his own interests is a valuable economic asset for the agent. Moreover, for a number of reasons, the least costly way for an agent to be able to convince others that he has certain moral

qualities (such as honesty) may be to actually cultivate those qualities, not merely to try to feign them.

In all of these areas of research, economists are expanding what has traditionally been regarded as the proper subject matter of economics to include moral behavior, not just self-interested behavior. In doing so, they are recognizing a more complex and mutually enriching relationship between economics and ethics.

Bibliography

Bowie, N. (1991). Challenging the egoistic paradigm. *Business Ethics Quarterly*, 1, 1–21.

Buchanan, A. (1985). *Ethics, Efficiency and the Market*. Totowa, NJ: Rowman & Allanheld.

Collard, D. (1978). *Altruism and Economy: A Study in Non-selfish Economics*. New York: Oxford University Press.

DeMandeville, B. (1714). *The Fable of the Bees*, ed. P. Harth. Harmondsworth: Penguin.

Etzioni, A. (1988). *The Moral Dimension: Toward a New Economics*. New York: Macmillan.

Fox, A. (1974). *Beyond Contract: Work, Power and Trust Relations*. London: Faber.

Frank, R. (1988). *Passions within Reason: The Strategic Role of the Emotions*. New York: W. W. Norton.

Guth, W., Schmittberger, R., & Schwarze, B. (1982). An experimental analysis of ultimate bargaining. *Journal of Economic Behavior and Organization*, 3, 367–88.

Hausman, D. & McPherson, M. (1993). Taking ethics seriously: Economics and contemporary moral philosophy. *Journal of Economic Literature*, 31, 671–731.

Isaac, R. M., Mathieu, D., & Zajac, E. E. (1991). Institutional framing and perceptions of fairness. *Constitutional Political Economy*, 2, 329–70.

Smith, A. (1776, 1976). *An Enquiry into the Nature and Causes of the Wealth of Nations*, (eds) R. H. Campbell & A. S. Skinner. Oxford: Clarendon Press.

ALLEN BUCHANAN

efficient markets   The operation of the market system that uses and allocates resources by means of the price mechanism so as to minimize cost while satisfying demand.

In a capitalist economy, markets for labor, capital, and goods will reach an equilibrium at the point where demand equals supply. The free movement of prices is the coordinating mechanism for the large and varied decisions made by buyers and sellers. This INVISIBLE HAND allows individuals in the market to fulfill their needs efficiently without the costly intervention of a central authority. A subset of this concept, the "efficient market theory" focuses on efficiency in capital markets, building on the assumption that the current price of an asset reflects all of the information available to buyers and sellers.

Vilfredo Pareto (1848–1923) refined and specified the criteria by which to evaluate the operation of the market under the direction of the invisible hand. He focused on the outcomes of the market in relationship to the well-being of the individuals within the total economy. PARETO OPTIMALITY (or Pareto efficiency) means that efficiency is achieved only if a change in the market leads to some people being better off without making anyone else worse off. Individuals will exchange with each other so that the ratios of the marginal utilities of goods are equal to the ratios of their prices. Pareto argued that the optimum point of exchange does not require any comparison between the total utility of each person involved.

Three conditions are necessary to achieve Pareto optimality (Pareto efficiency) – exchange, production, and product-mix efficiency (Stigler, 1993). Exchange efficiency means that goods are distributed among individual buyers to satisfy their preferences. The price system encourages continued exchanges up to the point where no further trade can take place. Production efficiency is achieved when it is no longer possible to produce more of some goods without producing less of others. The price system signals the scarcity of the resources needed by producers. This leads them to make more efficient use of resources and drives down costs. When the mix of products offered for sale in the economy fully reflects the preferences of consumers, product-mix efficiency is achieved. Increased demand for one product translates into higher prices, which leads producers to shift their production in order to gain greater profit.

Pareto's work laid the foundation for the development of the field of WELFARE ECONOMICS, which is concerned with defining the necessary conditions for efficiency because of market imperfection. The unequal distribution of income within an economy, which was not important to Pareto for assessing market efficiency, is a major point of contention in determining these conditions. Some contend that income inequity is an inevitable consequence of the operation of efficient markets. Any attempt to modify the market process will create inefficiencies. Others argue that significant differences in income have severe consequences for individuals and society. Therefore, it is necessary to alter the market operation to narrow this gap. The debate is often framed as a trade-off between efficiency and equality.

Bibliography

Okun, A. M. (1975). *Equality and Efficiency: The Big Tradeoff.* Washington, DC: Brookings Institution.
Pareto, V. (1971 [1927]). *Manual of Political Economy.* London: Macmillan.
Reiter, S. (1987). Efficient allocation. In J. Eatwell, M. Milgate, & P. Newman (eds), *The New Pelgrave: A Dictionary of Economics,* vol. 2. London: Macmillan, 107–20.
Sen, A. (1987). *On Ethics and Economics.* Oxford: Blackwell.
Stigler, J. E. (1993). *Economics.* New York: W. W. Norton.

D. JEFFREY LENN

egoism, psychological egoism and ethical egoism   The term "egoism" is ordinarily used to mean "exclusive concern with satisfying one's own desires, getting what one wants." Dictionaries tend to support this. They call "egoism," for instance, "1. selfishness; self-interest. 2. conceit" (*Webster's New World Dictionary*). The term "egotist" is often a substitute, although it's defined differently, for example, as "excessive reference to oneself." The ego is the self. But we should distinguish first between "selfishness," "self-interest," and "interest of the self." They usually mean, respectively, "concern exclusively and for indulging one's desires," "consideration based first on what is good for oneself without

the exclusion of others," and "that which motivates an autonomous person." These will help us appreciate what follows (*see* RATIONAL CHOICE THEORY).

"Egoism" is also used in ethical considerations of how human beings do or ought to live. It is thus often qualified by such terms as "ethical" and "psychological." So what determines the most sensible meaning of the term? It is crucial, first of all, what the *ego* is. If it is the unique identity of the individual human being or self, what exactly is this?

Some argue that everyone is, to use KARL MARX's term, a collective or *specie*-being. Others, in turn, hold that the human being is first and foremost related to a supernatural God and has a body (which is of this earth) and a soul (of the spiritual realm) combined in one person. Some others say a human being is an integral and unique whole, comprised of many diverse facets. Egoisms differ depending on which of these is taken to be true.

Psychological Egoism

Some hold we are all automatically selfish. So just as it is a constitutive part of us that we have certain physical organs and functions – a heart, brain, liver, blood circulation, motor behavior – so it is that we *will* act to advance our own well-being, that we will attempt to benefit ourselves at all times. We are supposed to be instinctively moved to act selfishly. Here is one way of giving expression to what seems to be the gist of this idea: "[E]very individual serves his own private interest . . . The great Saints of history have served their 'private interest' just as the most money grubbing miser has served his interest. The *private interest* is whatever it is that drives an individual" (Friedman, 1976, p. 11).

Egoism concerns itself with *benefiting oneself.* To do this is to provide oneself with what one requires for flourishing, excelling, developing in positive ways. Different explanations of what that comes to can be given. For example, some hold that to benefit oneself is to become satisfied. Benefiting oneself would be to obtain whatever one would like to have, or to enable one to do what one wants to do. Here is how THOMAS HOBBES put the point: "But whatsoever is the object of any man's Appetite or Desire, that is it which he for his part calleth Good: and the object of his Hate and Aversion,

Evill . . . For these words of Good and Evill . . . are ever used with relation to the person that useth them: there being nothing simply and absolutely so; nor any Common Rule of Good and Evill" (Hobbes, 1968, p. 120).

Yet, the above paradoxically implies that if someone were to want to do or have something obviously self-destructive, the person would be benefited. Being benefited, then, may be different from having one's desires satisfied or one's wants fulfilled. If so, then psychological egoism would mean that everyone does what one benefits from in terms of some objective standard of well-being, not based just on what one desires or likes.

We might make this more sensible by adding that what we desire or want is always something *we take to be* of benefit to ourselves. When we take a job, go on a vacation, seek out a relationship, or, indeed, embark on an entire way of life, we may be doing what *seems to us best*. Is this what is meant by the view that we are necessarily selfish?

Yet what is meant by "what seems to be best"? If one says, "This *seems* to me to be a vase," we know what is meant because we know what it *is* to be a vase. So could one tell what *seems to be of benefit* to oneself, *seems to contribute to one's well-being*, without any standard independent of what one desires or wants determining what *is to one's benefit, contributes to one's well-being*? No.

Some argue that despite its troubles, we can make good use of psychological egoism as a technical device, e.g., in the analysis of market behavior – of how people act when they embark on commercial or business tasks. By assuming that's how people act in markets, we can anticipate trends in economic affairs. In fact, however, when these estimates are made, usually certain assumptions are invoked about what *in fact is of benefit to us*. So even as an analytic device the psychological egoist position by itself seems to be difficult to uphold as a cogent doctrine.

Ethical Egoism

Ethical egoism states that one *ought to* benefit oneself, first and foremost. Yet, this by no means tells it all, as we have already seen in connection with psychological egoism. The precise meaning of ethical egoism also depends upon what the ego is and what it is to be benefited.

Subjective egoism. The most commonly discussed version of ethical egoism differs only in one basic respect from psychological egoism. According to this *subjective* egoism, the human self or ego consists of a bundle of desires (or drives or wishes or preferences) and to benefit oneself amounts to satisfying these desires in their order of priority, which is itself something entirely dependent upon the individual or, as it is often put, a subjective matter. Why this is still a type of *ethical* egoism is that everyone is supposed to *choose* to satisfy the desires he or she has – that is, one *ought to* attempt to satisfy oneself.

Criticisms: But this view is said to have serious problems, too. First, if John desires, first and foremost, to be wealthy; next, to be famous; then, to find a beautiful mate; then, to please some of his friends; then, to give support to his country; then, to conserve resources; and finally to assist some people who are in need, John ought to strive to achieve these goals in this order of priority. But how John ought to rank these goals cannot be raised. (Here is where the position is similar to the first version of psychological egoism: the desires are decisive in determining what benefits John.) Yet that is crucial in ethics.

Next, a *bona fide* ethical theory must be *universalizable* (i.e., needs to apply to all choosing and acting persons), *unambiguous* (provides clear guidance as to what one ought to do), *consistent* (does not propose actions which contradict one another), and is *comprehensive* (addresses all those problems that are reasonably expected to arise for a person). And this subjective egoist position fails to satisfy these conditions. For one, even for an individual, desires often oppose another. Any ethical theory has to avoid the problems cited above. Subjective egoism is, thus, often used as an example of a failed ethical theory. (Machan, 1983, pp. 185-202)

Classical egoism. A more promising ethical egoism states that each person should live so as to achieve his or her *rational self-interest*. (I have called this "classical" egoism to indicate its pedigree in Aristotelianism. It is also captured by the term "eudaimonist ethics.") Accordingly, as living beings we need a guide to conduct, principles to be used when we cannot assess the merits of each action from the start. As living beings we share with other animals the value of life. But life occurs in individual (living) things. And human living, unlike that of other animals, cannot be pursued automatically. We must learn to do it. And the particular life we can pursue and about which we can exercise choices is our own. By understanding *who and what we are*, we can identify the standards by which our own life can most likely be advanced properly, made successful, become a happy life.

In short, this ethical egoist holds that one's human life, the basis of all values, is to be lived with the aid of a moral outlook. Since (the value of) one's own life is the only one a person can advance in a morally relevant way (by choice), each person should live it successfully within that person's own context (as the individual one is, within one's circumstances). Even more briefly put, people should pursue their own individual happiness, and the principles that make this possible are the moral principles and virtues suited for leading a human life. The benefit one ought to seek and obtain is, then, not subjective but objective: it is one's own successful, flourishing human life.

The prime virtue in egoistic ethics is rationality, the uniquely human way of being (conceptually!) aware of and navigating the world. Success in life or happiness for any human being must be achieved in a way suited to human life. Accordingly, being *morally virtuous* consists of choosing to be as fully human as possible in one's circumstances, *to excel at being the human being one is*. Each person is a human being because of the distinctive capacity to choose to think, to attend to the world rationally (by way of careful and sustained principled thought); therefore, to succeed as a person, everyone should make that choice. All the specialized virtues in egoism must be rationally established (or at least capable of such establishment).

Egoism, unlike other ethical positions, considers the proper attitude in life to be informed selfishness – not, however, pathological self-centeredness (egotism). Pride, ambition, integrity, honesty, and other traits that are by nature of value to any human life are considered virtues. It is with regards to the sort of self that

is proper to a human being that one ought to be selfish, not just any sort of self. (Indeed, whether selfishness is to be thought of as good or bad depends on what the *self* is.) The worst, most reprehensible way of conducting oneself is to fail to think and exercise rational judgment, to evade reality and leave oneself to blind impulse, others' influence, the guidance of thoughtless clichés, and the like. Since knowledge is indispensable for successful realization of goals, including the central goal of happiness, failure to exert the effort to obtain it – thus fostering error, misunderstanding, and confusion – is most disastrous to oneself and, hence, immoral.

Finally, in classical egoism the goal, one's happiness, is something that should be sharply distinguished from pleasure, fun, or thrills. This type of egoism sets as our primary goal to be happy, which is a sustained positive reflective disposition, resulting from doing well in one's life *qua* the individual human being one is (Rand, 1964; Norton, 1976).

Business Ethics and Egoism

Egoism is of concern in the examination of business ethics, both when we use the latter to refer to how people in commercial and business endeavors ought to act, and what kinds of public policy should govern business and industry – to whit, capitalism, which arises from a legal system that respects and protects private property rights, and is an economic system that is closely linked to versions of egoism. ADAM SMITH, the founder of modern economic science, advanced something like a psychological egoist position about human motivation (although arguably Smith was not thoroughgoing in this – for example in his *The Theory of Moral Sentiments* he advances a different position). Many neoclassical economists incline toward psychological egoism when they discuss why people behave as they do, although since they refer to "utility maximization" rather than "the pursuit of self-interest," it is not always simple to classify their position (*see* SMITH, ADAM).

If there is something morally right about commerce and the profession of business, something along the lines of an egoistic principle must be included in the set of virtues human beings ought to practice. Thus some argue that *prudence* ultimately gives moral support to commerce and business (Den Uyl, 1991, and Machan, 1988).

Unless room is made for egoistic conduct as morally praiseworthy, commerce and business could be seen having nothing morally significant about them. In which case "business ethics" would be an oxymoron. (Many seem to believe just that, going on to require that corporate managers, executives, or owners do their morally good deeds apart from business – unlike the case with physicians, artists, or educators.) Indeed, in terms of classical egoism, commerce is a morally worthwhile undertaking and business an honorable profession. They are to be guided by both the general moral principles of human living and their specific professional ethics. The last posits the creation of wealth as its primary objective, to be pursued without violating principles of morality and through the effective achievement of prosperity with the appropriate enterprises selected accordingly. A banker ought to earn a good income from safeguarding and investing the deposits and savings of its customers, honestly, industriously, and with attention to the need to balance these undertakings with others that morality requires. So should an automobile executive, the CEO of a multinational corporation, or the owner of a restaurant. And this requires the institution of the right to private property and freedom of enterprise, lest the moral component – self-direction – be missing from how those doing business comport themselves.

Bibliography

Den Uyl, D. J. (1991). *The Virtue of Prudence.* New York: Peter Lang.

Friedman, M. (1976). The line we dare not cross. *Encounter*, **47**, (5), 11.

Hobbes, T. (1968). *Leviathan*, (ed.), with an intro. by C. B. Macpherson. Baltimore: Penguin.

Machan, T. R. (1983). Recent work in ethical egoism. In K. G. Lucey & T. R. Machan (eds), *Recent Work in Philosophy*. Totowa, NJ: Rowman and Allanheld. (For a discussion of this and other forms of ethical egoism).

Machan, T. R. (1988). Ethics and its uses. In T. R. Machan (ed.), , *Commerce and Morality*. Lanham, Md.: Rowman and Littlefield.

Norton, D. L. (1976). *Personal Destinies: A Philosophy of Ethical Individualism.* Princeton, NJ: Princeton University Press.

Rand, A. (1964). *The Virtue of Selfishness.* New York: New American Library.

TIBOR R. MACHAN

electronic surveillance   The term "electronic surveillance" currently has two distinguishable meanings of importance for ethical inquiry. The older, narrower, and more familiar meaning is exemplified in Presidential Order 12333 "United States Intelligence Activities" (Dec. 4, 1981) that states "electronic surveillance is acquiring nonpublic communications by electronic means without the consent of a person who is a party to an electronic communication or, in the case of nonelectronic communication, without the consent of a person who is visibly present at the place of communication, but not including the use of radio direction finding equipment solely to determine the location of a transmitter." Thus, wiretapping, bugging, and the use of directional microphones would be included but aircraft transponder signaling would not. Unless "informed consent" is taken loosely, this definition would include electronic tagging to monitor the whereabouts of offenders permitted to reside outside a prison and electronic monitoring of employees and customers.

Ethical issues involving electronic surveillance with this meaning include 1) violation of privacy in the sense of non-consensual and unwelcome presence of physical items placed by another party, 2) violation of privacy in the sense of non-consensual and unwelcome use of personal information and communciations, 3) the extent of morally permissible use of surveillance of suspect individuals and groups by government authorities for purposes of law enforcement and public defense, and 4) the extent of morally permissible use of surveillance of employees, customers, or competitors by business organizations in pursuit of competitive business interests or internal security. These issues have their non-electronic counterparts in a variety of cases involving stalking, mail tampering, unauthorized inspection of personnel records, clandestine photography, and employee drug testing. Because electronic surveillance in this narrower sense involves, by definition, a lack of unforced and informed consent by at least some of the parties being monitored, such activities are commonly judged *prima facie* immoral pending a satisfactory justification for them.

Electronic surveillance activities have been and are carried out by law-enforcement agencies, government intelligence agencies, business organizations, private investigators, and individual citizens or groups of citizens equipped with an increasingly efficient and numerous array of devices. Electronic monitoring of workers, including the monitoring of computer terminals, e-mail, observation or recording of worker activities, and telephone-call accounting, seems to be the topic attracting the greatest attention in business ethics. As Ottensmeyer and Heroux (1991) note, there is evidence that such worker monitoring is economically counter-productive as well as being ethically suspect. Marx and Sherizen (1986) have proposed guidelines to protect the interests of employees when electronically monitored by employers.

The second, broader, and more recent meaning of "electronic surveillance" does not immediately render a practice so designated as morally suspect although it may be open to a wider variety of moral concerns. Related to the increasingly common reference to modern life as being lived in a "surveillance society," "electronic surveillance" in this sense denotes the processes of obtaining, recording, storing, retrieving, matching, manipulating, analyzing, and transmitting personal and organizational information in electronic databases. From tax returns and social-security accounts to credit-card purchases and library checkouts, electronic records are made – and sometimes sold – containing data on people's health, education, employment history, travels, financial transactions, breaches of the law, consumer preferences, supported causes, and more.

While public discussion of databases has nominally focused on actual and potential violations of privacy, most writers seem basically concerned with the power to affect other's lives that database access gives. Stories abound involving erroneous data, misinterpretation of data, and mischievous use of data that lead in turn to terminated credit or medical insurance, exclusion from job candidate lists, or ruin of public reputation. Rothfeder (1992) details several such stories.

At least three non-exclusive types of organizational response have been made or proposed to deal with database misuse: governmental directives or legislation, business policies, and professional codes of conduct. Specific forms of all three types of remedies raise moral questions of informed consent, unwelcome consequences, personal or organizational responsibility for harm and the avoidance of harm, and extent of personal or organizational rights and authority.

Some codes of conduct for computer professionals have outlined society members' obligations regarding databases. The revised ACM Code (1992) cites obligations to "ensure the accuracy of data, as well as protecting it from unauthorized access or accidental disclosure," and others having to do with excessive collection of data, correcting inaccuracies, disposal policies, and handling electronic mail.

National legislation protecting personal information in databases dates back as early as Sweden's restrictive Data Act in 1973. *Guidelines on the Protection and Privacy of Transborder Flows of Personal Data* was published in 1980 by the Organization for Economic Cooperation and Development and subsequently adopted by all member countries. Having legal binding force on members, unlike the OECD *Guidelines*, is the Council of Europe's 1985 *Convention for the Protection of Individuals with Regard to Automatic Processing of Personal Data*. Such directives and legislation usually call for 1) the data subject to have knowledge of and to consent to the purpose of collection and subsequent use of the data, 2) restrictions on purposes and procedures of collection, 3) safeguards against loss, illicit use, and modification of the data, 4) the right of the data subject to be informed of the location or possessor of the data, to examine personal data, and to correct errors.

The basic US legislation governing federal databases is the 1966 Freedom of Information Act (amended in 1974 and 1986) and the 1974 Privacy Act (amended in 1988 and 1990). Similar legislation has been passed by some states (e.g. California and Massachusetts). The major US legislation that applies to private databases (credit bureaus) is the Fair Credit Reporting Act of 1970. Critics both in and out of government have argued that, given the magnitude of data collection and access, existing laws are either inadequate or under-enforced and additional legislation is needed.

See also **consent; ethical issues in computers and computer technology; ethical issues in information; ethical issues in technology; privacy; right to information**

Bibliography

Anderson, R., Johnson, D., Gotterbarn, D. & Perrolle, J. (1993). Using the new ACM code of ethics in decision making. *Communications of the ACM,* **36,** 98–107. (Contains the revised ACM Code adopted Oct. 1992.)

Donner, F. J. (1980). *The Age of Surveillance: The Aims and Methods of America's Political Intelligence System.* New York: Alfred A. Knopf.

Lyon, D. (1994). *The Electronic Eye: The Rise of Surveillance Society.* Minneapolis: University of Minnesota Press.

Marx, G. & Sherizen, S. (1986). Monitoring on the job. *Technology Review,* **89,** 63–72.

Ottensmeyer, E. & Heroux, M. (1991). Ethics, public policy, and managing advanced technologies: The case of electronic surveillance. *Journal of Business Ethics,* **10,** 519–26.

Privacy Rights Clearinghouse, The Center for Public Interest Law, 5998 Alcala Park, San Diego, CA 92110. E-mail: prc@teetot.acusd.edu. The PRC provides a website on privacy issues, accessible on the internet at http://www.acusd.edu/~prc/

Rothfeder, J. (1992). *Privacy for Sale.* New York: Simon & Schuster.

US Congress, Office of Technology Assessment. (1987). *The Electronics Supervisor: New Technology, New Tensions, OTA-CIT-333.* Washington, DC: US Government Printing Office.

US Department of Justice. (1992). *Freedom of Information Act Guide & Privacy Act Overview: September 1992 Edition.* Washington, DC: US Government Printing Office.

NEIL R. LUEBKE

emotions An emotion is a psychological process, state, or event, typically a reaction, virtually always accompanied by some sort of "affect" or feeling. The nature of emotions, however, is and long has been the subject of a lively debate by philosophers, psychologists, educators, and theologians, and various emotions have often been classified as great virtues (e.g., faith, love, compassion) or as vices (e.g., pride, envy, and anger). Not all emotions are reactions, and some may be durable features of a person's character. All emotions, however, are generally thought to be quite personal and potentially "irrational," that is, not sufficiently objective to be rationally effective.

Accordingly, emotions are often thought to be out of place in both business and BUSINESS ETHICS. Emotions are personal. Business is not. Business is considered a matter of hard-headed rationality, the province of the cool thinker, the calm and clever negotiator, the ingenious but not overly enthusiastic entrepreneur. Business ethics, accordingly, is typically presented as a matter of rationality, a matter of principles, beyond sentimentality. A boss who loses his or her temper displays signs of weakness or a lack or character. An employee or manager who weeps when fired is considered pathetic.

Yet, emotions lie at the very heart of both business and business ethics. In business, it is often noted that such emotional virtues as perseverance, courage, teamwork, and a certain amount of compassion for customers and employees are essential to good business. In business ethics, integrity is a central concern, but, as ARISTOTLE pointed out long ago, integrity is largely a matter of cultivating the right emotions. The idea that emotions get in the way of business and ethics is a dangerous if deep-seated prejudice.

The most successful people in business often say that they do it for the challenge, for the excitement, for the sense of competition, and camaraderie with others. Emotions are not "primitive" or "bestial" reactions, mere physiological disruptions, but indispensable motivations for whatever we do and would do well. Emotions provide the affections and sentiments that tie us to other people and prompt us to cooperate and care about them. Emotions have their own kind of "intelligence" and insight, not provided by the abstractions of rational DECISION THEORY or microeconomics. It is no accident that the greatest single defender of the free-enterprise system, Adam Smith, preceded his great work *The Wealth of Nations* with an equally substantial study of the "moral sentiments," the feelings that bind us together and make the cooperative competition of the market possible.

There are, of course, negative, destructive emotions, and emotions that can be destructive in the extreme. Some years ago, Helmut Schoeck (1966) wrote a book entitled *Envy*, in which he argued that this usually disdained emotion (one of the seven deadly sins) was in fact the psychological engine of capitalism. That may be true to a certain extent, but Schoeck underestimated the damage done by malicious envy, as opposed to the more healthy variety of aspiration that, for example, inspires advertisers and (they hope) their customers. So, too, a bit of ambition is indeed a good thing, but overweening ambition may be the greatest threat to integrity of all. There has been considerable debate ever since Machiavelli about whether it is better for bosses (or princes) to be "loved or feared," and the debate has raged ever since the days of Aristotle, over what place motivated self-interest, that is, what the medievals called "avarice," should play in human affairs. Today, of course, we call it "the profit motive," and in some quarters it is thought to have no proper ethical bounds. It does, however, have many emotional bounds. That which satisfies the profit motive may nevertheless leave persons deeply unsatisfied.

The most important and most neglected emotions in business and business ethics, however, are the most positive emotions, often dismissed as mere "sentimentality." Caring and compassion are not weaknesses but strengths in business. Several recent works on the subject of business and "caring" offer a more healthy (if somewhat exaggerated) alternative. True, an excess of compassion, pity, or personal affection can lead to some unfortunate business decisions, but the alternative is not cold and calculating ruthlessness, or what is often misidentified as "toughness." Business is not an impersonal game of wits and trades. It is a very personal, very human activity. To lose sight of that simple fact, not only in the excitement of the trading floor but also the friendship and genuine affection that is often (obviously not always) fostered between people who work together, is to miss the point of business, which is not only to "make a living" but to live well.

Bibliography

Calhoun, C., & Soloman, R., (eds) (1984). *What is an Emotion?* New York: Oxford University Press.

de Sousa, R. (1989). *The Rationality of Emotion.* Cambridge, Mass.: MIT Press.

Gibbard, A. (1990). *Wise Choices, Apt Feelings: A Theory of Normative Judgment.* Cambridge, Mass.: Harvard University Press.

Greenspan, P. (1988). *Emotions and Reasons.* New York: Routledge.

James, W. (1890). *What is an Emotion?* New York: Dover.

Neu, J. (1980. Jealous thoughts. In A. Rorty (ed.) *Explaining Emotions.* Berkeley: University of California Press.

Rorty, A. (1980). Explaining emotions. In A. Rorty, (ed.), *Explaining Emotions.* Berkeley: University of California Press.

Sartre, J.-P. (1948). *The Emotions: Sketch of a Theory.* New York: Philosophical Library.

Scheler, M. (1970). *The Nature of Sympathy,* New York: Archon.

Schoeck, H. (1966). *Envy.* New York: Harcourt Brace Jovanovich.

Smith, A. (1976). *The Theory of Moral Sentiments.* Oxford: Oxford University Press.

Solomon, R. C. (1976). *The Passions.* NewYork: Doubleday.

Solomon, R. C. (1988). *Ethics and Excellence: Integrity and Cooperation in Business.* Oxford: Oxford University Press.

Williams, B. (1973). Morality and the emotions. In *Problems of the Self.* Cambridge: Cambridge University Press.

ROBERT C. SOLOMON

employee stock ownership plans (ESOPs): a form of worker ownership of business firms recognized under the laws of the United States. Technically, an ESOP is a deferred benefit plan in which a company purchases shares of its own stock and places them in trust for its employees, who may claim their shares or sell them back to the company when they quit or retire. Companies may purchase shares for an ESOP either with cash or borrowed funds; in the latter case, the result is known as a leveraged ESOP.

Since 1974, when the first US enabling legislation was passed, the number of ESOPs in the US has grown rapidly. By late 1993, there were approximately 9,500 ESOPs in the US, covering over 10 million workers and controlling $150 billion in corporate stock. About 85 percent of ESOPs were in privately held companies, and employees controlled a majority of shares in less than 15 percent. Some of the best-known ESOPs included Publix (supermarkets), United Airlines, Avis (rental cars), Weirton Steel Corp., and W. L. Gore Associates (textiles).

Under US laws, ESOPs have a number of tax benefits. Company contributions to the plan are tax deductible, and employees owe no taxes until they claim their shares. In some cases, banks may deduct a portion of the interest received on loans to an ESOP.

Advocates have argued that in addition to the tax benefits, ESOPs help companies by aligning their interests with those of their workers. In this view, employee owners are likely to work harder and to be more committed to the firm, thus improving corporate performance. A review of empirical evidence (Quarrey & Rosen, 1994) found that employee ownership enhanced corporate performance, but only when linked with participative management practices. At Avis, for example, workers not only owned shares in the company but also participated directly in management decisions through "employee participation groups." Other companies with ESOPs used self-managed teams or had employee representatives on the board of directors. Companies with ESOPs that provided their employees with mechanisms for participation in decision-making significantly outperformed comparable non-worker-owned companies. Neither employee ownership nor participation alone, however, had a clear effect on performance.

Critics have argued that ESOPs represent a costly taxpayer subsidy to some workers and companies unwarranted by ESOPs' social or economic benefits. Other critics have contended that ESOPs are risky for employees because they concentrate retirement savings in investments in a single firm.

Most ESOPs are in the United States, although laws in England, Canada, Australia, Argentina, and the Philippines also permit the formation of employee stock ownership plans of some type. In the early 1990s, interest in various forms of employee ownership surged in Eastern Europe and in the former Soviet republics, where privatization laws encouraged the sale of formerly state-owned firms to their managers and workers.

Further information about ESOPs may be obtained from the National Center for Employee Ownership, a nonprofit research and information organization, at 1201 Martin Luther King Jr. Way, Oakland, Calif. 94612-1217; telephone 510-272-9461.

Bibliography

Blasi, J. R. & Kruse, D. L. (1991). *The New Owners: The Mass Emergence of Employee Ownership in Public Companies and What It Means to American Business.* New York: HarperCollins.
Kalish, G. I. (1989). *ESOPs: The Handbook of Employee Stock Ownership Plans.* Chicago: Probus.
National Center for Employee Ownership. (1993). *Employee Ownership Reader.* Oakland, Calif.: NCEO.
Quarrey, M. & Rosen, C. (1994). *Employee Ownership and Corporate Performance.* Oakland, Calif.: National Center for Employee Ownership.
Rosen, C. & Young, K. M. (eds). (1991). *Understanding Employee Ownership.* Ithaca: ILR Press.

ANNE T. LAWRENCE

employment at will   The principle of Employment at Will (EAW) is a common-law doctrine stating that, in the absence of law or contract, employers have the right to hire, promote, demote, and fire whomever and whenever they please. The principle was stated explicitly in 1887 by H. G. Wood, who wrote, "a general or indefinite hiring is prima facie a hiring at will" (Wood, 1887).

In the United States EAW has been interpreted as the rule that when employees are not specifically covered by union agreement, legal statute, public policy, or contract, an employer "may dismiss their employees at will . . . for good cause, for no cause, *or even for causes morally wrong*, without being thereby guilty of legal wrong" (Blades, 1967, p. 1405). Today at least 60 percent of all employees in the private sector of the economy, from part-time or temporary workers to corporate presidents, are "at will" employees.

EAW has been widely interpreted as allowing employees to be demoted, transferred, or dismissed without having a hearing and without requirement of good reasons or "cause" for the employment decision. This is not to say that employers do not have reasons, usually good reasons, for their decisions. But there is no legal obligation to state or defend their decisions. Thus EAW sidesteps the requirement of due process or grievance procedures in the workplace, although it does not preclude the institution of such procedures.

As a recognized common-law principle, traditionally EAW has been upheld in the US state and federal courts. However, in the last 15 years legal statutes have increased the number of employees who are protected from EAW, including those protected by equal opportunity and age discrimination legislation. Moreover, what is meant by "public policy" has been expanded. For example, cases in which an employee has been asked to break a law or to violate a stated public policy, cases where employees are not allowed to exercise certain constitutional rights such as the right to vote, serve on a jury, or collect worker compensation are all considered wrongful discharges. Employees won 67 percent of their suits on wrongful discharge during a recent three-year period. These suits were won, not on the basis of a rejection of the principle of EAW, but rather because of breach of contract, lack of just cause for dismissal when a company grievance policy was in place, or violations of public policy (Geyelin, 1989, B1).

EAW is often justified for one or more of the following reasons:

1 The proprietary rights of employers guarantee that they may employ or dismiss whomever and whenever they wish.
2 EAW defends employee, managerial, and employer rights equally, in particular the right to freedom of contract, because an employee voluntarily contracts to be hired and can quit at any time.
3 In choosing to take a job, an employee voluntarily commits herself to certain responsibilities and company loyalty, including the knowledge that she is an "at will" employee.
4 Extending due-process rights and other employee protections in the workplace often interferes with the efficiency and productivity of the business organization.
5 Legislation and/or regulation of employment relationships further undermine an already over-regulated economy.

On the other side, there are a number of criticisms of EAW. Perhaps the most serious is that while EAW is defended as preserving employer and employee rights equally, it is sometimes interpreted as justifying arbitrary treatment of employees. This is analogous to considering an employee as a piece of property at the disposal of the employer or corporation. When I "fire" a robot, I do not have to give reasons, because a robot is not a rational being; it has no use for reasons. On the other hand, if I fire a person arbitrarily I am making the assumption that she does not need reasons for the decision, a questionable logic. If I have hired persons, then I should treat them as such, with respect throughout the employment process. This does not preclude firing, but it does ask employers to give reasons for their actions, for reasons are appropriate when one is dealing with persons.

There are other grounds for not abusing EAW as part of recognizing equal obligations implied by freedom of contract. Arbitrariness, although not prohibited by EAW, violates the managerial model of rationality and consistency. This ideal is implied by a consistent application of this common-law principle, that EAW protects employees, managers, and employers equally and fairly. We expect managers, in their roles as employers, to act reasonably and consistently in their decision-making. Not giving reasons for employment decisions belies that expectation. Thus even if EAW itself is justifiable, the practice of EAW, when interpreted as condoning arbitrary employment decisions, is not.

Looking ahead, the signs are clear that the doctrine of EAW will continue to be refined and challenged. Within the corporation new approaches to work and organizational activity are bringing new modes of employee participation that encourage greater employee expression. The challenge for management and employees is to find creative ways to minimize burdensome litigation while at the same time balancing employer and employee rights.

Bibliography

Arvanites, D. & Ward, B. T. (1990). Employment at will: A social concept in decline. In J. J. Desjardins & J. J. McCall (eds), *Contemporary Issues in Business Ethics,* 2nd edn, Belmont, Calif.: Wadsworth Publishing, 147–54.

Blades, L. E. (1967). Employment at will versus individual freedom: On limiting the abusive exercise of employer power. *Columbia Law Review,* **67**.

Ewing, D. (1983). *Do It My Way or You're Fired!* New York: John Wiley.

Feinman, J. M. (1991). The development of the employment at will rule revisited. *Arizona State Law Journal,* **23**, 733–40.

Geyelin, M. (1989). Fired managers winning more lawsuits. *Wall Street Journal,* 7 Sept., B1.

Hutton v Watters. (1915). 132 Tenn. 527, S.W. 134.

Payne v. Western. (1884). 81 Tenn. 507.

Summers, C. B. (1980). Protecting *all* employees against unjust dismissal. *Harvard Business Review,* Jan./Feb.

Werhane, P. H. (1985). *Persons, Rights, and Corporations.* Englewood Cliffs, NJ: Prentice-Hall.

Wood, H. G. (1887). *A Treatise on the Law of Master and Servant.* Albany, NY: John D. Parsons.

PATRICIA H. WERHANE

empowerment may be defined in many specific ways, but in common is the idea of providing people the "power" necessary to fulfill their job responsibilities without having to secure approval from others (i.e., supervisors). With empowerment, control over the means of getting the job done is left with the person doing the job, creating greater control over the results produced. This responsibility for producing results leads to greater ownership on the individual's part for both the input and output of production.

Some argue that empowerment is nothing new, for example, just today's equivalent for previous management concepts such as participative decision-making, team building, job enrichment, and the like. Others argue that empowerment is "oversold," really nothing more than a buzzword or slogan; or that it is an overrated concept that ignores or minimizes, among other things, political realities and workload increases. Furthermore, failures in implementation have led to feelings ranging from disappointment to disillusionment and anger about empowerment.

Research has found that empowered employees, teams, and organizations outperform their less democratic and more bureaucratic counterparts. Some common misconceptions about empowerment are: (1) managers and leaders lose power by empowering others; (2) empowered people do not need leaders; and, (3) empowerment and delegation are synonymous.

"The problem with empowerment is that it suggests that this is something leaders magically give or do for others. But people already have tremendous power. It is not a matter of giving it to them, but of freeing them to use the power and skills they already have. It is a matter of expanding their opportunities to use themselves in service of a common and meaningful purpose. What is often called empowerment is really just taking off the chains and letting people loose" (Kouzes & Posner, 1993, p. 157). In essence, organizations can only create environments where people feel powerful and choose to create and use their power.

Research into the times when people feel powerful and powerless reveals that feeling powerful comes from a deep sense of being in control of one's life. When people feel able to determine their own destiny, when they believe they are able to mobilize the resources and support necessary to complete a task, then they will persist in their efforts. When people report feeling controlled by others, and when they feel that resources and support are lacking, they may comply but they experience little motivation or commitment to excel.

The initial challenge is to articulate a clear vision of what empowerment entails, including both boundaries and opportunities. Empowerment is akin to "guided autonomy" in which people feel that they not only can, but should, make a difference, and that consensus and strong feelings (values) exist about the right way to do things in the organization. The psychological process of empowerment involves enhancing individual's sense of self-efficacy. This is accomplished through role models, persuasion, and facilitating personal mastery.

The organizational process of empowerment is multifaceted and cannot flourish without institutional support and nourishment. Here are some essential management practices:

Developing Capacity: Organizations that invest more than the average amount of money on training and development activities enjoy higher levels of employee involvement and commitment, along with higher levels of customer service and productivity. Unless people know how, there is no "can do" possible. Educational activities are often needed to ensure that people have the capacity to handle additional responsibility and autonomy.

Facilitating Discretion: Given the latitude and opportunity to exercise choices and make decisions, people feel a sense of ownership – ownership as a state of mind resulting from having the knowledge and skills (education) necessary to make a decision, and then the motivation and will to act. Able to exercise discretion, people feel in control of their own lives: Broad job descriptions, multiple customers and suppliers, and tasks requiring a range of skills facilitate discretion.

Opening Communications: Being able to influence and see the results of their efforts, people will take great interest in what is happening. With detailed feedback, including such factors as quality, timeliness, and customer delight, people can become self-corrective. Information ensues from being involved and included in important planning and problem-solving efforts. Being "in the know" and understanding the premises on which decisions are based increases one's influence.

Building Confidence: Confident people feel powerful, and persist in the face of challenge and adversity. In a simulated series of management situations, managers led to believe that decision-making was an innate capability (rather than an acquired capability) lost their confidence in themselves when they encountered difficulties. Their problem-solving deteriorated, they lowered their aspirations, and organizational performance suffered – and they also tended to place blame for the situation on others. The most effective means of raising people's self-confidence is through the experience of performing successfully.

Fostering Innovation: In any new endeavor there is a learning curve; meaning that performance generally goes down before it goes up. A willingness to take risks and experiment with innovative ideas characterizes an empowered organization, as does making it safe for people to make mistakes, since this is the means for development. Discretion, as the ability to take non-routinized actions and exercise independent judgment, is the first cousin of innovation and the opportunity to be flexible, creative, and adaptive. Doing one's job the way it has always been done is the antithesis of empowerment.

Providing Recognition and Visibility: Power does not flow to unknown sources. Being noticed is a key precursor to developing key strategic alliances with others. Recognition for one's efforts and achievements, important in its own right, creates interest in being connected and having one included in relationships, as well as access to higher-level sponsors and to the increased resources which generally flow to successful people.

"It is common to think of empowerment," say organizational scholars, "as a principal quality of leaders" (Coffey, Cook, & Hunsaker, 1994, p. 153). However, it is ironic that so much of what leaders accomplish is through enabling their constituents to become leaders (empowered) themselves.

See also **autonomy; leadership; participatory management; managerial values; power; trust**

Bibliography

Blanchard, K., Carlos, J. P. & Randolph, W. A. (1995). *Empowerment Takes More than a Minute.* San Francisco, Calif.: Berrett-Kohler.

Coffey, R. E., Cook, C. W. & Hunsaker, P. L. (1994). *Management and Organizational Behavior.* Homewood, Ill.: Austen Press.

Kanter, R. M. (1983). *The Change Masters: Innovation for Productivity in the American Corporation.* New York: Simon & Schuster.

Kouzes, J. M. & Posner, B. Z. (1993). *Credibility: How Leaders Gain and Lose It, Why People Demand It.* San Francisco: Jossey-Bass.

Kouzes, J. M. & Posner, B. Z. (1995). *The Leadership Challenge: How to Keep Getting Extraordinary Things Done in Organizations.* San Francisco: Jossey-Bass.

Wood, R. E. & Bandura, A. (1989). Impact of conceptions of ability on self-regulatory mechanisms and complex decision making. *Journal of Personality and Social Psychology*, 56, 407-15.

BARRY Z. POSNER and JAMES M. KOUZES

energy, ethical issues in *see* ETHICAL ISSUES IN ENERGY

engineers and business ethics Engineers depend on their technical knowledge and skills to carry out research, design, development, testing, and maintenance of technological products and systems. Their tasks can include quality control, safety efforts, implementation of government regulations, and sales. A great majority of engineers practice in business organizations; they are so integral to so many areas of business that any comprehensive account of business ethics has to consider engineers' roles and responsibilities.

The surge in growth of the engineering profession from the last third of the nineteenth century onward coincided with the rise of modern large-scale business organizations. These organizations needed engineers to remove some of the guesswork from operations on a large scale, and they could afford the skills of large numbers of trained engineers. The process by which new industries arose in close association with the growth of fields of engineering continues to the present (Layton, 1986).

Engineers began organizing as a profession in the second half of the nineteenth century. They formed separate societies specific to areas of practice, e.g. civil, and they continued the process of forming professional societies and formulating standards as their numbers surged, in spite of their intimate ties with business organizations. Over this same period, the education of engineers in institutions of higher education assumed increasing importance. The engineering curriculum traces its origins to the late eighteenth century in the Ecole Polytechnique in France. With its emphasis on analytical methods, science, and mathematics, the French plan was the model for the first engineering school in the United States, West Point, established in 1802. The eighteenth-century

French model remains discernible in the technical core of engineering education in this country. Vestiges of engineering's military past also survive, perhaps in part because military organizations provided the model for early large business organizations, especially the railroads, and thereby for industrial organizations of the late nineteenth century.

By the second decade of this century, engineering already showed most of the features which mark occupations as professions. Engineers depended on knowledge that was difficult to acquire and had theoretical coherence. They had formed professional societies and announced that they serve the public. Eschewing the ordinary rough and tumble of the marketplace, they had adopted standards of education and performance, including codes of ethics, to help them serve the public welfare. In the intervening decades, engineers revised the codes of ethics in response to developments in the wider society and to internal pressures. A legal ruling in 1978 required elimination of provisions that barred consulting engineers from competing on the basis of price. The emphasis in 1912 on "gentlemanly" conduct and "due regard" for the public gave way to a "paramount" concern for the "safety, health, and welfare of the public," clearly announced in the First Canon of most codes after the revisions of the mid-1970s.

Professions are distinctive among occupational groups in creating communities of peers with standards that reach across and apply in the organizations that employ their members. Collegiality, with its emphasis on mutual support and reciprocity, constitutes a distinctive relationship among professional peers. Publications such as the Institute of Electrical and Electronic Engineers' *Spectrum*, which circulates to a large, international membership, help to create and maintain a sense of a peer community.

Other professionals (e.g. physicians, accountants, lawyers) are employed in business organizations, but engineers often constitute a larger proportion of the workforce and are usually more integral to generating the end product. Their professional standards set engineers apart from other employees of their organizations; similarly, the standards of other professionals in business organizations set them apart. Indeed, situations which require cooperation between members of different professions, e.g. between architects and engineers or between physicians and lawyers, likewise juxtapose separate standards, not necessarily comprehensible across professional boundaries. Their responsibility for safety is distinctive to engineers.

The engineer's overarching ethical task is to mesh the demands for cooperating in a business enterprise with professional requirements for maintaining an appropriate standard of care in generating the products of the enterprise. In general terms, the codes of ethics speak to both dimensions of this task, making the concern for the welfare of the public paramount, but emphasizing the obligations of a faithful employee. Engineers are left on their own to find specific mechanisms for making accommodations and to discover the advantages of allying with colleagues in support of responsible conduct.

Business organizations depend upon engineers for the reliable, uncompromised judgment of trained professionals; they and their engineer employees must, therefore, be concerned with threats to the reliability of judgment that conflicts of interest pose (see CONFLICT OF INTEREST). When employers protect information with claims of trade secrecy or for patent applications, they present distinctive problems of confidentiality for engineers (see TRADE SECRETS; INTELLECTUAL PROPERTY). Engineers must separate legitimate from exaggerated demands for secrecy and generic from locally specific knowledge, and they may have to weigh the claims of former employers when responding to certain demands of current employers (Frederick & Snoeyenbos, 1983).

Engineers must identify their ethical responsibilities in settings that are regulated by laws, codes, and government agency rules, at federal, state, and local levels, and by threats or outcomes of law suits. This means they must cooperate with government officials to meet standards. And they must recognize their own individual responsibility though they are generally not named in law suits. Plaintiffs target companies and firms. Government licensing is required for only a small number of engineering roles. Engineers, therefore, have to be mindful that they perform as *bona fide* engineers even though manufacturing businesses have influenced most states to exempt most engineer employees from licensing. As professionals, they must meet appropriate standards of care, based in our ordinary morality.

Business ethics should give attention to the situation of professional employees of business organizations. Professionals are needed and valued for the kind of informed judgment they bring to decision processes. It should be an important concern in business organizations to maintain climates conducive to the exercise of reliable judgment by professionals and mechanisms assuring incorporation of professional judgment, including "bad news", in decision processes.

Bibliography

Accreditation Board for Engineering and Technology. (1977). *Code of Ethics of Engineers.* New York: ABET.

Baron, M. (1984). *The Moral Status of Loyalty.* Dubuque: Kendall/Hunt Publishing. (Illinois Institute of Technology: Center for the Study of Ethics in the Professions).

Broome, T. H. Jr. (1987). Engineering responsibility for hazardous technology. *Journal of Professional Issues in Engineering,* 113, 139–49.

Davis, M., Weil, V., Hollander, R. & Gibson, K. (1994). Symposium on engineering and business ethics. *The International Journal of Applied Philosophy,* 8, (2), 1–21.

De George, R. T. (1981). Ethical responsibilities of engineers in large organizations: The Pinto case. *Business and Professional Ethics Journal,* 1, (1), 1–14.

Frederick, R. E. & Snoeyenbos, M. (1983). Trade secrets, patents, and morality. In Snoeyenbos, M., Almeder, R., & Humber, J. (eds), *Business Ethics: Corporate Values and Society.* Buffalo, NY: Prometheus, 162–9.

Layton, E. T. (1986). *The Revolt of the Engineers: Social Responsibility and the American Engineering Profession.* Baltimore: Johns Hopkins.

Vincenti, W. G. (1990). *What Engineers Know and How They Know It: Analytical Studies from Aeronautical History.* Baltimore: Johns Hopkins.

VIVIAN WEIL

entitlement theory   The term "entitlement(s)" as found in business texts normally describes a right to a governmental service. In legal and economic theory, the term is used to mean rights individuals have to control resources or take actions without infringement by others (Calabrasi & Melamed, 1972). "Entitlement theory," however, is a theory of DISTRIBUTIVE JUSTICE or PROCEDURAL JUSTICE. Most generally, it holds that a distribution is just if no one's rights (entitlements) were violated in bringing that distribution about. The theory is usually associated with the political writings of contemporary philosopher ROBERT NOZICK (1974) and sometimes with LIBERTARIANISM.

Entitlement theory is concerned with "holdings," that is, with the justice of what one has or acquires. Justice in holdings has three elements to consider: 1) how holdings were originally acquired, 2) how they may be transferred from one person to another, and 3) how problems related to 1 and 2 can be rectified. Most everyday issues of justice fall under the second consideration, or "justice in transfer." If one person transfers a good to another, for example, the second person is entitled to the good if the first was so entitled (had a right to it) and the transfer was voluntary. The first person was entitled to the good if that person in turn received it from someone who was entitled to it and so on. Usually goods are transferred in exchange for something else, but gifts would also be subject to justice in transfer. The transfer is just if (a) the parties were entitled to the goods they transferred, (b) the transfer was voluntary and (c) the terms of the transfer were adhered to. No further issues of effects, benefits, or the well-being of individuals or society are relevant to any stage of the transfer process. If, however, there were problems with the original acquisition of a good (justice in acquisition) or someone's rights were violated in the transfer itself, appropriate principles of rectification (justice in rectification) would have to be applied. Compensation is one possible way in which such problems are rectified.

Entitlement theory sees the issue of justice as strictly historical and procedural. There is no concern with the future outcome or end result of any distribution, nor is there a concern to structure society so that the distribution favors some particular value, such as need, merit, or marginal productivity. The only concern is whether persons under a given distribution are entitled to their respective holdings. If they are, the distribution is just.

The theory has been criticized for failing to provide an adequate foundation for rights (entitlements) and for failing to exclude the possibility of engineering certain social patterns or results by simply redefining what it means for a person to be entitled to something (Paul, 1981). Nevertheless, the characteristics of looking to entitlements rather than social outcomes or patterns, of thinking in terms of rights rather than welfare, and of basing transfers upon mutual consent alone remain as basic elements of this theory. Since not every conception of rights or justice will be compatible with these elements, entitlement theory does constitute a distinctive theory of justice.

Bibliography

Calabrasi, G. & Melamed, D. A. (1972). Property rules, liability rules and inalienability: One view of the cathedral. *Harvard Law Review*, 85, 1089–1128.

Lomasky, L. (1987). *Persons, Rights, and the Moral Community*. Oxford: Oxford University Press.

Nozick, R. (1974). *Anarchy, State, and Utopia*. New York: Basic Books.

Paul, J. (ed.). (1981). *Reading Nozick*. Totowa, NJ: Roman & Littlefield.

Sterba, J. (1980). *Justice: Alternative Political Perspectives*. Belmont, Calif.: Wadsworth.

DOUGLAS J. DEN UYL

entrepreneurship, ethics and   *see* ETHICS AND ENTREPRENEURSHIP

environment and environmental ethics
In the sense intended by "Environmental Ethics" (EE), "environment" refers specifically to the natural world of which humans are a part. It includes landscapes which function according to evolutionary natural processes. But, since humankind has substantially altered many natural systems, the "environment" also includes areas manipulated for the human use, including landscapes where agriculture, agroforestry, and cities are located.

EE appears at first to be a species of applied ethics, like business ethics or bioethics, applying ethics to the problems of human interaction with the environment. Unlike those disciplines, however, EE goes beyond the appropriate application of familiar doctrines to a certain species of practical problems: it requires that we extend or transcend our accepted moral doctrines because it forces us to rethink the boundaries of the morally considerable. Whatever our moral persuasion, we must go beyond the "anthropocentric" paradigm (that is, the position that only humans are morally considerable and that they are at the "center" of our moral reasoning), to establish who or what might possess moral standing (Van DeVeer, 1986). EE is broader, more inclusive than other practical ethics; hence it is, in some sense, a *new* ethic, addressing as it does totally new problems in many areas (Callicott, 1984; D. Scherer, 1990; L. Westra, 1994).

EE requires us to confront problems that cannot be easily resolved if we cling to pure anthropocentrism; they may remain intractable even if ours is a "weak" anthropocentrism, that is, one which admits environmental values beyond those of economic exploitation of nature (Norton, 1991). Thus the first question raised by EE, is where do we draw the boundaries of the moral community? Is sentience necessary for the inclusion of non-human animals (Singer, 1993)? Or should we consider all individual organisms equally, because of their individual teleology, their unique desire to realize themselves, which supports their intrinsic worth (Taylor, 1986)? And what of natural "wholes" such as ecosystems (Rolston, 1988; Leopold, 1949; Westra, 1994a)? Many philosophers argue that *all* these entities are valuable, hence merit inclusion in the moral community, whereas others draw the line at sentience only, or limit themselves to individual rights (Regan, 1983).

The approach we choose will dictate how we respond to the many environmental problems we encounter, problems of pollution, resource depletion, animal EXPLOITATION, waste disposal, population explosion, and erosion and depletion of soils; problems involving the air we breathe, the sun that warms the earth, the water and land we need to survive, and biotic impoverishment of habitats, loss of species, climate changes – all of which affect our life-support systems. Aside from the moral considerability question, other novel aspects of environmental problems predicate the need for a new ethic. All actions in regard to the environment can now be defined as "upstream/downstream," as all our activities have unprecedented effects through the future (in time) and globally (in space). Nothing we do, given our increasing technological powers, can be viewed as yielding limited, spatially circumscribed consequences. Thus our actions now require new social constraints, as "traditionally broad concepts of liberty," are no longer appropriate (Scherer, 1990).

Further, our environmental moral conflicts are no longer limited to disagreements about external constraints, or conflicts about group preferences. Internal conflicts are also unavoidable: we *know* that not all our preferences and choices are acceptable, as our very lifestyle has been called into question. Each one of us must thus resolve the internal conflicts between "consumer" and "citizen," learning to modify and restrain the former, while emphasizing the latter and our commitment to our community and to life on earth (Sagoff, 1989). A new understanding of what it means to be moral, and an ecological ethics which is "deep" rather than "shallow" (Seed et al., 1988), is required, and a changed lifestyle, based on reproductive and consumerist restraint, a changed diet, and new intellectual or spiritual goals.

EE is a relatively new field, but several conflicting approaches are already discussed in the literature. I alluded earlier to the anthropocentric/non-anthropocentric dichotomy. Some argue that to view purely human concerns as central is nothing but "speciesism" (that is, a position that is based inappropriately on the "superior" value of our species over others), whereas others respond that only humans can be moral or even appreciate or discuss questions of value, hence the moral view must be human. Another conflict is that between individualists and holists. Some ask whether individual animals or plants have value or even rights. Others argue that wholes such as species, ecosystems, the land, or the biosphere might represent the most appropriate locus of value instead (Rolston, 1988; Leopold, 1949; Westra, 1994a). Yet another debate centers on the role of science such as biology or ecology in environmental ethics.

Those who accept a holistic ethics tend to allow the scientific "is," uncertain and incomplete though it is, to provide the limits appropriate to the moral "ought" which dictates environmentally good actions (Rolston, 1988). Others prefer not to tie EE to the methodological difficulties and the predictive uncertainties of a young, science-like ecology, with its many approaches and varied scalar perspectives (Shrader-Frechette & McCoy, 1993).

In essence, EE is basic to social, political, and economic policy-making, and represents one of the major considerations required of business operations. Nowhere can the power and the reach of business have a deadlier impact on human and non-human life than through its interaction with the environment. By the same token, it is in the environmental realm that large corporate bodies, particularly multinationals, can make the greatest contribution to the public good, if their operation is seriously guided by an ecologically sound environmental ethics.

Examples of destructive business behavior are unfortunately more frequent and better known than their opposite actions. Bhopal and *Exxon Valdez* are names everyone has heard, whereas efforts like the funding of buffer zones sustainability next to Amisconde's Man-in-the-Biosphere project in Costa Rica, by MacDonald's Corporation, has never made front-page news (Lacher & Cesca, 1995). Another environmental problem connected with some business operations is only now being clearly recognized in all its implications, although it has a long and nefarious history: that of "environmental racism." Both "risky business" operations and hazardous-waste disposal facilities tend to permit economic considerations *only* to guide their siting policies, and thus most often choose poor areas where house and land values are lower. Hence they tend to choose existing "brownfields," already present in and around areas inhabited primarily by persons of color (Bullard, 1994; Westra & Wenz, 1995).

When business practices are hazardous to human beings, through their environmental impact, corporations may simply respond by appealing to traditional moral theories to evaluate their activities. For instance, utilitarian doctrines will dictate that the "good" of the many should represent the proper goal of moral agents; and, provided that the "good" is defined and understood in communitarian terms, rather than as aggregate preferences or purely as economic benefits, this approach may work,

at least in a limited manner. Deontological emphasis on respect for human rights, if it is based on Kant's doctrine of the absolute value of life, would not permit that human health and life be risked, no matter what other benefits might accrue to any of the parties involved. Finally, Rawlsian "fairness" might serve (a) to limit unjust burdens imposed on some stakeholders in the interest of business development or profit; and (b) to curtail the exploitation of the weakest and most powerless, and thus perhaps to attack "environmental racism" from another direction (*see* KANTIAN ETHICS; RAWLS, JOHN).

In fact, many of the consequences of their operations can be made environmentally sound, simply through a consideration of their possible effect on human beings (thus remaining within the ambit of traditional moral theory, for instance the harm principle). Business should monitor closely their products, their processes, and their practices, in regard to both their internal and their external stakeholders, in order not to impose unacceptable risks, often unknown by those exposed to such risks and uncompensated (Westra, 1994b).

But there are other, more far-reaching problems (e.g., questions of siting location or waste disposal), where guidelines reaching beyond present, existing human stakeholders, to the non-human environment, may provide a more inclusive perspective. In general, it is hard to quantify, specify, or defend in a court of law, hazards to human health which may take years to develop. But both non-human animals and the ecosystem habitat we share with other creatures, may already be affected, in a demonstrable, non-controversial way. It is in these cases that ethics that demand respect for the environment as such might be more effective from the moral standpoint and that of public policy. The same attitude may be found increasingly in new regulations and laws. For instance, land-use cases which might have been treated as a "taking" in earlier times, now may be dealt with under the heading of "police powers," to prevent owners' business choices and to protect some endangered and fragile ecosystems, such as wetland, for future generations, when all may depend on these ecosystems' "services."

At the international level, biodiversity treaties, or the ozone protocol, also indicate a trend to universal regulation, and away from the need to demonstrate harm to a specific individual before restraints may be instituted.

After all, even the Endangered Species Act demands the protection of *habitats*, in order to ensure their goals in regard to some species. Finally, even major economic players such as the World Bank, have also changed their practices to emphasize the importance of environmental impact, which is now the major consideration in their lending policies (Goodland & Daly, 1995).

Taylor, P. (1986). *Respect for Nature*. Princeton: Princeton University Press.

Van DeVeer, D. & Pierce, C. (1995). *People, Penguins and Plastic Trees: Basic Issues in Environmental Ethics*. Belmont, Calif.: Wadsworth.

Westra, L. (1994a) *An Environmental Proposal for Ethics: The Principle of Integrity*. Lanham, Md.: Rowman Littlefield.

Westra, L. (1994b). Corporate Responsibility and Hazardous Products, *Business Ethics Quarterly*, Vol. 4, No. 1, 97-110.

Westra, L., and Wenz, P. (eds) (1995) *The Faces of Environmental Racism: Confronting the Global Equity Issue*. Lanham, Md.: Rowman Littlefield.

LAURA WESTRA

Bibliography

Bullard, R. (1994). *Dumping in Dixie*. Boulder, Colo.: Westview Press.

Callicott, J. F. (1984). Non-anthropocentric value theory and environmental ethics. *American Philosophy Quarterly*, **21**.

Goodland, R., and Daly, H. (1995). Environmental sustainability: universal and non-negotiable. In L. Westra and J. Lemons (eds), *Perspectives on Implementing Ecological Integrity*. Dordrecht, The Netherlands: Kluwer Academic Publishers.

Lacher, T., and Cesca, R. (1995). Ethical obligations of multinational corporations to the global environment: McDonald's and conservation. InL. Westra and J. Lemons (eds), *Perspectives on Implementing Ecological Integrity*. Dordrecht, The Netherlands: Kluwer Academic Publishers.

Leopold, A. (1949). *A Sand County Almanac and Sketches Here and There*. New York: Oxford University Press.

Norton, B. (1991). *Toward Unity Among Environmentalists*. New York: Oxford University Press.

Regan, T. (1983). *The Case for Animal Rights*. Berkeley, Calif.: University of California Press.

Rolston, H. (1988). *Environmental Ethics*. Philadelphia: Temple University Press.

Sagoff, M. (1989). *The Economy of the Earth*. Cambridge, Mass.: Cambridge University Press.

Scherer, D. (ed.) (1990). *Upstream/Downstream: Issues in Environmental Ethics*. Philadelphia: Temple University Press.

Seed, J., Macy, J., Fleming, P., & Naess, A. (1988). *Thinking Like a mountain: Towards a Council of All Beings*. Philadelphia: New Society Publishers.

Shrader-Frechette, K., and McCoy, E. (1993). *Method in Ecology*. Cambridge: Cambridge University Press.

Singer, P. (1993). *Practical Ethics*. 2nd edn. New York: Cambridge University Press.

environmental risk The first meaning of risk in *Webster's Ninth New Collegiate Dictionary* (1986) is "possibility of loss or injury." To risk is "to expose to hazard or danger." The meaning of environment is, most generally, "the circumstances, objects, or conditions by which one is surrounded," including biophysical factors determining the form and survival of organisms or ecosystems, and socio-cultural factors influencing individuals and communities.

Environmental risk, then, as relevant to business ethics, encompasses those actions or inactions by which businesses give rise to and are affected by the possibility of biophysical or social loss or injury to entities of all kinds. This definition is more inclusive than that used in most discussion – where the environment and environmental risk are taken to be limited to biophysical, not social or cultural factors.

This entry examines several components of this definition, focusing primarily on loss to biophysical systems. It concentrates on questions concerning probability and uncertainty, the notion of what counts as loss or injury and the relationship of this to other desired or desirable phenomena, and the normative nature and policy dimensions of the construct of risk.

Risk as Probability

The likelihood of injury or harm may be well known or a subject of much dispute. In all but the most remote parts of the world, people know that the likelihood of serious harm from stepping immediately in front of a speeding car is very high. People understand and can estimate familiar, frequent risks. Although their very familiarity can lead to underestimation, individuals need not pursue elaborate exercises in quantification to make most of their decisions; nor need organizations do so in similar circumstances.

Away from this simple model, entire industries are built on such exercises. Consider mortality rates. An example of well-established probabilities are actuarial tables of human life expectancies in different parts of the world. Establishing such probabilities for particular categories of human lives or other elements of the environment is more complex. Whether we do it depends on the value we place on those elements and whether we have other acceptable ways of arriving at decisions.

Even well-established risks are subject to change that can come more or less rapidly, depending on social and environmental conditions. Many risks are subject to human influence or control. But the likelihood that individual, group, or organizational actions or inactions will result in increasing or decreasing risks to human lives or those of other species and ecosystems may not be well-established. There may be greater or lesser degrees of uncertainty. Other forms of harm than those resulting in premature mortality need consideration and may be subject to even more uncertainty. If this is so, many risks to humans, other species, and ecosystems cannot be accurately measured. Many species on the planet have not been identified, so risks cannot be assigned at all. Here rather than uncertainty there is ignorance.

Inability to assign well-founded estimates of life expectancies or rates of environmental succession or decay, however, cannot be used to justify the position that there are no risks. The risks are unknown. When risks are unknown, the question of where the burden of proof should lie arises. If this question can be answered, it will be through a process of social negotiation, not quantification, although the negotiation may include the question of further research, and its risks, costs, and benefits.

This last point is true of finding answers to all questions of environmental risk. Consider the possibility of injury or harm from the release of lead into the environment. Lead is a metallic chemical element. All lead compounds are poisonous. Lead has had and continues to have many important commercial uses. Human beings of different ages and ethnicities exhibit different sensitivities. Many kinds of injury or harm that can be attributed to lead are well established; some are subject to some dispute. Actions can be taken to change commercial and waste-disposal practices to get rid of, control, or minimize the use of lead so that the risk to the environment, in the plant, at home, or at large, is alleviated. Even with such a long-standing risk, about which a great deal is known, decisions will arise through an ongoing process of social negotiation.

Part of this negotiation process involves procedures called risk assessments. Scientists and engineers often undertake these assessments, under the auspices of businesses and industries that may perform them in deciding whether or not to develop or market a new product or continue an old one. They also undertake these assessments, as employees, under the auspices of governmental agencies charged to protect human or ecological health and safety; or, with grants and contracts from these agencies, in colleges and universities. Federal agencies support research to improve processes of risk assessment as well. These assessments are an important albeit controversial tool in the process by which organizations, groups, and individuals decide whether or not something poses risk and what to do about it.

Risk as Normative Construct

Although some risks are worth taking, people wish to avoid injury or harm. But care must be taken not to view this idea too simplistically. What exposures, actions, or inactions, at what levels, must be avoided? To whom? When? Whose responsibility is it to avoid exposing themselves or others to environmental risks, to alleviate results from such exposure, or to compensate? What evidence, of what kinds, suffices to establish risk? What kinds of regulation are appropriate? What about the international implications of risk exposures?

Business interests, among others, may accuse environmental or neighborhood groups or regulators of overreaction to environmental risks, pointing out that to some degree such risks are unavoidable, and the price of much that people hold dear. They may contrast environmental risks to economic risks. This particular normative construct of risk – the trade-offs view – is described further below, as are other normative approaches.

When risks are being debated, such as in considering the question of lead in the environment, it is useful to ask the following questions: Have persons' legitimate expectations for feasible control and due care been met or violated? Are there ways to improve the situation? According to what standards? (Hollander, 1994.) The use of the shorthand term "risk" here goes beyond counting how many organisms, in what environments, at what ages, are injured or harmed, and how. It goes to questions about what kind of world we wish to see: what kinds of outcomes, institutions, procedures, and behaviors we value.

a) Risk Priorities

Many people have strong views about the importance of environmental risk. In expressing these views, they often use arguments and develop positions that fall into categories identified by Aiken (1986): the top-priority, trade-offs, constraints, and interconnectedness views.

The top-priority view places an environmental risk at the top of a list of all kinds of risks – environmental and other – and insists that the proper way to proceed is to lower or overcome it. In this view, the top risk has priority even if another risk is increased by doing so.

The trade-offs view might agree to the list, but its proponents proceed by trying to compare what they take to be relevant risks in order to reduce the overall level of risk. This form of comparative risk assessment tends to be the approach of Federal regulators in the US Environmental Protection Agency (EPA). Risk assessments often presuppose this normative view. The trade-offs view has to find a way to measure different kinds of risk for these comparisons to be made. It is not always easy to do this. Economists tend to use this normative view, but they have difficulty setting a monetary value on ecologists' views about ecological risks or environmentalists' views about the value of wilderness, for instance. And microbiologists may disagree with ecologists, even about what the relevant risks are.

Persons with the constraints view identify such issues as human rights and informed consent; whatever the ranking scheme, they indicate concern about human exposures to chemical toxins without their knowledge and/or beyond their control. Regulators in the EPA and in the Food and Drug Administration often take this view, along with the trade-offs view. The concept of environmental justice, beginning to play an important role in social deliberations about environmental risks, often presupposes the constraints view, asking whether it is fair for poor or minority communities to be faced with more environmental hazards than richer communities, which tend to have fewer residents of color.

The interconnectedness view points out that the natural world does not operate like a balance sheet, which can only be completed after the fact. Rather, it operates more like business decision-making environments in which risk is unavoidable and positive as well as negative. Life requires evolution, predation, and death. Interconnectedness means a negative can't be simply traded off against a positive; it may be necessary to the maintenance of a desirable whole. The desire to return wolves to the American Northwest may be an example of this view.

b) Risk Policy

There is growing recognition that adequate answers to questions of acceptable risk and acceptable evidence of risk require acknowledging different positions groups take and behaviors they exhibit about what is risky and what to do about it. Adequate answers require attention to issues of process and conduct, as well as outcomes (Thompson, 1993).

The positions that different groups take about risk have consequences that themselves affect the risk. The groups include scientific and non-scientific institutions, business among them, in roles ranging from undertaking risk assessments; to attempting to bring different dimensions of risk to the attention of relevant scientists and policy-makers, in order to make them part of formal processes; to disputing the results of risk assessments or risk-management processes; to adopting or ignoring their results in policy or practice. Adequate risk assessment and management, and risk policy, will need to take these consequences into account.

Additionally, risk policy will need to be concerned with outcomes, structures, and procedures, and conduct or behavioral norms in order to understand the responses of individuals and organizations. In its initial forms exclusively and to a great extent now, quantitative risk assessment examines outcomes and distributions of outcomes. Assessments look for answers to questions of morbidity or mortality. As noted above, these are difficult questions to answer when limited to human beings, and questions concerning other species and ecosystems are even more complicated. Furthermore, environmental values go beyond concerns for morbidity and mortality, to those perhaps better viewed as bio- or enviro-aesthetic, and to feelings of awe or wonder. It is not clear that these values can be assimilated in a trade-offs analysis.

In addition to outcomes, issues of risk concern the structures and procedures by which risk decisions are made. These are not concerns about outcomes to humans or environments of exposures to putative hazardous substances or other factors influencing environmental degradation. They are concerns for the norms and procedures by which, and institutions in which, decisions get made. As in the constraints view, these are concerns for process and fairness in process and protection of human rights. They are concerns for integrity and public confidence in social systems, for feasible control and due care. The perception of risks from and to procedures and processes often lies behind people's reluctance to allow business, government, and other institutions to proceed as they would like and think they should be able.

A concern about conduct is a final element that should be considered in risk policy. This is a concern for how risk assessments get made and what their implications are for human behavior. It is a concern for the implications for humans and their impacts, that decisions are made in certain ways and not others. If decisions are made by one or another group of elites, or by democratic processes, what does that mean for how these individuals and groups will behave in the future? For how institutions will evolve, or how others will behave? To what

habits of character will these procedures lead? Will they result in more care, or more carelessness? Will they lead to efforts to improve in the future, or to complacency?

For instance, should procedures be used that try to quantify the value of an individual human life as a basis for making social decisions? The concern about this procedure may not be just for its influence on outcomes or structures, but about its influence on human beings' regard for each other. The refusal to place monetary values on individual human lives need not mean that decisions about scarce resources lack justification. It would mean that the grounds could not rely on a consequentialist procedure that assigns monetary values to individual lives. Such a refusal takes the position that questions about norms, structures, human character, and conduct need to be incorporated into decision procedures.

See also **acid rain; biodiversity; consequentialism; environment and environmental ethics; ethical issues in energy; ethical issues in investment; ethical issues in technology; ethics of marketing; externalities; fiduciary responsibility; future generations; global warming; greenmail; hazardous waste; multinationals; negligence; property, rights to; responsibility; risk; transnational corporations**

Bibliography

Aiken, W. H. (1986). On evaluating agricultural research. In K. A. Dahlberg (ed.), *New Directions for Agriculture and Agricultural Research: Neglected Dimensions and Emerging Alternatives.* Totowa, NJ: Rowman & Allanheld, 31–41. (Presents four normative views in the context of setting agricultural research priorities).

Brown, H. S., et al. (1993). *Corporate Environmentalism in a Global Economy: Societal Values in International Technology Transfer.* Westport Conn.: Quorum Books.

Cranor, C. F. (1993). *Regulating Toxic Substances: A Philosophy of Science and the Law.* New York: Oxford University Press.

Hollander, R. D. (1994). Is engineering safety just business safety? *The International Journal of Applied Philosophy,* 8 (2).

Krimsky, S. & Golding, D. (eds). (1992). *Social Theories of Risk.* Westport Conn.: Praeger Publishers. (Good introduction to different theories, approaches, models of risk assessment.)

MacLean, D. (ed.). (1986). *Values at Risk.* Totowa, NJ: Rowman & Allanheld.

MacLean, D. & Brown, P. (eds). (1983). *Energy and the Future.* Totowa, NJ: Rowman and Allanheld.

Mayo, D. G. & Hollander, R. D. (eds). (1992). *Acceptable Evidence: Science and Values in Risk Management.* New York: Oxford University Press. (Examines value dimensions in risk assessment processes and policies).

Thompson, P. (1993). Food labels and biotechnology: The ethics of safety and consent. Discussion Paper, Center for Biotechnology Policy and Ethics, Texas A&M University. (Differentiates the outcomes, procedures, and character concerns over policies).

RACHELLE D. HOLLANDER

envy   is a form of ill will that is directed against someone else because they possess more of some good thing than the envier possesses. I could never envy someone because they have less money or power or public esteem than I do – unless I think of them as bad things and their absence, consequently, as something good.

Envy is a unique sort of hostility. Typically, we are hostile toward others because of something about them that we see as bad: because they have treated us unjustly, for instance, or because they possess some odious trait of character. When we envy, however, we are hostile toward someone who possesses something that is not bad but good, and precisely on account of its goodness.

The hostility in envy appears to us, in consequence, as being in the typical case peculiarly undeserved and unprovoked. When envy prompts Cain to rise up against Abel and slay him, it is for no better reason than that Abel is more favored by God than he is. No doubt, this is why his act has stood for millennia as a paradigm of conduct that is evil beyond qualification or excuse. Among the traits that are commonly regarded as vices, envy has suffered over the centuries from an almost uniquely "bad press." Many other such traits – including selfishness, greed, jealousy, cowardice, and anger – have had defenders who claim that they are either good or morally neutral. Envy apparently has not.

Within the literature on envy, there has been little or no disagreement about its value. Controversy has generally focused, instead, on its social and political implications. These implications all have to do with the close and sometimes embarrassing connection between envy and equality.

One way to characterize this connection is this. If I envy you for having more money than I do, my hostility is not in any way based on a belief that you have taken your money from me. Any hostility that had such a basis would not be envy but, presumably, some sort of moral indignation. If I am envious, what upsets me is precisely the fact that what you have exceeds what I have. That is, the object of the envious person's attitude is inequality, and inequality that is perceived as *per se* bad, without regard to its source.

This means that the point of view the envious person takes is, thus far, indistinguishable from a certain sort of egalitarianism: namely, the sort that pronounces adverse judgments on unequal distributions of goods simply because they are unequal, and without regard to their source.

Various writers, including von Mises (1951), Rand (1957), and Schoeck (1966) claim that envy is what motivates this sort of egalitarianism and, in particular, that it is what lies behind egalitarian objections to the unequal distributions of wealth that capitalism permits. This idea is never argued for at length by its advocates, being stated instead as if it were more or less obvious. It is not difficult, however, to get an intuitive grasp of why it can seem obvious to them.

The intuitive appeal of this idea is partly due to the fact that, while envy bears a certain resemblance with the relevant kind of egalitarian indignation, it is quite compatible with it. The difference between them seems to lie mainly in this: if I am envious, what I am upset about is the fact that some individual has more than *I* do, while as a principled egalitarian what I would be upset about is that the individual has more than *someone* does. That is, in the latter case, the object of the upset is something more abstract: to the extent that this is my attitude, the identity of the disadvantaged individual does not matter.

The concept of envy is not the exclusive property of anti-egalitarian writers. Egalitarians sometimes use it in defense of their own cause. In one way or another, the suggestion is often made that radically egalitarian policies would eliminate envy from the world. Descriptions of egalitarian utopias typically follow the pattern of Bellamy's *Looking Backward* (1887), in which people live together in peace, without the rancor that envy brings, precisely because the social system has eliminated all material inequality. A corollary of this idea is a certain criticism of non-egalitarian systems of wealth distribution, one that Rawls (1972) takes some pains to answer. This is the notion that systems which (like that of Rawls) allow some inequality merely exacerbate envy.

The thought that lies behind this egalitarian line of reasoning seems to be that envy is caused by inequality. We can eliminate the problem of envy by eliminating its cause. On the other hand, to permit its cause to exist simply guarantees that the problem will have no solution. Is either of these approaches to envy correct? There is actually some room to doubt both of them.

On the face of it, there is an obvious difficulty in proving that the anti-egalitarian argument is true. The charge that some forms of egalitarianism are based on envy is an attempt to explain observed phenomena in terms of a cause that is of course not observed. In fact, this explanation itself implies that the cause it cites is not only unobserved but actively hidden. The point of these egalitarian principles, it seems to say, is to both satisfy and conceal the envious urges that lie behind them. This creates a problem about collecting evidence of a direct sort in favor of this explanation. Just in case the explanation is a true one, the people of whom it is true can be expected never to admit its truth, even to themselves.

The only sort of evidence that could be offered for such an explanation would be to show that it is the only way, or at least the best way, to explain the observed phenomena. Clearly, there *are* other explanations available: writers who believe in the relevant sorts of egalitarianism often suggest, in one way or another, that they take this position because some argument leads them to accept it. The anti-egalitarian charge, in that case, can only rest on the claim that these arguments are not the best explanations for the fact that these people take this position. Since there is no independent evidence for the envy explanation, this would have to mean that the explanation based on argument is weak on its own merits: that the

arguments are too weak to convince someone that justice requires the relevant kind of equality, perhaps because they covertly assume the obligatoriness of equality without actually arguing for it.

This claim about egalitarian arguments is, of course, not obviously true. The anti-egalitarian charge, then, ultimately rests on the notion that this claim *can* be supported somehow. That is, the charge must rely on a serious discussion of the philosophical foundations of egalitarian theories of justice. It is not, as its proponents sometimes seem to think, a substitute for such discussion.

On the other hand, while this claim is not obviously true, neither is it obviously indefensible. Conceivably, analysis of relevant egalitarian arguments might show that they rest on ideas, like "fairness" or "non-arbitrariness," which simply smuggle the idea of equality into the argument without actually giving it any logical support. In that case, these arguments would fail to explain why the people who use them believe in equality while other people do not. That would seem to mean that the explanation for their belief must be psychological rather than logical, and envy is one psychological force that seems potentially very relevant.

Regarding the anti-egalitarian use of the idea of envy, a certain amount of circumspection seems called for, but the same is true where the egalitarian use of the idea is concerned as well. There the idea, as I stated it, was that, since envy is caused by inequality, it can be eliminated by egalitarian redistributions of some sort. In this form, this idea seems to rest on a rather strong assumption about the nature of envy, one that might well be false. The assumption is that envy is in certain respects the same sort of emotion that fear is. Fear is often a completely inevitable response to observable phenomena of certain sorts. In the presence of a dangerous animal suddenly unchained, fear follows by irresistible necessity. Because of this, the only practicable way to eliminate the fear is to remove the beast that occasions it.

On the other hand, if the feeling is not inevitable when the occasion for it appears, there might well be some other way to get rid of the feeling, other than getting rid of the circumstances in which it arises. There is good reason for thinking that envy is this sort of feeling, that it is not in this way like fear. Some people burn with envy when they realize that someone they know has more money than they do. Other people are utterly indifferent to such knowledge. Why does envy flare up in some cases and not in others? There must be some other necessary causal condition, besides the perceived presence of inequality. If that is so, then perhaps the envy can be eliminated by removing this other cause. Depending on what this other cause is, this may be something that can be removed by means that are much easier to do – and less ethically problematic – than the complete elimination of inequalities of wealth and income.

For instance, it has been pointed out by Rawls (1972), among others, that knowing that others possess more than they themselves do seems to threaten the self-esteem of envious people. This suggests that the other necessary causal condition consists in the fact that the self-esteem of these people is peculiarly vulnerable at the outset, independently of the inequalities that ignite the envious response. If that it true, perhaps the envy can be removed or reduced by enhancing the self-esteem of those who suffer from envy, either by their own individual efforts or by some institutional reforms less drastic than egalitarian leveling would be.

This would mean that the egalitarian solution for the problem of envy may be unnecessary. Actually, a similar line of reasoning suggests that it may be worse than that. Envy, it is appropriate to recall, is a form of hostility which is directed at others simply because they have more of some good thing than one has oneself. One of the factors that might contribute to causing this response – aside from the mere fact that they do have more – could be various ideas and principles that imply that possessing more than one's neighbor is in itself a wrong, a wrong of which the neighbor is the victim. Given that one holds ideas that have such implications, a hostile response to more favored individuals can seem perfectly rational and moral. Of course, this is just the sort of thing that egalitarian ideas do imply. If we accept them, they transform the brute fact that one person has more than another into something with a moral meaning, and a negative one. It is but a short step from this perception to the further one that the more

favored person is responsible for this negative fact and thus worthy of the sort of bad feelings that moral blame brings with it, feelings which will have a special bitterness when the person who feels them is the one who is less favored. This, of course, is envy. That is, while egalitarian institutions whittle away at the occasions for envious hostility, the ideas that they are based on – and inevitably bring with them – might continually produce more of these same feelings of animosity.

Though it might be false to suggest that egalitarian ideas are a product of envy, it might nonetheless be true that there is another causal link between them, one that runs the other way: they might be a fertile source of envious resentment.

Bibliography

Bellamy, E. (1960 [1887]). *Looking Backward*. New York: New American Library.

Mises, L. von. (1951). *Socialism: An Economic and Sociological Analysis*. New Haven: Yale University Press.

Rand, A. (1957). *Atlas Shrugged*. New York: Random House.

Rawls, J. (1972). *A Theory of Justice*. Cambridge, Mass.: Harvard University Press.

Schoeck, H. (1966). *Envy: A Theory of Social Behavior*. New York: Harcourt, Brace and World.

LESTER H. HUNT

equal opportunity a standard of decision-making, stipulating that all people be treated the same, except when distinctions can be explicitly justified. This standard has been used to define FAIRNESS in lending, housing, hiring, wage and salary levels, job promotion, voting rights, and other concerns. Artificial barriers, prejudices, and personal preferences should neither restrict nor enhance the opportunities for anyone. AFFIRMATIVE ACTION PROGRAMS set goals and quotas for hiring, promotion, and suchlike, but equal opportunity focuses on breaking down the artificial barriers and stereotypes.

The standard of equal opportunity is a frequent theme in American culture and tradition. Perhaps the most basic notion of the American FREE ENTERPRISE economy is the value of equal opportunity. Thomas Jefferson used equal opportunity as the foundational theme of the Declaration of Independence: Jefferson's argument is that God made us equal, and that equality is protected for basic opportunities: life, liberty, and the pursuit of HAPPINESS. It is also at the core of Martin Luther King Jr.'s famous "I Have a Dream" speech. He dreamt that his four little children would someday "not be judged by the color of their skin but by the content of their character."

Major thinkers in intellectual history have championed equal opportunity as well. ADAM SMITH made it a necessary part of an efficient and fair economy. For JOHN RAWLS it is one of the three most elementary principles to which all rational beings should agree. Hilary Putnam, while acknowledging that the belief and practice of equality was first taught in the Bible, defends it as his model for "pragmatic realism."

The phrase "equal opportunity" contains two value-charged, ambiguous words. It seems "nice" to say that we are "equal," but there is no factual measure on which any two people are truly equal. "EQUALITY" in this case is a standard for decisions and policies, not a description. Moreover, it is difficult to be against any "opportunity," for example; nevertheless, how much personal responsibility should be required is a matter of debate.

Some distinctions between people are pertinent, and decisions based upon these distinctions can be justified in ways that are consistent with equal opportunity. For example, when evaluating applicants for a women's professional basketball team, the management may justifiably exclude all men as well as those women who are not skilled in basketball. Similarly, many jobs require special training or even licensing, and equal opportunity is not violated when these criteria are recognized. People without accounting training need not be considered on an equal basis with those who are trained, when accounting is an important part of a job opening. Also, banks and mortgage companies do not violate equal opportunity when loan applicants are evaluated by relevant criteria: credit records, income, job stability, and the like.

The critical question is: "What distinctions between people are pertinent without equal opportunity being compromised?" Overt and subtle standards need to be evaluated; both conscious and subconscious patterns ought to be scrutinized. Even the most self-conscious egalitarians will likely have some unjustified implicit assumptions that color or twist their perceptions and decisions.

Statistical analyses of personal and corporate decisions help to reveal patterns that are otherwise difficult to recognize. For example, even a very conscientious bank may discover that it demands a higher credit rating for Latinos and Blacks than it does for Asians and Whites for the same kinds of loans. This pattern might be an unconscious aspect of a partially subjective process, even when the loan officer is Black or Latino. Similarly, a statistical analysis of various corporate offices and levels may reveal a kind of "glass ceiling" for women and minorities. If, with few exceptions, there are no minorities or WOMEN IN LEADERSHIP and white men are exclusively promoted above a certain organizational level, equal opportunity is probably violated. Similarly, one can ask, Is the ethnic DIVERSITY of the organization similar to the geographic region around it? If not, there may be artificial barriers that restrain equal opportunity.

Why is equal opportunity an important value standard? There are at least five reasons: First, an egoistic reason: people owe it to themselves to have broad contacts and objective evaluations of others, in order to expand their own horizons and increase the quality of those whom they then select as special friends, employees, advisers, etc. Second, a utilitarian reason: an organization or a group of people is better off when everyone is given a full equal opportunity to thrive. Third, a rights-based reason: merely by virtue of being human, everyone deserves the right to equal opportunity, regardless of any benefit or cost. To restrict equal opportunity is to dehumanize people and institutions. Fourth, as a direct application of the GOLDEN RULE, equal opportunity is supported by JUSTICE reasoning. Any opportunity we enjoy we should want to be available to others, too, without prejudice. Fifth, there is a transcendent reason: every human being is an image of God, and is thereby an heir to certain privileges and opportunities that should not be arbitrarily restricted. Equal opportunity is every person's divine endowment which should be honored and protected with IMPARTIALITY.

See also **discrimination in employment; racism**

Bibliography

de Vries, P. (1990). Adam Smith's theory of justice. *Business and Professional Ethics Journal,* summer.

King, Martin Luther, Jr. (1986). *A Testament of Hope.* San Francisco: HarperCollins.

Putnam, H. (1987). *The Many Faces of Realism.* Chicago: Open Court.

Rawls, J. (1971). *A Theory of Justice.* Cambridge, Mass.: Harvard University Press.

Smith, A. (1976). *An Inquiry into the Nature and Causes of the Wealth of Nations.* Indianapolis, Ind.: Liberty Classics.

Sowell, T. (1990). *Preferential Policies.* New York: William Morrow and Company.

Stasz, C. (1981). *The American Nightmare: Why Inequality Persists.* New York: Schocken Books.

PAUL DE VRIES

equality   has long been a potent ideal, playing a prominent role in political argument. Views about equality inform debates about such wide-ranging issues as RACISM, sexism, obligations to the poor or handicapped, relations between developed and developing countries, and the justification of competing political, economic, and ideological systems. Unfortunately, equality defies easy characterization or definition.

If I give one piece of candy to Andrea, and two to Rebecca, Andrea will immediately assert "unfair!" This natural reaction suggests that equality is intimately connected with notions of fairness or justice. Arguably, concern about equality is that portion of our concern about fairness or justice that focuses on how people fare relative to others. Specifically, concern about equality reflects the view that it is bad – unfair or unjust – for some to be worse off than others through no fault of their own.

Understanding Equality

The notion of equality is widely assumed to be:

simple – we all know what equality is, that is where everybody has the same amount of x, for whatever x we are interested in;

holistic – we are concerned about (in)equality between groups or societies, for example, between blacks and whites, women and men, homosexuals and heterosexuals, or Ethiopians and Swiss; and

essentially distributive – concern is with how certain acts or goods are distributed among an outcome's groups, *ceteris paribus,* they should be distributed equally.

The conventional assumptions are questionable. Arguably, the notion of equality is:

complex – comparisons regarding inequality involve many considerations, for example, the extent of deviations from "perfect" equality, the inequality's "gratuitousness," or the extent to which individuals have a "complaint" regarding equality. Indeed, there may be twelve distinct elements, or "aspects" of equality, underlying people's judgments about equality (Temkin, 1993);

individualistic – *groups* or *societies* aren't the proper objects of moral concern, *individuals* are. So, for example, while, on average, whites may be better off than blacks, inequality between well-off blacks and poorly-off blacks, or whites, is objectionable; and

essentially comparative – equality is a *relation* between individuals, and the concern is for how individuals fare *relative to each other.*

Given that equality's different aspects often diverge in the judgments they yield, and that many of the aspects rest on contrary views, one may come to believe that the notion of equality is largely inconsistent and severely limited. Alternatively, one may conclude that it is complex, multi-faceted, and partially incomplete. Either way, once one understands what the notion of equality involves, many of one's common-sense judgments about equality will need to be revised.

Equality of What?

Much debate concerns what *kind* of equality is desirable. Should one be concerned about equality of income, resources, primary goods, welfare, opportunity, needs satisfaction, rights, or what? This issue is extremely important, since equality of one kind may require inequality of another. Thus, the handicapped may require more income than the healthy to be equal regarding needs satisfaction. Similarly, equality of opportunity may lead to inequality of welfare.

Many assume that concern for one kind of equality rules out concern for other kinds. On a pluralistic conception of morality, this assumption is dubious. Perhaps different kinds of equality matter in different contexts. Or perhaps even in the same context there are strong reasons for promoting different kinds of equality. Thus, the question "equality of what?" may have several plausible answers.

Amartya Sen suggests that most moral theories "want equality of *something*," what they differ about is "equality of *what*?"; thus, "income-egalitarians . . . demand equal incomes, . . . welfare-egalitarians . . . equal welfare levels, . . . classical utilitarians . . . equal weights on the utilities of all, and . . . libertarians . . . equality with respect to . . . rights and liberties" (Sen, 1992, p. ix) (*see* UTILITARIANISM; LIBERTARIANISM).

Sen's suggestion illuminates the importance of the question "equality of *what*?" However, to avoid confusion, one might distinguish between purely *formal* principles of equality – that require *impartiality* or *universality* – and *substantive* principles of equality – that condemn inequalities between better- and worse-off. Arguably, utilitarianism and libertarianism are only formal principles of equality, as both recognize constraints of impartiality or universality, yet may endorse increasing the gaps between better- and worse-off. Other formal principles of equality may include Aristotle's principle of equality, that likes should be treated alike, and unalikes should be treated unalike, and the widely accepted view that all persons should be treated with equal consideration and respect.

Arguments against Equality

Many arguments oppose equality. A sample follows.

1) Equality demands sameness, so differences wouldn't be allowed in size, strength, intelligence, talent, beauty, or effort. Such an outcome would be horrible, and would require totalitarianism.

2) Inequality is good, fueling intellectual and economic progress. In a world of scarcity, such "luxuries" as basic research, art, philosophy, and philanthropy, all depend on inequality.

3) Equality is incompatible with human psychology. We have natural and deep bonds with those closest to us, that we couldn't, and shouldn't, break. Moreover, given our numerous limitations, treating everyone equally would only mean treating everyone shabbily, not treating everyone well.

4) Equality is incompatible with liberty or freedom. It would not allow individuals to voluntarily improve themselves, or engage in mutually beneficial exchanges.

5) Equality requires "leveling down" the better-off, if we cannot benefit the worse-off. Similarly, equality favors wasting resources that would not benefit the worse-off.

Responses and Arguments for Equality

Equality is defended in many ways, including the following.

1) Opponents attack extreme positions. Nobody wants sameness in *all* respects. Some inequalities may be acceptable (e.g. regarding strength, beauty, or intelligence), while others are not (e.g. regarding income, resources, or opportunity).

2) Granted, inequality may have its advantages, but these may be outweighed by its disadvantages, or by its moral unacceptability. Not everything *useful* is *permissible*.

3) Equality is important, but it is only one ideal among others. So, in some circumstances, concern for equality is outweighed by other concerns. Also, equality is not the only ideal that would, if exclusively pursued, have terrible implications. The same is true of justice, freedom, utility, perfectionism, etc. This does not show each ideal is implausible, only that morality is complex.

4) Though human psychology impels us to give special consideration to those closest to us, it also impels us to regret undeserved inequalities. And we should not ignore the latter aspect of our nature, any more than the former. Thus, we must try to accommodate both elements, perhaps by expressing the former in the personal realm, and the latter in the social and political realms (see Nagel, 1991).

5) Against the "leveling down" objection, one might endorse a *person-affecting* principle of equality, that would only condemn inequality if it adversely affected individuals, rather than an *impersonal* principle, that would condemn inequality even when no one was harmed by it. Similarly, instead of a *teleological* principle of equality, that focused on assessing outcomes, one might endorse a *deontological* principle, that gave us a duty to *aid* the worse-off, but not to harm or hinder the better-off (see Temkin, 1993).

6) For many, equality is a central concern of both their pre-theoretical intuitions and their firm considered judgments. Correspondingly, any theory hoping to plausibly capture our moral judgments has to include a principle of equality.

7) Though freedom may promote some inequality, it may also require removing inequalities. Genuine freedom involves the autonomous formulation and effective implementation of a meaningful life plan commensurate with one's nature and capacities. This requires satisfaction of one's basic needs, and acceptable levels of income, resources, or primary goods, as well as freedom from social, economic, and political COERCION. This, in turn, is incompatible with many levels of inequality that are prevalent throughout the world.

8) Besides freedom, equality is instrumentally valuable for many other positions. For example, different kinds of inequality are incompatible with socialist goals, undermine the values of COMMUNITARIANISM, are often objectionable on efficiency grounds for both capitalism and utilitarianism, are unjust because they adversely affect the expectations of the worst-off group, and threaten the stability and legitimacy of democratic institutions.

Unfortunately, equality's instrumental value often leads to a conflation between the concern for equality and other concerns that equality may, under certain circumstances, promote. Thus, both proponents and opponents of equality may wrongly identify equality with socialism, or communitarianism – not recognizing that even if commitment to the latter entails commitment to the former, the reverse is not true. Likewise, Rawls's "maximin" principle (Rawls, 1971) is widely advocated as a principle

of equality, though it licenses vast *increases* in inequality, if necessary for improving – however slightly – the expectations of the worst-off group. Of course, in most cases promoting equality *will* improve a situation according to maximin; still maximin itself is *not* plausible as a *substantive* principle of equality, even if it is – like most plausible moral principles – acceptable as a *formal* principle of equality.

Important Questions Remaining

Does inequality matter more at high levels than low levels? Is it affected by population size? Does it matter *between* societies as much as within societies, between non-overlapping generations, between different species? Should the principle of equality focus on comparing people's whole lives, the simultaneous segments of their lives, or perhaps the corresponding segments of their lives (today's elderly with tomorrow's elderly, rather than today's elderly with today's youth)? These questions are important, and their answers may have a significant bearing on our understanding of morality as a whole, as well as equality.

It is no accident that appeals to equality are ubiquitous. Equality remains one of the most powerful of human ideals. Unfortunately, discussions of equality have been shrouded in error and confusion. Much careful work still needs doing, on this enormously complex topic.

See also **equal opportunity; gay rights; multinationals; women at work**

Bibliography

Atkinson, A. B. (1975). *The Economics of Inequality.* Oxford: Clarendon Press.

Dworkin, R. (1981). What is equality? Part 1: Equality of welfare. *Philosophy and Public Affairs,* 10, 185–246.

Dworkin, R. (1981). What is equality? Part 2: Equality of resources. *Philosophy and Public Affairs,* 10, 283–345.

Lucas, J. R. (1965). Against equality. *Philosophy,* 40, 296–307.

McKerlie, D. (1989). Equality and time. *Ethics,* 99, 475–91.

Nagel, T. (1991). *Equality and Partiality.* New York: Oxford University Press.

Rawls, J. (1971). *A Theory of Justice.* Cambridge, Mass.: Harvard University Press.

Schaar, J. H. (1967). Equality of opportunity and beyond. In R. Pennock & J. Chapman (eds), *Nomos IX: Equality.* New York: Atherton Press, 228–49.

Sen, A. K. (1973). *On Economic Inequality.* Oxford: Clarendon Press.

Sen, A. K. (1992). *Inequality Reexamined.* Cambridge, Mass.: Harvard University Press.

Temkin, L. S. (1993). *Inequality.* New York: Oxford University Press.

Temkin, L. S. (1995). Justice and equality: Some questions about scope. In E. F. Paul, F. D. Miller, & J. Paul (eds), *Social Philosophy and Policy,* 12. Cambridge: Cambridge University Press, 72–104.

Williams, B. (1962). The idea of equality. In P. Laslett & W. G. Runciman (eds), *Philosophy, Politics, and Society,* 2nd series. Oxford: Blackwell, 1962, 110–31.

LARRY S. TEMKIN

ethical issues in auditing At its most fundamental level, the objective of an audit is to render a professional opinion regarding the fairness (or lack thereof) of a set of financial statements in depicting a company's financial condition, results of operations, and cash flows. Such an opinion is based on an auditor's accumulation of evidence pertinent to the company's financial assertions and his/her own independent evaluation of that evidence. In the United States, and in most other industrialized countries, the company being audited is the buyer of the audit. That is to say, the company hires, pays the fees of, expects value from, and fires the auditor. Although this is the typical scenario, the audit of a publicly traded company is usually mandated by securities regulators or stock exchanges for the benefit of the investing public, not the company being audited. Thus, a fundamental tension exists as to this three-part relationship: the auditor, with a. FIDUCIARY RESPONSIBILITY to the public; the auditee, with a desire for cost-efficient value-added audits; and the investing public, with a desire for full and fair company disclosures. Given that there is an economy-wide benefit stemming from audits and that there is increased competition among audit firms for clients, it is a non-trivial auditor concern to meet the expectations and balance the needs of the engagement client (i.e., the auditee company) *and* the superordinate client (i.e., the investing public).

Springing from this tension, are two additional phenomena, each generating additional ethical issues. First, at the engagement-client level, auditors have attempted to redirect an auditee's value-added expectations (i.e., the desire for advice and ideas that extend beyond an auditor's mere rendering of an audit opinion) to the audit-firm's consulting divisions (this is often referred to as the cross-selling of services). As a byproduct of the audit, auditors frequently do offer company management a number of recommendations for how the auditee might improve various aspects of their financial reporting and control systems. In business circles there is an ongoing debate as to whether auditors are truly independent if they or their firms are also providing auditee management with recommendations for, and assistance in, implementing any number and type of improved business processes. Indeed, an auditor's opinion regarding the fairness of an auditee's financial statements is valuable, in large measure, because the auditor is perceived to be an independent, objective party qualified to render such an opinion. For example, if an audit firm's consulting division helps an auditee design and implement a new inventory control system and the audit, in part, calls for an evaluation of the company's controls over inventory, it is believed by some that the auditor is auditing his/her own firm's work and if the controls are not totally adequate, the auditor might refrain from being as critical as he/she might otherwise be. It is the perception of independence, as well as independence in fact, that is critical to the viability of the audit.

One other set of ethical issues occurs at the level of the audit profession. It is important to note that while a set of financial statements involves the adherence to many accounting guidelines, some of which are very prescriptive, they are also replete with many financial figures that are the result of management estimations and judgments. The performance of an audit and the evaluation of audit evidence entails a similar dual phenomenon for the auditors – i.e., adherence to professional guidelines and the constant exercising of professional judgment. In this context two more pervasive ethical issues exist.

One of these has to do with what is known as "opinion shopping" by clients. There are times when a company's management judges as acceptable and preferable a certain accounting treatment for a significant transaction in a way different from their auditor's judgment. Such differences of opinion may not be reconcilable, and client management may dismiss the current auditor and embark on a search for a new auditor who will agree with management's judgment. (A minimal control mechanism in this regard applicable to publicly held companies is that companies must file an 8-K statement with the Securities and Exchange Commission (SEC), spelling out the reasons for an auditor's dismissal. Many of these 8-Ks, however, are not very detailed or informative.) Clearly, at one level, if the original auditor was exercising extreme care and competency in his/her concern for fairness of the financial statements, all other similarly professional auditors should come to the same conclusion. For any number of reasons (e.g., propensity for risk-taking or competitive pressures), however, the reality is that company management may find an auditor who accepts their judgment, with or without any modification. Thus, both the current auditor and any prospective auditor are faced with a possible moral dilemma of doing what is right (i.e., insisting on a certain accounting treatment) and losing an audit client versus justifying what is perhaps not totally right or preferable and keeping/gaining a client.

The second ethical issue at the level of the audit profession's tension between judgment and guidelines has to do with the "liability crisis." Corporate managements and astute observers of business agree that reports on financial condition and performance are by nature relative and imprecise, not absolute and exact. Thus, an auditor must exercise judgment in rendering his/her opinion. Audit opinions are not the mechanical output of a series of precisely specified formulae and tasks. It is a fact, however, that auditors are increasingly being sued, for huge sums of money, on matters related to their exercising of professional judgment. As auditors face an increasing number of lawsuits, from a public seeking audit assurances that are looking more and more like guarantees of a company's reported financial results rather than opinions as to their

fairness, they are quite naturally interested in the safe harbors of more authoritative guidance on audit tasks and accounting treatments for a myriad of business transactions. The conundrum is that more authoritative guidance (e.g., from the SEC) generally means less need for the exercising of professional judgment which many would view as at the heart of the value of a professional audit. Auditors do not audit merely to serve the public need – they audit with the need to do so at a profitable level. Lawsuit costs are a substantial cost of the audit business. There may be a not too distant future in which professional, well-intentioned auditors cannot profitably conduct judgment-laden audits that satisfy an increasing public demand for assurances.

In summary, an auditor faces several ethical tensions at several levels. At the economy level, there is the issue of who is the real versus *de facto* client (i.e., the company being audited or the investing public). At the engagement level, there is the issue of auditor independence when the audit firm provides an audit and also advises auditee company management on ways to improve various business processes. At the audit profession level, there are the judgment-related issues of (1) auditee opinion shopping, and (2) the legal liability crisis.

Bibliography

Campbell, D. R. & Parker, L. M. (1992). SEC communications to the independent auditors: An analysis of enforcement actions. *Journal of Accounting and Public Policy*, winter, pp. 297–330.

Elliott, R. K. (1994). Confronting the future: Choices for the attest function. *Accounting Horizons*, Sept. 106–24.

The Expectation Gap Standards. (1993). New York: American Institute of CPAs.

Hanson, R. K. & Rockness, J. W. (1994). Gaining a new balance in the courts. *Journal of Accountancy*, Aug., 40–4.

Schultze, W. P. (1994). A mountain or a molehill? *Accounting Horizons*, Mar., pp. 69–75.

Wallace, W. A. (1980). *The Economic Role of the Audit in Free and Regulated Markets.* New York: Touche Ross & Co.

MARK E. HASKINS

ethical issues in bankruptcy The philosophy behind bankruptcy laws was to preserve assets for creditors, and allow debtors to have a "fresh start." This philosophy has changed recently to include a new reason for filing bankruptcy – use it as a business strategy to improve your bargaining position in restructuring debt. Three of the largest examples of bankruptcy filings addressing this newest philosophy occurred during the 1980s: 1) Manville Corporation trying to deal with class-action asbestos claims, 2) A. H. Robbins trying to deal with class-action Dalkon Shield claims, and 3) Texaco trying to deal with a $10 billion judgment for Pennzoil.

One could argue that bankruptcy laws are inherently improper because they do not promote one's moral obligation to satisfy their debts. By its very nature, these laws seem to allow individuals to avoid personal responsibility. Irrespective of these challenges, a discharge of one's debts in bankruptcy should allow that person to escape oppressive debt and have a second chance. The "fresh start" theory makes sense because there is little to be gained from debtors who are so burdened with bills that they have no hope of repayment. Since we no longer have debtor's prisons or sell people into slavery for failing to pay their bills, insolvents should be allowed to develop a payment plan which gives creditors the maximum amount available, and discharge the remainder. This way debtors can use their efforts to start new (more successful) ventures, or develop better spending and saving habits.

Bankruptcy as a Planning Tool

The newest debate focuses on the use/abuse of the bankruptcy laws to gain a strategic advantage in business negotiations. This is not suggesting that companies enter into the bankruptcy decision lightly, nor that they do not pay a price. Stockholders may suffer, management may lose their jobs, and the company will incur substantial legal fees. Even with these negatives, it may still be the best business decision to enter into bankruptcy. The question becomes whether the best business decision is the best ethical decision.

Bankruptcy filing used to carry the stigma of financial ruin and failure. With its increased usage and acceptance, bankruptcy is no longer shameful. Since a company or individual does not need to be insolvent to file bankruptcy, a strategic filing (or the threat of one) may be considered a savvy business decision. While the Manville, A. H. Robbins, and Texaco filings satisfied the letter of bankruptcy laws, one may question whether they met its spirit. These companies gained substantial profits respectively from: 1) selling asbestos, 2) selling Dalkon Shields, and 3) acquiring Getty, after it (Getty) had agreed in principle to be acquired by Pennzoil. In order to avoid or renegotiate their burdensome liabilities, each company declared bankruptcy. This strategy gives the debtor more time to deal with its creditors. Strategic filings may also give the debtor an unfair advantage by allowing it to bargain with creditors within the bankruptcy system, a system that typically favors compromise.

Other Ethical Issues

Two additional bankruptcy situations violating both law and ethics are fraudulent conveyances and preferential transfers. In a fraudulent conveyance, debtors attempt to cheat their creditors by selling assets, before filing for bankruptcy, to family members at deeply discounted prices. An example would be a President of a closely held corporation selling a company car valued at $15,000 to her daughter for $1,000, then filing for bankruptcy. Due to this scheme, the bankrupt estate has $14,000 less to pay its creditors. To complete the cycle, after the bankrupt's remaining debts are discharged in bankruptcy, the daughter who purchased the car would transfer use back to the discharged debtor.

Preferential transfers occur when a debtor wants to treat some unsecured creditors better than others. This desire is a clear violation of bankruptcy laws, but insolvents may have hopes of using their skills in similar businesses after the bankruptcy proceedings. They may need the goodwill of certain suppliers. These suppliers may extort "preferential" treatment from the debtor before they file for bankruptcy, by threatening to never do business with them in the future if *their* bills are not paid. These preferred creditors do not care whether the other unsecured creditors will receive less on their claims. The law and ethics concur on how to treat both fraudulent conveyances and preferential transfers. Bankruptcy laws allow the Trustee in Bankruptcy to invalidate both transactions and collect full value into the bankrupt's estate for a ratable distribution to all unsecured creditors.

Conclusion

Even if Manville, A. H. Robbins, and Texaco bankruptcy filings were both legal and ethical, will the bankruptcy filings of the future be the same? Will companies make short-term profits by cutting environmental costs, pollute the environment, then declare bankruptcy, leaving someone else to pay their bills? Will unscrupulous business-people enter into contracts they know they cannot afford, with the expectation that they can always declare bankruptcy and receive more favorable terms? The original intent was to allow bankruptcy laws to be used as a "defensive shield" against oppressive debt. The ethical question becomes whether its current application as an "offensive sword" frustrates this intent.

Bibliography

Ayer, J. D. (1986). How to think about bankruptcy ethics. *American Bankruptcy Law Journal,* fall 355–98.

Henwood, D. (1992). Behind the bankruptcy boom: Failures in the system. *The Nation,* Oct. 5, p. 345.

Hiltzik, M. A. (1987). Bankruptcy: Beyond failure; big business sees Chapter 11 shield as a potent tool. *Los Angeles Times,* July 26, business section, p. 1.

Moskowitz, D. & Ivey, M. (1987). You don't have to be broke to need Chapter 11. *Business Week,* Apr 27, p. 108.

Newborn, M. J. (1994). The new Rawlsian theory of bankruptcy ethics. *Cardozo Law Review,* 16, 111–46.

Schlangentstein, M. (1987). Pennzoil chairman denounces Texaco's bankruptcy filing. *United Press International,* Apr. 30.

Thompson, T., Tell, L. J., Vogel, T., Davis, J. E., Norman, J. R. & Mason, T. (1987). Bankruptcy court for Texaco: The lesser evil – barely. *Business Week,* Apr. 27, p. 102.

PAUL E. FIORELLI

ethical issues in computers and computer technology Many ethical issues have arisen as a result of the increasing use of computers and computer technologies. Most of the issues can be classified and analyzed using traditional ethical concepts such as property, responsibility, rights, and authority, and most involve relationships that exist independent of computers – employer/employee, citizen/government, producer/vendor/consumer, professional/client, professional/society. Nevertheless, when a situation involves computers it takes on special features which may transform its moral character or create uncertainty about norms, rights, and responsibilities. The special features of the situation necessitate a rethinking of traditional norms and values, a new understanding of how traditional values and norms apply. Hence, it seems fitting to call the issues new *species* of generic moral issues.

The new and old in computer ethical issues can be illustrated using the threat to personal privacy that computer technology seems to create. Information about individuals was being gathered and kept in increasing quantities by government and business for centuries before computers were invented. Still, the development of computer technology facilitated a radically increased *scale* of record keeping. It has facilitated: an increased level of exchange of information about individuals (increased speed of exchange, quantity of information being exchanged, and number of organizations exchanging); an increased endurance of such information (rather than being discarded, records remain because they take up little space); and, the creation of new kinds of information (especially transactional information produced when, for example, individuals use credit cards or automated teller machines). The new scale of activities needs to be evaluated morally, but when we do this we are *not* entering a wholly new domain; we are evaluating new versions of behaviors, relationships, and institutions that existed before computers.

Similarly, workplace monitoring made possible by computer technology illustrates the new and old in computer ethical issues. As a result of developments in computer technology, it is now possible for an employer to purchase software that will allow supervisors within the company to keep a complete record of everything that employees do while working on computers. The software allows supervisors to keep track of keystrokes so as to measure the speed or accuracy of work being done or simply to view work as it appears on a worker's computer screen. So, the software creates a new possibility for employers, but the ethical issue posed by this new possibility can be classified as a new version of the tension between employer and employee rights – a tension that has been in play for many centuries and has been addressed in law and in practice with regard to such matters as wages and safety conditions, political speech, and drug testing. Computer monitoring is a new species of an old issue.

Computer technology is now a fundamental part of doing business and its incorporation into the business world has created a wide variety of issues which can be understood to be new species of issues in business ethics. Indeed, one major change brought about by computer technology has been the creation of a whole new industry (or set of industries), producing computer hardware and software and other computer peripherals. As these new industries have developed, it has been necessary to work out laws, policies, and rules to ensure that the industry (and computer usage in general) is organized in ways that lead to beneficial consequences for society. One such area of concern has been defining property rights in the domain of computing – what should individuals and companies be allowed to own and what should be *un*ownable; that is, what should be proprietary and what not?

Property

Computer software is what makes computers the enormously powerful tools that they are. The stakes involved in successfully creating and bringing new and better software to the market-place are now extremely high. This has meant that companies and individuals want to lay claim to ownership of as much as they possibly can. In the domain of the "technological arts," the primary way to do this is by using the legal protection offered by patents, copyrights, and trade secrecy. These legal mechanisms, how-ever, were developed long before computers, and extending them to computer technology has been awkward and uncertain. Their applicability is being worked out primarily through legal suits, and the outcomes of these legal suits will define the "rules of the game" in computer and computer-related industries.

Our patent and copyright systems aim at encouraging development in the technological arts and sciences so that society benefits. The presumption is that individuals are more likely to create and invent *and* bring their inventions to the marketplace when they can profit from doing so. Inventors will not be able to profit from their useful inventions unless they have proprietary rights in them. Hence, the patent and copyright systems are designed to give such rights to inventors. However, both systems recognize that the benefits to society will be undermined if too much is owned by individuals. In particular, if the building-blocks of science and technology were owned, then the owners could restrict invention, making it difficult or expensive for others to use funda-mental knowledge to make yet newer inventions. For this reason, each system of legal protection restricts what can be claimed. The patent system does not allow ownership of abstract ideas, laws of nature, and mathematical formulas. One can only obtain a patent on an application or implementation of such. Simi-larly, the copyright system disallows ownership of ideas and grants copyright only in the expression of ideas.

Both the distinction made in patent law between an idea and the application of an idea, and the distinction in copyright law between idea and expression, have been problematic when used to protect computer software. In the case of patents, initially the problem was fear that granting ownership in software might, in effect, grant ownership of numerical sequences or mental steps – since all the steps in a computer program can, in principle, be done by an individual performing the steps mentally. More recently, uncertainty has centered on whether computer algorithms for solving abstractly defined problems can be patented; will this mean ownership of mathematical algorithms or of the building-blocks of comput-ing? Similarly, the distinction between idea and expression used in copyright has proved problematic for computer software. There is presently a good deal of uncertainty about the copyrightability of such things as the "structure, sequence, and organization" of a computer program, and the "look and feel" of a user interface. It is unclear whether such things constitute idea or expression. The copyright system also leaves a good deal of uncertainty about what is "fair use" when it comes to computer programming. One is allowed, in the copyright system, to use the ideas one learns from reading something. One is even allowed to use what another has created if one makes a significant improvement upon it and gives credit. These conditions do not, however, clarify whether one can use lines of computer code written by another. It does not make clear when one has stepped over the line between "fair use" and violation of copyright.

Legal problems aside, because of the nature of computer software, it is easy for individuals and companies to makes copies of what is proprietary. Rampant illegal copying has meant millions of dollars in lost revenues for the computer software industry. While software developers have developed a variety of techniques to protect their software from copying or at least to discourage it, illegal copying persists. Some compare software copying to drinking alcohol during Prohibition, claiming it is a form of behavior that cannot be stopped; hence we ought to give up and develop some other system for software.

In any case, the copying of proprietary software raises ethical questions for businesses as well as for individuals. For individuals the question seems straightforward: is it morally wrong for me to make a copy of proprietary software? For companies the issue is more complicated. Of course, the company should not intentionally break the law (for example, by buying one copy of a useful piece of software, making multiple copies, and distributing them throughout the company). But what responsibility does a company have for preventing illegal copying within the company? Does it have a responsibility to make internal policies which discourage employees from illegal copying? If so, how far should it go to enforce these policies? Should it periodically check what is stored on every computer and require employees to show proof of purchase for any software found on a corporate computer?

Privacy

The increase in the scale of information gathering facilitated by computer technology was mentioned earlier. Information about individuals is now big business. Databases containing financial information, address and telephone numbers, magazine subscription information, as well as information from government agencies (e.g. driver's license information), are now routinely bought and sold. The ethical issues surrounding this activity are generally placed in a framework of understanding that the need of organizations and institutions for information is in tension with the desires of many individuals for privacy. Organizations want and need the information in order to make better and more efficient decisions. They argue that individuals are the beneficiaries because the increased efficiency made possible by more and better information leads to better services and lower prices for individuals. At the same time, many individuals are uncomfortable with so much information about them being circulated without their knowledge or consent, and without their ability to check its accuracy.

Framing the issue as a tension between the need of organizations for information about individuals and the desires of individuals for privacy seems to tip the scales in favor of information gathering – at least in the US, where there is no explicit constitutional protection for personal privacy and no comprehensive legislative protection. The ethical issues surrounding the personal information industry (made possible by computers) may be better understood by thinking of them as issues of power in the relationship between individuals and the bureaucratic organizations which shape and determine their lives. Information gathering is part of the growing power of large bureaucracies (government agencies and private institutions) to dramatically affect the lives of individuals. Insurance companies, credit agencies, educational institutions, criminal-justice agencies, and welfare agencies all make decisions about individuals based on information stored in databases. Individuals do not have control over that information and, hence, do not know whether these agencies are basing decisions on accurate or appropriate information. Hence, individuals have very little power in relation to these organizations.

The differential in power raises a variety of ethical issues in business. First, and perhaps foremost, it raises questions about how we might better organize an information industry so as to benefit society and respect the desire for personal privacy. This is complex insofar as we want both efficient private and public institutions and a high degree of individual autonomy. Another set of privacy issues in business has to do with how businesses handle information about individuals with whom they deal. Shouldn't they have policies informing employees about the confidential nature of information and restricting how they use it? Shouldn't companies inform their customers as to how they will treat information the customers provide? Does the company gather more information than it needs? Does the company's use of personal information lead (directly or indirectly) to racial or gender discrimination?

Responsibility

Computer technology often changes or diffuses understanding of who is responsible for what. The legal liability of those who produce and sell software (mass-market software, custom systems, and hybrid systems) for errors and malfunctions in the software is still being worked out in the courts. Law aside, there are special issues of responsibility in software because of its power and complexity. Software that automates an activity such as an industrial process is based on a model of that activity. A computer system is then built on the basis of the model and may consist of millions and millions of lines of computer code. Those who design and program computer systems admit that they can never be sure that the software is perfect: the model may be incomplete and the code may have errors in it. While there may be ways to test a system, often it cannot be tested under every condition so as to eliminate the possibility of error. This, of course, must be figured into our understanding and use of computer systems, but its implications for responsibility are problematic. It seems to mean, for example, that errors and consequent accidents or harms will occur for which no one is responsible. What can be done to minimize accidents? What sort of system of liability or insurance can be worked out to compensate those who are harmed?

More and more decision-making is now being done by computer or based on complex computer analysis. Computers now manage industrial processes, monitor patients in hospitals, route airplanes, approve and assign credit limits, and so on. Even when computers do not make decisions, human decision-makers now routinely base their decisions on computer analysis – computer analysis that the decision-maker may not fully understand because he or she does not understand the inputs and algorithms used in the program. In such a situation the human decision-maker may feel compelled to act on the computer output because it justifies a decision. Imagine, for example, a person who manages funds for a pension plan. She believes this is not a good time to invest more money in bonds, but the computer system which her company uses regularly is recommending bonds. If she does not follow the system recommendations, she may be accused of mismanaging funds and the computer output can be used as evidence of her "incompetence." She does not understand how the system works but her years of experience tell her it is wrong this time. If she follows the advice of the computer system, is she abdicating responsibility or acting in a responsible way?

The Global Information Infrastructure

Computer technology in combination with our vast telecommunications system is now evolving to create what promise to be National Information Infrastructures and a Global Information Infrastructure. These systems will link individuals and companies across the world, making it possible to do business instantaneously, and to intensively manage companies, on *a global scale*. Individuals, industries, and governments will send and receive digitalized information in literary, audio, and video form. Property rights, privacy, and responsibility issues will arise between nations with a greater intensity than ever before. The security of the system will be a major problem, as businesses become more and more dependent on it at the same time as the potential for industrial espionage and terrorism reach a new scale. The development of such a global information infrastructure will shape the future of business and in so doing will create yet newer species of generic moral issues in business.

Bibliography

Dejoie, R., Fowler, G., & Paradice, D. (eds),. (1991). *Ethical Issues in Information Systems.* Boston: Boyd & Fraser.

Erman, M. D., Williams. M. B., & Gutierrez, C. (eds),. (1990). *Computers, Ethics, and Society.* Oxford: Oxford University Press.

Forester, T. & Morrison, P. (1990, 1994). *Computer Ethics, Cautionary Tales and Ethical Dilemmas in Computing.* Cambridge, Mass.: MIT Press.

Gould, C. (ed.). (1989). *The Information Web: Social and Ethical Implications of Computer Networking.* Boulder, Colo.: Westview Press.

Huff, C. & Finholt, T. (1994). *Social Issues in Computing.* New York: McGraw-Hill.

Johnson, D. G. (1985, 1994). *Computer Ethics.* Englewood Cliffs, NJ: Prentice-Hall.

Johnson, D. G. (1992). Computers. In L. C. Becker & C. B. Becker (eds), *Encyclopedia of Ethics.* New York: Garland.

Johnson, D. G. & Nissenbaum, H. F. (eds),. (1995). *Computers, Ethics, and Social Values.* Englewood Cliffs, NJ: Prentice-Hall.

Kallman, E. (1993). *Ethical Decision Making and Information Technology: An Introduction with Cases.* Watsonville, Calif.: Mitchell McGraw-Hill.

Oz, E. (1994). *Ethics for the Information Age.* Dubuque, Iowa: William C. Brown Communications.

DEBORAH G. JOHNSON

ethical issues in corporate finance   For many, the conjunction of corporate finance and ethics is oxymoronic. This reaction is justified by the financial scandals of recent years, when financial activities were reported with an intensity not seen since the Depression. In fact, for centuries financial activities of necessity have had to be conducted according to higher than existing normal standards of trust and responsibility. Of all human endeavors, financial transactions are most dependent on the exchange of intangible items (clay tablets, pieces of paper) and on the exchange of promises to perform at some time, often distant, in the future. This does not mean, of course, that finance has not attracted its share of charlatans – often the development of new financial tools has been accompanied by those eager to cash in on the desperation of the distressed and the naiveté of the ignorant. Many depositors lost money in the period of Wildcat Banking, and the early days of the insurance industry were characterized by widespread fraud.

Although particular institutions and structures are characteristic of each historical period, there is evidence that the basic functions have been in operation for over 5,000 years. The Code of Hammurabi, which dates to about 2,100 BC, contains provisions that indicate active business and financial sectors were already well developed. The ethical responsibilities of the parties have probably not changed since then, although they were undoubtedly much less complex in a less complex and interdependent society.

The Financial Function

The financial function, in its broadest sense, assists in the efficient allocation of scarce resources between those who hold surplus resources and those who can use the resources productively. The holders of surplus resources (who can be individuals, corporate bodies, or financial institutions such as pension funds) are often not in a position efficiently to allocate the surplus to those that can use it. Second, the principle of diversification (which virtually guarantees some small level of loss in order to avoid the overwhelming loss that can come from a concentration of investment) suggests that the surplus units may benefit from a mechanism that allows the surplus to be invested in many smaller positions. The costs of direct investment make accomplishing diversification prohibitively expensive on a small scale.

These requirements create a need for financial intermediaries to bring savers and investors together efficiently. The intermediaries can take virtually any form of legal structure. They can perform the task without any commitment of their own resources (although there is often some out-of-pocket expense at risk), or they can invest some of their own capital in the process. Banks are in the latter category, as are insurance companies. This type of intermediary accepts savers' funds, adds some of its own capital, and provides the mix to those whose earnings on the funds is expected to be greater than the cost (including an allowance for loss). If problems develop with the borrower, this type of intermediary is expected to bear the losses first out of the capital it contributed.

At the other extreme, investment banks traditionally have acted as agents, for a fee, and at most have their capital invested for a few days while an issue is being placed. The saver and the user are then placed in a direct relationship, with the saver bearing the entire risk of ultimate loss. The agent's potential loss is confined to that associated with the placement process.

Complexities of Modern Society

The nature of financial ethical violations and dilemmas has naturally changed over time as the economy has become more sophisticated and increasingly relies on intangibles as ways in which wealth is held and traded. The US government did not issue paper money until the Civil War; its transactions were largely in specie. Even after the first US Legal Tender Notes were issued, they were not valid for payment of interest on the US government debt nor for payments to the US government for excises and taxes. As late as the start of the twentieth century, the US economy was still primarily agrarian. The commercial ethical issues were largely physical: short measure, clipped coins, nondelivery. Even the management of inheritances was largely left to family, friends, or local attorneys, and the assets in the estates were primarily real assets.

With the growth of intangible assets (often merely impulses in a computer) and of financial intermediaries, ethical problems in finance have taken on correspondingly less physical and more characteristically financial dimensions: accounting fraud, misappropriation of funds, misleading information, and conflicts of interest in the handling of financial transactions and obligations.

The general ethical obligation in financial transactions, however, has remained honesty – although there is a buyer-beware clause. If the buyer asks the right question, the ethical mandate is for the question to be answered honestly. There has been little obligation until recently, however, to disclose what is not asked about.

Because of the perceived differences in modern society between the power of the individual investor and of the large intermediary or large user of savings, the legal system in the United States now requires that the user of savings disclose all material facts of its situation and interpret them for the small investor. This requirement, however, does not apply to transactions between large and presumably knowledgeable parties and institutions.

Financial Intermediaries

The most interesting questions in contemporary corporate financial ethics indeed relate to these large financial intermediaries. Following the end of the Second World War, pension and retirement plans became significant holders of funds for their beneficiaries. Between 1950 and 1991, the assets of pension funds grew six times as fast as the Gross National Product. In recent years, as individuals have been allowed to direct the investment of their share of these funds (rather than leaving these decisions to the plan trustees), equity and balanced mutual funds began to grow rapidly. Because of the regulatory structure of the banking system, money-market mutual funds were also established and eventually accounted for 15 percent of the deposits in commercial banks. In sum, institutional investors are now thought to hold some 70 percent of the value of the stocks listed on the New York Stock Exchange and probably a larger proportion of taxable corporate bonds.

At the simplest intermediary level, the securities broker or customer's representative is acting as an intermediary, often recommending investments to a client and then holding the assets in the broker's name until the client decides to sell them. What, for example, should the broker's (or the firm's) trading practices be with respect to the trades recommended for the broker's customers? Can the broker ever sell a stock that is being recommended for customer purchase (or vice versa)? Can the broker buy (or sell) in advance of recommendations to the firm's customers? Which customers get called first or have their transactions placed first? How hard does the broker work to get the best price for the customer?

Although the Securities and Exchange Commission and the securities exchanges themselves have many regulations (particularly with respect to use of inside information) attempting to prevent brokers from profiting at the expense of the investment community (and, to a lesser extent, from profiting at the benefit of the users of funds), these are minimal expectations. Some brokerage firms have established regulations that are considerably more demanding. For example, some firms allow their employees to invest only mutual funds managed by another firm. Some go as far as to restrict employees' investments to US government securities.

Similar regulations with similar intentions have been established in the United States for the users of funds, the issuers of securities, so they will provide investors with complete and accurate material information. Issuers of securities, particularly those corporations issuing securities to the public for the first time, are increasingly being subject to legal attack from disgruntled investors if the price of the security subsequently declines. Issuing the security at such a low price that a decline is improbable, however, penalizes the existing equity owners – another ethical problem.

The question of favoring existing owners over future owners is more easily settled than the issue of which customers a broker or other financial intermediary should favor. The general rule is to favor the existing owners subject to full disclosure but buyer-beware on the part of the new owners. As one corporate treasurer responded when asked if the company would issue shares if the treasurer believed them to be overvalued: "Yes, I'd issue the shares. The investors are entitled to their opinions, and mine may be wrong."

A much more complex set of ethical problems arises among the relationships of the investor, the intermediary, and the user of the funds when the investor is not making the ultimate buy-and-sell decisions. For example, what are the ethical responsibilities of a pension fund when the sponsoring employer encounters financial difficulties? Should the fund invest in the employer's securities, trying to help stabilize the situation and protect the company's current employees – the later beneficiaries of the fund? Or, is the responsibility of the fund to protect the fund's assets by putting them in safe investments so they will be more certain to be there to meet the eventual claims on the fund? The question is further complicated because some former employees may have already retired. What risks should be taken to protect the current employees? These are the difficult

questions faced by a number of labor unions and their pension funds during the financial problems of New York City in the late 1970s.

Ethical Aspects of the Socialization of Risk

Another emerging trend places on the economic sector and indirectly on the financial sector responsibility for activities that have been for several generations considered governmental responsibilities. This has been termed the "socialization of risk" (*see* RISK). Less genteelly phrased, it might be expressed as, "Somebody else has to pay!"

Starting with the economic problems of the 1930s, society accepted the government's obligation to step in to assist society in resolving major social problems and distributing the associated costs. It was considered fair to spread the costs over the whole society, usually through individual income tax, rather than to assess it against the segment of the society that had the problem.

The tax "revolt of the middle class" that appeared during the late 1980s, however, created serious problems with this consensus. The middle class, which pays the majority of the income taxes (and indirect taxes) by virtue of its large size in the United States, appears to have decided that it was paying too much and getting too little in return. On the other hand, the electorate did not wish to have services curtailed, particularly those services that involved transfer payments to the poor, the elderly, and the environment. The legislative response was to try to pass those costs on to the corporate sector.

The socialization of risk has been most evident in the retrospective establishment of liability for activities that were legal and not known to be harmful at the time they were undertaken. Judgments and settlements in these circumstances are then charged to insurance companies, whose rates had not been set with this knowledge and which were therefore much too low. The insurance company's owners are thus damaged (perhaps pension and retirement funds), its existing customers are damaged if the firm fails, and its future customers are damaged because their premiums are raised to allow the company to rebuild its equity. This latter may be difficult to accomplish in the face of competition from new companies and those that did not happen to write insurance in the problem area.

Risk socialization has also been evident in the effort to mandate actions for certain financial sectors, apparently on the presumption that the sectors are natural monopolies that can easily spread these additional costs over their existing customer base. One instance has been the demand that insurance companies provide health insurance for individuals who are sick at the time they request the insurance. This is akin to mandating that payment be made to a person whose car has been stolen even though the individual had not taken out insurance. The costs must be passed on to those who have taken out the insurance or who will be taking it out in the future. Another instance is the demand that financial institutions provide free services to designated economic sectors or allocate credit to sectors deemed not to have adequate access to credit.

In the case of true natural monopolies, such as electric power companies, such mandates may provide a substitute for direct governmental support. Mandates placed on institutions that do not have natural monopolistic power usually undermine those institutions because their customers find more efficient ways to obtain the desired services. The public is far less ignorant than legislators tend to assume when they put mandates into effect.

The effort to avoid having to balance in an ethical manner the demands of various segments of society is creating these serious new ethical financial issues for the corporate sector and financial intermediaries. Colleges, for example, must offer health-insurance coverage for pregnancy as part of the insurance provided to their students. Students who do not think they will require this coverage may find it less expensive to get insurance elsewhere that more nearly suits their needs. The smaller base then makes the cost of the college-sponsored insurance much more expensive. Those who really need the coverage may not be able to afford any. The effort to mandate that all college students should buy into the college-sponsored pool foundered for fear of the protest of parents whose children were already being covered by the parent's employer's plan.

Thus, although the core ethical precept in finance remains honest disclosure and dealing, the operational definition of these terms changes to reflect society's overall sense of who should be responsible to whom for what and in what priority. As of the late twentieth century, these norms are undergoing substantial changes. Whether the economy can provide the resources to support these new demands is not clear.

WILLIAM W. SIHLER

ethical issues in energy   The ethical issues surrounding energy use can be reduced largely to questions of DISTRIBUTIVE JUSTICE and intergenerational equity. The Brundtland Report on sustainable development, for example, exhorts industrialized countries to "recognize that their energy consumption is polluting the biosphere and eating into scarce fossil fuel supplies" (World Commission on Environment and Development, 1987). The World Council of Churches (WCC) offers an even more explicit assessment of the normative implications of energy use: "In a just society everyone would have access to the energy necessary to meet basic needs. Justice would also require fairer distribution of energy between rich and poor, [as well as] the equitable distribution of risks, benefits, and costs among and between groups in the population" (Albrecht, 1975, p. 87). These distributive and intergenerational concerns are examined in further detail below.

Distributive Justice

It has been suggested that the social costs of energy generation and distribution are borne disproportionately by the poor and ethnic minorities (Commoner et al., 1975). Consider, for example, the power-generating grid centered in the Four Corners area, where the borders of Arizona, Colorado, New Mexico, and Utah converge. There, a complex of six electricity generating plants are fueled by low-sulfur coal strip-mined from rich deposits located on Navajo and Hopi lands, including the Black Mesa region. The Black Mesa is sacred to the Hopi, who believe that its preservation is fundamental to human survival. The Peabody Coal Company's mining operations leave huge craters in the landscape, churn up coal dust that winds deposit for miles in every direction, and pollute streams and rivers with sulfuric acid and heavy metals borne by rain and melting snow that leaches it from tailing banks. The slurry pipeline that transports the coal to faraway power plants consumes thousands of gallons of water per minute, depleting ancient aquifers located far below the desert. The plants themselves require vast quantities of water to cool their generators, water which is redirected from the Colorado River, creating salinity problems for wildlife, native tribes, and other agricultural users down river. The haze of sulfur oxides, nitrogen oxides, and particulate matter generated by the plants can be seen for hundreds of miles, clouding and toxifying the otherwise pristine air of the region. Thermal pollution from the plants alters aquatic ecosystems, raises local air temperatures, and contributes to global climate change. The immediate costs of these adverse environmental impacts are borne largely by the residents of the area, who use little of the power generated, work at few of the jobs created, and receive nominal compensation for the use of their lands (Gordon, 1973). This situation, and analogous conditions that often exist in urbanized areas with high concentrations of economically disadvantaged and ethnic minorities, illustrates the vast disparities that can exist between populations who bear the costs of energy extraction, generation, transport, and use, and those who receive the benefits.

Ironically, efforts to require energy conservation and reduce the adverse health, ecological, and cultural impacts of energy use can lead to price increases that are particularly burdensome for low-income individuals. The poor spend a disproportionately high percentage of their incomes on energy, while consuming considerably less per capita than the middle and upper classes (Landsberg, 1979). They are generally less able to reduce transportation costs, relocate to milder climates, or invest in other forms of energy conservation in response to higher prices. On the other hand, the emerging literature on "environmental justice" suggests that low-income individuals would be net beneficiaries of policies designed to reduce the adverse environmental consequences of energy use (Mohai, 1992).

Intergenerational Equity

Intergenerational equity is one of the primary ethical concerns surrounding energy generation and consumption. Peet (1992, p. 190) contends that "We have an ethical responsibility to leave as many resources as possible, of both raw materials and ecosystem services, for future generations." When evaluating the sustainability of alternative resource consumption rates or energy technologies, the rate used to discount their relative costs and benefits can dramatically affect the welfare of future generations. Consider, for example, the case of atmospheric warming caused partly by the emission of greenhouse gases by electricity generating facilities. It has been estimated that without corrective action, warming is likely to continue for the next 250–300 years. Applying an artificially high discount rate will serve to understate future costs (in the form of health, ecological, and welfare impacts) associated with technologies using coal- and petroleum-based fuels, as well as understate the future benefits of regulations or investments designed to reduce greenhouse gas emissions. Cline (1992, p. 235) notes that "As the benefits of avoided greenhouse damage tend to be realized much later than the costs imposed on the economy from restriction of greenhouse gas emissions, a discount rate that is inappropriately high will bias policy toward inaction."

Many scholars argue that the appropriate rate for discounting costs and benefits of conservation and energy regulation is not the rate of return on private capital, but rather the *social discount rate* or *social rate of time preference* (SRTP). One reason is that market rates reflect only current individuals' impatience or time preference, while the SRTP accounts for the fact that future generations cannot be here to argue on their behalf. Another is that regulatory efforts to reduce greenhouse gas emissions draw societal resources primarily from consumption, rather than investment (Burton, 1993). A carbon tax, for instance, would raise revenue not from capital markets, where it would have to compete with alternative public and private uses for funds, but from everyday transactions spread throughout the economy. The SRTP approximates, in essence, the rate at which society is willing to trade current consumption for future consumption (*see* FUTURE GENERATIONS).

While many environmentalists argue that zero is the appropriate reference rate (Barry, 1977), economists sympathetic to the idea of using the SRTP have estimated rates of between 1 and 3 percent per annum (Kolb & Scheraga, 1990). Others argue that the rate should vary depending on the nature of gains and losses that are being valued (Lowenstein, 1992), or that the rate should decline as costs and benefits are projected into the distant future (Harvey, 1994). In virtually all cases, the SRTP is estimated to be far below prevailing rates of return on investment capital. Cost/benefit analyses incorporating the latter rate will tend to favor the interests of current over future generations.

Bibliography

Albrecht, P. (1975). *Faith, Science, and the Future*. Geneva: World Council of Churches.

Barry, B. (1977). Justice between generations. In P. Hacker & J. Raz (eds), *Law, Morality, and Society*. Oxford: Clarendon Press.

Burton, P. S. (1993). Intertemporal preferences and intergenerational equity considerations in optimal resource harvesting. *Journal of Environmental Economics and Management*, **24**, 119–32.

Cline, W. R. (1992). *The Economics of Global Warming*. Washington, DC: Institute for International Economics.

Commoner, B., Boksenbaum, H. & Corr, M. (eds). (1975). *Energy and Human Welfare – A Critical Analysis*. New York: Macmillan.

Gordon, S. (1973). *Black Mesa: The Angel of Death*. New York: John Day.

Harvey, C. M. (1994). The reasonableness of non-constant discounting. *Journal of Public Economics*, **53**, 31–51.

Kolb, J. A. & Scheraga, J. D. (1990). Discounting the benefits and costs of environmental regulations. *Journal of Policy Analysis and Management*, **9** (3), 381–90.

Landsberg, H. H. (1979). *Energy: The Next Twenty Years*. Cambridge, Mass.: Ballinger.

Lind, R. C. (ed.). (1982). *Discounting for Time and Risk in Energy Policy*. Washington, DC: Resources for the Future.

Lowenstein, G. (1992). *Choice Over Time*. New York: Russell Sage Foundation.

Mohai, P. (1992). Environmental racism: A review of the evidence. In B. Bryant & P. Mohai (eds), *Environmental Hazards: A Time for Discourse*. Boulder, Colo.: Westview Press.

Peet, J. (1992). *Energy and the Ecological Economics of Sustainability*. Washington, DC: Island Press.

World Commission on Environment and Development. (1987). *Our Common Future*. Oxford: Oxford University Press.

TOM E. THOMAS

ethical issues in finance   arise especially in transactions between parties characterized by unequal market powers and differential access to relevant information, particularly in areas where legal or regulatory rules are of uncertain effectiveness. Most financial transactions depend on implicit contracts and expectations of ethical behavior, and financial decisions are often made on behalf of principals by agents, agents that may have preferential access to information and who may face conflicts of interest in making such decisions. Ethical issues in finance are particularly important as they often involve conflicts between fiduciary responsibilities, self-interest, and responsibilities to other stakeholders.

Nature and Importance of Ethical Issues in Finance

While many social values are reflected in laws, many others are reflected only in ethical guidelines restraining self-interest and balancing the often conflicting interests of various stakeholders. Many actions that favor certain stakeholders or are self-serving may be legal, but are often considered unethical. Ethical guidelines are a reflection of values and mores that are considered important by society. Unfortunately, there is often considerable disagreement in a society about what is considered unethical in finance. A case in point relates to disagreements, since at least biblical times, about appropriate interest rates on loans.

In recent years there have been continuing instances of unethical behavior related to financial activities (often leading to significant losses for the firms involved). Highly publicized cases in the late 1980s where unethical behavior in finance resulted in illegal activity include those that led to government actions against Michael Milken, Ivan Boesky, Salomon Brothers, Bank of Credit and Commerce International, futures traders, mutual fund managers, a number of defense suppliers, and other firms. Some of these actions led to the liquidation and loss of independence of major investment banking firms such as Drexel Burnham and Kidder Peabody. Serious ethical and legal questions are being raised about the suitability of the sales of many derivative products, even to managers of major corporations who are presumably sophisticated investors. American companies operating overseas have to conform to the Foreign Corrupt Practices Act that outlaws bribery overseas; and US companies continue to be prosecuted for violating its requirements. However, unethical behavior in finance is not limited to US companies. In the early 1990s, banks and other financial firms in Europe, Asia, and Latin America have been implicated in widespread corruption and unethical behavior. Clearly, ethical issues in finance are important and not limited to any one country.

The Modern Setting of Ethics in Finance

Business organizations are replete with opportunities for behavior that is self-serving or that favors certain stakeholders at somebody else's expense. For example, employees control the use and disposition of business assets and, more generally, managers and directors act as agents for principals such as owners and other suppliers of capital. Further, principals and agents have differential access to relevant information, and agents often face ethical dilemmas relating to the disclosure of adverse information. As another example, many business relationships depend on implicit contracts between the company and its various stakeholders. In these cases, the expectation of ethical behavior is critical to the efficient operation of a business. Similarly, ethical and moral values also influence the relationship between employees, managers, and their firms and, thus, the relative efficiency of alternative approaches to the organization of a firm (this is contended to be one of the main reasons for the differences in how work is organized between, say, US and Japanese firms). Consequently, modern financial economics, and finance theory and practice, are intimately concerned with ethical issues and behavior as indicated by the importance of topics such as agency theory, financial contracting under information asymmetry, moral hazard and adverse selection, and reputation acquisition in finance.

Ethical behavior in the financial industry is particularly important since financial decisions may involve other people's money, accumulated wealth, and other savings. It is impossible to develop and impractical to implement, for every possible contingency in the financial industry, rules of behavior constraining self-serving behavior or behavior favoring certain stakeholders. Laws, regulations, and corporate rules of conduct consequently often have to leave many details undefined, and the players have to look for guidance to commonly accepted values and mores as reflected in social expectations of ethical behavior.

Continuing unethical behavior in finance generally has a contagion effect. Even for firms that do not face failure and are not directly associated with unethical behavior, unethical behavior in an industry can lead to higher operating costs for all businesses in that industry due to the increased regulatory and legal actions designed to curb such behavior. Each major epoch of unethical financial behavior in the past has been followed by new government regulations and laws designed to reduce or at least minimize such unethical behavior. Some have even argued that most government regulations related to the financial industry originated as reactions against episodes of significant unethical behavior among some financial market participants. Unfortunately, persistence of scandals and unethical behavior in financial markets can erode confidence in such markets, and lead to a reduction in the number of market participants and, thus, to reduced efficiency of such markets. Ethical behavior in finance is often a tug of war between self-interest, market efficiency, and various concepts of fairness.

Forces Impacting Ethical Behavior in Finance

Ethical behavior reflects the constraining role of social conventions, and ethical behavior in finance often presents many dilemmas and choices between personal, organizational, and societal goals. In a market-based economy, social conventions as guides to ethical behavior can be of uncertain value as they are often in conflict with the notion, associated with Adam Smith and others, that the pursuit of self-interest by individuals leads to the maximum social good. These uncertainties and conflicts become particularly evident and even critical in economies that are in transition from centrally planned socialist economies to market-driven economies.

However, the pursuit of self-interest associated with Adam Smith's "invisible hand" is somewhat mitigated by the need to allow for market failures. Such failures can arise due to externalities, costly and asymmetric information, high transactions costs, unequal bargaining powers, barriers to entry and exit, and other factors limiting market participation. Regardless of the reason(s) for market failure, it is contended that the pursuit of self-interest and corporate shareholder wealth maximization must be restrained by appropriate laws, regulations, and social expectations for ethical behavior that reflect society's shared values and beliefs (Adam Smith, in fact, also recognized society's dependence on virtue).

Ethical behavior in finance can also be promoted by detecting and punishing unethical behavior. Such efforts to prevent or minimize unethical behavior in finance are generally based on regulation and disclosure of such activities. Of course, to be effective, such regulations and disclosure rules must be enforced and violators punished. However, as discussed above, such regulations and laws are likely to impose higher dead-weight costs on all participants in financial transactions and may lead to less efficient markets. Thus, the need for ethical behavior in finance also arises from the recognition that its absence is likely to encourage new laws and higher levels of government regulations against such behavior.

In some cases, it may be possible to discourage unethical behavior by redefining property rights, internalization of previous externalities, or by the explicit recognition of implicit contracts between the various stakeholders in a firm. For example, many new regulations and class action lawsuits against unethical business practices are based on demonstrating that such a business is appropriating or damaging property belonging to others. As another example, public pressure may be used to make explicit the implicit contracts between a company and the commu-

nity in which it operates. However, redefinition of such property rights is often difficult, involves lengthy processes, or may be impossible in many cases in modern democratic societies. Of course, it is much more effective and economically efficient when ethical behavior is promoted (and unethical behavior constrained) by shared values and beliefs.

In addition, a reputation for ethical behavior can have many advantages. For example, firms build and maintain good reputations in order to convince clients that the risks of transactions are reduced. In doing so, they increase the value of implicit claims sold by the firm to its various stakeholders, and the firm's ability to attract and engage in profitable transactions. This is particularly important in finance as such transactions generally involve decisions about somebody else's assets. Trust and a good reputation are not only essential in such cases, but are also very efficient mechanisms for reducing and eliminating agency costs and costs of contractual enforcement. Finally, good reputations enhance the available opportunity set by reducing the risks faced by the parties in a transaction. Thus, firms with good ethical reputations gain access to wealth-enhancing opportunities not available otherwise.

Most finance professionals are taught that the overriding goal of the firm is to maximize shareholder wealth. Some contend that maximizing shareholder wealth in the long term is possible only with ethical behavior. Unethical behavior is costly as it damages a firm's reputation and, conversely, ethical behavior can be wealth enhancing. However, shareholder wealth maximization alone will prevent unethical behavior only if the firm's stock price reflects the extent to which the benefits of such unethical behavior are less than the expected present value of the future costs of unethical behavior (in the form of penalties or lost reputation that impact a firm's risk or return). This implies that unethical behavior is disclosed publicly in a timely manner and that capital markets are able to assess its impact on share value accurately. Consequently, the goal of shareholder wealth maximization by itself is unlikely to lead to ethical behavior other than in some special cases. Thus, most finance professionals accept that the pursuit of the shareholder wealth maximization goal has to be constrained by behavior that certainly must be legal and preferably also ethical.

Ethical Issues in Financial Management

Managers are agents for principals (owners and other stakeholders in a firm). Managers also have preferential access to information about the firm and its assets and liabilities. Members of a firm's board of directors share similar advantages relative to other owners. While managers and directors are restrained from taking advantage of their positions as agents by many laws and regulations, generally there is considerable room for unethical behavior. For example, accounting rules generally allow some flexibility and important information can be withheld. Similarly, the release of other material non-accounting information can also be withheld. Empirical evidence shows that the announcement of an issue of equity depresses the stock price as equity is sold to the public only when it is overpriced. Similarly, compensation of senior management is sometimes set by directors with insufficient attention to their fiduciary duties to stockholders allowing for overly generous stock options, golden parachutes, and other forms of managerial compensation.

Ethical Issues in Financial Transactions with Stakeholders

Managers can also take advantage of their preferential access to information in their dealings with other stakeholders such as suppliers, customers, the communities in which the firm operates, labor unions, and others. Problems arise when different parties in transactions between a firm and its stakeholders have different expectations regarding what is considered ethical. Suppliers and customers may behave opportunistically. A firm may ignore its implicit commitments to a community. A new owner may not accept many or all of the implicit contracts between a firm and its stakeholders. It has been suggested that the renegotiation of costly implicit contracts can be a major source of synergistic savings in a merger or acquisition. In these and other financial transactions between a firm and its stakeholders, implicit contracts are

impacted and ethical issues become very important and even critical in many cases.

Ethical Issues in the Financial Services Industry

Mandatory disclosure regulations as reflected in the 1933 and 1934 Securities Acts in the United States and in the 1900 British Companies Act are an attempt to reduce information asymmetry by requiring disclosure of certain minimum amounts of information and apply penalties for misrepresentation in all disclosures by issuers of securities. While it is possible that they may have reduced investor choice by increasing costs of security issuance and by reducing the choice set of available risky securities, these requirements have clearly increased the informational efficiency of financial markets.

Laws against insider trading in securities are another example of attempts to reduce information asymmetry among financial market participants. While there is some controversy regarding these laws and regulations, many of them are based on the notion that insider information does not belong to the person using it and, thus, its use is fraud or theft and is contrary to fiduciary responsibilities of insiders.

In recognition of the need to address the problems arising out of unequal market powers and asymmetric information, most professional associations in the financial services industry in the US have developed ethical guidelines for their members (e.g., the Chartered Financial Analysts Federation). In addition, many regulations and guidelines, such as the suitability rules regarding sales of securities, are an attempt to protect investors with low market power and knowledge from firms with greater market power and knowledge. Suitability rules require that brokers determine if potential buyers of certain risky securities are suitable owners of such securities. For similar reasons, issuers of securities are required to issue securities at prices that are "fair and equitable." Both the New York and the Tokyo Stock Exchanges have in recent years appointed study groups and panels to recommend ways to improve the fairness and efficiency of financial markets for individual investors.

Another ethical issue in finance relates to the desire of many investors to invest only in firms that engage in ethical businesses. These investors are willing to limit their universe of investments thus forgoing a possible better risk–return combination. A number of "socially responsible" mutual funds are available for the portfolio investment needs of such investors.

Conclusions

Ethical issues are ubiquitous and important in finance. Ethics act as important and cost-effective constraints on self-serving and other undesirable behavior by agents (such as managers) who have preferential information and who are responsible for the management of assets that belong to others (principals). Ethics in finance are especially important as it is impractical for laws, regulations, and corporate rules of behavior to cover every contingency in financial transactions between employees, managers, firms, and their various stakeholders. Financial transactions depend critically on implicit contracts, and the pursuit of shareholder wealth maximization must be constrained by expectations of ethical behavior. Further, unethical behavior in finance can lead to business failure and/or increased regulatory and legal costs for the industry, while a reputation for ethical behavior leads to an expanded opportunity set and can be wealth enhancing.

See also **Accounting ethics; Agency theory; Efficient markets; Ethical issues in corporate finance; Ethical issues in investment; Financial reporting; Foreign Corrupt Practices Act; Insider trading; Market for corporate control; Mergers and acquisitions; Risk; Stakeholder theory; White knight**

Bibliography

Aggarwal, R. & Chandra, G. (1990). Stakeholder management: opportunities and challenges. *Business,* **40** (4), 48-51.
Anand, P. & Cowton, C. J. (1993). The ethical investor: exploring dimensions of investment behavior. *Journal of Economic Psychology,* **14** (2), 377-385.
Baumol, W. (1991), *Perfect Markets and Easy Virtue: Business Ethics and the Invisible Hand.* Cambridge, Mass.: Blackwell.
Bear, L. A. & Maldano-Bear, R. (1994), *Free Markets, Finance, Ethics, and Law.* Englewood Cliffs, NJ: Prentice-Hall.
Dobson, J. (1993). The role of ethics in finance. *Financial Analysts Journal,* Nov./Dec., pp. 57-61.
Markowitz, H., (1992). Markets and morality. *Journal of Portfolio Management,* winter, pp. 84-93.
Noe, T. H. &. Robello, M. J. (1994). The dynamics of business ethics and economic activity. *American Economic Review,* **84** (3), 531-547.
Shefrin, H. & Statman, M. (1993). Ethics, fairness and efficiency in financial markets. *Financial Analysts Journal,* Nov./Dec., pp. 21-29.
Williams, O., Reilly, F. K. & Houck, J. W. (eds) (1989). *Ethics and the Investment Industry,* Savage, Md.: Rowman and Littlefield.

RAJ AGGARWAL

ethical issues in information   Information, narrowly defined, consists of descriptions, representations, and data that purport to be true. Broadly defined, information can include interpretation, speculation, prediction, and the like. Although orders, promises, and questions are not information in the narrow definition (since they are not evaluated as true or false), the fact that an order has been given (for instance to purchase a product at a stated price) is information. There are a broad range of ethical issues concerning access to information, proper use of information, and standards of accuracy when reporting information. The following issues have received considerable attention.

In many corporations, information flow crudely parallels corporate power structure, and access to information is often seen as a form of power. Managers, for instance, may ask for employment data on those below them, but not on those above them or outside their departments. The design of the flow of information within a corporation, therefore, affects the moral climate of the corporation. In corporations where information flow is largely computerized, this is an ethical component of the management information system (MIS). The system can be written to reflect or ignore corporate structure, or in the extreme to make all information open to all workers. Since such MIS choices bear on traditional power relations, they have serious ethical consequences. On a broader social level, the observation that privileged access to information can be a source of political power has justified moves to ensure "freedom of information" through open access to government data bases.

Proprietary interests can determine who may have access to or use information. The paradigm example is trade secrecy policy, which forbids certain practices for the discovery of a commercially valuable information (*see* TRADE SECRETS). This policy depends on the ethically charged notion of a "fair means" of discovery. Under present business standards, for instance, it is impermissible to tap into a telephone transmission of data, but it is fair practice to reverse engineer a product. These standards can change and are often controversial. Although other forms of intellectual property do not traditionally restrict access to information, they raise ethical and social questions over the value of open information. For instance, one popular justification for patent policy views patents as social contracts under which a monopoly on technical applications is exchanged for disclosure of trade secrets. There is also a long-standing debate over whether information may be kept secret during a patent application process. And there is a new debate over whether copyrights on machine-level computer code may be used to block access to information incorporated into the code.

There has been much discussion of a presumed right of individuals to limit access to "personal information," defined as information that is not publicly available and that an ordinary person might wish to keep private. This right is often seen as one aspect of a "right to privacy." (Other aspects of privacy do not concern information, e.g. rights to make personal medical decisions or to be free from nuisance telephone calls.) What information should be kept private is controversial. Income levels, for instance, are seen as private or public, depending on a number of factors. The US Privacy Act of 1974 placed constraints on information acquisition by federal agencies, some of which can be adapted to business organizations and corporations as well. These include: informing individuals that the information is held and whenever it is accessed; giving individuals a right to correct the information; and restricting dissemination of the information. Although in the 1970s, most discussion of privacy focused on access to sensitive databases (e.g. medical and criminal records), subsequent debates have focused on the possibility of "tracking" individuals through information that is automatically generated by credit-card use, telephone calls, etc.

A closely related series of issues concerns misuse of irrelevant information (even when there is no claim that the information is private in nature). In the context of legal trials, this bears on the "admissibility of evidence." In professional business contexts, it can involve guards against unethical biases. For instance, information on marital status, national origin, and religious affiliation may or may not be relevant to employee hiring or promotion (*see* ETHICAL ISSUES IN RECRUITING AND SELECTION). Similarly, it may or may not be relevant to a contract decision that a potential contractee has minority ownership, runs a charity, or has a foreign home office. The definition of "relevant" is highly controversial, and has many ethical consequences. In 1994, for instance, there was considerable public debate over the relevance of information about the sexual practice of soldiers to their military duty. In order to avoid the suspicion of improper bias, it is often wise to severely restrict the sort of information that is available to a decision-maker, even though this goes against an intuition that the best decisions are the most informed decisions.

There is a moral imperative to properly qualify the accuracy of information. Reports should distinguish between data, scientific prediction, and personal interpretation. In some cases, the attempt to ensure accuracy has led to the creation of standards by professional associations or law. Accounting practices for corporate reports, for instance, are largely mandated by the National Accounting Standards Board, whose authority is recognized by the federal regulatory agencies even though NASB is primarily a professional organization. Both the NASB standards and the authority of NASB to determine standards will seem unjust to those who wish to use alternative accounting procedures (*see* ETHICAL ISSUES IN FINANCE; FINANCIAL REPORTING).

The use of statistics in reporting information has generated a special subset of issues over the ethical imperative for accuracy. A wrong choice of statistical method or an error in application can be a serious professional lapse. And where there is consequential harm (e.g. from reliance on financial reports), it can justify a claim of fraud or negligence. Considerable attention has been paid to statistical reports that exclude "outlying" data items. In response, most scientific research has accepted the standard that all outlying data must be reported. Note that since statistics is a relatively new science, it is a mistake to fault past generations for failing to live up to present standards, just as it is a mistake to continue to use old methods when better ones become available.

Many professions recognize a duty to report all data sources and to keep source data for further analysis, or as a check on the accuracy of an interpretive report. Tax law, for instance, demands the maintenance of documentation that justifies financial reports for a period set by law (*see* TAX ETHICS). In all cases where information is based on prior reports or studies, there is a duty to fully report the provenance of the information, and a failure to do so may be condemned as "plagiarism." (The availability of information over the internet creates a new context for the provenance of information, and we have yet to establish standards for verifying those sources.) In scientific studies, many researches recognize a duty to keep basic data and laboratory notes "in perpetuity." However, the custodianship of the data, by the research sponsor or by members of the research team, can be controversial. And rights of access to scientific source data are highly controversial, especially when the information is a trade secret or bears on national security.

Finally, it is worth noting that the issues listed above frequently intersect and conflict. Thus, for instance, attempts to ensure freedom of information can easily conflict with attempts to ensure privacy. And trade secrecy policy often limits MIS options.

See also **right to information**

JOHN W. SNAPPER

ethical issues in investment   for the investment broker, require a consideration of the sometimes competing claims of those dependent upon her, the agency which employs her, the professional rules to which she has subscribed, and her client's interests, expressed or implicit.

Ethical codes have been drawn up to deal with such conflicts (e.g., Financial Analysts et al., 1988). The private investor himself, the broker's client, however, is generally encouraged to consider his investment decisions as if they were moves in a game. That game, like all games, requires a temporary self-contained world of its own. Ethical concerns outside the game are likely to feel awkward – to seem a violation of an implicit rule of silence. (For useful dialogues on the games metaphor see Carr, 1968 and Sullivan, 1984; Ladd, 1970 and Heckman, 1992; Hofstadter, 1986 and Solomon, 1993.)

Corporate investors, for whom investment is likely to involve managerial as well as financial responsibility, may find the claims of a variety of stakeholders intruding on this financial game. Obligations to these stakeholders are liable to complicate things – to make it difficult for the corporate investor to hold to the standard of a simple fiduciary obligation to maximize stockholder returns. (Whether or not they ought to complicate things in this way has been richly explored. See for example, Friedman: 1962, Donaldson: 1982, Nunan: 1988 and Carson: 1993.) (*See also* STAKEHOLDER THEORY; FIDUCIARY DUTY; FIDUCIARY RESPONSIBILITY).

For financial analysts in particular, but also for private investors, corporate investors, and the economy in general, healthy financial markets may be considered a commons. (Hartman, 1994 and Solomon, 1993 provide an engaging discussion of the usefulness of the term.) Like the traditional sheep-herder, we may seek to exploit the commons, in our case the financial market, and like them, we may be aware that we also need it to remain healthy. Financial markets, like any commons, require protection from those who regard them merely as private opportunities. Rules against the use of material information which has not been made public, rules requiring disclosure of conflicts of interest relating to the advice being proffered, rules against breaches of confidentiality, and rules requiring that investment advice be supported by diligent professional research, all protect financial markets in this way. The necessity of the rules is of course also an index of some breakdown in the normative understandings which must fundamentally underpin any commons.

Normative understandings cannot be relied on because one cannot assume a community which the investor and other stakeholders share. Even if the investor is moved by a sense of duty toward these others, it is difficult for her to know what to make of their circumstances and their commitments; difficult for the investor, an outsider, to make confident judgments that reject ongoing practice. The context of the investment is likely to be remote, difficult to understand, and inconvenient to think about. Neither the investor's sense of duty nor her calculation of the consequences of her investment is likely to be very sure. Reliance on his sense of virtue can in such circumstances seem strained and inappropriate.

Nonetheless, personal financial decisions can have large non-financial social consequences. Investments, especially in international contexts, may directly or indirectly support objectionable social systems. They may contribute to the production and distribution of morally questionable products. They may sustain unsavory hiring practices, or unscrupulous dealings with customers, suppliers, distributors, or regulatory agencies. The separation of ownership from management provides the private investor with insulation from these difficulties but it does not remove them. Perhaps the central ethical problem associated with private investment is the ease with which it permits us to imagine that we have been relieved of ethical responsibility.

Bibliography

Carr, A. (1968). Is business bluffing ethical? *Harvard Business Review* (Jan./Feb.), pp. 143–53.

Carson, T. (1993). Friedman's theory of corporate social responsibility. *Business and Professional Ethics Journal*, 12 (1), 3–32.

Donaldson, T. (1982). *Corporations and Morality.* New York: Prentice-Hall.

Friedman, M. (1962). *Capitalism and Freedom.* Chicago: University of Chicago Press.

Financial Analysts Federation and the Institute of Chartered Financial Analysts (1988). *Code of Ethics and Standards of Professional Conduct.* Charlottesville, Va.: The Financial Analysts Federation and the Institute of Chartered Financial Analysts.

Hartman, E. (1994). The commons and the moral organization. *Business Ethics Quarterly*, 4 (3), 253–69.

Heckman, P. (1992). Business and games. *Journal of Business Ethics*, 11, 993–38.

Hofstadter, D. (1986). *The Prisoner's Dilemma and the Evolution of Cooperation from his Metamagical Themas.* New York: Bantam Books.

Ladd, J. (1970). Morality and the ideal of rationality in formal organizations. *The Monist*, 54, 488–516.

Nunan, R. (1988). The libertarian conception of corporate property: A critique of Milton Friedman's views on the social responsibility of business. *Journal of Business Ethics* (Dec.), 891–906.

Solomon, R. (1993). The corporation as community: A reply to Ed Hartman. *Business Ethics Quarterly*, 4 (3), 271–85.

Sullivan, R. J. (1984). A response to "Is business bluffing ethical?" *Ethical Business and Professional Ethics Journal*, 3 (2), 1–17.

BARRY CASTRO and FRANK GRIGGS

ethical issues in organizational theory Organizational theory (OT) focuses on the behavior of companies or units, and their leaders and members. It examines those factors that determine the behavior of these groups and their consequences for organizational effectiveness. OT theorists have offered many insights into human motives and behaviors. They have also devoted considerable intellectual energy to the study of formal and informal organizations, and examining rational and political processes. Consequently, OT can enrich our understanding of the roots and consequences of business ethics.

Although OT scholars and business ethicists focus on many common issues, they espouse different views of organizational and human behaviors. While these views may occasionally conflict, they often complement one another. This essay explores areas of convergence and divergence between OT and business ethics by focusing on three levels of analysis. The first is the concept of the firm and its implications for human behavior. The second is inter-organizational relations. The third is the relationship between the company and society.

The Concept of Organization and its Implications for Human Behavior

The concept of the firm represents an important starting-point for scholars of both business ethics and OT. Whereas economics and finance theorists view the firm as a web of contracts, OT and business-ethics scholars espouse a broader and more complex definition. Both groups believe that formal contracts among organizational members, and ensuing rights and obligations, are only a part of the concept of the organization. A deeper appreciation of human behavior can be achieved by delving into the values of different organizational members, because these values undergird the choices made by individuals and groups. Differences in, and clashes of, values often induce differences in orientations, interests, and behaviors. Thus, by exploring the causes and manifestations of value differences, the stage is set to understand and explain the behavior of groups and individuals within the organization.

OT researchers further suggest that organizations are political entities, where individuals attempt to pursue their interests. To achieve organizational goals, formal and informal controls are needed. These controls help promote cohesion and unity of direction, thus reducing conflicts. Still, conflicts persist because of the divergence of interests and differences in power among members of the organization.

Nowhere is conflict more recognized in OT research than in the relationship between principals (owners) and agents (managers). A large body of research suggests that the rise of public corporations has resulted in the dispersion of ownership which, in turn, has resulted in loss of control by owners over their companies. Professional managers have become centers of power in the large contemporary organization. These managers own very little or no stock in the companies they run. Lacking connection to the company and its owners, managers may pursue goals that do not maximize shareholders' value or that undermine their property rights. Conflicts of interests are represented in a multitude of managerial actions such as over-diversification (Hoskisson & Hitt, 1994), excessive compensation (Zahra, 1995), and misdirecting corporate resources.

Conflicts between principals and agents are at the very core of scholarly conversation in OT and business ethics. Much attention has centered on governance systems that align the interests of the two groups, an interest that has generated a large number of studies (Zahra & Pearce, 1989). The company's board of directors is widely viewed as the ultimate means of corporate control. Yet in reality boards have often failed to align the interests of shareholders and managers. Instead, many boards have become subservient to managers. Moreover, attempts to empower boards have not been very successful (Pearce & Zahra, 1991).

Researchers in OT and business ethics have explored different ways to empower boards and make them true instruments of corporate governance. OT scholars have focused on restructuring the board composition, information flows, and decision-making processes. They have also explored ways to provide incentives to senior managers to place shareholders' interests ahead of other groups. Conversely, business ethicists have attempted to understand when and why conflicts of interests between principals and agents arise, outline guidelines to ensure alignment of their goals, and explore the effect of corporate and professional codes of ethics on this alignment. Clearly, contributions by business ethicists complement those offered by OT researchers (see also CONFLICT OF INTEREST; CODES OF ETHICS).

The relationship between individual employees and the organization is another key area of interest to both OT and business ethics. In OT, both the structuralist and Marxist schools have given this issue special attention. The Marxist view states that the separation of ownership of the tools of production from labor creates conflicts between owners and workers (employees). This happens because owners have an incentive to exploit their workers to maximize their profits. Structuralists view the organization somewhat differently. They assert that the formal structure perpetuates the domination of owners over labor. They also claim that work organizations often dehumanize employees, stifle their initiative and creativity, emphasize compliance and conformity, and foster feelings of anomie and alienation. The individual is thus exploited for the good of the owners.

Not all OT researchers accept the Marxist or structuralist views. Some have advocated several more enlightened views of the organization, conceiving more humanistic organizations that foster creativity, enhance individuality, and provide an environment conducive to human growth. Promoting these more humanistic organizations has become a central theme in the current research in OT. Managers have been admonished to build a wholesome quality of working life (QWL) in order to better integrate organizational and individual goals and needs.

One outcome of the debate on the nature of the relationship between the individual and the organization is a growing recognition of the rights and obligations of employees. Here, business ethicists have much to offer OT researchers. There is an obvious fundamental difference between OT theorists and business ethicists. Whereas ethicists appear interested in balancing different interests and promoting moral conduct, OT scholars are more interested in cultivating human capabilities and talents to improve performance and increase productivity. This subtle difference seems to permeate the current theoretical and empirical discussions of employee rights and responsibilities.

Some business ethicists build their arguments within philosophical discussions of human nature and values. They focus on stages of moral development and, accordingly, prescribe appropriate behaviors. Conceptual models of ethical behavior abound. According to Reidenbach and Robin (1990), these models converge empirically on three major dimensions. The first relates to moral equity which in turn embodies beliefs about the fairness, justice, morality, and acceptability of behavior. The second dimension is relativistic in nature and refers to whether or not a behavior is culturally acceptable. The third dimension is contractual in nature insofar as it indicates commitment to and consistency with formal and informal work contracts.

The above three-dimensional classification shows the potential contribution of business ethicists to the study of behavior in the organization. Yet, like other classifications, it also highlights the difficulty awaiting managers in attempting to ensure ethical behaviors: employees often have very different frames of reference, vary in their cognitive development, and may have different goals and expectations. Accommodating individual differences can sometimes create perceptions and feelings of inequity. Moreover, a group's agreement on a definition of acceptable behavior does not guarantee it is ethical.

The difficulty of prescribing ethical behavior in work organizations becomes apparent in discussions of employee rights and responsibil-

ities. There is no universal agreement on these rights, the approaches the company should take to support and protect them, the limits to be placed on these rights, or the conditions under which these rights can be changed. Further, balancing the rights and responsibilities of different employees may induce conflicts that paralyze the firm, lower productivity, and threaten the very existence of the organization (Werhane, 1985).

Doing what is ethically right can sometimes have unintended negative effects. Consider, for example, companies that have attempted to address past discriminatory hiring practices. These efforts have produced charges of reverse discrimination by groups traditionally favored in corporate hiring (*see* AFFIRMATIVE ACTION PROGRAMS). Likewise, corporate efforts aiming at helping women break through the "GLASS CEILING" have been criticized by male employees. Similarly, granting women maternity leaves has sparked controversy; leading to charges of favoritism. Some male employees have sued their employers to establish their right to paternity leaves. Doing the ethically right thing can sometimes fuel conflicts that divide the labor force. Of course, this does not mean that companies should not do the right thing; it merely suggests that sometimes business ethics are as hard to implement as they are hard to define. Therefore, occasionally, OT theorists have avoided discussions of the ethical implications of their strategies for organizational change.

The issues are as complex for the individual as they are for the company. Should an employee blow the whistle on her/his managers if they are engaged in unethical or illegal activities? (*see* WHISTLEBLOWING). Should they accept as a fact of life the special programs enacted to redress past corporate hiring practices? Should they comply with poorly designed work routines, rather than question their managers' authority? Answering these and similar questions requires considerable soul-searching because there are no absolutely correct answers.

Inter-organizational Relationships and Business Ethics

OT researchers also focus on inter-organizational relationships that affect the company's ability to secure resources and accomplish its goals. Companies develop joint ventures, join trade associations, and support lobbying on behalf of the industry. Companies also signal their moves to competitors to promote goodwill in the industry. OT theorists acknowledge the fact that some inter-organizational activities can stifle competition and reduce consumer welfare. This happens through interlocking directors, either directly or indirectly, to coordinate the activities of two or more companies. Inter-organizational links, while useful in many cases, can harm the competition in an industry.

Another area of interest is the growing use of competitive analysis where companies collect and analyze data about their rivals' operations and strategies. Competitive analysis is now widely viewed as a requirement for success. However, some companies use questionable techniques for this purpose. For example, they may spy on their competitors or bribe their employees to gain access to data on a rival's operations. A recent study concluded that managers believe that rising competition, concern over their company's survival, and careerism promote ethical violations in competitive analysis. Surprisingly, managers also indicated these actions can harm the competition in an industry, reduce trust, and inhibit the flow of information in the market (Zahra, 1994).

A third area that has received some attention in the literature is the mutual interdependence of companies. Increasingly companies are dependent on each other for survival; one company's products are inputs into another company's operations. With the ongoing massive restructuring of the US economy, for example, companies have divested and farmed out some of their operations. Will this interdependence stifle long-term competition and reduce consumer welfare? When are these actions ethical? Whose values should OT researchers use in evaluating the ethical nature of these transactions? Greater attention to these questions can enhance the contribution of business ethics to the study of OT.

OT researchers tend to view inter-organizational relationships as essential to competing in today's global economy. However, the ethical implications of these transactions are not clear. At a first glance, some transactions funnel information to competitors and may lead to tacit collusion. Others may strengthen the bargaining power of existing companies and can stifle the entry of new companies. Still other transactions may prolong the existence of marginally efficient companies, and may undermine the long-term interests of shareholders and society.

Clearly, the ethics of inter-organizational relations deserve greater attention in the literature. Guidelines on ethical versus unethical inter-organizational relations are needed. Business ethicists need to consider three questions that may determine whether an action is ethical or not: Will the action reduce competition in the market? Will the action reduce consumer satisfaction and welfare? Will the action inhibit industry evolution?

The Organization and its Society

OT and business ethics researchers have shown considerable interest in a company's relationship with its society. Both groups appear to accept the multiplicity of, and conflicts among, the company's goals. They disagree, however, on the importance of different organizational goals and how best to reconcile any trade-offs among them. The stakeholder approach (Freeman & Gilbert, 1988) has become the focal point in discussing these disparate views, including recent discussions of the environment in which the earth is recognized as the "ultimate" stakeholder (*see* STAKEHOLDER THEORY).

Business ethicists have contributed greatly to research into the relationship of the company and society. For instance, they have highlighted the important role of the firm in enhancing social welfare, improving living conditions, nurturing human growth, and protecting the environment and natural resources. This discussion has influenced companies' efforts to promote ethical behavior among managers and employees. Many of these recommendations have become an integral part of the corporate codes of ethics. OT scholars have accepted this view and incorporated it in their discussions of the organizational mission and goals.

The debate on the corporate social role has entered a new phase. In today's global economy, managers must deal with a complex array of stakeholders, with different goals, interests, and values. Business ethicists are therefore confronted by a number of challenging questions.

Whose values should dominate the mission and goals of the global corporations? Whose work ethics should guide employee behavior? If societies differ in their definition of ethical behaviors, can these different views be reconciled? What are the implications of cultural and ethnic diversity for corporate codes of ethics? These basic questions are now receiving some attention in the literature. However, as the globalization of the world economies continues, these issues are likely to become more complex. Transnational clashes of values will become a centerpiece in discussions of business ethics and OT (*see* GLOBALIZATION; INTERNATIONAL BUSINESS ETHICS; MULTINATIONALS).

Conclusion

This essay has focused on the role of business ethics in OT. It has suggested that business ethicists and OT theorists share many common interests, but still differ in their conclusions. Business ethics research has enriched OT discussions of the nature of the firm and its impact on employee behavior, inter-organizational relationships, and the role of the organization in society. While researchers have focused on the nature of the firm's relationship with society or individuals, many gaps remain in the literature on the inter-organizational relationships. The growing use of these transactions suggests a need for greater attention to their ethical implications. Moreover, there is need for understanding the ethical issues associated with transnational organizations. By giving greater attention to the changing dynamics and nature of competition in the global marketplace, business ethics can further enrich future OT research. Clearly, business ethicists and OT scholars have much to learn from each other.

Bibliography

Hoskisson, R. E. & Hitt, M. A. (1994). *Downscoping: How to Tame the Diversified Firm.* New York: Oxford University Press.
Freeman, R. E. & Gilbert, D. R., Jr. (1988). *Corporate Strategy and the Search for Ethics.* Englewood Cliffs, NJ: Prentice-Hall.
Pearce, J. & Zahra, S. (1991). Relative powers of CEOs and boards of directors: Associations with corporate performance. *Strategic Management Journal,* 12, 135–53.
Reidenbach, R. & Robin, D. (1990). Toward the development of a multidimensional scale for improving evaluations of business ethics. *Journal of Business Ethics,* 9, 639–53.
Werhane, P. (1985). *Persons, Rights & Corporations.* Englewood Cliffs, NJ: Prentice-Hall.
Zahra, S. (1994). Unethical practices in competitive analysis: Patterns, causes and effects. *Journal of Business Ethics,* 13, 53–62.
Zahra, S. (1995). The ethics of CEO compensation. *Journal of Business Ethics,* in press.
Zahra, S. & Pearce, J. (1989). Boards of directors and corporate financial performance: A review and integrative model. *Journal of Management,* 15, 291–334.

SHAKER A. ZAHRA and PEGGY CLONINGER

ethical issues in real estate sales   The field of real estate in the US is highly regulated at the state level. Additionally, federal and local laws affect various aspects of the brokerage operation. But there are many questionable actions which may or may not be viewed as ethically acceptable to different stakeholders in the environment, even if the actions are within the law (*see* STAKEHOLDER THEORY). The primary stakeholders in real estate sales are: buyer, seller, sales agent, managing broker, facilitating help (attorneys, closing agents, mortgage loan agents, appraisers, inspectors, and a variety of others who may be required to complete the transaction). If it is a new project, the building contractor and subcontractors would also be involved.

Any of these individuals may take an action that another stakeholder may feel is an unethical transgression against their respective interest. The first party may or may not feel the action was completely ethical within their personal code of behavior. To give the real estate professional more guidance and help in deciding if their actions are not only legal but reasonably ethical, a code of ethics is available to realtors (*see* CODES OF ETHICS). The word *realtor* is a trade name of the National Association of Realtors, which is the largest professional association of individuals involved in various types of real estate related activities. But the realtor group is a voluntary group, and a number of sale agents and brokers may not be realtors.

While ethical transgressions may be against anybody in the real estate related dealing, it is buyers and sellers that professional real estate brokers and agents wish to protect from inappropriate behavior. By maintaining the highest level of standards with buyers and sellers, the real estate agent and the whole profession ensures having an image that will encourage people to continue to use their services. For real estate professionals to only follow the law is not enough. The code goes beyond the law, so that buyers and sellers will have maximum confidence that they will be treated fairly.

The main ethical problem is in not fully representing the buyer or seller in a transaction. The agent listing a property for sale clearly represents the seller, but once in a while the listing agent is also the selling agent. The buyer just wants to believe this nice person (selling agent) must be working for his best interest. The other side is where a listing agent or another sub-agent reveals some information about the property or seller that compromises the bargaining position of the seller. Both of the above situations are highly unethical in that the buyer or seller is misled without full disclosure.

There are numerous other possible ethical transgressions that may take place, but the real estate agent or broker who does not treat his buyers and sellers ethically is in a small minority. Realtors do follow the code because it is the best behavior and results in a positive reputation and repeat sales.

Bibliography

NAR form 166-100; available from the National Association of Realtors, 430 North Michigan Avenue, Chicago, IL. 60611.

Pivar, W. H. (1979). *Real Estate Ethics.* Chicago, Ill: Real Estate Education Company, Inc.

DEAN ALLMON and JIM GRANT

ethical issues in recruiting and selection

A candidate files a complaint with her school's placement office when a hiring manager makes several racial comments at a campus presentation.

A company pressures a candidate into making a quick job-acceptance decision and is surprised when the individual later reneges on the decision.

A company withdraws a job offer once it determines that a candidate misrepresented his background on an employment application.

Do these situations, which actually happened at top-tier graduate business schools, represent illegal or unethical behavior, or simply poor judgment on the part of either the candidates and/or the hiring managers involved? In recruiting and selection, a myriad of opportunities exist for misrepresentation, misinterpretation, and outright violation of individual and organizational rights.

Recruitment and selection are defined respectively by Stoner and Freeman (1989, pp. 332, 339) as "the development of a pool of job candidates in accordance with a human resource plan," and "the mutual process whereby the organization decides whether or not to make a job offer and the candidate decides on the acceptability of the offer."

In the first situation, the candidate was excluded from consideration because of a hiring manager's bias against minority candidates. In the second case, the hiring organization decided to extend a job offer which the candidate first accepted but later rejected, once the candidate determined the offer was unacceptable. And in the third scenario, an applicant who was placed in the candidate pool had to be withdrawn from candidacy later because of receipt of information that affected eligibility.

These examples depict situations in which recruitment and selection decisions were made on the basis of inaccurate or insufficient information, and in which the rights of the individual or the organization were in jeopardy. As stated by Williams (1992, p. 42), the right of the individual is an imperative that must be maintained by organizations contemplating personnel actions. Similarly, as explained by the College Placement Council's document on the subject (1990), organizations also have rights that need to be maintained as personnel decisions are made.

Following are some specific guidelines for individuals and organizations that can be gleaned from the literature as potentially useful in determining ethical outcomes in recruitment and selection situations. These guidelines include:

- the right of the candidate to obtain accurate information about a prospective hiring organization, and, concurrently, of the organization to obtain the applicant information that is necessary for making effective employment decisions;

- the right of the individual to choose an organization that is consistent with his or her personal career objectives, and of the organization to hire the most suitable candidate for a given job;

- the right of the individual to withdraw acceptance of an offer due to a change in personal circumstances, and of the organization to withdraw a job offer due to a change in economic conditions or to acquisition of pertinent information about a candidate;

- the right of the applicant to obtain information that will help him or her gauge the potential for personal effectiveness on the job, and of the organization to obtain information that predicts an applicant's potential success on the job;

- the rights of both the individual and organization to expect that scheduling agreements for interviews and other recruitment arrangements will be honored;

- the rights of both the individual and organization to expect that government regulations that affect recruitment and selection, such as affirmative action, the Americans with Disabilities Act, and comparable worth will be honored in all recruitment and selection activities;

- the right of the individual to be made aware in advance of all employment criteria used in selection decisions such as testing, and of the organization to expect honest compliance with the requirements of testing in use;

- the right of the individual to expect that personal information transmitted as part of the recruitment and selection process will not be divulged outside of the process without permission from the candidate, and of the organization to expect that confidential company or client information shared with the applicant as part of the recruiting process will not be divulged to competitors; and

- the right of the candidate to have an adequate amount of time in which to make an employment decision, and of the organization to obtain a decision within a time-frame agreed upon ahead of time by both parties.

Individual candidates and representatives of hiring organizations are all involved in the important processes of recruitment and selection. By respecting the rights of both individuals and organizations as demonstrated in the guidelines above, the process is more likely to meet the needs of all involved.

See also comparable worth

Bibliography

College Placement Council. (1990). *Principles for Professional Conduct for Career Services and Employment Professionals.* Bethlehem, Penn.: College Placement Council, Inc.

Cunningham, W. P. (1993). Careful selection: Interviewing for ethics. *Manager's Magazine,* July.

Fletcher, C. (1992). Ethics and the job interview. *Personnel Management,* Mar.

Laabs, J. J. (1993). Does a bad driver make a good employee? *Personnel Journal,* Dec.

Stoner, J. A. F. & Freeman, R. E. (1980). *Management of Organizations and Human Resources.* Englewood Cliffs, NJ: Prentice-Hall, 332–44.

Williams, G. J. (1992). Employment and wages. In *Ethics in Modern Management.* New York: Quorum Books, 41–9.

KAREN O. DOWD

ethical issues in technology Technology is the intelligent organization and manipulation of materials for useful purposes (Unger, 1994, p. 3). Sometimes, however, this organization and manipulation of technologies – from airlines and cosmetics to plows and nuclear weapons – is both less intelligent and less useful than it ought to be. According to the World Health Organization, for instance, the application of chemical technologies annually kills at least 40,000 persons worldwide, often because of pesticide use in developing nations. As the pesticide case illustrates, the design and employment of technologies often raise ethical issues, that is, questions about rules of behavior or about right and wrong.

Most of the ethical issues concerning technology focus on questions of risk. Some of these questions include whether persons have been informed adequately about technological dangers, whether they have consented to them, whether the risks are equitably distributed, and whether risk imposers have been compensated for the threats they generate.

Technological risks can be divided into two main types, societal and individual. Societal risks (such as those from liquefied natural gas facilities) are largely involuntarily imposed. Individual risks (such as those from using a regulator to engage in scuba diving) are largely voluntarily chosen. Societal risks often raise greater ethical questions than individual risks because their potential victims typically have less choice regarding whether to accept them. For example, people choose whether to become scuba divers and what kind of breathing equipment to use. Usually, however, they have less choice over whether to allow a liquefied natural gas facility to be built near them.

Much ethical debate focuses on whether technological risks ought to be evaluated by members of the technical community (Cooke, 1992) or by laypersons who are most likely to be their victims (Freudenburg, 1988). Scientists and engineers often treat the assessment of technological risks as the paternalistic prerogative of experts, in part because they claim that the definitions of irrational, ignorant, or risk-averse laypersons could impede social and technological progress (Douglas and Wildavsky, 1982). Many moral philosophers argue, in response, that evaluations of technology are not only matters of scientifically defensible outcomes but also matters of just procedures, because they affect public welfare (Cranor, 1992; Shrader-Frechette, 1991). Also, because even scientists and engineers have well-known prejudices in defining and estimating technological risks – such as the over-confidence biases in estimates of nuclear risk (Cooke, 1992;

Kahneman et al., 1982) – ethicists claim that we need democratic, as well as technical, evaluations of technology.

Other ethical controversies concern what level of technological safety is safe enough. Utilitarian philosophers, who emphasize maximizing overall welfare, typically argue that we can serve the greater good by accepting low levels of risk and by not forcing industry to spend money to avoid unlikely hazards, such as nuclear core melts or chemical explosions. Harsanyi (1975), for example, argues that "worst cases" of technological risk rarely occur. He claims that forcing industry to avoid worst cases is too conservative, impedes social progress, and over-emphasizes small probabilities of harm. Egalitarian philosophers, who emphasize the equal rights of all persons to protection from harm, maintain that the people deserve protection, even from unlikely technological threats. Shrader-Frechette (1991, 1993), for example, argues that because the probabilities associated with technological risks are often uncertain, the public deserves protection from them, even if they are small. Their size is dwarfed by potentially catastrophic consequences such as global warming or toxic leaks (see Rawls, 1971). Some egalitarian philosophers also claim that fairness and equal treatment require technology assessors and decision-makers to reverse the burden of proof and place it on those who impose technological risks rather than on those likely to be their victims. They say that because causal chains of harm are difficult to prove – and because risk victims are less able than risk imposers to bear the costs of faulty technological evaluations – those who design, implement, apply, or benefit from a technology should bear its greatest risks (Cranor, 1992).

Still other ethical issues regarding technology address the criteria under which it is acceptable to impose some hazard (for example, chemical effluents) on workers or on the public. One important criterion for risk imposition is the equity of distribution of the risks and benefits associated with an activity. For example, Parfit (1983) argues that temporal differences among people/generations are not a relevant basis for discriminating against them with respect to risk. He and others maintain that a technological risk is less acceptable to the degree that it imposes costs on the future but awards benefits in the present. Commercial nuclear fission, for example, benefits mainly present generations, whereas its risks and costs – because of radioactive waste – will be borne primarily by members of future generations.

On the one hand, many economists evaluating technology follow the utilitarian philosophy. They question notions of distributive equity and argue that a bloody loaf of bread – earned through dirty or risky technologies – is better than none at all, because such technologies bring tax and employment benefits. On the other hand, egalitarian philosophers evaluating technology argue for "geographical equity" (Shrader-Frechette, 1993, 1985) and "environmental justice" (Bullard, 1993). They maintain that technological risks should be distributed equally across generations, regions, and nations. Otherwise, they claim, economically and socially disenfranchised persons will bear disproportionate burdens of technological risks. Economically, educationally, or socially disenfranchised persons also are less likely than others to be able to give genuine free informed consent to technological and workplace risks (MacLean, 1986; Rescher, 1983). Chemical facilities and hazardous-waste dumps, for example, tend to be located in areas where income, education, and political power are the lowest.

To such equity and consent arguments, some utilitarian ethicists have responded that no instances of distribution or consent are perfect. They claim that the greater good is achieved by risk-for-money trade-offs when workers accept jobs in dangerous technologies or when citizens accept the tax benefits of a hazardous technology in their community. Egalitarians like MacLean (1986) claim, however, that some values (like bodily health and environmental security) ought not to be traded for financial compensation. Gewirth (1982) also argues, for example, that persons have a moral and legal right not to be caused to have cancer. Such ethical debates over risk imposition and trade-offs generally focus on opposed views about rights, paternalism, human dignity, equal treatment, and adequate compensation for technological risk (Thomson, 1986).

Another aspect of the consent and compensation debate over technological risk concerns liability. Current US laws, for example, excuse nuclear power plant licensees from full liability for accidents on grounds of economic efficiency and the greater good. A number of ethicists argue that these exclusions violate citizens' rights to due process and to equal protection (Shrader-Frechette, 1993, 1991), whereas some economists claim that liability limits are necessary to promote essential, but dangerous, technologies.

As this discussion of equity, consent, and compensation reveals, the ethical issues associated with technology may be just as important as the scientific and safety issues. Once we understand the magnitude of these ethical issues, we are forced to ask about a technology, not only "how safe is safe enough?" but also "how safe is equitable enough?" or "how safe is voluntary enough?" or "how safe is compensated enough?"

Bibliography

Bullard, R. D. (1993). *Confronting Environmental Racism*. Boston: South End Press.

Cooke, R. (1992). *Experts in Uncertainty: Opinion and Subjective Probability in Science*. New York: Oxford University Press.

Cranor, C. (1992). *Regulating Toxic Substances: A Philosophy of Science and the Law*. New York: Oxford University Press.

Douglas, M., & Wildavsky, A. (1982). *Risk and Culture*. Berkeley: University of California Press.

Freudenburg, W. (1988). Perceived risk, real risk: Social science and the art of probabilistic risk assessment. *Science, 242*, 44–9.

Gewirth, A. (1982). *Human rights*. Chicago: University of Chicago Press.

Harsanyi, J. (1975). Can the maximin principle serve as a basis for morality? *American Political Science Review, 69*, 594–605.

Kahneman, D., Slovic, P., & Tversky, A. (eds) (1982). *Judgment under Uncertainty: Heuristics and Biases*. Cambridge: Cambridge University Press.

Kates, R., & National Academy of Engineering (eds) (1986). *Hazards: Technology and Fairness*. Washington, DC: National Academy Press.

Kneese, A. V., Ben-David, S., & Schulze, W. D. (1982). The ethical foundations of benefit–cost analysis. In D. MacLean & P. Brown (eds), *Energy and the future*. Totowa, NJ: Rowman and Littlefield, 59–74.

MacLean, D. (ed.) (1986). *Values at risk*. Totowa, NJ: Rowman and Allanheld.

National Research Council. (1983). *Risk Assessment in the Federal Government: Managing the Process.* Washington, DC: National Academy Press.

National Research Council. (1993). *Issues in Risk Assessment.* Washington, DC: National Academy Press.

Parfit, D. (1983). The further future: The discount rate. In D. MacLean & P. Brown (eds), *Energy and the Future.* Totowa, NJ: Rowman and Littlefield, 31–7.

Porter, A. L., Rossini, F. A., Carpenter, S. R., & Roper, A. T. (1980). *A Guidebook for Technology Assessment and Impact Analysis.* New York: Holland.

Rawls, J. (1971). *A Theory of Justice.* Cambridge, Mass.: Harvard University Press.

Rescher, N. (1983). *Risk: A Philosophical Introduction.* Washington, DC: University Press of America.

Sagoff, M. (1988). *The Economy of the Earth.* Cambridge: Cambridge University Press.

Shrader-Frechette, K. (1985). *Science policy, ethics, and economic methodology,* Boston: Kluwer.

Shrader-Frechette, K. (1991). *Risk and rationality: Philosophical foundations for populist reforms,* Berkeley: University of California Press.

Shrader-Frechette, K. (1993). *Burying Uncertainty: Risk and the Case Against Geological Disposal of Nuclear Waste.* Berkeley: University of California Press.

Shrader-Frechette, K. (1995). Technology assessment. In W. T. Reich (ed.), *Encyclopedia of Bioethics,* New York: Macmillan.

Srinivasan, M. (ed.) (1982). *Technology Assessment and Development.* New York: Praeger.

Thomson, J. J. (1986). *Rights, Restitution, and Risk.* Cambridge, Mass.: Harvard University Press.

Unger, S. H. (1994). *Controlling Technology: Ethics and the Responsible Engineer.* New York: John Wiley.

Winner, L. (1977). *Autonomous Technology: Technics Out of Control as a Theme in Political Thought.* Cambridge, Mass.: MIT Press.

KRISTIN SHRADER-FRECHETTE

ethical issues in the defense industry

Common charges levied against the defense industry include procurement and overbilling charges and violations of the FOREIGN CORRUPT PRACTICES ACT. Some factors potentially encouraging these practices include the complex legal and regulatory environment surrounding the defense industry, CONFLICT OF INTEREST and "revolving doors" between government officials and defense-industry leaders (Wrubel, 1989), a one-customer market, and the pressures to meet the contracted budget and schedule.

In light of the numerous scandals in the defense industry, the federal government responded in several ways: passing the amended False Claims Act of 1986, proposing mandatory ethics programs, and creating a blue-ribbon commission to investigate the scandals. The amended False Claims Act of 1986, through its "qui tam" provisions, grants monetary incentives to defense contractor employees who whistleblow (*see* WHISTLEBLOWING). Critics argue that this Act promotes bounty hunting (Singer, 1992). The Defense Acquisition Regulatory Council has called for mandatory ethics programs to become part of the Department of Defense's procurement rules. However, it still remains in the proposal stage.

In 1986, President Ronald Reagan created a blue-ribbon commission headed by Dave Packard to investigate defense procurement fraud. The commission's major recommendation was for defense contractors to adopt ethics programs, and it thereby created the Defense Industry Initiative (DII). The DII was drafted by 18 defense contractors, is voluntary, and wholly self-regulating.

On becoming a signatory company, a company must adhere to the following six principles of BUSINESS ETHICS and conduct (President's Blue Ribbon Commission, 1986, p. 251):

1 Each company will have and adhere to a written code of business ethics and conduct.

2 The company's code establishes the high values expected of its employees and the standard by which they must judge their own conduct and that of their organization; each company will train its employees concerning their personal responsibilities under the code.

3 Each company will create a free and open atmosphere that allows and encourages employees to report violations of its code to the company without fear of retribution for such reporting.

4 Each company has the obligation to self-govern by monitoring compliance with federal procurement laws, and adopting procedures for voluntary disclosure of violations of federal procurement laws and corrective actions taken.

5 Each company has a responsibility to each of the other companies in the industry to live by standards of conduct that preserve the integrity of the defense industry.

6 Each company must have public accountability for its commitment to these principles.

These six principles are intended to promote sound management practices, ensure that companies are in compliance with other complex regulations, and restore public confidence (*1990 Annual Report*, p. 3).

The DII remains one of the most ambitious attempts by an industry to implement ethics. However, its success in engendering ethical behavior remains undetermined (cf. Kurland, 1993 for a critique of the Initiative).

See also **codes of ethics**

Bibliography

1990 Annual Report to the Public and the Defense Industry. Defense Industry Initiative on Business Ethics and Conduct. Available on request from Alan Yuspeh, DII Coordinator, c/o Howrey & Simon, 1299 Pennsylvania Avenue N.W., Washington DC 20004.

Kurland, N. B. (1993). The Defense Industry Initiative: Ethics, self-regulation, and accountability. *Journal of Business Ethics*, **12**, 137–45.

President's Blue Ribbon Commission on Defense Management. (1986). *A Quest for Excellence: Final Report to the President*. Washington, DC.

Singer, A. W. (1992). The whistle-blower: Patriot or bounty hunter? *Across the Board*, **29**, 11, 16ff.

Wrubel, R. (1989). Addicted to fraud?: Why the Defense Industry just can't seem to clean up its act. Even when it tries. *Financial World*, June 22, 58–61.

NANCY B. KURLAND

ethics Broadly speaking, ethics has always been the study of What We Should Do.

First, "we": ethics has never been entirely self-addressed, but rather is a general inquiry: the question is, what should *one* do, where "one" is anyone. It may also, however, be any one belonging to some identified group.

Second, "should": ethics is a "normative" inquiry. It is about what to do, what it would be good or bad, right or wrong, wise or unwise, to do. It is not merely an inquiry into what we

actually do, into what makes us tick, the subject-matter of (human) psychology, rather than ethics. Nevertheless, ethical theories always say something about "human nature," in some way or other, as will be further noted below.

And third, the word "do": many ethical theories have concentrated on character, on what we should be like, rather than on the question of which actions we should perform. However, character is always presumed to have a bearing on action, to be borne out or exemplified in action. If it is separated from that practical interest, the study of character for its own sake would perhaps be found more nearly in aesthetics than ethics.

However, there is a narrower use of the term "ethics," one which applies to most of the moral philosophy of the past few centuries, though it is also applicable to much of the moral philosophy of earlier times as well. In this narrower use, ethics is concerned especially with norms for the conduct of people insofar as they are members of social groupings – of people *qua* members of society. In this more specialized use of the term, ethics is better referred to as "morals" or "morality." The philosophical study of morality has concerned itself especially with the project of finding, or at least determining whether it is in principle possible to find, a set of moral principles or rules that would hold good for all people, or (what is thought to be essentially equivalent) for all rational people. It is debatable whether there is or can be any such set of principles, and a historically prominent view called "relativism" holds that there cannot be, but that instead such sets of rules have to be fairly specific to individual societies or even individuals (*see* RELATIVISM, CULTURAL AND MORAL).

Morality is a set of rules for a group, but which groups, then? There are two answers. First, and primarily, there are what we may call "natural" groups, that is, groups which are together not by virtue of deliberate choice but by birth or happenstance: societies, cultures, and of course the group of all humans generally, which we may treat as a limiting case. The other sort of group, however, is the association, that is, groups whose members are such by virtue of having intentionally chosen to do what makes them members, or even intentionally chosen to become members as such. Thus doctors are a group in the first sense, while the American Medical Association is one in the second. So we may speak of "medical ethics," "business ethics," and so on (*see* BUSINESS ETHICS).

There is a large question about specific ethical codes of these latter types. Business ethics is the ethics pertaining to people in their roles as transactors of business: that is the definition of the term. But are the principles of business ethics to be conceived as subordinate principles to more general principles of ethics that apply to everyone in their general relations of life? Or does the business connection actually generate special new principles? Are business-people exempt from ordinary ethics and subject only to the special rules of their own calling? That is no longer a question of definition but of substantive theory (*see* CODES OF ETHICS).

Philosophical ethics is reflection about ethics in the above senses: attempts to think out the foundations of ethics, or its logical status, its basic ideas, or its basic principles. However, ever since the Middle Ages and perhaps before, philosophers have sometimes also attempted to apply these general principles to fairly specific real-life questions. That project was called "casuistry," a term widely used with some contempt. But, it in fact designates a perfectly real and legitimate task, that of applying principles of ethics to the complexities of real life.

Having noted various distinctions about domains and types of ethical theories and studies, let us, finally, consider the question of what morality is. This is a question about which there has been considerable dispute, and the explanation offered here must be understood in that light – that is, as a discussable idea about which people still differ. To understand the idea of morals, we need the idea of a social rule. Two elements go into this notion. First, it is "social" if it applies to the whole of society, or of the society whose morality it is. And it is a "rule" if it rules out certain kinds of behavior, and calls for other kinds. Moreover, these must be kinds of behavior that the people subject to them might well not do otherwise. Moral rules call upon us to refrain from doing merely whatever we want. Second, a moral rule for a society is social in the sense that its enforcement is social. What is meant by this is that it need not be enforced nor legislated by a specific body of

people designated or appointed for the purpose – that is law, not morals. Morality, however, is informal: there may be no authoritative setting down of these rules, and there is no designated, official enforcement. Rather, everyone participates in "enforcing" morality, by praising, blaming, rewarding, and punishing. The "morality" of a society, then, is that set of rules or principles or ideals such that people in that society generally accept that they apply to their own and others' behavior, and tend to reinforce the called-for behavior in others.

We can now make one more distinction, extremely important for philosophical purposes. The definition just supplied defines what we might call the "social-sciences sense" of the term: the ethics of Society X is the set of rules which the members of X do actually attempt to get each other to conform to. However, one might suppose that the prevailing rules of some society, or even of humans in general, are defective in some way; and one might suppose they could be improved upon. A set of rules that is proposed as being what a society should have, whether or not it actually does, would be what we might call an exercise in "ideal" ethical theory. And the very deep question this raises is whether it is really possible to do ideal theory in ethics. Can we actually conceive of rules that are still recognizably moral rules, and yet are only ideal rules that a society ought to have even though it does not (at least, as yet) actually have them, or not fully? Again, that large question is one philosophers must consider. But not only philosophers either. Especially in societies with extensive cultural diversity, there is substantial disagreement among its members about just what exactly to praise and blame, reward and punish, and emulate in one's own behavior. Inevitably many people will be in the position ascribed to philosophers: that is, of at least contemplating and very likely of promoting what is seen to be "reforms" of society's morality.

In the case of business ethics and similar more specific areas of ethical inquiry, the scope for reformative approaches is extensive. Business ethics is bound not to be well-defined. This is so for two reasons. First, it is a protean field encompassing very diverse activities, many of which are changing rapidly with the growth of technology. And secondly, business relations know no boundaries: people of the most diverse cultures engage in business interactions. These are bound to be affected by the differing ethical practices and expectations of the parties concerned. So there remains plenty of work for the philosopher concerned with business ethics, of both the analytical and the reformative type.

JAN NARVESON

ethics and entrepreneurship   Economist Joseph Schumpeter pointed out early in the twentieth century that entrepreneurial activities create change by challenging the *status quo* and throwing up new combinations in a process of "creative destruction." From Schumpeter's perspective, entrepreneurship consisted of events and processes outside the range of existing practice, a "creative response" to the economy instead of one that adapts to the existing framework (Schumpeter, 1934). Using Schumpeter's definition, entrepreneurship is a set of activities and processes that explain the dynamic and regenerative capacities of societies. These can be manifest by individuals, teams, an organization, or collaborative behavior by firms. This broad definition allows the following discussion to capture the change-oriented character of entrepreneurs and entrepreneurial activity regardless of particular players or settings, while retaining an emphasis on start-ups and innovative small and mid-sized organizations that are commonly the sites for entrepreneurial innovation. Furthermore, while entrepreneurship is typically viewed as a vehicle to create private wealth, it is at its best when, through its processes, societal benefits are realized, for example, such as increased or more meaningful employment, useful innovation, and improvements to the quality of life (Venkataraman, 1994).

At a more concrete level, entrepreneurship consists of the processes through which new products, markets, industries, technologies, and new organizational forms are created (Schumpeter, 1934). Entrepreneurs can be visionaries of new ways of living, but essential is the capacity of the individuals and teams to mobilize critical resources (capital, knowledge, technology, etc.) to exploit perceived opportunities. Entrepreneurs conduct this process often without ownership and direct control over resources. This requires considerable skill and persistence in engaging others in the process.

The intersection of ethics and entrepreneurship has only infrequently been addressed by writers. One approach to the topic has been to examine the elements of the entrepreneurial arena for which the application of ethical concepts is distinct compared to their application in non-entrepreneurial environments (e.g. no-growth smaller firms and stable, bureaucratic, large companies). Stated as a question, do distinctive ethical issues arise in the context of start-ups, rapidly growing smaller firms, and innovative/change-oriented pockets of large companies compared to other less entrepreneurial arenas? A broad discussion of this question was provided by Dees & Starr (1992) in which they identified three major areas within the context of entrepreneurial management (as opposed to administrative management) for considering the ethical implications of entrepreneurship: promotion, relationship, and innovations.

Promotion: entrepreneurs must promote their vision of change with persistence in order to engage a critical mass of others in the project. Yet the entrepreneur's vision is often at odds with standard practice, accepted design, or traditional definitions of markets and existing consumer preferences. Consequently, skepticism of investors and consumers must be overcome and resources gained to pursue risky and sometimes unprecedented paths. The successful entrepreneur will manage the risk and uncertainty by distributing it across stakeholders who are persuaded to join. In this way, each stakeholder will carry a part of the economic risk. But the entrepreneur as a promoter must walk a fine line between honestly presenting the vision and implementing a strategy without misrepresenting the risks and potential losses that may be incurred by stakeholders. Typically, others wait to see who else is committing capital or other assistance so that the entrepreneur must gain commitment and manage the risks without falsely representing the positions of others. In this environment the entrepreneur's unqualified enthusiasm for the idea can create a gray area with ethical implications.

Relationships: Prior relationships (friends and family) are relied upon frequently and can be viewed as the network of ties that provides the resources enabling the entrepreneurial venture to gain stable footing (Larson & Starr, 1993). These early relationships are often personal and trust-based with family members and close friends who control resources (investors, bankers, etc.), as well as early suppliers and customers who may be relatives or personal acquaintances. Ethical dilemmas easily arise as affective social and family ties expand to take in instrumental and utilitarian purposes, creating tensions around roles and expectations as the venture grows and falters. Dees & Starr (1992) talk about "transactional ethics" in which relationships that are mutually beneficial are valued, but when the entrepreneur decides the tie is no longer advantageous, it is severed. The necessity for this kind of calculated decision-making is often in conflict with the friendships and other personal ties that underlie the economic exchange relationships that enabled the entrepreneur to get started in the first place. This tension, combined with the propensity of entrepreneurial individuals to be highly optimistic about their prospects for success, may lead to an unwillingness to admit to realistic orders. In other words, the particular challenges of entrepreneurial initiatives combined with the determination and conviction of the entrepreneurial founder can create opportunities for what many would consider unethical behavior. While Bhide & Stevenson (1990) found that adherence to moral values was typical of entrepreneurs, and other studies have revealed entrepreneurs' awareness of their public visibility and a consequent higher adherence to personal ethical standards than non-entrepreneurial managers, the tales of less scrupulous behavior have created negative images of the entrepreneur. The common stereotype of the untrustworthy, self-promoting entrepreneur arises in part from the distinctive characteristics endemic to start-up circumstances and from certain entrepreneurial personality characteristics.

Innovation: Innovation is defined broadly by Dees & Starr to include technological, administrative, and social innovation. The cumulative effects of innovation can generate new institutional forms and alternative cultural values.

Breaking new ground through innovation carries with it risk of unanticipated consequences with ethical implications inside and outside the firm. Innovations in information, technology, genetic engineering, employee social contracts, organizational forms, or new definitions of leadership can create unprecedented ethical considerations that must be incorporated into the collective understanding of business management. Even when new goods, services, or institutional structures address real needs, the disruption caused to the *status quo*, and the ripple effects of the innovation, always have the potential for raising ethical concerns.

Social Relationships: As the research focus in the entrepreneurship field has shifted away from relatively unproductive studies of entrepreneurs' characteristics and cultural conditions to recognition that entrepreneurial processes are firmly embedded in social relations and networks of ties, ethical issues have been raised to central importance in explaining entrepreneurial phenomena. Granovetter (1985), Powell (1987, 1990), and others have highlighted this embeddedness of economic activity pointing to the need to understand the social structure within which economic exchange activity rests. These social structures, defined typically as family, friends, and contacts, provide the connections (the structural embeddedness) that enable the entrepreneurial initiatives to occur. From this perspective, non-economic factors such as trust and reputation are seen as significant determinants of entrepreneurial activity and are critical controlling mechanisms for successful management (Larson, 1992). This approach views the embeddedness of the entrepreneurial firm in a network of trust-based ties as key to firm survival, and that selective cultivation and management of embedded ties is central to successful economical strategies for innovative ventures and growing companies. Rather than peripheral or incidental to entrepreneurial action, they are the forces that permit and enhance the economic transactions. Uzzi (1994) suggested that they may be the elusive mechanisms unaccounted for by Schumpeter that explain entrepreneurial innovation and the creation and expansion of new markets. According to this perspective, the embeddedness of entrepreneurial firms in supporting network structures explains a great deal about their formation, growth, and innovative capabilities, and this framing of the issues in network relations terms has ethical dimensions as its core (trust, relationships, etc.). By logical extension then, ethical issues are not just part of the entrepreneurial story, but in fact, to a significant degree, explain the economic phenomenon of dynamic entrepreneurial innovation.

Under this conceptual architecture, the entrepreneur and the new, growing entrepreneurial organizations are seen linked into critically important and interdependent networks of relationships, individual to individual and community, and firm to firm or network of firms. As the field of entrepreneurship establishes clear theoretical foundations, the accumulated field-based empirical evidence argues strongly for a network model to explain firm formation and growth (Aldrich & Zimmer, 1986; Birley, 1985; Larson, 1992). The accumulated evidence and derived theory indicate that entrepreneurial activity cannot be understood without the incorporation of non-economic factors such as trust, relationships, and commitment. Furthermore, entrepreneurs and their teams, and ultimately their organizations, create networks of relationships and strategic alliances of various kinds, within which the economic transaction is central but only part of a densely layered exchange process in large part structured and controlled by the notions of trust and commitment.

The rapid proliferation of entrepreneurial companies committed to a broad definition of the bottom line provide opportunities for new insights about entrepreneurship and ethics. The broader bottom line refers to the incorporation into the philosophy and operations of the firm of a sustained, genuine, and explicit concern for employees, community, customers, suppliers, investors, as well as for the natural environment – all stakeholders on which the entrepreneurial initiatives depend. Firms and entrepreneurial individuals adhering to this vision and these operating assumptions tend to form networks and linkages that reinforce the legitimacy and strategic values of ethical principles related to a broader common good. Firms in this category in the 1990s are Levi Strauss, Stride Rite, Ben and Jerry's, The Body Shop, Stonyfield Farm, and Ecover. For these firms the topic of entrepreneurship and ethics is not just about avoiding questionable behavior in the conduct of establishing and growing a business. It is also about the practical integration of what is good for society and future generations throughout company operations and within the network of investors, suppliers, and customers with which the company is engaged. For example, a subset of these companies are at the leading edge in designing and implementing publicly available ecological and social audits of their business activity. To a greater degree than their less entrepreneurial counterparts, they make their firms transparent so that the public can examine and evaluate their behavior against an ethical ideal. Despite the challenges of this kind of public stance, an important phenomenon is at work. These entrepreneurial firms are based on a distinctive and non-traditional set of underlying assumptions. They exist within networks of interdependent relationships with communities and ecosystems as well as with customer, supplier, and investor stakeholders. Their definition of the firm and their obligations extend far beyond the neoclassical economic model based on stockholder returns. For example, earnings are a means to the ends of further service to customers, suppliers, employees, and the immediate community, as well as to the larger national and global communities and the natural ecosystems on which the economy depends. Within these forms and networks, ethical considerations play an explicit role in shaping corporate policies and facilitate the coordination of the network through shared values and competitive differentiation. As more investment dollars flow to these companies due to growing consumer interest and approval, their ethical stances are increasingly viewed as a strategic competitive advantage. While traditional corporations have paid lip-service, or even sincere attention in limited ways, to these issues, leadership from the entrepreneurial sector of the economy around these ethically laden concerns suggests an alternative model of conducting business has emerged.

The field of entrepreneurship has expanded dramatically in the last ten years. In the early 1980s the field was ill-defined and still hugely dependent on a small number of pioneer researchers and their ideas. As interest in entrepreneurship grew in the decade of the 1980s, the research efforts distinguished among a more diverse set of topics and concepts. More systematic studies of entrepreneurs proliferated, while other researchers focused on firm growth or interrelationships among entrepreneurs, resources, and economic opportunities (Brophy, 1986). The separability of entrepreneurship (growth oriented) and small business was accepted and research instruments and other methods were refined to provide more reliable empirical data (Churchill, 1992). Research subtopics such as corporate venturing, venture formation, women entrepreneurs, venture capital, high-tech entrepreneurship and processes of entrepreneurship (how to manage entrepreneurically) were established as legitimate categories for investigation, expanding the domain for research beyond the early focus on individual entrepreneurs. Churchill (1992) recognized several approaches to the study of entrepreneurship, each with its own objective, unit of analysis, and lens of perspective. The first approach viewed entrepreneurship as the founding of firms and an engine of broader economic and social change. Entrepreneurship thus defined produced jobs and mobilized resources, and was linked to national economic health. This research arena focused on the creation of new ventures and all factors that influence the event. A second approach focuses on the power of entrepreneurial activity to create innovation. Again, entrepreneurship was seen as an engine of change but the emphasis was on understanding how and why innovation occurred and how innovation moved into markets. Corporate venturing was a central concern to this group of researchers, as were the innovations from the growth-oriented and high-tech entrepreneurial sector. Churchill's third category defined entrepreneurship as an arena within which researchers from diverse disciplines attempted to apply and adapt the concepts from their disciplines (applied historically to large and non-entrepreneurial institutions) to start-up, innovative, and fast-growing businesses. For example, researchers steeped in the theoretical traditions of marketing, strategic management, organizational behavior, technology transfer, business ethics, and social networks tried to apply their ideas to explain entrepreneurial activity. These developments in the field, combined with the new models of business represented by entrepreneurial actors and firms, have opened up the entrepreneurship field to broader examination from diverse disciplinary viewpoints. The intersection of entrepreneurship and ethics is one area of this emerging research landscape that deserves greater attention due to its central importance both to the entrepreneur, the definition of the firm, and the character of commerce.

Bibliography

Aldrich, H. & Zimmer, C. (1986). Entrepreneurship through social networks. In D. Sexton & R. Smilor (eds), *The Art and Science of Entrepreneurship.* Cambridge, Mass.: Ballinger. 3–24.

Bhide, A. & Stevenson, H. (1990). Why be honest if honesty doesn't pay? *Harvard Business Review,* **68**, (5), 121–9.

Birley, S. (1985). The role of networks in the entrepreneurial process. *Journal of Business Venturing,* **1**, 107–17.

Brophy, D. (1986). Venture capital research. In D. Sexton & R. Smilor (eds), *The Art and Science of Entrepreneurship.* Cambridge, Mass.: Ballinger. 119–44.

Churchill, N. C. (1992). Research issues in entrepreneurship. In D. L. Sexton & J. D. Kasarda (eds), *The State of the Art of Entrepreneurship.* Boston, Mass.: PWS-Kent. 579–96.

Dees, J. G. & Starr, J. A. (1992). Entrepreneurship through an ethical lens: Dilemmas and issues for research and practice. In D. L. Sexton & J. D. Kasarda (eds), *The State of the Art of Entrepreneurship.* Boston: PWS-Kent. 89–116.

Granovetter, M. (1985). Economic action and social structure: The problem of embeddedness. *American Journal of Sociology,* **91**, 481–510.

Larson, A. (1992). Network dyads in entrepreneurial settings: A study of the governance of exchange relationships. *Administrative Science Quarterly,* **37**, 76–104.

Larson, A. & Starr, J. A. (1993). A network model of organization formation. *Entrepreneurship: Theory and Practice,* **17**, (2), 5–15.

Powell, W. (1987). Hybrid organizational arrangements: New form or transitional development? *California Management Review,* **30**, (1), 67–87.

Powell, W. (1990). Neither market nor hierarchy: Network forms of organization. *Research in Organizational Behavior,* **12**, 295–336.

Schumpeter, J. A. (1934). *The Theory of Economic Development.* Cambridge, Mass.: Harvard University Press.

Uzzi, B. (1994). Through the economic looking glass: Embeddedness and economic action in the New York apparel industry. Working paper, Department of Organizational Behavior, Northwestern University.

Venkataraman, S. (1994). Associate editor's note. *Journal of Business Venturing*, **9**, 3–6.

ANDREA LARSON

ethics of care Moral reasoning that derives from a concern for others and a desire to maintain thoughtful mutual relationships with those affected by one's actions. The concern of this approach is the responsibility of the individual to respond to another in the other's terms, acting out of care for the other person (Gilligan, 1982). This is distinct from conceptions of morality as justice in that it does not attempt to follow impartial rules or ensure equitable treatment. It focuses on responsiveness to another's needs. It also includes caring for oneself in a nurturing rather than a self-maximizing way. Because the voices expressing an ethic of care are most frequently women's voices, this orientation has become the focal point of extensive research and debate about whether men and women differ in their moral reasoning.

Distinct Moral Orientation

A moral orientation towards caring was initially observed by Carol Gilligan in her interviews of women facing abortion decisions (Gilligan, 1977, 1982). Gilligan's articulation of morality as care emerged in contrast to Kohlberg's stage theory of moral development, which Gilligan argued relied on a conception of morality as justice (*see* MORAL DEVELOPMENT).

In 1977 Carol Gilligan challenged the field of moral development to consider the sex bias inherent in Kohlberg's model. The longitudinal sample which had given Kohlberg his critical model-building data was composed of 84 males. Women, when measured on Kohlberg's scale, rarely reached the higher stages, and most often seemed to demonstrate stage three reasoning, that of helping and pleasing others.

In conducting interviews for a project with Kohlberg, Gilligan had found what she subsequently called "a different voice," the perspective, voiced more frequently by women, that morality was not defined by justice, fairness, or universal rights, as Kohlberg argued. Instead this perspective described a morality based on care, on responsibility to others, on the continuity of interdependent relationships.

Gilligan described this perspective as a morality of care and argued that it was a distinct moral orientation, not merely one of Kohlberg's stages of moral development. She believed that this orientation resulted in clearly different reasoning and unique ways of resolving moral conflict situations.

Kohlberg's response to Gilligan was to acknowledge the importance of recognizing the concept of morality which focuses on special relationships and obligations, but to deny that it was a distinct moral orientation. He saw it as a supplement rather than an alternative to justice solutions (Kohlberg, Levine & Hewer, 1983, p. 21).

The Relational Context of Care

Nell Noddings (1984) elaborated an ethic of care characterized by a fundamental grounding in relation. According to Noddings, the act of caring requires moving away from oneself and becoming engrossed in the reality of another's life. This ethic of care involves the "one-caring" and the "cared-for", in acts of giving and receiving, understanding and sharing, which establish their relatedness. Accepting this relationship as necessary to our existence and well-being is a premise for the ethic of care. Noddings suggests that we are not fundamentally alone in this world, driven by the anguish of isolation and motivated by self-interested individualism. Rather, we are most basically in relation to each other, and a deep and profound joy is the basic human affect. The ethical ideal is the nurturing of the understanding of our mutual interdependence. How ethically good any of us can be as the "one-caring" depends on the reception and response of each of us as the "cared-for." Education in ethics, therefore, should focus on both aspects of the caring relationship.

Similarly, the successful development and practice of an ethic of care demands a consistent integration of the awareness of our relatedness. That which creates difficulty and suffering for the cared-for is also suffered as a difficulty for the one-caring. The reality of the joys and pains of the cared-for is shared by the one-caring as she realizes the possibility of such reality. Ethical action is driven by the feeling of "I must" act in a way to alleviate the pain of another. This aroused sense of concern for another is our natural ethical self. We may learn to listen to that self or to silence it.

The emphasis on feeling rather than thinking as the key route to an ethical life, distinguishes the ethics of care from other formal systems of ethics which rely on rational thought and the ability to abstract the general from the specific. Noddings and Gilligan both argue the critical relevance of an emotional basis for ethical decisions. Rather than trying to create rules for ethical action that would hold in all similar situations, or to calculate the good or evil to the general population, the ethics of care encourage learning to respond to the uniqueness and context of each situation.

The ethics of care have frequently been considered to be an approach more natural for women, and as such, have contributed to substantial debate over the existence of measurable differences in the moral reasoning of women and men. Both Gilligan and Noddings identify women's experience as that which gives rise to the articulation of the ethics of care. Gilligan offers an extended argument for the inclusion of the morality of care in the social repertoire of ethical behavior, citing the systematic exclusion of and bias against women's logic, priorities, and concerns within the development of moral philosophy (Gilligan, 1982, p. 30).

Related Research

Numerous important contributions to ethical theory have emerged from the distinction of the ethics of care. Although these do not all support the entire conception of care reasoning presented by Gilligan or Noddings, each has derived significant impetus from the initial thesis. As a result, the ethics of care can be seen as an array of ideas, broadly encompassing such topics as: what care consists of, who engages in it and why, what an understanding of care teaches us about our society, how care is experienced, and how care is researched.

Seyla Benhabib develops a critical view of traditional moral philosophy by elaborating the relational self found in the ethics of care. She suggests that contractarian theories from HOBBES to RAWLS rely on a "generalized other." Universalistic moral theories hypothesize disembodied and disembedded rational beings in an attempt to establish a system in which all will be treated fairly and equally. In contrast, Benhabib argues for an understanding of "every rational being as an individual with a concrete history, identity and affective-emotional constitution" (Benhabib, 1987, p. 87). Only with this perspective of "the concrete other," are we able to make ethical decisions which are good for individuals as well as humanity. The relational self described by both Noddings and Gilligan is deeply embedded in personal feelings, values, and experiences. An individual's own "concreteness" as well as that of the people she cares about are critical components of her moral reasoning.

The importance of drawing on women's experience in the construction of theoretical models is one of the hallmarks of feminist research. Accordingly, Gilligan is recognized for listening to the voices of women in a field where the uniqueness of women's experience was unnoticed. In her discussion of feminist morality, Virginia Held (1993) acknowledges Gilligan's contribution of examining actual relationships in the lives of women. This methodology is critical for Held as she develops a "mothering person" model to replace the more abstract "rational economic man" paradigm. The mothering person, an ostensibly gender-neutral concept, looks to the maternal experience of women as a reliable guide for moral behavior. Held's model specifically values the integration of emotion to the process of moral reasoning.

The use of emotion and familial experience to develop moral theory stands in stark contrast to the insistence on impartiality and detachment found in theories articulated by most male philosophers and derived from men's experience and values.

Further drawing on the methodology of Gilligan, Jonathan Adler (1987) argues that the value placed on autonomous, universalizable moral reasoning by Kant and Kohlberg neglects the personal point of view. In doing so, it overlooks the importance of contextual variables in individual decisions and establishes a standard of consistency that undermines effective ethical action. Gilligan's articulation of care embraces the inconsistency in practical moral evaluations, thereby relinquishing the necessity of generalizing action to all similar situations. Adler suggests that abstraction from situational realities results in a "widening of the gap between theory and our actual moral practices" (1987, p. 206). By contrast, the ethics of care look deeply into contextual specifics to formulate a moral solution.

The use of context in moral reasoning is also addressed by Marilyn Friedman in her criticism of Kohlberg's theory of moral development. Friedman (1987) suggests that the essential aspect of contextual thinking is not the use of real as opposed to hypothetical moral dilemmas, as Gilligan proposes, but rather the presence of rich detail in the situational variables. Friedman challenges Kohlberg's emphasis on the primacy of justice and suggests that sometimes considerations of care and community, of special relationships, override considerations of justice and rights (1987, p. 195). Whereas justice reasoning envisions abstract persons crafting a mutually respected social contract, care reasoning envisions the unique bonds of an individual relationship. Therefore, care reasoning is most able to be articulated within a rich contextual framework. Friedman's insight suggests that research instruments for the assessment of care reasoning should enable reference to details and contextual variables.

Care and Business Ethics

There is a paucity of theoretical and empirical research applying the ethics of care to business ethics. Surveying ethics education for accountants, Sara Reiter signaled the need for full narratives, similar to those used in Gilligan's research, portraying real individuals in concrete situations. She argued that "The lack of research on the ethical problems of practicing accountants presents a barrier to development of appropriate narratives and cases" (Reiter, 1994, p. 27). Creating such models for business ethics education would encourage both professors and students to weigh contextual components in addition to the rights and duties found within cognitive moral development theory.

Thomas White (1992) noted the potential contribution of Gilligan's ethic of care to a better understanding of how women manage organizations. John Dobson and Judith White

further suggested that a "feminine-oriented relationship-based value system complements the essential nature of the firm as a nexus of relationships between stakeholders" (Dobson & White, 1995, p. 19). Each of these scholars urged extensive incorporation of the ethics of care into business ethics research.

The moral reasoning of a sample of men and women managers of a Fortune 100 company was investigated by Robbin Derry using interviews and real-life dilemmas (Derry, 1989). Finding little evidence of care reasoning among any of the participant managers, she suggested that the organizational culture and the promotional system in the conservative, high-tech organization may have fostered moral reasoning focused on rights and rules: strong components of justice reasoning. Those participants who used care reasoning in other areas of their lives seemed to believe that it was inappropriate at work. In addition, Derry argued that the lack of a reliable and valid research instrument to measure care reasoning, as readily as the Kohlberg or Rest instruments measure justice in moral development, has hampered the further investigation of the ethics of care.

The potential for the application of the ethics of care to business ethics is significant. As indicated above, such potential is evident in several distinctive features. First, the ethics of care emphasize the maintenance of relationships and their myriad commitments. In the corporate environment, there is an increasing demand for business to be attentive to its many stakeholders, particularly customers and employees, in caring ways. As organizations attempt to build such relationships, they must define the responsibilities of initiating and maintaining care. The ethics of care may be able to facilitate an understanding of these responsibilities. Second, the use of real-life dilemmas, or rich hypotheticals, would enable a broader definition of ethical issues, inclusive of the specifics of the market and work environments. This offers an alternative to the abstraction utilized in traditional philosophical models. Third, the ethics of care draw on women's lives and perspectives as informative and instructive. The much-heralded change in demographics over the next few decades, with an increasing number of women and minorities taking on significant roles in management, creates a greater need to build models and paradigms on the experience of these people. While the ethics of care may not be fully representative, understanding this perspective opens the way for inclusion of other "different" voices.

Bibliography

Adler, J. (1987). Moral development and the personal point of view. In E. F. Kittay & D. T. Meyers (eds), *Women and Moral Theory*. Totowa: Rowman & Littlefield, 205–34.

Belenky, M. F., Clinchy, B. M., Goldberger, N. R., & Tarule, J. M. (1986). *Women's Ways of Knowing*. New York: Basic Books.

Benhabib, S. (1987). The generalized and the concrete other: The Kohlberg-Gilligan controversy and feminist theory. In S. Benhabib & D. Cornell (eds), *Feminism as Critique*. Minneapolis: University of Minnesota Press, 77–95.

Derry, R. (1989). An empirical study of moral reasoning among managers. *Journal of Business Ethics*, 8, 855–62.

Dobson, J. & White, J. (forthcoming, 1995). Toward the feminine firm. *Business Ethics Quarterly*, **5** (3), 463–78.

Friedman, M (1987). Care and context in moral reasoning. In E. F. Kittay & D. T. Meyers (eds), *Women and Moral Theory*. Totowa: Rowman and Littlefield, 190–204.

Gilligan, C. (1977). In a diffferent voice: Women's conception of the self and of morality. *Harvard Educational Review*, **47**, 481–517.

Gilligan, C. (1982). *In a Different Voice*. Cambridge, Mass.: Harvard University Press.

Held, V. (1993). *Feminist Morality Transforming Culture, Society, and Politics*. Chicago: University of Chicago Press.

Kohlberg, L., Levine, C., & Hewer, A. (1983). *Moral Stages A Current Formulation and a Response to Critics*. New York: Karger.

Noddings, N. (1984). *Caring: A Feminine Approach to Ethics and Moral Education*. Berkeley: University of California Press.

Reiter, S. A. (1996). The Kohlberg–Gilligan controversy: Lessons for accounting ethics education. *Critical Perspectives on Accounting* **7**.

Tong, R (1993). *Feminine and Feminist Ethics*. Belmont: Wadsworth.

White, T. (1992). Business, ethics, and Carol Gilligan's "two voices." *Business Ethics Quarterly*, **2** (1), 51–61.

ROBBIN DERRY

ethics of competition   Ethical issues that arise from the rivalry between persons or firms striving for the same market. For instance, under capitalism workers compete with each other for jobs and promotions, salespeople compete against each other to obtain customers, and companies compete against each other in terms of product quality and desirability. Capitalist theory assumes that a perfectly competitive and efficient market system is "good" for society because it allows for *autonomy* and *liberty* on the individual level and achieves *general welfare benefits* on the communal level, all of which are highly valued (*see* EFFICIENT MARKETS).

The ethics of competition can be evaluated according to the ethical demands of both PROCEDURAL JUSTICE (FAIRNESS of practices) and DISTRIBUTIVE JUSTICE (fairness of allocating benefits and burdens). How are fair competitive practices and distributions to be determined? JOHN RAWLS provides the most useful method for undertaking an ethical analysis of competition. Go behind a "veil of ignorance" and enter the "original position," an initial position of equality that defines the fundamental terms of association. Now, without knowing whether you are the producer, consumer, general public, competitive winner, or competitive loser, what would be a set of fair rules? Two sets of rules that would be acceptable in a Rawlsian original position can be found in the writing of Freeman and Gilbert (1988). First, they provide a set of "common morality" principles that are derived by KANTIAN ETHICS and the GOLDEN RULE. Competitors should abide by the principles of promise keeping, non-malevolence, respect for persons, and respect for property (*see* PROMISES, PROMISING). These are some of the conditions necessary for a level playing field. It is unethical for competitors to violate these rules. Thus, competitors unethically violate the principles of justice when they break promises, inflict physical harms, exploit people, and damage property. ADAM SMITH in *Theory of Moral Sentiments*, used an impartial spectator theory to argue that these HARM-based injustices would be minimized in a capitalist system due to an appeal to either a person's CONSCIENCE or a nation's justice system (*see* IMPARTIAL SPECTATOR THEORIES).

Secondly, Freeman and Gilbert also construct a set of rules which they call "implicit morality of the marketplace." A perfectly competitive marketplace is characterized by perfect information, consumer sovereignty, price competition, no conscious attempts at rent-seeking, firms internalizing externalities, and free entry into markets. These are also some of the conditions necessary for a level playing field. It is unethical for competitors to violate these rules. Thus, competitors unethically violate the demands of justice when they engage in false advertising, price-fixing, BRIBERY, externalities, and creating market barriers, to name a few.

Capitalist theory maintains that there exists a competitive equilibrium which is ethically preferred. As summarized by Smith in *Wealth of Nations*, when demand exceeds supply, economic agents will enter the market, thus increasing aggregate competition and decreasing product price and firm profits. When supply exceeds demand, economic agents will leave the market, thus decreasing aggregate competition and increasing product price and firm profits. Smith concluded that "when the quantity brought to market is sufficient to supply the effectual demand and no more, the market price naturally comes to be either exactly, or as nearly as can be judged of, the same with the natural price" (Smith, 1776/1976, i, p. 64). According to Smith, placing restraints on competition in job and product markets is detrimental to laborers, consumers, and the aggregate wealth of a nation.

According to KARL MARX and Friedrich Engels, the competitive nature of capitalism is inherently unethical from both procedural and distributive justice perspectives. In order to maximize their own economic SELF-INTEREST, capitalists pay laborers subsistence wages rather than the actual economic value of laborers' contribution. When competition reduces product price, the capitalist maintains his own profit margins and responds by slashing the wages of laborers, or by demanding more hours for the same pay, further increasing worker alienation. The ultimate goal of many capitalists is to create monopolies and oligopolies (*see* MONOPOLY). As a result, the rich get richer and the poor get poorer. As poverty increases capital becomes even more concentrated. Once national markets

have been fully exploited, capitalists find other countries with even lower wage rates to produce and sell their goods.

Unfortunately, Marx's critique of capitalist competitive behaviors does have descriptive power. Not that all capitalists engage in unethical competitive activities all of the time, but almost all capitalists engage in unethical competitive activities some of the time. In his book *Capitalist Fools*, conservative-leaning Nicholas von Hoffman notes how many capitalists fail to heed the moral voices of utilitarianism and deontology in their pursuit of profits. Many of the great founders of American capitalism practiced very unethical competitive methods in their pursuit of increased market share. Diamond Jim Brady bribed customers with money, alcohol, and sex. William Hearst dragged the United States into the Spanish-American War to increase newspaper sales. Henry Ford was a cruel, anti-Semitic employer. Henry Frick hired thugs who killed unruly employees. John Patterson and Tom Watson established dummy stores on both sides of a competitor and cut prices until the competitor went out of business. Charles Schwab, J. P. Morgan, Jay Gould, and Sam Insull were corrupt people who bribed well-placed sources to enhance their profits. Firm survival in competitive battles over market share too often results in violations of common morality and the implicit morality of the marketplace. From the original position of initial equality, all of these competitive activities are unethical.

As a result of unethical Machiavellian games played by competitive capitalists pursuing profits in imperfect markets, all capitalist economies are to some degree regulated by government. For instance, in the United States there is a host of government REGULATION protecting employees (Equal Pay Act, Occupational Safety and Health Act, Age Discrimination in Employment Act), consumers (Fair Packaging and Labeling Act, Consumer Product Safety Act), communities (Air Pollution Control Act, Hazardous Material Transportation Act), people in other countries (Business Payments Abroad Act), the political system (Campaign Finance Amendments), and other businesses (Antitrust Amendments). Anticipating many of the unethical competitive practices listed above, Adam Smith argued that a capitalist system must have an independent, democratically controlled, accountable system of justice that derives impartial decisions and is authorized to impose its just and fair decisions on affected parties.

Bibliography

Braveman, H. (1974). *Labor and Monopoly Capital: The Degradation of Work in the Twentieth Century.* New York: Monthly Review Press.

Buchanan, A. (1988). *Ethics, Efficiency, and the Market.* Totowa, NJ: Roman Littlefield Publishers.

Freeman, R. E. & Gilbert, D. R. (1988). *Corporate Strategy and the Search for Ethics.* Englewood Cliffs, NJ: Prentice-Hall.

Marx, K. & Engels, F. (1848/1964). *The Communist Manifesto.* New York: Washington Square Press.

Rawls, J. (1971). *A Theory of Justice.* Cambridge, Mass.: Harvard University Press.

Smith, A. (1759/1976). *The Theory of Moral Sentiments.* Indianapolis, Ind.: Liberty Classics.

Smith, A. (1776/1976). *An Inquiry into the Nature and Causes of the Wealth of Nations,* 2 vols. Chicago: University of Chicago Press.

von Hoffman, N. (1992). *Capitalist Fools.* Doubleday: New York.

DENIS COLLINS

ethics of consulting deals with the responsibilities of individuals who serve as consultants to institutions and their members. Consulting can be defined as an intervention into an organization with the goal of helping that organization 1) understand its beliefs and practices and how they affect organizational outcomes, 2) design appropriate structures, systems, and processes to manage or change thoses beliefs and practices to result in more effective outcomes, and 3) implement the mechanisms designed.

The institutions served by consultants are in the private, public, and nonprofit sectors of our society. They can be business corporations or partnerships; they can be hospitals and other health-care facilities; they can be governments and government agencies; they can be foundations, charities, and other nonprofit organizations. Any organized setting in which individuals and groups work for a broad common purpose is a potential client for consultation.

Consulting in any field and under any circumstances requires a carefully honed sense of ethics, since by its very nature, any consultation involves intervening into the lives of individuals, having impact on a system simply by being present, and dealing with values in a way that could result in the inappropriate imposition of the consultant's values on the client institution.

In some ways, the consultant is similar to the health professional. The client institution, like a patient, is seeking remedy to a "condition" (or conditions) its members believe is preventing the institution's achieving "good health." Like the medical practitioner, the consultant is asked to "make things better." Therefore, to continue the medical analogy, the moral minimum of consulting must be: *Do No Harm.* This principle may be easier said than done. Unlike the medical profession in which there are licensing and accrediting bodies for members and the institutions in which they serve, the occupation of consulting, *per se*, is not monitored, reviewed, nor guided by any organization which sets standards or tests practitioners. In addition, there is no prescribed course of study; there are no standard "treatments" which clients may anticipate. (These descriptive statements provide the reasons one must call consulting an occupation and not a profession.) For the client, there can be only trust that the consultant is knowledgeable and well-trained, and is a responsible, ethical person. Given these realities, the principle "Do No Harm," requires the consultant to be critically cognizant of his or her own limitations.

To emphasize the importance of the "Do No Harm" rule, and the potential pitfalls to enacting it, consider the consulting field relevant to this volume: Business Ethics Consulting.

Business Ethics Consulting. As an occupation, business ethics consulting is in its adolescence, both in terms of its age and its characteristics. Business ethics consulting formally came into being in the early 1980s, so, in the mid-1990s, it can truly be called "teenaged." Further, it is an adolescent in that it has had some early successes and shows promise of having an impact on the world, but it is unpredictable, often self-centered, sometimes undisciplined, and very frequently hard to understand.

Practitioners. One of the effects of occupational adolescence is that the characteristics of the practitioner have not been specified. The business ethics consultant body is composed of individuals trained in a number of different academic disciplines with varied amounts of knowledge about and experience in the professions, industries, businesses, and organizations to which they consult. Many ethics consultants are trained in philosophy, theology, and related fields; others come from the social sciences: psychology, sociology, anthropology, and the like; some were trained in the professional area to which they consult: medicine, law, and engineering, among others. In addition, there are individuals marketing themselves as business ethics consultants who have taken one- or two-day programs offered by various organizations. Because there is no accrediting body for business ethics consultants (as is the case with many fields of consultancy), anyone choosing to act as a business ethics consultant may do so. Consequently, the mandate to "Do No Harm" at present must be paired with a client message of "*caveat emptor* – buyer beware."

Why Do Organizations Initiate an Ethics Consultation? Just as there are a variety of reasons a patient will seek medical assistance or guidance, there are several reasons an organization will choose to bring in a business ethics consultant: 1) The organization and/or its members or others in its industry have been found to have done something legally or ethically "wrong" and it wants to prevent future misconduct as well as generate positive public relations; 2) the organization or its industry is undergoing major regulatory or structural changes in which the new "rules" are unclear or significantly different than in the past and it wants to anticipate and, thus, prevent unintentional wrongdoing; 3) the organization engages in professional activities with acknowledged health and safety impact on the public – e.g., medicine, engineering – and it wants to manage the dilemmas of professional delivery of services; 4) there is a legal mandate, such as the 1991 US Corporate Sentencing Guidelines; and, 5) a soon-to-retire CEO or senior official wishes to leave a legacy of "Ethics."

These reasons that institutions seek ethics consultation further confirm the importance of the injunction to do no harm. In a majority of cases, client organizations consider themselves to be in reasonably good shape, seeking prevention or enhancement as much or more than remedy. While prevention or betterment may be impossible to promise, a commitment to not making things worse is imperative! If clients cannot feel assured that, at the very least, they will end up no worse than they started, then consultants cannot claim they are acting responsibly.

Ethical Obligations Beyond "Do No Harm." Beyond the avoidance of harm, ethical consulting demands other considerations. A critical ethical obligation of the consultant is *respect* for the client institution and its members. Respect means holding in regard the work that the members of the institution do and their knowledge related to that work. While consultants are brought in as outside "experts," they should never forget that the organization to which they are providing guidance is the expert in its business: Almost no consultant can know as much about an organization as its members.

Similarly, consultants are obligated to *not impose their values* on the institutions to which they consult. This injunction can become complicated, in that most guidance and advice is not value-free. Consequently, consultants must walk the line between *suggesting* and *imposing* ways of thinking and acting. A responsible consultant needs never to say to a client "You must see things my way."

However, respect for the client's values does not mean the consultant must always "follow orders." The ethical consultant must *recognize his or her personal bottom line*, and be willing to turn down or step aside from work with a client whose beliefs and actions fall below that line.

Respectful, responsible consultation must include listening to and hearing the concerns of the client institution's members, learning whatever is necessary to understand the business of the client organization, designing and implementing interventions that meet the client organization's needs, and valuing the skills, capabilities, and knowledge of the organization's membership. There is an old joke that goes: "A consultant is someone who borrows your watch to tell you what time it is." A wise consultant knows that comment contains more than a grain of truth – as well as an ethical mandate. As a consultant, one is being entrusted with the real and the emotional "property" of its client: 1) proprietary information, 2) hopes, fears, and beliefs of its membership, and, perhaps above all, 3) the institution's reputation and its image in the world. The responsible consultant employs that "property" (along with other tools) to reflect back to the client institution what it has not been able to see, and to help the institution use its resources to build its capabilities as a responsible and successful organization.

BARBARA LEY TOFFLER

ethics of management *see* MANAGERIAL ETHICS AND THE ETHICAL ROLE OF THE MANAGER

ethics of marketing   Marketing ethics is the systematic study of how moral standards are applied to marketing decisions, behaviors, and institutions. The moral standards aspect of this definition has to do with the application of ethical theories (e.g., UTILITARIANISM, DUTY-based, VIRTUE ETHICS) to marketing issues. Furthermore, implicit in this definition is the understanding that ethics contains a NORMATIVE aspect, that is what is right or correct. Ethical questions arise in many marketing decisions including whether to introduce a new product, the price to offer and choice of advertising strategy. The behavior of marketers like salespeople, who are often judged only on the amount of product sold without investigating the methods used to acquire those sales, comes under scrutiny. As marketing has become more commonplace at nonprofit institutions such as hospitals and museums, ethical questions now have surfaced which are rather similar to those faced by business firms.

Ethical issues in marketing have existed since the first things of value were traded. However, serious study of marketing ethics has only begun in the last 25 years. Marketing ethics sometimes is labeled as an oxymoron because certain marketing practitioners, like used car dealers, advertising copywriters, and telemarketers, commonly violate ethical precepts. This stereotypical judgment of marketing has been replaced with the understanding that most marketers not only hold to a higher standard

of ethics but also recognize that short-term financial payoff gained by ethical transgressions is often supplanted by long-term damage to both balance sheet and reputation.

Marketing Theory

Substantial effort has been expended by scholars to develop theoretical models that stipulate the factors leading to an ethical marketing decision. Most of this work employs one or more accepted ethical theories like utilitarianism, duty and rights, and virtue ethics. The thrust of these models has concentrated on individual moral development (Kohlberg's stages), organizational moral development (from amoral to highly ethical companies), contingency theory (opportunity to engage in unethical activity and relative importance of peers and top management), and the theory of reasoned action (rational persons must recognize ethical dimension of a decision and determine the potential consequences of it) (Laczniak & Murphy, 1993; Smith & Quelch, 1993). A recent article which proposes a "workable ethical philosophy" for marketing suggests three distinct characteristics – moral relativism, bounded/constrained relativism, and descriptive ethics (Robin & Reidenbach, 1993).

Another thrust of the research in theoretical work within marketing ethics is theory testing. Recent empirical studies have investigated the application of Kohlberg's theory in a study of marketing practitioners and testing the importance of commitment and trust in relationship marketing (emphasizing ongoing relationships with customers rather than short-term transactions). (See articles in *Journal of Marketing*, 1992–5.)

Marketing Practice

Although a myriad of marketing decisions contain ethical ramifications, several topics that are widely accepted as major areas of marketing practice are examined here. They are: market segmentation/targeting, marketing research, product development, pricing, distribution, personal selling, advertising, and international marketing.

Segmenting the market to appeal to smaller groups with more homogeneous needs is one of the major premises of marketing management. The needs of some segments like children and the elderly have long been protected by public policy makers. Growth in the new immigrant population in the US and increases in school dropout rates indicate that the segment of "market illiterates" likely will grow in the future. Furthermore, the segmentation strategy employed by R. J. Reynolds in marketing Dakota cigarettes to women (historically an acceptable segment) drew such criticism that the product was withdrawn from the market. Ethical questions can arise from both inclusion and exclusion of certain market segments (Smith & Quelch, 1993, pp. 188–95).

Marketing research techniques are used by all marketers. Research practitioners usually operate in an ethical manner because of their commitment to the scientific method and professionalism. The marketing researcher has several duties to respondents in any type of research (i.e., not to deceive, protect privacy and anonymity). Many marketing research firms operate as consultants to companies and a set of duties exist to be forthright with one another in financial dealings and research requirements. Researchers also have duties to the general public when the research results are disseminated in the media. One emerging ethical issue in the 1990s is corporate intelligence-gathering where companies attempt to gain information about their competitors (Laczniak & Murphy, 1993, ch. 3).

Product development and management is a cornerstone of marketing because the marketing process must begin with a product (defined as goods, services or ideas). Ethical questions are continually being asked about product safety and product counterfeiting. Laws do protect both consumers and marketers from abuse, but ethical issues sometimes arise when the law is being followed. Socially controversial products, like the "sin" categories of tobacco and alcoholic beverages and firearms, consistently are questioned from an ethical standpoint. The environmental compatibility or incompatibility of many products including all packaged goods, chemicals, plastics, and many others are being scrutinized by consumers and policy-makers. The whole "green-marketing" movement of the last several years where companies have promoted the environmental benefits of their products has raised suspicion on the part of

consumers and led to some state and federal regulatory restrictions. This issue is one likely to raise even more attention in the future.

Pricing of products within marketing is a central marketing decision. In an era of increasing competition in the retail sector, traditional guidelines on markups and pricing strategies are growing obsolete. Although price gouging of specific segments like the elderly and market illiterates does still occur, price sensitivity is the watchword for many consumers and most industrial buyers. Thus, ethical concerns seem to be arising more frequently since some marketers fail to disclose pertinent data about product quality or features in pricing their products to promote low prices. For example, a current strategy practiced by discount retailers is to offer very low prices on computer hardware and software without divulging they are last year's model or not expandable. Other pricing-related issues pertain to non-price price increases (reducing product quality or quantity while keeping the price the same) and pricing in the service sector where airlines, rental car firms, and some financial institutions have been criticized for not giving relevant information about prices being offered.

The distribution element of marketing contains a number of different firms, starting with suppliers to manufacturers, then to wholesalers and retailers, and finally to end consumers. At each point of interface in this "channel" of distribution, potential ethical issues arise. One of the most prevalent is the power and control within the channel, meaning that large members of the channel may coerce smaller ones into price concessions and unreasonable delivery demands. Another ethical issue pertains to gift giving or bribery, because most of these organizations employ buyers and purchasing agents who may be influenced by these techniques. Competition between firms within the same level (retailer vs. retailer) and different levels (manufacturer vs. retailer) of the channel cause some managers to rationalize unethical conduct when competition becomes intense (Laczniak & Murphy, 1993, pp. 110–13).

More people are employed in the personal-selling function than any other marketing area. Consequently, the issue of ethics in selling touches many marketing practitioners. Salespeople seem to be most prone to act unethically when one or more of the following situations exist. They are: competition is intense; economic times are difficult; compensation is based exclusively (or primarily) on commission; questionable dealings are common industry practice; sales training is nonexistent or abbreviated; the individual has limited selling experience. Sales managers operate in a position above the salesrep and are charged with administering the territories of salespersons, setting quotas, and evaluating competition. Ethical sales managers strive for fair treatment of salespersons and competitors as well as regular communication with their salespeople about company policies and personal ethical concerns.

Advertising is the most visible area of marketing and often charged with ethical abuse. Some observers argue that advertising often reaches unintended audiences who may view the ad as being misleading when the targeted segment understands the message. Advertising is inherently intrusive and causes irritation or suspicion even when conducted ethically. Some of the most pertinent ethical questions deal with the persuasiveness of advertising messages, the advocacy role played by advertising agencies, the responsibility to audiences, and the media's stance with respect to advertising. One of the curious features of ethics in advertising is that the involvement of several separate groups (advertiser, agency, and media) has led to generally lower standards for the field than one would expect. These issues and others are explored in more depth in ADVERTISING ETHICS.

The complexities of marketing in the international sphere have meant even greater ethical scrutiny of business. Different cultures, traditions, and values have added a new set of challenges to marketing managers interested in satisfying marketplace needs. Two of the factors associated with ethical problems in international marketing are cultural RELATIVISM and economic development. Historical activities like massive bribery of foreign government officials is not only unethical but illegal under the FOREIGN CORRUPT PRACTICES ACT, and "dumping" of products in Third World countries where many industries have codes making such practices unacceptable seem to be exceptions now. As multinational corporations have expanded their operations to even more far-flung countries, they have weighed the importance of consistent policies with sensitivity to local needs and customs (*see* MULTINATIONALS). This situation requires an even higher level of ethical concern, and this observer believes that multinationals must operate at the highest rather than lowest common denominator (see Laczniak & Murphy, 1993, ch. 8) (*see also* GLOBALIZATION).

Marketing Ethics in the Future

Several challenges facing marketing practitioners need to be tackled. First, ethical questions in small and medium-sized firms are equally important as those confronted by global marketers. Since most of the growth in the future is projected to be in these smaller operations, the founders and owners of these firms need to specify clearly their ethical position. For example, product development criteria, selling tactics, and pricing philosophy should be discussed with regularity from an ethical viewpoint. Barriers to communication are much lower than in large corporations, but a willingness to grapple with and discuss ethical issues must exist for meaningful interaction to occur in these businesses.

Second, codes of ethics must be tailored to the marketing function and be made more specific. The good news about codes is that 90 percent of large US companies have such a code, and an increasing number of multinationals headquartered in other countries have some written ethical policies. However, few codes offer meaningful guidance for salespeople and marketing executives. Such guidance should ideally go beyond policy manuals, and these marketing codes should be made available to all stakeholders. Less than 50 percent of current codes are public documents (Murphy, 1995). Another strategy that companies might use is a series of ethical audit questions pertinent to marketing (Laczniak & Murphy, 1993, pp. 292–7).

Third, most major ethical questions facing companies in the future will require both a philosophical and technical analysis. Some companies use trained ethicists that assist them with these issues. In addition, technical experts with strong scientific backgrounds are also needed to properly evaluate many of these questions. For example, environmental problems resulting from product use and disposal should probably be confronted in this manner.

Finally, the dynamic tension between ethics and competition must be kept in balance. Getting ahead and winning are part of the competitive nature of the marketplace. This tension will likely only be heightened in the increasingly competitive world of the late twentieth century. Companies must compete in an uncertain global market where the playing field is not always level. The top managers of large and small businesses need to assert their role as "leaders" to ensure that ethics has an important role to play in all companies (Murphy & Enderle, 1995).

Laczniak (1993) identified four challenges to academic researchers studying marketing ethics. The first one is to develop alternative paradigms to the past work which has applied normative ethical theories or proposed positive models of marketing ethics. A second challenge requires more cross-cultural evaluation. Increasingly, researchers are comparing consumer attitudes and/or marketing practices from several countries. Third, both societal and professional "performance gaps" exist between accepted behavior of marketers and the aspiration levels of society or the profession. Fourth, researchers should become informed advocates for improved ethical practice by marketing managers.

Bibliography

Laczniak, G. R. (1993). Marketing ethics: Onward toward greater expectations. *Journal of Public Policy and Marketing*, 12, 91–6.

Laczniak, G. R., & Murphy, P. E. (1993). *Ethical Marketing Decisions: The Higher Road*. Boston: Allyn and Bacon.

Murphy, P. E. (1995). Corporate ethics statements: Current status and future prospects. *Journal of Business Ethics*, 13, 1–14.

Murphy, P. E., & Enderle, G. (1995). Managerial ethical leadership: Examples do matter *Business Ethics Quarterly*, 5, 115–26.

Murphy, P. E. & Laczniak, G. R. (1981). Marketing ethics: A review with implications for managers, educators and researchers. In B. M. Enis & K. J. Roering (eds), *Review of Marketing 1981* (pp. 251–66). Chicago: American Marketing Association.

Murphy, P. E. & Pridgen, M. D. (1991). Ethical and legal issues in marketing. *Advances in Marketing and Public Policy*, 2, 185–244.

Robin, D. P. & Reidenbach, R. E. (1993). Searching for a place to stand: Toward a workable ethical philosophy. *Journal of Public Policy and Marketing*, 12, 97–105.

Smith, N. C. & Quelch, J. A. (1993). *Ethics in Marketing*. Homewood, Ill.: Irwin.

Tsalikis, J. & Fritzsche, D. J. (1989). Business ethics: A literature review with a focus on marketing ethics. *Journal of Business Ethics*, 8, 695–744.

PATRICK E. MURPHY

ethics of ownership   To own means "to have or to hold as property" (*Webster's Third New International Dictionary*, 1986). Ownership implies rights to control, but control rights are rarely unlimited or exclusive; they are shaped by the surrounding context and accompanied by duties. These rights and duties are defined differently in different communities and they reflect changing times.

The Cheyenne plains Indians were nomads inhabiting the North American Great Plains. They depended on hunting. A warrior's ownership rights extended even beyond his death: his best equipment – bows, arrows, guns, knives, and such – went with him to the grave. The rest of his property went to his widow.

The Hopi, on the other hand, an agricultural people living in villages on the table land above the Arizona desert, placed rigid constraints on their most valued possession – land. It was owned by the village, and divided into clan and family plots for cultivation. Ownership for them thus meant trusteeship (Beaglehole, 1968, p. 591).

Conceptions of corporate ownership found around the globe reflect these two approaches, one individualistic and the other communitarian (*see* INDIVIDUALISM; COMMUNITARIANISM). Both reflect and define a social morality, although their ethical precepts differ. Ownership in Japan is predominantly a communitarian concept. The corporation is owned by all its members. Its purpose is to serve those members and the larger community of which they are a part. In Chinese tradition, ownership is in the family and the purpose of the corporation is to serve the interests of the family throughout the ages.

On the other hand, Western individualistic tradition, for example, has historically tended to regard the right to own property as a natural right, coming in essence from God, and inherent in the human individual: the least interference with that right is the best. This notion conceived of the corporation as property, owned by its shareholders, each of whose individual benefit was the primary obligation of corporate managers. The manager was bound to hire and fire workers so as to ensure that the corporation satisfied consumer desires in a market kept as open as possible by antitrust laws. The moral justification of this arrangement derived from ADAM SMITH's conception that the good community would result from each individual's self-interested pursuit of his or her own welfare, a pursuit that was justified by the rights of private ownership.

This economic model – what might loosely be called unfettered capitalism – has for some time been eroding. It has come under attack from two quite unrelated sets of forces. The first is moral or ethical, the second is competition from more efficient systems.

The first was launched in the nineteenth century by European socialists, who, after having invented the term "capitalism" to embody all that they detested, set out to destroy it. For them, as well as for many non-socialists, the problem was that the sum of consumer desires did not always add up to what the community held to be its needs. These needs came to be expressed in a plethora of governmental rules and regulations as well as in the practice of labor relations and management generally. In recent years the community need that has shaken the old assumptions most profoundly is the preservation of our life-supporting ecosystem, recognizing that air and water are no longer free, inexhaustible goods, and that the rights associated with private ownership often conflict with what the community deems essential.

The second source of attack on old-time capitalism comes from the Asian economies which in the last 20 years have spawned corporations whose competitiveness is second to none and often is unequalled. These corpora-tions have as their purpose the long-term health and welfare of their employees and of their home communities. They enjoy a close and cooperative relationship with government and often with one another. For them the Western concept of ownership has little meaning.

American business for some time has been moving in a communitarian direction as a result of these two sets of forces. Examples of the transition include:

> The increasing recognition that devotion to the short-term interests of share-holders of large, publicly held companies – who incidentally in many cases have stopped being owners in any real sense – places the corporation at a disadvantage when competing with a business whose purpose is the long-run interests of the enterprise;

> The chemical industry's cooperative endeavors with government and local communities to safeguard the environment, called "Responsible Care";

> Relations between managers and managed in the steel, automobile, and other industries where employee involvement in management and employment security have, to some extent replaced the old ways;

> Government/business collaboration for high-tech development as in Sematech and the Clinton administration's technology policies embodied in the proposed Competitiveness Act of 1994.

The transition in the United States, however, has been slow and awkward, impeded by old assumptions, which are rooted in the old ethics of individualism. The ethical questions associated with business ownership for Americans in the future can be conveniently sketched in communitarian terms, and these questions seem to be as important for corporate competitiveness as they are for corporate virtue:

> How do managers best design the organization so as to provide employees with fulfillment and self-respect?

What is required to assure fairness throughout the corporate community as well as to respect and reward individual differences?

How do managers foster a consensus about corporate goals and the means to their fulfillment?

What are the rights of the corporation in the community, and what are its duties; and what are the rights and duties of corporate members? Should the CEO, for example, be paid ten times as much as the janitor, or more or less?

What are the community needs that the corporation serves and what are the most efficient procedures for assuring that those needs are served? Is it competition in the marketplace, or regulation by government, or is it some form of partnership with government? Might it even be a government charter?

What is the role of government that is best suited to an ethical use of property?

How is ownership most effectively harmonized with the holistic demands of the natural environment?

These questions strike a slightly discordant note in communities rooted in the individualistic tradition. They are, however, quite familiar to the Asian ear, and even to many continental Europeans. The special ethical problem for these communitarians, as it has always been for the individualists, will be to preserve and protect individual liberties and respect for the individual human being.

To oversimplify, those who have regarded ownership in individualistic terms are beginning to see it more in communitarian terms, and communitarians are feeling an ethical compulsion to have perhaps a higher regard for the individual than they have had in the past.

Bibliography

Beaglehole, E. (1968). Property. *International Encyclopedia of the Social Sciences*, vol. 12. New York: Macmillan.

Berle, A. & Means, G. C. (1932). *The Modern Corporation and Private Property*. New York: Macmillan.
Lodge. G. C. (1974). *The New American Ideology*. New York: Alfred Knopf.
Lodge, G. C. & Vogel, E. F. (eds), (1987). *Ideology and National Competitiveness*. Boston: Harvard Business School Press.
Vogel, E. F. (1979). *Japan as Number One*. Cambridge, Mass.: Harvard University Press.

GEORGE C. LODGE

ethics of pricing   A central tenet of the capitalist creed exhorts the wise businessperson to buy cheap and sell dear. But can it be unethical to sell a good or service at too high a price? In answering this question, it is helpful to distinguish between *legal* norms of conduct and alternative *ethical* concerns. As a general rule, the American common law permits the seller to seek his or her highest price. The common law focuses on CONSENT. So long as the buyer consents to the price, it is presumptively fair and enforceable. The law seeks to assure that the buyer's consent is meaningful through the doctrines of fraud, duress, undue influence, and unconscionability. It is illegal to lie, to coerce, or to abuse the trust of one's trading partner. However, if the buyer fails to prove fraud or the like, the courts will enforce the contract price, no matter how outrageous that price may appear to an outside observer (Ostas, 1992, p. 580).

Ethical analysis suggests alternative concerns. First, a "fair" price in an ethical sense may simply mean the market price. Under this view, a price that far exceeds the market would be unfair and unethical even if the buyer consented to it. Historically, the common law embraced such an ethic. Employing the doctrine of *laesio enormis*, American courts in the eighteenth and early nineteenth centuries routinely inquired into the substantive fairness of contractual prices (Horwitz, 1977, 173–80). Prices that significantly exceeded the market rate were not enforced. The market provided an objective benchmark by which to judge the fairness of pricing. By the mid-nineteenth century, the belief in an external notion of value had been discredited in favor of respect for individual autonomy, the parties alone could determine the value of the commodity or service traded.

Discrimination in pricing raises a second ethical concern. Perhaps it is unethical to discriminate between buyers, demanding a higher price from one class of buyers than another. For example, it is clearly unethical to discriminate between buyers on the basis of race, religion, or ethnicity. "Red-lining" in inner-city lending provides an example. Price discrimination can appear in other contexts as well. Consider the effects of a natural disaster such as a flood. Electricity is out and there is a sudden demand for gasoline-driven electric generators. Can a seller demand its highest price in such a setting? Traditionally, the common law answer is "yes"; so long as buyer and seller consent to the price, the price is fair. State legislatures, by contrast, typically answer "no." Responding to public outcries of "price gouging," state legislatures typically impose a more generous ethic, demanding that the seller not take undue advantage of the necessitous condition of its trading partners. Price discrimination also can be used as a competitive weapon. A large chain-store may charge an unusually low price in hopes of driving its smaller competitors out of business. Again, the common law permits such practices; both ethical analysis and antitrust legislation impose an alternative moral vision of "fair" competition.

The presence of monopoly power also affects the ethics of pricing. Perhaps if a seller has exclusive control over a needed product, fairness would demand that that product be offered at a price that reflects the monopolist's costs. For example, regulated monopolies, such as utilities, must justify price increases before regulatory commissions, where consumer groups have a right to air their concerns. Since the buyer and seller do not have equal bargaining power, the market is not trusted to generate an ethically acceptable price. Yet in other arenas the law permits the monopolist to seek its highest price. For example, a pharmaceutical company has no legal duty to offer its patented life-saving drug at an affordable price. Legally, the company can set its price so as to maximize its profits, even if this means that people in need will not get the drug. Again, ethical analysis suggests an alternative ethic.

Before condemning the common law too harshly, it is important to note that the law itself embodies an ethic. In fact, the common-law approach to pricing can be defended on either libertarian or utilitarian grounds (Epstein, 1975, p. 293). LIBERTARIANISM elevates the principles of individual AUTONOMY and individual liberty to positions of the highest order. Positive laws that interfere with the liberty and autonomy rights of individuals are impermissible and immoral. From a libertarian perspective, only the parties to a contract can determine whether a price is fair, and individuals have no duty to share their property rights with others. UTILITARIANISM will argue that a regime of FREEDOM OF CONTRACT generates the greatest good for the greatest number. To a utilitarian, personal autonomy and liberty are not ends in themselves, but rather, are means to generating prosperity for the greatest number. Borrowing from Adam Smith, a utilitarian may argue that attempts to regulate prices will interfere with the invisible hand of the market and lead to unintended negative consequences (*see* SMITH, ADAM; INVISIBLE HAND, THE). Given a competitive free market, the best public policy is one that firmly embraces the right of an individual or company to set its own price.

The common law rests on a presumption that individuals should be empowered to set the terms of their own bargains. Ethical analysis suggests some pragmatic limitations to this presumption. First, a price that exceeds the market price gives evidence that some sort of misrepresentation, duress, or abuse of trust may have occurred during the contract negotiations. Ethical reasoning demands that parties treat one another with respect, providing full disclosure of relevant information, and not taking undue advantage (Shell, 1991, p. 93). Second, although private autonomy and respect for private property are important ethical concerns, they are not the only ethical concerns raised by pricing. Price discrimination on the basis of prejudice (red-lining), to take advantage of a necessitous condition (flood), or to destroy a competitor (chain-store) all violate ethical standards of fair play. And finally, the presence of monopoly power generates an affirmative ethical duty to offer one's product at a price reasonably tied to one's costs. Such ethical concerns provide a useful supplement to traditional common-law principles.

Bibliography

Chamberlin, E. (1985). *The Theory of Monopolistic Competition.* Cambridge, Mass.: Harvard University Press.

Darr, F. (1994). Unconscionability and price fairness. *Houston Law Review,* **30,** 1819–91. (Explores the factors that lead common-law courts to find a price to be unfair and unenforceable).

Epstein, E. (1975). Unconscionability: A critical reappraisal. *Journal of Law & Economics,* **18,** 293–315. (Defends a general regime of freedom of contract on both utilitarian and libertarian grounds).

Fried, C. (1981). *Contract as Promise.* Cambridge, Mass.: Harvard University Press. (Links the legal duties of contracting with the ethical duties generated by promising).

Horwitz, M. (1977). *The Transformation of American Law: 1780–1860.* Cambridge, Mass.: Harvard University Press. (A seminal work on the history of the common law of contracts).

Macneil, I. (1980). *The New Social Contract: An Inquiry into Modern Contractual Relations.* New Haven: Yale University Press. (Identifies a communitarian ethic at the core of contractual endeavors).

Ostas, D. (1992). Predicting unconscionability decisions: An economic model and an empirical test. *American Business Law Journal,* **29,** 535–84. (Concludes that modern courts require evidence of some sort of negotiating impropriety to hold a price unenforceable).

Shell, G. (1991). When is it legal to lie in negotiations? *Sloan Management Review,* **32,** 93–101. (Explores the interface between law and ethics in contract negotiations).

DANIEL T. OSTAS

Europe, business ethics in *see* BUSINESS ETHICS IN EUROPE

excellence *see* TOM PETERS ON EXCELLENCE

executive compensation Executive compensation based on agency theory argues that equity holders (principles) delegate the responsibility of managing firms to top executives or agents, who are charged with using their specialized knowledge and the company's resources to generate the highest possible return to principals. Control problems often exist because the interests of agents and principals differ. Executives may exploit their privileged positions to gain excessive compensation or perks independent of the company's performance, at the expense of principals who may thereupon develop monitoring systems to counter the agent's avarice. The use of pay practices to align the interests of agents and principals is complicated by the difficulty of directly observing an executive's effort or behavior.

The executive compensation controversy can be addressed by trying to ensure that distributive justice, or the proper distribution of economic benefits and burdens, occurs. Following the principle of "to each according to merit," companies should hire, promote, and distribute bonuses to executives strictly on the basis of individual merit. Fair sales for most people are based on market competitiveness, meaning that salaries should be sufficient to attract and retain the number and quality of people needed to sustain the business in the long term.

In practice these ethical theories break down because there isn't any real competitive salary market for large company executive talent. A phantom market exists primarily in the minds of the CEO's hand-picked compensation committee. Hence the balancing of risk and rewards achieved in most occupations is nullified. The risk–reward profile of the American CEO is now heavily biased toward reward such that elements of risk have been virtually eliminated through stock options and golden parachutes.

In a truly free market those executives with a proven track record at one or more companies would be in demand, offering their services to the highest bidder. However, there is little evidence of such movement among CEOs. In fact, most executive jobs at top firms are filled from within where there is a high level of competition amongst the senior ranks of the corporation. Most competitors would probably take the CEO position, with its prestige and perks, for a reasonable pay raise of about 30 percent. However, the pay gap between the CEO and other senior-level executives is now much wider, with CEOs typically earning 60 percent more than the second-highest-paid executive.

Executives should be rewarded for decisions and judgments affecting the long-term future of the company. But, in fact, up to 90 percent of the pay of executives is geared to the current year's business results, and this leads to short-range rather than strategic decisions. Bonus schemes are not anchored to tough performance standards, which should be at least as difficult as those for division managers, plant managers, and other employees who are on incentive pay. CEOs and boards of directors should be evaluated regularly just like rank and file employees.

Responsibility can be restored to compensation committees of boards of directors by allowing shareholders to use the proxy system to nominate and elect independent directors who are more responsive and accountable to the long-term interest of shareholders. Investors could then get the information needed to better analyze performance pay plans and long-term income plans that executives now recommend for themselves. Executive salaries and their justifications should be unambiguously disclosed to stockholders and the general public. Performance control systems could then be better implemented to link pay with performance. No bonuses should be paid until earnings cover the cost of capital and surpass the rate of inflation. Revising methods of determining executive pay will help restore compensation levels that are fair and competitive.

PAUL G. WILHELM

exploitation Under the broadest interpretation, exploitation occurs whenever specific means are determined for accomplishing a task set by interest. The means then become instruments to be used in achieving interest-determined goals. Thus, human life itself is exploitative. However, given that exploitation is an inevitable consequence of human existence, it does not follow that all manifestations of it are necessary or morally acceptable.

To "exploit" is not merely to use, but to use to one's advantage. Although the origin of the word "exploit" goes back only to about the 1430s, the idea has its antecedents in ARISTOTLE's *Nicomachean Ethics*. Roughly, Aristotle maintained that the good of a being is attainable only from actions that accord with its nature as a unique natural kind. This fostered the view that virtue of a species is acquired from its participation in species-specific activities. In the case of persons, if such activities include choosing one's own ends, appropriating materials for producing ends, and participating in activities to assure success, then persons are wrongfully exploited when denied the possibility of attaining their happiness as decision-making entities. Moreover, since Aristotle esteemed human existence as the highest form of organic life, exploitation may involve a reduction in status of equals by those holding a monopoly on the materials of human flourishing.

Psychological Components

The concept of exploitation presupposes the existence of an ego, autonomy, freedom, interest, and a field of contingencies as modalities of interest. The ego establishes an interest in a subjectivity. The idea of human freedom is the condition that enables autonomy to manifest itself as a contingency. By virtue of the contingency displayed and expressed in individual autonomy, we may infer that interest as such, is not biologically given (*see* INTERESTS AND NEEDS). AUTONOMY asserts itself as an appropriating transcendence that transforms interest into an objectivity of some kind.

Metaphysics of Exploitation

As a metaphysical phenomenon, exploitation is a necessary condition for human agency. As Sartre argued, human consciousness is best understood as a desire for being, rather than as being as such. Consciousness is constituted only from its interests and desires. Hence, from the onset of human existence, consciousness is parasitic, and, therefore, necessarily exploitative (Sartre, 1973).

As "exploitative" beings, we are fully responsible for the character of a human existence fashioned from contingencies admitting indefinite possibilities (*see* RESPONSIBILITY). This is to say, the manner of human existence is at bottom choice-determined. Persons do not determine their status as exploitive creatures; they do choose, however, to orient their interest one way or another, and to contemplate whether to adopt principles to constrain the scope and categories of human choices.

Aspects of the Moral Conception of Exploitation

Considerations relating to "constraining principles" on exploitative propensities have traditionally fallen in the realm of political theory and ethics. It is only within the frameworks of such theories that a distinction between good and bad exploitative behaviors can be drawn. Most instances of "exploitation" are not morally objectionable. An even greater number of cases are borderline with respect to their moral permissibility. Among clear cases in which exploitation involves immorality are those that violate the Kantian dictum: "we must always treat persons as ends in themselves, and never as means merely," with special emphasis on the phrase, "as means merely" (*see* KANTIAN ETHICS). Kant believed that the supreme good of persons is their autonomy. Relations that subordinate autonomy can never be of benefit to persons as such, since a trade-off will necessarily involve giving up an absolute value for a conditional value. Kant was, of course, mindful that there may be "circumstances" when allowing oneself to be exploited or even to exploit oneself, may be advantageous for some purpose. However, since contingent objectives never change the "category" of human value, circumstances can never be used to justify exploitation considered immoral in the Kantian sense.

From a political perspective, it is frequently argued that where actions comply with sovereign laws, exploitative activities within legal constraints are acceptable. This method of interpreting exploitation is founded on the view that human value is defined by sovereigns. Where sovereign states manifest different conceptions of value, ideas of immoral exploitation are subject to relativity (*see* RELATIVISM, CULTURAL AND MORAL).

Exploitation Under the Pyramid Model of Organizational Structure

The Pyramid Model of organizational structure is frequently cited as a mechanism with systemic exploitive properties. Put simply, it is believed that only upper-level organizational interests can be realized under the Pyramid Model. The problem associated with this form of exploitation is that most people (since they will exist at the bottom of the organizational chart) are denied the opportunity to develop as interest-bearing subjects. This implies that subjects of equal value are regarded as if they are not. The elite are given primacy of expression solely because of their economic advantages and rank. Thus, their domination of the lower ranks of the pyramid is one of power, not of intrinsic worth.

An Egalitarian Conception of Exploitation

In contrast to the Pyramid Model, Marx and Engels argued that workers are necessarily disadvantaged since their only commodity is their labor (*see* MARX, KARL). The means of production belong to the ruling class. Workers must, for the sake of their survival, accept conditions of employment established by the ruling class, conditions often reducing the worker to the level of a product. To remedy this form of exploitation, Marx and Engels advocated a conception of PROPERTY that would virtually obliterate the Pyramid Model by making "property" a communal phenomenon.

Identifying Instances of Exploitation

The identification of unacceptable instances of exploitation is, at best, difficult. Since the roles of "ability," "interest," and "circumstances," in limiting human success cannot be fully determined, we can never be certain that social/political role assignments are not unduly restrictive. Our conception of "acceptable exploitation," therefore, could be derived from theory about "equality of opportunity" (*see* EQUAL OPPORTUNITY). If the theory permits frequent judgments of unjust exploitation, this would tend to give rise to theory modification or abandonment.

Bibliography

Becker, L. C. & Kipnis, K. (eds). (1984). *Property: Cases, Concepts, Critiques.* Englewood Cliffs, NJ: Prentice-Hall.

Carnoy, M. (1984). *The State and Political Theory.* Princeton: Princeton University Press.

Cohen, G. A. (1988). *History, Labour, and Freedom.* Oxford: Oxford University Press.

Edwards, R. C., et al. (eds). (1986). *The Capitalist System.* Englewood Cliffs, NJ: Prentice-Hall.

Machan, T. R. (Ed.) (1986). *The Main Debate: Communism versus Capitalism.* New York: Random House.

Marx, K. & Engels, F. (1959). *Basic Writings on Politics and Philosophy,* (ed.), L. S. Feuer. Garden City, NY: Doubleday.

Sartre, J.-P. (1973). *Being and Nothingness.* New York: Washington Square Press.

Schweickart, D. (1993). *Against Capitalism.* Cambridge: Cambridge University Press.

Terkel, S. (1974). Here I am a worker. In L. Silk (ed.), *Capitalism: The Morning Target.* New York: Quadrangle, 68–9.

JESSE TAYLOR

externalities are the consequences that one economic agent's actions have on the welfare of others that are not mediated by market prices. The neoclassical model of welfare economics uses prices as a means to motivate and achieve efficient resource allocation. Under a set of ideal conditions, self-interested behavior on the part of individuals and firms leads to an efficient (Pareto optimal) social outcome. This possibility, referred to as the Theorem of the Invisible Hand, emphasizes the mediating role of competitive prices in achieving both private and socially efficient resource allocation (*see* INVISIBLE HAND). If, however, the conditions necessary for the "invisible hand" to hold are not met, then market outcomes can result in inefficient and socially undesirable resource allocations. Externalities are one situation where market mechanisms can fail to provide for socially optimal resource allocations.

In effect, externalities arise when sources of social gain or loss are not translated into market prices. Frequently, this happens because externalities arise when economic activities do not involve legally recognized rights of compensation or liability. For example, water pollution is a classic example of a negative externality. A firm discharging waste into a body of water may detract from the recreational use of the water. The firm's failure to recognize the cost of the pollution (in terms of the clean-up efforts of the municipality or in the disutility caused to the public) leads to the overuse of this resource and a socially inefficient resource allocation. Alternatively, externalities can also have positive consequences. Consider a firm that is evaluating an investment in specialized technical training for employees. In this case the externality has aspects of a public good associated with it as the training is likely to increase the marketable skills of the employees and hence their wages and standard of living. This is a benefit to other firms and the local community. An externality exists because the firm providing the training does not fully capture all of the benefits associated with the decision. As a result, the firm may underinvest in the socially desirable level of training.

One solution to externalities, articulated in the Coase Theorem, is to assign well-defined and marketable rights to the resources in question. By assigning the local municipality the right to "clean water" in the example above, the locality can require that the firm pay for the costs of maintaining clean water. Because this requires the firm to explicitly recognize a cost for using the water, the end result is a more socially optimal resource allocation.

Bibliography

Hirshleifer, J. (1976). *Price Theory and Application.* Englewood Cliffs, NJ: Prentice-Hall.

Milgrom, P. & Roberts, J. (1992). *Economics, Organization and Management.* Englewood Cliffs, NJ: Prentice-Hall.

SUSAN CHAPLINSKY

F

fairness Exactly what constitutes fairness will depend on the specific nature of the decision process or institution in question. Consider, for example, a fair trial, a fair contest, a fair grade, a fair price, a fair agreement, a fair election. This variety of contexts entails a corresponding range of criteria of fairness. All of these, however, generally center on equal treatment of people, with departures from equality requiring justification.

The concept of fairness is closely related to a number of other moral concepts, such as EQUALITY, IMPARTIALITY, and JUSTICE. Like these other notions, it centers on how people are treated by others, especially the requirement that they be treated alike, in the absence of significant differences between them. The distinctive focus of fairness is decision-making processes or institutions that apply rules. For instance, in regard to the application of rules, a fair procedure is one that applies them similarly to all cases, unless there are strong reasons for making exceptions in particular cases. Accordingly, an examination is graded fairly when all papers are judged by the same standards. "Fairness" is generally appealed to in assessing both the means through which decisions are made or rules applied, and the outcomes that are brought about. The former is generally described as "procedural" fairness, the latter as "distributive" fairness. Though these two concerns frequently coincide (i.e., fair procedures give rise to fair outcomes and unfair to unfair outcomes), this is not always the case, and so procedural and distributive fairness should be distinguished. However, though the notion of fairness pertains to both concerns, it is more closely associated with procedures, while the notion of justice bears more particularly on outcomes (*see* DISTRIBUTIVE JUSTICE).

According to the *Oxford English Dictionary*, "fairness" and cognate words have been used in English, with their present sense at least as far back as 1460. But in other languages, closely related concepts are encountered many centuries earlier. For example, in Book V of Thucydides' *History of the Peloponnesian War* (late fifth century BC), the besieged people of Melos ask their besiegers to consider "that in the case of all who fall into danger there should be such a thing as fair play and just dealing (*ta eikota kai dikaia*)" between people (Thucydides, 1972, V, 90). Their request is that strong and weak peoples be treated similarly, regardless of differences in power. In his *Politics* (late fourth century BC), Aristotle makes the important observation that standards of justice or fairness are different in different regimes. In oligarchical regimes, ruled over by the rich, it is thought fair to treat people differently according to their merits, with amount of property constituting degree of merit. In democratic regimes, in contrast, it is considered fair to treat people alike – and so to distribute political offices through a lottery system – with free birth and citizenship constituting being alike (Book V, ch. 1). An important lesson of Aristotle's discussion is that there is no universally recognized standard of fair treatment, in terms of either procedures or distribution. Different ways of dealing with people can plausibly be represented as fair, as long as they treat people who are similar in important respects similarly.

Much of the attention "fairness" has received in recent years is because of the work of John Rawls and his theory of "justice as fairness." In his main work, *A Theory of Justice* (1971), Rawls argues that specific principles of justice can be justified by showing that they would be chosen by representative individuals placed in a carefully constructed, artificial choice situation. To ensure that the choice of principles is not influenced by people's particular interests, Rawls employs a hypothetical "veil of ignorance." Individuals are to make their decision without knowledge of their specific identities or attributes, e.g., economic or social position, religion, sex, age, etc. Because of the representative individuals' concern that, once the veil of ignorance is lifted, they might turn out to be disadvantaged members of society, Rawls argues that they will choose principles that protect the weaker or "least advantaged" members. Rawls calls his theory "justice as fairness," because this name "conveys the idea that the principles of justice are agreed to in an initial situation that is fair" (1971, p. 12).

The need to promote fair distribution in cooperative enterprises has been appealed to by recent scholars – including Rawls – to establish obligations to support such associations. The "principle of fairness" (or fair play) was developed by H. L. A. Hart, in 1955:

> When a number of persons conduct any joint enterprise according to rules and thus restrict their liberty, those who have submitted to these restrictions when required have a right to a similar submission from those who have benefited by their submission. (Hart, 1955, p. 185)

The moral thrust of the principle of fairness is the fair – or just – distribution of benefits and burdens. When a number of people engage in cooperative activity to produce and consume benefits, other people who enjoy the benefits but do not share the costs of providing them (i.e., free-riders) treat the cooperators unfairly. In order to correct this situation, they too should cooperate, in spite of their desire not to (when a number of further conditions are also met). As Hart and other theorists have argued, the principle of fairness can establish people's obligations to bear the burdens of citizenship – most notably obeying the laws of their countries – even if they have not consented to do so.

In recent years, the concept of fairness has also figured prominently in social psychology. Researchers have studied decision processes in judicial, political, business, and other settings, in order to ascertain people's views about procedural fairness – or procedural justice, in this context interchangeable terms. Procedural considerations have been found to have strong effects on research subjects, which are not only distinct from considerations of outcome but frequently more influential, even when outcomes are highly unfavorable. For instance, in assessing a variety of institutions – political, judicial, business – subjects have repeatedly been shown to place greater weight on their views of how decisions are made than on how the outcomes of the decisions affect them (see Lind & Tyler, 1988). Results of empirical tests have also complicated theorists' views concerning the nature of fairness. Subjects have been found to view a decision-making process as fair if it gives them the opportunity to be heard and treats them with respect, rather than focusing on the formal assurances of consistent treatment across cases on which philosophers have traditionally concentrated.

Bibliography

Aristotle. (1981). *The Politics,* Revised edn, eds T. A. Sinclair and T. Saunders. Harmondsworth: Penguin.

Bayles, M. (1990). *Procedural Justice: Allocating to Individuals.* Dordrecht: Kluwer.

Hart, H. L. A. (1955). Are There Any Natural Rights? *Philosophical Review,* **64,** 175-91.

Hochschild, J. (1981). *What's Fair: American Beliefs About Distributive Justice.* Cambridge, Mass.: Harvard University Press.

Klosko, G. (1992). *The Principle of Fairness and Political Obligation.* Savage, Md.: Rowman and Littlefield.

Lind, E. A. and Tyler, T. R. (1988). *The Social Psychology of Procedural Justice.* New York: Praeger.

Rawls, J. (1971). *A Theory of Justice.* Cambridge, Mass.: Harvard University Press.

Thucydides (1972). *History of the Peloponnesian War,* trans. R. Warner. Baltimore: Penguin.

Tyler, T. R. (1988). "What is Procedural Justice?: Criteria Used by Citizens to Assess the Fairness of Legal Procedures," *Law and Society Review,* 22: 103-35.

GEORGE KLOSKO

feminist ethics A diverse range of women-centered *approaches* to moral theory and practice which aim to reinterpret, supplement, and reconceive traditional ethics so that it (1) includes women's as well as men's moral experiences and perspectives and (2) values women as men's moral equals. *Feminine* approaches to ethics favor an ethics of care that emphasizes the importance of nurturant human relationships. Not surprisingly, *maternal* approaches to ethics identify a good mother–child (parent–child) relationship as the most promising paradigm for what counts as a nourishing human relationship. In contrast, *feminist* approaches to ethics emphasize issues of male domination and female subordination, and argue "against patriarchal domination, for equal rights, a just and fair distribution of scarce resources, etc." (Sichel, 1991, p. 90). Finally, *lesbian* approaches to ethics show how traditional ethics disciplines those who deviate from its norms, especially its norm of compulsory heterosexuality.

Although it is tempting to think that women-centered approaches to ethics are late twentieth-century developments, most of them have a long history. Mary Wollstonecraft, John Stuart Mill, Harriet Taylor, Catherine Beecher, Charlotte Perkins Gilman, and Elizabeth Cady Stanton all debated whether morality is or is not gendered. In large measure these eighteenth- and nineteenth-century thinkers set the stage for current discussions about whether "women's ethics" is indeed one of *care* and "men's ethics" one of *justice*, and whether women's traditional role as childbearers and childrearers has caused women, but not men, to think maternally.

Feminine Approaches

Rather than denigrating typically "feminine" characteristics (e.g., nurturing, caring, compassion, benevolence, and kindness) as "soft" virtues for "weak" people, *feminine* ethicists such as Carol Gilligan have presented them as just as morally demanding as typically "masculine" characteristics (e.g., justice, independence, and rationality) (*see* ETHICS OF CARE). In her book, *In a Different Voice*, Gilligan included a study of women making decisions concerning abortion. As she listened to these women's narratives, she heard a language of care that stressed intimate relationships and particular responsibilities instead of a language of justice that emphasized communal well-being and/or individual rights (*see* UTILITARIANISM; MILL, JOHN STUART; KANTIAN ETHICS). Although Gilligan has repeatedly denied that she regards an ethics of care as uniquely "female" and an ethics of justice as uniquely "male," most of her interpreters nonetheless insist that for Gilligan morality is thoroughly gendered. As they see it, Gilligan's work reflects her disagreements with educational psychologist Lawrence Kohlberg about men's and women's relative abilities to develop as full moral agents.

Supposedly, men routinely ascend to Stage Five on Kohlberg's six-stage scale of moral development ("the social contract legalistic orientation"), while women rarely climb past Stage Three ("the interpersonal concordance or 'good boy – nice girl' orientation") (Kohlberg, 1971, pp. 164–5). Instead of viewing this gender difference as evidence of women's moral inferiority, Gilligan interpreted it as a sign that Kohlberg's methodology provided an account not of *human* but of *male* moral development. According to Gilligan, women typically achieve full moral personhood in a way that men typically do not. Whereas men are inclined to measure their moral progress in terms of how autonomous they are becoming, women tend to assess their moral progress in terms of how strongly they are connected to others (Gilligan, 1982, pp. 76–92).

Another thinker who has developed a so-called feminine approach to ethics is Nell Noddings. She argues that ethics is about the overall goodness or badness of actual relationships between individuals. There are, she says, two parties in any relation: the "one-caring" and the "cared-for." When all goes well, the one-caring is motivationally engrossed in the cared-for, and the cared-for welcomes the one-caring's attention, spontaneously sharing his/her aspirations, appraisals, and accomplishments with him/her (Noddings, 1984, p. 9). For Noddings, caring is not a matter of being favorably disposed towards humankind in general. Instead, caring involves both continual communication with particular individuals and active engagement in their lives. Deeds count more than thoughts.

Noddings insists that caregiving is a fundamental *human* activity, something that men as well as women can and should do. She also claims that the one-caring can and should also be a cared-for. Nevertheless most of the carers Noddings describes are women, some of whom seem to care too much – to the point of imperiling their own identity, integrity, and even survival. As a result, a number of critics have faulted Noddings (and Gilligan) for their apparent overemphasis on *women's* capacities for caring. According to critic Sheila Mullet, for example, genuine caring between men and women cannot occur in a patriarchal society. Unless women become men's full political, economic, social, and psychological equals, women cannot care for men in a truly voluntary manner (Mullet, 1988, p. 199).

Maternal Approaches

Clearly related to feminine approaches to ethics are so-called maternal approaches to ethics. Virginia Held, Sara Ruddick, and Caroline Whitbeck stress that the paradigm of contractual transactions between equally informed and equally powerful autonomous men does not serve to illuminate our typical moral transactions. Most of our relationships are between unequals: the young and the old, the client and the professional, the student and the teacher, and so on. As maternal thinkers see it, a good mother–child (or, better, mothering person–child) is the best paradigm to use in assessing the moral quality of these inevitably imbalanced relationships. In the course of striving to preserve, help grow, and make socially acceptable their children, mothers/mothering persons teach themselves as well as their children how to be responsible persons sensitive to the needs and interests of others (Ruddick, 1983, p. 215).

Two sets of critics have challenged maternal approaches to ethics. *Non-feminist* critics object that it is doubtful whether any one human relationship, however good, either can or should serve as the paradigm for all human relationships. *Feminist* critics express similar reservations, underscoring the point that the mother–child relationship is a particularly problematic choice for a moral paradigm, freighted as it is with enough patriarchal baggage to weigh down even the strongest of

women. They reason that a better model for good human relationships is a successful friendship relationship. Created and maintained by a set of interlocking and reinforcing loves, trusts, and emotional commitments, the friendship relationship, like the mother–child relationship, strikes a wider range of moral chords than a legalistic rational-contractor relationship. It has the added advantage, however, of being more equal than a mother–child relationship.

Feminist Approaches

Given that feminine and maternal approaches to ethics have much in common with feminist approaches to ethics, it is challenging to specify what makes an approach to ethics "feminist" as opposed to "feminine" or "maternal." Ultimately, it might be the fact that feminist as opposed to feminine or maternal approaches to ethics tend to ask questions about women's *power*, even more than women's *goodness*, relative to men's. In other words, feminist approaches to ethics stress how traditional ethics mirrors and maintains systems, structures, and patterns of behavior that repress, suppress, and oppress women.

Among others, Alison Jaggar has claimed that traditional ethics contributes to women's subordination in at least five ways. First, traditional ethics shows little concern for women's as opposed to men's interests and rights. Second, it neglects women's issues on the grounds that few morally interesting questions arise in "women's world" – the realm of dishes and diapers. Third, traditional ethics frequently operates on the assumption that women's moral capacities are deficient compared to men's moral capacities. Fourth, it tends to overvalue allegedly masculine traits like "independence, autonomy, intellect, will, wariness, hierarchy, domination, culture, transcendence, product, asceticism, war, death" (Jaggar, 1992, p. 364) on the one hand and to undervalue allegedly feminine traits like "interdependence, community, connection, sharing, emotion, body, trust, absence of hierarchy, nature, immanence, process, joy, peace and life" (Jaggar, 1992, p. 364) on the other. Finally, traditionally ethics devalues women's moral experience by favoring "masculine" ways of thinking that focus on rules, universality, and impartiality over "feminine" ways of thinking that focus on relationships, particularity, and partiality.

Aware of the ways in which traditional ethics has disadvantaged women, Jaggar has concluded that, minimally, any feminist approach to ethics must proceed on the assumption that women and men do not share precisely the same situation in life; offer action guides "that will tend to subvert rather than reinforce the present systematic subordination of women"; provide strategies for dealing with issues that arise in private or domestic life; and "take the moral experience of all women seriously, though not, of course, uncritically" (Jaggar, 1991, p. 366). Women should not focus first and foremost on becoming more perfect carers. Rather, their primary aim should be to resist and overcome gender inequity.

Lesbian Approaches

That feminist approaches to ethics should be so bold as to focus on *women's* concerns is part of what makes them unique and controversial. In a similar vein, lesbian approaches to ethics dare to focus on lesbian concerns thereby taking "particularity" to what even some heterosexual feminists regard as a fault. Although it is difficult to make generalizations about lesbian approaches to ethics, they usually entail a transvaluation of traditional moral values. Mary Daly, for example, insists that she whom the patriarch calls "evil" is in fact good, whereas she whom the patriarch calls "good" is in fact bad. If a woman is to escape the traps men have laid for her – if she is to assert her power, to be all that she can be – then she must realize that it is not good for her to sacrifice herself for the sake of the men and children in her life. What *is* actually good for women is precisely what patriarchy identifies as evil for women – becoming their own persons (Daly, 1984, p. 275).

Additionally, lesbian approaches to ethics usually urge women to replace the question "Am I good?" with the question "Does this contribute to my self-creation, freedom, and liberation?" Just because lesbian ethicists emphasize the role of choice as opposed to duty in ethics does not mean that lesbian ethics is relativistic. On the contrary, Sarah Lucia Hoagland observes that in choosing for herself, a lesbian chooses for other lesbians who in turn choose for her. Lesbians do not weave value in isolation from each other; they weave value together. Ethics is not an individualistic quest. Moral value does not emerge from somewhere inside of one's self or from far outside of one's self, but from the space between one's self and others. A lesbian approach to ethics is about lesbians becoming persons "who are not accustomed to participating in relationships of domination and subordination" (Hoagland, 1988, p. 241). Such persons have "the ability to travel in and out of each other's world" (Lugones, 1987, p. 13). In Hoagland's estimation, an emphasis on "adventure, curiosity, desire" – "seems to take the power out of (traditional) ethics, of being able to make each other behave; ethics ceases to be a tool of control" (Hoagland, 1988, p. 246). Ethics becomes instead a series of open questions, the partial and provisional answers to which emerge as playful souls weave tapestries of meaning together.

Woman-Centered Approaches and Business Ethics

As described here, women-centered approaches to ethics have much to offer the field of business ethics. From *feminine* approaches to ethics, business persons can learn about the value of care and consider ways to restructure the business world so that it becomes more responsive to the concrete needs of particular persons. Similarly, from *maternal* approaches to ethics, business persons can gain the courage to imagine a business world ruled not by the dynamics of a competitive relationship between two rational adult contractors but instead by the dynamics of a cooperative relationship between a mothering-person and a child. Were the business world to adopt feminine and maternal values, it might learn how to pursue maximum profit at minimum human cost – that is, in ways that do not permit the intentional, reckless, or negligent infliction of harm on vulnerable persons such as overworked employees, uninformed consumers, or struggling rivals.

Business persons can also learn much from feminist approaches to ethics. Minimally, they can come to see the gender disparities that characterize the business world. Women and minority men are not paid as much or promoted as quickly and noticeably as men (particularly white men). The "old boys" coexist with the equal-opportunity employers; GLASS CEILINGS and "tokenism" are just as much the order of the day as effective AFFIRMATIVE ACTION PROGRAMS. Moreover, the business world is still organized in ways that make it much more difficult for women than for men to combine family and career. Without supportive maternal (or parental) leave policies and without adequate childcare facilities, businesswomen cannot hope to achieve what businessmen can. Finally, women are far more likely to be sexually harassed by their employers and co-workers than are men.

Ideally speaking, business persons can also learn much from *lesbian* approaches to ethics since structures and systems of male domination and female subordination undoubtedly impede the ability of business to produce quality goods, to provide excellent services, and to make substantial profits. Perhaps the best way for business to achieve its goals is for it to enable each and every person in its network of relationships to develop his/her talents fully. By encouraging all of their employees to be adventuresome, curious, and desirous and to welcome human difference as much as human similarity, employers might find themselves blessed with a fully productive workforce.

Critiques of Woman-Centered Approaches

Whether traditional ethics ultimately acknowledges feminist ethics as a *bona fide* moral enterprise partially depends on the ability of those developing women-centered approaches to ethics to persuade their non-feminist colleagues that ethics can legitimately focus on the concerns of a particular group of people: *women*. What distinguishes a feminist from a non-feminist moral perspective is a so-called feminist standpoint. Although feminists have not fully developed the concept of a feminist standpoint, most of them agree that it identifies women as oppressed persons whose status as victims gives them "access to understanding about oppression that others cannot have" (Bartlett, 1991, p. 385). Moreover, most feminists ground this privileged perspective in the contention that oppressed persons' pain, humiliation, and subordination motivate them to criticize "accepted interpretations of reality" and to develop "new

and less disturbed ways of understanding the world" (Jaggar, 1983, p. 370).

As defined above, a feminist standpoint is vulnerable to at least two lines of criticism. One set of critics object that it is based on the essentialistic notion "Woman" – the view that all women are the same (Tong, 1993, p. 10). In replying to this objection, feminist standpoint theorists emphasize that just because they believe that women are like each other by virtue of their sex does not mean that they deny the many differences among women (class, race, ethnicity, sexual identity, and age). Feminist standpoint theorists do not wish to promote the idea of women understood as a collectivity (who all think the same thought), but the idea of women understood as a plurality (who think different thoughts) (*see* DIVERSITY; MULTICULTURALISM).

Another set of critics object that feminist theory is "female-biased." Whereas traditional ethicists supposedly offered *everyone* objective truth, feminist standpoint theorists offer *women* subjective beliefs. To this criticism, feminist standpoint theorists respond that what traditional ethics identified as *the* truth was nothing of the sort. Like all knowledge, its knowledge was the product of a specific set of experiences – in its case, mostly the experiences of privileged white men. Largely missing from traditional ethics were the experiences of women as well as those of men of color and unprivileged white men. Therefore, far from being truly representative of human moral experience, traditional ethics was very selective.

Conclusion

What women-centered approaches to ethics share is a conviction that denial of perspective does not achieve neutrality; denial of plurality does not bring unity; denial of relationship does not achieve self-identity for the rational, autonomous self. Women-centered ethicists do not offer traditional ethics just another set of approaches, a set of pretty frames through which to view old moral sights. Rather, they offer traditional ethics a new set of spectacles to superimpose upon its old lenses, thus bringing into focus the full range of human moral experience in all its "gendered," "raced," and "classed" diversity.

Bibliography

Bartlett, K. T. (1991). Feminist legal methods. In K. T. Bartlett & R. Kennedy (eds), *Feminist Legal Theory: Readings in Law and Gender*. Boulder, Colo.: Westview Press, 370-403.

Beecher, C. E., & Stowe, H. B. (1987). *The New Housekeeper's Manual*. New York: J. B. Ford and Company.

Daly, M. (1984). *Pure Lust: Elemental Feminist Philosophy*. Boston: Beacon Press.

Gilligan, C. (1982). *In a Different Voice: Psychological Theory and Women's Development*. Cambridge, Mass.: Harvard University Press.

Gilman, C. P. (1979). *Herland: A Lost Feminist Utopian Novel*. New York: Pantheon.

Held, Virginia. (1993). *Feminist Morality: Transforming Culture, Society, and Politics*. Chicago: University of Chicago Press.

Hoagland, S. L. (1988). *Lesbian Ethics*. Palo Alto, Calif.: Institute of Lesbian Studies.

Jaggar, A. M. (1983). *Feminist Politics and Human Nature*. Totowa, NJ: Allanheld.

Jaggar, A. M. (1991). Feminist ethics: Projects, problems, prospects. In C. Card (ed.), *Feminist Ethics*. (Lawrence, Kan.: University Press of Kansas).

Jaggar, A. M. (1992). Feminist ethics. In L. Becker and C. Becker (eds), *Encyclopedia of Ethics*. New York: Garland Press, 363-4.

Kohlberg, L. (1971). From is to ought: How to commit the naturalistic fallacy and get away with it in the study of moral development. In T. Mischel (ed.), *Cognitive Development and Epistemology*. New York: Academic Press, 164-5.

Kourany, J., Sterba, P., & Tong, R. (eds), *Feminist Philosophies: Problems, Theories, and Applications*. Englewood Cliffs, NJ: Prentice-Hall.

Lugones, M. (1987). Playfulness, 'world'-traveling, and loving perception. *Hypatia*. **2**, 13.

Lugones, M., and Spelman, M. (1992). Have we got a theory for you!: Feminist theory, cultural imperialism and the demand for "the woman's voice."

Mill, J. S. (1970). The subjection of women. In A. S. Rossi (ed.), *Essays on Sex Equality*. Chicago: University of Chicago Press, 125-56.

Mullet, S. (1988). Shifting perspectives: A new approach to ethics. In L. Code, S. Mullet, & C. Overall (eds), *Feminist Perspectives: Philosophical Essays on Method and Morals*. Toronto: University of Toronto Press.

Noddings, N. (1984). *Caring: A Feminine Approach to Ethics and Moral Education*. Berkeley: University of California Press.

Ruddick, S. (1983). Maternal thinking. In J. Trebilcott (ed.), *Mothering: Essays in Feminist Theory*. Totowa, NJ: Rowman and Allanheld, 213-30.

Sichel, B. A. (1991). Different strains and strands: Feminist contributions to ethical theory, *Newsletter on Feminism*, **90**, 90.

Taylor Mill, H. (1970). Enfranchisement of women. In A. S. Rossi (ed.), *Essays on Sex Equality*. Chicago: University of Chicago Press.

Tong, R. (1993). *Feminine and Feminist Ethics*. Belmont, Calif.: Wadsworth.

Whitbeck, C. (1983). The maternal instinct. In J. Trebilcott (ed.), *Mothering: Essays in Feminist Theory*. Totowa, NJ: Rowman and Allanheld, 185-98.

Wollstonecraft, M. (1988). *A Vindication of the Rights of Women*, ed. M. Brody. (London: Penguin).

ROSEMARIE TONG

fiduciary duty is a duty of a person in a position of trust to act in the interest of another person without gaining any material benefit, except with the knowledge and consent of that other person.

The term describes the legal duty of trustees, guardians, executors, agents, and others who are in an explicit fiduciary relation, but a fiduciary relation may exist in law whenever one person has superior power or influence over another person and the other person places confidence in or relies on that person. Although it is primarily a legal term, *fiduciary duty* is also used to describe the purely ethical duty of a person in a position of trust. Thus, some breaches of fiduciary duty by lawyers (who are in a fiduciary relation with clients) constitute ethical but not legal misconduct.

In business, officers and directors of corporations are fiduciaries with a duty to act in the interest of the corporation and, to some extent, the stockholders (*see* STOCKHOLDER). Members of partnerships and joint enterprises are fiduciaries with respect to each other's interest; majority stockholders are considered in law to have a fiduciary duty similar to that of officers and directors; and minority stockholders in closely held corporations are fiduciaries under certain conditions. Corporations and their members may have a fiduciary duty toward employees, customers, and other constituencies in such matters as employee pension plans and client investment accounts, and the duty of loyalty that employees have to a firm is sometimes regarded as fiduciary in character.

The concept of fiduciary duty originated in common law for cases in which one person entrusts property to the care of another, and it remains a central concept in the law of trusts. Use of the concept has been extended over time to other trust-like situations in order to prevent abuse when one person has superior power over another. Historically, fiduciary duty belongs to the law of equity, in which courts decide cases on the basis of justice or fairness instead of strictly formulated rules, and the concept developed as a means for imposing duties where precise rules cannot be easily formulated. Fiduciary duties are further unlike the specific duties created by contracts in that they are imposed on all persons in fiduciary relations and cannot be easily altered by the affected parties.

Among the features of fiduciary duty, the most prominent are:

(1) *An open-ended duty to act in the interest of another.* The acts that a person in a fiduciary relation are required to perform are generally not specified in advance, so that a fiduciary has wide latitude in the means used to advance the interests of another. The standards for evaluating the performance of a fiduciary are commonly those of due care, good faith, and, in business, the business judgment rule, all of which can be satisfied by many different acts.

(2) *A closed-in duty to avoid acting in self-interest.* Generally, the acts in a fiduciary's self-interest that violate a fiduciary duty are clearly stated in the law. Among such specific legal prohibitions are self-dealing, acceptance of bribes, direct competition, and use of confidential information

(3) *Strongly mandatory, moralistic character.* Whereas much of corporate law can be altered by agreement or contract between the affected parties, fiduciary duties are relatively unalterable. An agent can engage in self-dealing, for example, with the knowledge and consent of the principal, but courts hold such departures from fiduciary duty to very stringent standards. However, the fiduciary duty of corporate officers and directors cannot generally be waived, even with stockholder approval. Courts have also used highly moralistic words, such as *loyalty*, *trust*, and *honor*, to describe fiduciary duty, thereby giving their rulings moral as well as legal force.

The importance of fiduciary duty for business ethics lies principally in the question, to whom do officers and directors owe a fiduciary duty? The standard answer is that management has a fiduciary duty to stockholders and to stockholders alone, so that corporations ought to be run solely in their interest, which is to say that managers should seek to maximize stockholder wealth (*see* FIDUCIARY RESPONSIBILITY). This stockholder view of the corporation has been challenged on two different grounds. Some critics argue that the ethical basis of a fiduciary duty to serve the interests of stockholders has been undermined by the changed nature of corporate property, caused in part by the separation of ownership and control noted by BERLE and MEANS. Stockholders, according to these critics, do not entrust their property to the managers of corporations but are merely investors who can be said to own only their stock, not the corporation. Thus, Dodd (1932) argued that corporate managers no longer had a strict fiduciary duty to serve the interests of stockholders but were free to operate the corporation for the benefit of diverse constituencies. In the famous Berle–Dodd debate, Berle (1932) agreed that the traditional ethical basis of management's fiduciary duty to stockholders had been undermined but argued against freeing managers to serve other interests because of the danger of unbridled management discretion.

Other critics of the stockholder view of the corporation contend that the same conditions which create a fiduciary duty to serve the interests of stockholders also apply to other constituencies, with the result that a fiduciary duty is owed to these other constituencies as well. Thus, officers and directors may have a fiduciary duty to other investors, such as bondholders, to protect their investments; to employees to maintain remunerative employment; to consumers to meet their needs and to protect them against harm from defective products; and so on. Such arguments lend support to STAKEHOLDER THEORY as an alternative to the stockholder view.

Recent developments in corporate law reflect both of these grounds of criticism, and shifting understandings of the fiduciary duty of management remain central to the ongoing debate over the purpose of corporations and the interests that they ought to serve.

Bibliography

Bayne, D. C. (1958). The Fiduciary Duty of Management: The Concept in the Courts. *University of Detroit Law Review*, **25**, 561–94.

Berle, A. A. (1932). For Whom Corporate Managers Are Trustees: A Note *Harvard Law Review*, **45**, 1365–72.

Bratton, W. W. (1992). Public Values and Corporate Fiduciary Law. *Rutgers Law Review*, **44**, 675–98.

Clark, R. C. (1985). Agency Costs versus Fiduciary Duties. In J. W. Pratt & R. J. Zeckhauser (eds), *Principals and Agents: The Structure of Business.* (pp. 55–79). Boston: Harvard Business School Press.

Dodd, E. M. (1932). For Whom Are Corporate Managers Trustees? *Harvard Law Review*, **45**, 1145–63.

Frankel, T. (1983). Fiduciary Law. *California Law Review*, **71**, 795–836.

Scott, A. W. (1949). The Fiduciary Principle, *California Law Review*, **37**, 539–55.

Sealy, L. S. (1962). Fiduciary Relationships. *Cambridge Law Journal*, 69–81.

JOHN R. BOATRIGHT

fiduciary responsibility   In the law, fiduciary responsibility arises whenever a trust is created. A trust is an arrangement whereby one party, called the trustee or fiduciary, agrees to maintain certain assets for the benefit of another party called the beneficiary. A fiduciary is required to act in good faith on the beneficiary's behalf and must maintain, if not enhance, the value of the assets under his or her care. If a trustee does not fulfill his fiduciary responsibility, the beneficiary has the right to file a lawsuit against the trustee. Common examples of a fiduciary relationship include:

pension manager: an individual or legal entity (e.g. a corporation) that is appointed to make investment decisions for a group of people like the employees of a corporation (see below for further explanation of a pension trust).

executor: an individual or legal entity that administers the estate of a person leaving a will.

guardian: a person appointed by the courts to care for the personal needs and property of another person, most commonly a minor.

An example of a fiduciary relationship is that created when a business firm establishes a trust to provide retirement benefits for its employees. The trust allows a professional money manager (the trustee) to make the investment decisions for the employees (the beneficiaries). Because of fiduciary responsibility, however, the pension manager is required to act solely in the interest of the employees. The US Employee Retirement Income Security Act (ERISA) of 1974 established a broad base of laws covering plan management and administration, standards of fiduciary conduct, and civil and criminal penalties for violations. According to ERISA fiduciary responsibility is defined as the obligation to execute decisions regarding a retirement plan solely in the interest of, and for the exclusive purpose of providing benefits to, the plan's participants and beneficiaries, and to minimize reasonable expenses for administering the plan. In other words, plan fiduciaries must act in the best interest of the plan and of those served by it. If fiduciaries are also plan participants, the fiduciaries must subordinate their own interests to those of the plan. ERISA further defines fiduciary responsibility as the obligation to exercise the "prudent man standard" of common law; i.e., to use the same care, skill, and diligence under the prevailing circumstances that a prudent person acting in a like capacity would employ. This standard of prudence also includes the obligation to consider the suitability of a plan's investment vehicles given the plan's goals and mission, and to diversify the investments of the plan so as to minimize the risk of large losses and protect the interests of the participants (*see* FIDUCIARY DUTY).

Bibliography

Chadwick, W. J. & Hass, L. J. (1978). *The Annotated Fiduciary: Materials on Fiduciary Responsibility and Prohibited Transactions Under ERISA.* Brookfield, Wis.: The International Foundation of Employee Benefit Plans.

Knorr, R. M., Schleifer, L. & Friedlob, G. T. (1993). Managing employee benefit plans: Is your role as fiduciary a personal liability? *Management Accounting (USA)*, **75** (5), 49–53.

McNamara, K. J. (1994). Plan sponsors seek ways to guard against fiduciary liability. *Pension World*, **30** (1), 14–16.

Melbinger, M. S. (1992). ERISA and tax-deferred retirement plans; Employee Retirement Income Security Act of 1974. *Healthcare Financial Management*, **46** (10), 74–5.

KENNETH M. EADES

finance, ethical issues in *see* ETHICAL ISSUES IN FINANCE

financial reporting   can be defined as the organized or systemic process of collecting, processing, and disclosing an organization's economic activity. Data and information in a financial reporting system are typically measured on a transactional basis (e.g., buying inventory or selling merchandise) in one functional currency (e.g., such as dollars, yen, or pounds sterling) using a set of standardized accounting practices known as generally accepted accounting principles (or GAAP). Three primary financial statements are the final outputs of a financial reporting system. This includes the balance sheet, which measures the assets, liabilities, and equity of an organization at a point in time; the income statement, measuring revenues and expenses of an organization over a time period lasting no longer than one year; and the statement of cash flows, measuring the sources and uses of funds over the same time period as the income statement.

The two primary objectives of financial reporting are: 1) to help ensure that the assets of an organization are safeguarded or controlled and 2) that the organization's financial reports are accurately prepared in accordance with GAAP and are provided to financial-statement users in a timely fashion. The beneficiaries of financial reporting include the organization's management, employees, stockholders, creditors, customers, vendors, governmental authorities, and labor unions. The ethical foundation of financial reporting is derived from the accounting principles that clearly specify what, when, and how transactions are or ought to be recorded and disclosed. The ethical implication of financial reporting stems from the general belief that financial statements generated from the system are objective, reliable, and capture the so-called economic reality of the organization. In other words, an ethical financial reporting system is one which provides all relevant users with truthful reports about the financial condition or health of an organization.

An unethical financial reporting system is one that does not meet its fundamental objective of control or reporting information in an ethical and objective fashion. Inaccuracies or errors in financial reports come about because of computational problems and mistakes in the system or because of intentional manipulation and fraud. An example of unintentional error in financial reporting would be an underestimate of a current liability on the balance sheet due to the duplicate payment to vendors because of data-entry problems in the accounts-payable department. The recording of fake or falsified sales invoices by the accounting manager to inflate a company's yearly earnings is clearly an intentional and fraudulent manipulation of financial reports.

While many parties can be influenced by nefarious accounting practices that cause fraudulent financial statements, the ethical domain of financial reporting usually involves two primary constituents: the organization's management and stockholders. In most cases, the organization's management is typically represented by the company's top executives whose performance is inextricably linked to financial results. Stockholders are those individuals and institutions who provide large-scale economic resources to the organization, typically represented by collective interests of major stockholders and board members.

Competing economic interests of different stakeholder groups, such as managers and stockholders, can cause actual and perceived ethical conflict within the organization, often motivating financial management of the company to behave in ways that can compromise the quality and integrity of financial reports (*see* STAKEHOLDER THEORY). Independent auditors and regulatory bodies such as the SECURITIES AND EXCHANGE COMMISSION (SEC) are becoming increasingly concerned about actual and perceived problems in financial reporting systems that can diminish the credibility of a company's financial-statement information. As a result of these concerns, the accounting and financial management communities have made a concerted effort in recent years to study ways of improving financial reporting in terms of its ethical objectives.

See also accounting ethics; ethical issues in corporate finance; ethical issues in finance

Bibliography

Treadway Commission, sponsored in 1987 by the US Financial Executive Institute, the Institute of Internal Auditors, and other organizations. See O'Reilly, V. M. & Committee of Sponsoring Organizations of the Treadway Commission (COSO) (1987). *Internal Control-Integrated Framework.* Available from the American Institute of Certified Public Accountants, Jersey City, NJ.
Kirk Commission

LAWRENCE A. PONEMON

Foreign Corrupt Practices Act (FCPA) A United States law passed in 1977 that prohibits publicly traded US corporations from making illicit payments to officials of foreign governments, to political parties and their officials, or to intermediaries for such purposes. The FCPA is an outcome of a series of investigations of the mid-1970s which revealed that some major US corporations maintained slush funds used for bribery and other dubious payment to officials of a number of foreign governments. Over 300 corporations admitted to hundreds of millions of dollars in such payments, one of which led directly to the fall of a Japanese government and imprisonment of its prime minister.

From the outset, the FCPA was criticized on a number of grounds, most prominently: vagueness, economic loss, and moral unsoundness.

Vagueness. Even after the 1988 amendments, still vague are: (1) what counts as acceptable payments to low-level officials for routine services such as clearance of customs, police protection, and utility service; (2) the extent of allowances for "reasonable and *bona fide* expenditure" – such as for travel and lodging – directly related to promotion of a product or execution of a contract; (3) the level of knowledge of intermediaries' activities that creates liability. It is generally agreed that the FCPA remains vague, perhaps as all laws must be, but

the effect is disputed: Does the vagueness chill honest business dealings, or does it open the door to wider abuses?

Economic loss. Perhaps the strongest objection is that since businesses from other countries are not similarly restricted, the FCPA merely puts US corporations at a competitive disadvantage, resulting in lost profits to shareholders, fewer US jobs, and reduced US tax revenues. Among responses to this objection are that bribery and extortion payments are not often really necessary and that as a matter of fact, US businesses have not lost much in sales; and that a reputation for honest business dealings will pay off in improved long-term economic and political relations with foreign governments and .citizens.

Moral unsoundness. Among moral objections, it has been argued that the FCPA imposes our moral standards on others, that morally valid concern for economic well-being outweighs prohibitions on bribery, and that the most common practice at issue is not bribery corruptly initiated by the US business, but rather extortion in which the business is the victim. Responses include that both bribery and extortion are illegal and judged immoral in virtually every country in the world, as confirmed by the secrecy of such dealings. And against any loss in short-term profit, it must be recognized that complicity in such illicit dealings corrupts the free market and moves international business closer to the state of nature.

The government has only infrequently laid charges under the FCPA and claims have been made that the 1988 amendments have emasculated the law. Large illicit transfers of funds may have become less frequent – or more cleverly disguised – but a law cannot have much impact without the general will that it be followed.

Bibliography

Alpern, K. D. (1983). Moral dimensions of the Foreign Corrupt Practices Act. In T. Donaldson & P. Werhane, (eds), *Ethical Issues in Business*, 4th edn 1993. Englewood Cliffs, NJ: Prentice-Hall. (Defends the morality of the FCPA)
Gillespie, K. (1987). The Middle East response to the US Foreign Corrupt Practices Act. *California Management Review*, summer, pp. 9-30. (Economic impact of the FCPA.)

Pastin, M. & Hooker, M. (1980). Ethics and the Foreign Corrupt Practices Act. *Business Horizons*, Dec., 43-47. Repr. in T. Donaldson & P. Werhane (eds), *Ethical Issues in Business*, 4th edn 1993. Englewood Cliffs, NJ: Prentice-Hall. (Argues that the FCPA is morally unsound.)

Pines, D. (1994). Amending the Foreign Corrupt Practices Act to include a private right of action. *California Law Review*, **82**, 185-229. (Contains a good general overview.)

US Government. (1988). 15 USC §§ 78m(b), 78dd-1, 78dd-2, 78ff (originally enacted as Pub. L. No. 95-213, 91 Stat. 1494 (1977), and amended by Foreign Corrupt Practices Act Amendments of 1988, Pub. L. No. 100-418, 5001-3, 102 Stat. 1107, 1415-25). (Codification of the FCPA.)

KENNETH D. ALPERN

free enterprise A system of organizing economic activity in which the owners of resources land, labor, and capital make the decisions determining how those resources are utilized. The basic assumption underlying free enterprise was articulated by Adam Smith (1776) and is that individuals and firms acting in their own self-interest within a competitive market will allocate resources in an efficient fashion. Efficiency in theoretical discussions or models is usually defined as a Pareto-efficient equilibrium in which resources cannot be reallocated to benefit one individual without reducing the welfare of another. In practice, efficiency is measured by such economic variables as productivity, growth in gross domestic product, or comparative standards of living (*see* SMITH, ADAM).

Outside of theoretical discussions no nation or society has a pure free-enterprise system. Every society imposes some restrictions on the use of economic resources. Restrictions are justified on the basis of market failures that lead to a sub-optimal or inefficient allocation of resources when individuals act without constraint or regulation. Market failures can be broadly classified into three types: lack of competition, the existence of externalities, or the presence of transaction costs.

Adam Smith was the first economist to call attention to the necessity to support a free-enterprise system by preventing non-competitive conditions. He commented on the tendency of manufacturers of the same product to collude in order to increase their profits through higher prices and lower production than would exist in a competitive market. This has led to antitrust laws and a broad range of restrictions that limit the scope of firms' actions. For similar reasons the determination that some industries are natural monopolies, and if left unregulated would lead to inefficient resource utilization, has led to the designation of public utilities as regulated industries in which outputs and prices are set through a political, legal, or governmental process and not by market forces.

Externalities exist when the costs or benefits to society are not fully reflected in the prices of goods or services. If the price does not fully include the cost then individuals will be led to overuse or overproduce a good because they do not have to bear the true or real burden of their actions. Environmental legislation is often proposed on the basis of arguments supporting the existence of externalities. Hardin (1993) uses externalities to show how public goods, those not owned by individuals, are under-invested in by society because the market fails to account for the externalities associated with them.

Finally, the cost of maintaining or participating in a market might lead to the need for restrictions or regulation. Schelling (1978) suggests that market activity entails a cost that cannot always be allocated to the individual and, therefore, some form of state involvement is made necessary. The need for traffic lights is a mundane but informative example of the difficulty of assigning the right of way through an intersection by reliance on price.

The determination that a particular market failure of any of the three types exists is subject to dispute. Coase (1960) has argued that markets are very robust and can adjust or internalize supposed market failures in many situations. Consequently he has argued for fewer restrictions.

The extent of state intervention is highly variable across nations and over time in any one nation. One way to describe whether a nation is disposed towards a free-enterprise system is to look at the nature of the legal system. Where free enterprise is the dominant system laws and regulations delineate what cannot be done. In a society where free enterprise does not exist laws and regulations state what is allowed.

Bibliography

Coase, R. H. (1960). The problem of social cost. *The Journal of Law Economics*, 3.

Hardin, G. (1993). The tragedy of the commons. *Valuing the Earth*. Boston: MIT Press, 127–43.

Schelling, T. C. (1978). *Micromotives and Macrobehavior*. New York: W. W. Norton.

Smith, A. (1776; 1976). *An Inquiry into the Nature and Causes of the Wealth of Nations*. New York and Oxford: Oxford University Press.

MARK EAKER

free speech in the workplace   Free speech is the ability to express oneself without seeking prior clearance and without fear of subsequent reprisal.

Free speech is one of the first rights enumerated in the United States Constitution. Its position in that document reveals the moral importance that its framers accorded to the free expression of ideas. In the US context, however, the right to free speech is a limited right possessed by citizens against their *government*. The constitutional protection of speech is a constraint only against government actions; it provides no bar even against a private employer's discharge of an employee for speaking, outside the workplace, on behalf of political causes opposed by the employer. (We should note, though, that such a discharge, while not unconstitutional, may be illegal according to statute in specific states.)

If the Constitution provides no protection for employee speech in the private sector, traditional US labor law provided scarcely much more. The doctrine of EMPLOYMENT AT WILL allowed employers to dismiss for any reason or for no reason (*see also* JUST CAUSE).

An employer's almost total employer discretion to discharge has been limited in the last few decades. For example, courts have held that firing for speech disclosing serious product safety hazards violates public policy. Courts have also limited the traditional duty of LOYALTY the employee owes as an agent by excepting actions (including speech) that are

illegal or unethical (*see* AGENCY THEORY). Perhaps the major legal protection for employee speech can be found in legislation. For instance, the Wagner Act (1935) makes it illegal to discharge employees for promoting unionization; the Occupational Safety and Health Act (1970) makes it illegal to discipline workers who request safety inspections of the workplace.

These protections notwithstanding, most commentators would accept that legal protection for employees' speech remains quite limited when compared to the more extensive constitutional protection from government interferences that citizens enjoy. The moral question is whether a more extensive right to free speech *ought* to apply to the workplace. The answer to that question will depend on the moral foundations that can be offered for a right to free speech.

Traditionally, rights to free speech have been justified as both instrumentally and intrinsically valuable. One instrumental defense of free speech holds that citizens' freedom of expression is required for the health of democratic government. If government can effectively control the speech of its citizens, it could prevent citizens from debating and criticizing government policy, effectively limiting democratic self-determination. If democracy has moral importance, so would a right to freedom of expression.

A second instrumental defense claims that the best hope for arriving at truth, if only in the long run, is through allowing competing opinions to be tested in a free marketplace of ideas.

A non-instrumental defense of free speech argues that it is a necessary condition for treating persons with due respect. Morality holds that human persons have a special moral status that requires they be treated with dignity. The source of that dignity is often explained by the fact that persons are unique in their autonomy, their ability to make reasoned choices about their lives. Respect for persons demands that they be able to engage in open discussion about important aspects of their lives.

Do these moral arguments justify an extension of free speech rights to the workplace? Some argue No. They would claim that (1) in a free competitive economy, employees can find alternative employment and avoid a specific corporation's restrictions on their speech; (2) rights against the government are necessary because the threat to the well-being of citizens from a totalitarian government is much greater and the avoidance costs much higher than for any specific authoritarian corporate policy (especially given (1), above); (3) strict control over the workforce is required for efficient production, and employee rights to free speech would undermine the necessary discipline.

Others find these reasons unconvincing in that (1) they overstate the difference, both in potential harm and avoidance costs, between governmental and corporate exercises of power; (2) alternative employment (a) requires forgoing time and firm-specific skills invested in one's job, (b) may not be readily available and, (c) in any case, may not be any different with regard to free speech; and (3) the need for efficiency has not been proven to preclude the possibility of carefully circumscribed employee rights (e.g., open communication may increase work satisfaction and productivity while threats of reprisal may dampen them). Most importantly, however, the proponents of employee rights to free speech will point out that the arguments critical of that right fail to address the crucial connection between respect and free speech.

Even those willing to defend employees' speech rights must admit that some limits on speech are necessary. For example, when, if ever, would outside political activities be grounds for corporate disciplinary action? Most proponents of employee rights would not accept an answer to that question that stated "whenever the political activities are in conflict with the economic interests of the firm," since that would threaten, say, an insurance company nurse from urging legislative passage of a single-payer health insurance system. Would support of racist policies by an employee of a firm with a large black client base be any different?

Similarly, proponents of employee rights to free speech still need to answer, with justifications, questions as the following: whether, and under what conditions, an act of WHISTLE-BLOWING ought to be protected; how far should a right to express grievances about corporate policy to co-workers and supervisors go?

Recently adopted corporate racial and SEX-UAL HARASSMENT policies raise questions about the range of employee speech rights as well.

Some have argued that these policies are vague in their definition of harassment and insufficient in their guarantees of due process for accused employees, with the effect that even acceptable speech is "chilled." So, even if one agrees that rights to free speech ought to extend to the workplace, much analysis remains before the specific content of that right can be identified.

Bibliography

Bingham, L. (1994). Employee free speech in the workplace: Using the First Amendment as public policy for wrongful discharge actions. 55 *Ohio State Law Journal* 341.

Blades, L. (1967). Employment at will vs. individual freedom: On limiting the abusive exercise of employer power. 67 *Columbia Law Review* 1405.

Ewing, D. (1977). *Freedom Inside the Organization*. New York: McGraw-Hill.

Martin, D. (1978). Is an employee bill of rights needed? In Johnson, M. B. (ed.), *The Attack on Corporate America*. New York: McGraw-Hill.

Novosel, v. *Nationwide Insurance Company*. 721 F. 2d 894 (3d Cir 1983).

Summer, C (1976). Individual protection against unjust dismissal: Time for a statute. 62 *Virginia Law Review* 481.

Werhane, P. (1985). *Persons, Rights and Corporations*. Englewood Cliffs, NJ: Prentice-Hall.

Westin, A. and Salisbury, S. (eds) (1980). *Individual Rights in the Corporation*. New York: Pantheon.

JOHN J. MCCALL

free will   Although the term is used in different ways, an individual has free will to the extent that he has the sort of freedom typically associated with moral responsibility. That is, free will is the freedom that is relevant to moral responsibility. There are various notions of freedom that might be relevant to moral responsibility.

The first kind of freedom is "freedom of the will." When one has freedom of the will, one has a certain sort of freedom with respect to certain motivational states, such as "willing," "trying," "choosing," etc. Regarding "choosing," when one has freedom of the will with regard to a certain act X, then one can choose to do X and one can choose not to do X. Thus, freedom of the will entails freedom to "will" (or, say, choose) otherwise; it implies the existence of a certain sort of alternative possibility.

Similarly, when one has freedom of action with regard to a certain action X, one can either do X or refrain from doing X. Freedom of action, like freedom of the will, entails the existence of alternative possibilities. When one has freedom of action, one has freedom to do otherwise.

Although we ordinarily suppose we sometimes do possess these sorts of freedom, can we be confident of this upon reflection? Perhaps the most disturbing challenge to our confidence comes from the possibility that "causal determinism" obtains. Causal determinism is roughly the claim that everything that occurs at any time is causally necessitated by prior states of the world and the laws of nature. More carefully, the doctrine of causal determinism is the thesis that, for any given time, a complete statement of the facts about the world at that time, together with a complete statement of the laws of nature, entails every truth as to what happens after that time.

It is not clear that causal determinism is true. But neither can we be certain that it is false. It may turn out that scientists in the future will develop a causally deterministic picture of the world. Given this possibility and the importance of freedom to moral responsibility, it is important to consider the relationship between causal determinism and freedom.

It is controversial what the relationship is between freedom and determinism. Some philosophers have argued for "incompatibilism" – the doctrine that freedom (of the type under consideration) is incompatible with causal determinism. On the other hand, some philosophers are "compatibilists": they believe that freedom and causal determinism are consistent.

Regarding the argument which purports to show that, if causal determinism obtains, then no one possesses either of the first two types of freedom, we begin by assuming that causal determinism obtains and that I do something quite ordinary, such as raise my hand at some time T. Because causal determinism obtains, we know that conditions in the past relative to T together with the natural laws entail that I raise my hand at T. Thus, if I am free to do otherwise at T, i.e., to refrain from raising my arm, then either I am free to so act that the past relative to T would have been different in some respect from what it actually was, or I am free to so act

that some natural law which actually obtained would not have obtained. But I cannot so act that the past would have been different from what it actually was. And I cannot so act that a natural law which actually obtained would not have obtained. That is, both the past and the natural laws are "fixed." Thus, if causal determinism is true, I am not free at T to refrain from raising my hand, and, in general, if causal determinism is true, I am never free to do (choose) otherwise. The Basic Argument for Incompatibilism proceeds from intuitive principles putatively capturing the ideas of the fixity of the past and the fixity of the natural laws to the conclusion that if causal determinism obtains, then we do not possess the sort of freedom that entails alternative possibilities. And if moral responsibility requires freedom of this sort, then the argument poses a threat to our confidence in our moral responsibility.

Is the Basic Argument for Incompatibilism sound (i.e., both logically valid and possessing all true premises)? The formulation can be sharpened so that it can be seen to be a valid argument. The crucial questions then are whether the premises expressing the fixity of the past and the fixity of the natural laws are true (and thus whether the argument is sound).

Some compatibilists, who might be dubbed "multiple-pasts compatibilists," deny the fixity of the past premise. They distinguish between two ways of capturing the insight that the past is fixed:

(FP1) No one can at any time initiate a backwards-flowing causal sequence issuing in the occurrence of some event in the past that did not actually occur.

(FP2) No one can at any time perform any action such that if he were to perform it, some event that did not actually occur in the past would have occurred.

The multiple-pasts compatibilist will claim that whereas (FP1) is true, (FP2) is not. Further, the claim is that (FP2) is required by the Basic Argument.

The multiple-pasts compatibilist will want to justify his distinction between (FP1) and (FP2) by insisting that, whereas it is clear that we cannot initiate backwards-flowing causal chains, there is no incoherence in the conjunction of a "can–claim" (I can at T refrain from raising my arm) and a "backtracking conditional" (If I were at T to refrain from raising my arm, the past would have been different in some respect from what it actually was). The incompatibilist, in contrast, will insist that if the pertinent "back-tracker" is true and thus is a necessary condition of performing the action in question to make the past different from what it actually was, it follows that the can-claim is false.

Other compatibilists, who might be dubbed "local-miracle compatibilists," deny the fixity-of-the-laws premise. They distinguish between two ways of capturing the insight that the natural laws are fixed:

(FL1) No one can ever do something which itself would be or cause a violation of a natural law.

(FL2) No one can ever do something which is such that were he to do it, some violation of an actually-obtaining natural law would occur at some time.

The local-miracle compatibilist will claim that, whereas (FL1) is true, (FL2) is not. Further, the claim is that (FL2) is required by the Basic Argument.

The local-miracle incompatibilist will want to justify his distinction between (FL1) and (FL2). He will claim that whereas it is obvious that (FL1) is true – no one can fly faster than the speed of light, etc. – it is not so obvious that (FL2) is true. In denying (FL2) the local-miracle compatibilist is asserting the coherence of a "can-claim" (I can at T refrain from raising my hand) and a certain sort of conditional (If I were to refrain from raising my hand at T, then some law which actually obtained would have been violated, perhaps immediately prior to T). Note that this sort of incompatibilist is not committed to the truth of obviously wild "can-claims," such as that I can jump to the moon, etc.

The incompatibilist, in contrast, will insist that (FP2) is no less appealing than (FP1). He will insist that if it is a necessary condition of performing a certain action that an actually-obtaining natural law be violated, then one cannot perform the action. He will claim that

our concepts of "natural law" and "freedom" imply that there is no important difference between (FL1) and (FL2).

The Basic Argument is, then, a powerful argument for the incompatibility of the alternative-possibilities types of freedom and causal determinism. Given that causal determinism might be true, if one wishes to protect moral responsibility from the threat posed by the Basic Argument, one must either take one of the compatibilistic tacks described above, or deny that moral responsibility requires the sort of freedom that entails alternative possibilities.

This brings us finally to the third kind of freedom pertinent to moral responsibility. This sort of freedom is exercised by an individual who acts (or "wills") freely. It is claimed by some philosophers that this sort of freedom (which can be applied either to motivational states, such as choosing, or to actions themselves) need not require genuine alternative possibilities. That is, it is alleged by some philosophers that one can freely choose to do X without having the freedom to choose not to do X, and that one can freely do X without having the freedom to refrain from doing X. The first types of freedom – freedom of the will and freedom of action – are "alternative-possibilities" notions of freedom, whereas the third type of freedom – acting freely – is an "actual-sequence" notion of freedom.

But this last kind of freedom might seem to be no genuine sort of freedom at all. If one does not have alternative possibilities, how can one be thought to have freedom with respect to one's choice or action? To help to motivate the view that there is indeed an "actual-sequence" notion of freedom, consider the following example (Frankfurt, 1969 and 1971). Imagine, if you will, that Black is a rather talented, experimental, and adventuresome neurosurgeon. In performing an operation on Jones to remove a brain tumor, Black inserts a mechanism into Jones's brain which enables Black to monitor and control Jones's activities. Jones, meanwhile, knows nothing of this. Black exercises this control through a sophisticated computer which he has programmed so that, among other things, it monitors Jones's voting behavior. If Jones were to show any inclination to vote for George Bush, then the computer, through the mechanism in Jones's brain, intervenes to ensure that he actually chooses to vote for Bill Clinton and does so vote. But if Jones chooses on his own to vote for Clinton, the computer does nothing but continue to monitor – without affecting – the goings-on in Jones's head.

Suppose that Jones chooses to vote for Clinton on his own, just as he would have if Black had not inserted the mechanism into his head. It seems that Jones freely chooses to vote for Clinton, and that Jones freely votes for Clinton. After all, Black's mechanism plays absolutely no role in Jones's deliberations and the process that leads to his action of voting for Clinton. Further, it seems that Jones can be held morally responsible for his choice and act of voting for Clinton, although he could not have chosen otherwise and he could not have done otherwise.

It is at least plausible then to suppose that the third type of freedom – the "actual-sequence" type of freedom – is sufficient for moral responsibility. Further, the claim would be that the Basic Argument does not produce any reason to think that causal determinism rule out *this* sort of freedom. Thus, according to this "actual-sequence approach," causal determinism does not pose a decisive challenge to our moral responsibility (Fischer, 1994).

So far the focus has been on the threat posed to freedom by causal determinism. But there is also a threat posed for freedom by the *lack* of causal determinism, as follows. If what I do is not causally determined by the past (including my deliberations), then it seems that I am not in control of what happens. If what I do is not causally determined, then it would seem entirely arbitrary that I behave in the way I actually behave rather than otherwise. Thus, the lack of causal determinism poses a threat to the idea that I have the kind of control (and freedom) required for moral responsibility.

Some philosophers have taken this threat to be a decisive reason to adopt incompatibilism about indeterminism and freedom. Others have attempted to generate an account of the pertinent sort of freedom according to which indeterminism is compatible with freedom. On such an approach, one claims that indeterminism need not entail randomness and arbitrariness, and thus, that indeterminism is consistent with the type of control required for the freedom that is relevant to moral responsibility.

So, finally, do we have free will? It depends on what one means by "free will," what sorts of claims one is willing to embrace, and how the world is. If free will implies alternative possibilities, then there is a strong challenge to our possession of it based on the possible truth of causal determinism. (There is a similar challenge, which I have not presented here, based on the existence of an omniscient God.) But if one adopts the "actual-sequence" picture of free will (according to which one can exercise freedom without having alternative possibilities), then the threat from determinism (or God) is not so worrisome.

Substantial portions of this entry appeared in Lawrence C. Becker and Charlotte B. Becker (eds) *Encyclopedia of Ethics* (pp. 358–88). New York: Garland Publishing, 1992.

Bibliography

Dennett, D. (1984). *Elbow Room: The Varieties of Free Will Worth Wanting*. Cambridge, Mass.: MIT Press.

Fischer, J. M. (ed.). (1986). *Moral Responsibility*. Ithaca: Cornell University Press.

Fischer, J. M. (1994). *The Metaphysics of Free Will: An Essay on Control*. Oxford: Blackwell.

Fischer, J. M. & Ravizza, M. (eds). (1993). *Perspectives on Moral Responsibility*. Ithaca: Cornell University Press.

Frankfurt, H. (1969). Alternative possibilities and moral responsibility. *Journal of Philosophy*, **65**, 828–39.

Frankfurt, H. (1971). Freedom of the will and the concept of a person. *Journal of Philosophy*, **68**, 5–20.

Ginet, C. (1990). *On Action*. Cambridge: Cambridge University Press.

Strawson, G. (1986). *Freedom and Belief*. Oxford: Clarendon Press.

van Inwagen, P. (1983). *An Essay on Free Will*. Oxford: Clarendon Press.

Wolf, S. (1990). *Freedom Within Reason*. New York: Oxford University Press.

JOHN MARTIN FISCHER

freedom of contract   The view that competent individuals should be at liberty to enter into private, consensual exchange agreements of their choosing, without interference from third parties, including governments. To the extent that government has an active role in economic life, it is to protect this freedom and to help enforce the contracts made under it. Belief in freedom of contract is generally accompanied by an endorsement of extensive individual PROPERTY RIGHTS.

This belief in individual liberty grew out of the major Western political and social transformations of the seventeenth and eighteenth centuries. The transformations were driven by doubts about external moral authority, increasing faith in individual rationality, and a new appreciation of the potential of freely functioning markets. Consent became the preferred ground for obligation in political and private life.

Freedom of contract is supported by two distinct, but often intertwined traditions: classical LIBERALISM and free-market economics. Classical liberalism has its intellectual roots in JOHN LOCKE's writing on civil government and JOHN STUART MILL's work on liberty. It has received recent expression in the LIBERTARIAN-ISM of ROBERT NOZICK. Classical liberalism emphasizes the inherent moral value of individual autonomy and private property rights. The core idea is that people should be free to govern their lives and their property, so long as they do not obstruct the rights of others to do the same. Free-market economics, on the other hand, derives the value of contractual freedom from a theory of social welfare (see WELFARE ECONOM-ICS). Often associated with ADAM SMITH, this line of reasoning has found more recent champions in FRIEDRICH HAYEK and MILTON FRIEDMAN. They argue that prosperity (or, more precisely, economic efficiency) is a social good of overriding importance, and that it is best achieved when people are free to seek their own gain. Just as liberals are skeptical about external moral authority, these economists are skeptical about centrally controlled social engineering.

Though few would deny that contractual freedom has some value, critics have raised a number of questions about its legitimate extent. Even the proponents of freedom of contract recognize a need for limits. All but the most radical add two qualifications. The first is that private contractual agreements should not unjustly harm third parties. The second is that neither party to an agreement should use force or fraud. Breach of either condition could provide a rationale for societal intervention.

For most proponents, these are the only conditions that justify interference with private contracts and they are to be interpreted very narrowly. Critics, however, support more extensive grounds for intervention. These may be simplified into three areas: remedying defects in voluntariness, protecting community interests, and preventing self-destructive behavior.

Defects in Voluntariness. Both the liberal and economic defenses of freedom of contract seem to rest on the idea that individuals make informed, rational, and free choices. The value of freedom is questionable when people make uninformed, irrational, or impaired choices. Critics argue that the prohibition against force and fraud does not go far enough. Even mentally competent adults who are not subject to force or fraud may lack crucial information and may not know they lack it; the costs of personally gathering missing information (search costs) may be very high; even if provided with the information, they may not have the education or capacity to understand it, especially with complex products; they may be pressed to make a decision without enough time to think it through; they may be in a state of mind that temporarily impairs their reasoning; they may be acting under some form of duress; they may be subtly manipulated in some way; or, they may have very little relative bargaining power. Some critics go so far as to suggest that the very idea of a free choice that is not corrupted by social conditioning and constrained by external circumstances is a chimera.

More moderate critics use common defects in voluntariness to assert that societies have an obligation to create favorable decision-making conditions and to protect people when these conditions do not obtain. They argue for a wide array of regulations and legal protections, from information disclosure requirements to "cooling off" periods in which parties have a right to rescind a contract. Proponents respond that individuals can and should learn to protect themselves from unfavorable conditions. *Caveat emptor* is a common corollary to freedom of contract.

Community Interests. Some critics go further to argue that communities have a legitimate interest in many private contracts. Proponents open the door to community interests by acknowledging that unjust harm to third parties may justify social intervention. Though it is not what proponents had in mind, interpreted broadly, harm to third parties could include intangible harms to the community, its social fabric, and its shared values. In this regard, communities often attempt to limit the kinds of things subject to market exchange (or "commodified"). Economic exchanges that have been outlawed include the sale, for example, of sexual services (prostitution and surrogacy), votes in an election, public offices, human organs, oneself into slavery, and babies. In many early societies, even land was not treated as a commodity to be owned or traded. Beyond blocking exchanges, communities might want to regulate them to preserve shared values and objectives. Examples of social values potentially threatened by private contracts include DISTRIBUTIVE JUSTICE, preservation of human dignity, community aesthetics, and the absence of discrimination against religious, ethnic, or gender groups. Social values of this sort have been used to argue for rent control, minimum wage laws, health and safety regulations, zoning restrictions, AFFIRMATIVE ACTION, and limits on the production and sale of pornography.

Communitarian critics of freedom of contract argue that harm to community values can justify social interference with private contracts. Proponents of contractual freedom counter this argument by pointing out the potentially oppressive results of allowing this type of restraint. Community values about the appropriate role and worth of women and minority groups have been used to justify discrimination. Proponents also point out the costs of these constraints. They argue, for instance, that minimum wage laws increase unemployment, and the absence of a market in human kidneys for transplants limits the supply and results in more deaths from kidney disease.

Self-Destructive Behavior. A few critics of freedom of contract go further. Even when conditions of informed voluntary choice are met, people may choose to engage in economic exchanges that are not judged to be in their own long-term interest. This judgment may be made by the individuals themselves in more reflective moments, by elders who have more life experience, or by some collective social assessment. Even if such contracts are isolated and do not negatively impact others in the community,

some would argue that society should play the role of protecting people from themselves. Examples in this area are difficult to identify because they often raise issues of voluntariness and community values as well. Common candidates, however, are drug laws, laws against assisted suicide, and laws against gambling. Liberal proponents tend to respond to paternalistic criticisms by arguing that it is none of society's business if individuals choose self-destructive paths that do not directly harm others. This is an objectionable form of *paternalism.* Economic proponents stress the fact that mentally competent adults are in a better position than anyone else to determine what is in their own best interest, even if their judgment is not perfect and even if it changes over time.

Courts and legislatures have been sympathetic to many of these criticisms, leading some observers to claim that freedom of contract is dead. However, others see this freedom expanding, as societies experiment with new commodities (such as sexual surrogacy and organ sales) and as former communist countries embrace free markets. What is certain is that the extent and limits of freedom of contract will continue to be a contentious and rich issue of debate for the foreseeable future.

See also **autonomy; coercion; economic efficiency; economics and ethics; efficient markets; externalities; free enterprise; individualism; liberty; rational choice theory**

Bibliography

Andre, J. (1992). Blocked exchanges: A taxonomy. *Ethics,* **103,** 29-47. (An extensive survey with references to the literature.)

Atiyah, P. S. *The Rise and Fall of Freedom of Contract.* Oxford: Oxford University Press.

Friedman, M. (1962). *Capitalism and Freedom.* Chicago: University of Chicago Press.

Hayek, F. (1960). *The Constitution of Liberty.* Chicago: University of Chicago Press.

Nozick, R. (1974). *Anarchy, State, and Utopia.* New York: Basic Books.

Paul, E. F., Miller F. D. Jr., & Paul, J. (1985) (eds), *Ethics and Economics.* Oxford: Blackwell. (Particularly the essays by Amartya Sen and Allan Gibbard.)

Trebilcock, M. J. (1993). *The Limits of Freedom of Contract*. Boston: Harvard University Press. (A comprehensive treatment.)

J. GREGORY DEES

Friedman, Milton   A Nobel laureate whose main contributions to business ethics are his defense of free-market capitalism and his theory about the social responsibilities of business.

Friedman on Government Regulation of Business

Friedman criticizes many ordinary forms of government regulation of business. Among other things, he attacks anti-discrimination laws, laws requiring that one possess a license to practice certain professions, minimum-wage laws, consumer protection laws, and occupational safety laws.

Friedman's Theory about the Social Responsibilities of Business

Friedman first states his theory about the social responsibilities of business in the following passage from *Capitalism and Freedom*:

> In such an economy ["a free economy"], there is one and only one social responsibility of business – to use its resources and engage in activities designed to increase its profits so long as it stays within the rules of the game, which is to say, engages in open and free competition without deception or fraud. (1963, p. 133)

In his later essay "Social responsibility of business" he states his theory as follows:

> In a free-enterprise, private property system, a corporate executive is an employee of the owners of the business. He has direct responsibility to his employers. That responsibility is to conduct the business in accordance with their desires, which will generally be to make as much money as possible while conforming to the basic rules of the society, both those embodied in law and in ethical custom. (1970)

These two formulations of his theory are *not* equivalent and have different implications for a wide range of cases (see Carson, 1993).

Friedman's Arguments

Friedman's arguments against various forms of government regulation assume that there is a strong moral presumption against coercion. His arguments also appeal to the following "factual" claims: 1) free markets tend to correct many of the problems addressed by government regulation, for example, discrimination and monopolies; 2) free markets can provide many of the services now provided by the government, for example, food inspection and consumer product safety information, and can do so without the objectionable paternalism that government regulation involves; 3) government regulation of business produces many bad consequences (for example, laws requiring the licensing of members of certain professions unfairly restrict entry into those professions and force the public to pay much higher prices than it would otherwise have to).

Friedman's defense of his theory of the social responsibilities of business also depends importantly on factual claims about the workings of the market. With some qualifications about "neighborhood effects" such as pollution, he thinks that businesses best promote the general welfare by aiming at their own interests (provided that they follow "the rules of the game"). He also proposes the following arguments: 1) Business executives have no special competence to directly promote the general welfare and are unlikely to do so when they aim at it directly. 2) Since they were not democratically elected and are not accountable to the general public, business executives should not impose their own visions of the public good on society. 3) When businesses sacrifice profits for the sake of promoting social ends, for example, contributing money to charitable causes, they are violating the rights of shareholders and, in effect, *stealing* their money.

See also **corporate philanthropy; fiduciary duty; invisible hand, the; Knight, Frank; managerial ethics and the ethical role of the manager; social responsibility**

Bibliography

Carson, T. (1993). Friedman's theory of corporate social responsibility. *Business and Professional Ethics Journal*, **2**, 3–32. (Notes inconsistencies in Friedman's formulations of his theory of corporate social responsibility. Criticizes Friedman's theory on several different grounds.)

Donaldson, T. (1982). *Corporations and Morality*. Englewood Cliffs, NJ: Prentice-Hall. (An excellent and thorough discussion of the social responsibilities of business; critical of Friedman.)

Friedman, M. (1963). *Capitalism and Freedom*. Chicago: University of Chicago Press.

Friedman, M. (1970). Social responsibility of business. *New York Times Magazine*, Sept. 13.

Friedman, M. (1972). Milton Friedman responds. (Interview with John McClaughry.) *Business and Society Review*, Spring, pp. 5-17. (Arguably contains a third version of Friedman's theory of corporate social responsibility.)

THOMAS L. CARSON

future generations The moral issue involved is the proper treatment of the people who will come after us as inhabitants of the earth.

This basic moral question can be expressed very simply: "What sort of world do we want to leave for our children?" Should we take what we need now in the way of the natural resources (scarce oil, ore, and timber), the public goods (clean air, water, and land) and the financial, social, and political capital that has been bequeathed to us, and leave the members of future generations to fend for themselves? Or, should we restrict our usage of those resources, goods, and forms of capital out of a sense of duty to those not yet born?

The ethical analysis of this basic moral question is not simple. It is a form of inquiry frequently termed transgenerational justice (though certainly concepts of rights, benefits, and duties are also relevant), and it is made complex by empirical uncertainties, finite limits, value disagreements, and symmetrical inconsistencies. This entry will take up each of these complicating factors first, and then briefly discuss the various forms of ethical inquiry that have been attempted.

Complicating Factors in Transgenerational Moral Issues

Most modern ethical theories assume a timeless world. It is a world limited to the interests of the persons living at a single period who make trade-offs between those interests. Once we add the dimension of time – and this is time extending beyond the immediately adjacent generations – we add a number of very severe complications:

Empirical uncertainties. Forecasting economic, social, and technological change over a period of three to four generations is an exceedingly imprecise art. We do not know what future conditions will be like, and therefore it is frequently unclear what actions might be taken now in the hope of improving those conditions. For example, should we conserve our supplies of carbon-based energy (coal, oil, and natural gas), or should we rely upon the hoped-for means of converting sunlight to electricity.

Finite limits. Regardless of technological advancements, most of the natural resources and public goods of this world are severely limited. Locke recognized this limitation with his proviso to the right of property ownership that "enough and as good be left for others." (*See also* LOCKE, JOHN.) Unless this proviso is accepted as a base for transgenerational issues, we are rapidly into the situation described by Hardin (1968) where the rational self interests of many individuals are shown to destroy the limited resources and goods held in common.

Value disagreements. Population control is frequently prescribed as the cure for finite resources. Fewer total people will obviously have lower total demands, but we are left to decide how many people are too many, and that depends upon the style of life that is desired. You may want beautiful vistas and abundant wildlife. I may prefer large extended families. Both are doubtless "good" in any rational sense of that word, yet how are we to decide between them?

Symmetrical inconsistencies. Trade-offs between contemporaries can be considered as contracts based upon mutual advantage or mutual agreement, and it is hard to fault either as being morally "wrong" in some way. This simplifying view is not valid for future generations. Here we encounter a one-way street, where no mutual advantage or mutual agreement is possible. We can determine the basic quality of life of those living in the future; they cannot help or harm us in any way.

Ethical Approaches to Transgenerational Moral Problems

It is generally recognized that we hold certain moral obligations to future generations. It is the extent of those obligations that is in question, because each increase in the natural resources and public goods reserved for those not yet born results in a decrease in the living standards of some of those here now. Conversely, policies that will improve the welfare of less-well-off contemporaries automatically entail some environmental risks or economic burdens for posterity. There have been three basic approaches to this problem, all of them generally unsatisfactory due to the special complications described previously:

Individual rights. It is easy to say the members of future generations have rights (*see also* RIGHTS). They obviously do. This approach, however, does not seem to help in the trade-offs between generations because there is no way of determining whose rights should predominate or whose values should hold sway. Even the most basic right to life, when applied to future generations, becomes merely a right to survival, which most would agree is not enough.

Economic benefits. It has often been suggested that future benefits and harms be discounted back to present value to make them more readily comparable to contemporary benefits and harms (*see also* SOCIAL COST-BENEFIT; ECONOMIC EFFICIENCY). The problem is that while the present cost of future benefits may legitimately be expressed in this way, it is morally awkward, at best, to attempt to think of a present value equivalent to such future harms as genetic ill-health or environmental destruction.

Distributive justice. Rawls attempted to overcome the symmetrical inconsistencies associated with future generations by proposing that each individual, choosing behind the veil of ignorance, was actually the head of a family with some degree of affection and concern for succeeding generations. This is an ingenious approach, but it presents difficulties, for we are not certain whether those succeeding generations – extended far enough to encounter both empirical uncertainties and value disagreements – will be better off or worse off than the present generation. If they are to be better off, then the "difference principle" would seem to preclude any sacrifice being made on their behalf. If they are to be worse off, then the amount of that sacrifice is still not clear (*see also* DISTRIBUTIVE JUSTICE; RAWLS, JOHN).

What ends are worth pursuing? this is the major issue confronted by consideration of individual rights, economic benefits/harms, and just agreements in the trade-offs between the welfare of present versus future generations. It is an area of inquiry that will receive continually increasing attention as we appear to approach the finite limits of our natural resources and public goods.

Bibliography

De-Shalit, A. (1992). Community and the rights of future generations: A reply to Robert Elliot. *Journal of Applied Philosophy*, **9**, 105–15.

English, J. (1977). Justice between generations. *Philosophical Studies*, **31**, 91–104.

Hardin, G. (1968). Tragedy of the commons. *Science*, **162**, 1243–8.

Hauerwas, S. (1974). The moral limits of population control. *Thought*, **49**, 236–49.

Jecker, N. (1992). Intergenerational justice and the family. *Journal of Value Inquiry*, **26**, 495–509.

Laslett, P. & Fishkin, J. S. (eds). (1992). *Justice between Age Groups and Generations*. New Haven: Yale University Press.

Mueller, D. C. (1974). Intergenerational justice and the social discount rate. *Theory and Decisions*, **5**, 263–73.

Sikora, R. L. & Barry, B. (eds). (1978). *Obligations to Future Generations*. Philadelphia: Temple University Press.

LaRue Tone Hosmer

G

gambling putting something valuable at risk in a process the end of which cannot be known to those whose risk it is.

Typically the activity of gambling centers on a "game" – of dice, cards, or randomly calibrated wheels in some mechanical array – called a "game of chance" in which the players are individuals who have no way of knowing how cards, dice, or wheels will fall and only goods in the form of cash are put at risk. The avowed purpose of the enterprise, properly called "gaming," is merely the entertainment of the individuals so engaged. Beyond that typical scenario, the word "gambling" generalizes to any activity in which there is risk (something valuable may be lost), and/or opportunity (something valuable may be gained), and the outcome is not knowable in advance. This entry will attend only to the central meaning of the term, participation in the gaming industry.

Gambling is very big business in the United States. According to *Gaming and Wagering Business*, a New York trade magazine, nearly $330 billion was wagered in 1992. By 1993, (legal) gambling had outstripped baseball in attracting visitors; it took in $30 billion in revenues in the same year. Thirty-seven states had lotteries in 1994; 23 had casinos, many of them run by Native American tribes (on federal lands, state anti-gambling legislation does not apply). Many states have off-track betting, video lotteries and casinos on riverboats. The income, jobs, and taxes supplied by gaming establishments keep many small cities in the black, take pressure off legislators to raise taxes on individuals, and bring real prosperity to the Native American tribes, most of them poverty stricken before the advent of gambling.

The problematic aspect of gambling is that most people sense that gambling is wrong, but almost no one knows why. We know that there are some "compulsive gamblers," persons with a personality disorder that makes it impossible to stop gambling before impoverishing themselves, and that these people gamble more if gambling is legal; but we do not ban the sale and use of alcohol because of alcoholics. For the normal person, the establishment of legal gaming facilities cannot be a violation of autonomy, since all participation in gambling is fully autonomous. It cannot be a violation of the duty to promote happiness and avoid causing pain, since the patrons insist that gambling makes them happy, the casino operators are clearly prosperous, and the larger community benefits from the revenues; and it cannot be a violation of justice, since the only injury sustained, loss of money, is voluntarily undertaken by the person who loses it.

Yet there are ethical problems. The most troubling one is that, however freely it may be chosen, gambling amounts to a very inequitable tax on the poor. More poor people gamble than rich, and since the odds of winning are very small, they lose almost all of the time; that is the money that pours into the coffers of the fortunate tribes and state governments. Beyond that clear injustice, there is a violation of the duty of STEWARDSHIP entailed by gambling. In throwing hard-earned money away at the gaming tables, the gambler seems to show imprudence with regard to his or her own or family needs, disrespect for the work that provided that money, and a culpable lack of awareness of cultural resources that might elevate taste and enhance sensibilities. On the other hand, if the money is the gambler's own, who are we to make such judgments?

Bibliography

Clines, F. X. (1994). The Pequots. Magazine section, *The New York Times*, Feb. 27, 49.

Dostoevsky, F. (1972). *The Gambler, with Polina Suslova's Diary.* Chicago: University of Chicago Press.

Fenster, J. M. (1994). Nation of gamblers. *American Heritage*, **45** (5), 34.

Gordon, J. S. (1994). Born in iniquity. *American Heritage*, **45** (1), 14.

Hirshey, G. (1994). Gambling nation. Magazine section, *The New York Times*, July 17, 34.

Newton, L. (1993). Gambling: A preliminary inquiry. *Business Ethics Quarterly*, **3** (4), 405.

Triplett, T. (1994). Marketers eager to fill demands for gambling. *Marketing News*, **28** (12), 1.

LISA NEWTON

game theory   the systematic study of *interdependent* rational choice. It may be used to explain, to predict, and (or) to evaluate human behavior in contexts where the choices of individuals depend on what others choose to do. The seminal works were *The Theory of Games and Economic Behavior* (1944) by von Neumann and Morgenstern and a couple of papers by John Nash in the early 1950s. Four decades later, game theory is used widely in all of the social and policy sciences, moral and political philosophy, linguistics, and biology. In 1994 the Nobel Prize for Economics was awarded to John Nash, John Harsanyi, and Reinhard Selten for their defining contributions to the field (*see* DECISION THEORY; RATIONAL CHOICE THEORY).

The theory of *independent* individual choice studies the decisions of a single individual choosing from a number of options or alternatives. The outcome of the individual's choice is understood to be the result of his or her choices and of the relevant intervening states of the environment or world (e.g., the weather). In contexts of decision-making *under certainty*, it is known exactly what outcome will be produced by each available choice or act. In these situations a rational choice will be one that maximizes the satisfaction of the agent's goals (or *utility*, a measure of the agent's values, goals, interests, or preferences). In contexts of *risk*, where only a probability can be assigned to any act bringing about a particular outcome, the most widely accepted view is that rational choice requires maximizing one's *expected* utility. (If no probabilities can be assigned, the decision problem may be thought of as one *under complete uncertainty* or *complete ignorance*. There is considerable disagreement about rational choice under uncertainty.) (*See* RISK.) In the basic neoclassical model of a competitive market, it is assumed that there are so many producers and consumers that none can influence the behavior of any other. This assumption, in effect, makes the decision problem facing any particular individual one of independent individual choice; if it is also assumed that every agent possesses full information, then the problem becomes one of individual choice under certainty.

Interdependent choice is more complex as the outcome is a result not only of the choices of the agent in question and the state of the world, but also the choices of other individuals. The problem is how to choose when the outcome is dependent on the choice of others? One cannot, as in individual choice under risk, assign a probability to the choices of others and maximize expected utility: one's choice depends on what the others choose, but their choice depends on what we choose. How then to form expectations regarding what others will do? A new element of *strategic* choice is introduced by interdependence. We may, then, think of game theory as the systematic study of strategic choice.

A problem of interdependent choice or a "game" consists of two or more agents (or "players"), each facing a choice of two or more acts or strategies ("moves"). An outcome results from the set of strategies chosen. Different sorts of games present different sorts of problems, and different conditions can facilitate the choice process. A particular set of "ideal" conditions simplifies game theory and made most of the early results possible: equal rationality (each agent is fully rational), complete information (each agent knows the rules of the game, the preferences of the other players), common knowledge (each knows that each knows the rules of the game, etc., and so on). Under these conditions there are, for certain types of games, sets of strategies that result in outcomes with attractive properties. One such property, which plays a crucial role in game theory, is that of an *equilibrium* outcome (or "Nash equilibrium"): a set of strategies (or outcome) is in equilibrium when no one can improve their position by unilaterally changing their strategy. Equilibria of this sort possess a type of stability: no one will rationally choose, by oneself, to upset it. If one is interested in *predicting* or *explaining* outcomes, the concept of an equilibrium outcome will be important, and, for normative purposes, it also proves significant.

It is important to distinguish games with two players from those with more ("*n*-person games"). The complexities introduced by having more than two players make *n*-person game theory more complicated and controversial. The second distinction that needs to be made is that between games where there is perfect conflict of interest and all others. The first are called "zero–sum" or "constant–sum" games, as the "sum" of the possible gains from interaction is zero or constant (e.g., two-person parlor games where one player wins, the other looses). With two–person zero–sum games, if we enrich the choice of strategies in certain ways, there is always at least one equilibrium outcome (and a convenient decision rule, the "minimax" rule).

Two-person zero-sum games are theoretically important but of less practical interest. Few choice problems facing humans, in spite of what is sometimes said about love and war, are genuine zero-sum or strictly competitive games. The class of "positive-sum" games is of greater interest for understanding human interaction. Here we must distinguish between situations where the interests or aims of individuals do not conflict at all, and situations of "mixed conflict" where there is some (but not complete) conflict. Situations with no conflict are games of "pure coordination" (e.g., the choice to drive on the right or the left of the road). With such problems it is thought to be desirable that outcomes not only be in equilibrium but that they be "optimal" or "efficient" in a particular sense attributed to PARETO, the second important possible property of outcomes. An outcome is *Pareto efficient* if and only if there is no change that would improve one person's situation without at the same time making another worse off. In other words, if an outcome is efficient in this sense, any change will make another worse off. In coordination games equilibria will often be efficient or "optimal" in this sense.

More troubling and perplexing are a variety of "mixed" games, with some conflict of interests. The well-known PRISONER'S DILEMMA (PD) is an example of such a game. A two-person PD is any situation facing two individuals, each with a choice of two acts or strategies, with four possible outcomes valued in a certain way. If we label the strategies "cooperate" and "defect", or "C" and "D", then the outcomes are such that each individual prefers joint cooperation (C,C) to joint defection (D,D). But each most prefers the outcome where he or she defects and the other cooperates (D,C) and least prefers the outcome where he or she cooperates and the other defects (C,D). In PDs played once, on the received conception of rationality (as well as many others), it is rational to defect whatever the other does. The result, then, is (D,D), an outcome which is an equilibrium but which is not Pareto efficient: (C,C) is mutually preferred to (D,D). Some find this result (and others like it) troubling – rational individuals do less well than they might. Others blame the situation or context and recommend that we focus our attention on the setting of choice (e.g., institutions). Yet others point to the fact that some PDs may have outcomes that are desirable to others, e.g., economic competition. It is games like these that may prove to be of most interest to students of economics and business. For instance, recently the idea of "corporate culture" has been fruitfully explored using game-theoretic models of "reputation" and related notions.

Bibliography

Axelrod, R. (1984). *The Evolution of Cooperation*. New York: Basic Books.

Eatwell, J., Milgate, M. & Newman, P. (1989). *Game Theory, The New Palgrave*. New York: W. W. Norton. (A useful set of articles from the new edition of the famous encyclopedia of economics).

Fudenberg, D. & Tirole, J. (1992). *Game Theory*. Cambridge, Mass.: MIT Press. (Advanced text).

Kreps, D. M. (1990). *Game Theory and Economic Modelling*. Oxford: Clarendon Press. (An accessible introduction, relatively non-mathematical).

Schelling, T. C. (1967). What is Game Theory? In. *Choice and Consequence*. Cambridge, Mass.: Harvard University Press, 213–42. (Introductory article, by a great writer).

CHRISTOPHER W. MORRIS

GATT The 1947 General Agreement on Tariffs and Trade (GATT) aims to develop and manage bilateral economic relations between countries to achieve freer and fairer trade.

In the case of GATT, this philosophy rested firmly on the theories of comparative and absolute advantage. In essence, these theories postulate that, given one central assumption, two countries can benefit from trade even if one country is more efficient in the production of all goods. The central assumption is that the relative efficiency of production between the two countries is not constant across goods. Thus the inefficient country will specialize in the production of the goods in which it is relatively less inefficient.

GATT also arose from a desire to escape the mercantilist protectionism that had characterized international trade in the years between the two world wars. International trade was recognized as a non-cooperative "Prisoner's-Dilemma type" game in which the optimum solution could be reached only through some form of cooperation between players, the primary players being governments of developed nations (*see* PRISONER'S DILEMMA).

In order to dismantle the cobweb of tariff barriers and achieve free trade, GATT was founded on three basic principles:

Non-Discrimination: a country is prohibited from levying different tariffs on the same good imported from different countries;

Reciprocity: reductions in tariffs should be balanced between countries;

Impartial adjudication of trade disputes: through processes developed and controlled by GATT.

For the first three decades of its existence GATT appeared to serve the international community of developed nations well. Trade barriers worldwide were reduced, and membership in GATT grew from 23 countries at its inception in 1947 to almost 100 countries today. The membership of GATT, therefore, has expanded from essentially a "club" for developed nations into an organization spanning all stages of the development life-cycle.

From an ethical perspective, GATT has been criticized recently on the grounds that its espoused ideology of free trade is merely a façade to conceal an underlying mandate of profit maximization for the world's large multinational corporations. Dobson (1993) has suggested the replacement of GATT with a hub-and-spoke network of regional trade organizations monitored by a single global trade organization. The regional trade organizations would comprise clusters of developmentally equivalent nations, and would perform the economic function of promoting free trade within these clusters. The overarching global trade organization would perform the moral role of ensuring fair trade between these regional trade organizations. Thus a clear distinction would be made between the economic ideology of free trade and the moral ideology of fair trade.

Bibliography

Dobson, J. (1993). TNCs and the corruption of GATT: Free trade versus fair trade. *Journal of Business Ethics*, **12**, 573–8.

JOHN DOBSON

gay rights Generally taken to mean bars against discrimination on the basis of sexual orientation in employment, housing, and public accommodations. Where they exist, gay rights give gay men, lesbians, and bisexuals the same rights afforded to racial, gender, and religious groups by the 1964 US Civil Rights Act. Sometimes "gay rights" is used in a broader, amorphous sense to encompass anything that benefits gays (say, arts funding, constitutional equal protection, speech right, privacy right, and affirmative action programs).

Current Status

As of 1996, nine US states and over a hundred cities have legislated gay rights in the narrow sense. In addition, hundreds of companies have specific policies banning discrimination based on sexual orientation, including IBM, Eastman Kodak, Harley-Davidson, Dow Chemical, Du Pont, and 3M. One-quarter of the Fortune 500 have such policies. Through Carter-era regulations and Clinton-era executive orders, the federal government bans discrimination against gays everywhere *but* in the military, where discrimination has been mandated by Department of Defense policy since 1942 and by federal law since 1993.

Arguments

What sort of case can be made for gay rights? No one can have much self-respect or maintain a solid sense of self, if she is, in major ways affecting herself, subject to whimsical and arbitrary actions of others. Work, entertainment, and housing are major modes through which people identify themselves to themselves. A large part of the misery of unemployment is not merely poverty and social embarrassment, but also a sense of loss of that by which one defines oneself. Work is also the chief means by which people in America identify themselves to others. America is a nation of doers. So, when job discrimination is directed at lesbians and gay men, it is a way of branding them as essentially un-American. It is a chief mode of expatriation from the national experience.

Gay rights also unclog channels between individual effort and the fulfillment of an individual's basic needs. For it is chiefly through employment that people acquire the things they need to assure their continued biological existence – food, shelter, and clothing. Employment is also the chief means by which people satisfy those various culturally relative needs which maintain them as credible players in the ongoing social, political, and economic affairs of the society into which they are born. Civil-rights legislation then helps people discharge through their own devices their presumptive obligation to meet their basic biological needs and other conditions required for human agency.

Social Benefits

Extending civil rights protections to gay men and lesbians is also justified as promoting general prosperity. By eliminating extraneous factors in employment decisions, such legislation promotes an optimal fit between a worker's capacities and the tasks of her prospective work. Both worker and employer are benefited by such a fit. Such legislation enhances the prospects that job slots are not filled by second bests.

Further, human resources are wasted if one's energies are constantly diverted and devoured by fear of arbitrary dismissal. The cost of life in the closet is not small, for the closet permeates and largely consumes the life of its occupant. Without civil-rights protections, society is simply wasting the resources that are expended in the day-to-day anxiety – the web of lies, the constant worry – that attends leading a life of systematic disguise as a condition for employment. A 1992 survey of 1400 gay men and lesbians in Philadelphia found that 76 percent of men and 81 percent of women conceal their orientation at work.

Domestic Partnership

The 1990s have seen a dramatic increase in attention paid to gay domestic partnership issues in the workplace. Society is beginning to realize that gays do not just come one by one, but, like other folk, typically come two by two. Even against oppressive odds brought on by the threat of discrimination, gay men and lesbians have shown an amazing tendency to nest. Acknowledging this fact, a number of the nation's largest cities, including New York and Los Angeles, some of the nation's most prestigious universities, including Stanford and Harvard, and several leading corporations, including Levi Strauss, Lotus Development, Warner Brothers, and Apple Computer, have extended to partners of their gay employees many of the same benefits extended to employees' legal spouses. Such "fringe benefits" on average mount up to about 16 percent of an employee's salary and so constitute a major issue of pay equity as well as an issue of moral fairness.

Some people have claimed that denying partners of gays such benefits does not constitute sexual-orientation discrimination, because the class of those denied the benefits includes both gay and non-gay people – the unmarried. This move overlooks the obvious fact that the law currently denies gays, though not straights, the opportunity to marry, and so simply bootstraps one discrimination off of another. If a country denied legal recognition to the marriages of members of a certain religious sect (as is the case with the Baha'i in Iran), everyone would agree that the denial of marital benefits to all members of the religious group constituted religious discrimination, even though the general class of those denied the benefits included some members of all religions. So too, then, consistency requires acknowledging that the denial of marital benefits to gays whose marriages are not legally recognized constitutes sexual-orientation discrimination.

Gay Marriage

Issues of equal access aside, what is marriage anyway? Marriage is intimacy given substance in the medium of everyday life, the day-to-day. To be poetic, marriage is the fused intersection of love's sanctity and necessity's demand. Marriages differ from "Great Loves," which burn brightly but too intensely ever to be manifest in a medium of breakfast and tyre changes. Neither, though, do we consider mere roommates, who regularly cook, clean, tend to household chores, and even share household finances, as married, because such relationships are not intimate ones. Marriage requires the presence and blending of both necessity and intimacy.

Ethnographic studies have shown that gay and lesbian relationships fulfill this definition of marriage in an exemplary way. The benefits that marriage accrues from the realms of law and business (for example, insurance benefits and bereavement leaves) are primarily directed at those occasions when necessity is inopportune, especially when life is marked by crisis, illness, and destruction. Gays' relationships are as deserving and as needful of such benefits as anyone's.

See also **affirmative action programs; AIDS; discrimination in employment; equal opportunity**

Bibliography

McNaught, B. (1993). *Gay Issues in the Workplace.* New York: St. Martin's.
Mohr, R. D. (1994). *A More Perfect Union: Why Straight America Must Stand Up for Gay Rights.* Boston: Beacon.
Weston, K. (1991). *Families We Choose: Lesbians, Gays, Kinship.* New York: Columbia University Press.
Woods, J. D. (1993). *The Corporate Closet: The Professional Lives of Gay Men in America.* New York: Free Press.

RICHARD D. MOHR

glass ceiling A metaphor that refers to the invisible barrier that blocks the advancement of women and minorities to upper-level leadership positions, especially in the world of business. This phenomenon can be reported objectively as a statistical fact. It was noted in the early 1970s that although women and minorities had been entering the workforce in record numbers for over a decade, very few were able to progress to middle- or upper-level management. The EEOC (Equal Employment Opportunity Commission) reported in 1966 that while over 40 percent of white-collar jobs were held by women, their representation in upper-level management was so small as to be statistically insignificant. *Harvard Business Review*'s 1964 study concluded that "the barriers [for women in upper management] are so great there is scarcely anything to study." Not surprisingly, at that time many experts urged patience. Without denying that discrimination was a factor of concern, it does take time, they suggested, for any group to work its way up through the ranks.

Twenty years later little progress is apparent. In 1987 the US Department of Labor published a report – *Workforce 2000* – that brought attention to dramatic changes in the workforce, including almost 50 percent participation by women overall, the fastest-growing segment being married women of childbearing age, and especially mothers of preschool children. Yet, the level of participation in upper management has remained virtually unchanged. A 1990 survey of the country's 1,000 largest corporations (see Korn/Ferry, 1990) reported that women and minorities now hold less than 5 percent of executive positions, representing a growth rate of less than 2 percent since 1979. This statistic has not changed in the most recent 1994 survey. The existence of the glass ceiling is clear, but its nature is nebulous and its causes controversial.

Insofar as it is the product of overt discrimination it is prohibited by law and actionable, if it can be proven. But much of the problem today seems to be a manifestation of subtle forces and pervasive presumptions that are very difficult to pinpoint in particular circumstances. Prejudices abound. For example, it is widely held that single women are bad investments for leadership training because they are more interested in marriage than a career (despite the fact that few women today stop working when they marry); and that women of childbearing age are similarly bad risks because they are likely to get pregnant (despite the fact that professional women take no more time off for preganacy than men take for sick leave). Many executives claim that women and minorities do not make it to the upper ranks because they lack the characteristics needed for leadership positions. A number of studies have corroborated this attitude. One, for example, (Basil, 1972) asked for a ranking of personal characteristics necessary for effective upper management and received the following top five: Decisiveness, Consistency and Objectivity, Emotional Stability, Analytical Ability, Perceptiveness and Empathy. All five of these characteristics were perceived by the executives and students surveyed as more common in men than in women. Thus, women as a class were perceived as lacking in leadership qualities, in drive and motivation, in strength and decisiveness. Similar studies have reviewed attitudes about minorities with similar results (e.g., Dickens & Dickens, 1982). The lack of scientific evidence for such attitudes in no way reduces their effects. And the perceptions are self-verifying. If women and minorities are preconceived as lacking leadership qualities, then they will quite naturally be passed over for the highest positions and channeled into support services. They will not be leaders, so they will not be perceived as leaders. Recent reports of the Department of Labor (*The Glass Ceiling Initiative*, 1991, 1994) noted that typical selection and grooming procedures for upper-level management, conducted by personal recommendation, informal meetings, and networking, tends to disadvantage women and minorities who remain outside the network. Yet, no discrimination is verifiable in such circumstances. It is likely to be unconscious. Business leaders tend to select and groom successors who are more or less like themselves, and they perceive women and minorities as importantly

different. For those being judged before they have a chance to perform, this creates and maintains an invisible barrier: the glass ceiling.

Bibliography

Basil, D. C. (1972). *Women in Management*. New York: Dunleen.

Catalyst. (1983). *Barriers to Women's Upward Mobility: Corporate Managers Speak Out*. New York, NY.

Catalyst. (1990). *Catalyst's Study of Women in Corporate Management*, New York, NY.

Dickens, F. & Dickens, J. (1982). *The Black Manager*. New York: American Management Association.

Korn/Ferry International and UCLA's Anderson Graduate School of Management. (1990). *Korn/Ferry International's Executive Profile 1990: A Survey of Corporate Leaders*. New York: Korn Ferry International.

Martin, L. (Secretary of Labor). (1991). *Report on the Glass Ceiling Initiative*. Washington, DC: US Department of Labor.

PATRICIA G. SMITH

globalization   Labels such as "global village," "global marketplace," "global factory," or "global corporation" are increasingly used and frequently imply that the world is becoming a single, homogenized place. Yet the "globalization" tag is often applied loosely and indiscriminately in describing a totally pervasive set of forces and changes with uniform effects on countries, regions, and localities (Dicken, 1992, p. 1). Therefore, a sensitive and discriminating approach is needed to understand and evaluate the fundamental and complex processes of globalization which characterize the world at the turn of the century.

Whereas the adjective "global" (meaning, strongly, worldwide; or, more loosely, "the whole") has been in use for a long time, the noun "globalization" has developed quite recently, influenced by Marshall McLuhan's idea of "the global village" (Carpenter & McLuhan, 1960) – the shared simultaneity of media, particularly televisual, experience in our time. Basically, "globalization" refers both to the compression of the world and the intensification of consciousness of the world as a single place (Robertson, 1992, p. 8). Although globalization of *economic* activities is of paramount importance and the main focus of this article, it would be shortsighted to conceive globalization in exclusively economic terms. Environmental as well as political (including legal and military) and sociocultural (see Robertson, 1992) aspects are equally relevant to the makeup of globalization.

There are two different approaches to globalization: the first describes and analyses "global unity" in relatively neutral terms with respect to the risks, costs, and benefits (interdependence, interpenetration, global consciousness, homogenization, etc.) associated with it; the second evaluates it in normative terms (world progress, global community, one-worldism, globalism, etc.). The following discusses basic features of the globalization of economic activities and reflects on its ethical implications.

Economic globalization can be understood as the widest geographic extension possible of international economic integration, either as a process or a state of affairs, that moves beyond provincial, sectoral, national, and regional (i.e., transnational but less than global) integration. What is often called "globalization" relates, in fact, only to the triad of the United States, European Union, and Japan, at the factual exclusion of the rest of the world. Taking the world as a single place, globalization's essential criterion is commonly seen in the equality of prices of equal goods and equal services (see Machlup, 1977) and includes three necessary conditions: (1) division of labor, (2) mobility of goods or factors of production or both, and (3) non-discrimination in the treatment of goods and factors (with regard to origin, destination, etc.). Since all economic activities are conceived to be (virtually or actually) interrelated and interdependent, all economic actors in charge of planning and allocation must make their calculations on the basis of opportunity costs (i.e., the costs associated with not choosing the alternative option). As long as prices of equal items in any market (of goods, services, labor, capital, currencies) are different, the pursuit of economic efficiency and competition tends to equalize those prices. So the globalization of the economy means that, as economic activities are increasingly interdependent worldwide, in order to survive each actor must compete. Yet in order to be competitive, productivity has to rise quickly. But raising productivity implies that

fewer jobs are being created, which means that growth has to be even faster.

Although this general picture of economic globalization needs several qualifications, it definitely influences the strategies of multinational enterprises and individual governments. Moreover, it has a strong empirical basis. Since the 1950s, a rapid growth in world trade occurred, and foreign direct investment spread in the 1960s, led by the United States. But only since the late 1980s, an array of internationalization processes have integrated in a more systematic fashion, covering a large set of parameters including inter-country investment, production, marketing, and trade, and increased interfirm alliances and collaboration, often due to the importance of research and development and its interconnection with globalization (see UN, 1991–5; Dicken, 1992; Hirst & Thompson, 1996; Howells & Wood, 1993). These recent developments are paralleled by international agreements on trade and investment (GATT, etc.), the creation of the World Trade Organization, reform discussions about the International Monetary Fund and the World Bank, and a host of other initiatives.

In order to understand and evaluate the globalization of economic activities from the perspective of a comprehensive conception of business ethics, the distinctions between the "macro" and "meso" levels and between "the choice of constraints" and "the choice within constraints," are of far-reaching relevance. Globalization challenges both national economies and business organizations. At both levels, actors have to cope with these new challenges and cannot delegate their responsibilities to government or corporations alone since they are "in the same boat" (which, by the way, would suggest a cooperative rather than an antagonistic relationship between them). Because either type of actor can establish constraints, and must accept constraints, each faces two kinds of choices, namely those about and those within constraints, which both necessarily involve an ethical dimension.

The liberal conception of globalization strives for a worldwide "level playing field" and thus advocates liberalization and non-discrimination (except for unrestrained movement of labor across borders), along with certain global institutions and policies. However, there are a number of serious, pervasive ethical questions, besides the controversial issue of what precisely makes up a "global level playing field." First, economic growth must be conceived in terms of "sustainability"; hence certain environmental standards should be constitutive of global trade and investment regulations (e.g., IISD, 1994). Second, the creation of jobs and the preservation of humane working conditions are not achieved automatically by growth and competition; they need to be targeted explicitly, as in global agreements, being the shared responsibility of all economic actors (e.g., ILO, 1992; UNDP, 1993). Third, the allocation of resources by global trade and production at both the macro and meso levels necessarily involves a distributive dimension which requires ethical justification. Fourth, to determine the role of global economic institutions within a global order is of great ethical importance. Fifth, global institutions and global corporations can be understood as "public goods," facing enormous cultural diversity and significant pluralism. They can only work in the long run if they stand atop a common ethical ground (see CPWR, 1993; ID, 1994; PfB, 1994; De George, 1993; Donaldson, 1989).

See also **ethics of competition; multinationals; global warming; international business ethics; justice; multiculturalism; political philosophy and business ethics; relativism, cultural and moral**

Bibliography

Carpenter, E. S. & McLuhan, M. (eds),. (1960). *Explorations in Communication*. Boston: Beacon Press.

Council for a Parliament of World's Religions (CPWR). (1993). *Towards a Global Ethic*. (An Initial Declaration). Chicago.

De George, R. T. (1993). *Competing with Integrity in International Business*. New York: Oxford University Press.

Dicken, P. (1992). *Global Shift: The Internationalization of Economic Activity*. 2nd edn, New York/London: Guilford Press.

Donaldson, T. (1989). *The Ethics of International Business*. New York: Oxford University Press.

Hirst, P. & Thompson, G. (1996). *Globalization in Question*. Oxford: Blackwell.

Howells, J. & Wood, M. (1993). *The Globalisation of Production and Technology*. London/New York: Belhaven Press.

An Interfaith Declaration [ID]: A Code of Ethics on International Business for Christians, Muslims and Jews (1994). London: British North American Research Association.

International Institute for Sustainable Development (IISD). (1994). *Trade and Sustainable Development Principles*. Winnipeg, Canada: IISD.

International Labour Office (ILO). (1992). *World Labour Report 1992*. Geneva: ILO.

Machlup, F. (1977). *A History of Thought on Economic Integration*. New York: Columbia University Press.

Principles for Business (PfB). (1994). The Hague: Caux Round Table Secretariat.

Robertson, R. (1992). *Globalization: Social Theory and Global Culture*. London: Sage.

United Nations (UN). (1991–5). *World Investment Report*. Annually. New York: UN.

United Nations Development Program (UNDP). (1993). *Human Development Report*, New York: Oxford University Press.

GEORGES ENDERLE

global warming   The likely consequences of a build-up of a variety of "greenhouse gases" in the earth's upper atmosphere. These gases, primarily water vapor, carbon dioxide, ozone, methane, nitrous oxide, and chlorofluorocarbons (CFCs), trap heat within the atmosphere, much as the glass of a greenhouse functions to allow warming sunlight in while preventing the warmer air from escaping. Well-confirmed through observation and experiments over the past century, the "greenhouse effect" is the prevailing scientific explanation of the atmosphere's role in regulating the earth's temperature.

Measurements have shown that the levels of many greenhouse gases have risen in recent decades, mostly as the result of human activities. Carbon dioxide accounts for most of the measurable increase (generally estimated at over 50 percent), with CFCs (25 percent), methane (15 percent), and nitrous oxide (5 percent) accounting for the remainder. Fossil-fuel use in automobiles, electric utilities, industry, and home heating is primarily responsible for the increase in carbon dioxide. At the same time, worldwide deforestation has decreased nature's ability to remove carbon dioxide from the atmosphere through photosynthesis.

While there is little scientific dispute concerning the greenhouse effect, there is some uncertainty regarding the consequences of the increase in greenhouse gases. Most scientific evidence suggests that the build-up of greenhouse gases will lead to an increase in the earth's surface temperature, or *global warming*. The specific details of global warming (How much will the temperature increase? How quickly? Are we already experiencing temperature increases?) and the climatic and ecological implications of this warming remain open questions. This uncertainty has led some critics to challenge environmental and regulatory policies aimed at reducing the emissions of greenhouse gases.

Many variables could affect the relationship between the increase in greenhouse gases and global warming. The climatic role played by oceans, the polar ice caps, and clouds, as well as human decisions concerning pollution, deforestation, fossil-fuel use, and agriculture, all have the potential for either increasing or decreasing global warming. Nevertheless, various experiments, including analysis of air bubbles trapped deep within the Antarctic ice sheet, indicate a long-term correlation between increases in the earth's temperature and the presence of relatively high levels of carbon dioxide and methane. Along with data generated from computer modeling, we have strong *prima facie* evidence that a continued build-up of greenhouse gases would lead to an increase in average global temperatures in the range of 1 to 5 degrees celsius over the next few decades.

The implications of this change range from a worst-case scenario of a major rise in ocean levels, climatic shifts, worldwide droughts and famine, and massive extinctions of plant and animal life, to a best-case scenario of a slow adaptation to higher temperatures, including significant shifts in population and agricultural centers.

Ethical issues raised by global warming include responsibility to future generations, justice questions concerning the allocation and distribution of resources and risks, responsibility to non-human life, and respect for the natural world. More generally, the questions of how one ought to act and what public policies are appropriate in the face of uncertainty about great risk are particularly pertinent when considering global warming.

See also **ethical issues in energy; environment and environmental ethics; future generations**

Bibliography

Miller, G. T., Jr. (1994). *Living in the Environment.* Belmont, Calif.: Wadsworth. (A comprehensive environmental science textbook.)

Schneider, S. (1989). *Global Warming: Are We Entering the Greenhouse Century?* San Francisco: Sierra Club Books.

Wyman, R. (ed.), . (1991). *Global Climate Change and Life on Earth.* New York: Routledge.

JOSEPH R. DES JARDINS

golden parachute A *contract* where a corporation agrees to provide a large *severance pay package* to a *key officer* of the corporation if the officer is *terminated*, such as after a *change of control* of the corporation. Although sometimes challenged in the courts, the "contract" is offered by the board of directors (as an agent of the shareholders) and is legally binding on future owners. The severance pay package generally consists of two or three years' salary plus accelerated stock options and retirement provisions, bonuses, and insurance benefits. A key officer is "any officer, shareholder, or highly compensated individual . . . who is one of the highest paid one percent of the employees of the corporation, or, if less, one of the highest paid 250 employees of the corporation" (US *Internal Revenue Code*, 1994). Termination must usually occur within two years of a change of control and may be either involuntary (dismissal from the company) or constructive (change in job title, responsibilities, job location, or salary). A change of control may involve the acquisition of a substantial number of shares (normally 20 percent) or a turnover of more than half of the board of directors within a specified period (usually six to twelve months). As illustrated by the precision of terms in the definition of a golden parachute (GP), legalism now dominates this previously controversial financial compensation instrument.

GPs became prevalent as a CORPORATE GOVERNANCE issue in the early 1980s (see Cochran and Wartick, 1984). Amid the emerging TAKEOVER frenzy of the 1980s, GPs were offered to: (a) insure executive objectivity and loyalty to shareholders, (b) encourage executive retention after a change of control, and (c) increase the acquisition cost of a takeover target. Critics of GPs contended that the contracts were: (a) nothing more than rewards for *poor* management performance, since being a take-over target implied an undervalued firm, (b) not "arm's-length" transactions, since executives controlled the boards of directors that offered the packages, (c) questionable application of fiduciary responsibility, since after an acquisition every dollar of GP money means one less dollar for shareholders, and (d) a public relations nightmare, since executives can walk away from a takeover with millions of dollars of the acquired firm's cash (for example, after Pantry Pride acquired Revlon in the mid-1980s, Michael Bergarac left Revlon with a $15 million GP). Early GPs were particularly controversial because they included a "ripcord" provision that permitted executives to unilaterally choose to leave the employment of an acquired firm and exercise the GP payments. This provision was abandoned in most GPs after legislative and tax law changes in the mid-1980s stated that companies paying excessive GP payments would not be able to deduct the expenses, and that recipients of the payments would be subject to a 20 percent excise tax on the total amount of compensation received in excess of their base salary (see Feldman, 1992, for additional qualifications).

Although more than half of all large American corporations still provide GP contracts to their senior management, GPs, along with GREEN-MAIL and other "SHARK repellents," are far less controversial than in the 1980s. "Tin parachutes" (see Robertson and Bassick, 1989), "bronze parachutes," "golden handshakes," and various other severance packages have become commonplace as corporate compensation tools.

Bibliography

Cochran, P. L. & Wartick, S. L. (1984). Golden parachutes: A closer look. *California Management Review,* summer, 111–25. (Good review of early GPs).

Feldman, C. F. (1992). Golden parachutes remain popular despite strict rules *Taxation for Accounts,* Oct., 204–11. (Excellent for current laws).

Robertson, D. C. and Bassick, E. W. IV. (1989). Beyond golden bailouts: The tin parachute is landing *Sloan Management Review,* fall, 43–52. (For more on "tin parachutes").

US Government, *Internal Revenue Code,* Section 280G (c) (2), 1994.

STEVEN L. WARTICK

golden rule, the   "Treat others as you want to be treated." In Matthew 7: 12, Jesus gave the rule as the summary of the Jewish tradition. The Rabbi Hillel had earlier said much the same thing. Even earlier, Confucius had used the rule to summarize his teachings. All the major religions and many non-religious thinkers teach the rule as being of central importance; and it is influential among conscientious people in very diverse cultures. All this suggests that the rule may be an important moral truth.

The golden rule is best interpreted as saying: "Treat others only in ways that you're willing to be treated *in the same exact situation.*" To apply it, you should imagine yourself in the exact place of the other person on the receiving end of the action. If you act in a given way toward another, and yet you are unwilling to be treated that way in the same circumstances, then you're violating the rule.

To apply the golden rule adequately, we need knowledge and imagination. We need to *know* what effect our actions have on the lives of others. And we need to be able to *imagine* ourselves, vividly and accurately, in the other person's place on the receiving end of the action. With knowledge, imagination, and the golden rule, we can progress far in our moral thinking.

The golden rule is best seen as a consistency principle. It does not replace regular moral norms. It is not an infallible guide on which actions are right or wrong. It does not give all the answers. It only prescribes consistency – that our actions (toward another) not be out of harmony with our desires (toward a reversed-situation action). It tests our moral coherence. If we violate the golden rule, then we're violating the spirit of fairness and concern for people that lies at the heart of morality.

The golden rule, with roots in a wide range of world cultures, is well suited to be a standard to which different cultures could appeal in trying to resolve conflicts. As the world becomes more and more a single interacting global community, the need for such a common standard is becoming more urgent.

See also altruism and benevolence; fairness; impartiality; moral imperatives; moral reasoning; multiculturalism; reciprocity; universalizability

Bibliography

Cadoux, A. T. (1912). The implications of the golden rule. *Ethics*, 3, 272–87.
Gensler, H. J. (1986). Ethics is based on rationality. *Journal of Value Inquiry*, 20, 251–64.
Gensler, H. J. (1996). *Formal Ethics*. New York and London: Routledge.
Hare, R. M. (1963). *Freedom and Reason*. New York: Oxford University Press. (esp. chs 6 and 11)
Hertzler, J. O. (1934). On golden rule. *Ethics*, 44, 418–36.
Singer, M. G. (1963). The gold rule. *Philosophy*, 38, 293–314.
Wattles, J. (1966). *The Golden Rule and Human Kinship*. New York: Oxford University Press.

Harry J. Gensler

goodwill is the monetary value placed on a firm due to its past reputation and anticipated future financial opportunities. The concept of goodwill as it pertains to business ethics has its roots in the fields of accounting and finance. The goodwill value placed on a firm's financial statement normally is represented by the difference between the actual costs of the enterprise's net worth and the market value of the firm at a time of contemplated sale or merger. A business firm that builds up desirable characteristics that are especially attractive among its stakeholders is able to realize an increased monetary value beyond the actual costs of its net assets.

According to Swanda (1990, p. 752), morally based efforts on the part of the organization's management are one of the major contributors to this enhanced value or goodwill. Along with moral factors, other conditions such as the firm's location, production system, marketing apparatus, and economic advantages also contribute to the firm's goodwill value. But it is the moral rightness within the business organization that provides a base from which to gain respect and credibility among its external and internal constituents. Hence, future improved sales income, market size, worker efficiency, and financial rates of return are all connected directly and indirectly to the firm's overall state of moral conduct.

Goodwill is portrayed by early authorities in the field of accounting (Moonitz & Littleton, 1965) as an embodiment of respected ideals and practices by the firm. More recently, Norton Bedford (1990), while referring to goodwill valuation suggested that "These undervalued or unrecorded assets may arise from advertising and represent a type of deferred advertising cost *from proper business conduct and represent the cost of building a reputation for moral and fair action*, or from chance developments and represent a type of unrealized appreciation of recorded assets or such unrecorded assets as a favorable location or a differentiated product." There is this strong suggestion among earlier pioneers from the field of accounting theory that the firm's reputation, shaped by its moral climate, has a significant impact on the goodwill value of a business organization. Hence, professional managers are obligated to maintain this positive linkage between the moral and financial integrity of the firm.

Swanda (1990, p. 753) explains that the recognized moral climate within a business organization implies the presence of a unique long-term financial advantage. Strong moral elements within the firm contribute to its reputation and ultimately its financial value described as goodwill.

The concept "goodwill," as it is viewed by professional accountants and financial analysts, can be to a certain degree a representation of the consequence of recognizable fair treatment of customers by business personnel, the maintenance of trusting relationships with clients or consumers, the carrying out of previous agreements without any intent of abusing vulnerable parties, and engaging in other similar types of noble behavior.

The reduction or absence of reported goodwill on the financial statements of a firm that has been sold may be attributed to unethical behavior on the part of the business's personnel via dishonest consumer treatment, rude or dehumanizing treatment of parties with whom the firm does business, sale of known unsafe products, and other questionable behavior which may reduce the reputation of the business firm.

The actual establishment of the goodwill value on the balance sheet of the firm also is subject to possible abuses to the uninformed investor or user of financial information. Such possible abuses may include arbitrary write-downs of the firm's assets prior to the sale of the business, misstatement of the sale price of the firm (especially when there is an exchange of stock), and the sale of a business that is not consummated at an arm's-length bargained exchange. In essence, misuse of accepted accounting principles in reporting goodwill value can reflect a kind of questionable moral behavior that detracts measurably from any legitimate and deserved goodwill value attributed to the firm.

Bibliography

Bedford, N. M. (1990). Goodwill. In S. Davidson (ed.), *Handbook of Modern Accounting*. New York: McGraw-Hill.

Moonitz, M. & Littleton, A. C. (eds). (1965). *Significant Accounting Essays*. Englewood Cliffs, NJ: Prentice-Hall, 479–80.

Swanda, J. (1990). Goodwill, going concern, stocks and flows: A prescription for moral analysis. *Journal of Business Ethics*, 9, 751–9.

JOHN R. SWANDA, JR.

government agencies and stakeholders
Major decisions by government agencies impact a broad range of constituents, many of which can thwart that organization's ability to carry out its decisions. Authority assigned by law may prove inadequate to overcome political and legal initiatives by aggrieved parties. Therefore, in addition to their express authority, decision-makers must earn political and legal authority by meaningfully involving all parties before making final decisions. Only then will their major decisions count.

The process of public participation to help solve complex problems is much more than public relations and education, which so often become propaganda serving more to justify ourselves than to seek critical input from others. Nor is it confined to an exercise in seeking compromise or consensus. The real thrust of public involvement is to find superior, creative, and enduring solutions. Properly conducted public participation fosters just such results.

Public involvement constitutes a new discipline indispensable to executives today, particularly those responsible for government institutions. Few investments will bear greater returns. Rewards manifest in a better educated and more understanding public, superior decisions, overall reduced time and costs, improved understanding between affected parties, more authority for decision-makers, and greater institutional credibility.

With troubled customers and the public now exerting more influence, conflict is inevitable. Executives can either attempt to dodge this controversy or learn to harness it. If they elect to harness it by including third parties rather than trying to vanquish them, they will have the opportunity to consider new possibilities and to test out new ideas in the heat of dialogue. While others are mired in disputes and litigation, astute practitioners of public involvement will have hammered out an understanding and gotten on with the project. In short, they will have made better decisions, decisions that will count.

Bonneville Power Administration (BPA): An Illustration

Established in 1937, BPA, a $2.3 billion agency of the US Department of Energy, had earned a good reputation for transmitting and marketing hydro power from the Federal Columbia River Power System. The agency had constructed over 15,000 miles of high-voltage transmission line linking 30 large federal dams and several thermal resources to markets throughout the 11 western states and British Columbia. However, by the early 1980s, respect for BPA was waning, and in some situations, the agency was outright reviled. For example, while trying to construct a high-voltage transmission line tying coal-fired generating plants in eastern Montana to the agency's grid in Washington State, angry farmers prevented surveyors from entering their property at gun point and accused the agency of being insensitive to their interests. In addition, the collapse of a $24 billion nuclear power-plant construction debacle, where BPA had guaranteed the financing of three of five of the plants, further damaged BPA's reputation and contributed to the erosion of the agency's authority to shape energy policy.

About that time, BPA published a comprehensive seven-foot-high, court-mandated Role Environment Impact Statement, which offended almost everyone, because it was ponderous and prepared by consultants without meaningful participation by affected customers and other stakeholders. Progressively, the agency had lost the credibility it previously enjoyed and decisions by the Administrator were frequently challenged politically or were taken to court (*see* STAKEHOLDER THEORY).

BPA's assistant for external affairs and a public-involvement specialist suggested that BPA could re-earn its authority by inviting the public into the decision-making process. But the head of the BPA was initially against the idea, having been an executive in the private sector for 20 years. BPA attorneys reinforced those fears. They argued that public involvement would force the premature release of important documents and jeopardize the attorney–client privilege, that BPA would forfeit its flexibility and become hostage to its own policies and guidelines, that outsiders would have the leverage to make unreasonable demands, and that BPA would become vulnerable to lawsuits right and left. Concurrently BPA management began to realize that while there may be some legal risks in involving the public, it had to balance those risks against the risks of not involving customer and public stakeholders in the process.

The transmission lines BPA was constructing in Montana (where a farmer's rifle had stopped surveyors from entering upon his land) had been stopped by a flurry of lawsuits and an angry public. That project was selected to begin putting BPA's new philosophy in action. Dozens of meetings were held with individuals,

groups, state and county executives, and the governor. During these meetings, most of which were open to anyone wishing to attend, unwarranted assumptions yielded to new knowledge and deeper understanding. As a direct result of those discussions, BPA relocated transmission lines off scenic lowlands and behind forested ridges. It reduced the visibility of towers. BPA discovered that if it had not already made some investments in the original route, the new routing would have been less costly. Consulting with external stakeholders had broken the logjam and fostered a new attitude of cooperation.

But it seemed that not all the agency's offices were really taking the new approach to heart, and some customers were getting mixed messages. So BPA hired the foremost professional in public participation to assess the new agency-wide program. He found that the public perceived BPA as "arrogant, insensitive, and uncaring." Despite fears that the media would use the report's harsh findings against the agency, it was released to the public along with a letter outlining the steps being taken to address the findings. To BPA's relief, the press praised it for being forthright.

Next BPA began the hard work of restoring public confidence. Two tasks lay ahead: to change the internal attitudes at BPA and to develop practical skills in dealing with the public. They added public involvement to employee performance requirements, and those who did an outstanding job were recognized in the BPA newsletter and given cash awards. Mandatory training programs were set up for employees and required managers to prepare a public-involvement plan for each major decision. Each plan was developed by the function within BPA that was likely to carry out that decision. However, before the plan could be initiated, it had to meet the approval of BPA's new public-involvement specialist.

By letting the whole organization help shape the formal policy, employees would take ownership of it and bring about the culture shift BPA needed. Some employees fought back and served as a counterpoint to the agency's multiplying successes employing their new discipline – public participation. It took two years to get the policy in final form. During that period, BPA invited customer and public participation in all major decisions to test and improve the idea. Successes reinforced employee commitment.

On all major decisions, management prepared and distributed "backgrounders" and "issue alerts" which communicated the information people needed to participate meaningfully. Some ratepayer advocates and environmental groups continued agitating, complaining that they wanted to meet one-on-one with top management, including the Administrator. They wanted to set the agenda for those meetings, and the meetings could not be costly for them to participate in. As a result, an elaborate telecommunication system was set up in the Administrator's conference room, which allowed anyone who could not be physically present to participate by phone.

Every critic, including those who staff had labeled as "crazies," was invited to participate. Although tense in the beginning, over time people realized they could have a frank discussion on any subject. Tensions dissipated, and mutual trust and respect increased. Some of BPA's best ideas came out of these informal give-and-take discussions. BPA's public involvement program was proving to be a practical alternative to litigation as it produced innovative solutions to very difficult problems. Solutions that all of BPA's stakeholders had helped to craft.

In one case public participation helped BPA turn a nasty problem into an opportunity. A highly contentious, $2.5 billion lawsuit had been filed against BPA in connection with the mothballing of a nuclear power plant. BPA could either allow the courts to set energy policy or could seize the opportunity to settle the dispute and control the destiny of the electric utility industry in the Pacific Northwest. In the beginning this attempt at settlement through an open public process was considered an impossible undertaking by just about everyone outside the agency. The successful outcome, however, illustrates what can be accomplished through public participation.

If there was ever to be a settlement all interested parties and stakeholders had to buy into the agreement. This included the investor-owned utilities (IOUs) that had filed the lawsuit, the public power utilities, the Northwest's congressional delegation, governors, industrial groups, and public interest groups. And the agreement had to be both fair and perceived as fair. The only way to accomplish this was ultimately to engage in an open public process. BPA first met separately with the IOUs and the public power group. Although public power was not a direct party to the lawsuit, as the preferred customers of BPA by law, their interests were at stake, a situation intensified by long-standing mutual suspicion and mistrust between public and private power. Later when a settlement appeared possible, open public meetings were held to educate and seek comment from other interested parties. This strategy pleased no one, particularly the IOU community.

As BPA staff, including the general counsel and the chief lawyer representing the Department of Justice, shuttled back and forth from one group to the other over a period of months, people gradually began to understand that there were intelligent people with good ideas on both sides of the public power–private power divide. Reconciliation seemed a less remote possibility. Admittedly, the willingness to reach a resolution was partly attributable to the fact that if a preliminary agreement was not reached, BPA would take its own proposal to the public. If they wanted the public to review a settlement that they found generally acceptable, they had to reach a tentative agreement.

By early 1985 after about a dozen meetings, a settlement package looked feasible. The proposal stipulated that BPA would agree to exchange surplus hydropower in the spring for output at other times from the IOU's combustion turbines which were frequently idle. Having reached this threshold it was time to open the process to all interested parties, including the general public. Press releases were issued that explained the lawsuit, the tentative settlement, and the commencement of the open process, including planned forums. BPA staff contacted hundreds of people who would be interested in the outcome. Written records of each contact were kept and BPA made that information public.

By the time the settlement documents were signed in September 1985, BPA's investment in public involvement had paid off handsomely. All utilities were satisfied. The politicians were comfortable, as were their constituents. BPA had saved the investor-owned utilities from serious financial stress, and had avoided wasteful legal battles. The utility community had maintained control over its destiny, converting a problem into an opportunity through consultation with all stakeholders, a task that many had in the beginning thought impossible.

This and many other successes, including the adoption, following a year-long public process, of a creative variable rate that saved the aluminum industry in the Northwest, have enabled BPA to again play its important role in the western United States. The agency's credibility and authority were restored as all stakeholders became convinced that they would be consulted before major decisions were made.

Conclusion

BPA's example is illustrative. The executive leadership of any organization must see the need for a major cultural shift in how they make major decisions affecting many stakeholders. Public participation must never be used as an on-again, off-again expedient, nor as a gimmick to be lightly adopted and then cast aside when results begin to improve. Once initiated, the commitment must be continuously appraised and renewed. Only an unwavering commitment will produce enduring benefits.

Bibliography

Creighton, J. L. (1992). *Involving Citizens in Community Decision Making.* Washington, DC: Program for Community Problem Solving (13-1 Pennsylvania Avenue N.W., Suite 600, Washington, DC 20004).

Johnson, P. T. (1993). How I turned a critical public into useful consultants. *Harvard Business Review,* Jan./Feb.

PETER T. JOHNSON

Great Britain, business ethics in *see* BUSINESS ETHICS IN GREAT BRITAIN

---

greenmail A financial maneuver associated with the turbulent contest for financial control that distinguished corporate finance and stock-market trading in the US during the mid-1980s, creating inevitable echoes in European and Japanese markets as well. Typical greenmail issues from a relatively recent buyer of a large block of one company's stock who sends a threatening message to the company's managers: buy my stock (usually at a premium price not available to other stockholders) or suffer an aggressive effort to take over the firm. The greenmailer commonly is a speculative financial entrepreneur, not another corporate entity. By 1984 greenmail reached a peak in impact on US financial markets, with American corporations paying an estimated $3.5 billion to buy off unwelcome suitors at above-market prices. Thereafter the greenmail maneuver foundered: paying greenmail seldom sufficed for keeping a company or its management intact; major corporations amended their charters to create anti-greenmail barriers; and the US Congress began considering restrictive legislation (*see* ETHICAL ISSUES IN CORPORATE FINANCE).

Greenmail in its heyday drew some moral support from the claim that corporate raiders and the general increase in tender offers worked to improve the value of shareholdings and to discipline otherwise self-satisfied managers. Greenmail also presented itself as a version of legitimate stock repurchase by corporations. The term "greenmail," however, associates the practice with blackmail. That the pejorative quickly overwhelmed use of softer or redemptive words represents the prevailing opinion of the business establishment, which emphasized the ethical questions of fairness to the body of stockholders and the public's interest in thwarting buccaneers out for the quick hit.

See also **corporate governance; fairness; mergers and acquisitions; stockholder; takeovers**

Bibliography

How to foil greenmail. *Fortune,* Jan. 21, 1985, 157–8.

Is greenmail obsolete?. *Institutional Investor,* May 1985, 208–10.

Strategies of takeover attack and defense. *Mergers and Acquisitions,* winter 1985, 24–50.

Vermaelen, T. (1984). Repurchase tender offers, signaling, and managerial incentives. *Journal of Financial and Quantitative Analysis,* **19,** 163–81.

LAWRENCE G. LAVENGOOD

guilt the state of being deserving of punishment in virtue of having culpably done something wrong. Its opposite is innocence. Guilt and innocence are the chief concerns of a system of retributive justice, and punishment, in such a system, is seen as merited evil inflicted for the purpose of exacting just requital for wrongdoing. The fundamental principles of retributive justice are that only the guilty deserve punishment and that the guilty deserve punishment in proportion to the degree of their guilt. Accordingly, it is a rank injustice to punish the innocent. Innocent people do not deserve punishment because either they have done nothing wrong or, though they have done something wrong, it was not their fault. It is also an injustice to punish the guilty excessively. Guilty people deserve only as much punishment as is warranted by the seriousness of their wrongdoing and the egregiousness of their fault. Wrongdoing and fault are therefore the principal factors in understanding guilt.

Wrongdoing can be understood as either the transgression of a limit on conduct imposed by an authority to whom the agent owes obedience or the violation of a norm of conduct that governs the legal or moral relations of the society to which the agent belongs. In either case, wrongdoing represents a breach in the relations between the agent and another or others, and as a result the agent owes reparations or amends to the person or persons relations with whom he has breached. Making amends is the means to his repairing the breach. If the agent was not at fault, then amends are made by giving an explanation that excuses. But if the agent was at fault, then he incurs some guilt and, consequently, must do more to make amends. The guilt, in this case, must be expiated by the agent's suffering evil, which is either self-inflicted through, for example, penance or inflicted by an external authority through submission to punishment.

Fault can be understood as blamable responsibility. It is attributed to wrongdoers in virtue of their having either freely and knowingly chosen to act wrongly or ignorantly chosen to do so when they should have realized the nature of their action. Attributions of fault can thus be defeated by showing that one acted under such duress or compulsion that one was unable to act otherwise. They can also be defeated by showing that one misapprehended the circumstances of the action or lacked foresight of its consequences, provided of course that one's misapprehension or lack of foresight does not itself qualify as blamable ignorance. Duress, compulsion, mistake, and accident are the standard defenses that wrongdoers offer to block the attribution of fault and thus absolve themselves of blame for their act.

In addition, showing that one was not a responsible agent at the time of the action can absolve one of blame. Intoxication, somnambulism, and insanity are defenses that, if cogent, defeat an attribution of fault. Responsible agency, in other words, is a necessary condition of guilt. For this reason, small children and animals cannot incur guilt. Whatever punishment they may duly receive for their misbehavior is needed to reform their character or correct their habits rather than deserved as just requital. In other words, it is disciplinary rather than retributive.

Corporate agents, by contrast, can incur guilt. They too exemplify responsible agency, notwithstanding the collective nature of their deliberations or of the actions that execute the plans those deliberations yield (*see* CORPORATE MORAL AGENCY). Cases of corporate guilt raise questions about whether the guilt falls on the shoulders of any or all of the individuals involved in the agency and, if it does, how it is apportioned among them. These are some of the thorniest questions that a theory of guilt must answer.

Bibliography

Feinberg, J. (1970). *Doing and Deserving: Essays in the Theory of Responsibility*. Princeton: Princeton University Press.

Hart, H. L. A. (1968). *Punishment and Responsibility: Essays in the Philosophy of Law*. Oxford: Oxford University Press.

May, L. (1987). *The Morality of Groups*. Notre Dame, Ind.: University of Notre Dame Press.

Morris, H. (1976). *On Guilt and Innocence: Essays in Legal Philosophy and Moral Psychology*. Berkeley: University of California Press.

JOHN DEIGH

H

happiness 1) The quality or state of being happy, delighted, pleased, glad, joyous, blithe, cheerful, merry, contented, blissful, satisfied. 2) Good fortune; pleasure, enjoyment, satisfaction.

In the history of philosophical thought about happiness, several major, competing accounts may be identified. Hedonists have sought to identify happiness with pleasure, and then have debated whether to characterize pleasures sensually in straightforward quantitative ways or to opt for qualitatively different pleasures and then debate their relative merits and importance in a happy life. Aristotle sided with the qualitative account, and argued that the happy life was one of balance between extremes of each of a number of qualitatively different pleasures, excess and deficiency of which across the course of one's life both contribute to unhappiness.

Stoics held that the proper exercise of reason and recognition of the ephemeral character of the emotions associated with pleasure and pain should lead us to the view that happiness comes with living in accordance with and resignation to the universal, lawful determinants of one's fate. Even Epicureans such as Lucretius argued for a kind of hedonism that disvalued sensuality in favor of the calmer contemplative life of resignation to an existence without punishment or reward after death.

In contrast to the equation of happiness with experience of quantity of sensual pleasures, happiness as a balance between extremes of qualitatively different pleasures, and happiness as resignation to the limits of existence, a fourth, dynamic view characterizes happiness as constituted by an active process of self-realization through a variety of activities. No one formula exists for the happy life on this view; rather, as we might put it, the pursuit of happiness consists in setting and achieving a series of challenging goals; such goals may be set for one by a general, cultural image of a full life, or by the particular set of talents and happenings that set one's "personal destiny" (Norton, 1976; Werkmeister, 1957); but whatever their source, the dynamic view holds that happiness consists in the exercise of a range of competencies.

As struggle to achieve goals is often fraught with frustrations and set-backs, such a dynamic view is, on the face of it, incompatible with hedonistic accounts; and, as the pursuit of goals involves risk-taking and striving against limits, such a view seems incompatible with Stoic resignation. But a deeper reflection shows such incompatibilities to be only apparent and superficial, and shows the dynamic view to be both a synthesis of and an advance over the others.

The dynamic view of happiness is, of course, one which contains a measure of realism. Constant striving towards unattainable goals involves only frustration, and a life filled with frustration cannot be a happy one. So, an appropriate recognition and acceptance of one's limits is essential to happiness on this view, provided that such a resignation is not a quiet counsel of despair. As for hedonism, the wisdom of the dynamic view is that pleasure is most satisfactory and most secure when it is the accompaniment of the achievement of other goals, rather than when it is the goal.

Insofar as business, broadly construed, comprises the full range of human goal-directed activities, the dynamic view seems most appropriate as a characterization of happiness for business ethics. Heidegger emphasized the importance to full humanness of work; and work, properly structured, involves the dynamic setting of goals, striving to realize them, and the satisfaction of (even partial) success in such endeavors. Hence, happiness is central to business ethics, well conceived.

Bibliography

Aristotle,. *Nicomachaean Ethics*, Books I and X. Many editions are available.

Mill, J. S. (1863). *Utilitarianism*, ch. 2. Many editions are available.

Norton, D. (1976). *Personal Destinies: A Philosophy of Ethical Individualism*. Princeton: Princeton University Press.

Werkmeister, W. H. (1957). History and human destiny. *The Personalist*, 38, 117–29.

Zeller, E. (1962 [1870]). *The Stoics, Epicureans, and Sceptics*, trans. O. J. Reichel. New York: Russell & Russell.

RICHARD T. HULL

harm   To say that *A* has harmed *B* is to say that *A* has set back *B*'s interests and thereby wronged *B*. What *A* did to *B* was at once both to cause him harm by setting back his interests, and also to wrong him by violating his right not to be harmed without justification or excuse. There are many ways in which the concept of harm is of central importance for business ethics. For example, in lawsuits between private litigants over property, unfulfilled contracts, or damage done to body, mind, or property, it is usually a necessary condition for liability that some specifiable harm was done to the plaintiff for which he seeks compensation, and indeed, for which compensation, as a matter of public policy, is appropriate. But even in this familiar legal context, misunderstandings of the concept of harm can occur. A judge or jury must decide whether mere offense (like that caused by a leer, an unwanted kiss, or an insult) can ever count as a harm, or whether monetary fines should be greater when the lawbreaker is a wealthy person than when he is not, so as to allocate the "harm" of the punishment in an equal or proportionate way as required by justice. When a friendly passerby actually improves the property of a landowner while trespassing on his land, in what sense, if any, does he harm the landowner's interest in land? Is there an important distinction between the objective harm caused a person and the subjective *hurt*, if any, he suffers either from the harm or from the "very idea" that he is being harmed?

In political philosophy the concept of harm is primarily associated with the work of John Stuart Mill (Mill, 1985; first publ. 1859) whose famous "harm principle" legitimizes only one class of criminal prohibitions, namely, those that are necessary to prevent harm to persons other than the actor. And in ethics generally, it is a challenge to think of any kind of human conduct that can plausibly be condemned as immoral but that does *not* cause harm to someone or other. What are the basic types of harm? Should invasion of privacy be classified as a fourth basic kind of human harm, to be added to the list that includes physical, psychological, and economic harm? And how should one deal with the "moral harm" (harm to one's own character), which, according to Plato's *Republic* (Grube trans. 1974), is the worst kind of harm there is. In what does the "harm" of death consist? While alive a person cannot suffer this particular harm, and the moment he dies he no longer exists to be the subject of the harm. Clearly, when we talk or write of harm, riddles abound.

When we turn toward unspecialized language, we find three senses of harm in general circulation. The first ordinary concept of harm causes great confusion, and probably should be properly labeled by a philosopher and then dismissed. In this extended or transferred sense of the word "harm," any kind of thing can be harmed. Our reference to "harm" when we apply that notion to automobile engines and the like, is elliptical for the harm done to those who have interests in the maintenance or improvement of the engine, those who, in a manner of speaking, have invested some of their own well-being in some condition of inanimate objects.

The second ordinary sense of "harm" is the original from which the first is derived. This is harm conceived as thwarting, setting back, or defeating (even destroying) an interest. In turn, a person has an interest in *x* (whether *x* be a company, a career, or some kind of issue of events) when he stands to gain or lose depending on the nature or condition of *x*. A person's total set of interests, or perhaps more accurately, the things those interests are *in*, are distinguishable components of a person's well-being. He flourishes or languishes as they flourish or languish. So in the second sense, "harm" refers to setback to interest. The next problem for a philosopher is to list in some sort of priority order what the basic human interests are, and how they must be related to one another if they are to be harmoniously satisfied.

The third sense of "harm" is one we must ascribe to John Stuart Mill's "harm principle," if that principle is to play any important role in political theory. In this third sense, the word "harm" merges interests and rights. Harming another person in this sense means "adversely affecting" his interest in a way that wrongs him or, equivalently, wronging him in a way that adversely affects his interest. There are numerous advantages to the third sense of "harm." Without it, for example, much of Mill's *On Liberty* would be extremely implausible. Since we are justified in using the criminal law, for example, to prevent people from harming other people, and to punish those persons and only those persons who have violated statutes meant to prevent harm, it would seem to be justifiable to punish a professional boxer for breaking his opponent's jaw in a licensed boxing match. In general, all types of competitive situations in which, whatever the outcome, one competitor must win and another must lose would pose the hazard of criminal punishment for the winner or for any participant inadvertently injured during the fray. Even sales competitions between rival retailers might seem to be endangered when the word "harm" is used only in its second sense in the formulation of Mill's harm principle. The interest-rights definition of "harm" often obviates these unwelcome results, but the most important philosophical tactic is the one that generates one person's rights from other peoples' *consent*. *A* does not harm *B* in this third sense if he persuades her without coercion or fraud to engage in a fair wager with him. If she then loses the wager she will be harmed in the sense that her pecuniary interest will be set back, but she will not be wronged, since she freely assumed the risk of loss from the beginning. Thus she will not be harmed in the third sense, which merges setback to interest with wrong. One class of harms must certainly be excluded from those that are properly called wrongs, namely those to the risk of which the injured party had freely consented.

See also **consent; Mill, John Stuart**

Bibliography

Aristotle. (1985). *Nicomachean Ethics,* trans. T. Irwin. Indianapolis, Ind.: Hackett.

Feinberg, J. (1984). *Harm to Others.* New York: Oxford University Press.

Kleinig, J. (1978). Crime and the concept of harm. *American Philosophical Quarterly,* **15,** 31–125.

Mill, J. S. (1985 [1859]). *On Liberty.* Indianapolis, Ind.: Hackett.

Plato. (1960). *Gorgias,* trans. W. Hamilton. Harmondsworth, England: Penguin.

Plato. (1974). *Republic,* trans. G. M. A. Grube. Indianapolis, Ind.: Hackett.

JOEL FEINBERG

Hayek, Friedrich A. (1899–1992)   was one of the twentieth century's most forceful defenders of classical liberalism and critics of socialism. Hayek's central contentions turn on his contrast between two conceptions of social order. The exogenous, designed conception of social order is the root of socialist aspirations. It sees order as the conscious creation of the social engineer who knows what end should be promoted and knows how to marshall society's human and extra-human resources to advance this *summum bonum*. A society is rational only insofar as it is consciously constructed or reconstructed by an authority who expertly surveys the ways in which people's lives may be organized, identifies the best organization, and effectively directs people toward it.

The endogenous, non-designed conception sees order emerging, as though directed by an INVISIBLE HAND, out of the interactions and accommodations of individuals, each of whom has particular knowledge about his own values, circumstances, skills, and opportunities, which no central planner could gather or utilize. Coordination vastly more subtly adjusted to people's diverse values and circumstances arises when individual planning is not overridden by authorities afflicted with the conceit that they know society's purpose and how to mobilize for it. For Hayek, people's diverse purposes are best served by reliance on fragmented knowledge and endogenous orders. This, however, requires that authority be restricted to "delimiting distinct individual rights (the rights of property, for example) and [thereby] designating domains within which each can dispose over means known to him for his own ends" (Hayek, 1988, p. 63).

Bibliography

Hayek, F. A. (1944). *The Road to Serfdom*. London: Routledge and Sons.

Hayek, F. A. (1948). *Individualism and Economic Order*. London: Routledge and Sons.

Hayek, F. A. (1960). *The Constitution of Liberty*. Chicago: University of Chicago Press.

Hayek, F. A. (1973, 1976, 1979). *Law, Legislation, and Liberty*, 3 vols. Chicago: University of Chicago Press.

Hayek, F. A. (1988). *The Fatal Conceit*. Chicago: University of Chicago Press.

ERIC MACK

hazardous waste are wastes (solids, sludges, liquids, and containerized gases) other than radioactive (and infectious) wastes, which, by reason of their chemical activity or toxic, explosive, corrosive, or other characteristics, cause danger or likely will cause danger to health or the environment, either alone or when coming in contact with other wastes. Waste here refers to a movable object that has no direct use and is discarded permanently. (Lagrega, Buckingham, & Evans). Wastes are an unintended byproduct of production processes. With the increasing use of toxic substances in production (both goods and services), many wastes are hazardous to human health and the natural environment. The definition of what exactly constitutes "hazardous" waste, is highly debated and varies widely, depending on the country's laws. Most industrialized nations have laws (developed in the past 20 years) defining hazardous wastes, and specifying mechanisms for their containment, transportation, and disposal.

The true scale of the hazardous waste problem facing the world in this last decade of the twentieth century, is not known for several reasons. First, there is definitional variability across countries. Even within each country the definition of "hazardous" keeps changing continuously, as new information about toxicity of substances and interaction effects between substances is developed. Second, there is paucity of good data on how much hazardous waste is generated. Moreover, there is very incomplete information about where past toxic wastes are stored or buried.

The USA alone generates annually 250 to 280 million tons of regulated (under the Resource Conservation and Recovery Act) hazardous wastes, and an additional 320 million metric tons of waste not regulated under this act. There are over 37,000 known hazardous waste sites that need remediation. 2,000 to 3,000 new waste sites are created each year. Over 1,275 toxic waste sites are considered active dangers to public health and are on the Environmental Protection Agency's National Priority List (Likens, 1987).

These figures pertain only to the civilian sector. Little information is available on toxic wastes production and storage by defense establishments. These were kept secret until recently. The scale of the defense-related toxic waste problem may be larger than the civilian sector.

The causes of toxic waste production are many. Production technologies today use more toxic substances than ever before. Chemicals, mining, heavy manufacturing, power generation, and nuclear technologies are major sources of hazardous wastes. Our knowledge of toxicity is expanding very fast. With rapid advances in the science of toxicology, what was considered nontoxic a few years ago, is turning out to be intolerably toxic today (National Toxicology Program, 1984). As the number of chemicals in the atmosphere increase, so do the interactions between them. These chemical interactions are complex and a source of hazard to ecosystems. For example, sulfur and nitrogen oxides released by burning of fossil fuels interact to create acid rain. This acidic water accumulates in lakes and groundwater tables, which also receive agricultural runoffs rich in fertilizer and pesticide residues. The resulting chemical interactions create lakes that cannot support marine life.

The consequences of hazardous waste proliferation include damage to ecosystems, detrimental health effects, and widespread blight on the landscape. While there is much scientific controversy on exact level of damages, there is wide recognition of the presence of this problem among public and corporate policy-makers, media, and citizens. The secondary effects of these damages include decline in real estate values around hazardous waste sites and community resistance to creating new waste sites in their midst (Postel, 1987).

There are several ethical issues raised by the hazardous waste problem. The first ethical concern involves the inequitable distribution of risks posed by these wastes. There is some preliminary evidence that hazardous waste sites are often located in poor sections of communities. The poor bear a disproportionately high amount of health risks created by toxic wastes. The not-in-my-backyard attitude serves to concentrate hazardous waste sites in powerless communities and neighborhoods (Portney, 1991). A second ethical issue is the intergenerational transfers of impacts of hazardous wastes. We are creating wastes that will last for generations and impose health and ecological burdens on future generations. Some nuclear wastes will have deleterious effects for thousands of years. The morality of this practice is questionable.

The third ethical issue is the export of toxic wastes. Despite the Basel Convention banning the export of toxic wastes, many countries continue to ship toxic wastes to poor developing countries (Vallette, 1989). These countries lack the technological and financial capacity to safely deal with these wastes, and eventually they harm both the natural environment and humans.

The long-term ecologically sustainable solution to the toxic waste problem lies in not producing them in the first place. This will require development of cleaner production technologies, abandonment of certain inherently toxic substances, and changes in consumption habits (Commoner, 1990). Bringing about these changes in individuals, corporations, and government institutions is the ethical challenge facing us all.

Bibliography

Commoner, B. (1990). *Making Peace with the Planet*. New York: Pantheon.

Lagrega, M. D., Buckingham, P. L., & Evans J. C. (1994). *Hazardous Waste Management*. New York: McGraw-Hill.

Likens, G. (1987). Chemical wastes in our atmosphere – An ecological crisis. *Industrial Crisis Quarterly*, 1, (4), 13–33.

National Toxicology Program. (1984). *Toxicity Testing: Strategies to Determine Needs and Priorities*. Washington, DC: National Academy Press.

Portney, K. E. (1991). *Siting Hazardous Waste Treatment Facilities: The NIMBY Syndrome*. New York: Auburn House.

Postel, S. (1987). Diffusing the toxics threat: Controlling pesticides and industrial wastes. Worldwatch Paper 79. Washington, DC: Worldwatch Institute.

Shrivastava, P. (1995). *Greening Business: Profiting Corporations and the Environment*. Cincinnati, Ohio: Thompson Executive Press.

Vallette, J. (1989). *The International Trade in Waste: A Greenpeace Inventory*. Washington, DC: Greenpeace.

PAUL SHRIVASTAVA

health-care ethics and business ethics Health-care ethics, which is a more specialized branch of the field widely known as bioethics, deals with ethical issues that arise in the health-care setting. Some of the more significant subjects in health-care ethics are the moral traditions and directives of health-care workers, the health-care worker/patient relationship, the rights and responsibilities of patients, access to health care, and the allocation of resources (Beauchamp & Childress, 1994).

One of the most interesting similarities between the fields of health-care ethics and business ethics is their relatively recent emergence. A wide array of writings dating from ancient times can be found on ethics in both business and medicine. The writings and traditions of medicine, in particular, have a rich and extensive grounding in ethics. However, it is only within the past 40 years that both business ethics and bioethics have become distinct academic disciplines which also correspond to wider social movements designed to reshape their respective practices. Although it is difficult to determine precisely when they came into being, the "Birth of Bioethics" has been traced by historians and bioethicists to the year 1962, when a Seattle hospital faced the problem of allocating a scarce life-saving medical treatment (kidney dialysis) (Jonsen, 1993). Business ethics is a newer field and has no such defining movement. In the US, it has origins in the movement for corporate social responsibility in the 1970s, and Watergate, and developed critical mass during the 1980s amid the popular reaction to the perceived excesses of that period – what some commentators called "the decade of greed." Numerous theories have been put forward as to why these movements have taken root. The factor which seems to be most commonly cited by researchers as the impetus for their emergence is the pluralistic character of modern American culture. However, there is considerable disagreement as to whether the diversity of values that allegedly gives to the need for "business ethics" and "bioethics" represents a healthy culture or a society in a state of moral decay (MacIntyre, 1984; Stout, 1984; Walzer, 1983). Other factors that have been cited include: the increasing complexity of society (as well as health care and business), broader social changes, the rapid expansion of technology, the increased effectiveness and importance of medical treatment, and the growing influence of business on medicine. Finally, as these movements have grown, there is an ongoing ambiguity about the appropriate role for ethicists, particularly as they are being drawn into more practice-related roles as consultants and policy advisers. The question of what "expertise" ethicists have has been raised, but the status and function of ethicists is far from resolved in either field.

Another connection between business ethics and health-care ethics is the alleged influence of business on the practice of medicine. This has become particularly evident in the past several decades. A number of studies have indicated a powerful interaction between medicine and business, especially as health care becomes more dependent on high technology, pharmaceuticals, private medical insurance, and other resources which are both directly and indirectly connected to business (Starr, 1982). While there is disagreement regarding the extent to which business has reshaped medicine, there is widespread agreement that business has become an increasingly powerful influence in how medicine is practiced. E. Haavi Morreim has argued that the traditional model of the health-care encounter found in the Hippocratic tradition, that of a doctor and patient, has been under pressure to change for some time and must

include a wider array of interested parties or stakeholders in health-care related decision-making (Morreim, 1992). Private businesses, which provide the technology and resources that enable health-care workers to provide care, are among the array of groups she believes deserve a legitimate role in how health-care resources are allocated and delivered. Some authors have argued that the increasing influence of business is an alarming recent trend. Implicit in their argument is a belief that medicine has retained much of its distinctiveness and independence from business (Relman, 1992; Dougherty, 1990). However, as health-care costs rise and the use of technology increases it appears that this interaction will be expanding for the foreseeable future. As a result, it will be increasingly difficult to sharply distinguish health care from business; both at the institutional level and in terms of practitioners. Evidence for this can be found in the mission statements and practices of a number of health-related businesses, particularly the pharmaceutical industry.

There are also alleged connections between the central moral norms of both fields. Although little has been done to compare the moral traditions and concepts which structure the inquiry of ethicists in both fields, recent research makes a case that there are fundamental similarities between the two (Wicks, 1995a). Furthermore, if one can make a case that the line between health care and health-related businesses is becoming blurred, then it strengthens the basis for connecting the normative core of each field. Some authors are deeply suspicious of business and fear the traditions of medicine will be eroded or destroyed by any wholesale interaction between these institutions and their respective ethics (Relman, 1992; Dougherty, 1990). Others argue that a comprehensive meshing of (the ethics of) medicine and business (ethics) is necessary to serve the needs of society (Morreim, 1992; Agich, 1990; Wicks, 1995b).

Finally, both fields are influenced by other disciplines. Philosophy and religious studies have proven to be particularly important resources to develop vibrant accounts of applied ethics. More specifically, business ethicists and bioethicists draw on these broader resources to develop a more systematic base from which to generate moral insights or theories that can be related to specific human activities.

Bibliography

Agich, G. (1990). Medicine as a business and profession. *Theoretical Medicine*, 11, 311-24

Beauchamp, T. L. & Childress, J. F. (1989). *Principles of Biomedical Ethics*, 3rd edn, New York: Oxford University Press.

Dougherty, C. (1990). The cost of commercial medicine. *Theoretical Medicine*, 11, 275.

Jonsen, A. R. (1993). The birth of bioethics. Special Supplement of *The Hastings Center Report*, (Nov./Dec.): S1-15.

MacIntyre, A. (1988). *After Virtue*, 2nd edn, Notre Dame: University of Notre Dame Press.

Morreim, E. H. (1992). *The New Medical Ethics of Medicine's New Economics*. New York: Klewter.

Reich, W. T. (ed.) (1978). *Encyclopedia of Bioethics*. New York: The Free Press.

Relman, A. (1992). What market values are doing to medicine. *Atlantic Monthly*, Mar., 106.

Starr, P. (1982). *The Social Transformation of American Medicine*. New York: Basic Books.

Stout, J. (1988). *Ethics After Babel*. Boston: Beacon Press.

Walzer, M. (1983). *Spheres of Justice*. New York: Basic Books.

Wicks, A. C. (1995a). Albert Schweitzer or Ivan Boesky? Why should we reject the dichotomy between medicine and business. *Journal of Business Ethics*,14 (5), 6339-51.

Wicks, A. C. (1995b). The business ethics movement: Where are we headed and what can we learn from our colleagues in bioethics. *Business Ethics Quarterly*, 5 (3), 603-20.

ANDREW C. WICKS

Hinduism, business ethics and   *see* BUSINESS ETHICS AND HINDUISM

history of business ethics   Concern about ethical issues in business goes back as far as history itself; there has always been some form of mandate for people in commerce. The Egyptians were not to take money for passage across the river until after the passenger was safely there. In the Old Testament interest was not to be taken on loans. For ARISTOTLE interest was also not to be levied on loans because money was "consumed" in its first use (like fruit) and therefore had no other use for which interest could be extracted. Cicero asked about price justice for goods in a starving city. Dionesian Roman Law prescribed that justice requires to grant to each person what is his/her due.

Arguments against the position of the Roman Catholic Church towards business can be traced to scholastic theologians, especially to Thomas Aquinas. Some claim that for Aquinas a just price was determined by the inherent nature of the product and not by the market forces of supply and demand, although subsequent studies have shown that the medieval scholars acknowledged market forces in determining business ethics. In the medieval period the guilds furnished protection and standards for their respective groups. The Reformation and the trade in the new world opened new horizons for business and its practices, including slavery, an upcoming middle class of merchants, and a rising sense of nationalism. Much later, ADAM SMITH's *Wealth of Nations* fits well into the overall surge into developing an industrial society and setting minimum standards for business behavior. Ethical principles such as Kant's categorical imperative, and Bentham's utilitarianism also served the industrial revolution and its new ethical choices (*see* KANTIAN ETHICS; UTILITARIANISM). However, no set of ethical principles or practices emerged to guide business practices of employers and employees. In the late nineteenth century the underpinning concepts of business ethics – power and rights – were exercised in such interacting arenas as courts of law, unions, trade associations, and professional societies (*see* POWER; RIGHTS). Social DARWINISM, with its new evolutionary social ideology of progress in an industrial society, became prominent. In 1881, Pope Leo XIII reacted by writing his famous social encyclical (letter) on capital and labor. He used natural-law principles and the theories of Thomas Aquinas to fortify his arguments for the rights of labor. The 1886 Haymarket riots in Chicago, however, exemplify conflict between employer and employees during this period of industrial growth.

In the early twentieth century, most of the books on business ethics were general in approach and provided an overview on an issue or a specific aspect or problem. For example, they did not deal with an overall problem of business ethics. The exception was Sharp and Fox (1937), who covered pricing, lying, and other topics which related to the economics of business in their book. Issues dealing with employee rights, the environment, and international ethics would come at a much later date.

The first breakthrough for a general interest in business ethics came in BAUMHART's revealing 1961 study, "How Ethical Are Businessmen?" Baumhart's study was published in 1961 when the electrical industry price-fixing scandal shook the United States. It was the first empirical study which showed that ethical issues and problems were found in every industry, in most companies, and on all levels of the managerial pyramid. This revelation came at a time when business enjoyed an outstanding reputation for providing goods and services, where it was assumed that executives and managers acted in an ethical manner.

Following Baumhart's study, the principle-to-solution approach to ethical problems in business was frequently, but not exclusively, pursued through NATURAL LAW concepts in conferences, textbooks, and general interest books. Furthermore, the manager was himself (sic) responsible and accountable: business ethics was personal and individual – it was not corporate. The issues and the problems were generally perceived from an individualistic viewpoint. For example, the highest executives of the General Electric Corporation believed that the company did not have any responsibility for the managers who fixed prices. Padded expense accounts, bribery, "call girls," cheating, lying, pricing, and wages were some of the popular topics which were discussed and written about. Most of the concerns were personal, not corporate: how was this executive or manager responsible for his ethical problem? Courses in institutions of higher learning were generally called Business Ethics and were frequently taught in the philosophy departments, although some were given by business law or management departments (see BUSINESS ETHICS).

The 1964 US Civil Rights Act and subsequent social legislation triggered an awareness of concerns which affected employees, the environment, and the community, both local and national. The term business ethics was frequently replaced with the phrase "the social responsibilities of business," thus incorporating prevailing social norms and expectations. The change of name reflected the shift in emphasis from the personal ethics of the manager to the overall position of the company on such issues as racial and sexual discrimination, air and water pollution, plant closing, and employee rights, the companies became legally and ethically responsible for implementing these changes. "Responsibility" as such implies having assumed an obligation and is thus accountable and prescriptive in nature. Responsibility also refers to rights as well as to obligations (see RESPONSIBILITY). Furthermore, the philosophical approach to business ethics shifted from natural law to utilitarianism and Kant's categorical imperative. RAWLS' theory of distributive justice became a necessary tool in the teaching of business ethics. By 1975, US colleges and universities offered over 550 undergraduate and graduate courses on business ethics, although most institutions used titles such as "Business and Society." Text books and case books on business ethics proliferated, written primarily by philosophers who specialized in applied ethics. Bowie, Cavanagh, Davis, Donaldson, De George, Frederick, Garrett, Goodpastor, Sethi, Steiner, Velasquez, Walton, and Werhane are just a few of the authors who published anthologies and textbooks on business ethics. Centers for research and programs on business ethics as well as endowed chairs multiplied; business ethics became recognized as a distinct discipline in academia. Indeed, in 1976 the prestigious Academy of Management added a "social issues in management" division.

The Watergate Affair and payoffs to foreign government officials in the 1970s shifted emphasis once again in business ethics. Media attention on questions about who told subordinates to act illegally and\or unethically pierced the corporate veil of secrecy; personal accountability within institutional structures became the arena of concern. The question was: "Who told whom to do what as it affected society?" At the same time, payoffs to foreign government officials precipitated the 1977 FOREIGN CORRUPT PRACTICES ACT. It also set the stage of discussing not only the issue of personal accountability but also the question of cross-cultural differences and incompatible legal systems: Whose ethics does a business person follow when she/he is in a foreign country? Finally, business ethicians became concerned with political and social structures that permitted humans to be treated in an inhumane manner, such as apartheid, child labor, and land division. These changes led to a newer view of business decision-making in the form of what authors refer to as "social responsiveness" which both requires a reaction of social pressures but also the "long-run role in a dynamic social system" (Sethi, 1974), which in turn should be anticipatory and preventative. Frederick (1978) calls corporate social responsibility CSR_1, which has a philosophic underpinning. He names corporate social responsiveness CSR_2, which refers to the capacity of the corporation to respond to social pressures; it is a more pragmatic effort in reacting to the corporate environment. While social responsibility relates more clearly to rights and obligations, social responsiveness reacts to pressures which are in effect various forms of power exercised by different groups affecting the corporation. Davis and Blomstrom, Post, Sethi, Wilson, and others have developed various categories to illustrate social responsiveness. Carroll has combined social responsibility, social responsiveness, and social issues to produce the "corporate social performance model."

Two sets of events in the 1980s encouraged business ethicians to consider 1) insider trading and 2) an unprecedented number of acquisitions and mergers. The former challenged the ethical as well as the legal practices of the financial community. First of all, using insider information unbalanced the competitive environment, but discussion on what constituted insider information left much gray area, while the law challenged violators like Boesky (*see* INSIDER TRADING).

Freeman (1984) and others developed the notion of stakeholders: "an individual or group who can affect or is affected by the actions, decisions, policies or goals of the organization." The notion of stakeholder broadened the relationship of the firm to different, and perhaps previously disregarded, elements in society, such as special-interest groups, social activists, environmentalists, and institutional social investing (*see* STAKEHOLDER THEORY). The

proliferation of mergers and acquisitions occasioned "downsizing," "rightsizing," and "reorganization" which resulted at times in massive terminations of employees, including executives and managers. Middle management positions were frequently eliminated, employees felt a loss of job security, and they redirected their loyalty in the firm. Furthermore, the term "business ethics" now included the broader view of social issues. Authors included the social responsibilities of business, business and society, and perhaps even public policy under the now more generic "business ethics." Indeed, the founding of the Society for Business Ethics resolved the concern of individual and social issues of business once and forever. Business ethics included both.

In the late 1980s and 1990s business ethics assumed an international flavor. European philosophers and business school professors in particular began to develop their own approaches. Up to this time, the Europeans and others depended primarily on material produced by American scholars. The political and economic changes in the Eastern European countries and the forming of the European Community raised specific issues in business ethics that had not been adequately treated previously by Americans, such as language and cultural changes when working in foreign countries. The European approach has strong philosophical tenets as well as interests in dealing with the ethics of economics. It also questions the moral individualism of American decision-making which is closely linked to individual persons. Indeed, these new problem-type approaches should have a greater interdisciplinary analysis. The European approach is more collegial and investigates long-term interests of all concerned. Business ethics is thus conceived as a consensual ethic, possibly a result of the different variations of European social democracy. EBEN (the European Business Ethics Network) is the institutionalized network for European ethicians. Enderle, Mahoney, Ryan and van Luijk are familiar names in the European setting.

Political events raise business ethics issues: NAFTA (North American Free Trade Agreement) and GATT (General Agreement on Tariffs and Trade) (*see* GATT). These agreements have international implications for business ethics in terms of jobs, relocation, investing, environment, and discrimination, both racial and sexual. It is too early to determine the precise ethical application of these issues, which standards will apply, and how they will be implemented. Furthermore, the legal disintegration of apartheid raises new problems in business ethics, such as ownership of property, foreign investing, and equal job opportunity (see EQUAL OPPORTUNITY).

International business ethics is different from national business ethics inasmuch as there is no sovereign power to settle claims; there are different derivative values from different cultures; there are problems of communication; and there are differences in interpretation and application.

The one constant in the history of business ethics has been change: in emphasis, in philosophy, in topics, in cases. Change is also noticeable in accountability: from the individual to the corporation and then returning to the individual within the corporation. Changing economics, financial, and marketing functions shifted production and distribution, which in turn brought new and sometimes different ethical problems. Business ethics has also broadened its scope from national and regional issues to international and global concerns. All this change has produced a complexity in business ethics that requires thorough inquiry and innovative solutions.

Bibliography

Baumhart, S. J., & Raymond C. (1961). How Ethical Are Businessmen? *Harvard Business Review*, **39** (4).

Beauchamp, T. L. & Norman E. Bowie, (eds) (1993). *Ethical Theory and Business*, 4th edn. Englewood Cliffs, NJ: Prentice-Hall.

Buchholtz, R. A. (1992). *Business Environment and Public Policy*, 4th edn. Englewood Cliffs, NJ: Prentice-Hall.

Cavanagh, G. F. (1976). *American Business Values in Transition*. Englewood Cliffs, NJ: Prentice-Hall.

Carroll, A. B. (1993). *Business and Society: Ethics and Stakeholder Management*, 2nd edn. Cincinnati, Ohio: South-Western.

Davis, K. & Blomstrom, R. L. (1971). *Business, Society and Environment: Social Power and Social Response*, 2nd edn. New York: McGraw-Hill.

De George, R. T. & Pichler, J. A. (eds) (1978). *Ethics, Free Enterprise and Public Policy*. New York: Oxford University Press.

Donaldson, T. & Werhane, P. H. (eds) (1993). *Ethical Issues in Business: A Philosophical Approach*, 4th edn. Englewood Cliffs, NJ: Prentice-Hall.

Frederick, W. C. (1978). From CSR$_1$ to CSR$_2$: The Maturing of Business-and-Society Thought. Graduate School of Business, University of Pittsburgh, 1978. working paper No. 279.

Frederick, W. C., Post, J., & Davis, K. (1992). *Business and Society: Corporate Strategy, Public Policy, Ethics*, 7th edn. New York: McGraw-Hill.

Freeman, R. E. (1984). *Strategic Management: A Stakeholder Approach*. Boston: Pitman.

McMahon, T. F. (1975). *Report on the Teaching of Socio-Ethical Issues in Collegiate Schools of Business/ Public Administration*. Charlottesville, Va: University of Virginia Press.

Sethi, S. P. (ed.) (1974). *The Unstable Ground: Corporate Social Policy in a Dynamic Society*. Los Angeles: Melville Publishing.

Sharp, F. C. & Fox, P. G. (1937). *Business Ethics: Studies in Fair Competition*. New York: Appleton-Century.

van Luijk, H. J. L. (1990). Recent Developments in European Business Ethics. *Journal of Business Ethics*, **9**, 537-44.

Velasquez, M. G. (1982). *Business Ethics: Concepts and Cases*. Englewood Cliffs, NJ: Prentice-Hall.

THOMAS F. MCMAHON

Hobbes, Thomas (1588–1679): Describing himself as the "twin of fear" because his premature birth was supposedly caused by rumors of the Spanish armada off the coast of England, Thomas Hobbes made fear of death the centerpiece of his political and moral theorizing. In a series of works culminating in *Leviathan* (1651), Hobbes argued for the institution of an absolute sovereign as a way to further the peace of the community and thereby promote the preservation and comforts of its citizens. To reach this conclusion he forged a social contract argument, a type of argument popular among some intellectuals of his day but which he revolutionized in a way that powerfully influenced the political thinking of subsequent contractarians such as LOCKE (1632–1704), Rousseau (1712-1778), and Kant (1724-1804) (see SOCIAL CONTRACT THEORY; KANTIAN ETHICS).

Imagine, says Hobbes, a "state of nature" prior to the creation of all governments: in this state of nature, he argues, human nature is such that before long there would be "a war of everyone against everyone" so that every person's life would be "solitary, poor, nasty, brutish and short" (*Leviathan*, ch. 13). To remedy such war, Hobbes argues that people would contract with one another to create a government with a sovereign holding absolute power, because only absolute power is sufficient to resolve disputes that otherwise would precipitate conflict dissolving the commonwealth. Such an argument is meant to show the kind of government that we would be rational to create and sustain, lest we descend into a state of war analogous to the one that would exist in the state of nature.

Hobbes also published other works tackling issues in metaphysics and epistemology (including ontology, scientific method, and FREE WILL), and topics in science and mathematics (including optics, geometry, and human physiology).

Bibliography

A longer version of this entry appeared in Becker, L. C. & Becker C. B. (eds) (1992). *Encyclopedia of Ethics*. New York: Garland, 543–9.

Gauthier, D. (1969). *The Logic of Leviathan*. Oxford: Clarendon Press.
Hampton, J. (1986). *Hobbes and the Social Contract Tradition*. Cambridge: Cambridge University Press.
Hobbes, T. (1965). *Leviathan*, (ed.), C. B. MacPherson. Harmondsworth, England: Penguin.
Kavka, G. (1986). *Hobbesian Moral and Political Theory*. Princeton: Princeton University Press.
Watkins, J. W. N. (1965). *Hobbes's System of Ideas*. London: Hutchinson.

JEAN HAMPTON

humanities and business ethics

> Novels and stories are renderings of life; they can not only keep us company, but admonish us, point us in new directions, or give us the courage to stay on a given course. (Coles, 1989, p. 159)

A central issue in teaching a theoretical discipline, such as philosophy or ethics, involves exemplifying and connecting theory to the common and often complex realm of human experience. This is especially true in the case of business ethics. Generally speaking, the problem of connecting theory and experience in undergraduate-level business ethics classes is compounded by two salient but seldom-articulated factors. (1) In most, but certainly not all, cases the class is taught by an instructor who probably has no, or at best, limited business experience. (2) In a traditional undergraduate setting, the course is taught to individuals who have yet to begin their careers in business. Additionally, there is the issue of how business ethics is taught and presented in the classroom. Studies indicate that the materials used fall into four major categories (Kennedy & Lawton, 1992): monographs on business ethics; collections of case studies; classic treatises on ethics; and anthologies and texts that combine elements of the former categories.

We are not arguing that these texts and their standard pedagogical presentations are wrong, but rather that they remain limited in their ability to infuse theory with experience. As one important study has pointed out, there remains "a sad lack of dialogue in business ethics courses between theory and case analysis" (Derry & Green, 1989, p. 531).

While these traditional texts can adequately unpack the theoretical framework of ethics, most cases offered are often only fact-driven snapshots of heroic "war stories" that overlook the fundamental human issues that lie at the core of every ethical dilemma: personality, character development, as well as the texture and nuances of the story-line that envelope the particular incident in question.

William J. Bennett has correctly pointed out that what is at stake in any *ethics* course is the "formation of character" (Bennett, 1993, p. 13), or perhaps more modestly, the development of ethical sensitivity and sensibility. In particular, what is at stake in a *business ethics* class is the development of ethically sensitive businesspeople and managers who, as yet, lack managerial experience. How then can instructors best fill in or offer a substitute for their students' as well as their own lack of experience? How do we give business ethics students a sense of what it is like to be a manager confronted by ethical dilemmas?

This issue is analogous to a problem raised by Thomas Nagel in his influential paper "What is it like to be a bat?" Nagel argues that in order to correctly attribute consciousness to an organism, there has to be "something that it is like to *be* that organism." That is, every conscious organism experiences the world from a unique conscious perspective. In order to properly understand an organism's consciousness, one has to adopt its point of view, and experience the world from its unique conscious perspective. The trick is to give up one's own perspective entirely, and get inside the "point of view" of that organism. Nagel's point is a variation on the old chestnut about walking a mile in another's shoes before judging him/her. In essence he is asking us to adopt the other's perspective, rather than merely add our own to it. While it is debatable if this is ever totally possible, we contend that this perspective shifting can best be approximated through the pedagogical use of narratives.

Fundamentally, narratives are stories, fictional tales, or accounts of human encounters, interactions, emotional experiences, commonplace occurrences, and critical dilemmas. According to Amos N. Wilder, the call of stories is deeply entrenched in the evolution of the human psyche and heart. Storytelling helps fulfill our natural quest for orientation, it facilitates our "mapping of experience." We orient ourselves to our own experience of life, to the unknown and to the experiences of others by the stories we know and share with others. For Wilder the appeal of a story is grounded in the natural curiosity of the human condition. How did it begin? What happened? How does it unfold? What is it getting at? How does it end? What does it mean? Does any of it apply to me? (Wilder, 1983, p. 354). The story and its characters, said Wilder, can capture our attention, expose us to new knowledge, explain things, and offer insight into ourselves and others. Stories can give us differing textures and motifs of various cultural contexts and differing horizons (Wilder, 1983, p. 357).

For Wilder, stories hold us because they "light up our own adventures." Under the disguises of false-realism, theatrical drama, and action, our attention is riveted and our imagination is challenged by a combination of surprises (novelty), and familiarity (recognition) (Wilder,

1983, p. 358). Fiction (even science fiction) never really takes us out of the world. In following along with the foibles and follies of the story line a kind of charting occurs (p. 359). The imagination is offered a staged rehearsal of possible lived experience. Readers (or listeners) themselves are voyeurs and tacit interlocutors in the performance; participants in the world-making going on (p. 358). The "orientation exercise" of a story is complete when fiction offers us insight into others as well as ourselves.

Robert Coles believes that literature stirs the "moral imagination." Novels (stories), said Coles, nudge us to think about what we want – and at what cost (1987, p. 14).

> The point of reading . . . fiction, is to stir . . . the students and teachers alike to take stock of themselves: what they believe in, what they want out of life, how they want to live that life. Fiction can be infectiously engaging, can prompt us to sift and sort, to consider ups and downs, desirable possibilities and potentially harmful impasses or dead-end streets. The point, ultimately, is to stir the moral imagination – to encourage us as readers to look inward as we keep moving through our days and ways. (Coles, 1987, p. 12)

Echoing the works of William Carlos Williams, Coles argues that when we immerse ourselves in a world of stories replete with moral drama, the hope is that when the reader closes the book his/her own character is influenced. And, he suggests, if you don't get nudged into practicing what you read, then you are at a moral standstill (1987, p. 9). If "character is fate," as Heraclitus suggested, then studying the "character" of others may help us to better understand and improve our own "fate."

It is our contention that the use of narratives, novels, or stories broadens the intellectual venue for a dialogue between the issues, the players, the setting, and the moral risks at stake in an ethical decision-making process, especially regarding business ethics. Traditional teaching methods often remove the study of business ethics from the broader fabric of social life. Literature, by its very nature, weaves the problems of business ethics into the fabric of social life.

At the very least, as Robert Coles has suggested, even if you don't find specific answers in stories, you will find lots of questions, lots of detailed contextual data, which will offer some insight into the ideas, values, and behavior of the characters involved.

> Novels don't (always) supply the intellect its prized formulations, but rather, suggest various moral, social, and psychological possibilities – stimulate the mind's capacity to wonder, to dream, to put itself in all sorts of situations, and to be shaped by such imaginative experiences. (Coles, 1987, p. 12)

For these reasons, we believe that literature is at the very least an important supplement to case studies and philosophical treatises in aiding the student manager's search for virtue. As Kennedy and Lawton (1992) have argued:

> through reading imaginary and imaginative dramatizations of business dilemmas, students will develop new and perhaps greater awareness of the complexity of the ethical and moral dilemmas contained therein than they achieve through either essays or through the use of case studies. Narratives also provide students with a clear picture of a problem; through the heightened realism of a story, we are able to see very clearly what the main characters are struggling with.

Ten Contemporary Suggestions

In addition to the list of obvious classics in the area (*The Great Gatsby, Babbitt, The Jungle, The Man in the Grey Flannel Suit, Billy Budd, Death of a Salesman, Catch-22, Grapes of Wrath, Seize the Day*), we would like to suggest ten recent publications for classroom use.

Bibliography

Ethan Canin, *The Palace Thief* (novella) (1993). If "character is fate," then what can be expected from a person driven by fear, ambition, power, and the need to be in the public eye?

Charles Dickenson, *Rumor Has It* (1991). Is there a line between personal ethics and professional responsibility? What happens when you pursue your job but forget about integrity?

Peter Drexter, *God's Pocket* (1983). The quality of life and the burdens of work from the viewpoint of a lower-middle-class construction worker.

Kazuo Ishiguru, *Remains of the Day* (1989). How does one balance life, work, love, role-playing, loyalty, and employer–employee responsibility?

Robert Robin, *Above the Law* (1992). The story of one man's attempt to balance secret deals, hidden finances, accounting gimmicks, the law, family commitments, and greed.

Robert Rodi, *Closet Case* (1993). A boardroom-bedroom farce of a closeted homosexual's desperate attempt to hide his homosexuality from his co-workers and clients.

Scott Smith, *A Simple Plan* (1993). Pretend for a moment that you have come upon $4 million – but it's not yours. Just how far would you go to keep it? Would you betray a brother or a mate? Would you kill?

Jerry Sterner, *Other People's Money* (play) (1989). A story of high finance, hostile takeovers, loyalty, tradition, employer–employee rights, and, of course, money.

John Updike, *Rabbit is Rich* (1981). Harry Angstrom is middle-aged, successful, and financially well-off, but happiness yet eludes him.

Brent Wade, *Company Man* (1992). The struggles and problems of African-Americans in Corporate America.

For our limited purposes, "Humanities" can be defined as non-scientific, non-fact-driven narrative. We have argued that such materials can bolster and better inform a more effective course in business ethics. Thus, teaching business ethics might prove the cliché that literature is the next best thing to being there.

Bibliography

Bennett, W. J. (1993). *The Book of Virtues*. New York: Simon & Schuster.

Carson, T. L. (1994). Corporate moral agency: A case from literature. *Journal of Business Ethics*, 13, 155–6.

Coles, R. (1987). Storytellers' Ethics. *Harvard Business Review*, March–April, 8–14

Coles, R. (1989). *The Call of Stories*. Boston: Houghton Mifflin.

Derry, R. & Green, R. M. (1989). Ethical theory in business ethics: A capital assessment. *Journal of Business Ethics*, 8, 512–33.

Kennedy, E. J. & Lawton, L. (1992). The manager seeking virtue: Lessons from literature. *Journal of Business Ethics*, 11, 627–34.

Nagel, T. (1974). What is it like to be a bat? *Philosophical Review*, 83, 435–50.

Wilder, A. N. (1983). Story and story-world. *Interpretation*, 37, 353–64.

AL GINI and MARK D. SCHNEIDER

human resource management as a profession Human resource management may be defined as the planning, organizing, and coordinating of a corporation's most valuable resource (and the provisions and services necessary to support this resource) – the people, the employees who breathe life into the organization, who make the product or provide the service. A human resources manager has the unique opportunity to influence the management process of this valuable resource while occupying a position which affords a view of the organization both as a whole and as the sum of its parts. Caring for the employees, providing them with fair compensation and benefits, and ensuring they have a safe environment in which to work, all come under the purview of the human resources manager.

Like other "emerging" professions, human resource management exhibits some of the central features of professions defined by Bayles (1989). There is a significant intellectual component to the study of human resources involving communication, human development, an understanding of systems and operations, certain principles of accounting and finance, and legal trends, to name a few. Extensive training and experience is required for entry into the field, which takes on greater meaning with the growing trend of gradually returning the care of individuals from the responsibility of government and society to the corporation. In striving to emerge as a profession, human resources management has assimilated other common features of a profession mentioned by Bayles, including the organizing and credentialing of members, provided through professional societies like the Society for Human Resources Management and the American Society for Training and Development.

To assist professionals and further the image of the profession, the Society for Human Resources Management advances a code of ethics which members agree to abide by. The code states that the human resources manager should, through effective employment practices, increase the corporation's profitability and public confidence in the profession. The human resources manager should uphold laws relating to the employer's activities and maintain loyalty to the employer. And the human resources manager should maintain the confidentiality of privileged information. This implied contract of maintaining confidentiality benefits employers by allowing them to seek help from a professional when they may otherwise fear to ask and it strengthens the professional's capacity to help by obtaining all necessary information (Bok, 1988).

Much of the information and data (the "raw materials") used in human resources management is confidential. Personnel records, compensation and payroll information, medical records, and benefits information must be treated as confidential either under prescribed legal procedures or a general respect of an individual's right to PRIVACY. In short, what is confidential becomes the everyday in human resources management. Yet confidential information or confidentiality can create conflicts for the human resources manager, when such information may affect the company's wellbeing.

Can the concepts and tenets of professional ethics provide direction for resolving the conflict? Larry May's interpretation of SOCIAL RESPONSIBILITY offers some guidance. He writes, "the concept of responsibility seems especially well suited to problems in professional ethics because it has an inherently social dimension – responsive to specific features of people and relationships" (May, 1995). Tying social responsibility to vulnerability, May explains that when people are depending on us (as when they approach a professional human resources manager) then the vulnerability of these people must be given greater weight than others whom we could help but who do not have a dependency relationship with us. The question then becomes, who is more dependent on the human resources manager – the employees who look upon that manager as a professional, or the corporation who has given the human resources manager the responsibility to act as a professional for its benefit, as spelled out in the Society of Human Resources Management Code of Ethics?

Whenever facing a quandary in the practice of professional ethics, William May (1980) suggests that the professional ask five questions:

1 What is going on in the case?
2 By what criteria should decisions be made?
3 Who should decide?
4 For whose benefit does the professional act?
5 How should the professional decide and act?

Number 4 specifically addresses the scenario described above. For whose benefit does the human resources manager act? As an accepted part of the job responsibility, the human resources manager is a point of contact for all employees and serves to influence management decisions by representing the voice of the employees collectively concerning not only their compensation and benefits but how they are treated and nurtured within the corporate setting. At the same time, the human resources manager is also an employee of the corporation. This problem of double agency creates dissonance for the human resources manager. Whose voice does the human resources manager represent?

See also conflict; ethical issues in information; professional ethics; social responsibility

Bibliography

Bayles, M. D. (1989). *Professional Ethics.* San Francisco, Calif.: Wadsworth.

Bok, S. (1988). The Limits of confidentiality. In J. Callahan (ed.), *Ethical Issues in Professional Life.* New York: Oxford University Press, 230–9.

May, L. (1995). Social responsibility. *Midwest Studies in Philosophy,* **20.**

May, W. F. (1980). Professional ethics: Setting, terrain, and teacher. In D. Callahan & S. Bok (eds), *Ethics Teaching in Higher Education.* New York: Plenum Press, 212–19.

Society of Human Resources Management,. *Code of Ethics.* Alexandria, Va.

LORRI E. COOPER

I

impartial spectator theories constitute a school of moral theories that all identify the appropriate standard or moral right and wrong, good and bad, as the reaction, the felt or rational judgment of an observant but uninvolved, thus "impartial" spectator.

Such moral theories were first well-developed in the eighteenth century, advocated by such famous philosophers as Francis Hutcheson, David Hume, and ADAM SMITH. Impartial spectator theories have enjoyed a revival in the twentieth century as well, beginning with an exchange of articles by Richard Brandt and Roderick Firth.

Impartial spectator theorists agree that there is more to moral judgment and action than some purely rational activity. Computers are highly logical – rational in a sense – but it makes no sense to speak of computers as behaving morally or immorally. Morality is also *affective*, that is, it is something *felt*. It is bound up with the human spirit. In a sense, we *feel* moral approval or disapproval and are motivated by our *affections*. As Adam Smith writes:

> To be the proper and approved object either of gratitude or resentment, can mean nothing but to be the object of that gratitude, and of that resentment, which naturally seems proper, and is approved of. . But these, as well as other passions of human nature, seem proper and approved of, when the heart of every impartial spectator entirely sympathizes with them, when every indifferent bystander entirely enters into, and goes along with them. (Smith, 1976)

The chief difficulty of any such theory of morality is that as individual human agents, we have limited knowledge as well as emotional PARTIALITY. Rationalistic philosophers of ethics have used these limitations as a reason to reject or marginalize the affective component of morality. The response of advocates of impartial spectator theories is to emphasize that they are pointing to the reactions of a *well-informed* and *impartial* spectator. Indeed, Brandt (1955) goes so far as to speak of an "ideal observer," seeking to emphasize that he is referring to the judgment of someone who has *all* the relevant knowledge and is not subject to *any* inappropriate partiality. More traditional impartial spectator theorists, however, prefer to keep this hypothetical impartial spectator as human as possible. Hence, they do not require the spectator to be omniscient nor without human passion. Rather, the spectator is a reasonably well-informed, temperate, moderate, well-socialized, individual human being.

Bibliography

Brandt, R. (1955). The definition of an "ideal observer" theory in ethics. *Philosophy and Phenomenological Research*, **15**, 407–13.

Firth, R. (1952). Ethical absolutism and the ideal observer. *Philosophy and Phenomenological Research*, **12**, 317–45.

Raphael, D. D. (1975). The impartial spectator. In A. S. Skinner & T. Wilson (eds), *Essays on Adam Smith*. Oxford: Oxford University Press, 83–99.

Smith, A. (1976). *The Theory of Moral Sentiments*, eds D. D. Raphael & A. L. Macfie. Oxford: Oxford University Press.

Werhane, P. (1991). *Adam Smith and His Legacy for Modern Capitalism*. Oxford: Oxford University Press.

MARK H. WAYMACK

impartiality involves the willingness to treat people fairly and in accordance with general principles arrived at independently of the influence of one's own personal preferences or interests. It is a key feature of morality stressed by almost all leading moral theories. Although widely assumed to be a crucial feature of moral reasoning, impartiality raises philosophical questions of some importance to the field of business ethics.

The requirement of impartiality is present in both ancient and modern approaches to moral theory. "Golden Rule" formulations of ethics found in many religious and ethical traditions embody it in their stress on "reciprocity" or "reversibility" in moral reasoning. The Christian formulation, "Do unto others as you would have them do unto you," is an example. It expresses impartiality by asking us to put aside attention to our own interests in order to evaluate our conduct in terms of its impact on the other persons we affect. The philosopher Immanuel Kant assumed impartiality in his well-known formulation of the categorical imperative, "Act only according to that maxim by which you can at the same time will that it should become a universal law" (Kant, 1785, p. 39) (*see* KANTIAN ETHICS). According to Kant, one must try to transcend one's own perspective and evaluate one's proposed course of conduct (maxim) as a general principle of behavior (a universal law) that is open to everyone and which all persons might accept. UTILITARIAN thinkers also repeatedly underscore the role of impartiality in their approach to moral reasoning. For example, JOHN STUART MILL insisted that as between a person's own happiness and that of others, "utilitarianism requires him to be as strictly impartial as a disinterested and benevolent spectator" (Mill, 1861, p. 218).

The requirement of impartiality is given graphic expression in the work of the modern contract theorist John Rawls. In his book *A Theory of Justice*, Rawls offers the device of the "original position of equality" in which rational agents select the basic moral principles governing society from behind a "veil of ignorance." This deprives them of all merely particular personal knowledge such as information regarding their race, sex, age, or natural abilities. Working only with general information available to everyone, Rawls' hypothetical contractors are presumed able to arrive at a fair and enduring ordering of social disputes.

Against this background, we can sketch how impartiality works in the context of moral decision. Impartiality is meant to remove the accidental or contingent features of our situation that distort our judgment. The aim is to arrive at basic moral rules or principles which *anyone* might reasonably accept. Reasoning impartially, we must take into account the interests of *all* persons affected by our moral decisions. This extends to the impact on such persons both of our immediate actions and the public rules of conduct they imply. Impartiality does not mean that we must omit attention to our own interests, but these interests are not privileged. They are placed on a plane of equality with those of all other affected persons. These persons' interests, in turn, are assessed from the standpoint of each individual, as far as possible using that person's own terms of reference and preferences. When interests conflict, the impartial person strives for objectivity, balancing claims and examining issues against the background of such facts as are available and in the light of the best available evidence.

Conceived in this way, impartiality raises two questions that can be acute for the business manager. The first is whether impartiality really is possible. Each of us is called on to make decisions amidst the real circumstances of our lives. We do not inhabit a Rawlsian "original position of equality." Does this mean that the theoretical concept of impartiality is irrelevant to people's actual moral decision-making?

A reply to this is the understanding that "impartiality" is "an ideal of reason" meant to be approximated in conduct but likely never to be fully achieved. A judicial and mediatory procedure can sometimes be used to maximize impartiality by selecting as judges people who are removed from the immediate circumstances of conflict, but moral decision-makers rarely have the luxury of this procedure. They are at once judges and full participants in the situations and choices they must evaluate. Although it is impossible for such decision-makers to put aside purely personal preferences and not allow self-interest to color their judgment, impartiality nevertheless calls on them to minimize the influence of these factors and to strive toward objectivity of judgment. Managers often evidence objectivity in non-moral or purely technical areas of their work, as when they choose among suppliers or business strategies. A similar exercise of objectivity is also required in their moral reasoning.

A second question concerns the moral appropriateness of impartiality in light of the importance of managers' obligations to their firm and its owners. There are circumstances when we recognize that acting impartially is not required and may even be morally wrong. A parent would be more likely to be blamed than applauded if he gave other children equality with his own in the allocation of his time or resources. Do not managers stand in a similar situation? Do they not violate their fiduciary obligations to shareholders if they place other companies or other corporate STAKEHOLDERS on a footing of equality? (see FIDUCIARY DUTY; FIDUCIARY RESPONSIBILITY).

An answer to this question lies in the recognition that, while we are always called upon to be impartial in arriving at the basic moral rules and principles that govern our conduct, these principles sometimes allow and even require our attention to particular duties and obligations. Although it appears paradoxical, *impartial moral reasoning* frequently *authorizes partiality* in specific instances of conduct. For example, in thinking impartially about what we shall require of parents, it makes good sense to require them in most circumstances to privilege the welfare of their own children and not to insist that they always provide other children with the same degree of care. By respecting and employing the force of natural parental feelings this rule maximizes the care of children generally. Of course, there are limits to such partiality. We would not impartially choose to allow parents actively to injure or kill other people's children in order to benefit their own.

The same reasoning applies to the world of business. Impartially regarded, it is wise to authorize business managers to privilege the needs of the company they are paid to manage and to seek to maximize owners' return. This rule promotes efficiency far better than one requiring them to promote equally the welfare of other firms. It is also probably better than a rule requiring them to promote equally the

interests of all corporate stakeholders. Nevertheless, impartially regarded, there are limits to this rule. There are many things that we cannot allow to be done in the name of competition. It would also not make sense to permit managers to seek to maximize shareholder wealth when doing so leads to very serious and avoidable harms to employees, consumers, communities, or other stakeholder groups. Although managers will most of the time devote their energies to their particular obligations, when broader issues or conflicts arise, moral theory tells us that managers must be prepared to set aside their own interests and those of their firm, and strive to reason impartially about the rules and principles on which they act.

Bibliography

Gert, B. (1988). Impartiality. In *Morality*. New York: Oxford University Press., 77–95

Gert, B. (1992). Impartiality. *Encyclopedia of Ethics*, vol. 1, pp. 599–600.

Graham, A., Kolakowski, L., Marin, L., Montefiore, A., Taylor, C., Ten, C. L., & Weinstein, W. L. (1975). *Neutrality and Impartiality*. Cambridge: Cambridge University Press.

Kant, I. (1785). *Foundations of the Metaphysics of Morals*, trans. Lewis White Beck. Indianapolis: Bobbs-Merrill.

Mill, J. S. (1861). *Utilitarianism*. In *Collected Works of John Stuart Mill*, 4th edn, vol. 10. Toronto: University of Toronto Press and Routledge & Kegan Paul, 203–59.

Rawls, J. (1971). *A Theory of Justice*. Cambridge, Mass.: Harvard University Press.

RONALD M. GREEN

individualism Any theory, doctrine, meaning, or attitude that focuses on the individual person in contrast to a group, a collective, an organization, or a state. Sometimes the term refers to individual character or to unique or peculiar characteristics of an individual phenomenon. Individualism is often confused with egoism, and sometimes identified with atomism, the view that only individuals exist and count as meaningful entities. But few terms in the political vocabulary have borne as many meanings, and as widely divergent normative charges, as individualism (Lukes, 1973).

Like many other political expressions, individualism was first used as a term of reproach, only to be adopted later on as a badge of honor by its devotees. The sources of individualism have been traced, *inter alia*, to the Epicurean and Stoic philosophies, Roman law, the Christian gospels, medieval nominalism, the Renaissance, Protestantism (especially the dissenting sects in England), and the expanding market economy in the early modern period (Macpherson, 1962). All have been credited with – or accused of – fostering the release of the individual from the ties of the traditional, *Gemeinschaft* social order and the elevation of his rights to the central position in modern politics and political philosophy. The historical growth of individualism in the West, it is widely held, can be tracked by the transition (to use Henry Maine's celebrated typology) from *status* to *contract* as the regulative social principle.

The word itself was first used by the theocratic conservative, Joseph de Maistre, becoming in France a standard term of abuse deployed by the reactionary school. In this context, it represented "an attempt to strike at the roots of the philosophy of the Enlightenment, its rehabilitation of the principle of self-interest, [and] its belief in the power of reason" (Swart, 1962). But it was eagerly taken up and disseminated by the early French socialists, particularly the Saint-Simonians. Thus, the enemies of the emerging order of formal equality and the unfettered market economy on both the "right" and the "left" found individualism a useful focus for their critiques of modern society, or "modernity."

The first use of the term in English was in Henry Reeve's 1840 translation of the second part of Tocqueville's *Democracy in America*. Elaborating on the insight of Benjamin Constant, Tocqueville held that the tendency of modern society to break down "intermediate groups" (between the individual and the state) and proliferate sources of hedonistic enjoyment produced a novel phenomenon, which he called "individualism." He defined it as a "mature and calm emotion, which disposes each member of the community to sever himself from the mass of his fellows and to draw apart with his family and his friends, so that after he has thus formed a little circle of his own, he willingly leaves society at large to itself." For Tocqueville, the chief danger of individualism lay in its perfect complementarity to the state-bureaucratic thrust toward domination of social life. From the same starting point, modern communitarians (Bellah et al., 1985) have by and large focused on the market economy as the root of the pathologies allegedly associated with individualism.

With the spread of collectivism (paternalistic interventionism and socialism) in the later nineteenth century, individualism was increasingly used as a synonym for laissez-faire liberalism (*see* PATERNALISM; LIBERALISM). Individualism, in the words of one French liberal, was "a neologism" that had "become indispensable" to express the protest "against the tendency of the legislator to enervate the human personality through governmental tutelage" (Follin, 1899). In Britain, HERBERT SPENCER's "Law of Equal Freedom" – "Every man has the right to do all that he wills, provided he infringes not the equal freedom of any other man" – became the credo of a school of self-styled "individualists" whose most radical spokesman was Auberon Herbert (Greenleaf, 1983). As the title of Spencer's collection of essays, *The Man Versus The State*, suggests, these writers discerned the antagonist of the individual not in "society," but in the hypertrophic state. This approach dovetailed with the insistence of the economic liberals that their doctrine conduced to the long-run interests of "society" *as well as* the "individual."

The emergence in the twentieth century of totalitarian movements and ideologies, which entailed the diminution or even annihilation of the autonomous individual on behalf of some "higher" entity (class, nation, or race), helped generate a reaction in favor of individualism. Early in the century, A. V. Dicey (1963) was influential in firmly anchoring the term in the concepts of freedom of contract and private property. In Britain, and, especially, America, individualism was generally seen as the energizing principle of civil society, as against the state. Thus, while there have been attempts to reshape the concept of individualism to encompass social-democratic values and methods (Dewey, 1930; Lukes, 1973), individualism has retained its identification with opposition to state intervention and control.

F. A. HAYEK, perhaps the best-known classical liberal thinker of the twentieth century, emphatically rejected the dichotomy of "individual" and "society" that has been the mainstay of critiques of individualism (Hayek, 1948). The idea of preformed, "atomistic" individuals who "enter into" social relations was, Hayek maintained, a component of a "false" individualism. This had no essential connection with the "true" individualist tradition descending from David Hume and ADAM SMITH, which, while cognizant of the social dimensions of personality formation, etc., remained the primary philosophical foundation for a social order based on the free market and the rule of law.

Bibliography

Bellah, R. N., et al. (1985). *Habits of the Heart: Individualism and Commitment in American Life.* Berkeley: University of California Press.

Dewey, J. (1930). *Individualism Old and New.* New York: Minton, Balch.

Dicey, A. V. (1963 [1914]). *Lectures on the Relation of Law and Public Opinion in England During the Nineteenth Century,* 2nd edn. London: Macmillan.

Dumont, L. (1987). *Essays on Individualism: Modern Ideology in Anthropological Perspective.* Chicago: University of Chicago Press.

Follin, H.-L. (1899). Quelle est la veritable definition de l'individualisme? *Journal des économistes,* 5th series, vol. 38.

Greenleaf, W. H. (1983). *The British Political Tradition,* vol. 2 of *The Ideological Heritage.* London: Methuen.

Hayek, F. A. (1948). *Individualism and Economic Order.* Chicago: University of Chicago Press.

Lukes, S. (1973). *Individualism.* New York: Harper and Row.

Lukes, S. (1992). Individualism. In L. Becker & C. Becker (eds), *Encyclopedia of Ethics.* New York: Garland Publishing.

Macpherson, C. B. (1962). *The Theory of Possessive Individualism, Hobbes to Locke.* Oxford: Oxford University Press.

Morley, F. (ed.). (1977 [1958]). *Essays on Individuality.* Indianapolis, Ind.: Liberty Press.

Morris, B. (1991). *Western Conceptions of the Individual.* New York and Oxford: Berg.

Moulin, L. (1955). On the evolution of the meaning of the word "individualism". *International Social Science Bulletin,* 7, 181–5.

Schatz, A. (1907). *L'Individualisme économique et social: Ses origines, son évolution, ses formes contemporaines.* Paris: Armand Colin.

Swart, K. W. (1962). "Individualism" in the mid-nineteenth century (1826–1860). *Journal of the History of Ideas,* 23 (1), 77–90.

Tocqueville, A. de. (1945 [1840]). *Democracy in America,* vol. 2, trans. H. Reeve, rev. F. Bowen, (Ed.), P. Bradley. New York: Knopf.

Williams, R. (1953). *Free and Unequal: The Biological Basis of Individual Liberty.* Austin, Tex.: University of Texas Press.

RALPH RAICO

information and international insider trading While there are many issues that arise in international finance, the most persuasive has to do with the use of information. Information is a valuable commodity. Generally information in a financial context is of two types. The first is public information. This is information that is in the public domain. This does not mean that it is known to everyone, but that it is available to anyone. There may be a fee to obtain the information but the key is its availability. Broadly in an international context there is no issue about using this information to formulate and execute financial transactions.

The more important distinction has to do with non-public or insider information. This is information that is not available to everyone. The issue in this context is whether this information can be used to formulate and execute financial transactions. There is a great deal of evidence both in the United States and internationally that this type of information can be used to generate profits in financial transactions. This profit comes at the expense of those individuals or institutions that do not have access to the information. A key question is whether this is fair, and whether trading on such information should be barred either legally or ethically. Regrettably this is viewed differently in different cultures.

The international view is the central issue which financial managers face when operating in different countries. In general, standards which apply to the use of non-public information come in three forms. The first is legal restrictions or prohibition. The second are rules governing the standards of practice of professional societies. Finally, there are individuals' own ethical standards that are the result of the individuals' cultural identity. In those cases where any or all of these conflict, the actions of the individual should be governed by the highest standard. This is true both domestically and in an international context.

The United States has taken the position that insider trading is inappropriate and has established legal prohibitions against using insider information. Moreover, prohibitions against using material non-public information are included in many professional societies' standards of practice. As such, in the United States there is a clear prohibition against such trading.

In an international context, the laws and customs in different countries can be quite varied. An individual can find that the local laws and customs are at variance with the established norms that had governed their actions in the past. Usually the dilemma is that the laws and customs allow practices that would be prohibited in their normal operating environment. The logical question is, what norms should the individual follow? In the case where the individual subscribes to a set of standards of practice that specifically prohibits insider trading, this prohibition should supersede the local law and customs.

In the absence of such guidelines the individual must make his/her own determination. If an individual believes that insider trading is wrong, then the local law and customs cannot relieve that individual of the responsibility to act in a way that is consistent with his/her own internal value system. On the other hand, if an individual does not hold the opinion that activities such as insider trading are wrong, then to the extent that the individual operates within the guidelines of local law and customs, such activities would be reasonable.

See also **insider trading**

ROBERT CONROY

information, ethical issues in   *see* ETHICAL ISSUES IN INFORMATION

information, right to   *see* RIGHT TO INFORMATION

innovation   The creation of new value. As distinct from invention, which is the creation of new ideas, innovation is the development of new ideas into things of value: new or improved products, processes, or services. Innovation provides the vitality that makes a firm's offerings of continuing interest to customers and thereby assures continuing health of the enterprise from the viewpoint of shareholders, employees, suppliers, and the community at large.

Yet, innovation involves more uncertainty and risk than most other activities in business. Despite our best efforts, the innovation process is often chaotic and unpredictable, and is not easily planned or controlled. As Professor Edward Roberts has said, "The farther a company tries to go in innovating, the greater the likelihood of that innovation effort failing; yet the less the company seeks to innovate, the greater the likelihood the company itself will fail." Innovation affects all of the stakeholders of a business. Innovation is the most complex social process in business. It involves all functions from technology, marketing, and manufacturing to sales, distribution, and finance. It involves all levels from factory workers, laboratory technicians, and designers, to project and product managers, division managers, and right on up to senior management. It involves creative people, big egos, extended time-frames, and high levels of uncertainty and risk. It involves distribution systems and customers, especially early adapters. And finally, it involves shareholders, who must accept the uncertainty in the interest of future rewards.

The ethical issues involved in innovation can be examined by considering both the inputs and the outputs of the innovation process from the standpoint of the various stakeholders. Ideally, one would want the beneficial outputs to be of greater value than the inputs, and there to be no undesirable side-effects. Although business strives for this ideal, in reality most attempted innovations do not achieve it. Even for the most successful innovative firms, a small proportion of their innovations are far more successful than the rest, and provide the benefits that justify the whole portfolio of innovations.

The main inputs to the innovation process are the efforts of the people involved and the cost of these efforts in money and time. Of these, the most important costs are the indispensable efforts of specialists and particularly those creative people who are always in short supply and whose talents are often needed on other projects. The key, then, is project selection, and the development of a portfolio of projects that strikes a balance between risk and expected gain, between projects that pay off in the short term, and those with longer-term but higher-return prospects. Why is this an ethical issue? Short-term payoff, incremental innovations involve lower risks simply because there is less uncertainty about them. Usually, however, they have limited potential to create major benefits for the customers or for the firm. Too much emphasis on this low-risk approach makes the firm and all of its stakeholders vulnerable. On the other hand, major innovations take a longer time to implement, although when successful can yield major value for customers and all other stakeholders. Uncertainty and risk are higher, however, and too much emphasis on such long-shots can put the whole enterprise at risk. The crucial managerial judgment, then, is to strike the right risk/reward balance appropriate to the business and to the capabilities of the firm. This is the essence of innovation stewardship. Of course, it is obvious that short-term projects with high expected returns should definitely be pursued and long-term projects with low expected returns should be avoided.

Similar ethical issues are involved when considering the outputs of the innovation process. The new value provided by a particular innovation should benefit as many of the stakeholders as possible (*see* STAKEHOLDER THEORY). Ideally, customers will enjoy new products with improved quality or lower prices, shareholders will receive higher dividends or stock appreciation, suppliers will prosper, and employees will receive higher wages and job security. Often, however, the benefits are not distributed in a balanced way. Competition in the product market may dictate that all of the benefits go to customers. Or competition in financial or labor markets may steer most of the benefits to shareholders or employees. These are familiar ethical issues in business. As applied to the innovation process, they suggest that a portfolio of innovations should be pursued so as to satisfy all stakeholders over the long run.

This may require restructuring the business at substantial short-term cost to employees and shareholders.

The indispensable ultimate need is for innovations to provide outputs that are valued by customers. For products or services intended for individual consumers such as clothing, personal-care products, toys and leisure activities, consumers should have wide discretion to decide what they consider "value," moderated only by issues of safety and reliability. This is an area where the ethical behavior of businesses varies widely and which has engendered much oversight and regulation by government and industry organizations. Regulation of over-the-counter drugs is widely accepted, as is regulation of medical devices and foods. In advanced countries with open political systems, an active media, and an open legal system, consumer concerns about safety and reliability have led to increasing regulation of a wide variety of products and services. For the individual firm, however, the ethical obligation remains, regardless of the regulatory environment: innovations of consumer products and services must be developed and tested to be safe and reliable, and the consumer must be adequately informed about the products' intended use and limitations. Discharging this ethical obligation has an important impact on one of the firm's most valuable assets: its reputation.

For new products and services the benefits of which are widely distributed, such as new transportation systems, new sources of electric power, and other improvements in infrastructure, as well as widely shared products and services such as broadcast television and telecommunication systems, a broad consensus must be developed to confirm the value of such innovations. Such support is often developed through the political process. Government regulations and industry standards are relied upon to assure that such major innovations are cost-effective, safe, and reliable.

For all innovations, a continuing concern is the possibly harmful side-effects that may come along with the benefits of the innovation. Innovating firms have an obligation to identify, evaluate, and minimize harmful side-effects. Some of these possibly harmful effects are confined to the user of the new product or service. For example, a new electric appliance may present an electrical hazard if not properly grounded or sealed. Or, more dramatically, a new drug to suppress leukemia may cause hair loss and skin rash. Although undesirable side-effects should always be minimized, total elimination is almost impossible. When the benefits are important, as in curing a life-threatening disease, we have a higher tolerance for undesirable side-effects than we would for less beneficial innovations such as a new toaster or a new toy. The same principles apply to innovations whose benefits are widely shared: harmful effects should be minimized, and tolerance of them should be in proportion to the importance of the benefits.

An especially difficult ethical dilemma is presented where innovations that provide value to individual consumers have undesirable side-effects that are broadly distributed. A new and convenient form of product packaging may be valued by individual consumers, but aggravate an already serious societal problem of solid-waste disposal. Similarly, new alcoholic beverages or new cigarettes may be valued by individuals but be recognized to lead to increased auto accidents and serious health problems, putting an increased burden on the health-care system. Or a new manufacturing process for high-quality and low-cost paper may increase the discharge of process chemicals into the water system. These are familiar problems in DISTRIBUTIVE JUSTICE, for established products and services as well as for innovations. What makes such problems more difficult for innovations is that by definition we have no long-term experience with the new product or service and therefore may not be able to anticipate undesirable side-effects that may manifest themselves in the future. Further, with an active mass media and a responsive political system, public awareness of broadly distributed undesirable environmental health, safety, and other side-effects has been greatly increased, and public tolerance for such effects has decreased. As a result, the public is wary of innovations based on technologies that they do not understand or feel confident about, bringing about a new balance in the relationship between the perceived value of new products and services and the perceived costs in undesirable effects. New products involving chemistry, nuclear radiation, and genetic engineering often face such ethical dilemmas.

The obligation of innovating firms is to be sensitive and responsive to evolving ethical norms of the consuming public by fully exploring and minimizing undesirable side-effects from new products, processes, and services. At the same time, innovating firms and industry groups working with government agencies, the medical community, and the media, should help to educate the public so as to improve understanding and acceptance of innovations where the perceived undesirability is more imagined than real.

THOMAS C. MacAVOY

insider trading   The practice of buying or selling securities with reliance upon information that is not available to the public. Insider trading is also defined as trading by true corporate insiders, such as directors or officers of a firm, or by outsiders who are privy to non-public information and who trade in contravention of a FIDUCIARY DUTY.

Insider trading was prohibited in the United States under common law early in the twentieth century. This prohibition was codified under the Securities and Exchange Act of 1934, under a broad proscription of fraud in the purchase or sale of securities (*see* SECURITIES AND EXCHANGE COMMISSION). Under present judicial interpretation of the Act, insiders or outsiders who have a fiduciary duty to another must either disclose their inside information to the public or abstain from trading on the information. A second section of the Securities and Exchange Act of 1934 purports to mitigate insider trading practices more indirectly, by requiring disgorgement of short-swing profits by certain classes of insiders, regardless of whether trades have been made with the advantage of any inside information. Specifically, beneficial owners, directors, and officers must return any profits gained by a sale of stocks within six months of purchase, or a purchase of stocks within six months of sale. Through the 1970s, the United States was the only nation that both prohibited insider trading and vigorously prosecuted violators. More recently, industrialized nations in Asia and

Europe have strengthened their insider trading laws and have begun to prosecute violators with some consistency.

Whether insider trading is unethical, and whether it is appropriate to outlaw insider trading behavior, are highly controversial questions. Those who support insider trading as ethically defensible tend to posit arguments of economic efficiency. Some contend that trades made on accurate inside information support an efficient market by contributing to the most rapid market assimilation of information, which drives stock prices closer to an equilibrium that accurately represents true asset values. Commentators supporting the practice have also argued that insider trading by directors and officers can benefit a company by providing an incentive for the most highly qualified candidates to fill high-level management positions. Finally, critics of the climate which presently disfavors insider trading have suggested that no one is harmed by the practice, and therefore it is morally supportable.

Those who condemn insider trading as unethical rely on arguments of both economic function and fairness. Some suggest that insider trading does in fact harm buyers or sellers who deal with the insider. They reason that innocent buyers or sellers who trade with insiders purchase stocks at higher prices or sell them at lower prices than they would agree to under parity of information, and are harmed to the extent of the difference between actual price and the price they would be willing to set under informational parity. Other critics of insider trading focus on potential negative effects on the market at large rather than the potential harm to individual transactors. They reason that proliferation of selective insider advantage will tend to erode faith in the marketplace as a level playing field, causing anything from market sluggishness to market crash as disadvantaged investors withdraw their support. Some suggest that ethical consideration of insider trading must either supplant or supplement economic concerns with consideration of fairness issues. They contend that insider trading is wrong because transactions under disparate conditions of informational access are inherently unfair transactions.

These challenging ethical questions are exacerbated by both legal and pragmatic complications. Under present federal law in the United States, the statutory prohibition neither uses nor defines the term "insider trading," relying instead upon a more general ban on "fraud." Accordingly, cases arise in which a trader is uncertain whether particular practices at the margin are legal or illegal. The present lack of clarity under federal law presents several kinds of ethical problems. First, many consider laws unfair when they hold persons civilly and criminally accountable for behaviors that have not been clearly defined. This issue of due process under law is also an issue of fundamental fairness of the legal system. Second, from a utilitarian standpoint, systematic discouragement of economic investment by enacting vague legal prohibitions that may tend to have a chilling effect on transactions, detracts from the greater social good. Among both supporters and critics of the practice of insider trading, many commentators agree that the present imprecision of the state of the law is unethical.

The problems of inadequate definition of insider trading are compounded by conceptual ambiguities, which suggest that precise circumscription of an unethical sphere of activity is pragmatically troublesome. For example, if we define insider trading as trading on information to which the public does not have access, we must then define the boundaries of public access. Yet information can exist in practice on a continuum, from "accessible to one person" to "accessible to all persons." The difficulties associated with trying to fix insider trading somewhere along the access continuum quickly become evident. Likewise, difficulties exist in regard to defining precisely what is inside "information," as opposed to opinion or speculation. While some believe that information must be factual and verified to yield an unfair edge in trading, others contend that inside opinions confer unfair advantage to the extent that they are expert or well-informed. What comprises "inside information" is therefore a complicated question, which to date remains largely unresolved by both legal and ethical scholars.

Bibliography

Bagby, J. (1987). The evolving controversy over insider trading. *American Business Law Journal,* **24,** 571–620.

Levmore, S. (1988). In defense of the regulation of insider trading. *Harvard Journal of Law and Public Policy,* **11,** 101–9.

Macey, J. (1984). From fairness to contract: The new direction of the rules against insider trading. *Hofstra Law Review,* **13,** 9–64.

Moore, J. (1990). What is really unethical about insider trading? *Journal of Business Ethics,* **9,** 171–82.

Salbu, S. (1992). The misappropriation theory of insider trading: A legal, economic, and ethical analysis. *Harvard Journal of Law and Public Policy,* **15,** 223–53.

Shaw, B. · (1990). Shareholder authorized insider trading: A legal and moral analysis. *Journal of Business Ethics,* **9,** 913–28.

Werhane, P. (1989). The ethics of insider trading. *Journal of Business Ethics,* **8,** 841–5.

STEVEN R. SALBU

integrity   Integrity, in the sense relevant for business ethics: the quality of moral self-governance. Derived from the Latin word *integritas,* meaning wholeness, completeness, or purity, integrity has been widely praised both as a virtue and as a quality essential for personal well-being and social effectiveness. Psychologists have found integrity to be essential to an individual's sense of identity and self-worth, enabling the successful navigation of change and challenge. Links between integrity and the ability to gain and maintain the trust of others have often been noted. Many purveyors of practical advice, including Cicero and Benjamin Franklin, have counseled that integrity is the cornerstone of worldly success. According to Franklin, "no Qualities [are] so likely to make a poor Man's Fortune as those of Probity & Integrity" (quoted in Beebe, 1992, p. 8).

Although integrity has been defined in a variety of ways, it is generally identified with one or more of the following related characteristics:

Moral Conscientiousness. Integrity involves moral conscientiousness and a desire to do what is right. Persons of integrity are trustworthy and resistant to corruption. They can be relied on to be truthful, to be fair, to stand by their promises, to follow the rules – or, at least, to challenge them openly and fairly. Such persons are faithful to the moral requirements of the roles in which they serve. When acting as a fiduciary for others, for example, they can be counted on to exercise independent judgment unbiased by personal advantage (*see* FIDUCIARY DUTY; FIDUCIARY RESPONSIBILITY).. They are scrupulous in dealing with CONFLICT OF INTEREST or improper influences which might taint their judgment.

Moral Accountability. Integrity involves personal accountability. Persons of integrity accept responsibility for themselves and what they do. They rarely appeal to external forces to explain or justify their behavior. They do not pass the buck or seek exculpation in excuses such as "He made me do it," "I was just following orders," "I had no choice." Nor do they see themselves as slaves of their own desires. Integrity is associated with a high degree of self-control and self-awareness.

Moral Commitment. Integrity is often identified with having a set of distinctive and strongly held commitments. Persons of integrity have a set of anchoring beliefs or principles that define who they are and what they believe in. They stand for something and remain steadfast when confronted with adversity or temptation. In some instances – for example, Gandhi's commitment to non-violent resistance or Martin Luther King's commitment to civil rights – their anchoring beliefs become the driving force of their lives. Individuals who have no defining commitments, who are too easily swayed by the crowd, who tailor their beliefs to their audience, or who capriciously change their fundamental values are generally thought to be lacking in integrity. While integrity is incompatible with dogmatic adherence to unexamined belief, it does imply constancy of purpose and willingness to take a principled stand.

Moral Coherence. Integrity connotes coherence or consistency in a variety of senses: among commitments, among moral judgments, between belief and expression, and between word and deed. Hypocrisy, dishonesty, and self-deception, perhaps the most common failures of integrity, all involve forms of incoherence. Although perfect coherence in all the above senses is unattainable – and perhaps undesirable

– persons of integrity generally strive for harmony between principle and practice and for coherence among who they are, who they perceive themselves to be, and how they present themselves to the world. AUTHENTICITY and sincerity are often regarded as hallmarks of integrity.

These different aspects of integrity, though related, can sometimes conflict, creating difficult moral dilemmas for decision-makers. For example, managers' role-related obligations may conflict with their personal commitments. Conscientious persons may be torn between blowing the whistle on misconduct they observe and adhering to the conventional bounds of their assigned responsibilities. Despite its associations with harmony and personal well-being, integrity requires that individuals deal with such conflicts and overcome the tensions inherent in them.

While philosophers and psychologists have approached integrity from different perspectives, it is tempting to speculate that the moral expressions of integrity may rest on the psychological foundation of a well-integrated personality. If true, this connection would lend credence to Aristotle's view that virtue and personal well-being are closely linked and rooted in human nature (see ARISTOTLE). In this regard, it is interesting to note that Erik Erikson (1950), the well-known psychoanalyst and developmental psychologist, regarded integrity as encompassing ethical and psychological wholeness and as the final and highest stage of personal development.

Though integrity has been widely admired, some philosophers have questioned its usefulness as a moral standard. The philosopher JOHN RAWLS, for example, has called integrity a secondary moral concept, one of form rather than content, with no moral purchase until informed by a theory of right and wrong. According to Rawls (1971, p. 519), integrity is compatible with almost any guiding principles or commitments; even a tyrant, he says, could exhibit a high degree of integrity.

Others have argued that while integrity allows for some latitude in content, it is not entirely open-ended. Integrity-conferring commitments must be important, and they must be morally sound (McFall, 1987). There is a note of irony in attributing integrity to the mafioso who only

"takes out" those who deserve it. Similarly, a "tyrant with integrity" would appear to be a contradiction in terms insofar as a tyrant is someone who exercises absolute power brutally and in flagrant violation of law and morality. According to this line of thought, integrity is a powerful moral concept precisely because it focuses on form as well as content and because it is compatible with a range of personal commitments.

Whether moral integrity can be properly ascribed to entities other than individual persons has been a matter of debate. In recent years, however, executives and management theorists have become concerned with corporate or organizational integrity. New US standards for sentencing corporations convicted of wrongdoing have reinforced this concern. Under the 1991 Federal Sentencing Guidelines, organizational culpability was made a critical factor in determining corporate fines, thus giving managers added incentives to promote moral self-governance in their companies.

While organizational integrity is sometimes thought to require nothing more than the personal integrity of the organization's members, research suggests that organizational strategies, structures, and systems are important factors in supporting organizational integrity. Research also suggests that individual integrity is best thought of not as a stable personality trait established once and for all in early life, but as a process of interacting with the world which can be supported or inhibited by the context in which the individual acts. These findings imply that executives concerned about organizational integrity should focus both on developing the personal capabilities of individuals in their companies and on establishing the organizational conditions required for moral self-governance.

Bibliography

Badaracco, J. L., Jr., & Ellsworth, R. R. (1989). *Leadership and the Quest for Integrity*. Boston: Harvard Business School Press. (Executive perspectives).

Beebe, J. (1992). *Integrity in Depth*. College Station: Texas A&M University Press. (A psychological perspective).

De George, R. T. (1993). *Competing with Integrity in International Business.* New York: Oxford University Press. (A philosophical perspective).

Erikson, E. H. (1950). *Childhood and Society.* New York: W.W. Norton. (A developmental perspective.)

Halfon, M. S. (1989). *Integrity: A Philosophical Inquiry.* Philadelphia: Temple University Press. (A philosophical perspective).

McFall, L. (1987). Integrity. *Ethics,* **98**, 5–20 (A philosophical perspective).

Paine, L. S. (1994). Managing for organizational integrity. *Harvard Business Review,* Mar./Apr., 106–17 (An organizational perspective).

Rawls, J. (1971). *A Theory of Justice.* Cambridge, Mass.: Harvard University Press. (A philosophical perspective).

Srivastva, S. & Associates. (1988). *Executive Integrity: The Search for High Human Values in Organizational Life.* San Francisco: Jossey-Bass. (Organizational and executive perspectives).

Taylor, G. (1985). *Integrity: Pride, Shame, and Guilt.* Oxford: The Clarendon Press, 108–41. (A philosophical perspective).

LYNN SHARP PAINE

intellectual property Intellectual property refers to patents, copyrights, trademarks, and trade secrets and is distinct from tangible property, such as land, buildings, or commodities (*see also* PROPERTY).

Patents generally protect inventions of new processes and products. Since patents are published with the description of the underlying research, they eventually spread innovations around the globe as well as spur further innovation. The fact that critical information is published, however, makes it extremely easy for people to pirate the innovations straightaway.

In distinction to patents, copyright protects the expression or concrete representation of ideas. Copyright covers many forms of expression, notably literary and artistic works and, most recently, computer programs (*see also* COPYRIGHT).

A trademark is a symbol, word, or figure used by a company to designate its goods and distinguish them from others. It is usually registered with a government agency to assure its use exclusively by the owner. Cashing in on another's valuable trademark hits all sorts of markets from fashion to medical, agricultural, and computer industries.

TRADE SECRETS represent a company's product or process innovations, but they are not legally registered as patents, copyrights and trademarks are. Increasingly trade secrets are targets of industrial espionage (*see also* TRADE SECRETS).

Means to Acquire and Protect

Approaches to the acquisition of intellectual property differ according to whether one defines technology as either a private or a common good. For example, the green revolution agricultural technologies are generally considered to be a common good, while at the same time a specific seed strain could be a private good. Private business interests generally view technology itself – not just a specific product – as a private good and a commercial commodity. In contrast, developing countries often view technology as a common good and, because it is non-applied, as non-commercial.

If technology is viewed as a common good, the information it embodies is open to all. It is not a commodity to be bought and sold. Only specific applications of a technology in terms of products and processes can be considered a commercial commodity or private property.

If technology is viewed as a privately owned commodity, however, the approach to its acquisition is a contractual agreement between the owner and acquirer. This may take the form of direct sales or licensing (*see* ETHICS OF OWNERSHIP).

The means to protect technology are straightforward enough and encompass economic sanctions against violators, legal action, ideological struggles over legitimation, and a variety of political measures, including lobbying and political action committees, domestically; and diplomacy, internationally.

Management and Social Policy

To patent scientific ideas and information as property is a very new development in human history, indeed. Such social policy stems primarily from the West in the late eighteenth and nineteenth centuries. Traditionally, intellectual ideas have been treated as part of the public domain – much like the alphabet or nuclear physics. While applications, such as a particular keyboard or a nuclear plant design, might be patented or copyrighted, the idea itself could not be. If ideas, not simply applications, can become privatized in the context of an incentive and reward system, then the very foundations of further technological innovation become entangled in the perpetuation of entrenched interests.

The management of intellectual property poses special problems for two reasons. First, intellectual property possesses economic characteristics not found in tangible commodity property. It is readily divisible and transportable and can be easily appropriated by many parties at once. With intellectual property violations, the owner does not lose property but, rather, the exclusive rights to its imputed stream of economic benefits. Owners do not lose the property itself but their monopoly control over it. Secondly, intellectual property plays such a pivotal role in the development prospects of many countries that they cannot afford to be excluded from access to it.

Protection of intellectual property is thought to stimulate economic progress in several ways: by providing an incentive for people to spend money on research and innovation, by improving the quality of competition, by enhancing an economy's prospects for growth and development, by providing the consumer with better products over time, and by providing new jobs through the continual dynamic transformation of the economic structure. The latter point is especially problematic for it posits the necessity of continual retraining of the workforce as an economy moves from the age of Pony Express to the age of Federal Express and beyond to global electronic communication networks (e.g., Internet).

International copyright protection is afforded by the Berne Convention, which originated in 1886 and has been expanded through 5 subsequent Berne Acts (the latest being Paris 1971). The United States ratified the Convention in 1988 and joined in 1989. The Paris Convention of 1883 covers patents as well as trademarks. The area of trade secrets is the least protected of all. Business enterprises usually meet threats in this area by taking measures to tighten up internal security and by placing restrictive clauses in contracts of those who deal with sensitive proprietary information. In the United States the theft of trade secrets and other misappropriated information is covered by State laws rather than Federal law. The Paris, Berne, and other conventions mentioned above are vague to the extent that their interpretation in a particular case depends upon local case law.

Ethical Issues

The social questions presented above raise a number of ethical issues. First, with respect to what society considers legitimate forms of property, it is not all that clear that intellectual property rights are really "rights" (*see* RIGHTS). Four general sets of philosophical arguments emerge to legitimate a set of property rights: 1) rights to liberty and self-realization; 2) rights to livelihood; 3) rights to the fruit of one's labor and effort; and 4) efficiency and social benefits flowing from such rights as part of the common good (*see* ECONOMIC EFFICIENCY). In the intellectual property debate it is often forgotten that the property rights advocated by multinational companies are primarily based upon modern Western values and culture (*see* MULTINATIONALS). In different cultural settings they do not find the same legitimacy.

Secondly, one finds two principal disputes over how intellectual property is to be acquired and protected: (a) who should hold the rights and (b) whether the owner should enjoy exclusive monopoly power. In the United States, the person "first to invent" enjoys the property rights, whereas in Europe and most other countries it is the person "first to file." At issue is who is entitled to enjoy the fruits of scientific labor. The problem is further complicated by the fact that many inventors work in corporate and government organizations, which demand that researchers sign away any such rights as a condition of employment.

The owner's interests are usually protected by the grant of unconditional monopoly power. The argument put forward is essentially utilitarian: such protection provides strong incentives for researchers to produce a rich stream of social benefits (*see* UTILITARIANISM). This argument is countered by many developing countries, that insist monopoly power should be mitigated by social mandates. For example, a country's law may stipulate that a patent be "worked" or face "compulsory licensing;" that is, a patent must be fully exploited so as to speed the rapid and wide diffusion of new technologies. Developing countries tend to insist on widespread social mandates in technologies that they determine to be vital. Monopoly powers raise a third issue: that of a fair price and a just rate of return. Traditionally, the pricing of intellectual property is legitimated in terms of incentives to expend the effort to innovate and, in so doing, provide a wide array of social benefits, and as a way to cover the costs of wide-ranging research efforts over the long term, especially given the fact that many such efforts end in failure. In the end, monopoly control and pricing as well as social mandates are generally disputed on the grounds of *social* benefits and costs. The first group emphasizes INDIVIDUALISM, utilitarianism, and procedural justice (liberty, opportunity, incentives, fruits of one's labor), while the latter emphasizes communitarian bonds and broader patterns of distributive justice (*see* COMMUNITARIANISM).

A third major moral problem arises from the above and focuses upon the legitimate rights of third parties. There is not much of a conceptual problem of fairness, when the innovation in question causes harm to a third party, and the owner is then held morally and legally liable for damages. The main moral problem pits the moral principle that the inventor(s) have the right to the fruits of their labor versus the principle that priority be granted to fulfilling the basic needs or rights to livelihood of those who cannot afford the [monopoly priced] innovation in question, such as a vital drug. This point raises the question of whether (if, indeed, there is a moral obligation to aid the disadvantaged, reminiscent of RAWLS) it is the obligation of the property owner or, rather, of society at large to do so.

In the pluralistic cultural setting that characterizes the global economy, none of these issues are easy to resolve. In practice, there are three general types of solutions to intellectual property problems that are usually employed in tandem: legal, political, and economic. Each has a mixed record in terms of efficacy and portends different ethical and socio-economic consequences.

Bibliography

Besen, Stanley M. & Raskind, Leo J. (1991). An introduction to the law and economics of intellectual property. *Journal of Economic Perspectives,* 5 (1), 3–27.

Brown, Carole Ganz & Rushing, Francis W. (1990). Intellectual property rights in the 1990s: Problems and solutions. In Rushing, F. W. & Brown, C. G. (eds), *Intellectual Property Rights in Science, Technology and Economic Performance.* Boulder, Colo.: Westview Special Studies in Science, Technology and Public Policy.

Deardorff, Alan V. (1990). Should patent protection be extended to all developing countries? *The World Economy,* 13 (4), 497–506.

Emmert, F. (1990). Intellectual property in the Uruguay Round – Negotiating strategies of the Western industrialized countries. *Michigan Journal of International Law,* summer, 1317–99.

Gadbaw, R. Michael & Richards, Timothy J. (1988). *Intellectual Property Rights – Global Consensus, Global Conflict? Boulder, Colo.: Westview Press.*

Geller, Paul. (1989). Copyright protection in the Berne Union – Analyzing the issues. *Intellectual Property Journal,* 5 (1), 1–10.

Harvard International Law Journal (1992). Recent intellectual property trends in developing countries. Vol. 33, 277–90.

Magrab, E. Brendan. (1992). Computer software protection in Europe and the EC Parliamentary Directive on Copyright for Computer Software. *Law and Policy in International Business,* 23 (3), 709–24.

Maskus, Keith E. (1993). Intellectual property rights and the Uruguay Round. *Federal Reserve Bank of Kansas City Economic Review,* Nov., 11–25 .

Siebeck, W., Evenson, R. E., Lesser, W. & Primo Braga, C. A. (eds). (1990). *Strengthening Protection of Intellectual Property in Developing Countries: A Survey of the Literature.* Washington, DC: World Bank.

Spector, H. M. (1989). An outline of a theory justifying intellectual and industrial property rights. *European Intellectual Property Review,* 11, 270–3.

Wallerstein, M. B., Mogee, M. E., & Schoen, R. A. (eds). (1993). *Global Dimensions of Intellectual Property Rights in Science and Technology.* Washington, DC: National Academy of Sciences.

PAUL STEIDLMEIER

intentionality The term "intentionality" has two senses in philosophical writing: 1) the property that distinguishes intentional from non-intentional behavior; 2) the property, possessed by many mental states, of being about, or directed at, something. The first sense is pertinent to ethics. There is an important connection between intentional conduct and conduct for which we are morally accountable. Although we are morally accountable for some unintentional behavior, as in cases of negligence, ethical assessment of actions is focused primarily upon intentional actions.

Proposed analyses of intentional action divide broadly into two kinds: causal and non-causal. According to a representative causal analysis, actions are intentional in virtue of being suitably caused (in part) by appropriate intentions. The primary task borne by proponents of such analyses is to specify, in broad terms, the relevant causal role of intentions. Non-causal analyses of intentional action also tend to feature agents' intentions, but as loci of agents' purposes in doing what they do, not as causes.

Proposed analyses also divide over cases of "double effect." Suppose that, for financial reasons only, an entrepreneur buys a small company and moves it to another state. She gives the employees the option of moving with the company, but she is virtually certain that some have commitments that preclude their moving and that at least a few will suffer temporary unemployment. Given what she knows, does she intentionally render employees temporarily unemployed, or is this rather a non-intentional consequence of her intentionally moving the company? As yet, there is no consensus on the extent of intentionality in cases of double effect. Some theorists limit intentional conduct to actions that are intended, either as ends or as means. Others argue that intentionality extends even to some foreseen behavioral consequences that are not themselves intended.

Intentions themselves, conceived as genuine states of mind, have been the subject of fruitful study. Functions plausibly attributed to intentions in the literature include initiating and sustaining intentional actions, guiding intentional behavior, helping to coordinate agents' behavior over time and their interaction with other agents, and prompting and appropriately terminating practical reasoning. Theorists have advanced characterizations of intention designed to accommodate these functions. According to a representative characterization of this kind, intentions are executive attitudes toward plans. Plans – which range from simple representations of "basic" actions to complex strategies for achieving remote goals – constitute the representational contents of intentions. What distinguishes intentions from other practical attitudes – e.g., desires – is their distinctive practical nature. Although one can harbor a desire to do something without being at all settled upon doing it (e.g., one may be deliberating about whether to perform the desired action), to intend to do something is, in part, to be settled upon doing it (but not necessarily irrevocably). Such settledness upon a course of action constitutes a psychological commitment to executing the pertinent plan of action.

Bibliography

Brand, M. (1984). *Intending and Acting.* Cambridge, Mass.: MIT Press.

Bratman, M. (1987). *Intention, Plans, and Practical Reason.* Cambridge, Mass.: Harvard University Press.

Davidson, D. (1980). *Essays on Actions and Events.* Oxford: Clarendon Press.

Mele, A. (1992). *Springs of Action.* New York: Oxford University Press.

Wilson, G. (1989). *The Intentionality of Human Action.* Stanford: Stanford University Press.

ALFRED R. MELE

interactional justice   A person's perception that she or he or others have been treated *interpersonally* fairly, that is, with sensitivity, consideration, honesty, and respect.

This term was introduced by Bies and Moag (1986) who said: "By interactional justice we mean that people are sensitive to the quality of interpersonal treatment they receive during the enactment of organizational procedures" (p. 44). They introduced this term during a time when much was being published on issues pertaining to PROCEDURAL JUSTICE, or perceptions of the fairness of procedures, such as dispute-resolution procedures, including court, and other decision-making procedures in general, such as allocation procedures in organizations (see Lind & Tyler, 1988, for a review). Bies and Moag (1986) explained that, although aspects of procedure (e.g. neutrality) matter to people when they are assessing fairness, the interpersonal aspect of procedure (e.g., the degree of respect shown to grievants) influences perceived fairness, too. Specific behaviors associated with interactional justice, which are discussed more elaborately in Shapiro (1993), include:

- Discussing issues in an honest and candid manner,

- Giving an adequate explanation for an authority's decision,

- Taking grievants' views into consideration before making an authoritative decision,

- Responding to questions and concerns in a sensitive manner.

The importance of the interpersonal aspect of procedural enactment has been relatively neglected in the theoretical and empirical literature pertaining to justice. More recently, however, justice researchers have begun to recognize – both theoretically and empirically – the importance of interactional justice in understanding, and predicting, people's perception of justice (see reviews by Shapiro, 1991; Shapiro, 1993). Attention to interactional justice-related behaviors has been found to have practical importance, too. Specifically, in studies where authorities (e.g., court judges, managers) were more, rather than less, attentive to interactional justice during their communication of unfavorable decisions (e.g., guilty verdicts, job rejections, layoffs, pay cuts), those affected by these decisions were significantly less likely to engage in the negative affect and behaviors that typically accompany the receipt of bad news (see reviews by Shapiro, 1991; Shapiro, 1993). The negative behaviors examined by researchers include complaining (Bies, Shapiro, & Cummings, 1988), withdrawal of leader support (Tyler, 1987), reduced organizational commitment (Brockner et al., 1990), stealing (Greenberg, 1990), and resistance to new management initiatives (Kirkman et al., 1996). And consequently, an understanding of interactional justice, and its mitigating effect on these behaviors, has important cost-saving implications for organizations.

Bibliography

Bies, R. J. & Moag, J. S. (1986). Interactional justice: Communication criteria of fairness. In R. J. Lewicki, B. H. Sheppard & M. H. Bazerman (eds), *Research on Negotiation in Organizations*. Greenwich, Conn.: JAI Press, 43–55.

Bies, R. J., Shapiro, D. L. & Cummings, L. L. (1988). Causal accounts and managing organizational conflict: Is it enough to say it's not my fault? *Communication Research*, 15, 381–99.

Brockner, J., DeWitt, R. L., Grover, S. & Reed, T. (1990). When it is especially important to explain why: Factors affecting the relationship between managers' explanation of a layoff and survivors' reactions to the layoff. *Journal of Experimental Social Psychology*, 26, 389–407.

Greenberg, J. (1990). Employee theft as a reaction to underpayment inequity: The hidden cost of paycuts. *Journal of Applied Psychology*, 75, 561–8.

Kirkman, B. L., Shapiro, D. L., Novelli, L. & Brett, J. M. (1996). Employee concerns regarding self-managing work teams: A multidimensional justice perspective. *Social Justice Research*, 9, 47–67.

Lind, E. A. & Tyler, T. R. (1988). *The Social Psychology of Procedural Justice*. New York: Plenum Press.

Shapiro, D. L. (1991). The effects of explanations on negative reactions to deceit. *Administrative Science Quarterly*, 36, 614–30.

Shapiro, D. L. (1993). Reconciling theoretical differences among procedural justice researchers by re-evaluating what it means to have one's views "considered": Implications for third-party managers. In R. Cropanzano (ed.), *Justice in the Workplace: Approaching Fairness in Human Resource Management*. Hillsdale, NJ: Lawrence-Erlbaum, 51–78.

Tyler, T. R. (1987). Conditions leading to value expressive effects in judgments of procedural justice: A test of four models. *Journal of Personality and Social Psychology*, 52, 333–44.

DEBRA L. SHAPIRO

interests and needs People's interests consist in provisions for meeting needs: maintaining or increasing the provisions is in their interest; reducing the provisions is against it. Needs are conditions that must be met if people are to go on living, with normal prospects of happiness, or else they are conditions of success in contingent projects (going fishing, playing tennis). In the latter cases they figure in people's interests (if at all) only if they are consistent with meeting basic needs.

Buying something and consuming it is in a person's interest if it meets a need. Earning an income is in a person's interest because it increases the person's capacity to provide for needs. Economists, determined to take preferences as given, at least when the preferences have been consistently stabilized, incline to reject any distinction between preferences answering to needs and preferences not so answering. Thus they get no further to needs than to confuse wants having a footing in them with other wants, and no closer to interests than to embrace all a person's wants expressed in preferences (so long as the personal pattern of expression is consistent). The result is a sharp conflict with any definition appropriately based on the ordinary conception.

For according to the ordinary conception of interests, it is possible (indeed commonly the case) that a person's preferences and needs are at odds. Janis prefers to smoke two packs of cigarettes a day and to drink a fifth of bourbon while she is smoking, practices that are flagrantly not in her interest, because they thwart providing a whole range of things that she needs, ranging from adequate diet and exercise to mental alertness and dependable companionship. True, this assumes that it is in her interest to live a long and healthy life and meet the needs that go along with it. But this is in her interest, even if she wants to destroy herself, and therefore deliberately disregard her needs, refusing to take needs as the basis for making her preferences consistent. She destroys herself by acting against her interest and rejecting provisions for her needs.

Claims by business to be serving consumers' interests are too easy to make if the claimants discard the ordinary conception in favor of the notions of economists and other social scientists who accept interests as well enough defined by preferences. Every product that a consumer can be persuaded to buy is on this view something that it is in his or her interest to buy. Nor can there be any objection, on this approach, arising from that interest, to inducing in him or her a preference that he or she would not have had otherwise. Given the legal conditions for its operation, the market (with or without advertising), heeds all preferences that come with money attached to them, whatever their basis and however arrived at. A market can thus be efficient, according to the notions of economists, in reaching optimum results when every street is a cluster of ginshops doubling as sources of cigarettes, with life expectancy in the society declining precipitously year by year. Few social

scientists – few merchants or manufacturers – would contemplate such results entirely comfortably, but that is the direction in which their ideas lead, when they abandon the ordinary conception of interests.

Suppose that education, including warnings about misleading advertising, led most people to discriminate between preferences answering to needs and other preferences; and to act, of their own volition, to give priority to preferences answering to needs. In a free society, competent adults who do not do so might be left to other practices, so long as they did not harm others. For such a society, claims that a competitive market serves people's needs become less paradoxical. On the consumption side, provisions for needs will be available more cheaply than they would be otherwise; and hence consumers will be able to do more to meet their needs and put more money aside to make sure of buying provisions later. Thus their interests will be better served. On the production side, a competitive market might give everyone a chance to insist upon high wages and safe, even comfortable conditions of work. Thus people's needs would be provided for, and their interests respected. (In the real world, the virtues of competition may be even harder to realize here, because of the degree to which workers are immobile and in a weak bargaining position with powerful employers.)

The more advantages that consumers or workers are able to realize in the market, the more agreeable they will be able to make things for themselves, in the sense of acting on some of the harmless preferences not answering to their needs. Is it in their interest to be able to do this? It is certainly in their interest to have the opportunity to choose between increasing their holdings in resources and laying out resources to act on harmless preferences. Moreover, once they have made prudent savings arrangements, there is no compelling objection on the ground of their interests against using in this way whatever surplus they have after meeting needs. On the other hand, it seems too heavy-handed to maintain that it is in their interest to do so. Going back to needs to claim that people may need to have some of their harmless preferences heeded (a charming dress, an afternoon at the beach) would cover only part of the ground, as would the need for recreation, unless this were extravagantly inflated. The concept of interest may just not apply here one way or the other. We are not bound to have it embrace every choice that is not self-destructive, whether to meet a need or not.

See also **needs**

Bibliography

Barry, B. (1965). *Political Argument*. London: Routledge. (Contains a helpful discussion of interests, 174–86; a not so helpful discussion of needs, 47–9.)

Beckerman, W. (1968). *An Introduction to National Income Analysis*. London: Weidenfeld and Nicolson. Also, by the same author: (1974). *In Defence of Economic Growth*. London: Cape.Braybrooke, D. (1987). *Meeting Needs*. Princeton: Princeton University Press. Also, by the same author: (1992). Needs and interests. In Lawrence C. Becker & Charlotte B. Becker (eds), *Encyclopedia of Ethics*. New York: Garland, 894–7. (The present article is complementary to the *Encyclopedia*, one rather than reduplicative; both articles answer the economists.)

Mansbridge, J. (1980). *Beyond Adversary Democracy*. New York: Basic Books. (Contains (24–8, 342–4) an attempt, subtler and more judicious than most, to reduce interests to preferences.)

Thurow, L. (1973). Toward a definition of economic justice. *The Public Interest*, 31, 56–80. (Sets forth (p. 66) succinctly the reasons characteristically advanced by economists to dismiss the concept of needs. Answered in Braybrooke, *Meeting Needs*.)

DAVID BRAYBROOKE

international accounting Can international codes of professional ethics be developed to successfully regulate professional behavior? Put differently: are the rules of the game the same in Boston, Berlin, and Tokyo? There is evidence that local "customs" may override universal principles, thus making for ethical "diversity." By identifying and understanding the factors which make local cultures unique, and addressing their requirements, the potential effectiveness and acceptability of an "international" code might be enhanced. There is no guarantee of success in this venture: to illustrate the problems, we will examine the code of conduct or guidelines used by the International Federation of Accountants (IFAC) in July 1990.

On the face of it, there are two major reasons why worldwide acceptance of the current version of this Guideline may be problematic. First, societies tend to resist guidelines imposed from without where they are perceived as inconsistent with a society's entrenched cultural norms. Second, as socio-economic conditions vary dramatically from country to country, so, too, do levels of professional proficiency in the countries in which guidelines are to be implemented. While all accountants encounter ethical conflicts, those arising in the context of the high technical proficiency required of accountants in a developed country may be entirely different in kind from those encountered by accountants in developing countries. In this article we will concentrate on highlighting the cultural issues.

Cultural Influences on Ethical Conduct

We will argue that culture plays an important role in relation to ethical standards. If we restrict the meaning of culture to a national or local unit of analysis, as opposed, say, to ethnic or corporate cultures, Hofstede's (1980b) definition provides a useful framework. Culture in his sense is "the collective mental programming of the mind which distinguishes the members of one human group from another" (p. 25). As he considered cultures, he concluded that four measures – power distance, uncertainty avoidance, poles of individualism and collectivism, and poles of masculinity and femininity – could be used to differentiate the "collective mental programming" which is culture.

Power distance, a construct originally identified by Mulder (1977), measures how less a powerful subordinate perceives the degree of inequality in power which separates him or her from a more powerful superior.

Uncertainty avoidance, which indexes tolerance for uncertainty in culture, considers three indicators: rule orientation, employment stability, and stress. *Reluctance to break rules*, even when doing so is in the interests of the company, indicates an aversion to uncertainty. *Employment stability* captures a collective tolerance of the risks associated with job change. (Long-term employers who hold scrupulously to rules would measure high on the uncertainty

Figure 1   A framework for evaluating international codes of conduct applied to IFAC's "Guideline on Ethics"

	Consistency with Cultural Values			
	Power Distance	*Individualism/ Collectivism*	*Uncertainty/ Avoidance*	*Masculinity/ Femininity*
Integrity	Loyalty to supervisor	Conflicting loyalties	Compromising professional standards	Exaggeration of ability
Objectivity	Loyalty to supervisor	Value of others' opinions		
Confidentiality	Willingness to follow instructions	Loyalty to family and friends		Acceptability of self-promotion
		Loyalty to professional colleagues	Resolution of ethical conflicts	"Lowballing" and aggressive promotion of the firm
	Professional behavior		Independence of audit	Sex discrimination

avoidance scale.) While recognizing that *stress* certainly reflects organizational and personality variables, Hofstede attributes some part of it to culture and sees it as reflecting the level of anxiety in a society.

The poles of *Individualism* and *Collectivism* form the third dimension of national culture. Put simply, this dimension captures the extent to which a culture values individual achievement over group cohesion. Individualist societies, such as the United States, regard achievement as personal; collective contributions to one's success tend to be discounted. In contrast, collectivist cultures prize group well-being and group achievement over individual self-interest.

The poles of *Masculinity* and *Femininity* form the final dimension of national culture. This dimension measures the extent to which a culture emphasizes assertive ("masculine") rather than supportive ("feminine") values and also captures the degree to which a culture identifies jobs as gender-based.

Where cultures differ, international codes of ethics, even for a relatively homogenous profession such as accounting, may encounter difficulties. Two broad difficulties suggest themselves: lack of consensus as to what

constitutes acceptable behavior and divergent interpretations of the code.

Lack of consensus on acceptable behavior. Since cultures embody generally held beliefs and norms of appropriate behavior in a country, they have consequences for ethical behavior. Consider bribery. Pressure on a subordinate to cover up a supervisor's illegal action, such as accepting bribes, might be evaluated differently by Japanese than Americans because of cultural influences. While an American might interpret this pressure as coercion, a Japanese might willingly participate in a cover-up for collective motives – to save face and protect the reputation of the group.

Intellectual property presents another interesting contrast. In the typically collectivist cultures of Asia, the individual artist or writer is expected to share his or her creation. In contrast, individualist societies emphasize protecting the artist or writer by establishing copyright and patent laws.

Diversity of interpretation. Cultural differences, in the second place, might limit the application of an international code by spawning a diversity of interpretations of the code, with corresponding consequences for implementation. The ideal of a self-regulating profession, in which members identify not with the organization by which they are employed but instead with the code of a profession may be based on an individualist value system. Several researchers have argued that individualist values prize allegiance not to a group of people, but to a set of standards. As a consequence, practitioners in an individualist society may assume that if a professional chooses in light of the profession's guidelines, this will produce the best long-term results for that profession and for the society. But such an assumption may be antithetical to a collectivist culture.

An Evaluation of the IFAC Guideline

The Guideline identifies six principles fundamental to the accounting profession: Integrity, Objectivity, Professional Competence and Due Care, Confidentiality, Professional Behavior, and Technical Standards. Some of these could conflict with some cultural norms, and others are geared more toward the needs of developed economies than those of less-developed countries. Figure 1 shows a matrix consisting of Hofstede's cultural dimensions and the IFAC Guideline: cells with text identify areas where cultural diversity might create problems.

Power Distance and the dilemmas of the faithful follower. Power Distance captures the extent to which subordinates in an organization expect to be instructed by superiors, and willingly obey those instructions. In a "high" Power Distance culture, the International Guideline's requirements on integrity, objectivity, and confidentiality are likely to create cultural conflicts for subordinates. Consider the first column of Figure 1: a subordinate in such a culture would be likely to acquiesce to a superior's unauthorized request for confidential information, and such acquiescence would be regarded as acceptable behavior. A subordinate would also be more likely to remain loyal to his or her supervisor out of respect for the supervisor's position, even when the supervisor acts unethically, or even illegally. More important, such behavior on the part of the subordinate would be culturally acceptable.

Individualism/Collectivism and the dilemmas of personal loyalty. The integrity principle requires the professional accountant to be "straightforward and honest in performing professional services," and the Objectivity principle requires that "a professional accountant should be fair and not allow prejudice or bias or influence of others to override objectivity" (IFAC, 1990, p. 8). If we take "straightforward and honest" to involve a willingness on the part of individuals to be open to non-members of their group, then cultures will differ markedly. As the second column indicates, a member of a Collectivist culture would value the opinion of peers, and indeed would be unwilling to make a decision without their input. A code of conduct which forces individuals to compromise relationships with group members in favor of client confidentiality also conflicts with Collectivist cultural norms.

The Confidentiality principle states that a professional accountant "should respect the confidentiality acquired during the course of performing the professional services and should not use or disclose any such information without proper and specific authority" (IFAC, 1990, p. 9). If a professional discovered that his or her client was close to bankruptcy, the Guideline requires that this information be withheld from close friends and family. However, in a Collectivist culture, a failure to warn family and friends who were owed money would be a serious breach of collectivist norms.

Uncertainty Avoidance and the dilemma of being "professional". In the process recommended for the solution of an ethical conflict, the Guideline recommends a hierarchical approach whereby the professional is to review the conflict with his or her superior, or a higher authority if the superior is involved in the conflict problem. While this hierarchical approach might be suitable for a strong Uncertainty Avoidance culture, with its preference for written rules and intolerance of deviance, a weak Uncertainty Avoidance culture would be more tolerant of WHISTLEBLOWING. Furthermore, a professional from a Collectivist culture would value the advice of colleagues rather than superiors.

Masculinity/Femininity and the question of professional "presentation". The Masculinity dimension has important implications for the accounting profession, in which Western norms of professional conduct include restrictions on advertising and promotion. A Masculine culture might be more tolerant of exaggerated self-promotion, and aggressive bidding for new clients.

The norms of a Masculine culture which include acceptance of gender-based work-role differences in a country such as Japan (which has the highest Masculinity score) would be interpreted as sex discrimination by members of a more Feminist culture (such as Sweden).

Toward Internationally Acceptable Ethical Guidelines

As our review of the IFAC's guidelines suggests, "international" professional guidelines may turn out to be ethnocentric, reflecting the ethical and cultural standards of the developed countries whose organizations are most influential in writing them. They therefore risk failing to address ethical dilemmas found primarily in developing countries. Truly international guidelines must be sensitive to the need for guidance of the profession in its normal practice in all countries in which the code will operate.

Bibliography

Hofstede, G. (1980a). *Culture's Consequences*. Beverly Hills, Calif.: Sage.

Hofstede, G. (1980b). Motivation, leadership, and organization: Do American theories apply abroad? *Organizational Dynamics*, summer, 42–63.

International Federation of Accountants. (1990). *Guidelines on Ethics for Professional Accountants.* New York: IFAC.

Mulder, M. (1977). *The Daily Power Game.* Leiden, Netherlands: Martinus Nijhoff.

JEFFREY COHEN
LAURIE PANT
DAVID SHARP

international business ethics   Ethical issues surrounding transnational corporations are numerous and fall into at least eight major categories: bribery and sensitive payments, employment issues, marketing practices, impact on the economy and development of host countries, effects on the natural environment, cultural impacts of transnational operations, relations with host governments, and relations with the home countries.

While discussions of the responsibilities of transnationals has occurred for decades, few analyses cast explicitly in terms of ethics occurred until the late 1970s. It was then that moral philosophers and business academics began exploring specific issues in international business ethics. Since then, two distinct schools of thought have arisen concerning transnational responsibilities: they may be called "minimalist" and the "maximalist" schools. The "minimalist" school argues that a transnational's moral responsibilities are tied directly to its economic purposes: i.e., to make profits for its investors and products or services for the public. Minimalists deny that it is the responsibility of the corporation to help the poor, encourage the arts, or contribute to social causes – except insofar as doing such things is consistent with its more fundamental mission of making profits. Minimalists assert that transnationals have moral responsibilities, but that these are largely subsumable under the heading of "not harming" and not directly violating the rights of others. In contrast, the maximalist believes that corporations are unique in their level of organization and ability to control wealth, and that, in turn, they have the duty to reach out and help others. If housing and water supplies are substandard in the local area, then the company should work toward their improvement. And if malnutrition is a serious problem, the transnational should both develop nutrition programs and facilitate their implementation. Both minimalists and maximalists agree that transnationals should meet certain minimum ethical standards in conducting their business, but they disagree about whether transnationals should exceed this minimum.

The most often-used means of expressing minimum standards is through the moral language of rights. Many international documents which articulate rights, including the United Nations' *Universal Declaration of Human Rights*, have gained broad acceptance among nations. A list of rights to which most nations and individuals would agree is the following:

1 The right to freedom of physical movement.
2 The right to ownership of property.
3 The rights to freedom from torture.
4 The right to a fair trial.

5 The right to non-discriminatory treatment (i.e., freedom from discrimination on the basis of such characteristics as race or sex).
6 The right to physical security.
7 The right to freedom of speech and association.
8 The right to minimal education.
9 The right to political participation.
10 The right to subsistence.

All individuals, nations, and corporations are understood to have correlative duties in connection with these rights. Moreover, most experts agree that these duties include not only refraining from depriving people of the objects of their rights directly, but also, at least in some instances, helping protect people from being deprived of their rights. For example, a transnational operating in a developing country has correlative duties regarding the right to minimal education. In turn, the transnational would violate the right to minimal education if it hired 8-year-old children for full-time, ongoing labor and thus deprived them of the opportunity to learn to read and write. Here the violation would be passive rather than active; it would happen not through the company's actively removing the means for minimal education, but by passively failing to protect the right from deprivation.

Another example of failing to honor a right by failing to protect it from deprivation involves the prospective purchase of land in a Third World nation by a transnational corporation, where the intent is to convert the land to the production of a cash, export crop. Suppose the land in question is owned by absentee landlords but worked by tenant farmers. Suppose further that the tenant farmers each year have been able to take a portion of the crop barely sufficient for their own nutritional needs, but that the conversion of the land to a cash crop (forced by the transnational's purchase) will have the effect of driving the farmers to the slums of a nearby city where they will suffer malnutrition as a result. If this were true, then the transnational may violate the farmers' right to subsistence by its actions, even though it would not have taken food from anyone's mouth. The violation of the right would be passive; it would occur as a result of not honoring the duty to

protect the right to subsistence from deprivation.

An approach that is satisfied with merely honoring rights, such as the above, is a "minimalist" approach to international business ethics. In contrast, De George's book, *Competing with Integrity in International Business* (1993), is a good example of the "maximalist" approach. De George advances ten guidelines that he believes apply to American multinationals operating in less-developed countries. According to him, such multinationals should:

1 Do no intentional direct harm.
2 Produce more good than harm for the host country.
3 Contribute by their activity to the host country's development.
4 Respect the human rights of their employees.
5 Respect the local culture and work with and not against it.
6 Pay their fair share of taxes.
7 Cooperate with the local government in developing and enforcing just background institutions.
8 Recognize that majority control of a firm carries with it the ethical responsibility for the actions and failures of the firm.
9 Make sure that hazardous plants are safe and run safely.
10 When transferring hazardous technology to less-developed countries, be responsible for redesigning such technology so that it can be safely administered in the host country.

As De George's rules imply, one of the most difficult contexts for transnational ethics involves clashes between home- and host-country norms or laws. The problem is especially acute when the norm or law appears substandard from the perspective of the transnational's home country. When wage scales, pollution standards, norms prohibiting bribery, and treatment of minorities appear substandard in a foreign country, should the transnational take the high road of adhering to the home-country standards, or should it take the expedient route of embracing the host-country standards?

Embracing either extreme would be morally problematic. Always to adopt the home-country standard would sometimes disadvantage the host country. For example, a transnational that always paid workers in host countries the same wage rates as paid in the home country could damage foreign development in the host country, since attractive wage rates are often the principal incentive for transnational investment overseas. Furthermore, the trade-offs among competing economic and social goods may be different in the host than in the home country. A Third World country barely able to feed its malnourished population may prefer somewhat higher levels of pollution and more productivity (say, of food and fertilizer) than would a developed nation.

On the other hand, always to adopt the host-country standard would be pernicious. Laws and regulations in many developing countries are frequently unsophisticated, and a lack of technological knowledge coupled with inefficient bureaucratic mechanisms may preclude effective government control of industry. Blindly to adopt a developing country's standards for asbestos or for the dumping of hazardous waste could have tragic human consequences. While no simple answers exist, Donaldson, De George, and others have argued that certain principles can be articulated for the purpose of addressing such problems of norms in conflict.

In a directly practical vein, coalitions of governments and transnational corporations are increasingly articulating shared responsibilities in formal documents. Sometimes the responsibilities are formalized as the result of voluntary efforts by companies who are members of the same industry, as in the instance of the World Health Organization's Code on Pharmaceuticals and Tobacco, and the World Intellectual Property Organization's Revision of the Paris Convention for the Protection of Industrial Patents and Trademarks. Sometimes they are formalized as the result of international economic arrangements, as in the instance of the principles of intellectual property circumscribed by the General Agreement on Tariffs and Trade (GATT). And sometimes they are formalized as a result of decisions by truly global institutions, as in the instance of the OECD's *Declaration on International Investment and Multinational Enterprise.*

Bibliography

DeGeorge, R. T. (1993). Competing with Integrity in International Business. (New York: Oxford University Press).

Donaldson, T. (1989). The Ethics of International Business. (New York: Oxford University Press).

Donaldson, T. (1991). The ethics of conditionality in international debt. *Millennium: Journal of International Studies,* **20** (2), 155–69.

Enderle, G. (1989). The indebtedness of low-income countries as an ethical challenge for industrialized market economies. *The International Journal of Applied Philosophy,* **4** (3), 31–8.

Guidelines for Multinational Enterprises. (1984). Added to the 1976 *OECD Declaration.* In *International Investment and Multinational Enterprises: Revised Edition 1984.* Paris: Organization for Economic Cooperation and Development, 11-22.

Kline, J. (1985). *International Codes and Multinational Business: Setting Guidelines for International Operations.* Westport, Conn.: Quorum Books.

Moran, T. H. (1977). *Multinational Corporations and the Politics of Dependence: Copper in Chile.* Princeton, NJ: Princeton University Press.

O'Neill, O. (1986). *Faces of Hunger: An Essay on Poverty, Justice, and Development.* London: Allen & Unwin.

Preston, L. E., & Windsor, D. (1991). *The Rules of the Game in the Global Economy: Policy Regimes for International Business.* Dordrecht, The Netherlands: Kluwer.

Shue, H. (1980). *Basic Rights.* Princeton, NJ: Princeton University Press.

Waldman, R. J. (1980). *Regulating International Business Through Codes of Conduct.* Washington, DC: American Enterprise Institute.

THOMAS DONALDSON

invisible hand, the The assumption that society benefits most when individuals are allowed to define and pursue their own self-interests, with minimal interference from governments or other authorities. However, this assumption also presumes there is some guiding natural force – seldom mentioned and almost never defined – that ensures a just equilibrium will result from such self-interested behaviors.

The concept of the invisible hand first emerges in the work of ADAM SMITH, who mentions it in two brief passages in his two major books. Nowadays the term has been captured by the economists, but, originally, it had more to do with Smith's moral philosophy than it did with merely his economic ideas. It is this larger, moral conception that is of greatest interest for business ethics.

Smith, profoundly influenced by Stoicism, believes the invisible hand is a beneficent force of nature, operating without human intention and within a system of natural liberty, which allocates social goods in a rough and ready, but generally fair, distribution. This eventually results in the greatest happiness for the greatest number, a concept he borrows from his mentor, Francis Hutcheson.

Some argue that Smith's ideas about the invisible hand come from the rather unsavory philosophy of unmitigated SELF-INTEREST advocated by his contemporary, Bernard Mandeville, who argued that the pursuit of "private vices" resulted in "publick benefits." But Smith devoted a hefty chapter in his first book, *The Theory of Moral Sentiments* (1759), to discrediting Mandeville's ideas. Indeed, it can be argued that Smith's conception of the invisible hand was his answer to Mandeville.

Turning to Smith's writings, aside from a casual and contradictory reference in an early essay, "The history of astronomy," the two major references to the invisible hand are in his two major books. The most famous and frequently quoted passage, in his second book, *The Wealth of Nations* (1776), is actually the least explanatory of the two. In a section discussing the "natural balance of industry," Smith notes that investors like to keep their capital close to home, which works to the advantage of the local community. Further, the main reason they invest is to increase their profits. Thus:

> As every individual, therefore, endeavours as much as he can both to employ his capital in the support of domestick industry, and so to direct that industry that its produce may be of the greatest value; every individual necessarily labours to render the annual revenue of the society as great as he can. He generally, indeed, neither intends to promote the publick interest, nor knows how much he is promoting it. (Smith, 1776, p. 456)

The important point here is that intelligent individuals, who possess capital, direct the full force of their intelligence to improving domestic industry so as to make a profit. Even though their motive is profit, the entire society benefits from that collective application of intelligence. As a result:

> By preferring the support of domestick to that of foreign industry, he intends only his own security; and by directing that industry in such a manner as its produce may be of the greatest value, he intends only his own gain, and he is in this, as in many other cases, led by an invisible hand to promote an end which was no part of his intention. (Smith, 1776, p. 456)

This passage might seem to support the popular, but erroneous, argument that Adam Smith was the precursor of economic Social Darwinism (*see* DARWINISM AND ETHICS). But that is far off the mark, as can be seen in his earlier and longer explication of the term in *The Theory of Moral Sentiments*.

Here Smith presents his moral philosophy, intending that all of his later works would be interpreted in terms of it. The foundation of that system rests upon the primacy of sympathy, which is the ability of all individuals to understand one another. Moreover, Smith knows that society is a mixed bag: some people are unabashedly self-interested, but others are both virtuous and caring. It is upon the latter that he constructs his ideal society.

The main issue that leads Smith to the notion of the invisible hand is the incomprehensible complexity of society. It is impossible for any individuals or groups, including the government, to comprehend society well enough to allow them to systematically plan and guide the society toward good ends. Indeed, he notes that he had "never known much good done by those who affected to trade for the publick good. It is an affectation . ." (Smith, 1776, p. 456).

Smith wants to free humankind from the paternalism of those individuals and groups who believe they can direct and control society for its own best good. The villain is "the man of system": the individual who believes that he or she can devise and execute plans which will guarantee desired social benefits.

Smith recognizes the impossibility of any human plan being able to encompass the fullness and complexity of society. Thus, organizational systems, externally imposed, are bound to fail, and people will suffer as a result. Smith advises us to let the human chess pieces move of their own volition, guided primarily by their individual virtue, and an invisible hand will lead them all toward a just outcome.

It is significant that the concept of the invisible hand is introduced in a passage attacking the "splenetic philosophy" of Mandeville. Smith begins by condemning the silly ostentation of the wealthy: "If we consider the real satisfaction which all these things are capable of affording, by itself and separated from the beauty of that arrangement which is fitted to promote it, it will always appear in the highest degree contemptible and trifling" (Smith, 1759, p. 183). He knew, however, that the rich would continue to spend lavishly, out of "their natural selfishness and rapacity." But since the stomachs of the wealthy can contain no more than the stomachs of the poor, what do the wealthy hope to obtain? The answer is clear: most of them serve only their vanity.

However, out of such self-indulgence will often come social good. The wealthy

> are led by an invisible hand to make nearly the same distribution of the necessaries of life, which would have been made, had the earth been divided into equal portions among all its inhabitants, and thus without intending it, without knowing it, advance the interest of the society, and afford means to the multiplication of the species. (Smith, 1759, p. 184)

Thus, without intending it, and in an economic system of natural liberty, such spending provides indirectly for the working men and women. As H. B. Acton writes: "An unintended result of action is thus something that is not specifically aimed at by any member of a group of agents but that arises as a result of each agent's successful pursuit of his particular aim" (Acton, 1993, p. 174).

So, ordinary people are employed in building the mansions of the rich; they tend their fields, flocks, and gardens; they run their industries; they manufacture and repair their goods; and so on. For these services, they are compensated, and this brings about a relatively just distribution of material benefits. Smith clearly understands the savage inequities of tyrannies and monopolies, but he attacks them at other places in his books.

The most important thing for Adam Smith is the happiness of all individuals, which is not necessarily related to their comparative shares in economic goods. Thus, he continues his description of the invisible hand by pointing to its moral significance:

> When Providence divided the earth among a few lordly masters, it neither forgot nor abandoned those who seemed to have been left out in the partition. These last too enjoy their share of all that it produces. *In what constitutes the real happiness of human life, they are in no respect inferior to those who would seem so much above them.* In ease of body and peace of mind, all the different ranks of life are nearly upon a level, and the beggar, who suns himself by the side of the highway, possesses that security which kings are fighting for. (Smith, 1759, p. 184–5, emphasis added)

In the ideal, then, the invisible hand concerns much more than economics: it concerns the moral happiness of all individuals encompassed within a larger society.

Such happiness comes through virtuous character. Throughout *The Theory of Moral Sentiments*, Smith repeats the admonition that for the ideal to exist, all individuals must act virtuously. What is not clearly understood by too many contemporary readers is how much Smith's ideal rests upon individual virtue, and that is certainly the case with the invisible hand: it only works as it should when all participants play fair. For Adam Smith, the optimal functioning of the invisible hand is predicated upon widespread virtue (Smith, 1759, pp. 82–91).

However, that ethical conception has been lost to modernity, and the invisible hand has been reduced down to an unintentional (and largely inexplicable) ordering factor among rational utility maximizers competing in free markets, which results in a reasonable distribution of economic goods within that society. This view of the invisible hand relies more upon the

UTILITARIANISM of JEREMY BENTHAM and his followers than it does upon Adam Smith.

For them, the primal motivation for each individual is the minimization of pain and the maximization of pleasure. Since such pleasures and pains come mostly from the physical needs of individuals, it follows that citizens serve society best by following their material instincts. Adam Smith conceives of the invisible hand quite differently. For him, it operates best as the result of intentional and voluntary virtue. The greatest contribution individuals can make to the collective good is the development and actualization of their own virtue.

Bibliography

Acton, H. B. (1993). *The Morals of Markets and Related Essays*, (eds) D. Gordon & J. Shearmur. Indianapolis, Ind.: Liberty Classics.

Morrow, G. R. (1923). *The Ethical and Economic Theories of Adam Smith*. Clifton, NJ: Augustus M. Kelley.

Muller, J. Z. (1993). *Adam Smith in His Time and Ours*. New York: Free Press.

Smith, A. (1759; 1790). *The Theory of Moral Sentiments*, (eds) D. D. Raphael & A. L. Macfie. Indianapolis, Ind.: Liberty Classics.

Smith, A. (1776). *An Inquiry into the Nature and Causes of the Wealth of Nations*, (eds) R. H. Campbell & A. S. Skinner. Indianapolis, Ind.: Liberty Classics.

Werhane, P. H. (1991). *Adam Smith and His Legacy for Modern Capitalism*. New York: Oxford University Press.

DAVID KIRKWOOD HART

Israel, business ethics in *see* BUSINESS ETHICS IN ISRAEL

J

Japan, business ethics in *see* BUSINESS
ETHICS IN JAPAN

Judaism, business ethics and *see* BUSINESS
ETHICS AND JUDAISM

just cause is a policy requiring that dismissal
of employees be for just or good reason.

A just cause dismissal policy is best understood in contrast to a strict EMPLOYMENT AT
WILL (EAW) rule which allows employers
absolute discretion to fire an employee. The
essence of just cause policies, on the other hand,
is to limit the employer's authority to discharge.
While there may be many different instantiations of just cause policies, all will address the
following: reasons, procedures, and remedies.

What constitutes a good or just reason for
dismissal is impossible to define exactly in a
brief policy or statute. Typically, "just cause" is
defined loosely (e.g., as reasonable and job-
related grounds for dismissal) and left to
arbitrators or labor courts to define more
precisely through their decisions. It is, however,
clearly understood that union membership,
race, sex, personal bias, political opinions,
religion, or ethnicity are invalid reasons; theft,
fighting on the job, drug use on the job,
excessive absenteeism, or substandard performance are acceptable reasons.

There are interesting corollaries of requiring
good reasons: 1) If inadequate performance is a
valid reason for discharge, then employers must
specify what counts as adequate performance. 2)
More broadly, a just cause policy must understand "valid reason" as requiring more than an
employer's subjective belief, say, that an

employee stole or used drugs at work. Some
substantial evidence must be available to make
such a belief reasonable. Failure to require these
things of employers will obviously make a
demand for just cause ineffectual in protecting
employees from unfair dismissals.

Just cause policies will also require that some
procedures be available to review discharge
actions. At the very least, some mechanism for
external and independent assessment of the
merits of the employer's reasons must be made
available to the employee. Arbitrators or labor
courts usually fill this role. While not essential,
less formal internal pre-termination hearings or
appeals mechanisms are consistent with the
spirit of just cause in that these will help prevent
unfair discharges. Once the employee completes
the probationary period required for coverage,
most just cause policies also require prior notice
of intent to dismiss and written provision of the
reasons.

Finally, all just cause policies must include
some remedy for those cases where a firing is
found to be unjust. Possible remedies include
reinstatement and/or monetary damages. In
jurisdictions governed by just cause, monetary
damages are usually limited by statute to some
small multiple of wages.

While most Western industrialized nations
have adopted some form of just cause policy,
US state laws almost universally represent a
modified EAW rule. In the US, employer
discretion to discharge is no longer absolute,
having been limited incrementally by judicial
precedents or statutes that identify impermissible grounds for dismissal. However, aside
from those enumerated exceptions, US employers may still fire for any or no reason.
Exceptions to this are public employees and
union workers, both of whom enjoy protections

similar to "just cause," and those who work for corporations that have voluntarily adopted a just cause policy.

Interestingly, some employer groups in the US are urging the adoption of a just cause standard because they find state law so uncertain and because firings found to violate the law can bring damage awards far greater than those allowed by just cause statutes. For these reasons, the Billings Chamber of Commerce supported Montana's 1987 just cause law.

Since 1980, just cause statutes have been introduced in ten states. The debate over these proposals is in part a moral debate involving issues of FAIRNESS, justice, and collective welfare (see JUSTICE, CIRCUMSTANCES OF; UTILITARIANISM). Proponents of such statutes are moved by the substantial harms that can accompany job loss. In addition to lost income, workers and their families suffer insecurity, depression, loss of self-respect. They argue that it is unfair to impose these costs on the estimated 150,000+ workers a year discharged without just cause and due process.

Opponents of just cause claim that broad employer authority to dismiss is necessary for workplace discipline and motivation. (Implicit in this argument is the belief that job security and work output are inversely related.) They also point to the need for employer flexibility in the competitive global economy. They argue that just cause is not required by fairness since workers and employers have equal ability to terminate the relationship. Finally, they claim that just cause must be inefficient since if it were efficient, the labor market would force employers to provide it.

Defenders of just cause respond to these challenges by arguing that: 1) The motivator under EAW is fear of job loss and psychological literature is unanimous on fear being a poor motivator. At most, fear will assure that workers conform to minimum external standards. It will probably also assure workers who lack innovation and who are dispirited. 2) Those who point to drones as the paradigm of workers with job security need to show that is typical under job security, and if it is, that security and not some other variable (e.g., lack of autonomy) is the cause of low productivity. 3) The appeal to needed flexibility in a competitive economy is a red herring since all just cause policies accept

layoffs due to economic conditions. 4) While formally equal, individual employees and employers are not often in positions of equal bargaining strength. As a result, it is not surprising that the private labor market does not typically provide job security. It is also not surprising that grievance procedures are one of the first demands of organized workers.

It remains to be seen which set of arguments carries the day in the continuing US debate. It also remains to be seen whether European labor rules experience any great change as a result of increased global competition and local unemployment. (Through 1994, changes have been small and limited mainly to increased allowance for temporary workers.)

See also due process; free speech in the workplace; freedom of contract; right to work

Bibliography

Beerman, J. & Singer, W. J. (1989). Baseline questions in legal reasoning: The example of property in jobs. 23 Georgia Law Review 911.

Edwards, R. (1993). Rights at Work: Employment Relations in the Post Union-Era. New York: Twentieth Century Fund.

Epstein, R. (1984). In defense of the contract at will. 51 University of Chicago Law Review 947.

Krueger, A. (1991). The evolution of unjust dismissal legislation in the United States. 44 Industrial and Labor Relations Review 644.

Paull, K. (1991). Employment termination reform: What should a statute require before termination – some lessons from the French, German, and British experiences. 14 Hastings International and Comparative Law Review 619.

Singer, W. J. (1988). The reliance interest in property. 40 Stanford Law Review 614.

Summer, C. (1976). Individual protection against unjust dismissal: Time for a statute. 62 Virginia Law Review 481.

Werhane, P. (1985). Persons, Rights and Corporations. Englewood Cliffs, NJ: Prentice-Hall.

JOHN J. McCALL

justice   Any inquiry about "the circumstances of justice" is ultimately one about the scope of justice. It is, in other words, a part of the broader search for the conditions which must obtain for questions of justice to have meaning. Clearly some such conditions must obtain. To ask whether last year's weather treated my house justly is nonsense, but to ask whether the rich citizens of second-century Rome treated their poorer fellow citizens justly makes sense. But what, precisely, gives sense to the latter question while denying it to the former? The practical implications of this question may be significant, for it appears that one must determine the conditions of justices in order to confront a host of vexing issues: Can one nation treat another unjustly? Can one generation treat a future generation unjustly? Can people treat animals unjustly?

While discussion about the "circumstances of justice" are cut from the larger cloth of the inquiry into the scope of justice, they encompass a narrower range of issues. The phrase "circumstances of justice" refers implicitly to a key set of disputed issues about the conditions of justice, and to specific "circumstances" asserted by the British philosopher, David Hume (1711–76). Indeed, it was Hume who coined the phrase "circumstances of justice." Hume argued that people usually find themselves in circumstances manifesting four general characteristics which limit the possibility of justice: dependence, moderate scarcity, restrained benevolence, and individual vulnerability

1 *Dependence.* According to Hume, individual human beings are not entirely self-sufficient. In addition to requiring nature's cooperation in the form of, for example, air and water, they rely upon the cooperation of their fellows to achieve certain critical goods.

2 *Moderate scarcity.* Most people find themselves confronted neither by a dramatic material abundance, which would make a conflict of material interests impossible, nor by a dramatic scarcity which would make decent life impossible.

3 *Restrained benevolence.* Humans tend neither to be saints nor devils; they manifest generosity, but only to a point. While they frequently sacrifice on behalf of family, friends, nation, and humankind, they tend over the long term to reveal a deep-seated and resilient self-interest.

4 *Individual vulnerability.* Humans are vulnerable to one another. No matter how powerful or intelligent, an individual may succumb to attacks by weaker fellows.

The twentieth-century American philosopher, JOHN RAWLS, has made use of Hume's interpretation of the circumstances of justice in his well-known account of distributive justice, *A Theory of Justice* (1971). He explicitly states that his own account adds "nothing essential" to Hume's "much fuller" discussion, and proceeds to employ Hume's insights in establishing limits on the scope of distributive justice. He refers to the circumstances of justice as "the normal conditions under which human cooperation is both possible and necessary," and gives special attention to the condition of modern scarcity, which he defines as the existence of natural resources "not so abundant that schemes of cooperation become superfluous," nor "conditions so harsh that fruitful ventures must inevitably break down."

But even if Rawls' account is identical to Hume's – a claim questioned by many observers – one may wonder whether the so-called circumstances of justice are, in truth, necessary either for the meaningful application of such terms as "just" and "unjust" or for the existence of just institutions.

For example, it seems at first glance that if people have either an extravagant abundance of material goods, or an extreme scarcity, then issues of justice will not arise. But first impressions may be misleading. Suppose that an extravagant abundance of material goods exists. Might not questions of justice nonetheless arise over, say, the bestowing of awards in public contests, or in structuring systems of seniority and status? Or, alternatively, suppose that a dramatic scarcity of goods exists: Might not questions of justice arise in determining, say, who should be utterly deprived in order for others to survive?

Much turns on the sense of "necessary" intended. If the circumstances of justice are said to be necessary for the term "justice" even to have meaningful application to states of affairs, then obvious counter-examples must be considered. For example, imagine a society populated by utterly selfish people – rational brutes preying on one another. Might such a society not still be labeled "unjust" from the perspective of an external observer? Hence, some critics argue that while the condition of restrained benevolence may be practically necessary for the emergence of just institutions, it is unnecessary for the meaningful application of concepts of justice even to societies that lack such institutions.

Even the presumably less stringent test of being "necessary for the emergence of just institutions" is subject to controversy. Extending the example mentioned above, some argue that even conditions of dramatic scarcity are compatible with the existence of cooperative schemes used to effect damage control and maximize human survival.

It should be added that controversy sometimes also surrounds the meaning of key terms specifying the circumstances of justice. Rawls, for example, believes that distributive justice is inappropriate in international contexts owing to the low level of international dependence. While asserting that distributive justice concerns the distribution of the fruits of cooperation, he proceeds to note that nations are more or less self-sufficient schemes of social cooperation. "The boundaries" of the cooperative schemes to which the principles of distributive justice apply, Rawls argues, "are given by the notion of a self-contained national community." But how much dependence is necessary? Might it be enough simply that the wealth of developed industrial nations owes itself, at least in part, to dealings with industrially underdeveloped nations? Or is it perhaps enough that the financial destinies of most nations are currently intertwined by mutual systems of money, commerce, and regulation? That distributive justice has international application in this sense is precisely the claim made by many contemporary philosophers.

Hence, while the discussion of the "circumstances of justice" belongs to the historical stream of discussion about the conditions of justice generally, it reflects the special focus given to it by Hume in the eighteenth century. For this reason, even appealing to the "circumstances of justice" may imply adopting a particular approach to the broader issue of the scope of justice.

See also **distributive justices; economic justice; interactional justice; Nozick, Robert; Rawls, John**

This entry is reprinted from Lawrence C. Becker and Chaarlotte B. Becker (eds), *Encyclopedia of Ethics* (pp. 653–5), New York: Garland Publishing, 1992, where it appeared under the title "Justice, circumstances of".

Bibliography

Beitz, C. (1979). *Political Theory and International Relations*. Princeton, NJ: Princeton University Press.

Hubin, D. C. (1979), The Scope of Justice. *Philosophy and Public Affairs*, **9**, 3–24..

Hume, D. A. (1988 [1737]). *Treatise of Human Nature*, ed. L. A. Selby-Bigge, Oxford: Oxford University Press.

Hume, D. (1977 [1751]). *An Inquiry Concerning the Principles of Morals*. London.

Rawls, J. (1971). *Theory of Justice*. Cambridge, Mass.: Harvard University Press; see pp. 127–8.)

THOMAS DONALDSON

K

Kantian ethics   The moral theory of Immanuel Kant (1724–1804); or, any theory that incorporates some of Kant's central claims, or claims similar to Kant's.

Kant's Moral Theory

Kant's most basic claim is that nothing can be conceived to be good unconditionally and without qualification except a good will. This he explicates and defends in the *Foundations of the Metaphysics of Morals* (1785) and in the *Critique of Practical Reason* (1788). He argues along the following lines.

The Hypothetical Imperative

We (human beings) have needs, desires, reason, and a will. Our will is our capacity to act in accordance with rational principles (that is, to act for reasons). When we will any action we act on more or less general principles (maxims); these contain a description of our action, a description of our purpose, and a (putatively) justifying rationale. If, for example, the maxim of my action is to return library books in order to accommodate other users, then although there are indefinitely many true descriptions of what I am doing as I return a book, this is the description under which and the purpose with which I act. My rationale might in turn refer to a more general maxim, for example, my maxim to do my part in mutually advantageous cooperative schemes – my maxim of fairness. As it happens, our maxims often fail to contain fully justifying rationales, even when they appear to us to do so. They often fail, that is, to conform to relevant principles of rationality. In this respect our maxims are unlike those of a perfectly rational will. For us, then, the principles of rationality are imperatives and expressed with an "ought."

One valid principle of rationality is *the* hypothetical imperative – that we ought to do what is necessary to achieve our goals. If my goal is health and a long life, for example, then this imperative declares invalid maxims of taking no exercise and eating rich foods. All maxims this imperative declares as valid, on the other hand, are themselves hypothetical imperatives. Should we agree there were no principle of rationality other than *the* hypothetical imperative, then all valid imperatives would be based on our desires and inclinations and a perfectly rational will would be good only conditionally – good only as a means.

The Good Will and the Categorical Imperative

If a perfectly rational will is to be good unconditionally, therefore, there must be some principle of practical rationality other than *the* hypothetical imperative. That there is such a principle (or that we believe there is) is contained in the concept of duty. For to act from duty is not to act from inclination or desire; indeed, to act from duty may require acting contrary to all inclination. To illustrate: consider the difference between the merely warm-hearted Good Samaritan and the Good Samaritan who acts from duty. Both make the well-being of others their end. The maxim of the former, however, is a hypothetical imperative. For him the needs of the stranger in distress are reasons to act only conditionally on his warm-hearted nature. For the Samaritan who acts from duty, by contrast, the stranger's needs are unconditional reasons for acting; his maxim is therefore a categorical imperative, chosen simply because it is a law. One who chooses maxims on this basis acts from respect for law as such. The basic principle of all action from duty, therefore, is one that sets out the conditions under which a maxim could be a categorical imperative. This formal principle of all categorical imperatives is called *the* categorical imperative: "I ought never act in such a way that I could not will that my maxim should be a univeral law" (IV 402). This is the supreme regulative principle of the good will.

Autonomy, Dignity, and the Realm of Ends

If all imperatives were hypothetical then the condition of the human will would be (as many moral theorists assume) heteronomy, a will always bound to serve inclination. But if the condition of our will were heteronomy, then one with effective power could always coerce us to do his will by making the price of non-compliance higher than we can pay. If, for example, self-preservation is my strongest inclination and heteronomy the condition of my will, then death is a price I cannot pay. I could not, for example, resist the threat of my sovereign to kill me should I refuse to bear false witness against an innocent man whom he wishes, on some plausible pretext, to execute. On the other hand, if I know that I ought to resist him – that resistance is duty – then I know that I can resist him and know that the condition of my will is autonomy. If, therefore, the categorical imperative is valid then autonomy is the condition of our will.

What is more, as the example illustrates, if I take the categorical imperative to be valid, I also take myself to have dignity, a value beyond any price (or exchange value); furthermore, I must grant that what holds for me holds for moral agents generally. The validity of the categorical imperative entails that moral agents are ends in themselves, each having a value that limits the value of anything that can be produced through action. That moral agents have dignity implies, negatively, that we are never to act on maxims to which others could not freely and rationally consent and, positively, that we are to make the morally permissible ends of others our own ends. Thus, beginning with the idea that the supreme principle of morality is a categorical imperative, we arrive at the formula of humanity: "Act so that you treat humanity, whether in your own person or in that of another, always as an end and never as a means only" (IV 429).

The idea that we are all ends in ourselves leads to the conception of a realm of ends, an ideal of moral community in which we are united under common moral laws to which we freely consent (each having a veto), laws which define equal rights to freedom from interference by others (external freedom) and which establish social and political conditions favorable to individual development and happiness. This conception of a realm of ends interprets the concept of a categorical imperative: our maxim is a categorical imperative if and only if it could serve as a law in a realm of ends. (This interpretation of the idea of a categorical imperative has inspired recent work in contractarian moral theory.)

Defense of the Categorical Imperative

Up to this point it has been shown only that if the concept of duty is not a vain delusion, then (a) the categorical imperative is a valid rational principle for us, (b) we are agents with autonomy, (c) we are ends in ourselves. It remains to defend the categorical imperative. The key is autonomy of the will. In the final analysis, Kant's defense comes to this: the autonomy of the will is the inescapable fact of our own reason; we reject it on pain of rational incoherence.

The System of Duties

In the *Foundations* Kant sketches a decision procedure – the law-of-nature test – for determining what our specific duties are. The test itself is not the categorical imperative, but an adaptation of it. It requires first that we form a universalized counterpart of our personal maxim, for example, the maxim of the liar would become the law of nature: all lie when it suits their purposes. Then we are to ask whether this could be conceived or willed as a law of nature. If not, then action on that maxim is morally impermissible. The test seems (satisfactorily) to rule out lying promises and ignoring the needy. We cannot conceive the maxim of the lying promiser as a universal law, for a lying promise is a possible means to one's ends only if it is the *exception* and not the universal rule. Similarly, we cannot rationally will not to be helped when we cannot achieve our ends without aid (this would contradict the hypothetical imperative), so we cannot consistently will the universal law of no help. Thus, to help the needy is a law we must, on pain of contradiction, legislate for ourselves. Unhappily, as critics have noted, the test can seem also to have counter-intuitive results. The fact of the matter, however, is that there is no consensus in the critical literature about what precisely the test is, how it is supposed to work, or what it is designed to accomplish. Since in *The Metaphysics of Morals* (1797), where Kant sets out his system of duties, he does not use the law-of-nature procedure, this late work sheds no light on it.

The Metaphysics of Morals divides duties into two sets: duties of justice (*Recht*) (also called juridical duties), concerned with enforceable external freedom, and duties of virtue, concerned with unenforceable internal freedom. Each set has a fundamental principle derivable from the categorical imperative. The universal law of justice enjoins us not to interfere with the morally permissible activity of others (VI 231). An act is wrong if it violates this law (or its derivatives); yet since coercive prevention of wrongdoing is not wrong, these duties can be enforced. It follows that such duties are duties to perform or not to perform certain acts. If I refrain from assaulting you or if I honor my contract, I perform my duty, even if I act solely from self-interest. Indeed, it is because we are naturally inclined to act from self-interest that these duties can be enforced. (In connection with the juridical duty not to steal, Kant develops a theory of original entitlement to land different from Locke's labor-theory.)

The fundamental principle of duties of virtue is to act in accordance with a maxim of ends that we can will as a universal law. Like the universal law of justice, this is directly implied by the humanity formula (VI 395). Since duties of virtue are duties to adopt ends, they leave us some latitude in deciding how they are to be achieved. (They are duties of wide requirement.) For example, in fulfilling the duty of benevolence I may permissibly be guided by personal attachment in my choice of beneficiary. They divide further into duties to ourselves – to make our own natural and moral development our end; and duties to others – to make their well-being and happiness our end. Some duties of virtue, however, are of narrow requirement, e.g., duties not to lie or willingly to end our lives. (Kant's view that lying is a violation of a duty to oneself and is never permitted is controversial.) *The Metaphysics of Morals* is not a tidy book; yet only in it do we find the substantive morality Kant believes follows from his claim that the good will is the single unqualified good.

Kantian Theories

A theory may be labeled Kantian if it displays some of the distinguishing marks of Kant's theory: that moral rules or moral reasons are categorical, that persons are ends in themselves, that moral agents are self-governing (i.e., have autonomy), that the value of consequences of action is conditional on the value and integrity of moral agents, that moral principles are universalizable, that the fundamental principle of morality is formal, absolute, and grounded in our rationality, and that substantive morality is a rational construction. Theories described as Kantian for one or other of these reasons may nonetheless diverge from Kant's theory in other ways. Some contemporary accounts of moral reasons agree with Kant's that these are not conditional or agent-desire dependent, but reject Kant's doctrines of the categorical imperative and of autonomy. Others stress the value of agent integrity as a bulwark against consequentialism, but they reject Kant's interpretation of agent integrity. Many contemporary theorists follow Kant in saying that moral rules must be universalizable and impartial, while at the same time they reject Kant's view that moral rules command categorically. In the theory of R. M. Hare, a theory frequently described as Kantian, the universalizability thesis is defended on narrowly linguistic grounds – an appeal to ordinary meaning – and the moral use of "ought" is subordinated to prudential rationality (the only principle of rationality Hare accepts), with the un-Kantian result that moral imperatives which are categorical in form, command hypothetically.

Kant's own theory is often described as rigorist, absolutist, formalist, and deontological. Kant is rigorist in insisting on the purity of the moral motive (respect for law) unmixed with inclination; still he believes that we have a duty to cultivate, e.g. "the compassionate natural feelings in us," and to rid ourselves of feelings of envy, ingratitude, and malice (VI 456–62). Kant is absolutist in that he holds the moral law, which is a strictly formal (contentless) principle, to be absolutely valid for all moral agents, but only on some interpretations of Kant's substantive system of duties does he endorse absolute duties, e.g., never to lie, never to torture, never to kill an innocent human being, whatever the consequences. Kant is a deontologist in this sense, that the categorical imperative sets formal conditions that outcomes of possible actions must meet in order to have value and to be worth promoting. Yet unlike standard deontological theorists, he does not share with consequentialists the view that there is a way to rank outcomes from best to worst independently of how they might be achieved or by whom. He also rejects the standard deontologist's view that there is a set of moral rules (absolute or *prima facie*) presented to us directly by our reason (or moral intuition) and demanding our obedience. In Kant's view, such rules could command only hypothetically and the rationality of obedience would presuppose some inclination, e.g., an implanted or acquired desire to follow rules of this kind. The substantive morality of *The Metaphysics of Morals* is, to be sure, anti-consequentialist, but only in its theory of justice do we find even an approximation of a deontological ethics and even this part of the theory derives from the theory of the good will. Finally, a theory is rightly labeled Kantian if it builds on the idea that we are all free and equal moral persons with autonomy (in something like Kant's sense of autonomy). This conception of persons goes hand-in-hand with the (constructivist) idea, the organizing idea of Kant's realm of ends, that the system of duties, rights, and virtues is the legislative product of mutually harmonious willing of free and equal moral persons.

Bibliography

Works by Kant:

Kant, Immanuel. (1902–). *Gesammelte Schriften.* Prussian Academy Edition. 28 vols. Berlin: Walter de Gruyter. (In most translations of Kant's works one can find page numbers referring to this edition. Under the editorship of Paul Guyer and Allen Wood, Cambridge University Press is currently preparing new translations of Kant's works.)

(1785). *Grundlegung zur Metaphysik der Sitten.* Contained in volume 4 of the Prussian Academy Edition. Several translations are available. Trans. by Lewis White Beck as *Foundations of the Metaphysics of Morals.* (Library of Liberal Arts, 1959); by H. J. Paton as *Groundwork of the Metaphysics of Morals.* (Harper, 1964), and by James Ellington as *Grounding for the Metaphysics of Morals.* (Hackett, 1983).

(1788). *Kritik der praktischen Vernunft.* Contained in volume 5 of the Prussian Academy Edition. Trans. by Lewis White Beck as *Critique of Practical Reason.* (Library of Liberal Arts, 1956).

(1797). *Metaphysik der Sitten.* Contained in volume 6 of the Prussian Academy Edition. Trans. by Mary Gregor as *The Metaphysics of Morals.* (Cambridge, 1991).

Works about Kant:

Beck, Lewis White. (1960). *A Commentary on Kant's Critique of Practical Reason.* Chicago: University of Chicago Press. (A classic work by one of America's most distinguished Kant scholars.)

Herman, Barbara. (1991). *The Practice of Moral Judgment.* Cambridge, Mass.: Harvard University Press. (Excellent discussion of the role of the categorical imperative in moral judgment).

Hill, Thomas, Jr. (1991). *Dignity and Practical Reason.* Ithaca, NY: Cornell University Press. (Collection of essays, especially clear and readable, on a range of topics in Kant's ethics).

Nell (O'Neill), Onora. (1975). *Acting on Principle: An Essay on Kantian Ethics.* New York: Columbia University Press. (Excellent study of the law-of-nature procedure for testing maxims).

O'Neill, Onora,. (1989). *Constructions of Reason: Exploration of Kant's Practical Philosophy.* Cambridge: Cambridge University Press. (Collection of illuminating, interpretive essays, some dealing specifically with practical problems).

Paton, H. J. (1971). *The Categorical Imperative: A Study in Kant's Moral Philosophy.* Philadelphia: University of Pennsylvania Press. (Commentary on the *Groundwork*).

Sullivan, Roger J. (1989). *Immanuel Kant's Moral Theory.* Cambridge: Cambridge University Press. (Comprehensive).

JOHN MARSHALL

Knight, Frank (1885–1972): One of the century's most eloquent proponents of market competition. In his three decades at the University of Chicago, he defended laissez-faire as the best form of social organization, and was the intellectual inspiration to liberal economists such as Milton Friedman.

Unfortunately, Knight's legacy as champion of economic freedom has obscured his career-long struggle with the market; his epistemological observations about uncertainty and incomplete knowledge challenged both the supposition of free-market optimality and the very methodology with which economics should be studied.

Knight did not advocate laissez-faire economics because it was ideal; indeed, his concerns about the concentration of economic power, the need to preserve the family unit, and the importance of universally available education led him to support a considerable role for state social spending. However, he also concluded that free-market capitalism was the best solution for the central problem of all economic activity – uncertainty.

While Knight grudgingly acknowledged the need for mechanical models of economic behavior as a useful but highly imperfect tool of social inquiry, he forcefully argued that unmeasurable "human" factors must be considered to confront real-world problems of risk and uncertainty. Because people often do not even know their own preferences, much less those of other people, one of the most important variables in the study of economic activity is "judgment." Knight passionately attacked the emerging school of positivism in the 1930s, rejecting what he considered arrogant and unethical efforts to prove economic hypotheses with an empirically based theory-testing methodology borrowed from the natural sciences.

See also **Friedman, Milton**

Bibliography

Hammond, J. D. (1991). Frank Knight's antipositivism. *History of Political Economy*, **23** (3), 359–80. (Review of Knight's methodological criticism).

Kasper, S. D. (1993). Frank Knight's case for laissez faire: The patrimony of the social philosophy of the Chicago School. *History of Political Economy*, **25** (3), 413–33.

Knight, F. H. (1964). *Risk, Uncertainty and Profit*. New York: Augustus M. Kelley.

Langlois, R. N. & Cosgel, M. M. (1993). Frank Knight on risk, uncertainty and the firm: A new interpretation. *Economic Inquiry*, **31**, 456–65. (Sophisticated interpretation of Knight's theory of uncertainty).

Raines, J. P. (1989). Frank H. Knight's contributions to social economics. *Review of Social Economy*, **47**, 280–92. (Brief review of Knight's non-laissez-faire side).

DAVID VOGEL

L

labor union an organization of employees whose primary purpose is to improve its members' economic conditions at. WORK through COLLECTIVE BARGAINING with an employer or an industry association of employers.

Brief History

Cyclical instabilities of the early market system intermittently ravaged industrial communities with unemployment and depressed wages (*see* ETHICS OF COMPETITION; EMPLOYMENT AT WILL). In response, desperate workers sought some form of job protection through unions. Continuing competitive pressure on both a "living wage" and "fair standards of work" encouraged employees to form unions and to demand specified, written terms of work (*see* FAIRNESS). By the early nineteenth century, they had focused on fixed rates of pay, regularized hiring and layoff standards, and maximum hours of work, applicable over a fixed period of time (*see* DISCRIMINATION IN EMPLOYMENT; FREEDOM OF CONTRACT). As they strengthened their organized power, unionists increasingly sought limits on employers' arbitrariness in hiring, firing, and managing the production process at the place of workshop, assembly line, mill, factory, or office.

Grievance procedures: Once unions and management established a stable relationship, they discovered the need and use of regular procedures to settle disputes *under* the agreement. Gradually they created joint grievance processes, where the parties peacefully determined the applicability and interpretation of agreement terms through judicial appeals arrangements. These usually involved multiple steps of appeal, ending in neutral, third-party arbitration (*see* DUE PROCESS). In the United States, the grievance process is uniquely developed, pro-

viding on-the-job service to all employees within a bargaining unit (a group of workers, duly recognized and certified by the National Labor Relations Board, exclusively represented by a chosen, designated union). Unions expend more resources in grievance handling than any other single activity, making it the daily core of union service for members.

Unions, Politics

Union leaders, particularly in Europe, have supported and often been intimately involved in political parties. Major purposes were to advance the interests of laboring people and, in the past, to promote socialist forms of ownership. Historically in many developing countries unions provided the base for political organizations, whose members sought independence from colonial powers. American unions have usually played a political role primarily as interest groups, particularly at local and state levels, to win legislative favors. In federal politics, unions have generally limited their efforts to providing support for laws and programs that provide national minima, in wages, conditions of work, old-age pensions, occupational health and safety protection, and affirmative action (*see* WORKER SAFETY).

Unions in the United States

Labor unions have long been important, publicly recognized American institutions, but many groups distrusted their means as well as their ends. Well into the twentieth century, farmers disliked them as creatures of corrupting cities where agrarian freedom and independence did not flourish; native-born Americans found all too many immigrant workers bringing foreign doctrines and un-American ideologies with them; employers saw in them threats to their PROPERTY and authority. While individuals might properly strive to raise themselves, Americans generally did not favor large organizations whose members challenged authority in ways deemed violent and also espoused a relatively egalitarian wage ethic. From early in the nineteenth century, courts defined unions as combinations, dangerous to property owners and the free, competitive market. Nevertheless courts found ways to transform business combinations, as corporations, into constitutional *persons*. The courts never raised combinations of workers in unions to such a legal eminence. Even after unions won legal recognition through legislation in the 1930s, the public and courts remained concerned that unions would subvert workers' individual rights. Both also perceived an aura of violence and intimidation around unions which convinced them that union activities had to be constrained, if not contained (*see* CONFLICT). In some industries, such as garments, longshoring, trucking, and other highly competitive trades, racketeering, corruption, and anti-democratic union governance often prevailed – and persisted. The public image of unions was thus surrounded until recent years by an ambience of disorder, lawlessness, and illicit behavior. Its persistence has made unions vulnerable to their critics and hindered organizing efforts, especially among white-collar workers in private employment.

Employers and managers typically have viewed unions with great suspicion, treating them adversarially, if not with hostility. Union participation in workplace decisions is still widely interpreted as a challenge to managers' power and autonomy (*see* FREE SPEECH IN THE WORKPLACE). Confronted since the 1960s with greatly increased competitive economic pressures from deregulation and increased global trade, to lower costs and prices, managers have feared that unions would – or at least, could – impede necessary adjustments required by the continual shifting of demand. From experience they knew that union-sponsored rules and regulations limited their flexibility in introducing new work methods and new means of production. Managers seldom had encouraged cooperation, but pursued policies that provided workers ever-rising economic benefits but left essentially intact authoritarian and confrontational control of the workforce. The policies

often perpetuated an oppressive workplace environment and sometimes an alienated workforce. Both conditions kept American industry from matching the PRODUCTIVITY gains and product quality that foreign industries provided through the 1970s and 1980s.

Managers' typical adversarial approach to unions helped create and maintain antagonistic collective bargaining in the three decades after World War II. Union–management cooperation was minimal and mutual trust low. Strikes and other disruptions of production slowly declined over the decades after the 1950s, but more as a result of declining union membership and ebbing strength than as a development of cooperation (*see* COERCION). Despite waning union power, members typically enjoyed a substantial wage and benefit margin over non-union members. By the late 1980s both parties recognized the need to break old patterns of interaction. Increasingly managers realized that global competition demanded they persuade employees to contribute unprecedentedly to productive efficiency; it had become increasingly obvious that only cooperative workers could and would make that contribution.

More widely than ever before, American managers in the nineties are experimenting in developing cooperative relationships with their workers. Their historic insistence on controlling employees has become obsolete where factories are decentralized, and the workforce more skilled and technically trained than in the past (*see* MEANINGFUL WORK). Union–management cooperation, assurance of dignity at the place of work, and peaceful resolution of disputes provide a morally satisfying and practical means to winning those efforts (*see* PARTICIPATORY MANAGEMENT). They offer the nation morally sounder relationships at the place of work than unions and management have known in the past.

Bibliography

Commons, J. R. (1966). *History of Labor in the United States*. New York: A. M. Kelly. (The first significant history of unions up to the 1920s).

Dickman, H. (1987). *Industrial Democracy in America: Ideological Origins of National Labor Relations Policy*. LaSalle, Ill.: Open Court.

Dunlop, J. T. (1990). *The Management of Labor Unions: Decision Making With Historical Constraints.* Lexington, Mass.: Lexington Books.

Freeman, R. B. (1989). *Labor Markets in Action: Essay in Empirical Economics.* Cambridge, Mass.: Harvard University Press.

Industrial and Labor Research Association. (1993). *Employee Representation: Alternatives and Future Directions.* Madison, Wis.: Industrial Relations Research Association.

Montgomery, D. (1988). *Workers' Control in America: Studies in the History of Work, Technology, and Labor Struggles.* New York: Cambridge University Press.

Perlman, S. (1979). *Theory of the Labor Movement.* Philadelphia: Porcupine Press. First published 1928.

JAMES W. KUHN

leadership Leadership has often been contrasted with management. Indeed, Warren Bennis and Burt Nanus (1985) claimed that "organizations are over-managed and under-led." While endorsing the validity of the distinction, John Kotter (1990a) claims that effective management and inspired leadership are both necessary in an increasingly complex and volatile business environment. In this view, good management provides the degree of order and consistency necessary in large, complex organizations through planning, structuring jobs and relationships, staffing, directing and delegating, comparing behavior with plan, and problem-solving and taking corrective action. By contrast, inspired leadership is about envisioning alternative futures, enrolling and aligning people in a common direction, and "satisfying basic needs for achievement, a sense of belonging, recognition, self-esteem, a feeling of control over one's life, and the ability to live up to one's ideals" (Kotter, 1990b).

However, this view of leadership is a relatively recent one. Historically, there have been three main schools in the study of leadership: the trait, behavioral, and situational/contingency approaches. These and related perspectives have spawned thousands of definitions of leadership, most of them implying that leadership is about influencing an individual or group to do what "the leader" wants done in a superior/subordinate relation-

ship. After examining briefly the methodologies and tenets of the main schools, we will explore more recent work, and the forces calling for a new paradigm of thinking about leadership.

An early approach to the study of leadership at the beginning of the twentieth century is the "great person" theory, which attempted to identify the traits or qualities which separated leaders from non-leaders by studying "great people" in history (Bass, 1990). This approach spawned interest in examining the lives of exemplary individuals, as if the unique accomplishments of those leaders were expressions of some underlying traits or extraordinary personal "gifts," not to be found in the general public. As this research failed to identify a generalizable set of traits that could be used to identify leaders, it confirmed a belief by others that leaders were born and not made. Or, as one researcher put it: leaders have a "natural unlearned power" with an instinct for the "propitious moment" (Hillman, 1995). But however inspiring the lives of people like Lincoln, Gandhi, Churchill, and others were to study, for the average person, there seemed to be little chance to enhance one's own effectiveness as a leader by exposure to their lofty example.

A more practical approach was the notion that leadership was perhaps learnable. Behavioral theorists at the University of Michigan in the late 1940s (e.g. Rensis Likert (1961) and fellow researchers at the Institute for Social Research) attempted to identify patterns of leadership behavior associated with high- and low-performing groups in various organizations. In general, they asserted that "employee-centered" managers who emphasized the well-being of their subordinates had more productive work groups than "production-centered" managers who focused on getting work done. Much related research in the 1950s was predicated on similarly notions of sharply contrasting styles of leadership, e.g., autocratic vs. democratic, task-oriented vs. relationship-oriented, etc.

However, subsequent research by Ralph Stogdill and his associates at Ohio State University (Stogdill, 1974) suggested that a leader's style wasn't a discrete point on a continuum, but rather two independent dimensions: "initiating structure" and "consideration." Those high on the first dimension tended to be primarily concerned about influencing subordinates to set goals and produce results, while those high on the latter dimension were primarily concerned with establishing supportive relationships with people they led.

While initially the Ohio State researchers believed that a leader high on consideration would have more highly satisfied and/or more highly performing subordinates than a leader high on initiating structure, later research suggested that both were important. This led Robert Blake and Jane Mouton (1978) to suggest that "concern for people" and "concern for production" were two independent dimensions of leadership behavior and could be measured by a 9-by-9 "managerial grid." They also implied that there was one best leadership style, the so-called "9,9" team-manager style, who was high on both dimensions.

The premise of "one best style" was challenged by Fred Fiedler and his associates (Fiedler & Chemers, 1984), who argued that the effectiveness of a leader was based upon "situational contingency," that is to say, a match between the leader's style and the requirements of the situation. In their classic popular article on "How to choose a leadership pattern," Tannenbaum and Schmidt (1973) argue that the degree to which a leader invites others to participate in making decisions depends upon the leader's assumptions about his/her own and others' abilities, the skill and education of the subordinates, and other elements of the circumstances.

A variation on this theory included Paul Hersey and Ken Blanchard's (1988) "situational leadership" theory in which the authors argue that a leader needs to adjust his/her relative emphasis on "task behaviors" (e.g., providing guidance and direction) and "relationship" behaviors (e.g., providing emotional support) according to the "readiness" of the followers, viz., their willingness and ability to perform a particular task.

A significant shift away from the trait, behavioral, and situational contingency approaches to the study of leadership was pioneered by Kouzes and Posner (1987), who analyzed the patterns and themes in the "personal best" leadership experiences of some 550 managers. Rather than focusing on "style," they identify five common behavioral practices that managers are engaging in when they are

leading vs. managing: 1) challenging the process, 2) inspiring a shared vision, 3) enabling others to act, 4) modeling the way, and 5) encouraging the heart.

At the threshhold of the twenty-first century, as leadership is increasingly about responding to and creating often discontinuous change, leading inevitably requires relentlessly questioning the status quo or "business-as-usual." At the simplest level, leadership is a challenge to how people have behaved in the past. For example, a "quality revolution" may require people to spend more time in "quality improvement teams" and learn new skills in group problem-solving or statistical process control. More fundamentally, however, leadership often represents a challenge to deeply held assumptions or beliefs, e.g., that "individuals are more effective than groups." And finally, when organizational transformations are required, leadership must challenge people at the level of their worldview – and the organization at the level of its shared worldview or "paradigm," e.g., that "low cost and high quality" are not necessarily mutually exclusive.

As Einstein has said, "the world that we have made by the level of thinking we have done thus far creates problems that we can't solve at the level of thinking we were at when we created them." Thus, leadership will increasingly require leaders to challenge people to think and act in new ways, to reflect on and question their own deeply rooted assumptions, and ultimately confront the unexamined premises which have shaped the history of their enterprise.

Increasingly leadership is mostly closely associated with the notion of vision. By contrast to managerial goals, which are often an extension of what has been done in the past and/or a prediction of what is to come, vision is value based, engages people emotionally, and presumably inspires people to extraordinary accomplishment. Leaders devote a significant amount of time in conversations (Shaw & Weber, 1990) with key stakeholders in developing a shared image of a future state that their team and/or organization could and should become. (*see* STAKEHOLDER THEORY). When this is crystallized, leaders see it as their responsibility to engage the energies and enthusiasm of all stakeholders in this view of the future through speaking passionately for their vision, listening openly to what others say and for what is in the "unsaid," so as to facilitate the reshaping of the vision in ways that broadly capture the imagination and spirit of everyone.

Developing and communicating a shared vision not only provides opportunities for leaders to challenge others to think and act in new ways, but to find ways to empower individuals, groups, and organizational units to translate the vision into action. In doing so, they must confront their own managerial assumptions and practices concerning others' capacity to assume responsibility.

However, the flattening of organizations and the creation of self-managed work groups means that not only do managers need to be willing to give up control and empower others, but fundamentally rethink the nature of leadership (Ghoshal & Bartlett, 1995). Similarly, re-engineering and redesigning organizations around horizontal processes such as "order fulfillment" and so-called business transformation, have promoted the notion that leadership, rather than being rooted in hierarchical authority, is increasingly shifting to one's capacity to influence peers and others over whom one lacks formal authority. Similarly, changing demographics and diversity in the workplace, globalization of business, deregulation of markets, telecommuting, accelerating technological change, and the impact of information technology on emerging network models of organization call for paradigm shifts in how we think about leadership (*see* WOMEN IN LEADERSHIP).

The world is changing so rapidly, the stakes are so high, and issues are so complex, that one person can no longer lead an organization. Rather, leadership and the freedom to exercise initiative needs to be exercised throughout the organization to serve customers better, to dramatically increase productivity, decrease cycle times, spur innovation, and to help people find meaning in their work. And as organizations increasingly require the exercise of discretion, it can only happen when leaders work to align members on a set of guiding principles.

Several years ago a friend gave me a beautiful quotation from George Bernard Shaw's *Man and Superman* that included the following line: "This is the true joy in life, the being used for a purpose recognized by yourself as a mighty one." While it clearly speaks to man's universal search for meaning, it speaks to the opportunity that leadership provides to inspire people to go beyond ordinary limits of service and accomplishment, to enable people at all levels of the enterprise to transcend the frustrations of organizational life and achieve a sense of purpose through their work, and to align people throughout the enterprise on a set of shared values.

In their classic study of America's best-run companies, Peters and Waterman (1982) note that "the excellent companies are the way they are because they are organized to obtain extraordinary effort from ordinary human beings." (*See* TOM PETERS ON EXCELLENCE). In attempting to explain this phenomenon, the authors point to what Burns (1978) called "transforming leadership": leadership that builds on man's need for meaning, and creates an engaging and widely shared sense of institutional purpose. Under this view, leadership is an opportunity to personally exemplify and call forth the commitment and urge for transcendence that we all seek. Since we dream about but rarely find this kind of leadership, the task is ours.

Bibliography

Bass, B. M. (1990). *Bass and Stogdill's Handbook of Leadership*, 3rd edn. New York: Free Press.

Bennis, W. & Nanus, B. (1985). *Leaders: The Strategies for Taking Charge.* New York: Harper & Row.

Blake, R. R, & Mouton, J. S. (1978). *The New Managerial Grid.* Houston: Gulf.

Burns, J. M. (1978). *Leadership.* New York: Harper & Row.

Fiedler, F. E. & Chemers, M. (1984). *The Leader Match Concept,* 2nd edn. New York: John Wiley.

Ghoshal, S. & Bartlett, C. A. (1995). Changing the role of top management: Beyond structure to processes. *Harvard Business Review,* Jan./Feb., 86–96.

Hersey, P. & Blanchard, K. (1988). *Management of Organizational Behavior.* Englewood Cliffs, NJ: Prentice-Hall.

Hillman, J. (1995). *Kinds of Power: A Guide to Its Intelligent Uses.* New York: Currency/Doubleday.

Kotter, J. P. (1990a). *A Force for Change: How Leadership Differs from Management.* New York: Free Press.

Kotter, J. P. (1990b). What leaders really do. *Harvard Business Review*, May/June, 3, 103–11.

Kouzes, J. M. & Posner, B. (1987). *The Leadership Challenge: How to Get Extraordinary Things Done in Organizations*. San Francisco: Jossey-Bass.

Likert, R. (1961). *New Patterns of Management*. New York: McGraw-Hill.

Peters, T. J. & Waterman, R. H., Jr. (1982). *In Search of Excellence: Lessons from America's Best Run Companies*. New York: Harper & Row.

Shaw, G. & Weber, J. (1990). *Managerial Literacy: What Today's Managers Must Know to Succeed*. Homewood, Ill.: Dow Jones-Irwin.

Stogdill, R. (1974). *Handbook of Leadership*. New York: Free Press.

Tannenbaum, R. & Schmidt, W. (1973). How to choose a leadership pattern. *Harvard Business Review*, May/June, 3, 3–11.

JACK WEBER

legal ethics   The history of legal ethics is often traced to a retired Presbyterian Sunday School teacher, George Sharswood, who went on to become the Chief Justice of Pennsylvania and founder of the law school at the University of Pennsylvania. In the midst of the tumultuous 1850s, Sharswood observed that the moral temptations and perils were great, perhaps too much for lawyers to resist: "There is no class . . among whom moral delinquency is more marked and disgraceful" (Sharswood, 1854, p. 170). In prescribing a set of professional ethics for members of the bar, he reasoned that "[t]he responsibilities, legal and moral, of the lawyer, arise from his relations to the court, his professional brethren, and to his client" (Sharswood, 1854, p. 174). "It is the duty of counsel," Sharswood wrote, "to be the keeper of the conscience of the client; not to suffer him, through the influence of his feelings or interest to do or say anything wrong in itself, of which he would afterward repent" (Sharswood, 1854, p. 175). The ethical principles found in the writing of Sharswood, as well as the scholarship of David Hoffman (1836) and Thomas Goode Jones (1899), laid a foundation for the development of early state codes of ethics for lawyers (Alabama adopted one of the first codes in 1887), and the passage of the American Bar Association's (ABA) Canons of Professional Ethics (1908) (Papke, 1986).

For nearly a century, the pioneering work of Sharswood, Hoffman, Jones, and the Canons of Professional Ethics served as a guide and reference for the ethical challenges and controversies. By mid-twentieth century, however, there was a need for an elaborate set of ethical principles reflecting the bar's collective interest in self-regulation. Without a modern recodification of ethical principles, there was a fear that wayward lawyers would be increasingly vulnerable to external regulation and sanction (Wilkins, 1992). This need was addressed with the passage of the ABA's Model Code of Responsibility (1969/1992) ("Model Code"), the first comprehensive model codification of legal ethics. The Model Code was adopted in nearly every state with only a few changes. Following criticism by scholars, jurists, and members of the bar, the ABA issued a new codification in 1983, called the Model Rules of Professional Conduct (1983/1992) ("Model Rules"). Unfortunately, the Model Rules were not well received by all jurisdictions. Some states rejected the Model Rules and others modified them. Some retained the Model Code, and a few adopted sections of both (Hazard & Hodes, 1994). All states await the completion of the Restatement Third of the Law Governing Lawyers drafted by the American Law Institute. At present, the professional regulation of lawyers is a matter of idiosyncratic state law. Not surprisingly, commentators have called for a creation of national ethical standards for lawyers, uniform standards codified in federal law that would apply across all states.

With all of the differences in ethics laws, there are five core ethical issues that capture much of the variance in state ethics codes and reflect a common set of problems facing the business and practice of law: 1) ethics in the profession of law, 2) ethics in our adversary system, 3) conflicts of interest, 4) perjury and confidentiality, and 5) ethics in the provision of legal services (Davis & Elliston, 1986). In Table 1, the substance of these five issues are compared with the coverage of the Model Code and Model Rules.

Ethics in the Profession of Law

Legal ethics and business ethics differ in scope and specificity. Legal ethics is underwritten by a very limited set of professional requirements

Table 1

Core issues in legal ethics	Coverage of ABA Model Code (1992)	Coverage of ABA Model Rules (1992)
Ethics in the profession of law	Integrity of profession	Competence
Ethics and the adversary system	Making counsel available	Scope of representation
Conflicts of interest	Unauthorized practice of law	Diligence
Perjury and confidentiality	Confidences and secrets	Communication
Ethics in the provision of legal services	Independent judgement	Confidentiality of information
	Competence	Prohibited transactions
	Zeal within the law	Imputed disqualification
	Improving the legal system	Successive government and private employment
	Appearance of impropriety	Former justice or arbitrator
		Organizations as client
		Disabled client
		Safekeeping property
		Declining or terminating representation
		Adviser
		Intermediary
		Meritorious claims and contentions
		Expediting litigation
		Candor toward tribunal
		Fairness to opposing party counsel
		Advocate in nonadjundicative proceedings
		Truthfullness in others
		Communication with represented persons
		Dealing with unpresented persons
		Respect for rights of third person
		Responsibilities of a partner or supervisory lawyer
		Responsibilities of a subordinate lawyer
		Responsibilities regarding nonlawyer associates
		Professional independence of lawyer
		Unauthorized practice of law
		Restrictions on right to practice
		Pro bono public service
		Accepting appointments
		Membership in legal services organization
		Law reform activities affecting client interests
		Communicating concerning lawyer's services
		Advertising
		Direct contact with prospective clients
		Communication of fields of practice

and norms, such as requirements relating to competence and integrity. The legal profession is given significant responsibility for enforcement of ethical requirements and norms through a special system of adjudication that disciplines those who violate ethics rules (cf. Hazard, 1991). Business ethics, in contrast, reflects a host of diverse professional, industry, and corporate norms that are both internally and externally regulated. The distinction is made clear by the fact that there are only two formal mechanisms for the ethical regulation of attorney conduct: 1) a fitness test as an entry requirement, and 2) state code disciplinary proceedings for the sanctioning of unprofessional behavior. The former (1) requires that all candidates for admission to the bar of a particular jurisdiction be of "good moral character." Fitness boards evaluate fitness in light of community standards (Elliston, 1986).

The latter (2) appears in the authority given to the state bar associations to self-regulate, discipline, and sanction, through private reprimand, censure, probation, suspension from practice, and disbarment. Professional self-regulation, for example, often requires inquiries into attorney integrity and competence. It is no coincidence that the first canon of the Model Code mandates that: "A lawyer should assist in maintaining the integrity and competence of the legal profession" (Model Code, 1992). This canon not only makes attorney competence and integrity an individual responsibility (the breach of which is subject to disciplinary actions), but also requires the disclosure of any member of the bar who falls short of its strictures (see also Model Code, Canon 6). The Model Rules specify explicit standards relating to legal knowledge and skill; thoroughness and preparation; and the need to maintain competence over time (Model Rules, Rule 1.1). Legal ethics in both the Model Rules and Model Code are reflected in a self-regulating set of professional norms (aspirational "ethical considerations") with explicit disciplinary rules governing misconduct.

Ethics and the Adversary System

Lawyers representing different or opposing clients generally have adverse interests. They approach the law and the legal system as adversaries. The active participation of attorneys in shaping, reshaping, and framing facts and arguments in the courtroom stands in sharp contrast to the inquisitorial system of justice (Laufer, 1995). Notably, to some moral philosophers, the adversary system promotes an amoral view of life (see Wasserstrom, 1975; Bayles, 1983; and Luban, 1983). To many lawyers and legal ethicists, the adversary system is fundamental to our system of justice, reflecting certain core values and rights, such as the right to personal autonomy and equal protection of the laws (Freedman, 1992).

Central to the adversary system are lawyers in the role of the advocate. As Fuller and Randall (1958) noted some years ago: "In a very real sense it may be said that the integrity of the adjudicative process itself depends upon the participation of the advocate. This becomes apparent when we contemplate the nature of the task assumed by the arbiter who attempts to decide a dispute without the aid of partisan advocacy." Partisan advocacy is required under both the Model Rules and Model Code. The former requires that an attorney, as an advocate, "zealously asserts the clients under the rules of the adversary system" (Model Rules, 1992, Preamble). Even though lawyers must act with "zeal in advocacy," the Model Rules do not require the taking of every advantage or opportunity on the client's behalf. Professional discretion allows for limits to be placed on efforts to vindicate a client. The Model Code, however, is less forgiving. Canon 7 requires that "A lawyer should represent a client zealously within the bounds of the law." Short of pursuing frivolous litigation, this may be accomplished through any permissible means to seek any lawful objective (Model Code EC-7-1). Disciplinary rules allow for sanction of those who fail to zealously represent a client's interests (Model Code, DR 7-101 and DR 7-102).

Conflicts of Interest

Conflicts of interest are unavoidable in a profession that promotes multiple and often conflicting roles. As the preamble of the Model Rules states, "A Lawyer is a representative of clients, and officer of the legal system and a public system having special responsibilities for the quality of justice" (Model Rules, Preamble). Multiple responsibilities and multiple obligations (to client, the court, and the system of justice) can create significant conflicts. These conflicts may be confounded by situations that require the simultaneous representation of divergent interests; problems arising from successive representations; and problems that arise from personal conflicts (Hejmanowski, 1993).

The Model Rules prescribe a fundamental loyalty to the client underwritten by an independence of professional judgement (see also Canon 5, Model Code). Model Rule 1.7, for example, requires the declination of withdrawal of representation where an impermissible CONFLICT OF INTEREST arises before or during representation. Adverse interests, whether personal or professional, are not permitted. To gauge the existence or extent of a conflict in situations that are not explicitly covered by Model Rules, lawyers must consider the "duration and intimacy of the lawyer's relationship with the client or clients involved, the functions being performed by the lawyer, the likelihood that the actual conflict will arise and the likely prejudice to the client from the conflict if it does arise" (Rule 1.7, Comment, Other Conflict Situations).

Conflict of interest provisions apply to individuals and institutions alike. Some critically important conflicts occur at the institutional level between and among large, often decentralized, law firms (Epstein, 1992). Firm structure and firm practices may create additional conflicts. Problems related to specialization in law are particularly troublesome (Schneyer, 1991; Rhode, 1985).

Perjury and Confidentiality

In a now classic paper published in 1966, Professor Monroe H. Freedman (1966) raised three of the hardest questions facing the criminal defense lawyer: 1) Is it proper to cross-examine for the purpose of discrediting the reliability or credibility of an adverse witness whom you know is telling the truth? 2) Is it proper to put a witness on the stand when you know he will commit perjury? 3) Is it proper to give your client legal advice when you have reason to believe that the knowledge you give him will tempt him to commit perjury?

The controversy over confidentiality, perjury, and disclosure is made far more complex by the conflicting provisions found in the Model Code and Model Rules. The former *allows* for only certain disclosures and breaches of lawyer–client confidentiality. The latter *permits* or *requires* a far greater disclosure (Landesman, 1980). According to the Model Rules, the central task of the advocate – to zealously and persuasively present the client's case – is qualified by the primacy of the advocate's duty of candor to the court. Thus, according to the Model Rules, "A lawyer shall not knowingly: 1) make a false statement of material fact or law to a tribunal; 2) fail to disclose a material fact to a tribunal when disclosure is necessary to avoid assisting a criminal or fraudulent act by the client, 3) fail to disclose to the tribunal legal authority in the control jurisdiction known to the lawyer to be directly adverse in the position of the client and not disclosed by opposing counsel; or 4) offer evidence that the lawyer knows to be false. If a lawyer has offered material evidence and comes to know of the falsity, the lawyer shall take reasonable remedial measures."

Ethics in the Provision of Legal Services

Legal commentators have engaged in an interesting but largely academic debate on the merits and limitations of mandatory *pro bono* service, i.e., requiring lawyers to donate services for free to represent those in need of legal services who cannot afford to retain counsel. Mandatory *pro bono* service is more than a personal duty, it is a duty owed to the courts; it is a duty arising from the privilege of licensure; it is a duty of an officer of the court (Strossen, 1993; Coombs, 1993; Macey, 1992). Mandatory *pro bono* representation amounts to involuntary servitude; it is taking of property without just compensation, and it violates the equal-protection rights of those required to give service. The parallels to debates over corporate SOCIAL RESPONSIBILITY are nothing short of remarkable.

The Future of Legal Ethics

In reflecting on the core ethical issues and the future of legal ethics, Hazard (1991) observes that the historical or traditional function of the legal profession has undergone significant change in recent years. The narrative that once defined the legal profession (i.e., an attorney is an advocate who defends a client threatened with the loss of life and liberty by government oppression) is tired and dated. Courts, legislators, and administrative agencies have interposed themselves in matters that were once the exclusive province of the profession.

The result for legal ethics? Legalized regulation of ethics will increasingly replace professional self-regulation; case law and statutory law will become increasingly intrusive; and the "bar" will lose its time-honored normative status to the normative power of courts and regulatory agencies. According to Hazard, it is simply a matter that leadership goes where the action is. Law practice is increasingly specialized. It is found in large firms, law departments, government agencies, and corporations. The professional relationships of the "bench and the bar" are a thing of the past. The client is now the business organization, not the indigent; the transaction is regulatory in nature, not criminal; the outcome will have as its remedy money or property, not freedom; and justice will be all but incidental. If Hazard is right, and much evidence supports his view, business and legal ethics may soon face many of the same challenges as the regulation and narrative of law and business converge.

Bibliography

Bayles, M. (1983). Professionals, clients and others. In W. L. Robison et al. (eds). *Profits and Professions.* Clifton, NJ: Humana Press. 65–73.

Coombs, M. (1993). Your money and your life: A modest proposal for mandatory pro bono services. *Boston University Public Interest Law Journal,* 3, 215–38.

Davis, M. & Elliston, F. A. (eds). (1986). *Ethics and the Legal Profession.* Buffalo: Prometheus.

Elliston, F. A. (1986). The ethics test for lawyers. In M. Davis & F. A. Elliston (eds), *Ethics and the Legal Profession.* Buffalo: Prometheus.

Epstein, R. A. (1992). The legal regulation of lawyers' conflicts of interest. *Fordham Law Review,* 60, 579.

Freedman, M. H. (1966). Professional responsibility of the criminal defense lawyer: The three hardest questions. *Michigan Law Review,* 64, 1469.

Freedman, M. H. (1992). Professionalism in the American adversary system. *Emory Law Review,* 41, 467.

Fuller, L. L. & Randall, J. D. (1958). Professional responsibility: Report on the joint conferences. *American Bar Association Journal,* 44, 1159–1218.

Hazard, G. C., Jr. (1991). The future of legal ethics. *Yale Law Journal,* 100, 1239.

Hazard, G. C., Jr. & Hodes, W. (1994). *The Law of Lawyering: A Handbook on the Model Rules of Professional Conduct,* 2nd edn. Englewood Cliffs, NJ: Prentice-Hall.

Hejmanowski, L. E. (1993). An ethical treatment of attorney's personal conflicts of interest. *Southern California Law Review,* 66, 881.

Landesman, B. M. (1980). Confidentiality and the lawyer–client relationship. *Utah Law Review,* 54, 765–86.

Laufer, W. S. (1995). The rhetoric of innocence. *Washington Law Review,* 70, 329–421.

Luban, D. (1983). The adversary system excuse. In Luban (ed.), *The Good Lawyer: Lawyers' Roles and Lawyers' Ethics.* 83–122.

Macey, J. R. (1992). Collective discharge of duty or compelled free service? *Cornell Law Review,* 77, 1115–23.

Marks, F. R. & Cathcart, D. (1974). Discipline within the legal profession. *University of Illinois Law Forum,* 34, 193–236.

Papke, D. R. (1986). The legal profession and its ethical responsibilities: A history. In M. Davis & F. A. Elliston (eds), *Ethics and the Legal Profession.* Buffalo: Prometheus.

Rhode, D. L. (1985). Symposium on the law firm as a social institution: Ethical perspectives on legal practice. *Stanford Law Review,* 37, 589.

Schneyer, T. (1991). Professional discipline for law firms? *Cornell Law Review,* 77, 1–46.

Sharswood, G. (1854). *An Essay on Professional Ethics.* Philadelphia: T. & W. Johnson.

Strossen, N. (1993). Pro bono legal work: For the good of not only the public, but also the lawyer and the legal profession. *Michigan Law Review,* 91, 2122.

Wasserstrom, R. (1975). Lawyers as professional: Some moral issues. *Human Rights,* 5, 1.

Wilkins, D. B. (1992). Who should regulate lawyers? *Harvard Law Review,* 105, 801–87.

WILLIAM S. LAUFER

leveraged buyouts   A leveraged buyout (LBO) is a transaction which transforms a publicly traded corporation into a privately owned firm through the use of newly issued debt. A typical LBO begins when an investor or group of investors determines that a firm's assets are undervalued; that is, when market value drops below asset book value. Investors can then reap rewards by buying the firm's stock at a premium from shareholders and redeploying its assets. Funds for the buyout are often obtained through the issuance of high-risk, high-interest bonds, called "junk bonds" when they do not meet the standards of investment-grade bonds. LBOs can be big business; in 1988, $64 billion worth of LBOs were undertaken (Sherrid, 1989).

In order to realize the profit potential of LBOs, investors must either sell off assets (i.e., divisions of the firm) to reduce the debt burden taken on by the "leveraging" of the buyout, or employ them more efficiently through various cost-cutting measures. The pressure to make interest payments on large amounts of newly acquired, high-interest debt magnifies the importance of efficient operation.

Ethical Issues

Attempts to cut operating costs introduce some thorny ethical issues. Employees often lose their jobs as firms tighten their economic belts; employees who are retained often become demoralized and suffer psychological stress. When plants are consolidated, entire communities may suffer significant losses. Buyers of sold-off divisions may repudiate pension obligations, warranty claims, and/or supply contracts, thus harming retired employees, customers, and/or suppliers.

"Junk bonds" add another ethical issue. Bond rating services, noting that the firm has taken on large amounts of high-risk debt, reduce the rating on the firm's previously existing investment-grade bonds, resulting in losses for the firm's pre-LBO bondholders. For conservative investors, who bargained for high-grade (low-risk, low-interest) corporate bonds, such losses may be particularly painful.

LBOs also play a role in the economy as a whole. The increased debt load taken on by leveraged firms increases the risk of defaults and bankruptcies. In an economic downturn, the failure of highly leveraged firms could exacerbate, or even precipitate, a major recession. Further, LBOs represent a major factor in what has become a highly volatile and speculative stock market, itself a major contributor to what has been called a "casino" society.

Management-led LBOs

A significant proportion of LBOs are initiated not by investors outside the firm, but by managers of the firm itself. This phenomenon is not surprising since insiders are well positioned to determine that the firm's assets are undervalued. Managers, with the financial backing of junk bonds underwritten by investment bankers, offer to buy company stock at a premium over the market price. To some authors (Houston & Howe, 1987), the existence of this premium fulfills the ethical duties of participating managers because social wealth is increased. To others (Bruner & Paine, 1988), the premium must be *fair*, which means that it is based on a "synthetic" buyout price.

Other authors (Stein, 1985, 1987; Jones & Hunt, 1991) identify additional ethical issues raised by *management-led* LBOs. First, since the brokerage firm which attests to the virtues of the planned buyout and the fairness of the offer is hired by the firm's managers, an "unfair" judgment is highly improbable. Second, managers may manipulate the firm's earnings downward in order to reduce the cost of the buyout (Stein, 1987). While some financial manipulation is routinely done for corporate purposes, thus benefiting STOCKHOLDERS (Briloff, 1981), manipulation for the benefit of managers at the expense of stockholders is ethically unsound.

A third ethical problem arises with respect to the valuation of the firm. Unlike outside investors, managers can gauge the value of the firm after "restructuring" with considerable precision. Stein (1985) argues that managers are thus: (1) trading on inside information; and (2) violating disclosure rules, when they buy "their" firm without disclosing its true value. The conflict of interest in management-led LBOs is also readily apparent. As fiduciaries of shareholders, managers should seek the highest possible price for company shares; as bidders, they may seek the lowest possible price (*see* FIDUCIARY DUTY; FIDUCIARY RESPONSIBILITY).

The principal problem many observers have with management-led leveraged buyouts is that participating managers often reap enormous returns on relatively small investments. Large returns are often justified in terms of high risk. Since highly leveraged investments are often quite risky, high potential returns may be deserved. When managers, who know the financial capabilities of the firm with substantially more certainty than do outside investors, bid for the firm, their "deserved" return would seem to be substantially smaller.

The Ethics of Leveraged Buyouts

A short list of key considerations for judging the ethics of individual LBOs is in order. First, in any UTILITARIAN analysis, costs to non-stockholder constituents of the firm – especially bondholders, employees, customers, suppliers, and neighboring communities – must be included. Second, the FAIRNESS of enriching investors (especially managers) and shareholders at the expense of these groups must also be considered. Further, the fairness of the bid to stockholders must be judged in view of the fact that most actions which managers could undertake to enhance their wealth after an LBO could also be undertaken to enhance shareholder wealth before (or instead of) an LBO. Managerial MOTIVES are also at issue; using corporate constituents merely as means to managerial ends violates Kantian principles. A LIBERTARIAN perspective (Nozick, 1974) would call into question the potentially coercive nature of LBOs from the perspective of employees or bondholders (*see* NOZICK, ROBERT). In short, LBOs, like many complex transactions, are morally complex. Recourse to simple formulae such as "creating shareholder wealth" is rarely appropriate.

Bibliography

Briloff, A. (1981). *The Truth about Corporate Accounting*. New York: Harper & Row.

Bruner, R. F. & Paine, L. S. (1988). Management buyouts and managerial ethics. *California Management Review*, **30**, (2), 89–106.

Houston, D. A. & Howe, J. S. (1987). The ethics of going private. *Journal of Business Ethics*, **6**, (7), 519–25.

Jones, T. M. & Hunt, R. O. (1991). The ethics of leveraged management buyouts revisited. *Journal of Business Ethics*, **10**, 833–40.

Nozick, R. (1974). *Anarchy, State, and Utopia*. New York: Basic Books.

Sherrid, P. (1989). Debt on trial. *US News and World Report*, Feb. 13.

Stein, B. J. (1985). Going private is unethical. *Fortune*, Nov. 11, 169–70.

Stein, B. J. (1987). Shooting fish in a barrel. *Barron's*, Jan. 12, 6–7, 20, 22, 24.

Note: This entry is based on Jones & Hunt (1991) above.

THOMAS M. JONES

liability in accounting   Sole practitioners to large public accounting firms face potentially devastating legal liabilities. Since the mid-1980s there has been a dramatic increase in lawsuits against public accounting firms resulting in billions of dollars in legal settlements, proposed congressional legislation to change the US tort system, and the bankruptcy of Lavanthol and Horwath, the seventh largest public accounting firm. The legal basis of accountants' liability primarily lies in the US Securities Acts of 1933 and 1934 and the common-law theories of fraud, breach of contract, and negligence.

The 1933 Securities Act imposes liability for actions related to initial public offerings of securities. It imposes civil and criminal liability for false statements or omissions in registration statements or if securities are sold without an accurate prospectus. The 1934 Securities Act regulates purchases and sales of securities. It imposes civil and criminal liability for false or misleading statements filed with the Securities and Exchange Commission, or if an accountant intentionally deceives others through oral or written misstatements or omissions in connection with a sale or purchase of securities. Prior to 1994, the 1934 Act imposed liability for aiding and abetting; however, in April 1994, the US Supreme Court eliminated aider and abettor liability in the *Central Bank of Denver* v. *First Interstate Bank of Denver* case.

Common-law theories impose contract liability, criminal liability, and tort liability on the accounting profession. When accountants or public accounting firms enter into contracts with clients, they agree to act as reasonable, prudent professionals and to perform all terms of the contract. If they fail to do so, they can be sued for either breach of contract or negligence. Breach of contract suits fall under contract liability and are usually brought by the client against the accountant. Accountants are subject to criminal liability for willfully certifying false documents, altering or tampering with records, forgery, and so forth.

Fraud involves the intentional misstatement of material information. Most accountants do not purposefully misstate facts on behalf of clients. The most devastating legal liability for accountants is the tort theory of negligence. Negligence involves the failure to act as a reasonably prudent professional under the circumstances. Lawsuits for negligence may be instigated by clients or non-clients. The litigation by non-clients is based on the extent to which accountants should be held liable to third-party financial statement users. This responsibility to third parties varies by state, with three major approaches being utilitized: Credit Alliance, Restatement of Torts, and Reasonable Foreseeable User. Some states do not follow a specific, prescribed approach.

Under the Credit Alliance approach the accountant is not liable for negligence to third parties unless the accountant is aware that the third party intended to rely on the auditor's opinion and the financial statements. The third party must be specifically identified to the accountant. This is the most conservative approach and the most favorable for the accounting profession. This approach is based on the rulings in the *Credit Alliance* v. *Arthur Andersen & Co.* case and the landmark case of *Ultramares* v. *Touche*, and is followed in nine states.

Restatement of Torts subjects accountants to more liability by permitting recovery by foreseen third parties even if they are not specifically identified. The accountant must only be aware that the audited financial statements will be used by a third party. This approach is followed in nineteen states.

The Reasonable Foreseeable User approach subjects accountants to the highest degree of liability exposure. It permits recovery by all parties that are reasonably foreseeable recipients of financial statements. There is no privity requirement, and in effect the accounting profession is viewed as the public watchdog. This approach is currently only followed in three states.

The concept of joint and several liability applies in all of the above three theories. A successful plaintiff is permitted to collect an entire judgment against any defendant regardless of the degree of fault attributable to the individual defendant. Joint and several liability is the primary concern of those seeking tort reform. The six largest US firms and the American Institute for Certified Public Accountants are actively campaigning for legislative action to replace joint and several liability with a proportionate liability standard that would assess damages against each defendant based on degree of fault and would permit recovery of legal fees by a defendant from a plaintiff who brings meritless lawsuits.

In addition to liability in audit and tax roles, a recent California court ruling opened a new avenue of liability for accountants doing expert witness and other litigation support services. A $42 million judgment for litigation support negligence and fraud was awarded in the *Mattco Forge* v. *Ernst & Young* case. The case is currently under appeal, but may break the precedent of litigation protection for expert witnesses that has been followed under common law. This case also has implications for all accountants who testify in litigation as an expert witness, since it severely limits immunity protection.

The organizational structure of public accounting firms also affects the extent of the individual accountant's liability exposure. Historically accounting firms have been organized as proprietorships or partnerships, resulting in unlimited personal liability for the partners. In 1992, the AICPA changed its bylaws to permit CPAs to practice in any organizational form allowed by state law. Limited Liability Partnerships (LLPs) and Limited Liability Corporations (LLCs) are emerging as states change their restrictions. LLCs and LLPs remove much of the partners' personal liability for other employees' negligent or wrongful acts. Most large accounting firms are converting to LLP status since state laws usually permit LLPs to practice in non-LLP states, and the conversion to a LLP from a general partnership is much less complicated.

Accounting liability will remain at the forefront of the accounting profession. One goal of the profession will be to systematically work toward the elimination or alteration of the present rules on joint and several liability.

See also **compensatory justice; fairness; justice; negligence; responsibility; risk**

Bibliography

Arthur Andersen, Coopers and Lybrand, Deloitte and Touche, Ernst and Young, KPMG Peat Marwick, Price Waterhouse (1992). *The Liability Crisis in the United States: Impact on the Accounting Profession.* Position Paper.

Epstein, M. & Spalding, A. (1993). *The Accountants Guide to Legal Liability and Ethics.* New York: Richard D. Irwin.

Hanson, R. & Rockness, J. (1994). Gaining a new balance in the courts. *Journal of Accountancy* (Aug.), 40–4.

Hanson, R., Rockness, J., & Woodard, R. (1995). Litigation support liability – the Mattco decision. *The CPA Journal* (March).

Simonetti, G. & Andrews, A. (1994). A profession at risk/a system in jeopardy. *Journal of Accountancy* (April), 45–54.

JOANNE W. ROCKNESS

liberal–communitarian debate, the The liberal–communitarian debate, which took its present form in the early 1980s, can be traced back to the beginning of the modern age, when liberalism emerged as a political and philosophical movement. JOHN LOCKE in seventeenth-century England and Immanuel Kant in eighteenth-century Prussia developed theoretical views of society and human nature that stressed equality, personal autonomy, individual rights, and universalizable moral principles. Considering the now-familiar preference within liberalism for autonomous reasoning rather than unquestioning acceptance of received opinions, it is not surprising that their own views were at odds with the pre-Enlightenment political philosophies then prevailing, all of which assumed the legitimacy and necessity of traditional political authority and hierarchical social structures. Thus Locke, Kant, and other early liberals can be thought of as reacting against the communitarianism, or proto-communitarianism, of their day, which culminated in William Blackstone's outrageously complacent belief that in English law and society "All is as it should be," and echoed ARISTOTLE's ancient notion that the *polis* is the natural normative base of all human activity. However, that proto-communitarian theory grew out of theological conceptions of society (Christendom, the divine

right of kings, etc.), whereas today's communitarian views (including those most friendly to religion) begin with the relatively secular psychological insight that social affiliation is not only a profoundly urgent human need but also the ground for all thinking, valuing, and self-awareness. (*See* LIBERALISM; COMMUNITARIANISM; KANTIAN ETHICS; UNIVERSALIZABILITY.)

Contributors to today's liberal–communitarian debate generally take the publication of JOHN RAWLS's *Theory of Justice* in 1971 as the starting-point of the contemporary discussion, since in that work Rawls attempted to replace then-current utilitarian rationales for liberal democratic systems with more recognizably Kantian principles such as impartiality, universalizability, and respect for persons. (*See* UTILITARIANISM.) Using his heuristic device of an "original position" in which perfectly rational individuals deliberate and choose the most adequate (i.e., most just) institutions for distributing burdens and benefits, Rawls effectively projected his vision of the American political system onto a timeless, transcultural intellectual screen.

The most important early reactions to Rawls's book were Michael Sandel's *Liberalism and the Limits of Justice* (1981) and ALASDAIR MACINTYRE's *After Virtue* (1984), each of which argued against Rawls's model of an individual moral agent as a solitary, autonomous, utterly rational holder of desires and beliefs, and replaced this model with that of a self which is culturally embedded and socially engaged from its first moments of self-awareness to its most sophisticated achievements of selfhood or personal identity. Over the next several years other important contributors to the communitarian literature emerged, most notably Charles Taylor (1989a, 1989b) and Michael Walzer (1983, 1987). Predictably, this literature has evoked counter-replies from Rawls (1993) and other partisans of liberalism, such as Ronald Dworkin (1985) and Will Kymlicka (1989), as well as from Jürgen Habermas (1994). As the debate continues in the 1990s, some convergence seems to be taking place, or at least some softening of the rhetoric. Thus Daniel Bell (1993) and others have begun to use such phrases as "the communalization of liberalism."

The contemporary liberal–communitarian debate operates at several levels. At the level of political theory, it is a debate over the relationship between legal or governmental structures and cultural structures such as religions or ethnic groups. At the level of moral theory, it is a debate over the relationship of values and obligations, or more specifically, over whether conceptions of what is good can logically ground principles about what is right, or vice versa. Finally, at the level of what is sometimes called philosophical psychology, it is a debate over the nature of the self.

Political Theory. At the first level, liberals argue that laws and other social institutions are neutral with respect to individual persons' conceptions of the good or even conceptions of the good that are specific to a cultural group. The liberal position is that these institutions, as well as the political system as a whole, exist to enable each person to pursue the good life as long as doing so does not interfere with that of other persons. Communitarians, on the other hand, argue that political structures are inevitably shaped by conceptions of the good, even though these conceptions are culture-specific: in other words, not only is there nothing wrong with the state giving special support to particular traditions and values (e.g., stamping "In God we trust" on coins), but in some cases doing so is vital to the well-being of the state itself (e.g., preserving a sense of national identity that can hold the country together in times of crisis). Between these two positons is an intermediate one, which has emerged over the last few years in the writings of Taylor and Walzer, viz., that democratic liberalism is itself "a fighting creed" constituting a conception of the good as well as a principle of justice.

Moral Theory. At the second level, that of ethics or moral philosophy, liberals hold that morality is primarily a matter of procedural rightness, such that it would be immoral to use unfair or otherwise unacceptable procedures in order to attain substantive goods or ends, no matter how worthy these goals are in themselves. This is an essentially deontological (duty-oriented) conception of morality, in contrast to the teleological (goal-oriented) conceptions of communitarianism and, in a quite different sense, classical utilitarianism. As with most if not all deontological conceptions, the central principle of rightness is that of impartiality, or in Kantian terms, the Categorical Imperative. Moral judgments about the rightness of an action are made from a perspective that transcends the perspective of the individual agent, such that their validity can be recognized by any competent reasoner, regardless of his or her historical circumstances and regardless of how he or she would be affected by the action in question. So construed, personal morality is seen as a set of universalizable moral rules, corresponding to the Rights of Man celebrated in the political doctrines of the Enlightenment. Communitarianism, on the other hand, refuses to adopt the detached perspective of the impartial reasoner, insisting instead that all perspectives, including moral perspectives, are inherently historical and hence relative to one's socialization history. For communitarians, moral principles express the community's sense of its own history and its own conception of the good, which can be thought of as the common good or individual flourishing, or some combination thereof. Communitarians generally distance themselves from the rather simplistic cultural relativism which was popular in the 1960s, though there are obvious similarities between the two views. Unlike most relativists, many communitarians adopt a hermeneutical theory of moral knowledge, according to which it is possible for someone outside a moral tradition to "fuse horizons" (Gadamer, 1976) and thereby come to a significant, albeit partial, understanding not only of what it is like to have another moral perspective but also of how one's own moral perspective appears to outsiders. However, few liberals would count this as a genuinely middle position between universalism and moral relativism.

Philosophical Psychology. At the third level, that concerned with the moral self, the liberal–communitarian debate turns on the question of whether human personality is best thought of individualistically, which is to say in terms of autonomy and its correlates (freedom, critical thinking, self-realization) or, in contrast, collectively, which is to say in terms of historical embeddedness and its correlates (relationships, cultural identity, loyalty, sense of the common good). Each side is able to mount telling objections against the other's position in terms of abuses all too common in our own century.

For instance, liberals point to the conformism characteristic of "authoritarian personalities" whose tendencies toward fascism are now well documented (Adorno et al., 1950), and communitarians decry the rootlessness and anomie of decontextualized individuals as "the malaise of modernity" (Taylor, 1991). However, many contributors to the discussion of moral selfhood actually combine elements of both positions, understanding socialization both as a necessary condition for the possibility of any experience whatever and also as an intrinsically historical process riddled with ethnocentricity and other sorts of contingency. In this middle view, attachments to other persons and groups are seen as prior to choice (I simply find myself as a member of a family, nation, etc.), but those groups and attachments are not thereby immune to criticism. True, such criticism can be launched from without as well as from within: from without, as when one criticizes one's legal system in terms of a "higher law," or from within, as when one criticizes one's legal system in terms of other statutes and judicial decisions that are part of the system itself. But however it is launched, it *is* criticism, and for that reason these contributors believe the old liberal objection to communitarianism as mindless conformism and personal stultification fails.

Bibliography

Adorno, T. W., Frenkel-Brunswik, E., Levinson, D. J., & Sanford, R. N. (1950). *The Authoritarian Personality.* New York: Harper and Row.

Aristotle. (1985). *Nicomachean Ethics,* ed. and trans. T. Irwin. Indianapolis, Ind.: Hackett.

Bell, D. (1993). *Communitarianism and Its Critics.* Oxford: Clarendon Press. (A good non-technical introduction to the whole liberal–communitarian debate, with special sympathy for the communitarian position).

Blackstone, Sir W. (1979). *Commentaries on the Laws of England.*, 4 vols. Chicago: University of Chicago Press. (Facsimile of 1st edn of 1765–9).

Dworkin, R. (1985). *A Matter of Principle.* Cambridge, Mass.: Harvard University Press.

Gadamer, H.-G. (1976). *Philosophical Hermeneutics.* Berkeley: University of California Press.

Habermas, J. (1994). The new conservativism: Cultural criticism and the historians' debate. In A. Gutmann (Ed.), *Multiculturalism and the Politics of Recognition,* 2nd edn. Princeton: Princeton University Press.

Kant, I. (1959 [1785]). *Foundations for the Metaphysics of Morals.*, ed. and trans. L. W. Beck. Indianapolis, Ind.: Bobbs-Merrill.

Kymlicka, W. (1989). *Liberalism, Community and Culture.* Oxford: Clarendon Press.

Locke, J. (1924). *An Essay concerning the True and Original Extent and End of Civil Government.* Book Two of *Two Treatises of Government.* London: Guernsey Press. (Originally published in 1690).

MacIntyre, A. (1984). *After Virtue.* South Bend, Ind.: Notre Dame University Press.

Rawls, J. (1971). *A Theory of Justice.* Cambridge, Mass.: Harvard University Press.

Rawls, J. (1993). *Political Liberalism.* New York: Columbia University Press.

Sandel, M. (1981). *Liberalism and the Limits of Justice.* Cambridge: Cambridge University Press.

Taylor, C. (1989a) Cross purposes: The liberal–communitarian debate. In N. Rosenblum (Ed.), *Liberalism and the Moral Life.* Cambridge, Mass.: Harvard University Press.

Taylor, C. (1989b). *Sources of the Self: The Making of the Modern Identity.* Cambridge, Mass.: Harvard University Press.

Taylor, C. (1991). *The Ethics of Authenticity.* Cambridge, Mass.: Harvard University Press. (Originally published in Canada in 1991 under the title *The Malaise of Modernity.*)

Walzer, M. (1983). *Spheres of Justice.* Oxford: Blackwell.

Walzer, M. (1987). *Interpretation and Social Criticism.* Cambridge, Mass.: Harvard University Press.

THOMAS E. WREN

liberalism   can be understood in two separable but related ways. On the one hand it is a porous and fluctuating political or ideological tendency and force. As such it has promoted freedom, rights, privacy, pluralism and – at its best – a robust individuality. On the other, it is a fractious family of theories whose authors share the values just mentioned while disagreeing as to how best to construe and implement them.

In the first perspective, liberalism is a disposition of belief and thought that, from the seventeenth century forward in Western Europe and North America, challenged religious intolerance, authoritarianism, mercantilism, and *dirigisme*, and – if less insistently – entrenched social inequalities. Having achieved wide albeit contested acceptance throughout much of the Western world, liberalism is now a political and moral outlook located uneasily between Left and Right oppositional forces.

Leftist critics of liberalism object to its acceptance of the structural inequalities that disfigure contemporary liberal democracies. In their turn, traditional conservatives complain of its voluntarism and suspicion of hierarchy and authority, a criticism that communitarians and classical republicans extend to what they regard as liberalism's overly abstract but nevertheless community-dissolving individualism. By contrast, those self-styled recent "conservatives" who associate themselves with Adam Smith and free-market economics deride the statist and "tax and spend" proclivities of welfare-state liberalism (see SMITH, ADAM). In much of the rest of the world liberalism continues as a source of dissent against tendencies similar to those that animated early liberal thinking.

In the second, more resolutely theoretical perspective, liberal thinkers can be differentiated in various partly complementary, partly competing ways. A schema given prominence by John Rawls features a distinction between justice- and rights-oriented liberalisms as distinct from utilitarian or otherwise teleological formulations that give pride of place to conceptions of the human good. Rawls claims that the former type of theory, which he traces to John Locke and Immanuel Kant, best secures the liberal value of respect for individual persons. If liberalisms of this kind have difficulty accommodating ambitious conceptions of the common good – hence perhaps also active participatory democracy – they support procedural considerations such as the rule of law and constitutionalism. By contrast, utilitarian liberalisms, associated with John Stuart Mill and recent welfare economics, privilege substantive conceptions of the general welfare. If the latter jeopardize justice and individual rights, they may encourage a vigorous democratic process (see RAWLS, JOHN; LOCKE, JOHN; KANTIAN ETHICS; WELFARE ECONOMICS; MILL, JOHN STUART).

The distinctions on which this account depends, valuable in signalling tensions internal to both liberal theory and practice, invite amendment along various lines. Mill struggled to provide a well-protected place for justice and rights, an effort continued by his "rule-" and "indirect-" utilitarian successors. Numerous welfare-state liberals are strongly committed to rights such as those enshrined in the United States Constitution, including rights to privacy as regards familial, vocational, sexual, and other matters of "lifestyle." Conversely, rights- and justice-oriented liberal theorists accept the desirability of a domain of end-directed public policy and tacitly acknowledge that conceptions of ends or goods are necessary to delineating and construing justice and rights. Notions of justice and rights are given priority in the "basic structure" (Rawls) of society, but utilitarian considerations operate freely within the constraints of the latter.

An alternative account, which seeks to encompass liberal thinkers and tendencies that are difficult to classify in the terms just discussed, features a distinction between agency- and virtue-oriented liberalisms. Theories of the first of these two types foreground individuals as actors, initiators, and creators. Agency liberals do not deny that reasoning should play a role in action, but they stress that acting involves desires and intentions, imagination and will. As Hobbes famously put it, reason is a "scout" for the passions, not their master (see HOBBES, THOMAS). In tolerably favorable circumstances human beings form and satisfy a diversity of incommensurable desires and interests, thereby distinguishing themselves one from the other.

Agency liberals manifest a non-dogmatic skepticism concerning the power of reason to arrive at uncontestable truths about morals and politics. Accordingly, they fear misbegotten but often determined attempts to subject thought and action to the rule of reason. Diversity and dissonance invigorate activity and heighten the prospects for individual and collected gratification. Because interests and desires frequently conflict, restrictions on conduct are necessary. But for this purpose agency liberals look first and foremost to "adverbial" *virtus* rather than end-directed principles or rules. The primary political *virtu* is civility, and agency liberals emphasize qualities of character such as magnanimity and fastidiousness, courage and free-spiritedness.

Classically formulated by Hobbes, the elements of agency liberalism are evident in thinkers such as Benjamin Constant, Wilhelm von Humboldt, in the individuality-affirming aspects of the thinking of Mill, and in recent writers such as Isaiah Berlin and Stuart Hampshire.

For virtue liberals, human affairs can be just and humane only if they are disciplined by virtues firmly grounded in deliberative rationality. Ends that are shareable because based on reason are superior to those that divide, and some ends are categorically inadmissible. There is a realm of activity that is properly private, but its scope should be determined by public reason; the distinction between public and private circumscribes the authority of the state but not of reason and morality. Of persons who "find that acting justly is not a good," "their nature is their misfortune" (Rawls, 1971, p. 576). Political society, acting coercively as it judges necessary, is entitled to discipline and punish such unfortunates.

The classic proponents of this version of liberalism are Kant and T. H. Green. Among contemporary thinkers, John Rawls and Jürgen Habermas are the most influential representatives of this orientation. The large body of writing affirmatively influenced by these thinkers gives virtue liberalism great prominence in the current literatures of political and moral philosophy.

These important differences noted, and recognizing that liberalism as both force and idea is currently on the defensive, Jose Ortega y Gasset was correct to say that liberalism is "the noblest cry that has ever resounded in this planet" (1932, p. 84).

See also communitarianism; individualism; liberal–communitarian debate, the; utilitarianism

Bibliography

Arblaster, A. (1984). *The Rise and Decline of Western Liberalism*. Oxford: Blackwell.

Berlin, I. (1969). *Four Essays on Liberty*. Oxford: Oxford University Press.

Constant, B. (1988). *Political Writings*. Cambridge: Cambridge University Press.

Flathman, R. E. (1992). Liberalism. In L. Becker (Ed.), *Encyclopedia of Ethics*. New York: Garland Publishing. (The above entry borrows from this publication.)

Flathman, R. E. (1992). *Willful Liberalism*. Ithaca, NY: Cornell University Press.

Freeden, M. (1978). *The New Liberalism*. Oxford: Clarendon Press.

Gasset, Jose Ortega y (1932). *The Revolt of the Masses*. New York: W. W. Norton.

Green, T. H. (1986). *Lectures on the Principles of Political Obligation and Other Writings*. Cambridge: Cambridge University Press.

Hampshire, S. (1989). *Innocence and Experience*. Cambridge, Mass.: Harvard University Press.

Hayek, F. A. (1960). *The Constitution of Liberty*. Chicago: University of Chicago Press.

Hobbes, T. (1955). *Leviathan*. Oxford: Blackwell.

Humboldt, W. von (1969). *On the Sphere and Duties of Government*. Cambridge: Cambridge University Press.

Kant, I. (1948). *Groundwork of the Metaphysics of Morals*, trans. H. J. Paton, as *The Moral Law*. London: Hutchinson.

Kant, I. (1964/5). *Metaphysics of Morals*. Most of the first part trans. J. Ladd, as *The Metaphysical Elements of Justice*. Indianapolis, Ind: The Library of Liberal Arts, 1965. The second part trans. Mary Gregor, as *The Doctrine of Virtue*. New York: Harper & Row, 1964.

Locke, J. (1948). *A Letter Concerning Toleration*. Oxford: Blackwell.

Locke, J. (1960). *Two Treatises on Government*. Cambridge: Cambridge University Press.

Mill, J. S. (1951). *On Liberty, Utilitarianism, and Representative Government*. New York: E. P. Dutton.

Rawls, J. (1971). *A Theory of Justice*. Cambridge, Mass.: Harvard University Press.

Rawls, J. (1993). *Political Liberalism*. New York: Columbia University Press.

Ruggerio, G. de. (1927). *The History of European Liberalism*. London: Oxford University Press.

Smith, A. (1937). *The Wealth of Nations*. New York: Modern Library.

RICHARD E. FLATHMAN

liberation theology and business ethics Liberation theology is a religious ideology born in the climate produced by the Castro revolution in Cuba, on the one hand, and the impetus toward religious renewal stimulated by the Second Vatican Council (1962–5), on the other hand, in the Roman Catholic Church in Latin America. As part of their regional effort to implement the reforms of Vatican II, the Catholic bishops of Latin America met at Medellin, Colombia, in 1968. The documents ratified at that conference were seen as conferring the Church's blessing upon libera-tion theology, particularly, on the so-called "preferential option for the poor," which was believed to warrant an approach to economic and social development far to the left, for example, of the Kennedy–Johnson administra-tion's Alliance for Progress.

The innovative program of theological reflec-tion that has won for liberation theology countless sympathizers and imitators in Chris-tian communities worldwide, takes it cues, not from inherited Roman Catholic doctrine, but from the lived experiences of religiously committed social activists, gathered together in "base communities" (*communidades de base*), who search the Scriptures for guidance in their struggles for social justice. The premises operative in this program are anything but otherworldly, for they do entail constructive engagement with secular ideologies such as Marxism that are valued for their capacities for exposing various forms of systemic injustice. Though liberation theologians usually see their works in substantive continuity with the main-stream of Roman Catholic social teaching, they tend to promote a religious commitment to socialism that is a significant departure from the tradition's attempt at even-handed ethical criti-cism of both socialism and capitalism. A close inspection of the writings of liberation theolo-gians, however, suggests that this commitment, though rhetorically impressive, is rarely elabo-rated in coherent strategies for political and social change.

If all one had to go on were the translated works of the Latin American founders of liberation theology, one could easily conclude that liberation theology is simply irrelevant to the development of business ethics, either in North America or anywhere else that it has attracted a following. Its widely publicized hostility to capitalism logically ought to dis-qualify it from any further say in the ethical assessment of business management and routine business practice. A more discerning response, however, might entail exploring the concrete ways in which certain social movements inspired by liberation theology have actually helped to promote ethical responsibility in business.

In order to do this, one should consider the pragmatic consequences of a commitment to, or

sympathy with, liberation theology, and not just its logical structure. In addition to the perspec-tives of the Latin American theologians, there is the Black Theology that emerged from the struggles of African-Americans for civil rights, and economic and social equality. Another form of liberation theology by the same name was developed indigenously in South Africa as part of Christian resistance to apartheid. Most Christian feminists identify their own critique of sexism and sexist institutions as a form of liberation theology. Other parallels can be found in the empowerment struggles specific to some Native American peoples, as well as Mexican-Americans, and in various forms of social activism in South Korea, the Philippines, India, and throughout Sub-Saharan Africa. Each of these local variants of liberation theology can be shown to have contributed significantly to the common effort to hold business corporations accountable to the full range of ethical and social concerns.

The assumption that those who sympathize with liberation theology are not interested in reforming the ethics of business management is demonstrably false. Despite their penchant for Marxist rhetoric, or perhaps because of it, these sympathizers have been active in virtually every recent campaign to improve corporate social responsibility in North America. The work of religious organizations in the historic Nestlé boycott, for example, or in the various mobiliza-tions of support for the United Farmworkers, or in movements to end apartheid in South Africa through increased economic pressure – includ-ing, by the way, both the Sullivan Principles and various divestment strategies – each of these examples shows how liberation theology has awakened the social conscience of many Chris-tians, especially middle-class professionals work-ing within the churches, governmental agencies, as well as in the business community. The most striking outcome of all this social activism has been the formation of the Interfaith Center for Corporate Responsibility (ICCR) and related denominational organizations, which have insti-tutionalized the learning curve that is implicit in the liberationist process of conscientization.

Though critics would hardly have predicted it, the ICCR and related organizations are clearly evolving away from principled confron-tation and toward pragmatic collaboration, whenever possible. Such religiously affiliated activist organizations may once have conducted themselves merely as external stakeholders, as if lobbying and exerting various forms of social and political pressure were the most effective ways to improve corporate social responsibility. ICCR, however, assists its member organizations to position themselves as internal stakeholders, who can use their investments (through endowment and pension fund portfolios) to leverage ethical debate within the corporations, if not actually mandate changes in corporate policy. Granted, the exercise of this internal role was, at first, confrontational, as ICCR affiliates were left with little choice but to dramatize their ethical concerns at the annual stockholders' meetings. But more recently some management teams have learned how to avoid dramatic confrontation by consulting socially activist stockholders, like the ICCR affiliates, on a routine basis.

The ICCR affiliates, in turn, have been learning to appreciate both the strategic constraints that corporate managers routinely experience, and the ethical values that are operative within sound corporate cultures. It is not unusual today to find knowledgeable religious activists collaborating with managers in formulating codes of business ethics, and devising strategies for monitoring their enforcement, both internally within the individual corporation, and externally on an industry-wide basis. The tendency of these organizational developments, in both camps, suggests, among other things, that managers are not well served by polarizing – and misleading – distinctions between business ethics and corporate social responsibility.

To be sure, not all supporters of liberation theology are active in the religious wing of the corporate social responsibility movement. But the connection between the two is sufficiently well established to suggest that liberation theology has contributed to the development of contemporary business ethics, and will continue to do so in the future. In order to understand this evolution as anything more than pragmatic accommodation, one must acknowledge, as Cornel West has usefully done (1982), the diversity of perspectives that have emerged within history of Marxist social analysis and how this diversity is reflected in the range of political strategies espoused by activists inspired by liberation theology. It remains true that Marxist social analysis tends to assume the paradigmatic status of a dualistic view of the struggles between oppressed groups and their oppressors. Nevertheless, to the extent that liberation theology has actually stimulated new commitments to Christian social activism, those involved inevitably experience the intractable complexity of real social change, which may stimulate revisionist suspicions about the validity of the inherited paradigm. The experiential learning going on within the ICCR and related organizations thus may tend to confirm the necessity of organizing various forms of countervailing social and political power in order to hold business corporations publicly accountable. But it will also suggest that countervailing power need not be either hostile or wholly external to the business community as such.

The enduring significance of liberation theology for business ethics, particularly in the context of an emerging global economy, is that it marks the historic shift from otherworldly to this-worldly forms of asceticism in certain Christian communities, especially Roman Catholic, in Latin America, Sub-Saharan Africa and Asia. This shift, which Max Weber first identified as an ethical precondition for the emergence of modern capitalism in European history, is now occurring as part of a broad pattern of religious and cultural change in the so-called Third World. The recent gains in Latin America by Protestant evangelicals, Pentecostalists, and Mormons are part of this same trend. Not all of those affected by it will automatically end up in the growing ranks of the cosmopolitan middle classes, but among them those particularly influenced by liberation theology are likely to be at the forefront of indigenous movements for economic and social justice, which is hardly a priority in religious cultures still preoccupied with otherworldly concerns. It is not unrealistic to expect liberation theology eventually to have as positive an impact on movements for corporate social responsibility in developing countries as it, demonstrably, already has had in North America.

Bibliography

Cone, J. H. (1975). *God of the Oppressed*. New York: Seabury Press.

De George, R. T. (1986). Theological ethics and business ethics. In D. P. McCann (Ed.), "Religious Ethics and Business Ethics: New Directions in an Emerging Field," special issue of the *Journal of Business Ethics*, 5 (6), 421–32.

Freire, P. (1970). *Pedagogy of the Oppressed*, trans. Myra Bergman Ramos. New York: Seabury Press.

Gutierrez, G. (1973). *A Theology of Liberation*, trans. and eds Sister Caridad Inda & John Eagleson. Maryknoll, NY: Orbis Books.

Lernoux, P. (1980). *Cry the People: United States Involvement in the Rise of Fascism, Torture, Murder and the Persecution of the Catholic Church in Latin America*. Garden City, NY: Doubleday.

McCann, D. P. (1981). *Christian Realism and Liberation Theology: Practical Theologies in Creative Conflict*. Maryknoll, NY: Orbis Books.

McCann, D. P. & Strain, C. R. (1985). *Polity and Praxis: A Program for American Practical Theology*. Minneapolis, Minn.: Seabury Books/Winston Press.

Novak, M. (1987). *Will it Liberate? Questions about Liberation Theology*. New York: Paulist Press.

Rubenstein, R. L. & Roth, J. K. (eds) (1988). *The Politics of Latin American Liberation Theology: The Challenge to US Public Policy*. Foreword by US Senator Dave Durenberger. Washington, DC: The Washington Institute Press.

Ruether, R. (1975). *New Woman New Earth: Sexist Ideologies and Human Liberation*. New York: Seabury Press.

Stackhouse, M. L., McCann, D. P. & Roels, S., with William, P. (eds) (1995). *On Moral Business: Classical and Contemporary Resources for Ethics and Economic Life*. Grand Rapids, Mich.: Eerdmans Publishing.

Weber, M. (1958). *The Protestant Ethic and the Spirit of Capitalism*, trans. Talcott Parsons. New York: Harper & Row.

West, C. (1982). *Prophesy Deliverance! An Afro-American Revolutionary Christianity*. Philadelphia: Westminster Press.

DENNIS P. McCANN

libertarianism

Pedigree and Essentials

Libertarianism emerged from the classical liberal tradition, as a purified or more consistent version of its pedigree. The focus is on the political priority of individual (negative) liberty. Libertarianism views the basic rights of every (adult) individual to life, liberty, and property as the central normative claim underlying the political, legal, economic, and social system most suitable for human community life.

Although there are several strains of libertarianism, the differences concern mainly the philosophical argument from which the conclusion emerges that each individual possesses the basic rights to life, liberty, and property. Some of these strains use somewhat different terms, some eschewing talk of rights, some stressing the utility of efficiency or practical value, or, again, the progressive prospects to be obtained from regarding individual liberty as the highest public good.

Still, the conclusions of these different lines of argumentation issue in the affirmation of the political value of a system of laws that focus on establishing and protecting the sovereignty of the individual citizen in all spheres of his or her life – religious, artistic, economic, scientific, and so forth.

Libertarianism stresses, perhaps somewhat misleadingly, the fundamentality of the right to private property. Here, too, different strains of arguments for this kind of polity will advance somewhat different grounds for why this right is to be recognized and legally protected. Two major views appear to have emerged as prominent: a more or less descriptive or positivist line of argument, and one that involves normative or prescriptive considerations.

Positivist (Economic) Libertarianism

The positivist line of argumentation focuses on the common human objective of prosperity or wealth, something preeminently likely in a society wherein private property rights are respected and protected. Prosperity, along these lines, is determined subjectively – that is, by reference to how citizens perceive themselves to be satisfied, enriched, fulfilled, successful, etc.

As in the tradition of most non-cognitivist approaches to values, this (neo-Hobbesian, *homo economicus*) version of libertarianism regards only a value-free approach to understanding society as intellectually defensible (*see* HOBBES). Value judgments are non-cognitive, except in the limited sense that one can identify, by reference to what people do (i.e., their revealed preferences) what is good for them. From within this framework, negative individual liberty – identified as the absence of physical intrusion by others upon the person and property of any individual – would most effectively secure mutual, widespread progress toward what is taken to be the common objective of everyone, namely satisfaction of preferences.

Normative (Moral) Libertarianism

The normative libertarian takes value judgments to be objectively determinable, albeit most often agent relative (i.e., depending upon many individual, social, and other aspects of the individuals involved). Among the few universalizable objective values is the central condition – to be secured by everyone within a community – of individual self-determination, personal sovereignty, or autonomy. This value, as others, is established by reference to what and who the individual is, namely, essentially self-directed, in possession of the unique capacity of free will.

Because the morally successful individual must, first and foremost, take the initiative to do the right thing, to act ethically, the condition of liberty (spelled out by the set of basic individual rights) is an indispensable precondition for everyone's moral development. Private property, in turn, is viewed here as the concrete implementation of the condition of moral autonomy and political sovereignty – it is supposed to constitute the precondition for a life guided by one's own moral choices, for better or worse. Private property pertains to one's life and what one acquires or obtains in it without force or fraud. This is taken to enable one to make free determination of the course one's life will take while others are no less enabled, so far as human choices make a difference for this purpose.

Individualism

Individualism – also referred to as psychological or ethical egoism – is often taken to be a crucial component of libertarianism, although strictly it would play a role at the foundations underlying this political outlook (see INDIVIDUALISM; EGOISM). Some version of individualism, but not necessarily the type referred to (mostly by critics) as atomistic, is closely linked to libertarianism.

The crucial individualist element is personal determination of or responsibility for one's conduct, so that the individual person is taken to be decisively (though not exclusively) involved in initiating judgment and shaping conduct. Sociability is compatible with the position, even as an essential component, provided it is not coercively imposed. Because of the nature of human beings as basically self-directed, the social or COMMUNITARIAN dimension of life is introduced by libertarianism as requiring freedom of choice (e.g., in the selection of social ties among adult human beings).

Justice, Equality, etc., via Libertarianism

Whether one approaches the libertarian framework from a positive or normative framework, the concrete socio-economic result would be a constitutional system that stresses the supreme significance of individual liberty. Such notions as "justice," "equality," "order," "welfare," etc., have a significant role in the development of the libertarian's basic legal framework or constitution, albeit never superseding the right to individual liberty.

Thus libertarian justice consists in a system's focus upon the standards of due process that disallow any policy involving involuntary servitude, regardless of how worthy the objective might be (e.g., fighting crime, defending the county, fostering the arts, sciences, health care, education, recreation, etc.). It is not that such objectives necessarily lack widespread acceptance or even objective value. Yet, the precondition of having to reach them without the violation of individual rights (for example, by means of taxation, universal conscription, transfer, or redistribution of wealth) is the central prerequisite of justice. Equality, too, is understood by reference to the mutual condition of liberty that every citizen must enjoy – that is, everyone is equal in respect of having the right to life, liberty, and property, regardless of whether equality prevails in natural assets, good fortune, health, well-being, sexual appeal, etc. Thus libertarianism tolerates various types of social injustice, such as personal betrayal, economic exploitation, and racial discrimination, so long as no force and fraud are involved. Furthermore, while it is egalitarian at the political and legal levels of community life, there is no insistence upon the political priority of equality in economic, educational, athletic, or similar opportunities, let alone equality of conditions or results, level playing fields, etc. The main reason is, briefly, that to establish such equality is a pipe dream – clearly those attempting to establish the equality in question would always fail to be equal to others in the central respect of being authorized to violate individual rights.

Libertarianism is concerned with political – not social or economic or racial or ethnic – justice and equality. While the latter are not, by at least some libertarian lights, incapable of being identified and sought out, they must be pursued without recourse to the violation of individual rights to life, liberty, and property. Order, progress, cultural diversity, ethnic, racial, and gender harmony are similarly regarded as possibly valid but never primary values for a good political community.

Comparative (Non-utopian or Idealistic) Assessment

There is no room here to consider the innumerable theoretical objections, let alone aversions, expressed against libertarianism. Put simply, libertarians take most of them to stem from utopian or idealistic thinking.

Indeed, at the level of comparative political thinking the libertarian may be distinguished by a lack of utopianism. (This is especially true of the normative libertarian, who does not see human nature as conducive to perfectibility or any institutional guarantee against immoral conduct – imprudence, dishonesty, stinginess, greed, sloth.)

Accordingly, when it comes to assessing the merits of libertarianism, it is argued that it should be done comparatively: which polity is most likely or highly probable to do justice to the most rational assessment of human good. Utopian or idealistic thinking judges political theories by impossible standards and, thus, encourages misguided public policy and legal measures. Because individuals are fallible and cannot be engineered to be morally good, the utopian aspirations of many competing political, social, and economic frameworks need to be set aside. When this is done, so the libertarian holds, the polity of individual liberty comes off as superior to all live options and contenders.

When it comes to the libertarian approach to business ethics, what stands out is the principled insistence on the public policy of *laissez-faire*, not embarking on any type of prior restraint (analogously with the public policy of respecting and protecting the right to freedom of the press or religion). Yet this does not tell the whole story because libertarians are people who do not confine their interest to politics alone. As far as libertarianism is concerned, business ethics – albeit not strictly speaking concerned with politics and public policy but with answering the specialized question "How ought a person embarking on commerce, as an amateur or professional, to conduct themselves?" – draws on ethical not political theory. Whatever sound ethical theory human beings ought to live by will have implications for the various roles human beings take on in their lives, including the role they have as commercial or business agents. Libertarianism is not directly concerned with what ethical theory is sound, although in the defense of libertarianism it is usually stressed that commercial and business activities are morally at least unobjectionable if not outright morally proper (as per the exercise of the virtue of prudence in a social context).

Bibliography

Friedman, M. (1962). *Capitalism and Freedom.* Chicago: University of Chicago Pres.

Hayek, F. A. (Ed.), . (1954). *Capitalism and the Historians.* Chicago: University of Chicago Press.

Hospers, J. (1971). *Libertarianism.* Los Angeles: Nash.

Machan, T. R. (Ed.), . (1988). *Commerce and Morality.* Lanham, Md.: Rowman & Littlefield.

Machan, T. R. (1995). *Private Rights and Public Illusions.* New Brunswick, NJ: Transaction Books.

McGee, Robert W. (Ed.), . (1992). *Business Ethics and Common Sense.* Westport, Conn.: Quorum Books.

Narveson, J. (1991). *The Libertarian Idea.* Philadelphia: Temple University Press.

Nozick, R. (1974). *Anarchy, State, and Utopia.* New York: Basic Books.

Rand, A. (1967). *Capitalism: The Unknown Ideal.* New York: New American Library.

Rasmussen, D. & Machan, T. R. (eds),. (1996). *Liberty for the 21st Century.* Lanham, Md.: Rowman & Littlefield.

Rothbard, M. N. (1973). *Power and Market.* New York: Macmillan.

von Mises, L. (1951). *Human Action*. New Haven: Yale University Press.

TIBOR R. MACHAN

liberty is commonly regarded as one of the fundamental values or principles of modern western society. Ideally, it characterizes individuals within both political and economic systems (*see* ECONOMIC LIBERTY,). Though there is widespread agreement that liberty is highly desirable, there is much less agreement as to what it is.

The word "liberty" has a Latin origin and captures the same ideas as "freedom," which has a Germanic derivation. Liberty is usually taken, most simply, to be the situation of individuals who are not constrained by others (or the state) in their choice of goals or course of action. This liberty of nonconstraint, or negative liberty, is one of two standard views of liberty. The term "negative liberty" is not pejorative. It simply refers to the lack of constraint.

However, a complete view of negative liberty requires definition of both the nature and extent of such constraint. First, does constraint refer simply to physical impositions placed upon a person by the intentional actions of others? There have been various objections to this external and intentional interpretation of constraint. Some have argued that the constraint which limits one's freedom may be unintentionally imposed. If a night custodian locks a door, unintentionally leaving a manager inside the building, the custodian has reduced the manager's liberty. Similarly, a person's freedom, it is argued, may also be reduced by psychological pressures and threats, as when a supervisor demands that a subordinate act in certain ways subject to possible dismissal. Finally, others have maintained that even the internal, psychological states of individuals, for example great fears or anxieties created in a working situation, may also limit their liberty.

Thus, interpretations of negative freedom as simply the lack of intentional, physical constraint are of disputable adequacy. Suppose, however, that the preceding disputes can be resolved. Another crucial issue remains. Since people must live together and by their actions may constrain each other, what is the extent of the lack of constraints required for freedom? At what point may a person's actions be restricted so as to secure freedom for others (or themselves)?

There are several prominent responses. Some claim that a person's actions may be limited when they HARM another person, though "harm" has itself received various interpretations: (i) violating a person's important human interests; (ii) violating individual rights (to religion, opinion, expression, property); and (iii) impairing practices and systems in the public interest. Others maintain that grave offense to other persons (e.g. pornography), or even the immorality of one's actions (e.g. prostitution) are grounds for limiting a person's behavior so as to secure freedom. Each of these responses has its own advantages and disadvantages. However, the appeal to harm has been thought by many to be the least controversial response.

Accordingly, negative freedom exists when people are relieved of a broad range of constraints and those that are imposed on them derive from one of the liberty-limiting principles just noted. Since people may choose under such conditions to act in a variety of ways, such freedom is sometimes linked with equality of opportunity (see Friedman & Friedman, 1980; Berlin, 1969). In any case, the enjoyment of negative liberty requires a social and legal system in which some actions are restrained. Absolute freedom, in the sense of a total lack of constraints, would destroy itself.

It should be noted that liberty, as so far described, characterizes a passive condition of an individual. Certain constraints do not exist; various opportunities or alternatives are present. It is an individualistic view, not necessarily connected with democracy or self-government. An enlightened despot, for example, might allow a greater extent of negative freedom than a democratically run fundamentalist society.

Some have argued that negative freedom is an incomplete or inadequate account of liberty. They contend that liberty is not simply a lack of certain forms of constraint ("freedom from"), but that it is the self-determination (or self-realization) by individuals of their affairs ("freedom to"). Liberty, on this view, is a positive and active condition of a person. This is the second standard view of liberty, commonly referred to as "positive freedom." It is closely related to the notion of AUTONOMY. Berlin claims that this form of freedom answers the question, who or what controls one's actions? For Berlin this is a different question from the one negative freedom asks, namely, what is the extent of the area within which one is/is not constrained? Others, however, claim that liberty requires both negative and positive aspects. Those who defend positive freedom admit that one's self-determination is fostered by the lack of constraints, but they place their emphasis on the self-determination, not the lack of constraints.

This positive view of liberty also requires additional clarification and qualification. It would appear that even those individuals, who set their course based on irrational emotions or desires and inadequate knowledge, have engaged in a form of self-determination. Nevertheless, many defenders of positive freedom are reluctant to characterize such acts as free. Accordingly, they specify that only certain kinds of self-determination, e.g. those embodying particular forms or degrees of rationality, are instances of freedom.

However, some have argued that this opens the door for others (including the state) to determine when people's self-determinations fulfill these additional conditions for freedom and to impose those conditions on them. In short, they undertake to force people to be free. There is, however, no necessity to this. It is one thing to claim that people do not fulfill certain conditions of positive freedom. It is another to force them to fulfill those conditions and, hence, to be free.

Finally, defenders of positive freedom must also specify the relation of an individual's own self-determinations to those of other members of one's society. Frequently this has been done by means of theories of participation in a democratic order in which each individual is to have a say in those issues which significantly affect him or her. The manner in which this is possible within large, urban societies is a crucial issue for positive freedom.

Traditionally, both views of liberty have been applied to political states and their relations to their citizens. Within such views, negative liberty requires exemption from various forms of interference or constraint. Positive liberty requires some form of participation in the determination of the affairs of state. Within economic organizations, both forms of liberty have traditionally been realized more fully by entrepreneurs, owners, and (perhaps) upper management. In recent years, however, there has been an attempt to extend both forms of liberty more broadly to employees (see Ewing, 1977). Demands for negative liberty have taken the form of demands for employee rights such as freedom of expression and privacy. Positive liberty has been linked with due process and various forms of participation within the firm.

Positive and negative freedom carry different implications for the relation between freedom and economic (and political) resources. If one adheres to negative freedom, the absence (or presence) of resources which enable one to engage in various activities may be desirable, but does not detract from, or add to, one's freedom. Various resources may make one's freedom more valuable, but do not alter the extent of one's freedom. However, resources play a necessary role in positive freedom. One cannot be self-determining, for example, if one does not have the wherewithal to do so.

When freedom is linked with economic resources, questions of the relation of freedom and equality arise. Freedom is sometimes said to be opposed to equality. This view assumes that equality requires that limits or constraints be placed on some to promote the resources of others (hence, greater equality). Defenders of this view tend to assume that liberty is defined by the lack of restraints and that equality requires the elimination of differences (see Friedman & Friedman, 1980). Neither assumption must be made. Defenders of equality may allow for various justified differences. Proponents of liberty may opt for positive liberty as a form of self-determination which recognizes the interdependence of individuals in a society. When liberty and equality are so viewed, liberty may itself require that resources be apportioned equally rather than enjoyed disproportionately by various parts of society. In these circumstances, freedom and equality need not be opposed (see Norman, 1987).

Liberty is frequently connected to rights. For example, individuals are often said to have a right to liberty. This is a global claim regarding liberty. It implies that a person's (positive or negative) liberty is entitled to certain protections. On the other hand, and more specifically, liberty is also often said to consist of a number of rights, whose protection is often supposedly guaranteed by constitutions. The nature of these rights, whether positive or negative, reveals the nature of liberty being defended.

In modern times, a common distinction has been drawn between political and civil liberties. Political liberties consist of rights that individuals have to participate in the political realm: for example, the rights to vote and to run for office. Civil liberties, then, consist of rights one might have outside a political realm, such as rights to religion, to free speech, and not to be tortured.

The liberties guaranteed by the constitutions of nations and states extend to the citizens and individuals within the authority of those political entities. Such guarantees do not necessarily hold between private individuals, or employers and employees. Thus, though a government may be prohibited by its constitution from interfering with a citizen's freedom of speech, privacy, and due process, these protections do not thereby extend to the workplace. The attempt to extend the protection of individual liberties to the workplace is a movement which has gained considerable momentum in recent decades (see Ewing, 1977).

Finally, though liberty is often viewed as an unambiguous good, this is too simple. The constraints or limits of a social, political, or economic system may also serve to give individuals a sense of security and identity. Lack of such limits, it has been argued, creates people who may feel isolated and anxious (see Fromm, 1965). In this situation, they may be willing to surrender their freedom to others. Accordingly, liberty is one value, albeit a very important one, amongst others such as justice, equality, community, fraternity, and security. A healthy society and workplace will accord liberty a significant place. However, they must also weigh it against other important values.

Bibliography

Berlin, I. (1969). Two concepts of liberty. In I. Berlin (ed.), *Four Essays on Liberty*. Oxford: Oxford University Press. 118–172.

Ewing, D. W. (1977). *Freedom Inside the Organization*. New York: McGraw-Hill.

Friedman, F. & Friedman, R. (1980). *Free to Choose*. New York: Avon Books.

Fromm, E. (1965). *Escape from Freedom*. New York: Avon Books.

Gray, T. (1991). *Freedom*. Atlantic Highlands, NJ: Humanities Press International, Inc.

Hayek, F. (1960). *The Constitution of Liberty*. Chicago: University of Chicago Press.

Mill, J. S. (1956). *On Liberty*. Indianapolis, Ind.: Bobbs-Merrill.

Norman, R. (1987). *Free and Equal*. Oxford: Oxford University Press.

GEORGE G. BRENKERT

lobbyists   persons whose primary function is to influence the outcome of the public-policy process. The origin of the term derives from the room outside of a legislative chamber in which the "lobbyists" waited for an opportunity to speak to the legislators.

Historically, to some citizens, the label "lobbyist" has carried a negative connotation. Public opinion has typically been suspicious about the combination of politics and money. Some lobbyists have been assumed to supply money – in the form of bribes, gifts, or campaign funds – to politicians who serve the interest group's favored agenda.

Political theorists and constitutional scholars emphasize the free-speech aspects of lobbying activity. In a democratic society, political activity is a legitimate function of individuals and groups, including business organizations. Active participation by all segments of society contributes to a strong system of checks and balances. Most importantly, lobbyists exercise their basic right to free speech.

Efforts to control lobbying activities have been proposed for at least a hundred years. The free-speech arguments have prevailed in moderating zealous reform attempts. The US Foreign Agents Registration Act of 1938 and the Federal Registration of Lobbyists Act of 1946 have been the notable reforms. These acts basically require lobbyists to register themselves as such with Congress and to report significant lobbying expenditures. During the 1993/4 period, Congress debated The Lobbying Disclosure Act. A final bill had not yet been agreed upon in late 1994. The primary emphasis of this legislation was to limit severely the amount of gifts and campaign donations that could be given to legislators and to close loopholes in the rules requiring disclosure of a lobbying activity (Congressional Quarterly Almanac, 1993, pp. 50–2).

The scope of lobbying activity increased greatly during the post-World War II period. The number of lobbyists registered with Congress in 1961 was 365 and had risen to 23,011 in mid-1987 (Smith, 1988, p. 29). This was an adaptation to new media and technology. The ability to communicate at grassroots levels and to conduct mass marketing campaigns altered the possible influence channels for interest groups. Information about supporters of members of Congress became available through information technology. This allowed lobbyists an opportunity to use indirect influence to affect the positions of legislators. These channels supplemented the traditional direct lobbying efforts of face-to-face contact. Even these direct efforts became more complicated as the size of Congressional staffs grew rapidly during the same time period.

A sensitive issue for lobbyists is the so-called "REVOLVING DOOR" of public service. Former government officials often land positions in which access to those who succeeded them in office is a valuable commodity. Restrictions exist that limit former officials from doing business in their area of public responsibility for a period of one year. These restrictions are often difficult to define; access created for colleagues can frequently substitute for direct contact.

The term "lobbyist" once referred only to those who sought to influence Congress. It now is applied to broader public-policy activities, including the activities of the executive branch in influencing Congress, foreign governments influencing one another, and state and local governments influencing the federal government. It also applies to actions taken to influence regulatory agencies.

Bibliography

Congressional Quarterly. (1994). Stiff limits on gifts to members will ride on final lobby bill. Sept. 24, 2656–7.
Congressional Quarterly Almanac. (1993). Senate passes lobbying disclosure bill. 50–2.
Mack, C. S. (1989). Lobbying and Government Relations. New York: Quorum Books.
Smith, H. (1988). The Power Game. New York: Ballantine Books.

ALAN R. BECKENSTEIN

Locke, John (1632–1704), probably the most influential seventeenth-century British philosopher, made important contributions in nearly every area of philosophy. But he is best known for his defenses of empiricist epistemology (in *An Essay Concerning Human Understanding*), religious toleration (in *A Letter Concerning Toleration*), and (what we now call) classical political LIBERALISM (in *Two Treatises of Government*). As the foremost philosophical spokesman for Whig political principles, Locke helped shape the Glorious Revolution of 1688 and the later revolutions in America and France. His theory of property profoundly influenced both socialist and laissez-faire economic theorists and continues to inspire much contemporary libertarian thought (*see* LIBERTARIANISM).

Though an empiricist in epistemology, Locke argued for rationalist principles in his moral, political, and religious theories. Locke's moral philosophy has the shape of a relatively traditional, Thomistic NATURAL LAW theory; but his addition of a strong theory of natural rights moves him in a distinctly individualist direction (*see* INDIVIDUALISM). Locke's political philosophy is dominated by this defense of individual rights to LIBERTY and PROPERTY and by his consequent case (against Hobbes and Filmer) for limited government (*see* HOBBES, THOMAS). Private property rights, Locke argues, can be acquired prior to the existence of political society by laboring on unowned land or natural resources. Individuals may not legitimately be deprived of their property or have limited their innocent liberties without their own CONSENT. The authority of a legitimate society thus rests on a social contract among that society's members. And legitimate governments, Locke maintains, hold their powers in trust from the societies they rule, with the consequence that governments may be removed (by force if need be) whenever the people judge this to be necessary (*see* SOCIAL CONTRACT THEORY).

See also **property, rights to**

Bibliography

Ashcraft, R. (1987). *Locke's Two Treatises of Government*. London: Unwin Hyman.

Ayers, M. R. (1991). *Locke*. London: Routledge.

Dunn, J. (1969). *The Political Thought of John Locke*. Cambridge: Cambridge University Press.

Simmons, A. J. (1992). *The Lockean Theory of Rights*. Princeton: Princeton University Press.

Tully, J. (1980). *A Discourse on Property*. Cambridge: Cambridge University Press.

A. JOHN SIMMONS

loyalty   A willingness to sacrifice. Loyalty does not refer to exceptional performance while the boss is looking, it does not refer to action that is intended to lead to gain for the subject. Rather, a loyal individual is willing to act for the benefit of someone or something else. Therefore loyalty carries with it the notion of sacrifice, of willingness to risk personal loss. The varieties of loyalty change with 1) how willing the subject is to sacrifice, 2) how much is to be sacrificed, and 3) the beneficiary of the sacrifice.

For an employee, workplace relations may involve loyalty to fellow employees, to individual managers, to the enterprise (business, corporation, institution). For management, obvious questions that arise involve loyalty to employees, to senior management, to stockholders (if any), and to customers. For customers there may be a pattern of brand loyalty.

For and Against Workplace Loyalty

When is loyalty admirable, and when is it foolish? Suppose an employee has an opportunity to move to another enterprise at a higher salary: loyalty to the enterprise suggests sacrificing and remaining with the first employer. Suppose that a manager can replace a long-time employee by someone who will do the same job at a lower salary: loyalty to the employee suggests keeping the long-time employee even at a financial cost. It appears to be irrational to make such sacrifices, to take such losses.

Are the above sacrifices ever "justified," or are they merely sentimental stupidity? The argument against loyalty in such cases may hold that individuals should have more than one loyalty; they should also be loyal to themselves and their families. Such personal interests are morally legitimate, and being "rational" and avoiding personal loss is an appropriate move. This holds for both managers and employees. Each individual not only has a right to be "selfish," but according to Adam Smith's assumption "an invisible hand" will produce the best result for the community when individuals are free to act for personal benefit. Loyalty, on this account, is economically inefficient for the community. In addition, to have only one loyalty may be a sign of single-minded fanaticism (*see* INVISIBLE HAND, THE).

The argument in favor of loyalty is put in various ways. To sacrifice is to create a special and unique value. Examples are easily found: parental sacrifice for children's welfare, loyal soldiers sacrificing their health or life for country, lovers or friends sacrificing for each other, people sacrificing for a cause. There are cases in which the individual understands that something is not a fair market exchange, that more may be given up than ever returned. Why, then, do it; why sacrifice? Because one wants to, because one wants or needs the "value" thus created. Because to have no such values is to be an empty though rational computer. Humans sacrifice; computers don't.

There are two risks of error in choosing loyalties. Error I: Being loyal when the beneficiary is not worth it. Error II: Not being loyal when the beneficiary is worth it. How can we know in advance if a beneficiary will turn out to be a desirable value? While the risk of error cannot be eliminated, our culture gives us guides. Life without loyalties is eyed suspiciously. We are made to feel that we must have friends, and that we must have some degree of loyalty to our associates, country, institutions, neighborhood, etc. We understand the shame involved in the taunt that King Henry IV (of France) gave to Crillon, one of his captains: "Hang yourself, brave Crillon! We fought at Arques, and you were not there!"

Alienation and Traitors

As Oldenquist put it, one "would normally be expected to have community loyalty if [one] has lived in a community for a long time, it has at least roughly identifiable boundaries and a name, and if [one] works there and knows its people and byways" (Oldenquist, 1982, p. 187). He takes the term "alienation" to describe a case in which loyalty is to be expected but does not exist. There are situations in which one ought to be alienated, for example, from a company producing a lethal product.

Beyond mere alienation, we have a stronger term for one who is expected to be loyal and yet betrays the trust: traitor. Suppose someone carries business plans, strategies, training, patents to a competitor. Even if such moves are legal, to betray an expected and acknowledged loyalty is to be a traitor. Of course, the military world, the political world, and the business world have each had their histories of traitors. To the other side, the term may be "hero," not traitor. A whistleblower may be a hero to one party and a traitor to the other (see WHISTLEBLOWING).

Industrial espionage, like other forms of spying, ordinarily involves lying to people and betraying those cultivated as loyal friends. While spies may be honored secretly by their employers, the public understands that such people cannot be trusted (see RIGHT TO INFORMATION; TRUST; TRUTHTELLING).

Loyalty versus Impartial Morality

As a recent author put it (Fletcher, 1993, p. 172), "Impartial morality and loyalty remain independently binding; neither reduces to the other." When the objects (beneficiaries) of our loyalty have committed crimes, we are torn in two directions. The tradition of universal morality presses us to apply the rules impartially; personal loyalties ask us to make exceptions for those we love. We ought to be sensitive to both demands. Which gets our loyalty tells the world something of our character. Perhaps neither side should always win. A *locus classicus* was the response that Aristotle made to a question about his friendship with Plato: "though both are dear, it would be wrong to put friendship before the truth." On the other side we find Albert Camus answering a question about his loyalty to principle when his family was involved in the Algerian rebellion: "I care about the truth, but I will not abandon my mother!"

That we can name-drop on each side does not answer the problem: there may be no answer that covers all situations.

Loyalty Oaths

There exists, occasionally, the practice of requiring a signed statement binding the future behavior of an employee. A business or government agency may use this means (a contract) to try to limit or deny their employees the ability to sell their skills or knowledge to competitors or to the public for personal gain. There is a rough analogy here to the pattern of "giving parole" in prisoner-of-war camps. To do so is to give your word that you will not escape during a certain specified period. The US Armed Forces tells our soldiers not to give parole, except under certain very limited conditions: but that if they do give their word not to escape . . then they must stick to their word. Even during war we tell soldiers, "Don't lie to the enemy," and there are good reasons for that position. In parallel, either we should refuse to sign a statement promising loyalty to a particular business or other institution, or we should stick to our agreement. Of course, duress can provide an exception.

Varieties of Loyalty

There are four different sorts of loyalty. These vary with the willingness and size of the sacrifice and with the objectives of that sacrifice.

Type 1. Absolute loyalty for any goal of the beneficiary.
Type 2. Absolute loyalty for some goals of the beneficiary.
Type 3. Some loyalty for some goals of the beneficiary.
Type 4. Some loyalty for any goal of the beneficiary.

In loyalties of Types 1 and 2, the subject is willing to make any sacrifice required to help reach any or certain goals of the beneficiary. Such willingness to do anything for the goal is ordinarily called fanaticism. In Types 3 and 4, the loyal subject is not fanatic, is willing to make some but not any sacrifice for the beneficiary.

Hachiko and absolute loyalty. The objection to the absolute loyalties, at least so far as this author is concerned, comes from the lack of dignity in having only one loyalty. To be *completely* devoted to a beneficiary is to be close to the example of Hachiko. As Japanese schoolchildren learn, a dog named Hachiko accompanied his master to the Shibuya railroad station in Tokyo every workday and came back to the station to meet him in the early evening. In 1925, his master died while at work, and Hachiko waited at the station for him to return for the next ten years. This "loyalty" became well known (concerned people fed him), and after his death a statue of Hachiko was set up and remains at the place of his vigil.

A human who behaved like Hachiko would be considered either retarded or mentally ill. Healthy people are not dedicated to one beneficiary alone. The honor that we give to loyalty depends on having more than one beneficiary, and then choosing between them unselfishly.

Where does this leave the matter? While loyalties of Types 1 and 2 come too close to inhuman mechanical responses, we have Types 3 and 4 that allow limited loyalty. Limited loyalty is all that a decent individual or business can or should ask of someone.

Conclusions

Ideally, loyalty (like friendship) is symmetrical. Actually, it may not be. Can we expect that employer and employee will each have the same degree of loyalty to the other? Will each sacrifice for the other? Is that desirable? In his *seminal book* Josiah Royce (1916) put it this way:

> critics have only to turn to the recent history of corporate misdeeds and of the unwise mismanagement of corporations in this country, in order to be reminded . . that what we want, at present, from some of the managers of great corporate interests is more loyalty, and less of the individualism of those who seek power . . precisely the same sort of loyalty is what we want both from the leaders and from the followers of organized labor. There is here one law for all.

Royce, and fairness, call for loyalty – willingness to sacrifice – from both management and labor.

Bibliography

Business Ethics Quarterly and the *Journal of Business Ethics*, frequently have articles on aspects of business loyalties.

Criminal Justice Ethics. (winter/spring 1993). This issue has papers on the relations between loyalty and tolerance, identity, and universal morality.

Ethics. (July 1991). This issue has a symposium on impartiality versus loyalty.

Fletcher, G. P. (1993). *Loyalty, An Essay on the Morality of Relationships.* New York: Oxford University Press.

Nathanson, S. (1993). *Patriotism, Morality, and Peace.* Lanham, Md.: Rowman and Littlefield. (A strong argument for "moderate" loyalty.)

Oldenquist, A. (1982). Loyalties. *The Journal of Philosophy,* **79** (4), 173–93.

Pfeiffer, R. Owing loyalty to one's employer. *Journal of Business Ethics,* 11, 535–43.

Royce, J. (1916 [1908]). *The Philosophy of Loyalty.* New York: Macmillan.

SIDNEY AXINN

M

MacIntyre, Alasdair (1926–): introduced VIRTUE ETHICS into modern ethical theory. MacIntyre contends that business has its own internal standards for achieving its ends, but that these standards are morally deficient and incoherent. Problems arise because MacIntyre understands corporate modernity as requiring strict adherence to ROLES AND ROLE MORALITY. Corporate existence requires separating business from other spheres of life and maintaining moral distance between social roles. Managers do not make moral decisions as we customarily understand them. They seek the good for their role, focusing on efficient achievement of their predetermined ends (for example, profit and production of goods and services), rather than focusing on the good for humanity (*see* PROFIT, PROFITS). The structure of corporate modernity thus precludes moral judgments.

In contrast to the ethics of corporate modernity, MacIntyre defends virtue ethics, especially as discussed by ARISTOTLE and found in various traditional, pre-capitalist societies. Pre-modern societies unify social roles under a shared, comprehensive notion of the good, and so allow for moral judgments. It is not clear, however, that any kind of business could fit the virtue model developed in MacIntyre (1984). He distinguishes between the internal and external goods of practices. The virtues help us to achieve the internal goods of a practice (e.g., effective teaching in academia); external goods, such as wealth, inhibit the development of those virtues. Business necessarily involves a focus on the external good of wealth, and so precludes the virtues, except for their simulacra.

Bibliography

MacIntyre, A. (1977). Corporate modernity and moral judgment: Are they mutually exclusive? In K. E. Goodpaster & K. Sayre (eds), *Ethics and Problems of the 21st Century.* Notre Dame, Ind.: Notre Dame Press, 122–35.

MacIntyre, A. (1977). Why are the problems of business ethics insoluble? *Business Values and Social Justice: Compatibility or Contradiction? Proceedings of the First National Conference on Business Ethics.* Waltham, Mass.: Center for Business Ethics, Bentley College. 99–107.

MacIntyre, A. (1984). *After Virtue,* 2nd edn. Notre Dame, Ind.: Notre Dame Press.

GEORGE D. RANDELS, JR.

Madisonian leadership James Madison defined and managed events at every phase of the enterprise that became the United States of America. In the Continental Congress, he directed key projects like funding for the War of Independence. After the war, he mobilized state representatives to meet and begin planning a federal government. At the Philadelphia Convention of 1787, he introduced a plan of his own that formed the basis for the eventual Constitution. He then led the campaign for ratification, explaining the framers' intent in a classic series of *Federalist Papers.* In the US Congress, he went on to design specific organizations and procedures called for in the constitutional blueprint. Once the machinery of government was in place, he built the first national political party, the Democratic-Republican movement, to check imperious officials and preserve the spirit of the Constitution. As Jefferson's Secretary of State and his successor as President, he conducted a controversial but principled foreign policy that finally made the United States a respected member of the family of nations.

James Madison was not only a practical politician and administrator, he was also a scholar. Contemporaries described Madison as learned all his life. Later generations recognized him as a social theory builder in a class with Adam Smith, Karl Marx, and other pioneers of the social sciences. Today, political scientists and moral philosophers claim him as a father of modern liberalism. Some of Madison's best ideas have relevance beyond the political arena – to business ethics.

In *Federalist* No. 10, Madison writes that all societies are divided into different interest groups or factions: rich and poor, debtors and creditors, inhabitants of various regions, disciples of one religion or another, followers of this leader or that, and parties to all sorts of commercial dealings. These factions tend to pursue their own welfare at others' expense, resulting in conflict. Unless managed in some way, conflicts get settled by force: policies are made by those with the most power at the time. This leads, ultimately, to injustice and instability. How, then, to manage factional conflict and minimize its potential for harm?

According to Madison, there are two ways of curing the mischiefs of faction: one, by removing its causes; the other, by controlling its effects. There are, in turn, two ways of removing the causes of faction: the first, by suppressing the freedom of persons to advance their own interests; the second, by persuading persons to share the same interests. Madison questions both methods of avoiding the causes of faction. The first, denying personal freedom, he considers unwise. It stifles initiative, destroys social life, and is even worse for individuals than the condition it is meant to remedy. The second, inducing common interests, Madison considers impractical. He argues that, if nothing else, the varying abilities and fortunes of individuals will divide them into haves and have-nots, whose interests diverge in matters of social policy. He adds that "different leaders ambitiously contending for preeminence and power" will be more apt to inflame and exploit such societal divisions than to reconcile them.

Madison, therefore, sought ways to control the effects of faction, instead of its causes. He proposed dividing social power and purpose – to let factions check and balance one another – thus limiting the capacity of the strong to take advantage of the weak. Government was to play a big role in this checking and balancing act; but Madison did not suppose that the limited government created by the US Constitution would do the trick of adequately protecting minority rights (even as amended with a Bill of Rights). Minority interests would still need protection from majorities in private associations, which in turn need checks and balances of their own to control the effects of faction.

Madison's views run counter to traditional theories of organization and leadership, which prescribe *common* purposes to eliminate the *causes* of faction. Madison's approach can be contrasted, for instance, with theories of transforming leadership as represented by James MacGregor Burns (*Leadership*, 1978). Burns differentiates "lower" needs, such as physical survival and economic security, from "higher" needs, such as moral purpose and "participation in a collective life larger than one's personal existence." The lower needs are addressed by *transactional* leaders, who may at best defuse conflict by meeting the separate demands of their different constituents. The higher, more "authentic" needs are engaged by *transforming* leaders who can refocus attention – with much greater effect – on common goals that have transcendent value. The greater the goal, the greater the energizing force: "the leader who commands compelling causes has an extraordinary potential influence over followers. Followers armed by moral inspiration, mobilized and purposeful, become zealots and leaders in their own right" (Burns, 1978, p. 34).

Madison could have accepted most of this; he was certainly not ignorant of the transforming potential of leadership. But he thought beyond it, to the problems that zealots – armed by moral inspiration, mobilized and purposeful – might create for persons who disagreed with them. Madison concentrated on a fact about human motivation that proves troublesome for transformational leadership theories: not everyone is attracted to the same goals or leaders. Madison realized that, because individuals and their circumstances differ, minority ideas about the value of particular goals and interests are likely to exist within large social groups – even where leaders are able to transform many individual views into a majority vision. "However erroneous or ridiculous these grounds of dissension and faction may appear to the enlightened Statesman or the benevolent philosopher," Madison says, "the bulk of mankind who are neither Statesmen nor Philosophers, will continue to view them in a different light. It remains then to be enquired whether a majority having any common interest, or feeling any common passion, will find sufficient motives to restrain them from oppressing the minority."

Here is the crux of things. If not all social participants have the same goals, if transforming leaders are not able to persuade *everyone* to voluntarily accept a common vision, what is the likely status of people who prefer their own goals and visions? Non-conformists have been targeted for criticism by leadership theorists since Plato (see his *Republic*), and many have been subjected to *real* injury by historical leaders with single-minded majorities on their side. What, asks Madison, will stop majorities from taking advantage of anyone who opposes them? Madison considers possible restraints, such as concern for the public good, fear of negative public opinion, and personal moral standards. He rejects each as ineffective: The public good is no use, since majorities (and their leaders) define it for themselves. Similarly, public opinion supports their actions, by definition. And personal morality falls victim to groupthink.

Madison concludes that, if differences in individual interests exist within social systems, and if a majority united by a common interest cannot be restrained from harming minorities, then the only way to prevent harm is to keep majorities from uniting around common interests – the *reverse* of what transforming leaders are supposed to do. In other words, unless leaders are able to transform everyone and create absolute unanimity of interests (a very special case), transforming leadership produces simply a majority will that represents the interests of the strongest faction. Sometimes this will is on the side of good – as in Gandhi's case. Sometimes it is on the side of evil – as in Hitler's. In any case, might is an arbitrary guide to right, as Madison clearly understood.

This, then, is why the Madisonian system of organization divides power and purpose, and why it restrains leadership in the pursuit of "collective" goals. In proposing social structures that would impact people's daily lives, Madison recognized a responsibility to build in checks and balances as protections against abuses of power. While not denying the value of voluntary ethical codes, or the possibility of virtuous leaders (like George Washington), Madison refused to rely on them. He felt that flesh-and-blood persons who might suffer from misconduct by public officials deserved better than parchment barriers and hypothetical defenses. Persons vulnerable to corporate officials, Madison would have thought, deserve better too.

Bibliography

Burns, J. M. (1978). *Leadership.* New York: Harper & Row.

Keeley, M. (1995). The trouble with transformational leadership: Toward a federalist ethic for organizations. *Business Ethics Quarterly,* 5, 67–96.

Ketcham, R. (1990). *James Madison: A Biography.* Charlottesville, Va.: University of Virginia Press.

Miller, W. L. (1992). *The Business of May Next: James Madison and the Founding.* Charlottesville, Va.: University of Virginia.

Rossiter, C. (Ed.), (1962). *The Federalist Papers.* New York: Mentor.

MICHAEL KEELEY

managerial business ideology *see* CLASSICAL AND MANAGERIAL BUSINESS IDEOLOGIES

managerial ethics and the ethical role of the manager   The ethical dimension of management is determined by the social role that managers are understood as playing. Three possibilities are especially worthy of consideration. They are that managers are agents acting on behalf of a principal or client, that managers are trustees for various corporate constituencies, and that managers are partners with governmental officials in an integrated system of political authority.

If managers are agents acting on behalf of a principal/client, the moral dimension of management is the same as in any agency relationship (*see* AGENCY THEORY). In such a relationship, the agent consents to act on behalf of and under the direction of the principal, who in turn consents to have the agent's actions count as the principal's for moral or legal purposes. The duties of an agent are performance (to do what he or she has undertaken to do), obedience (to accept the reasonable directions of the principal, which may involve performing the undertaken task in what seems to be a mistaken way), and loyalty (not to act contrary to the interests of the principal).

The moral strength of these duties is influenced by the intrinsic moral importance of the task the agent has undertaken to perform, but is not exhausted by it. The duties of an agent can have considerable moral force even when the task undertaken has no intrinsic moral importance if the interests of the principal would be seriously damaged by failure to perform the task, or to perform it well. Of special significance here is the case where the principal is not knowledgeable enough to determine whether the agent is performing well or to instruct the agent on how to proceed. The problem of the control of an expert agent by a relatively inexpert principal is sometimes called an "agency problem."

The model of agency is applicable to the provision of many professional services, and it is characteristic of paradigmatic professions such as the law that the agent is much more knowledgeable than the principal/client. Thus the moral problems that arise when an agent has expertise that the principal lacks are central to PROFESSIONAL ETHICS. In addition to prohibitions against exploiting the vulnerability of the principal/client, professional ethics may call for the abridgment of the duty of obedience. If employing the means suggested by an inexpert client would, in the judgment of the agent, be extremely foolish, the agent may have no duty to comply.

Managers of corporations are often thought to be agents of the shareholders, but this claim is not supported by the law. The law of corporations does not regard the directors (or the other managers) as having the same duties to the shareholders that agents have to principals. For example, one of the duties of agents is obedience to the reasonable directions of the principal or principals, but although shareholders sometimes make corporate decisions directly by voting

their shares, corporate constitutions usually provide no way that the shareholders as a group can routinely give instructions to managers. And while legal relations do not necessarily determine moral relations, the lack of an institutional mechanism that would enable shareholders to give instructions to managers also argues against the view that managers function morally as the agents of the shareholders. The difficulties encountered in regarding the managers of corporations as agents of the shareholders leads to the second way of characterizing the moral dimension of management. This approach can be introduced by noticing that the idea that the primary moral task of managers is to serve the shareholders can be accommodated without regarding managers as agents of the shareholders. They can be regarded instead as trustees. A trustee has a FIDUCIARY DUTY to advance the interests of the beneficiary of the trust, but has no duty to obey the beneficiary. Even if legally managers are not trustees for the shareholders, the model of trusteeship may provide a more accurate representation of the moral relation between managers and shareholders than the model of agency.

The primary importance of the model of trusteeship, however, is that it provides an alternative way of accommodating the fact that the interests of the shareholders are not the only interests that managers must take into account. The model of agency accommodates this fact by saying that an agent may not do on behalf of a principal anything that would violate the rights of other people. A similar point can be made in connection with the model of trusteeship. A trustee may not advance the interests of a beneficiary in any way that would violate the rights of other people. But the model of trusteeship also seems to allow another possibility. We can say that, morally, managers have the status of trustees not only for the shareholders but also for some other groups.

This is the core of the "stakeholder" model of managerial ethics (see STAKEHOLDER THEORY). The fact that the interests of certain groups other than the shareholders – most importantly, employees, customers, suppliers, and neighbors of corporate facilities – are routinely affected by managerial decisions is registered by regarding them as having, like the shareholders, a "stake" in managerial decisions. And the idea of trusteeship is used to explain how these interests are to be reflected in managerial decision-making. Morally, managers are trustees for all routinely affected groups, with the same duty to protect or advance their interests (without violating the rights of people who fall outside them) that they have to protect or advance the interests of the shareholders.

This way of representing the moral significance of the interests of non-shareholders for managerial decision-making is not free of difficulty, however. There is no transaction that establishes a relation of trusteeship between non-shareholder groups and managers. Apparently, then, the possession by managers of this role must be derived from some general moral principle according to which each moral agent is a trustee for all others – or all others whose interests he or she routinely affects. But this drains from the role of trustee any distinctive content capable of distinguishing it from other relations in which individuals might stand to each other, and reveals the stakeholder view as a variant of the moral theory of UTILITARIANISM, according to which each is required to maximize the total aggregate satisfaction of all affected interests.

Whether or not the stakeholder view is best regarded as a variant of utilitarianism, it shares an important defect with utilitarianism. It provides no way of regarding some, but not all, interests routinely affected by managerial decisions as creating legitimate moral claims. If we wish to characterize routinely affected interests in a way that reflects such distinctions, the conceptual apparatus of rights or fairness with which we started is preferable. Some interests are such that frustrating them violates stringent rights or constitutes serious unfairness, while others, equally strongly felt by those whose interests they are, lack this feature. So a right-based way of representing the moral claims of non-shareholders, whether routinely affected or not, actually yields a subtler view than the stakeholder theory. The members of routinely affected groups sometimes have rights that constrain what managers may do to promote narrower organizational goals.

There is a third way of understanding the social role of managers. Managers can be regarded as serving not the shareholders, or all the stakeholders, but rather as serving the employees. On this view, the shareholders join consumers, suppliers, and neighbors as an affected group that has a right to fair treatment in the course of managerial efforts to promote narrower organizational goals. To be more precise, they become investors, understood as suppliers of a certain kind – suppliers of capital – who have a right to a fair price for what they provide, which in this case means an adequate return on investment. But they have no right that managers derive organizational goals from their interests. These goals are rather determined by the concerns, especially the moral concerns, of the employees.

The justification for this way of looking at the social role of managers arises from an important difference between employees and other groups affected by managerial decisions. Managers have AUTHORITY over employees. But where there is authority, consideration must be given to what makes it legitimate. In the governmental sphere, legitimate authority is authority that serves the interests of those over whom it is exercised. Legitimate rulers rule in the interests of the governed. That is, they have the job of facilitating mutually beneficial cooperation among the governed. If managerial authority is relevantly similar to governmental authority, then managers should be regarded not as servants of the shareholders or all the stakeholders, but as servants of the employees with the task of facilitating mutually beneficial cooperation among them.

If managers have this social role, their primary moral duty is to exercise authority in a way that enables the employees more successfully to achieve their moral aims in their work (while appropriately respecting the rights of other groups). To the extent that managers are understood as exercising the legal property rights of non-employee owners, these must be defined so that the directive power they confer on managers does not exceed legitimate authority.

This approach can be challenged by questioning whether managerial authority is relevantly similar to the authority of governments. Earlier we saw that the law of corporations does not regard managers as agents of the shareholders. But legally, employees often have the status of agents of their employers. In corporate contexts, this means that employees are agents of the corporation that employs them. Managers are supervising agents to whom the corporation's authority as principal has been delegated. Viewed in this way, managerial authority is different from the authority of governments. On standard contractarian political theories, for example, the people are not the agents of the state; rather the government is an agent or trustee of the people. Defenders of this third view of the social role of managers must, then, do more than simply point out that managerial authority has to be legitimate. They must vindicate the claim that what makes managerial authority legitimate is the same thing that makes the authority of governments legitimate. One way of doing this is explored in McMahon (1994).

In the political sphere, it is generally accepted that cooperation-facilitating authority should be democratically exercised, at least in the sense that those exercising it should be elected by those over whom it is exercised. So this third approach points to the conclusion that managers should be elected by the employees. But legitimate social purposes may be served by corporate constitutions that also give investors some role in choosing managers – as in the system of codetermination – and strong unions may provide a way of satisfying the demand for democracy without instituting the election of managers by employees.

On all of these ways of understanding the social role of managers, the moral structure of managerial decision-making is the same. There is some goal that managers are understood as responsible for promoting, and there are constraints, deriving from rights, on what managers may do to promote these goals. The three views differ only on what the goal of managers is: either to advance the interests of the shareholders, to advance the aggregate interests of all the stakeholders, or to facilitate mutually beneficial cooperation among the employees. Ordinarily, constraints deriving from rights limit absolutely what can be done to promote non-moral goals, but it may be possible to regard some managerial goals as underwritten by deeper moral considerations. In cases of this sort, the constraints on managerial action provided by rights may have to be balanced

against the moral benefits associated with the goals. Many moral problems have this structure.

A further question can be raised about the moral dimension of management. Are the moral considerations that managers face the same as those faced by ordinary citizens, or are the requirements of morality strengthened or weakened in the domain of management? Two possibilities must be distinguished here.

The first is that although the moral considerations that managers face in their capacity as managers are the same as those faced in ordinary life, the factual situation of managers combines with these considerations in such a way that actions that would be impermissible for ordinary citizens become permissible for managers. For example, the closing of a plant may devastate a whole town, and an ordinary citizen would not normally be justified in doing something that had this effect. But managers may be faced with a situation in which the failure to take this step would result in greater losses to the employees and others down the road, and thus the balance of ordinary moral considerations may justify it.

The second way that managerial morality could depart from ordinary morality is that managers could face a different set of moral considerations than ordinary citizens. Of particular interest here is the idea that in the world of business, some ways of treating people that would ordinarily be prohibited are permissible. This point must be distinguished from the previous one. The claim is not that moral considerations applicable to all sometimes justify managers in performing actions that ordinary citizens would not be justified in performing, but rather that certain moral considerations applicable to ordinary life are inapplicable to the business world.

This claim is dubious, however. Managerial ethics depends on the social role of management, and it is hard to think of any legitimate social purposes that would be served by regarding the world of business as one in which some ordinary moral considerations do not apply. The closest we can come is to make the converse point. There is a class of moral considerations that identify social states of affairs the promotion or maintenance of which is important from the moral point of view. These morally important social values include the preservation of the environment, the advancement of knowledge, the development of culture, the fostering of community, the promotion of social prosperity, and the protection of public health. Considerations of this kind have little significance outside organizational contexts since nothing much can be done to affect them. Thus they are not a part of the morality of ordinary life. But like governmental officials, the managers of large non-governmental organizations must take these values into account, and the moral desirability of promoting them may sometimes outweigh – and thus justify departing from – more familiar moral considerations. To say this, however, is to say that managers must be sensitive to more, rather than fewer, moral considerations than ordinary people.

Bibliography

Dahl, R. (1985). *A Preface to Economic Democracy*. Berkeley: University of California Press.

Frascona, J. (1964). *Agency*. Englewood Cliffs, NJ: Prentice-Hall.

Goldman, A. (1980). *The Moral Foundations of Professional Ethics*. Totowa, NJ: Rowman and Littlefield.

Mason, E. (Ed.), . (1959). *The Corporation in Modern Society*. Cambridge, Mass.: Harvard University Press.

McMahon, C. (1994). *Authority and Democracy: A General Theory of Government and Management*. Princeton: Princeton University Press.

Nagel, T. (1978). Ruthlessness in public life. In S. Hampshire (Ed.), *Public and Private Morality*. Cambridge: Cambridge University Press, 75-91.

CHRISTOPHER McMAHON

managerial values Unobservable, enduring beliefs of ideally acceptable or preferable modes of conduct or end-goals held by managers.

Values are different from other psychologically based notions, such as attitudes, social norms, needs, traits, and interests (see Rokeach, 1973, pp. 18–22). They are typically integrated by the individual into a system, which may be part of a shared managerial value system. Managers then might use their value system or value orientation as a guide for determining behavior, or in developing standards, general plans, or motivators for use in their decision-making processes.

The Measurement of Values

Three generally accepted and widely used value instruments have been created. In 1931, Gordon Allport and his associates developed the *Study of Values* instrument. By presenting 45 value-laden statements for the individual to make either forced-choice or rank-order decisions, researchers using the Study of Values instrument categorized an individual's responses into value types. Six value types or orientations were presented: the theoretical man, the economic man, the aesthetic man, the social man, the political man, and the religious man (these value types are defined in Guth & Taguiri, 1965, pp. 125–6). Research using the Study of Values to assess managerial value orientations consistently found that managers exhibited a strong economic type, along with some preference for the theoretical and political orientations (see Naumes & Naumes, 1994).

A second managerial value instrument was developed, in 1967, by George England – the *Personal Values Questionnaire* (PVQ). This instrument has been widely accepted among researchers investigating the value systems of business employees. The PVQ used business-context values, such as high productivity, profit maximization, boss, and labor unions, as value statements. From an analysis of the respondents' ratings of 66 values, four modes of evaluations were possible: a pragmatic (or successful) mode, an ethical-moral mode, an effective or feeling mode, or a combination of the three modes. US managers generally clustered toward the pragmatic mode. The values of managers from four non-US countries have also been assessed and some significant differences were found. For example, Japanese managers were more pragmatic than US managers, although Australian and Indian managers demonstrated a balance between a pragmatic mode and an ethical–moral mode (England, 1975). Posner, Randolph, & Schmidt (1993) used the PVQ to assess managerial value differences across business disciplines. Although they found some differences, strong similarities generally existed among managers from all areas of a business organization.

The final major value instrument used in managerial value research was developed by Milton Rokeach (1973) – the *Rokeach Value Survey* (RVS). Rokeach presented two sets of 18 values – the first set consisted of "terminal" or end-states of existence values, and the second set were "instrumental" or modes of conduct values. Individuals were asked to rank order the set of values, indicating the importance of the value in their lives. The Rokeach Value Survey was adapted to form the Chinese Value Survey, which enabled researchers to compare American managers' values with Chinese and Hong Kong managers' values (Bond, 1988).

Typically, researchers using the Rokeach Value Survey attempted to discover differences between specific value rankings or performed a factor analysis of the responses to cluster value preferences into groups. Weber (1990) constructed a *Personal Value Orientation* typology based on Rokeach's 36 values. He presented four value orientations: Personal–Competence, Personal–Moral, Social–Competence, and Social–Moral. His conclusions were consistent with other researchers' factor analysis results: most US managers exhibited a value orientation that emphasized a concern for personal values and a quest for competency or achievement.

Linking Values to Behavior

Linking an individual's value preferences to actual behavior is a complex research challenge. The assumption that values influence behavior was found in early works on managerial values – for example, Baumhart's classic (1961) survey of manager's opinions and Guth & Taguiri's (1965) investigation of managerial strategic decision-making. In general, researchers isolated specific values and investigated the possibility of a correlation between the importance of the value with the propensity toward behavior. For example, De Vries & Walker (1986) found that higher stages of moral reasoning were related to the opposition of capital punishment; Zahra (1989) focused upon individual's valuing a concern for life; Vitell & Davis (1990) emphasized the value of corporate social responsibility; and Terpstra, Reyes, & Bokor (1991) investigated the influence of valuing competitiveness in relation to unethical behavior. More comprehensive investigations concerning the relationships between value orientations and ethical reasoning or behavior have emerged. For example, Weber (1993) empirically links his four value orientations with various stages of moral reasoning.

See also **Business ethics; Conscience; Organizational culture; Integrity; Managerial ethics and the ethical role of the manager; Moral reasoning; Self-interest; Values**

Bibliography

Baumhart, R. C. SJ (1961). How ethical are businessmen? *Harvard Business Review*, July/ Aug., 6.

Bond, M. H. (1988). Finding universal dimensions of individual variation in multicultural studies of values: The Rokeach and Chinese Value Surveys. *Journal of Personality and Social Psychology*, **55**, 1009–15.

De Vries, B. & Walker, L. J. (1986). Moral reasoning and attitudes toward capital punishment. *Developmental Psychology*, **22**, 509–13.

England, G. W. (1967). Personal value systems of American managers. *Academy of Management Journal*, **10**, 53–68.

England, G. W. (1975). *The Manager and His Values*. Cambridge, Mass.: Ballinger.

Guth, W. D. & Taguiri, R. (1965). Personal values and corporate strategy. *Harvard Business Review*, **43**, (5), 123–32.

Naumes, W. & Naumes, M. J. (1994). A comparison of values and attitudes toward risk of Greek and American entrepreneurs. *International Journal of Value Based Management*, **7**, 3–12.

Posner, B. Z., Randolph, W. A., & Schmidt, W. H. (1993). Managerial values in personnel, marketing, manufacturing, and finance: Similarities and differences. *International Journal of Value Based Management*, **6**, (2), 19–30.

Rokeach, M. (1973). *The Nature of Human Values*. New York: Free Press.

Terpstra, D. E., Reyes, M. G. C., & Bokor, D. W. (1991). Predictors of ethical decisions regarding insider trading. *Journal of Business Ethics*, **10**, 699–710.

Vitell, S. J. & Davis, D. L. (1990). The relationship between ethics and job satisfaction: An empirical investigation. *Journal of Business Ethics*, **9**, 489–94.

Weber, J. (1990). Managerial value orientations: A typology and assessment. *International Journal of Value Based Management*, **3**, (2), 37–54.

Weber, J. (1993). Exploring the relationship between personal values and moral reasoning. *Human Relations*, **46**, (4), 435–63.

Zahra, S. A. (1989). Executive values and the ethics of company politics: Some preliminary findings. *Journal of Business Ethics*, 8, 15–29.

JAMES WEBER

market for corporate control   refers to the role that capital markets play in disciplining the management of firms to take actions to improve shareholder value. Free and well-functioning capital markets provide an ongoing assessment of a firm's performance through the value that investors are willing to pay for a firm's securities. The security of most relevance in this context is equity or common stock because control of a firm usually requires that a party obtain a majority of the outstanding equity shares. Theoretically, the firm's common stock represents the fair value of the net benefits that investors foresee accruing on the stock over all future years. The returns or benefits received by shareholders arise from dividends or other cash payments and from the price appreciation of the shares (capital gains). Because investors can compare how a particular firm fares in relation to peer firms, they are able to use capital market information to identify "under-performing" and "over-performing" firms. Depending on the reason for and the extent of under-performance, a firm may find itself subject to takeover pressure. Takeover pressure is often prompted by a bidder's belief that the current market value of a target firm is less (i.e., its current stock price is low) than what it would be worth if the assets were deployed differently. For example, a bidder might believe that the target's share price would increase if it sold off some unrelated lines of business and instead concentrated on its core business. However, since this strategy may be at odds with the one pursued by the existing management, implementing these changes may require that a bidder gain control of the firm and oust management. Regardless of whether a bidder is ultimately successful in gaining control, the actions of the bidder and even the threat of takeover often are sufficient to prompt management to reassess its own performance and make changes to improve shareholder value. In this way, the market for corporate control provides an "external review" of management's actions which works to enhance the incentives to increase shareholder value.

An important related issue is why managers appear to require an external force – such as the discipline of the capital markets – to maximize shareholder value. Berle and Means (1932) first noted that the ownership and the control of assets is separated in many publicly held US corporations. This separation results because managers who have decision-making authority over the day-to-day operations of the firm typically did not have large ownership or equity stakes in the firms they manage. Jensen and Meckling (1976), following on this observation, argue that costs arise because managers and shareholders have different incentives. For example, when managers are paid a fixed salary their decisions have different consequences for them than for shareholders who are residual claimants. Thus, a manager may overspend on certain items that enhance his or her welfare (e.g., fancy carpeting for the office, a corporate jet) which reduce the available earnings that could be paid to shareholders. In general, the differing incentives can lead managers to pursue their own self-interest at the expense . of maximizing shareholder value. The principal–agent literature puts forth a number of suggestions to improve the firm's internal control process to reduce the potential for agency costs. These include: (1) giving managers a larger ownership stake in the firm, (2) tying executive compensation to stockmarket performance, and (3) increasing the oversight provided by boards of directors. For a variety of reasons, the firm's internal control process may still fail to offer sufficiently strong incentives to maximize shareholder value (Jensen, 1993). When this happens the capital markets remain a powerful, disinterested check on the management's actions – a court of last resort. Some argue, therefore, that the greatest protector of shareholder interests is a free and unfettered market for corporate control.

Bibliography

Berle, A. & Means, G. (1932). *The Modern Corporation and Private Property*. New York: Macmillan.
Jensen, M. (1993). The modern industrial revolution, exit, and the failure of internal control systems. *Journal of Finance*, July.

Jensen, M. & Meckling, W. (1976). Theory of the firm: Managerial behavior, agency costs and ownership structure. *Journal of Financial Economics*, **3**, 305–60.

SUSAN CHAPLINSKY

marketing and the consumer Marketing is defined, in part, as an open and non-coerced exchange of values between the marketer and the consumer. The consumer is the final user of the utility he or she derives from the exchange and is the focus of marketing efforts developed to create enough perceived consumer value to precipitate the exchange.

Overview

Society has set very broad limits on the freedom of choice in these exchanges in an effort to maximize consumer satisfactions and the utility created by them. During his term as US President, John F. Kennedy announced a consumer bill of rights, and one of the four rights he created focused on the consumer's opportunity to choose from among several available goods and services. Legal constraints have been developed throughout the twentieth century to prevent business combinations that would reduce the available choices.

Marketers have responded with a large and widely varied array of goods and services, offered at differing prices, available in many locations, and with a range of available consumer information. Generally, marketers have developed this mix in order to maximize the value that they receive from the exchange process. However, because consumers have options, they must also focus on the wants and needs of the consumer.

Fortunately for society, the marketing exchange is not a "zero sum game," and in most (but certainly not all) exchanges, positive value or utility is created when the exchange occurs. Specifically, both parties are usually better off after the exchange than before it occurred. This outcome can exist because the marketer and the consumer differently value that which is exchanged. Typically, the mar-keter gains economic utility, while the consumer gains a functional and/or psychological utility.

Opportunities for Ethical Problems

Perhaps the most fundamental opportunity for ethical problems to develop occurs because of consumer's inability to evaluate the market basket available to them on dimensions that they would consider important. The plethora of exchange opportunities available to the consumer creates options that cannot reasonably be evaluated in all important dimensions because (1) the consumer lacks the technical skill, or (2) the consumer is overwhelmed by the task and chooses not to evaluate opportunities beyond a very basic list of characteristics. Consumers often overcome this sometimes massive ignorance about important factors in an exchange by placing trust in the producer or retailer.

Marketers seldom have perfect information about the important characteristics of the products and services they sell. Nevertheless, their information is usually far superior to their customers' level of knowledge. For convenience in this discussion, this difference in level of information between the marketer and the consumer is called the "knowledge gap." The abuse of the knowledge gap is the basis for a variety of unethical behaviors by marketers.

To some degree, the remaining three "rights" in President Kennedy's consumer bill of rights are concerned with abuses of this knowledge gap. One of these rights is for the consumer "To be informed and protected against fraudulent, deceitful, and misleading statements, advertisements, labels, etc.; and to be educated as to how to use financial resources wisely." A second right is for the consumer "To be protected against dangerous and unsafe products." And a third right is for the consumer "To be heard by government and business regarding unsatisfactory or disappointing practices." With perfect knowledge and understanding of all important characteristics of the marketing exchange, the consumer shouldn't need any of these "rights." However, consumers are often closer to total ignorance than perfect knowledge even in the case of regularly purchased items, and when the trust is broken, the marketer has acted unethically and the consumer must be protected. Note that marketers may not understand that they have broken consumers' trust.

While abuses will undoubtedly continue to exist, many marketers seem to understand that long-term profitability can be achieved and maintained by not abusing the knowledge gap and honoring the consumers' trust. Consumers tend to look for marketers they can trust, and they can become extremely loyal to those who attempt to act in accordance with that trust. Alternatively, should consumers find out that their trust has been violated, it becomes very difficult for a marketer to win them back. The outcome of most marketing exposés supports that contention. However, opportunities to take advantage of the knowledge gap can frequently produce at least short-term profits, and vigilance is necessary. Perhaps the most important role of government and consumer advocates in preventing unethical behavior is to fill the knowledge gap with relevant information.

Most good basic marketing textbooks will have a section or chapter on marketing's ethical interface with the consumer.

Bibliography

Evans, Joel R. & Berman, B. (1994). *Marketing*, 6th edn. New York: Macmillan, esp. ch. 5.

Laczniak, G. R. & Murphy, P. E. (1993). *Ethical Marketing Decisions: The Higher Road.* Boston: Allyn and Bacon.

Pride, W. M. & Ferrell, O. C. (1989). *Marketing: Concepts and Strategies*, 6th edn. Boston: Houghton Mifflin, ch. 2.

Smith, N. C. & Quelch, J. A. (1993). *Ethics in Marketing.* Homewood, Ill.: Richard D. Irwin.

DONALD P. ROBIN

marketing, anti-competitive practices in *see* ANTI-COMPETITIVE PRACTICES IN MARKETING

marketing, ethics of *see* ETHICS OF MARKETING

Marx, Karl   (1818–83), German revolutionary critic of capitalism, was influenced in his thought by British economics, German philosophy, and French social theory. Together with Friedrich Engels, Marx formulated the theory of historical materialism, which held that a society's political and ideological structures are ultimately determined by its economic base (though there are reciprocal influences). Human productive labor is at the crux of the economic base, which has developed through different socio-economic historical stages: Asiatic, ancient, feudal, and modern capitalist. Marx argued that this revolutionary process has been driven by class conflict and the development of the material forces of production, and would eventually lead to a free, unalienated, classless society. Central to this argument was an analysis of modern capitalism as the production and exchange of commodities whose value is determined by the amount of labor required to produce them (the labor theory of value). Under capitalism, workers are a unique kind of commodity. They are able to create more value in their products than is required to produce their own labor. This "surplus value" is appropriated by the capitalist and constitutes an exploitation of the worker. Though the processes by which this occurs are viewed by many as operating according to natural, unalterable laws, in fact they are alterable social processes involving the supremacy of one class over another, as well as the control of all humans by their productive system. A rational, free society would eliminate these forms of domination. Marx anticipated that conflicts within capitalism would create worsening crises of alternately expanding and contracting production. The resolution of these crises – whether violent or peaceful – would ultimately lead to a free, communist society.

Bibliography

Elster, J. (1985). *Making Sense of Marx.* Cambridge: Cambridge University Press.

Heilbroner, R. L. (1980). *Marxism: For and Against.* New York: W. W. Norton & Co.

Singer, P. (1980). *Marx.* New York: Hill and Wang.

Sowell, T. (1985). *Marxism.* New York: William Morrow.

Tucker, R. C. (1978). *The Marx-Engels Reader*, 2nd edn. New York: W. W. Norton & Co.

GEORGE G. BRENKERT

meaningful work is work that is worthwhile, significant, satisfying, and conducive to personal growth, worth, and well-being. As a social construction, the idea of meaningful work reflects the value that a culture places on the activity of work and the value and status of various kinds of work. As a personal construction, meaningful work reflects the aspirations, ideals, and values that comprise a person's view of him or herself and a satisfying life. The British social commentator and craftsman William Morris offers this characterization of meaningful work: "Worthy work carries with it the hope of pleasure in rest and the hope of pleasure in our daily creative skill" (Morris, 1885, p. 21).

History of the Meaning of Work

People have not always thought that work should play the central role in a person's life (de Grazia, 1962). For the ancient Greeks, work itself had little value and the good life was a life of leisure. In *The Politics*, Book II, Aristotle says that work is best done by slaves, because it ties them to necessity. He says that slaves are not human because they lack the freedom to decide, deliberate, and plan the future. Greek myths depict boring repetitive work as the worst punishment – Sisyphus is doomed to push a rock up a hill and the Dianides spend eternity filling leaking water jars.

The craft guilds of the Middle Ages endowed craft work with new meanings. Guilds tied the identity of a person to his craft, hence came the proliferation of occupational last names such as Baker, Carpenter, and Goldsmith. Guilds gave craftsmen and women affiliation to a specific community, privileged technical knowledge, standards of workmanship, and ethical norms of behavior.

The Renaissance gave us the Promethean view of work that exalted human ingenuity and the image of humans as inventors and creators of their own destiny; whereas the Reformation promoted the idea that all of work was inherently meaningful in that it was a calling that demonstrated one's worthiness to God (*see* PROTESTANT WORK ETHIC).

Meaningful Work and Industrialization

The intrinsic value of work as a calling stands in sharp contrast to the instrumental view of work that came with industrialization (Clayre, 1974).

One way to understand meaningful work is by understanding alienation. For Karl Marx work is the central human activity. Marx believed that wage labor under capitalism led to alienation because it did not pay people for what they produced, but rather compensated them for the freedom that they lost at work. In the *1844 Manuscripts*, Marx argues that capitalism alienates people from themselves, each other, their product, and their creativity (*see* MARX, KARL).

The scientific approach to management focused on increased productivity. Scientific management stripped work of many elements that give it meaning. It broke down the social relationships of workers and systematized work so that it required little skill or knowledge. Managers did the thinking and workers performed the physical motions. The goal of scientific management was to replace expensive labor with cheap labor and gain absolute control over production. The sole meaning of work under scientific management was manifested in the pay that a worker received for producing the most goods in the least amount of time (*see* TAYLOR, FREDERICK W).

Models of Meaningful Work

One major assumption about meaningful work is that mental labor is more meaningful than physical labor (*see* ARENDT, HANNAH). Technology rids us of difficult physical labor and repetitive work, but it also deskills some kinds of work (Braverman, 1980). One way that management mediates the affects of deskilled labor is by redesigning jobs. Implicit in job redesign are assumptions about meaningful work, such as the need for variety, creativity, and EMPOWERMENT.

Today's ideal of meaningful work is often based on the professions. That is why more work groups call themselves professionals. The professional has autonomy, respected identity with other professionals, and pride in the notion of using specialized knowledge to help others. Norman Bowie argues that companies should focus on providing meaningful work and treating employees as professionals. He suggests that by treating employees as the primary stakeholder, companies might be more profitable than if they only focused on profits (Bowie, 1990) (*see* STAKEHOLDER THEORY).

Meaningful Work and Business Ethics

The concept of meaningful work raises these questions about the ethics of business: Do people have a right to meaningful work? Do employers have an ethical obligation to provide meaningful work to their employees?

To answer these questions, we have to ask: Is it possible for a company to create meaningful work for all employees?

A job may be meaningful to one person and a form of daily humiliation to another (Terkel, 1974). In the popular management book *In Search of Excellence* (1982), Peters and Waterman assert that the role of managers is to "make meaning." However, their approach raises questions as to whether this kind of management is a form of psychological manipulation. Meaning can be found in the aesthetic qualities of a job, its end product, or its usefulness. It can also be derived from the relationship of the worker to others in the organization.

The right to meaningful work is difficult to establish, because it cannot be clearly defined for everyone. However, we can use ethical principles like negative harm and respect for persons to argue that employees have a right to work that does not degrade them physically and mentally and respects their dignity and autonomy as a person. Similarly, an employer's obligation to supply meaningful work is difficult to support. However, one may argue that an employer has an obligation to provide conditions conducive for finding meaning in work (Ciulla, 1990). These conditions include a healthy moral environment where all employees are treated fairly and with respect and appreciation, open communication between management and employees, ongoing training and job enrichment, employee involvement in the structure and organization of their job, and a safe workplace (*see* WORKER SAFETY).

In liberal societies people also have the right to seek meaning outside of the workplace. This means that employers have an obligation to provide working hours and conditions that do not impair a person's ability to seek a meaningful life (Ciulla, 1990) (*see* WORK AND FAMILY). Despite its abstract nature, meaningful work is central to ethical management. It focuses attention on how people's experience in the workplace contributes or detracts from their non-economic ideal of the good life.

Bibliography

Bowie, N. E. (1990). Empowering people as an end for business. In G. Enderle, B. Almond, & A. Argandoña (eds), *People in Corporations: Ethical Responsibilities and Corporate Effectiveness.* Dordrecht: Kluwer Academic Publishers, 105–12.

Braverman, H. (1980). *Labor and Monopoly Capital: The Degradation of Work in the Twentieth Century.* New York: Monthly Review Press.

Ciulla, J. B. (1990). On the demand for meaningful work. In G. Enderle, B. Almond, & A. Argandoña (eds), *People in Corporations: Ethical Responsibilities and Corporate Effectiveness.* Dordrecht: Kluwer Academic Publishers, 113–18.

Clayre, A. (1974). *Work and Play: Ideas and Experience of Work and Leisure.* London: Weidenfeld and Nicolson. (Good discussion of nineteenth-century ideas of work and life).

Gini, A. R. & Sullivan, T. J. (eds) (1989). *It Comes with the Territory: An Inquiry Concerning Work and the Person.* New York: Random House. (Excellent collection of classic and contemporary readings on work).

Grazia, S. de. (1962). *Of Time, Work and Leisure.* New York: The Twentieth Century Fund. (One of the best books on this topic).

Morris, W. (1885). *Useful Work and Useless Toil.* London: Socialist League Office, Socialist Platform Number 2.

Schwartz, A. (1982). Meaningful work. *Ethics, 92,* 634–46.

Terkel, S. (1974). *Working.* New York: Pantheon Books. (Wonderful interviews on work).

Werhane, P. (1985). *Persons, Rights and Corporations.* Englewood Cliffs, NJ: Prentice-Hall, ch. 7.

JOANNE B. CIULLA

Means, Gardiner Coit (1896–1988): Before entering Harvard to major in economics, Gardiner Means had two experiences that profoundly shaped his outlook. The first was work with a relief agency in post-World War I Turkey which gave him a good understanding of a pre-factory economy. The second shaping experience came with his establishment of a blanket-manufacturing plant in Lowell, Massachusetts, where he learned how relatively easy it was to minimize market influences when setting prices. If he, a small entrepreneur, could establish administered prices, why could not large corporations do the same thing? His professors' silence on this fact convinced Means that, though he might be ignorant of economic theory, his teachers were innocent of economic reality.

Means became prominent when, with Columbia colleague A. A. BERLE, he published the 1932 landmark study, *The Modern Corporation and Private Property*, which identified the separation of ownership from control as the dominant characteristic of American business. The book caught the attention of Henry Wallace who, determined to make the Agricultural Adjustment Act a centerpiece of New Deal legislation, needed expert advice from someone who understood Big Business. Means provided an answer in *Industrial Prices and Their Relative Inflexibility*, demonstrating how large corporations followed administered-pricing policies. The thesis stirred controversy. While the highly respected mathematical theorist, Charles Roos, said that Means wrote "out of ignorance," others, notably Keynes, felt his distinction between market and administered prices was of major theoretical importance. The Keynesian, rather than the Roosian, assessment has prevailed.

Means explained how he came to his heterodox views when he received the Veblen-Commons Award in 1975:

> By 1939 I had laid down the basic postulates for the new general theory. The first is that a large part of production is carried on by a few great corporations in which final ownership is widely dispersed, ownership and control are largely separated, and management is largely a self-perpetuating body. The second postulate is that most prices are administered privately (or by agencies of government) and behave in a fashion quite different from that indicated by traditional theory. The third is the non-Keynesian and nonclassical postulate that changes in the money stock have two quite different and important direct effects on aggregate demand, a process effect as the quantity is changed and a continuing effect which arises once the quantity has been changed. This I added

to the Keynesian liquidity postulate and the classical postulate of a simple direct effect.

Although Means considered himself neither an institutionalist nor an ethicist, he raised important questions for both: Are small businesses too vulnerable before concentrated economic power? Is justice served when corporations, to meet predetermined profit goals, meet declining demand by dismissing workers? Are consumers essentially helpless before price-fixing producers? Is private power out of control? Is greater government intervention in business justified? If so, what are the moral implications for a free society?

Bibliography

Means, G. (1935). *Industrial Prices and Their Relative Inflexibility*. Senate Document No. 13, 74th Congress: First Session, Washington, Jan. 17.

Means, G. (1936). *The Structure of the American Economy*. Washington, DC: National Resources Committee. (Often considered his *magnum opus*.)

Means, G. & Berle, A. A. (1932). *The Modern Corporation and Private Property*. Chicago: Commerce Clearing House.

CLARENCE C. WALTON

media ethics   may seem to be an oxymoron, particularly to anyone who has felt misused by media. But "media," even when the discussion is confined to the United States, refers to a diffuse collection of corporations. The media include profit and not-for-profit companies and companies that take as their primary description one of three basic thrusts: news/information, persuasion in the form of public relations or advertising, and entertainment. Each kind of company has its own social function and resulting moral responsibilities.

"Media" also include two major divisions in medium – print and electronic – that impact on their capabilities and methodologies, though not necessarily on their responsibilities. Broadcasting live events, for example, raises questions of appropriateness of material for the audience as well as questions of privacy for the individuals involved in the event. Privacy and appropriateness of material are ethical issues for news coverage by print media as well, but they rarely require the split-second decision-making required in "live" broadcast coverage.

Sometimes charges of unethical behavior are based on a misunderstanding of the specific media role rather than on actual malfeasance, as when a local auto dealer condemns a newspaper for running an article that tells consumers how to be savvy car buyers. Other times, lowered expectations of a particular medium – "what can you expect from television?" – derail needed analysis of media behavior.

As different kinds of media have different social functions, understanding those functions is vital to making judgments concerning the ethics of practitioners' actions. In any profession, acting in a morally acceptable way means meeting one's moral obligations and not causing unnecessary harm in the process of doing so.

Entertainment Media

The social function of entertainment media is self-explanatory. Those media practitioners exist to produce written, audio, or visual programming and materials that will appeal to designated audiences. This social function is accompanied by an economic function that all other for-profit companies share, namely to make money for the stockholders or owners. But neither the social nor the economic function alone provides justification for action that could be predicted to cause harm to individuals or identifiable groups.

The element of harm becomes important in determining the morality of entertainment media when one considers the effect of violence on children, the effect of pornography on women, and the effect of promoting unattainable lifestyles to vulnerable audiences. Whether groups or individuals are depicted in ways that continue a history of discrimination is also a matter of ethical concern. The question of whether violence, pornography, unattainable lifestyles or stereotypical depiction cause harm is a matter of debate in the scholarly literature. Whether harm caused is "unnecessary," and thus unjustified, and in need of regulation is a matter of debate among advocacy groups, media representatives, and policy-makers.

Persuasive Media

Persuasive media, which include public relations and advertising, exist to sell their clients' ideas or images to designated publics. The editorial or opinion pages of a newspaper are also examples of persuasive media, but the intent is slightly different in that here the rationale is to create a public forum or a showcase of informed opinion on important issues of the day. The newspaper *showcases* ideas; public relations and advertising practitioners *sell* them. The persuasive message is necessarily one-sided and distorted by its lack of completeness. That is not, in itself, an ethical concern, but the line between withholding information in the name of advocacy and the withholding of information in what counts as deception is not clear.

The designated public for advertising is consumers targeted for product use. More directly than entertainment media, advertisers sell status and fantasy. One doesn't merely buy a particular brand of toothpaste or running shoe, one also buys an image, that will inspire love, acceptance, or envy. If the product is out of the price range of the targeted consumer (such as designer footwear targeted to inner-city youth), or if the consumer is unable to separate fantasy from product (such as children and advertised toys), then the advertiser may be causing unnecessary harm in marketing the product.

When the product itself has questionable merit, such as tobacco, then any marketing becomes an ethical issue. In this debate, the legality of tobacco use and of free speech in promoting legal, albeit dangerous, products, is set against the ethical precept of "do not cause unnecessary harm."

Public relations practitioners who work as "information agents" or "public information officers" for corporations or governmental agencies also target consumer audiences, but many public relations practitioners target news media as a way of achieving a larger audience and as a way of adding credibility to their message. If news media report the message developed by public relations in a way that does not expose the bias of the information, it is more likely to be accepted as accurate and complete than information that the public understands originates with a biased, self-interested source.

News Media

News media in the US have the social function of telling citizens what they need to know for self-governance. The information that we need to know for self-governance is a varied lot and includes information about our governmental processes, the bureaucrats who facilitate the process, and the leaders we elect; it includes information about our economic structure and pragmatic information about how our tax dollars are spent. It includes information about our community and our fellow citizens.

But, as with the other media, news media are restrained in meeting this social function by the moral dictate that they ought not to cause unnecessary harm. Harms caused to sources, story subjects, and consumers in the process of reporting the news include the causing of pain through undesired attention or intrusion, depriving people of freedom or pleasure by turning the spotlight of public scrutiny their way. The harms include the breaking of promises to sources who have been promised anonymity. The harms include the deception of story subjects by use of undercover reporting and the deception of consumers when information is illegitimately or incorrectly left out of a story. Whether the news organization is meeting its social function of telling people what they need to know for self-governance serves as a basis for determining when the harm caused is "necessary" and when it is not.

The Special Problem of Enforcement in Media Ethics

Media organizations and professional societies, particularly those related to news presentation, have shown increasing interest in ethics issues over the past two decades. Attention to ethical transgressions by individual organizations and professional societies is particularly important, because media constitute the only industry with US First Amendment protections. The law limitations provide after-the-fact sanctions for the publication of libelous material or material that fits the very narrow definition of legal invasion of privacy. Codes of Ethics articulated by professional societies can only be accepted by their members, not enforced. The First Amendment precludes the regulation of the press by anything other than voluntary means. Codes of ethics developed within news organizations may be enforced in the respect that an individual's unwillingness to subscribe to an organizational policy may result in discharge. But no journalist can be barred from the profession; no news

organization can be prevented from printing or broadcasting what it terms news (*see also* CODES OF ETHICS).

Blurred Distinctions Create Hybrid Moral Problems

The distinctions between the three types of media become blurred, creating new ethical concerns. Different media have different jobs to do. If one cannot identify a media product as informative, persuasive, or entertaining in primary intent, there is no basis upon which one can argue that the medium is failing to meet its moral responsibility.

The blurring between entertainment and opinion-writing becomes an issue in the publication of cartoons that have a strong political message. Some newspapers call these comics, forms of entertainment; some put politically charged cartoons on the editorial page, considering them to be persuasive products; others refuse to run such hybrids, charging that the creation of such cartoons is a misuse of the cartoonist's fame and influence.

The blurring between news and entertainment becomes a factor in trying to decide if television magazines such as *Hard Copy* and *Untold Story* are news or if they are entertainment. Producers for these segments certainly don't hold themselves to the journalistic standards of "news" programs, yet their saleability is their believability. And their interviews look and sound enough like news interviews that all but the most sophisticated viewer may be tricked into believing that the shows are "news."

The blurring between entertainment and persuasion becomes a factor when children's television programming is created as a marketing tool for merchandise. Watchdog groups have convinced Federal agencies of the special vulnerability of children to advertising and have succeeded in curtailing advertising that wraps around children's programming. But, when the product *is* the show, few limitations apply. Creators of such merchandise-propelled programming counter that there is no important difference between the selling of dolls or toys that spin-off from a popular program and creating a program to stimulate children's interest in particular dolls or toys.

Finally, the lines between news and persuasion blur when news media provide press releases or video news releases without appropriate warning to the reader or viewer. Without identification of the author or producer of the piece as an advocate, the audience is likely to accept the piece as information produced by a disinterested party.

Bibliography

Baker, L. (1993). *The Credibility Factor: Putting Ethics to Work in Public Relations.* Homewood, Ill. Irwin.

Black, J.,. & Barney, R. (1993). *Doing Ethics in Journalism.* Greencastle, Idaho: Society of Professional Journalists.

Blyskal, J. & Blyskal, M. (1985). *PR: How the Public Relations Industry Writes the News.* New York: William Morrow.

Christians, C.,. Rotzoll, K.,. & Fackler, M. (1991). *Media Ethics: Cases and Moral Reasoning.* 3rd edn. New York: Longman.

Cooper, T. (1988). *Television and Ethics: A Bibliography.* Boston: G. K. Hall.

Ellul, J. (1973). *Propaganda.* New York: Vintage.

Goodwin, G. (1994). *Groping for Ethics in Journalism.* 3rd edn. Ames, Iowa: Iowa State University Press.

Gross, L.,. Katz, J.,. & Ruby, J. (eds) (1988). *Image Ethics: The Moral Rights of Subjects in Photographs, Film, and Television.* New York: Oxford University Press.

Jaksa, J. & Pritchard, M. (1994). *Communication Ethics: Methods of Analysis.* 2nd edn. Belmont, Calif.: Wadsworth.

Johannesen, R. (1990). *Ethics in Human Communication.* 3rd edn. Prospect Heights, Ill.: Waveland Press.

Limburg, V. (1994). *Electronic Media Ethics.* Boston: Focal Press.

Montgomery, K. (1989). *Target Prime Time. Advocacy Groups and the Struggle over Entertainment Television.* New York: Oxford University Press.

Patterson, P. & Wilkins, L. (1994). *Media Ethics: Issues and Cases.* 2nd edn. Madison, Wis.: Brown and Benchmark.

Schudson, M. (1984). *Advertising: The Uneasy Persuasion.* New York: Basic Books.

DENI ELLIOTT

mentoring   "A one-to-one relationship between a more experienced person and an inexperienced person, and only until the latter reaches maturity" (Collin, 1979); "an experienced person [who] provides guidance and support in a variety of ways to the developing novice" (Bolton, 1980); who "in addition to being a role model, acts as a guide, a tutor or coach, and a confidante" (Bolton, 1980). Levinson and his colleagues (1978) offer the richest source of insights and hypotheses about the mentor relationship: "The mentor relationship is one of the most complex and developmentally important [relationships], a man can have in early adulthood. The mentor is ordinarily several years older, a person of greater experience and seniority in the world the young man is entering. No word currently in use is adequate to convey the nature of the relationship we have in mind here. Words such as 'counsellor' or 'guru' suggest the more subtle meanings, but they have other connotations that would be misleading. The term mentor is generally used in a much narrower sense, to mean teacher, advisor, or sponsor. As we use the term, it means all these things, and more."

The term mentor and the reasons for its use can be found in Greek mythology. When Odysseus went off to fight the Trojan war, he entrusted the education and development of his son, Telemachus, to his trusted house manager, Mentor. This education covered all aspects of life and human development. Mentor served as a teacher, coach, confidant, task master, counsellor, and friend.

The last ten years have witnessed increasing interest in the mentoring relationship. This has resulted, in part, from the belief that mentoring contributes significantly to one's career development. Popular and academic literature have drawn attention to the benefits that mentoring relationships can offer to protégés, mentors, and organizations (Kram, 1983). Having a mentor has been linked to career advancement (Whitely, Dougherty, & Dreher, 1991), higher pay (Roche, 1979), and greater career satisfaction (Burke, 1984). Moreover, the mentoring relationship may be critical to the advancement of women in organizations (Morrison, White, & Van Velsor, 1987). For mentors, the relationship is an opportunity to make productive use of knowledge and expertise in middle age (Dalton, Thompson, & Price, 1977) and to learn in new ways. The organization also benefits, as leaders are prepared (Zaleznik, 1977) and they may find that employees who are mentored are more satisfied and committed than those who are not (Hunt & Michael, 1983).

Mentors are helpful to their protégés in a variety of ways. These have been grouped into career development (instrumental) functions and psycho-social functions. The former would include such things as providing career advice and counselling, feedback, training and development opportunities, providing sponsorship and visibility to the protégé, and providing a protected environment in which the protégé could learn without risking his or her job. Psycho-social functions include such things as providing counsel and moral support to protégés under stress, showing confidence in the protégé, providing support and encouragement, believing in and supporting the career aspirations of the protégé, and providing friendship. Both types of mentor functions or benefits are important to protégés. But only instrumental or career-development functions may facilitate career advancement. There is also some evidence that women mentors and protégés report more psycho-social functions.

Mentor–protégé relationships typically emerge spontaneously. Kram (1983) identified four phases in the development of mentor relationships:

Initiation: a period of six months to one year, during which time the relationship gets started and begins to have importance for both individuals. Expectations of both parties become firm and realized. Opportunities exist for work-related interaction. Mentors provide coaching, challenging work, and visibility; protégés provide technical assistance, respect, and a desire and willingness to be coached.

Cultivation: a period of two to five years, during which the number of career and psycho-social functions provided by the mentor increase to a maximum. Both continue to benefit from the relationship. More frequent and meaningful interactions occur. Both become more emotionally linked.

Separation: a period of two months to two years after a change in the structural role relationship (transfer, promotion) or in the emotional parts of the relationship (feelings of independence, threat, betrayal). Protégés may no longer need coaching; mentors may be psychologically or physically unable to provide career or psycho-social functions.

Redefinition: an indefinite period, during which time the relationship ends or takes on a more peer-like friendship quality. Peer status may result from diminished resentment and anger, and increased thankfulness and appreciation.

These phases are typically found when mentor relationships develop informally or spontaneously in organizations. But some organizations, interested in developing a greater number of mentor relationships, or in deriving the benefits from them, have developed formal mentoring programs. Several strategies are used. One is education. This includes training and development that foster an awareness and understanding of mentoring in career development. The second strategy is structural change. This involves modifying (or creating) structures in the organization (reward systems, tasks, performance appraisal systems) to foster the desired behaviors from staff.

As the workforce becomes increasingly diverse, issues of race and gender become more important in mentoring. It has been suggested that it is easier for white males to develop mentorships. In addition, cross-gender mentoring has unique challenges (Clawson & Kram, 1984). These include finding a balance of intimacy/distance in the relationship, dealing with sexual attraction and perceptions of favoritism by outsiders. Other barriers exist for women and racial minorities (lack of access to information networks, tokenism, stereotypes, and attributions). Thomas (1993) considered how racial dynamics influenced the mentor–protégé relationship. He was specifically interested in the question of whether such relationships were more effective when the individuals confronted their differences openly or when they denied them. The most common strategy to manage cross-racial differences was denial and suppression. The other strategy, direct engagement, was used less often. Thomas reported that the most effective mentor relationships were those where both pair members had similar strategy preferences.

There may also be ethical dimensions to mentoring in organizations. Such relationships can be elitist, in dividing staff into the "ins" and the "outs." When these relationships are influenced by sex, race, ethnic background, age, or sexual orientation, concerns about fairness and unearned privilege can legitimately be raised.

Bibliography

Bolton, E. B. (1980). A conceptual analysis of the mentor relationship in career development of women. *Adult Education*, **30**, 195–207.

Burke, R. J. (1984). Mentors in organizations. *Group and Organization Studies*, **9**, 353–72.

Clawson, J. G. & Kram, K. E. (1984). Managing cross-gender mentoring. *Business Horizons*, **17**, 22–32.

Collin, A. (1979). Notes on some typologies of management development and the role of mentors in the process of adaptation of the individual to the organization. *Personal Review*, **8**, 10–14.

Dalton, G. W., Thompson, P. H. & Price, R. I. (1977). The four stages of professional careers – A new look at performance by professionals. *Organizational Dynamics*, **5**, 19–42.

Hunt, D. M. & Michael, C. (1983). Mentorship: A career training and development tool. *Academy of Management Review*, **8**, 475–85.

Kram, K. E. (1983). *Mentors in Organizations.* Chicago: Scott Foresman.

Kram, K. E. (1983). Phases of the mentor relationship. *Academy of Management Journal*, **26**, 608–25.

Levison, D.J., Darrow, C.M., Klein, E.G., Levison, M. H. & McKee, B. (1978). *The Seasons of a Man's Life.* New York: Knopf.

Morrison, A. M., White, R. P. & Van Velsor, E. (1987). *Breaking the Glass Ceiling.* Reading, Mass.: Addison-Wesley.

Roche, G. R. (1979). Much ado about mentors. *Harvard Business Review*, **57**, 14–28.

Thomas, D. (1993). Racial dynamics in cross-race developmental relationships. *Administrative Science Quarterly*, **38**, 169–94.

Whitely, W., Dougherty, T. W. & Dreher, G. F. (1991). Correlates of career-oriented mentoring for early career managers and professionals. *Journal of Organizational Behaviour*, **13**, 141–54.

Zaleznik, A. (1977). Managers and leaders: Are they different? *Harvard Business Review*, **55**, 67–78.

RONALD J. BURKE

mergers and acquisitions Corporate mergers have played a prominent role in shaping the structure of business. Technically speaking, there are many different ways two (or more) firms can combine. For example, in a statutory merger, when two or more firms combine, one company survives under its own name, and the others cease to exist as legal entities. In a statutory consolidation, on the other hand, all the combining companies cease to exist as legal entities, and an entirely new, consolidated corporation is created. Some mergers are consummated after amicable negotiation between managers of acquiring and acquired firms. Other business combinations occur despite bitter disagreement between two sets of managers. In such hostile TAKEOVERS, the acquiring firm often goes over the heads of the acquired firm's management to the shareholders by means of a tender offer. A tender offer is an offer to pay existing shareholders some specified amount of cash or securities if these shareholders will sell (tender) their shares of stock to the acquiring firm. For present purposes, we will use the broader term *merger* to refer to combinations of firms without making these detailed distinctions (see RESTRUCTURING).

Mergers have motivated intense public debate about their effects and desirability. Much of this debate is ultimately grounded in fundamental ethical and value judgments. Almost inevitably, mergers raise issues about the rights of a wide spectrum of stakeholders in the modern corporation (*see* STAKEHOLDER THEORY). Does the merger create value to owners, or does it simply serve managerial interests? Are there detrimental consequences to employees, communities, or consumers? Are decision-makers who craft mergers compromised with conflicts of interest?

Many of the issues raised by mergers and acquisitions stem from the complex set of interrelationships in a corporation. In the simplest sense an acquisition involves a buyer purchasing an asset (or assets) from the existing owner for some agreed-upon compensation. If an individual purchases a used car from another person, there are issues about truthful representation of the quality and legal ownership of the car; however, a single individual buyer typically negotiates directly with a single individual seller with relatively little effect on others not directly party to the negotiation. Like a car sale, a corporate acquisition involves basic issues of TRUTHTELLING, but the rights to property and the effects on many parties (who are not empowered legally to participate in the

acquisition negotiation) are much more complicated (*see* PROPERTY, RIGHTS TO).

Insights as to why corporate mergers take
place and the ethical issues they raise can be
sharpened by realizing that a merger results in a
new set of legal and other contracts among
economic interests (*see* CONTRACTS AND CON-
TRACTING). These contracts (and their pre-
decessors), however, involve only a subset of the
stakeholders affected by the corporate combination. The legal, regulatory, and political context
will shape the powers and responsibilities of
specific stakeholders in the recontracting process involved in a merger and, as a result,
influence the effects a merger may have on a
particular group. A society's structure of
CORPORATE GOVERNANCE cedes certain decision-making powers to management and the
board of directors, who in turn have certain
responsibilities. This command system (the
shape of which may vary dramatically across
political and cultural boundaries) replaces direct
market transactions for a wide array of important economic decisions. In effect, the governance structures set down the rules of the
MARKET FOR CORPORATE CONTROL.

This perspective highlights a number of
points: (1) The interests of people with decision
authority determine incentives for merger (*see*
AGENCY THEORY, MORAL HAZARD). (2) These
interests are shaped by provisions of contracts.
(3) Such contracts are incomplete and do not
cover all contingencies. (4) Mergers may lead
both to changes in total value and redistribution
of such value. As a result, mutual understandings (implicit contracts and "goodwill")
play a crucial role inside and between firms –
even though such understandings are often not
written, legally enforceable contracts. The legal
system sets the context for trade-offs among
particular stakeholder interests in a merger. At a
more fundamental level, however, the society
and its political process will ultimately shape
legal and other standards. Generally market-
based, capitalistic views favor the rights of
owners, but the fabric of corporate governance
is a complicated balance of rights and interests
of different groups. These interests work their
way through the business, legal, and political
system.

Some of the principal ethical concerns raised
in mergers surround the rights, duties, and
obligations of the following stakeholders:

- Consumers – When two firms combine to
  increase market power, the result may be
  higher prices and profits as competition is
  lessened. While such profits are beneficial to
  owners, consumers may be worse off. In part,
  to protect consumer interests, governments
  often pursue regulatory and antitrust policies
  designed to foster competition.

- Employees – Mergers may lead to job
  reductions and revamping (or elimination)
  of contracts with employees. Particularly
  troubling are the status of promises about
  future compensation (e.g. through pension
  plans) and the status of implicit contracts
  between the firm and employees. For
  instance, the workers and prior management
  may have had unwritten agreements (implicit
  contracts) about job advancement and security.

- Managers – As prime decision-makers in
  mergers, managers may have conflicts of
  interest arising from concerns about their
  own job security and compensation. These
  pressures may lead them to pursue acquisitions of other firms and perhaps resist
  takeovers of their own company (*see* POISON
  PILL; WHITE KNIGHT; GREENMAIL). On the
  other hand, managers may receive large
  payments (GOLDEN PARACHUTES) upon
  completion of a takeover while their employees lose jobs. Furthermore, managers (and
  the board of directors) must deal with the
  disparate effects a merger may have on
  different stakeholders.

- Communities – Sometimes a merger may
  result in the postmerger company planning to
  lay off workers and close facilities. A specific
  closure may be inevitable for a firm to remain
  competitive, or it may be only one of many
  management options. What are the rights and
  responsibilities of communities in such a
  context?

- Boards of Directors – Boards are often the
  final arbiter of the merger and must conclude
  whether the merger agreement is in the best
  interests of the corporation and what con-

stitutes such best interests. The legal context of corporate structure and governance shapes specific board responsibilities to consider different stakeholder views.

- Advisors and Financial Intermediaries – With their compensation often contingent on an agreement being struck, such parties may not have incentives consistent with sound advice and performance.

- Classes of Security Owners – A great number of conflicts may arise among classes of security holders. For instance, equity holders may see a benefit from increasing debt in part to siphon off value from existing debt claimants who have inadequate legal protection from value downgrades due to the increased risk of default. Different generations of security holders may also have disparate interests. For instance, INSIDER TRADING laws are written expressly to prevent someone with privileged information from profiting from such information by exploiting the ignorance of existing owners. The structure and desirability of such laws raises a host of issues about rights and privileges of different groups.

A more detailed list of issues is beyond the scope of this entry. What is clear is that through the conduct of many decision-makers, society will develop a governance context for mergers to accommodate its view of the claims of different parties. Once such a context is set, pressures will exist for debate among different claimants, and that debate will likely engender a reassessment of the context over time.

Bibliography

Coase, R. H. (1937). The nature of the firm. *Economics*, **4**, (A classic treatment of the firm as an organizational structure.)

Copeland, T. E. & Weston, J. F. (1988). *Financial Theory and Corporate Policy*. Reading, Mass.: Addison-Wesley. (A survey of corporate finance with chapters detailing the financial theory of and empirical evidence about mergers).

Freeman, R. E. (1984). *Strategic Management: A Stakeholder approach*. Boston: Pitman. (An explication of the stakeholder perspective).

Hanly, Ken. (1992). Hostile takeovers and methods of defense: A stakeholder analysis. *Journal of Business Ethics*, **11**, 895–913 (An example of a stakeholder analysis).

Jensen, M. C. (1993). The modern industrial revolution, exit, and the failure of internal control systems. *Journal of Finance*, **48**, 831–80 (A view of a transformation in organizational form).

Jensen, M. C. & Meckling, W. H. (1976). Theory of the firm: Managerial behavior, agency costs, and ownership structure. *Journal of Financial Economics*, **2**, 305–60 (An influential article on ownership structure).

Kester, Carl W. (1991). *Japanese Takeovers*. Boston: Harvard Business School Press. (An interesting look at the Japanese context).

Williamson, O. E. (1985). *The Economic Institutions of Capitalism*. New York: Free Press. (A view of economic organizational forms).

ROBERT S. HARRIS

merit (noun) worth, importance; (verb) to deserve, to earn.

Most references to merit in contexts of interest to students of business ethics occur within discussions about DISTRIBUTIVE JUSTICE, especially concerning employment, promotion, and compensation practices.

Merit typically refers to a quality by virtue of which an employee or manager will tend to advance the goals of the organization. Such qualities may be competence, skill, experience, conscientious effort, contribution, talent, or potential. When benefits are to be awarded on the basis of *merit*, it is thought that the criteria for the award should not be arbitrary or discretionary, should be made public in advance of the decision, and be impartially applied.

Some standards, like nepotism or random selection, would not be termed merit, but much else can be comprehended under the term. An institution which uses merit as a standard will invest the term with a specific content and specify rules for applying the term. To have merit, then, or to merit an award, will mean to have successfully competed under the rules of that system.

Systems of *merit pay* are intended to replace or supplement other compensation schemes such as those based on seniority, percentage increases, or fixed-sum awards. Merit pay is the most frequently used method of linking pay to performance. Merit pay systems have been defined as systems in which 1) pay ranges with minimum and maxima are established for each job; 2) individual progression within the pay range depends at least in part on observations of the employee's performance; 3) performance is usually operationalized through performance appraisal systems; and 4) the pay increment obtained in any one time period is retained over time by building it into the employee's base pay (Schwab & Olson, 1990, pp. 2385–95).

Merit system refers to the system used by the United States federal government, among other institutions, for appointing and promoting civil-service personnel. The system was intended to protect employees from adverse treatment due to their political affiliation or loyalty. One of its hallmarks is the use of standardized exams.

Merit is sometimes contrasted with membership in a protected class in discussions of Affirmative Action or preferential treatment. One author, for example, denounces the "widespread perception that all Affirmative Action measures conflict with merit criteria" (Ezorsky, 1991, p. 88). *Merit* here refers to competence produced by effort. It is assumed that Affirmative Action violates the rights of maximally qualified workers who have "exerted effort to attain positions under an accepted and just rule" (ibid., p. 90) (*see* AFFIRMATIVE ACTION PROGRAMS; PREFERENTIAL TREATMENT).

It is sometimes suggested that an economy of perfectly competitive free markets would result in a *meritocracy*, a system in which advancement is based on individual ability or achievement. Those at the top would have an earned status, based on superior competence. One author recommends that *merit* here be understood as a combination of effort and intelligence, with intelligence measured by IQ scores and effort measured by modern time and motion studies (Young, 1961) (*see* MERITOCRACY).

Others, like Rousseau and MARX, argue that capitalist society actually rewards only the talent for making money. What people possess is not proportionate to what they deserve or *merit* but to what they can buy. Social inequality results from four sorts of differences, "wealth, nobility or rank, power and personal merit" (Rousseau, 1970, p. 17), but in bourgeois society these are all reduced to wealth.

Bibliography

Ezorsky, G. (1991). *Racism and Justice: The Case for Affirmative Action*. Ithaca, NY: Cornell University Press.

Rousseau, J. J. (1970, 1964). *The First and Second Discourses*, (Ed.), R. D. Masters, trans. R. D. Masters & J. R. Masters. New York: St. Martin's Press.

Schwab, D. P. & Olson, C. A. (1990). Merit pay practices: Implications for pay–performances relationships. *Industrial and Labor Relations Review*, **43**.

Young, M. (1961). *The Rise of Meritocracy*. Baltimore: Penguin Books.

JANE F. UEBELHOER

meritocracy a social system in which merit or talent is the basis for sorting people into positions and distributing rewards, such that the positions of highest authority are occupied by those of greatest merit. The term "meritocracy" is a satirical invention of Young (1958), who wrote a fable about a future society that could not abide the perfect meritocracy it created. The term is now applied, without the irony, to advanced capitalist systems of status attainment and reward allocation, usually to distinguish them favorably from aristocratic or class-based systems, where birth or family privileges determine an individual's status (Bell, 1972). A meritocracy relies on three principles (Daniels, 1978): 1) merit is a well-defined and measurable basis for selecting individuals for positions, 2) individuals have equal opportunity to develop and display their merits and to advance, and 3) the positions into which individuals are sorted are mapped to stratified levels of rewards (such as income or status). An organization or an entire society might espouse and try to operate on meritocratic principles.

Proponents of meritocracy highlight several advantages. A meritocracy is fair in that everyone has an opportunity to advance and rewards are proportional to meritorious contributions; merit is distinguished from equality or need, other fair bases of reward. Meritocracy motivates people. Functional sociologists argue that meritocracy directs the most talented people into the most functionally important positions and thereby enhances a society's survival and efficiency

The idea of meritocracy enters into ethical discussion about social systems – whether societies or organizations – in two ways, which are addressed in the following sections. First, a social system can be evaluated for the extent to which it lives up to meritocratic promises. Second, the moral basis of meritocracy as a distributive system can be assessed. This critical stance is less common, because meritocracy is accepted as a fair and legitimate principle and deeply woven into the culture and political rhetoric in many advanced capitalist societies and organizations.

The Pursuit of Meritocracy as Fairness

In societies, debate rages over whether equal opportunity and meritocracy have been achieved. One position is that class and privilege, not talent, determine who gets ahead, so the society is not a true meritocracy. It follows that programs should be created to improve opportunities for the disadvantaged, redistribute wealth, and assist the undeservingly poor. An opposing position is that talent and hard work drive advancement and that the society is a meritocracy or a close enough approximation. It follows that no redress is needed and people in the lowest positions should work harder. At stake in this debate is the question of whether a society is just.

In organizations, reward systems that are variations on meritocracy, such as pay-for-skills or pay-for-performance, are assessed from the standpoint of the three principles of meritocracy. There are discussions about whether chosen measures of merit are appropriate and measurable, whether biases compromise equality of opportunity, and how steeply and how high the reward curve should rise (*see* AFFIRMATIVE ACTION PROGRAMS). At the societal and organizational levels, the focus is often fine-tuning a meritocracy.

The Moral Tenor of Life in a Meritocracy

A second ethical approach to meritocracy probes whether a perfectly fine-tuned meritocracy has undesirable implications, three of which are considered here – privileging a dominant class while denigrating the poor, amplifying unearned differences in merit, and

potentially compromising cooperation. First, meritocratic ideology legitimates inequality, by painting a picture where "success comes to those whose energies and abilities deserve it, failures have only themselves to blame" (Mann, 1970, p. 427). Meritocracy is a "ruling ideology" (Marx & Engels, 1978, p. 64) that may serve the privileged by justifying their status and curbing resistance. Weber (1978, p. 953) writes that "every highly privileged group develops the myth of its natural superiority." The concomitant feelings of inferiority among those in lower positions have been called "the hidden injuries of class" (Sennett & Cobb, 1972). However, empirical evidence suggests that people in the lowest positions are not necessarily overcome by belief in meritocracy and have ways of making sense of their position other than blaming themselves (Scully, 1993). While meritocratic ideology may not fully legitimate inequality, it may raise enough uncertainties about distributive justice that resistance is not mobilized.

Second, the links between merit and reward may be difficult to justify on the grounds of moral desert inasmuch as merit may be unearned or a weak basis for special treatment. Historically, the Protestant ethic justified the link between hard work (as an indicator of moral rectitude) and wealth (as a possible indicator of salvation) (*see* PROTESTANT WORK ETHIC). However, merit, whether ability (such as I.Q.) or the capacity to exert effort and achieve goals, may be inherited or beyond an individual's control (Sher, 1979). If so, it becomes difficult to argue that a person's very "life chances" (income, housing, education) should be linked to their merits. For example, a society where people with mental handicaps routinely receive fewer resources seems cruel. Moreover, a meritocracy seems to assume that performance must be coaxed from the talented, which suggests they are more petulant than morally deserving. An alternative system, which may be more idealistic than practical, might be designed around the talented sharing their gifts without extra rewards; MEANINGFUL WORK can be its own reward.

Third, merit-based differences are divisive. They can create a climate where cooperation and concern for others are mitigated and where smug success and embarrassing failure charge the tenor of social life. For example, organizations are discovering that the individualistic and competitive spirit of merit-based rewards can undermine teamwork. Because meritocracy is such a taken-for-granted ideal, the search for alternative reward systems for societies and organizations has been difficult (Donnellon & Scully, 1994). A less competitively individualistic society, perhaps based on COMMUNITARIANISM, might distribute occupations and tasks by merit but not skew rewards in other domains by merit (Walzer, 1983). The inclusion of meritocracy in the lexicon of business ethics is a reminder to evaluate the very assumptions about fairness and the social contract that guide the everyday operations of individuals and organizations.

Bibliography

Bell, D. (1972). On meritocracy and equality. *Public Interest*, **29**, 29–68.

Daniels, N. (1978). Merit and meritocracy. *Philosophy and Public Affairs*, **3**, 206–23.

Donnellon, A. & Scully, M. (1994). Teams, merit, and rewards: Will the post-bureaucratic organization be a post-meritocratic organization? In A. Donnellon & C. Hecksher (eds), *The Post-Bureaucratic Organization*. Thousand Oaks, Calif.: Sage Publications.

Mann, M. (1970). The social cohesion of liberal democracy. *American Sociological Review*, **35**, 423–39.

Marx, K. & Engels, F. (1978). *The German ideology*, (Ed.), C. J. Arthur. New York: International Publishers.

Scully, M. (1993). *The Imperfect Legitimation of Inequality in Internal Labor Markets*. Working Paper 3520-93, Sloan School of Management, MIT, Cambridge, Mass.

Sennett, R. & Cobb, J. (1972). *The Hidden Injuries of Class*. New York: Vintage Books.

Sher, G. (1979). Effort, ability and personal desert. *Philosophy and Public Affairs*, **8**, 361–76.

Walzer, M. (1983). *Spheres of Justice: A Defense of Pluralism and Equality*. New York: Basic Books.

Weber, M. (1978). *Economy and Society: An Outline of Interpretive Sociology*, vol. 2, (eds) G. Roth & C. Wittich. Berkeley, Calif.: University of California Press.

Young, M. (1958). *The Rise of the Meritocracy*. New York: Penguin Books.

MAUREEN A. SCULLY

methodological individualism   the view that all of the concepts of the social sciences may be analyzed into the dispositions and characteristics of individuals. There is a tendency to confuse this position with what may be called ontological individualism, which maintains that societies are constructed of individual human beings and that there are no non-individual social entities which impose their histories and values on people. Since it is likely that no one has ever denied the ontological thesis, in discussing the thesis of methodological individualism it is best to put ontological individualism aside.

There are two purposes to be served by the use of social concepts, one descriptive and the other theoretical or explanatory. The first attempts to describe actual social situations as they appear to observers who see them taking place. The second attempts to render intelligible social behavior or social change. These are quite unlike each other, but methodological individualism argues that the concepts used in either project must be susceptible to the same sort of analysis.

There is some social-scientific research which suggests that the tendency for people to think individualistically or collectively is a matter of culture, and that specific cultures incline those who have been socialized within them in one direction or another (Kim et al., 1994). There are persistent features of what we may call the culture of empiricism that make methodological individualism seem reasonable to many. *One such feature* is its atomism, a commitment to the belief that there are only particulars. In dealing with the social world, that belief translates into the view that societies are made up of individuals and are to be understood only and fully as sums of the individuals who make them up. Even before the emergence of modern social science, we find this reflected in a way in which social-contract political theorists such as HOBBES and LOCKE take it that the commonwealth comes into being by the purposive decision of individuals. According to Hobbes and Locke, individuals are fully formed before the commonwealth comes into being; hence in no way are they shaped by non-individualistic social factors. Thus the being of the commonwealth is entirely exhausted by the sum of its individuals. It is not that we cannot speak of social wholes or political entities, e.g., the

English state, but we must always remember that "the English state . . is a logical construction out of individual people" (Ayer, 1950, p. 63) (*see* SOCIAL CONTRACT THEORY).

The other feature of the culture of empiricism is the view that *all facts are grounded in what is given to senses.* Hume, for example, takes it that our ideas are faint refections of impressions, and impressions are all sensory. Either we have had appropriate sense impressions or we have no adequate basis for any particular factual belief. The presumption is that one has only to open one's perceptual apparatus to discover the presence of individuals. But no sensory experience can enable us to detect the presence of social classes and other institutions that the non-individualist claims must be taken into account when describing and explaining social change and human action (cf. Knorr-Cetina & Cicourel, 1981, pp. 83ff). It may be noted that physics makes use of concepts – say, the electron – which are not grounded in sense impressions. Yet empiricist philosophers of science have long stopped being concerned about this. We may wonder why social science must be forced to labor under more severe restrictions or why the sort of things that occupy its attention, such as social classes or economic systems, are dismissed as "dubious entities." (See Knorr-Cetina & Cicourel, 1981, p. 144.) A number of issues emerge from this, and it seems best simply to raise them seriatim.

First of all, what are the particulars (the individual human beings), that the culture of empiricism, as that informs the philosophy of social science, seems to find so much more easily handled and accepted than those so-called collective entities or the concepts which refer to them? If one looks at what purports to be an instance of such a particular and limits one's apprehension to the givens of sense only, one does not perceive an individual person. At the level of the sensory, all one perceives is a collection of sensa. The special kind of unity which is the individual human being *qua* human being is not given to the senses. That it is known to the sense-data empiricists themselves is clearly evident from the fact that for more than two centuries they have been trying to show that our knowledge of the otherness of the other – what they call other minds – may be derived inferentially from an argument that

leads from the sensorily given to the other. That the argument never succeeds is not to the present point. What is to the point is that those who offer the argument know that the otherness of the other is given non-sensorially, but given their epistemological commitment to the primacy of the sensory they try to show that the knowledge in question may be reconstructed in sensory terms. Because he could find no impressions of substance, Hume claimed that the idea is not epistemologically grounded. His followers do not seem open to doing that to the idea of the other. The primacy of the sensory, it seems, need not be the last word.

The next issue has to do with what social science is all about. If one surveys the literature of social science one discovers attempts to deal with institutions, social classes, economic systems, systems of kinship nomenclature, etc. But one never finds mention of such things in the examples discussed by methodological individualists. Rather, the focus of their attention is on how to explain why some given individual did or sought to do something or other. By dealing with that sort of made-up example, methodological individualists make it appear that the individual – the only thing that one can experience empirically – is all that the social sciences deal with. But such examples overlook the fact that individual action takes place within an institutional framework which is non-individual. In a now classic example, Maurice Mandelbaum shows that no one not familiar with the institution of banking could perceive an individual making a deposit. He would perceive the individual and the movements of his body, but the banking transaction cannot be reduced to those (O'Neill, 1973, p. 224). Thus, even if sometimes one wants to explain individual action and deems it relevant to point to the motives and interests of individuals, it doesn't follow that that is all there is.

A third issue concerns the nature and existence of collective entities. Methodological individualism denies that such entities exist. Tables and chairs exist, but societies are not like them. The presumption is that to think of societies as existing is to think of them as being like tables and chairs. That would imply that they possess casual properties which would result in their being imposed on individuals in ways incompatible with the freedom of individuals. (See Wisdom, 1970, pp. 271–96.) Thus, the non-individualist position not only rejects collective entities from the standpoint of the culture of empiricism, but also as incompatible with the freedom of individuals. Of course, no one who takes seriously the collective entities that interest social science believes that they have the same sort of being as tables and chairs, and to suggest otherwise is merely a polemical ploy.

What is in reality the case is that methodological individualism and its opponents advocate two radically unlike ontologies of "social being." Implicit in the position of the former is the view that existence requires spatial extension, that is, to be like tables and chairs. Since, clearly, social entities do not have such a characteristic, methodological individualism denies that they could exist. Human individuals do have spatial extension, and that seems to be why methodological individualists take it that what is alleged to be talked about social entities can only be analyzed so that what is asserted is seen to be said about collections of individuals with no remainder. The non-individualist position takes it that there are social classes and social institutions, that they have histories, and that those histories are not to be confounded with the histories of individuals. It has been said that a statement about the battle of Hastings must be analyzed into or reduced to statements about individuals who participated in the battle (MacIver, 1947, pp. 33–50), but while historians know that such a battle took place, what its outcome was, and what the consequences were of the battle, except for the leading participants they have no idea at all as to who the soldiers were who fought the battle. Thus it would seem that we can talk about social entities and collective events without having first to amass collections of statements about individuals. It may be difficult to characterize the nature of social being on the non-individualist view of it in a way that would be analogous to the individualist view that existence requires spatial extension, yet there does seem to be a sense in which the social does seem to exist, persist, and change.

In sum it seems reasonable to conclude that while the controversy over methodological individualism is a dispute over what the subject-matter of the social sciences is and how the concepts used in them are to be analyzed, it is likewise reasonable to conclude that what lies behind the controversy is independent of the social sciences and is rooted in differences of opinion as to what sorts of things exist and how what exists may come to be known.

See also **individualism**

Bibliography

Ayer, A. J. (1950). *Language, Truth and Logic*. London: Gollancz.

Kim, N., et al. (eds). (1994). *Individualism and Collectivism*. Thousand Oaks, Calif.: Sage.

Knorr-Cetina, K. & Cicourel, A. V. (eds). (1981). *Advances in Social Theory and Methodology*. Boston: Routledge and Kegan Paul.

MacIver, A. M. (1947). The character of a historical explanation. *Aristotelian Society Supplementary Volume,* **21,** 33–50.

O'Neill, J. (Ed.), (1973). *Modes of Individualism and Collectivism*. London: Heinemann.

Wisdom, J. O. (1970). Situational individualism and the emergent group-properties. In R. Borger & F. Cioffi (eds), *Explanation in the Behavioural Sciences*. Cambridge: Cambridge University Press, 271–96.

LEON J. GOLDSTEIN

methodologies of business ethics research comprise the variety and justification of methods by which business ethics research is undertaken. Business ethics research conventionally is divided into two approaches: normative and descriptive. Normative research is concerned with evaluating or prescribing the behavior of business persons and organizations. Descriptive research, by contrast, focuses on describing individual and organizational behavior so that it can be explained and possibly predicted. This conventional division of business ethics into two fairly distinct fields can be criticized as theoretically untenable and ethically undesirable (see below). But the distinction between normative and descriptive business ethics research *at least* captures a variety of important *surface* differences of current practice in the field, even if those differences fade at a deeper level of scrutiny.

Normative research focuses on what ought to be, and typically is the province of persons trained in philosophy, religious studies, or related liberal arts subjects. Such persons may see themselves filling the role of external critic of established business practices. By contrast, descriptive business ethics research usually is performed by applied social scientists, and often takes place within business organizations and business schools. It displays a more pragmatic approach to issues, and arguably is less prone to take a critical stance toward the established norms and goals of business. More importantly, mainstream social science theory (at least in the US) generally forgoes questions of what ought to be in favor of queries into what is. The goal is to explain the behavior of business organizations and their members. Business policies and practices are studied to discover what influences them and what they in turn influence. Although questions of their ethical propriety may be important, those are questions which range beyond the scope of conventional social science inquiry.

Language and Style

These different institutional homes and academic outlooks incorporate significant differences of style and language. Mainstream empiricists utilize the consensually agreed upon methods of their social scientific training, whether it be laboratory experimentation, business database studies, or surveys. Research is guided by relatively formal design criteria which, if judiciously followed, are thought capable of supporting explanatory models of business behavior. Data typically are analyzed utilizing a variety of quantitative statistical methods (e.g. regression analysis).

By contrast, philosophically driven research includes nothing like the highly specified research methods of social science. Although there is methodological self-reflection in normative ethics generally, it tends to be individualized to the task and author at hand. Any generally applicable normative method is best described informally in terms of intellectual virtues such as consistency, clarity, avoidance of emotional manipulation, etc. Thus, whereas descriptive work has relatively standardized forms of method and presentation, normative work is much more eclectic and idiosyncratic.

Differences of language and presentation, plus different attitudes toward methodological uniformity, can contribute to misunderstanding. For example, normative theorists usually use the phrase "ethical behavior" to refer to behavior which in fact is ethically proper. Descriptive researchers, however, use the term "ethical" in a non-normative sense. For them, "ethical behavior" denotes the behavior of a person or organization confronted with ethical issues or choices, regardless of whether or not the behavior in question is normatively proper.

Assumptions about Human Agency

The normative and descriptive domains invoke explanatory models that rest upon distinct and sometimes unstated assumptions about human agency. The normative approach typically assumes that actions are performed with some degree of autonomy and responsibility. For some (metaphysical – as distinct from political – libertarians), this assumption entails a denial that ethical action easily can be placed in the kind of causal or nomological nexus empiricists usually seek. For other normative theorists (sometimes called "soft" determinists), the assumption of autonomy and responsibility attendant to ethical de(eds) suggests that not all causal factors are on equal footing. Autonomous and responsible actions involve the agent's choices, *even if* those choices are causally determined. Thus only causal factors that work through a person's choices preserve autonomy and moral responsibility.

Searches for the causal antecedents of behavior, then, can be problematic to normative theorists, as the goal of such a search conflicts with a normative assumption about human agency. To some normative theorists, success on the part of the empiricist in finding the sources of behavior risks compromising one's ability to impute normative significance to the behavior. Moreover, to some normative theorists, ethically proper action is self-explanatory, needing no additional explanation in social scientific terms.

In contrast, management researchers – even if they admit that in some sense individuals should be considered ethically responsible for their actions – nevertheless are more interested in finding causal determinants of ethical behavior (e.g. reward systems, codes of conduct, individual characteristics). External determinants of behavior are more interesting and useful for study because they are factors a manager can control. For example, a manager can manipulate reward systems in order to influence subordinates' behavior. In the descriptive approach, both ethically proper and improper actions are viewed as complex phenomena that should be explained by a combination of causal factors. Even whistleblowing, often presumed to be an example of autonomous, ethically proper action, is understood by social scientists to be the product of multiple internal and external causal factors.

Role of Abstraction vs. Empirical Detail

Modern normative ethical theory typically (though not universally) pursues a standard of moral reasoning or action which holds for persons in general. Consequently, normative theory often is framed at an abstract level, and is distanced from the specifics of any particular social setting. Even though normative inquiries often rely on the detailed study of real-life cases in business ethics, that kind of empirical detail often merely provides a venue for applying normative theories or unearthing implicit counter-intuitive implications of such theories. It is only at the level of dealing with particular issues that normative theory is context sensitive; its general principles typically are framed in context-neutral fashion.

While normative business ethics thus displays a bias toward abstraction, descriptive business ethics leans in the opposite direction. Even though the abstract concepts of empirical psychology and sociology may play key roles in empirical business ethics research, those concepts are expected at some point to be empirically or observationally defined so that they can be concretely measured. Thus, the social scientist may devalue the philosopher's moral judgments because they cannot be evaluated by standardized empirical tests, nor be used to predict or explain behavior. But the social scientist's statements about "ethical" behavior may seem of secondary value to a normative theorist, because they do not address the evaluative questions of right and wrong.

Basis for Evaluating Theoretical Claims

The "method" of normative ethical theory – insofar as there is a common one – involves achieving what Rawls (1971) calls a reflective equilibrium between theoretical constructions (i.e., general normative principles) and persons' considered moral judgments. Everything from the formal sciences to common norms and intuitions is relevant in this process. Importantly, actual moral practice functions among the criteria for evaluating moral theories; were a normative theory to prescribe gratuitous punishment, we would have at least *prima facie* grounds for rejecting the theory. But these grounds are only *prima facie*; inconsistency with current moral practice in no way *necessitates* the rejection of a normative principle. After all, the point of such principles is to guide and possibly correct current practice. Normative claims and principles, in short, are to be evaluated according to an open-ended array of evidence, concerns, and insights, all tied together by generalized standards of good argument (e.g. no unseemly emotional appeals, no efforts to intimidate, etc.) rather than by some precisely defined methodology.

In descriptive business ethics, the initial stages of theory development may proceed in somewhat intuitive fashion. However, on the conventional account an acceptable theory ultimately must contribute to one's ability to explain and predict. Thus, theory justification is accomplished via a putatively natural scientific model of empirical confirmation or disconfirmation, or through the theory's pragmatic ability to predict behavior and solve problems. Although critics of this conventional view of science argue that (a) the ideas of empirical confirmation and disconfirmation are beset with conceptual problems, and (b) that a variety of non-rational factors enter into the acceptance or rejection of a theory, the bulk of descriptive research on business ethics maintains this traditional empiricist (or neo-positivist) view of the goals and methods of inquiry.

Conventional Empirical Approaches

The prominent research methods within conventional descriptive business ethics fall within two broad categories: experimental and correlational research. Within both categories, researchers are expected to begin with hypotheses rooted in social science theory. They then are to design a study that will test the hypothesized relationships.

Experimental approaches are used when the researcher wants to investigate a causal relationship between two variables, essentially investigating whether some phenomenon, X, "causes" another, Y. Experiments can be conducted in laboratory or field settings. The experimenter manipulates one or more independent variables (X, above), and then measures variations in the dependent variable (Y, above). The two major criteria for evaluating experimental research are *internal* and *external* validity. If an experiment is internally valid, the researcher can be confident that the independent variable "caused" the dependent variable. Laboratory experiments are generally thought to be higher in internal validity because the investigator has maximum control over the independent variables. For example, a laboratory experimenter might hypothesize that individuals would be more likely to steal under certain circumstances, and then randomly assign subjects to conditions that represent either the presence or absence of those circumstances. External validity has to do with the generalizability of the research results. Laboratory experiments are lower in external validity because they are conducted in artificial settings that strip away much of the complexity of real-life settings. Field experiments are higher in external validity because they are conducted in actual organizational settings, but they are lower in internal validity because the antecedent conditions (the Xs) are more difficult to control.

Correlational approaches are used when the research has hypothesized relationships among variables which cannot be manipulated by the researcher. Data to test the hypotheses may come from archival sources, or from surveys the researcher administers. For example, the researcher might hypothesize that individuals' cynicism toward business ethics will be higher for business school students and lower for older, more experienced members of the business community. A survey could be conducted of members of both groups, and their responses could be compared. Or, the research might hypothesize that corporate crime is higher in firms that are in financial difficulty. In this case, archival data about convictions and financial performance could be collected and subjected to correlational analysis.

Alternative Empirical Approaches

There is, however, descriptive business ethics research which departs from the standard, quantitatively oriented methods. These approaches involve a variety of qualitative techniques which eschew numerical analysis for some form of in-depth verbal description or textual and verbal analysis. This research does not claim to provide generalizable claims in the fashion of quantitatively oriented research, but often is presented as a basis for building theories which can then be tested by more conventional quantitative techniques. Constructing a robust theoretical model of some category of phenomena may require intimate familiarity with it, familiarity best obtained by extensively talking to, observing, or living among the people involved. Qualitative research, in the fashion of interviews and ethnographic research such as participant observation, provides the basis for that kind of in-depth understanding.

The theoretical account resulting from qualitative research *may* be shaped into a formal model and then subjected to quantitative empirical test. But more radical non-quantitative research questions this possibility, and argues for the unavoidably malleable, interpretive character of all social or behavioral phenomena. In this view, any efforts to quantitatively assess phenomena by "objective" means (such as survey research) disguise the fact that the resulting portrait is *artificially* static. Quantitative methods, according to this alternative view, treat essentially interpretive phenomena as considerably more fixed and objective than we are entitled to claim.

More importantly, radically interpretive empirical research rejects the assumption of a normative/empirical distinction which underlies the conventional approaches to business ethics research. Rather, it argues that even the mainstream empiricist methodology imposes a normative standard on its subjects. Conventional empiricists may go so far as to admit that normative concerns lead them to study some phenomena rather than others (e.g. ethical concerns may prompt one to study the effects of certain forms of organizational discipline). But conventional empiricists would argue that standardized empirical methods guarantee that any conclusions will be value-neutral, favoring no particular ethical position. To the critic of conventional methodology, however, such "objective" methods inherently favor a particular set of ethical claims (usually held to be those of the status quo or dominant power structure). For example, conventional empirical research on the effects of punishment on employees focuses on whether or not punishment is effective in changing behavior. But in doing so, this ostensibly neutral research assumes a consequentialist view of punishment (i.e., behavioral consequences are all that matters), and defines the relevant consequences from a managerial standpoint (rather than from the standpoint of, e.g., a labor union organizer). To the critic, then, empirical business ethics research – despite its methodological and stylistic differences from normative research – does not avoid normative issues so much as hide them.

Integrative Approaches

The more radically interpretive approach to empirical methodology, then, suggests the possibility of more integrative approaches to business ethics inquiry, in which normative and empirical considerations are not so readily isolated. Various types of integrative methods are well known in other fields. Kohlberg's work on moral development, to take just one example, uses normative principles or categories not only to label levels of moral development, but also to carry out some of the explanatory work in accounting for an individual's transition from one type of moral reasoning to another. (In Kohlberg's view, people move toward higher levels of moral reasoning in part *just because* they are higher, i.e., morally preferable.)

Within business ethics research, however, integrative methodologies are rare. Most typically, they occur when the empirical methods used are of the more interpretive, qualitative sort. (Jackall's *Moral Mazes* (1988) exemplifies this approach, simultaneously describing the ethical assumptions and standards of managerial work *and* the normative ethical problems attendant to those standards.) Integrative empirical work in the conventional quantitative tradition is rarer, however, as the underlying assumptions of that approach usually work

against integrative tendencies. Extant work which attempts such integration generally uses normatively articulated categories to initially frame issues and phenomena, which then are analyzed according to conventional empirical methods (e.g. Victor & Cullen, 1988).

See also **Business ethics; Business ethics periodicals; Business ethics research centers**

Bibliography

Donaldson, T. (1994). When integration fails. *Business Ethics Quarterly*, **4**, (2), 157–71.

Jackall, R. (1988). *Moral Mazes: The World of Corporate Managers*. New York: Oxford University Press.

Rawls, J. (1971). *A Theory of Justice*. Cambridge, Mass.: Harvard University Press.

Trevino, L. K. (1992). Experimental approaches to studying ethical/unethical behavior in organizations. *Business Ethics Quarterly*, **2**, (2), 121–36.

Trevino, L. K. & Weaver, G. R. (1994). Business Ethics/Business Ethics: One field or two? *Business Ethics Quarterly*, **4**, (2), 113–28.

Victor, B. & Cullen, J. (1988). The organizational bases of ethical work climates. *Administrative Science Quarterly*, **33**, 101–25.

Victor, B. & Stephens, C. U. (1994). Business ethics: A synthesis of normative philosophy and empirical social science. *Business Ethics Quarterly*, **4**, (2), 145–57.

Weaver, G. R. & Trevino, L. K. (1994). Normative and empirical business ethics: Separation, marriage of convenience, or marriage of necessity? *Business Ethics Quarterly*, **4**, (2), 129–33.

GARY R. WEAVER
and LINDA KLEBE TREVINO

Mill, John Stuart (1806–73), British philosopher, economist and political theorist, was the foremost utilitarian of the nineteenth century, and his essay, *Utilitarianism*, is today the most widely read statement of utilitarian ethics. UTILITARIANISM is a variety of CONSEQUENTIALISM, judging acts to be right or wrong on the basis of their foreseeable consequences, and in its formulation in the nineteenth-century tradition established by JEREMY BENTHAM and followed by Mill, "acts are right in proportion as they tend to promote happiness, wrong as they tend to produce the reverse of happiness" (Mill, 1861, ch. 2). Both Bentham and Mill analyzed

HAPPINESS in terms of pleasures and pains, but whereas Bentham judged the value of a pleasure or pain to consist of the two quantitative dimensions of intensity and duration, Mill believed that pleasures and pains also differ in "quality" and that some pleasures are qualitatively superior to others even if not more intense or longer lasting. Mill's test for the qualitative superiority of one pleasure in comparison with another is the preference of persons qualified by knowledge of both. Mill's utilitarianism is thus not a calculus of given preferences, regardless of ignorance and prejudice, but of happiness as indicated by informed and enlightened preferences.

In the twentieth century a distinction has been made between act-utilitarianism and rule-utilitarianism (*see* MORAL RULES). Mill's theory does not fit neatly into either category. On the one hand he says that morality may be defined as the rules and precepts by the observance of which the greatest possible happiness for all mankind and even for the whole sentient creation may be secured. But when discussing any particular rule, such as that prohibiting the telling of lies, or prohibiting the infringement of a person's liberty, he says that it may admit of exceptions to prevent some greater harm. Although subordinate to utility as the ultimate standard of morality, Mill also has a place for rights and justice, and for the role of conscience and virtue, in his ethical system.

According to Bentham and Mill, laws, policies, and political and social institutions as well as personal acts are to be evaluated by their consequences, and reformed if there is a feasible alternative with better, or less bad, consequences. Mill advocated what at the time were radical proposals: equal rights for women, restrictions on the rights of inheritance of property, and LIBERTY of individuals to pursue their own lifestyles so long as they do not infringe on the rights of others. His essay *On Liberty* is a classic statement advocating complete freedom of thought and expression of opinion, and freedom of action when it does not harm others. His *Principles of Political Economy* paid unusual attention, for its time, to the effects upon the working classes of alternative economic policies, and it contains chapters debating the merits of private property versus forms of utopian socialism.

Bibliography

Mill, J. S. (1963–91). *Collected Works of John Stuart Mill*, 33 vols. Toronto: University of Toronto Press. (Complete edition of Mill's writings.)

Mill, J. S. (1848). *Principles of Political Economy*, 2 vols. Various editions. In *Collected Works*, **vols. 2 and 3**.

Mill, J. S. (1859). *On Liberty*. Various editions. In *Collected Works*, **vol. 18**.

Mill, J. S. (1861). *Utilitarianism*. Various editions. In *Collected Works*, **vol. 10**.

West, H. R. (1992). Mill, John Stuart. In L. C. Becker (ed.), *Encyclopedia of Ethics*. New York and London: Garland, 811–16.

HENRY R. WEST

monopoly   is exclusive control over producing or selling a commodity or service. By definition, when a monopoly exists there are not numerous sellers in a market, each having a share, but only one seller having 100 percent of the market. Also, by definition, a monopoly is a market in which new sellers are, by one means or another, barred from entering. A monopoly may be held by the state or by a private interest. It may be due to the nature of the commodity itself or it may be established by some form of legislation. Additionally, such factors as original patents and sizable initial investment in start-up costs may effectively bar or discourage other sellers from entering a market – at least for a time. Monopoly may also be created in effect by mergers (Gonsalves, 1989; Velasquez, 1988).

Monopolies raise at least three closely related moral issues: 1) a basic issue of justice in price (commutative justice); 2) the issue of efficiency of the economic system amid concentration of power (distributive justice); and 3) the issue of corruption and other negative effects on economic society.

1. Commutative Justice

In the nineteenth and early twentieth centuries giant corporations began to have great control over the economy of a country. The United States was certainly an example.

The Interstate Commerce Act (1897) and the Sherman Anti-trust Act (1890) were introduced to combat these effects. These measures, together with the Clayton Act and the Federal Trade Commission Act (both 1914), eventually succeeded in gaining control over these problems. After 1930, extensive regulation of business on all governmental levels developed, as well as an ongoing debate over the usefulness and appropriateness of government regulation as opposed to self-regulation of business (Beauchamp & Bowie, 1988).

The classic focus of concern on justice and pricing distinguishes the possibility of a just monopoly, when the control by monopoly is for the common welfare, from an unjust monopoly, which damages the common good. Competitive pricing to undercut competitors is not seen as wrong, but pricing below or above the level of a just price through monopolistic power is seen as wrong (Gonsalves, 1989). The determinants of just price and the factors that ought to be considered in this judgment are highly disputed, but the standard of "whatever the buyer is willing to pay" is manifestly insufficient. Monopoly sellers can, for example, limit supply sufficiently to secure an artificially high price. The seller violates a principle of commutative justice by selling the commodity at more than it is actually worth to him and by forcing the buyer to pay more than it is worth to him (Velasquez, 1988).

Additional producers and sellers are interested in there being additional supply. Otherwise the economic system is forcibly restricted to limiting the agency of those involved in the system to mere utility in producing profits. (See Sen, 1987, on utility and agency.) Such a restriction is morally questionable in view of larger considerations. Increased competition has been the cumulative effect of antitrust actions through the decades. Antitrust action has also restrained mergers among competitors (Shepherd, 1986).

2. Distributive Justice

On the level of larger questions of distributive justice, monopolistic practices damage the efficiency of an economic system and undercut the moral arguments arising for the distribution of resources under that system. The general justification of profit maximization cannot be widened to include monopoly (Arrow, 1973). Monopoly, or even oligopoly, increases the difficulty to the level of impossibility for survival of small businesses in an economy. Control over a series of products in one industry

– the food industry, for example – can effectively squeeze the consumer through the total costs of the market basket cumulatively by small increases over numerous items (Shaw & Barry, 1992). Monopolies can influence the efficiency of the distribution of goods in an economy through controlled shortages to produce higher prices, through a disinclination to efficient consumption of resources to produce a commodity, through disinclination of efficiency to reduce costs of production, through the maneuvering of some products unnecessarily to the level of high-priced luxuries, through requiring purchasers to purchase other items in order to be able to purchase some desired commodity, etc. (Velasquez, 1988).

One of the largest antitrust cases involved AT&T. AT&T agreed to divest itself of all its regional Bell operating companies. AT&T has increasingly been competing aggressively and successfully in a host of new endeavors (Stewart, 1993).

The victim or beneficiary in such situations is the system itself as an instrument of not only economic efficiency, but also of social justice. The choice of a social system is important to economic justice, but, in both private-property and socialist systems, markets exist and true competition militates against price wars and other abuses of market power (Rawls, 1971) (see DISTRIBUTIVE JUSTICE).

3. Corruption and Negative Effects

Monopolies are open to the kinds of concerns that characterize a general corruption of the system and a wounding of society. Monopolistic practices deviate from justice by producing a gravely exaggerated inequality of power over the consumer, allowing sellers to dictate terms to the consumer instead of responding to the market (Velasquez, 1988).

Monopolistic practices are among the factors contributing to the overweening power of corporations in dangerous areas of concern, nationally and internationally. Giant corporations can effectively negotiate by themselves with governments and influence legislation to serve their interests in franchising, tariffs, and other matters (Shaw & Barry, 1992).

At base, what is at stake is an inequality of knowledge poisoning the moral foundation of bargaining in an economy (Fried, 1979). Knowledge is important to genuine determination of preference by a consumer. Neither the supplying of this knowledge, nor the responsible shepherding of it in the interests of the economic society and the consumer, is likely to occur in the case of monopoly or in the similar effects of oligopoly.

Bibliography

Andrews, E. L. (1994). A.T.M. case on monopoly settled. *The New York Times*, April 22, p. D1+.

Arrow, K. J. (1973). Social responsibility and economic efficiency. *Public Policy*, 21. Reprinted in Shaw & Barry, 1992.

Beauchamp, T. L. & Bowie, N. E. (1988). *Ethical Theory and Business*, 3rd edn. Englewood Cliffs, NJ: Prentice-Hall.

Fuhrman, P. (1987). Do it big Sammy. *Forbes*, **140**, 278–80.

Fried, C. (1979). *Right and Wrong*. Cambridge, Mass.: Harvard University Press.

Gonsalves, M. A. (1989). *Right and Reason, Ethics in Theory and Practice*. Columbus, Ohio: Merrill.

Rawls, J. (1971). *A Theory of Justice*. Cambridge, Mass.: Harvard University Press.

Sen, A. (1987). *On Ethics and Economics*. Oxford: Blackwell.

Shaw, W. H. & Barry, V. (1992). *Moral Issues in Business*, 5th edn. Belmont, Calif.: Wadsworth.

Shepherd, W. G. (1986). Bust the Reagan trustbusters. *Fortune*, **114**, 225–7.

Stewart, J. B. (1993). Whales and sharks. *The New Yorker*, **68**, 37–43.

Velasquez, M. G. (1988). *Business Ethics, Concepts and Cases*, 2nd edn. Englewood Cliffs, NJ: Prentice-Hall.

SAMUEL M. NATALE
WILLIAM O'NEILL
TARA M. MADDEN

moral agency   is not so much a single concept as a cluster of concepts having to do with moral action, at the heart of which is the notion of RESPONSIBILITY. Closely related to responsibility are the concepts of moral motivation, moral cognition, and personal AUTONOMY. Each of these, as well as less central but important concepts such as virtue, moral weakness, self-esteem, shame, and guilt, is the subject of much debate in ethical theory, philosophy of action, and moral psychology.

Responsibility

In ordinary parlance, the belief that someone, including oneself, is responsible for an action supposes that the person in question has acted not only purposively but freely, which in turn usually supposes that he or she could have acted otherwise. However, there is a large and contentious philosophical literature on the topic of freedom, much of which takes a determinist line in suggesting either that "freedom" should not be understood in terms of the allegedly meaningless counterfactual expression "could have acted otherwise," or that freedom itself is an illusion (*see* FREE WILL). From this perspective, the concepts of responsibility and, accordingly, moral agency no longer refer directly to the moral agent. Instead, they are regarded as social constructs, oftentimes useful (albeit culture-specific) but still only a kind of mental shorthand for saying in retrospect that the agent did something of positive (or negative) worth to the society, was at least minimally aware of what was being done, and had no extraordinary determinants such as hypnotism or drugs. Under this account, typified by H. L. A. Hart's theory of "ascriptivism," the reason that it is useful to call such a person responsible and, by extension, guilty, heroic, etc., is not that doing so points to some special sort of human causation at work in the behavior: rather, the reason is that when we call someone responsible we serve notice that he or she is held to certain expectations and, by serving this notice with its implicit sanctions, we provide additional incentives for moral action. Thus at the individual level, a would-be criminal is deterred from criminal action by the foreknowledge that society will react to such behavior *as though* it could have been avoided, regardless of whether it really could be avoided in the absence of this deterring consideration. At the social level, it is useful to ascribe responsibility to agents because doing so simplifies the task of social control: regardless of how well designed a society's legal or moral code might be, it is difficult or impossible to sort out all the circumstances and motivating factors in an individual person's conduct. Society usually allows certain excusing mental conditions, as noted above, though not ignorance of the law, intoxication, resentment, and other relatively unacceptable excuses. Sometimes (more often in some societies than in others) the social code allows virtually no excuses, as in strict liability statutes such as the rule against homicide on the high seas violated by Melville's Billy Budd, who though undeniably well-intentioned had to be hanged forthwith. What these rather harsh special cases illustrate is the general point that ascriptivist theories of human responsibility and moral agency have a utilitarian base: excusing or mitigating conditions are counted as relevant features of human action if and only if the general practice of counting them serves the common good (see UTILITARIANISM).

In contrast, the more familiar (Western) view is that such conditions should be counted not because it is convenient to do so but because it is correct to do so, i.e., because these conditions are somehow inherently relevant to the action under evaluation, or to the agent's state of mind. This view of responsibility as something really "in the agent" corresponds to the retributivist theory of punishment whose classic spokesman is Immanuel Kant, just as the aforementioned ascriptivist view corresponds to the deterrence theory associated with Jeremy Bentham and John Stuart Mill (see KANTIAN ETHICS; BENTHAM, JEREMY; MILL, JOHN STUART). For Kant and others who hold a causal or quasi-causal view of human freedom, responsibility is a capacity that an agent *has* and ascriptions of responsibility are based on the recognition of that fact. Correspondingly, ascriptions of diminished responsibility are based on the recognition that an ignorant, mentally ill, or otherwise dysfunctional person really has less capacity or even no capacity at all for acting in the desired way.

Moral Motivation

Moral agency is inconceivable without some notion of the motivational springs of human action. Every moral philosophy has some more or less explicit psychology of moral motivation, though it is only in modern times that psychology has emerged as a discipline in its own right (see MOTIVES). In the English-speaking countries during the twentieth century, psychologists have generally emphasized

the external incentives that control behavior (Thorndike, Skinner, Aronfreed, Bandura), though psychodynamic accounts of intrapsychic factors such as drives (Freud, McClelland) have also been influential. During the second half of the century, especially over the last three decades, somewhat more cognitive accounts of motivation have emerged (Piaget, Kohlberg, Gilligan), with special relevance to moral action and the philosophical literature on that topic (see MORAL DEVELOPMENT).

Corresponding to these three general approaches to human motivation are three metaethical accounts of moral motivation and moral judgment (see MORAL REASONING). The first approach, characteristic of social learning theory, regards judgments of the form "X is wrong" as epiphenomena of the more basic experiences of aversion or attraction toward certain kinds of action, these experiences being in turn the results of social conditioning (modeling, punishment, etc.). In this sense, moral judgments reflect moral motivations but do not produce them. The second approach assigns a causal role to moral judgments, but the content of those judgments is thought of not as a statement but rather as an internalized admonition by a parent or some comparable figure constituting one's superego. Thus "X is wrong" is really a parental voice uttering "Don't do X!" and only indirectly a statement about the moral worth of X itself (see MORAL IMPERATIVES). The third approach regards the cognitive judgment as efficacious because of its truth value (real or imagined), in roughly the same way that judgments about the physical world ("That is a poisonous snake") motivate actions. When the link between judgment and action breaks down, three retrospective explanations are possible: the judgment was not sincere in the first place, the agent revised the judgment at the last minute, or some countervailing motive outweighed the less powerful motivation provided by the moral judgment. The first explanation points to the problem of self-deception, the second to the problem of matching general principles with concrete situations, the third to the problem of weakness of will. Each of these problems is much discussed in the literature of moral philosophy as well as in the psychology of personality.

Autonomy

Since Kant, Western moralists have generally assumed that morality involves self-rule, or as modern psychological literature puts it, self-regulation. The classic contrast here is between an autonomous will, which imposes moral rules on itself, and a heteronomous will, which is ruled by "the other" in that it reacts to external pressures – including the passions, which for Kant and his descendants are outside the realm of moral agency. A more complex account of personal autonomy has recently emerged in the philosophical literature, inspired by H. Frankfurt's hierarchical model of second-order desires. In this and similar models, an agent's desires are, or should be, subject to other "meta-level" desires, i.e., the desire to have or not to have certain first-order desires, and these meta-desires are typically shaped by moral considerations on the one hand and one's deepest wants and tendencies on the other. Autonomous agents are those who have, and act upon, the desires they want to have.

In its classical, Kantian formulation autonomy did not admit of degrees, but it is now generally recognized by philosophers and psychologists that people are more or less autonomous and that for most people there is a developmental sequence such that personal maturation can be described as a process of increasing autonomy. In the philosophically nuanced moral psychology of Piaget and Kohlberg, this point is expanded into a stage-structural account, whereby children's moral judgments and moral motives are "moral" in the minimal sense that they deal with right and wrong but are nonetheless heteronomous (X is deemed wrong because of the results it produces, especially those involving punishment). As the child matures, judgments are keyed to socially constructed norms rather than the results of actions (X is deemed right because it is the sort of thing a loyal son, sibling, friend, citizen, etc., would do), a shift which reflects the older child's greater ability to take perspectives other than his or her own. At the highest, most cognitively adequate stages, the moral agent goes beyond the socially constructed norms handed down by others, and instead uses his or her rational powers to adopt multiple points of view corresponding to the various parties who would be affected by the moral decision. At this point autonomy, cognitive adequacy, and moral maturity coincide and even in formal philosophical analyses are often indistinguishable, as illustrated in the work of JOHN RAWLS.

Virtues

Both utilitarian and duty-oriented ethics focus on moral *actions*, though in the first case actions are thought to derive their ultimate importance from the states of affairs they produce. However, in the early 1980s a backlash appeared, which aimed at restoring the Aristotelian emphasis on virtue, or, in the language of certain educators, "moral character" (*see* VIRTUE ETHICS). Moral agency was understood by these authors (MACINTYRE, Nussbaum, Slote) as a way of being, i.e., as a kind of life rather than as a way of acting or making decisions. The role of moral judgment was reduced, that of moral EMOTION and intuition expanded. Moral education was construed as developing the right kinds of habits rather than as developing greater powers of principled thinking and perspective taking. Willingness to live within a tradition was prized over readiness to take a point of view (critical or otherwise) on that tradition, and so moral agency was thought of as conformity to standards (often admitted to be culture-specific) rather than as personal, rational autonomy. This contrast is reflected in the current debate in political philosophy about liberalism, which sees morality as part of a cultural heritage (*see* LIBERAL-COMMUNITARIAN DEBATE). It is also reflected in the contrast, noted above, between cognitive developmental and social learning psychologies. In each of these contrasts, a similar pattern can be found in the scholarly literature: one view dominates for a generation or two, a backlash emerges and holds sway for about a decade, and then the lines of difference are blurred as new, more comprehensive theories emerge. In the case of moral agency, this probably means that the cognitive dimensions of human action and evaluation will soon become integrated more closely with the affective dimensions, and that the shape of this integration will vary considerably from culture to culture, perhaps giving rise to a new subdiscipline, moral anthropology.

THOMAS E. WREN

moral development a rational process of acquiring moral VALUES. According to moral development theory, we do not adopt moral values uncritically; rather, we adopt moral values only if we have the conceptual and emotional resources to understand them, and only if they help us resolve interpersonal problems. Moral autonomy is possible because we have some choice over which values to adopt and how to interpret them.

Moral development theory is associated with three names: Jean Piaget, Lawrence Kohlberg, and Carol Gilligan.

Piaget: Morality and Rationality

Piaget published *Le Jugement moral chez l'enfant* in 1932, the heyday of psychoanalysis and the beginning of behaviorism. Psychoanalysis and behaviorism, though different in many ways, both view morality as a set of *external rules* imposed on individuals.

Piaget rejected the external-rule interpretation of morality. Studying the behavior of young males, Piaget argued that morality develops as a result of *internal rational processes* (*see* KANTIAN ETHICS). We develop morally as we become involved in increasingly complex social arrangements. We adopt moral rules and principles because they help us cope with these complex social environments. While embraced by those in education, Piaget was largely ignored by research psychologists until Kohlberg devised more precise ways to measure moral development.

Kohlberg: An Ethic of Rights

In the late 1950s, Lawrence Kohlberg began an 18-year study of 50 men and boys to evaluate and refine Piaget's theory. On the basis of that and many subsequent studies, Kohlberg argued that there are three levels of moral development, each of which has two stages.

Level I: The Pre-Conventional Level. Individuals have a limited understanding of, but not loyalty to, social or MORAL RULES, which are valuable only if they promote self-interest.

Individuals make moral judgments in terms of concrete consequences to themselves (*see* CONSEQUENTIALISM).

Stage 1: The Punishment and Obedience Orientation. Right acts are those that are not punished. Punishment consists of either corporal punishment or the loss of a privilege. Authorities are obeyed because of their power to punish.

Stage 2: The Instrumental-Relativist Orientation. Right acts promote self-interest now or in the future. Individuals understand how RECIPROCITY can justify current loss to secure greater rewards later.

Level II: The Conventional Level. Individuals understand how moral rules bind groups together. They make moral judgments in terms of rule-following and the concrete consequences to their group, and so can justify self-sacrifice. One's group is viewed as morally superior to others.

Stage 3: The Interpersonal Concordance of "Good Boy/Nice Girl" Orientation. Right acts promote the good of a small group, such as a family. Reciprocity is valuable because it holds a group together. There is loyalty to the group, its rules, and authorities.

Stage 4: The Law and Order Orientation. Right acts follow group rules or promote the good of a large group, like a nation. There is loyalty to the large group, its laws, and leaders.

Level III: The Post-Conventional Level. Individuals use universal ethical standards. The PARTIALITY of Levels I and II is rejected in favor of IMPARTIALITY, which views all human beings, groups, and societies as equally valuable.

Stage 5: The Social-Contract Legalistic Orientation. Right acts and policies are those that are fair or promote the good of the group. Laws can be unjust. Principles of SOCIAL CONTRACT THEORY and UTILITARIANISM are not clearly distinguished. There is loyalty to laws or groups that respect human beings.

Stage 6: The Universal Ethical Principle Orientation. Right acts and policies respect human dignity. Utilitarianism is rejected. There is loyalty to universal principles, not to laws or groups.

People move through these stages serially. Each stage provides the foundation for the next, integrating the values of previous stages. Stage

5, for example, reinterprets the values of self, family, and nation in terms of fairness and the good of all. Value adoption is rational: people move to later stages because they are better for resolving problems.

Gilligan: An Ethic of Care

Carol Gilligan argues that Piaget and Kohlberg ignore the moral importance of interpersonal relationships. She argues that up to one-third of women, but virtually no men, define moral responsibility in terms of caring relationships (*see* ETHICS OF CARE)..

Care reasoning has three levels. Women move to later levels because later levels are better for resolving problems. In the *first level* of care reasoning, right actions promote one's own interests, but self-interest is understood in terms of successful interpersonal relationships. As women become more empathetic and dependent on how others view them, they move to the *second level* of care reasoning, in which right actions promote the good of others, as dictated by conventional expectations. These expectations can lead women to neglect themselves, making them unable to serve the interests of others. If women perceive this conflict, they move to the *third level* of moral reasoning, in which right actions nurture all people and relationships as much as possible. Level three balances caring for oneself with caring for others.

Although the view that only women use care reasoning is widely disputed, many now accept that these two kinds of reasoning exist. The nature of these two types of reasoning and their relationships to each other and to gender is far from settled.

Implications for Business

Since we use moral reasoning to evaluate and understand relationships and conflicts, it occurs in all aspects of life, including business. The issue, then, is not whether ethics has a role in business decision-making, but what that role is. *Descriptively*, we can ask "What kind(s) of moral reasoning do people use in business?" *Normatively*, we can ask "What kind(s) of moral reasoning should people use in business?" Moral development theory can help us answer the first question by giving us research categories and procedures; it is less helpful in

answering the normative question, except insofar as it can help us design effective reasoning strategies (*see* PRACTICAL REASONING).

Bibliography

Dienhart, J. (1992). *A Cognitive Approach to the Ethics of Counseling Psychology*. Lanham, Md.: University Press of America. (An assessment of rational and non-rational theories of moral acquisition).

Duska, R. and M. Whelan. (1975). *Moral Development: A Guide to Piaget and Kohlberg*. New York: Paulist Press. (An excellent introduction to moral development).

Gilligan, C. (1977). Conception of the self and of morality. *Harvard Educational Review*, 47, (4), 481–517.

Gilligan, C. (1992). *In a Different Voice*. Cambridge, Mass.: Harvard University Press. (Gilligan's major work).

Gilligan, C., Ward, J. V., & Taylor, J. M. (eds) (1988). *Mapping the Moral Domain*. Cambridge, Mass.: Harvard University Press.

Friedman, M. (1987). Beyond caring: The demoralization of gender. In Hanen, M. & Nielsen, K. (eds), *Science, Morality and Feminist Theory*. Calgary, Alta.: University of Calgary Press, 87–110. (An insightful discussion of how care and rights reasoning fit together).

Kohlberg, L. (1981). *Essays on Moral Development vol.1: The Philosophy of Moral Development;* and (1984). vol. 2: *The Psychology of Moral Development*. San Francisco: Harper and Row.

Piaget, J. (1965). *The Moral Judgment of the Child*. New York: The Free Press (first published in 1932).

JOHN W. DIENHART

moral dilemmas   are situations where moral requirements conflict, and *neither* requirement is *overridden*. Different people have very different kinds of situations in mind when they talk about moral dilemmas. If a contractor could gain a large profit by deceiving a customer, some might call this a moral dilemma, even if the moral factors all fall on one side and conflict only with self-interest. Similarly, conflicts between morality and law or religion are sometimes called "moral dilemmas."

People even talk about moral dilemmas when it is *not clear* whether morality is relevant at all. A manufacturer, for example, might be said to be in a moral dilemma if she suspects but does not know that a certain customer is using her products in harmful and illegal ways. What makes this a moral dilemma is that it is hard to tell whether there are moral reasons against selling to this customer.

Moral philosophers have recently discussed a narrower set of situations as moral dilemmas. They usually define moral dilemmas as situations where an agent morally *ought* to do each of two (or more) acts but cannot do both (or all). However, it often seems that one ought to do something (such as give to a certain charity) that one is not morally required to do. The most common examples of moral dilemmas include moral obligations or requirements, so it is natural to limit "moral dilemmas" to situations where an agent cannot fulfill all applicable moral *requirements*.

Some philosophers refuse to call a situation a moral dilemma when one of the conflicting requirements is clearly stronger, such as when one must break a trivial promise to avoid a serious harm. To exclude such resolvable conflicts, "moral dilemmas" can be defined, as in the original, formal definition, to include all and only situations where an agent cannot fulfill all applicable *non-overridden* moral requirements.

It is also common to define moral dilemmas as situations where every alternative is morally *wrong*. This is equivalent to the two previous definitions if an act is morally wrong exactly when it violates a moral requirement or a non-overridden moral requirement. However, we usually do not call an act "wrong" unless it violates an overriding moral requirement. Then the definition in terms of "wrong" makes moral dilemmas impossible, since overriding moral requirements cannot conflict. So it is preferable to define moral dilemmas in terms of non-overridden moral requirements.

Some would object that this definition includes trivial requirements and conflicts, so one might require that the conflicting moral requirements to be *strong*. One also might want to add that the agent must be *aware* of the moral requirements and must be *able* to satisfy each by itself. But such additions will not affect the basic logical issues about whether it is possible for moral requirements to conflict without resolution.

Bibliography

Gowans, C. W. (Ed.), (1987). *Moral Dilemmas*. New York and Oxford: Oxford University Press.

Gowans, C. W. (1994). *Innocence Lost: An Examination of Inescapable Wrongdoing*. New York and Oxford: Oxford University Press.

Morton, A. (1991). *Disasters and Dilemmas: Strategies for Real-Life Decision Making*. Oxford, UK and Cambridge, Mass.: Blackwell.

Sinnott-Armstrong, W. (1988). *Moral Dilemmas*. Oxford, UK and Cambridge, Mass.: Blackwell.

WALTER SINNOTT-ARMSTRONG

moral hazard Moral hazard is a term originally developed in the insurance industry, which now has broad application to many contracting (principal–agent) situations. Moral hazard is the risks or costs ("hazard") that an agent bears (i.e., an insurer) when individuals change their behavior in light of the *purchase* of insurance. Some have referred to moral hazard as "post-contractual opportunism" (Milgrom & Roberts, 1992). Consider an insurance-related example of moral hazard where a world-renowned pianist purchases insurance to protect against the loss in earnings if his/her hands are injured. Prior to the purchase of insurance, the pianist self-insures against the loss of earnings by avoiding activities that could cause harm to his/her hands. Purchasing the insurance, however, shifts the risk of lost earnings from the pianist to the insurer, thereby reducing the pianist's incentives to avoid harmful activities. Hence, the insurer is at risk (and future claims may be higher) because an individual is now more likely to engage in harmful activities he/she previously avoided. If an insurer could "costlessly" monitor individuals to anticipate the changes in behavior, moral hazard could be eliminated. Consequently, moral hazard results from the inability of agents to costlessly write and enforce contracts that cover all eventualities.

The term moral hazard has now broadened to include situations beyond the direct purchase of insurance. In some cases, the extension of the principle is as simple as seeing the equivalence between certain activities and the purchase of insurance. For example, some studies show that individuals who use their seatbelt tend to drive faster than those who do not. Because fastening a seatbelt reduces the possibility of being seriously injured or killed in an accident, individuals may change their behavior and drive faster. In an individual's mind the act of fastening a seatbelt may be the equivalent of purchasing insurance, and, consequently, any ensuing movement toward riskier driving habits exposes the car insurance company to moral hazard.

Moral hazard can also arise in the context of corporate control transactions. In the 1980s concerns were raised that LEVERAGED BUYOUT (LBO) transactions were motivated by shareholders' attempts to expropriate bondholder wealth. In some of these transactions, pre-LBO bondholders lent to the firm on terms that did not foresee all of the consequences of the LBO. The pre-LBO bond indenture attempted to "insure" the conditions of debt repayment. However, the covenants may not have been sufficient to prevent the loss in value of pre-LBO debt claims once the large amount and type of LBO debt was issued. Thus, pre-LBO bondholders are subject to moral hazard through the potential for opportunistic behavior by shareholders in raising the LBO debt.

Bibliography

Milgrom, P. and Roberts, J. (1992). *Economics: Organization and Management*. Englewood Cliffs, NJ: Prentice-Hall.

SUSAN CHAPLINSKY

moral imperatives Moral imperatives are moral commands or prescriptions. They tell us what we morally must do or not do, e.g. "Keep promises," "Do not punish the innocent." Moral imperatives also tell us what we morally should be or not be, or what character traits we should have or not have, e.g. "Be an honest person," "Do not be a malicious person." Acts that are commanded by moral imperatives are morally right. Those forbidden by moral imperatives are morally wrong (*see* ETHICS). Character traits prescribed by moral imperatives are virtuous, while those forbidden by moral imperatives are vicious (*see* VIRTUE ETHICS).

The "must" or "necessity" of moral imperatives can be defined by permissibility, or what may or may not be done. If it is morally imperative that I act (i.e. I am obligated to act), then I am not permitted to refrain from acting. If it is morally imperative that I not act, then I am not permitted to do the act. Morally right acts are those acts that I am not permitted to

refrain from doing. Morally wrong acts are those acts that I am not permitted to do. Morally permissible acts are those acts that I may or may not do and are therefore morally allowable. The moral imperative "Honor your contracts" says that I am not permitted to ignore or break my contractual obligations on a whim. If I violate the must of this moral imperative by breaking the contract, I am doing a wrong act.

How are moral imperatives justified? How does one determine which imperatives to follow? Moral theorists are in disagreement as to the justification of moral imperatives. Some theorists view God as justification. On this approach, morally right and wrong acts are those that God commands and forbids respectively, e.g. "Honor thy father and thy mother," "Thou shalt not steal." (*see* RELIGION AND BUSINESS ETHICS). Other theorists regard the use of unaided human reason as justification for moral obligation. On this approach, what is morally obligatory or necessary is what is reasonable or what can be applied consistently to all moral agents. Thus, I am not permitted to do what cannot be done by everyone (*see* KANTIAN ETHICS). Breaking promises cannot apply to all moral agents because present and future agents would no longer accept promises if they had all been broken in the past. Still other theorists attempt to justify moral imperatives by appealing to the culture from which they arise. This position is a version of moral relativism (*see* RELATIVISM, CULTURAL AND MORAL). In this approach, the only justification for moral imperatives is their use in their culture of origin. Moral imperatives, then, are relative to culture in their range of application. This means that a culture's imperatives cannot apply to any other culture. Thus, cultures may like or dislike the practices of other cultures, but they cannot morally praise or condemn those practices.

Some theorists have defended a version of moral relativism as the appropriate moral theory for business. Albert Carr (1968) defends this version of moral relativism by use of an analogy between the context of business and the game of poker. For Carr, the ethics of business are best viewed as rules of accepted strategy like those in poker and which differ from the ethics of "civilized human relationships," so bluffing is accepted in poker as well as business. Thus, in

Carr's view, "Tell the truth" may be an imperative in some contexts, but it does not apply to the game of business or poker.

Are moral imperatives always absolute? Are there exceptions? Is their moral force ever conditional? Kant distinguished hypothetical from categorical imperatives. The must or necessity of hypothetical imperatives is conditional or dependent upon a want or desire. The ought in the imperative "If I want the reward, then I ought to tell the truth" is dependent upon wanting the reward. Categorical imperatives are those whose ought is not dependent upon having a want or desire, e.g. "Always tell the truth." Kant thought that only categorical imperatives were moral. Some philosophers disagree with Kant and argue that moral imperatives are hypothetical (see Foot, 1972). In this view, it is the way moral imperatives are taught that gives them their categorical character rather than anything about morality *per se*.

Philosophers wanting to avoid hypothetical imperatives, while seeing the necessity for allowing exceptions to moral imperatives, came to view them as *prima facie* (see Ross, 1930). This means that, all things being equal, we should follow the imperative. But where there is a conflict of imperatives in a particular situation, one will override the other (*see* DUTY). This is decided by assessing the strength of the competing imperatives. The imperative that we determine as obligatory in a particular situation is our actual duty. Most moral theorists view moral imperatives as *prima facie* in order to resolve situations where moral imperatives conflict.

Are moral imperatives really imperatives? Some philosophers have argued that the correct way to view moral imperatives is to see them as either descriptions of likes or dislikes of the speaker, or as expressions of emotion. On the first approach, called subjectivism, the moral imperative "Tell the truth" really means "I (the speaker) like or approve of truth telling." On the second approach, called emotivism, the moral imperative "Tell the truth" means "Hooray for the truth." Philosophers that defend these positions believe that we are mistaken to think that there is really anything imperative about moral statements (*see* TRUTHTELLING).

Thus, moral imperatives have several interpretations when attempts are made to justify them. They include appealing to God, reason, and culture. There are also different interpretations of the strength and structure of moral imperatives. They are seen as categorical, hypothetical, *prima facie*, and as statements of individual approval or expression. Competing arguments are made and seem sound for each of these, but such is the nature of most topics in philosophy.

Bibliography

Carr, A. Z. (1968). Is business bluffing ethical? *Harvard Business Review*, **46**, 145–53.

Foot, P. (1972). Morality as a system of hypothetical imperatives. *Philosophical Review*, **84**, 305–16.

Frankena, W. K. (1973). *Ethics*, 2nd edn. Englewood Cliffs, NJ: Prentice-Hall.

Rachels, J. (1993). *The Elements of Moral Philosophy*, 2nd edn. New York: McGraw-Hill.

Ross, W. D. (1930). *The Right and the Good*. New York: Oxford University Press.

ROBERT T. SWEET

moral mazes The metaphor "moral mazes" refers simultaneously to the labyrinthine structure of large bureaucratic organizations and to the ethical quandaries that such organizations regularly create for men and women who work in them.

Bureaucracies not only rationalize work, but behavior and attitudes as well. Though each organization has its own constructed "institutional logic," and its own ethical standards, bureaucracies, whether public or private, share certain structural features that shape the moral ethos of big organizations. Typically, bureaucracies require and create patterns of predictable routine, impersonal rules and procedures, and patterns of delimited authority in order to maximize organizational efficiency. In the process, bureaucracies bring together people who have little in common with each other except the impersonal rules that govern their behavior. Since these rules are not given but made, they vary widely not only between different organizations, but even within the same organization, depending on who has the authority and power to make the rules. Moreover, authority and power shift in organizations, depending on changes in the markets or external exigencies that determine organizational frameworks and fates.

Bureaucracies place powerful premiums on certain behavior, and reward those able to discern those premiums and behave accordingly. Both the premiums themselves and conformance to them are ambiguous because they are constantly subject to peers' and superiors' interpretations, making compulsive sociability in an attempt to discern and shape those interpretations an occupational virtue. Though specific premiums and requisite conformance to them vary considerably depending on the nature and purpose of particular bureaucracies and on organizational leadership, all bureaucracies require varying degrees of self-rationalization of their members. Voluntary self-rationalization produces the deepest internalization of organizational goals, creating relatively enclosed social worlds that cause people to bracket moralities to which they might adhere in their homes, churches, or other social settings. Occupational rules-in-use gain ascendancy over more general ethical standards. Moral choices become inextricably tied to organizational fates.

Within such a context, bureaucracies typically separate men and women from the human consequences of their actions. For instance, top managers rarely meet workers fired because of their decisions; they rarely visit communities devastated economically because of their reallocation of resources; they rarely encounter consumers inadvertently injured by their companies' products; they rarely meet specific men or women who have become "cases" under procedures they have authorized. Such insulation heightens rational decision-making according to the impersonal criteria at the core of every modern bureaucracy, even as it makes notions such as the "ethics of brotherhood" irrelevant. Further, despite claims to the contrary, bureaucracies also separate people from internal accountability for their actions. Bureaucratic hierarchies generally encourage superiors' usurpation of credit for the work of subordinates. Moreover, few bureaucracies have formal tracking systems to allot blame for mistakes; men and women who are upwardly mobile can outrun their mistakes, leaving others to bear blame for them. At the upper levels of organizations, among men and women of proven and relatively equal abilities, the allocation of credit and blame, and corresponding success and failure, is thus very often experienced as arbitrary, indeed capricious. In short, big organizations often seem to be vast systems of organized irresponsibility – even, perhaps especially, to those within them.

Organizational leaders can attempt to impose standards of moral evaluation and practical moral reasoning to guide their charges' actions. But since there is no necessary connection between the good of a particular individual, the good of an organization, and the common good, every set of standards that leaders might assert is arbitrary to some extent and subject to constant negotiation and reinterpretation by competing organizational interests. Leaders can impose certain standards by dint of effort and authority and sometimes those standards become deeply institutionalized in a particular organization. Typically, however, standards last only as long as leaders themselves do. When looking up provides little direction, men and women in large organizations look around. They turn to each other for moral cues for behavior and come to fashion specific situational moralities for specific significant others in their world. As it happens, the guidance that they receive from each other is as profoundly ambiguous as the social structure of big organizations. Moral rules-in-use for all issues become indistinguishable from the rules for achieving success or avoiding failure. Ethical issues often get translated into problems of public relations. Men and women in large organizations thus often find themselves caught in an intricate set of moral mazes, unable even to discern the terms of their quandaries, let alone a way out of the thicket.

Bibliography

Bensman, J. (1983). *Dollars and Sense: Ideology, Ethics, and the Meaning of Work in Profit and Nonprofit Organizations*. New York: Schocken Books, rev. edn.

Jackall, R. (1988). *Moral Mazes: The World of Corporate Managers*. New York: Oxford University Press.

Weber, M. (1946). Religious rejections of the world and their directions. In *From Max Weber*, trans., ed., and with an intro. by H. H. Gerth and C. Wright Mills. New York: Oxford University Press.

ROBERT JACKALL

moral projection, principle of is formulated as follows: "It is appropriate not only to describe organizations (and their characteristics) by analogy with individuals, it is also appropriate normatively to look for and to foster moral attributes in organizations by analogy with those we look for and foster in individuals" (Goodpaster, 1982). The intuitive idea is straightforward: to explore the analogy between persons and organizations to determine whether and how it might guide descriptive and normative ethical thinking about either.

Critics of the principle of moral projection (Ranken, 1987) have argued that the analogy between persons and organizations is not only imperfect in certain respects, but dangerous in that it could have the effect of reducing needed attention to individual responsibility in corporate settings. Defenders reply that affirming corporate responsibility is not inconsistent with affirming individual responsibility as well in situations where both apply.

Put in its simplest terms, the principle of moral projection states that we can and should expect no more and no less of our institutions (taken as moral units) than we expect of ourselves (as individuals). In particular, moral responsibility is an attribute that we should look for and try to foster in individuals. The principle of moral projection, therefore, invites us to explore the analogues of moral responsibility for organizations. "Corporate responsibility" could then be seen as the moral projection of the idea of responsibility in its ordinary (individual) meaning, viz. perception, reasoning, and action rooted in a basic concern for stakeholders (Stone, 1976, p. 114).

See also **moral status of corporations**

Bibliography

Goodpaster, K. E. (1982). The concept of corporate responsibility. *Journal of Business Ethics*, **2**, (An earlier formulation appears in Goodpaster & Matthews (1982). Can a corporation have a conscience? *Harvard Business Review*, Jan.–Feb).

Ranken, N. (1987). Corporations as persons: Objections to goodpaster's "principle of moral projection." *Journal of Business Ethics*, **6**, (8), 633–7. (Also see Goodpaster (1987). The principle of moral projection: A reply to professor ranken *Journal of Business Ethics*, **6**, (4), 329–32).

Stone, C. (1976). *Where the Law Ends: The Social Control of Corporate Behavior*. New York: Harper & Row, 1975.

KENNETH E. GOODPASTER

moral realism Ethical theories of moral realism assert the objective reality of moral facts about good and evil and right and wrong. According to moral realists, moral facts, being objective, exist regardless of whether or not human beings believe that they do. An act may be wrong even though no one thinks that it is in the same way that the earth is round regardless of our beliefs about it. Likewise, objective moral facts are independent of how people feel about moral issues or what attitudes or emotions they have regarding them. The fact, for example, that a certain form of behavior offends the members of a community has no bearing on whether this behavior is wrong. Moral realism stands in opposition to any theory claiming that morality amounts to the expression of subjective states of feeling or emotion, and in opposition to any theory maintaining that morality is relative to the beliefs and customs of people. For realists, moral facts are as real as any facts in the world, scientific or otherwise.

It is only recently that the term "moral realism" has come into vogue – to describe ethical theories of realism developed in the United States and Britain during the 1970s, 1980s, and 1990s. Realist theories of morality, however, have appeared throughout the history of Western philosophy. Theories of moral realism, past and present, differ greatly in the way they describe the specific nature of moral facts. They also differ in their views about the manner in which one has knowledge of these facts. We shall consider several realist theories of morality and examine their claims about both the ontological status of moral facts (what they are) and their epistemological status (how they are known).

The first great moral realist was the ancient Greek philosopher Plato (427–347 BC). Plato believed that there are independent and ideal standards (what he called *forms*) of such things as goodness and justice, and he claimed that these standards or forms are eternal and unchanging. He placed them in a non-physical world where they have reality outside of space and time. People, actions, and governments are good or just (or virtuous in other ways) insofar as they reflect or copy the form of goodness or justice (or the form of some other virtue). But good people and just governments are never to be confused with goodness and justice themselves. For one thing, neither perfect goodness nor justice exists in the spatio-temporal world of actual people and governments – the ideal forms are never copied exactly. For another, although good people and just governments come and go – emerge, change, and suffer deterioration – goodness and justice in their ideal nature never change.

For Plato, it is through the exercise of a faculty of *reason* that we apprehend the moral forms. We do not observe them with one or more of our five senses; our senses only put us in contact with spatio-temporal things. Just as a geometer is able to use reason to grasp the nature of the true triangle (the form of a triangle, whose sides are perfectly straight lines unlike the ever-so-slightly wavy ones we encounter in experience), so a person who has rational insight into the nature of goodness, justice, and other virtues possesses moral knowledge.

ARISTOTLE (384–322 BC) denied that moral forms exist in a non-physical realm. They are, rather, the structures or essences of actual persons, states, or events. While reason is still needed to grasp them, perception is also needed. One grasps the nature of a virtue by apprehending through reason the essential nature of the virtuous individuals and character traits presented to us in experience. For Aristotle, the "good for man" is essentially happiness, and happiness in turn is essentially virtuous activity in accordance with reason. What happiness is is an objective matter; it is *not* what makes one feel good or a matter of one's attitudes about human life.

In the history of ethics following Aristotle, we find moral realists asserting a number of other theories about the specific nature of goodness, justice, and the like. Some, for instance, claim that morality consists of facts about what is conducive to human survival; others point in the direction of facts about human freedom; and still others insist that morality is a matter of acting in accordance with a universal law of nature, God, or reason. Some moral realists attempt to provide a general theory showing what moral facts have in common (e.g., their evolutionary advantage); others are pluralistic in perspective and deny that moral facts have some general nature in common.

After a period in recent intellectual history in which philosophers favored subjectivist and relativist theories, moral realism has reappeared and asserted itself vigorously. There are two varieties of current moral realism, one developed primarily in Great Britain and the other in the United States. The former is "intuitionist moral realism," the latter "scientific moral realism" (*see* RELATIVISM, CULTURAL AND MORAL).

The British variety is pluralistic in nature. According to it, there are many different kinds of moral facts – facts, for instance, about a person being kind, courageous, just, or generous; or, negatively, cruel, unjust, or cowardly. In ordinary life we make a great variety of moral distinctions among people and forms of behavior, and in describing them in terms of these distinctions we frequently get things right: as a matter of fact, some people *are* kind, others *are* cruel. These moral features are no less objective than the features of height and weight. Furthermore, a moral person, one who is attuned to the moral dimensions of the world, can detect these moral features with a perception-like intuitive capacity. One can directly "see," for instance, that children torturing a dog are acting cruelly; one can immediately "observe" the kindness of a gesture. Moral awareness, like all perception, can be dulled or blinded by a number of factors – self-interest and intense desire often prevent us from seeing the facts as they are. But with attention and care, we are often able to attain knowledge of moral facts about people and situations.

The American variety of moral realism has a more scientific and theoretical conception of moral facts and moral knowledge. First of all, moral facts must be understood naturalistically: any change in the moral nature of things reflects a change in their physical features. Thus moral features are said to *supervene* on natural features. Second, just as a scientist posits the reality of entities like subatomic particles – entities no scientist has directly observed – in order to explain phenomena that can be observed, so in the moral realm we must posit unobservable moral features and facts in order to explain our everyday moral experience. If we say that Hitler behaved as he did (e.g., advocated genocide) because he was morally depraved, we posit a form of immoral character that explains Hitler's actions. Moral knowledge is achieved by putting forth a moral hypothesis – by positing a moral cause – that provides the best explanation of events within our experience. Thus the form of moral knowledge is the same as that of scientific knowledge.

Bibliography

Aristotle. (1985). *Nichomachean Ethics*, trans. T. Irwin. Indianapolis, Ind.: Hackett.

Arrington, R. L. (1989). *Rationalism, Realism, and Relativism*. Ithaca: Cornell University Press.

Brink, D. O. (1988). *Moral Realism and the Foundations of Ethics*. Cambridge: Cambridge University Press.

Lovibond, S. (1983). *Realism and Imagination in Ethics*. Oxford: Blackwell.

McNaughton, D. (1988). *Moral Vision*. Oxford: Blackwell.

Plato. *The Republic*. Many editions currently are available.

Platts, M. (1979). *Ways of Meaning*. London: Routledge and Kegan Paul, ch. 10.

Sayre-McCord, G. (Ed.), . (1988). *Essays on Moral Realism*. Ithaca: Cornell University Press.

ROBERT L. ARRINGTON

moral reasoning   A process or form of thinking by which humans arrive at judgments about moral standards and the evaluation of behavior, persons, institutions, or policies as measured by these standards.

The traditional concern of moral reasoning has been to rationalize the moral life, to establish clear normative directives and clear standards of rational justification for guiding and evaluating the moral life. Traditionally, some moral judgments are taken as basic, while others are derivative, though controversy arises concerning the issue of which kinds of judgments are basic and which are derivative. For example, deontologists, such as Kant, hold that judgments about what is right are basic, and judgments about what is good are derivative, while teleologists or consequentialists, such as

Mill, generally hold that what is good is basic and what is right is derivative (*see* KANTIAN ETHICS; CONSEQUENTIALISM; MILL, JOHN STUART).

There is also disagreement about the way in which moral reasoning takes place and what kind of moral reasoning is actually involved in arriving at basic moral decisions. For example, Mill's utilitarian approach involves rational calculation of sensible consequences, consequences which must focus on taking account of the good of the whole rather than the good of individuals *qua* individual (*see* UTILITARIANISM). Kant's position is based on the rational grasp of a first moral principle, which he calls the "categorical imperative," that there are certain rights and duties to which all humans, as humans, have claim. The practical work of reason then consists in enabling us to work out the dictates of reason which tell us how to act, operating solely on reverence for the law. Our moral reasoning is guided by duty to the law, not by fulfillment of desire.

Sometimes the basic moral percepts by which one reasons to moral conclusions are concerned not with utilitarian consequences or what is good for the group as a whole, or Kantian rights and duties of individuals, but on what is just or fair. Rawls' position on justice is the most widely discussed today (*see* RAWLS, JOHN). His method of reasoning consists in determining what principles a group of rational, self-interested individuals would choose to live by if they knew they were to live in a society which utilized those principles, but knew also that they must choose these principles through a "veil of ignorance" in which none of them yet knew what role or place any of them would have within that society, such as race, station in life, etc. Our moral convictions or intuitions must then be placed in a coherent whole, and once the system is established, its principles are unconditional. Rawls thus develops a theory in which detached rationality provides the measure for justice and for all moral principles. In this type of development, all rational beings will come to embrace the same basic principles.

It can be seen that in these three examples, which are those most widely applied in understanding moral reasoning, its function is to rationalize and provide clear standards of rational justification for directives by which to live the moral life and evaluate the moral life of other individuals, institutions, and practices. Further, in all of these instances, it is presumed that if people use reason to approach moral problems, and avoid the mistake of letting emotion, desires, or personal interests get in the way, they will arrive at the same position concerning moral principles and judgments. There is the common assumption that people are essentially rational beings who have the possibility of reasoning their way to universally acceptable moral standards. In this way, the tradition attempts, through different avenues, to provide rational legitimacy for moral claims. Morality is in some sense postulated in moral rules and moral reasoning is by and large the application of the rule to the particular case. Moral reasoning thus works itself downward from first principles to specific cases which fall under the rule either directly or through intermediate steps of reasoning. It can be seen also that all of the above examples involve reasoning toward fixed ends in some sense. Further, while Mill's position stresses the good of the whole, Kant's position stresses the moral autonomy of the individual, and Rawls' position the self-interest driven principles of abstract justice, they all begin with the assumption that individuals are atomic or discrete units isolatable from the social contexts in which they develop. The paradigm is that of discrete events obeying universal laws. And, they all use moral reasoning to transcend individual desires, interests, or inclinations.

VIRTUE ETHICS, the most famous example of which is ARISTOTLE's position, is sometimes thought to exclude moral reasoning, since virtue ethics is concerned with the cultivation of virtuous traits of character as among the primary functions of morality. A virtue is a state or disposition to act in a certain way, and moral virtue is promoted by regular practice, which provides the inculcation of dispositions or habits. In insisting on a state, rather than a pattern of behavior, Aristotle shows that he is concerned with virtues as something more than means to virtuous action. Actions may be virtuous even though they are not done for the virtuous person's reasons. But agents are not virtuous unless they do the virtuous action because they have decided to do it for its own sake. For example, people who act solely from a sense of duty can very grudgingly fulfill moral obligations. An ethics based on virtues depends on an evaluation of selected traits of character and is very different from one based on principles or statements of what ought to be done. But moral reasoning plays an important role. Indeed, since a human being is essentially a rational agent, the essential activity of a human being, according to Aristotle, is a life guided by practical reason.

Moral virtue, which is promoted by regular practice, involves following a mean course between extremes. But action is not virtuous because it follows a mean course – it is virtuous because it is in conformity with reason, and as a result it will in fact involve a mean. Virtue of character is inseparable from virtue of intellect.

Practical wisdom discovers what is right in action and makes it possible for desire to conform to reason by discovering ends and then relating means to ends. For Aristotle, moral reasoning is a form of practical reasoning which involves a type of syllogism called the practical syllogism. The conclusions of such practical syllogisms are not propositions but dispositions. The conclusion is not a proposition stating what I ought to do, but an intention to do something. But the ultimate end, living well, is not a matter of deliberation or choice but rather is something given in the nature of the human *qua* human. Humans tend to realize a pre-given teleology. There is a pre-ordained end determining the continuity of character or dispositions. The good for humans is the fulfillment of their function.

More recent variations of virtue ethics have distanced themselves from the particulars of Aristotelian teleology, but they all depend on an assessment of selected traits of character as opposed to principles or statements of what ought to be done. All those who hold to the primacy of virtue ethics believe that morality is not obedience to abstract moral principles but rather morality is the expression of a virtuous character internal to the dispositions of an individual and needing no external rules specifying what ought to be done. Correct choices that are made out of a sense of duty do not necessarily indicate that a person is virtuous. We might judge their acts to be good, but not their character. In virtue ethics, moral ideals are directed toward the kind of person it is commendable to become, but they do not indicate what one ought to do in particular circumstances. What is judged moral is the character and the intentions from which an act flows, not specific actions and their empirical consequences or their conformity to "the moral law" grasped by reason.

Each of the above ways of providing a moral evaluation of actions, persons, institutions, or situations is held by its proponents to be absolute and applicable to the full range of problems and issues which occur in moral experience. But more and more today it is being recognized that no one of them captures all the factors that must be taken into account in making moral decisions. Rather, sometimes the rules of Kant's position which emphasizes the autonomy of the individual should be put to use, and sometimes the utilitarian principles which stress the aggregate social welfare. Actions done with the best of intentions by virtuous people may nonetheless be misguided, and can only be so judged by something other than intentions. Further, the application of a moral rule to a specific case can be used by ill-intentioned individuals to justify all sorts of behavior which common sense judges to be immoral. Rules seem to judge intentions, yet bad intentions can misuse rules.

What is operative in this recent view that none of these moral positions can be taken as absolute is moral pluralism, the view that no single moral principle or overarching theory of what is right can be appropriately applied in all ethically problematic situations. There is no one unifying, monistic principle from which lesser principles can be derived. Different moral theories are possible depending upon which values or principles are included. Moral pluralism generally advocates two different approaches to moral reasoning: first, that each relevant principle be considered in every instance; or, second, that one principle be operative in one type of domain or sphere of interest, and another principle be operative in another type of domain or sphere of interest. The right act is the one which is subsumed under the proper balance of rules or principles. But, in none of these theories can there be guidance in deciding when to use a particular theory, for each theory is self-enclosed or absolute; no principle or rule can provide any

guidance for the moral reasoning that underlies the choice among the principles or rules. The basis for this choice, which now becomes the heart of moral reasoning, remains mysterious.

A position is emerging on the contemporary scene, called classical American pragmatism, and best represented by the philosophy of John Dewey, that attempts to provide a basis for moral reasoning as inherently pluralistic. It involves not a synthesis of existing theoretical alternatives but a radical reconstruction of the understanding of what it is to think morally. In place of the traditional understanding of moral reasoning as abstract and discursive it is now understood as concrete and imaginative. Moral reasoning as concrete is not working downward from rules to their applications, but working upward from concrete moral experience and decision-making toward guiding moral hypotheses. Moral reasoning as imagination is not to be understood in terms of classical philosophy which viewed it as the faculty of providing copies of sensible objects, or the romantic view of it as an arbitrary, quasi-irrational power of creating the totally new. Rather, for Deweyian pragmatism, rationality itself is imaginative, for imagination provides the capability of understanding what is actual in light of what it is possible to bring forth, of seeing conflicting fragments in light of a projected creative synthesis. Moral reasoning is not the inculcation of a past, either in terms of rules or dispositions. But, it is inherently historical, for moral reasoning involves a creative reorientation of the present toward the future in light of the past. It involves dealing with a changing world which manifests stabilities and possibilities to be utilized. It does not ignore the lessons of the past, or past relations between theory and data, but reinterprets, reappropriates them in light of an imaginative grasp of what might be based on possibilities operative in the present. One grasps a situation historically not just in terms of the past but in terms of the future.

Moral reasoning is not ultimately guided by fixed ends but rather it involves an ongoing process in which the means–end distinction becomes purely functional, for any chosen end is a means to something further, and any end chosen is value laden with the means with which it is intertwined. In this ongoing process rigorous dialectical criticism is replaced by the dynamics of experimental method. Our moral claims are about something that requires experimental integration: the emergence of concrete valuings of humans in their specific situational concrete interaction with their world. Just as scientific hypotheses emerge as ways of organizing the diversity of physical data and must be judged by their workability in organizing the data into an integrated, meaningful whole, so we create and utilize norms or ideals in the moral situation as working hypotheses by which to organize and integrate the diversity of concrete valuings. But where the scientist deals with abstractions, the moral realm is one of concrete situations, and what works is dependent upon the emergent but real domain of valuings which need integration and harmonizing. Workability cannot be understood in terms of one fixed end, but rather workability involves the enrichment of experience in its entirety.

In this view, moral reasoning involves an enrichment of the capacity to perceive moral dimensions of situations rather than a way of simplifying how to deal with what one does perceive. It involves sensitivity to the rich, complex, value ladenness of a situation, and to its interwoven and conflicting dimensions, the ability to utilize creative intelligence geared to the concrete situation, and an ongoing evaluation of the resolution. And, decisions which change a situation will give rise to new problems requiring new integrative solutions. One cannot just "put the problem to bed" and forget about it. The goal is not the most unequivocal decision, but the richest existence for those involved. In this process, we are often reconstructing moral rules. Principles are not directives to action but are rather suggestive of actions, are tools for getting hold of diverse strands operative in complex situations. Just as hypotheses in the technical experimental sciences are modified through ongoing testing, moral principles are hypotheses which require ongoing testing and allow for qualification and reconstruction.

Further, the individual and the community, on this view, are not isolatable entities, but rather they are inextricably interwoven. Given this inherent interrelatedness, neither individuals nor whole systems are the bearers of value. Rather value emerges in the interactions of individuals, and wholes gain their value through the interactions of individuals, while the value of individuals cannot be understood in isolation from the interrelationships which constitute their ongoing development. When we slide over the complexities of a problem, we can easily be convinced that categorical moral issues are at stake. And, the complexities of a problem are always context dependent.

Given this view, the resolution of conflicting moral perceptions cannot be resolved by appeal to abstract principles but through a deepening sensitivity to the demands of human valuings in their commonness and diversity. Such a deepening of course does not negate the use of intelligent inquiry, but rather opens it up, frees it from the products of its past in terms of rigidities and abstractions, and focuses it on the experience of value as it emerges within concrete human existence. This allows us to grasp different contexts, to take the perspective of "the other," to participate in dialogue with "the other." Morality is not postulated in moral rules but discovered in concrete moral experience. The vital, growing sense of moral rightness comes not from the indoctrination of abstract principles but from sensitivity to concrete situations. This pragmatic pluralism of course rules out absolutism in ethics. But what must be stressed is that it equally rules out subjectivism and relativism, for it is rooted in the conditions and demands of human living and the desire for meaningful, enriching lives. While the experience of value arises from specific, concrete contexts shaped by a particular tradition, this is not mere inculcation, for the deepening process offers the openness for breaking through and evaluating one's own stance.

Thinking morally is not merely applying rules of community interest, self-interest, universalizability and so on, to some specific act, nor is it acting according to some ultimate value, or to some set of ultimate values within which all others can be seen as subsets; rather, it is acting to bring about enriching growth within concrete situations. In this way growth is not mere accumulation but has an inherently moral and esthetic quality, for it involves the enrichment of human living. What is needed for moral reasoning is the development of the reorganizing and ordering capabilities of creative intelligence, the imaginative grasp of authentic possibilities, the vitality of motivation, and a deepened sensitivity to the sense of concrete human existence in its richness, diversity, and complexity. The importance of this latter cannot be over-stressed. As Dewey holds, a problem cannot be stated until it is felt. It is this "felt" dimension that regulates the way one selects, weighs, and conceptually orders what one observes. It is this which gives vitality to the diverse and changing abstract principles as working hypotheses embodied in concrete moral activity. Humans cannot assign priority to any one basic value, nor can their values be arranged in any rigid hierarchy, but they must live with the consequences of their actions within concrete situations in a process of change.

See also **Justice; Moral development; Moral dilemmas; Moral imperatives; Moral rules; Motives; Relativism, cultural and moral; Situation ethics; Values**

Bibliography

Aristotle. (1985). *Nicomachean Ethics,* trans. Terence Irwin. Indianapolis, Ind.: Hackett.

Dewey, J. (1983). *Human Nature and Conduct.* In *The Middle Works,* vol. 14, ed. Jo Ann Boydston. Carbondale: Southern Illinois University Press.

Dewey, J. (1990). *Logic: The Theory of Inquiry.* In *The Later Works,* vol. 12, ed. Jo Ann Boydston. Carbondale: Southern Illinois University Press.

Kant, I. (1959). *Foundations of the Metaphysics of Morals,* trans. W. W. Beck. New York: Library of Liberal Arts.

Rawls, John. (1971). *A Theory of Justice.* Cambridge, Mass.: Harvard University Press.

Rosenthal, S. (1986). *Speculative Pragmatism.* Amherst: University of Massachusetts Press, ch. 8.

Ryan, Alan. (1974). *John Stuart Mill.* London: Routledge and Kegan Paul, ch. 4.

Schneewind, J. B. (ed.) (1965). *Ethical Writings.* New York: Collier.

SANDRA B. ROSENTHAL

moral rules   Rules that everyone is required to obey unless they have some justification for not doing so. JOHN STUART MILL claimed that almost all philosophers accept the same moral rules even though "they differ as to their evidence, and the source from which they derive their authority" (1863, ch. 1, para. 3). In fact, not only most philosophers, but most people, regard such rules such as "Don't kill," "Don't cause pain," "Don't deceive," and "Keep your promise," as paradigm cases of moral rules. Mill also says "The moral rules which forbid mankind to hurt one another (in which we must never forget to include wrongful interference with each other's freedom) are more vital to human well-being than any maxims, however important, which only point out the best mode of managing some department of human affairs" (ch. 5, para. 3).

Mill seems to be right not only in claiming general agreement on the moral rules and their importance, but also in claiming that there is disagreement about the evidence for these rules and the source from which they derive their authority. Many claim divine authority for the moral rules, and use religious writings as evidence for them. The Ten Commandments are sometimes taken to be a list of moral rules. However, on the standard view of moral rules, it is quite clear that some of the Ten Commandments are not moral rules. Since no one can be required to obey a rule of which they are completely ignorant, the standard view entails that the moral rules be known to everyone. "Remember the Sabbath, to keep it holy," cannot be a moral rule, for some people have no idea that one day of the week is to be distinguished from all of the others; indeed, many do not even have the concept of a week.

There is also considerable disagreement on the way in which the moral rules are to be understood. Some have interpreted Kant as claiming that these rules can never be justifiably violated. Others have interpreted Mill as claiming that moral rules are merely well-established guidelines for promoting the general happiness, and may be justifiably violated whenever the general happiness would be better served by that particular violation. However, the most common understanding of these rules is that although they can sometimes be justifiably violated, they are more than simply guidelines for achieving some purpose.

It is generally recognized that there is some difference between those precepts which prohibit harming others and those enjoining one to help others, as shown by the often-made distinction between perfect and imperfect duties, or negative and positive duties. However, the significance of the distinction between those rules which prohibit harming others directly, e.g., rules prohibiting killing and causing pain, or indirectly, e.g., rules prohibiting deception and breaking promises, and those moral precepts which enjoin us to help others, has not been sufficiently appreciated. This distinction is sufficiently important to use the term "moral rules" to refer only to the prohibitions, and use a phrase like "moral ideals" to refer to the precepts enjoining us to help others.

Unlike moral ideals, everyone is morally required to obey the moral rules impartially. Everyone is morally prohibited from killing or deceiving anyone unless they would be willing for everyone to know that they are allowed to kill and deceive in the same circumstances, e.g., kill in self-defense and deceive to save the life of an innocent person. "Help the needy" and other moral ideals do not need to be followed impartially. It is morally acceptable to concentrate on helping the needy with whom one has some special relation, e.g., those in the same town where one has a business.

The reason for this is that rules prohibiting causing harm, directly or indirectly, can always be obeyed impartially, whereas ideals encouraging helping others cannot. When I obey the moral rule prohibiting deception, I do not deceive anyone and so I obey it with regard to all impartially. When I follow the moral ideal encouraging me to help the needy, I have to follow it with regard to some particular person or persons, I cannot follow it with regard to all needy people. This explains why the claim that morality requires impartiality is correct only when it is limited to a claim about following moral rules; impartiality is not required when following moral ideals.

Neglect of the distinction between moral rules and moral ideals, together with the view that morality requires impartiality, leads some to make bizarre claims about what morality requires, e.g., claiming that when two people's lives are in danger, my wife's and some stranger's, morality requires me to regard them impartially in deciding whom to rescue. Distinguishing between moral rules and moral ideals explains why accepting that one is not morally allowed to kill a stranger in order to save one's wife does not require accepting that one is not morally allowed to choose to rescue one's wife rather than a stranger.

Taking moral rules as general and universal rules, e.g., "Don't kill," and "Don't deceive," which prohibit doing those kinds of actions that everyone knows cause harm to others either directly or indirectly, allows one to account for most of what has been said about them. Such rules form the core of the kind of public morality that everyone would want taught to all members of a society, and to be enforced by the law.

Bibliography

Baier, K. (1965). *The Moral Point of View.* abridged edition. Ithaca, NY: Cornell University Press. New York: Random House.

Gert, B. (1988). *Morality.* New York: Oxford University Press. (See chs. 4, 6, and 7 on moral rules and their justification.)

Hennessey, J. W. Jr., & Gert, B. (1985). Moral rules and moral ideals: A useful distinction in business and professional practice. *Journal of Business Ethics,* 4, (2), 105–15.

Kant, I. (1785). *Grounding for the Metaphysics of Morals.* Numerous editions are available.

Mill, J. S. (1863) *Utilitarianism.*, esp. ch. 5, "On the Connection between Justice and Utility." Numerous editions are available.

Rawls, J. (1971). *A Theory of Justice.* Cambridge, Mass.: Harvard University Press.

Ross, Sir D. (1930). *The Right and the Good.* Oxford: Oxford University Press.

BERNARD GERT

moral status of corporations   The moral status of the corporation is dependent on the moral features of the corporation and dependent on the moral status of the members of the corporation. At the heart of the philosophical sub-field called business ethics are central questions of metaphysics, ethical theory, and social philosophy related to the status of the business corporation. Of chief concern are these questions: Is the corporation ontologically distinct from the individual persons who compose it? Does the corporation have responsibilities, and to whom? Does the corporation have moral rights and are they equivalent to those of individual humans? Does the regulation of corporations pose special moral problems?

Questions of ontology, responsibility, and rights have always been the proper purview of philosophy and so it is easy to understand why philosophers have gravitated recently to these questions in business ethics.

The moral status of the corporation is intimately linked with its metaphysical status, for only if the corporation is a distinct moral entity, specifically a moral agent, does the corporation have a distinct moral standing, separate from the entities (individual human persons) who make it up. Of course, the corporation could have an auxiliary or dependent moral status even if the corporation was not a moral agent. While this is in itself an important point, most of what follows will ignore this alternative. Instead, the focus will be on questions of agency, responsibility, and rights of a corporation *per se*.

The corporation exists, but what kind of existence is this? There are at least three ways to answer this question. First, the corporation may exist in the way that a "heap" exists, as merely the category which stands for the collection of entities which happen to compose it. Second, the corporation may exist as a "unity," where the form of the corporation (its organizational structure) is what renders it unique, but where the substance of the corporation is entirely made up of other things. Third, the corporation may exist somehow in its own right, as a formally and substantially "unique thing."

The question of whether the corporation is an agent can be addressed in a similar way to the question of whether the corporation exists. First, a corporation may be an agent in the sense that "corporate action" is merely a shorthand way to refer to how discrete individual human persons act. Second, a corporation may be an agent vicariously through the various actors who make up the corporation and who are facilitated in their actions by the corporation's organizational structure. Third, a corporation may be an agent in its own right, perhaps as much an actor as is the collection of body parts that make up a human actor. The law treats corporations as full-fledged legal persons that can act in their own right. This is commonly known as "the legal fiction of the corporate person," and hence it is not necessarily useful in determining whether the corporation is a moral person.

One way to approach the question of corporate agency is to ask whether the common-sense understanding of corporate actions can be reduced to individual human actions. In this context the corporation cannot really act on its own; only individual human persons can act. But it is very difficult to make sense completely of corporate actions, such as "Gulf Oil Company acquired XYZ Company," without referring to corporations, or to features of individual human persons. Of course, merely because it is hard to make these complete reductions does not yet tell us that corporate agents should be admitted into our moral universe. But until complete reductions are made, it is intelligible to think of corporations as moral agents.

If corporations are moral agents, what kind of agents are they? Corporations may be full-fledged moral agents or they may be partial or vicarious agents. In order to be full-fledged moral agents there must be some sense in which they can act in a morally significant way on their own. Following the model of individual human action, a locus of choice or intention must be found from which moral actions could issue. The corporate boardroom is the most obvious place to look for such choice or intention. Here the individual choices or intentions of the board members are transformed so that what emerges is a collective choice or intention. For the choices to be the choices of a full-fledged moral agent they must at least resemble the choices that a single human individual would make. But there is a wide diversity of viewpoints about what constitutes choice for a single human individual, and it is not clear what criteria must be satisfied for a collective choice to be ascribable to a corporation. Nonetheless, the more these choices and intentions resemble those cases of individual human choice or intention, the stronger the case for thinking that a corporation is a full-fledged moral agent.

Vicarious or secondary agency is a weaker form of corporate agency than full-fledged agency. One way to understand vicarious agency is in terms of individual humans who have been authorized to represent the corporation, thereby providing the corporation with a way in which it can act *through* the actions of these individuals. It is common to speak of an employee "acting within the scope of his or her authority." Such expressions belie a moral fact: that for certain previously established purposes, a given act can be given two descriptions. The act always remains primarily an act of a discrete individual human; and the act is secondarily (or vicariously) also an act of a corporation. Whenever authority has been so conveyed, then it is relatively easy to establish this weaker sense of moral agency on the part of a corporation.

Corporations may be morally responsible for harms in several different ways. Most obviously, if a person is harmed directly as a result of a corporate intentional decision, then the corporation is morally responsible for this harm. Responsibility may also apply to corporations for harms that result from negligence, recklessness, or simple omission. Such cases are more or less problematic, depending on the difficulty of telling whether the corporation's contribution to a harm was in some sense morally faulty. In Anglo-American law there are three main types of fault: intentional wrongdoing, negligence, and recklessness.

Corporations can engage in intentional wrongdoing and hence be morally responsible and blameworthy on this basis. It is rare that a corporation sets out to do wrong to a person in the same way that an individual agent might intend to do harm to another out of revenge or anger. The most obvious explanation for the rarity here is that corporations do not have any recognized way of displaying or feeling anger or revenge. The corporation can make decisions, and those decisions may be based on the emotional reactions of the members of the board of directors. Nonetheless, corporations could decide to harm a person especially if it would advance the interests of the corporations to do so. But normally the threat of adverse publicity will make this very unlikely. Far more common is that corporations decide to do things which will risk harm to persons so as to more expeditiously advance their interests.

Corporate negligence is the most common basis upon which corporate moral responsibility can be based. Negligence is the failure to display due care, that is, care which a reasonable person would take. Decision-making in the corporate domain is so focused on serving the goals of the charter, or the interests of investors, etc., that it is relatively common for corporations to fail to take into account the possible harms of their decisions. But for these failures to constitute

moral negligence, it must also be the case that reasonable people would have taken those possible harms into account. An interesting example concerned a decision by the Boeing Company to build their 727 line of aircraft so that all of the backup electrical systems were in the same part of the plane. In the event of an accident it was possible that all of the backup systems could be disabled at once, leaving the plane unmaneuverable and the passengers on the plane in great peril. Of course, no one at Boeing intended to harm anyone by making this decision. But it did seem unreasonable for them to have done this, given the risks of harm to their passengers. This is a fairly straightforward case of corporate moral negligence.

An example of corporate moral recklessness concerned a decision by the Ford Motor Company to place the gas tank on the Ford Pinto in a position so close to the back of the car that it could explode upon fairly low-speed collisions. What made this case one of recklessness was that key members of Ford's management knew of the problem and knew that it would cost very little to fix it, but decided to take the risk. Here a rare internal memorandum surfaced which indicated that Ford had actually calculated how many people were likely to die and how much Ford would be likely to lose in wrongful-death lawsuits, compared to how much it would cost to fix the Pintos so that it was far less likely the gas tanks would explode. This was judged in a court of law in Indiana to be reckless because of the decision to go ahead with a known risk that no reasonable person would inflict on the populace. The moral assessment would be similar.

In addition to the responsibilities to individual persons, corporations also have more broadly based social responsibilities. While it is controversial how extensive these responsibilities are, nearly everyone recognizes the responsibility that corporations have not to harm or risk harm to the larger society, by such acts as discriminatory hiring or polluting the water sources in a particular locale. MILTON FRIEDMAN, a well-known critic of most social responsibilities for corporations, has said that the chief social responsibility of business corporations is to make a profit. But even this view supports the general idea that there are various customs in each locale, concerning what are appropriate and inappropriate actions which affect the overall well-being of a society.

On the other side of the balance sheet from corporate moral responsibilities, are corporate moral rights. Corporate moral rights can be divided into commercial and non-commercial rights. Commercial rights generally concern rights to property, rights to profit, and generally rights to determine how the corporation is run. Non-commercial corporate rights concern such things as rights to free speech, and generally rights to exert influence in the public domain. The basis of rights can come from the moral agency of the corporation, or from the moral interests of the corporation. In either case, the ascription of moral rights to corporations is based on an analogy to the ascription of moral rights to persons.

Commercial rights of corporations are moral if they affect moral duties, liberties, privileges, or immunities. The property rights of corporations are moral rights if, for instance, they restrict the range of moral options that individuals or groups have in behaving toward that corporation. Property rights generally are rights to the exclusive (or nearly exclusive) ownership and use of a given thing. In most modern corporations, ownership and control are divided to the extent that, while the shareholders own the corporation, it is normally management (in a sense employed by the shareholders) which controls the activities of the corporation. The property rights of a modern corporation create moral options related to control for managers and moral options related to ownership for shareholders, but the divided nature of corporate property makes it often hard to tell who should be afforded what moral privilege or immunity.

Corporate rights to profit are even harder to ascertain morally. While it seems reasonable that corporations are morally entitled to keep whatever surplus value is generated from their production processes, things get cloudier when these profits are generated by windfalls or exploitative conditions. Indeed, the moral right to profit seems to virtually everyone to be limited based on how that profit was generated. The same could be said of all commercial corporate rights. Since commercial rights themselves are justified by their social productiveness, when the overall social effect is negative,

rights may be restricted as well. The corporation generally has the right to decide how it is run as long as its being run this way is not likely to be harmful to the overall social welfare.

Non-commercial rights of corporations derive their moral force from analogy with similar rights for individual humans. The Anglo-American legal tradition recognizes corporations as legal persons with very similar rights to other persons. Morally, to the extent that corporate agents resemble human agents, corporations will have a basis for rights to free speech similar to that which human persons have. But the problem with this strategy is that corporations are not the kind of agents whose voices necessarily add to the political process when they participate. Indeed, corporations have a history of drowning out the rest of the voices in a political debate. And these corporations are rarely the kind of agents who are vulnerable and hence in need of the kind of protection which free-speech rights afford. For these reasons, most corporations will not have the same, or as weighty, non-commercial rights as will individual humans.

Finally, corporations may be considered morally virtuous or morally evil, but from a more roundabout route. While a plausible case can be made for seeing corporations as limited agents, it is far harder to see them as having characters that can be morally assessed except in a very derivative form. But the leading members of a corporation may convey a character to a corporation by the way these members conduct themselves while acting on the behalf of the corporation. It is also possible for a succession of virtuous leading members of a corporation to convey good character to a corporation over many years. But should the moral characters of the leading members change, then so will the "character" of the corporation. The regulation of corporations does not pose the same sort of moral problems as it does for individual humans, except in limited cases of rights violation, since the lack of distinct moral character of the corporation means that there is no *prima facie* basis for respecting corporate autonomy.

Bibliography

Berle, A. A. & Means, G. C. (1933). *The Modern Corporation and Private Property.* New York: Macmillan.

Copp, D. (1979). Collective actions and secondary actions. *American Philosophical Quarterly,* **16,** 177–86.

De George, R. (1990). *Business Ethics,* 3rd edn. New York: Macmillan.

Donaldson, T. (1982). *Corporations and Morality.* Englewood Cliffs, NJ: Prentice-Hall.

French, P. A. (1984). *Collective and Corporate Responsibility.* New York: Columbia.

Fuller, L. L. (1967). *Legal Fictions.* Stanford, Calif.: Stanford University Press.

May, L. (1987). *The Morality of Groups.* Notre Dame, Ind.: Notre Dame University Press.

Soloman, R. C. (1992). *Ethics and Excellence: Cooperation and Integrity in Business.* New York: Oxford University Press.

Velasquez, M. (1983). Why corporations are not morally responsible for anything they do. *Business and Professional Ethics Journal,* **2,** 1–18.

Werhane, P. (1985). *Persons, Rights, and Corporations.* Englewood Cliffs, NJ: Prentice-Hall.

LARRY MAY

moral subjectivity The states of mind and capacities that structure moral perception and moral judgment constitute moral subjectivity. Relevant states of mind include cognitive states, emotional states, and behavioral dispositions. Traits of character, occurrent emotions, standing attitudes, moral convictions, factual beliefs, and interpersonal bonds are among the states of mind that shape moral perception and judgment. Relevant capacities include empathic skills, introspective skills, imaginative skills, interpretive skills, and reasoning skills. To understand morally significant situations, one must register others' needs, expectations, and hopes, and one must grasp one's own resources and values. To decide how to act, one must envisage alternative courses of action, anticipate the likely outcome of each, and assess the available options in light of moral considerations.

One's state of mind may facilitate insightful moral perception and sound moral judgment, or it may cloud perception and judgment. Likewise, the degree to which one's various capacities are developed and one's adeptness at summoning and coordinating one's skills have a tremendous impact on moral perception and moral judgment. Although there is no single formula for a desirable form of moral subjectivity, philosophers have sought to explicate some of the elements of moral subjectivity.

Reasoning skills and the structure of moral rationality have received a great deal of attention from philosophers. Kantians contend that moral principles must be universalizable; that is, it is wrong to act on a principle that one could not agree that everyone else should follow too (*see* KANTIAN ETHICS; UNIVERSALIZABILITY). Social contract theorists devise fair bargaining situations and speculate about what principles free and equal contractors would endorse (*see* SOCIAL CONTRACT THEORY). Utilitarians consider how individual happiness should be gauged and how predictions of individual happiness should be aggregated into calculations of expected social welfare (*see* UTILITARIANISM). Recently, this traditional inventory of rationalistic approaches to moral deliberation has been augmented by a more improvisational care-based approach. The ethic of care stresses the need to take responsibility for minimizing harm and exploitation and for maintaining relationships with particular others without betraying one's own needs and integrity (*see* ETHICS OF CARE).

Still, until one perceives a situation as requiring a moral response, and until one notices the morally significant features of a situation, deliberative skills have nothing to do. Thus, some philosophers focus on the prior question of moral perception (Blum, 1991). Some hold that cultures impart rules that identify morally salient features of experience and that individuals rely on them to construe situations (Herman, 1985). Others contend that emotional openness and attunement give people access to the moral dimensions of life (Nussbaum, 1990). What is clear from these discussions is that individuals enter situations endowed with cognitive and emotional templates through which they perceive the world and which structure their interpretations of interpersonal encounters, social relations, and institutional structures.

That moral perception is so structured raises the possibility that a person's preconceptions or emotional condition may block or distort moral perception. In particular, the dangers of prejudice come to the fore. For example, people often perceive women and members of minority groups through derogatory stereotypes, and these stereotypes are often cognitively and emotionally entrenched (Piper, 1990). As a result, people may regard unjust practices and policies as reasonable and fair, and they may refuse to credit the protests of individuals who suffer from these wrongs. Particularly when cultures implicitly perpetuate race, gender, and similar prejudices, and when these prejudices operate unconsciously, they are resistant to rational criticism and extremely difficult to overcome (see DISCRIMINATION IN EMPLOYMENT).

Prejudice and other obstacles to insightful moral perception and sound moral judgment have led some philosophers to inquire into the process of critical moral reflection. Some invoke epistemic virtues, such as objectivity, breadth, and depth (Kekes, 1989). Some advocate cognitive psychotherapy designed to correct errors of fact and iron out inconsistencies (Brandt, 1979). Others highlight the social dimensions of critical moral reflection. One theme is the role of consciousness-raising as a basis for developing emancipatory social theory (Young, 1990). Another theme is the importance of empathically listening to the voices of individuals from different social groups and imaginatively reconstructing their point of view (Meyers, 1994).

Moral subjectivity is devilishly complex, and it is seldom, if ever, morally unalloyed. Amalgamating morally equivocal and even objectionable beliefs, attitudes, and dispositions with morally admirable and humane ones, an individual's moral subjectivity is indebted to a cultural heritage that is likely to be enriching in some respects and troubling in others; it is conditioned by interpersonal ties of affection and trust, but also by personal enmities and group insularity; it is idiosyncratic in some ways and never altogether transparent. Yet, imperfect though it may be, moral subjectivity is the foundation of all moral thought. Only by cultivating the capacities and refining the states of mind that are constitutive of moral subjectivity can moral sensitivity be enhanced and sound moral judgment secured.

Bibliography

Blum, L. (1991). Moral perception and particularity. *Ethics,* **101**, 701–25.

Brandt, R. B. (1979). *A Theory of the Right and the Good.* Oxford: Clarendon Press.

Herman, B. (1985). The practice of moral judgment. *Journal of Philosophy,* **82**, 414–36.

Kekes, J. (1989). *Moral Tradition and Individuality.* Princeton: Princeton University Press.

Meyers, D. T. (1994). *Subjection and Subjectivity: Psychoanalytic Feminism and Moral Philosophy.* New York: Routledge.

Nussbaum, M. C. (1990). *Love's Knowledge.* New York: Oxford University Press.

Piper, A. M. S. (1990). Higher-order discrimination. In O. Flanagan & A. O. Rorty (eds), *Identity, Character, and Morality.* Cambridge, Mass.: MIT Press.

Young, I. M. (1990). *Justice and the Politics of Difference.* Princeton: Princeton University Press.

DIANA TIETJENS MEYERS

motives You have a motive for performing an act if and only if there is something to be said for it from your point of view. You have a motive for doing anything that is in your interest, though in some cases you may have a stronger motive for not doing something of that kind. Motives can be causes of behavior even though we sometimes identify them through the behavior they cause, and usually cannot identify the law-like regularities that link cause and effect.

Philosophers have long argued over whether one has any motivation to be moral. "Why should I be moral?" is a standard question in moral philosophy. Some philosophers who have posed it have thought moral behavior to be costly in itself – for example, to involve sacrifices and missed opportunities – and so to need some compensating justification. Religions have promised post-mortem rewards: some people have held that honesty and other virtues, for organizations as well as individuals, constitute the best policy. Game theorists have demonstrated that universally selfish behavior may make everyone in a community worse off than all would be if all were unselfish (see GAME THEORY).

One assumption common to nearly all the philosophers of the Western tradition, with ARISTOTLE as the most notable exception, is that narrow self-interest is the motive behind all or most intentional actions, and the most comprehensible reason for acting. Psychological egoism, the doctrine that all intentional actions are that way, can defend itself finally only by retreating into tautology. There is no good reason to deny that many acts are motivated by charity, concern for one's family and friends, patriotic sentiment, or compassion: in some instances it would be extraordinary for an agent to put personal convenience ahead of the chance to avert disaster for someone else.

Kant, much influenced by Christian pietism, suggests that moral action is a matter of goodness winning out over the agent's natural selfishness. Some of Kant's successors in business ethics have been read as arguing that moral action is necessarily unselfish, even if it must be opposed to one's own best interests – to put it crudely, that being moral must hurt (see KANTIAN ETHICS).

One's interests are in fact primary motivators; in the sense that they may encompass the prosperity of one's friends, the happiness of one's children, the success of one's organization or even one's favorite charity. For some people these are components of happiness. Aristotle states that the surest sign of character is what gives one pleasure: good people find pleasure in good deeds, bad ones in bad. The one who manages to resist temptations to be immoral is less praiseworthy and less reliable; the one who does the right thing in hope of some reward is worse yet. Worst is the agent for whom morality is no motivating consideration at all.

Among the philosophers who believe that morality can be a motive for acting are so-called internalists, who argue that an agent has no moral obligation to do anything that he or she has no motive for doing. One assumption that supports internalism is that moral obligation is something one may accept or not. Internalism suggests a contract theory of morality, but not all contract theorists are internalists. The more common view is externalism, according to which whether an act is morally good is a matter of whether it meets moral standards that are separate from (external to) the agent. Moral realism, the view that there are actual moral facts that our moral theories seek to state or explain, implies externalism, but not the other way around.

One of the abiding questions of ethics is whether a good act is necessarily done out of good motives, as opposed to selfish ones, for example. Consequentialists like Mill answer negatively, deontologists like Kant affirmatively. Kant goes so far as to claim that only the good will really counts in morality, and that one is not in the fullest sense responsible for the consequences of one's good intentions. Few moral philosophers and fewer managers would agree that it is enough to be well-meaning (see CONSEQUENTIALISM; MILL, JOHN STUART).

I may have a motive for an action and yet not do it. For example, I may find there is reason to fire an employee because of bad performance, but may refrain out of personal loyalty. Or I may fire the employee on account of both incompetence and dishonesty. A corporate decision to support a local charity may have multiple motives in a similar way. The two motives are then jointly sufficient conditions of the behavior, whether or not either by itself would suffice.

A manager who wants a moral organization might prefer that the employees do the right thing for the best possible reason, but would likely settle for one in which morally good behavior is the result of incentives carefully designed to motivate the selfish. To a manager who wants employees to be motivated by moral considerations a strong corporate culture is an attractive vehicle, for it can to some degree socialize employees to want to be honest, loyal, and so on – that is, to be people of good character in Aristotle's sense .

It is a largely empirical question whether and when an appropriate corporate culture is a more effective device for ensuring moral behavior than are the incentives of money and status. The former way well be more effective and the latter less so for large, diversified organizations in turbulent environments: for in these, position descriptions and performance criteria will not form a valid or reliable basis for incentives, especially where teamwork is essential to production. There it is more effective to get employees to identify with the organization's success, which will then be itself a motivator. In any case, if employees are as selfish as Kant suggests all people are, managers will have great difficulty in creating a moral organization no matter what they do.

Bibliography

Aristotle. (1985). *Nichomachean Ethics*, trans. T. Irwin. Indianapolis, Ind.: Hackett.

Davidson, D. (1980). *Essays on Actions and Events.* New York: Oxford. (Contains an influential defense of the view that reasons are causes of actions.)

Kant, I. (1959). *Foundations of the Metaphysics of Morals*, trans. L. W. Beck. New York: Liberal Arts Press.

Mill, J. S. (1957). *Utilitarianism.* Indianapolis, Ind.: Bobbs-Merrill.

Sen, A. K. (1987). *On Ethics and Economics.* Cambridge, Mass.: Blackwell. (Includes a critical analysis of psychological egoism).

EDWIN HARTMAN

motives and self-interest A *New Yorker* cartoon once depicted a distinguished-looking gentleman taking his grandson for a walk in a woods. "It's good to know about trees," he tells the boy, adding: "Just remember, nobody ever made big money knowing about trees." This advice nicely captures the modern economist's view of human nature. Unselfish motives may exist, the economist reluctantly concedes, but in our bitterly competitive world, people indulge them at their peril.

Cynical though it is, the self-interest model has yielded important insights. It tells us, for example, why car pools form in the wake of rising fuel prices; why divorce rates are higher in countries that have liberal welfare benefits; why energy use is lower in apartments that have separately metered utilities; and so on.

Yet many other behaviors do not fit the me-first caricature. When traveling, we leave tips in restaurants we never expect to visit again. We donate anonymously to private charities. We often incur costs to dispose of unwanted pesticides properly rather than simply pour them down the drain. Soldiers dive atop hand grenades to save the lives of their comrades. Seen through the lens of modern self-interest theory, these behaviors might seem the human equivalent of planets traveling in square orbits.

Recent research, however, suggests how noble human behaviors might not only survive the ruthless pressures of the material world, but might actually be nurtured by them as well. This research builds on the observation that people often confront problems in which the conscious, direct pursuit of self-interest is self-defeating.

An example is the case of the owner of a profitable business who is currently weighing an opportunity to open a branch in a distant city. He knows that if he hires an honest manager the branch will return high profits, but that otherwise it will lose money. One of his employees wants the job and is fully qualified for it. The owner would be willing to double her current salary if he could be sure that she would manage honestly. He knows, however, that if she manages dishonestly, she will be able to make three times her current salary.

In standard economic models, this option spells doom for the branch operation. Reasoning from the self-interest model, the owner concludes that since the employee could earn more by managing dishonestly, she will do so. And since this means the branch will be a loser, the owner does not open it. The irony, of course, is that this choice leaves both the owner and his employee worse off than if the owner were to open the branch and the employee were to manage it honestly.

In this scenario we have what economists call a "commitment problem." This problem could be solved if the employee could credibly commit herself to manage honestly. In situations like these the pursuit of material self-interest proves self-defeating.

Traditional economic models try to solve commitment problems by changing the material incentives people face. For example, the owner might try to hire an investigator to monitor the branch manager's performance. But in many cases, the relevant behavior simply cannot be monitored. In such cases, traditional models suggest that solutions do not exist.

Yet commitment problems can often be solved even when behavior cannot be monitored. Solutions require that we relax the assumption that people are motivated only by narrow self-interest. Suppose, for example, that the owner had some means of discovering that his employee was a trustworthy person, and would manage his branch operation honestly even though she could earn much more if she cheated. He could then open the branch with confidence, even though he could not monitor his manager directly. Both the owner and the manager would gain.

This solution relies on two premises: first, that there are people who behave honestly even when they could earn more by cheating; and second, that reliable means exist for identifying these people. The first premise is uncontroversial, but the second invites scrutiny. After all, all managerial candidates have strong incentives to portray themselves as trustworthy, so personal declarations of honesty cannot carry much weight. Investigating a candidate's past record will be illuminating only in those cases where someone has actually been caught doing wrong. It will reveal little about the many cheaters who were shrewd enough to avoid detection. If these methods fail, how can trustworthy persons be identified?

The key is to recognize that honest behavior is motivated not by rational calculations but by emotions – by moral sentiments, to use Adam Smith's term. The employee who walks away from a golden opportunity to cheat is motivated by her sympathy for the owner's interests, and by her feelings of self-esteem, which depend strongly on right conduct. The problem for the would-be cheater is that the emotions that motivate honest behavior are difficult to fake. Once we get to know a person well, we are able to make reliable judgments about her character. The cheater's goal is to appear trustworthy, but given our ability to detect the presence of the emotions that motivate trustworthiness, the easiest way to *appear* trustworthy is actually to *be* trustworthy.

The irony is that the *homo economicus* caricature that populates conventional economic models often does worse, even in purely material terms, than his genuinely trustworthy counterpart. In his single-minded quest to further his own material interests, he becomes unattractive as a partner in situations that require trust. By contrast, the trustworthy person values honest behavior for its own sake, and therefore is much in demand in these situations. The material rewards he reaps are no less valuable for having come unbidden.

Bibliography

Akerlof, George, (1983) Loyalty Filters. *American Economic Review*, 73, 54-63.

Frank, R. H. (1988). *Passions Within Reason*. (New York: W. W. Norton.

Frank, R. H., Gilovich, T. D., & Regan, D. T. (1993). The evolution of one-shot cooperation: An experiment. *Ethology and Sociobiology*, 14, 247–56.

Gauthier, D. (1985). *Morals by Agreement*. (Oxford: Clarendon.

Hirshleifer, J. (1987). On the emotions as guarantors of threats and promises. In J. Dupre (ed.), *The Latest on the Best: Essays in Evolution and Optimality*. (Cambridge, Mass.: MIT Press, 307–26.

Schelling, T. (1978). Altruism, meanness, and other potentially strategic behaviors. *American Economic Review*, 68, 229–30.

Sen, A. K. (1985). Goals, commitment, and identity. *Journal of Law, Economics, and Organization*, 1, 341–55.

Skyrms, B. (forthcoming). Darwin meets *The Logic of Decision*: Correlation in evolutionary game theory. *Philosophy of Science*.

ROBERT H. FRANK

multiculturalism an appreciation of diversity, which may range beyond ethnic or racial identities to diverse lifestyles or health-challenged individuals; openness and acceptance of alternative lifestyles; people of different backgrounds living constructively together, cooperating, and getting things done together; and cultures sharing power. Cultural power-sharing promotes ideal multiculturalism as the opposite of such negative "isms" like "racism," "ethnocentrism," "sexism," and "xenophobism" which stress the fragmented relationship of negative prejudice and power, and racial, cultural, sexual, and domestic/foreign imbalances.

Within larger groupings or society, ideal multiculturalists consist of people in multicultural organizations genuinely committed to a diverse representation of their membership; sensitive to maintaining open, supportive, and responsive environments; working toward and purposefully including elements of diverse cultures in their ongoing operations; and authentic in their responses to issues confronting them with equal power-sharing as a primary goal. Gudykunst and Kim identify a model for multicultural human development: "If strangers successfully overcome the multitude of challenges and frustrations that invariably accompany the process of cultural adaptation, they develop a mental and behavioral capacity more adaptable, flexible, and resilient than that of people who have limited exposure to the challenges of continuous intercultural encounters" (Gudykunst & Kim, 1992, p. 253).

Multiculturalists are uniquely a heritage of the late twentieth century, shaped as much by intercultural and international travel and exchange, computers, internets, and satellites as by their own personality traits. Peter Adler notes that these new people cannot be defined by the languages they speak, though they are more and more likely to be bilingual or multilingual, nor by their professions, places of residence, nor cognitive sophistication. Instead, they are recognized by their developing inclusive outlooks and worldviews, by how they see the universe as a dynamically moving process, by their reflection on the interconnectedness of life and their cultural ecology in their own thoughts and actions, and by how they remain open to new experiences. Adler suggests that the universal character of multicultural persons is an abiding commitment to essential similarities between people everywhere, while paradoxically maintaining an equally strong commitment to their differences. He stresses their psychocultural adaptiveness, always undergoing personal transitions; maintaining indefinite self-boundaries; and continuously living in a state of creative tension (cited in Prosser, 1989, pp. 70–3). Thus, the ideal multicultural society serves as a symbol of acceptance and protection for all, including those who least have power.

Multicultural persons often find themselves working in multinational organizations with a dominant home country or cultural base where the major organizational decisions are made, or in international organizations where power is shared more evenly among cultural groups (see MULTINATIONALS). Geert Hofstede suggests that since power-sharing is an important ingredient of effective multicultural relationships, there are common challenges in managing multicultural, multinational, or international organizations. These include the necessity to create their own strong and unique subcultures, especially with considerable cultural diversity in the organizations themselves; choosing partner cultures very carefully while deciding how much power and decision-making is to be shared; organizing international headquarters sensitively with organizational rewards facing outwards rather than inwards to the center; forming well constructed international teams, for example, with members who themselves have the potential of exemplifying ideal multicultural characteristics; and deciding whether to accept or try to change local cultural habits in host countries and cultures which affect the constructive aspects of the organizations (Hofstede, 1984, pp. 273–6).

Contemporary ethical issues for multicultural persons and multinational and international organizations are significant. Among the strongest cross-cultural sets of ethics developed since World War II has been the 1948 Universal Declaration of Human Rights with officially accepted principles by all nations joining the United Nations, but honored often only in the breach. Because ethical principles typically are culture specific, multiculturalists tend to form their ethical perspectives either from the viewpoint of their own cultures, or seek to accommodate the opposite culture's ethical precepts. Dean Barnlund states that current ethical questions which influence intercultural/ multicultural encounters are entirely new, and call for a metaethic to be used by people from different cultures when ethical dilemmas arise (1992, cited in Gudykunst & Kim, pp. 264–5). Such a metaethic remains still only an outline.

Gudykunst and Kim stress that the final goal of all multicultural persons is to build community, for the good of the whole, with a full recognition of cultural diversity, and initiated both by societies and individuals, whether at a domestic or international level. To this end, these authors recommend those seeking truly multicultural lives to attempt to live their own lives by following seven community-building principles: *be committed, be mindful, be unconditionally accepting, be concerned for themselves and others, be understanding, be ethical, and be peaceful* (Gudykunst & Kim, 1992, pp. 267–8). The end goal of the ideal multicultural person would seem to aspire toward becoming a "citizen of the world," acknowledging with Socrates that "I am neither a citizen of Athens, nor of Greece, but of the world."

Bibliography

Prosser, M. H. (1989). *The Cultural Dialogue: An Introduction to Intercultural Communication.* Washington, DC: SIETAR International.

Gudykunst, W. B. & Kim, Y. Y. (1992). *Communicating with Strangers: An Approach to Intercultural Communication,* 2nd edn. New York: McGraw Hill.

Hofstede, G. (1984). *Culture's Consequences: International Differences in Work-Related Values,* abridged edn. Beverly Hills, Calif.: Sage Publications.

MICHAEL H. PROSSER

multinational marketing is marketing across national boundaries, often by companies whose manufacturing operations are also multinational. Multinational marketing has generated some specific ethical issues that are represented by well-known cases. These cases relate to particular products, such as pesticides, pharmaceuticals, armaments, and infant formula. They also concern the methods used to promote them, ranging from the sales and advertising techniques employed to the extent of the existence of bribery and corruption. The concerns focus especially on the impact of Western multinational corporations on less-developed countries; and, as a consequence, embrace the role of corporate, industry, home-government, and international codes in regulating the process of multinational marketing.

A Western multinational's marketing and promotion practices in less-developed countries were at the heart of the Nestlé infant formula case. An exhaustive account of the controversy has been given by Prakash Sethi (Sethi, 1994). Critics argued that Nestlé irresponsibly persuaded poor mothers to buy an artificial food that they could not afford, and that they could not use safely in conditions of low water quality and hygiene. By encouraging a move away from breast-feeding, and the use of an infant formula product that was likely to be diluted and contaminated, the critics claimed that the company was adding to the incidence of infant disease and death. The marketing and promotion methods used included:

> direct promotion to mothers, consumer advertising, free samples in hospitals, inducive packaging and labeling, promotion to doctors and other health care workers, saleswomen dressed as nurses to "promote" or "educate" mothers of newborn babies in hospitals, and commission-based compensation systems. (Sethi, 1994, p. 120)

Nestlé's position was that the company was a legitimate and accepted participant in the multinational market for a product that was safe and useful, and that they used marketing practices that were both legal and ethical.

The multinational marketing of pharmaceuticals and pesticides presents industrial corporations with some fundamental ethical challenges. A pharmaceutical product may be banned in the home country, for example, the United States, but less-developed countries may not have the means to regulate or effectively monitor the pharmaceuticals market. A multinational marketer has the opportunity to exploit the situation by deceptive changes in the product's formulation, name, or country of origin. But it might be argued that conformity to home-country regulations is not an ethical requirement for a corporation in its multinational marketing. For example, the potential net social benefits of a product's use may be different in the different circumstances of a less-developed country; the effectiveness of the pesticide DDT in combatting malaria could well be regarded as outweighing the increased risk of human cancer in a DDT-contaminated environment – a consideration that caused it to be banned in some countries. But in what forum can such a decision legitimately be made? The absence of an institutional framework for making such decisions in the host country, or internationally, means that corporations and industries cannot escape the necessity to confront issues of business ethics and regulate themselves. In his book, *Competing with Integrity in International Business,* Richard De George argues that "not to cause direct harm and to produce more good than harm to the host country remain the operating ethical norms, together with the general prohibition against deception and lying" (De George, 1993, p. 62).

De George's principles might also be applied to the multinational marketing of banking and financial services. Snoy (1989) illustrates the ethical issues in international lending to less-developed countries – to what extent should banks accept responsibility, or a share of it, for the social impact of the selection of projects to be funded, or of the efficiency and honesty with which the funds are applied to those projects; and where development projects fail, what represents a fair sharing of the burden of financial adjustment? De George (1993) quotes the example of the Bank of Commerce and Credit International to epitomize the harm a bank can do – "Beyond facilitating fraud and embezzlement, it provided a financial conduit for illegal drug and arms traffic, laundered illegally acquired moneys [and] supplied secret accounts for illegal flight capital" (De George, 1993, p. 68).

Bibliography

De George, R. (1993). *Competing with Integrity in International Business.* New York: Oxford University Press.

Sethi, S. P. (1994). *Multinational Corporations and the Impact of Public Advocacy on Corporate Strategy: Nestlé and the Infant Formula Controversy.* Boston: Kluwer.

Snoy, B. (1989). Ethical issues in international lending. *Journal of Business Ethics,* Aug., 635–9.

BRIAN HARVEY

multinationals Corporations that have operations in more than one country (host countries) but are controlled by a headquarters in a home country.

Multinationals have been the focus of three groups of ethical disputes.

1) By which rules are multinationals bound: those of the home country or those of the host country? One view defends the position that "when in Rome, do as the Romans do." This is rejected by those who equate this view with ethical relativism and argue that although a company should obey local laws and customs whenever possible, a multinational may not, e.g., employ forced labor or discriminate on the basis of race or gender, even if these practices are locally accepted.

2) The differential in power between large, powerful multinationals and less developed countries has led to such charges as exploiting labor and resources; undermining local cultures; raising expectations that cannot be fulfilled; ignoring the safety and health of host countries; and causing malnutrition and starvation by buying up the most productive land for cash crops. Multinationals have an obligation to take special care when operating in less-developed countries.

3) Because of the lack of adequate international institutions and laws, some charge that multinational companies can fix prices in transfer payments, avoid taxes, and circumvent national legal restrictions. The problems and temptations of multinationals have led to international and industry codes and other attempts at international control. Many companies of integrity, conscious of the ethical pitfalls facing multinationals, have adopted their own codes or guidelines to ensure ethical activity.

Bibliography

Barnet, R. J. & Ronald, E. M. (1974). *Global Reach: The Power of the Multinational Corporations.* New York: Simon & Schuster.

De George, R. T. (1993). *Competing With Integrity in International Business.* New York: Oxford University Press.

Donaldson, T. (1989). *The Ethics of International Business.* New York: Oxford University Press.

Hoffman, W. M., Lange, A., & Fedo, D. A. (eds),. (1986). *Ethics and the Multinational Enterprise.* Lanham, Md.: University Press of America.

RICHARD T. DE GEORGE

N

narrative and business ethics   What a company ought to do about a decision it is faced with or with a question about what direction it should take, can be illumined by its giving attention to where it has come from and to the ethos that has guided it to become what it is. Every company has a story that it tells itself and any who would like to know about it. That story might be more fiction than fact and used for public relations or to explain itself to its own personnel. Or it can be true and used to throw light on its historical ethos and ethics. Business is beginning to appreciate the ethical value of revisiting the business's own story, a story that laces together sequentially and, at times, causally, events and characters that otherwise remain disconnected.

Businesses do not exist in a historical vacuum. They all have a beginning, a middle, and possibly a new beginning or even an end. They are narratively constituted. Their narratives will have founding moments and a founder. Original entrepreneurs who launched the enterprises, and subsequent refounders had purposes, methods, resources, ideas and ideals, opportunities, and a market whose demand they supplied or created. All of these constitutive parts had and still have an ethical component to them, in the sense that they affected people for good or ill.

Like the person in Montaigne's essay who learned that he had been speaking prose all his life, so businesses have been doing their ethics narratively ever since there have been businesses. This means that they have been making their decisions on the basis of the stories their decision-makers have internalized, with particular attention, presumably, to the founding though ever-evolving story of the business itself. Or they have been correcting the mistakes

their forebears made. In either case, narratives are key to the business's ethics.

Our choices are made on the basis of our present perceptions but these will have been shaped by the stories or narratives we have identified with and allowed to swim into our affections. Of course, the effect the stories we internalize have on us might be ethical or unethical, depending on their character. Whichever, narrative is the usual medium within which choices are made. Narratives are formative of what choosers choose. Granted, we can extricate ourselves from these formative influences and act out of some other medium like rationality or abstract principle or passion or opportunity or imagination. But even these alternate sources of choice usually have a narrative basis to them if one reflects on their genesis in the moral agent. Furthermore, insofar as the moral agents of a given company are steeped in its narratives, the less likely they are to shape policies and decisions on the basis of influences inimical to or abstracted from the particularities of the company.

Businesses can be communities of memory or of amnesia. The latter type of community will make for poor business and probably poor ethics. When a business's narratives grow remote or irretrievable its decisions are far more likely to be wholly pragmatic, *ad hoc*, and normless. Discontinuity from a business's memory pool makes its decisions susceptible to ignorance or indifference to its past, and vulnerable to memoryless managers driven by short-term gain. This condition heightens the likelihood that decisions will be made out of self-interest, or the personal preference and style of its present managers. While it is true that businesses must be ready to change and change often and, that tradition can act as a weight, nonetheless a business that disregards its traditions and customs will put its customers, its employees, and the public on notice that it lives opportunistically. Opportunists focus on the occasion rather than on those impacted by it.

A narrative approach to ethics is not a recommendation against either rationality or economic rationality, but a recommendation that this rationality be exercised attentive to the recent and past history from which the company has emerged. This is saying more than that each company has a history. It is saying that its respective history is more than its profits, strategies and goals. This more which is accessible through its remembered narratives is a trove of experience, example, norm, continuity, precedent, and ideals.

But the narrative approach to business ethics is not only retrospective, it is prospective. A business's projections, goals, strategic plans are a story waiting to be acted on. Its projections will have to be made in terms of its past narratives since these will have shaped the present in varying degrees. It is not only the present that charts the future course but what the present has done with the past. Scenario building doesn't come from materials created *ex nihilo* but from materials that have developed over time.

But all of the above assumes that the narratives we are investing with so much ethical content are ethical. They might, in fact, be unethical. A business might have developed an unethical practice or taken on the shady character of one of its founders or subsequent leaders. So narrativity of itself is not a guarantee of ethicality.

What makes the difference is the overall character of the business's narratives. These can be of a good or an evil character. But that judgment presumes there is a measure beyond the business that can be used to judge the moral character of the business narrative. There are such measures and norms. These come from the classical moral traditions that have been developed over time to discern the good, the ethical, and their opposites. These culturally communicated moral traditions are either religious or philosophical. But even these traditions are narratives and are dependent on carriers who have knowledge of the past and can transmit them to the present and to those prepared to be enriched and enlightened by their contents. A business ethics that is attuned to its own narratives will inevitably be connected to and aligned with these larger, deeper, older moral traditions.

Bibliography

Boje, David. (1991). The story telling organization. *Adminstrative Science Quarterly*, **36**, 106–26.

Gabriel, Yiannis. (1991). Turning facts into stories and stories into facts: A hermeneutic exploration of organizational folklore. *Human Relations*, **44**, 857–75.

Gergen, Kenneth. (1990). Affect and organization in postmodern society. In S. Srivastva & David Cooperider (eds), *Appreciative Management and Leadership*. San Francisco: Jossey-Bass, 153–74.

Hauerwas, Stanley. (1981). *A Community of Character: Towards a Constructive Christian Social Ethic*. Notre Dame, Ind.: University of Notre Dame Press.

Hauerwas, Stanley & Jones, L. Gregory. (1989). *Why Narrative? Readings in Narrative Theology*. Grand Rapids, Mich.: Eerdmans.

Schein, Edgar. (1983). The role of the founder in creating organizational culture. *Organizational Dynamics*, **12**, (1), 13–28.

Strine, Mary & Pacanowsky, Michael. (1985). How to read interpretive accounts of organizational life: Narrative bases of textual authority. *The Southern Speech Communication Journal*, **50**, 283–97.

JOHN C. HAUGHEY

natural law Principles of right human conduct that can be discovered in "nature" by the use of human reason – without needing to be received directly from a divine source, as through the Bible or some other revelation. The advantage of this approach is that such principles could, in theory, define universally valid principles, and in a universally accessible moral language persuasive to all reasonable persons regardless of their religious or ethnic identity.

What is meant by the term "nature" has shrunk considerably between antiquity and the modern era. Originally, Stoic philosophers (300 BCE–200 CE) asserted that the natural order of the universe expressed a perfect moral order as well, and that human happiness and duty converged in conforming to this order. ARISTOTLE (384–322 BCE) and Thomas Aquinas

(1225–74 CE), grounded natural law in quasi-scientific claims about the "functions" and purposes of human existence, viewed from the vantage point of whole organisms, whether the individual, the community, or society. In Thomistic thinking, societies by their nature are oriented towards collective health, which requires just government, just as individuals are oriented to a comprehensive well-being, mandating the principle of "do good and avoid evil."

Confidence that nature expresses moral order and value collapsed under the withering attack of modern philosophers, who turned away from natural law to concepts of "natural rights." (*see* HOBBES, THOMAS). Most familiar are the civil and political rights expressed in the US Declaration of Independence ("We hold these truths to be self-evident, that all men are by nature created equal . . ") and the Bill of Rights. Beginning with Immanuel Kant, philosophers have sought to ground rights claims in distinctive features of individual persons as thinking and acting beings (*see* KANTIAN ETHICS). The contemporary proposal by Finnis (1980, chs 3 and 4) is the most detailed and comprehensive.

The natural-rights tradition is criticized for expressing a bias for the individual (especially in the extreme view, LIBERTARIANISM). Contemporary philosophers and sociologists have sought to redescribe humans as concrete historical beings formed in and by particular communities (*see* COMMUNITARIANISM). This description of humans as inherently social resonates closely with traditional natural law, as reasserted by Roman Catholic theologians and ethicists since the nineteenth century. For example, David Hollenbach (1979) seeks to leaven natural-rights thinking with concern for the "common good," or the welfare of individuals understood to be members of a social whole rather than isolated individuals.

It is such hybrid thinking which has been most visible in business ethics, due to recent vigorous Roman Catholic efforts to engage businesspeople in dialogue. The widely influential 1986 Pastoral Letter issued by the US Bishops asserts that economic systems and institutions have moral value to the extent that they protect human "dignity," a value not only revealed in the Bible but founded upon the claim that human personhood is fulfilled in community. Individuals therefore have not only rights but "responsibilities": specifically, the obligation to be "active and productive participants in the life of society" (NCCB, paras 61–95, esp. 71). The Bishops tap the non-sectarian language of natural rights, while avoiding an individualistic bias. Thus they are able to appeal to non-Catholics and non-Christians, reflecting the aim of natural law to provide a universal language of moral reasonableness.

Few contemporary business-ethics textbooks are explicitly based upon natural law. Closest to the classic model of Aristotle and Aquinas stand Thomas Garrett and Richard Klonoski, who posit "full human perfection" (Garrett & Klonoski, 1986, p. 3) as the goal from which sheer human reason can derive precise moral judgments. Far more common is the eclectic approach taken by other philosophical business ethicists who argue that making correct decisions in specific cases involves applying a variety of moral considerations anchored in societal conventions as well as the enduring "nature" of individuals claimed by the natural-law and natural-rights traditions (*see* UTILITARIANISM; SOCIAL CONTRACT THEORY). Most radically skeptical of both traditions is the emerging postmodernism in business ethics, which rejects the idea that any moral language can be universally accessible and binding (*see* POSTMODERNISM AND BUSINESS ETHICS).

Bibliography

Finnis, John. (1980). *Natural Law and Natural Rights*. Oxford: Clarendon.

Garrett, T. M. & Klonoski, R. J. (1986). *Business Ethics*, 2nd edn. Englewood Cliffs, NJ: Prentice-Hall.

Hollenbach, David. (1979). *Claims in Conflict*. New York: Paulist.

National Conference of Catholic Bishops (1986). *Economic Justice for All*. Washington, DC: United States Catholic Conference.

STEWART W. HERMAN

needs   Commonly conceived in either of two ways: 1) as a means required for some end; or 2) as a biological or psychological requirement which, if unmet, will damage some organism in question. The first sense of need is often called the relative conception of need, since it understands the existence of any need as depending on its relation to some particular end at issue. The second sense of need is often called the absolute conception, since it commonly concerns basics such as food, water, shelter, and healthcare, which are unconditionally required for survival.

Some have tried to reduce all needs to either one or the other of these conceptions, but there is no consensus about either of these reductions. But there is a significant consensus that needs can be not only natural (e.g., food) but also conventional. ADAM SMITH wrote: "By necessaries I understand, not only the commodities which are indispensably necessary for the support of life, but whatever the custom of the country renders it indecent for creditable people, even of the lowest order, to be without" (Smith, 1976, bk 5, ch. 2). KARL MARX discussed the conventional swelling of needs in "keeping up with the Joneses" by suggesting that many will feel a need for a bigger house once the house next to theirs is expanded.

This capacity for needs to swell so quickly and easily has led many libertarians and other capitalists to have ambivalent, inconsistent, or even hostile attitudes toward emphatic efforts to meet needs (*see* LIBERTARIANISM). On one hand, capitalists often emphasize the greatness of capitalism in using the profit motive to give ambitious producers an incentive to meet consumers' needs more efficiently than any other economic system known. On the other hand, facing massive starvation and poverty in a world largely dominated by capitalism, capitalists often deny that emphasizing meeting needs *per se* is useful or even tolerable. For example, Antony Flew states "an emphasis upon needs as opposed to wants cannot but appeal to those who would like to see themselves as experts qualified both to determine what the needs of others are, and to prescribe and enforce the means appropriate to the satisfaction of those needs" (Flew, 1981, p. 117). Humorists ridicule capitalism somewhat by advising the ambitious that the best way to get a bank loan is to show that you do not need one. Capitalists, however, fear envious demands for rights to realize Marx's famous goal "from each according to his ability, to each according to his needs!" (Marx, 1977, p. 569). These capitalists praise ambition but condemn ENVY, though both

ambition and envy seem fundamentally similar needs to outdo others.

To escape this ambivalence about needs, some try to reduce needs to mere preferences (wants or desires). Economists often clash with psychologists here, since many economists want to reduce the urgency and rhetorical force of meeting needs to merely some preferences among many others, while many psychologists follow Abraham Maslow in accepting a hierarchy of needs, ranked in order of importance. For example, the longer one can go unharmed without an item, the less likely that item is to be a high-ranking need. Further, the greater the damage incurred without an item, the more likely it is to be a high-ranking need.

David Braybrooke argues against reducing all needs to preferences. He writes: "There is no contradiction between a person having a set of needs and her preferring not to have any of them met; people can and do prefer on occasion not to go on living, and they act on the preference precisely by disregarding their needs" (Braybrooke, 1987, p. 202). But his example fails, since he overlooks the needs to relieve suffering or save money for one's family, assuming the case he has in mind is rational euthanasia rather than irrational suicide.

Reducing needs to preferences seems more feasible with a relative conception than with an absolute conception of needs. Preferences serve as ends and the required means to that end are needs in the relative sense. But absolute needs often seem irreducible to preferences. For example, a baby or an unconscious adult often needs medical care, but do they prefer the medical care? It seems not, unless one counts hypothetical conditions, what one would prefer under certain ideal conditions. But explaining needs in terms of hypothetical preferences seems unsatisfactory, since hypothetical preferences are much more inexplicable, abstract, and speculative than needs were in the first place. Complicating the analysis here is that needs and preferences are matters of degree. For example, we can sensibly ask, "How badly to you need a new car?" or "How great is your need to buy that?" Absolute needs are often more important than a mere preference, but even these needs will often shade off by degrees into actual preferences.

At the most fundamental level, needs are equalizers, since even though some have special needs or even embarrassing needs, we all have many basic needs in common. For example, a tycoon in a palace and seemingly without a need or care in the world one moment can the next moment easily be reduced (e.g., by an earthquake) to a charity case in dire need of medical care.

The relevance of needs to business ethics goes beyond the debates over capitalism and socialism. For example, on the value of the products of business, Diogenes Laertius said of Socrates: "Often when looking at a mass of things for sale, he would say to himself, 'How many things I have no need of!' " (quoted in Bartlett, 1992, p. 70). Further, our common needs and the ups and downs of business make many reflect on the old saying "There but for the grace of God or good fortune go I." Some emerge from this reflection optimistically, or perhaps idealistically, in adopting a business ethics of trying to reduce dramatically the role of luck in determining the meeting of needs. Others emerge pessimistically, or perhaps realistically, by fatalistically resigning themselves to a business ethics accepting the inevitability of a larger role for luck in meeting needs. These are two ends of a spectrum along which many approaches appear in business ethics.

Bibliography

Bartlett, J. (1992). *Bartlett's Familiar Quotations*, 16th edn. Boston: Little, Brown, & Co.

Braybrooke, D. (1987). *Meeting Needs*. Princeton: Princeton University Press.

Flew, A. (1981). *The Politics of Procrustes*. Buffalo, NY: Prometheus Books.

Ignatieff, M. (1984). *The Needs of Strangers*. London: Chatto & Windus.

Leiss, W. (1976). *The Limits of Satisfaction: An Esssay on the Problem of Needs and Commodities*. Toronto: University of Toronto Press.

Marx, K. (1977 [1875]). *Critique of the Gotha Programme*, in D. McLellan (Ed.), *Karl Marx: Selected Writings*. Oxford: Oxford University Press.

Maslow, A. (1973). *Dominance, Self-Esteem, Self-Actualization: Germinal Papers of A. H. Maslow*, (Ed.), R. Lowry. Monterey, Calif.: Brooks/Cole Publishers. (A classic work in psychology).

Smith, A. (1976 [1776]). *An Inquiry into the Nature and Causes of the Wealth of Nations*. Chicago: Chicago University Press.

Soper, K. (1981). *On Human Needs: Open and Closed Theories in a Marxist Perspective*. Brighton, Sussex: Harvester Press.

Wiggins, D. (1985). Claims of need. In T. Honderich (ed.), *Morality and Objectivity: A Tribute to J. L. Mackie*. London: Routledge & Kegan Paul.

STERLING HARWOOD

negligence   The failure to take reasonable care regarding a duty created by an ethical obligation. Negligence is not a willful violation of duty, but rather the omission of an act which a reasonable person would take to honor a duty or the commission of an act which a reasonable person would refrain from, given the duty.

Thus negligence may be either passive or active. Passive negligence results from the failure to act when an act is required to honor a duty. For example, the right to privacy is generally considered a human right. The right to privacy carries a corresponding duty for others not to violate willfully that privacy. One may be negligent by failing to act, thus allowing one party's private information to become known by other parties. A private letter carelessly left where others – competitors, superiors, peers – can read it is a case of ethical negligence.

Deception created by the failure to disclose important information is another example of passive negligence. In June 1994, Intel Corporation discovered a flaw in its new Pentium computer chip which caused division errors in complex calculations. Although affecting few users, the flaw could have significant consequences for some. In November 1994, Thomas Nicely from Lynchburg College discovered the flaw and notified colleagues via the Internet. The news media picked up the discovery and made it public knowledge. Because the flaw could create serious problems for some users, the failure to disclose the flaw when discovered made Intel guilty of passive ethical negligence.

Active negligence occurs when an act committed for some other purpose incidentally violates a duty. The act would not be performed by a reasonable person due to its breaching of the ethical duty. Another human right, for example, is free speech; it carries corresponding duties. A discussion with others – competitors, superiors, peers – which inadvertently creates a false, harmful image of a person or company is a case of ethical negligence.

The American Express Company was guilty of active ethical negligence when it supplied travel and telephone records in response to a subpoena from the Philip Morris Company. The subpoena was for the records of two ABC producers for the month of January 1994 in connection with a libel suit against ABC. American Express immediately provided the travel and telephone records of the two producers for a period of seven years. They also included the records for half a dozen other journalists. Thus the privacy of the other journalists was violated as well as the privacy of the two producers for the period not covered by the subpoena.

Bibliography

Black, H. C. (1979). *Blacks Law Dictionary*, 5th edn. St. Paul: West Publishing Company.

Cavanagh, G. F. (1990). *American Business Values*, 3rd edn. Englewood Cliffs, NJ: Prentice-Hall.

Clark, D. J. (1994). Some scientists are angry over flaw in Pentium chip, and Intel's response. *The Wall Street Journal*, Nov. 25, B6.

Cohen, L. P. & Freedman, A. M. (1995). American Express sends a statement that's quite wrong. *The Wall Street Journal*, Feb. 24, A1, A4.

DAVID J. FRITZSCHE

negotiation and bargaining A joint decision-making process in which two or more parties, whose interests conflict, attempt to reach an agreement. Generally, the two terms are used interchangeably. Negotiations take place in a wide variety of contexts: buying (and selling) a home, establishing employment contracts, dividing up tasks in a group project, and even quelling highly emotional disputes among nations. In all of these cases, the parties decide what each will give and take in an exchange in an attempt to resolve the CONFLICT and improve the situation for everyone. As a dispute-resolution technique, therefore, negotiation reflects the parties' preferences for working together to craft a mutually agreeable solution as opposed to deferring to an authority, giving up and reaching an impasse, or even fighting openly.

Despite its broad application in human affairs, negotiation tends to be conceptualized by scholars primarily in economic terms. Economists, some of the first scholars to study the topic, analyze negotiations in terms of the outcomes that should emerge in multiparty decision-making assuming that everyone acts rationally (von Neumann & Morgenstern, 1944). In this *game-theoretic approach*, negotiators are believed to be fully informed – i.e., they have perfect information about their own preferences, about all possible outcomes and about the expected utility or value associated with those outcomes – and to make choices based on self-interest; that is, each negotiator is believed to act so as to maximize his or her individual outcome (Nash, 1950) (*see* RATIONAL CHOICE THEORY).

Many scholars challenge this rational model, however, claiming that it fails to capture the actual experiences of negotiators and that it makes prescriptions that may be unrealistic and, arguably, unethical in some circumstances. For example, negotiators rarely have ample time or ability to imagine all possible outcomes and to assess each's expected utility; empirical research shows that people's preferences shift quite dramatically in response to factors that are considered irrelevant from a game-theoretic perspective (e.g., Bazerman, Loewenstein, & White, 1992; Tversky & Kahneman, 1986). In addition, the approach also fails to acknowledge the social context of negotiation (Thompson, 1990), the prevalence of negotiating teams (Thompson, Peterson, & Brodt, 1996), and various factors that "bound" decision-making and choice, such as societal rules and customs, as well as personal relationships and ethics (March & Simon, 1958).

Raiffa's (1982) *decision analytic approach* provides a modest alternative that emphasizes the situation as understood by actual negotiators who often have incomplete and perhaps biased information, and limited cognitive capacity to remember facts and imagine possible alternatives. According to Raiffa (1982, p. 21), the approach describes how "erring folks like you and me actually behave." The approach's key components include two assessments: (a) each party's *alternative to a negotiated agreement* (i.e.,

Figure 1   Amount of $500,000 budget allocated to Manager A (in $1000s). Bargaining zone is noted by x's

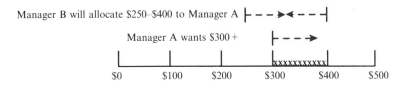

Manager B will allocate $250–$400 to Manager A

Manager A wants $300 +

$0 $100 $200 $300 $400 $500

"best alternative to a negotiated agreement," (BATNA)) and (b) each party's *interests*, including the relative importance of their interests. The utility of a party's BATNA (Fisher & Ury, 1981) places a lower bound on the negotiation and establishes a negotiator's *reservation point*, meaning the point at which he or she is indifferent between settlement and impasse. Presumably, a negotiator should not accept an agreement that leaves him or her worse off than his or her BATNA.

To assess one's interests, a negotiator must determine what issues really matter. You may decide, for example, that it is very important to provide for your daughter's college education and so your annual bonus and salary (raise) become key issues during your annual performance review. The specific *position* you take in the negotiation (e.g., request for $5000 bonus and $2500 salary increase) should reflect your underlying interests. Finally, you may decide that your interest in additional vacation time pales in comparison to the importance of the financial issues. These differences in the relative importance among issues allow you to make decisions about trade-offs and concessions you are willing to make as well as take during a negotiation (Northcraft, Brodt, & Neale, 1995). Taken together, the assessment of one's BATNA and interests define the structure of the negotiation. It is within this (psychological) context that negotiators attempt to craft mutually agreeable outcomes.

There are two primary tasks in negotiation: (a) *distribution* or the division of existing resources, and (b) *integration* or the creation of additional resources. When managers haggle over the size of their budgets, they are negotiating the division of a resource "pie." Each manager wants a bigger piece of the pie

and yet a bigger piece for one manager necessarily means a smaller piece for another manager. In distributive bargaining, therefore, the parties' interests are presumed to be in direct conflict and disputants typically focus on a limited number of issues (e.g., price).

A *bargaining zone* framework (Raiffa, 1982; Walton & McKersie, 1965) is often used to represent the distribution task. In the case of two managers haggling over the allocation of a $500,000 resource pie, the one from the larger division (Manager A) wants to claim $400,000 (and yet would settle for at least $300,000 – Manager A's reservation point) while the manager from the smaller division (Manager B) wants to claim $250,000 (and yet would settle for as little as $100,000 – Manager B's reservation point). Figure 1 diagrams the situation in terms of Manager A's allocation. The bargaining zone – i.e., the set of solutions that the managers would prefer over impasse – ranges from $300,000 to $400,000. That is, the managers should settle for any distribution between $300,000 for Manager A (and $200,000 for Manager B) and $400,000 for Manager A (and $100,000 for Manager B).

To reach a mutually agreeable settlement, negotiators generally engage in a give-and-take process and settle on a compromise somewhere within the bargaining zone (*see* RECIPROCITY). Because of the nature of the distribution task (i.e., "win–lose"), typical bargaining tactics include: misrepresentation, silence, extreme positions, threats to walk away, and BLUFFING AND DECEPTION. Distribution comprises the competitive aspect of negotiation. Generally speaking, when managers talk about negotiation, they are referring to distributive bargaining.

Integration contrasts sharply with distribution. When a conflict involves multiple issues, which are valued differently by the disputants, there is the potential for integrative bargaining or problem-solving. The quintessential example of integrative bargaining comes from Follett (1940), who describes the case of two sisters in conflict over one orange. Conceiving of the situation as a pure conflict, the sisters face a seemingly intractable situation; there is no division of the orange that is acceptable to both sisters. After each discloses her reasons for wanting the orange (i.e., her interests), however, the situation is transformed: one sister wants the orange juice while the other wants the orange rind. A simple, mutually beneficial solution becomes clear – one sister takes the juice and the other takes the rind. Integrative agreements that are crafted out of complementary interests tend to maintain and even strengthen the long-term relationships among parties.

To reach a mutually agreeable settlement, negotiators must understand clearly what others value (i.e., each other's interests) and look for creative ways of structuring an agreement that meets each party's interests; not surprisingly, integrative bargaining often is referred to as joint problem-solving. Because of the nature of the integration task (i.e., "win–win"), typical bargaining tactics include: honesty, openness, ample time to bargain, information sharing, and TRUST. Integration comprises the cooperative aspect of negotiation.

Negotiations that involve both integration and distribution are called *mixed-motive* negotiations; these situations include both cooperation and competition. In general, most negotiations are mixed-motive. Even a negotiation such as buying (selling) an automobile, which may seem to be a purely distributive task, typically involves both integration and distribution. At some point in the negotiation, one of the parties begins to expand the set of issues beyond price, to include: financing, new tires, floor mats, sound-system upgrades, extended warranty, and other issues that may be valued differently by the two parties. By adding issues to the negotiation, the resource "pie" increases; these resources still need to be divided, however, between the buyer and seller.

Perhaps one of the greatest challenges for disputants is to realize the integrative potential in their negotiations and to create mutually-beneficial agreements. Many managers feel uneasy about sharing information about their interests, which is an important part of identifying complementary interests and crafting integrative agreements. In cases of protracted union–management negotiations, the low level of trust between the parties may cripple integrative bargaining. Researchers have identified several cognitive impediments such as the "mythical fixed pie" perception and the framing of negotiator judgments (see Bazerman, 1994, ch. 8, and Northcraft, Brodt, & Neale, 1995, for additional cognitive limitations). According to the mythical fixed-pie perception, negotiators assume at the onset of the negotiation that their interests necessarily and directly conflict with the other party's interests (Bazerman, Magliozzi, & Neale, 1985). This initial "win–lose" bias, along with its associated "hard-ball" tactics, emphasizes the competitive aspect of the negotiation and inhibits a problem-solving approach.

Also, the framing of disputants' judgments biases negotiation, which may stymie problem-solving. Depending on a negotiator's frame of reference, a potential agreement may be viewed as a loss or a gain. In comparison to the initial listing price, for example, a seller may perceive an interested buyer's offer as a loss, whereas the same offer may be considered a gain in light of the price the seller paid for the house just five years earlier. Because peoples' choices differ dramatically in response to prospects involving gains versus losses – i.e., people tend to be risk averse for gains and risk seeking for losses (Kahneman & Tversky, 1979) – their negotiating behavior also is affected by how prospects or offers are framed. Specifically, when a choice is framed in terms of a potential gain, a negotiator is more likely to choose the risk-averse option and show a general willingness to settle. In contrast, the riskier option of holding out for a better offer would be more likely to result if the identical choice were framed in terms of a potential loss. By interpreting offers in light of different perceptual anchors, disputants may overlook potentially beneficial agreements.

The preceding analysis reflects the generally accepted approach to negotiation analysis, which dominates teaching and research in most major US business schools. The approach appeals to many researchers and practitioners and it enjoys a substantial scholarly tradition. Several important and thoughtful critics have emerged, however, and their voices and concerns raise serious questions about key assumptions of the dominant approach. Specifically, some scholars question the approach's underlying assumptions, particularly the presumption of SELF-INTEREST (i.e., the goal of maximizing one's individual outcome). Because of the changing nature of business relationships, namely the popularity of negotiating joint ventures between organizations and cooperative labor–management arrangements within organizations, scholars have begun to question the individualist focus of traditional approaches. Other critics challenge the entire traditional conceptualization of negotiation. As a result, some criticisms slightly modify the traditional approaches while others boldly assert that a fundamental change is needed in the conceptualization of negotiation.

Responding to the highly individualistic nature of these traditional approaches, Pruitt and Rubin (1986) propose the *dual-concern model*, which recognizes a negotiator's concern for the other party's outcomes as well as one's own. Regardless of whether this concern is genuine or strategic, it has a distinct effect on negotiations and, according to Pruitt and Rubin, it should be part of negotiation theory. Specifically, negotiators who are more concerned about the other party's outcomes than they are about their own, often yield or defer in negotiations; those who are equally (strongly) concerned about both parties' outcomes typically adopt problem-solving strategies (see Pruitt & Carnevale, 1993, for a review). The dual-concern model quietly introduces the concept of relationships into the analysis of negotiator cognition and behavior.

Other scholars, particularly feminist theorists, assert the need to reconsider traditional conceptualizations and to propose fundamentally different ones. Morely (1992), for example, rejects the view of negotiation as a series of tactics employed by the parties as they converge on an agreement. Rather, he considers negotiation as a process within a relationship whereby people decide whether and in what manner the relationship will change. The goal is to come to a "collective rationale, linking what is happening now to what has happened in the past and what needs to happen in the future" (1992, p. 206).

Finally, Gray's (1994) feminist critique highlights the male-gendered assumptions underlying negotiation research and points out key elements missing from current conceptualizations. She argues that "[t]he male-gendered orientation of negotiations [theory and research are] . . directly manifest in (1) the transactional nature of negotiations, (2) the overly rational, instrumental goals attributed to negotiators, (3) the absence and delegitimization of human emotions (or their instrumental use), (4) intergroup competition and distrust, (5) inflation of negotiators' predictions of success, (6) justification for international violence, and (7) a rationale for nuclear deterrence" (1994, pp. 18–19). The components of a new theory of negotiations, according to Gray, should include: valuing of DIVERSITY, reclaiming EMOTION, reconceptualizing POWER, and an ETHICS OF CARE.

Bibliography

Bazerman, M. H. (1994). *Judgment in Managerial Decision Making*. New York: Wiley.

Bazerman, M., Loewenstein, G., & White, S. (1992). Psychological determinants of utility in competitive contexts: The impact of elicitation procedure. *Administrative Science Quarterly*, 37, 220–40.

Bazerman, M. H., Magliozzi, T., & Neale, M. A. (1985). The acquisition of an integrative response in a competitive market. *Organizational Behavior and Human Decision Processes*, 35, 294–313.

Fisher, R. & Ury, W. (1981). *Getting to Yes*. Boston: Houghton Mifflin.

Follett, M. P. (1940). Constructive conflict. In H. Metcalf & L. Urwick (eds), *Dynamic Administration: The Collected Papers of Mary Parker Follett*. New York: Harper & Row, 30–49.

Gray, B. (1994). The gender-based foundations of negotiation theory. In R. J. Lewicki, B. H. Sheppard, & R. Bies (eds), *Research on Negotiations in Organizations*, vol. 4. Greenwich, Conn.: JAI Press, 3–36.

Kahneman, D. & Tversky, A. (1979). Prospect theory: An analysis of decisions under risk. *Econometrica*, 47, 263–91.

March, J. & Simon, H. (1958). *Organizations*. New York: Wiley.

Morely, I. E. (1992). Intra-organizational bargaining. In J. F. Hartley and G. M. Stephenson (eds), *Employment Relations*. Cambridge, Mass.: Blackwell.

Nash, J. (1950). The bargaining problem. *Econometrica*, 18, 155–62.

Northcraft, G., Brodt, S., & Neale, M. (1995). Negotiating with non-linear subjective utilities: Why some concessions are more equal than others. *Organizational Behavior and Human Decision Processes*, **63**, (3), 298–310.

Pruitt, D. G. & Carnevale, P. J. (1993). *Negotiation in Social Conflict*. Pacific Grove, Calif.: Brooks/Cole.

Pruitt, D. & Rubin, J. (1986). *Social Conflict*. New York: Random House.

Raiffa, H. (1982). *The Art and Science of Negotiation*. Cambridge, Mass.: Harvard University Press.

Thompson, L. (1990). Negotiation behavior and outcomes: Empirical evidence and theoretical issues. *Psychological Bulletin*, **108**, 515–32.

Thompson, L., Peterson, E., & Brodt, S. (1996). Team negotiation: An examination of integrative and distributive bargaining. *Journal of Personality and Social Psychology*, **70**, 66–78.

Tversky, A. & Kahneman, D. (1986). Rational choice and the framing of decisions. *Journal of Business*, **59**, 251–94.

von Neumann, J. & Morgenstern, O. (1944). *Theory of Games and Economic Behavior*. Princeton, NJ: Princeton University Press.

Walton, R. & McKersie, R. (1965). *A Behavioral Theory of Labor Negotiations*. New York: McGraw-Hill.

SUSAN E. BRODT

networking   is a phrase used to represent the activity of making connections and establishing relationships with others for mutual benefit. Consider going to a cocktail party, meeting several individuals through whom you meet other fascinating people or learn of new and interesting activities. The activity just described is an example of networking: meeting people who will open up the possibilities and connections for meeting others.

Networking is an important individual career-development skill. Many jobs are found not by answering advertisements in newspapers, but by whom one knows or to whom one can be introduced. Thus, the larger one's network, the more personal relationships or contacts one might call upon for information or resources.

Networking is also a crucial skill for managerial excellence and effectiveness, and one whose importance is growing. Managers derive power from the number of individuals they know and who know of them and their abilities. These contacts represent people to call upon for resources, support, information, and assistance. Research has suggested that the larger an individual's network, the greater are that person's chances of being promoted or being influential. More importantly, as companies become flatter in hierarchy and more involved in creating strategic alliances and internal partnerships, the more managers and other employees will need to interact with and influence others over whom they have little or no line authority. Strong networks can substitute for line authority in getting the job done.

Networking has ethical implications. There are scholars who contend that networks can be exclusionary, and therefore of benefit to only a few. Because networks are based on personal relationships, there may be segments of the population, often minorities or women, who do not have immediate or ready access to key networks. If networking is equated to power and influence, and networking is not equally available, then benefits are also unequal. It is no wonder that one key organizational network has been called the "old boys network."

Bibliography

Arthur, M., Hall, D. & Lawrence, B. (eds). (1989). *Handbook of Career Theory*. New York: Cambridge University Press.

Feldman, D. (1989). Careers in organizations: Recent trends and future directions. *Journal of Management*, **15**, 135–56.

Hall, D. T. (1976). *Careers in Organizations*. Pacific Palisades, Calif.: Goodyear.

Schien, E. (1978). *Career Dynamics: Matching Individuals and Organizational Needs*. Reading, Mass.: Addison-Wesley.

LYNN A. ISABELLA

New Zealand, business ethics in   *see* BUSINESS ETHICS IN NEW ZEALAND

normative/descriptive   The field of business ethics explores the antecedents and consequences of moral behavior in the economic sphere. To do so, the field draws upon two distinct theoretical bases: philosophy, and social sciences – most often social psychology and organization theory. The former base is normative, prescriptive, and held to represent values. The latter is descriptive, empirical, and held to represent "value-free" facts. Within business ethics, a distinct division of labor appears to exist between scholars who were trained in the normative, philosophical tradition and those in the descriptive, social-science tradition.

The normative/descriptive distinction in business ethics has its roots in the fact/value split articulated in ancient Greek philosophy and nineteenth-century European logical positivism. This schism is problematic for two reasons: First, it is philosophically questionable. Second, even if it were predicated upon sound theory, it would be inappropriate in a field that definitionally comprises both prescriptive and descriptive elements.

For the pre-Socratic Greek philosophers (sixth century BC), there was no fact/value distinction, because the two categories corresponded – the normative and the descriptive were assimilated through the assumption that value (e.g. justice) was founded on nature. Knowledge of fact and value was based upon reason, and observation of the natural world. The fact/value dichotomy began to arise with the Sophists (fifth and fourth centuries BC), but they too developed a correspondence theory of truth for statements about values: since value of any kind is determined by human convention, it is factual for those who agree on the truth of a value. In other words, truth is determined by logic and argumentation. The Socratic tradition (fifth and fourth centuries BC) was a reaction to the ethical relativism of the Sophists. By taking an absolutist stance, Socrates, Plato, and Aristotle resolved the fact/value problem. According to their theory, value is determined by nature and can be ascertained through the use of reason. Plato found value (e.g. justice, courage, wisdom, temperance) in the other-worldly *forms* that exist beyond empirical observation. Although ARISTOTLE rejected Plato's other-worldly theory of the *forms*, he believed that value existed in nature and could be discovered, albeit imperfectly, through deliberation based on the use and refinement of practical wisdom.

Values and empirical forms became further distinguished in the nineteenth century, with the advent of Comtean positivism, which later developed into logical positivism. A very strong paradigm in the contemporary social sciences, logical positivism assumes that (a) facts are entirely distinct from values, and (b) social scientists discern truth that is independent of any value judgments and has no normative implications (Comte, 1854; Ayer, 1946).

Yet despite Comte and the logical positivists, a number of thinkers argue that there is no absolute demarcation between fact and value. All science entails value-laden decisions about what to study and how to study it, and – as the social constructionists (e.g. Berger & Luckmann, 1967) have argued – social reality is inarguably open to multiple, value-based interpretations. Pirsig (1991, p. 66) draws upon Socratic philosophy and William James's radical empiricism to argue:

> Values are not outside of the experience logical positivism limits itself to. They are the *essence* of this experience. Values are *more* empirical, in fact, than subjects or objects. Any person of any philosophic persuasion who sits on a hot stove will verify without any intellectual argument whatsoever . . that the *value* of his predicament is negative. This . . is not just a vague, woolly-headed, crypto-religious, metaphysical abstraction. It is an *experience*. It is not a description of experience. As such it is completely predictable. It is verifiable by anyone who cares to do so. It is reproducible, of all experience it is the least ambiguous, least mistakable there is.

The evasion of normative content is untenable in the field of business ethics, since ethics, by definition, advances moral claims. Hence the field cannot be purely non-normative, studying the causes and impacts of organizations' moral behavior without specifying, in philosophical terms, what constitutes morality. Neither can the field be strictly normative. Although the objective of moral philosophy is finding and defending normative positions, philosophers nonetheless have always utilized implicit models of human behavior. Throughout history, much of what we have come to understand about ourselves has had its bases in philosophical inquiry. In recent times, these models of human behavior have been explicitly enhanced by the empirical social sciences. For instance, John Rawls' (1971) *A Theory of Justice* – widely deemed to be one of the great works of twentieth-century philosophy – drew heavily upon the empirical findings of developmental psychologist Lawrence Kohlberg (1969). Rawls' extensive theory of the principles undergirding the construct of justice includes psychologically descriptive discussion of which system of distribution an individual would choose if he or she did not know what his or her natural endowments and position in the social structure would be. The theory's compelling power derives, in part, from Rawls' use of a psychologically tenable decision model: He notes empirical evidence that the principles embedded in his model of justice do indeed serve as decision heuristics for people at high stages of moral development (*see* RAWLS, JOHN).

However, social-science research on topics related to ethics must elucidate constructs as defined by. *philosophers* if such research is to have any claim to studying what it purports to. For instance, psychological research on moral development would be invalid and logically impossible in the absence of a specification of morality – a definition of what ought to be rather than what is.

When the normative/descriptive distinction in business ethics is dissolved, single works of scholarship may draw upon both bases. Under such a method, the specification of ethicality is a philosophical one – for example, Kantian deontology (*see* KANTIAN ETHICS). Social-science theories and techniques then are used to determine how this condition of ethicality may be brought about, and/or what its consequences are. Questions such as how organizations may be designed to foster goals of corporate social performance, and what occurs when businesses behave unethically, are at the heart of business ethics research. Such questions cannot be fully addressed without both normative and empirical components. To ignore the normative aspects is to risk amoral social science, and to ignore the descriptive aspects is to risk unreal philosophy.

Bibliography

Ayer, A. J. (1946). *Language, Truth, and Logic.* London: V. Gollancz.

Berger, P. & Luckmann, T. (1967). *The Social Construction of Reality.* New York: Doubleday.

Comte, A. (1854). *The Positive Philosophy,* trans. H. Martineau. New York: D. Appleton & Co.

Donaldson, T. (1994). When integration fails. *Business Ethics Quarterly,* **4**, (2), 157–70.

Frederick, W. (1994). The virtual reality of fact vs. value. *Business Ethics Quarterly,* **4**, (2), 171–4.

Kohlberg, L. (1969). Stage and sequence: The cognitive-developmental approach to socialization. In D. Goslin (Ed.), *Handbook of Socialization Theory and Research.* Chicago: Rand McNally.

Pirsig, R. (1991). *Lila: An Inquiry into Morals.* New York: McGraw-Hill.

Rawls, J. (1971). *A Theory of Justice.* Cambridge, Mass.: Belknap Press.

Trevino, L. & Weaver, G. (1994). Business *Ethics/ Business* Ethics: One field or two? *Business Ethics Quarterly,* **4**, (2), 113–28.

Weaver, G. & Trevino, L. (1994). Normative and empirical business ethics. *Business Ethics Quarterly,* **4**, (2), 129–44.

Werhane, P. (1994). The normative/descriptive distinction in methodologies of business ethics. *Business Ethics Quarterly,* **4**, (2), 175–80.

Victor, B. & Stephens, C. (1994). Business ethics: A synthesis of normative philosophy and empirical social science. *Business Ethics Quarterly,* **4**, (2), 145–56.

CARROLL U. STEPHENS
and JON M. SHEPARD

Nozick, Robert   (1938–), a philosopher whose main contribution to business ethics is his defense of markets and the libertarian state. Of Robert Nozick's major works, *Anarchy, State, and Utopia* (1974) has the most relevance for business ethics. In it Nozick wrote that after Rawls one must either work within a Rawlsian framework or explain why not. Both Nozick and Rawls reflect the revival of interest in normative philosophy and the attempt to find an adequate alternative to UTILITARIANISM within the social contract tradition. Rawls employs a hypothetical contract argument to defend a modest welfare state, while Nozick also uses a hypothetical contract argument, one based on natural rights and modeled on John Locke. He attempts to defend the claim that a minimal (libertarian) state and nothing more extensive is morally legitimate (*see also* SOCIAL CONTRACT THEORY; LOCKE, JOHN).

Nozick's LIBERTARIANISM rests on a very short list of natural rights, most importantly the natural right of liberty to do whatever one wishes (e.g., give away, buy, sell, trade) with one's person, possessions, and property, provided that one does not harm another in her liberty, person, possessions, or property. Additionally, the list includes the right of self-defense, and the rights to punish and receive compensation from rights violators.

Since only individuals possess natural rights, Nozick claims that governments have rights only insofar as individuals would hypothetically transfer rights (would consent to give up rights) to government. And, because of significant inconvenience associated with a life without government, Nozick believes that rational, self-interested individuals would freely contract together to form a minimal state, but nothing more extensive. Hence, a minimal state and nothing more extensive is legitimate.

In a minimal state, the sole functions of government are to protect individual rights, to punish those who violate rights, and to force compensation when appropriate. Thus, not only a welfare state, but even a state which attempts to promote the public good is illegitimate. Nozick is most concerned, however, to demonstrate the illicit nature of any redistributive functions of a welfare state. Consequently, Nozick devotes one entire part of his work to a criticism of Rawls's principle for distribution and to the development of an alternative entitlement theory of property.

While Milton Friedman provides the most widely known defense of the ideas of the classical business ideology, namely, that the sole responsibility of business is to maximize profit, and the government's function should remain minimal, leaving the free market alone, Nozick offers a natural-rights alternative to utilitarian defenses (see FRIEDMAN, MILTON). Within Nozick's framework, corporations are organizations created by individuals exercising their rights of liberty by contracting together, and have as much right as any individual to do whatever they wish, including profit maximize, provided they violate no one else's rights. Managers may be obligated to profit maximize because they may have contracted with others to perform this role. The right of liberty also guarantees that the minimal state would have no

right to interfere in voluntary contracts between individuals, which would rule out virtually all government regulations establishing minimal wages, working conditions, taxation for safety nets, etc.

Bibliography

Nozick, R. (1974). *Anarchy, State, and Utopia*. New York: Basic Books.
Nozick, R. (1981). *Philosophical Explanations*. Cambridge, Mass.: Harvard University Press.
Nozick, R. (1989). *The Examined Life: Philosophical Meditations*. New York: Simon & Schuster.
Nozick, R. (1993). *The Nature of Rationality*. Princeton: Princeton University Press.
Nozick, R. (Ed.), (1981). *Reading Nozick: Essays on Anarchy, State, and Utopia*. Totowa, NJ: Rowman and Littlefield.

JOHN R. DANLEY

nuclear power Energy released from a nuclear reaction. Nuclear power controversies in America center around complex issues involving safety – nuclear power plants, nuclear waste disposal, and weapons-grade materials. Acting responsibly requires that we learn to distinguish between three general and very different types of problems: "tame," "messy," and "wicked" (Rittel and Webber, 1973; Ackoff, 1974). Nuclear power involves all three.

We *solve* tame problems through analytical methods. First we break a system into its parts, relate them through "linear" (A causes B) logic, then improve the system by improving various of its parts. Tame problems presuppose that reasonable people of good will agree on *why* and on *how*. Solving them has been the great forte of science for several hundred years.

Sorting out messes is complementary but qualitatively different from analysis. First we examine patterns of interactions among the parts, the behavior of the system itself over time, then seek to improve the performance of the system through systemic leverage points. Messes presupposes that we agree on *why* but not on *how*. Such "systems thinking" is a relative newcomer to science.

A simple example illustrates why it is irresponsible to attempt to tame a mess. Asking which of your kids started the argument and then blaming one of them mistakes a mess for a tame problem, and typically makes things worse. Analogously, we have long assumed that probability risk assessments provide reasonable safety estimates. However, assigning probabilities to *known* sequences of failures leading to one of several known nuclear disasters assumes tameness. In stark contrast, incidents documented in the Nuclear Regulatory Commission's regularly published *Nuclear Safety* provide "endless, numbing fascination as they describe all the things that can go wrong in these awesome plants" (Perrow, 1984, p. 46). Messiness increases when we include such unpredictable events as earthquakes, terrorist attacks, and the proliferation of weapons-grade materials.

Systemic problems require systemic remedies. Instead of trying to predict which straw will break the proverbial camel's back, we lighten the load on the camel by simplifying the system, by increasing our capacity to stop disasters once they start, or both.

Nuclear power also involves wickedness, for even given "inherently safe" reactors, reasonable people of good will still radically differ over the *why* of nuclear power. This is primarily because nuclear power entails very different configurations of power than, say, passive solar. Specifically, while pro-nuclear "cornucopians" believe we can manage powerful, modern technologies, anti-nuclear "catastrophists" do not; and while the former reinforce a cultural orientation of "mastery over nature," the latter advocate "harmony with nature."

Such issues are inescapable. But if we pretend otherwise – if we insist on taming wicked problems, we must conclude that our antagonists are ignorant, morally corrupt, or both. This undermines conditions of trust which are our only hope for coping with wickedness. Alternatives include oppression, anarchy, and culture wars.

Wicked problems demand unique strategies which are as ancient as they are imperative in our modern times. The master virtues of integrity and compassion combine in the GOLDEN RULE. As Hillel pointed out long ago, "all else is mere commentary" (King, 1993).

Bibliography

Ackoff, R. L. (1974). *Redesigning the Future: A Systems Approach to Societal Problems.* New York: John Wiley & Sons. (Ackoff coined the term "mess").

King, J. B. (1993). Learning to solve the right problems: The case of nuclear power in America. *Journal of Business Ethics*, 12, 105–16. (An elaboration of this entry).

Perrow, C. (1984). *Normal Accidents: Living With High-Risk Technologies.* New York: Basic Books. (Very readable, excellent analysis).

Reason, J. (1990). The contribution of latent human failures to the breakdown of complex systems. *Philosophical Transactions of the Royal Society of London (Series B)*327, 475–84 (Updated, European variant of Perrow).

Rittel, H. W. J. & Webber, M. M. (1973). Dilemmas in a general theory of planning. *Policy Sciences*, 4, 155–69 (Increasingly relevant analysis of "tame" versus "wicked" problems).

JONATHAN B. KING

O

obedience, to authority and to the law
Obedience: behavioral compliance with a set of
standards or rules formulated by an individual
or by a group. In either case, an individual is
being obedient to authority when he or she
behaves in a manner prescribed by these
standards or rules.

Authority refers to the right or power of the
individual or group who formulated the standards to ensure compliance. Such authority is
generally conveyed by the capability to enforce
the standards. Authority is a function of the
perceived legitimate power of the group or
individual who formulated the standards. Legitimate power is power derived from the position
or role of the group or individual. For example,
typical sources of legitimate power and authority can be found in the roles of parent,
supervisor, teacher, and various law enforcement and judicial positions. The law can be
considered a formal set of rules and standards
that is associated with significant legitimate
power and authority in society.

The psychological and moral implications of
obedience to authority have been investigated
by various researchers. Milgram (1974), for
example, examined why individuals abandon
their responsibility when obeying their supervisor inside a hierarchy. He suggested that the
hierarchical structure of organizations causes
individuals to deny responsibility for their
actions because they are following orders
(obeying authority). Carroll (1978) and Jackall
(1988) both described how difficult it can be for
managers to behave morally inside a hierarchical
business organization when obeying a supervisor may be a condition of continued employment or advancement (*see* MORAL MAZES).

The moral implications of obedience to the
law have also been discussed by numerous
scholars. A useful distinction between *moral
legalism* and *pure legalism* can be found in
Beauchamp and Bowie (1993), as well as a
variety of other business ethics texts. Moral
legalism refers to using the law as a moral
standard or rule. That is, the moral thing to do
is to obey the law.

Pure legalism refers to obeying the law as a
means to help coordinate social activities, but
does not always constitute moral behavior. The
morality of an individual's action is determined
by a moral rule or standard which supersedes
the law. Therefore, although morality and law
are closely connected, they are distinct. Obeying
the law does not necessarily result in moral
behavior.

See also **Legal ethics; Organization ethics;
Organizational theory; Managerial ethics
and the ethical role of the manager; Guilt;
Justice; Responsibility**

Bibliography

Beauchamp, T. L. & Bowie, N. E. (1993). *Ethical
Theory and Business,* 4th edn. New Jersey: Simon
& Schuster.
Carroll, A. (1978). Linking business ethics to
behavior in organizations. *SAM Advanced Manage-
ment Journal,* **43,** 4–11.
Jackall, R. (1988). *Moral Mazes: The World of
Corporate Managers.* New York: Oxford University
Press.
Milgram, S. (1974). *Obedience to Authority.* New
York: Harper & Row.

DAWN R. ELM

omissions   In applied ethics generally, three
issues have come to dominate discussion of
omissions. First, the act/omission distinction is
not simply that between acting and failing to act,

since not all failures to act are omissions. A non-swimmer who does not leap into the ocean to save a drowning man does not have the ability to save one. A swimmer who never comes across a drowning man does not have an opportunity to save one. A swimmer who is not a lifeguard may not be expected or required to save one, just as, because Smith is not expected or required to feed Jones's baby, Smith does not omit to feed it. Ability, opportunity, expectation: these conditions must be satisfied for a failure to act to become an omission.

Omissions are not *ipso facto* immoral omissions. One reason we expect a lifeguard to plunge in is because he seems morally/legally obliged to; one reason we expect the man's son to plunge in, if he is a swimmer, is because he seems morally obliged to. Unless we can establish on *moral* grounds that there is a general duty of rescue, however, we may not expect a member of the general public who is a swimmer to plunge in. (In the United States, a number of state legal codes explicitly lack any general *legal* duty of rescue.) So, in order to be guilty of an immoral omission, the reason one is expected to plunge in must run through, e.g., a moral or legal duty. With this fourth condition met, one needs to defend one's failure to act, if one is to avoid moral and/or legal censure.

Second, is the act/omission distinction morally significant? Today, this has come to be the question of whether there is a significant moral difference between killing and letting die. If one strangles the starving poor, one intentionally kills them, and this is wrong; but is it any less wrong intentionally to omit to feed them and let them starve to death? Either way, they end up dead, and since so many of the consequences of both acts can appear to be the same, consequentialists will be inclined to find little moral difference between killing and letting die. Deontologists, however, typically want to find such a difference, for example, between intending a death and "allowing" or "permitting" one, between actively intervening and intentionally bringing about a death and letting "nature" or some causal sequence run its course, between causing a death and not preventing one, between a stringent duty to avoid harm and a less stringent one to render aid, and so on (*see* CONSEQUENTIALISM).

Third, are omissions causes? If one omits to save a drowning man, and the man dies, it certainly looks to a consequentialist as if the omission plays a causal role in the man's death. Deontologists have wanted to resist this view, not merely through querying, if acting is a doing or a doing-something, how not acting, or a not-doing or a doing-nothing, can cause anything, but also through suggesting that there is a different causal structure associated with death by killing than with death by letting die. If one strangles the starving poor, one directly causes their deaths; if they are "allowed" or "permitted" to die, malnutrition causes their deaths. One is not the direct agent of their demise, a fact which will then be held to have moral import. Consequentialists will likely see the affair as one in which we can kill or cause death by acting or not acting.

Bibliography

D'Arcy, E. (1963). *Human Acts.* Oxford: Clarendon Press.

Denton, F. E. (1991). The case against a duty to rescue. *Canadian Journal of Law and Jurisprudence*, 4, 101–32.

Feinberg, J. (1984). *Harm to Others.* Oxford: Clarendon Press. ch. 4.

Kamm, F. M. (1986). Harming, not aiding, and positive rights *Philosophy and Public Affairs*, 15, 3–32.

Steinbock, B. (Ed.), (1980). *Killing and Letting Die.* Englewood Cliffs, NJ: Prentice-Hall.

R. G. FREY

opportunity cost Opportunity cost exists whenever choosing one alternative precludes the choice of another alternative in a world of scarcity. It is an important principle of rational DECISION THEORY. It arises when some alternatives are not formally considered in a rational analysis.

For example, suppose a person is faced with the choice of whether to play a colleague in handball for an hour. In making a rational choice, if this person made the choice by considering only the value (utility) received from playing handball, the analysis would be incomplete because the opportunity cost of the next best alternative (perhaps working on a revision of a book) was not considered. In making the choice of whether to play handball, one must consider the cost of the lost opportunity (working on the book revision).

Samuelson and Nordhaus define opportunity cost in the following way: "The value of the next best use for an economic good, or the value of the sacrificed alternative. Thus, say that the best alternative use of the inputs employed to mine a ton of coal was to grow 10 bushels of wheat. The opportunity cost of a ton of coal is thus the 10 bushels of wheat that *could* have been produced but were not" (Samuelson & Nordhaus, 1992, p. 743).

The idea of "best alternative" recognizes there may be many alternative uses of a resource, but that the opportunity cost is determined by the most valuable benefits sacrificed. This implies that the correct opportunity cost can only be determined by considering the specific details of a specific problem situation.

The concept of opportunity cost serves to remind us that the out-of-pocket dollar outlays are not a complete measure of the cost. The concept is sometimes misapplied and misunderstood in practice because of the practical difficulty of determining the value of the next best alternative. As an example consider the cost of getting an MBA degree. The out-of-pocket costs for tuition, fees, books, room and board might total $60,000. However, the true cost of getting the MBA degree must also consider the cost of the next best alternative, e.g., working as a financial analyst. Suppose one could earn $40,000 by working as a financial analyst during the same amount of time it takes to get the MBA degree. Then the true cost of getting the MBA is actually $100,000. One way to avoid having to consider the opportunity cost in this way is to formally consider the choice between two alternatives: 1) get an MBA degree, or 2) work as a financial analyst. The cost of 1) is $60,000. This should be compared to the cost of 2) which is the most valuable benefit sacrificed.

Bibliography

Heymann, H. G. & Bloom, R. (1992). *Opportunity Cost in Finance and Accounting*. New York: Quorum Books.

Samuelson, P. A. & Nordhaus, W. D. (1992). *Economics*, 14th edn. New York: McGraw-Hill.

JAMES FREELAND

organization ethics The study of ethical issues in organizations. From a behavioral perspective, ethical issues in business, government, and nonprofit organizations are much more similar than they are different. Equally, the bureaucratic and organizational causes of unethical behavior in business, government, and nonprofit organizations are more similar than they are different. This is why organizational scholars study organizational ethics phenomena and not solely business ethics, government ethics, or nonprofit organization ethics issues.

For example, problems of fair treatment of employees, occupational health and safety, product/service safety, abuse of power, responsibility to external constituencies, pollution, bribery, privacy, conflict of interest, equal opportunity, preferential treatment, unjust discharge, etc., exist across business, government, and nonprofit organizations. Similarly, causes of unethical behavior such as greed for money and/or power, fear of upper-level powerful managers, organizational requirements to obey orders, organizational isolation, routinized "in the box" job behavior, and thinking that does not include the ethical as part of "my job," lack of organization civil liberties that might protect employees from retaliation for raising ethical issues, etc., exist in business, nonprofit, and government organizations.

Organization ethics may be following a developmental path similar to that of organization behavior. Organization behavior is taught in schools of management, business, public administration, education, engineering, nursing, public health, and medicine. This was not always the case. The behavioral sciences were introduced into business schools in the 1920s and it took almost 50 years for organization behavior to be taught in professional schools across economic sectors. Organization ethics may be following a similar pattern. In the 1980s organization ethics was introduced into schools of management and business. Since then a few schools of government and public administration have begun to teach it, and it is spreading to other professional schools. The day may come when most ethics courses in management schools are called organization ethics instead of business ethics.

Bibliography

Ewing, David W. (1977). *Freedom Inside the Organization: Bringing Civil Liberties to the Workplace.* New York: McGraw-Hill.

Hirschmann, Albert O. (1970). *Exit, Voice, and Loyalty: Responses to Decline in Firms, Organizations, and States.* Cambridge, Mass.: Harvard University Press.

Nielsen, Richard P. (1993). Organizational ethics from a perspective of action (praxis). *Business Ethics Quarterly,* **3**, (2), 131–51.

Nielsen, Richard P. (1996). *The Politics of Ethics: Methods for Acting, Learning, and Sometimes Fighting Others in Addressing Ethics Problems in Organizational Life.* New York: Oxford University Press.

RICHARD P. NIELSEN

organizational culture a distinctive characteristic of a community having a significant history, consists of shared assumptions and fundamental beliefs validated over time as essential to the group's successful handling of problems relevant to its internal cohesiveness and external adaptations. Taken for granted as the most realistic way to view the organization and its environment, such beliefs and assumptions are automatically transmitted to new employees as guides for their acting, thinking, and feeling toward the entity's operation.

Situated at the intersection where many disciplines (anthropology, sociology, psychology, philosophy, history, and ORGANIZATIONAL THEORY) meet to offer diverse definitions of organizational culture, it is not surprising that the term seems surrounded by ambiguities.

Previously ignored – even considered as irrelevant – organizational culture had clearly come of age when *The New York Times* (Jan. 7, 1983) described it as the catchphrase "management consultants are breathing into the ears of American executives." An even surer sign of the term's acceptance came when companies followed the lead of Ford, Polaroid, TRW, Proctor and Gamble, and Pacific Telesis in investing millions in efforts to define more precisely their respective cultures. Since culture is the organization's foundation, architects of change had to understand how much restructuring the foundation could support.

Organizational cultures are developed in various ways: World War II gave a Rosie-the-Riveter culture to war-production facilities; IBM's outstanding past performances made the Big Blue a model for other cultures; charismatic founders in the mold of Thomas Watson of IBM, General Johnson of Johnson & Johnson, and Harley Proctor of Proctor and Gamble, who, convinced that the lives and productivity of their employees were shaped by the workplace, sought to build an environment in which both could thrive. An intriguing historical footnote is the question whether Sears-Roebuck surpassed arch-rival Montgomery-Ward because Sears' General Robert Wood had more humanistic values than MW's Sewell Avery. There are, of course, other heroes – Thomas Edison, Charles Steinmetz, and Gerald Swope at General Electric, Knute Rockne at Notre Dame, Theodore Vail and Walter Gifford at American Telephone and Telegraph, and hundreds of others.

On the other hand, hard-driving and successful executives like Harold Geneen of International Telephone and Telegraph, and Richard Snyder of the Simon & Schuster publishing house, left their respective companies with badly battered cultures. The hero-hellion tale suggests that a culture's making may be more than the company's maker. Job security, high wages, aesthetically pleasing workplaces, on-site health and recreational facilities are among the ways new leaders and employees enrich and redefine the culture.

Within organizations are subcultures. The sales division, for example, may have a "gung-ho" ideology; research and development, a visionary "can do" outlook; and engineering, a careful, meticulous approach. But all subcultures partake of the essential qualities of the entity's larger culture that serve as both an integrative and control agent over the various parts.

Distinctions are now in order. *Organizational culture* is not the same as *corporate structure*, which may reflect (a) Weberian bureaucratic models that provide impartial treatment of people and standardized procedures, or (b) patrimonial structures that emphasize personalities, an emphasis that often results in politicking, Machiavellian intrigues, and discreet maneuvering to win the boss's favor.

A more important distinction exists between *culture* and *climate*. The *organizational climate*, often determined by taking the pulse of employees, seeks to answer such questions as these: What are the workers' expectations of the enterprise? Do they find their expectations being met? Are they proud of being an Organization X's employee? The climate is more like public opinion – transitory, subject to sudden change, and an uncertain base for judging the company's underlying character.

Culture's Importance

That culture plays a significant role in business is illustrated by the way company breakups and corporate mergers are handled. The most dramatic example of breakup came in 1984 in the court-ordered division of AT&T. To dismantle efficiently, the company established headquarters in Basking Ridge, New Jersey. On the center's walls were posted every conceivable item: schedules, charts, alternatives and options, and the like. Missing was the word *culture* – an omission that added confusion to the dismantling process.

A second example of culture's importance occurs during mergers or takeovers. Postmortems of failures have tended to focus on such factors as over-inflated purchase prices, unrealistic projections for earnings, or potential economies of scale. Ignored was the possibility of a mismatch of corporate cultures. One example occurred in 1984 when General Motors purchased Electronic Data Systems from H. Ross Perot. At the time it was thought that EDS's hard-driving entrepreneurial spirit would be crushed by the bureaucracy of the giant purchaser. In reality, the reverse occurred: loyalty to the boss became the prime requisite for employees.

Ethical Questions

By its very nature, organizational culture raises important moral questions: Are individuals trustworthy or not? More prone to good or to evil? Capable of increasing their understandings of right and wrong? On another level is the question of truth: Is it what most people say truth is? Is it what the boss declares? Is everyone's opinion as good as everyone else's?

On the institutional plane the question centers around the meaning of the corporate person – a definition used in the American legal system. What does *person* mean? (*See* CORPORATION, MORAL STATUS OF.) While many terms have been coined to describe the perspective of the disputants on this issue, one useful distinction is that between (1) the moral person's view and (2) the structural-restraint paradigm. Under the first, all agents are moral agents because they behave *intentionally* – and organizations act with intent, an intent that may differ from the intention of even certain directors and officers. Corporations are, therefore, full-fledged members of the moral community on equal standing with humans. The organization is not simply an agency among agencies; it is the stage on which actors perform. As role-holders their actions might be quite different from their personal behavior and beliefs.

Firmly opposed to this position is the structural-restraint camp who insist that individuals, not entities, act. Simply establishing goals implies that other moral considerations are either automatically excluded or considered irrelevant. Persons alone have intellects and free wills and only they can bear moral responsibility for their actions. Hiding under a collective cloak is no excuse for evading individual responsibility.

While scholars debate, managers act. Perhaps leadership's most important function is to know when and how to create, recreate, and, when necessary, destroy the organization's culture.

Bibliography

Deal, T. W. & Kennedy, A. A. (1982). *Corporate Cultures*. Reading, Mass.: Addison-Wesley.

Frost, P. J., et al. (1985). *Organizational Culture*. Beverly Hills, Calif.: Sage.

Hofsteder, G. (1980). *Culture's Consequences*. Beverly Hills, Calif.: Sage.

Ott, J. S. (1989). *The Organizational Culture Perspective*. Chicago: Dorsey.

Schein, E. H. (1985). *Organizational Culture and Leadership*. San Francisco: Jossey-Bass.

Walton, Clarence. (1992). *Corporate Encounters*. New York: Dryden.

CLARENCE C. WALTON

organizational decay   a process in which an organization shifts its focus from coping with the real world to dramatizing a fantasy about itself. It is a progressive condition that builds upon itself, enlisting more and more of the organization's energies and resources, until the capability of the organization to deal with the real world becomes problematic.

Psychology of Organizational Decay

In the beginning of psychological life, the fusion of infant and mother creates for the infant a sense of being the center of a loving world. Freud (1955, 1957; Chasseguet-Smirgel, 1985) refers to this experience as *primary narcissism*. Inevitably, the fact of the world's indifference presents itself to us, resulting in anxiety. To defend against anxiety, we develop a fantasy of the return to the state of narcissistic fusion. Freud called this fantasy the *ego ideal*. It represents for us a life free of anxiety.

Our projection of the ego ideal into organizations is what lies behind their attraction for us. In doing this, we picture ourselves in our organizational roles as being the center of a loving world – perfectly good, free of tension, able to do what we want and be loved for it. When we do this, we have taken the organization as our ego ideal. An image of the organization functioning as an ego ideal is called the *organization ideal*. Unfortunately, we are not the center of a loving world. The ego ideal, whether in the form of the organization ideal or any other form, is never realized.

Organizations attempt, in various ways, to preserve the fantasy of the ego ideal, while registering that it has not been attained. In corporate life, the most common means for this is through the idea of hierarchy. Hierarchy explains how the organization can be the ego ideal, while our lives as organization participants are not perfect. It is because those who really represent the organization, its high officials, have attained the organization ideal, even if we have not. In this way, the organization enlists our anxiety as a powerful motivational force, which it can direct by specifying criteria for promotion.

To maintain the fantasy of the organization ideal as a motivational force, the corporation must dramatize its own perfection and the perfection of its high officials. But the organization and its officials are not perfect. Hence, the organization that operates this way must shift its focus toward the creation and embellishment of

a fantasy of perfection, and deny the reality that stands at variance with it. This is the root of organizational decay.

Some Aspects of Organizational Decay

(1) *Commitment to bad decisions* The organization ideal, being perfect, makes only perfect decisions. An organization in a state of decay compels the belief that its decisions have been perfect, no matter how imperfect they may have been. The subsequent policies of the organization amplify this error, degrading the organization's capacity to make good decisions in the future and leaving the original problems unresolved.

(2) *Advancement of participants who detach themselves from reality, and discouragement of reality-oriented participants who are committed to their work* As the organization's capacity to make good decisions erodes, successful idealization of the organization becomes increasingly difficult. At the same time it becomes increasingly urgent as an organizational priority. Promotion criteria shift toward those who are best at advancing and maintaining this fiction, in the face of increasing variance with reality. These people can either be cynics, whose elevation degrades the moral character of the organization, or individuals with a high capacity for self-delusion, who simply do not have much engagement with reality at all. Reality-oriented participants tend to become discouraged and alienated.

(3) *The narcissistic loss of reality among management* When the organization becomes the dramatization of its own perfection and that of its high officials, individuals are subjected to organizational pressure to maintain this performance. Those in positions of power, who are central in exerting this pressure, often having been assisted in their rise to power by the lack of a firm connection with reality, can easily take this performance as an authentic reflection of their real perfection. In this way, they may lose touch with reality altogether (*Business Week*, 1991).

(4) *Transposition of work and ritual* In the decaying organization, productive work loses its meaning; work becomes a ritualized performance. At the same time, rituals associated with the process of promotion, increasingly divorced as they are from the organization's function,

come to be supercharged with meaning. Employees' energy is redirected accordingly.

(5) *Creation of the organizational jungle* Progress through the hierarchy, which is supposed to mean increasing freedom from anxiety, may make it worse. The cause of the anxiety cannot be acknowledged, and the necessity of maintaining the fantasy of the organization ideal means that one has to deal with it in isolation. Often, individuals attribute its cause to others, who are experienced as threats to their security, threats that may be dealt with by gaining hierarchical advantage over those seen as posing them.

(6) *Creation of the enemy without* Another way of dealing with anxiety is by attributing it to forces outside the organization, seen as bad, who make demands on the organization, seen as all good. This may be the source of some of the antisocial activity of otherwise perfectly decent organizational citizens.

Morality is not a matter that affects organizational life only occasionally. It is always present in the obligation to do good work. Organizational decay, by construing the organization as its own moral universe, interferes with the morality of the work process. This places many organizational participants in a condition of sustained moral dilemma, torn between what they need to do to get their work done, and what they need to do to advance within the organization. Resolution of this continuing dilemma requires a realistic sense of what life has to offer and a deep appreciation of the meaning of our relationships to others.

Bibliography

Business Week (1991). Cover story: CEO Disease: Egotism can breed corporate disaster – and the malady is spreading. 1 April, pp. 52–60

Chasseguet-Smirgel, J. (1985). *The Ego Ideal: A Psychoanalytic Essay on the Malady of the Ideal.* New York: Norton.

Freud, S. (1955). *Group Psychology and the Analysis of the Ego.* Standard edition, ed. L. Strachey, vol. 18. London: Hogarth Press.

Freud, S. (1957). *On Narcissism: An Introduction.* Standard edition, ed. L. Strachey, vol. 14. London: Hogarth Press.

Jackall, R. (1988). *Moral Mazes: The World of Corporate Managers.* New York: Oxford University Press. (Organizational decay processes from a sociological perspective.)

Schwartz, H. S. (1990). *Narcissistic Process and Corporate Decay: The Theory of the Organization Ideal.* New York: New York University Press.

Trento, J. J. (1987). *Prescription for Disaster: From the Glory of Apollo to the Betrayal of the Shuttle.* New York: Crown. (Organizational decay processes at NASA.)

Wright, J. P. (1979). *On a Clear Cay You Can See General Motors: John Z. De Lorean's Look Inside the Automotive Giant.* New York: Avon. (Organizational decay processes at General Motors.)

HOWARD S. SCHWARTZ

organizational dilemmas   A dilemma is a choice between two conflicting alternatives where both cannot be realized. In an ethical context of a business setting, "organizational dilemmas" may be choices faced by business decision-makers in which to choose to behave ethically is also to choose to behave in ways that may harm a corporation's profit margins or even threaten its continued existence.

These are the sorts of decisions faced when, for instance, asbestos manufacturers received medical reports that asbestos inhalation caused lung cancer in workers, tobacco manufacturers received scientific reports on the cancer-causing properties of cigarette smoking, or the Robbins corporation received reports that its contraceptive device, the Dalkon Shield, drew dangerous bacteria into the bodies of its users.

The Causes of Unethical Resolutions to Organizational Dilemmas

When episodes of corporate malfeasance are discovered, and large numbers of persons are involved, a great deal of public anger is generated. While the public condemnation is appropriate, it is also worth carrying out a close examination of the organizational dynamics that led to these results; an examination that might allow for the reduction of these incidents. The first result of such an examination suggests that organizations that engage in harm-doing to their workers, the consumers of their products, or the general public fall into two categories: in the first category the corporate leaders intend to commit the practice, in the second they do not, but, as we will see, complex organizational processes often cause it to happen.

Organizations that seek to do harm.   In the first category, it becomes obvious that the organizational principals plan to commit the unethical or illegal actions in order that they personally or the organization gains what profits can be made. The assumption is that the nature of the actions can be concealed, or the consequences of its detection minimized. Examples of this abound: "boiler room" stock-brokerage houses that push dreadful stock on customers, siding contractors who disappear with customers' deposits. Some large and apparently respectable companies have also engaged in these practices: for example, newspaper reports on the settlements that the Prudential Corporation is making with investors lured into "safe investments" that tumbled in value. Nor is it always customers that are the target of such behaviors; the Film Recovery System Corporation hired illegal immigrant workers who could not read English in order that they would not know their health was being endangered by the toxic chemicals they were required to handle without safety precautions.

If the corporate management intends that unethical or illegal solutions to organizational dilemmas be chosen, then how is it that they make certain that the corporate subordinates resolve dilemmas in the direction of acting unethically or illegally when they face concrete choices to do so? Broadly, this is accomplished in two ways. First they recruit workers who will act questionably. Investigators of businesses running swindles by telephone reveal that the average telephone swindler has worked for a number of such operations before, moving to new ones as legal prosecution closes down the old ones. Second, the corporation uses techniques for the "socialization" of ordinary individuals into acting unscrupulously. These methods of socialization can be specified by organizational social scientists; here we simply mark that they change the individuals involved, generally making them active participants in unethical actions, thus adding to the pool of those who are recruitable for similar actions in the future, and who will independently engage in those actions without organizational pressures to do so.

The social control of organizations in which the top management is complicit in harm-doing actions can take three general forms: voluntary change in the corporate structure to eliminate inappropriate pressures, government monitoring to detect wrongdoing, followed by fines,

criminal prosecutions, or interventions to force changes in corporate structure, or consumer boycott actions. Many scholars (e.g. Clinard & Yeager, 1980, pp. 229–325) who have examined the actual workings of these social controls on corporate behavior do not find them altogether effective, although some think that they could be strengthened and made effective.

Organizations that get entrapped in wrongdoing. In other cases, the wrongdoing in a corporation is not condoned by the management; instead it begins at some lower level within the organization. These cases deserve considerable analytic interest because, unlike the cases in which the top of the organization intends unethical actions, it seems that corporate practices could be effective in detecting and stopping these actions. While no definitive surveys identify frequencies, it is clear that in a number of cases in which unethical actions begin in some unit of a corporation, those practices capture the acquiescence of those higher in the hierarchy, and moves are made to cover up the practices. A number of factors bring this about: loyalties to subordinates, superiors' feelings of negligence and mismanagement for not detecting the practices earlier, corporate commitments to the quality of the product now discovered flawed or to the industrial practice now discovered dangerous, and/or costs incurred to date that would be wasted if the wrong were to be corrected; perhaps most importantly, the humiliation of being a part, although not an unwitting part, of an unethical action. For these reasons, corporations sometimes attempt to cover up the unethical actions. In doing so, they often encourage behaviors that are as unethical as the actions that they cover up, and as a second consequence, continue the initial unethical actions, such as when defective and dangerous products have been marketed by corporations long past the point when they discovered that they were dangerous.

How this can be avoided is a question that calls for a good deal of attention. Corporate CODES OF ETHICS are helpful if the corporation has a history of taking them seriously. Protected mechanisms for reporting violations to corporate authorities that will take them seriously also have been recommended; outside directors may be used in this fashion. Other mechanisms for supporting those within the organization who "blow the whistle" are important because traditionally WHISTLEBLOWING is frequently a punished activity.

Bibliography

Clinard, M. & Yeager, P. (1980). *Corporate Crime.* New York: Free Press.
Schlegel, K. & Weisburd, D. (eds). (1992). *White Collar Crime Reconsidered.* Boston: Northeastern University Press.

JOHN DARLEY

organizational influence, perceived legitimacy of *see* PERCEIVED LEGITIMACY OF ORGANIZATIONAL INFLUENCE

organizational moral climate   shared perceptions of prevailing organizational norms for addressing issues with a moral component. These issues include (a) identifying moral problems, (b) choosing criteria for resolving moral conflicts, and (c) evaluating the moral correctness of outcomes that ensue (Cohen, 1995). The terms *ethical climate* (Victor and Cullen, 1988) and *moral atmosphere* (Kohlberg, 1984) are also commonly used.

The current interest in moral-climate research among organizational scholars is an outgrowth of a large literature documenting the effects of situational factors on moral conduct in organizations. Featuring prominently in this literature are the works of social psychologists who studied the effects of *moral atmosphere* on behavior in school and prison settings (Kohlberg, 1984). These studies showed that making changes in organizational practices, policies, and procedures created a positive moral atmosphere that, in turn, contributed to improvements in individual moral development and moral judgment, as well as to reductions in cheating, stealing, and other antisocial activities.

In the last several years, business researchers have extended this line of inquiry by studying how certain types of moral climate evolve in business firms, how moral climate affects employee behavior, and how moral climate can be transformed. These studies indicate that a firm's moral climate affects the way employees

exercise moral judgment, make moral choices, and, ultimately, how they act to resolve a moral problem. This research has also shown moral climate to be the product of several organizational and environmental factors. Environmental factors include cultural values, religious beliefs, external threats or opportunities, and industry characteristics. Organizational factors include strategy, structure, culture, and, most importantly, managerial expectations (see Cohen, 1995; Victor and Cullen, 1988; Wimbush and Shepard, 1994). Recently, academics have also looked at the role of business-school moral climate for educating responsible managers (Trevino and McCabe, 1994).

In terms of evaluating a firm's moral climate, two methods of assessment have been developed. The first involves classifying moral climate according to the implicit moral philosophy that appears to prevail in organizational decisions, as well as whose interests are typically considered to be most important when these decisions are made (Victor and Cullen, 1988). The second method, designed primarily for managing change, entails examining key organizational activities such as setting goals, administering rewards, and allocating resources to determine how widely norms prevail in the firm for treating employees and external stakeholders in a trustworthy manner (Cohen, 1995).

The growing literature on moral climate, combined with other research exploring the effects of organizational processes on moral conduct in business firms, has had a major impact on the way both managers and public policy-makers address the problem of unethical business practice. Rather than seeking to change behavior by trying to change employee attitudes, managers have begun to recognize that transforming organizational policies and procedures will have a more lasting impact on moral conduct in the firm. Managers are also becoming aware of how their own actions affect the organization's moral climate overall. Meanwhile, new laws, such as the organizational sentencing guidelines, are demanding greater corporate accountability for individual misconduct and at the same time acknowledging the good-faith efforts of organizations to encourage responsible business practice through procedural and structural change. These developments reflect a new and promising understanding of the complexity of moral behavior in the workplace that will advance both the study and the practice of ethics in the business community.

See also **Organizational culture; Procedural justice; Leadership**

Bibliography

Cohen, D. V. (1995). Creating ethical work climates: A socio-economic perspective. *Journal of Socio-economics*, **24**, (2), 317–43.
Kohlberg, L. (1984). *The Psychology of Moral Development*. San Francisco: Harper and Row.
Trevino, L. & McCabe, D. (1994). Meta-learning about business ethics. *Journal of Business Ethics*, **13**, (6).
Victor, B. & Cullen, J. (1988). The organizational bases of ethical work climates. *Administrative Science Quarterly*, **33**, 101–25.
Wimbush, J. & Shepard, J. (1994). Ethical work climates and behavior: An agenda for a neglected area of research. *Journal of Business Ethics*, **13**, (8), 637–48.

DEBORAH VIDAVER COHEN

organizational theory, ethical issues in *see* ETHICAL ISSUES IN ORGANIZATIONAL THEORY

OSHA The US Occupational Safety and Health Administration, authorized . by the OSHA Act of 1970 (29 USC 651 *et seq.*). OSHA's functions are to: develop and promulgate occupational safety and health standards, develop and issue regulations; conduct investigations and inspections to determine the status of compliance; and issue citations and propose penalties for non-compliance (*US Government Manual, 1994/1995*, pp. 420–1).

OSHA regulations apply only to businesses with 11 or more employees and do not apply to government agencies, self-employed persons, family farms, and workplaces protected by other federal agencies (*Federal Regulatory Directory*, 1994, p. 388).

The Act was passed in 1970 after a long history of debate over safety in the workplace. The early years of OSHA were very controversial. Business interests complained about arbitrarily-set standards and unnecessary interference with business practices.

Beginning with the Carter Administration, the agency was streamlined. During the Reagan and Bush administrations, an anti- regulatory posture emerged. Cost–benefit principles were applied to all regulations, particularly by the Office of Management and Budget. Court decisions rendered such practices inappropriate in situations of extreme health risk (*see* SOCIAL COST–BENEFIT).

Organized labor has favored strict enforcement of OSHA. "OSHA has conveyed rights and hopes which workers now hold as fundamental in their workplace" (Kirkland, 1984, p. 1). Employers generally have opposed strict enforcement and tough standard-setting by the agency. The broader debates over regulation and cost–benefit analysis, in general, have occasionally overshadowed the specific debates about regulations for workplace safety and health.

Bibliography

Federal Regulatory Directory. (1994). Washington, DC: Congressional Quarterly Inc.
Kirkland, L., et al. (1984). *OSHA: A 10-Year Success Story*. Washington, DC: AFL-CIO (American Federation of Labour and Congress of Industrial Organizations.)
The US Government Manual. (1994/1995). Office of the Federal Register, National Archives and Records Administration, Washington, DC.

ALAN R. BECKENSTEIN

ownership, ethics of *see* ETHICS OF OWNERSHIP

P

Pareto optimality A Pareto-optimal allocation is one from which it is impossible to
improve any party's share without diminishing
the share of another party.

When allocating resources, whether through
a negotiation process, political process, or
simply by edict, the question arises: How do
you know whether the final allocation is a
"good" one?

Regardless of one's philosophy, a necessary
condition for "goodness" with which few people
would argue is Pareto optimality. One would
never want to accept a non-Pareto-optimal
allocation, because such an allocation could
always be improved upon for at least one party –
if not for all parties – without requiring any
sacrifice from any other party.

This idea is presented graphically in Figure
1. The figure depicts the collection of possible

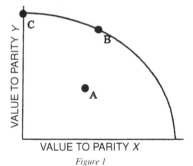

Figure 1

resolutions of a two-party allocation decision, as
measured by the value each party derives from
each possible resolution. The points on and
within the curve represent the values to the
parties of the possible allocations. Because no
allocations are mapped to points outside the
curved boundary, that boundary represents the
collection of Pareto-optimal allocations. No

allocation represented by a point within the
curved space is Pareto optimal because there is
always another allocation on the curved boundary that is preferred by both parties.

For instance, compare the allocations whose
values to the parties are depicted by points A
and B. No matter what the value systems are to
which the individuals subscribe, as long as the
individual's values are measured accurately,
then both parties must prefer allocation B to
allocation A. It follows immediately, therefore,
that all "good" allocations are Pareto optimal.

But, are all Pareto-optimal allocations good?
Consider allocation C. This allocation could be
described as "Y gets everything; X gets
nothing." In a multiparty allocation decision,
equivalent allocations are those where one party
or a few parties get everything, and everyone
else gets nothing. Few would welcome such
outcomes. And, the reason is clear: *Pareto
optimality says nothing about fairness.* In other
words, while few would disagree with the idea
that Pareto optimality is a *necessary* condition for
assessing the "goodness" of allocations, few
would argue that it, alone, is *sufficient* (*see*
FAIRNESS).

There is also an additional problem with
Pareto optimality. When one moves from few
parties to many, the concept itself becomes less
useful. The reason is that, as the number of
parties increases, the probability increases
dramatically that at least one party would be
made worse off whenever one allocation is
replaced by another. In other words, in multiparty allocation decisions, a far greater percentage of the collection of possible allocations are
Pareto optimal. And, in the extreme, when all
allocations are Pareto optimal, Pareto optimality
cannot discriminate among allocations. Hence,

as the number of parties increases, the Pareto optimality condition loses its power.

Nevertheless, the condition is still necessary. One should never accept an allocation – no matter how many parties – that is not Pareto optimal. Furthermore, in two-party allocation decisions, like one-on-one negotiations, Pareto optimality is a powerful tool for discriminating among alternatives.

Bibliography

Deutsch, M. (1975). *Distributive Justice*. New Haven: Yale University Press.

Clyman, D. R. (1995). Measures of joint performance in dyadic mixed-motive negotiations. *Organizational Behavior and Human Decision Processes*, **64**, 38–48.

Clyman, D. R. (1996). Measuring cooperation in negotiations: The impossible dream. In Zeckhauser, R. J., et al. (eds), *Wise Choices: Decisions, Games and Negotiations*. Boston: Harvard Business School Press, 388–99.

Lax, D. A. & Sebenius, J. K. (1987). Measuring the degree of joint gains achieved by negotiators. Unpublished manuscript, Harvard University, Cambridge, Mass.

Lind, E. A. & Tyler, T. R. (1988). *The Social Psychology of Procedural Justice*. New York: Plenum Press.

Raiffa, H. (1982). *The Art and Science of Negotiation*. Cambridge, Mass.: Harvard University Press.

Tripp, T. M. & Sondak, H. (1992). An evaluation of dependent variables in experimental negotiation studies: Impasse rates and Pareto efficiency. *Organizational Behavior and Human Decision Processes*, 51, 273–95.

DANA R. CLYMAN and THOMAS M. TRIPP

partiality The favoring of one interest, person, or group more than another, for example, favoring loved ones more than other persons.

All philosophers share the common–sensical view that partiality toward family members and friends has great value. Partiality is essential to sustaining those close relationships, which, in turn, are necessary for personal identity, integrity, and fulfillment in life. Many philosophers similarly see great value in communal and group loyalties. Philosophers disagree, however, about the best way to account philosophically for those values.

The dominant theoretical traditions of modern moral philosophy, UTILITARIANISM and KANTIAN ETHICS, define the moral point of view as requiring *impartial* concern for all persons. Impartiality seems either to imply that partiality is morally prohibited or to call for attitudes that make it psychologically impossible. An impartial moral reasoner is detached from her personal concerns and loyalties and gives equal consideration to the interests of all persons as abstract moral equals. These attitudes seem ill-suited to personal relationships and group loyalties.

"Partialists" reject these theories to at least some extent. They regard partiality toward loved ones as having an intrinsic value which cannot be overridden by the impartial moral requirement to give equal consideration to the interests of all persons. On this view, people are often justified in simply giving top priority to their own projects and loved ones. Some partialists believe that partiality toward loved ones is not a part of morality at all. Others regard it as a part of morality, but one which does not call for an impartial viewpoint; impartiality is required only for moral interactions in the public sphere, for example, when acting as an official with the duty to be "fair." Still other partialists insist that impartiality is never required by morality since impartiality is a psychologically rare, perhaps impossible, attitude. On this view, all morality is based on some sort of partiality (e.g., to loved ones, to one's own community, to humanity in general but not to non-human animals).

Moral "impartialists" believe, by contrast, that all of morality must rest on fundamental principles which are determined without giving any special weight to one's own interests or commitments. One may, however, show partiality toward loved ones in living one's daily life – so long as those choices are consonant with the fundamental, impartial principles of morality. Devotion to one's own children, for example, is morally legitimate so long as it is impartially morally right that all parents devote themselves each to their own children. On this view, impartialist moral principles remain the best basis for determining which forms of partiality are wrong – for example, nepotism, misogyny, and white supremacism.

Partialists thus modify and limit impartial moral theory when accounting for partiality. Impartialists instead reinterpret impartial moral theory in order to show that it already justifies (legitimate forms of) partiality. One other recent view is that both of these approaches have so far failed, and that we have not yet developed the moral theory which adequately recognizes and interrelates the fundamental moral importance of both partiality and impartiality.

Bibliography

Baron, M. (1984). The alleged moral repugnance of acting from duty. *Journal of Philosophy*, **81** (4), 197–220.

Blum, L. A. (1980). *Friendship, Altruism and Morality.* London: Routledge & Kegan Paul.

Brink, D. O. (1986). Utilitarian morality and the personal point of view. *Journal of Philosophy*, **83** (8), 417–38.

Kittay, E. F. & Meyers, D. T. (eds). (1987). *Women and Moral Theory.* Totowa, NJ: Rowman and Littlefield.

MacIntyre, A. (1984). *After Virtue,* 2nd edn. Notre Dame, Ind.: University of Notre Dame Press.

Nagel, T. (1991). *Equality and Partiality.* New York: Oxford University Press.

Scheffler, S. (1982). *The Rejection of Consequentialism.* Oxford: Clarendon Press.

Symposium on impartiality and ethical theory. (1991). *Ethics,* **101** (4), 695–864.

Williams, B. (1981). *Moral Luck.* Cambridge: Cambridge University Press.

MARILYN FRIEDMAN

participatory management   The concept of participatory or participative management has been used in the context of traditional hierarchical industrial organizations or bureaucracies. It means that, to a greater or lesser extent, managers share their power with employees, managers, or non-managers, who are lower in the structure. The opposite of participative management is autocratic or dictatorial management.

This overview first describes the experience of participative management in traditional industrial organizations and then reports recent organizational initiatives that have redefined participative management in terms of empowerment and interactive management.

Within the traditional organizational framework, there are three degrees of participative management: consultation, value-based influence, and formal power sharing.

Consultation is the form of participation wherein a manager seeks the viewpoints of subordinates before making a decision. There is no commitment by the manager to act according to the wishes or suggestions of subordinates (Weber, 1964).

Value-based influence implies a commitment by management to take account of subordinates' viewpoints before making decisions. Typically, there is agreement that managers will honor explicitly stated values. In some of the most effective companies, these values try to balance the interests of a number of stakeholders, in particular, owners, customers, and employees (Kotter & Heskett, 1992) (*see* ORGANIZATIONAL CULTURE).

Formal power-sharing entails a more democratic form of governance in which some, but not necessarily all, so-called managerial decisions are made by consensus or vote. This type of participation or co-determination is not usually adopted freely but is typically forced on management by the political system or stakeholder power (e.g. unions, environmental groups). It is then up to management to make good use of co-determination by adopting a participatory style of leadership.

An example is the German Works Council where members elected by the employees can make some decisions concerning changes in work rules and also influence top management's strategic decisions. Another example is the General Motors Saturn factory in Spring Hill, Tennessee, where union officials, elected by workers, formally share power with plant management.

Participatory management often implies that while managers may listen to or even share power with those lower in the hierarchy, they reserve the right to make the final decisions. Exceptions to this rule are those cases where through collective bargaining there is a contractual agreement with a union to share power – for example, in setting wages and evaluating working conditions. In some organizations, there is a mixture of consultation, influence, and power-sharing, depending on the type of decisions involved.

Why Does Management Invite Participation?

The purposes of practicing participatory management are to arrive at better decisions, to achieve employee buy-in for implementing management decisions, and to increase employee motivation. By listening to frontline employees, managers gain information and ideas. Workers and service technicians may find processes ineffective, inefficient, or cumbersome. They may offer suggestions for improvement. Especially in the age of service, frontline employees are in the best position to hear customer complaints and ideas for improvement. Experience demonstrates that at all organizational levels, when people feel they have been heard and their views given serious consideration, they are more likely to support management decisions and implement management plans.

Beginning with the pioneering research on worker morale at the Western Electric Hawthorne plant in Chicago in the 1930s, there has been evidence that by giving employees a say in how work is performed, satisfaction with work usually improves. (See the discussion of resistances to participation, below, for exceptions.) Recent surveys indicate that a majority of employees believe that participation in these areas will improve organizational effectiveness and quality. Employees in the US want to have a say in deciding how to do their jobs and organize the work; deciding what training is needed for their jobs; setting work schedules including breaks, overtime, and time off; setting goals for their work group; deciding how to work with new equipment or software; and setting safety standards and practices.

Japanese industries took the lead in the 1960s and 1970s by integrating participative management into a total quality management system including the idea that all workers have internal and external customers they must satisfy. Workers are encouraged to participate in continuous improvement and rewarded for ideas adopted by management. At Toyota Motors, in the early 1990s, there were about 50 ideas per worker per year proposed and of these 80 percent were adopted, with workers rewarded with bonuses for those adopted.

Japanese management also allows workers to experiment with changing work methods. In most large Japanese companies, worker representatives are consulted on strategic decisions.

The participation of unions as institutions in management decisions is required by law in Germany and Sweden, where union representatives sit on supervisory boards. This participation can range from a more perfunctory information sharing, with minimal consultation, to significant involvement in shaping and implementing policies. In the US, in some companies the United Autoworkers (UAW), United Steelworkers (USW), United Needletrades Industrial and Textile Employees (UNITE), and Communication Workers of America (CWA) have reached contractual agreement to participate with management in decisions ranging from market strategy to process changes. In these cases, the unions also encourage management to involve frontline employees in decision-making.

Limits to Participatory Management

The ability to participate in a meaningful way depends on such factors as size of group, participants' knowledge of the situation, and speed of decision-making required. There are occasions when management wants to limit the number of people involved in sensitive negotiations, because of possible negative consequences if the information becomes known publicly.

There are also cases where employees reject invitations to participate. For example, union representatives have refused to participate in decisions which might adversely affect their members. Although generally union members want their leaders to participate with management, there are instances in which participation could erode their political support. Crozier (1964) showed that many French bureaucrats rejected opportunities to participate in order to protect autonomy and the right to object, or in the case of union members, grieve a management decision.

An issue is the fear by employees that by volunteering ideas to improve productivity, they may no longer be needed and lose their jobs. In the large Japanese companies, participation has been reinforced by promises of employment security. In the US, some unions have bargained for employment security, while others in industries undergoing continual restructuring and rationalization, have negotiated programs for retraining and continual learning to enhance employability.

Effective participatory management requires a high level of mutual trust. Otherwise managers will not share information and their subordinates will not want to open themselves to possible manipulation or exploitation. The most effective participative management is based on practicing values such as respect, honesty, and an attempt to obtain mutual benefit from decisions. (Participatory management also requires that employees are educated sufficiently about management goals so that they can contribute meaningfully to decisions. Equally, it requires facilitative skills and the willingness to listen to employees on the part of managers. Maccoby (1988) has found that managers with an "expert orientation" have a hard time learning from subordinates.)

In 1994, the Communications Workers of America studied examples in which they had participated with the management of telecommunication companies. They found that when participation was value based and information was shared sufficiently, there were significant benefits to both management and employees. However, they also found cases of pseudo-participation and promises for participation made by a manager who then left his or her position and was replaced by someone who took advantage of the trust previously developed.

Beyond Participative Management

A new organizational model is emerging. It is flatter than the traditional industrial bureaucracy, with fewer middle managers. The ideal is that top management determines strategy and the frontline is empowered to implement and adapt it (*see* EMPOWERMENT). To some degree, these elements have been part of good management in the past. What is most different is the movement from autonomous functions to interactivity and heterarchical cross-functional teams.

The new organizational model has resulted from four factors: the shift to service industry, the lessons of total quality management, the competitive demand for speed in bringing new products to market, and the significant development in the 1980s and 1990s of information

and telecommunications technology (IT). IT allows manufacturing processes to be automated and information to be shared rapidly to and from the front lines that deal with customers. Furthermore, the new IT has allowed management to "re-engineer" processes to cut out layers of control and communication.

Under this model, instead of following directions, the frontline employees are "empowered" to use judgment and make decisions that will both satisfy customers and implement management strategy. In the case of complex technology, quick decisions must be made for purposes of safety and to avoid losses.

In the hierarchical, cross-functional team, leadership shifts according to who has the appropriate knowledge. An example is a concurrent design process which replaced a linear design process that moves from design to engineering to production. Instead designers, engineers, marketing experts, and frontline production employees, and in some cases, customers work together, share different types of knowledge, and make decisions by consensus. The results are better products, produced more rapidly.

The management model proposed by Ackoff (1994) redefines participatory management as interactive management, based on the concept of the organization as a social system with the goal of satisfying the main stakeholders: customers, employees, and owners. The interactive planning process requires that management design an "ideal future" which is interpreted and implemented by people in different parts of the system. A continual dialogue is led by management concerning how to close the gaps between the present state and the organization's ideal design.

This interactive approach to continual transformation and employee empowerment has been the basis for AT&T's Workplace of the Future and was agreed to by its unions – CWA and IBEW – in their 1992 contract. Each business unit and division has a planning council which includes union representatives who are there not because of their demand for power, but because they add value. They facilitate communication, and by emphasizing employee needs and protecting their contractual rights, they increase trust in the process. The planning council is led by management with the value-based participatory approach. The council designs the ideal future, develops an education program with the aid of Rutgers University, and interactively supports attempts by the various workplaces to interpret and implement it.

In the new interactive model, participatory management no longer depends on a few innovative skillful managers. It engages everyone in the organization in learning what is needed for success by all stakeholders. Interactive management becomes the most effective way of developing a customer-responsive, efficient, and highly motivated organization.

Bibliography

Ackoff, R. (1994). *The Democratic Corporation: A Radical Prescription for Recreating Corporate America and Rediscovering Success.* New York: Oxford University Press.
Crozier, M. (1964). *The Bureaucratic Phenomenon.* Chicago: University of Chicago Press.
Kotter, J. & Heskett, J. (1992). *Corporate Culture and Performance.* New York: Free Press.
Maccoby, M. (1988). *Why Work: Leading the New Generation.* New York: Simon & Schuster; 2nd edn. Arlington, Va.: Miles River Press.
Weber, M. (1964). *The Theory of Social and Economic Organization.* New York: Free Press.

MICHAEL MACCOBY

paternalism An activity undertaken by one party (e.g., an individual, organization, or government) for the supposed "good" of a second party without the consent of the second party or in direct violation of the second party's stated wishes. Examples of paternalistic laws would include those prohibiting the use of drugs or alcohol, restricting the activities of minors, or requiring the use of automobile seat belts or motorcycle helmets. In the area of business, many companies establish and enforce paternalistic regulations upon their employees in order to ensure the safety of those employees in the workplace. Such regulations are sometimes mandated by government agencies (such as the US OSHA), while others originate within the company. More controversial are regulations which appear to mandate a set of moral, political, or religious principles which may not be shared by all. Thus, rules requiring employees to conform to standards of appearance or behavior which seem to imply such principles have on occasion been challenged legally.

Paternalistic practices are often grounded on a claim that the first party is in possession of some special knowledge or virtue which places that party in a better position to recognize the true interests or needs of the second party in a manner which exceeds the abilities of that second party. In the history of Western philosophy, paternalists tend to be cognitivists who believe that it is possible for some individuals to come to know the truth in metaphysical areas (such as ethics, religion, politics, and aesthetics), and that those individuals have a moral obligation to ensure that others act in accordance with those truths even when they are unable or unwilling to see the value of such actions.

Perhaps the most famous example of a paternalistic society is the republic described by Plato in his dialogue of the same name in which a group of wise and good guardians establish and enforce the laws to be followed by those in the lower classes who are unable to understand the justification for such laws. Plato's paternalism extends even to the extent of justifying the use of the "noble lie," i.e., propaganda which is used to manipulate individuals into following such laws by means of trickery and deceit.

Opponents of paternalism tend to make reference to notions of AUTONOMY and individual LIBERTY. The philosopher Immanuel Kant argued that only acts committed autonomously (without the interference of any outside party) could possibly fulfill the minimal requirements for moral behavior (*see* KANTIAN ETHICS). One famous formulation of his Categorical Imperative requires that individuals always be treated with respect, i.e., that they always be treated as "ends," and never as "means" to an end.

Utilitarians who follow the principles established by the nineteenth-century British philosopher JOHN STUART MILL believe that one should always assume that all mature individuals are competent to determine their own best self-interest and should be allowed to do so without interference from others (*see* UTILITARIANISM). Mill's Harm Principle states that the activities of individuals in society should not be restricted unless it has been proven legally that such activity caused harm to others in society. While the exact interpretation of this principle is open to debate (especially on the issue as to what constitutes "HARM"), there is consensus that Mill's theory strongly defends the RIGHTS of individuals to act however they see fit unless their actions manifestly injure others in some measurable fashion.

More extreme defenders of individual liberty (such as the nineteenth-century American writer Lysander Spooner) are often labelled as libertarians for their belief that there should be as little interference with the autonomy of individuals as possible (*see* INDIVIDUALISM; LIBERTARIANISM). Such theorists agree with Thomas Jefferson's claim that "the government which governs best governs least." Libertarians often oppose many forms of involuntary taxation as well as laws restricting such activities as drug use, gambling, and prostitution.

Contemporary defenders of paternalism sometimes argue that the apparent decline in respect for "traditional values of family and hard work" is at least partially due to a permissiveness in society which derives from a failure on the part of responsible individuals and organizations to impose such values on the rest of society (*see* WORK AND FAMILY).

Bibliography

Beauchamp, T. L. & Bowie, N. E. (1983). *Ethical Theory and Business*. Englewood Cliffs, NJ: Prentice-Hall.

Devlin, P. (1965). *The Enforcement of Morals*. Oxford: Oxford University Press.

Feinberg, J. & Gross, H. (eds) (1991). *Philosophy of Law*, 4th edn. Belmont, Calif.: Wadsworth.

Gert, B. & Culver, C. (1976). Paternalistic behavior. *Philosophy and Public Affairs*, 6, 45–57.

Grube, G. M. A. (1974). *Plato's Republic*. Indianapolis, Ind.: Hackett.

Mill, J. S. (1956). *On Liberty*. Indianapolis, Ind: Bobbs-Merrill.

Nozick, R. (1974). *Anarchy, State, and Utopia*. New York: Basic Books.

Spooner, L. (1972). *Let's Abolish Government*. New York: Arno Press.

Wasserstrom, R. A. (ed.). (1971). *Morality and the Law*. Belmont, Calif.: Wadsworth.

SANDER LEE

perceived legitimacy of organizational influence   Something every person attempting to exercise authority (whether formal or informal) wants to possess, and to which every participant subject to influence wants to respond. For the influencer (manager, say, or senior associate), perceived legitimacy makes cooperation more likely and requires fewer inducements and less surveillance to affect behavior. For the participant, subject to another's authority (again, whether or not that authority is formal), perceived legitimacy of influence allows for cooperation without feelings of having been "bribed" or "coerced."

Introduction

"Legitimate" has been defined as "necessary and proper" (Becker et al., 1961, p. 41). A shorthand that is easily comprehended is "appropriate." Of course, this begs a series of questions. Necessary for what? Proper by whose standards? Clearly, in an organization where behavior is shaped by authority (formal or informal), views as to legitimacy of that authority may not be shared between the person wishing to be in authority ("influencer") and the person who is the target of influence ("target"). Under these circumstances, a negotiation (in the broadest sense of that term) may be engaged in to modify the influence attempt and/or socially construct, via linked reciprocal behavior, the target's perception of the legitimacy of that particular influencer for that particular task.

It is a commonplace to attribute unethical behavior in organizations to selfishness, motivated by hope of reward or fear of punishment. However, one of the most troubling forms of unethical behavior is that which seems to the participants to be appropriate at the time but, when exposed to the light of day, is found by those not involved to be unacceptable by society at large. In the US context, the Tailhook scandal, various price-fixing indictments, the post office excesses by congressmen – these all appear to be examples of the participants believing they were engaging in legitimate (even if illegal) activity. How are we to account for this disparity between what is seen as legitimate (necessary and proper, or appropriate) in an organization but seen as unethical by those outside of it?

This article will address this question by focusing on factors that bring about perceived legitimacy of influence attempts in organizations. When one looks at a workplace scene, be it a factory floor or an office environment, from a worker's standpoint, one is struck by the quantity of suggestions, rules, and commands passing between participants, and by the ability of workers to sort these into an orderly set that influences how they proceed with their tasks.

The worker heeds some of the these potential controls on his behavior, disregards others, and proceeds with the tasks that make up his job. What actually occurs may be considered to be the net product of this multitude of rules, suggestions, and commands, plus habituated and customary procedures.

When organizational behavior is viewed in this way, a question naturally arises: "Why is a particular command (or rule or suggestion or other form of influence) heeded and another disregarded?" Two dominant schools of thought give an explanation. One considers the subjective assessments of rewards and penalties associated with a particular behavior, and assumes the participant acts to increase rewards and decrease penalties. This approach is often referred to as a "needs" or "expectancy" model of explaining behavior (Lawler, 1973).

Another approach (Weber, 1947), seeks an explanation as to which command is obeyed (again, using command in its broadest sense) in the perceived legitimacy of the commands as well as the payoffs associated with them. Of course, commands seen as not legitimate may still be obeyed if the contingent payoffs or penalties associated with them are sufficiently powerful. This second approach to understanding responses to influence has not received as much scholarly attention as has the "needs" or "expectancy" approach. Indeed, explanations of human behavior in general have focused on what feels good or bad, often overlooking explanations that involve calculations of "right" or "wrong."

Importance of Perceived Legitimacy

Figure 1 shows the possibilities when the target complies with influence from the influencer under conditions of reward or punishment, and with the influence perceived as legitimate or not legitimate.

Affective consequences of response to influence under different conditions of sanction and perceived legitimacy.

	not legitimate	legitimate
rewarded	bribed	committed
punished	coerced	martyred

Figure 1

Persons operating in the upper right quadrant (legitimate and rewarded) act with more "commitment," and are more likely to persist in the behavior, do so without close supervision, contribute beyond minimum expectations, and are not likely to be seen as unethical by others from their own peer group. The affective reaction to complying with authority under other circumstances has been (exaggerating to make the point) described as "bribed," "coerced," or "martyred."

Antecedents of Perceived Legitimacy

But where does a perceived legitimacy of an influence attempt come from? Both structural and task-related factors affect the initial assessment of legitimacy. An example of a structural factor is the nature of the relationship between the influencer and the target of the influence attempt. A highly charismatic relationship renders almost any influence attempt legitimate. One only need think of the Davidians in Waco, or the mass suicides in Jonestown. On the other hand, a totally soured relationship will cause any influence attempt to be seen as not legitimate, and examples are not hard to think of. Parents of adolescent children sometimes seem to face this phenomenon on a daily basis.

For most situations, however, task-related factors will be important to an initial assessment of legitimacy. The relevant competence of the influencer for the task at hand, and the commitment of the influencer to the purpose being served by accomplishing the task, all as seen by the target person, are the most important task-related factors in the initial assessment of legitimacy of an influence attempt. Of course, the perceived competence and commitment of the influencer may be different for different groups. That difference may be expected to be especially apparent across hierarchical groups. Upper management's perception of the competence and commitment of a middle manager may be very different than that of the group of individuals being managed.

More subtle, but of equal importance to perceived legitimacy, is the idea that work performed may be engaged in to further the goals of a profession or craft just as much as to further organizational goals. If behavior being shaped by an influencer affects the profession or craft involved, legitimacy of that influence attempt may be salient. Without commitment to the professional or craft objectives involved, organizational objectives notwithstanding, the influencer may have initial difficulty in establishing perceived legitimacy. For example, if the purpose of the task is to make a process more efficient, a person exercising authority will be seen to be legitimate if he is seen as technically competent and as committed to the outcome. If he is seen as not having the technical skill to analyze the situation and/or is seen as one who cares little about efficiency, the initial assessment of the legitimacy of his influence attempt is likely to be problematic.

If the influence attempt is seen as important to the person being influenced, or if the influence attempt is seen as legitimate, committed cooperation ensues. If, however, the attempt is viewed as not legitimate for an activity seen as important, there is a problem for all concerned. Thus, both the person attempting to exercise authority and the person being influenced by that authority have a vested interest in having the influence perceived as legitimate.

The influencer may revise the nature of his influence attempt, and/or engage in one of several linked behaviors that may serve to legitimate the influence attempt. Examples of linked reciprocal behavior to negotiate legitimacy are:

1. Listen/explain. The simple act of explanation can legitimate an influence attempt perceived as illegitimate. Administrative practice has long recommended "explaining why." Of course, in the process of listening and explaining, some modification of the behavior being requested may occur, further facilitating perception of legitimacy.

2. Sharing the burden of unpleasant work. Willingness to work alongside can legitimate influence. The senior nurse who helps her trainee empty a bedpan can more easily secure the legitimacy of a direction to do so at that moment, and later on when working alongside may not occur.

3. Appeal to a superordinate goal. "This may be unpleasant for us, but it is essential for the department." While we may make cynical gibes about "for God, for Country and for (whatever)," the influence of shared superordinate goals on organizational behavior is undeniable and profound. Under some circumstances, especially under the momentum of commitment from past success in achieving organizational goals, and when employed by an authority that has a reputation of being skilled and committed, this legitimation technique can be very effective.

This is not an exhaustive list, and every situation, every context, will have its characteristic linked reciprocal social negotiating behaviors that attempt to construct the perception of legitimacy. What is important here is the idea that when perceived legitimacy is problematic, there is a shared vested interest in achieving it when possible. Perceived legitimacy will depend on competence and commitment appropriate to the task as seen by the target of the influence attempt, and linked social behaviors may be engaged in to negotiate and construct it.

Suggestions for Management

We now can specify how management, interested in keeping unethical behaviors from being perceived as legitimate behaviors, can enter into, and affect, this process at several points. To wit:

1. Beware of overly charismatic leadership. Unquestioned perception of legitimacy of an influencer, while enormously effective when appropriate, is a setup for blind behavior deemed by others to be unethical.

2. The perceived legitimacy of an influencer can be reinforced or diminished by affecting the perceived appropriateness of the influencer's competence to deal with the task, and commitment to the purpose of the task. Of course, it is important to remember

that this is as perceived by the participant being influenced, and that individual may not perceive the same purpose of task that management has in mind. These differences can be exploited by those wishing to legitimate influence-encouraging behavior that may be unethical in the eyes of others.

3 Enter into the reciprocal behavior that affects the perceived legitimacy of possible future influence attempts. Role playing can sensitize people to legitimation attempts that may be inappropriate from the organization's larger viewpoint. The technique has been used successfully, for instance, to awaken managers to the risks of sexual harassment charges, or of unconscious discrimination against one or another minority group.

4 Legitimize proactively that which is desired via ceremony and other group activity. For instance, if one wishes to legitimate the influence of high-seniority persons, a ceremony celebrating length of service might be appropriate.

Conclusion

Organizations are socially interactive systems that can and do construct perceived legitimacy within themselves, without necessarily taking into account the way their behaviors will be regarded by the segment of society in which the organization is embedded. Behavior that is perceived as being legitimate and rewarded will be likely to be engaged in with enthusiasm, even without close direction, and be endorsed as ethical by the peer group of the participants. By realizing the importance of perceived legitimacy, and the mechanisms by which it is constructed in an organization, management can be forewarned and adopt interventions which will make inappropriate legitimating processes less likely.

See also authority; coercion; distributive justice; just cause; meaningful work; mentoring; obedience, to authority and to the law; organizational culture; participatory management; psychology and business ethics; corporate punishment; rational choice theory; situation ethics; social contract theory; supererogation; trust; utilitarianism; values.

Bibliography

Barnard, C. I. (1938). *The Functions of the Executive.* Cambridge, Mass.: Harvard University Press.

Becker, H. S., Greer, B., Hughes, E. C., & Strauss, A. L. (1961). *Boys in White.* Chicago: University of Chicago Press.

Cobb, A. T. (1980). Informal influences in the formal organization: Perceived sources of power among work unit peers. *Academy of Management Journal,* 23 (1), 155–61.

French, J. R. P. & Raven, B. (1960). The bases of social power. In D. Cartwright and A. Zander (eds), *Group Dynamics.* Evanston, Ill.: Row, Peterson, 607–23.

Glaser, B. G. & Strauss, A. L. (1967). *The Discovery of Grounded Theory.* Chicago: Aldine.

Kusterer, K. C. (1978). Know how on the job: The important working knowledge of "unskilled workers." Boulder, Colo.: Westview Press.

Lawler, E. E., II. (1973). *Motivation in Work Organizations.* Belmont, Calif.: Brooks/Cole.

Michener, H. A. & Burt, M. R. (1975). Components of "authority" as determinant of compliance. *Journal of Personality and Social Psychology.* 18 (3), 364–72.

Umbach, L. C. (1983). Antecedents and consequences for morale of perceived legitimacy of task direction among skilled blue collar workers. Unpublished doctoral dissertation, Northwestern University business school, Evanston, Ill.

Weber, M. (1947). *The Theory of Social and Economic Organization.* New York: Free Press.

L. CUTLER UMBACH

poison pill An option given to shareholders of a company to purchase on usually favorable terms the shares of the company. Such options are "triggered" or enabled only in specific circumstances, such as a raider purchasing more than a certain percentage of the target's shares. Typically, only the shareholders other than the raider are permitted to exercise their option. This imposes value dilution on the raider, making the poison pill a relatively costly defense for the raider to surmount. To date, the poison pill has functioned exclusively as a deterrent: no pill has been triggered intentionally. By 1990, more than 1,000 publicly traded corporations had adopted shareholder-rights plans. These firms then constituted 43 percent of the companies listed on the major public stockmarkets in the United States, and accounted for (conservatively) $2 trillion of market value of equity. Virtually all major hostile tender offers of the late 1980s involved litigation about poison pills. The "pill" is widely regarded to be the most effective anti-takeover defense available (*see* TAKEOVERS).

The adoption of a shareholder-rights plan raises numerous ethical issues for a company, its managers, and board of directors. First, it is sometimes claimed that the pill is a device for *management entrenchment*. The adoption of a pill virtually blockades an unwanted takeover of a public corporation. The potential agency costs arising from this entrenchment are numerous. Second, the *costs to shareholders* of management entrenchment appear to be material. Scholarly research reveals a one-day loss in share value of 0.5 percent to 2.5 percent on the date of announcing the adoption of a pill – this is after netting out the movements of the overall stockmarket on those days, and given the size of companies involved, amounts to shareholder losses in the millions of dollars in one day. The exception to this wealth loss occurs where outside directors comprise a majority of the board; in that case, shareholders gain. Third, the pill *discriminates among owners of the firm*. The unwanted suitor who purchases enough shares to trigger the pill is not permitted to participate in the favorable terms of a share purchase and thus succumbs to an *involuntary transfer of wealth* from the suitor to the other shareholders of the firm. This involuntary or coercive aspect of the pill is the key to its effectiveness. Fourth, the pill appears to *subvert the governance process* whereby dissident shareholders denied other means of expressing their displeasure with management, are also denied the opportunity to replace management by purchasing a majority of shares, and voting them out of office (*see* CORPORATE GOVERNANCE). Finally, pills are almost always emplaced *without the consent of shareholders*.

In the defense of pills, proponents (Lipton, 1987) reply, first, that it does not rule out takeovers, but rather permits boards and managers to give studious consideration to a takeover and all its alternatives, rather than be stampeded into action. This, they argue, has the effect of eliciting higher bid premiums from corporate raiders. Second, pills deter self-dealing transactions by large shareholders who might use a large (but not majority) bloc of shares to coerce managers. And finally, pills do not change the firm structurally or change its earning capacity, unlike certain other kinds of anti-takeover defenses.

Bibliography

Brickley, J. A., Coles, J. L. & Terry, R. L. (1994). Outsider directors and the adoption of poison pills. *Journal of Financial Economics*, **35**, 371–90.

Bruner, R. F. (1991). *The Poison Pill Anti-takeover Defense: The Price of Strategic Deterrence*. Charlottesville, Va.: The Research Foundation of the Institute of Chartered Financial Analysts.

Lipton, M. (1987). Corporate governance in the age of finance corporation. *University of Pennsylvania Law Review*, **136**, 1–72.

Ryngaert, M. D. (1988). The effect of posion pill securities on shareholder wealth. *Journal of Financial Economics*, **20**, 377–417.

ROBERT F. BRUNER

political action committees   legal, tax-exempt entities through which interest groups raise and contribute money to political candidates. PACs are an increasingly important source of funds for political campaigns in the United States, especially in congressional elections where public funding is not available.

Since 1907 corporations have been prohibited from making contributions to Federal elections. For several decades the lack of the precedent for such endeavors and the absence of conclusive judicial rulings kept corporations and other institutions from engaging in the election processes. Interestingly, PACs were developed in the 1940s by labor unions because of the prohibition of union contributions to federal elections enacted by a 1943 statute. Thus, unions began to establish separate segregated funds to conduct their campaign fundraising and contribution activities. By the mid-1970s many legislative, judicial, and administrative actions paved the way for other groups to explore the PAC process. By late 1975 decreasing legal barriers spurred the PAC process, because of a perceived decline in the strength of political parties and increased government involvement in people's lives.

Political Action Committees have become a major force in political campaigns, affording a modern methodology for persuasion and influence. In 1974 the number of PACs was 608; by 1993 there were 3,210. The totals by Committee Type are as follows: Corporate: 789; Labor: 337; Trade/Membership/Health: 761; Non-Connected: 1,121; Cooperative: 56; Corporations without stock: 146.

Contribution Limits

Federal law affords different sets of limits for the two broad types of political action committee structures. Limits are listed as follows: $1,000 to any candidate for Federal office, per election; $20,000 to the national committee of a political party, and $5,000 to any other political committee.

Within the law political committees and the individual are treated equally. However, political committees are not subject to an aggregate annual limit on political contributions. The law affords those committees a higher per-candidate contribution by meeting the requirements of a "multi-candidate committee." A multi-candidate committee is a political committee registered with the FEC (Federal Election Commission) for a minimum of six months. The committee must have received contributions from 50 persons and contributed to at least five candidates for Federal office. A "multi-candidate political action committee" is subject to the following contribution limits: $5,000 to any candidate for Federal office, per election; $15,000 to the national committee of a political party, and $5,000 to any other political committee.

Summary and Conclusions

The Jefferson ideal of democracy which demands that citizens become engaged in government has always been the foundation of the great American Experiment. Public-interest reforms open the processes of government decision-making to alert the citizenry. The citizenry must protect the fundamental principles of accountability and responsibility of elected officials to the *governed*. Democratic expression should never be allowed to become so expensive as to remove the people from this process. Democracy fails when power to decide shifts from the *majority* to a collective *few*. Do PACs affect the rights of the majority to self-govern?

Bibliography

Bowers, J. (1993). Political Action Committees (PACs): Bibliography-in-Brief, 1991–1993. CRS Report for Congress, Congressional Research Service, The Library of Congress, Washington, DC.

Cantor, J. E. (1984). Political Action Committees: Their Evolution, Growth and Implications for the Political System. CRS Report Number 84-78 GOV. Washington, DC.

Cantor, J. E. (1993). Campaign Financing in Federal Elections: A Guide to the Law and its Operations. Congressional Research Service, The Library of Congress, Washington, DC.

Federal Election Commission. (1994). FEC Releases Year End PAC Count. Press release, FEC Press Office, Washington, DC, Feb. 11.

Frazier, J. B. (1992). Political Action Committees (PACs): Sources for Lists of PACs. CRS Report for Congress, Congressional Research Service, The Library of Congress, Washington, DC.

Greider, W. (1992). *Who Will Tell the People*. New York: Simon & Schuster.

Swift, A. (1994). Campaign reform debate dominated by sheer malarkey. *Roll Call*, July 14, p. 5.

JOHN F. LOBUTS

political philosophy and business ethics

I. The definition of "political philosophy" is itself a matter of controversy, especially among those who identify themselves as political philosophers. There is perhaps even less agreement on proper methodology than on what constitutes the subject matter of political philosophy. However, most if not all of the following questions are widely recognized to be the proper concern of political philosophy.

A. Under what conditions, if any, is political authority and, in particular, the authority of the state, legitimate? What are the scope and limits of state authority – what are the legitimate functions of the state? What is the proper division between the public and private sectors in a society – which functions are best performed by government, which by the private sector (including the market and nonprofit organizations)?

B. Assuming that the state is to be the ultimate guarantor of justice, through the threat of coercive enforcement of principles of justice, which principles of justice are appropriate (under which sorts of circumstances, for which types of societies)?

C. What is the nature of political obligation? When can persons rightly be said to have an obligation to obey the law or the commands of those in positions of political authority? What are the scope and limits of political obligation – when is resistance to political authority justifiable?

D. What are the moral justifications for various forms of government, including democracy and federalism?

E1 What sorts of conduct are ethically permissible or obligatory for government officials? (To what extent, if any, can appeals to the higher good of the country or "national security" justify behavior on the part of officials that would otherwise be immoral?)

E2 More generally, how, if at all, does the ethics of governmental organizations differ from the ethics of individuals or of private-sector organizations? Under what conditions can members of political units (citizens) or officials (in government bureaucracies) be said to be collectively, as distinct from individually, responsible for outcomes resulting from their actions or omissions?

F. What are the rights and duties of membership in political units (especially states)? What are the moral justifications for various proposals for determining criteria for membership (e.g., ethnicity, religion)? What is the moral case for a rights of immigration and emigration, rights of political sanctuary, etc.?

G. What are the moral constraints that bear on war, considered primarily as an activity of states? (Traditional political philosophy distinguishes between the moral justification for going to war and the morality of what is permissible in the conduct of war.)

H. To what extent are the legitimate goals of political association (the establishment of justice, security, etc.) best served by a state-centered system as opposed to one in which other political units (regional associations such as the European Community, confederations, etc.) have a more prominent role?

This list of questions, which is not intended to be exhaustive, should make it clear that political philosophy is primarily concerned with normative issues, even though the exploration of normative questions invariably requires conceptual analysis and rests on empirical assumptions about institutions and human nature as well. If there is a theme that unifies these questions, it is the investigation of the *morality of the institutionalized uses of power, and ultimately of coercive power.*

II. Business Ethics: The proper definition of "business ethics" is, if anything, even more contested than that of "political philosophy." As with political philosophy, there are contrasting views on both methodology and subject matter. The following alternative conceptions of business ethics are among those currently most prominent in the field, although a number of them have come under strong criticism. As we shall see, each has important, though usually unstated, implications for what the relationship between business ethics and political philosophy is.

Rule-egoism

According to this conception, business ethics is concerned exclusively with the ethical conduct of business people as they go about their business activities. In other words, like most of the other conceptions listed below, the rule-egoist model limits business ethics primarily if not entirely to the consideration of ethical questions *within* the sphere of business, without explicitly investigating ethical issues concerning the *institution* of business as a whole. More specifically, according to the rule-egoist model it is the task of political philosophy, not of business ethics, to investigate the justifications for using markets as the basic institution for producing and distributing the material requirements of human welfare. Instead, it takes the existence of the market, and hence of a distinct sphere of business activity, for granted and asks: Why should people engaged in business act ethically? The answer this view gives is disarmingly simple: Business people should act ethically because it is in their long-term interest to do so. The assumption is that business activity is purely self-interested and that by following moral rules business people can, at least in the long-run, best serve their self-interest.

One prominent variant of rule-egoism is the "social responsibility" view of business ethics. The defining thesis of the social responsibility view is that business people can best serve their interests (and the common interest of the business community as a whole) by acting ethically so as to preempt regulation imposed by government upon business. The idea is that by acting ethically (and making the public aware that they are doing so) business people can convince the public and their legislative representatives that such external controls are not necessary because business people can be counted on to do what is right without the threat of government coercion.

The rule-egoist conception is flawed on a number of counts. First, it provides no guidance whatsoever in cases in which there is not a close congruence between self-interest and what is ethical – and is quite implausible if it claims that the two never diverge. Second, the rule-egoist position simply assumes that there is an independent and adequate list of moral principles available in society at large which business people can simply follow in order to maximize their own interests. In this sense it adopts an uncritical attitude toward received moral principles. Indeed, rule-egoism is not properly described as an ethical theory at all. Instead, it is only a theory of why business people should be ethical – taking it for granted that there is no problem of determining what being ethical requires.

Third, rule-egoism tends to overlook entirely (or at least to minimize) the fact that corporate interests (for example, the interest in maximizing profit or growth or market share) and the interests of a given individual within the corporation can and do diverge. Indeed some of the most vexing ethical dilemmas in business have to do with the conflict between loyalty to organizational interests and a proper regard for one's own interests as an individual, including one's interests in the well-being of one's family. Political philosophy takes this general type of conflict as one of its central problems, especially in its investigation of the scope and limits of the individual's obligation to obey the law and the duties of government officials to comply with institutional policies. Saying that business people ought to act ethically because it is in "their interest" sheds no light on these issues.

Fourth, rule-egoism, at least in its "social responsibility" version, begs important questions by assuming that existing conceptions of self-interest (or corporate interests, or the interests of the business community as a whole) are legitimate and beyond ethical criticism.

Questions about the moral character of business institutions as a whole, or of the market system, are never broached within this model. Because of this exclusion, the rule-egoist model divorces questions of political philosophy entirely from the domain of business ethics. In particular, the justice of market systems is never an object of inquiry. Yet whether behavior within a given institution is ethically permissible generally depends at least in part upon whether the institution itself is compatible with the requirements of justice. By offering a conception of business ethics that is entirely independent of political philosophy's concern about the justice of institutions, the rule-egoist model presents an unduly foreshortened picture of the domain of ethical issues concerning business (see EGOISM, PSYCHOLOGICAL EGOISM AND ETHICAL EGOISM).

The Simple Legalist/Loyal Agent Model

This conception of business ethics is suggested by a widely cited article by MILTON FRIEDMAN entitled "The Social Responsibility of Business is to Increase its Profits" (Friedman, 1970). The central claim is that the only ethical obligation of business people, who are viewed as agents of the corporation's shareholders, is to maximize profits, subject only to conformity to legal requirements (contract law, antitrust law, etc.). Legal requirements are seen as "rules of the game" necessary for preventing fraud and theft and avoiding anti-competitive practices that interfere with well-functioning of the market in the production of human welfare. Clearly, this view, like rule-egoism, fails to consider either the possibility that a market institution within which corporations operate is subject to ethical criticism (for example, on grounds of justice), or to consider the problem of determining exactly what moral constraints ought to be observed, in what circumstances, in the pursuit of profit. In addition, the simple legalist/loyal agent conception of business ethics assumes without argument that (a) all shareholders are concerned exclusively with maximizing profit (rather than with the pursuit of ethical values) and that (b) managers have no ethical responsibilities to try to educate or convince shareholders that certain ways of pursuing profit are inappropriate. Here again, an unduly restricted conception of business ethics overlooks important ethical issues that are the stock-in-trade of political philosophy, in particular the moral obligations of persons in positions of authority within institutions to dissent from policies they regard as unethical and to be a voice for reform within the organization.

Friedman suggests that the pursuit of profit-maximization is subject to the constraint of "ethical custom" as well as the law. However, his view here is subject to the same criticism advanced above against rule-egoism, namely, that it adopts a wholly uncritical attitude toward what are commonly taken to be valid ethical principles, assuming that there is no problem of determining what ethics requires. In effect, Friedman is able to conclude that the only moral obligation of business people is to maximize profits only by assuming that there are no cases in which there are serious questions about whether the means by which profit maximization is pursued are ethical. Most importantly, Friedman's conception of business ethics lacks any plausibility unless it is assumed that the institution of the market is itself beyond any serious ethical criticism. In that sense, the simple legalist/loyal agent view is able to exclude issues of political philosophy from the domain of business ethics only by assuming that political philosophy has already provided an adequate justification for the "rules of the game" of the market, including the overriding commitment to profit-maximization.

The Casuistry Model

According to this conception of business ethics the proper subject matter of ethical inquiry is the concrete case in which an ethical problem arises; and the proper method of inquiry is to argue by analogy from cases in which we have a confident consensus on what the right thing to do is, to those cases in which we are unsure about what is ethical. The casuistry model does not deny the role of general principles in business ethics (or in ethics generally). However, it does include a substantial degree of

skepticism about the possibility of systematic ethical theory, and insists that whatever general principles we eventually endorse should emerge from reflection on the concrete realities of particular cases.

The casuistical approach suffers from two main limitations. First, by its own admission, it is not helpful for exploring ethical issues about large-scale institutions, whose characteristics are necessarily more abstract than the features of particular cases, and about whose legitimacy we may have no clear moral intuitions. Second, and more importantly, the casuistry model assumes, quite implausibly, that the nature of our ethical responses to particular cases that arise within a framework of institutions are not themselves influenced – and possibly distorted by – morally questionable features of the framework itself. For this reason, there are serious doubts about the reliability of the results casuistry yields even in its attempt to cope with particular ethical problems, quite apart from its apparent inability to engage larger issues of the justice of the institutional framework within which these particular problems arise.

Managerial Professionalism

A fourth conception tacitly restricts the domain of business ethics to the ethical problems encountered by managers. Indeed the fact that much, perhaps the greater part of the contemporary business ethics literature is addressed exclusively to managers shows the pervasiveness of this conception. In effect this constitutes a reduction of business ethics to a particular kind of role morality or a species of professional ethics.

One obvious flaw of this approach is that it either denies the fact that employees who are not managers face serious ethical problems in business or facilely assumes that the solution to all such problems lies primarily in the hands of managers. Quite apart from this indefensible elitism, the managerial professionalism view has another grave defect, one which it shares with each of the preceding conceptions of business ethics: It precludes inquiry into the ethical status of the institutions within which the role of manager exists. Once again, an impoverished conception of business ethics results from the exclusion of the sorts of larger institutional issues that are the subject of inquiry in political philosophy.

III. An Alternative Conception of Business Ethics – Blurring the Boundary Between Business Ethics and Political Philosophy: A more fruitful conception of business ethics recognizes that for a number of reasons it is implausible to make such a sharp separation between business ethics and political philosophy. Instead, we should think of these as being fields which are in part complementary and in part overlapping.

The preceding critical analysis of several influential conceptions of business ethics reveals that what political philosophy and business ethics have in common is this: Both are concerned with *the morality of the uses of collective power in organizations operating in the public sphere*. There are differences, of course, the most important being that the power of political institutions, at least of the most inclusive of these, includes the explicit and legally sanctioned use of coercion. In spite of this difference, however, there are many important similarities. In both business and government, there are complex issues concerning the ethics of WHISTLEBLOWING and, more generally, of the permissibility and obligatoriness of dissent, conscientious refusal, and of obligations to work for reform within the organization. In both business and government, ethical codes and principles are often invoked to cope with conflicts of interest that are inherent in principal/agent relationships, due to the asymmetry of knowledge between principal and agent and in recognition of the fact that assuring a perfect congruence of interests between principal and agent through material incentives (or through monitoring and the threat of penalty) is often impractical or too costly. Furthermore, a growing body of social science research indicates that moral commitments and values (including honesty and fairness) play a crucial role in achieving stable cooperation within organizations, regardless of whether they are in the private or the public sector. Finally, business competition and war are similar in that they are both zero-sum interactions (in which one party's gain is another's loss). To that extent both business ethics and political philosophy are concerned with the ethical constraints on competition in which the stakes, in terms of welfare and power, are high.

Given that both political philosophy and business ethics are concerned with the ethics of institutions and with the moral uses of institutionalized power in the public sphere, researchers in both should be willing and able to borrow from one another. In addition, recent developments in the evolution of the global economy make the case for cooperation even stronger and may even call into question our ability to distinguish the two fields. Increasingly we are witnessing the emergence of extremely powerful transnational institutions that are partly economic and partly governmental in nature. Examples include the European Community and the World Bank (whose leaderships include both officers of banks and representatives of national governments). For this reason as well, business ethics and political philosophy are becoming even more closely linked.

Bibliography

Clegg, S. (Ed.), . (1989). *Organization Theory and Class Analysis: New Approaches and New Issues.* New York: Walter de Gruyter.

De George, R. T. (1993). *Competing with Integrity in International Business.* New York: Oxford University Press.

Donaldson, T. & Werhane, P. (1988). *Ethical Issues in Business: A Philosophical Approach,* 3rd edn. Englewood Cliffs, NJ: Prentice-Hall.

Freeman, R. E. (1991). *Business Ethics: The State of the Art.* New York: Oxford University Press.

Friedman, M. (1970). The social responsibility of business is to increase its profits. *New York Times Magazine,* 13 Sept.

Goodin, R. & Pettit, P. (1993). *A Companion to Political Philosophy.* Oxford: Blackwell.

Kymlicka, W. (1990). *Contemporary Political Philosophy: An Introduction.* Oxford: Clarendon Press.

Pateman, C. (1970). *Participation and Democratic Theory.* London: Cambridge University Press.

Velasquez, M. G. (1992). *Business Ethics: Concepts and Cases,* 3rd edn. Englewood Cliffs, NJ: Prentice-Hall.

ALLEN BUCHANAN

pornography the sexually explicit depiction of persons, in words or images, done with the primary, proximate aim, and reasonable hope, of eliciting significant sexual arousal on the part of the consumer of such materials.

Etymologically, "pornography" meant writing about, or depictions of, female prostitutes or whores. Today the core meaning tends to be: sexually explicit depictions (including writing) of people, typically females or children. Hence, the core meaning has been extended much beyond the original sense. Some define "pornography" evaluatively as involving the endorsement of, or approving portrayal of, women being subordinated and wrongfully treated in some sexual manner; consider, for example, a non-condemnatory film of a woman with her nipples being cut off with a chain saw. Thus, *among* the materials referred to as "pornographic" are those which, although they may induce sexual excitement in some, are misleadingly described as "merely erotic" and which are found objectionable on other grounds (e.g., brutality).

The difficulty with the evaluative definition is that it requires settling moral issues *in order* to apply the term. Second, common usage allows one to refer to films of happily committed couples voluntarily engaging in explicit (beyond "foreplay") sexual activity as "pornography." Arguably, the woman or man is not exploited here. So, the evaluative definition is at odds with common usage.

If we reconstruct the meaning of pornography, it is preferable to abandon the restrictive, evaluative definition. We need a reasonably precise definition that accords with prevailing usage and which is morally neutral. A neutral definition will allow all disputants over the morality of producing such materials, disseminating them, or censoring them, to agree on which materials are the subject of discussion. The failure to separate the tasks of *identifying* which practices are at issue and the *moral evaluation* of those practices leads to unnecessary confusion.

The definition with which this entry began is more adequate. The dominant goal of most pornography-makers is to profit, but that fact is compatible with our definition. The definitional feature that one aim is to elicit sexual arousal normally will distinguish pornography from, e.g., nude photographs in a medical text. Assuming no intention by Michelangelo to elicit sexual arousal, his statue of David is not pornographic, even if its effect on some is to arouse. Further, the "reasonable hope" clause in our definition implies that lovely, vivid photographs of juicy red strawberries normally, or always, fail to qualify as pornography.

The term "erotic" means what arouses, or tends to arouse, sexual desire or love. Hence, all pornography would seem to be erotic (though none may arouse love). However, not all the erotic is pornographic. Seeing a juicy strawberry may be erotic but its representation is not pornography given our restriction of the latter term to denote only sexually explicit depictions of persons.

The pornographic (and the erotic) tend to arouse sexual desire. To be obscene is to be repellent. Hence, it is not obvious that anything can be both pornographic and obscene, contrary to much discussion. The ethical and political disputes over what to do about pornography are naturally much affected by what range of materials we are referring to when we speak of it. What has preceded is conceptual sorting. If it is on the right track, the path to a moral evaluation of pornography (its production, dissemination, or restrictions on dissemination) is clearer.

See also **autonomy; feminist ethics; harm; liberty; sexual harassment**

Substantial portions of this entry appeared in Becker, L. C. & Becker, C. B. (eds) (1992). *Encyclopedia of Ethics.* New York: Garland Publishing.

Bibliography

Copp, D. & Wendell, S. (eds). (1983). *Pornography and Censorship.* Buffalo: Prometheus Books.
Feinberg, J. (1985). *Offense to Others.* Oxford: Oxford University Press.
MacKinnon, C. (1993). *Only Words.* Cambridge, Mass.: Harvard University Press.
Schauer, F. (1982). *Free Speech: A Philosophical Inquiry.* Cambridge: Cambridge University Press.
Tucker, D. (1985). *Law, Liberation, and Freedom of Speech.* Totowa, NJ: Rowman and Allanheld.

DONALD VANDEVEER

postmodernism and business ethics To what extent can a position that characterizes itself as postmodern be ethical? This is the question that business ethics must address if it wishes to characterize itself as postmodern. The modernity/postmodernity debate is over the possibility of an ethic. Before allying business ethics with postmodernity one must first answer this more fundamental question regarding the alliance of ethics with postmodernity.

In order to define the term "postmodernity" it is necessary to define "modernity." Although the term "postmodernity" entered into modern discussion through architecture, its roots are philosophically determined by a certain reading of the history of modern philosophy. The reading of the history of modern philosophy that legitimates postmodernity over modernity must be contrasted with another reading that rehabilitates the project of modernity. Although this scenario can be played out in many ways, the real issue has to do with an evaluation of two major figures in the history of modern philosophy, Heidegger and Nietzsche. The point of departure for postmodernity given this scenario would be Nietzsche's critique of philosophy which began in his *The Birth of Tragedy*, resulting in a return to antiquity for the rehabilitation of philosophical truth claims. Heidvolegger, particularly the middle and later Heidegger, followed Nietzsche in his return to antiquity. If one chooses to abandon modernity, on what can one base an ethic? This may seem a peculiar question if it were not the case that modernity has within it a normative status that harbors an ethic. In their respective critiques of modernity both Heidegger and Nietzsche abandon the claims to autonomy and responsibility that were implicit in modernity's emphasis on the subject and subjectivity. Nietzsche was quite willing to abandon the claims to individualism and particularity associated with modern subjectivity in favor of an attempt to reunite alienated humanity with nature. Heidegger followed him in this quest but with a somewhat different agenda.

In the current modernity/postmodernity debate one cannot overlook Heidegger's political agenda and his readiness to associate himself with the cause of National Socialism, as well as his later attempts to avoid assuming responsibility for his action. One finds little room in his later philosophy for the assumption of either guilt or responsibility. Hence, the price of returning to antiquity has been to undercut the normative claims of modernity without replacing them. To the extent that one sides with the claims of postmodernity one will find it difficult to construct an ethic.

Before showing how one might make ethical claims on the basis of a position that identifies itself with postmodernity, let us turn to normative claims of modernity. The paradigm for modernity in this reading of the history of philosophy would find its representation in the philosophies of Kant, Hegel, Descartes, Fichte, even Hobbes, Hume, Locke, Machiavelli, and Rousseau (*see* KANTIAN ETHICS; HOBBES, THOMAS). The basic assumption of modernity as represented in various ethical positions is that normative claims must be self-referential. In other words, reason without reliance on a metaphysical tradition must justify itself. Implicit in this process of justification is the assumption that the rational subject has been emancipated from tradition, able to establish reasons on autonomous grounds for her own actions. Hence, rational activity presupposes ethical autonomy. Whether one follows Kant's discourse on practical reason, Hegel's philosophy of history (which presupposes a certain progress toward human emancipation), Fichte's theory of rights, or even Rousseau's social contract, there is a basic normative assumption implicit in the definition of modernity (*see* SOCIAL CONTRACT THEORY). It is that normative assumption that can either be rehabilitated after the critique of philosophy that has dominated the twentieth century, or abandoned as with Nietzsche and Heidegger. However, if one abandons the claim for ethical autonomy, on what basis can one establish an ethic? Of course, the reverse is no less difficult. If one is to sustain the claim for ethical autonomy, it is necessary to rehabilitate the project of modernity, while taking into account the critique of subjectivity that is at the heart of the turn toward postmodernity.

If the debate between modernity and postmodernity is a debate over the possibility of an ethic to what extent can a position that characterizes itself as postmodern be ethical? Jacques Derrida, with his method of "deconstruction," is the prime spokesperson for an answer to this question for a number of reasons. First, among the various postmodernists, it seems Derrida is unique in having made this case on philosophical grounds. From his early critiques of Husserl and Saussure to the present, he has attempted to think through a position that would result as a consequence of the limits imposed by a foundationless philosophy. Second, Derrida has been sensitive to the critiques of his position that suggest that the reactivation of philosophical programs of justification applies to questions of normativity and validity as well. In other words, Derrida is sensitive to those whose claim that his attempt to think through Heidegger's project of *destruction* of Western metaphysics as *deconstruction* leads to ethical autonomy as it did with Heidegger.

In *Racism's Last Word* (1986) his debate with Anne McClintock and Rob Nixon, Derrida attempts to show how deconstruction can take an ethical turn. The debate centers on the use and effectiveness of the term *apartheid* as a term that characterizes South African racism. Although deconstruction can be characterized by its opponents as anemic and apolitical, in this debate Derrida shows how deconstruction can be justified as precisely an ethico-political practice. In his words the term *apartheid* "would have been impossible, unthinkable without the European discourse on race – its scientific pseudoconcept and its religious roots, its modernity and its archaisms – without Judeo-Christian ideology, and so forth" (Derrida, 1986, p. 364). In other words, Derrida's claim is that deconstruction can, by its very attempt to unearth the dichotomies in discourse, unearth the latent metaphysics implicit in the use of apartheid. Behind deconstruction is the imminent prioritizing of discourses, which leads to forms of political organization that emphasize discrimination. The term *apartheid* exists within a discourse about race. As such it is part of a text. Deconstruction is said to be less an analysis and more an *intervention*. These are *political* and *institutional* interventions, "that transform context without limiting themselves to theoretical or constative utterances even though they must also produce such utterances" (Derrida, 1986, p. 364).

Here, Derrida makes the crucial point upon which the modernity/postmodernity debate in

ethics should rest. His claim against Husserl as shown in his critique of Husserl, was that Husserl's attempt to conceive of phenomenology as an idealization independent of language was impossible. This led to his conceptualization of deconstruction as a reading of a text, with the text being conceived as a field of forces from which there is no escape either back to an idealized foundation or forward to an idealized future. It would appear that deconstruction as a mere reading of a text would lead to a relativization of normative assumptions. However, and this is the central point, Derrida would want to abolish the assumed distinction between text and action. There is no getting behind or going beyond the text. By separating text from action, Derrida's critics on both the political left and the right have represented "deconstruction as a turning inward and an enclosure by the limits of language, whereas in fact," claims Derrida, "deconstruction *begins* by deconstucting logocentrism, the linguistics of the word and this very enclosure itself" (Derrida, 1986, p. 367). As Derrida would have it, deconstruction is a kind of strategy that would lead to the exposition of ethical claims, a practice that when placed in the right hands would lead presumably to the disclosing of the latent metaphysics that would leave undisclosed the foundations of discrimination within the larger text that contains both text and action.

Derrida has done an admirable job of showing how deconstruction can be reconstructed along the lines of an ethical paradigm. Whether or not this pairing of deconstruction and normativity can adequately be called an ethic remains debatable; at best, deconstruction reconceived as an ethic can be understood as a strategy. In a discourse about ethics that has been shaped by modernity one could ask for more. Modernity's assumptions about the necessity for a deontological ethic requires a mechanism for the derivation of normative rules, normative procedures, and normative validity, which deconstruction as a strategy can only either assume at the price of abandoning its critique of modernity, or deconstruct. If deconstruction chooses the former way, it would have to retreat to a kind of foundationalism; while, if it chooses the latter, it must question the very possibility of there being an ethic. In both cases it must abandon claims to moral autonomy, the achievement of modernity. In the end Derrida's critique of apartheid is persuasive. But Derrida's arguments are appealing not because of deconstruction but because of his questioning of basic assumptions about moral autonomy, democratic procedures, and necessary equality – all of which are central to ethics.

Bibliography

Derrida, J. (1986). Racism's Last Word. In Gates (Ed.), *Race, Writing, and Difference*. Chicago: University of Chicago Press, 320–69.

Gates, H. L., Jr. (Ed.) (1986). *Race, Writing, and Difference*. Chicago: University of Chicago Press.

DAVID M. RASMUSSEN

power No single definition of power seems adequate to convey its many forms and aspects (Lukes, 1986). One important conception sees it as paradigmatically a capacity to cause others to do what they would otherwise not do. A gunman, for example, may have the power to force a victim to hand over money, and a police officer may have the power to arrest the gunman. In cases such as these power is used to bring about behavior that is against the will of the person over whom power is exercised. But even if a person's will is broken, as by long imprisonment, power may still be what keeps the person in prison where she would otherwise not be. Power, however, is not the same as force, and is not always used coercively.

A person's persuasive argument may have the power to change another's behavior. Sometimes power rests on authority to which others have agreed, as when an elected official has the power to affect policy through voting for or against a given measure. Power can also be exercised by controlling what is on the agenda for decision, and by bringing it about that various issues are accepted uncritically as not subject to debate. Structures of what are taken to be forms of knowledge, as when psychiatric interpretations classify certain behavior as indicative of mental illness, also constitute power to control what people may do (Foucault, 1980). And the media, along with other social institutions not usually associated with power, can be said to have the power to shape consciousness, to affect what is thought about and wanted (Held, 1989). Power, on some views, may be the capacity to affect the outcomes of any issues.

Where a situation is interpreted in terms of conflicting desires and interests, power may be thought of as power over others. To have power is to be able to further one's own interests and to avoid having others further theirs at one's expense (Lasswell & Kaplan, 1950). Liberal political theory standardly sees the state as incorporating the power to compel compliance with its laws amid the conflicting interests of its citizens. But there can also be the power to empower others in contexts seen as cooperative, as when parents use their power to empower their children to increasingly take care of themselves, and teachers empower their students to learn on their own. Feminists, especially, urge increased attention to these forms of power, and strive for a decrease of the power over others that can so easily be used to dominate (see FEMINIST ETHICS).

Marxist conceptions of power see it as exercised within a structure in which domination and subordination characterize relations between classes in society (Poulantzis, 1973) (see MARX, KARL). Examinations of racism and imperialism also focus on the power of groups rather than merely individuals. Privileged groups dominate other groups through a multiplicity of forms of power, including the power to silence and to marginalize (Williams, 1991).

"Power," like most important social and political and economic terms, has been contested. There has been especially sharp disagreement over the nature of economic power. Libertarians have claimed that while political power is coercive, economic power is not (Friedman, 1962) (see LIBERTARIANISM; FRIEDMAN, MILTON). This claim rests on an assumption, thought clearly false by others, that one can always refrain from entering into an economic exchange against one's will, as when one chooses not to buy a product one does not want. Critics of such a view point out that where jobs are scarce and persons not independently wealthy, they have little choice but to accept the wages and working conditions available. With no other means of support open to one, one will be effectively forced to accept conditions that may be exploitative and dehumanizing. Many persons experience the economic power of others as coercive: there may be few possibilities persons experience the economic power of others as coercive: there may be few possibilities for defying one's boss, and the powers of corporations to determine the conditions in which we are employed or not, or in which we prosper or not, are obviously very great (Galbraith, 1984). Many multinational corporations control resources, and affect outcomes, that are many times more influential in determining people's lives than are the powers of many governments (see MULTINATIONALS).

Theories of democracy traditionally argue for the equal political power of citizens. Contemporary interpretations advocate that one person should have one vote, regardless of wealth or social standing, and anyone elected or appointed to a position of greater political power must ultimately be subject to democratic control. But most societies with capitalist economic systems have not extended democratic principles to the economic sphere and have not sought an equality of economic power among citizens. Many advocates of democracy argue that democratic principles cannot be respected without a great deal more "economic democracy" than exists in most capitalist states, especially the United States (Dahl, 1970). Advocates of social democracy favor: democratic control over corporate investment, worker participation in corporate management, and greater equalization of wealth and income in order for society to be democratic. Others argue that at least the political system should be insulated from various distortions caused by wealth; these distortions include candidates able to vastly outspend their rivals and to dominate campaign debates with media advertisements, media conglomerates whose primary interests are commercial yet who largely determine the parameters of political debate, and interest groups which spend vast sums to influence legislation and policies to serve their own economic interests.

Those concerned about the power of the commercial media to shape consciousness and thus to control the culture of society may argue for the liberation of culture from the grip of commercial control. This could be furthered by increased public funding for independent non-commercial broadcasting, and by increased public support for other forms of non-commercial cultural production.

Theories differ regarding which forms of power, if any, are most fundamental. Marxists often argue that economic power is determinative of most other aspects of society. Some feminists hold that gender domination is fundamental to most other kinds of domination. Environmentalists criticize the scientific paradigm of "man's control over nature" (see ENVIRONMENT AND ENVIRONMENTAL ETHICS). Conservatives are often aware of the powers of traditions and religious beliefs. Liberals characteristically advocate governments of limited power, with a "balance of power" between branches of government (see LIBERALISM).

Bibliography

Dahl, R. A. (1970). *After the Revolution? Authority in a Good Society*. New Haven: Yale University Press.

Foucault, M. (1980). *Power/Knowledge: Selected Interviews and Other Writings, 1972–1977*, (Ed.), C. Gordon. New York: Pantheon.

Frazer, E. & Lacey, N. (1993). *The Politics of Community: A Feminist Critique of the Liberal–Communitarian Debate*. Toronto: University of Toronto Press.

Friedman, M. (1962). *Capitalism and Freedom*. Chicago: University of Chicago Press.

Galbraith, J. K. (1984). *The Anatomy of Power*. London: Hamish-Hamilton.

Held, V. (1989). *Rights and Goods: Justifying Social Action*. Chicago: University of Chicago Press.

Lasswell, H. & Kaplan, A. (1950). *Power and Society*. New Haven: Yale University Press.

Lukes, S. (Ed.), (1986). *Power*. New York: New York University Press.

Poulantzas, N. (1973). *Political Power and Social Classes*, trans. T. O'Hagan. London: New Left Books.

Williams, P. J. (1991). *The Alchemy of Race and Rights*. Cambridge, Mass.: Harvard University Press.

VIRGINIA HELD

practical reasoning   a goal-driven, knowledge-based, action-guiding species of reasoning that meshes together goals with possible alternative actions that are means to carry out these goals, in relation to an agent's given situation as he or she sees it, and concludes in a proposition that recommends a prudent course of action. Practical reasoning is a defeasible kind of argumentation, in that it is tentative in nature

– subject to revision as new information concerning the agent's changing circumstances comes to be known. Practical reasoning is crucial to the underlying framework of virtue ethics, where it defines the right personal characteristics needed to undertake a prudent course of action in relation to an agent's ethical goals as applied to a given situation (*see* VIRTUE ETHICS).

An example would be the case of a manufacturer who wants to market a drug, but knows that satisfying the regulatory safety requirements will involve costly testing of the drug. To arrive at a prudent line of action, the manufacturer might take a close look at how the drug would be tested, including such factors as who would carry out the tests, how much this would cost, what options are available, how long it would take, and so forth. They would then put this information together with their goals in manufacturing, making a judgment of how much of a priority that manufacturing this particular drug should be for them. Their deliberations on the question should take the form of practical reasoning that meshes their general goals as a company with specific information about this drug, and the means necessary to manufacture it under current, or reasonably predictable circumstances.

Practical reasoning, in its simplest form (Walton, 1990), is an inference with a goal premise and a means premise: "*G* is my goal ; carrying out action *A* is the means, in this situation, to realize *G*; therefore I should carry out *A*." Although this simple structure gives the reader a basic idea of how practical reasoning works, other factors need to be taken into account. In Walton (1991, p. 109), these other factors are expressed in the form of critical questions that should be asked in a given case. One factor is that there may be more than one means available, so that the various possible alternative lines of action may need to be compared. Another factor is that the agent may have multiple goals, so that it may be necessary to decide which goals have priority over others. There may even be practical conflicts, i.e. conflicts between carrying out one goal and carrying out another, where the line of action required to carry out one goal would interfere with, or cancel out the line of action required to carry out the other. Another factor is that of side-effects. The practical

reasoner needs to ask critical questions about the likely consequences, both positive and negative from the point of view of her goals, of carrying out a contemplated action. A final factor is that the contemplated action may require prior actions to carry it out. Often a number of preparatory actions are needed. Thus in complex practical reasoning, it is not just a single action in isolation that needs to be considered. Typically it is a connected sequence of actions that leads toward the goal.

Bibliography

Walton, D. N. (1990). *Practical Reasoning: Goal-Driven, Knowledge-Based, Action-Guiding Argumentation.* Savage, Md.: Rowman and Littlefield.
Walton, D. N. (1991). *Begging the Question: Circular Reasoning as a Tactic of Argumentation.* New York: Greenwood Press.

DOUGLAS WALTON

pragmatism   A distinctly American approach to philosophy which, in its most general form, holds that the meaning of a word or concept lies solely in its experimental and practical consequences. Its practitioners have identified this idea as distinctly American because it rejects the traditional European preoccupation with the origins of ideas. C. S. Peirce (1839–1914) and William James (1842–1910) were co-founders of pragmatism; it then enjoyed further development and broadened application in the work of John Dewey (1859–1952). Although it went into eclipse during the years that followed Dewey's death, pragmatism is now enjoying a major renaissance in many fields, including philosophy, political science, jurisprudence, psychology, literary criticism, and public administration.

What came to be known as "the pragmatic maxim" received its first formulation by Peirce. "The rational purport of a word or other expression," he wrote, "lies exclusively in its conceivable bearing upon the conduct of life" (Peirce, 1982, p. 102). Peirce's version of pragmatism was motivated in part by his criticism of the work of René Descartes (1596–1650). Descartes had attempted to place knowledge on an unshakable foundation by claiming to have been able to doubt everything except his own existence. He then claimed to have deduced certain knowledge from his innate ideas.

Peirce thought that Descartes had committed four major mistakes. First, since doubt is an involuntary response to what is actually experienced as unsettled, universal doubt is not possible. Second, since an idea of anything is exhausted by its sensible effects, there can be no innate ideas. Third, since all knowledge is fallible, there can be no absolute foundation of certainty; knowing is a natural activity that evolves. Fourth, successful inquiry is social, and not the activity of a solitary thinking self.

Peirce thought of the pragmatic maxim as a generalization of the method of experimental science. He held that inquiry is successful insofar as it removes doubt by establishing new habits which are satisfactory in the sense that they have universality of application and are therefore able to control future action.

William James applied the pragmatic maxim somewhat differently. For James, pragmatism meant that "the effective meaning of any philosophic proposition can always be brought down to some particular consequence, in our future practical experience" (James, 1978a, p. 124). So whereas Peirce had emphasized the role of the pragmatic maxim in the discovery of universal habits or laws, James emphasized its role in assessing the consequences of specific beliefs. Put negatively, James argued that if two apparently contradictory hypotheses yield no conceivable practical difference of consequence to anyone at any place or time, then the two hypotheses are functionally the same. More positively, James thought that "the ultimate test for us of what a truth means is indeed the conduct it dictates or inspires" (James, 1978a, p. 124).

James's version of pragmatism, like that of Peirce, stressed fallibilism, anti-foundationalism, and evolutionary naturalism. Unlike Peirce, however, James thought the pragmatic maxim applicable to particular religious and ethical beliefs that lie outside of what is scientifically universalizable. "The whole function of philosophy," he wrote, "ought to be to find out what definite difference it will make to you and me, at definite instants of our life, if this world-formula or that world-formula be the true one" (James, 1978b, p. 30). James thus claimed that a person has the right to choose a religious or ethical belief even if there is no evidence for it. If such beliefs are meaningful, however, they will produce results that can be tested.

John Dewey's version of pragmatism, which he called "instrumentalism," also stressed fallibilism, anti-foundationalism, and evolutionary naturalism. But whereas Peirce had thought that the norms of inquiry are discovered as independent of what anyone thinks them to be, Dewey held that norms of all types – scientific, ethical, and political – are constructed as byproducts of actual inquiry. And whereas James had focused on application of the pragmatic method to the emotional and spiritual life of the individual, Dewey sought to render more precise the general structures of inquiry as it applies to every area of life, including the social and political.

Two of Dewey's ideas are particularly relevant to business ethics. The first is his claim that "efficiency" must be defined more broadly than has historically been the case. True efficiency, he argued, involves consideration of consequences that extend beyond quarterly balance sheets. It requires cooperative ventures among stockholders, managers, employees, customers, and even regulators, that enhance the aesthetic value of every area of business activity, including working conditions, products, packaging, and marketing. He argued that the social consequences that follow from each of these areas of business practice are as much the products of business activity as are automobiles or insurance policies.

Second, Dewey rejected reductionistic models of decision-making in business. He criticized deontological ethical views, such as the one held by Kant, which privilege absolute duties and norms (see KANTIAN ETHICS). He also criticized teleological ethical views, such as UTILITARIANISM, which privilege outcomes of actions. Synthesizing what he considered to be the best elements of these traditional positions, he argued that the methods of successful ethical deliberation are similar to those used in the sciences. Problems are articulated, hypotheses are proposed on the basis of what is already known to be the case, and outcomes are tested. Accepted norms are tested against outcomes, and outcomes are tested against norms. In ethics, as in science, norms and outcomes evolve together. The result is a move from subjectivity to objectivity and enhanced bases for common action.

Because of its fallibilism, pragmatism has been attacked by some who fear the loss of absolute truth. Some of its critics, including religious fundamentalists, have attacked pragmatism as immoral. Others have objected that pragmatism makes action an end in itself. To all of these critics Dewey responded that absolute truth is unattainable and that intelligent experimentation constitutes the best means so far devised to control outcomes that would otherwise be random or unsatisfactory. He argued that the pragmatic method has proven superior to all competing methods, including reliance on luck, tradition, authority, and supernatural directives.

Because of its identification of the truth of an idea with "what works," some of its critics have accused pragmatism of justifying crass commercialism. Dewey responded that even though commerce is noble, commercialism tends to be evil in the degree to which it is dominated by private interests instead of attempts to promote the common good. He thus saw a need for more, not less commerce, lamenting the fact that "commerce in knowledge, in intelligence, is still a side issue." He termed this condition "ragged individualism," and suggested that as long as it continues, "pragmatic faith walks in chains, not erect" (Dewey, 1983, p. 310).

Bibliography

Dewey, J. (1983). Pragmatic America. In Jo Ann Boydston (ed.), *The Collected Works of John Dewey: The Middle Works*, vol. 13. Carbondale and Edwardsville: Southern Illinois University Press.

Dewey, J. (1984). *The Quest for Certainty*. In Jo Ann Boydston (ed.), *The Collected Works of John Dewey: The Later Works*, vol. 4. Carbondale and Edwardsville: Southern Illinois University Press.

Dewey, J. (1985). *Ethics*. In Jo Ann Boydston (Ed.), *The Collected Works of John Dewey: The Later Works*, vol. 7. Carbondale and Edwardsville: Southern Illinois University Press.

Hickman, L. (1990). *John Dewey's Pragmatic Technology*. Bloomington and Indianapolis: Indiana University Press.

James, W. (1978a). The pragmatic method. In *The Works of William James: Essays in Philosophy*. Cambridge, Mass.: Harvard University Press.

James, W. (1978b). *Pragmatism and the Meaning of Truth*. Cambridge, Mass.: Harvard University Press.

Peirce, C. S. (1982). What pragmatism is. In H. S. Thayer (Ed.), *Pragmatism: The Classic Writings*. Indianapolis, Ind.: Hackett.

LARRY A. HICKMAN

praxis   theory and method of appropriate action for addressing ethics issues and developing ethical organizations.

The difference between theoria and praxis in organizational ethics is not the same as the difference between theory and application. Organizational ethics praxis focuses on ways of acting in addressing concrete ethics situations. Its units of analysis are not the ethical issues themselves, but rather the action methods for addressing and influencing concrete ethics issues and developing ethical organizations.

The perspective of praxis (theory and method of action) is important and different from the perspectives of theoria (theory of understanding), epistemology (ways of knowing/learning), and ontology (ways of being/existing). Praxis is the least developed area within the field of organization ethics.

Within the area of organizational ethics praxis theory, the approaches that have received the most attention, are: (a) forcing, e.g., top-down punishment-based ethics codes and different types of bottom-up forcing methods such as various forms of secret and public WHISTLE-BLOWING, obstruction, and adversarial processes. Types of organizational ethics action approaches that have received considerably less, but nonetheless significant, attention are: (b) organization DUE PROCESS systems such as grievance and arbitration procedures that include ethics cases in the due process systems; (c) integrating, for example, win-win problem solving negotiating methods and integrative ethics organizational change and development methods; and, (d) dialogue methods. The distinction between integrating and dialogue may seem a bit ambiguous here, but it will be considered in more detail later in the paper. A key to the difference is that dialogue has a priority concern for the ethical while integrating has a more or less equal concern for ethical and other organizational effectiveness criteria.

In classical philosophy, a contrast is made between two dimensions of life within the whole person, understanding (theoria) and action (praxis). There can be some confusion in the Greek to English translation from praxis to practice. Praxis/practice does not refer to the mundane, or to an anti-intellectual person or to a person who is not concerned with ideas or theory. The end of the praxis dimension of life is living well or living appropriately within the polis, within the community, within the organization. According to Bernstein (1971, p. x), "'Praxis' in this . . sense signifies the disciplines and activities predominant in man's ethical and political life" within the polis, within the community, within the organization. In contrast, the end of the theoria dimension of life is knowing or wisdom for its own sake. Within the whole person, both dimensions and perspectives are important, can and should inform one another.

While classical, scholastic, modernist, postmodernist, and hermeneutic discourse ethics philosophers all consider the concept of praxis somewhat differently, the basic contrast between a perspective of understanding more or less for its own sake (theoria) with a perspective of acting and living appropriately (praxis) is maintained.

In an organizational ethics context, for example, theoria focuses on whether or not it is ethical to expose workers to certain levels of a particular chemical. Praxis focuses on how to act in addressing the worker chemical exposure issue, for example: 1) through such forcing methods as punishment-enforced safety codes, whistleblowing, etc.; 2) through internal due process, grievance, and arbitration systems; 3) through integrative, win-win negotiating or participative organizational development efforts, for example, with and between those more concerned with safety and those more concerned with reducing costs; 4) through dialogue among managers, or dialogue among managers, workers, and health experts about what the ethical thing to do is; or, 5) through some sequence or combination of the above praxis methods.

As referred to above, both perspectives can inform one another. For example, interpretation and explanation theories can precede action and theories of action; and conversely, experiences and theories of action can precede and inform interpretation and explanation theories. That is, one can first theorize about the content of an ethics issue and as a result of such theorizing then theorize about how to act well in addressing the issue in the concrete case, and then act appropriately. Conversely, one can act well in addressing an ethics issue in the concrete case and later theorize about how one acted in addressing the ethics issue, as well as theorize about the content of the ethics issue based on the experience. However, there can also be discontinuities. For example, one can through theoria understand that a particular, concrete organizational behavior that one sees and even is part of is unethical. Nonetheless, one can choose not to theorize about how to act in addressing the issue and also not act at all because of lack of interest, concern, courage, and/or constraints, etc. Similarly, one can act well or poorly in addressing an important ethical situation and nonetheless not theorize much or at all about the issue or how to act.

Why should we be concerned about differences in perspectives of theoria and praxis? The more we understand that there are different and multiple action/praxis methods, the more our degrees of freedom and choices increase so that we can potentially live and act better and more appropriately with respect to the ethical. If we know we have action choices with their relative and contingent strengths and weaknesses, potentially we can live and act better, more appropriately, more fully.

Confusion or inattention to differences between the theoria and praxis perspectives can lead to needless, cognitive either/or controversies with respect to ideas with implicitly different emphases on the learning and action dimensions, when those ideas might be complementary rather than antagonistic. In addition, such either/or interactions in the praxis dimension can needlessly alienate and render ineffective on the praxis dimension potentially fruitful and cooperative interpersonal relationships and interactions that could help advance theoria concerns. Understanding these differences can facilitate potential integration, at least to some extent, of apparently mutually exclusive models when differences between theoria and praxis are attended to.

A serious problem that is often overlooked and that sometimes occurs is that what is effective as an ethics learning method is not always effective as an ethics action method. For example, whether we approach dialogue from perspectives of learning, action, or combined learning–action can be important. While Socratic dialogue can be used from both learning and action perspectives, its strength can be more as learning than action. For example, in the case of Roger Boisjoly and the Challenger Launch, at the time the events of this case were unfolding Boisjoly, in effect, was not able to distinguish and separate dialogue as learning from dialogue as action. He incorrectly assumed that since dialogue was effective as a way of learning and knowing what was ethical, it would be equally effective as interpersonal and inter-organizational praxis method. At the time, the correspondence between dialogue as learning and action appeared so obvious and direct that he was unable to consider alternative praxis methods such as negotiating, and secretly or publicly blowing the whistle. With an understanding of the praxis limitations of Socratic dialogue, Robert Greenleaf, in the case of gender discrimination within AT&T, successfully used Woolman dialogue to build upon and correct this potential praxis weakness in Socratic dialogue by intentionally and specifically including and combining praxis-focused elements with epistemological elements. This is not to suggest that Socratic dialogue is always more effective than Woolman dialogue from a learning perspective or that Woolman dialogue is necessarily more effective than Socratic dialogue from an action perspective. While this may be the case and a potential area for empirical research, the point is that it can be very important to recognize and attend to differences in the perspectives of epistemology and praxis in organizational ethics contexts.

There are great opportunities for research and theory-building in this area. First, as referred to above, organizational ethics praxis has not been studied nearly as much as organizational ethics theoria and epistemology. It is an area in relative need of development. Second, from an epistemological perspective, we can study how different praxis methods can combine epistemological and praxis elements that can then be more and less effective relative to learning and knowing about the ethical. This can help us make appropriate choices of learning/knowing methods. Third, from a praxis perspective, we can try to learn more about how there are different and multiple action methods that can increase our degrees of freedom and choices so that we can potentially live and act better and more appropriately with respect to the ethical. If we know how we have action choices with their relative and contingent strengths and limitations in organizational ethics contexts, potentially we can live and act better, more appropriately, more fully. Fourth, we can try to learn more about how epistemology and theoria can inform praxis and praxis can inform epistemology and theoria in organizational ethics contexts. Potentially, these are three dimensions of the whole person that may be able to mutually strengthen each other and the whole person. There are opportunities for considering how these distinctions among dimensions within the whole person can be inseparable parts of the same whole, both with respect to a whole and healthy person, and the whole and healthy organization and organizational community.

Bibliography

Bernstein, R. J. (1971). *Praxis and Action.* Philadelphia: University of Pennsylvania Press.

Ewing, D. (1989). *Justice on the Job: Resolving Grievances in the Nonunion Workplace.* Boston: Harvard Business School Press.

Nielsen, R. P. (1990). Dialogic leadership as ethics action (praxis) method. *Journal of Business Ethics,* 9, 765–83.

Nielsen, R. P. (1993). Organizational ethics from a perspective of action (praxis). *Business Ethics Quarterly,* 3 (2), 131–51.

Nielsen, R. P. (1993). Woolman's "I am we" triple-loop, action–learning: Origin and application in organization ethics. *Journal of Applied Behavioral Science,* 29 (1), 117–38.

RICHARD P. NIELSEN

preferential treatment typically refers to selecting or promoting a less "qualified" minority candidate over a more "qualified" non-minority applicant. Qualification is defined in terms of job-relevant merits. Job-relevant merits can include objective performance indices or test scores that have been proven to be valid predictors of job performance. In the academic literature, preferential treatment is alternatively termed preferential selection, preferential hiring, reverse discrimination, or diversity-based hiring.

Preferential treatment should be clearly distinguished from the practices of either "equal opportunity" or "affirmative action" in personnel functions. Equal opportunity ensures that all potential candidates are given equal chance and treatment in the competition for the limited job vacancies. Equal opportunity is not a race- or gender-conscious practice and the final allocation decision is based solely on proven job-relevant merits. In theory, preferential treatment is then the opposite to equal opportunity in that not all candidates are treated equally and that certain groups of job candidates are given preferences over the others.

Affirmative action, as defined by Seligman (1973), can take on any of these four meanings: (a) pure or passive non-discrimination, (b) pure affirmative action, (c) affirmative action by preferential treatment, or (d) quota hiring. With reference to this definition, preferential treatment involves both (c) and (d). Preferential treatment therefore can be considered as a subset of affirmative action.

The main characteristics of preferential treatment are: 1) it is race- or gender-conscious; 2) it is redistributive in nature as a means of resources allocation; 3) it is intended for specified target groups; and 4) it is intended as a temporary measure.

The justifications for and against preferential treatment are well documented in the philosophical literature. The most frequently cited justification is that preferential treatment obeys the COMPENSATORY JUSTICE principle in providing compensations to minorities for past discriminations they suffered. Other justifications have been put forward by proponents of preferential treatment: the practice helps to equalize life chances so that minorities can compete with non-minorities on equal terms; it helps to broaden the talent pool of organizations; it ensures having minority role models in the workforce; and it ultimately helps to reduce inequality and to achieve justice in society.

Opponents of preferential treatment argue that proponents of the practice misinterpret the principle of compensatory justice. Compensa-

tion for past discrimination should not be required of all members of non-minority groups, nor should reparation go to all minority group members. Further, opponents argue that preferential treatment itself violates the principle of justice by discriminating against non-minority candidates; and that allocation of employment resources should be based on job-relevant merits rather than personal characteristics.

In the United States, the legal status of preferential treatment has not been clear. The Civil Rights Act of 1964 and Title VII of the Act prohibited the use of pre-set hiring quotas or the use of any non-job-relevant factors as criteria for employment practices. The Supreme Court has ruled, on several occasions, that a numerical hiring or promotion quota is a lawful remedial action aiming at rectifying employers' past discriminations against minorities. However, between 1964 and 1991, the Supreme Court was not consistent in its interpretation of the Act, and consequently inconsistent in its rulings over alleged cases of preferential treatment in employment practices. These inconsistencies were partly due to, and closely tied to, the inconclusive and often conflicting findings in psychometric research on differential validity, test fairness, subgroup differences in job-related abilities, subgroup norming, as well as validity and accuracy in performance predictions (e.g., Sackett et al., 1991; Gottfredson & Sharf, 1988). Under the current Civil Rights Act of 1991, employment discrimination is defined in terms of "disparate hiring outcome" rather than "disparate treatment of individual candidates." The Act also stipulates that subgroup norming is unlawful. Based on current psychometric data on the accuracy of predicting job performance, it has been argued that subgroup norming could significantly improve prediction accuracy. However, it remains to be seen how the Court will interpret the Act regarding preferential treatment.

Employing utility analysis, researchers have addressed the question of the economic consequences of preferential treatment in hiring practices. Findings suggest that, relative to the net gains of hiring based on merits, preferential hiring would result in less gains, or a loss in overall workforce efficiency in the economy. However, this effect could be reduced by adopting the "top-down within-group" method of selection, which appears to result in the least amount of productivity loss and at the same time, significantly increases the minority hiring rate (e.g., Hartigan & Wigdor, 1989).

Social-psychological research has shown that preferential treatment may have adverse consequences for individual beneficiaries whom the practice intends to benefit (e.g., negative self-perception and self-evaluation of own abilities or performance). Preferential treatment may also have negative influence on relations between minority and non-minority groups. However, other authors have noted positive social-psychological consequences of preferential treatment (e.g., feelings of being more respected by others, or raising minorities' expectations of being able to "make it").

The perceived fairness of preferential treatment in employment practices has received increasing attention in recent psychological literature. For this practice to achieve its intended goal of social justice, it "must be, and also must appear to be, fair" (Crosby & Clayton, 1990, p. 73). Although people in general perceive the practice as unfair, researchers have delineated various conditions under which preferential treatment may be seen as less unfair or even fair (e.g., framing the practice in different terms, the discrepancy in merits between candidates, or personal experience with unfair employment-related treatments). More recent research tends to take the perspective of organizational justice theories (e.g., Opotow, 1992; Singer, 1993). This perspective enables researchers to examine the very core of the issue: concern for social justice in any multicultural society.

See also **affirmative action programs; discrimination in hiring; equal opportunity; ethical issues in organizational theory; multiculturalism; organization ethics; women at work**

Bibliography

Crosby, F. & Clayton, S. (1990). Affirmative action and the issue of expectancies. *Journal of Social Issues*, **42**, 1–9.

Gottfredson, L. S. & Sharf, J. C. (eds). (1988). Fairness in employment testing. *Journal of Vocational Behavior (Special Issue)*, 33 (3).

Hartigan, J. A. & Wigdor, A. K. (1989). *Fairness in Employment Testing*. Washington, DC: National Academy Press.

Opotow, S. (Ed.), (1992). Affirmative action and social justice. *Social Justice Research (Special Issue)*, **5** (3).

Sackett, P., DuBois, C., & Noe, A. W. (1991). Tokenism in performance evaluation: The effects of work group representation on male–female and White–Black differences in performance ratings. *Journal of Applied Psychology*, 76, 263–7.

Schmidt, F. L., Ones, D. S. & Hunter, J. E. (1992). Personnel selection. *Annual Review of Psychology*, **43**, 627–70.

Seligman, D. (1973). How "equal opportunity" turned into employment quotas. *Fortune*, March, 160–8.

Singer, M. (1993). *Diversity-Based Hiring: An Introduction from Legal, Ethical and Psychological Perspectives*. London: Avebury.

M. SINGER

pricing, ethics of   *see* ETHICS OF PRICING

Prisoner's Dilemma   The Prisoner's Dilemma is an analytical device that is designed to demonstrate difficulties inherent in voluntary human cooperation.

William Poundstone (1992) locates origins of the Prisoner's Dilemma in the cold-war era. The Prisoner's Dilemma quickly became popular, he argues, among game theorists who doubted that American and Soviet leaders could practice nuclear self-restraint (*see* GAME THEORY). The Prisoner's Dilemma is customarily defended as a fact of human societies. Robert Frank (1988, p. 257) claims that prisoner's dilemmas abound. A species of game theory, the Prisoner's Dilemma frequently has been applied to problems of business competition (Oster, 1990; McMillan, 1992; Murnighan, 1991; Dixit & Nalebuff, 1991; Frank, 1988).

The Prisoner's Dilemma story-line involves two prisoners who are suspected of committing a single crime. The prisoners sit in separate prison cells awaiting interrogation. The prisoners are pure egoists who rationally prefer less jail time to more jail time. The story also includes, in the background, a district attorney who lacks sufficient evidence to obtain any conviction without a confession from at least one of the prisoners.

The key ingredients in the Prisoner's Dilemma framework are the payoffs that the district attorney offers the prisoners. Each prisoner is enticed with an offer of little, or no, jail time *if* s/he confesses *and* the other does not confess (Murnighan, 1991). If both confess, they both can expect lengthy prison terms. If both remain silent, they receive shorter prison terms than if both had confessed. The long-standing moral of the Prisoner's Dilemma is that it is better for the prisoners to cooperate with each other by each keeping silent. Yet, this moral continues, each prisoner's egoism undermines the likelihood of such a solution. Each, as an egoist, goes for the "sucker offer": cooperate with the district attorney by confessing in anticipation of a reward.

Numerous commentators use the Prisoner's Dilemma to make a point about the prospects for human cooperation (Murnighan, 1991; Axelrod, 1984; Frank, 1988). In so doing, they venture into the territory of ethics and, in particular, the territory of any ethics that deals with human communities (*see* ETHICS OF CARE; COMMUNITARIANISM). In this regard, the Prisoner's Dilemma is ripe for four kinds of ethical scrutiny. Each deals with the suitability of the Prisoner's Dilemma as a way of talking about human community (*see* PRAGMATISM).

First, there is reason to question whether the Prisoner's Dilemma supports any ethical conception of the "good life." The nameless prisoners have no known pasts, no known ties to one another, no known ties to others (such as family members), and no known life aspirations (Gilbert, 1995; Solomon, 1992). These are characters who simply prefer more to less. At issue is whether this austere view of humanity can serve as a useful guide for living in association with other human beings (Taylor, 1991; Poundstone, 1992). Frank (1988, p. xi) tries to add "more noble motives" to such a conception of human beings.

Second, there is reason to question whether cooperation is taken seriously in the Prisoner's Dilemma account. Robert Axelrod (1984, p. vii) introduces his application of the Prisoner's Dilemma with this question: When should a person cooperate, and when should a person be selfish in an ongoing interaction with another person? Cooperation, on this view, is *one* among several, optional actions that an *individual* could take in relation to another party. On this view, defection from cooperation is also a feasible alternative for the parties to the Prisoner's Dilemma. This conception of cooperation differs from the customary ethical premise that human cooperation is a jointly created result.

Third, there is reason to question whether human community, as something more than reciprocity, is taken seriously in the Prisoner's Dilemma account (*see* FEMINIST ETHICS). Axelrod (1984) takes the Prisoner's Dilemma to the doorstep of human community. He argues that if each prisoner takes a so-called *tit for tat* approach in an iterated Prisoner's Dilemma, then a self-sustaining process of reciprocity will result. Still, there is no common good, no shared sense of "us," in the Prisoner's Dilemma framework, no matter how long and how frequently the two parties interact.

Fourth, there is reason to question whether voluntary human cooperation is taken seriously in the Prisoner's Dilemma account. The payoffs are controlled by the district attorney. Neither prisoner has any way of knowing what the other is saying or what payoffs were offered to the other. The critical question then is whether the Prisoner's Dilemma contains room for anything other than a solution that is imposed by someone acting outside the two prisoners' cells (Gilbert, 1995; Poundstone, 1992). All of Axelrod's (1984) proposals for promoting cooperation involve third parties' interventions in the prisoners' lives.

The Prisoner's Dilemma is increasingly vulnerable to challenge from a group of BUSINESS ETHICS scholars who work in a social contract tradition (*see* SOCIAL CONTRACT THEORY). Among these contractarian projects are the works of Donaldson & Dunfee (1994) regarding integrative social contracts theory; Freeman (1984; 1994) regarding a stakeholder theory of the firm; Evan & Freeman (1987) regarding "Kantian capitalism"; and Gilbert (1992) regarding strategy, ethics, and conventions.

As contractarians, these writers each start from the premise that human beings are inevitably connected in the patterns of human relationships called communities. They then move to consider what humans should do to protect and to enhance their associations, toward the elusive goal of human solidarity

(Rorty, 1989). In so doing, these writers challenge a premise that is central to the Prisoner's Dilemma: persons can live meaningfully by behaving uncooperatively. These contractarians, in short, are working to replace "prisoner" with new metaphors for human beings (Rorty, 1989).

Bibliography

Axelrod, R. (1984). *The Evolution of Cooperation.* New York: Basic Books.

Dixit, A. & Nalebuff, B. (1991). *Thinking Strategically: The Competitive Edge in Business, Politics, and Everyday Life.* New York: W. W. Norton.

Donaldson, T. & Dunfee, T. (1994). Towards a unified conception of business ethics: Integrative social contracts theory. *Academy of Management Review,* 19, 252–84.

Evan, W. & Freeman, R. E. (1987). A stakeholder theory of the modern corporation: Kantian capitalism. In T. Beauchamp & N. Bowie (eds), *Ethical Theory and Business,* 3rd edn. Englewood Cliffs, NJ: Prentice-Hall, 97–106.

Frank, R. (1988). *Passions Within Reason The Strategic Role of the Emotions.* New York: W. W. Norton.

Freeman, R. E. (1984). *Strategic Management A Stakeholder Approach.* Boston: Pitman.

Freeman, R. E. (1994). The politics of stakeholder theory: Some future directions. *Business Ethics Quarterly,* 4 (4), 409–21.

Gilbert, D., Jr. (1992). *The Twilight of Corporate Strategy: A Comparative Ethical Critique.* New York: Oxford University Press.

Gilbert, D., Jr. (1995). The prisoner's dilemma and the prisoners of the prisoner's dilemma. *Business Ethics Quarterly,* 145–78.

McMillan, J. (1992). *Games, Strategies, and Managers.* New York: Oxford University Press.

Murnighan, J. K. (1991). *The Dynamics of Bargaining Games.* Englewood Cliffs, NJ: Prentice-Hall.

Oster, S. (1990). *Modern Competitive Analysis.* New York: Oxford University Press.

Poundstone, W. (1992). *Prisoner's Dilemma John von Neumann, Game Theory and the Puzzle of the Bomb.* New York: Doubleday.

Rorty, R. (1989). *Contingency, Irony, and Solidarity.* Cambridge: Cambridge University Press.

Solomon, R. (1992). *Ethics and Excellence: Cooperation and Integrity in Business.* New York: Oxford University Press.

Taylor, C. (1991). *The Ethics of Authenticity.* Cambridge, Mass.: Harvard University Press.

DANIEL R. GILBERT, JR

privacy is the state of being free from intrusion or disturbance in one's private life or affairs (Flexner, 1987). One's private life is considered to be that which is not of an official or public character, that solitary or secluded part of life that does not include the presence of others. The private part of life is the most intimate and personal part of life that is not exposed to the public or available to outsiders for whatever reason. Privacy refers to that sphere of life where one's behavior, thoughts, feelings, etc., are unknown to others and are not available for their scrutiny.

The self requires a space of its own to be what it is, and this space is the private world. While people play many social roles in the context of a society, the underlying self, the so-called real person, is seen as the ultimate moral unit, deserving of protection and respect in its own right, and not just because of the functional role it occupies. Its sources of dignity are detachable from the specific social fields it occupies. Because the self is not dependent on any particular context for its value, it implicitly imposes a limit on what can be done to beings to achieve any particular social objective. It is capable of standing in opposition to society or taking a critical attitude toward things going on in society, even if this critical attitude is unwelcome.

Yet the self is not an atomic unit independent of other selves. Our dependence on others accounts for most of our moral qualities and accounts for most of what we are and can hope to become. This susceptibility to others is a prime and salutary feature of being human, but it also threatens us in ways that need to be limited. In different historical settings, and in different contexts, different levels of susceptibility to others are appropriate. The concept of privacy limits the amount and effectiveness of social control over an individual. In various settings, different levels of self-direction are appropriate. Privacy protects the individual by limiting scrutiny by others and the control some of them have over our lives (Schoeman, 1992).

On the narrow end of the spectrum, privacy relates exclusively to personal information and describes the extent to which others have access to this information. A broader conception extends beyond the informational domain and encompasses anonymity and restricted physical access. The most embracing characterizations of privacy include aspects of autonomy, particularly those associated with control over the intimacies of personal identity. For advocates of this interpretation, privacy is the measure of the extent an individual is afforded the social and legal space to develop the emotional, cognitive, spiritual, and moral powers of an autonomous agent (Schoeman, 1992).

As social beings, we may be more vulnerable to social than to legal coercion, and the strategies that we construct to combat social coercion will be different from those that insulate us from legal coercion. The strategies that protect individuals from the overreaching power of government are mostly dependent on legal remedies. In the social realm, the defenses will have to be of a more nuanced and informal character as represented in social norms. Given the awareness of the danger of social control, it is curious that so little mainstream philosophical attention is placed on rights and wrongs of social control mechanisms (Schoeman, 1992).

With respect to privacy, it is interesting to note that the US Constitution does not explicitly mention a right to privacy, although the Bill of Rights does protect what could be called zones of privacy including the free exercise of religion and security from unreasonable searches and seizures. Not until 1966, however, did the Supreme Court affirm that a right to privacy exists in a case involving a Connecticut law restricting contraception. While this case pertained to marriage and the family, it wasn't long before this right to privacy was transformed into an individual right that has had many permutations. In *Roe* vs. *Wade*, Justice Blackmun had the following to say about the constitutional right to privacy:

> The constitution does not explicitly mention any right of privacy. In a line of decisions, however . . the Court has recognized that a right of personal privacy, or a guarantee of certain areas of zones of privacy, does exist under the Constitution. In varying contexts, the Court of individual Justices have, indeed, found at least the roots of that right in the First Amendment . . in the Fourth and Fifth Amendments . . in the penumbras of the Bill of Rights . . . in the Ninth Amendment . . or in the concept of liberty guaranteed by the first section of the Fourteenth Amendment. . These decisions make it clear that only personal rights deemed "fundamental" or "implicit in the concept of ordered liberty" . . are included in this guarantee of personal privacy. (*Roe* vs. *Wade*, 410 US 113, 1973)

The Fourth Amendment to the Constitution guarantees the right to be secure in one's person, houses, papers, and effects against unreasonable search or seizure. The First Amendment affords people free exercise of religion and freedom of speech, the press, and assembly – freedoms we associate with freedom of conscience. The Fifth Amendment ensures that people cannot be required to testify against themselves, and the Fourteenth Amendment provides that they cannot be deprived of life, liberty, or property without due process of law. In tort law there are four categories of individual protection: (1) intrusion upon a person's seclusion, solitude, or private affairs; (2) disclosure of private, embarrassing facts; (3) public disclosure of a person in a false light; and (4) appropriation of another's name, image, or other aspect of identity, for one's advantage or profit, without that person's consent (Schoeman, 1992, p. 12).

Privacy has been held to be the most comprehensive of all rights and the right that is most cherished by civilized individuals. It has also been described as the kernel of freedom and as the most basic right from which all other freedoms stem (Rotenberg, 1993). Whether privacy is this basic is subject to debate, but there seems no doubt that privacy serves some basic human need, that there is some kernel to the self that needs to be protected from intrusion and from scrutiny by other people. There apparently are some things that must be kept inviolate and unknown in order for humans to have some space that is entirely their own and is unavailable to others.

The question in an advanced society with all kinds of interconnections between people, and where people are dependent on one another for the performance of certain jobs, is: where does the sphere of privacy end and the public's need to know begin? Many of the issues that involve privacy in our society can be stated in terms of the individual's right to privacy versus the society's need to know. Other issues, particularly with regard to private property, can be stated in terms of the right to use things in one's own interests versus the public's right to regulate that usage in the public interest. These questions are complex and have no easy answers.

The rapid advances in computer and telecommunications technology have taken individual records and individual papers from the home and private safes and out of the control of the individual. The record-keeping explosion of the computer age has prompted both government and the private sector to keep previously unimagined records and papers relating to the individual (Freeman, 1987). The right to privacy is not absolute in an organized society, for society's need to know must always be balanced against the individual's right of privacy in most democratic societies.

With regard to business organizations, privacy is an issue relating to drug testing, testing for AIDS, computer privacy, and other issues. Drug abuse constitutes a significant problem in the workplace, contributing to impaired productivity and job performance, increased accidents and injuries, violations of security, theft of company property, and diminished employee morale. Highly focused programs such as drug testing can be a valuable deterrent in discouraging non-users from beginning to use drugs, deterring experimental users from graduating to more serious abuse, motivating non-addicted users to discontinue using drugs for fear of getting caught, and challenging addicted users to seek medical help.

Drug testing is especially appropriate in safety-related work, particularly where public safety is involved. In 1994, new US federal regulations doubled the number of workers that needed to be tested for drug and alcohol use at work. Government required both random alcohol and drug testing each year for 25 percent of transportation workers in such safety-sensitive areas as trucking, aviation, railroads, and pipelines. Only random drug testing was required before. The rules also covered mass-transit workers, and expanded drug testing to intrastate truckers and bus drivers (Newman, 1994).

These new rules were expected to cover 7.5 million workers as compared with 3.5 million before. In addition to the new coverage required by these rules, testing for drugs was on the rise generally as more companies were testing job applicants and employees. An American Management Association survey reported that in 1993, 85 percent of the 630 companies surveyed had drug-testing programs, including 73 percent of manufacturers and 66 percent of financial service companies. Since 1987, the number of companies with drug-testing programs had tripled (Newman, 1994).

Drug tests can be applied to many different kinds of samples and materials, but most often urine is tested because of the ease of getting a sample, the speed of conducting the analysis, and the low cost involved. But urine tests can be considered an invasion of privacy because the tests can disclose numerous other details about one's private life, such as whether or not an employee or applicant is pregnant or being treated for various medical conditions in addition to evidence of illegal drug usage. Drug testing is less intrusive if the actual giving of the sample is not observed, since most people using the toilet or urinal usually have an expectation of privacy. However, the absence of supervision means that an employee who does use drugs is able to substitute someone else's "clean" urine or otherwise tamper with the sample.

Testing for AIDS has many of the same problems with regard to privacy, but is different in many important respects. For one thing, there is as yet no cure for AIDS, so identifying people who have the disease will not help them to get on some rehabilitation program to get over the disease. AIDS sufferers also run a greater risk of discrimination than do people on drugs, because the same elements of fear are not present. Once identified as a carrier of the AIDS virus, an individual runs the risk of losing friends, employment, housing, and insurance, despite laws protecting them from discrimination. Another problem is that the results of testing can be misleading as well as inaccurate and lead to unjust treatment of individuals. In spite of these problems, however, many people in the general public believe mandatory testing is necessary, particularly in those instances where there is a risk of exposure where they are willing to set the right to privacy aside in the interests of protecting public health.

Problems in the computer field traditionally had to do with security breaks into the computer network, the accuracy of credit information, and other such problems. Technological changes have brought other issues on the agenda of concern, such as monitoring of electronic mail (e-mail) and employee performance. Do employers have the right to read employees' electronic mail correspondence, or do employees who work on the equipment own the data even though the employer owns the infrastructure or pays for the service? Is it an invasion of privacy to monitor employees' performance using computer technology without their knowledge? Companies have been encouraged to develop policies on these issues and legislation has been introduced into Congress to require companies to alert workers in advance if they regularly monitor e-mail messages and place limits on how many times a worker could be monitored for performance.

These examples are only a few of the many areas in the workplace where privacy is a concern. The issue, as mentioned before, is generally stated as the employer's or public's need to know versus the individual's right to privacy. This way of stating the issue looks on the surface to be some collective body such as the public pitted against the individual who want privacy to be respected. But in the final analysis, the issue is really one individual or set of individuals against another individual or set of individuals. People who fly in airplanes are at risk under normal circumstances, and they want to know if they are faced with an additional risk involving pilots who may be on drugs and not able to function properly. Individual managers may want to know what kind of conversations are taking place between employees over electronic mail, but employees want to keep these conversations private as they do other conversations with fellow employees.

In all of these cases, decisions have to be made about where the zone of privacy ends and where other members of the public have a legitimate right to know in order to protect their own interests. What protections are needed to preserve that core of the individual and protect that space that is necessary for human beings to function, and what intrusions on this space are valid to promote other people's legitimate interests in knowing something about that individual and what he or she is doing? These are difficult questions that any society and its institutions have to continually grapple with as technology and society changes to bring up new issues that were not previously of concern.

Bibliography

Coombs, R. H., & West, L. J. (1991). *Drug testing: Issues & Options.* New York: Oxford University Press.

DeCew, J. W. (1994). Drug testing: Balancing privacy and public safety. *Hastings Center Report,* **24** (2), 17–23.

Fay, J. (1991). *Drug testing.* Boston: Butterworth-Heinemann.

Flexner, S. B. (1987). *The Random House Dictionary of the English Language,* 2nd edn. New York: Random House.

Freeman, W. (1987). *The Right of Privacy in the Computer Age.* New York: Quorum.

Furchgott, R. (1992). Invasion of privacy. *Self,* **14** (12), 128–31.

Handlin, O. (1993). The Bill of Rights in its context. *American Scholar,* **62** (2), 177–86.

Newman, A. (1994). Drug testing firms face pluses, minuses in new rules. *Wall Street Journal,* Mar. 15, p. B4.

Peterman, L. (1993). Privacy's background. *Review of Politics,* **55** (2), 217–46.

Pillar, C. (1993). Privacy in peril: How computers are making private life a thing of the past. *Macworld,* July, p. 124.

Rotenberg, M. (1993). Communications privacy: Implications for network design. *Communications of the ACM,* Aug., p. 61.

Schoeman, F. D. (1992). *Privacy and Social Freedom.* New York: Cambridge University Press.

Viles, Peter. (1994). Privacy a murky area in First Amendment law. *Broadcasting and Cable,* **124** (3), 70–4.

Worsnop, R. L. (1993). Privacy in the workplace. *CQ Researcher,* **3** (43), 1011–24.

ROGENE BUCHHOLZ

privatization   A term encompassing a set of policies whose common objective is to reduce the influence of the state in the economy and to strengthen the role of market forces. Most often included under the privatization rubric are liberalization, deregulation, contracting out, and divestiture (sometimes called denationalization). Liberalization, deregulation, and divestiture result in a different, and possibly diminished, role for the state in the economy, while contracting out privatizes the delivery mechanism but clearly retains the ultimate responsibility for provision of the good or service in the sphere of the state.

Liberalization and deregulation are policy programs that serve to remove or reduce market regulation and introduce or increase competitive forces in the market. The elimination or reduction of price controls, investment restrictions, and barriers to international trade such as tariffs and quotas are all liberalization policies that are expected to result in greater competition, lower prices, and expanded production. Contracting out allows a private management team to accept the commercial risk and operational responsibility for the firm while maintaining asset ownership in the hands of the state. The competitive bidding for the management contract substitutes for the competition absent in the output market and provides an incentive for operational efficiency and quality service.

Divestiture is the sale of publicly owned assets and has been the cornerstone of privatization efforts in Europe and Latin America. As a result, responsibility for delivery of many basic services including telephones, electricity, water, garbage, gas, oil, transportation services, and pension systems has shifted to the private sector. At the national level in the United States, privatization to date has consisted principally of deregulation and liberalization, but policy discussions have included consideration of the sale of national parks, prisons, highways, airports, and the education and pension systems. Divestiture reduces the size of the state in terms of assets, employment, and revenues, but may have little effect on competition if monopolies are sold without regulatory changes.

The motivation for privatization varies across countries but more often reflects economic than ideological considerations. The most frequently cited justification for privatization is the gain in efficiency that is said to result from reduced political interference, exposure to competition, and increased competitive pressure on management, arising from the fear of takeover or bankruptcy. Financial adversity has also motivated some governments to sell assets to generate funds that can be used to repay outstanding public debt. This one-time exchange of physical assets for financial ones is especially appealing to developing countries with large debt burdens. In the longer run, the transfer of ownership of a loss-making public enterprise to the private sector eliminates the need for continuing subsidies and thus reduces government current expenditures. Technological capability is another argument used to justify privatization and is an especially important one for such industries as telecommunications and informatics. Many public enterprises have been unable to finance new investments during the last decade, creating a technological backlog.

While the promise of privatization policies is great, there are limitations. Privatization is unlikely to generate major efficiency gains unless it is accompanied by reforms which alter prevailing relative prices. For example, the sale of a monopoly will generate more revenue for the state than the sale of an enterprise subject to competition, but a private monopoly is unlikely to be more efficient than a public one. If efficiency is the goal and the public monopoly is statutory, the mere repeal of the law may make the enterprise more efficient even if new firms never enter the market and government ownership is maintained.

In terms of implementation and impact, privatization presents numerous economic, political, and social difficulties. Divestiture is often associated with a social objective, the decentralizing of asset ownership. Yet an international study of privatization revealed that while privatization had increased the number of individual and employee shareholders, ownership in most stockmarkets remained predominately in the hands of large domestic investors (Seth, 1989). For developing countries (which were under-represented in the study) the results are likely to be similar, with large foreign investors being more predominant in some countries.

Weak or nonexistent capital markets, inadequate operating data for the firm under consideration, and difficult macroeconomic environments can make the valuation of a public enterprise extremely difficult. Undervaluation, which seems to have been the more frequent case in both developing and developed countries, results in windfall gains for the new owners at the expense of other taxpayers. Moreover, loyalty bonuses and special incentives for employee ownership of shares in privatized firms have distorted stock prices, reduced market liquidity, and misrepresented the behavior of a capitalist equities market to new investors.

Some countries have resorted to the private placement of public-enterprise assets when interest in the company is limited or the size of the stockmarket precluded a successful public sale. In such cases, privatization has resulted in the transfer of public assets to a small group of wealthy elites or individuals with privileged access. Instead of the oft-touted benefits of the dispersion of ownership and the development of small capitalists, wealth has been further concentrated. In some cases, existing enterprise management has been given preferential treatment in the purchase of the firm. While this may mitigate the concentration of wealth in the economy, it raises many of the same ethical issues associated with other privatization transactions and insider trading.

Whatever the economic impact, the popularity of privatization seems to reflect society's changing philosophical and ideological perspectives. The 1980s have seen an increase in emphasis on the individual and a declining confidence in the ability of government to act in the public interest and to effectively address social concerns. While privatization policies have sought to reduce the role of government in the economy, declining public employment and labor standards, concentration of ownership among domestic elites, foreign ownership and control of key sectors of the economy, and the erosion of sovereign control which often accompanies the transfer of ownership from the public to the private sector create significant policy challenges for the newly redefined state.

Bibliography

Houston, Douglas A. & Howe, John S. (1987). The ethics of going private. *Journal of Business Ethics*, **6**, 519–25.

Seth, Rama (1989). Distributional issues in privatization. *FRBNY Quarterly Review*, summer, 29–43.

Starr, Paul. (1990). The limits of privatization. In Dennis J. Gayle & Jonathan N. Goodrich (eds), *Privatization and Deregulation in Global Perspective*. New York: Quorum Books, 109–25.

Stein, Benjamin. (1985). Going private is unethical. *Fortune*, Nov. 11.

Vickers, John & Yarrow, George. (1988). *Privatization: An Economic Analysis*. Cambridge, Mass.: MIT Press.

MELISSA H. BIRCH

procedural justice   The doctrine that justice is not fairness of outcome but fairness of procedure in arriving at the outcome. A procedural definition of the just goes back to John Locke (b. 1632), and behind him to ancient Roman law. "Procedural" justice stands against "substantive" justice, Roman law against Greek philosophy. In the vocabulary of the philosopher Robert Nozick, who in 1974 revived procedural justice, substantive justice is an "end-state" principle. According to end-state or substantive definitions of justice, if someone is now a millionaire, and you regard great wealth as obscene in a world of poverty, you will regard the outcome as unjust. By contrast, Locke and Nozick start and end with private property, to which someone is entitled. "A distribution is just," writes Nozick, "if it arises from another just distribution by legitimate means" (1974, p. 151), such as a market or a court in a republic. The theory is historical, looking back to the origins of wealth.

Thus, Andrew Carnegie the steelmaker was entitled to his wealth if he acquired it by legitimate means from people who had in turn acquired it by legitmiate means, back to the Flood. Procedural justice would not, for example, acknowledge the justice of a gospel of wealth, commonly defended on the grounds that the millionaire should "give back to the community some of what he has taken" (the gospel of wealth could be defended perhaps on other grounds, such as magnanimity). The free exchanges in which Carnegie partook to acquire his wealth were legitimate, not takings. Nozick makes the point in his famous Wilt Chamberlain example. Four million people each voluntarily pay a quarter to see exhibitions of Chamberlain's prowess as a basketball player. Chamberlain therefore becomes a millionaire. According to an end-state theory such as that of Nozick's colleague at Harvard, John Rawls, Chamberlain's wealth is just only if allowing it to accumulate will improve the welfare of the least-advantaged person in the community. On the contrary, Nozick replies, Chamberlain has a natural right to the fruits of his labor. He is entitled to his wealth if he acquired it without force or fraud. Procedural justice therefore fits smoothly with libertarianism, anarchism, classical liberalism. It is hostile to utilitarianism (and other theories of the just that urge the government to adjust end states). "Commutative justice" (the term is from Aquinas) is justice in market exchanges, with the proviso that the exchanges take place at the just price. For modern economics and for libertarian philosophers like Nozick, the just price is any price voluntarily contracted. In the words of H. B. Acton, "Commutative justice is found when freely made agreements are kept, and it is maintained when there are laws for punishing fraud and for enforcing the fulfillment of contracts" (1993, p. 125). In English legal terms, procedural justice is that of common-law courts, as against equity. In economic terms, it is that of markets as against governments.

See also **Communitarianism; Justice; Libertarianism; Locke, John; Natural law; Nozick, Robert; Rawls, John; Utilitarianism**

Bibliography

Acton, H. B. (1993). *The Morals of Markets and Related Essays*, (eds) D. Gordon & J. Shearmur. Indianapolis, Ind.: Liberty Fund.
Nozick, Robert. (1974). *Anarchy, State, and Utopia*. New York: Basic Books.

DIEDRE N. MCCLOSKEY

productivity   is the relationship between the output of a production process and the inputs – labor, capital goods, and natural resources – required to produce that output.

It is important to distinguish between productivity and production. Production, which is the output of a production process, depends on the volume of resources used (inputs) and the efficiency with which they are used. When the ratio of output to total input rises, it indicates an increase in productive efficiency, or productivity. Production can rise simply because more inputs are used, without any necessary increase in productivity. Productivity increases occur only when (1) more output is produced with no increase in inputs, or (2) more output is produced without a corresponding increase in inputs. However, if less output is produced, productivity could still increase if inputs decrease by more than the reduction in output.

Productivity is a relationship between output and the associated inputs, where both outputs and inputs are measured in physical volume terms, unaffected by price changes. Measuring productivity is not as straightforward as its definition would lead one to believe. While one might be able to count the number of units of output produced in a particular period of time, how does one determine the output of a plant that produces multiple products, such as a farm that produces corn and wheat? Similarly, how does one add together units of several inputs, such as labor, land, and capital equipment? By convention, constant prices as of one period are multiplied by the units of different outputs and inputs in order to combine them into aggregate measures. The resulting aggregate measures are typically converted to an index where the base year is set equal to 100. The ratios may relate to the entire national economy, to a particular industry, or to a specific company.

At the national level, the broadest measure of output is the gross national product (GNP), that is, the market value of the final goods and services produced by the nation's economy for a given period of time. When GNP is adjusted for price changes through deflation, the resulting real GNP measures the total physical volume of final goods and services, combined by means of constant prices as of one period. Real GNP can be broken down by industry of origin so that real product (output) can be related to factor inputs for each industry and productivity compared for different industries.

The inputs to the production process are labor, land, and capital – the three factors of production. Labor inputs are usually measured by the number of hours worked. It is desirable to measure hours worked in each major occupation and/or industry and then combine the hours on the basis of the relative compensation per hour, held constant as of a particular base period. In this way the relative importance of the various kinds of work is taken into account, just as prices are used to indicate the relative importance of the different products. Non-human inputs – land and capital – can conceptually be measured in physical units, such as acres for land and units of equipment for capital. To arrive at a measure of total input, these units must be combined into a single measure of input on the basis of their relative contribution to the production process.

Total productivity, or total factor productivity, relates output to all inputs used in production. Output may also be related separately to each major class of inputs used in production. Such measures are known as partial productivity ratios. Examples of partial productivity ratios are output per man-hour, output per acre, and the output/capital ratio. These partial productivity ratios reflect changes in input proportions, or factor substitutions, as well as changes in productivity efficiency. So caution must be used in interpreting partial productivity ratios. For example, when output per man-hour rises, that may be the result of the substitution of equipment or other non-labor inputs for labor, rather than any increase in overall productive efficiency.

In the short run, changes in productivity may reflect changes in the rate of utilization of fixed plant and equipment, and possibly, changes in labor efficiency. In the long run, increases in total productivity are the result of many factors, including technological progress, investment, and the organization of production – the state of the art. Technological progress and investment are closely related. The technological advances that reduce unit real costs and raise productivity usually require investments in basic research to create new knowledge and know-how. That in turn feeds into applied research designed to develop new products and processes. To produce the new products and use the new processes requires 1) investments in education to incorporate them into labor and 2) investments in non-human productive agents – new buildings and equipment. New technology thus becomes embodied in producers' goods and is diffused through investments in successive generations of capital goods and workers. How the production process is organized can also affect productivity. Recent history is replete

with examples of companies that have increased (and decreased) production by "re-engineering" the process.

The level of a productivity ratio for any one period, for any one firm, for any one industry, or for any one country is not meaningful. Significance comes from comparisons of the ratios for particular firms, industries, or countries over time, or comparisons between levels of productivity between similar firms or between the same industry in different countries.

Increasing productivity provides a number of benefits to society. 1) It allows a society to improve the economic well-being of its people, since it provides for an increase in output per capita. 2) It results in conservation of resources per unit of output. 3) It helps to mitigate inflation by offsetting increases in the prices of inputs. 4) It increases the ability of domestic producers to compete internationally. At the same time, changes in productivity can lead to changes in the structure of the economy, resulting in reallocations of resources. Specifically, new technology is likely to involve the growth of new industries and the decline of old ones; the growth of certain occupations and the decline of others; the growth of certain regions and the decline of others. The reallocation of resources is not a painless process and imposes real costs on society. This raises important policy issues about how to mitigate the human and other costs associated with increasing productivity. But it should be noted that the costs associated with reallocation of resources is usually only a fraction of the gains to income attributable to the increase in productivity

The earliest efforts at measuring output for the national economy developed out of the work of the National Bureau of Economic Research in the 1930s and 1940s. In the 1950s, when trying to relate the observed growth in output with the growth in inputs, economists discovered that the growth in conventional inputs explained little of the growth in output. "This finding of large residuals was an embarrassment, at best a measure of our ignorance" (Abramovitz, 1956, p. 11). But by attributing it to technical change and other sources of improved efficiency they turned it "from a gap in our understanding into an intellectual asset, a method for measuring technical change" (Griliches, 1994, p. 1). Subsequent research concluded:

> The major sources of productivity growth were seen as coming from improvements in the quality of labor and capital and from other, not otherwise measured, sources of efficiency and technical change, the latter being in turn the product of formal and informal R&D investments by individuals, firms, and governments, and the largely unmeasured contributions of science and other spillovers. (Griliches, 1994, p. 1)

Bibliography

Abramovitz, M. (1956). Resource and output trends in the US since 1870. *The American Economic Review*, **46** (2), 5–23.

Fare, R., Grosskopf, S., Norris, M. & Zhang, Z. (1994). Productivity growth, technical progress, and efficiency change in industrialized countries. *The American Economic Review*, **84**, 66–83.

Griliches, Z. (1994). Productivity, R&D, and the data constraint. *The American Economic Review*, **84**, 1–23.

Kendrick, J. W. (1961). *Productivity Trends in the United States*. National Bureau of Economic Research, Number 71, General Series. Princeton: Princeton University Press.

Kendrick, J. W. (1973). *Postwar Productivity Trends in the United States, 1948–1969*. National Bureau of Economic Research, Number 98, General Series. New York and London: Columbia University Press.

Kendrick, J. W. (1977). *Understanding Productivity: An Introduction to the Dynamics of Productivity Change*. Baltimore and London: The Johns Hopkins University Press.

Kendrick, J. W. & Grossman, E. S. (1980). *Productivity in the United States: Trends and Cycles*. Baltimore and London: The Johns Hopkins University Press.

Measuring Productivity: Trends and Comparisons from the First International Productivity Symposium. (1984). Sponsored by Japan Productivity Center. New York: UNIPUB.

CHARLES MEIBURG

products liability An area of law determining the conditions under which a manufacturer/seller is required to provide financial compensation for injuries caused by defective products.

Prior to the industrial revolution, products liability law was effectively governed by a principle of *Caveat Emptor* (Buyer Beware). That principle precluded injured consumers from ever recovering damages in court. At the beginning of this century, the ruling legal doctrines were a conjunction of Privity of Contract and NEGLIGENCE. The Privity Doctrine allowed consumer suits only against parties with whom they had direct contractual relations; this requirement effectively insulated manufacturers from suits since manufacturers were removed in the chain of distribution from the end purchaser. The Negligence standard required that successful consumer suits had to prove the defendant seller was negligent for letting a defective product into the marketplace. (A defective product is one that is judged to be "unreasonably dangerous.")

In 1916, a New York court case, *McPherson* v. *Buick Motors*, eliminated the privity requirement and thus exposed manufacturers to increasing numbers of product liability suits. Other state jurisdictions gradually followed New York's lead in establishing simple Negligence as a standard for manufacturer liability. However, by the 1960s, that standard was challenged as a number of states began to recognize a consumer's cause of action even in cases where negligence was not established. In California, a 1963 ruling in *Greenman* v. *Yuba Power Products* established a doctrine of Strict Liability. Under this standard, manufacturers would be held strictly liable for injuries caused by defective products. The plaintiff is under no burden to establish negligence. Strict Liability has become the norm for product liability in most states and for most product categories.

The shift to Strict Liability and away from a Negligence standard signifies an important change in the function of product liability law. Prior to the adoption of Strict Liability, the decision to compensate an injured consumer was, at least arguably, based on a finding that the defendant was at fault and liability could be seen as a penalty for negligent behavior. Once Strict Liability was adopted, however, the conception of product liability law shifted from a fault-finding exercise to an attempt to provide a mechanism of compensation for consumers injured by defective products. The law became a scheme of no-fault insurance where the premiums for that insurance are paid by the manufacturer.

An obvious result of the loosened requirements on consumer suits is an increased frequency of consumers bringing suits and recovering damages. This is not to suggest that business is without available legal defenses, however. A corporation may block or diminish monetary judgments by showing consumers voluntarily assumed risk, misused, or were contributorily negligent; or by establishing that the risk of the product is outweighed by its social benefits.

Given the increased financial exposure of corporations under strict liability, it is not surprising that they, and their insurance carriers, are lobbying hard for state and federal legislation to change the law and return to the Negligence standard. The arguments used in this lobbying effort raise issues of morality and public policy. Some of the arguments assert that Strict Liability is harmful to society. Others claim that Strict Liability is unfair to business because it imposes liability in cases where the business is not at fault.

The first line of argument concentrates on the social costs of Strict Liability. Opponents claim that it has led to an explosion of liability suits and damage awards, with drastically increased insurance premiums. This in turn leads, they claim, to increased product prices, products being withdrawn from the market, decreased investment in research and development of new products, and depressed employment.

Those defending Strict Liability question the data on the "explosion" of liability suits and awards. (They indicate that in recent years the number of suits and the size of awards, once three exceptional instances are excluded, has shadowed the general rate of economic growth.) Proponents must admit, however, that there is some effect on prices, research, and employment and they must also admit that some producers have withdrawn products because the potential liability did not justify continued marketing (some vaccines and birth-control products are clear examples). This forces those

favoring Strict Liability to argue that 1) the general decrease in accidents because manufacturers have greater safety incentives under Strict Liability outweighs the other harmful economic effects; and 2) the law can make exceptions for product categories if Strict Liability leads to the unavailability of socially essential products (as California courts have done for prescription pharmaceuticals).

Defenders of Strict Liability also challenge the charge that it is unfair to impose liability on faultless manufacturers. Since even opponents of Strict Liability will accept the propriety of manufacturer liability where there is negligence, the issue at hand is essentially a question about how to assign the costs for injuries from defective products when no one is at fault. If we abandon Strict Liability, its proponents argue, and return to Negligence, then the full cost of the accident falls on the injured party, who of course bears no responsibility for the defect. They contend that it would be fairer to allocate the cost to a corporation, which is also faultless, because the corporation can spread the cost of the accident broadly among the consumers of its product.

Some critics of the current approach accept the foregoing defenses of Strict Liability as a standard but they suggest reforms in how it functions. These critics propose changes such as limits on lawyers' fees (as a way of decreasing frivolous suits and "fishing expeditions"), dollar limits on monetary awards, and/or the elimination of awards for pain and suffering. While these reforms are not as far reaching as the proposal that we return to a Negligence approach, each of these public-policy choices will also raise questions of morality and fairness. For instance, in discouraging frivolous suits or excessive awards, would we be unfairly limiting some worthy plaintiffs?

See also **compensatory justice; fairness; responsibility; risk**

Bibliography

Brenkert, G. (1984). Strict products liability and compensatory justice. In W. M. Hoffman & J. M. Moore (eds), *Business Ethics: Readings and Cases in Corporate Morality*. New York: McGraw Hill.

Calabresi, G. (1970). *The Costs of Accidents: A Legal and Economic Analysis.* New Haven: Yale University Press.

Coleman, J. (1976). The morality of strict tort liability. 18 *William and Mary Law Review,* 259.

Coleman, J. (1992). *Risks and Wrongs.* Cambridge: Cambridge University Press.

McCall, J. (1990). Fairness and strict liability. In J. DesJardins & J. McCall (eds), *Contemporary Issues in Business Ethics.* Belmont, Calif.: Wadsworth.

Miller, A. (1982). *Miller's Court.* New York: Houghton Mifflin.

Posner, R. (1973). Strict liability: A comment. 2 *Journal of Legal Studies.* 205.

Thomson, J. J. (1986). *Rights, Restitution and Risk.* Cambridge, Mass.: Harvard University Press.

JOHN J. MCCALL

professional codes   generally shorthand for "code of professional ethics," a set of standards governing the conduct of members of a certain occupation. Whether or not a business has its own code of ethics, many of its employees or contractors may. There are, for example, codes of ethics for lawyers, accountants, and actuaries, for engineers, chemists, and computer scientists, for professionals in purchasing, marketing, and personnel. A professional code is neither a (purely) personal code, ordinary morality, nor (mere) law. What then is it?

A professional code states ("codifies") *standards of practice*, whether by describing preexisting practice (as a dictionary definition does) or by creating the practice (as a definition in a statute does). A code that does not state an actual practice (more or less) is a possible code, not an actual one.

A professional code need not be *written*. An oral formulation will do. But, in any society where writing is common, most professional codes are in writing for the same reason most technical standards are. Writing makes them easier to recall, easier to transmit to newcomers, and so on.

A code of ethics, any code of ethics, states standards of practice for a *group*. For example, a corporate code states how employees of a certain business should conduct themselves. It does not apply to everyone. In this respect, codes of ethics resemble laws rather than morality. They *are* relative.

Codes of ethics are nonetheless part of morality in at least two ways. First, *their standards must be morally permissible.* (A "torturer's code of ethics" could only be ethics in scare quotes, an ethic or ethos much as counterfeit "money" is money only in a degenerate sense.) Second, *the standards in question must morally oblige members of the relevant group.*

A code of ethics cannot, however, oblige because it restates common moral standards or applies them to new circumstances. A code of ethics must require something ordinary morality merely permits. A code of ethics, by definition, always sets a standard of conduct "higher" (that is, more demanding) than ordinary morality. How can a code of ethics be both a morally obliging standard and a standard higher than ordinary morality?

The answer is simple: a code of ethics must be part of morality because of some (morally obliging) convention, for example, an oath or contract. The convention must, in conjunction with some ordinary moral standard (e.g. "Keep your promises"), add a new moral standard.

Here then, is a crucial difference between codes of ethics and law. Law as such achieves order by threatening liability, legal restraint, or punishment; a code of ethics achieves order by getting novel moral commitments from people who take such commitments seriously. A code of ethics is, therefore, always a personal code; its claim results from a person's commitment, not from external force. A code of ethics is nonetheless never merely a personal code; the commitment in question must be shared with others, the rest of the group.

A *professional* code is the code of ethics of a certain kind of group, a *profession*. What is a profession? For our purposes, a profession is a group of people organized to earn a living by providing a service at a standard higher than law, market, and (ordinary) morality demand.

A profession must be a group. There can no more be a profession of one than a club of one. A profession must be organized. Without organization, there is only a particular occupation. But not any organization will do. The organization must be designed to help its members earn a living. An organization concerned only to help others would be a charity or other service group, not a profession.

The service a profession provides may be of any (morally permissible) sort from which its practitioners can earn a living (though in fact professions tend to be organized by relatively well-educated occupations). The professional need not be an independent consultant (for example, the traditional lawyer). The professional may be an employee, whether of government or private business. Indeed, even such occupations as plumber, secretary, or peddler could organize as a profession. All they need to do is adopt (and generally follow) standards for earning a living higher than law, market, and morality impose. (Without such higher standards, the resulting organization would be a trade association, labor union, or similar organization of self-interest.)

Why would any occupation want to be a profession? Why, in other words, would rational people voluntarily burden their livelihood with demands neither law, market, nor morality make? The answer, of course, must be that the people in question believe that they benefit overall from taking on those burdens. One profession may organize to protect its members from market pressure to do what law and morality forbid. The code of such a profession would emphasize the aid each member owes those who do what law and morality require when client, employer, or government try to get them to do something else. Another profession may organize to protect the reputation of its members. Its code would emphasize practices designed to prevent the appearance of wrong-doing. And so on. Most professional codes reveal a mix of such purposes.

A professional code cannot achieve its purpose unless members of the profession in fact generally do as the profession's code requires. Professional codes thus create a cooperative practice: each participant benefits (primarily) from what the others do and would not do did they not believe the rest were generally doing the same. Since the standards of a cooperative practice are morally obliging if participation in the practice is voluntary and the standards themselves are morally permissible, each person who voluntarily maintains membership in a profession, is morally obliged, even without oath or contract, to practice it as its code says.

Bibliography

Bayles, M. (1989). *Professional Ethics*. Belmont, Calif.: Wadsworth.

Davis, M. (1987). The moral authority of a professional code. *Authority Revisited: NOMOS XXIX*. New York: New York University Press.

Kultgen, J. (1988). *Ethics and Professions*. Philadelphia: University of Pennsylvania Press.

MICHAEL DAVIS

professional ethics The terms "professional" and "profession" have a variety of different meanings. In one familiar meaning, "professional" is contrasted with "amateur." In another meaning, "professional" is used to extol the quality of a performance or of a piece of work – "it was a professional job"; here "professional" is contrasted with "unprofessional." Things are made even more complicated by the sociological fact that recognized professions have a lot of social prestige and their members enjoy a distinctly superior social, economic, legal, and political status. Because of this, there is an understandable scramble among occupational groups, especially the newer ones, for the title of profession.

Bearing in mind the ambiguity and flexibility of the terms "profession" and "professional," as related to ethical issues, this entry is confined to traditional models of the so-called "higher" professions of law, medicine, divinity, and academic scholarship. Using these as models, social scientists have identified a number of elements as paradigmatic of a profession. They are:

(1) the provision of "esoteric" services that require practitioners to complete a lengthy period of academic training, usually including an advanced degree. The underlying assumption is that the professions incorporate an "intellectual" component.

(2) Professions call for an "altruistic orientation" on the part of practitioners. That means that the *primary* objective of professional practice is zealously to serve the needs of others, notably individual clients (patients, students) and society in general. The commitment to the service of others and of society is paramount.

(3) In a profession all individual practitioners are considered to be members of a professional body, organized or unorganized, that, as an autonomous self-governing collective group, is responsible for determining standards of acceptable professional practice, for providing guidance for professional education, and for controlling the licensing of its members.

(4) Finally, professions are characterized by a unique relationship to society, which grants them an array of special privileges and powers, often amounting to monopolies, on the assumption that such privileges are necessary to enable members to practice their profession effectively and for the public interest. In addition, society (i.e. the state) provides subsidies to the professions at large, such as educational assistance, libraries, hospitals, equipment, research facilities, etc. The mutual advantages gained by a profession from society and by society from a profession are often taken to imply that there exists a sort of social contract between the state and the professions, which, as such, provides a moral basis for their relationship and for the special moral responsibility that professionals owe to society.

At the heart of the ethics of the traditional model of professionalism is the idea of unqualified moral commitment on the part of professional practitioners in the area of their expertise to the welfare of their clients and to the common good. That means that any personal benefits coming from professional practice, such as income, status, and power, are secondary to the principal aims of the profession. In theory at least, personal advantage to the individual professional can never serve as the primary or direct motive justifying, for example, a particular medical decision or a particular legal intervention. In this regard professionals are significantly different from business people (or other groups and workers), who may frankly admit that profit is their main motive and that they are in the business to make money (commercialism). The seriousness of the charge of a conflict of interest in a professional's relationship with a client underlines the unconditional nature of the professional commitment to a client.

Another distinguishing feature of the professional–client relationship, is the peculiar character of professional services. Neither the aim nor the evaluation of professional services is defined by its success in bringing about a desired outcome. Good doctors have patients whom they cannot cure or who even may die, and good lawyers lose cases. It is clear that the service provided, for instance by a doctor or a lawyer, may be professionally exemplary and morally praiseworthy for reasons other than success. The specification of what good professional service is when it is conceived as person-oriented rather than as goal-oriented needs further examination. There is already a considerable ethical literature on the subject. One promising approach draws on so-called "virtue theory" and focuses on virtues like compassion, caring, concern, trust, and responsibility as central ingredients of the professional–client relationship.

Some reservations are in order. First, it should be kept in mind that the professional–client–society relationship portrayed here is an ideal. As is inevitable, there is a wide discrepancy between the ideal and the actual. Moreover, in many renderings of it, the ideal itself is controversial; thus, it is often attacked as supporting monopolistic practices, paternalism, and authoritarianism. Other critics charge that it encourages professionals to be hypocritical or even dishonest.

Second, the analysis presented leaves out many other groups claiming to be professions. In response, it should be pointed out that the characteristic open-textured and cluster-like quality of ethical concepts, which include that of a profession, allows for the legitimate use of a loaded term even when not all the constituent elements are present. Thus, if we wish to discuss, for example, engineering as a profession, we need to ask which elements are present and what ethical difference it makes whether particular elements are absent or present.

Once again, the assessment of professionalism needs to take into account the additional fact that, like other institutions in contemporary society, the professions are rapidly and radically changing. Commercialism has crept into all walks of life and has made traditional relationships and institutions, including law, medicine, religion, and education, into commercial enterprises. This trend has been reinforced by what might be called the "erosion of public morality," that is, the loss of a sense of personal integrity and of social responsibility, which are the cornerstones of professional ethics. Future generations, it may be hoped, will develop new institutions and new ethics to take the place of those that have been lost.

Bibliography

Callahan, J. (Ed.), . (1988). *Ethical Issues in Professional Life*. New York: Oxford University Press.
Flores, A. (Ed.), . (1988). *Professional Ideals*. Belmont, Calif.: Wadsworth Publishing Co.

JOHN LADD

profit and the profit motive   Profit: the return to owners of business firms or investors in other financial ventures after the cost of operations, including taxes, have been paid. These net returns or net earnings may be distributed to the owners/investors in the form of dividends or they may be retained and reinvested in the business entity to produce additional profit.

For accounting purposes, cost will include internal or "book" cost only. These are the business-related obligations attributable to the firm for a specified accounting period. Economists will add "external" or "social" cost to that figure. For example, suppose an audited accounting statement shows costs of $500,000 and a net profit of $100,000. An economist would further reduce that profit figure on the basis of credible evidence that the firm failed to "account for" or to "internalize" the harm that it caused to the environment, to occupational health and safety, or to consumers. These harms are called social costs – costs that could have been avoided with the expenditure of extra time, effort, and money (*see* SOCIAL COST-BENEFIT). In economic theory, business entities are supposed to cover their full range of costs. Those that do not cover these costs and produce a profit comparable to rival firms are expected to fail. This permits the capital that has been tied-up in an unproductive firms to be available for investment in more efficient and profitable opportunities.

In a business context, the *profit motive* is roughly equivalent to self-interest in economics and philosophy. A string of synonyms such as incentive, inducement, influence, force, or drive add very little to the common understanding that a motive is something that moves or causes a person to act. It is scarcely a controversial proposition that owners of businesses and investors in other economic enterprises are influenced or induced to invest by the prospect of financial returns in the form of profit.

Given the diversity of literally millions of owners and investors, however, it is unsurprising that the profit motive ranges across a full spectrum of intensity. Some profit seekers pursue that goal in the short term, others in the long term. Some are content to "satisfice" or to settle for profits that are less than the maximum that (theoretically) could be produced. Others are content with whatever profit results from the major thrust of their efforts – the pursuit of "socially responsible" investments, customer satisfaction, or meaningful employment.

In these different but significant ways, the profit motive impacts the decisions and the expectations of owners and investors all over the globe. Business people from entrepreneurs and managers to stockholders and Wall Street professionals are energized by the prospect of making a profit because profit represents, for most people, a significant component of the "good" life.

Accumulated profit translates into material goods (some degree of wealth and affluence) and into intangible goods (some measure of public regard and self-esteem). These goods are seen by many people, but by no means everyone, as prerequisites of the good or flourishing life. In the overall scheme of things, these material and intangible goods take their place along with health, knowledge, friendship, play, aesthetics, justice, practical rationality as constituent elements of the good life.

A countervailing view of profit, or of "money" as a close proxy for accumulated profit, is that money is the root of evil. If money is understood to be the "root" of evil, rather than evil-in-itself, then it is capable of being used for good as well as evil purposes. As an instrumental good, it can never approach the unqualified good of Aristotelian "happiness" or of Kantian "good will," but it is a convenient, if imprecise, yardstick in calculations of the public welfare (*see* ARISTOTLE; KANTIAN ETHICS).

Whether one is influenced by the Aristotelian, the Kantian, or the utilitarian point of view, a principal concern is that individual moral agents will become so attached to material goods, so warped by acquisitiveness and the pursuit of wealth, that they will embrace the credo, "Greed is good." Marxists, of course, equate capitalism with greed, but, within free enterprise, the moral challenge is to strike some responsible balance between the pursuit and acquisition of material goods and intangible goods (*see* UTILITARIANISM).

From the perspective of VIRTUE ETHICS, the process of striking a balance, of recognizing and identifying with the appropriate balance of material and intangible goods, is something that begins in the home. It begins with parents, family, and friends nurturing, tutoring, and disciplining the child in ways that are calculated to produce, over time, a harmonious and proportionate blend of material and intangible goods. A community of responsible citizens – citizens of strong moral character who have been taught from childhood to identify their own good with the good of others – is the most formidable defense against the "greed credo."

In summation, *profit* and the *profit motive* are at the core of a free-enterprise economic system. Profit is the return to owners and investors after all costs of operations are accounted for. The profit motive is a manifestation of self-interest, and it is capable of producing both tangible and intangible goods. Within bounds, the profit motive will be regarded as an important good. If it is not contained, virtue ethicists – with their emphasis on good character – will regard this form of acquisitiveness as a vice. Kantians will see it as destructive of a "good will," and utilitarians will view it as an obstacle to their pursuit of "the greatest good for the greatest number."

BILL SHAW

profit, profits In popular usage, profit is loosely associated with a "markup" of merchandise or a rate of return on capital. The average person typically thinks of profit as what is left over from revenues after all the bills have been paid. A "normal profit" is often defined as "the implicit cost of the resources contributed by the owners." A more technical definition of "profit" becomes quite elusive, and probably no concept in economics is used with such a wide range of meanings.

Profit in Economic Theory

The history of economic thought regarding the word "profit" is important to the field of business ethics. What generally makes the issue of profit an ethical issue are distributional questions such as "Who gets to profit?" and "How much do they deserve?" Answers to these questions depend on being able to determine the source of profits. Many factors enter into the profitable business venture: available capital, competent management, entrepreneurial ideas, skilled labor, market advantage, and sheer luck. Ethically speaking, profit should be distributed to the most deserving source, and economists have argued for 200 years over the nature of profit.

Adam Smith was one of the first to articulate a theory of profit. He argued that social classes were partly defined by their source of income: landlords collected rent, laborers received wages, and businessmen earned profits. Smith was one of the first to see that profit was a major motivating force in economies. Indeed, he saw that it was often potential for profit that attracted resources into those activities that produced goods and services most desired by buyers. But why should profit exist at all? Why would anyone want to pay more for a product than what it cost to produce it? There are several answers. Smith mentions two. One is that profit represents the surplus value created by labor returning to the capitalist as profit after wages are deducted. Both Ricardo and Marx articulated this view more fully, referring to profit as a form of exploitation of one social class over another. The other view mentioned by Smith is the idea that profits are related directly to the cost of production and are, therefore, a fixed component of price.

There are more factors in profitable business activity than either labor or the costs of production. Alfred Marshall lists money capital, physical capital, management, land, and labor as the productive factors in economies. His view of the factor most deserving of profit was management: Management provides business ability, energy, and organization; and management takes the risks associated with business ventures. Therefore, since management takes the risks, it should earn the profit (and take the losses).

Of course, any RISK that can be estimated or measured can also be insured. Therefore, if profit arises from risk-bearing, profit should disappear as the cost of insurance against loss. Frank Knight pointed out, however, that there is a difference between risk and uncertainty. Risk is insurable; uncertainty is unmeasurable and is, therefore, uninsurable. Therefore, according to Knight, profit arises from the bearing of uncertainty, not just risk. He was less clear about who, exactly, bears uncertainty. To say that entrepreneurs, creditors, or managers bear uncertainty is to view the matter too narrowly. Indeed, entrepreneurship and innovation are diffused throughout organizations, as all levels of personnel assume uncertainty in various forms. For example, good ideas often are generated by labor, yet they may be least likely to realize a profit from their contribution. Also bearing the burden of innovation are the suppliers of previously needed inputs to production who have lost their market, and the suppliers of new equipment who need to redesign. Paradoxically, those most likely to profit from innovation are often those with the weakest claim to such an improvement – shareholders and management.

So, profit can be attributed to a variety of sources, and deciding the equitable distribution of profits has been one major theme in business ethics. Various profit-sharing programs are popular among organizations that assume employees contribute strongly to profit.

Profit in Social Theory

Social theory has also contributed to this discussion. Foremost among the contributors in recent decades are Robert Nozick and John Rawls. In his *A Theory of Justice* Rawls argues that economic and social inequalities are justified only when they ultimately result in benefits to those most in need. Because markets frequently fail to accomplish this, government functions to provide for the redistribution of profits. Like health and education, wealth is the product of a social context, without which it could not occur, and upon which all citizens begin with an equal claim. But society can do better for all its citizens by encouraging the use

of skills and talents on behalf of society. Thus, corporations are chartered, managers are given executive compensation, and entrepreneurs are made wealthy *so long as those least advantaged in society are made better off in the process*. Thus, for Rawls, profit (or wealth accumulation) is directly linked to the production of social good at all social levels.

Robert Nozick countered with a more individualistic view of profit-making. His "Wilt Chamberlain example" (1974, pp. 161–4) is famous for attempting to demonstrate that great wealth is just, so long as it derives from a history of just transactions. His view is that the moral status of wealth accumulation should be judged, not by some ideal distributive pattern of social justice, but at the micro level by the moral status of the individual economic transactions that gave rise to the wealth. His *Anarchy, State, and Utopia* (1974) has come to be regarded as a major modern statement of libertarian philosophy.

Not only might profit-making be socially allowed, to some it is the prime moral imperative for business activity. Milton Friedman has argued that it is the sole social responsibility of business to increase its profits ("lawfully," I might add). Thus, profit maximization is frequently mentioned as both a socio-economic and a moral imperative for modern business, to the exclusion of other felt responsibilities. Part of the attraction of this view is its simplicity. In contrast with this view is STAKEHOLDER THEORY, which holds that businesses have greater responsibilities than simply making a profit.

See also **Friedman, Milton; Knight, Frank; Marx, Karl; Nozick, Robert; Rawls, John; Smith, Adam**

Bibliography

Arnold, N. S. (1987). Why profits are deserved. *Ethics*, **97**, 387–402.

Friedman, M. (1970). The social responsibility of business is to increase its profits. *New York Times Magazine*, Sept. 13, 32–3, 122–6.

Knight, F. (1971). *Risk, Uncertainty, and Profit*. Chicago: University of Chicago Press.

Marshall, A. (1948). *Principles of Economics*. New York: Macmillan.

Nell, E. (1987). On deserving profits. *Ethics*, **97**, 403–10.

Nozick, R. (1974). *Anarchy, State, and Utopia*. New York: Basic Books, Inc.

Obrinsky, M. (1983). *Profit Theory and Capitalism*. Philadelphia: University of Pennsylvania Press.

Rawls, J. (1971). *A Theory of Justice*. Cambridge, Mass.: Harvard University Press.

F. NEIL BRADY

promises, promising Promising: Taking what was not previously obligatory and turning it into our obligation; for example, we promise to attend a meeting; or, taking what was already our obligation and making it stronger by a promise; for example, we promise to tell the truth by taking an oath. Promising has a personal and creative aspect unlike the freestanding moral obligations. One cannot, however, turn what is forbidden into an obligation by a promise; thus the contract killer has no moral obligation to commit a murder even though he had said he would. While it is a matter of our voluntary choice whether we ever create for ourselves any concrete duties based on the principle of fidelity to promises, it is not a matter of choice whether we should keep our promises once we make them. We have placed ourselves under an obligation by our act.

There are times when promising is wrong to do even though what one promises, such as attending a meeting, might be quite innocent in itself. One may not be sincere about keeping the promise or know that inevitably it will be misleading to others. This observation about what one may or may not do allows us to see that *the promise* is itself both a kind of (speech) act, viz., a promising, as well as something that has a content, viz., what is promised. The content or substance of the promise of action considered alone purports to inform another person of one's future plans. Now giving this kind of information to someone is not yet a promise; it is nothing more than a statement of intention. To have made a promise, a moral obligation must be created around that intention. Indeed – in the light of this requirement – the ability to place oneself under an obligation by communicating one's intention to do this is sometimes thought to be mysterious.

Promises naturally purport to be that upon which reliance can be placed by the promisee. One is invited to count on them. For this reason it might seem that defeating someone's reliance would show the sort of wrongdoing involved in breaking a promise. There is no mystery. But is the promisor's obligation to keep his promise grounded in the reliance of a promisee? Say that the promisee is properly convinced that the promisor is utterly insincere; hence she does not rely in the least upon what was said. Would it follow that an obligation will never have existed for the promisor? Of course, a promisee can *release* the promisor from the obligation, but that is consciously a different process from the one being considered. Has the foreknowledge of insincerity, in effect, freed the promisor of an obligation even as he spoke? Surely the obligation persists, whatever the promisee does.

That said, one should probably admit that a *completely* unrelied-upon promise does not carry as strong an obligation (or its breach is not so culpable) as one upon which out-on-a-limb reliance has been placed. But the fact remains that the right to rely comes into existence with (or after) the promissory obligation arises and so reliance is not the basis of the obligation. Villagers, who came to depend for the time of day on the great philosopher's afternoon walk, did not have him under an obligation to be punctual. The basic observation here is that reliance can be an obligation-influencing reason only if the person who relies had a *right* to rely. How does such a right arise?

Here one must speak of a moral power or ability resting in the conventions of human communication to create an obligation (or greater obligation) to an addressee where no (or a lesser) obligation had existed before. It is to give the act a moral power to put oneself under an obligation to the party with whom one communicates. Promises need not only concern actions to be performed; they may be made about states of affairs or facts as well. The salesperson promises, that is, warrants, that the rug is antique and made in Anatolia. Warranting some thing as something has a large presence in business settings; promising facts might even be more common than promising actions.

All promising is a kind of voluntary action; there can be attached no straightforward meaning to the phrase "making an involuntary promise." Even promises that we are compelled to make, as under a threat, are voluntarily chosen from within the options available. Of course, they are made under such unjustly manipulated conditions as usually to weaken, perhaps to virtually nothing, the force of their obligation. While always voluntary, the decision to "never promise anything" would be most unusual. Promising is such a useful thing to do – even under pressure. Someone who eschews promising could not make business contracts or deal in credit. Without promises, nothing but the most primitive form of exchange, that is, barter, could be conducted.

Though many say – perhaps many in business say – "My word is my bond," the obligation of promises is not absolute, especially with regard to actions promised. Conditions of performance can change dramatically, so much so that it would now be unreasonable to demand the performance envisioned. Thus, while promises are important reasons, they are not the only reasons in the world. Furthermore, promises depend importantly on communication and are vulnerable to mistake. What if the hearer understands the promise differently from what the speaker intended to communicate? What has been promised? In the strictest sense, only the intentions of the speaker control the content of the promise; it is these intentions that he sought to communicate as he undertook an obligation to the other. Yet what if any reasonable hearer would probably have misunderstood what was said? He sent buttons; she (as anyone would) understood it would be bows. At this point, the moral discussion must shift its ground from fidelity to promises to what it would be just to do: the situation being one of mutual and reasonable misunderstanding.

See also **contracts and contracting; moral reasoning; moral rules; justice**

Bibliography

Atiyah, P. (1981). *Promises, Morals, and the Law.* Oxford: Clarendon Press.

Fried, C. (1981). *Contract as Promise.* Cambridge, Mass.: Harvard University Press.

Kant, I. (1785). *Groundwork to a Metaphysics of Morals.* (Numerous editions are available.)

Patterson, D. M. (1992). The value of a promise. *Law and Philosophy,* 11, 385–401.

Prichard, H. A. (1928). The obligation to keep a promise. In his *Moral Obligation.* Oxford: Clarendon Press.

Raz, J. (1977). Promises and obligations In P. Hacker & J. Raz (eds), *Law, Morality and Society.* Oxford: Clarendon Press.

Robins, M. (1984). *Promising, Intending, and Moral Autonomy.* Cambridge: Cambridge University Press.

Scanlon, T. (1990). Promises and practices. *Philosophy & Public Affairs,* 19, 199–226.

RICHARD BRONAUGH

property refers both to (a) a normative relationship between agents and things and (b) the things that stand in that normative relationship to agents. In the paradigm case of property, an individual is related to some physical object, e.g., a sheep or a knife, by having an exclusive right to use, control, transform, consume, and exchange or donate that object as he chooses. In virtue of that property relationship, that object is the property of that agent. It is his to do with as he sees fit. In the paradigm case, the property-holder's right of disposition is only subject to the constraint that he not dispose of his property in ways that violate others' rights. The owner of the knife may not thrust it into anyone else's chest or sheep. However, many instances of property diverge in one or more respects from this basic paradigm. An agent's property need not be a physical object, but can instead be a more abstract thing such as a flow of water, a segment of the electromagnetic spectrum, an industrial process, or a number of shares in corporation X. Distinct agents may have property in different aspects of the same thing, e.g., one may have the usual land ownership rights while another may hold the subsurface mineral rights. And distinct agents may jointly own particular things, e.g., the "community" property of married couples.

The paradigm presented and its variants are all cases of *private* property. Yet it is often claimed that property can be communal, state (i.e., public), or private and that no one of these is the privileged form of property. What is classified as communal property exists when numerous individuals are each free to use and consume some common resource. For example, each hunter in the tribe is free to reconnoiter the tribal territory and take what game she finds

– as long as that game is not already being taken by another hunter. What is classified as state property exists when the use, control, transformation, and consumption of certain things is governed by explicit political decisions about public schemes of use, control, etc., or about who shall be charged with formulating such schemes. While communal "property" and state "property" do share with private property the feature that non-owners (e.g., members of other tribes or other states) are excluded, it is plausible to view all these relations as property relations only if one insists on classifying every set of norms which govern the use, control, etc., of things in a given society as property rules. Such an insistence tends to obscure the special character of property rules and of societies in which property rules largely govern the disposition of things.

The distinctive character of genuine, i.e. private, property regimes can be illustrated by means of a case discussed by Harold Demsetz (1967). Demsetz describes the emergence of property rights in beaver-hunting areas among a number of Indian tribes in Eastern Canada during the eighteenth century. Prior to the advent of the beaver-pelt trade, the hunting territory of each tribe and the beaver it contained was communal "property." Each hunter had the right to hunt anywhere within that territory and to take any beaver he first found. However, when European demand for beaver pelts caused a vast increase in the value of these pelts, a continuation of this communal system would have led to the destruction of the beaver population. For each hunter then had a strong incentive to take as much as possible from the commons and had very little incentive to bear costs to conserve or enhance the beaver population. Any hunter's efforts to conserve or enhance the population would immediately be exploited by some other hunter.

One solution which might have been attempted to avert a tragedy of the commons would have been the conversion of the beaver and their habitat to public "property" to which a politically determined scheme of conservation and exploitation would be applied. This would have required widely shared and articulated knowledge of the whole habitat, of the best methods and schedules for harvesting beaver furs throughout it, and of the human and non-human resources available for effective use in the public scheme of beaver exploitation. It would also have required effective mechanisms to enforce the rulings of the Beaver Production Council. However, the actual solution which emerged was a system of family-owned, private rights to beaver-producing sub-regions. This allowed particular hunters to reap the rewards of their own conservation and enhancement of the beaver populations within their own protected domains and to attune their hunting of the beavers to the special conditions they individually faced. No collective decision had to be reached about any comprehensive scheme, and enforcement costs were limited to ensuring that neighboring property-holders did not trespass on one another's domains.

Unlike the public "property" solution to communal "property" problems, this private rights solution displays the essential features of a property scheme. Decision-making is radically decentralized because distinct agents enjoy secure discretionary control over particular things. This allows them to reap the benefits of their own investments in attention, effort, and resources and requires them to suffer the costs of their own failures of investment. Economic coordination among agents arises not from any collectively adopted or imposed plan, but rather through multiple, interconnecting, bilateral, market and contractual accommodations.

Is private property morally justified? The tale of the beavers and like narratives suggest a consequentialist vindication, viz., private property facilitates rational economic decisions (*see* CONSEQUENTIALISM). But many have opposed private property regimes precisely because they undercut communal or public life. Many others charge that such regimes, unless augmented by redistributive programs, yield grave distributive injustices. On the other hand, defenders of private property argue that property is a fundamental right, that private holdings which emerge from peaceful acquisition, production, and trade are, for that very reason, just, and often even deserved.

See also **ethics of ownership; economic liberty**

Bibliography

Demsetz, H. (1967). Toward a theory of property rights. *American Economic Review*, **57**, 347–59.

Epstein, R. (1985). *Takings: Private Property and the Power of Eminent Domain*. Cambridge, Mass.: Harvard University Press.

Honor, A. M. (1961). Ownership. In A. G. Guest (ed.), *Oxford Essays in Jurisprudence*. Oxford: Oxford University Press, 107–47.

Munzer, S. (1990). *A Theory of Property*. Cambridge: Cambridge University Press.

Paul, E. (ed.). (1990). *The Monist*, **73** (4), (Issue on Property Rights).

Pennock, J. R. & Chapman, J. W. (1980). *NOMOS XXII: Property*. New York: New York University Press.

Waldron, J. (1988). *The Right of Private Property*. Oxford: Clarendon Press.

ERIC MACK

property, rights to

Possession and Property

Property rights are a complex, socially constituted bundle of obligations and permissions. It is a common mistake to think of PROPERTY as one thing and the rights that attach to it as another. We can think of a baseball as part of a system of rules and practices within which it is used. If we found such an object in an ancient tomb, we could say it was *just like* a baseball. But if we knew the game wasn't played when the object was buried, we couldn't say that is what it was.

Similarly there is a critical difference between the way the squirrel is in possession of its acorns and the way the corporation owns the forest. Unlike the mere possession of things, the ownership of property presupposes an elaborate system of rules governing the social allocation of things to persons. Just as our ancient artifact does not become a baseball until it is fitted into the practices of the game, so the things it is possible to possess – songs, lands, genetically engineered species, inventions, crops, manufactured items, mineral deposits, airplane tickets, stock certificates, trademarks, taxicab licenses, secret recipes, dolphins, human cell lines, news reports, athletic teams, and so on – do not become property until they are fitted into a complex system of legal arrangements.

In 1919, Wesley Newcomb Hohfeld tried to show how complex legal arrangements could be built out of four fundamental relationships: what are now called claim-rights, liberties, powers, and immunities. Each of these "Hohfeldian rights" specifies a unique reciprocal relationship involving at least two parties. When you owe me a dollar, I have a *claim-right* against you that you pay me and, reciprocally, you have the duty to pay. The claim-right and the duty are part of a single relationship: The one entails the other. Likewise, if I am at *liberty* to eat in the cafeteria, then, reciprocally, everyone else lacks the right that I not eat there. If I have the *power* to permit people to take the short cut through my backyard, then, reciprocally, whether another person is at liberty to take the short cut or not is subject to my decision-making authority. Everyone else is liable to me in that way; i.e., is subject to my power to give or withhold permission. And lastly, if I have *immunity* as an official representative of a foreign government, then I am not subject to arrest in the way everyone else is. Reciprocally, the police lack that legal power in my case: nothing they do to me can count as a valid arrest. A claim-right correlates with a duty. A liberty to do something correlates with the absence of a right that one not do that thing. A legal power correlates with a liability. And an immunity correlates with the absence of a power. Much as atoms make up molecules, so Hohfeld thought that complex social practices could be constructed out of these elements.

In its original sense, property connoted all that was proper to some person. John Locke (1689), for example, included as property one's life and one's liberties in addition to one's estates. C. B. Macpherson (1977) has noted that since ARISTOTLE, the concept of property has traditionally included the right not to be excluded from those things society had designated as common: for example, access to and right to use public parks and waterways. It was not until the seventeenth century – not until the rise of capitalism and those market systems that have come to dominate social life in the West – that conceptions of property have more narrowly focused on goods that can be exchanged in market transactions. What makes market systems – i.e., the practices of business –

possible are, in part, socially backed understandings of exchangeable entitlements.

The Analysis of Ownership

In a 1961 article, A. M. Honoré analyzed the familiar concept of ownership into its "incidents." Much of what he says about ownership can be understood in terms of Hohfeldian rights. At the foundation is the right to possess: a claim-right to be in exclusive control coupled with the liberty to exercise "such control as the nature of the thing admits." Stories, lands, and groceries admit to different sorts of control. If one owns a story, a movie producer may not adapt it without permission. Hikers may not trespass across one's land. It is a crime to steal another's groceries. This liberty to exercise control over one's property is exclusive: all others are prohibited from interfering unless the owner exercises a power of permission. Honoré notes that the practices of ownership entail the existence of remedies available to the owner in the event that the right to exclusive control is violated. If the groceries are stolen, the owner/victim has the power to summon the police and, if it is provably known who did it, to have the thief charged with a crime.

Three additional rights are closely related: the right to use, the right to manage, and the right to the income. One is at liberty personally to enjoy one's property at one's sole discretion: this is the right to use. One has the liberty and unique power to decide how and by whom one's property shall be used: this is the right to manage. And one comes to own whatever fruits, rents, or profits one's property generates: this is the right to the income. The right to the capital includes the power to give away one's property and the liberty to consume, waste, or destroy it. The right to security involves an immunity from expropriation: generally, property is transferred only with the consent of the owner. Honoré adds what he calls the "incident of transmissibility": at the death of the owner, what has been owned as property can pass to the owner's successors.

The foregoing discussion should make it clear that there is no singular "right" to property. Rather, ownership is best understood as a package of claim-rights, liberties, powers, and immunities. It is commonplace that these elements can be divided and reassembled in a myriad of ways. A trust, for example, can be set up so one party – the beneficiary – has the right to the income while a second party – the trustee – has the right to manage. When one rents an apartment, one has the right to use it for a fixed period during which many of the owner's rights are suspended. Corporations, as fictional persons, own property themselves, but corporate officers manage the business as agents of the corporation (see AGENCY THEORY). The STOCKHOLDER, as owner of the corporation, has rights to the income. This separation of management rights from the other rights of ownership is a striking feature of many contemporary business organizations.

Honoré discusses duties and liabilities associated with ownership. Chief among these is the prohibition against harmful use: owners have a duty not to use their property in ways that harm others. Likewise the general immunity against expropriation will not protect owners against having their property taken from them following non-payment of debts, bankruptcy, or as a consequence of state expropriation (as, for example, when lands are condemned to build a highway). Those who lose property in this last way may have a claim-right to just compensation. Rights are often shaped by regulations and exceptions conceived in the public interest. Zoning laws may restrict what I can construct on my land. And although owners ordinarily have exclusive control, under exigent circumstances government officials (police and firefighters, for example) and even ordinary citizens may be at liberty, without consent, to enter private premises or take into their possession the property of others.

The Justification of Property Rights

Conceived in this way, a system of property rights is a complex social artifact empowering owners to make socially enforceable claims. It is not much of an exaggeration to think of ownership as a kind of sovereignty. Morris Raphael Cohen (1927) has written: "In a régime where land is the principal source of obtaining a livelihood, he who has the legal right over the land receives homage and service from those who wish to live on it." Much as the justification of political authority has long been a central concern of philosophy, so philosophers have worried about the legitimacy of property rights.

Lawrence Becker (1977) distinguishes between general and specific justifications of property. The former explains why there ought to be any property rights at all. The latter explains why there ought to be some specific sort of property right: Should beaches be private property down to the water? While it is not possible to provide a comprehensive overview of this literature, two important strands of the debate are worth sketching.

John Locke in Chapter 5 of the *Second Treatise of Government* (1689) sets out the classic exposition of what has become known as the labor theory of property. Even prior to the establishment of law, Locke argues, there is a natural right to property. When, for example, a fisherman catches a fish in the ocean, it seems plain enough that the fish properly belongs to him. Locke would point out that the value of the fish in the boat is far greater than its value while it was in the ocean. The fisherman's labor makes the difference, for the fish in the boat is the original fish "mixed" with that labor. For this reason it would be wrong for a bystander to seize the fish in the boat, unjust to take for oneself "the benefit of another's pains, which he had no right to . .." Locke adds that the argument justifying appropriation applies only when the fisherman takes no more than he can make use of and only provided there is "enough and as good left in common for others." This latter condition – the "Lockean proviso" – grows in importance as the world's resources are depleted. Many critics have pointed out that Locke's general justification cannot specifically justify the ownership of land. Robert Nozick (1974) wonders why mixing one's labor with an unowned thing isn't simply a way of losing one's labor.

While, in justifying property, Locke tends to look backward at the laborer's initial appropriation, utilitarian and economic theorists see regimes of property rights as engineered mechanisms that, if well designed, can promote the general happiness or the broadest satisfaction of preferences (*see* UTILITARIANISM). JEREMY BENTHAM (1830), for example, builds his general justification of property upon the precariousness of mere possession. "Without law there is no security," and where there is no security, disorder and impoverished misery are, according to Bentham, inevitable consequences.

Law creates "a fixed and durable possession" and so encourages people to labor now for that which they may reasonably expect to enjoy in the future. Property, in at least some of its implementations, can promote human well-being by securing a more efficient – and, therefore, a more affluent – social order.

It may be useful to take note of the social perspectives underlying these two approaches to justification. While Locke appeals to justice, utilitarians and economic theorists appeal to a concern for the general well-being. There is more than a kernel of truth in each perspective. For our choices in configuring the claim rights, liberties, powers, and immunities that are associated with property will affect the justice of our economic institutions and the general well-being of those in our community. Although, in our individual pursuits of property and the good life, we may fixate upon what we want for ourselves, we might also do well to reflect on how our historically contingent, evolving regime of property rights could be improved and how accommodations to emerging circumstances might further shared aspirations for a more perfect community.

See also **Economic efficiency; Economic justice; Locke, John; Justice; Nozick, Robert; Rights; Entitlement theory**

Bibliography

Becker, Lawrence C. (1977). *Property Rights: Philosophic Foundations.* London: Routledge and Kegan Paul. (An important overview and analysis of the major arguments for and against property rights.)

Becker, Lawrence C. (1979). Property theory and the corporation. In Michael Hoffman (Ed.), *Proceedings of the Second National Conference on Business Ethics.* Washington, DC: University Press of America.

Bentham, Jeremy. (1830). *Principles of the Civil Code.* (Chapters 7–12 set out Bentham's account. The text is available in Bentham's *The Theory of Legislation,* ed. C. K. Ogden. London: Kegan Paul, 1931.)

Cohen, Morris Raphael. (1927). Property and sovereignty. *Cornell Law Quarterly,* **13**, 8–29.

Hohfeld, Wesley Newcomb. (1919). *Fundamental Legal Conceptions.* New Haven: Yale University Press.

Honoré, A. M. (1961). Ownership. In A. G. Guest (Ed.), *Oxford Essays in Jurisprudence.* Oxford:

Clarendon Press, 107–47. (The standard analysis of ownership.)

Locke, John. (1689). *Second Treatise of Government*. (Chapter 5 sets out Locke's account. The text can be found in Locke's *Two Treatises of Government*, 2nd edn. (Ed.), Peter Laslett. New York: Cambridge University Press, 1967.)

Macpherson, C. B. (1962). *The Political Theory of Possessive Individualism*. Oxford: Clarendon Press. (An important study of the Lockean account of property.)

Macpherson, C. B. (1977). Human rights as property rights. *Dissent*, **24**, 72–7.

Nozick, Robert. (1974). *Anarchy, State, and Utopia*. New York: Basic Books.

KENNETH KIPNIS

Protestant work ethic   The Protestant work ethic is a set of principles of conduct and values including a preference for hard, physical labor, working regularly because it is one's obligation to society, having obedience and respect for authority, and rejecting leisure time. These principles of conduct and values are drawn from a rationalistic and religious philosophy about work and the importance of human activity associated with, or as a consequence of, work (Wayne, 1984).

These traditional values were strongly held by a majority of people in the United States until about 1955. They were based upon several beliefs: One of primary concern is that the land holds unlimited potential; another is that each individual is capable of moving up the socio-economic ladder. Each generation of a family was expected to achieve more than its past generations. By achieving more, the family would accumulate more of society's rewards (e.g., money, possessions, and status). All individuals had to do was work hard, be dedicated to the task, and conform to the rules, and the family would reach a higher standard of living.

The Industrial Revolution in America had a strong negative influence on the traditional Protestant work ethic, specifically the corresponding intensification of the division of labor with increasing productivity as a primary purpose. The division of labor caused an increasing fragmentation of specific work processes that removed workers from direct participation in the final products. This factor and others resulted in a change in worker attitudes away from those that had existed in previous generations.

See also **contemporary work values**

Bibliography

Labovitz, S. S. (1992). A study of Protestant ethic beliefs and laboratory task behavior. Ph.D. dissertation, Ohio State University.

Lehman, H. & Roth, G. (eds). (1993). *Weber's Protestant Ethic: Origins, Evidence, Contexts*. New York: Cambridge University Press.

Wayne, F. S. (1984). An instrument to measure adherence to the Protestant ethic and contemporary work values. Ph.D. dissertation, Arizona State University.

F. STANFORD WAYNE

prudence   the rational concern of the individual for the practical, day-to-day affairs of his or her own life. It is the "practical wisdom" that enables individuals to connect with their world, to live in security, with reasonable comfort, and decent reputation. Prudence, along with justice, courage, and temperance constitute the four cardinal virtues. In traditional VIRTUE ETHICS, three religious virtues – faith, hope, and charity – are often added to the list, and the cluster becomes the seven classic virtues (*see* JUSTICE, CIRCUMSTANCES OF).

Many philosophers have focused upon virtue: from ARISTOTLE and Cicero, through Hume and Kant, but few have dealt with the virtue of prudence as well as Adam Smith, especially in his first book, *The Theory of Moral Sentiments* (1759; 1790) (*see also* KANTIAN ETHICS; SMITH, ADAM). He defines prudence as:

> The care of the health, of the fortune, of the rank and reputation of the individual, the objects upon which his comfort and happiness in this life are supposed principally to depend, is considered as the proper business of that virtue which is commonly called Prudence. (Smith, 1759, p. 213)

As such, he argues that prudence is, "of all the virtues that which is most useful to the individual" (Smith, 1759, p. 189), because it is the virtue that connects us to the empirical world wherein we live out our lives.

Nowadays, unfortunately, a diminished interpretation of prudence predominates. As Josef Pieper writes: "In colloquial use, prudence always carries the connotation of timorous, small-minded self-preservation, of a rather selfish concern about oneself (Pieper, 1966, p. 4). In this version, prudence is an individual's calculating ability to choose the most effective means to achieve a narrow range of practical ends. Thus, the prudent individual seeks the most reliable occupations, the most profitable ways to invest money, the safest ways to deal with risk, and the path that leads to a secure future. As mundane and unexciting – let us term it "inferior" prudence – as it may seem, Smith does not treat it lightly, for it provides the foundations for a stable social, economic, and political order. But while these are not ignoble attitudes, nonetheless they are, in Adam Smith's words, only worthy of "a certain cold esteem."

The great mistake made by too many business theorists and practitioners is their failure to look beyond that inferior prudence. Smith, along with most virtue theorists, does not limit prudence to an essentially utilitarian role. He follows the classic philosophers in granting prudence a much grander role – a "superior" prudence which,

> when carried to the highest degree of perfection, necessarily supposes the art, the talent, and the habit or disposition of acting with the most perfect propriety in every possible circumstance and situation. It necessarily supposes the utmost perfection of all the intellectual and of all the moral virtues. It is the best head joined to the best heart. It is the most perfect wisdom combined with the most perfect virtue. (Smith, 1759, p. 216)

Putting the two manifestations of prudence together, they become "perfect prudence," and it is perfect prudence that should be of greatest interest for BUSINESS ETHICS.

Traditionally, perfect prudence is seen as the *sine qua non* of all the other virtues, because it provides the conditions for the expression of the other virtues. To illustrate, while some virtues can be exercised in an environment of social chaos (courage, for instance), most require a stable, ongoing society (justice and temperance, for instance). Perfect prudence is the virtue that creates the optimal social order.

Six aspects of perfect prudence should be mentioned. First, prudent behavior frees society from the need to allocate time and resources to care for the fecklessly imprudent, which allows all citizens to engage in actions of greater moral import.

Second, perfect prudence assumes that all individuals, through introspection and study, can know what is in their own best interests. As Smith notes: "Every man is, no doubt, by nature, first and principally recommended to his own care; and as he is fitter to take care of himself than of any other person, it is fit and right that it should be so" (Smith, 1759, p. 82). This confirms our innate human need to live within a system of natural liberty, for it is only there that we can discover our individual needs.

Today, we refer to this as "self-actualization," and its advocates argue that it is only through the combination of finding and expressing our uniqueness, along with the development of a virtuous character, and all within a just society, that allows individuals to live "fully human lives." Thus, through perfect prudence, individuals can overcome the alienation that accompanies the division of labor, which makes us at home in our world – and, by living fully human lives, we become ideal citizens.

Third, prudence is subject to the same conditions as the other virtues: in order to affect the moral CHARACTER, all virtuous actions must be both intentional and voluntary. Intentionality means, as the Stoics argued, that individuals must always do the right things for the right reasons: we intentionally pursue clearly understood virtuous ends. Further, all prudent actions must be voluntary, for it is the self-willing of the individual that makes the action a part of the good character of the individual.

Fourth, since perfect prudence requires interaction with others, it also requires honorable ways of obtaining the cooperation of others. In all human transactions, such cooperation is best obtained through friendship, honesty, gratitude, and impartiality. For that reason, Smith argues that perfect prudence must always be guided by the impartial spectator (*see*

IMPARTIAL SPECTATOR THEORIES). The ultimate reward of perfect prudence is its contribution to the most noble of all virtues, benevolence.

Fifth, with respect to business ethics, perfect prudence requires that honorable means must always be chosen to achieve honorable ends: one must play fair. Smith praises competition, but always subjects it to the conditions of fair play:

> In the race for wealth, and honours, and preferments, he may run as hard as he can, and strain every nerve and every muscle, in order to outstrip all his competitors. But if he should justle, or throw down any of them, the indulgence of the spectators is entirely at an end. It is a violation of fair play, which they cannot admit of. (Smith, 1759, p. 83)

Because fair play is central to Smith's concept of justice, it can be seen again how all of the virtues unite within perfect prudence.

Thus, perfect prudence demands that no one should wish for more than they can rightfully use, for that offends temperance; no one must ever deceive another, for that offends justice; no one must ever allow another to be harmed, for that offends courage; and so it goes. The attainment of perfect prudence requires success in all of the other virtues. As Smith writes: "As prudence combined with other virtues, constitutes the noblest; so imprudence combined with other vices, constitutes the vilest of all characters" (Smith, 1759, p. 217).

Sixth, perfect prudence requires self-trustworthiness throughout the lifetime of each individual, a moral constancy which is the necessary foundation of the virtuous society. The constancy of the good society allows the full development of all of the virtues among all citizens, and that is the definition of the good society.

To conclude, most virtue theorists argue that perfect prudence is the first of the virtues, because it is the precondition for the exercise of all other virtues. The perfectly prudent individual is the best of all citizens, and we can conclude with John Stuart Mill:

> and if it may possibly be doubted whether a noble character is always the happier for its nobleness, there can be no doubt that

it makes other people happier, and that the world in general is immensely a gainer by it. (Mill, p. 14)

Bibliography

Mill, J. S. (1950). *Utilitarianism, Liberty and Representative Government*. New York: E. P. Dutton (Everyman Library).

Morrow, G. R. (1923). *The Ethical and Economic Theories of Adam Smith*. Clifton, NJ: Augustus M. Kelley.

Pieper, J. (1966). *The Four Cardinal Virtues: Prudence, Justice, Fortitude, Temperance*. Notre Dame, Ind.: University of Notre Dame Press.

Sherman, N. (1989). *The Fabric of Character: Aristotle's Theory of Virtue*. Oxford: Clarendon Press.

Smith, A. (1759, 1790). *The Theory of Moral Sentiments*, eds D. D. Raphael & A. L. Macfie. Indianapolis, Ind.: Liberty Classics.

Werhane, P. H. (1991). *Adam Smith and His Legacy for Modern Capitalism*. New York: Oxford University Press.

DAVID KIRKWOOD HART

psychology and business ethics Psychology is the scientific study of human thought and action. An informal survey of several texts on business ethics suggests that Lawrence Kohlberg (1981) stands out from all other psychologists in his impact on this field. Kohlberg's influence is also great in the study of moral psychology. But in business ethics, as in moral psychology, to focus on Kohlberg to the exclusion of others would seriously confine the ways in which psychological research illuminates the moral nature of humans generally and in business contexts specifically. We note, for instance, that Kohlberg's theory is developmental, internal, normative, and rule based. Following Piaget, Kohlberg proposes that humans undergo a fixed developmental sequence in the way they reason about moral issues. The sequence of stages is presumed to be invariant; people differ in the rate at which they progress through the stages; and people stop at different stages. Higher stages in the sequences are "better" than lower stages in that they represent more mature concepts of morality and justice. Morality, in Kohlberg's theory, is a quality of mind, and it is a cognitive quality that characterizes one's reasoning about moral dilemmas.

Kohlberg's theory is, at best, an incomplete account of the psychology of human morality. For instance, it ignores the chasm that separates the way people reason about ethical dilemmas from the way they actually behave therein. It downplays the role of the environment in determining behavior and tends to portray judgments as rule based rather than context based. It privileges some ethical principles to the exclusion of others (e.g., justice as opposed to caring). It has little room for the emotional side of morality, for moral outrage directed at violators, for instance, or for sympathy, pity, shame, or guilt. Finally, Kohlberg's theory tells us little about how people perceive the causal texture of behavior that underlies judgments of praise and blame.

There is a voluminous research literature on a number of psychological issues that are relevant to business ethics. These include empathy and sympathy, altruism, cooperation, social influence, social conflict and its management, behavioral decision-making, lying, aggression, social comparison, prejudice, discrimination and intergroup relations, illusions and self-deception, distributive justice, procedural justice, and risk perception and communication to mention only a few. In this chapter, I will describe three of these areas. I have chosen the three areas for their pertinence to problems in business ethics. They are intergroup relations, social influence, and cooperation.

Intergroup Relations

As business becomes more global and the demographics of the labor force change, it becomes critical to understand the dynamics of intergroup processes, especially those that occur in the minds of individuals. Recent social-psychological research has made progress understanding the interrelated phenomena of prejudice, discrimination, ethnocentrism, and stereotyping (Fiske & Taylor, 1991). All of these phenomena involve reacting to persons on the basis of their group membership rather than on information about them as individuals. Stereotyping consists of responding to a person in terms of presumed qualities of the group to which the person belongs – women, African-

Americans, Italians, Jews, or men, for instance. The content of stereotypes for all of those groups will generally be different but the ways in which stereotypical information seeps into judgments and decisions about people will be the same. Ethnocentrism, on the other hand, refers to the distinction that we draw between "us" and "them." Recent work on the cognitive underpinnings of ethnocentrism suggest that we see and react to "outgroups" differently from ingroups even though the classification into ingroups and outgroups is not stable. At this moment an ingroup can be your gender and the next it can be your country or your firm.

The ways in which stereotypes and ethnocentric views of outgroups work are subtle, especially in a time in which discrimination and bias are viewed as unacceptable and indeed illegal in many contexts. Managers know that it is illegal to deny a promotion to an employee because the person is a woman or a Catholic. However, that does not mean the effects of stereotypes are non-existent. The use of stereotypical information is especially likely in a couple of circumstances. First, when the person is the only or one of just a few of the type, he or she is especially likely to be responded to stereotypically. A black employee who is the only black in the office will have her "blackness" highlighted more than if there were many other black employees. Thus the first person of "their" type to move into a position in a firm can expect to be labeled with "their" stereotype. Second, stereotyping is likely to occur when the criteria for evaluation are vague, ambiguous, or subjective. Being "able to get along with people" is more vague and subjective than "generating $100,000 of business a month." Stereotypes are more likely to influence the former than the latter judgment.

Like stereotypes, ethnocentric decisions or judgments are often subtle. A promotion is given to someone who is like "us" because one feels uncomfortable with "them." There is good evidence (Brewer, 1979) that discrimination often works through a process of ingroup favorability rather than through outgroup derogation. We make little exceptions to aid ingroupers that we fail to make for outgroupers. This is a plausible hypothesis to explain why blacks and Hispanics are denied home loans proportionally more often than white applicants.

Even when "equated" for credit-worthiness, minority applicants are refused more often than whites. The ingroup favorability idea suggests that the difference may be less a matter of qualified minorities being refused than of unqualified whites being granted loans. Racial, gender, or ethnic discrimination in business settings may well work through the subtle ways of favoring the ingroup (otherwise known as white males) rather than by derogating or harming the outgroup.

Social Influence

Most experimental psychologists place great weight on the environment as a cause of human behavior and this is nowhere more important than with the social environment. A line of research that was begun more than 50 years ago has demonstrated the importance of the social surround. Milgram's (1974) disturbing experiments on obedience to authority demonstrated how incorrect people's beliefs were (and probably still are) about how difficult it would be to induce one person to harm another merely through the urging of a legitimate authority. Milgram coaxed his subjects to deliver what they believed to be exceedingly painful and possibly fatal electric shocks to another participant. He noted that the single most important consequence of submitting one's self to the legitimate authority is the loss of the sense of responsibility. The subordinate becomes a pawn with no sense of moral responsibility for the harm that he is inflicting.

Latane & Darley (1970) and others found a somewhat paradoxical effect of the social environment that they called the *bystander effect*. This phenomenon refers to the finding that people are less likely to intervene in an emergency to help another person if they witness the emergency with other bystanders than if they witness it alone. In other words, the bystanders inhibit people's natural tendencies to come to the aid of a person in need. (It does not follow because each person in a group is less likely to help than they would be alone, that the victim is less likely to receive help when witnessed by a group. All it takes to get help is one volunteer.) This bystander effect has several causes. One is that we learn about the world by observing how other people respond to it. If we witness an emergency and see that no

one else is doing anything, we may interpret the situation as one that does not merit intervention. A second cause may be that we (self-servingly) diffuse our responsibility and assume that someone else will take care of the problem. If there are multiple witnesses then we cannot be personally blamed (either by ourselves or others) for doing nothing.

Social circumstances that foster poor decision-making are profoundly unethical in that poor decision-making will squander resources and put people in harm's way. One syndrome of this sort has been described as *Groupthink* (Janis, 1982). Groupthink is a pattern of group decision-making that results when a group places undue emphasis on conforming to the culture of the group and spends too little of its resources on getting the decision right. Groupthink represents the disastrous implosion of conformity pressures whose features include illusions of invulnerability, illusions of the group's morality (and the immorality of outgroups), and a powerful tendency to censor group members who appear to disagree with the group. Such suffocating social climates interfere with the accurate processing of information, with the exploration of alternative courses of action, and with the thorough appraisal of the risks and benefits of the options. Janis has attributed some of the worst political decisions of this century to groupthink, decisions including the disastrous Bay of Pigs invasion and the failure to prepare for the Pearl Harbor attack.

Finally, Cialdini (1988) has written about the psychological processes that subtend the strategies and tactics that are used to influence people's behavior. He identifies six principles of social influence that are manifested in business applications ranging from selling cars to soliciting contributions to charitable organizations. Cialdini discusses the ways in which these six principles (they are reciprocation, commitment, authority, social validation, scarcity, and liking) can be and are used to attain compliance with the influencer's goals. One interesting aspect of these ideas is that they all stem from basic social-psychological processes. Reciprocation, for instance, appears to be a universal feature of human social interaction. People tend to return favors and to reciprocate harm. Such a principle is one of the cornerstones of our social nature. This principle is exploited, however, principle is one of the cornerstones of our social nature. This principle is exploited, however, when a charitable organization sends addressed mailing labels to prospective contributors. Sending an inexpensive gift like mailing labels evokes the reciprocal favor of returning a cash contribution. The tactic is used with the intention of generating money, not with the intention of maintaining the fabric of a social community. The question is raised: When are such tactics manipulative and improper and when are they acceptable?

Most psychologists would look to the social environment to explain unethical behavior in business and other organizations. Darley (1992) offers an extreme position that most evil is organizationally grounded.

Cooperation in Social Dilemmas

Social dilemmas are situations in which there is a conflict between what is good for a group and what is good for the individual. More precisely, they are situations in which each individual in a group has a clear incentive to behave in a way which, if engaged in by all, produces less desirable outcomes than would have been achieved if all members did what was *not* in their individual interest. To illustrate a social dilemma, the world's fisheries are critically depleted, partly because each nation's interests are best served by harvesting as much as possible from the sea. The collective consequence is overharvesting that is the fault on no single nation. Corruption exists in some organizations because it is in no individual's interest to report it. However, the corruption will eventually stain everyone in the organization, including those who declined to report it, and the damage may be far worse than the cost of blowing the whistle. Inducing people to cooperate in such situations, to act against their individual short-term interest to achieve individual and collective long-term benefits, is at the heart of the problem of cooperation (Messick & Brewer, 1983; Komorita & Parks, 1994).

Psychological research on cooperation has focused on two interrelated strategies – changing the people or changing the structure. The first of these strategies attempts to promote cooperation by altering individuals' values, motives, expectations, or trust in the others in the group. It has been shown that in some

circumstances people are willing to act on behalf of their group when there are no possible individual interests to be served. One factor that is essential to developing that level of cohesion and trust is the ability of the members to communicate about the task. Communication allows promises to be made, intentions to be expressed, and a sense of community to develop. Communication also promotes empathy and friendship among group members.

Communication among members is not feasible in many contexts. In cases where the group is too large, dispersed, or diffuse, structural solutions can be sought. Structural solutions may involve changing the payoffs to individuals to enhance the incentive to cooperate, for instance. Appointing a single individual or agency to make decisions on behalf of the group, or changing the nature of the alternatives that the people have are other types of structural changes. Regulation of one sort or another may be called for. Some states, for instance, require teachers to pay a "fee" even if they are not members of the public teachers union, to eliminate the incentive for teachers to free-ride on the union dues of those teachers who are union members. Proposals for California citizens to install catalytic converters voluntarily were dismal failures because citizens could not justify the cost of more than $100 when the impact of their single acts on the quality of the air in California would be negligible. California state law now mandates that all cars have these pollution control devices. This is a good structural solution to a behavioral problem of cooperation.

Bibliography

Brewer, M. B. (1979). In-group bias in the minimal intergroup situation: A cognitive motivational analysis. *Psychological Bulletin, 86*, 307–324.
Cialdini, R. B. (1988). *Influence: Science and Practice.* Glenview, Ill.: Scott Foresman.
Darley, J. M. (1992). Social organization for the production of evil. *Psychological Inquiry, 3*, 199–218.
Fiske, S. T. & Taylor, S. E. (1991). *Social Cognition.* Reading, Mass.: Addison-Wesley.
Janis, I. L. (1982). *Groupthink.* Boston: Houghton Mifflin.
Kohlberg, L. (1981). *The Philosophy of Moral Development.* New York: Harper & Row.

Komorita, S. S. & Parks, C. D. (1994). *Social Dilemmas*. Madison, Wis.: Brown & Benchmark.

Latane, B. & Darley, J. M. (1970). *The Unresponsive Bystander: Why Doesn't He Help*. New York: Appleton-Century-Crofts.

Messick, D. M. & Brewer, M. B. (1983). Solving social dilemmas: A review. *Review of Personality and Social Psychology*, 4, 11–44.

Milgram, S. (1974). *Obedience to Authority*. New York: Harper & Row.

DAVID M. MESSICK

public/private distinction   The view that there is a line to be drawn between areas of human life open to social inspection or regulation, and areas of human life immune to such scrutiny.

Since the publication of J. S. Mill's *On Liberty* in 1859, the distinction between public and private spheres has been a mainstay of liberal political theory. The distinction has figured prominently in arguments such as Mill's that special kinds of information or choices ought to be protected from government interference. In business ethics, for example, the distinction plays a central role in controversy over whether aspects of an employee's life outside the job are proper subjects of employer intervention. The public/private distinction has also been crucial to the view that a range of social institutions – markets, families, or churches, for example – can and should operate without government interference.

The line between public and private has been drawn descriptively, legally, and normatively, and there have been frequent confusions among these levels of delineation. Mill drew the line descriptively in terms of the effects of actions: actions which affect only oneself are self-regarding, but actions which have consequences for others are other-regarding. Noting that there are few actions utterly without ripple effects, others have drawn descriptive lines between what is seeable by others and what is hidden or unseen, or between what has been traditionally regarded as intimate and what has not.

In law, the public/private distinction has served to identify actors of different types. In the United States, for example, state employees' managers have special constitutional obligations to respect rights and may be sued for damages if they do not. The public/private line has also been used to characterize places. Again in the US, if a shopping center is a public forum, then it is subject to constitutional claims, such as the right of free speech on the premises. The public/private distinction also has been drawn between types of law: contract law, property law, and tort law are generally characterized as "private law," governing arrangements among individual actors; criminal law, administrative law, and environmental law are matters of "public law," structuring affairs between individuals and the government.

There are many different normative accounts of what ought to be protected as private. One view of privacy centers on information about the individual that ought to be immune from scrutiny by others: health records, financial information, information about group affiliations and friendships, juvenile offense records, and the like (*see* ETHICAL ISSUES IN INFORMATION). Another account focuses on spaces – homes, bodily cavities, cars, purses, or desk drawers – that ought to be protected from intrusions without consent. Still another account looks to liberties, such as choices about marriage, reproduction, education, art and literature, or religion, for insulation from interference.

The public/private distinction, in all of its permutations, has come under fire from both the left and the right as a problematic manifestation of liberal individualism. Some critics argue that the distinction is meaningless; others that it marks out many different continua on which we might locate social relationships. Other critics contend that insistence on a line between public and private results from and protects certain entrenched interests against others. Communitarian critics argue that decisions often defended as private, such as what movies to see or whether to have an abortion, threaten the fabric of community and contribute to modern alienation. Economic leftists argue that the market is not a private affair; legal choices such as whether to treat employer/employee relationships as matters of private law have important consequences for the structure of public labor relations. Feminists argue that institutions such as the family have oppressed women, and that insulating these institutions from public scrutiny deepens that oppression.

Liberals reply that recognition of a private sphere in some form is crucial to the protection of liberty and self-respect. Perhaps the most difficult question for liberals, and the one on which they most disagree, is how to view social but non-governmental institutions such as markets or churches in terms of a public/private dichotomy (*see also* COMMUNITARIAN-ISM; FEMINIST ETHICS; LIBERALISM).

Bibliography

Benn, S. I., and Gaus, G. F. (eds) (1983). *Public and Private in Social Life.* New York: St Martin's Press.

Crittenden, J. (1992). *Beyond Individualism: Reconstituting the Liberal Self.* New York: Oxford University Press.

Daly, M., (ed.) (1994). *Communitarianism: A New Public Ethics.* Belmont, Calif.: Wadsworth.

Fox-Genovese, E. (1991). *Feminism Without Illusions: A Critique of Individualism.* Chapel Hill: University of North Carolina Press.

Gavison, R. (1992). Feminism and the public/private distinction. *Stanford Law Review,* 3, 1-45.

Kymlicka, W. (1989). *Liberalism, Community, and Culture.* Oxford: Clarendon Press.

Mill, J. S. (1859). *On Liberty.* Numerous editions are available.

Moore, M. (1993). *Foundations of Liberalism.* Oxford: Clarendon Press.

Singer, B. J. (1993). *Operative Rights.* Albany, NY: State University of New York Press.

Symposium on the Public/private Distinction. (1982).*University of Pennsylvania Law Review,* 130, 1289-1608.

LESLIE FRANCIS

public relations ethics   Historically, the role of public relations as a practice has had three major interpretations: controlling publics, responding to publics, and achieving mutually beneficial relationships among all publics (Newsom & Scott, 1985). Within the first interpretation lies the roots of the belief that all public relations is persuasive by nature. Within the last two are the seeds of modern public relations. However, all three approaches are still in use today. One of the myriad definitions of public relations explains this dichotomy of persuasion versus mutual ·understanding common to the field:

Public relations is a process aimed at adjusting organizations to their environments, and at adjusting environments to the organization.

The first part of the definition assumes that an organization is willing to adjust to the needs and desires of its constituencies. The second part admits that those same constituencies may sometimes need to be persuaded to the organization's point of view. Grunig and Hunt (1984) formalized these two environments as two-way symmetric (balanced communication based on mutual understanding), and two-way asymmetric (persuasive communication unbalanced in favor of the organization).

Additionally, public relations ethics is generally studied from two perspectives, not necessarily overlapping: corporate SOCIAL RESPONSIBILITY, and professionalism. The notion of social responsibility implies that the practitioner of public relations will seek out opportunities for mutual cooperation between an organization and its publics as well as suggest appropriate behavior or point out inappropriate behavior. The recent movement of corporation's toward "green" causes is one example of public relations as social responsibility.

Professionalism suggests that the practitioner will strive to uphold standards specific to the profession of public relations. The Public Relations Society of America's (PRSA) Code of Professional Standards supposedly governs the ethical actions of its membership. PRSA seeks to professionalize its membership and the practice of public relations. Accreditation of members and an enforcement mechanism for their code of standards are part of PRSA's approach.

While the social-responsibility model places the onus of ethical behavior on the organization itself and leaves the public relations practitioner in a more supporting role, the professional model places ethical responsibility squarely on the practitioner.

While role defines function in most cases, it is purpose that defines ethical behavior. For example, the function of a technician entails technical skills and may be simply to produce a persuasive piece of writing. The function of the manager who uses the writing as part of an overall campaign may be to solve an image problem. The manager's purpose, however, might be to persuade. Within the purposes of public relations, therefore, lie the real ethical considerations.

Those who study public relations ethics must admit to the differences between the persuasive and mediatory functions of public relations. Practitioners who accept the persuasive nature of public relations incur the special obligations of professional advocates: loyalty to client, and respect for the laws governing communication. Those who practice the mediatory role are further obligated to parties beyond the client and must be willing to present all sides of an issue along with recommendations that will be beneficial to all concerned.

Bibliography

Bayles, M. D. (1989). *Professional Ethics.* Belmont, Calif.: Wadsworth. (Detailed taxonomy of professional ethics.)

Christians, C. G., Rotzoll, K. B. & Fackler, M. (1987). *Media Ethics.* New York: Longman.

Grunig, J. E. & Hunt, T. (1984). *Managing Public Relations.* New York: Holt, Rinehart and Winston. (Excellent theoretical background in PR.)

Kultgen, J. H. Jr. (1988). *Ethics and Professionalism.* Philadelphia: University of Pennsylvania Press. (Excellent critique of professions and professionalism.)

Newsom, D. & Scott, A. (1985). *This is PR: The Realities of Public Relations.* Belmont, Calif.: Wadsworth.

THOMAS H. BIVINS

punishment the institutional infliction of harm upon an individual or organization which has violated one of society's rules of acceptable behavior. The institutionalization of punishment, which occurs in organizations such as the church, academy, and corporation as well as the state, has been justified by kinship, religion, jurisprudence, and philosophy (*see* CORPORATE PUNISHMENT).

Baker (1979) notes that punishment was originally rooted in kinship vengence. Later it was socialized and mitigated by the *lex talionis* (the famous eye-for-an-eye principle), often associated with religion. In eighteenth-century England, the legal system mixed theological notions of infamy with a maturing Hobbesian

justification of punishment (*see* HOBBES, THOMAS). Thus, while Blackstone (1983 [1764]) justified harsh punishments for crimes against "the immediate command of God" or against nature, he prescribed lighter punishments for those things made crimes by human authorities.

By the late 1800s, however, the secularization of the state allowed Holmes (1982 [1881]) to categorize three philosophical theories of punishment that remain standard today: retribution, deterrence, and reformation.

Kant, articulating a retributionist theory, argued that punishment should not promote a good for the criminal or for society, but follow the character of the crime itself. Since crime hinders freedom (the criteria for Kant's justice), punishment metaphysically hinders the crime itself (*see* KANTIAN ETHICS). Hegel followed Kant by speaking of a "negation of the negation" which "annuls" the crime. Such an evening process carries with it the requirement for the *lex talionis*. Contracts often use "evening" measures in terms of amounts deducted (punished) for delays in, for instance, delivery or construction.

While Ewing (1970 [1929]) agreed with Kant that one must first be found deserving of punishment, he disagreed with Kant and Hegel's metaphysical equating of wrongdoing and punishment because a wrongdoing can never be "annulled." Further, Bedau (1978) argued that in some instances, such as rape, *lex talionis* makes no sense.

The deterrence rationale, prominently argued by Beccaria (1963 [1764]), argued that the sole purpose of punishment was to prevent the criminal from repeating crimes and deter others through the application of proportionate punishments. Ewing argued that punishments must exceed the advantages of crimes, so as to discourage the criminal act. The civil law's imposition of punitive tort damages against a corporation is a non-criminal example of the deterrence theory. A major criticism of deterrence is determining whether given punishments in fact discourage wrongdoing. Further, as Malloy (1982) argued, deterrence's utilitarian justification risks sacrificing an innocent individual for the societal good.

The rehabilitation theory also reflects religious origins in that prisons were centers for conversion after penitence (hence the name penitentiary). Since then, psychological and sociological theories have predominated, arguing that retribution and deterrence do not take into account the wrongdoer's sociological and psychological obstacles. Corporate programs to rehabilitate an employee who has failed a drug test are business examples of the rehabilitation approach. As far back as Holmes, however, commentators have doubted the likelihood of rehabilitating or reforming a criminal, even though probation and parole are also examples of the theory's influence.

Bibliography

Baird, R. M. & Rosenbaum S. E. (eds). (1988). *Philosophy of Punishment*. Buffalo, NY: Prometheus Books.

Baker, J. H. (1979). *An Introduction to English Legal History*, 2nd edn. London: Butterworths.

Beccaria, C. (1963 [1764]). *On Crimes and Punishments*. Indianapolis, Ind.: Bobbs-Merrill.

Bedau H. A. (1978). Retribution and the theory of punishment. *Journal of Philosophy*, **75**.

Blackstone, W. (1983 [1764]). *Commentary on the Laws of England*, special edn. Birmingham, Ala.: Legal Classics Library.

Ewing, A. C. (1970 [1929]). *The Morality of Punishment*. Montclair, NJ: Patterson Smith.

Gerber, R. J. & McAnany, P. D. (eds). (1972). *Contemporary Punishment: Views, Explanations, and Justification*. Notre Dame, Ind.: University of Notre Dame Press.

Hegel, G. W. F. (1952). *The Philosophy of Right*. Oxford: Oxford University Press.

Holmes, O. W., Jr. (1982 [1881]). *The Common Law & Other Writings*, special edn. Birmingham, Ala.: Legal Classics Library.

Kant, I. (1965). *The Metaphysical Elements of Justice*. Indianapolis, Ind.: Bobbs-Merrill.

Malloy, E. A. (1982). *The Ethics of Law Enforcement and Criminal Punishment*. Washington DC: University Press of America.

Norrie, A. W. (1991). *Law, Ideology and Punishment*. Norwell, Mass.: Kluwer.

TIMOTHY L. FORT

Q

quality may be described by phrases such as conformance to requirements, defining external and internal customer expectations, finding problems and preventing their recurrence, and reducing process variation. Since the early 1980s, when scores of US businesses heard the wake-up messages of quality practitioners Crosby, Deming, Feigenbaum, Ishikawa, and Shewhart, the applications of TQM (Total Quality Management) principles have grown exponentially. As a result, quality may be described by phrases such as conformance to requirements, defining external and internal customer expectations, finding problems and preventing their recurrence, and reducing process variation. The Malcom Baldrige National Quality Award and the ISO 9000 quality system requirements have been important frameworks guiding organizations in managing for improved quality.

The Commitment to Quality

> Quality requires a commitment on the part of an organization's individual and collective employees to meet and, at appropriate times, exceed customer expectations.

The hallmark of quality-management systems has been the clarion call for never-ending improvement. By emphasizing continuous improvement of a firm's processes, employees of an organization are expected to be dissatisfied, as every accomplishment is followed with a new and higher set of expectations. But what keeps the ethic of quality improvement thriving in an organization? What stimulates employees to accept a way of thinking that encourages and stimulates everyone to challenge continuously

and change the way day-to-day activities are performed? More than anything, it is the commitment of employees to serve customers.

It is the men and women of an organization who make the final determination about the set of customer needs that will be the next business opportunity. They design the product and service characteristics that will be offered competitively by their organization in the service of its customers. In a total-quality-managed organization, employees at multiple levels are expected to create the greatest value for customers, while operating the business processes in ways that will cut operating costs *and* affect customers' buying decisions. Many service-intensive corporations manage for total quality by empowering employees to act immediately, fix problems, and do what it takes to retain customers. Although customers make the final determination of quality, the actions of employees throughout the creation-of-value cycle – needs assessment, product-and-process design, and delivery – become the true drivers of total-quality schemes.

Initiating the Commitment to Quality

An important, fundamental precept is that quality management is a senior executive design and resource-allocation responsibility. Senior executives must initiate and lead the development of new management behaviors and create a work environment that is a catalyst for continuous improvement. Despite the wealth of principles and guidelines that are now readily available, many executives do not understand how a set of supporting principles, policies, tools, and management processes come together in a system that can transform employee commitment into actions. As with any organizational system, senior executives must pick from a number of elemental design choices to shape a work climate that stimulates each member to excel at contributing to market growth and business profitability. The system-design tasks in quality management are guided by three overarching principles.

1 All efforts of employees are to be channeled toward continually improving customer satisfaction and removing waste in internal processes; benefits must be projected and converted into financial returns.
2 Quality management is a people-intensive process. Collaborative relationships within the organization and with key suppliers and customers are stressed as a way to enrich improvement activities. Costs of collaborative work strategies must be estimated and evaluated on a cost–benefit basis.
3 Quality-management capabilities must be built to deal with the implications of continuous change in customer expectations and competitive realities. Senior executives of the company must create an environment that values and rewards process changes.

What are the Characteristics of a Quality Management System?

A quality-improvement culture that synthesizes customer focus and employee empowerment can be created from the following four components:

Executive Leadership needs to have a vision for the value-added role of quality in the firm's business strategy. They must share the principles of and expectations for quality-management leadership at all levels and provide quality goals. Executive leaders are also responsible for defining employees' roles in the quality-management process, establishing policies dealing with employee relations, and establishing parameters for supplier/customer alliances.

A Performance Management Checklist systematically ensures that the quality-management process is on track.

● Put a strategic quality-planning process in place.

● Establish measurement systems for external and internal performance assessments.

● Establish a reward-and-recognition process for all stakeholders in the quality process (*see* STAKEHOLDER THEORY).

● Establish two-way communications subsystems that provide channels from the bottom to the top of the organization.

● Establish a project management and control subsystem, perhaps with a quality officer in charge.

● Use a quality-assessment process to check progress (ISO, Baldrige, or Benchmarking are commonly used quality-assessment tools).

Product/Service/Process Tools Necessary for Design and Improvement:

● Principles and tools of market-segment analysis and customer-perceptions measurement.

● Tools for robust product and services design.

● Tools to reduce process variability.

● Benchmarking to discover better practices.

● Information systems that contribute to improvement as a systematic process.

Human Resources should be responsible for developing leadership skills and creating effective teams through training programs and personal growth plans for each associate. Subsequently, they should establish a way of holding associates accountable and assessing their performance.

Realizing the Payoff

The design and evolution of a quality-management system should be thought of as a company's investment in renewing and building new operational capabilities into processes. Because a quality-management system is an investment decision, executives must insist that organizational returns be defined and estimated in the language of business operations – customer loyalty, employee productivity and retention, market share, pricing strengths, new market opportunities, and asset utilization. These factors then translate into improved sales, decreased costs, or both. Some of the payoffs are not obvious and are a considerable challenge to measure, but senior management must insist that the success of a quality initiative be measured against real business performance indicators – no matter how difficult the measurement process may be.

In view of the pressures to continually adjust and anticipate changing customer expectations and competitive strategies, it is imperative that a quality-management system be designed with flexibility. In order to succeed in meeting changing needs, new operating strengths and capabilities must be forecasted and developed five to seven years in advance. If employee empowerment is a key to organizational improvement, then anticipating and equipping the employees with new capabilities becomes a critical design requirement. Today this challenge is being met by emphasizing organizational learning and renewal. This continuous learning ethic places even greater financial demands on executives, as the results of educational investments may be extremely difficult to quantify. Executives may always struggle as they try to determine which investments provide certain financial outcomes and which are truly speculative in terms of organizational development.

ROBERT D. LANDEL

R

racism A belief that one's ethnic stock is superior. The term "racism" is an evaluative offspring of the concept "race." In spite of the parental relationship, however, racism is an independent phenomenon that has flourished in the midst of controversy surrounding "objectivity" with respect to the concept of "race" (Zack, 1993) itself. Conceptually, the idea of "race" is concerned merely with metaphysical or biological classifications of people in accordance with attributes or characteristics considered usually ascribable as group-identifying properties. By contrast, racism assigns VALUES and stereotypes to those race categories in order to fix race relations along a continuum of "superior-race-to-inferior-race." From this perspective, we understand racism primarily from what it seeks to accomplish as a value thrust, rather than as an action with independently definable properties. In this context, racism is viewed as an "occasional phenomenon" (Gadamer, 1993, pp. 144–59) of actions that are not intrinsically racist. However, the lack of tangible characteristics do not obstruct the fact that the display of racism in many practices and attitudes is frequently undeniable (Gault, 1992).

Racist: A member of a racial group considered elite as determined by political, social, economic, etc., powers, and, who willfully participate in practices designed to maintain the elite status of the racial group of which one is a member. There is an element of controversy associated with this conception of a racist. It eliminates blacks, for instance, as possible racists. But, since one could not claim social, political, or economic benefits from their black racism, it seems pointless to suppose that such racism exists. It is conceivable that what is considered "black racism" is merely a conditioned response to "white racism," thus not racism at all.

Epistemology of Racism: Our judgments that some actions are racist are open to debate for the same reasons a "held to be work of art" may be subject to debate over whether or not it is actually "art." As in art, disputes concerning racism will be settled with a heavier emphasis on "value" rather than "factual" considerations. That is, since racism is not definable as an independent act (Austin, 1956), its being is understood as the outgrowth of judgments about purposes and consequences of actions that are in fact fully definable. There are clear cases of racism, that tend to reinforce a "pecking order" among racial groups so as to give privilege to the so-called elites. At bottom, we understand "racism" as a commitment to that pecking order, or, to ones involvement in practices that help to maintain privileges of those considered racial elites.

Science and Racism: It is unlikely that science will ever settle disputes concerning racial superiority. Debates on this issue involve judgments that are immune to sensory input by virtue of their roles in constituting frameworks for judgments. In this respect, racism is viewed as a phenomenon of reflective consciousness. As such, it belongs to the Kantian realm of "art" as opposed to that of "science." On the other hand, even if racial superiority could be established scientifically, it may yet be morally wrong to oppress human beings since inferiority would not change nature's requirement to function in accordance with the full gamut of their humanity (Williams, 1991).

Equality and Racism: Racism is antithetical to prevailing conceptions of equality. Thriving on the idea of race as a "great-making quality," racism views the worth of a person as constrained within the scope of their racial identity. The interest of a race considered superior (generally as defined by those holding political and economic power) will supersede the interests of all others without regard to questions of justice or to impact upon the victims. Such subordination of interest persist in spite of its incompatibility with conceptions of equality advanced by Locke, Kant, Rawls, and other prominent social/political scholars (*see* LOCKE, JOHN; KANTIAN ETHICS; RAWLS, JOHN). For them, human equality is not to be defined in terms of abilities as such, since they vary from person to person and even with respect to a particular person at different times or circumstances. Equality is concerned with dispositional aspects of humanity that are universal; not with relative manifestations of those dispositions in individuals or in groups. This conception of equality evokes a kind of "form over function" standard for personhood. This standard forbids applying restraints to one's natural or metaphysical identity based on a notion that some should not be allowed to exist as fully human, since others are considered "better fit" to achieve the same metaphysical task. On this issue, Locke, Kant, and Rawls have clearly taken the position that it is morally impermissible to restrain the natural dispositions of persons to exist as such.

Universality of Racism: Slavery and its consciousness have made it impossible to live in America without the residual effect of racism having some influence on how our judgments of others and ourselves are determined. Racism has also become institutionalized to the degree that many of us participate in racist practices without our knowledge (Appiah, 1990). Persons actually viewed as racist, however, are among those privileged to the advantages of the racial elite, and who support the stereotypes that establish a hierarchy among racial groups.

Color and Racism: Color alone is not a race problem for persons of color. Blind persons would perhaps choose to be sighted if the means were available to them, but one's color is not an impediment to their human potential. Under Rawls' "veil of ignorance," for example, it is perfectly conceivable that as many persons would choose black as a color of preference as those disposed to choose to be white (among those wishing to express a color preference at all). The idea of color as a cause of racial problems gives rise to the view that color is a qualitative aspect of humanity. Once it is clear that color problems stem from a socially created color criterion, rather than from color itself, it is clear that racism has nothing to do with color as such.

Racism as Vice: Although racist sentiments tend to vary with political and economic climates, most people reject racism as an admirable human quality. Just as persons who find themselves "selfish" in undesirable respects can foster a better sense of altruism from practice, persons who are discontented with their racism can participate in practices that can help to reduce their racism considerably. In this sense, we can think of racism as a vice and the absence of it a virtue. So conceived, it is possible to cultivate non-racist potential that exists in actual racists, provided that they are unhappy with their racism. There are no assurances that racism will ever be fully eliminated. However, with general agreement that racism and selfishness are not good human qualities, the elimination of both can be espoused as worthy goals.

Bibliography

Appiah, K. A. (1990). Racisms. In D. T. Goldberg (Ed.), *Anatomy of Racism*. Minneapolis: University of Minnesota Press.

Austin, J. L. (1956). A plea for excuses. In W. T. Jones, F. Sontag, et al. (eds), *Approaches to Ethics*. New York: McGraw-Hill.

Cashmore, E., Banton, M., et al. (1994). *Dictionary of Race and Ethnic relations*, 3rd edn. New York: Routledge & Kegan Paul.

Feagin, J. R. (1992). The continuing significance of racism: Discrimination of black students in white colleges. *Journal of Black Studies*, **22**, 546–78.

Fredrickson, G. M. (1988). *The Arrogance of Race: Historical Perspectives on Slavery, Racism, and Social Inequality*. Middletown, Conn.: Wesleyan University Press.

Gadamer, H.-G. (1993). *Truth and Method*, 2nd edn. New York: Continuum.

Gault, Charlayne H. (1992). *In My Place*. New York: Harper-Collins.

Giovanni, N. (1994). *Racism 101*. New York: William Morrow & Company.

Williams, P. (1991). *The Alchemy of Race and Rights*. Cambridge, Mass.: Harvard University Press.

Zack, N. (1993). *Mixed-Race and Anti-Race.* Philadelphia: Temple University Press.

JESSE TAYLOR

rational choice theory   a body of literature that explores the idea that humans can and sometimes do make choices that are based on principles of rationality. Rational Choice Theory encompasses a large body of work including much of modern economics. This brief essay is confined to the use of rational choice theory in ethics (*see* DECISION THEORY; GAME THEORY).

Sometime during the 1950s moral philosophers became concerned with a question that is as old as Plato and Aristotle: Why should one be moral? Plato believed that if a person knew the right thing to do she would automatically do the right thing. Aristotle held out the possibility of weakness of will or *akrasia*, that a person could know the right but fail to do it because of some defect of character. Marked by Kurt Baier's *The Moral Point of View*, published in 1958, philosophers began to ground an answer to "Why be moral" in theories of reason and rationality.

At the same time John Rawls (1971) and later David Gauthier (1986) picked up the social contract tradition begun by Hobbes and began to develop theories of social institutions that grounded the morality and justice of institutions in theories of rationality. Thus, ethics and political philosophy merged around the notion that humans could rationally choose the ethical point of view and design political and social institutions that were based on principles of rational choice (*see* RAWLS, JOHN; HOBBES, THOMAS).

The publication of Rawls' magisterial *A Theory of Justice* is the landmark event in the application of rational choice theory to ethics. Rawls asked us to imagine an original position of hypothetical contractors behind a "veil of ignorance" trying to decide which principles of justice were rational to accept. Suppose that no one knew the position that she was likely to occupy once the veil was lifted, and hence no rational chooser would make an exception for herself. The principles chosen, according to this argument, would be in line with the rational choice principle called "minimax." Under conditions of total uncertainty, where the consequences of choice are important, rationality dictates choosing the alternative which has the least worst outcome.

The important point here is not whether or not Minimax is the correct principle, it is that Rawls connected ethical and political philosophy with an entire stream of research in economics in a manner that was novel. A whole body of scholarship on Rawls began to appear in economics journals. Psychologists who studied how people actually make decisions began to become relevant to ethicists. In short, ethics based on rational choice theory became more interdisciplinary, and Rawls became required reading in many graduate seminars in a number of academic disciplines.

Rational choice theory consists of a number of different decision or choice problems. The first could be called "decision-making under uncertainty," and consists of the principles or axioms or theories that a decision-maker should or does use when she has several alternatives each of which is probabilistically determined by states of nature. Sometimes the decision-maker has no control over the state of nature, and sometimes she can act as if she can influence which state actually occurs. In a famous example Leonard Savage supposes that a chef has already cracked five eggs into a bowl that will contain the eggs for a six-egg omelet, and wants to proceed rationally with the sixth egg. If she cracks the sixth egg into the bowl with the others and it is rotten, then all eggs will have to be discarded. Alternatively if it is a good egg, the omelet will proceed quickly. Or, she can crack the sixth egg into a separate bowl, sparing the five good eggs, but incurring a cost of washing the bowl. One theory, Bayesian Decision Theory, asks the chef to put a probability judgment on the state of nature that is defined by whether or not the egg is rotten, and to maximize her utility taking into account the costs of washing the bowl, etc. Now there are certain problems for which probability assignments make little or no sense. Rawls argued that the basic problem of choosing principles of justice was just such a problem. These special cases of uncertainty have been called "decision problems under ignorance."

A second kind of rational choice problem is one of interdependent choice, whereby two or more decision-makers determine the final outcome of a situation. This is the province of game theory. A third kind of rational choice problem is called "the social choice problem." Suppose that individuals in a society must decide on a voting rule by which to make social decisions. Which voting rules are rational to choose? Kenneth Arrow (1963) showed that there is no voting rule that obeys a few very simple conditions of rationality. And, the subsequent research on social-choice theory for the past 45 years has led to a new understanding of the conditions of rationality.

The so-called Arrow Paradox illustrates a strategy in much of rational choice theory. Axioms or conditions are proposed and general possibility theorems are proved which show that certain decision rules can be derived or not from the axioms. If one can prove an impossibility result, then new conditions or modified axioms are proposed and the process begins anew. Daniel Ellsberg, Maurice Allais, and Robert Nozick have each proposed paradoxes that occur with regard to one foundational principle of rational choice theory, the "sure thing principle." The PRISONER'S DILEMMA illustrates a paradox about the interdependence of certain choices in game theory.

Rational choice theory continues to be a wealth of insight for moral philosophers, but among some philosophers, questions have been raised about its foundations. Why, for instance, must morality be grounded in individual choice in general and rational individual choice in particular? What normative work is the term "rational" doing in such a theory? The attempt to ground ethics in rationality is just one more attempt to reduce all of human behavior to mere reason, negating or minimizing other kinds of behavior. This critique of rational choice theory argues that the primacy of the individual ignores the view that the very best of human activity may well be a function of human communities and the capacity to care for others, rather than a function of individual self-interested choices.

Bibliography

Arrow, Kenneth. (1963). *Social Choice and Individual Values*, 2nd edn. New Haven: Yale University Press.

Baier, Kurt. (1958). *The Moral Point of View*. Ithaca, NY: Cornell University Press.

Campbell, R. & Snowden, L. (eds). (1985). *Paradoxes of Rationality and Cooperation*. Vancouver: University of British Columbia Press.

Gauthier, D. (1986). *Morals By Agreement*. Oxford: Oxford University Press.

Luce, D. & Raiffa, H. (1957). *Games and Decisions*. New York: John Wiley and Sons.

Rawls, John. (1971). *A Theory of Justice*. Boston: Harvard University Press.

R. EDWARD FREEMAN

rationality and ethics   Rationality and ethics, as fields of inquiry, concern many diverse principles and problems of behavior, set in social and economic contexts. This brief entry focuses upon their interrelatedness, i.e., rationality *and* ethics.

Any contemporary account of this most ancient philosophical association, however brief, must start by recognizing the profound impact that technological and social change is now having on the nature of rational and moral *agents*. The attendant notions of deciding, trusting, promising, or harming are increasingly being interpreted as applicable not only to individuals or firms, but also to genetically engineered entities, distributed-cognition-systems, or new types of organization, such as networks, coalitions, virtual or hollow corporations.

There are also many rationalities. More than 40 distinctive forms have been identified. Collectively, these comprise a rationality-set, or *plural*-rationality. The *general theory* of rationality is concerned not only with the specification of members of this set, but also with the development of 1) meta-rational and meta-ethical criteria for classifying and evaluating the forms (e.g. perfect vs. imperfect; belief vs. means vs. ends orientation; forward vs. backward looking; local vs. global), and 2) natural and formal arguments that place the forms of rationality in relation to each other (e.g. RUM-capture; beliefs–ends relations, etc.).

Rationality, thus conceived, becomes an interwoven fabric. As such, it demonstrably wraps up much of moral philosophy. Many apparently ethical concerns, involving awareness of other entities with their interests, become incorporated into the general theory. For example, ethical egoism as a principle of behavior is partly captured by rational utility maximization (RUM), or satisfaction of the entity's own consistent preferences. The social ramifications and justifications of RUM then comprise the theory of Welfare Economics. Many other forms of substantive-ends rationality are RUM-captured, to a degree determined by various meta-rational arguments. Such forms embrace other interests in various ways, thus emphasizing the rationality of cooperative ventures for mutual advantage, rather than pure market competition. These forms include sympathy, commitment, interdependent-utility, sociality, and constrained-maximization. In business, they are manifest in diverse strategy concepts such as stakeholders-as-constraints, not-for-profit missions, and cooperative strategy (*see* EGOISM, PSYCHOLOGICAL EGOISM AND ETHICAL EGOISM; WELFARE ECONOMICS; STAKEHOLDER THEORY).

Rationality and ethics inhere in *processes* of formulating goals and beliefs. Much of the theory of procedural rationality, is framed in terms of individuals, but seems also to apply to many, if not all, other types of entity. *Deliberative* rationality sees an entity reconsidering its goals in relation to social-justice concerns. Morals by agreement sees reflective entities tacitly accepting constraints. Postmodernist (or neo-pragmatist) forms such as *contextual* rationality depict a process of achieving consensus about knowledge, or belief, within an ideal speech situation. *Rational-interaction* is similar, involving partial convergence toward consensus over a proposed course of action, or policy. The focus here is upon resolution, settlement, or dissolution of conflict without resort to coercion. In business, these forms of rationality are manifested in available approaches to strategy formulation.

Expressive rationality assigns value to the search *per se* for goals. This search underscores the sense of self, or autonomy, itself a carrier of value. Whilst this form is not RUM-captured, it is also manifest in business, for example in the Japanese management practice of *Ringi*. In a similar vein, *posterior* rationality refers to the emergence of goals, over time, as an historical process. In business, this corresponds to the emergence of a strategic vision.

The major schools of ethical reasoning also fall within the general theory. Teleological, or consequentialist ethics are associated with instrumental forms, or choosing means. Utilitarianism invokes the (ambiguous) goal of the greatest calculated good for the greatest number. In business, this is manifest as social cost–benefit analysis, either within predetermined policy parameters (i.e. rule-utilitarianism) or else applied *ad hoc* to an isolated business decision (act-utilitarianism). Rational deliberation is again quite central to deontological ethics. In the Kantian form, rational deliberation leads to the categorical imperatives (*see* CONSEQUENTIALISM; UTILITARIANISM; SOCIAL COST–BENEFIT; KANTIAN ETHICS).

Many of the associated meta-rational and meta-ethical arguments are found in formal GAME THEORY, with its meta-theory. For example, the PRISONER'S DILEMMA game (PDG) provides a clear rationale for Kantian ethics, linking it with strategic-belief rationality. Computer simulations with PDG have also yielded explanations of other moral principles, such as returning favors, forgiving, and not harming. Experimental games have further succeeded in incorporating moral sentiments such as guilt and gratitude into a rational calculus.

In sum, the evolving general theory of rationality, together with moral philosophy (and business strategy) is continually engaged in shaping principles of behavior most appropriate to the current changing economic, organizational, social, cultural, and personal spheres. As stated at the outset, even the words "personal" and "organizational" must now be interpreted with considerable caution.

See also **ethics; moral agency; rational choice theory; socio-economics; decision theory**

Bibliography

Etzioni, A. (1988). *The Moral Dimension: Towards a New Economics*. New York: Free Press.

Gautier, D. (1990). *Moral Dealing*. Ithaca: Cornell University Press.

Hamlin, A. P. (1986). *Ethics, Economics, and the State*. Brighton: Wheatsheaf.

Hargreaves-Heap, S. (1989). *Rationality in Economics*. Oxford: Blackwell.

Sen, A. K. (1987). *On Ethics and Economics*. Oxford: Blackwell.

Singer, A. E. (1994). Strategy as moral philosophy. *Strategic Management Journal*, **15**, 191–213.

ALAN E. SINGER

Rawls, John   One of the most prominent American moral philosophers of the second half of the twentieth century. Born on February 21, 1921, in Baltimore, Maryland, Rawls received his doctorate from Princeton University in 1950, and did a year of postgraduate work at Oxford University in 1952. He taught at Princeton University, Cornell University, and the Massachusetts Institute of Technology, before moving to Harvard University in 1962, where he later became James Bryant Conant University Professor.

Rawls's work has been widely discussed by social and political theorists, especially his first book, *A Theory of Justice*, which has exerted considerable influence in many areas of APPLIED ETHICS, including BUSINESS ETHICS. There he advances a form of the SOCIAL CONTRACT THEORY that harkens back to Locke, Rousseau, and Kant, as an alternative to UTILITARIANISM (*see* LOCKE, JOHN; KANTIAN ETHICS). Rawls seeks to identify principles for impartial, rational, autonomous individuals that will promote what he calls justice as fairness. He argues that free agents in an original position that includes a "veil of ignorance," which prevents them from seeing their positions in society, would select two lexically ordered principles that meet conditions of finality, generality, and publicity:

First Principle: "Each person is to have an equal right to the most extensive total system of equal basic liberties compatible with a similar system of liberty for all."

Second Principle: "Social and economic inequalities are to be arranged so that they are both: (a) to the greatest benefit of the least advantaged, consistent with the just savings principle, and (b) attached to offices and positions open to all under conditions of fair equality of opportunity." (Rawls, 1971, p. 302)

Throughout *A Theory of Justice*, Rawls offers political LIBERALISM support that many in academia have welcomed.

Among Rawls's early papers, "Two Concepts of Rules" and "Justice as Fairness" have been widely anthologized. His more recent "Kantian Constructivism in Moral Theory" has been incorporated in his second book, *Political Liberalism*. More recently, he has turned to issues of JUSTICE for international law and practice in "The Law of Peoples."

Bibliography

Rawls, J. (1955). Two concepts of rules. *The Philosophical Review*, **64**, 3–32.

Rawls, J. (1958). Justice as fairness. *The Philosophical Review*, **67**, 164–94.

Rawls, J. (1971). *A Theory of Justice*. Cambridge, Mass.: The Belknap Press of Harvard University Press.

Rawls, J. (1980). Kantian constructivism in moral theory. *The Journal of Philosophy*, **77**, 515–72.

Rawls, J. (1993). *Political Liberalism*. New York: Columbia University Press.

Rawls, J. (1993). The law of peoples. *Critical Inquiry*, **20**, 36–68.

THOMAS MAGNELL

real estate sales, ethical issues in   *see* ETHICAL ISSUES IN REAL ESTATE SALES

reciprocity   a tit-for-tat response to the actions of others: a fitting and proportional return of benefit for benefit, harm for harm. In business ethics, reciprocity is of special interest for three reasons: it is a fundamental, cross-cultural social and ethical norm; it is congruent with the general justifying aims of business, and with a very wide range of entrenched business practices; and when it is restricted to the context of business transactions, the most vexing philosophical difficulties with norms of reciprocity, including problems of moral motivation and application, are greatly reduced.

Powerful social norms in every society of record define and mandate forms of reciprocal conduct in a wide range of human interactions, from rules of hospitality and ritual gift-giving among individuals to international relations. Such norms have prompted a great deal of descriptive and theoretical behavioral science – from biological hypotheses about reciprocal altruism to exchange theory in anthropology and psychology, and to the testing of game-theoretic strategies for handling iterated prisoner's dilemmas, where a tit-for-tat strategy works very well indeed (*see* GAME THEORY; PRISONER'S DILEMMA). Solutions to cooperation and coordination problems of all sorts, at all levels of social complexity, typically appeal to or enforce norms of reciprocity: "I will if you will" agreements; "returning the favor" policies; the practice of taking turns; retaliation against free riders and cheaters.

The existence of norms of reciprocity is not a recent discovery, of course. Such norms have prompted a great deal of work in ethics from antiquity to the present. Secular accounts of the GOLDEN RULE may be seen as attempts to motivate (and perhaps to justify) reciprocity in terms of rationality or self-interest. Accounts of fairness, deservingness, retributive and compensatory justice are intimately connected to reciprocity – to the notion of a fitting and proportional response to benefit or harm. Discussions of gratitude, trust, fair play, and fidelity are also frequently linked to the notion of reciprocity.

In ethical theory, reciprocity (unlike altruism, for example) has always won general, even if wary, endorsement. The wariness comes from the lack of consensus about the solution to several deep problems. One is the question of the scope of the receipts for which people should reciprocate. Should principles of fair play and reciprocity apply only to voluntary social arrangements – to "games" people join willingly, knowing the rules before deciding to play? Or are people obligated to reciprocate for benefits they did not ask for, in games they did not willingly join? Another problem is specifying what counts as a fitting and proportional return. It is notoriously difficult to calibrate reciprocal punishments, for example, since what constitutes a meaningful penalty varies so widely with individuals. And in situations of great inequality of resources, norms requiring reciprocal exchanges of gifts can be quite destructive.

In business ethics, reciprocity is of special interest despite those problems, however. In the first place, any field of applied ethics can make good use of a powerful, fundamental ethical and social norm that is genuinely cross-cultural, and is generally accepted by both ordinary moral agents and ethical theorists. Second, reciprocity is a norm about *exchange*, and is thus directed to matters that are right at the core of business dealings. Third, reciprocity does not depend upon a principle of benevolence, where that is understood as an active concern for the welfare of others. Rather, reciprocity is grounded in strategies of rational self-maximization and total or average utility maximization, and in deontological concerns for desert, fairness, and UNIVERSALIZABILITY – all of which can be defended without invoking benevolence. This means that a principle of reciprocity can be applied rather directly in a business context, without adding premises about when doing business should involve active concern for the welfare of others as well as oneself.

Finally, from a theoretical point of view, an even more interesting advantage for business ethics is that the deepest philosophical difficulties of reciprocity are muted in a business context. For one thing, our economic, political, social, and ethical ideals for business transactions are for their being fully voluntary exchanges, where there is broad consensus that norms of fair play and reciprocity may govern. Thus the problem of using reciprocity to justify non-voluntary obligations, such as fundamental familial and political obligations, does not arise in business ethics with the same persistence that it has in other areas. For another thing, appealing to a principle of reciprocity in a business context is not likely to evoke objections to its "moral score-keeping" aspect, as often happens when reciprocity is invoked in other settings. (We often object to keeping strict accounts in friendships, for example.) And in a business context, because our dealings with each other usually have a clarity of definition and purpose lacking in moral life generally, it is often fairly easy to define what would count as a fitting and proportional return – and thus, for example, to identify the sorts of overtures one should not invite or accept precisely because they would establish a *prima facie* obligation to reciprocate in a way that is objectionable on other grounds.

See also **altruism and benevolence; compensatory justice; fairness; justice; rational choice theory; utilitarianism**

Bibliography

Axelrod, R. (1984). *The Evolution of Cooperation*. New York: Basic Books.

Becker, L. (1986). *Reciprocity*. Boston and London: Routledge. Paperback repr. Chicago: University of Chicago Press, 1990.

Blau, P. M. (1964). *Exchange and Power in Social Life*. New York: John Wiley. Repr., with a new introduction, New Brunswick: Transaction Books, 1986. (Political theory).

Bowie, N. (1991). New directions in corporate social responsibility: Moral pluralism and reciprocity. *Business Horizons*, **34** (4).

Ekeh, P. P. (1974). *Social Exchange Theory: The Two Traditions*. Cambridge, Mass.: Harvard University Press. (Social theory).

Gewirth, A. (1978). The golden rule rationalized. *Midwest Studies in Philosophy*, 3, 133–47.

Gouldner, A. (1960). The norm of reciprocity. *American Sociological Review*, **25**, 161–78 (Sociology).

Simmons, J. (1979). *Moral Principles and Political Obligations*. Princeton: Princeton University Press. (Material on gratitude and fair play).

Singer, M. G. (1963). The golden rule. *Philosophy*, 38, 293–314.

Singer, M. G. (1985). Universalizability and the generalization principle. In N. Potter & M. Timmons (eds), *Morality and Universality: Essays in Ethical Universalizability*. Dordrecht: Reidel, 47–73.

LAWRENCE C. BECKER

recruiting and selection, ethical issues in *see* ETHICAL ISSUES IN RECRUITING AND SELECTION

reflective equilibrium is a coherentist method of explanation and justification used in ethical theory, social and political philosophy, philosophy of science, philosophy of mind, and epistemology. Its initial articulation was made by Nelson Goodman. But its more familiar and extensive utilization is in moral and social philosophy, where it was initiated by JOHN RAWLS and Stuart Hampshire and was later amplified by Norman Daniels and Kai Nielsen.

Its most forceful critics are Richard Brandt, David Copp, Joseph Raz, Jean Hampton, and Simon Blackburn.

As a method of justification in ethics it starts with a society's, or cluster of societies', most firmly held considered judgments (principally their moral judgments) and seeks to forge them into a consistent and coherent whole that squares with the other things that are reasonably believed and generally and uncontroversially accepted in the society or cluster of societies in question. The considered judgments appealed to can be at all levels of generality, though the point of departure will usually be from particular considered judgments which in turn will be placed in a coherent pattern with more general moral principles, middle-level moral rules and with, as well, moral practices. (More strictly with the verbal articulations of the practices.) Suppose a particular moral belief fails to be compatible with a general moral principle in turn supported by many other firmly held particular considered judgments, other general moral principles, and middle-level moral rules. Then that particular considered judgement should either be modified until it is so consistent or be excised from the corpus of considered moral judgments and the moral repertoire of that society. If, by contrast, a general, moral principle (say the principle of utility) is incompatible with a considerable number of firmly held considered judgments, then it should also be either similarly modified or rejected. The idea is to shuttle back and forth between particular moral judgments, general principles, medium-level moral rules, and moral practices, modifying, where there is an incompatibility, one or the other, until we have gained what we have good reason to believe is the most consistent and coherent pattern achievable at the time. When this is attained a reflective equilibrium has been attained.

The idea is to seek to maximize the coherence of our moral beliefs and practices. But there is no assumption that any reflective equilibrium that has been attained will be *final* and will not subsequently be upset. It will be upset (and this is something we should expect to happen, historically speaking, repeatedly) if either we come to have a still more coherent pattern, or because, as the situation changes, new moral judgments enter the scene which conflict with some of the beliefs in the reflective equilibrium which has been established. When that is so we need to get a new consistent cluster of beliefs and moral practices. So, in such situations, the extant reflective equilibrium is upset. In that case, a new, more adequate one, has to be brought into existence which will contain either a larger circle of coherently related beliefs and practices or will instead, while not enlarging the web of belief, articulate a more coherent package of beliefs and practices. The expectation is that this pattern of reasoning will continue indefinitely, and, in doing so, yield, if it is pursued intelligently, ever more coherent conceptions of moral belief and practice, while never attaining final closure.

Fallibilism is the name of the game. No ultimate critical standards are sought and no principles or beliefs, not even the most firmly held, are, in principle, free from the possibility of being modified or even abandoned, though some moral truisms may always *in fact* be unquestioningly accepted. But this non-Absolutism is not skepticism, for, if a reflective equilibrium is achieved, we will have found a rationale for our moral beliefs and practices by seeing how they are in a consistent and coherent pattern. Justification, on this conception, is attained in this way.

The coherentist pattern of explanation and justification described above is still a narrow (partial) reflective equilibrium. It collects together moral and like considered judgments, moral practices, medium-level moral rules and, as well, moral principles, including very general ones. But this would simply be coherentism that does not take into consideration facts about the functioning of economies and other parts of the social structure, conceptions of human nature, social facts, political realties, and scientific developments. Rawls, Daniels, and Nielsen seek a wider reflective equilibrium which takes these matters into consideration as well. It is called wide (broad) reflective equilibrium. Besides seeking to forge a coherent pattern of the moral matters mentioned above, it seeks – continuing to seek to maximize coherence – an equilibrium which takes into account our best corroborated social-scientific theories and theories of human nature, firmly established social and psychological facts, and political realities,

such as the extent and intractability of pluralism in the society or cluster of societies where the reflective equilibrium is sought. It also should take into consideration what it is reasonable to believe in the society or societies in question and whether the *de facto* pluralism in question is a reasonable pluralism. The thing is to achieve a consistent cluster of moral, factual, and theoretical beliefs that would yield the best available account of what the social situation is, what possibilities obtain in the society, and of what it is reasonable and desirable to do. Such an account is through and through coherentist and holistic, justifying our beliefs and practices by showing the coherency of their fit with each other.

In taking one account of such beliefs and practices to be superior to another, we do so by ascertaining which account yields the superior fit of our beliefs and practices. But, wide reflective equilibrium accounts do not suffer from the defects of pure coherentist theories where any consistent set of beliefs, no matter how unrealistic, is justified simply in virtue of the fact of being a consistent system. In reflective equilibrium, we seek a cluster of *considered judgments* in wide reflective equilibrium. We do not seek just any consistent cluster of beliefs, for we start with considered judgments and return to them as well.

Some critics of reflective equilibrium have argued that there is no coherent system of moral beliefs and practices *to be discovered* by careful reflection and analysis. Instead we have inherited from history a mass of conflicting views, unreflectively gained, held, and persisted in. These views are views which are not infrequently ideological. They often are the non-principled result of brute compromises between contending parties, of religious biases and class, ethnic, racial, and gender prejudices. This unrationalized mélange is not supportive of (the objection goes) the idea of there being an underlying coherent whole, whose deep underlying structure is to be unearthed by careful investigation. What we have instead is simply a clutter of conflicting beliefs and practices revealing a jumble rather than a coherent pattern. To this it has been, in turn, responded that philosophers who are defenders of reflective equilibrium are also *constructivists*. The pattern of consistent beliefs, including very centrally moral beliefs, is *not* a structure to be discovered or unearthed, as if it were analogous to a deep underlying "depth grammar" of language, but something to be *forged* – constructed – by a careful and resolute use of the method of reflective equilibrium. We start from our considered judgments which involves the seeing of things by our own lights. Where else could we start? We can hardly jump out of our cultural and historical skins. But that is no justification or excuse for remaining there. If we use the method of reflective equilibrium, we will, after careful examination, reflection, and a taking of the relevant moral considerations to heart, modify or excise some considered judgments, persistently seeking a wider and a more coherent web of beliefs and practices. We will so proceed until we have constructed a consistent and relevantly inclusive cluster of beliefs and practices. But it is not a question of discovering some underlying moral structure that has always been there. Such "moral realism" is mythical.

Other critics of reflective equilibrium have argued that reflective equilibrium, both narrow and wide, is ethnocentric, relativist, and conservative. Similar responses to those made to the previous criticism can be relevantly made here. There is no escaping starting with our considered judgments. But the very fact of such a starting point is not a manifestation of ethnocentrism. In seeking to maximize coherence and to get the full range of relevant considerations into as coherent and inclusive a pattern as we can, the moral and empirical beliefs and conceptions of others – sometimes, culturally speaking, very different "others" – need to be taken into consideration. If our particular considered judgments are in conflict with either well-established factual claims, well-grounded and established social theories, or carefully articulated moral theories, they must be up for critical inspection and for at least possible rejection. If they conflict with the considered judgments of other peoples whose considered judgments square better with a careful appraisal of the facts or the most carefully articulated social, biological, and natural-scientific theories as well as with reflectively articulated general moral principles, then we have good reasons to accept these considered judgments rather than our own. This is true even of our more general considered judgments where they conflict with

such massively supported considered judgments. The method of reflective equilibrium is a *self-correcting* method which gives us, as we repair or rebuild the ship at sea, a *critical* morality. So, though we start inescapably with our considered judgments, if we apply reflective equilibrium resolutely, our account will not be, or at least need not be, ethnocentric. Similar considerations obtain for the claim that reflective equilibrium is relativistic or inherently conservative.

A somewhat different criticism of reflective equilibrium claims that it does not push questions of justification far enough. It does not come to grips with the foundational, or at least fundamental, epistemological issues that would show us what moral knowledge really is or what warranted moral beliefs really are, so that we could defeat a determined global ethical skepticism. An underlying *assumption* of reflective equilibrium is that our considered judgments have an *initial credibility*. But unless we can show how we could establish these considered judgments to be true or warranted that assumption will not be justified and we will not really have faced the epistemological questions that need to be faced if we are to come to have a genuinely objective ethical theory philosophically defended. Defenders of reflective equilibrium will in turn respond that such a foundationalist quest is both impossible and unnecessary. There is no just knowing moral propositions to be true or warranted. There is no just noting that they rest on some direct correspondence of moral propositions to the facts (moral or otherwise). There are no such fact-like entities for moral propositions to correspond to. But the recognition of this should not, they argue, lead to the abandonment of all notions of objectivity in morality. Cross-culturally agreed-on considered judgments set in a wide reflective equilibrium give us an inter-subjectivity, reflectively sustainable, that is all the moral objectivity we can get and all that we need.

This brief account cannot do justice to the complex issues that divide defenders of wide reflective equilibrium and their critics. These issues are now at the forefront of discussions concerning justification and explanation in ethics and social philosophy. Rawls and Hampshire provide the classical articulations of reflective equilibrium and Brandt and Hare the classical statements of its critique. Daniels, Nielsen, and Rorty provide cutting-edge defenses of wide reflective equilibrium and Raz, Copp, and Hampton cutting-edge statements of its critique. It is to these writings that the reader should turn for a more thorough analysis of these issues.

Bibliography

Blackburn, R. (1993). Can philosophy exist? In J. Couture & K. Nielsen (eds), *Méta-Philosophie: Reconstructing Philosophy?*, Calgary, Alberta: University of Calgary Press, 83–106.

Brandt, R. (1979). *A Theory of the Good and Right.* Oxford: Clarendon Press.

Copp, D. (1985). Considered judgements and moral justification. In D. Copp & D. Zimmerman (eds), *Morality, Reason and Truth: New Essays on the Foundations of Ethics.* Totowa, NJ: Rowan & Allanheld, 141-68.

Daniels, N. (1996). *Justice and Justification.* Cambridge: Cambridge University Press.

Hampshire, S. (1983). *Morality and Conflict.* Cambridge, Mass.: Harvard University Press.

Hampton, J. (1989). Should political philosophy be done without metaphysics? *Ethics*, **99**, 791–814.

Hampton, J. (1993). The moral commitments of liberalism. In D. Copp, J. Hampton, & J. E. Roemer (eds), *The Idea of Democracy.* Cambridge: Cambridge University Press.

Nielsen, K. (1982). On needing a moral theory: Rationality, considered judgements and the grounding of morality. *Metaphilosophy*, **13**, 97–116.

Nielsen, K. (1991). *After the Demise of the Tradition: Rorty, Critical Theory and The Fate of Philosophy.* Boulder, Colo.: Westview Press.

Nielsen, K. (1994). How to proceed in social philosophy: Contextualist justice and wide reflective equilibrium. *Queen's Law Journal*, **20**, 89–138.

Rawls, J. (1971). *A Theory of Justice.* Cambridge, Mass.: Harvard University Press.

Rawls, J. (1974). The independence of moral theory. *Proceedings and Addresses of the American Philosophical Association*, **48**, 5–22.

Rawls, J. (1993). *Political Liberalism.* New York: Columbia University Press.

Raz, J. (1982). The claims of reflective equilibrium. *Inquiry*, **25**, 307–30.

Rorty, R. (1988). The priority of democracy to philosophy. In M. D. Peterson & R. C. Vaughan (eds), *The Virginia Statute For Religious Freedom.* Cambridge: Cambridge University Press, 257–82.

KAI NIELSEN

regulation   As defined in the classic treatise of Alfred Kahn (1970, p. 3), "regulation is the explicit replacement of competition with governmental orders as the principal institutional device for assuring good performance" (from an industry). Several aspects of this definition are important. First, systems of regulation are imposed by law through the political-choice process because some segments of the population prefer the outcomes that emerge from an administrative process to those resulting from the operation of unfettered markets. These groups may also prefer some aspects of the regulatory process itself, such as their sense of its fairness, to the market process of resource allocation.

Second, industries, and the businesses and consumers who comprise those industries, are regulated in order to improve upon the performance of the industries, at least as measured or perceived by some segments of the population. WELFARE ECONOMICS focuses on policies for maximizing social efficiency defined as the sum of the benefits to consumers and companies from markets, whereas political economists tend to stress the distributional gains and losses resulting from regulation.

Finally, regulation operates through agencies who act as the agents of the administrative and legislative branches of the government in carrying out laws. Regulatory agencies are constrained by their enabling statutes, by procedural restrictions such as the US Administrative Procedure Act (in the US context), and by the political forces which act upon the agencies. They carry out their missions through setting rules, or regulations, and by adjudicating requests from affected parties such as an electric utility company.

One of the most famous results in economics is ADAM SMITH's (1776) observation that economic welfare can be maximized by organizing the distribution of goods and services through perfectly competitive markets. Much regulation can be justified as responses to so-called "market failures," that is, social inefficiencies arising from the operation of imperfectly competitive markets. From a political point of view, the logic is straightforward. If a market fails due to a market imperfection, then society can improve aggregate economic welfare by imposing regulations that force the market to operate as if it were perfectly competitive. Political forces can impose regulations on an economy even if those regulations only benefit the groups in political power at the expense of other groups, sometimes with an overall decrease in the aggregate level of economic welfare in the economy. In the latter case, the regulations stay in place until the political coalition behind them disintegrates or is beaten by another coalition, at which time the regulations are dismantled or the industry is deregulated (e.g., the American airlines industry was deregulated in 1978 after forty years of regulation).

Based on the theory of market failure or the pursuit of political aims other than economic efficiency, several justifications for regulation can be identified (see Breyer, 1982):

Natural Monopoly. If the number of companies in a market is small and if barriers to entry into the industry limit the competition from potential rivals, then the producers in the industry can raise their prices above the competitive levels without fear of a large loss of sales and profits. One of the entry barriers that limits the number of firms in an industry is due to increasing returns to scale. If the average cost of production falls dramatically at high volumes and industry demand is only strong enough to support one, or at most a few firms at this high rate of production, then small companies are unable to enter and compete in the market because of their marked cost disadvantage. Local telephone companies, electric utilities, and natural-gas distribution companies provide good examples of this kind of "natural monopoly" for which rate regulation limits the price charges to consumers of their products.

Spillover Costs. When the costs of producing some product, such as paper, spill over to other producers (e.g., in the form of polluted water that must be cleaned before use) or to consumers (e.g., in the form of air pollution which causes respiratory problems), then markets fail to maximize economic welfare. Without facing sufficient incentives to bear the costs of the spillovers, companies tend to produce too much of the products or they devote too few resources to reducing the spillover effects. Hence the potential justification for government regulation such as standards on the levels of

hydrocarbon emissions from automobiles, emission taxes on hydrocarbons emitted by electric utilities, and allocations of radio broadcast frequencies to avoid the spillover costs (namely, the interference) that would be imposed upon existing stations from new stations broadcasting on the same frequencies.

Inadequate Information. For markets to function smoothly, consumers and producers must possess accurate information about the availability of goods, their prices, and their quality. However, it is difficult to exclude others from the use of product information once it is produced or discovered, making information itself a good which is under-supplied in markets and thus a candidate for government programs that encourage further supply. The US National Weather Service provides information directly, while EPA's gas mileage labeling requirements ensure that this information is available to new car buyers. (See Viscusi & Magat, 1987, and Magat & Viscusi, 1992.)

Paternalism. Regulation is sometimes justified on the basis that consumers sometimes make decisions which are not in their own best interests. This argument can easily become a slippery slope quickly overriding freedom of choice in many economic decisions, but for certain classes of decisions government paternalism is at least arguable. State regulation of alcohol sales to minors and inebriated adults is one commonly accepted example of a paternalistic regulation. There is strong evidence that even well-educated adults have difficulty in accurately assessing the risks of health and safety risks, and in making self-protection decisions concerning these low probability risks. Both of these risks provide a potential justification for banning the direct sales to consumers of certain chemical and pharmaceutical products (*see* PATERNALISM).

Moral Hazard. Markets cannot function well without contracts written over private exchanges, and efficient contracts cannot be written unless the actions of parties involved in the contract are observable. Otherwise the problem of MORAL HAZARD arises. Employers may underinvest in the safety levels of their work environments if these safety levels are not observable by employees, consumers may use products carelessly if the products are covered by warranties and other forms of insurance, and doctors and their patients may agree to excessive levels of medical care if a third-party insurer pays without the ability to observe levels of care. In all of these cases government regulation has been suggested as a way of correcting the market failure.

Redistribution. Regulation is a political response by groups of citizens to override the outcomes of the market process. Given the ability of every level of government to create winners and losers from regulatory action, it is not surprising that much government regulation is motivated at least in part by efforts to redistribute resources, whether it be set-aside provisions for women and minority firms in government contracts and spectrum sales, grandfathering or relaxed pollution standards for existing versus new sources of pollution, or regulatory barriers to entry into long-distance telephone markets. (For further discussion see Noll, ch. 22 in Schmalensee & Willig, 1989; Magat, Krupnick, & Harrington, 1986; and Cohen & Stigler, 1971.)

While the examples in this entry are based on American regulatory institutions, the general principles behind the political causes and economic justifications for regulation are shared by all market-based economies.

See also **corporate social performance; efficient markets; environment and environmental ethics; ethical issues in information; global warming; hazardous waste; nuclear power; OSHA; Securities and Exchange Commission; social responsibility; worker safety**

Bibliography

Baumol, W. J. (1977). On the proper cost test for natural monopoly in a multiproduct industry. *American Economic Review*, 67, 809–22.

Breyer, S. (1982). *Regulation and its Reform*. Cambridge, Mass.: Harvard University Press.

Cohen, M. & Stigler, G. (1971). *Can Regulatory Agencies Protect Customers?* Washington, DC: American Enterprise Institute for Poliy Research.

Derthick, M. & Quuirk, P. J. (1985). *The Politics of Deregulation*. Washington, DC: Brookings Institution.

Kahn, A. E. (1970). *The Economics of Regulations: Principles and Institutions*. New York: John Wiley.

Magat, W. A., Krupnick, A. J. & Harrington, W. (1986). *Rules in the Making*. Washington, DC: Resources for the Future.

Magat, W. A. & Viscusi, W. K. (1992). *Informational Approaches to Regulation*. Cambridge, Mass.: MIT Press.

Noll, R. G. & Owen, B. M. (1983). *The Political Economy of Deregulation*. Washington, DC: American Enterprise Institute.

Schmalensee, R. & Willig, R. D. (eds). (1989). *Handbook of Industrial Organization*. Amsterdam: North-Holland.

Smith, A. (1776). *An Inquiry into the Nature and Causes of the Wealth of Nations*. London: W. Strahan, T. Cadell.

Spulber, D. F. (1989). *Regulation and Markets*. Cambridge, Mass.: MIT Press.

Viscusi, W. K. & Magat, W. A. (1987). *Learning About Risk: Consumer and Worker Responses to Hazard Information*. Cambridge, Mass.: Harvard University Press.

Viscusi, W. K., Vernon, J. M. & Harrington, J., Jr. (1992). *Economics of Regulations and Antitrust*. Lexington, Mass.: D. C. Heath.

WESLEY A. MAGAT

relativism, cultural and moral *Cultural relativism* is a descriptive claim that ethical practices differ among cultures; that, as a matter of fact, what is considered right in one culture may be considered wrong in another. Thus truth or falsity of cultural relativism can be determined by examining the world. The work of anthropologists and sociologists is most relevant in determining the truth or falsity of cultural relativism, and there is widespread consensus among social scientists that cultural relativism is true.

Moral relativism is the claim that what is really right or wrong is what the culture says is right or wrong. Moral relativists accept cultural relativism as true, but they claim much more. If a culture sincerely and reflectively adopts a basic moral principle, then it is morally obligatory for members of that culture to act in accordance with that principle.

The implication of moral relativism for conduct is that one ought to abide by the ethical norms of the culture where one is located. This position is captured by the popular phrase "When in Rome, do as the Romans do." Relativists in ethics would say

"One ought to follow the moral norms of the culture." In terms of business practice, consider the question, "Is it morally right to pay a bribe to gain business?" The moral relativist would answer the question by consulting the moral norms of the country where one is doing business. If those norms permit bribery in that country, then the practice of bribery is not wrong in that country. However, if the moral norms of the country do not permit bribery, then offering a bribe to gain business in that country is morally wrong. The justification for that position is the moral relativist's contention that what is really right or wrong is determined by the culture.

Is cultural relativism true? Is moral relativism correct? As noted, many social scientists believe that cultural relativism is true as a matter of fact. But is it?

First, many philosophers claim that the "facts" aren't really what they seem. Early twentieth-century anthropologists cited the fact that in some cultures, after a certain age, parents are put to death. In most cultures such behavior would be murder. Does this difference in behavior prove that the two cultures disagree about fundamental matters of ethics? No, it does not. Suppose the other culture believes that people exist in the afterlife in the same condition that they leave their present life. It would be very cruel to have one's parents exist eternally in an unhealthy state. By killing them when they are relatively active and vigorous, you insure their happiness for all eternity. The *underlying* ethical principle of this culture is that children have duties to their parents, including the duty to be concerned with their parents' happiness as they approach old age. This ethical principle is identical with our own. What looked like a difference in ethics between our culture and another turned out, upon close examination, to be a difference based on what each culture takes to be the facts of the matter. This example does, of course, support the claim that as a matter of fact ethical principles vary according to culture. However, it does not support the stronger conclusion that *underlying* ethical principles vary according to culture.

Cultures differ in physical setting, in economic development, in the state of their science and technology, in their literacy rate, and in many other ways. Even if there were universal moral principles, they would have to be applied in these different cultural contexts. Given the different situations in which cultures exist, it would come as no surprise to find universal principles applied in different ways. Hence we expect to find surface differences in ethical behavior among cultures even though the cultures agree on fundamental universal moral principles. For example, one commonly held universal principle appeals to the public good; it says that social institutions and individual behavior should be ordered so that they lead to the greatest good for the greatest number. Many different forms of social organization and individual behavior are consistent with this principle. The point of these two arguments is to show that differences among cultures on ethical behavior may not reflect genuine disagreement about underlying principles of ethics. Thus it is not so obvious that any strong form of cultural relativism is true.

But are there universal principles that are accepted by all cultures? It seems so; there does seem to be a whole range of behavior, such as torture and murder of the innocent, that every culture agrees is wrong. A nation-state accused of torture does not respond by saying that a condemnation of torture is just a matter of cultural choice. The state's leaders do not respond by saying, "We think torture is right, but you do not." Rather, the standard response is to deny that any torture took place. If the evidence of torture is too strong, a finger will be pointed either at the victim or at the morally outraged country: "They do it too." In this case the guilt is spread to all. Even the Nazis denied that genocide took place. What is important is that *no* state replies that there is nothing wrong with genocide or torture.

In addition, there are attempts to codify some universal moral principles. The United Nations Universal Declaration of Human Rights has been endorsed by the member states of the UN, and the vast majority of countries in the world are members of the UN. Even in business, there is a growing effort to adopt universal principles of business practice. In a recent study of international codes of ethics, Professors Catherine Langlois and Bodo B. Schlegelmilch (1990) found that although there certainly were differences among codes, there was a considerable area of agreement. William Frederick has documented the details of six international compacts on matters of international business ethics. These include the aforementioned UN Universal Declaration of Human Rights, the European Convention on Human Rights, the Helsinki Final Act, the OECD Guidelines for Multinational Enterprises and Social Policy, and the United Nations Conduct on Transnational Corporations (in progress) (Frederick, 1991). The Caux Roundtable, a group of corporate executives from the United States, Europe, and Japan, are seeking worldwide endorsement of a set of principles of business ethics. Thus there are a number of reasons to think that cultural relativism, at least with respect to basic moral principles, is not true, that is, that it does not accurately describe the state of moral agreement that exists. This is consistent with maintaining that cultural relativism is true in the weak form, that is, when applied only to surface ethical principles.

But what if differences in fundamental moral practices among cultures are discovered and seem unreconcilable? That would lead to a discussion about the adequacy of moral relativism. The fact that moral practices do vary widely among countries is cited as evidence for the correctness of moral relativism. Discoveries early in the century by anthropologists, sociologists, and psychologists documented the diversity of moral beliefs. Philosophers, by and large, welcomed corrections of moral imperialist thinking, but recognized that the moral relativist's appeal to the alleged truth of cultural relativism was not enough to establish moral relativism. The mere fact that a culture considers a practice moral does not mean that it is moral. Cultures have sincerely practiced slavery, discrimination, and the torture of animals. Yet each of these practices can be independently criticized on ethical grounds. Thinking something is morally permissible does not make it so.

Another common strategy for criticizing moral relativism is to show that the consequences of taking the perspective of moral relativism are inconsistent with our use of moral language. It is often contended by moral relativists that if two cultures disagree regarding universal moral principles, there is no way for that disagreement to be resolved. Since moral relativism is the view that what is right or wrong

is determined by culture, there is no higher appeal beyond the fact that culture endorses the moral principle. But we certainly do not talk that way. When China and the United States argue about the moral rights of human beings, the disputants use language that seems to appeal to universal moral principles. Moreover, the atrocities of the Nazis and the slaughter in Rwanda have met with universal condemnation that seemed based on universal moral principles. So moral relativism is not consistent with our use of moral language.

Relativism is also inconsistent with how we use the term "moral reformer." Suppose, for instance, that a person from one culture moves to another and tries to persuade the other culture to change its view. Suppose someone moves from a culture where slavery is immoral to one where slavery is morally permitted. Normally, if a person were to try to convince the culture where slavery was permitted that slavery was morally wrong, we would call such a person a moral reformer. Moreover, a moral reformer would almost certainly appeal to universal moral principles to make her argument; she almost certainly would not appeal to a competing cultural standard. But if moral relativism were true, there would be no place for the concept of a moral reformer. Slavery is really right in those cultures that say it is right and really wrong in those cultures that say it is wrong. If the reformer fails to persuade a slaveholding country to change its mind, the reformer's antislavery position was never right. If the reformer is successful in persuading a country to change its mind, the reformer's antislavery views would be wrong – until the country did in fact change its view. Then the reformer's antislavery view would be right. But that is not how we talk about moral reform.

The moral relativist might argue that our language should be reformed. We should talk differently. At one time people used to talk and act as if the world were flat. Now they don't. The relativist could suggest that we can change our ethical language in the same way. But consider how radical the relativists' response is. Since most, if not all, cultures speak and act as if there were universal moral principles, the relativist can be right only if almost everyone else is wrong. How plausible is that?

Although these arguments are powerful ones, they do not deliver a knockout blow to moral relativism. If there are no universal moral principles, moral relativists could argue that moral relativism is the only theory available to help make sense of moral phenomena.

An appropriate response to this relativist argument is to present the case for a set of universal moral principles, principles that are correct for all cultures independent of what a culture thinks about them. This is what adherents of the various ethical traditions try to do. The reader will have to examine these various traditions and determine how persuasive she finds them. In addition, there are several final independent considerations against moral relativism that can be mentioned here.

First, what constitutes a culture? There is a tendency to equate cultures with national boundaries, but that is naive, especially today. With respect to moral issues, what do US cultural norms say regarding right and wrong? That question may be impossible to answer, because in a highly pluralistic country like the United States, there are many cultures. Furthermore, even if one can identify a culture's moral norms, it will have dissidents who do not subscribe to those moral norms. How many dissidents can a culture put up with and still maintain that some basic moral principle is the cultural norm? Moral relativists have had little to say regarding criteria for constituting a culture or how to account for dissidents. Unless moral relativists offer answers to questions like these, their theory is in danger of becoming inapplicable to the real world.

Second, any form of moral relativism must admit that there are some universal moral principles. Suppose a culture does not accept moral relativism, that is, it denies that if an entire culture sincerely and reflectively adopts a basic moral principle, it is obligatory for members of that culture to act in accord with that principle. Fundamentalist Muslim countries would reject moral relativism because it would require them to accept as morally permissible blasphemy in those countries where blasphemy was permitted. If the moral relativist insists that the truth of every moral principle depends on the culture, then she must admit that the truth of moral relativism depends on the culture. Therefore the moral relativist must admit that at least the principle of moral relativism is not relative.

Third, it seems that there is a set of basic moral principles that every culture must adopt. You would not have a culture unless the members of the group adopted these moral principles. Consider an anthropologist who arrives on a populated island: How many tribes are on the island? To answer that question, the anthropologist tries to determine if some people on some parts of the island are permitted to kill, commit acts of violence against, or steal from persons on other parts of the island. If such behavior is not permitted, that counts as a reason for saying that there is only one tribe. The underlying assumption here is that there is a set of moral principles that must be followed if there is to be a culture at all. With respect to those moral principles, adhering to them determines whether there is a culture or not.

But what justifies these principles? A moral relativist would say that a culture justifies them. But you cannot have a culture unless the members of the culture follow the principles. Thus it is reasonable to think that justification lies elsewhere. Many believe that the purpose of morality is to help make social cooperation possible. Moral principles are universally necessary for that endeavor.

Bibliography

Benedict, R. (1934). *Patterns of Culture*. New York: Penguin Books.

Bowie, N. (1988). The moral obligations of multinational corporations. In S. Luper-Foy (Ed.), , *Problems of International Justice*. Boulder, Colo.: Westview Press.

Frederick, W. C. (1991). The moral authority of transnational corporate codes. *Journal of Business Ethics*, **10**, (3).

Harman, G. (1975). Moral relativism defended. *The Philosophical Review*, **84**, 3–22.

Hatch, E. (1983). *Culture and Morality*. New York: Columbia University Press.

Krausz, M. & Meiland, J. (1982). *Relativism: Cognitive and Moral*. Notre Dame: University of Notre Dame Press.

Ladd, J. (1973). *Ethical Relativism*. Belmont, Calif.: Wadsworth.

Langlois, C. & Schlegelmilch, B. B. (1990). Do corporate codes of ethics reflect national character? Evidence from Europe and the United States. *Journal of International Studies*, **21**, (9), 519–39.

Mackie, J. (1977). *Ethics: Inventing Right and Wrong.* Harmondsworth: Penguin Books.

Rachels, J. (1993). *The Elements of Moral Philosophy,* 2nd edn. New York: McGraw-Hill.

Sayre-McCord, G. (1991). Being a realist about relativism (in ethics). *Philosophical Studies,* **61**, 155–76.

Wong, D. (1984). *Moral Relativity.* Berkeley: University of Californina Press.

NORMAN E. BOWIE

religion and business ethics Business ethics is the product of religion's interest in business and business education's concern with social issues. In the West, Protestantism (in particular, Calvinism and Lutheranism), Roman Catholicism, and Judaism have been the most influential.

Judaism, the root of Christianity, provided business ethics with an operative set of norms. These norms, the most prominent being the Ten Commandments (Ex 20: 1–17), are an admixture of judgment (*mishpat*) and lovingkindness (*hesed*) and are reflective of God's covenant with the Israelites. They continue to influence and regulate the behavior of contemporary businesses as the basis of the "blue laws" that regulate business hours ("Remember the sabbath day, and keep it holy"), as the source of the idea that transactions should involve proper entitlement ("You shall not steal"), and as the basis for the expectation of TRUTHTELLING in negotiations ("You shall not bear false witness against your neighbor").

Coming out of this tradition, Christians believe that Jesus Christ fulfilled ("I have come not to abolish but to fulfill," Mt 5: 17) and reinterpreted Jewish law ("the sabbath was made for humankind, and not humankind for the sabbath," Mk 2: 27). The New Testament is replete with examples of how Jesus interpreted the law to pertain to business transactions and the economy. In it Jesus addresses business's relationship to worship (the story involving the money-changers in the temple, Mt 21: 12–13 and Jn 2: 14–16), he calls into question the relationship of work to wages (the story of the vineyard laborers, Mt 20: 1–16), he considers the worthiness of risk-taking and enterprise (the parable of the talents, Mt 25: 14–30), and he recognizes the propriety of tax payment (in encouraging Jews to pay the taxes due Caesar, Mt 22: 20–1). Scripture relates too how, prior to his arrest and conviction, Jesus himself was an object of barter in being sold by a traitorous disciple (see the story of Judas's blood money, Mt 27: 3–8).

Early Christian leaders tried to emulate Jesus by carrying on his concern for the justice of economic transactions, especially as they applied to the needy. St Paul, for one, emphasized the idea of labor as a form of worship, that is, a way by which we might participate in creation and the building up of God's Kingdom. Paul referred to early Christian disciples as ones who "work with me in Christ Jesus" (Rom 16: 3) and repeatedly encouraged his audiences to excel in "the work of the Lord" (1 Cor 15: 58).

Later, Saints Ambrose and Augustine considered different aspects of labor, in particular, the link between work and entitlements. St Ambrose's (333–397) theistic property ethic, for example, held that certain entitlements are part of our birthright. He argued that since we share a common natural poverty at birth and death, we have a justified claim to nature's wealth-producing resources. The wealthy, he claimed, because they have resources in abundance, have a duty to make restitution to the needy among us who have been deprived of this birthright.

Following Ambrose, St Augustine (354–430) asserted that the poor are the result of Adam's Fall and original sin (Gen 3). The poor are poor, he argued, because the propertied few have denied them access to the wealth that belongs to all. In paradise, Augustine reasoned, Adam was gifted with the wisdom to fulfill God's created order and was able to recognize that society should hold resources in common. After the Fall, however, attempts to live according to a system of common ownership were undermined as significant numbers of people insisted on remaining attached to an "earthly city" and a life regulated by personal and selfish desires.

Centuries after Augustine, St Thomas Aquinas (1225–74) considered the theological and philosophical implications associated with commutative justice (the justice between two equals in regard to private transactions) and distributive justice (the rendering of rewards according to proportion). Thomas's Aristotelian- and Augustinian-based virtue theory, for example, held justice to be a personal characteristic of habitual action that enables people to flourish in accord with God's plan. This Thomistic theory became the cornerstone of most Christian teaching for the following three hundred years.

With the Protestant Reformation, however, Christian ethics bifurcated into two branches: 1) a Protestant branch that sought to be prophetic and strove to discern the moral status of current practices, and 2) a Roman Catholic branch that sought to prescribe and proscribe specific acts. The difference between the two approaches is evident in Max Weber's and Pope Leo XIII's writings on the economy (*see* PROTESTANT WORK ETHIC; CATHOLIC SOCIAL TEACHING).

Max Weber (1864–1920) is considered to be the voice of the "Protestant work ethic." His larger body of work described the evolution of the modern institutional and organizational order of "rational bourgeois capitalism" from the Western European family-firm, and his *Protestant Ethic* investigated the psychological conditions that made possible the development of these large-scale business enterprises. In this latter essay, Weber considered the connections between religious affiliation and social stratification. He observed that business leaders and the owners of capital in Germany were overwhelmingly Protestant. He then looked to the four principal forms of ascetic Protestantism (Calvinism, Pietism, Methodism, and the sects growing out of the Baptist movement) for an explanation, and posited that the development of an economic spirit (an *ethos* attaching to an economic system) could be found in 1) Luther's notions of "the call" and the moral justification of worldly activity, and 2) Calvin's spirit of Christian asceticism and notion of a relationship between prosperity and salvation.

Largely adopted by business ethicists, Weber's provocative thesis impelled subsequent Protestant educators (Reinhold Niebuhr, John Howard Yoder, and others) to offer important and influential criticisms of capitalism. Yoder's notion of "servant strength," for example, calls into question the ethics of power that underly the connections that Weber observed.

During and after the Reformation, the Roman Catholic Church remained immersed in casuistry and scholasticism. In the nineteenth century it began to apply these methodologies to issues associated with capitalist economies. Due to the work of German-speaking Catholics

such as Adam Müller (1779–1829), Franz Von Baader (1765–1841), Adolph Kolping (1813–65), and Wilhelm von Ketteler (1811–77), the Church began to consider the issue of worker alienation and the social suffering that attended the transition from a feudal crafts system to a modern industrial order. Ketteler, in particular, was influential in an ability to move Pope Leo XIII (papacy: 1878–1903) to promulgate *Rerum Novarum* (*The Condition of Labor*, 1891), the Catholic Church's first major social encyclical on the economy. *Rerum Novarum*, which considered the dignity of labor, the rights and just wages of workers, and workmen's associations, has been celebrated subsequently in a number of anniversary encyclicals, the most recent being Pope John Paul II's *Centesimus Annus* (*On the Hundredth Anniversary of "Rerum Novarum"*, 1991).

In the US, prominent Catholic lay and clerical leaders who addressed economic and business concerns in the recent past include Orestes Brownson (1803–76), Dorothy Day (1897–1980), Peter Dietz (1878–1947), and John A. Ryan (1869–1945). In addition, in this century the US Catholic Bishops have produced two major pieces on the economy: *The Pastoral Letter of 1919* and *Economic Justice for All* (1986), the latter being a collaborative and inclusive venture that addressed a broad sweep of economic issues with particular attention paid to the economically needy.

Bibliography

Avila, C. (1983). *Ownership, Early Christian Teaching*. Maryknoll: Orbis Books.
Clifford, R. J., SJ (1990). Exodus. In R. E. Brown, SS, J. A. Fitzmyer, SJ, & R. E. Murphy, O.Carm (eds), *The New Jerome Biblical Commentary*. Englewood Cliffs, NJ: Prentice Hall, 44–60.
De George, R. T. (1987). The status of business ethics: Past and future. *Journal of Business Ethics*, 6, 201–11.
Gordon, B. (1994). Theological positions and economic perspectives in ancient literature. In H. G. Brennan & A. M. C. Waterman (eds), *Economics and Religion: Are They Distinct?* Boston: Kluwer Academic Publishers, 19–40.
Gustafson, J. M. (1981). *Ethics from a Theocentric Perspective*. Chicago: University of Chicago Press.
Marshall, G. (1982). *In Search of the Spirit of Capitalism*. London: Hutchinson & Co.

Naughton, M. (1992). *The Good Stewards: Practical Applications of the Papal Social Vision of Work.* Lanham, Md.: University Press of America.

O'Brien, D. J. & Shannon, T. A. (eds) (1992). *Catholic Social Thought – The Documentary Heritage.* New York: Orbis Books.

Weber, M. (1958 [1920]). *The Protestant Ethic and the Spirit of Capitalism* (student's edn). New York: Charles Scribner's Sons.

Yoder, J. H. (1984). *The Priestly Kingdom.* Notre Dame: University of Notre Dame Press.

Zweig, M. (ed.) (1991). *Religion and Economic Justice.* Philadelphia: Temple University Press.

MARTIN CALKINS

responsibility   "Responsibility" has a number of related meanings.

Causal responsibility: this involves something (an object or state or event) being the cause of something else (a state or event). For example, we might say that the beer, or Andy's drinking the beer, was responsible for Andy's drunken condition.

Personal responsibility: (a) prospective and (b) retrospective. To bear *prospective* responsibility for something is to have a responsibility – a duty, an obligation – to see to it that that thing occurs. For example, Andy might be responsible for remaining sober (from this moment on). To bear *retrospective* responsibility for something is to be such that the occurrence of that thing is something in virtue of which one is to be assessed and, possibly, treated. For example, Andy might be responsible – that is, deserving of blame (an unfavorable assessment) and, possibly, of penalty or punishment (an unfavorable treatment) – for getting drunk (in the past). Retrospective responsibility can also be positive. For example, Flo might be responsible – that is, deserving of praise (a favorable assessment) and, possibly, of recognition or reward (a favorable treatment) – for persuading Andy to attend the next AA meeting.

Personal responsibility, whether prospective or retrospective, can be of many different sorts. One's duty or obligation may be moral, legal, or professional; similarly, blame and praise may express a moral, legal, or professional assessment and the attendant treatment, if any, may be sanctioned by moral, legal, or professional norms.

Although causal, prospective, and retrospective responsibility are all related, they must not be confused. In particular, we should note that it is possible that someone be causally responsible for something without being retrospectively responsible for it (a child may have spilled some milk without being to blame for doing so), and it is also possible that someone can have failed to fulfill a prospective responsibility without being retrospectively responsible for this (for one can have an excuse for doing wrong).

Questions of personal responsibility are central to ethics in general and to business ethics in particular. Here is a sampling of such questions. No answers will be proposed here; the purpose of their presentation is to indicate the sorts of issues having to do with personal responsibility that philosophers have long grappled with.

With respect to prospective responsibility, one may ask the following questions:

1) What is the relationship between moral and non-moral duties or obligations? Can they conflict and, if so, how is the conflict to be resolved? Suppose that Judy is the account executive for Kleen cigarettes at the Show and Tell Advertising Agency. Her professional responsibility, we may suppose, is to promote this product as best she can. Moreover, she has a legal responsibility not to reveal confidential information. But what if it is clear that Kleen's CEO is intent on increasing the company's share in the teenage market? Does loyalty render Judy morally obligated to help achieve this goal? Might she even be morally obligated to try to prevent this goal from being achieved (by exposing the plan, perhaps)?

2) Is one's moral duty a function only of the consequences of one's action – does the end justify the means – or are there side-constraints (such as the rights of other people) on what one may do? Even if Judy may, morally, seek to promote Kleen cigarettes, are there moral limits (there are clearly legal limits) on how she may go about doing so?

3) Is one's moral duty a function of what one will actually achieve (either in terms of consequences produced or in terms of rights violated or respected) or of what one will probably achieve? Part of what makes Judy's participation in the campaign to promote Kleen cigarettes morally problematic is presumably the

risk of disease that smoking cigarettes apparently poses. But risk of disease is one thing, actually contracting a disease is another.

4) To what extent, if any, must an outcome be in someone's control for that person to have a moral obligation concerning it? To what extent, for example, is Judy able to affect whether or not teenagers smoke Kleen cigarettes? Can she ensure this? Presumably not; the teenagers themselves will make the final choice. Can she prevent this? Perhaps not; if she refuses to participate in the campaign, someone else may be found to replace her, and this person may approach the work even more zealously.

5) Are there actions that are morally supererogatory – that go beyond the call of duty – or is one always morally required to take the high road? (See SUPEREROGATION.) It might be that, if Judy refuses to participate in the campaign, she will lose her job, and she can ill afford this.

With respect to retrospective responsibility, one may ask these questions:

1) Just what mental capacities and qualities must a person possess in order to bear such responsibility for something? Suppose that it would be morally wrong for Judy to help promote Kleen cigarettes but that she believes otherwise. Would she then be to blame for promoting them?

2) Is it possible to have the freedom of will, and hence the control over one's actions, that retrospective responsibility appears to presuppose? If Judy is driven by ambition, or fear, or greed when she decides to participate in the campaign, is her decision, and hence her participation, really up to her? If instead she is moved by sympathy, or squeamishness, or moral scruples when she decides not to participate, is her decision, and hence her non-participation, really up to her?

3) Can luck play a role in how persons are to be assessed? Suppose that Judy decides to participate in the campaign but the campaign is subsequently cancelled by someone else. Does she thereby avoid the responsibility that she would otherwise have incurred? What if she is about to decide to participate but the campaign is cancelled before she can make this decision?

4) Does someone who is blameworthy (or praiseworthy) for something deserve some form of punishment (or reward)? Suppose that Judy decides to participate in the campaign, that this

is a morally wrong thing to do, and that she is to be blamed for doing so. Does she deserve some form of punishment for doing so? What form? Should her friends ostracize her? Would justice be served if the campaign fizzled and she lost her job?

With respect to personal responsibility, both prospective and retrospective, the following question should also be addressed: is it necessary that the bearers of such responsibility be individuals, or can collections of individuals, such as corporations, also bear such responsibility? Might not the Show and Tell Advertising Agency *itself* be responsible (prospectively) for ensuring that its advertising is non-deceptive and also be responsible (retrospectively) for any deceptions that it has already perpetrated? Corporations are often treated as legal persons in their own right; can they also be moral persons? While many philosophers deny that they can be, some insist that they can.

See also **consequentialism; corporate punishment; duty; free will; guilt; Kantian ethics; loyalty; moral dilemmas; punishment; rights; social responsibility; whistle-blowing**

Bibliography

Feinberg, J. (1980). *Doing and Deserving*. Princeton: Princeton University Press. (Essays on several issues concerning responsibility).

French, P. A. (1984). *Collective and Corporate Responsibility*. New York: Columbia University Press. (Extended defense of the moral personhood of corporations).

Hart, H. L. A. (1968). *Punishment and Responsibility*. Oxford: Oxford University Press. (Essays on several issues concerning responsibility).

Zimmerman, M. J. (1988). *An Essay on Moral Responsibility*. Totowa, NJ: Rowman and Littlefield. (General discussion of retrospective moral responsibility).

Zimmerman, M. (1992). Responsibility. In L. C. Becker & C. B. Becker (eds), *Encyclopedia of Ethics*. New York: Garland Publishing, 1089–95.

MICHAEL J. ZIMMERMAN

restructuring   Organization structure designates formal (a) hierarchic reporting relationships, (b) groupings of tasks into jobs and departments, and (c) systems intended to ensure effective communication, coordination, and control (Child, 1984). Restructuring involves changes in these structural components. Ostensibly, it becomes a project when organizational performance is questioned, when decision-making is delayed or deficient, when conflict inhibits effective organizational functioning, and/or when there is an insufficient or maladaptive response to the environment of the organization. Restructuring may be initiated by management or others. The pace of restructuring may be incremental or quantum. One way to analyze the ethics of restructuring is to apply the Utilitarian, Rights, Justice, Caring framework (Cavanagh, Moberg, & Velasquez, 1995).

A Utilitarian Analysis of Restructuring Projects

The social science discipline that informs restructuring projects is organization theory. A dominant concern among organization theorists is organizational effectiveness. Additionally, organization theory concerns itself with the efficiency or directness with which particular restructuring projects result in such levels of effectiveness. These are, of course, classic utilitarian concerns. Adam Smith, for example, had much to say about the necessary restructuring of a pin factory (*see* UTILITARIANISM).

A utilitarian problem is that evaluating the benefits of restructuring projects is both enormously complex and uninformed by the results of empirical research. Findings that show a relationship between structures and performances lack both definitiveness and robustness. Some evidence shows that redesigners often ignore research, basing their decision instead on fashion and the mindless aping of common practice (DiMaggio & Powell, 1983). Moreover, there is a school of organization theory (organizational ecology) that argues that restructuring is utilitarian folly – that restructuring cannot overcome the natural tendency of markets to select the fittest organizations for survival.

The costs of restructuring are more accessible. Reconfigured relations between employees consume energy as do the altered practices toward outside constituencies (e.g., customers, organizational partners, regulators, etc.). For these reasons, utilitarians are quite conservative about restructuring projects. In the absence of

good estimates of the benefits of restructuring and with the certain expense in disrupted work relationships, utilitarians often conclude (with Shakespeare) that "in trying to better, oft we mar what's well."

A Justice Analysis of Restructuring Projects

While organization theory gives voice to a Marxist element, its dominant paradigm mutes most justice concerns. Yet, restructuring projects create benefits and burdens that are not always distributed in a just fashion. Of particular concern is that restructuring decisions are usually made by the top management "elite" of an organization (Daft, 1978). That "elites" reserve restructuring to themselves constitutes a *prima facie* case for a blanket indictment of injustice against restructuring projects, and this needs to be taken seriously by organizational designers and their advisers. One resolution to this problem lies in an application of professional ethics. If the designers of restructuring projects abide by professional standards of diligence, disinterestedness, and disclosure, this can be taken as a measure of "good faith" that they are discharging their authority to restructure ethically (Moberg, 1994).

Nevertheless, it is not uncommon to hear cries of injustice about particular restructuring projects from groups that have historically been under-represented in work organizations in general, or the focal organization in particular. Restructuring projects that do not grant authority to members of groups that have historically been granted little authority are especially suspect according to commonly accepted canons of distributive justice.

A just restructuring must also meet the standards of procedural justice. Attention here should focus on notification, due process, and restitution regarding those immediately affected by the restructuring. When a corporation eliminates a division, the employees should receive advance notice, have an opportunity to be heard on the issue, and be given restitution should it create an unjust outcome (Pompa, 1992). Similarly, customers of a public utility deserve procedural protections from restructuring decisions that are precipitous, unilateral, and indifferent to their needs.

A Rights/Duties Analysis of Restructuring Projects

Rights claims may be advanced by parties affected by particular restructuring projects. Claims that particular restructuring projects trample the entitlements of employees, customers, suppliers, and other claimant groups are not extraordinary. Employees might contend that a provision of a restructuring that requires proof of residence as a condition of employment is a violation of a right of freedom of association, privacy, or physical movement. Similarly, suppliers might object to a provision of restructuring that requires them to disclose confidential information as a condition of being paid for services rendered.

Those who design restructuring projects must respect widely accepted standards of individual entitlements. The Bill of Rights and the UN Declaration of Human Rights are good starting-points. More arcane but nonetheless crucial is Kant's Categorical Imperative that defines a standard of respect for individuals that is fundamental in American values (*see* KANTIAN ETHICS). This standard holds that no one should *use* another for his/her ends *only*, in short an admonition against approaching human relationships as exclusively instrumental. Clearly, the literature that contends that restructuring requires neutralizing the resistors (Kotter & Schlesinger, 1979) through co-optation or manipulation is ethically questionable on the most fundamental grounds.

Rights and duties are created when parties make promises to one another about their future dealings. Relations with organizations leave such promises open-ended, allowing them to "flow" as situations change. Restructuring almost always requires a revision of these promises. Whether these revisions are part of the *necessary* or *expected* flow of dealing with organizations is critical to determining whether duties have been abrogated or rights defiled. Take the case of a long-term employee who trusts that her employer will employ her until she retires in six months. A restructuring that ends her employment before she expects will create a betrayal, but if such a restructuring was found to be unnecessary, the betrayal would be immoral as well. Similar cases might arise

among any parties with established relationships with an organization that is undergoing a restructuring.

A Caring Approach to Restructuring Projects

Within this view, relationships have intrinsic rather than instrumental value, and one ought to intervene only to enrich their quality. It is clear that restructuring projects consonant with a value on caring make work relationships more primary (e.g., smaller units), more familiar (e.g. more systems devoted to selection and indoctrination), and less stratified (e.g., more decentralized; fewer levels of authority). Moreover, caring implies a protective stance toward community. Disturbing an organizational community without a very significant cause is considered antithetical to these aims. At the same time, caring has less to do with structures in general than it does with emergent relationships, so one finds this approach less robust than the others in informing how particular restructuring projects should be designed or enacted.

See also **caring organization; change; ethical issues in organizational theory; justice; power; Smith, Adam; trust**

Bibliography

Cavanagh, G., Moberg, D. & Velasquez, M. (1995). Making ethics practical. *Business Ethics Quarterly*, **5** (3), 399–418.

Child, J. (1984). *Organization*. London: Harper & Row.

Daft, R. (1978). A dual-core model of organizational innovation. *Academy of Management Journal*, **21**, 193–210.

DiMaggio, P. & Powell, W. (1983). The iron cage revisited. *American Sociological Review*, **48**, 147–60.

Kotter, J. & Schlesinger, L. (1979). Choosing strategies for change. *Harvard Business Review*, **57**, 106–14.

Moberg, D. (1994). An ethical analysis of hierarchic relations in organizations. *Business Ethics Quarterly*, **4**, 205–20.

Pompa, V. (1992). Managerial secrecy. *Journal of Business Ethics*, **11**, 147–56.

DENNIS J. MOBERG

RIGHT TO INFORMATION

revolving door a commonly used metaphor that represents the fluid and continuous movement of individuals in and out of organizations. Imagine a steady stream of people from two directions passing through a spinning door. Their entrance as well as their exit is easy, quick, and relatively unencumbered; individuals are constantly in motion passing through. But, because hiring, training, and retraining individuals is costly, a constant revolving door of personnel has serious financial implications.

Revolving doors can exist in different ways for different reasons. Specific jobs or positions can become known as places where individuals quickly come and go; alternatively, the culture of an organization can come to be known as one where the tenure of people within the company is short. For example, a number of companies have jobs that become known as "stepping stones" within an organization. These are positions through which people rotate on their way somewhere else. One is never expected to remain long; one rarely sees the consequences of actions initiated. At the organizational level, companies can become known as "revolving-door" cultures. These are companies who expect (consciously or unconsciously) that employees will remain for short periods of time and then move on. These companies are extremely demanding of people's time and energies, workloads are heavy, and the atmosphere intense. Such a company may have an unintended (or intended) philosophy of people as expendable resources: use them as long and as hard as one can, then hire another to begin the cycle again.

The revolving-door phenomenon can have ethical implications for companies and for the individuals who work in them. For companies, as individuals pass through their doors quickly, so can company secrets, client data, and other proprietary information. Companies as a result often go to great lengths to protect that data. It is not uncommon for employees, especially high-level executives, when leaving or being asked to leave, to do so immediately and under guard or to be asked to sign an agreement limiting industry access. At the individual level, the "revolving door" may represent a constant supply of fresh talent for a company, but at the expense of perhaps unwitting but eager employ-

ees, who believe they are being hired into a position of promise.

Bibliography

Arthur, M., Hall, D. & Lawrence, B. (eds). (1989). *Handbook of Career Theory*. New York: Cambridge University Press.

Feldman, D. (1989). Careers in organizations: Recent trends and future directions. *Journal of Management*, 15, 135–56.

Hall, D. T. (1976). *Careers in Organizations*. Pacific Palisades, Calif.: Goodyear.

Schien, E. (1978). *Career Dynamics: Matching Individuals and Organizational Needs*. Reading, Mass.: Addison-Wesley.

LYNN A. ISABELLA

right to information The right to information involves access to information that is necessary for the effective discharge of stakeholders' duties. Stakeholders are entitled to information that permits them to function in roles defined by society or by agreement with others who have a mutual interest in outcomes affected by stakeholder actions. Information is power; it may be used in controlling others or empowering them. To the degree that the free flow of information is restricted by certain stakeholders, the potential for ethical violations of other stakeholders' rights will tend to increase (*see* STAKEHOLDER THEORY).

Information has become a "currency" for exchange between the organization and its stakeholders. As such, a central issue concerning the right to information is ensuring that an equitable balance is struck among parties in the information exchange process. Though moral and legal principles can be used to help in such determinations, the subjectivity involved in various stakeholders' perspectives precludes finding clear *a priori* boundaries between the right to know and the right to privacy. The following is an overview of the information rights of key organization stakeholders. It is based on the idea that stakeholder rights are important if organizations are to function effectively.

Employee as Stakeholder

Employees should have access to information that is needed to function effectively in their organizational roles. Because of salary- and career-related factors, employees have an interest in performing at a satisfactory or greater level. Insufficient access to job-relevant information may unfairly inhibit job performance.

Performance, personnel, and other career-relevant data that are maintained as part of employees' permanent records (excluding some information involving other parties' confidentiality) should be open to inspection. When personnel decisions are made about employees, they should have adequate access to information that helped shape the decision. Employees who are demoted, transferred, or terminated have a right to know why such action was taken.

Maintaining PRIVACY safeguards requires that employees be informed of monitoring efforts by the organization. Employees should also be informed of how personal information that may be collected by the organization will be kept confidential.

Employers also have certain information rights in the context of the employee–employer relationship. In general, employers are entitled to information pertinent to gainful organizational interests. Information employees possess that could affect organizational competitiveness should be communicated. Assuming it has been acquired ethically, information about competitors or unsolicited ideas from outsiders should also be communicated to the employer.

Organizations have the right to information concerning employees' acquisition of conflicting or competing interests. This right may also apply in cases where employees' immediate family members are involved in addition to or instead of the employees themselves. If employees have or have been asked to engage in behavior that violates organizational ethics codes, organizations are entitled to information bearing on the behavior. Given proper respect of employees' privacy rights, organizations have the right to information about unsafe employee behavior (e.g., drug use) in safety-sensitive jobs. They also may monitor workplace behavior where employees are informed and monitoring protects the organization's property and trade (see ORGANIZATION ETHICS).

Consumer as Stakeholder

Consumers have the right to be truthfully and accurately informed of a product's or service's content and purpose. This allows consumers to make rational choices among products. Advertising is a principal means of providing consumers with product information. Though advertisements may be designed to influence and persuade, the information communicated by them to consumers should accomplish this end in a manner that does not deceive, conceal, or withhold the truth (see ADVERTISING ETHICS).

Any information about potential safety defects or health hazards should be disclosed in such a way that is readily understood by the consumer. Organizations should inform consumers about means of registering valid complaints, and about procedures to be followed for obtaining compensation for faulty products.

Shareholders and Other Stakeholders

Organization shareholders have a right to information about financial and other related information (e.g., pending lawsuits). They should expect the organization to provide them with reports of how well it has followed the law and protected shareholder investments. Other stakeholders having various information rights with respect to the organization may be identified through stakeholder analysis. Unions, suppliers, trade associations, political and advocate groups, the media, and the general public among other entities comprise the potential stakeholder pool. The legitimate information rights of various stakeholder groups should be determined when such groups are identified.

Information Rights and the Law

There are many laws governing information access in organizations. For example, a partial listing of the US laws pertinent to employee stakeholders could consist of the following: Freedom of Information Act, Fair Credit Reporting Act of 1971, Worker Adjustment and Retraining Notification Act of 1988, Polygraph Protection Act of 1988, and ERISA. When identifying stakeholder groups, an organization should be attentive to legal responsibilities they have regarding information availability. Not all rights will be addressed by law; however, applicable laws can help define where organizations can begin the process of meeting the information rights of its stakeholders.

Organizations must continually adapt to the environments in which they operate. In the "information age," an important part of this process necessarily includes addressing stakeholder rights to information. Interconnections through various electronic media will likely increase the scope of information demands on organizations. Given this circumstance, information rights and access will likely expand as an area of focus within the field of business ethics.

See also **ethical issues in information**

Bibliography

Weiss, J. W. (1994). *Business Ethics.* Belmont, Calif.: Wadsworth.

KEVIN W. MOSSHOLDER

right to work   The United Nations *Universal Declaration of Human Rights* (1948) declares a right to work: "Everyone has the right to work, to free choice of employment, to just and favourable conditions of work and to protection against unemployment." An effectively implemented right to work would guarantee the availability of remunerative productive activity.

Is it morally imperative to provide work to people who are unemployed? This is the question posed by the idea of a right to work. There are, however, two other ways in which the phrase "right to work" is used. Sometimes this phrase is used to refer to the freedom to choose and refuse employment, the freedom from forced labor. This freedom is an important human right, and is widely recognized as such. The phrase "right to work" is also sometimes used to refer to freedom from compulsory union membership.

There are proven measures available to ameliorate the problem of unemployment. Free public schools allow each person to prepare for participation in the economy. Work programs for young people that combine work experience and job training can be created. Tax and other incentives to hire more people can be given to industries. Economic policies designed to run the economy at a rapid rate can be adopted. Protection can be provided to the temporarily unemployed through universal unemployment insurance. And government

can become the employer of last resort, guaranteeing a job to every person who is able to work, wants a job, and has been unable to find one. It is unlikely that a right to work can be fully implemented without government becoming the employer of last resort.

Why would anyone think that access to productive employment is something that is, or ought to be, a matter of right? The recognition of rights is often spurred by the recognition of serious problems, and unemployment has been an extremely serious problem for contemporary societies. Unemployment in the range of 5 to 15 percent is not uncommon, and unemployment among youths and minorities is often much higher. For most people inescapable unemployment has very bad consequences. It deprives them of what is usually the most important source of income; it denies them the opportunities for self-development that employment provides, and it makes unavailable one of the main areas in which they can gain respect from self and others. Extended involuntary unemployment typically stigmatizes its victims. The longer unemployment lasts, the worse its consequences tend to be (Kelvin & Jarrett, 1985).

To put the case positively, access to employment is extremely important because remunerative work provides the most prevalent, reliable, and acceptable means of providing for one's survival, flourishing, and self-respect. Non-financial benefits include the satisfaction of self-sufficiency; the satisfaction of doing a task skillfully; friendly relations with one's co-workers; producing goods or services that benefit society; and escaping from unwanted freedom due to the fact that one's job schedule structures one's activities and time (Arneson, 1990).

An argument based on the claim that work is one of the most important areas for gaining self-respect and the respect of others is usually used by advocates of the right to work. Although abilities and dedication can be demonstrated in areas other than employment (for example, in games or volunteer work), it is in the performance of useful activities carrying monetary rewards that self-esteem and respect for others are most likely to be created and maintained.

Another argument for guaranteed access to employment suggests that a system of private property cannot pass tests of fairness if it consigns many people to inescapable unemployment. If unemployed people find that current economic arrangements allow them neither to appropriate property that will support their lives and liberty (because all valuable property is already owned by individuals or the state) nor to find paid employment, these economic arrangements are unfair because they deny to some the means of survival, respect, and self-development, while providing access to those means to others who lack stronger claims.

One may be receptive to people's claim to assistance in meeting their vital needs while rejecting the right to work. It may be argued that guaranteeing people a minimum income will be less expensive and produce less inefficiency and corruption than guaranteeing them jobs. Economists generally prefer distributions of money or vouchers to in-kind provision because this allows for more efficient use of resources by the recipient (see Thurow, 1976, for a critical assessment of this preference). But a person with a minimum income who wants a job will find it very difficult to buy one, and voters may find public provision of employment more palatable than income grants. Arneson sees an advantage in providing minimum-wage jobs rather than income grants because doing this will benefit those members of the unemployed who are most needy while excluding "non-needy bohemians" (Arneson, 1990).

Jon Elster objects to a politically implemented right to work on the grounds that it is self-defeating to create a right to work for the purpose of promoting self-respect (Elster, 1988). To engender self-respect work must result in the production of a good or service that is considered valuable. A right to government jobs that were visibly supported by heavy subsidies and that produced few social benefits would do little to promote self-respect. (See Arneson, 1990, for a criticism of this argument.)

Bibliography

Arneson, R. (1990). Is work special? Justice and the distribution of employment. *American Political Science Review*, **84**, 1127–47.

Elster, J. (1988). Is there (or should there be) a right to work? In Amy Gutmann (ed.), *Democracy and the Welfare State*. Princeton: Princeton University Press.

Ginsburg, H. (1983). *Full Employment and Public Policy: The United States and Sweden*. Lexington, Mass.: Lexington Books.

Kelvin, P., & Jarrett, J. (1985). *Unemployment: Its Social Psychological Effects*. New York: Cambridge University Press.

Nickel, J. (1978). Is there a human right to employment? *The Philosophical Forum*, **10**, 149–70.

Nickel, J. (1987). *Making sense of human rights*. Berkeley: University of California Press.

Thurow, L. (1976). Government expenditures: Cash or in-kind aid? *Philosophy and Public Affairs*, **5**, 361–81.

JAMES W. NICKEL

rights   The claiming of rights is one of the strongest ways of demanding protection of persons' interests. At the same time, many aspects of the appeal to rights are intensely controversial. The controversies bear not only on the normative and substantive issues of who has rights to what, but also on basic conceptual issues.

Hohfeld's Distinctions

The standard starting point for dealing with the conceptual issues is Wesley N. Hohfeld (1879–1918), who saw that the phrase "a right" was used with different meanings in the legal literature. To avoid the resulting confusion, he distinguished four meanings of this phrase. First, if A has a *claim-right* to X against B, then B has a correlative *duty* to A to refrain from interfering with A's having or doing X, or, in some situations, a duty to give X to A or to help A to have or do X. Thus, A has a claim-right to life against B and all other persons in that they have a correlative duty to refrain from taking A's life; and if B promised to meet A at the bookstore at noon, then A has a claim-right against B that B meet him there and then, and B has a correlative duty to meet A as promised.

Second, if A has a *liberty-right* (or *privilege*) to X against B, then B has a correlative *no-right* (i.e., no claim-right) that A not do X. Hence A has no duty to refrain from doing X; but also, in contrast to the case of claim-rights, B has no duty to refrain from interfering with A's doing X. Thus, if A and B simultaneously engage in a footrace, each has a liberty-right to win the race if he can – neither has a duty to refrain from winning it – and each has no right that the other not win. The liberty-right is hence the opposite of a duty, just as the no-right is the opposite of a claim-right.

Third, if *A* has a *power* (or *power-right*) to *X* with regard to *B*, then *A* is in a legal or other justified position to effect a change in some relevant status of *B*, and *B* has a correlative *liability* to undergo this change. Thus a religious official has a power-right to perform a marriage ceremony between a man and a woman, so that their legal status is changed from being unmarried to being married to each other.

Fourth, if *A* has an *immunity* (or *immunity-right*) to *X* against *B*, then *A* is free or exempt from *B*'s legal or other justified power or control with regard to *X*, and *B* is under a correlative *disability* to affect the legal or other relevant status of *A*. Thus, *A* has an immunity to being forced to testify against himself in a criminal case, and the state has a correlative disability to force him to testify. The immunity is the opposite of a liability, and the disability is the opposite of a power (power-right).

These distinctions clarify many of the diverse usages of the phrase "a right"; but they also leave many conceptual problems unresolved. For example, what do all these types of "rights" have in common? Hohfeld said they are all "legal advantages"; but this is vague.

The Elements of Claim-Rights

Despite the possible interconnections between Hohfeld's types, it is generally agreed that claim-rights are the most important kind of rights, especially because of their stringency as entailing strict duties to forbear or assist. The general structure of a claim-right is given by the following formula: *A* has a right to *X* against *B* by virtue of *Y*.

There are five main elements here: first, the *subject (A)*, of the right, the right-holder; second, the *nature* of the right, what being a right consists in or what it means for someone to have a right; third, the *object (X)* of the right, what it is a right to; fourth, the *respondent (B)* of the right, the duty-bearer, the person or group

that has the correlative duty; and fifth, the *justifying ground (Y)* of the right.

The Problem of Redundancy

This formula with its elements helps to elucidate some of the chief conceptual problems that have been raised about rights. One is the problem of redundancy, which takes two forms. The first form concerns the relation between the subject's rights and the respondent's duties. Since rights and duties are correlative, this is taken to mean that the right of *A* against *B* is the "same relation" as (or, as Hohfeld said, is "equivalent" to) the duty of *B* to *A*. But if they are the "same relation," then isn't one of them redundant?

A main answer is that claim-rights and strict duties have objects that differ in valuational content. Rights are justified claims to certain benefits, the support or protection of certain interests of the subject or right-holder. Duties, on the other hand, are justified burdens on the part of the respondent or duty-bearer: they restrict his freedom by requiring that he conduct himself in ways that directly benefit not himself but rather the right-holder. But burdens are for the sake of benefits, and not conversely. Hence duties, which are burdens, are for the sake of rights, whose objects are benefits, so that rights are the justifying reasons for duties. Thus, rights and duties are distinct, and neither is redundant.

In opposition to this answer, it is sometimes contended that the objects of rights are not always benefits to the right-holder. Examples are the right to smoke excessively and the right to have a promise to oneself kept that will benefit not oneself but only some third party. There are at least three replies: (a) The right to smoke and to engage in other self-harming actions may be taken as species of the right to freedom, which is in general a good to the right-holder. Thus the objects of rights are general goods for the right-holder, even if all their specific varieties may not be good for her. (b) Rights would not be *claimed* unless the claimant *thought* there was some value in her having the object of the right. (c) In the case of third-party beneficiaries, the person to whom a promise is made also has an interest in the promise's being kept, so that to this extent she too derives benefit from it.

These considerations lead to a second form of the problem of redundancy. In the formula given above, the object (X) of the right – the object consisting in certain benefits or interests – seems to do most or all of the work for which the right is invoked, so that the concept of rights is again declared to be redundant. For if what is so important about rights is the support or protection of certain benefits or interests, then why isn't such protection sufficient; why do we also need rights to these interests?

There are several more answers. All involve that rights, especially when they are moral, provide certain indispensable normative additions to simply having or being protected in certain interests or benefits. To begin with, A's having a moral right to X adds to his having X or his being protected in having X the important qualification that there is strong justification both for his having X and for his being protected in having X. This justification, moreover, is of a special sort, in that, when A has a right to X, this means that he is personally entitled to have X as his due, as what belongs personally to him, so that it is normatively necessary that A be protected in having or doing X.

Rights as Normatively Necessary Personal Entitlements

These aspects of personal entitlement and normative necessity bear on three specific relations among the elements of rights distinguished above. First, rights are normatively necessary in the relation between the subject and the object, in that the subject has personal property in, and thus justified personal control over, the object, so that it is personally owed to him as his due and for his own sake, not because it adds to overall utility. Second, rights are also normatively necessary in the relation between the subject and the respondent, in that the former is in a position to make a justified personal claim or demand, not merely a request or a plea, against the latter for the support or protection of his having the object of his right. In this way the respondent has duties that are personally owed to the subject. Third, rights are normatively necessary in the relation between the subject and the object, on the one hand, and the justifying ground, on the other, in that this ground supplies the warrant or title, and thus the necessitating premise, for the object's being personally owed to the subject and hence for the requirement that the subject have, and be protected in having, the object to which he has a right. In view of these stringent aspects of normative necessity, the question arises whether rights can ever be overridden. This will be discussed below.

The Nature of Rights

These three diverse relations between the subject, on the one hand, and the respondent, the object, and the justifying ground, on the other, also have a direct bearing on the conceptual question of the nature of a right. Two different theories focus on different elements in the structure of a right given above. The "benefit theory" emphasizes the relation between the subject and the object of rights. Since the object consists in certain benefits or interests of the subject, the benefit theory holds that for a person to have a right is for him to be the directly intended beneficiary of someone else's performance of a duty, or, in a further version, that some projected benefit or interest of his is a sufficient ground for other person's having duties. The "choice theory," on the other hand, emphasizes the relation between the subject and the respondent of rights. The theory holds that to have a right is to be in a justified position to determine by one's choice how other persons (the respondents) shall act.

Each theory is plausible, but each also incurs difficulties. It has been held that the choice theory does not explain how children and mentally deficient persons may have rights; but this could be taken care of by the consideration that such persons can be represented by other persons who make claims for them. Another, perhaps more serious difficulty for the choice theory is that it implies that subjects may waive their rights; but some rights, such as those provided by the criminal law or by welfare legislation, cannot be waived. On the other hand, it seems to follow from the benefit theory, unlike the choice theory, that animals have rights, since they have certain interests and thus are capable of being benefited. Some thinkers have endorsed this conclusion, and have used it to reject the choice theory. At the same time, however, the choice theory has the distinct advantage that it views the right-holder as an active claimant on her own behalf, and thus as having an indispensable element of autonomy and dignity, in contrast to the passive recipience that the benefit theory seems to attribute to right-holders. This defect of the benefit theory can, however, be substantially remedied if it can be shown that a full justification of the theory involves that all morally justified rights have, as their most general objects, the fulfillment and support for each right-holder of the necessary conditions of action and of generally successful action. This will be further discussed below. It seems, then, that despite the possible divergences of the benefit and choice theories, the most acceptable account of the nature of rights must involve some combination of the two theories that incorporates the strong points of each while omitting its negative features.

The Nature of Moral Rights

The justifying ground of legal rights consists in the statutes and other provisions of positive municipal law. But it is also often said that persons have certain rights even if these are not recognized or enforced by positive laws, such as when it is asserted that slaves have a right to be free. In such cases the having in question, like the rights themselves, is moral, not legal.

There are two different views on the nature or existence of moral rights. On one view, for such rights to exist means that, while they fulfill certain moral criteria, they are embodied in positive laws or other social rules. On another view, moral rights exist or are had even when they are not so embodied; it is sufficient that they fulfill or derive from justified moral principles or other morally relevant considerations. Against this latter view it is objected that because of the diversity and conflicts of moral principles, there would be no way of definitively determining whether anyone has moral rights, in contrast to the determinate answers provided by positive laws. This point is often adduced in criticism of the undisciplined proliferation of rights-claims that are invoked by various protagonists in political and legal controversies. But against the former, positivist view it is objected not only that it incurs the same difficulty of ascertainment when it seeks to evaluate positive laws by moral criteria, but also that it makes unintelligible the recognized practice of appealing to rights even when they are not embodied in positive laws or ongoing social rules, and even in opposition to such laws and rules. Against the specifically legal positivist view it is further objected that it does not provide for those moral rights which, by general agreement, are not and should not be embodied in positive laws, such as the rights, in ordinary interpersonal relations, not to be lied to and not to be subjected to broken promises, as well as the rights of children to receive loving care from their parents.

The Justifying Ground of Moral Rights

To ask who has what moral rights to what is to ask a normative and substantive question, not only a conceptual one, although conceptual considerations also figure in the answers one gives. If for moral rights to exist, they must be justified by sound moral principles or other morally relevant grounds, where do we look for such principles or grounds? An important emphasis has been that human beings have interests. But not all interests generate rights. In view of the normative necessity involved in rights, it would seem that the interests that ground them must also involve necessity. Such necessity could be obtained if the interests consisted not in contingent, dispensable desires or goods, but rather in the goods that are necessary for human action or for having general chances of success in achieving one's purposes by action.

For such a general grounding of general moral rights to be successful, the necessary conditions of actions and of generally successful action would have to be carefully specified. The two main such conditions are freedom and well-being. Freedom is the procedural necessary condition of action; it consists in controlling one's behavior by one's own unforced choice while having knowledge of relevant circumstances. Well-being is the substantive necessary condition of action; it consists in having the general abilities and conditions needed for achieving one's purposes. Since the agency-needs that are here called "necessary" pertain not only to bare action but also to generally successful action, the necessity in question can accommodate the varying degrees in which practical abilities and conditions are needed for action. Thus, well-being falls into a hierarchy of goods ranging from life and physical integrity to education and opportunities for acquiring wealth and income. According to the general substantive theory here sketched, all actual or prospective agents have equal moral rights to freedom and well-being, and their having these rights is grounded in their enduring needs for the necessary conditions of their action and generally successful action. An argument can be given for the moral principle that grounds this thesis.

Moral Rights as Solely Negative

According to one libertarian view, all moral rights are negative: they set absolute "side constraints" on actions in that their correlative duties require refraining from actions that interfere with persons' freedom. A difficulty with this view is that it cannot handle conflicts of rights. Suppose A is going to murder B, and the only way to prevent this is for C to steal the car of D, who is entirely innocent in relation to A's murder-project. Here the absolute rights not to be murdered and not to be stolen from come into unresolvable conflict.

To deal with such cases, it has been suggested that rights construed as side constraints should be supplemented by "consequential analysis" that trades off the lesser badness of infringing one right by the greater badness of infringing another. A related suggestion is the general idea presented above that rights fall into a hierarchy according to the degree of their objects' needfulness for action, so that the right not to be stolen from is overridden by the right not to be murdered when these rights are in conflict.

Such a procedure has been called a "utilitarianism of rights." But this phrase is misleading if it implies a constant readiness to interfere with rights for the sake of regularly achieving some sort of weighted minimization of rights-violations. A "utilitarian" approach of this sort is different from considerations that are restricted to wide disparities in degrees of importance between the interests that are the objects of the respective rights, as in the above example

What, however, of situations where the rights that are in conflict have objects that are of the same degree of importance? A recurrently adduced example is the one in which a casual bystander can save ten innocent persons from being murdered only if he murders one of the persons himself. It has been suggested that, since the function of rights is to protect justified personal interests, and since the interests in this example are on a par, the rights-theorist must seriously consider participating in this abominable project.

The rejections of such participation can, however, be justified on grounds of rights. For the rights to life of the nine other innocent persons do not extend to the right to life of the tenth person. In general, if a person has a right to X, then he has a right to anything else Y that may be necessary for his having X, *unless* someone else already has a right to Y and Y is as important for action as is X. For example, if Jones is starving and cannot obtain food by his own efforts, while Smith has abundant food, then Jones's right to life overrides Smith's property right in the food, so that Jones has a right to as much of Smith's food as he needs in order to prevent starvation. But if Smith has only enough food to prevent his own starvation, then Jones does not have a right to it because Smith's not starving is as important for his action as Jones's not starving is for his. It is for such a reason that the nine other innocent persons do not have a right that the tenth person be murdered in order to prevent their being murdered. Hence, if the casual bystander were to murder the tenth person, he would be violating that person's right to life, while if he were to refrain from the murder, he would not be violating the others' rights to life, since they do not have a right that the tenth person be murdered in order to prevent their murder.

Positive Rights

A second view of the contents of moral rights is that they are positive as well as negative. If the ultimate justifying ground of rights is the needs of agency, including well-being, then positive welfare rights are justified when persons cannot fulfill their needs of well-being by their own efforts so that positive assistance by other persons is required, in cases ranging from relief of starvation to provision of educational resources. As in the case of negative rights, the application of the positive-rights model requires consideration of degrees of needfulness for action, so that, for example, taxation that removes a relatively small part of affluent persons' wealth is justified, and is not a violation of the taxed persons' rights, if this is needed in order to prevent other persons' starvation or to provide opportunities for education. More than in the exclusively negative theory of rights, the positive theory requires recourse to institutional, especially state, provision for various rights, as against leaving such provision solely to individual initiative. Thus on this view moral rights are social and economic as well as political and civil.

Utilitarianism and Rights

Utilitarianism raises two kinds of questions for theories of rights. One is whether it can "accommodate" rights, i.e., whether the requirements of rights can be justified by the utilitarian principle that the rightness of actions is to be determined by consequentialist considerations about the maximizing of total or average utility. It has been contended that utilitarianism can require that special protection be provided for the special interests and needs that are the objects of rights. A chief reply to this thesis is that, since the aim of utilitarianism is ultimately aggregative, to maximize utility, the distributive protections provided by even the most important rights would be at best only contingently maintained, since the rights could be overridden whenever the maximization of utility required this.

A second question about the relation of utility to rights goes in the reverse direction. Even if utilitarianism cannot adequately accommodate rights, is this always a fault? Isn't it also true that rights cannot accommodate utilitarianism, in that the insistence on individual rights may block the fulfillment of important communal goals? This question underlies the charge, which goes back at least to JEREMY BENTHAM (1748–1831) and KARL MARX (1818–83), that rights are egoistic because they involve claims for the fulfillment of individual interests, so that they may operate to submerge the values of community or society.

Two replies can be given to this charge. The first relies on the thesis sketched above about the varying degrees of importance or needfulness of the objects of rights. Thus the theory of rights may allow for the exercise of eminent domain where an important community project like the building of a new public school requires that some persons be forced to give up their property rights in their houses at a certain location (with due compensation). But the theory cannot allow, for the reasons indicated above, that an innocent person be killed in order to prevent certain even severe harms from befalling the community as a whole.

A second reply is that human rights, which are universally distributed moral rights, require of each person that he act with due regard for other persons' interests as well as his own. For since, in principle, each person has human rights against all other persons, every other person also has these rights against him, so that he has correlative duties toward them. The concept of human rights thus entails a reciprocal universality: each person must respect the rights of all the others while having his rights respected by all the others, so that there must be a mutual sharing of the benefits of rights and the burdens of duties. The human rights thus involve mutuality of consideration and, thus, a kind of altruism rather than egoism. By requiring mutual aid where needed and practicable, the human rights make for social solidarity and a community of rights.

An earlier version of this entry appeared in Becker, L. C. & Becker, C. B. (eds) (1992). *Encyclopedia of Ethics.* New York: Garland.

Bibliography

Dworkin, R. (1977). *Taking Rights Seriously.* Cambridge, Mass.: Harvard University Press. (Rights as "trumps").

Feinberg, J. (1973). *Social Philosophy.* Englewood Cliffs, NJ: Prentice-Hall. (Analysis and conflict of rights).

Feinberg, J. (1980). *Rights, Justice, and the Bounds of Liberty.* Princeton, NJ: Princeton University Press. (Importance of rights; their relation to claims).

Finnis, J. (1980). *Natural Law and Natural Rights.* Oxford: Clarendon Press. (Rights account for the requirements of practical reasonableness).

Flathman, R. E. (1976). *The Practice of Rights.* Cambridge: Cambridge University Press. (Rights are adversarial; communitarian objections).

Gewirth, A. (1978). *Reason and Morality.* Chicago: University of Chicago Press. (Rights based on necessary conditions of action).

Gewirth, A. (1986). Why rights are indispensable. *Mind,* **95,** 329–44. (Answers conceptual and moral objections against rights).

Hohfeld, W. N. (1964 [1919]). *Fundamental Legal Conceptions as Applied in Judicial Reasoning.* New

Haven and London: Yale University Press. (Classic fourfold typology).

Lyons, D. (ed.). (1979). *Rights*. Belmont, Calif.: Wadsworth Publishing, 1979. (Good collection, including Lyons's "Rights, Claimants, and Beneficiaries" (58–77), which argues for the benefit theory).

Martin, R. & Nickel, J. W. (1980). Recent work on the concept of rights. *American Philosophical Quarterly*, 17, 165–80. (Extensive bibliography).

Melden, A. I. (1977). *Rights and Persons*. Berkeley and Los Angeles: University of California Press. (Rights based on personhood).

Sen, A. (1982). Rights and agency. *Philosophy and Public Affairs*, 11, 3–29. (Discusses "goal rights system" wherein the fulfillment or non-fulfillment of rights is included in the consequential evaluation of states of affairs).

Shue, H. (1980). *Basic Rights: Subsistence, Affluence, and US Foreign Policy*. Princeton, NJ: Princeton University Press. (Basic Rights include subsistence as well as security and liberty).

Sumner, L. (1987). *The Moral Foundation of Rights*. Oxford: Clarendon Press. (Argues against natural-law and contractualist theories of rights and for consequentialist theory).

Thomson, J. (1990). *The Realm of Rights*. Cambridge, Mass.: Harvard University Press. (Examines what rights are and which rights there are).

Tuck, R. (1979). *Natural Rights Theories: Their Origin and Development*. Cambridge: Cambridge University Press. (Histories of rights theories from twelfth to seventeenth centuries).

Waldron, J. (ed.). (1984). *Theories of Rights*. Oxford: Oxford University Press. (Good introduction and bibliography).

Wellman, C. (1985). *A Theory of Rights*. Totowa NJ: Rowman and Allanheld. (A right is a complex structure of legal positions having a central core).

Wolgast, E. H. (1980). *Equality and the Rights of Women*. Ithaca, NY: Cornell University Press. (Women's rights based not on egalitarian reasoning but on distinctiveness and interdependence).

ALAN GEWIRTH

risk *To be at risk*: To be subject to harm from some process or activity. The degree of risk is a function of the probability and severity of that harm. Given the multitude of ways in which people can be harmed, most people are at risk to some degree most of the time. In addition, since things other than people can be harmed – for example, property, animals, the natural environment – these things can also be described as being at risk from certain processes or activities.

Safety is defined in terms of risk. It is sometimes said that something is safe if it is free from risk, but nothing can be absolutely risk-free. Both risk and safety, therefore, come in degrees and involve decision problems as to whether something is too risky or safe enough. So a thing is thought to be safe only if its risks are judged to be acceptable, quite often by a person or group empowered to make that decision for a larger society.

In making a decision about safety, two necessary and distinct activities come into play: measuring risk and judging the acceptability of that risk. The measurement of risk involves an objective scientific assessment of the probabilities and consequences of events. A risk estimate can predict the likelihood that some event will happen, but is unable to pinpoint the occurrence of any specific harmful event.

Unlike the empirical activity of measuring risk, judging safety or the acceptability of risk is a normative activity. This brings up the question: Who makes the judgment that a certain risk is acceptable, and by what criteria? And since risk implies the probability of harm to persons, to say that a risk is acceptable implies that the justification for undertaking the risk, or not avoiding it, overrides the moral rule "do no harm." Thus, judgments about acceptable risk for persons are necessarily moral judgments, at least in part.

The remainder of this entry will concentrate on acceptable-risk decision criteria, and will sometimes use environmental risk for the purposes of illustration, although in the field of business ethics, product and workplace safety are equally important areas of risk assessment.

Two essential components of any plan to deal with risk problems are clarity about the goals the decision is intended to achieve and the means proposed to achieve them. But before this can be done by a corporation, for example, risk problems, such as those about pollution or hazardous waste, are other difficulties that need to be addressed.

The first difficulty is problem definition. If there is uncertainty about how to define the problem, there will be uncertainty about the goals and what would constitute solving the problem. It has been claimed that plant species are diminishing because of business activities such as logging and large-scale farming. Is this a risk problem, and if so, what kind of risk? What would count as a solution to the problem?

The second difficulty is disagreement about which facts are relevant to the problem. Is the loss of plant species a problem because of their possible use in healing, because such loss affects the ozone layer, or because the loss of plant variety is a bad thing in itself? How the risk problem is defined will have a major influence on which facts are taken to be relevant, and vice versa.

Finally, there often is a conflict of values, or even confusion about what values we hold or ought to hold. Many claim that the environment is intrinsically valuable. Others argue that it has value only because it serves human ends. Difficulty over values affects how we define the risk problem and how we identify relevant facts.

There are certain characteristics that any acceptable solution to a risk problem must possess – characteristics that are also helpful with problem definition, identification of facts, clarification of values, determination of goals and the means to those goals. The following criteria have been suggested for any acceptable judgment about a risk problem. Unacceptable decisions fail to meet one or more of the criteria. A proposed solution to an environmental risk problem is acceptable only if it is:

1. Politically implementable: proposed solutions that do not take account of the political situation are not realistic.
2. Economically feasible: if the plan places unreasonable burdens on corporate productivity and profitability, it will destroy the base from which successful action is possible.
3. Legally defensible: there is a fundamental obligation to obey the law, except in extreme situations; law is necessary for social order and constructive action.
4. Technically plausible: if the technical means to accomplish the solution are not available or if they are excessively problematic, then any proposed solution becomes pure speculation.

5. Environmentally manageable: the proposed solution should be one that does not result in catastrophic or irreversible harm to the environment.
6. Ethically responsible: a decision to a risk problem is ethically responsible only if:
a) It poses no unreasonable threat to human life or health. People should not be exposed to foolish risks – those with goals that are unworthy of the potential harm. To act negligently is to act so as to cause harm by taking unreasonable risk.
b) It fairly distributes benefits and burdens. No solution is ethically acceptable, for example, if it allocates all benefits to some, and all burdens to others, or if it treats people unequally.
c) It neither unjustifiably violates moral rights nor unjustifiably forces a dereliction of moral duties. A moral right can justifiably be set aside only by other, more stringent moral rights.
d) It gives due consideration to the values and interests of all those affected. It will often be necessary to act against the values and interests of some, but only after serious consideration is given to every possible way to accommodate them.
e) It provides compensation in the event of unexpected or excessive harm. Victims must not be expected to bear such harm with no prospect of reparation.
f) It is voluntarily accepted, to the extent possible, by those affected, or, at least, those affected are given a fair opportunity to participate in the decision-making process. The only exceptions are where people voluntarily give up the opportunity to participate.
g) It treats persons not merely as means to some goal, but as ends in themselves. All human beings must be treated with dignity and respect and not as simply tools for others to use.

Bibliography

Fischhoff, B., Lichtenstein, S., Slovic, P., Derby, S. L. & Keeney, R. L. (1981). *Acceptable Risk*. New York: Cambridge University Press.

Frederick, R. E. & Hoffman, W. M. (1990). The individual investor in securities markets: An ethical analysis. *Journal of Business Ethics*, **9**, 579–89.

Frederick, R. E. & Hoffman, W. M. (1994). Environmental risk problems and the language of ethics. *Business Ethics Quarterly*, **5**, 699–711.

Fried, C. (1987). Imposing risks upon others. In G. Sher (ed.), *Moral Philosophy: Selected Readings*. San Diego: Harcourt, 699–710.

Hoffman, W. M. (1984). The Ford Pinto. In W. M. Hoffman & J. M. Moore (eds), *Business Ethics: Readings and Cases in Corporate Morality*. New York: McGraw-Hill, 585–92.

Hoffman, W. M. & Fisher, J. V. (1984). Corporate responsibility: Property and liability. In Hoffman & J. M. Moore (eds), *Business Ethics: Readings and Cases in Corporate Morality*. New York: McGraw-Hill, 176–82.

Lowrance, W. W. (1976). *Of Acceptable Risk*. Los Altos, Calif.: William Kauffman.

Mayo, D. G. & Hollander, R. D. (eds). (1991). *Acceptable Evidence: Science and Values in Risk Management*. New York: Oxford University Press.

Shrader-Frechette, K. S. (1991). *Risk and Rationality*. Berkeley: University of California Press.

W. MICHAEL HOFFMAN

roles and role morality Roles are positions in business or the professions to which different social functions attach; role morality is the assumption of different normative ethical systems for different roles. The central issue here is whether different social roles require distinct norms or moral frameworks to guide their behavior. For there to be truly distinct role moralities, it is not sufficient that those in different social roles or professions enter into unique relations with others. All social roles involve relations that uniquely define them to be the roles they are. Instead, moral considerations that arise elsewhere must be weighed differently, must be systematically augmented or diminished in their weight, against opposing considerations in proper moral deliberations in these social contexts. An occupant of the role, for example a lawyer or business manager, must be called upon to ignore certain moral rights, or certain utilities or disutilities, that would otherwise be morally decisive.

Often such special norms reflect some value central to the definition of the social role in question, and the norm gives that value extra weight for the occupant of the role. Lawyers are called upon to ignore the interests of third parties in zealously pursuing the legal objectives of their clients within the bounds of law. Journalists routinely ignore what others might properly perceive as rights to privacy in developing news stories for their reading publics. In business, the central values lie in efficient use of resources in providing desired goods to the consuming public and in providing stockholders a good return on their investments. Thus, some have argued (e.g. Friedman, 1979) that business managers ought not to forgo profit (which measures efficiency and provides returns) on perceived moral grounds.

From the point of view of moral theory, however, the basic question is how such special norms can be morally acceptable, how the concept of distinct role moralities is even coherent. From the point of view of a rights based or individualist moral theory, it seems that we can override moral rights only for the sake of protecting more central or important rights in the context in question. Otherwise, rights must be voluntarily waived or previously forfeited by wrongdoing in order to be safely ignored. This fundamental demand of the moral framework seems to hold in all social contexts. From the point of view of a utilitarian or collectivist moral theory, it seems that we can impose costs or forgo benefits only to prevent greater harm or realize greater collective good, and once more this constraint appears to govern all contexts to which the theory applies. Thus, if business managers perceive that pursuit of maximal profit imposes serious harm on the public (say in decisions regarding product safety, waste disposal, or relocation), how can it be morally coherent to suggest that such pursuit is their proper role?

The answer is that such norms are at least possible, or coherent, given sufficient complexity in a moral framework. In a multi-leveled framework there can be a distinction between an agent's perception of a morally required course of action and her authority to act on that perception. This distinction exists in several moral theories, including Mill's (1955), and it rests on the fact of fallibility in moral perception and moral reasoning (*see* MILL, JOHN STUART). A major argument by defenders of adversarial legal systems to the conclusion that lawyers ought not to restrain their clients on extra-legal moral grounds is that their moral perceptions may be eccentric or incapable of objective justification. Similarly, if a business manager seeks to sacrifice style or raise prices in order to impose safer products on the public, despite market research that indicates contrary preferences, the result may be not what she predicts, but loss of market share to the competition.

In other cases the justification of special norms does not appeal to fallibility in gauging the consequences of actions considered one at a time, but instead to the results of every occupant of the social role reasoning directly from those consequences. Waste disposal provides a good example here. Each small business may reason correctly that the effect of its disposing of wastes in the cheapest way possible is negligible. But if all reason in the same way, the result can be disastrous to the health of the entire community. Here it seems that a special norm restricting the pursuit of maximum profit is in order. Norms governing other roles may be justified in the same way. A teacher should grade based only on quality of work submitted, even though the effect of taking other considerations into account in individual cases might be known to be utility maximizing. A journalist's passing up a single story because of qualms about privacy might not harm the public, but the cumulative effect of all journalists forgoing stories because of such qualms might be significant deprivation of information to the public. Such norms result in a consistency or uniformity in the behavior of role occupants beyond that achievable without them.

It can be argued that norms of the type just considered are either not special or not necessary. A Kantian will hold that moral reasoners must always think of everyone's acting in the way proposed (see KANTIAN ETHICS). But this test is not always relevant. Telling a lie in order to avoid a greater evil can be justified, even though if everyone lied in similar circumstances, the strategy might be useless and hence unjustified. It is permissible not to vote in a local election even though the result of no one's voting would be disastrous. The universalizing test is relevant only when many individuals would act in a cumulatively harmful way on the basis of (individually) correct consequentialist reasoning in the absence of special constraint. This criterion does apply to various social roles, as indicated above, generating special norms and hence role moralities.

It can be argued, as in the pollution example, that a business manager ought not to impose higher costs on his corporation unless these are required by law. The appeal here would be to a moral division of labor (between managers and legislators), and it would reinstate the profit principle as the sole fundamental norm for business. Those who defend special-role moralities often make such appeals, but they must be closely scrutinized. Any justification of special-role moralities, even if coherent, must be carefully criticized, given the sacrifice of normally important moral factors involved.

See also **professional ethics**

Bibliography

Bayles, M. (1989). *Professional Ethics.* Belmont, Calif.: Wadsworth, ch. 2.

Fried, C. (1978). *Right and Wrong.* Cambridge, Mass.: Harvard University Press, ch. 7.

Friedman, M. (1979). The social responsibility of business is to increase its profits. In T. Donaldson & P. H. Werhane (eds), *Ethical Issues in Business.* Englewood Cliffs, NJ: Prentice-Hall, 191–7.

Goldman, A. H. (1980). *The Moral Foundations of Professional Ethics.* Totowa, NJ: Rowman & Littlefield.

Kadish, M. R. & Kadish, S. H. (1973). *Discretion to Disobey.* Stanford, Calif.: Stanford University Press, chs 1, 2.

Mill, J. S. (1955). *On Liberty.* Chicago: Gateway.

Wasserstrom, R. (1975). Lawyers as professionals: Some moral issues. *Human Rights,* 5, 1–24.

ALAN H. GOLDMAN

Russia, business ethics in   *see* BUSINESS ETHICS IN RUSSIA

S

safety in the workplace *see* WORKER SAFETY

Securities and Exchange Commission The SEC was established as part of the Roosevelt administration's response to the crises of the 1929 depression. The Commission is primarily responsible for administration of the laws governing the purchase and sale of securities in interstate commerce and the operation of securities exchanges in the United States.

When the securities laws were originally debated, some argued that the SEC should evaluate each security offered for sale and express an opinion as to its safety. However, Congress was evidently concerned that the power implied in that judgment might be abused, and so the federal securities laws – and the activities of the SEC – require only that investee companies provide full disclosure of relevant facts. Caveat Emptor was retained as a bulwark of the market, but with the understanding that the buyer was entitled to full and fair information (Loss & Seligman, 1989, pp. 171–80).

Even with that conceptual limitation, the Commission has considerable power. It exercises its authority in two primary ways (Phillips & Zecher, 1981, p. 9):

1 by establishing standards for the DISCLOSURE documents which companies are required to file when they want their securities sold to the public, and
2 by initiating civil enforcement actions against companies and their officers, alleging either fraud or failure to comply with the laws and filing standards.

The Commission does not have authority to bring criminal charges, but may ask a civil court to bar individuals from acting as an officer of a publicly held company, and to assess fines and recover damages. More commonly, an enforcement action results in an injunction, which orders the defendant to comply with the law in the future, or an order to cease and desist from certain practices. The theory behind those apparently innocuous sanctions is that the financial community will be reluctant to do business with those who have been stigmatized by such a court order, and so the activities of those people will be circumscribed. That theory may work for those who stumble into trouble, but it appears to be less effective for those who intend to abuse the markets for their own benefit (see for example the front page article in the May 12, 1995 issue of the *Wall Street Journal*).

The SEC was established in part to correct abuses in the securities markets and in part to restore confidence in the market and thereby get the economy moving again. The dichotomy of that dual role – police chief/confidence builder – has plagued the Commission since its founding. It is apparent in the current controversy over the disclosures that should be required of foreign companies. Some foreign companies, especially from Germany, argue that because they comply with the disclosure requirements established by their own financial communities, the SEC ought to accept those disclosure documents as a basis for selling securities in the United States. The SEC is under considerable pressure to agree, because those international securities transactions would promote world trade, would enhance the United States as a world leader in capital formation, and would provide opportunities for US investors to diversify their portfolios. The Commission has so far insisted that foreign firms comply fully with the requirements imposed on domestic companies, arguing that the current disclosure system in the United States is the best in the world, and that protection of the US investor is the SEC's first priority. However, in an increasingly global economy that is an increasingly difficult argument (AAA/SEC Liaison Committee, 1995, p. 82).

Some argue that the SEC is unnecessary because market forces will do a more efficient job of enforcing disclosure by companies who wish to sell securities (Kitch, 1994, explores this idea thoroughly). The theory behind that argument is that – in the long term – a company that provides above-average disclosures will have below-average costs of capital, because its shareholders will enjoy less information risk. That relationship has not been proven, however, at least in part because there are few companies who provide more than the required disclosures. In any event, those arguments have been largely academic: there seems to be an understanding in the securities industry (and in Congress) that the pressures of the marketplace will tempt some companies and managers beyond their ethics, and that a legitimized restraining authority serves the interests of all (Seligman, 1982, pp. 563–8; Beatty and Hand, 1992).

Bibliography

AAA/SEC Liaison Committee. (1995). Mountaintop issues from the SEC. *Accounting Horizons*, **9** (1), 79–86.

Beatty, R. P. & Hand, J. R. M. (1992). The causes and effects of mandated accounting standards: SFAS No. 94 as a test of the level playing field theory. *Journal of Accounting, Auditing and Finance*, **7** (4), 509–30.

Kitch, E. W. (1994). *The Theory and Practice of Securities Disclosure*. Working Paper, University of Virginia School of Law, Charlottesville, Va.

Loss, L. & Seligman, J. (1989). *Securities Regulation*. Boston: Little, Brown & Co.

Phillips, S. M. & Zecher, J. R. (1981). *The SEC and the Public Interest*. Cambridge, Mass.: MIT Press.

Seligman, J. (1982). *The Transformation of Wall Street: A History of the Securities and Exchange Commission and Modern Corporate Finance*. Boston: houghton Mifflin.

Skousen, K. F. (1983). *An Introduction to the SEC*. Cincinnati, Ohio: Southwestern Publishing Company.

ROBERT SACK

self-deception   (a) The activity of avoiding acknowledgment to oneself of unpleasant realities and (b) the resulting mental state of ignorance, false belief, unjustified attitudes, or emotional distortion. The expression "self-deception" is sometimes applied to unintentional biases and wishful thinking, but purposeful and intentional types of avoidance are more intriguing. Can we successfully "lie to ourselves," purposefully getting ourselves to believe what we know (deep down) is false? It would seem we can – by systematically using such (unconscious or partly conscious) tactics such as denial, repression, rationalization, pretense (to ourselves and others), selective attention to evidence favorable to what we want to believe, and selective ignoring of contrary evidence. Such tactics help explain the convoluted reasoning of otherwise highly intelligent managers who excuse or even try to justify their white-collar crimes ("No one was really hurt"), production of harmful products ("If we don't do it someone else will"), exploitation of employees ("Business is business"), sexual harassment of subordinates ("They were free to decline my offers"), racism ("They are all like that"), sexism ("She's only got the job because of affirmative action"), harm to oneself and one's family ("I'm not a workaholic; I'm just committed"), and disregard for the environment ("We're only doing our job in maximizing profits"). Such forms of dishonesty with ourselves (and with others) about wrongdoing may undermine integrity and compound guilt. Yet not all self-deception is immoral. Some "vital lies" are helpful and even necessary in coping with harsh realities. As in deceiving other people, deceiving ourselves can be a morally ambiguous activity.

See also **authenticity; bluffing and deception; integrity; truthtelling**

Bibliography

Fingarette, H. (1969). *Self-deception*. London: Humanities Press.

Lockard, J. S. & Paulhus, D. L. (eds) (1988). *Self-deception: An Adaptive Mechanism?* Englewood Cliffs, NJ: Prentice-Hall.

Martin, M. W. (1986). *Self-Deception and Morality.* Lawrence: University Press of Kansas.

Martin, M. W. (ed.) (1985). *Self-Deception and Self-Understanding: New Essays in Philosophy and Psychology.* Lawrence: University Press of Kansas.

McLaughlin, B. P. & Rorty, A. (eds) (1988). *Perspectives on Self-Deception.* Berkeley: University of California Press.

MIKE W. MARTIN

self-interest The motivational element in human action that relates any interest to the self to whom the interest belongs. With regard to the object of a self's interest, however, the phrase is ambiguous. It may refer to whatever any self may be interested in or it may mean that people are interested only in themselves. The former is nicely expressed in the couplet "the world is so full of a number of things, I am sure we should all be as happy as kings," and the latter expresses the doctrine of Egoism, commonly known as selfishness (*see* EGOISM, PSYCHOLOGICAL EGOISM AND ETHICAL EGOISM).

Historically, actions arising from desire or passion as sources of interest were well understood in both the Ancient (Plato, *Republic*, 434–40; *Phaedrus*, 248–57) and Medieval (Dante, *Inferno*) worlds. But it was not until the seventeenth and eighteenth centuries, with their this-worldliness and their emphasis upon the individual, coupled with the attempt to develop a science of man suggested by and modeled upon Newtonian mechanics, that self-interest and egoism became the measure of human motion. The specification of such self-interest varied widely; self-preservation in HOBBES; raising the power of one's being in Spinoza; acquiring pleasure and avoiding pain in LOCKE and early Utilitarians, such as BENTHAM; the aesthetic feeling in free, creative activity in Shaftsbury; the greatest happiness for the greatest number in J. S. MILL; and competitive success in the free-market system of ADAM SMITH. This emphasis upon "interest-in-the-self" has tended to make the narrow understanding of the phrase dominant in our tradition almost to the exclusion of any "social interests" a self may have. At the same time,

such a selfish ethic was considered to be no ethic at all because of its lack of any "other-regarding" interests. Attempts have been made to modify the "selfish" aspect through the use of an "enlightened self-interest" that counselled consideration for others, but this merely uses others as instruments for the ends of self and is morally objectionable. It won't do unless the others are treated as ends in themselves and then the object of interest is no longer the self. Thus, the narrow meaning has come to express basic human concern coupled with a sense of moral disapproval to such a degree that the mere presence of self-interest in any activity tends to poison whatever other-regarding interests may be involved in that activity. On these grounds, since every interest belongs to a self, it would be next to impossible for purely altruistic activity to occur (Broad, 1949, pp. 105–14) (*see* ALTRUISM AND BENEVOLENCE). An adequate conception of "self-interest" must be found in order to protect the moral value of INDIVIDUALISM.

Considered in itself, "self-interest," whether of the self-regarding or other-regarding variety, is a type of activity founded upon the capacity of our consciousness to be aware that we are aware, to have ends and purposes as objects for ourselves, be they of ourselves or of something else. Within the context of management and considering the vast power corporations exercise in communities, the question becomes, How can we be reasonably sure that such power will be exercised in the public interest? (Silk & Vogel, 1976, pp. 128–9). As long as the distinction between ownership and management was not recognized (Berle & Means, 1934, p. 348) the problem was not difficult; owners could be held directly responsible. But when corporations went public and shareholders were seen as owners, then the problem became more difficult, for, while management must satisfy many interests, including those of the shareholders, there is often very little to guard the interests of the public, and even those of the corporation itself, from the self-interest of the managers. In the last century, to protect the public we have increasingly used government to make laws and public agencies to apply them, only to discover that the people we elect to do the job are just as subject to considerations of self-interest in the narrow sense as are managers. It has become a very difficult problem.

A large portion of the difficulty arises from our failure to consider any other aspect of our activity of self-interest than its consequences; all decisions are to be made in terms of the bottom line, the end result. But self-interested activity involves more than just results and consequences (*see* CONSEQUENTIALISM). It requires freedom of choice and continuous concern. It requires structured alternatives and it requires consistency (Wilbur, 1992, pp. 16–19, 29, 44–5). And the degree to which these enabling conditions are present and maintained is the degree to which self-interest as an activity is possible. So, no matter what object your self-interest may have, there are some interests you ought to have, the conditions that enable self-interested activity. And the conditions that enable your self-interested activity are the same for everyone's self-interested activity. When you maintain them for yourself, you maintain them for everyone. For example, these considerations are what make freedom of choice such a terribly important human condition, and they help to constitute an adequate and morally acceptable conception of self-interest. In a famous passage, often held to be obviously false, Adam Smith held that if everyone pursues their own self-interest, then "as if led by an INVISIBLE HAND" they will promote the good of society. The conception of an adequate self-interest suggested here casts a different light upon what Adam Smith said (Smith, 1930, p. 421). In another famous passage, Kant said "act so that you treat humanity, whether in your own person or that of another, always as an end and never as a means only" (Kant, 1959, pp. 75–6), and the only way to treat someone as an end is to maintain the enabling conditions of self-interested activity (*see* KANTIAN ETHICS). They constitute the limitations within which self-interested activity for anyone can be maintained without destroying it for everyone.

Bibliography

Berle, A. A. & Means, G. C. (1934). *The Modern Corporation and Private Property*. New York: Macmillan.

Broad, C. D. (1949). Egoism as a theory of human motives. *Hibbert Journal*, **48**, (Oct.).

Dante (Alighieri). (1977). *Divine Comedy, Part I, The Inferno*, trans. J. Ciardi. New York: W. W. Norton & Co.

Kant, I. (1959). *Foundations of the Metaphysics of Morals*, trans. L. W. Beck. New York: The Liberal Arts Press, Inc.

Plato. (1961). *Collected Dialogues*, eds E. Hamilton & H. Cairns. New York: Bollingen Foundation, Princeton University Press.

Silk, L. & Vogel, D. (1976). *Ethics and Profits: The Crisis in Confidence in American Business*. New York: Simon & Schuster.

Smith, A. (1930). *Wealth of Nations*. London: Cannon, Book IV, ch. ii.

Wilbur, J. B. (1992). *The Moral Foundations of Business Practice*. Lanham, Md.: University Press of America.

JAMES B. WILBUR

self-respect The mark of self-respect is a positive moral attitude towards oneself regarding one's moral worth. The root idea is that, irrespective of physical features or economic standing, or even intellectual abilities or accomplishments, all individuals are warranted in regarding themselves as having and being worthy of full moral standing *vis-à-vis* one another. Self-respecting persons do not just see themselves as having full moral standing, they also conduct themselves in a manner that is appropriate with that self-assessment. In this regard, self-respect is closely aligned with moral dignity.

Self-respect is considered to be a prized moral good that can and should be possessed by all. Just the same, not all persons are thought to have self-respect. The idea behind self-respect is not to deny differences that are real and important, but to draw attention to a most basic and fundamental way in which all persons are equal before one another. If all that a person should be able to do well is push a broom, that individual nonetheless deserves to be treated fairly and with moral respect. And if that person has self-respect, then the individual believes this as well. Presumably, our broom-pusher is not capable of running a country or heading a corporation. Realizing this is thought to be compatible with the individual's possessing self-respect.

Self-respect can also be an issue for the well-off. The intellectually talented person who thinks that the quality of her mind is the only basis that others have for treating her fairly lacks self-respect, as does the person who believes that his wealth is the only basis that others have for respecting him. And the strikingly beautiful may lack self-respect if they regard their beauty as the basis for their moral worth. While anyone may not realize that she or he lacks self-respect, the well-off are perhaps particularly vulnerable to this error, since they in fact enjoy the esteem of others. The possibility of error here underscores the point that self-respect is a self-regarding attitude with a very special content.

As with other self-evaluative attitudes, a person's self-respect can be more or less secure; hence, persons can differ widely in the degree to which they have self-respect. A multitude of factors affect the extent to which a person's self-respect is secure. Foremost among these, if only because of its premiere place in every individual's life, is the overall quality of the familial experience. A loving familial environment is most conducive to a person's having enormous self-respect, a hostile one is most conducive to a person's having little or no self-respect. Every individual, however, is also part of a larger social environment, which may enhance or undermine her or his self-respect. It is generally thought that a just society is conducive to everyone having self-respect, and that an unjust society favors some and disfavors others. While favoring and disfavoring can track some readily identifiable physical feature such as gender or ethnicity, it need not.

Of course, neither justice nor injustice is experienced in the abstract, but in the day-to-day lives of individuals. And it is rarely a single instance, one way or the other, that affects the self-respect of individuals. Rather, it is the accumulative effect of the overall timbre of a person's experiences that makes the difference. Businesses (including service institutions such as hospitals and schools) are very much a factor in this regard, because of both their prevalence in society and their role in two areas in which the issue of fairness necessarily arises, namely employment and the rendering of services (public schools) or the sale of products and/or services (hospitals and institutions of higher learning). Should wages and salaries simply be dictated by market forces? Or does being mindful of the self-respect of persons impose certain restraints, especially in the case of basic goods? So even in the case where no formal rights and liberties are violated, one can ask whether a society is generally conducive to the self-respect of all of its citizens if wages and prices are such that large segments of the population regularly lack the means to secure basic goods. An affirmative answer would indicate the fragility of the moral good of self-respect; a negative one, its ruggedness.

Bibliography

Dillon, R. S. (ed.) (1995). *Dignity, Character, and Self-Respect*. New York: Routledge.

Hill, T., Jr. (1973). Servility and self-respect. *The Monist*, 57.

Rawls, J. (1971). *A Theory of Justice*. Cambridge, Mass.: Harvard University Press.

LAURENCE THOMAS

sexual harassment   The abuse of one's position of authority over an employee in order to exact sexual favors from the employee or to discomfort or humiliate the employee because of his or her sex.

Sexual harassment is a term with both a legal and a moral meaning, which, although related, are unfortunately not identical. The tendency to conflate these meanings has been the source of much confusion and indicates the need to clearly distinguish between the term's legal and moral ranges of application.

Legally speaking, sexual harassment is a form of sex discrimination. This is because, although the federal government is empowered by the Civil Rights Act of 1964 to prohibit employment discrimination on the basis of an individual's race, color, religion, sex, or national origin, it possesses no statutory authority to directly regulate interpersonal relationships in the workplace (*see* DISCRIMINATION IN HIRING). Therefore, the only forms of sexual harassment that are legally actionable are those that discriminate against an employee because of his or her sex.

As the law is currently interpreted, there are two types of prohibited sexual harassment: *quid pro quo* harassment and hostile-environment harassment. *Quid pro quo* harassment occurs when an individual's employment opportunities are conditioned upon his or her entering into a sexual or social relationship with an employer, i.e., when the opportunities are given or withheld as the *quid pro quo* for the relationship. *Quid pro quo* harassment may consist in either threats of adverse employment consequences if one does not enter the relationship, or offers of advancement if one does. It should be noted that if such threats or offers are equally directed toward individuals of both sexes, as they might be by a bisexual supervisor, they would not constitute legally actionable sexual harassment because they would not be discriminatory in nature.

Hostile-environment harassment occurs when an employer engages in conduct that has the purpose or effect of creating a working environment that is intimidating, hostile, or offensive to the members of one sex. Hostile-environment harassment consists in unwelcome behavior of a sexual nature that is sufficiently distressing to interfere with an individual's ability to perform his or her job, even when the behavior is not designed to elicit sexual favors. Such behavior must be severe and pervasive enough to alter the conditions of the victim's employment and may not consist in merely a few isolated incidents. It should be noted that unlike *quid pro quo* harassment which requires intentional conduct, hostile-environment harassment may consist in any course of action, intentional or not, that has the effect of creating a hostile working environment.

Morally speaking, sexual harassment consists in intimidating conduct directed toward individuals in subordinate employment positions by those with power over them for the purpose of exacting sexual favors that would not otherwise be granted (May & Hughes, 1987). This definition could reasonably be extended to include intimidating conduct that is designed to belittle or denigrate an employee because of his or her sex. From the moral perspective, sexual harassment is an abuse of power in the employment relationship and, as such, is objectionable primarily because of its oppressive, rather than discriminatory, nature. Thus, the actions of a bisexual harasser would constitute morally objectionable sexual harassment, even though they would not be legally actionable. Further, isolated instances of

oppressive, sexually degrading conduct that would be inadequate to make out a legal case of hostile-environment harassment could still constitute morally objectionable sexual harassment. However, because the evil of sexual harassment is its oppressive nature, and because oppression requires intention, there can be no negligent or inadvertent sexual harassment in the moral sense. Unlike legal sexual harassment, conduct that unintentionally creates an offensive working environment for the members of one sex would not lie within the moral significance of the term.

Bibliography

Dodds, S. M.; Frost, L., Pargetter, R., Prior, E. W. (1988). Sexual harassment. *Social Theory and Practice*, **14**, 111–30.

Estrich, S. (1991). Sex at work *Stanford Law Review*, **43**, 813–61.

MacKinnon, C. (1979). *Sexual Harassment of Working Women*. New Haven, Conn.: Yale University Press.

May, L., & Hughes, J. C. (1987). Is sexual harassment coercive? In Gertrude Ezorsky (ed.), *Moral Rights in the Workplace*. Albany, New York: State University of New York Press, 115–22.

Thomas, L. (1987). On sexual offers and threats. In Gertrude Ezorsky (ed.), *Moral Rights in the Workplace*. Albany, New York: State University of New York Press, 123–6.

US Supreme Court. *Meritor Savings Bank*, vs *Vinson*, 477 US 84 (1986).

York, K. M. (1989). Defining sexual harassment in workplaces: A policy-capturing approach. *Academy of Management Journal*, **32**, 830-50.

JOHN HASNAS

shame is, first of all, the painful, personal recognition that one has broken the communal code. Indeed, the painfulness of shame should be understood not as a psychological analogue of physical pain but rather as the humiliation and disgrace of exclusion, the awful sense that one has let other people down in a profound and not merely embarrassing way. Shame is a particularly painful emotion, but it is also an essential ingredient in ethics. Sociologist Thomas Scheff calls it "the emotional pivot of social life" and "a basic mechanism of social control." The great philosopher ARISTOTLE 2,500 years ago discussed shame as a "quasi-virtue," in the sense that although shame was not desirable in itself, the absence of shame in the face of dishonor proved a person to be a wicked character indeed. So, too, according to an old Ethiopian proverb, "without shame, there is no honor."

In business ethics, shame plays an essential role in sanctioning corporate and commercial behavior. Although the practices of "FREE ENTERPRISE" allow and even encourage a certain lack of rigidity concerning the mutual expectations and standards of behavior in business, there are, nevertheless, communally agreed-upon even if not always explicit rules of decent and honorable behavior. Shame is an essentially social emotion. In business, it forms the basis of ethical behavior insofar as it is vitally concerned with behavior within a community practice. This is true of both individual and corporate behavior, both within and outside of the context of a particular company or industry. Particularly within the corporate community, shame provides a much more effective deterrent than do external threats and sanctions. This is, in part, because the other side of shame consists of the very positive emotions of pride and a sense of belonging. It is the loss of pride and the damaged sense of belonging that provides the pain. A corporation without shame is very likely without ethics as well. That is why some of the harshest complaints and indictments against corporate malfeasance are aimed not so much at the original damage but at the subsequent lack of shame, for example, a refusal to apologize. One aspect of business ethics, accordingly, is the instillation of a keen sense of shame.

This can easily be misunderstood, however, in part because shame is often confused with GUILT. Guilt, of course, is also an important moral emotion, but it is easily conflated with legal guilt – which is rather a different topic – and with the neurotic, unjustified feeling of guilt (discussed at length by Freud, for example). Shame also has its pathological exaggerations, but in itself it is usually a justified and desirable response to one's own unethical behavior. Gabrielle Taylor even argues that genuine shame is *always* justified. Guilt, on the other hand, has acquired an intriguing connection with religion (especially in Judaism and Christianity). Guilt also tends to be a more individualistic emotion. Anthropologists often distinguish between guilt and shame societies, namely, those which are more tribal or communal and those which place more emphasis on the individual.

Corporations, accordingly, might well be conceived as "shame societies," more or less tight-knit communities with a shared identity, shared values, and common interests. Shame depends on the judgments of others, or, more accurately, one's self-condemnation reflecting the perceived or expected condemnation of others. In this, shame is extremely self-consciousness as well as social. Thus the French existentialist Jean-Paul Sartre emphasizes "the look" of shame, the piercing gaze of others which "pins us down" for our transgressions. Yet shame remains first of all self-reflective, a form of self-condemnation, and in this we recognize, as Aristotle did, its status as a "quasi-virtue."

Shamelessness is clearly a vice, a sign of viciousness. Thus it is extremely important that the much-touted business virtue of "toughness" must not be confused with shamelessness. In shame, one at least takes the blame for what one has done and thus admits responsibility. One might try to avoid or deny this responsibility by insisting that his or her actions were only "foolish" or "incompetent" or, of course, blame their behavior on others, but we can thus appreciate the virtue of shame. Ironically, shame is an emotion that presupposes a sense of responsibility. It also presupposes the importance of the group and assumes the validity of corporate or community values. Thus Aristotle rightly recognized the quasi-virtuous nature of shame and its essential importance in any ethical community or corporation.

Bibliography

Aristotle. (1925). *Nicomachean Ethics,* trans. D. Ross. Oxford: Clarendon Press, Book IV, ch. 9.

Isenberg, A. (1980). Natural pride and natural shame. In A. Rorty (Ed.), *Explaining Emotions.* Berkeley University of California Press.

Kekes, J. (1988). Shame and moral progress. In French (Ed.), *Ethical Theory: Character and Virtue.* Notre Dame, Ind.: University of Notre Dame Press.

Sartre, J.-P. (1956). *Being and Nothingness.* New York: Simon & Schuster. Part III, ch. iii sec. 4.

Scheff, T. (1990). Socialization of emotions: Pride and shame as causal agents. In T. Kemper (Ed.), *Research Agendas in the Sociology of Emotions*. Albany: State University of New York Press.

Solomon, R. C. (1993). *The Passions*. Indianapolis, Ind.: Hackett Publishing.

Taylor, G. (1985). *Pride, Shame and Guilt*. Oxford: Oxford University Press.

ROBERT C. SOLOMON

shark   a corporate raider given to the practice of hostile buyouts initiated solely for the purpose of liquidation and profit for the shark. This practice occurs only when the management is unable or unwilling to close a significant gap between the market value of the company's shares and the breakup value of the company. Thus, these buyouts are usually "hostile" to the intentions of the current management. The corporate raider (dubbed by management as "the shark"), after buying a significant percentage of the company's shares, then offers to buy the shares from the other shareholders at a price considerably higher than current market value, buys the company, and then makes a profit by selling off the underlying assets of the company. The raider may or may not take on a significant amount of debt in order to buy the target company. Such debt-based takeovers are called "leveraged," and takeovers can be more or less leveraged or not leveraged at all. Procedures created by management to stop such takeovers are called "poison pills," and often involve taking on great corporate debt to minimize the profit from such takeovers (*see* TAKEOVERS; LEVERAGED BUYOUTS; POISON PILL).

Such hostile buyouts by sharks are often thought to be immoral because they can produce much pain from unemployment, and they can destroy large and profitable companies. From a consequentialist point of view, the practice is sometimes thought to produce little other than pain and increasing unemployment (*see* CONSEQUENTIALISM). Some rule-consequentialists have argued in favor of the practice, however, on the grounds that, *in the long run*, the capital produced by the activity is more efficient in producing efficiencies of scale and competition, and hence wealth. In fact, it may be argued that such a practice is good because in the long run it is in everybody's interest that

capital be allowed to move where it can make the most profit.

Bibliography

Almeder, R. & Carey, D. (1992). In defense of sharks: Moral issues in liquidating buyouts. In M. Snoeyenbos, R. Almeder, & J. Humber (eds), *Business Ethics*, rev. edn. Buffalo, N.Y.: Prometheus Press.

Reich, R. (1992). Leveraged buyouts: America pays the price. In M. Snoeyenbos, R. Almeder, & J. Humber (eds), *Business Ethics*, rev. edn. Buffalo, N.Y.: Prometheus Press.

ROBERT ALMEDER

situation ethics   is an ethical theory developed as a contribution to Christian moral theology. It is an alternative to natural law and other rule-conceptions of morality, and was given its name by Joseph Fletcher in his popular book, *Situation Ethics: The New Morality* (Fletcher, 1966) (*see* NATURAL LAW; KANTIAN ETHICS). As presented by Fletcher, situation ethics has three major elements: a rejection of the idea that morality involves the following of rules; a positive account of moral requirements as rooted in the command to love thy neighbor as thyself; and, a substantive morality on sexual and other matters which is more permissive than orthodox Christian accounts. I will treat each of these in turn.

Most conceptions of morality hold that there are MORAL RULES governing particular types of acts, for example that promises ought to be kept and one ought not to injure others. Rules, however, can be understood in different ways. One view is that some or all of these rules are absolute, in the sense that they may never be broken. Kant is supposed to have held that it is never right to lie, even to save a life; many Catholic theologians take it as an absolute rule never to kill an innocent person.

A second, and weaker, conception is that moral rules lay down serious moral reasons for actions such that one must act on these reasons, unless there are also moral reasons against the action, which are weightier. The reasons against the action will be given by other moral rules. Thus all rules permit exceptions when rules conflict and one rule is overridden by another.

When a rule is overridden, however, it still has an important moral status. It structures the context of moral deliberation and correctly lays down moral reasons which, though overridable, can't be ignored and are not annulled. Even if an action contrary to a rule is right "all things considered," there is still a moral reason against it.

A third, even weaker, view is that moral rules are mere guidelines or "rules of thumb." They are based on past experience and tell us what in a given situation is likely to be right. But they may be mistaken and, if so, they have no applicability to the situation at all. They are not overridden, just discarded as irrelevant. A fourth view is that rules have no applicability at all. Every moral situation is different and one must simply figure out what is right in each situation without any help from rules or guidelines. The best-known expression of this "act-intuitionist" view is the French philosopher Jean-Paul Sartre's existentialism.

Fletcher dismisses strong accounts of rules as "legalism" that simply cannot work since real-life situations are too complex to be captured by rules. Situation ethics accepts the third view of rules as guidelines and rules of thumb. This is because there is a more fundamental principle of right, which is to do what love requires. Rules help us with this, but in a given situation what the rules say and what love requires may diverge. In such a case we should do what love requires and set the rules aside. Since we are to do what the situation requires, situation ethics is often identified with the fourth view – that no rules are required, just judgment in the situation. Fletcher, however, strongly rejects this "antinomian" stance. Rules are important. A person should come to a situation, he says, "armed with the ethical maxims of his community and its heritage," that "he should treat with respect as illuminations of his problems" (Fletcher, 1966, p. 26). But, while rules are important at the start, what love demands in the situation is the ultimate determinant of right.

The requirement to do what love demands is the requirement to do in each situation what *love of one's neighbor* requires. It is this which makes Fletcher's depiction of situation ethics a version of Christian moral theology. Its main claim is that the supreme value of Christianity is love or *agape*. To love one's neighbor is what Fletcher calls its "Great Commandment" and

"Summary" of all the other ethical teachings of the New Testament. To establish this, Fletcher gives many examples of where Jesus was willing to set aside the law in order to promote human good. Situation ethics is thus grounded in an interpretation of Christian scripture.

What exactly does love require? Fletcher says that the demand is to love not just one neighbor, but all neighbors, that is, all people. But how can we turn that into something more precise and usable? An obvious answer is to see situation ethics as akin to act-utilitarianism, that each act should produce the greatest total amount of human well-being or happiness. CONSEQUENTIALISM; UTILITARIANISM). He is not opposed to such an identification and speaks of a "genuine coalition" with Mill and Bentham (Fletcher, 1966, p. 95) (*see* BENTHAM, JEREMY; MILL, JOHN STUART). Seeing situation ethics as a version of act-utilitarianism enables us to illuminate two points about it. First, rules really are rules of thumb, strategies for maximizing happiness, to be laid aside when acting against a rule does that better. Second, situation ethics becomes a defense of utilitarian ethics on the theological ground that it is the best interpretation of scriptural injunctions.

If we accept this equivalence, situation ethics now has all the problems of utilitarianism: many things which produce the greatest happiness do not seem right because they violate commitments to particular people or are unjust. Fletcher answers these questions by urging that the Christian love appealed to is not a matter of feeling. It is not romantic love or liking, but what Kant called "practical love," a matter of attitude towards all humankind. It is love "using its head, calculating its duties, obligations, opportunities and resources" (Fletcher, 1966, p. 95). On this basis Fletcher argues that love and justice are the same; what we are due on the basis of love is only what we in justice have a right to and vice versa. This, however, seems to empty love of all meaning. Surely what we want to give someone on the basis of love can conflict with what we take them to deserve on grounds of justice. If we say that the love here in this conflict is not the sort of intellectual love the situationist has in mind, then we have in effect turned that love into nothing more than an intuition or judgment of what is right. Rather than love being the ground of what is right, we decide what is right in some independent way and call that love. For this reason, the appeal to love as the grounding of right is too vague to be of real help.

In his defense of situation ethics, Fletcher frequently expresses particular moral views. He clearly is not generally opposed to such things as abortion, extra-marital sex, homosexuality, prostitution, single parenthood through artificial insemination, polygyny, suicide, and euthanasia. These are all things condemned by many orthodox versions of Christianity on the basis of an appeal to fundamental moral rules found out through natural law, reason, revelation, or biblical interpretation. His general attitude is a pragmatic and "humanistic" one. If something "works," makes people happy, and no one is hurt, it is not wrong. According to Fletcher Jesus said nothing about

> birth control, large or small families, childlessness, homosexuality, masturbation, fornication or premarital intercourse, sterilization, artificial insemination, abortion, sex play, petting and courtship. Whether any form of sex (hetero, homo, or auto) is good or evil depends on whether love is fully served. (1966, p. 139)

It is very likely that these normative commitments are really what motivates situation ethics. If so, what is most important about it may be its challenge to conventional forms of Christian moral theology, not its vague and unpersuasive ethical theory.

Bibliography

Cox, H. (Ed.), . (1967). *The Situation Ethics Debate.* Philadelphia: The Westminster Press.

Fletcher, J. (1966). *Situation Ethics: The New Morality.* Philadelphia: The Westminster Press.

Fletcher, J. (1967). *Moral Responsibility.* Philadelphia: The Westminster Press.

Fletcher, J. & Wassmer, T., with May, W. E. (Ed.), . (1970). *Hello Lovers: An Introduction to Situation Ethics.* Washington, DC/Cleveland: Corpus Books.

Frankena, W. (1963). *Ethics.* Englewood Cliffs, NJ: Prentice-Hall. ch. 3.

Robinson, J. (1963). *Honest to God.* London: SCM Press.

BRUCE LANDESMAN

slavery A social institution characterized by ownership, subjection, and exploitation of a certain human being by another human being or human agency. A slave is one who is owned, whose will is subject to the owner's authority, and whose labor is coerced. The essence of slavery is ownership and loss of rights and freedom, hence the term chattel slave. A chattel slave is personal property just as a horse, cart, windmill, or tractor is personal property. In the ancient world where laws defined and regulated slavery, the slave was legally defined as a thing and as such could be purchased, sold, mortgaged, leased, traded, bequeathed, presented as a gift, used to pay debts, and seized in a bankruptcy. As an article of property a slave would not be under the jurisdiction of laws that protect citizens even though in some societies certain regulations have stipulated their treatment and behavior.

Slavery is a universal and perennial phenomenon having existed in nearly every kind of society and economic system from the ancient world to the latter days of the twentieth century. Slavery is not unique to any particular type of economy. It has appeared among nomadic Arabs, native American Indian tribes, nomadic pastoralists of Asia, seafaring Vikings, settled agriculturists, sophisticated agricultural societies (such as the American South where after the introduction of the cotton gin the demand for slaves increased), urban centers such as Bangkok with its sex slaves, to the slave labor in the free-market economy of Nazi Germany and in communist Russia.

Historically, there have been several sources of slavery. Warfare, where the vanquished were frequently enslaved, was the earliest and most common source of slaves. Purchasing slaves from captors was another major source. Other sources of slavery have been debt slavery (where children and wives have been sold to pay off debts), piracy, kidnapping, breeding, selling children and wives for economic survival, punishment for an offense, and birth by a slave parent.

Slavery is an issue of business ethics because it is an economic institution involving such business issues as the acquisition of laborers, labor relations, workplace quality, workplace safety, competitive advantage, and business as an agent of exploitation and oppression. It is a subject of business ethics because at issue are such deontological principles as justice and the regulative norms of justice – equality and freedom, the principle of non-maleficence, the principle of beneficence, and the second formulation of Kant's categorical imperative – "Treat humans as ends and not as means only." As an institution subject to ethical evaluation, it also raises utilitarian questions. Would slavery ever be justified if a greater balance of utility could be produced than the harm inflicted? (*See* JUSTICE; EQUALITY; KANTIAN ETHICS; UTILITARIANISM.)

The ethical evaluation of slavery involves two major considerations. The first and primary consideration is an ethical evaluation of the institution of slavery looking at the practice itself and the fact that some human beings are owned by others. This is a systemic approach focusing on the basic structures of a slave system. This approach raises the question of this system's moral legitimacy and to what extent the system inhibits human flourishing, harms human beings, and prevents people from realizing their potential as moral beings. The second ethical consideration is the practice of slavery, focusing on the relations between slaves and their owners. Even though one might argue that slavery is, by definition, an immoral institution because it violates most of the core deontological principles and cannot withstand a rigorous utilitarian critique, nevertheless, one may make judgments about the less or more moral quality of master–slave relations. For instance, it seems clear that there is a moral difference between the master–slave relationship in ancient classical Greece, where Athenian slaves were philosophers and policemen with manumission as a condition, in contrast to the master–slave relationship in twentieth-century Nazi slave-labor camps, where death was the typical outcome.

In the latter part of the twentieth century slavery is dead on paper. Virtually all governments have signed a series of abolitionist pledges going back to the League of Nations' Slavery Convention of 1926 and the 1948 Universal Declaration of Human Rights. However, human-rights specialists have been documenting widespread violations of the agreements for many years, and estimate that more than 100 million people around the world

are held in human bondage and suffer as slaves in the last decade of the twentieth century. The plight of these millions of people held as property for the purpose of productive labor begs for continued concern and ethical reflection. Slavery, as subject of ethical reflection, is of historic and contemporary concern.

Bibliography

Davis, D. B. (1966). *The Problem of Slavery in Western Culture*. Ithaca: Cornell University Press.

De George, R. T. (1994). Justice and economic systems. In *Business Ethics*. New Jersey: Prentice-Hall, 141–65.

Garver, E. (1994). Aristotle's natural slaves: Incomplete praxis and incomplete human beings. *Journal of the History of Philosophy*, 32, 173–95.

Genovese, E. (1965). *The Political Economy of Slavery*. New York: Pantheon Books.

Hare, R. M. (1979). What is wrong with slavery. *Philosophy and Public Affairs*, 8, 103–21.

Rubenstein, R. L. (1975). The modernization of slavery. In *The Cunning of History*. New York: Harper and Row, 36–47.

Stampp, K. M. (1978). *The Peculiar Institution: Slavery in the Ante-Bellum South*. New York: Knopf.

DONALD G. JONES

Smith, Adam   (1723–90): Born in Kirkcaldy, Scotland, Smith attended Glasgow University and Balliol College, Oxford. After briefly lecturing at the University of Edinburgh on rhetoric and literature, he accepted a chair at the University of Glasgow where he lectured on jurisprudence and moral philosophy. His most significant writings grew out of these lectures. *The Theory of Moral Sentiments* (1759) was the mainstay of Smith's reputation during his lifetime. He resigned the chair at Glasgow after a dozen years, devoting over a decade to travel and writing. The product was the *Wealth of Nations* (1776). This was the subject of immediate and continuing acclaim, not the least from his fellow philosopher and lifelong friend, David Hume (1711–76).

The *Wealth of Nations* is widely and justly acclaimed as one of the foundation stones of capitalism. In it Smith presented historical as well as theoretical arguments supporting a policy of substantial relaxation in government controls on trade and commerce. Directed primarily to legislators and monarchs, the book's main thesis is that the welfare of a nation is better served by permitting, within broad limits, entrepreneurs to pursue their own SELF-INTEREST through market transactions than by constraining them by unnecessary and counter-productive governmental supervision and REGULATION. Instead of relying either on the wisdom of governments or the integrity of merchants, Smith urged, as had Bernard Mandeville (1670–1733), reliance on the unintended, yet beneficial consequences of collective action. This emphasis is captured in the central metaphor of the work, "the INVISIBLE HAND."

Bibliography

Lindgren, J. R. (1973). *The Social Philosophy of Adam Smith.* The Hague: Nijhoff.

Lindgren, J. R. (1992). Smith, Adam. In L. C. Becker & C. B. Becker (eds), *Encyclopedia of Ethics.* New York: Garland, 1160–3.

Muller, J. Z. (1993). *Adam Smith in His Time and Ours.* New York: Macmillan.

Smith, A. (1976–80). *Works and Correspondence of Adam Smith,* 7 vols. Oxford: Oxford University Press. (Simply the best available edition).

Werhane, P. H. (1991). *Adam Smith and His Legacy for Modern Capitalism.* New York: Oxford University Press.

Winch, D. (1978). *Adam Smith's Politics.* Cambridge: Cambridge University Press.

J. RALPH LINDGREN

social contract theory In business ethics social contract theory involves the use of hypothetical implied contracts to establish ethical rights and obligations for business firms, professionals, and managers. The legitimacy of these ethical rights and obligations is based upon the assumed consent of the group members to the terms of the social contract. Social contract theory focuses on a community or group of rational, self-interested individuals who are presumed to consent to the terms of a hypothetical agreement because it is in their rational interest to do so. Specific ethical obligations and rights are then deduced from this contract. Social contract theory may therefore be thought of as a communitarian, norm-based approach to ethics. The device of a social contract has been used in business ethics since the early 1980s.

I. A Brief History

The concept of a social contract or covenant goes back to Socrates and the Greek Sophists and even earlier. The Old Testament refers to a covenant between God and every living thing for all generations (Genesis 9). Social contract is associated with political theory as a device for understanding the role of government within a society. The use of social contract in political theory reached its apex in the Enlightenment writings of JOHN LOCKE, THOMAS HOBBES, and Jean-Jacques Rousseau. Their ideas about the relationship between government and the governed were very influential in the American and French revolutions and in the establishment of a constitutional form of government in the United States. Hobbes envisioned a social contract in which citizens gave over their liberty to an absolute sovereign as the only solution to the "warre" of man against man in Hobbes' imagined state of nature, where life was "solitary, poor, nasty, brutish and short." In Hobbes' social contract citizens have no right to resist the sovereign; because if there were such a right, society would quickly disintegrate into the feared state of nature.

Locke, who had great influence on the founders of the US government, assumed that humans have natural rights to life and property. Unfortunately, in a state of nature, these rights may go unprotected. Locke's solution is a social contract in which citizens form a civil government for the purpose of securing these natural rights. Locke's civil government has a defined responsibility and its subjects have a right to resist if the government interferes with their natural rights.

Rousseau envisions a moral community in which natural freedom and equality is transferred to civil society, based upon the consent of the governed reflected in the "general will" of the people. More recently, in 1971, JOHN RAWLS uses the idea of social contract as the foundation for his influential book, *A Theory of Justice*. In 1986, David Gauthier, in *Morals by Agreement*, develops a rational-choice argument that self-interested parties will want to participate in a social contract recognizing certain principles of cooperation. Although business is not his primary focus, Gauthier recognizes the implications of his work for economic life: "Market interactions are a network of contractual arrangements, and this network is itself founded on an overall social contract, expressive of the two-sided instrumentality that constitutes society from the standpoint of economic man" (1986, p. 318).

II. Core Issues in Social Contract Theory

To be fully satisfying, social contract approaches must resolve certain core issues including: (1) explaining why it would be rational for everyone to agree to the terms of the social contract, (2) justifying the use of devices outside of the social contract itself as part of the theory, (3) explaining why individuals, in fact, would be willing to act consistently with the terms of the social contract, and (4) demonstrating that the espoused social contract is realistic and is based upon an accurate understanding of the nature of humanity.

Most of the issues result from the attempt to derive real world standards from a hypothetical or imaginary agreement. As a starting-point, a social contract theory must offer a plausible explanation as to why rational humans would agree to the terms of the proposed agreement. One approach, similar to that used by Rawls, is to rely upon critical extra-contractual assumptions that the contracting parties come together to set up the contract under very special conditions. Rawls (1971) and Donaldson (1982) both use such devices. Rawls' contract is made by people who act behind a veil of ignorance in which they do not know their particular endowments or preferences. In Donaldson's application of the social contract idea to business ethics, the original contractors are imagined as existing in a state of prehistory in which they know the characteristics of the organizations they wish to create, but they have control in the sense that they have complete flexibility in designing the surrounding legal and social environment. The devices of a veil of ignorance and a prescribed condition in prehistory come from outside the social contract itself and therefore require some type of independent justification. Some critics of social contract theory note this problem and conclude

that the social contract approach is incapable of providing a satisfactory moral theory on its own.

A more common approach to answering the question of why self-interested individuals would agree to a particular social contract is to demonstrate that the contract is the only plausible solution to an acknowledged problem. This approach is used by Hobbes, Locke, and Donaldson/Dunfee. Each theorist starts with a definition of the problem (e.g. Hobbes: without society life is nasty, brutish, and short) and makes certain assumptions about the nature of humanity (people are self-interested egoists). Then, a particular vision of a social contract is proffered as a realistic solution to the problem.

After offering a plausible argument why the original contracting parties would agree to a particular set of social contract terms, the theorists then must suggest reasons why individuals within the contracting communities would continue to comply with the terms of the agreement. After all, once they actually face a conflict between their self-interests and the terms of the social contract, they may wish to deviate from the agreement. Various explanations have been offered by theorists, for example, that self-interested community members will nonetheless continue to comply with the contract in the reciprocal expectation that others will similarly comply. Other theorists argue that humans possess an intuitive moral sense that promises should be honored.

Many contractarians, particularly Hobbes and Gauthier, assume that humans are egoists acting purely in their own self-interest. Others, including some business ethicists, assume that humans may be naturally altruistic. The choice of these assumptions will, of course, influence whether the derived social contract terms appear to be realistic.

The concept of an informal agreement setting standards for society appears to be intuitive to many people. References to specific, existing social contracts are commonplace in the general business literature. For example, the term is frequently found in the human resource management literature in references to a social contract between employers and employees. Social contract terminology is also found in the public utility regulation, accounting, and capital gain taxation literature. Writers often refer to "the social contract" of a particular nation state. (See generally Dunfee, 1991.)

III. Social Contract Theory and Business Ethics

Social contract theory can be used to identify rights and obligations pertaining to business ethics. Thomas Donaldson develops a special social contract theory for issues of business ethics in Chapter 3 of his book, *Corporations and Morality* (1982). In this seminal effort, Donaldson focuses on the issue of corporate rights and obligations. Following the classical social contract tradition of using a hypothetical agreement as a device for parsing specific rights and obligations, Donaldson imagines the terms of an agreement that could be rationally entered into between all productive cooperative enterprises (firms) and the individual members of a given society in the aggregate prior to the beginnings of their economic system. He assumes that the parties would want the benefits of specialization of labor, output and distribution, increased wages, and the ability to pay for harms that would result from having corporations. On the other hand, the parties to the agreement would also want to limit pollution, depletion of natural resources, destruction of personal accountability, and worker alienation. Representatives of productive organizations want the members of society to agree to provide them with an environment conducive for them to provide needed goods and services, resulting, in turn, in reasonable profits. The terms of the resulting social contract require that the harms be minimized and that when the inevitable trade-offs are made, they be made consistently with "the general canons of justice" (1982, p. 53).

Donaldson broadens his theory (1989), and considers all economic actors, not just corporations, employees, and consumers. He also extends his focus beyond a single society to explicitly consider issues of cultural relativism. Donaldson envisions a global social contract setting a minimal floor of responsibility for all business firms. Specifically, global firms have an obligation to enhance the long-term welfare of employees and consumers, minimize the drawbacks of large productive organizations, and refrain from violating minimal standards of justice and human rights. These obligations are defined in terms of ten fundamental rights (e.g.

freedom of physical movement, property ownership, minimal education, political participation, subsistence) which global firms should avoid depriving others of; and in some very limited circumstances, should protect against deprivation by others.

Others followed Donaldson in using the social contract device in the context of business responsibility. Keeley (1988) employs social contract as a metaphor to describe business firms as a series of contract-like agreements about social rules. Emphasizing the voluntary nature of agreements, Keeley relies upon a rights-based approach (personal claims based on a system of rules, such as rights to equal concern and respect, or to avoid personal harms). His approach is contrasted with an "organismic" model of the firm, which subordinates the welfare of individuals to the welfare of the organization.

In two joint articles, Donaldson and Dunfee (e.g. 1994) have set forth a social contract theory called Integrative Social Contracts Theory (ISCT) which is specifically applicable to business ethics. The term "integrative" is used to illustrate that ISCT is based upon a hypothetical social contract whose terms allow for the generation of binding ethical obligations through the recognition of actual norms created in real social and economic communities. A hypothetical social contract is thereby integrated with real or extant social contracts. The plural "contracts" is used to emphasize the fact that ISCT envisions literally millions of local-community-based social contracts establishing ethical norms for those local groups.

The hypothetical social contract is derived from an imagined attempt by all humanity to design a global agreement concerning business ethics. The terms of the contract are based upon the contractors' recognition of two factors. First, they realize that significant bounded moral rationality exists for economic actors. That is, they would recognize the limits of their own ability to comprehend, interpret, and apply moral concepts. Similarly, they do not expect that a formal moral calculus can be designed in advance for all of the contexts in which diverse humanity faces ethical choices. Second, they recognize the need for a community-based moral fabric to enable them to satisfy their individual economic and social interests.

In response to these assumptions, Donaldson and Dunfee hypothesize that global-level contractors would design a universal or macrosocial contract with the following terms

1. Local communities may specify ethical norms for their members through microsocial contracts (called moral free space).
2. Norm-generating microsocial contracts must be grounded in informed consent buttressed by a right of community members to exit and to exercise voice within their communities.
3. In order to be obligatory, a microsocial contract norm must be compatible with hypernorms.
4. In case of conflicts among norms satisfying principles 1–3, priority must be established through the application of rules consistent with the spirit and letter of the macrosocial contract.

Hypernorms entail principles so fundamental to human existence that they should be reflected in a convergence of religious, philosophical, and cultural beliefs. The priority rules are derived from conflicts of laws principles found in international and US law. Through the application of ISCT it is possible to identify authentic ethical norms within communities (that bribes should not be paid), to test these under hypernorms, and against conflicting norms from other communities (that bribes of a certain character are acceptable), and to then determine which norms should be given priority.

Social contract approaches have been applied to specific issues in business ethics. A prime example is found in Scheppele's (1993) advocacy of restrictions on insider trading based upon a claim that there is a social-contract-based justification for providing equal access to financial markets. Other efforts include the application of Donaldson's original social contract to the agribusiness industry and the evaluation of the exportation of hazardous products under an unwritten social contract (see Dunfee, 1991, p. 31).

IV. Limitations and Advantages of a Social Contract Approach

Critics of social contract argue that it fails to provide an independent basis for moral obligation. They reason that many of the results of contractarian approaches can be achieved through the use of other ethical theories. Others are concerned about coercion, particularly in the case of the use of actual consent as occurs with the microsocial contracts under ISCT. They worry that organizations will be able to impose group values upon individuals which will then be sanctioned by social contract theory. Another set of criticisms, particularly directed at ISCT, reflects concern that social contract theory cannot adequately protect important rights, such as freedom from gender-based discrimination.

Social contract theorists are refining their approaches in response to these criticisms. They note that social contract theory has great potential as a realistic, contextual basis for making normative judgments in business ethics. The realism must come from consistency of the contractarian assumptions with the empirical literature in the social sciences and moral psychology. The social contract approach is contextual by its very nature due to the emphasis on specific agreements. It explicitly recognizes the role of professional ethical norms and the understandings of right behavior that permeate business interactions. Ultimately, the distinguishing feature of social contract theory is its emphasis on the uncoerced, informed consent of those who will be bound by the ethical norms thereby established.

Bibliography

Business Ethics Quarterly. (1995). Special issue on social contracts and business ethics: **5** (2).

Donaldson, T. (1982). *Corporations and Morality.* Englewood Cliffs, NJ: Prentice-Hall.

Donaldson, T. (1989). *The Ethics of International Business.* New York: Oxford University Press.

Donaldson, T. & Dunfee, T. W. (1994). Toward a unified conception of business ethics: Integrative social contracts theory. *Academy of Management Review,* **19,** (2), 252–84.

Dunfee, T. W. (1991). Business ethics and extant social contracts. *Business Ethics Quarterly,* **1,** (1), 23–51.

Gauthier, D. (1986). *Morals by Agreement.* New York: Oxford University Press.

Gough, J. W. (1957). *The Social Contract,* 2nd edn. New York: Oxford University Press. (Historical summary of the use of social contract).

Keeley, M. (1988). *A Social-Contract Theory of Organizations.* Notre Dame, Ind.: University of Notre Dame Press.

Rawls, J. (1971). *A Theory of Justice*. Cambridge, Mass.: Harvard University Press.

Scheppele, K. L. (1993). "It's just not right": The ethics of insider trading. *Law and Contemporary Problems*, 56, (3), 123–73.

THOMAS W. DUNFEE

social cost–benefits   Economists in the 1940s and 1950s, who developed cost–benefit analysis, analogized the government to a firm. They thought that public-works projects, such as dams, should return a profit to society on its investment. The Flood Control Act of 1938 required a weighing of economic pluses and minuses, for example, the value of irrigation and electricity against the amortized capital cost of building a dam. It permitted the government to finance water projects only when "the benefits to whomsoever they accrue [are] in excess of the costs."

A cost–benefit approach is uncontroversial in relation to governmental projects – including "pork barrel" projects – that provide goods and services, such as electricity and irrigation, for which ordinary markets set prices. It becomes controversial, however, insofar as it replaces public deliberation and legislative intent in the administration of laws that express public values and morality. When Congress outlawed child labor, for example, it regulated markets for moral not economic reasons.

Similarly, Congress has passed environmental laws largely because of ethical concerns, for example, about the extinction of species and the protection of public safety and health. Can the cost–benefit approach apply to public policy in the area of the environment, civil rights, education, the support of the arts, and so on? These policies at present follow from political deliberation through which we form and express our values as a nation. Should they be based instead on the preferences of individuals determined and aggregated by the techniques of cost–benefit analysis?

Cost–benefit aggregation presupposes that all values are subjective. It assimilates ideals and moral commitments to wants and preferences of the sort individuals satisfy in markets. The cost–benefit approach enters these preferences into a social welfare calculus on which policy is then based. Moral deliberation, in contrast, is supposed to be educative. Rather than depend on the "given" or "exogenous" consumer preferences of individuals, it seeks to inform, educate, and constitute public opinion within legitimate democratic political institutions and processes. According to this approach, the public consists not of consumers seeking to promote their own welfare, but of citizens deliberating over shared values, objectively grounded moral beliefs, or conceptions of the common good.

The cost–benefit approach begins with an answer to the moral question: What is the goal of public policy? The goal of public policy, it assumes, is the same as that of the market, namely, to elicit and satisfy consumer wants and preferences. The theory of welfare economics on which cost–benefit analysis rests, equates the public good with the maximum satisfaction of preferences that individuals are willing to pay to satisfy. The theory defines "welfare" or "well-being" in terms of the satisfaction of those preferences.

Critics of the cost–benefit approach, including many environmentalists, believe, on the contrary, that democracy is seized with ethical questions not just economic ones. Environmentalists argue, for example, that persons and property should be protected by right from pollution, as from any form of invasion or coercion. Accordingly, legislation seeks to minimize pollution rather than to maximize welfare. What is more, environmentalists do not believe that smoking, pollution, and other assaults on health improve welfare even if people voluntarily smoke, accept risky jobs, and so on. The role of government may be to create new options and to educate and improve preferences, rather than simply to take them as they come.

Those who defend cost–benefit analysis reply that if people are assumed to be the best judges of their own well-being, the economically efficient outcome – that is, the one that maximizes the satisfaction of preferences weighted by willingness-to-pay – will (tautologously) maximize the well-being or welfare of those individuals. A perfectly competitive market – that is, a market in which all goods are fully owned and people can trade costlessly – would allocate resources to those willing to pay the most for them, and it would therefore reach the welfare-maximizing, efficient outcome. If the role of the government is the same as that of a perfectly competitive market, that is, to allocate resources to those willing to pay the most for them, then cost–benefit analysis is a legitimate basis for public policy. Since markets often fail to capture all willingness to pay, especially in relation to the environment, managers trained in cost–benefit analysis should determine these "unpriced" preferences and allocate resources accordingly.

Many economists are developing techniques to "price" ethical values and political convictions as if they were subjective or personal "consumer" preferences. The primary technique, "contingent valuation methodology," involves asking people how much they are willing to pay for outcomes to which they are morally committed (for example, the existence of an endangered species or a wilderness area they do not expect to visit). Even if citizens would pay only a few dollars each for these "existence" values, the aggregate sum might be substantial.

Cost–benefit analysis, insofar as it treats principled beliefs, moral commitments, and reasoned positions as "externalities" consumer markets have failed to "price," raises several difficulties. First, preferences, being mental states, are unobservable. Analysts must infer them from what a person says or does. However, anything a person says or does – including the answers he or she gives on surveys – can be interpreted in any number of ways. Accordingly, cost–benefit analysis greatly extends the power of governmental officials who, by asking questions and interpreting answers in one way rather than another, obtain the results they want. Since market "failures," "existence" values, and other "unpriced" preferences are pervasive and ubiquitous, moreover, the cost–benefit approach, for all its insistence on free markets, opens the door to centralized planning.

Second, the worth of an ideal or a principle cannot be determined by asking what people are willing to pay for it. Nobody asks economists how much they are willing to pay for their view that social welfare, as they define it, should be a basis of regulatory policy. Why should willingness-to-pay measure the importance of opposing principled positions and moral theories?

People who believe that it is wrong to accelerate the extinction of species, for example, do not express a subjective preference. They affirm a policy position opposed to the assumptions of a cost–benefit approach.

Third, having a preference, however ill-informed or poorly considered, may give the individual a reason to try to satisfy it, but what reason has the government to seek to satisfy that preference? The reply that the satisfaction of preference maximizes well-being is trivially tautological if "well-being" or "welfare" is defined in terms of preference satisfaction. Otherwise, it is false. For example, people as a rule do not report they become happier when their incomes rise, and they can satisfy more of their preferences.

Plainly, cost–benefit analyses have an important role to play in reviewing "pork barrel" public-works projects and subsidies to industry. One may question the applicability of cost–benefit analysis to regulatory policies, however, in which a nation attempts to do what is right but not necessarily what cost–benefit analysts say is efficient.

Bibliography

Hart, H. L. A. (1979). Between utility and rights. *Columbia Law Review*, **79**, 828–31.

Kelman, S. (1981). Cost – benefit analysis: An ethical critique. The American Enterprise Institute for Public Policy Research, Washington DC.

Posner, R. (1979). Utilitarianism, economics, and legal theory. *Journal of Legal Studies*, **8**, 103–19.

Sagoff, M. (1981). At the shrine of Our Lady of Fatima *or* why political questions are not all economic. *Arizona Law Review*, **23**, 1283–96.

Sagoff, M. (1984). On preserving the natural environment. *Yale Law Journal*, **297**, 205–67.

MARK SAGOFF

social ethics The term "social ethics" is used primarily in Judeo-Christian ethics and has become prominent only in the nineteenth and twentieth centuries, paralleling the development of the social sciences. Its concerns are those addressed in philosophical ethics under rubrics such as political philosophy and ethics, social theory, and social philosophy. Social ethics lacks a precise, broadly accepted definition. The term implies a critical reflection, either normative or descriptive, on the social or public aspects of morality as opposed to its strictly personal or interpersonal aspects. It is often used to refer especially to critical study of the morality of the large and complex social, economic, and political arrangements of society (what JOHN RAWLS (1971) has called society's "basic institutions"). BUSINESS ETHICS is a social ethics (in this narrow sense of the term) when it concerns itself with comparative description and ethical evaluation of various political and economic systems or the ethical evaluation of some particular political economy. Many also regard professional and institutional ethics as aspects of social ethics because professions and institutions have social or public character, and behavior within them is structured socially rather than determined in a strictly individual or personal manner. According to this usage, business ethics is a particular type of social ethics.

Social ethics is thus concerned more with social or institutional and professional policies and practices than with individual behavior. Thus, the question of corporate or governmental policies with reference to WHISTLEBLOWING, for example, is a social ethical question, but an individual's decision about whether or not to blow the whistle on an unsafe practice within her corporation may be considered a question of personal, not social, ethics. Some, however, also consider questions of individual behavior in an institutional or professional context to be matters of social ethics as well. Thus, an individual, reflecting critically about whether or not to blow the whistle on unethical behavior by an institution to which she is related, is engaged in social ethics. According to this broad understanding of social ethics, the only moral questions that are not social ethical are those about individual acts which do not affect others, or when the interaction between persons is strictly interpersonal and is not mediated by social, institutional, or professional roles.

Yet, even this restricted range of human action and interaction might fall within the purview of social ethics, because the term is also used simply to refer to the study of the moral life of any definable society or community. This includes the personal or interpersonal dimensions of moral life within the community to the degree that these are socially structured. Ethical reflection influenced by Marxist thought emphasizes the way in which all human actions and relationships are determined by the particular economic or other "class" standing of the individuals involved (see MARX, KARL). FEMINIST ETHICS, as reflected in the slogan "the personal is the political," suggests that even the most personal and intimate human relationships are determined in important ways by the economic and power differentials between the relating individuals. The more recent communitarian movement emphasizes the fundamental social character of human nature and identity and seems to deny that there is any human activity that is purely or absolutely autonomous or individual (see COMMUNITARIANISM).

The distinction between personal and social ethics or between personal, institutional, and professional ethics and social ethics reflects the assumption that human activity has both individual and social (or corporate) dimensions and that both have moral dimensions which are subject to the critical scrutiny of ethics. Human beings may act individually, but much, if not all, of our acting is organized, regulated, and routinized by cultural practices (such as greeting, dating, and eating "rituals," initiation and marriage rites, etc.), social institutions (such as hospitals, schools, armies, churches, etc.), and the law (which formalizes the basic terms of political, economic, and social relationships). Each of these reflects fundamental convictions that define the character of a particular society, though in complex and pluralistic societies – such as postmodern Western societies – agreement about fundamental convictions may be shallow and fragile (see POSTMODERNISM AND BUSINESS ETHICS). As a result, a variety of cultural practices and social institutions (or sets of each) coexist in greater or lesser tension with one another. Both individual and social activities are appropriately evaluated with respect to the typical categories and questions of morality and ethics: values (Is the activity appropriate to the well-being or flourishing of human beings and others?), respect (Does the activity treat others with moral status properly, protecting or promoting their interests appropriately?), and character (How does the activity reflect and serve to inoculate virtue in the actor or actors?).

Social ethics raises questions of value, respect, and character with reference to social activity.

The question of values: According to ARISTOTLE, all human activity is directed toward some *telos*, that is, some end, goal, or purpose which is an aspect of human well-being or flourishing. In other words, human activity is oriented by values. By their actions, individual human beings realize, pursue, or bear witness to distinct or individualized values or their own individualized conceptions of well-being or flourishing. Social activity is also value oriented. The political economy of a society enables persons within it to flourish with respect to some values, possibly at the expense of others; communities and societies gain their unity on the basis of shared values; cultural practices serve basic values by routinizing behavior that is appropriate to such values in an efficient and sustained manner. Thus, schools, colleges, and universities may be said to exist in order to serve the individual and social value attached to knowledge or wisdom. And business enterprises may be understood as gaining their purpose from the way in which the particular goods and services they produce and sell serve important human values or contribute to human flourishing. For example, farms, food-processing enterprises, and grocery stores serve the value placed on the ready and regular availability of both physical nourishment and a variety of foods and beverages pleasing to the palate.

Social ethics evaluates political-economies with respect to the values which basic political and economic arrangements are meant to embody and fulfill. It attends to the broad question of how the basic economic arrangements of society promote human well-being or flourishing. For example, social ethics critically evaluates the claim that free-market arrangements best serve the values of autonomy and material security and comfort, as opposed to the counter-claim that such values must be supplemented by social solidarity which is better served in systems such as socialist ones which promote greater economic equality. It may also concern itself with the question as to whether the organization and practices of various institutions (including business enterprises), are morally valid within some normative social-ethical framework, and with disagreements about whether the values which define the moral purposes of various types of institutions (including business enterprises), are morally valid within some normative social-ethical framework and with disagreements about the values which define the moral purposes of various types of institutions. For example, consider the debate in business ethics about "meaningful work." One way to understand this debate is in terms of the values which define the purpose of business enterprises. If the moral purpose or *telos* of business is defined exclusively by the values served by its products, businesses may not be obligated to organize work in ways that are satisfying to workers, to provide democratic or participatory decision-making processes, or to attend to the way in which business life enhances or diminishes human relationships or friendships. Some might argue that to regard businesses as obligated to provide "meaningful work" is to require them to abandon their attention to the values which more appropriately define their purposes. To deny such obligations is not to deny the values associated with "meaningful work," but to deny that such values define business institutions; other institutions properly serve those values. Others might want to broaden the value-orientation of business enterprises to include the values associated with meaningful work.

The question of respect: Social ethics also critically evaluates social activity in terms of the question of respect. Western philosophical and religious traditions generally affirm that human beings are equal in that each of us, by virtue of certain features we share as human beings, are equal sources of moral claims upon each other. Each of us commands respect from others, and this respect requires particular treatment by others and/or sets definite limits on their value-oriented activities. The respect that is owed to each of us is typically defined in terms of the natural or human rights we are said to hold. In addition to these general or equal rights, we may hold special rights which depend upon various particular roles we play or relationships with others. Debates over whether fetuses, animals, natural entities (rocks, trees, rivers), ecosystems, or communities have rights are debates as to whether these are entitled to respect or are sources of moral claims, which require particular treatment by us and/or sets definite limits on our value-oriented activities.

Whomever is thought to be owed respect and however respect is defined, both individual and social activity is directed and constrained by such respect. Individuals are morally obligated to respect others, but so are institutions and professionals. Moreover, basic social, economic, and political arrangements are subject to ethical critique in terms of whether or not they protect and promote such respect; this is a basic task of social ethics. For example, the defenders of democratic capitalism typically claim that such societies best respects the natural rights of human beings, including the right to participate in their own governance, to own property, and to pursue their own autonomously developed conception of human flourishing. Social ethics analyzes and critiques such claims considering whether or not respect is adequately defined and institutionalized in democratic-capitalist societies.

According to the broader understanding of social ethics, it will also consider the activity of specialized institutions and professions within a society with respect to the question of rights. For example, on this view the debates about what obligations are owed the various business "stakeholders" (the types of persons related in one way or another to a typical business enterprise – stockholders, managers, employees, suppliers, customers, local and wider communities), including the debates about whether employers may hire, fire, promote, or demote employees at will or whether employees are protected by rights requiring due process in employment decisions, are debates within the field of social ethics (*see* EMPLOYMENT AT WILL; STAKEHOLDER THEORY).

The question of character: Human individuals have their own distinctive character traits that are the source of behavior and that produce habits that are often repeated almost unconsciously or unintentionally. Virtues are morally praiseworthy traits of character, traits which typically and habitually produce right actions. Vices are morally inappropriate traits of character. While each of us may have a distinct character, that character is largely shaped by the society, communities, professions, and institutions of which we are a part. Thus, societies produce certain types of characters, and certain types of character are formed by particular institutions, practices, and professions. Moreover, professions and institutions typically attempt to inculcate virtues that are especially appropriate to the goods and values they serve and are necessary to prevent succumbing to the temptations that are prominent given the distinctive expertise and power required by the profession or institution. Indeed, part of what is meant by the "corporate culture" in a particular business enterprise is the way in which such an enterprise routinizes behavior so as to inculcate the virtues thought to be appropriate to the values it attempts to serve. Social ethics concerns itself, then, with the ways in which the basic social, economic, and political arrangements of a society shape character, and with the ways the types of character are encouraged by routinization of behavior in particular institutions, such as business enterprises.

Bibliography

Etzioni, A. (1993). *The Spirit of Community: Rights, Responsibilities, and the Communitarian Agenda.* New York: Crown Publishers.

Feinberg, J. (1973). *Social Philosophy.* Englewood Cliffs, NJ: Prentice-Hall.

Rawls, J. (1971). *A Theory of Justice.* Cambridge, Mass.: Harvard University Press.

Sandel, M. (1982). *Liberalism and the Limits of Justice.* Cambridge and New York: Cambridge University Press.

Stackhouse, M. (1968). *Creeds, Society and Human Rights.* Grand Rapids, Mich.: W. B. Eerdmans.

Stackhouse, M. (1993). *Communitarian Agenda.* Grand Rapids, Mich.: W. B. Eerdmans.

Winter, G. (1966). *Elements for a Social Ethic.* New York: Macmillian.

Winter, G. (1968). *Social Ethics: Issues in Ethics and Society.* New York: Harper & Row.

BARRY PENN HOLLAR

social responsibility (or corporate social responsibility): The concept that business has an obligation to society that extends beyond its narrow obligation to its owners or shareholders. The idea has been discussed throughout the twentieth century, but it was Howard R. Bowen's book *Social Responsibilities of the Businessman* (1953), which originated the modern debate on the topic. Bowen reasoned that there would be general social and economic benefits that would accrue to society if business recognized broader social goals in its decisions.

Eels & Walton (1961) furthered the concept's development with their view of social responsibility: "When people talk about corporate social responsibility they are thinking in terms of the problems that arise when corporate enterprise casts its shadow on the social scene, and of the ethical principles that ought to govern the relationship between the corporation and society."

Davis & Blomstrom (1975, p. 23) gave a more pointed definition of social responsibility with their assertion: "Social responsibility is the obligation of decision makers to take actions which protect and improve the welfare of society as a whole along with their own interests." They suggested two actions that business should take to invoke their social responsibility. First, business should *protect*, which implies avoiding negative impacts on society. Second, business should *improve* the welfare of society, which implies creating positive benefits for society.

A view that places business's social responsibilities in the context of its economic and legal obligations is provided by McGuire (1963): "The idea of social responsibility supposes that the corporation has not only economic and legal obligations, but also certain responsibilities to society which extend beyond these obligations." It is not clear from this definition what these obligations are, beyond the economic and legal. Sethi (1975) alluded to what these responsibilities were when he argued that social responsibility "implies bringing corporate behavior up to a level where it is congruent with the prevailing social norms, values, and expectations."

To build upon the McGuire and Sethi definitions and to help reconcile business's economic responsibilities with those that are social, Carroll (1979, p. 500) proposed a definition that sought to combine the two and give more clarity to business's obligations beyond the economic and legal: "The social responsibility of business encompasses the economic, legal, ethical and discretionary expectations that society has of organizations at a given point in time."

This definition provides us with categories in which to qualitatively state the nature or kind of obligation that business has towards society. First, business has an *economic* obligation to society. Business has a responsibility to produce goods and services that society wants and to sell them at a profit. Unless a business is economically viable, its other responsibilities become moot. To achieve its economic responsibilities, business must be effective, efficient, and make wise strategic decisions.

Another major part of business's social responsibility is *legal* in nature. Business is expected to be economically viable while obeying the laws of the land – federal, state, and local. Just as society has sanctioned the economic system by permitting business to assume a productive role of producing goods and services at a profit, it has also laid down the ground rules – the laws and regulations – under which business is expected to operate. These laws create a form of "codified ethics" in the sense that they formalize certain expectations of business decisions, actions, and practices.

A third kind of social responsibility of business is *ethical* in nature. Though there are ethical dimensions to business's economic and legal responsibilities, the ethical category goes beyond these and identifies an obligation to embrace those activities and practices that are expected, or prohibited, by societal members even though they may not be codified into law. Ethical responsibilities, therefore, embody the range of norms, standards, or expectations about business activity that reflect a concern for what major stakeholders such as consumers, employees, owners, the community, and others regard as fair or just (*see* BUSINESS ETHICS). The ethical responsibility of business includes the dictum to "do no harm" by such activities as polluting the environment, discriminating against workers, producing dangerous products, engaging in misleading advertising, and so on. To be sure, some of these practices are governed by the legal responsibility of business, but some are not. The ethical responsibility embraces a response to the "spirit" of laws and regulations and helps guide business actions in those decision arenas in which regulations are ill-defined or nonexistent. Some view the law as the ethical minimum or "floor" on business behavior, whereas the ethical manager or firm is often expected to operate above the minimum required by law. Ethical leadership would be a manifestation of this kind of business obligation.

The fourth part of business's social responsibility is *discretionary* in nature. Perhaps it is a misnomer to call the discretionary category a responsibility. However, it is clear from the history and practice of business over the decades that society expects business to be a good corporate citizen by contributing to the well-being of the community, through business giving or philanthropy (*see* CORPORATE PHILANTHROPY). The discretionary category of responsibility might well be named the philanthropic category, because the best examples of business fulfilling this expectation typically are considered philanthropic: giving money or other resources to charitable causes, initiating adopt-a-school programs, employing executive loan programs in the community, conducting in-house programs for drug abusers, sponsoring civic events, and so on. The distinction between ethical and discretionary responsibilities is that the latter are typically "desired" by society and not expected in a moral or ethical sense.

In summary, this four-part perspective on social responsibility holds that business should simultaneously fulfill its economic, legal, ethical, and discretionary (or philanthropic) responsibility to society, or business's stakeholders (*see* STAKEHOLDER THEORY). Stated in more pragmatic and managerial terms, the socially responsible firm should strive to make a profit, obey the law, be ethical, and be a good corporate citizen (*see* CORPORATE SOCIAL PERFORMANCE). Though the social responsibility concept is normative in that it proposes what business ought to do, it is also descriptive because it captures the essence of what socially responsible business organizations are doing today.

Bibliography

Bowen, H. R. (1953). *Social Responsibilities of the Businessman*. New York: Harper.

Carroll, A. B. (1979). A three-dimensional conceptual model of corporate social performance. *Academy of Management Review*, **4**, 497–505.

Carroll, A. B. (1991). The pyramid of corporate social responsibility: Towards the moral management of organizational stakeholders. *Business Horizons*, **34**, 3948.

Carroll, A. B. (1993). *Business and Society: Ethics and Stakeholder Management*, 2nd edn. Cincinnati, Ohio: South-Western Publishing Co.

Davis, K. & Blomstrom, R. (1975). *Business and Society: Environment and Responsibility*. New York: McGraw-Hill.

Eels, R. & Walton, C. (1961). *Conceptual Foundations of Business*. Homewood, Ill.: Richard D. Irwin.

McGuire, J. W. (1963). *Business and Society*. New York: McGraw-Hill.

Sethi, S. P. (1975). Dimensions of corporate social responsibility. *California Management Review*, **17**, 58–64.

ARCHIE B. CARROLL

social sciences and business ethics It is convenient to think of the social sciences as the organized pursuit of law-like regularities and theories regarding human action, and to think of BUSINESS ETHICS as the theory and practice of human action aimed at securing a good life in a market, a mixed market, or an exchange economy. Perhaps the most important word in the preceding brief definition of our headword is "convenient," because it emphasizes the fact that what is being offered is merely a stipulative definition or conventional understanding about the key words designating this subject-matter.

Although there is no general agreement about the proper way to define the social sciences and its diverse disciplines, there are different identifiable, self-defined, specialized research communities (i.e., professional or learned societies), academic departments, and scholarly journals. So, one way to proceed to an exhaustive analysis of our subject would be to list the appropriate social-science societies, types of academic departments, and journals, and then examine their particular relations to business ethics. One would still have borderline cases, one of the oldest being history and one of the newest being evaluation science (Michalos, 1992). Among the social sciences, one would include family studies, geography (especially economic and social geography), political science, policy science, planning (urban, rural, and regional), sociology (especially criminology, quality of work life, sociology of work or labor studies, industrial relations and social indicators, psychology, economics, organizational behavior) and anthropology.

Unfortunately, the suggested strategy of approaching our subject is oversimplified because it assumes that we are confronted with a many–one relation, many disciplines to one business ethics, when in fact we are faced with a many-to-many relationship, because different people construe ETHICS and business ethics in different ways. One theoretical approach in the study of ethics is CONSEQUENTIALISM (including UTILITARIANISM as a particular species). However, it too comes in many forms, which increases the variety of subheadings on the business ethics side of the relationship to be correlated with the social-sciences side. A few examples will suffice to illustrate the great importance of social-scientific research to consequentialism. Ruut Veenhoven published three fine collections of research studies on HAPPINESS, any one of which shows a world of difference between the primitive musings of JEREMY BENTHAM, with his felicific calculus and contemporary research. The first, Veenhoven (1993a), is a bibliography of 2,472 studies on the "subjective appreciation of life," and the second, Veenhoven (1993b) is a review of national surveys on the same topic for 56 countries in the 1946 to 1992 period. These were an extension of work begun earlier. Michalos (1991a, 1991b, 1993a, 1993b) reviews the research literature for the past twenty years on happiness and satisfaction with life as a whole and on satisfaction in a dozen domains of life (e.g., satisfaction with one's job, housing, family relations, etc.), and reports the results of testing his explanatory Multiple Discrepancies Theory (MDT) on over 18,000 undergraduates in 39 countries. MDT was designed to provide a new empirical foundation for consequentialist ethics, choice and DECISION THEORY, and microeconomics.

In Michalos (1991a) it was reported that biennial computer searches of the research literature carried out over the past dozen years on the key words "happiness" and "satisfaction" had revealed an average annual publication rate of over 1,100 titles for nearly 20 years. In February 1994 a search was made through Social SciSearch for the single year of 1990 using the original two key words plus "social indicators," "well-being" and "quality of life." To the researcher's astonishment, 11,256 titles were discovered. Electronic databases often

have duplicates and other kinds of "noise" in them, but most of the titles would have some relevance to one or another of the key words which, depending on one's particular project, may or may not be useful.

Although few philosophers have ventured into this empirical work in the consequentialist moral tradition, social scientists have been very active and social scientists working on business ethics are increasingly drawing on this tradition. For example, inspecting the most recent past 12 months of publications in the *Journal of Business Ethics* (*JOBE*, July 1993–June 1994), one finds that 34 (23 percent) of the total 151 articles appearing employed some sort of consequentialist analysis.

Another way to assess the impact of social science on business ethics was suggested by Robertson (1993). She reviewed the articles in *JOBE* in the years from 1982 to 1990, and found that 2.9 percent of them were empirical in the former year compared to 32.6 percent in the latter year. In the three years for which she presented detailed classifications of topics considered, 1988, 1989, and 1990, the most frequently mentioned was "theory." At the end of her review, she offered eight recommendations, including giving more care to connecting empirical research to normative assumptions, emphasizing behavior instead of mere attitudes as a dependent variable, testing theoretical models of ethical decision-making, building more and better theories, developing longer-term research programs, using more diverse experimental designs, and building "links to managerial and public policy applications".

A third way to measure the impact of social science on business ethics is by means of the most recent issue of the *Journal Citation Reports* of the *Social Sciences Citation Index*. Examining the "Cited Journal Listing" for 1992 (Grid: M5), one finds that only one (8 percent) of the 12 journals that are listed as citing *JOBE* in 1992, 1991, and 1990 was not a social science journal. Going in the other direction, one finds that every one of the 48 journals cited by authors in *JOBE* was a social-science journal (Grid: H9, I9).

A fourth way to assess the impact of social science on business ethics is to examine the empirical studies attempting to measure the influence of personal and situational factors on people's ethical decision-making in business contexts. Besides providing information that is interesting in itself, such information has significant instrumental value in helping people understand and train ethical decision-makers. Ford and Richardson (1994) published a splendid analysis of precisely this issue based on a review of 62 articles drawn from a wide variety of journals. Among other things, they found that one study showed that "strength of religious belief was significantly and positively related to strength of ethical standards," 7 studies found that "females are more likely to act more ethically than males," and 7 others found sex had no significant influence on ethical beliefs, a couple of studies found "managers were more ethical than students," 3 studies found Machiavellian managers "perceive ethical problems as less serious than others," 11 studies reported that "respondents saw themselves as more ethical than their peers, supervisors, or other people they knew," 5 studies found that people believed the "behavior of superiors" most influenced their own ethical behavior, 4 studies found a positive "relationship between rewards and the ethical behavior of the individual decision maker," and 2 studies found ethical decision-making inversely related to organization size and 3 others to a person's occupational level. As one would expect, there were often conflicting findings, but the preceding list of findings tended to be most representative of the total set.

Finally, then, it is worthwhile to mention that although the focus of the present essay was on different ways of measuring the impact of social science on business ethics, the causal arrows of influence obviously run in both directions. Business ethics has had and will likely continue to have a profound impact on social science. Indeed, it does not seem to be an exaggeration to say that we have not witnessed such a morally provocative influence on the social sciences since the turn of the century when virtually all of these sciences were driven by reform-minded researchers committed to improving the human condition with the help of their new tools of social analysis.

Bibliography

Ford, R. C. & Richardson, W. D. (1994). Ethical decision making: A review of the empirical literature. *Journal of Business Ethics*, 13, 205–21.

Michalos, A. C. (1980). Philosophy of science: Historical, social and value aspects. In P. T. Durbin (ed.), *A Guide to the Culture of Science, Technology and Medicine*. New York: The Free Press, 197–281.

Michalos, A. C. (1991a). *Global Report on Student Well-Being, vol. I: Life Satisfaction and Happiness*. New York: Springer-Verlag.

Michalos, A. C. (1991b). *Global Report on Student Well-Being, vol. II: Family, Friends, Living Partner and Self-Esteem*. New York: Springer-Verlag.

Michalos, A. C. (1992). Ethical considerations in evaluation. *The Canadian Journal of Program Evaluation*, 7, 61–75.

Michalos, A. C. (1993a). *Global Report on Student Well-Being, vol. III: Employment, Finances, Housing and Transportation*. New York: Springer-Verlag.

Michalos, A. C. (1993b). *Global Report on Student Well-Being, vol. IV: Religion, Education, Recreation and Health*. New York: Springer-Verlag.

Robertson, D. C. (1993). Empiricism in business ethics: Suggested research directions. *Journal of Business Ethics*, 8, 585–600.

Veenhoven, R. (1993a). *Bibliography of Happiness: 2472 Contemporary Studies on Subjective Appreciation of Life*. Rotterdam: Erasmus University, Dept. of Social Sciences, Center for Socio-Cultural Transformation.

Veenhoven, R. (1993b). *Happiness in Nations: Subjective Appreciation of Life in 56 Nations 1946–1992*. Rotterdam: Erasmus University, Dept. of Social Sciences, Center for Socio-Cultural Transformation.

ALEX C. MICHALOS

societies of business ethics   Organizations that promote the study and practice of business ethics.

Business ethics societies provide a forum in which the moral, legal, and philosophical issues of business ethics are openly discussed and analyzed and a means by which research centers, schools, colleges, universities, and individual faculty, as well as representatives from business organizations concerned with business ethics, may exchange ideas. They also facilitate joint ventures among these groups and promote research and scholarship through the regular publication of professional journals. Societies encourage the development of business ethics curricula to include the theory, application, and impact of business ethics and foster improvement in the teaching of business ethics in academic and business settings by promoting a better understanding between the administrators, managers, and/or executives in these settings and those engaged in teaching and research in the field of business ethics. Societies help develop ethical organizations by establishing and maintaining friendly relationships among teachers and scholars in the field of business ethics and those responsible for organizational ethics.

Membership is by application and payment of annual dues. Services provided to members usually include a subscription to the society's journal and reduced registration at the annual meeting. Most societies also distribute a newsletter that may include calls for manuscripts, position openings, upcoming conferences, information about other national and local professional societies and associations related to ethics, listings of recent publications on business ethics, as well as periodicals, videos, newsletters, and other materials. Societies are usually led by an executive board of officers who serve as volunteers and are elected from among the membership.

Examples of Societies of Business Ethics

The Society for Business Ethics
American College
Bryn Mawr, PA 19010 USA

Association for Practical and Professional Ethics
410 North Park Avenue
Bloomington, IN 47405 USA

Eur. Business Ethics Network c/o EFMD
40 rue Washington
B-1050, Brussels, Belgium

Int. Society of Business, Economics, and Ethics
Dept. of Philosophy, Wescoe Hall
University of Kansas
Lawrence, KS 66045 USA

Int. Assoc. for Business Society
Univ. of South Carolina
171 University Parkway
Aiken, SC Z9801

Bibliography

Society for Business Ethics. (1992). *Bylaws.* Department of Philosophy, Rosemont College, Rosemont, Penn.

PETER J. DEAN

socio-economics   The neoclassical paradigm assumes that people have one overarching goal: the satisfying of their wants. Historically, these wants were depicted as materialistic; more recently, satisfaction derived from other sources has been added, such as the pleasure gained from helping the poor, but the core concept remains self-centered and hedonistic and Me-istic: people are propelled by *their* wants, *their* self-interest, *their* profits. Research in this tradition further assumes that a person's various "tastes" can be neatly ordered into one unitary pattern of desire, with a common denominator to "trade-off" various items (apples for oranges, etc.), a notion at the heart of economics. In contrast, my finding is that people have several wants, including the commitment to live up to their moral values, and that these wants cannot be neatly ordered or regulated by prices. This finding provides a starting-point that is fundamentally different from that of the neoclassical premises.

Socio-Economic Based on the I–We Paradigm

This paradigm assumes a divided self, which *does* have the hedonistic urges assumed by the neoclassical paradigm (albeit those too are affected by the values of the society in which the person lives). However, far from mindlessly pursuing these desires, the person is viewed as a judging self which examines its urges and evaluates them by various criteria, the most important of which are moral/social values. A struggle ensues: under some conditions urges win out; in others, morals triumph.

There are many ways of classifying ethical positions. Socio-Economic is moderately deontological, where a deontological position is the notion that actions are morally right when they conform to a relevant principle or duty. Deontology stresses that the moral status of an act should not be judged by its consequences, the way utilitarians do, but by the intention. Moderate deontologists take consequences into account but as a secondary consideration (*see* UTILITARIANISM).

The significance of incorporating this moral dimension into the concept of human nature is that it is perhaps the most important feature that separates us from animals. Our moral commitments and our urges do not often pull us in the same direction. Much of human life is explainable as a struggle between the two forces, and a study of the conditions under which one or the other prevails. Even a modicum of introspection provides first-hand evidence of this significant, perpetual inner conflict. Those who never experience such conflict are either born saints – or utterly debased (Etzioni, 1988).

Having resolved the conflict and decided upon a goal, how does a person go about selecting a course, the means to the goal? Neoclassicists say, *rationally*; that is by using empirical evidence and logical inference. Some of the problems with this approach are contradicted by the observation that most choices are influenced heavily by normative/affective (N/A) factors, that is by people's values and emotions. These factors shape to a significant extent the information that is gathered, the ways it is processed, the inferences that are drawn, the options that are considered, and the options that are finally chosen.

Entire categories of means, whether "efficient" or not, are judged to be unacceptable and *automatically* ruled out of consideration. Thus, most reasonably competent daughters and sons of the American middle class consider it unthinkable not to attend college. About a third of those entitled to collect welfare refuse to apply, because it's "not right." Furthermore, emotions (e.g. impulse) cut short deliberation (when it does occur). While emotions and values have often been depicted as "distorting rationality," which they can do, they also agitate against using means that may be efficient in the narrow sense but are indecent or hurtful to others or the community. Furthermore, N/A factors can often play a positive role in decision-making, especially by mobilizing or inhibiting action or generating or communicating information. In short, the moral order deeply affects not

merely what we seek to accomplish but also the way we proceed.

The Individual in Community

The neoclassical paradigm draws on and contributes to the Whiggish tradition of investing all moral rights in the individual; the legitimate decision-maker is assumed to be the individual. All attempts to modify a person's tastes are viewed as inappropriate interventions (hence the term "consumer sovereignty"). Moreover, the government is usually blamed for attempts to redirect individuals, and such redirections are treated as intrinsically coercive. In contemporary terms, the neoclassical paradigm is essentially libertarian (*see* LIBERTARIANISM)..

A recent philosophical trend, the communitarian movement, attempts to correct this radical individualism. COMMUNITARIANISM builds on the observation that individuals and communities are mutually dependent, and that certain "public goods," not just the individual, are fundamentally of merit – for example, defense, basic research, public education. Some extreme communitarians entirely neglect individual rights in the name of societal virtues, the motherland, or some other such cause. A much more defensible position may be found in recognizing that both individual rights *and* duties to the community have the same basic moral standing, hence, the I & We paradigm. It follows, for example, that we need to both recognize the individual *right* to a trial by jury of peers, and the individual's *obligation* to serve on a jury; to be defended, and to pay for defense; to benefit from the savings of past generations, and to save for future ones.

The voice of the community is typically moral, educational, and persuasive. If coercion is relied upon, this indicates that the community has been weakened, with too many members engaged in activities previously considered unthinkable. The more effective policy is not to enhance the government but to rebuild the social and moral community. This shift starts with a change of paradigms, from the neoclassical to a new approach that encompasses rather than ignores the concept of community, one that balances (*not* replaces) individualistic tendencies with concern for community, and one that reaches beyond the realm of material incentives and sanctions to the role of values, particularly shared values, as long as they are *freely endorsed and not imposed*.

Empirical work on the role of community has shown unequivocally that social collectivities are major decision-making units, often providing the context within which the individual decisions are made. Moreover, in many areas collectivities, if properly structured, can both render more rational decisions than their individual members (though not necessarily highly rational ones) and account for more of the variance in individual decision-making than do individual attributes (see Etzioni, 1988).

Another crucial function of community is to contain the conflict and limit the scope of market competition. This social context is not merely a source of constraints on the market but a precondition for its ability to function. Three types of elements sustain market competition in this way:

- Normative factors, such as a commitment to fairness in competition and to trust that this commitment will be shared by others.

- Social bonds, reflecting the fact that competition thrives, not in impersonal systems of independent actors unbound by social relations, as implied by the neoclassical paradigm, not in the socially tight world of communal societies, but in the middle range where social bonds are strong enough to sustain natural trust and low transaction costs, but not so strong as to suppress exchange orientations.

- Governmental mechanisms as the arbiter of conflicts, where normative factors and social bonds have proved insufficient constraints, and the enforcer of judgments. These crucial roles illustrate the need to move beyond the conceptual opposition between "free competition" and "governmental intervention," which implies that all interventions are injurious and that unshackled competition can be sustainable.

The essential capsule of competition is thus best considered an intertwined set of normative, social, and governmental mechanisms, which have a distinct role but also can, within limits, substitute for one another.

Bibliography

Etzioni, A. (1988). *The Moral Dimension: Toward a New Economics*. New York: Free Press.

AMITAI ETZIONI

South Africa, business ethics in   *see* BUSINESS ETHICS IN SOUTH AFRICA.

South America, business ethics in   *see* BUSINESS ETHICS IN SOUTH AMERICA.

speculation, speculator   A speculator is a person or institution who purchases an asset, not intending to use it or consume it, but to resell it at a favorable price. The better price might be fetched by selling the good at a different location or at a future time. Thought by some to be a form of gambling or "profiteering," the process of speculation actually benefits sellers and users by dampening inter-regional or inter-temporal price differences. For example in the case of some agricultural products, speculation deters wasteful consumption at the harvest season when supply is great. Speculators bid some of the output away from consumption (thereby increasing the market price); then offer the good in the off-season when it otherwise would be very scarce (thereby decreasing the market price). Speculation can enhance economic efficiency. When goods are held off the market during a period of abundance, the value of additional consumption will be relatively low. Sold later, in what otherwise would be a time of relative scarcity, the value of additional consumption will be relatively high. Thus, speculators move consumption from periods of low utility to periods of high utility (*see* UTILITARIANISM).

The motives of the speculator are no different from other buyers: to purchase a product on favorable terms. So long as the practice is not monopolized, competition among speculators for profitable opportunities will prevent the activity from generating economic returns in excess of the value of the service. Excessive profits from speculation will be corrected by more speculators (not fewer). Speculation can occur with regard to a variety of assets, but is more common in commodities and financial markets.

Bibliography

Lerner, A. P. (1964). What would we do without the speculator? In *Everybody's Business.* New York: Harper Torchbooks. ch. 6.

KENNETH G. ELZINGA

Spencer, Herbert   (1820–1903): was the foremost defender of libertarian political theory during the second half of the nineteenth century (*see* LIBERTARIANISM). In *Social Statics* and *The Principles of Ethics*, Spencer formulated a "Rational Utilitarianism" which accepted the greatest (aggregate) happiness as the ultimate good but rejected the direct promotion of this *summum bonum* (*see* UTILITARIANISM). Spencer held that the greatest happiness will be attained only if each person achieves his own happiness, and this requires each person's free adaptive exercise of his own faculties. Thus, the greatest happiness requires that no one's exercise of his faculties interfere with another's exercise of his faculties. Moreover, only if individuals enjoy the benefits of their chosen actions and suffer their costs will the exercise of their faculties become duly adaptive. Thus, the greatest happiness necessitates acceptance of the Law of Equal Freedom, viz., "Every man is free to do that which he wills, provided he infringes not the equal freedom of any other man" (Spencer, 1978, p. 62).

This Law entails moral rights, including the rights to physical integrity, freedom of movement, legitimately acquired property, free exchange and contract, and freedom of belief and speech. Government's special task is to enforce these rights. This enforcement protects the freely adaptive processes which generate the mutually benefical social and economic relationships of "industrial" society. In *The Man Versus The State* especially, Spencer adamantly opposed governmental regulation of social and economic life as a throwback to an earlier "militant" stage of history characterized by force and the sacrifice of the individual to society.

Bibliography

Spencer, H. (1970). *Social Statics.* New York: Robert Schalkenbach Foundation. (Text of the original 1851 edn.)
Spencer, H. (1978). *The Principles of Ethics,* 2 vols. Indianapolis, Ind.: Liberty Classics. (Originally published 1892 and 1893.)
Spencer, H. (1981). *The Man Versus The State.* Indianapolis, Ind.: Liberty Classics. (Includes the text of the 1884 edn plus six additional essays in political ethics.)
Taylor, M. W. (1992). *Men Versus The State: Herbert Spencer and Late Victorian Individualism.* Oxford: Clarendon Press.

ERIC MACK

stakeholder paradox   is formulated as follows: "It seems essential, yet in some ways illegitimate, to orient corporate decisions by ethical values that go beyond strategic stockholder considerations to a concern for stakeholders generally" (Goodpaster, 1991, p. 63). The paradox is that ethics seems both to forbid and to demand a profit-oriented mindset.

The argument behind the paradox focuses on the board's and management's FIDUCIARY DUTY to shareholders, essentially the duty to keep a profit-maximizing promise, and a concern that the impartiality of the so-called "stakeholder" approach simply cuts management loose from certain well-defined bonds of shareholder accountability. Impartiality is thus seen on the one hand as a *virtue* and on the other as a *betrayal of trust.*

Critics of the concept of a stakeholder paradox (Boatright, 1994) have argued that the paradox can be eliminated if stockholder claims are seen as one kind of claim among others (employees, customers, etc.) using a broadly utilitarian idea of property rights (*see* UTILITARIANISM). Defenders have replied that basing property rights on a utilitarian principle creates problems of justice and that the corporation remains and should remain in the paradox (Goodpaster and Holloran, 1994).

The paradox is not of merely academic interest. Managers and boards of directors must confront it in practice due to the increasing attention paid to "constituency statutes" in US corporate law state by state, as well as the 1991 Federal Sentencing Guidelines, which mandate ethics and compliance programs for corporations seeking to avoid severe strict liability sanctions for individual management misconduct. It has been suggested that the way out of the stakeholder paradox lies in appreciating that investors cannot expect of managers behavior what would be inconsistent with the reasonable ethical expectations of the community.

See also **fiduciary responsibility; stakeholder theory; stockholder**

Bibliography

Boatright, J. (1994). Fiduciary Duties and the shareholder–management relation: Or, what's so special about shareholders? *Business Ethics Quarterly,* **4,** 393–407.
Goodpaster, K. (1991). Business ethics and stakeholder analysis. *Business Ethics Quarterly,* **1** (1), 63.
Goodpaster, K. & Holloran, T. (1994). In defense of a paradox. *Business Ethics Quarterly,* **4,** 423–9.

KENNETH E. GOODPASTER

stakeholders and government agencies *see* GOVERNMENT AGENCIES AND STAKEHOLDERS

stakeholder theory A *stakeholder*: any group or individual which can affect or is affected by an organization. This wide sense of the term includes suppliers, customers, stockholders, employees, communities, political groups, governments, media, etc. A more narrow definition is that the stakeholders in a firm are designated as suppliers, customers, employees, financiers, and communities.

Stakeholder theory: a set of propositions that suggest that managers of firms have obligations to some group of stakeholders. Stakeholder theory is usually juxtaposed with STOCK-HOLDER theory: the view that managers have a FIDUCIARY duty to act in the interests of stockholders. "Stakeholder" is an ironic twist of "stockholder" to signal that firms may well have broader obligations than the traditional economic theory has assumed.

The recent history of stakeholder theory has been well documented by Donaldson & Preston (1995). One can find vestiges of the concept in

many areas of business from finance, strategic management (cf. Mason & Mitroff, 1982); organization theory (cf. Thompson, 1967; and Dill, 1958); and ethics (cf. Freeman, 1994). The actual word "stakeholder" first appeared in the management literature in an internal memorandum at the Stanford Research Institute (now SRI International, Inc.) in 1963. The term was meant to generalize the notion of stockholder as the only group to whom management need be responsive. Thus, the stakeholder concept was originally defined as "those groups without whose support the organization would cease to exist." Stemming from the work of Igor Ansoff and Robert Stewart in the planning department at Lockheed, and later Marion Doscher and Stewart at SRI, the original approach served an important information function in the SRI corporate planning process. The Swedish management theorist Eric Rhenman, who is perhaps the originator of the term, was instrumental in the development of stakeholder thinking in Scandinavia, where the concept became one of the cornerstones of industrial democracy. (See Nasi (1995) for the history of the concept in Scandinavia.)

Donaldson & Preston suggest the research on stakeholders has proceeded along three often confused lines. First, there is instrumental stakeholder theory, which assumes that if managers want to maximize the objective function of their firms, then they must take stakeholder interests into account. Second, there is the descriptive research about how managers, firms, and stakeholders in fact interact. Third, there is a normative sense of stakeholder theory that prescribes what managers ought to do. *vis à vis* the stakeholder. To this framework we can add a fourth dimension, the metaphorical use of "stakeholder" which depicts the idea as a figure in a broader narrative about corporate life. We shall combine the first two senses of stakeholders and call that "the analytical approach to stakeholder theory," while the second two senses can be called "the narrative approach to stakeholder theory."

The Analytical Approach to Stakeholder Theory

Any business needs to be understood at three levels of analysis. The first concerns how the business as a whole fits into its larger environment, or the *rational* level. The second concerns

Table 1 Specific Stakeholders in a Large Operation

General	Specific
Owners	Shareowners
	Bondholders
	Employees
Financial Community	Analysts
	Investment banks
	Commercial banks
	Federal Reserve
Activist Groups	Safety and health groups
	Environmental groups
	"Big business" groups
	Single-issue groups
Suppliers	Firm no. 1
	Firm no. 2
	Firm no. 3
	etc.
Government	Congress
	Courts
	Cabinet departments
	Agency no. 1
	Agency no. 2
Political Groups	Political part no. 1
	Political party no. 2
	national League of Cities
	National Council of Mayors
	etc.
Customers	Customer no. 1
	Customer no. 2
	etc.
Customer Advocate Groups	Consumer Federation of America
	Consumers' Union
	Council of Consumers
	etc.
Unions	Union of workers no. 1
	Union of Workers no. 2
	etc.
	Political action committees of unions
Employees	Employee segment no. 1
	Employment segment no. 2
	etc.
Trade Associations	Business Roundtable
	NAM
	Customer trade organization no. 1
	Customer trade organization no. 2
	etc.
Competitors	Domestic competitor no. 1
	Domestic competitor no. 2
	Foreign competitor no. 1
	etc.

Table 2 Stakes of Some Special Stakeholders

Stakeholder	Stake
Customer Segment no. 1	High users of produce
	Improvement of product
Political Parties nos. 1 and 2	High users of product
	Able to influence regulatory process
	Able to get media attention on a national scale
Customer Segment no. 2	Low users of product
	No available substitute
Consumer Advocate no. 1	Effects of XYZ on the elderly
Employees	Jobs and job security
	Pension benefits
Consumer Advocate no. 2	Safety of XYZ's products
Owners	Growth and income
	Stability of stock price and dividend

executes actual *transactions*, or deals or contracts with those individuals who have a stake.

An example of the rational level is to think of business strategy as a game played, for example, between IBM and AT&T. IBM does action X and AT&T responds with action Y. An example of what we mean by the process level would be to look internally and see how the performance and reward procedures work at both AT&T and IBM. An example of the transactions level would be to closely examine the behavior of IBM and AT&T salespersons to see how each treats customers, and to examine the terms of various contracts, deals, promises, and individual motivations of each player. Obviously these three levels of analysis are connected. In fact, we argue that in successful businesses they fit together in a coherent pattern.

The rational level. The rational level of the stakeholder framework must give an accurate picture of the place of a business in its larger environment. It must identify those groups who have a stake, and it must depict the nature of the relationship between stakeholder and firm.

Stakeholder Identification: Who are those groups and individuals who can affect and are affected by the achievement of an organization's purpose? How can we construct a stakeholder map of an organization? What are the problems in constructing such a map? Ideally, the starting-point for constructing a map for a particular business is a historical analysis of the

how the business relates to its environment as a matter of standard operating procedures and routine management processes, or the *process* level. The third concerns how the business

Figure 1: Stakeholder Map of a Large Organization

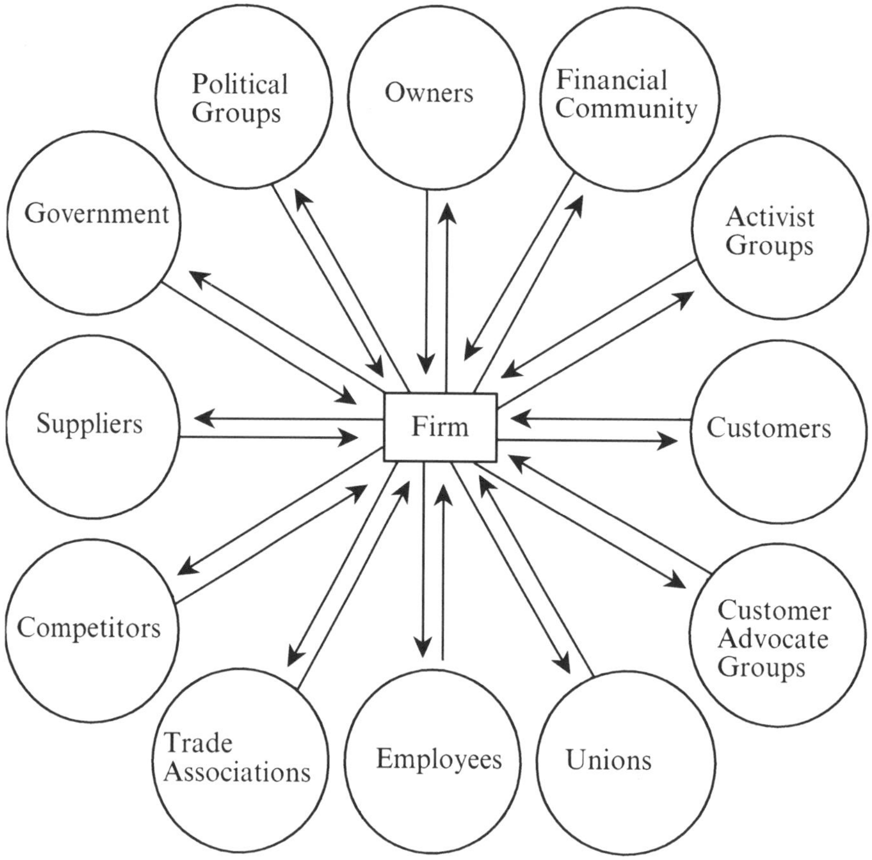

Figure 2: Stakeholder theory

	A. Corporations ought to be governed . . .	B. Managers ought to act . . .	C. The background disciplines of "value creation" are . . .
Doctrine of Fair Contracts	. . . in accordance with the six principles. (Freeman, 1994)	. . . in the interests of stakeholders	– business theories – theories that explain stakeholder behaviour
Feminist Standpoint Theory	. . . in accordance with the principles of caring/ connection and relationships (Freeman, 1994)	. . . to maintain and care for relationships and netrworks of stakeholders	– business theories – feminist theory – social science understanding of networks
Ecological Principles	. . . in accordance with the principle of caring for the earth. (Freeman, 1994)	. . . to care for the earth.	– business theories – ecology – other

environment of that particular firm. In the absence of such a historical document, Figure 1 can serve as a checkpoint for an initial generic stakeholder map.

Figure 1 depicts a stakeholder map around one major strategic issue for one very large organization, the *XYZ* Company, based primarily in the United States. Unfortunately, most attempts at stakeholder analysis end with the construction of Figure 1. The primary use of the stakeholder concept has been as a tool for gathering information about generic stakeholders. Table 1 is a chart of specific stakeholders to accompany Figure 1 for the *XYZ* Company. Even in Table 1 some groups are aggregated, in order to disguise the identity of the company. Thus, "Investment Banks" would be replaced by the names of those investment banks actually used by *XYZ*. Table 2 is an analysis of the stakes of some of those specific stakeholder groups listed in Table 1. Thus, the stake of Political Parties no. 1 and no. 2 is as a heavy user of *XYZ*'s operations, and as being able to elevate *XYZ* to national attention via the political process. Customer Segment no. 1 used a lot of *XYZ*'s product and was interested in how the producer could be improved over time for a small incremental cost. Customer Segment no. 2 used only a small amount of *XYZ*'s product, but that small amount was a critical ingredient for Customer Segment no. 2, and there were no readily available substitutes. As shown in Figure 1 and Tables 1 and 2, the construction of a rational stakeholder map is not an easy task in terms of identifying specific groups and the stakes of each. The figure and tables are enormously oversimplified, for they depict the stakeholders of *XYZ* as static, whereas in reality, they change over time, and their stakes change depending on the strategic issue under consideration.

The process level. Large, complex organizations have many processes for accomplishing tasks. From routine applications of procedures and policies to the use of more sophisticated analytical tools, managers invent processes to accomplish routine tasks and to make complex tasks routine. To understand organizations and how they manage stakeholder relationships, it is necessary to look at the standard operating procedures – the organizational processes that

are used to achieve some kind of fit with the external environment.

Organizational processes serve multiple purposes. One purpose is as a vehicle for communication and as symbols for what the corporation represents. Standard operating procedures depict what activities are necessary for success in the organization. And, the activities necessary for success inside the organization must bear some relationship to the tasks that the external environment requires of the organization if it is to be a successful and ongoing concern. Therefore, if the external environment is a rich multistakeholder, the strategic processes of the organization must reflect this complexity. These processes need not be rigid analytical devices, but rather existing strategic processes that work reasonably well with a concern for multiple stakeholders.

The transactional level. The bottom line for stakeholder management has to be the set of transactions that managers in organization have with stakeholders. How do the organization and its managers interact with stakeholders? What resources are allocated to interact with which groups? There has been a lot of research in social psychology about the so-called transactional environment of individuals and organizations, and we shall not attempt to recapitulate that research here. Suffice it to say that the nature of the behavior of organizational members and the nature of the goods and services being exchanged are key ingredients in successful organizational transactions with stakeholders.

Corporations have many daily transactions with stakeholder groups such as selling things to customers and buying things from suppliers. Other transactions are also fairly ordinary and unexciting, such as paying dividends to stockholders and negotiating a new contract with the union. Yet when we move from this relatively comfortable zone of transactions to dealing with some of the changes that have occurred in traditional marketplace stakeholders and the emergence of new stakeholder groups, there is little wonder that transactions with the corporation's stakeholder map become a real source of discontent.

If corporate managers ignore certain stakeholder groups at the rational and process level, then there is little to be done at the transactional level. Encounters between corporation and stakeholder will be, on the one hand, brief, episodic, and hostile, and on the other hand, nonexistent if another firm can supply stakeholders' needs. Successful transactions with stakeholders are built on understanding the legitimacy of the stakeholder and having processes to routinely surface their concerns. However, the transactions themselves must be executed by managers who understand the currencies in which the stakeholders are paid. There is simply no substitute for thinking through how a particular individual can win and how the organization can win at the same time.

The Narrative Approach to Stakeholder Theory

"The stakeholder theory" can be unpacked into a number of stakeholder theories, each of which has a "normative core," inextricably linked to the way that corporations should be governed and the way that managers should act. On the narrative approach, "stakeholder theory" is thus a genre of stories about how we could live. A "normative core" of a theory is a set of sentences that includes, among others:

(1) Corporations ought to be governed . .
(2) Managers ought to act to . .

where we need arguments or further narratives which include business and moral terms to fill in the blanks. This normative core is not always reducible to a fundamental ground like the theory of property, but certain normative cores are consistent with modern understandings of property. Certain elaborations of the theory of private property plus the other institutions of political liberalism give rise to particular normative cores. But there are other institutions and other political conceptions of how society ought to be structured so that there are different possible normative cores. Such a "reasonable pluralism" is what is meant by the idea of "enterprise strategy," but even that concept is too much in the instrumental/descriptive mode.

One normative core of a stakeholder theory might be the doctrine of Fair Contracts. Another might be Feminist Standpoint Theory, rethinking how we would restructure "value-creating activity" along principles of caring and connection. A third would be an Ecological (or

several ecological) Normative Principles. Figure 2 is suggestive of how these theories could be developed.

Any normative core must address the questions in columns A or B, or explain why these questions may be irrelevant, as in the ecological view. In addition each narrative must place the normative core within a more full-fledged account of how we could understand value-creating activity differently (column C).

Research is proceeding along both the analytical and narrative lines. The rich panoply of concepts that is stakeholder theory threatens to replace, once and for all, the old way of thinking about the publicly held business as the sole property of stockholders, and offers the opportunity to build a wider shared vision of business into the twenty-first century.

Bibliography

Dill, William. (1958). Environment as an influence on managerial autonomy. *Administrative Science Quarterly*, **2** (4), 409–43.

Donaldson, T. J. and Preston, L. E. (1995). The stakeholder theory of the corporation: Concepts, evidence, and implications. *Academy of Management Review*, **20** (1), 65–91.

Freeman, R. E.. (1984). *Strategic Management: A Stakeholder Approach*. Boston: Pitman.

Freeman, R. E. (1994). The politics of stakeholder theory: Some future directions. *Business Ethics Quarterly*, **4** (4), 409–21.

Mason, R. & Mitroff, I. (1982). *Challenging Strategic Planning Assumptions*. New York: John Wiley and Sons.

Nasi, J. (1995). *Understanding Stakeholder Thinking*. Helsinki: LSR-Julkaisut Oy.

Thompson, J.. (1967). *Organizations in Action*. New York: McGraw-Hill.

R. EDWARD FREEMAN

stewardship is a duty of care and conservation with regard to property. It derives from an ancient practice of a property owner's appointment of someone other than himself to watch out for his property in his absence or preoccupation with other cares. That appointee, the steward, had the duty of attending to the preservation, repair, and enhancement of that property, and when the master returned or had time, there would be a strict accounting for that period of care (*see* PROPERTY).

The duty of stewardship is an example of *fiduciary* duty: it was the steward's job to place the interests of the master first in all dealings with the property, setting aside his own interests. Although the duty was owed strictly *to* the master, the steward's tasks focuses on the property itself, to guard and increase it, and so became in effect a duty to that property (*see* FIDUCIARY DUTY).

The obligations of *corporate officers* are clearly duties of stewardship. The shareholders, owners of the corporation and its property, entrust the management of that property to the corporation's employees, especially the higher rank of officers, whose duty it is to make sure that the property increases in value. They are accountable to the shareholders for that stewardship, just as any property manager is accountable to the owner.

But the notion of stewardship goes well beyond clearly defined employer–employee or owner–manager relationships. In certain understandings of property, especially those based on a transcendent religion, the duty of stewarding applies indifferently to all property. If the earth is first and foremost the Lord's, and we are but tenants in it, we are bound to exercise stewardship on behalf of the Lord over all of creation. That duty has two major areas of application, areas not covered by other ethical standards.

First, we must be good stewards over whatever property is legally our own; we are under duties of care and of frugality – not to waste, not to discard unnecessarily, not to allow to be damaged, and not to use any resource more than is absolutely necessary for its purpose. On this understanding, the duty of stewardship curtails the exercise of property rights, and puts a firm limit on our freedom to do what we like with our income and our objects, even those that belong only to us, natural or manmade. Thus stewardship entails a critical posture toward all but the most minimal participation in gambling or gaming (weekly Bingo games to raise money for a church might pass muster), all purchases of unnecessarily expensive items to indulge vanity or machismo, and all industries that cater to preferences not based on real human need (e.g. cosmetics).

Second, that duty generalizes immediately to Creation as a whole: if the earth is the Lord's, we must care for and preserve all that the Lord created. Environmental preservation is a universal duty, counter to all motives of profit that would lead to exploitation and overuse of natural resources. The duty of stewardship limits our freedom to do what we like with the natural world, even as the duty of justice limits our freedom to do what we like with other people.

Invoked in a corporate context, the duty of stewardship requires every employee up to the CEO to be careful to waste no resources: to conserve money (avoiding unnecessary purchases), materials (finding ways to conserve even if a cost–benefit analysis shows that it is cheaper to throw away), and the natural environment in the surrounding community (curtailing emissions of all kinds, working diligently to prevent spills and accidents) (*see* SOCIAL COST–BENEFIT).

Stewardship is invoked in a variety of public contexts, to denounce practices that are wasteful of natural or other resources, in the absence of other ethical objections to those practices. It entails strong environmental preservationism, requiring that each practice destructive of the natural environment be closely regulated for that reason alone, in the absence of a showing of any human detriment or injury; it demands that gambling not be publicly encouraged, even where no one is shown to be harmed by the practice.

The centrality of individual rights in an ethic of business enterprise tends to marginalize the duty of stewardship. It is best understood, in such an ethic, as a form of long-term UTILITARIANISM, arguing for the conservation of all resources as a putative course toward the maximization of human happiness in the very long run.

Bibliography

Stackhouse, M. (1995). *Christian Social Ethics in a Global Era*. Nashville: Abingdon Press.

LISA H. NEWTON

stockholder The owner of one or more shares of the authorized common stock issued by a corporation; also called shareholder. Share certificates specify the number of shares owned, which entitles the holder to a proportionate share of any distribution of the corporation's residual equity, after the payment of the claims of creditors, employees, and governments. The shares are not assessable and the stockholder has no liability for claims against the company. The stockholder's return on investment may be realized through dividends or an increase in the value of the shares. But there may also be no dividends and the company's shares may decline in value or become worthless.

Stockholders have rights, such as voting for directors and auditors, attending annual or special meetings, and voting on changes in the capital structure of the company. However, the stockholders do not "own the company." The corporation is not a piece of property. The board of directors, elected by the stockholders, is legally responsible for the management of the corporation. The FIDUCIARY DUTY of the board is to the corporation itself and not solely to the stockholders in order to maximize their wealth. "Constituency statutes," now enacted in over forty states, recognize explicitly that the board may consider the best interests not only of stockholders, but also of the corporation's other stakeholders, such as the employees, customers, suppliers, and communities.

The corporation is a legal construct of society for accomplishing economic and social ends through the attraction and employment of private capital. Economic theory as commonly taught asserts that the relationship between the stockholder and the management of a publicly held corporation is a simple extension of the relationship between an entrepreneur (as principal) and a hired manager (as agent). This leads to the erroneous notion that "managers are agents of the stockholders." Managers are in fact and in law agents of the corporation.

MAX CLARKSON and MICHAEL DECK

stockholders as stakeholders Stockholders are those individuals or institutions who own a share of a corporation or other business venture. Ownership of the business is divided into a number of portions, or shares. Stockholders purchase these shares, thus gaining a percentage of the business and providing capital for the business to function.

A major controversy in business ethics concerns the conflict between managers' duties to stockholders and managers' duties to employees, vendors, customers, and others who are affected by business decisions (the "stakeholders"). Since stockholders are affected by business decisions, stockholders are also stakeholders. Milton FRIEDMAN and Kenneth Goodpaster argue that a manager's primary duty is to benefit stockholders; the "contract" between stockholders and management requires managers to give priority to the financial interest of stockholders. A manager who decreases profits in pursuit of social goals imposes a "tax" on stockholders, argues Friedman, and only the legislature has the authority to impose taxes. Other writers (such as Anshen, Freeman, Kavanaugh, and Schlossberger) contend that concern for stockholder's interests must be tempered by concern for other stakeholders or social welfare. Arguments offered to support this view include: (a) SOCIAL CONTRACT THEORY sets limits to the legitimate pursuit of profit – an implicit "contract," to which citizens consent by remaining in the state, requires businesses to respect society's needs and welfare; (b) UTILITARIANISM, the view that ethical action aims at the greatest good for the greatest number, sometimes requires limiting profits in order to achieve social welfare; (c) society, which provides businesses with the infrastructure, knowledge base, and other valuable "capital" without which businesses could not operate, is owed a good return on its "investment"; and (d) STAKEHOLDER THEORY.

More broadly, socialists challenge the legitimacy of private ownership of corporations. MARX saw the essential characteristic of human beings as our ability to remake the world in accordance with our vision of a better future. Thus, for Marx, the central moral imperative is freedom of labor. As a result, Marx views the system of private corporations, in which employees' labor is owned by stockholders, as a form of slavery.

Defenders of private ownership, such as ROBERT NOZICK, invoke JOHN LOCKE's theory of property rights (*see* PROPERTY, RIGHTS TO).

Like Marx, Locke begins with the importance of human labor in transforming nature. Locke's conclusion, however, is that, provided one leaves as much and as good for others, anything with which a person mixes his or her labor becomes that person's property, and may be kept or traded freely. Supporters of capitalism also invoke ADAM SMITH's INVISIBLE HAND argument: because, they argue, the market maximizes individual choice and people best know their own needs, free-market forces lead to an optimal outcome as if affairs were guided by an "invisible hand."

A third controversy involves the proper role of stockholders within a corporation: an AUTONOMY-based approach suggests that managers should solicit and be responsive to stockholder views, while a paternalist-based approach suggests that managers should exercise their own judgment in advancing the interests of stockholders (*see* PATERNALISM).

Other issues concerning the acquisition and holding of stock include INSIDER TRADING and socially responsible investing (*see* ETHICAL ISSUES IN INVESTMENT; STOCKHOLDER).

Bibliography

Buchanan, A. (1988). *Ethics, Efficiency and the Market*. Totowa, NJ: Rowman and Littlefield.

Donaldson, T. (1982). *Corporations and Morality*. Englewood Cliffs, NJ: Prentice-Hall.

Freeman, E. & Reed, D. (1983). Stockholders and stakeholders: A new perspective on corporate governance. *California Management Review*, **25**, 88–106.

French, P., Nesteruk, J., Risser, D., & Abbarno, J. (1992). Directors and shareholders. In *Corporations in the Moral Community*. Fort Worth: Harcourt Brace Jovanovich.

Schlossberger, E. (1994). A new model of business: Dual-investor theory. *Business Ethics Quarterly*, **4**, 459–74.

EUGENE SCHLOSSBERGER

strategy and ethics is a genre of management thought that deals with the question: whose voices should be taken seriously, and on what terms, with regard to the future course of an organization? *(See* CORPORATE GOVERNANCE.*)* Strategy and ethics is a liberal challenge to long-standing beliefs about the legitimacy of business and organizations. Strategy and ethics occupies a position on an educational margin between business policy and strategic management, on one hand, and BUSINESS ETHICS and BUSINESS AND SOCIETY, on the other.

A Genealogy of Strategy and Ethics

A genealogy of thinking about strategy and ethics can be traced across four "generations," each of which is distinguished by a particular meaning of "good" management policy.

First, strategy and ethics emerged as an expression of the premise that it is "good" policy for executives to know themselves. "Know and admit to your own voice" is the imperative. Kenneth Andrews (1980, p. 85) argued that executives should pay close attention to the values by which they can live: "Strategy is a human construction; it must in the long-run be responsive to human needs. It must ultimately inspire commitment. It must stir an organization to successful striving against competition. Some people have to have their hearts in it." (*See* VIRTUE ETHICS).

Second, strategy and ethics evolved as an expression of the premise that it is "good" policy for executives to pay attention to other voices raised outside their organizations. "Listen to the rhetorics of other general views of the world" is the imperative here. This imperative is manifest in the competitive strategy approach to strategic management, where Michael Porter (1985) has identified the "five forces" of buyers, suppliers, rivals, new entrants, and purveyors of substitute products. These are generic voices in the vicinity of an organization. This imperative is also manifest in the study of business and society, where Lee Preston and James Post (1975) argued that business organizations are one part of a pattern of "interpenetrating systems."

Third, strategy and ethics has taken a new turn on the premise that it is "good" policy for executives to listen carefully, and to be prepared to respond, to specific persons expressing their own voices. "Listen to what specific persons are saying about their specific stakes" is the imperative here. These persons are called stakeholders. R. Edward Freeman (1984, p. 46) defined a stakeholder as "any group or individual who can affect or is affected by the achievement of the organization's objectives."

Freeman (1984, p. 249) argued that a stake-holder approach to strategy should involve considerations of "distributive justice" (*see* STAKEHOLDER THEORY; DISTRIBUTIVE JUSTICE).

Fourth, strategy and ethics has evolved more recently on the premise that it is "good" policy for executives to justify corporate strategies in accordance with certain common ethical principles. "Think carefully about the specific terms of your relationships with others and find ways to agree on those terms" is the imperative here. Freeman and Daniel Gilbert (1988) give the name "Personal Projects Enterprise Strategy" to one version of this imperative. Freeman and Gilbert (1988) propose that strategies should honor, among others, a principle of personal autonomy and a principle of voluntary agreement.

Gilbert has gone further to argue that strategy is inseparable from a person's ethical responsibility to contribute to human solidarity. He calls this account "Strategy Through Convention" (Gilbert, 1992). Edward Stead and Jean Stead (1992) have extended this particular generation of strategy and ethics by linking strategic management to an environmental ethics.

An Opposing View to Strategy and Ethics

Strategy and ethics should not be confused with strategic ethics. Strategic ethics is an argument that institutions can be structured to safeguard the rights of a strategist against the encroachment of other people. Strategic ethics is based on the assumption that trust is fleeting in human relationships, because people are prone to opportunism unless they are given incentives to act otherwise. Oliver Williamson (1985) proposed one set of safeguards based on minimizing transactions costs. Robert Axelrod (1984) proposed a "tit for tat" strategy as a workable safeguard.

Strategic ethics is an antithesis of the strategy and ethics genre of management thought. On the strategic ethics view, the praiseworthy strategist is adept at rationally maximizing the gains from relationships with others (*see* EGOISM). On the strategy and ethics view, the praiseworthy strategist is adept at bringing different voices into strategic deliberations and actions (*see* SOCIAL CONTRACT THEORY).

Strategy and Ethics, and Feminist Ethics

Three FEMINIST ETHICS themes are prominent in the strategy and ethics genre. First, strategy and ethics educators create a prominent place for new and distinct voices in their accounts about business and organizations. This emphasis parallels a feminist concern with giving voice to those who have previously been silenced in modern institutions. This facet of strategy and ethics challenges a traditional view that the history of an organization can be explained in terms of the exploits of one more-or-less-omniscient mastermind, usually the chief executive.

Second, strategy and ethics educators create an account in which new and different voices participate in debates about the legitimacy of modern business institutions. This emphasis parallels a feminist concern with empowering those who were previously powerless. This facet of strategy and ethics challenges the traditional view – for example, articulated by Andrew Carnegie (1920) – that ordinary citizens should trust business leaders to practice as wise stewards who have the good of society foremost in their minds.

Third, strategy and ethics educators spread a belief that some liberal conception of a common good can be advanced as a direct consequence of management practice. This emphasis parallels a feminist concern with empathy and human connection. This facet of strategy and ethics challenges a traditional view from neoclassical economics – sustained in strategic management – that the greatest social good will come as a by-product of the market mechanism.

Bibliography

Andrews, K. (1980). *The Concept of Corporate Strategy*, rev. edn. Homewood, Ill.: Richard D. Irwin.

Axelrod, R. (1984). *The Evolution of Cooperation*. New York: Basic Books.

Carnegie, A. (1920). *The Autobiography of Andrew Carnegie*. Boston: Houghton Mifflin.

Freeman, R. E. (1984). *Strategic Management: A Stakeholder Approach*. Boston: Pitman.

Freeman, R. E. & Gilbert, D. R., Jr. (1988). *Corporate Strategy and the Search for Ethics.* Englewood Cliffs, NJ: Prentice-Hall.

Gilbert, D. R., Jr. (1992). *The Twilight of Corporate Strategy: A Comparative Ethical Critique.* New York: Oxford University Press.

Porter, M. (1985). *Competitive Strategy: Techniques for Analyzing Industries and Competitors.* New York: Free Press.

Preston, L. & Post, J. (1975). *Private Management and Public Policy: The Principle of Public Responsibility.* Englewood Cliffs, NJ: Prentice-Hall.

Stead, W. E. & Stead, J. (1992). *Management for a Small Planet.* Thousand Oaks, Calif.: Sage Publications.

Williamson, O. (1985). *The Economic Institutions of Capitalism: Firms, Markets, Relational Contracting.* New York: Free Press.

DANIEL R. GILBERT, JR.

subliminal advertising   Advertising that contains images or messages that are below the threshold of perception, consciousness, or apprehension, or too slight to be consciously perceived.

The subliminal threshold in early studies was defined as the stimulus intensity correctly perceived by the individual 50 percent of the time (Weiner & Schiller, 1960). Silverman (1976) defined subliminal as "the absence of evidence that the individual is aware of the impinging stimulus before its effect is felt" (p. 311). By this definition, any stimulus can be subliminal if the observer is not attending to it consciously.

Three areas have been examined to determine subliminal effects: psychological, physiological, and behavioral (choice) responses, the last of which is of particular interest to advertising specialists.

Choice Behavior in Advertising and Marketing

Advertising research has focused on whether subliminal suggestion can be choice specific, thereby prompting the purchase of refreshments or the selection of particular merchandise. Vicary in 1957 claimed to increase concession sales in a movie theater through the tachistoscopic presentation of the phrases "Eat Popcorn" and "Drink Coca Cola" at 1/2000 of a second (Bevan, 1964). However, the few controlled studies of the impact of sub-

liminal suggestion on choice have been contradictory (George & Jennings, 1975).

Zuckerman (1960) elicited increased writing when an experimental group received tachistoscopic instructions superimposed on pictures they were asked to describe, and elicited less writing when instructions were "don't write." Dixon (1981) and Moore (1982) suggested these results were due to a "ceiling effect" prompted by fatigue. Other research has shown that a subject's attitudes toward unfamiliar subliminally presented stimuli become more positive with repeated exposures (Bornstern et al., 1987).

Wilson Bryan Key contended that advertising in which messages are subliminally embedded stimulates an emotional response as well as identification with the brand name. Further, he suggested advertisers commonly use this mechanism as an effective selling device. Key tested over 1,000 male and female adults who were shown a gin advertisement that contained subliminally embedded sexually oriented messages. Subjects were asked to describe their feelings as they looked at the ad. Key reported that 62 percent of the subjects claimed feelings of sexual stimulation (Key, 1980).

Bagley and Dunlap (1980) found a significantly higher response to two ads that contained subliminally embedded sexually oriented messages than to two others that did not. The study was criticized as failing to measure the degree of effect ads had on subjects and of the effect on brand attitude, purchase intentions, or brand recall. Kilbourne et al. (1985) found that galvanic skin response measurements were heightened for versions of ads with such embedded messages, which may influence viewer's evaluations of ads. Yet subliminally embedded, sexually oriented stimuli do not appear to influence consumer preference, or brand name and ad recall others report (Kelly & Kessler, 1978; Gable et al., 1987).

DeFleur and Petranoff (1959) found communication with subliminal messages over closed circuit and commercial TV to be possible, but messages are ineffective as persuasive devices. Vokey and Read (1985) found no evidence of impact of subliminal messages in popular music and in advertising. They found evidence that the apparent presence of backward messages in popular music is a function more of the active construction of the perceiver than of the existence of the messages themselves.

Krugman (1977), writing in support of subliminal effects, suggested that advertising research should pay attention to the different functions of brain hemispheres, asserting that the right brain absorbs images while the left brain controls verbal recall. Cuperfain and Clark (1985) tested a model of subliminal stimulation based on studies of information-processing by the right hemisphere and found significant effects on stated preference for highly advertised products. They warned advertisers not to discount subliminal messages too quickly. Consumer attitudes may be positively affected regarding image creation, preference, or some other objective short of actual purchase.

See also **advertising ethics; ethics of marketing; marketing and the consumer; media ethics; situation ethics**

Bibliography

Bagley, G. S. & Dunlap, B. J. (1980). Subliminally embedded ads: A turn on? *Southern Marketing Proceedings,* 296–8.

Bevan, W. (1964). Subliminal stimulation: A pervasive problem for psychology. *Psychological Bulletin,* **61** (2), 81–99.

Bornstern, R. F., Leone, D. R., & Galley, D. J. (1987). The generalizability of subliminal mere exposure effects: Influence of stimuli perceived without awareness on social behavior. *Journal of Personality and Psychology,* **53** (6), 1070–9.

Cuperfain, R. & Clark, T. K. (1985). A new perspective of subliminal perception. *Journal of Advertising,* **14** (1), 36–41.

DeFleur, M. L. & Petranoff, R. M. (1959). A televised test of subliminal persuasion. *POQ,* **23,** 168–80.

Dixon, N. F. (1971). *Subliminal Perception: The Nature of a Controversy.* New York: McGraw-Hill.

Dixon, N. F. (1981). *Preconscious Processing.* London: Wiley.

Gable, M., Wilkens, H., Harris, L., & Fernberg, R. (1987). An evaluation of subliminally embedded sexual stimuli. *Journal of Advertising,* **16** (1), 26–30.

George, S. G. & Jennings, L. B. (1975). Effect of subliminal stimulation on consumer behavior: Negative evidence. *Perceptual Motor Skills,* **41,** 847–53.

Kahneman, D. (1973). *Attention and Effort.* Englewood Cliffs, NJ: Prentice-Hall.

Kelly, S. & Kessler, B. (1978). Subliminal seduction: Fact or fantasy. *Southern Marketing Proceedings.*

Key, W. B. (1980). *Clam-Plate Orgy: And Other Subliminal Techniques for Manipulating Your Behavior.* Englewood Cliffs, NJ: Prentice-Hall.

Kilbourne, W., Painton, S., & Ridley, D. (1985). The effects of sexual embedding on responses to magazine advertisments. *Journal of Advertising,* **14,** 48–55.

Krugman, H. E. (1977). Memory without recall, exposure without perception. *Journal of Advertising Research,* **17,** 7–12.

Moore, T. E. (1982). Subliminal advertising: What you see is what you get. *Journal of Marketing,* **46,** 38–47.

Silverman, L. H. (1976). Psychoanalytic theory: The reports of my death are greatly exaggerated. *American Psychologist,* **31** (9), 621–37.

Taylor, J., Rosenfeldt, D., & Schulz, R. W. (1961). The relationship between word frequency and perceptibility with a forced choice technique. *Journal of Abnormal Social Psychology,* **62,** 491–6.

Theus, K. (1994). Subliminal advertising and the psychology of processing unconscious stimuli: A comprehensive review of research. *Psychology and Marketing,* **11** (3).

Vokey, J. R. & Read, J. D. (1985). Subliminal messages: Between the devil and the media. *American Psychologist,* **40,** 1231–9.

Weiner, M. & Schiller, P. H. (1960). Subliminal perception or perception of partial cues. *Journal of Abnormal and Social Psychology,* **61** (1), 124–37.

Zuckerman, M. (1960). The effects of subliminal and supraliminal suggestions on verbal productivity. *Journal of Abnormal and Social Personality,* **60** (3), 4–11.

KATHRYN T. THEUS

substance abuse, drug testing, advertising substances   Substance abuse is the deliberate use of a drug in a manner that damages one's health or one's ability to function. Substance abuse does not depend on the type of drug used. Legal, illegal, and prescription drugs can all be abused. Professionals who study and treat substance abuse routinely include alcohol and tobacco among the major drugs of concern.

A drug can be considered "any substance that, when taken into the body, alters the way we function" (Schlaadt, 1992, p. 3). Drugs include medicines, illegal substances like cocaine, heroin, and marijuana, and legal substances like alcohol, nicotine, and caffeine.

Substance abuse is widely recognized as a major social problem, one that affects the quality of life in society and in the workplace. In terms of the US economy, the total cost of drug abuse is estimated to be between $100 and $200 billion a year, much of it attributed to lost productivity.

Employee assistance programs are one response by business to the problem of substance abuse. Such programs promote the identification and referral for treatment of employees whose performance suggests substance abuse. While the administration of these programs requires sensitivity to concerns like confidentiality, EAPs have generally not been ethically controversial.

Drug Testing of Employees and Job Applicants

The absence of controversy is clearly not characteristic of another employer response to the problem of substance abuse: mandated routine or random drug testing of employees and job applicants.

Employers have an interest in identifying drug users for a variety of reasons: maintaining a safe working environment and protecting public safety; creating a drug-free workplace; maintaining a productive workforce; reducing healthcare costs. While reasons advanced for opposition to drug testing are many, including questions about the accuracy of the tests, the primary concern is the privacy of individuals tested.

Privacy may be threatened in two different ways. The actual procedure for collecting the sample may require urinating on demand, under surveillance. In addition, there is the gaining of information about the person's private life that the employee or job applicant does not wish to reveal. Does the employer have a legitimate claim to information about (prospective) employee use of certain drugs outside of the workplace, especially where there is no evidence of inadequate job performance? A positive test does not clearly identify impairment (though residual effects of drugs may continue longer than the immediate desired effect); it simply provides evidence of recent use of a drug being tested for. It is essential that employers be able to insist that employees not be impaired on the job; it is not immediately clear that employers

should demand access to information about off-the-job drug use.

It is generally agreed that individual privacy, while very important, is not an absolute value. It does not "trump" all other considerations. Privacy objections carry less weight when there is a reason to suspect drug abuse (for example, a demonstrated performance problem) or when the particular occupation has a direct impact on the safety of others. In these situations, public safety or the need to identify the reason for poor performance provides a stronger justification for gaining information about the individual's off-the-job behavior than the simple desire to screen out users of some drugs. Workplace drug testing raises basic questions about the nature, extent, and limits of employee privacy.

Alcohol and Tobacco Advertising

Smoking is related to a broad range of diseases (including coronary heart disease and many forms of cancer) and is the leading cause of avoidable death in the United States. Alcohol-related motor vehicle accidents are the No. 1 public health problem for young people in the United States. Alcohol use is involved in most reported cases of child abuse and spouse abuse and in nearly half of all homicides. Most of the lost productivity caused by drug abuse is attributed to alcohol abuse (though alcohol is rarely tested for in drug-testing programs). The overall cost to society of the abuse of tobacco and alcohol is enormous; these two legal drugs cost the United States more in lives and economic losses than all illegal drugs combined.

Concerned about the widespread public health implications of the use of tobacco, some organizations (including the American Medical Association) have recommended a ban on the promotional advertising of cigarettes. They argue that the public health interest is incompatible with the active promotion of smoking through advertising. The discussion of a possible ban has included two very different considerations: 1) whether it is appropriate to understand cigarette advertising as directed toward getting smokers to change brands and not as attempting to entice non-smokers to begin; and 2) whether a ban or other severe restrictions on advertising a legal product is an acceptable restraint on free speech. In the process of addressing the specific issue of restrictions on the advertising of tobacco and alcohol, the general question of appropriate restraints on commercial speech in a democracy has emerged as an issue requiring serious attention.

Alcohol and tobacco are among the most widely advertised of all commodities in the United States, and a variety of questions are being raised about socially responsible advertising of these drugs. One major concern has been whether adolescents are being influenced by advertising to begin drinking or smoking. Young people may be especially susceptible to the active and glamorous images of alcohol and cigarette users presented in advertising, often in publications or associated with events popular among the young. The use of cartoon-like characters has also led some to conclude that advertising is being directed toward the young.

Research has not clearly demonstrated that advertising directly affects behavior in regard to drinking or smoking, but some researchers conclude that a small but significant correlation exists between exposure to advertising and drinking or smoking beliefs and behaviors among youth. The ethical issue is determining what is responsible advertising in view of the possibility that young people could be influenced by advertising to use drugs that have serious problems associated with their abuse.

Bibliography

DeCew, J. W. (1994). Drug testing: Balancing privacy and public safety. *Hastings Center Report*, **24** (2), 17–23.

DesJardins, J. & Duska, R. (1990). Drug testing in employment. In Des Jardins & J. J. McCall (eds), *Contemporary Issues in Business Ethics*. Belmont, Calif.: Wadsworth. 202–7.

Dunn, W. (1993). Government-mandated warnings on alcohol advertisements: Unnecessary, ineffective, harmful and unconstitutional. *Vital Speeches of the Day*, **59**, 749–51.

Dupont, R. L. (1993). Mandatory random testing needs to be undertaken at the worksite. In R. Goldberg (Ed.), *Taking Sides: Clashing Views on Controversial Issues in Drugs and Society*. Guilford, Conn.: Dushkin, 62–7.

Gostin, L. O. & Brandt, A. M. (1993). Criteria for evaluating a ban on the advertisement of cigarettes. *Journal of the American Medical Association*, **269**, 904–9.

Grube, J. W. & Wallack, L. (1994). Television beer advertising and drinking knowledge, beliefs, and intentions among schoolchildren. *American Journal of Public Health*, **84**, 254–9.

Novello, A. C. (1993). Alcohol and tobacco advertising. *Vital Speeches of the Day*, **59**, 454–8.

Schlaadt, R. G. (1992). *Drugs, Society, & Behavior*. Guilford, Conn.: Dushkin.

LEONARD J. WEBER

supererogation A supererogatory act is an act that is beyond the call of duty. It is something that is morally good to do but not obligatory. Examples of supererogatory acts are donating blood, volunteering on a rape crisis hotline, babysitting (without accepting recompense) a friend's two-year-old triplets for the afternoon, or throwing oneself on a live hand grenade in order to save one's buddies' lives.

Arguably it is important in business contexts (and indeed any work context) to distinguish what is morally obligatory from what is supererogatory. Just as one needs to know what is morally off-limits, one needs to know what is beyond duty. One needs to know what others count on one to do, as distinct from what would be appreciated but is by no means a job requirement. Outside of such a context it is less clear that this distinction is crucial.

In an influential article, "Saints and heroes," J. O. Urmson argued that this distinction is indeed crucial for ethics. He objected to ethical theories which classify all acts as either forbidden, merely permissible, or obligatory, pointing out that this threefold classification fails to capture saintly and heroic acts. Saintly and heroic acts are not obligatory (nor, usually, are they forbidden); and to classify them as merely permissible is to miss their special goodness. What is needed, Urmson suggested, is another category: that of supererogatory acts. Ethical theory needs to distinguish sharply, he argued, between acts which go beyond duty, and acts required by duty.

Some critics question the utility of the "baseline" approach to ethics (according to which everything below the line is strictly required, and everything above is strictly beyond duty) that Urmson advocates. Thus Christopher New argues that we have a duty to do whatever act (of those open to us) will produce the most good. True, heroic and saintly acts are not possible for those of us who are weak or cowardly; but, New suggests, we have a duty to be, and to become, as good as we possibly can, and to try to become saintly and heroic. Rather than say that our duties extend only to a set of "minimal duties," as Urmson favored, we should say that we all have a duty to do (and be) the best we possibly can.

Elizabeth Pybus advances a similar but slightly weaker thesis. She holds that we have a duty to be as good as we possibly can, but, unlike New, does not defend the utilitarian thesis that we ought to do whatever act will produce the most good (*see* UTILITARIANISM). Emphasizing ideals and virtues and the variety of ways in which these can be exemplified, she holds that we all have a duty to be, for example, courageous, but points out that this does not entail that we all have a duty to do the same courageous acts.

It is helpful to see how Immanuel Kant's (1724–1804) distinction between perfect and imperfect duty provides a reply to Urmson's thesis, and motivates either Pybus's position or a slightly weaker view. Kant's ethics arguably constitute a counter-example to Urmson's claim that without expanding the threefold classification of acts to recognize a separate category of supererogatory acts, ethics fails to capture the moral phenomena of the heroic and saintly. Kant's imperfect duties are duties to adopt certain ends, specifically the happiness of others and one's own perfection. Indirectly they require one to perform some acts or other of a general type – to help others and to develop one's talents – but they do not specify exactly what one is to do. In Kant's scheme, acts which most contemporary ethicists would classify as supererogatory are not really beyond duty, since one must perform some such acts. They are ways of "fulfilling" imperfect duties. ("Fulfill" needs scare quotes since the duties are never discharged, but rather are to guide and direct one all one's life.) (*See* KANTIAN ETHICS.)

Their differences aside, these alternative views raise the question of whether the category of supererogatory acts is, as Urmson claims it is, crucial to ethical theory. Do we need to draw a line, in ethical theory, between those acts which are morally required, and those which it would be good to do, but which one is in no way required to do?

Disagreements on this will depend partly on what one thinks our duties are: is it that we are morally required to do only a minimum (possibly, but not necessarily low), such that all good deeds beyond that minimum are essentially optional? Those who hold that we are obligated to do as much good as we possibly can or to try to be as good as we possibly can (New) will respond in the negative, as will Kantians who maintain that we have an imperfect duty to improve ourselves morally and that this duty precludes drawing a line and saying, "This much is required; anything more is optional" (Baron).

The disagreement can be traced to meta-ethical differences. Many of those who believe that ethics does need to recognize a category of the supererogatory construe duty on a legalistic or institutional model, holding that it is part of the concept of duty that we have a right to demand that others fulfill their duties (Urmson). Others distance themselves from this view, but tacitly assume (as does David Heyd, when he claims that a refusal to do a favor cannot be criticized as morally wrong since one can ask for a favor but never claim it) that x cannot be wrong unless it wrongs someone. Those who construe "duty" more broadly tend to be less sympathetic to the view that a line can and should be drawn, in ethical theory, between duty and the supererogatory.

Urmson's arguments reflect these and other disagreements. Here are some of the arguments he offers in defense of his claim that our "moral code" must distinguish between morality's basic requirements and "the higher flights of morality." 1) We need to know precisely what our duties are and such precision is not possible with respect to (e.g.) alleged duties to help others. 2) It is imperative that people not fall below a minimum of decency; but if more than that minimum is presented to us *as* morally required, we will be less willing to abide by morality's minimal requirements. 3) It is preferable that people be free from pressure, including moral pressure; it is best, therefore, that our duties be kept to a minimum.

To reply: argument (1) is based on an assumption that many philosophers (e.g., Kant) reject, the assumption that all duties are such that we may, indeed should, exact them like debts. In addition, as New has argued, the "precision test" is open to question. New also points out that (2) is a dubious psychological claim; it is no less likely that loftier expectations would result in better conduct. But (3) merits more serious consideration. One might reply that the fact that x is a duty for S does not entail that it is appropriate to pressure S to x. But (3) can be recast, and indeed has been by Heyd and others. The point, they suggest, is that moral constraint (with or without pressure to conform) limits freedom. Since the notion of a duty does entail moral constraint, it is desirable to keep our duties to a minimum. This argument has found favor with many philosophers; it hinges, however, on the assumption that moral constraints limit freedom, an assumption that some, notably Kant, would reject.

Urmson's article was influential both in that it convinced many readers that ethical theories which do not have, and cannot accommodate, a category of supererogatory acts are *ipso facto* defective, and in the interest it generated in related questions. Related questions include the following: (a) What are the necessary and sufficient conditions for an act's being super-erogatory? (b) At what point can we say that we have done enough, that the rest is beyond duty? (c) What ethical theories can best accommodate the supererogatory?

On (a), there are disagreements as to whether an act must, to qualify as supererogatory, be performed from altruistic motives or whether, as Heyd contends, the motive need not be altruistic as long as the intention is. Alternatively, one might argue that motive and intention are both irrelevant. Another issue concerning (a) spills over into (b): Must the act involve considerable self-sacrifice to be supererogatory?

Disagreements on (b) abound, particularly within discussions in applied ethics, such as the debate over our obligations to alleviate famine and poverty. Peter Singer advocates a very high cut-off and has sparked a flurry of dissent. The more popular (and personally less demanding) views favor drawing the line fairly low, and often appeal to the desirability of keeping moral requirements from "limiting our autonomy." They reject the suggestion that to qualify as supererogatory the act must involve self-sacri-fice, and maintain that non-spectacular acts, such as those of doing a small favor for a neighbor, should qualify (*see* AUTONOMY).

Regarding (c), rule-utilitarianism is often held to be especially suited to accommodate the supererogatory, the idea being that utility is maximized not by requiring individuals to do all they can to maximize utility – since the burden would generate unhappiness for each of them – but rather by requiring something less onerous. Deciding just what degree of beneficences should be required has thus been a task for rule-utilitarians: at what point is too much asked of people, so that the disutility of having to conform to demanding moral rules (or disutility generated by moral problems) lowers the net utility?

One other issue, closely related to (a) and (b), deserves mention: what is the basis for the claim that despite being so very good, supererogatory acts are not obligatory? Is it, as some familiar arguments suggest, (just) that many people are incapable of living up to tougher demands, that is, that they cannot perform many supereroga-tory acts? If we could all be saints or heroes, would there cease to be a need for the category of the supererogatory? Heyd argues that the need would remain. Even if we could all be saintly and heroic, it is preferable, he maintains, to regard a range of good deeds as beyond duty. In support of his claim, he cites the value of being free from moral constraints. He thus defends "unqualified supererogationism": its value is not contingent on human limitations.

See also **altruism and benevolence; duty; excellence; moral imperatives; moral rules; roles and role morality; whistleblowing**

An earlier version of this entry appeared in L. C. Becker & C. B. Becker (eds), *Encyclopedia of Ethics.* New York: Garland, 1992.

Bibliography

Baron, M. (1995). *Kantian Ethics Almost Without Apology.* Ithaca: Cornell University Press, chs 1-2.

Fishkin, J. S. (1982). *The Limits of Obligation.* New Haven: Yale University.

Heyd, D. (1982). *Supererogation.* Cambridge: Cam-bridge University Press.

Hill, T. E., Jr. (1971). Kant on imperfect duty and supererogation. *Kant-Studien,* **62**, 55–76. Reprinted in Hill (1991). *Dignity and Practical Reason.* Ithaca: Cornell University Press.

Mellema, G. (1991). *Beyond the Call of Duty: Supererogation, Obligation and Offense.* Albany: State University of New York Press.

Montague, P. (1989). Acts, agents and super-erogation. *American Philosophical Quarterly,* **26**, 101–11.

New, C. (1974). Saints, heroes and utilitarians. *Philosophy,* **49**, 179–89.

Pybus, E. (1982). Saints and heroes. *Philosophy,* **57**, 193–9.

Singer, P. (1972). Famine, affluence and morality. *Philosophy and Public Affairs,* **1**, 229–43.

Urmson, J. O. (1958). Saints and heroes. In A. I. Melden (Ed.), *Essays in Moral Philosophy.* Seattle: University of Washington Press. 198–216. Reprinted in J. Feinberg (Ed.), (1970). *Moral Concepts.* Oxford: Oxford University Press, 60–73.

MARCIA W. BARON

surveys Structured efforts to identify and understand the propriety of individuals', groups', and organizations' attitudes and behaviors in business settings.

Surveys of business ethics are designed to accomplish a variety of goals using a number of information gathering techniques. The complex and, sometimes, sensitive nature of the information sought can increase the potential for drawing incorrect conclusions from the data collected.

Business ethics surveys accumulate information about the behavior and attitudes of: business people in general; industry members, entire organizations; areas/departments/functions; professions; and various job classifications. For example, in 1992 the national Harris poll asked a general public sample whether business executives and small business owners had unethical standards of conduct (Harris Poll of 1,256 adults printed in "USA Snapshots," *USA Today,* Sept. 3, 1992).

The goals of business ethics surveys vary depending on the interests and concerns of the survey users and designers. Many surveys are created simply to describe the current situation in a particular setting or group, while others seek to compare the past with the present. It is common for business ethics surveys to be used to measure performance and as benchmarks against which future performance may be evaluated. The use of a business ethics survey

can signal to those surveyed that there is concern about the correctness of some behavior(s), which may then lead to a reduction in or avoidance of possible ethical problems.

Business ethics survey data is gathered: by using questionnaires; by conducting interviews; and by examining published records and data. By far the most extensively used survey technique is the prepared, written questionnaire which is sent or given to a sample of the targeted population (e.g., 500 employees out of the total number of employees in the manufacturing group of Ford Motor Company). Such questionnaires ask for respondents to self-report a variety of information about their business ethics attitudes, ethical dilemma solutions, and actual on-the-job behaviors. The structured interview method (where the same set of questions are asked of each respondent) is used to allow more extensive probing of responses to provide broader or more detailed information. The surveying of secondary sources (i.e., published materials reporting on behavior, action, or attitudes) is a third way to gather information about business ethics. For example, the Justice Department publishes reports describing the number of business organizations which have been convicted of violating various Federal laws.

Any attempt to draw inferences about the business ethics attitudes or behaviors from a survey is fraught with a number of pitfalls, including: non-response bias, reported versus actual behavior, and under-specification of the situation. In any survey situation those who choose to respond may hold different opinions (or may have engaged in different behaviors) than those who choose not to respond. This can create an improper description of the survey's results and thus erroneous conclusions. Where respondents are asked about the propriety of their own behaviors there can be a conscious or unconscious attempt to either tell the survey(er) what the respondent believes will make the survey(er) happy or will make the respondent look "good." In either case the data will not be correct, possibly leading to wrong conclusions. When respondents are presented with an ethical dilemma for solution, under-specification of the situation can lead to differential sets of assumptions by respondents. Should a significant proportion of respondents assume facts about the situation different from those made by the survey designers, then improper conclusions could be drawn.

Bibliography

Baumhart, R. (1980). How ethical are businessmen? *Harvard Business Review*, **39**, 6-12.

Brenner, S. & Molander, E. (1977). Is the ethics of business changing? *Harvard Business Review*, **55**, 57–71.

Posner, B. & Schmidt, W. (1989). Values and the American manager: An update. *California Management Review*, **26**, 202–16.

STEVEN BRENNER

T

takeovers A takeover is the acquisition of one firm, called the target, by another. A hostile takeover is one opposed by the target. Intense takeover activity occurs periodically in advanced capitalist countries. In late nineteenth and early twentieth-century America, it created huge firms that dominated the oil, tobacco, and steel industries. In the 1980s a record wave of takeovers engulfed the corporate world, prompting the business press to use such neologisms as GREENMAIL, LEVERAGED BUYOUTS, POISON PILL, SHARK, and GOLDEN PARACHUTE to describe the new practices associated with hostile takeovers and defenses against them.

Takeovers generate MORAL DILEMMAS and conflicts of interests among different stakeholders (*see* STAKEHOLDER THEORY). Takeovers can increase the efficiency of a company through the economies of scale, but they can also make it a near MONOPOLY by eliminating competitors, a result that may further STOCKHOLDER interests but hurt consumers by leading to higher prices. Whose interests ought to take precedence? Most countries opt for consumer protection through REGULATION and antitrust legislation. Takeovers may advance the interest of a foreign firm while threatening perceived national interests. Many countries restrict or review takeovers by foreign firms in such areas as culture, finance, and natural resources, but international trade agreements have eroded these types of restrictions and freed the flow of capital.

Much ethical debate revolves around problems created by leveraged buyouts. While some authors defend the eighties wave of leveraged buyouts for having restored international competitiveness by making companies leaner and meaner (Jensen, 1989), others claim that it created nothing of value and saddled firms with crippling debts (Wise, 1990). Stockholders usually gain in such takeovers, but other stakeholders may lose. Cities lose factories and workers lose jobs as companies reduce size or sell off assets to reduce debt or increase competitiveness.

Some stakeholders may be able to protect their interests in a takeover but others may not. Managers often negotiate golden parachutes that guarantee them special benefits if they lose their jobs because of a takeover. Usually, these benefits are not in the interest of stockholders; and workers, who may also lose their jobs, seldom have any parachutes at all! Leveraged buyouts by management protect management jobs but may create excessive debt.

In countries with powerful unions and labor-oriented political parties, plant-closing and layoff regulations offer communities and workers considerable protection from the negative EXTERNALITIES of takeovers. In the United States, where the level of unionization is low, labor legislation is weak and provides little protection for workers (Bluestone & Harrison, 1982, p. 236). Occasionally, employee buyouts have protected worker interests. Increasingly, however, the weight of global competition pressures firms to reduce costs, making it ever more difficult for workers in developed industrial nations to retain rights they have gained let alone promote them further.

Takeovers are an essential part of the process of capitalist development, which Joseph Schumpeter has aptly termed creative destruction. Defenders of takeovers stress the creative aspects; critics stress the destruction.

Bibliography

Bluestone, B. & Harrison, B. (1982). *The Deindustrialization of America.* New York: Basic Books.

Hanly, K. (1992). Hostile takeovers and methods of defence: A stakeholder analysis. *Journal of Business Ethics*, **11**, 895–913.

Jensen, M. (1989). The eclipse of the public corporation. *Harvard Business Review*, **89**, (5) 61–75. A defense of leveraged buyouts).

Walton, C. (1992). *Corporate Encounters.* Dryden Press: Orlando. (Chapter 5 is entirely about takeovers).

Wise, J. (1990). Junk bond overdose. *Dollars and Sense*, **154**, 6–9. (A leftist critique of leveraged buyouts).

KEN HANLY

tax ethics

> Any one may so arrange his affairs that his taxes shall be as low as possible; he is not bound to choose that pattern which will best pay the Treasury; there is not even a patriotic duty to increase one's taxes. (Judge Learned Hand, *Helvering* v. *Gregory*, 69 F.2d 809, 810 (2d Cir. 1934))

The code of conduct that passes for tax ethics in the United States has been described by one commentator as an "uneasy truce between notions of personal avarice and good citizenship" (Holden, 1991). Perhaps because of the additional difficulties of arranging such a truce in the context of complex yet ambiguous tax rules, the parameters of acceptable taxpayer behavior have been more fully explored in the context of the federal income tax than any other. This entry focuses on the standards developed in the income tax context and allows readers to extrapolate from them to other situations.

I. Standards for Tax Return Reporting

Although the Internal Revenue Service has extensive audit powers, it has never had the resources necessary to investigate more than a small fraction of the returns filed. The vast majority of taxpayers must therefore self-assess their tax obligations. It is plainly illegal, and not simply unethical, to lie to the Internal Revenue Service by filing a tax return containing false statements. Fraud on, and making false statements to, the Internal Revenue Service are felonies which can lead to the imposition of substantial monetary penalties as well as incarceration. Similarly, taxpayers may on their returns take only positions that they believe in good faith to be correct. Though incorrectly reporting the tax consequences of transactions (as opposed to misreporting factual issues, such as the existence of transactions) rarely leads to criminal charges, substantial civil penalties can be invoked for "negligence" (which includes the failure to make a reasonable attempt to comply with the tax law) and the disregard of rules and regulations (including careless, reckless and intentional disregard of the same). The traditional baseline for acceptable (and perhaps "ethical") tax behavior has been that necessary to avoid the imposition of this civil penalty.

Good faith does not require resolving all ambiguous questions in favor of the government. Taxpayers may take any position for which they believe in good faith a "reasonable basis" exists under the law. Because taxpayers often lack detailed knowledge of the tax laws, they may rely on a professional tax preparer's conclusion as to the merits of a particular tax position. The professional organizations that regulate lawyers and accountants allow their members to advise tax-reporting positions where there exists "some realistic possibility of success if the matter is litigated." The professional need not believe that the position will prevail if the matter is actually litigated. A lawyer, for example,

> may advise the statement of positions most favorable to the client if the lawyer has a good faith belief that those positions are warranted in existing law or can be supported by a good faith argument for an extension, modification or reversal of existing law. A lawyer can have a good faith belief in this context even if the lawyer believes the client's position probably will not prevail. (ABA Op. 85-352 (1985))

In drafting its standards for enrolling and disciplining agents practicing before it, the Treasury Department concluded that the realistic possibility standard would be satisfied if "a reasonable and well-informed analysis by a person knowledgeable in the tax law would lead such a person to conclude that the position has approximately a one in three, or greater, likelihood of being sustained on its merits" (Circular 230, 10.34). A professional return preparer, according to these same standards, may sign returns incorporating such positions, as well as positions which, though not "frivolous," fail the realistic possibility standard but are adequately disclosed to the Internal Revenue Service on the return. Preparers should not sign returns incorporating weaker positions in the absence of disclosure nor should they advise taking such positions without first explaining to their clients the penalties they risk incurring, as well as any opportunities of avoiding such penalties through disclosure. As of 1994, however, full disclosure of non-frivolous positions which fail the realistic possibility standard no longer protects a taxpayer from the negligence penalty. This means that no "ethical" way exists to take such non-frivolous positions. "Realistic possibility of success" has become the standard.

II. Post-Return Behavior

Concerns about acceptable behavior do not end with the filing of tax returns. One perennial issue is whether taxpayers who discover errors on previously filed returns are obligated to file correct, amended returns. There is no statutory or regulatory authority requiring taxpayers to file amended returns; nonetheless, lawyers believe that they have an ethical obligation to advise their clients to file such returns and that they may be required to withdraw from further representation with regard to the matter should the client decide not to file such a return. The precise extent of such a required withdrawal can be uncertain due to the multi-year effect of some tax decisions.

Once unlucky enough to be the targets of audits, taxpayers and their agents should cooperate with the tax authorities. Both taxpayers and their advisers should provide records and other information requested by the Internal Revenue Service unless they have reasonable cause to believe that such material is covered by a legal privilege. The criminal penalty against fraud and perjury continues in effect; furthermore, if a taxpayer is represented by an attorney, the attorney is prohibited by legal canons (as well as by the Treasury Department's disciplinary rules which apply to all taxpayer agents, not just attorneys) from "mislead[ing] the Internal Revenue Service deliberately, either by misstatements or by silence or by permitting the client to mislead" (ABA Op. 85-352 (1985)). As attorneys are also forbidden from revealing client confidences, when confronted with a client intent on misleading or lying to the Internal Revenue Service, an attorney must withdraw from representing the client. Whether a given course of conduct (or silence) rises to the level of "misleading" can be the subject of dispute.

It again bears repeating that the above discussion summarizes a minimalist definition of acceptable tax behavior. Those who ascribe to Justice Holmes' aphorism that "taxes are what we pay for civilized society" believe that far more candor and cooperation is required before taxpayers can call their actions with regard to the tax system "ethical." On the other hand, because tax laws are designed in part to influence behavior, even the most conscientious taxpayer will have trouble deciding when legal strategies to minimize taxes are appropriate responses to economic legislation and when they merely exploit tax "loopholes."

Bibliography

American Bar Association. Comm. on. Ethics and Professional Responsibility, Formal Op. 85-352. (1985). Available from ABA, 750 N. Lake Shore Drive, Chicago, Ill.

American Institute of Certified Public Accountants Statements on Responsibilities in Tax Practice No. 1. (1985). Available from AICPA, 1211 Avenue of the Americas, New York, NY.

Cooper, G. (1980). The avoidance dynamic: A tale of tax planning, tax ethics, and tax reform. *Columbia Law Review*, **80**, 1553–1622.

Holden, J. P. (1991). Practitioners' standard of practice and the taxpayer's reporting position. *Capital University Law Review*, **20**, 327–44.

Holden, J. P. & Friedman, R. E. (1992). Income tax return accuracy: Taxpayer responsibility and practitioner responsibility. *USC Law Center Tax Institute series on Major Tax Planning.* **44 (1)**, 10-1-10-22. (Slightly expanded version of first article).

Schenk, D. H. (1991). Conflicts between the tax lawyer and the client: Vignettes in the law office. *Capital University Law Review*, **20**, 387–420.

US Treasury Department Circular No. 230. Available from the Treasury Dept., Main Treasury Building, Washington, DC.

JULIE A. ROIN

Taylor, Frederick W.   During the first quarter of this century Frederick W. Taylor (1856–1915) developed a new management system which is described in his book, *Scientific Management.* In his youth a vision impairment forced Taylor to abandon his planned Harvard law education. Instead, he advanced up the factory job hierarchy from journeyman to engineer and consultant. Through night study he completed a mechanical engineering degree at Stevens Institute.

Taylor believed that it was the duty of management to examine the workplace scientifically through method and time studies. It was also management's responsibility to "study the character, the nature and the performance of each workman" and to "train and help and teach this workman" (Taylor, 1947, p. 42). In addition, management should measure the worker's output and establish an economic incentive by setting a higher wage rate for production above standard.

In his theory Taylor took a utilitarian view that production efficiency was in the long-run interests of management, workers, and society (*see* UTILITARIANISM). However, scientific management generated considerable opposition with some managers and workers resisting the necessary changes. The labor unions also opposed it and pressured the US Congress into holding hearings before the House Social Committee (see Taylor, 1947, for transcript).

Today many behavioral scientists oppose the "traditional" form of management that developed from the pioneering work of Taylor. They advocate "participative" management that gives the worker greater influence and control over his or her work and workplace (Belcher, 1987, p. 73). This shift results from changes in the economic environment, differences in the education and expectations of workers, and new understanding of motivation. However, aspects of Taylor's work which increased efficiency and productivity in manufacturing remain an important contribution in the history of management.

Bibliography

Belcher, J. G., Jr. (1987). *Productivity Plus.* Houston: Gulf: 72–4. (Changes from traditional to participative management).

Coffey, R. E., Cook, C. W., & Hunsaker, P. L. (1994). *Management and Organization Behavior.* Homewood, Ill.: Irwin & Austen. (Current appraisal of scientific management).

Hays, D. W. (1994). Quality improvement and its origin in scientific management. *Quality Progress,* 27 (5), 89–90. (Impact of scientific management on current manufacturing).

Taylor, F. W. (1947). *Scientific Management.* New York: Harper. (Excellent and highly readable source).

JOHN E. FLEMING

teaching business ethics   provides instruction in the cognitive and habitual skills needed to make ethical judgments on business matters. ETHICS is a system of moral principles for distinguishing right from wrong, and the methods of applying them. The purpose of ethics is to enable one to make better moral decisions and to develop into a better person. Business ethics treats the ethics of the individual, the firm, and the market system. The word "ethical" has a more cognitive meaning, and "moral" more explicitly includes behavior, but the two terms are often used interchangeably.

Business ethics provides the language, concepts, and models that aid an individual in making moral judgments. Teaching business ethics requires practical guidance through three steps: 1) gathering relevant factual information; 2) determining the moral norm(s) that are most applicable; and 3) making the ethical judgment on the rightness or wrongness of the act or policy. The facts gathered must be appropriate and sufficient for judging (*see* METHODOLOGIES OF BUSINESS ETHICS RESEARCH.). The moral norms most often used in cases in business ethics are UTILITARIANISM, RIGHTS, and JUSTICE.

The flow chart in Figure 1 presents one approach to teaching business ethics.

The moral norm of utilitarianism enables us to judge that an act is right if it produces the "greatest good for the greatest number", or the greatest net benefit when all the costs and benefits are taken into account. The decision process is similar to a cost–benefit analysis applied to all parties who would be touched by the decision.

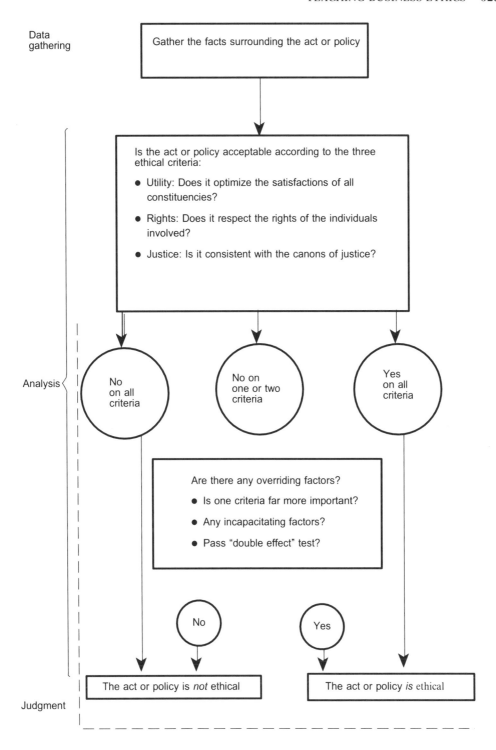

Figure 1

The moral norm of individual rights indicates a person's entitlement to something. Rights stem from the human dignity of the person, and enable individuals to pursue their own interests. Rights also impose duties or correlative prohibitions or requirements on others.

Justice requires all parties to be guided by fairness, equity, and impartiality. Justice from this perspective calls for even-handed treatment of groups and individuals: in the distribution of the benefits and burdens of society, in the administration of laws and regulations, and in the imposition of sanctions. Justice considers how all parties are impacted by the consequences of a business act, including: workers, supervisors, firms, the poor, and unemployed.

Business ethics is not LEGAL ETHICS, although both are built upon ethical principles. Law specifies the minimum requirement. To provide an even playing field in a healthy society, legislation is necessary. For example, if pollution control were not legislated, unethical firms would benefit financially. However, ethics often calls us to actions beyond what the law requires.

Pedagogy for Business Ethics

Teaching business ethics demands that one deal with substantive business issues. First, issues internal to the firm, such as WORK, employee rights, worker satisfaction, WORKER SAFETY, and DISCRIMINATION IN EMPLOYMENT are often treated. Second, the environment external to the firm: consumers, media, advertising, energy, pollution and the environment (*see* ADVERTISING ETHICS; ETHICAL ISSUES IN ENERGY; ENVIRONMENT AND ENVIRONMENTAL ETHICS.). Finally, the strengths and weaknesses of the business system itself are examined. Crediting the positive ethical outcomes of capitalism and the market system, such as, jobs, goods, freedom, and innovation, we aim and strive to lessen the negative outcomes, such as suppression of wages, and the encouragement of greed and selfishness.

Teaching business ethics in today's competitive world also demands that one understand other cultures and values. Cases that demonstrate a variety of world values enhance sensitivity to other cultures, broaden one's perspective, and help the individual and the firm develop more realistic future goals (*see*

MULTICULTURALISM; BUSINESS ETHICS IN AFRICA, CHINA, EUROPE, GREAT BRITAIN, JAPAN, RUSSIA, SOUTH AFRICA, SOUTH AMERICA; BUSINESS ETHICS IN BUDDHISM, ISLAM, JUDAISM, HINDUISM).

Good teaching demands active learning and interaction (see Piper et al., 1993). Some standard methods of teaching business ethics include: input (reading, lecture, film), business cases (actual or simulated), written assignments, discussion, interactive computer programs, projects (often with teams to teach cooperation). For individuals or classroom use, there are excellent business ethics texts available, such as Velasquez, 1992; De George, 1995; Cavanagh, 1997. Films are available from university and public libraries.

Analysis and discussion of cases is generally considered the most effective method for teaching business ethics (*see* CASE METHOD). This is true for university teaching, as well as for short programs. There are numerous casebooks available (see, for example, Donaldson & Gini, 1996; Sethi, 1991). The Business Enterprise Trust publishes written and filmed cases of ethical business-people.

Personal Values, Character, and Moral Development

Ethics provides the skills to decide specific ethical acts or policies. Teaching business ethics and encouraging ethical values also influences ethical behavior and personal values (*see* VALUES). Studying ethics generally deepens a lasting belief that a certain goal or mode of conduct is morally better than the opposite goal or conduct, and thus encourages more ethical behavior. This can then develop better MANAGERIAL VALUES and support a more ethical climate within the organization.

Bibliography

Cavanagh, G. F. (1997). *American Business Values.* 3rd edn. Englewood Cliffs, NJ: Prentice-Hall. (Historical and behaviorial overview of values, along with ethics and cases).

De George, R. T. (1995). *Business Ethics.* New York: Macmillan. (Clear, philosophical approach).

Donaldson, T. & Gini, A. (eds) (1993). *Case Studies in Business Ethics.* 4th edn. Englewood Cliffs, NJ: Prentice-Hall. (Comprehensive, readable collection).

Donaldson, T. & Werhane, P. H. (eds) (1996). *Ethical Issues in Business.* 5th edn. Englewood Cliffs, NJ: Prentice-Hall. (Excellent collection of philosophical articles and cases).

Hosmer, L. T. (1995). *The Ethics of Management*, 3rd edn. Homewood, Ill.: Irwin. (Ethics cases by strategic management expert).

Mahoney, J. (1990). *Teaching Business Ethics in the UK, Europe and the USA: A Comparative Study.* London: Athlone Press. (Status and techniques of teaching business ethics in various countries.)

Piper, T. R., Gentile, M. C., & Parks, S. D. (1993). *Can Ethics Be Taught? Cambridge, Mass.: Harvard University Press.* (Survey of students and content of Harvard Business School short non-credit ethics course.)

Sethi, S. P. (1991). *Up Against the Corporate Wall: Modern Corporations and Social Issues of the Nineties*, 5th edn. Englewood Cliffs, NJ: Prentice-Hall. (Social responsibilities of the corporation).

Velasquez, M. G. (1992). *Business Ethics: Concepts and Cases*, 3rd edn. Englewood Cliffs, NJ: Prentice-Hall. (Comprehensive, engaging text with cases interwoven.)

GERALD F. CAVANAGH

teaching business ethics to executives
The process of adding ethical concerns to the decision-making processes of executives. Executive education in business ethics has evolved to where it now appears in several diverse venues. In-house corporate training, university-based executive development and executive MBA programs, management conferences and workshops, and seminars conducted by various institutes and centers have all been used as vehicles.

Educational programs are available from academics specializing in the field who offer their teaching services as corporate consultants, from nonprofit organizations that have sprung up in response to the perceived need for ethics education and from for-profit training companies who have added business ethics to their usual corporate training services. As executive education *per se* has grown over the recent past, so too has the teaching of business ethics to executives proliferated.

Moreover, the educational content of these programs has become richly varied and diverse. In many corporate classrooms, general topics and issues in MANAGERIAL VALUES that one typically might find in any college textbook on business ethics are addressed. Other programs deal with very specific ethical issues that arise in given functional areas such as marketing or purchasing. Still other organizations provide ethics training in a thematic way with single or multiple sessions that focus on an array of topics, including: executive INTEGRITY, CONFLICT OF INTEREST, TRUTHTELLING, WHISTLEBLOWING, SEXUAL HARASSMENT, managing DIVERSITY in the workplace, ENVIRONMENT AND ENVIRONMENTAL ETHICS, SOCIAL RESPONSIBILITY, and INTERNATIONAL BUSINESS ETHICS, among others.

Although there are varieties of programming, it is possible to categorize them into training experiences that emphasize either conduct or cognition. Thanks in large part to regulations set by the US Sentencing Guidelines Commission, which allow federal judges to use their favorable discretion in handing down penalties to corporate wrongdoers that have instituted ethics training, a number of firms now have major compliance programs that emphasize an executive's obligations with respect to legal and ethical matters. Such compliance training focuses upon professional conduct, the ethics of wrongdoing, corporate CODES OF ETHICS, and policies and legal statutes. This form of training can be taken as a "rules and regulations approach" in that executives learn standards that govern their behavior in the workplace.

Alternatively, many firms see ethics training as a way to prepare managers for the numerous MORAL MAZES encountered in organizational life. Typically, these APPLIED ETHICS sessions outline traditional ethical theories and urge executives to incorporate them into their everyday management decision-making. The assumption is that no code or law is broad enough to cover the many ethical intricacies that executives encounter and that they can benefit from a problem-solving ethics CASE METHOD approach, which develops their cognitive reasoning abilities. And while corporations tend to offer either compliance training or training in moral mazes, there are some that combine both within a single program.

Teaching business ethics to executives is not without controversy. Questions about its efficacy, the independence of instructors, and whether or not corporations conduct ethics programs solely as "window dressing" have been raised in the literature of business ethics.

See also **teaching business ethics**

Bibliography

Jones, D. G. (Ed.) (1982). *Doing Ethics in Business: New Ventures in Management Development.* Cambridge, Mass.: Oelgeschlager, Gunn & Hain.

Kohls, J., Chapman, C., & Mathieu, C. (1989). Ethics training programs in the *Fortune 500. Business and Professional Ethics Journal,* 8, (2), 55.

Madsen, P. (1992). Human resources and ethics: Ethics training. *Ideas and Trends in Personnel,* 273, 60.

Powers, C. W. & Vogel, D. (1980). *Ethics and the Education of Business Managers.* Hastings-on-Hudson, NY: Institute of Society, Ethics and the Life Sciences, the Hasting Center.

Rice, D. & Dreilinger, C. (1990). Rights and wrongs of ethics training. *Training and Development Journal,* 44 (5), 103.

PETER MADSEN

teams   A team refers to a special sub-class of cooperative scheme characterized by a particularly high degree of interdependence and close-knittedness and often focused on a single goal. While sports examples abound, a good, non-athletic example may be a project team within a manufacturing firm. Although the members may all be employees of the same corporation and thus have obligations to that organization and the economy at large as members of these respective cooperative schemes, they are also part of a team with the concomitant increase in ethical content. They spend many hours a day together, they share a common goal, they are more likely to go out of their way to assist teammates, and they depend upon one another more than the organization at large. The concept of a team, on this understanding, indicates a higher level of commitment than many other similar cooperative schemes and therefore will contain a higher level of ethical content.

The necessity of cooperation in value creation and exchange relationships (i.e., virtually all economic interactions) is readily apparent. This need to cooperate leads inexorably to the demand that individual economic entities work as parts of teams. There are many things that can only be done by teams and many others which can be done better by teams than by individuals. Further evidence of the importance of teams can be seen in the preeminent role of building "team skills" in most business schools. One's ability to work as part of a team is, more often than not, vital to success in the business world.

However, insofar as most issues with high ethical content occur in interpersonal contexts – indeed, some would argue that ethics for a hermit is an empty or meaningless concept – the benefits of cooperative behavior carry with them a great deal of ethical baggage. A good starting-point is to ask the question, "Does a person have greater obligations to a 'teammate' than to society at large? If so, what is the source and nature of this increased obligation?"

Philosophical justification for behavior within teams can be found (in addition to its utility for those of consequentialist leanings) in the concept of FAIRNESS or fair play (*see* CONSEQUENTIALISM). Alluded to by JOHN LOCKE (1690) and ADAM SMITH (1790), and later by H. L. A. Hart (1955), the principle of fairness finds its most sophisticated defense in the work of JOHN RAWLS. The "principle of fairness," combined with certain natural duties, represents the moral rules for individuals in Rawls' much-acclaimed *A Theory of Justice* (1971). As Rawls puts it in another work:

> The principle of fair play may be defined as follows. Suppose there is a mutually beneficial and just scheme of cooperation, and that the advantages it yields can only be obtained if everyone, or nearly everyone, cooperates. Suppose further that cooperation requires a certain sacrifice from each person, or at least involves a certain restriction of his liberty. Suppose finally that the benefits produced by cooperation are, up to a certain point, free: that is, the scheme of cooperation is unstable in the sense that if any one person knows that all (or nearly all) of the others will continue to do their part, he will still be able to share a gain from the scheme even if he does not do his part. Under these conditions a person who has accepted the benefits of the scheme is bound by a duty of fair play to do his part

and not to take advantage of the free benefit by not cooperating. (Rawls, 1964)

The principle takes as one of its major concerns the issue of free-riders within a cooperative scheme. One of the greatest problems with using teams is that there are often members of a team who fail to do their share. Free-riders hope to be carried along by the success and effort of others within the cooperative scheme while themselves contributing far less than their role and the benefits they receive would dictate. The principle of fairness provides a moral foundation for the obligations of individuals within a cooperative scheme as well as the obligations of the scheme to the individual in the form of provision of a fair-share of the benefits of the scheme.

Although providing solutions to the myriad ethical issues would be rather difficult (if not impossible) in the abstract, it might nonetheless be useful to at least point out some of the possible areas of controversy inasmuch as the recognition of ethical content in a situation may help properly frame the issues. Can the majority (ethically) force their will on the minority or an individual for the sake of the team goal or purpose? Should the individual *voluntarily* yield to the team for the sake of the goal? Should such a goal or purpose come from within or from outside the team and will the source make a difference in the level of commitment required? What about the assignation of responsibility and accountability both within teams and for the effect of the team as a whole on the rest of the world? Where is the line between team leadership and coercion? What are the obligations of being a follower? These are but a few of the possible ethical pitfalls to be aware of when thinking about teams, especially in a business context.

Bibliography

Hart, H. L. A. (1955). Are there any natural rights? *Philosophical Review*, **64**.

Katzenbach, J. R. & Smith, D. K. (1993). *The Wisdom of Teams*. Boston: Harvard University Press.

Locke, J. (1690). *Second Treatise of Government*, para. 130. Numerous editions are available.

Rawls, J. (1964). Legal obligation and the duty of fair play. In S. Hook (Ed.), *Law and Philosophy*. New York: New York University Press, 9–10.

Rawls, J. (1971). *A Theory of Justice*. Cambridge, Mass.: Harvard University Press, 108–17, 333–55.

Smith, A. (1790). *Theory of Moral Sentiments*, Part II, Section II, ch. II. Numerous editions are available.

ROBERT A. PHILLIPS

technology, ethical issues in *see* ETHICAL ISSUES IN TECHNOLOGY

teleopathy The unbalanced pursuit of purpose in either individuals or organizations (*Teleo* in Greek meaning "goal, target, purpose," and *pathos* meaning "disease, sickness"). This mindset or condition has been described as a key stimulus to which business ethics is a practical response (Goodpaster, 1991). The principal symptoms of teleopathy are fixation, rationalization, and detachment.

Fixation

There is a difference between determination, courage, perseverance, and tenacity (each a virtue to be applauded in persons and organizations), and addiction, dependency, or fixation (which are not to be applauded). When determination is celebrated, we are confident that the person owns the goal. When fixation is lamented, we sense that the goal owns the person. The difference is between "management by objectives" and being managed by one's objectives. Investing in goals beyond our capacity for critical judgment is, in the language of philosopher Immanuel Kant, treating the self as a means, not an end (*see* KANTIAN ETHICS.). Examples of the "harvest" of fixation in business life are as plentiful as they are in the government sector. When NASA overrode a safety recommendation against launching the Challenger in 1986, leading to fatal results, we saw a pattern not unlike various corporate scandals during the 1980s.

Rationalization

The human psyche seems attuned to the problem of fixation at some fairly deep level – both individually and institutionally – explaining the persistence of denial and "reinterpretation" so characteristic of drug addicts and other fixated actors. Saul Gellerman (1987) argued that the common denominator in white-collar crime during the 1980s was rationalization in its many forms. Two principal types of rationalization dominate the landscape in the context of business and worklife: loyalty (appealing to fiduciary obligations to shareholders in the face of market competition) and legality (appealing to the permissibility of a behavior or policy within the constraints of the law) (*see* FIDU-CIARY DUTY; FIDUCIARY RESPONSIBILITY). Each provides an excuse for questionable business behavior, though not always plausibly.

Detachment

Repeating the fixation/rationalization "loop" becomes a habit. This habit leads eventually to a kind of callousness, what some observers have called a separation of head from heart (Maccoby, 1976). Competitiveness and goal seeking eventually drive out compassion and generosity, making more serious compromises easier as time goes on. Insulation from moral responsiveness sets in under banners like "jungle," "tough-ness," and "real world." The detached organiza-tion, like the detached individual, loses the ability to connect its behavior to the larger human picture.

Possible Illustrations

Some cigarette companies insist that respons-ibility means responding to the market, perhaps rationalization and detachment simultaneously. Or consider a remark by a former head of a prestigious American consulting firm, describ-ing those his company sought to hire: "The real competition out there isn't for clients, it's for people . . and we look to hire people who are first, very smart; second, insecure and thus driven by their insecurity; and third, competi-tive" (*Fortune*, Nov. 1, 1993, p. 72). Karl Marx seems to have believed that the capitalistic system itself was fundamentally hostage to something like this pathology, inevitably infect-ing institutions and individuals within it. Avoiding teleopathy as an occupational hazard of business life is no small challenge. Winston Churchill is supposed to have said, "First we shape our institutions; then they shape us."

See also **egoism, psychological egoism and ethical egoism; moral hazard; partiality; self-deception**

Bibliography

Gellerman, S. (1987). Why "good" managers make "bad" ethical choices. *Harvard Business Review*, **64**, 85–90.
Goodpaster, K. (1991). Ethical imperatives and corporate leadership. In Andrews (Ed.), *Ethics in Practice*. Cambridge, Mass.: Harvard Business School Press. Originally presented as a Ruffin Lecture at the Darden School, University of Virginia, 1988.
Maccoby, M. (1976). *The Gamesman*. New York: Simon & Schuster.

KENNETH E. GOODPASTER

Tom Peters on excellence   Ethics is a hot business topic, and that is a potential boon to us all. Unfortunately, the heightened awareness has spawned an industry of mindless, "do good, be good" writings. But dealing with ethics is not so easy.

1. Ethics is not principally about headline issues – responding to the Tylenol poisoning or handling insider information. Ethical concerns surround us all the time, on parade whenever we deal with people in the course of the average day. How we work out the "little stuff" will determine our response, if called upon, to a Tylenol-sized crisis. When disaster strikes, it's far too late to seek out ethical touchstones.

2. High ethical standards – business or otherwise – are, above all, about treating people decently. To me (as a person, businessperson, and business owner) that means respect for a person's privacy, dignity, opinions, and natural desire to grow; and people's respect for (and by) co-workers.

3. Diversity must be honored. To be sure, it is important to be clear about your own compass heading; but don't ever forget that other people have profoundly different – and equally decent – ethical guidance mechanisms.

4. People, even the saints, are egocentric and selfish; we were designed "wrong" in part from the start. Any ethical framework in action had best take into account the troublesome but immutable fact of man's inherently flawed character.

5. Corporations are created and exist to serve people – insiders and outsiders – period.

6. By their very nature, organizations run roughshod over people. Organizations produce

powerlessness and humiliation for most participants, with more skill than they produce widgets.

7. Though all men and women are created equal, some surely have more power than others. Thus, a central ethical issue in the workplace (and beyond) is the protection of and support for the unempowered – especially the frontline worker and the customer.

8. For employees and managers alike, fighting the impersonal "they"/"them" (the/every bureaucratic institution) is almost always justified on ethical grounds.

9. While one can point to ethically superior (and profitable) firms, such as Herman Miller, most of us will spend most of our working life in compromised – i.e., politicized – organizations. Dealing with "office politics," "brown-nosing," etc., is a perpetual ethical morass. A "pure" ethical stance in the face of most firms' political behavior will lead you out the door in short order, with only the convent, monastery, or ashram as alternatives. The line between ethical purity and arrogant egocentricism (i.e., a holier-than-thou stance toward the tumult of everyday life) is a fine one.

10. Though I sing the praises of an "action bias," ethical behavior demands that we tread somewhat softly in all of our affairs. Unintended consequences and the secondary and tertiary effects of most actions and policies far outnumber intended and first-order effects. As a manager, and a "change agent", dropping out may be the only decent/ethical path; our best-intended plans so often cause more harm than good. (Think about it: Leaving the world no worse off than when you arrived is no mean feat.)

11. The pursuit of high ethical standards in business might well be served by the elimination of many business schools. The implicit thrust of most MBA programs is that great systems and great techniques win out over great people.

12. Can we live up to the spirit of the US Bill of Rights in our workplaces? Can "good business ethics" and "good real-life ethics" – and profit – coincide on a routine bases? One would hope that the answer is yes, although respect for the individual has hardly been the cornerstone of American industry's traditional approach to its workforce.

13. Capitalism and democracy in society are messy. But capitalism has far fewer downsides and far more upsides than any alternative so far concocted. The same can be said for the firm – where "democracy" and "capitalism" are served by wholesale worker participation and widespread ownership.

14. Great novels, not management books, might help. There are no easy answers, but there are fertile fields for gathering ideas. If you wish to be appropriately humbled about life and relationships and the possibility of ethical behavior, read Dostoyevsky, Forster, or Garcia Marquez instead of Drucker, Blanchard, or Peters. Then reconsider your latest magisterial proclamation.

15. Each of us is ultimately lonely. In the end, it's up to each of us and each of us alone to figure out who we are, who we are not, and to act more or less consistently on those conclusions.

Anyone who is not very confused all the time about ethical issues is out of touch with the frightful (and joyous) richness of the world. But at least being actively confused means that we are actively considering our ethical stance and that of the institutions we associate with. That is a good start. (1989 TPG Communications. All rights reserved.)

TOM PETERS

trade secrets   Information a firm reserves for its exclusive use, or for use by other firms to which it grants a license. In this respect trade secrets and patents are similar. But trade secrets differ from patents in four important ways.

First, while a patent is an official grant of certain rights from the US government to the patent holder, and patent cases are tried in federal courts, trade secrets are governed by state law and cases are usually tried in state courts. Second, patents expire after 17 years. The information can then be used by anyone. But trade secrets can be maintained indefinitely. The Zildjian family, for example, has kept its trade secret for manufacturing cymbals since 1623. Third, patented information must meet strict standards of novelty and unobviousness, and must represent a genuine advance in a particular field. The requirements for something to qualify as a trade secret are much less strict. In most states as long as information has some degree of novelty, cannot be readily discovered by public inspection, has genuine commercial utility, and, most importantly, is actively protected from disclosure by the firm that holds it, then it can qualify as a trade secret. Finally, although the information in a patent is public, patent law protects it from any use not authorized by the patent holder. But trade-secret law is quite different. A trade secret cannot be used if it is acquired by improper means, e.g. industrial espionage or unauthorized disclosure by an employee. However, if a firm X independently discovers Y's trade secret, then X can legally use the information. Y cannot sue to prevent X from using it, nor can Y require that X pay a licensing fee.

Unpatentable proprietary information, such as customer lists and marketing plans, can be held as trade secrets. But so can patentable information. Whether to hold such information as a trade secret or apply for a patent is a matter for the firm to decide. In some cases keeping information secret, whether patentable or unpatentable, seems clearly justified. But is it always justified? Suppose, for instance, that a utility firm discovers a pollution-free fusion process for making electricity cheaply, but decides to keep the process secret. Or suppose a pharmaceutical firm discovers and keeps secret an inexpensive and effective cure for AIDS. In both these cases it seems obvious that the information ought to be disclosed, even if unpatentable, because the public benefit of disclosure would greatly outweigh anything the firm gains by keeping the secret. If this is right, then on some occasions a decision about whether to keep information as a trade secret has a moral as well as a commercial dimension. If benefit to the public could be significantly increased by revealing the secret, or if harm to the public could be significantly decreased, then the firm may have a moral obligation to disclose the information that overrides considerations of profit or other business advantage.

Bibliography

Baram, M. (1968). Trade secrets: What price loyalty? *Harvard Business Review*, **6**, 66–74.

Del Mar, D. (1974). *The Security of Industrial Information*. New Hope, Penn.: The Chestnut Hill Press.

Frederick, R. & Snoeyenbos, M. (1983). Trade secrets, patents, and morality. In Snoeyenbos, M., Almeder, R., & Humber, J. (eds), *Business Ethics*. New York: Prometheus Books.

Rosenberg, P. D. (1982). *Patent Law Fundamentals*, 2nd edn. New York: Clark Boardman Company, ch. 3.

Unkovic, D. (1985). *The Trade Secrets Handbook: Strategies and Techniques for Protecting Corporate Information*. Englewood Cliffs, NJ: Prentice-Hall.

R. E. FREDERICK

transforming justice may be defined as a theory on the interaction between rights and power that makes justice operative. Transforming justice is a conceptualization of justice which seeks to incorporate the vitality of power in the very definition of justice (*see* POWER). Although transforming justice does have human rights for its basis, it does not subscribe to the strengths or weaknesses of other theories of justice (*see* RIGHTS).

How does transforming justice differ conceptually from the more traditional theories of justice and rights? The fundamental difference rests in the concept that justice cannot, and therefore will not, become an existential reality unless its theory also contains the notion of power. Power is what makes justice "transforming" – for example, moving away from inequality in fact towards equality in deed (*see* EQUALITY).

The "interaction" between rights and power in transforming justice challenges the traditional view that rights and power are to be treated as parallel factors in human behavior. It is in the practical order – not necessarily in abstract notions – where rights and power interact to produce transforming justice.

Rights

Rights are claims by one entity for or against another entity, either human or corporate. A right is a relationship; it is not a thing. In a way, a right is a means to an end, such as the equality of justice (*see* JUSTICE). Rights are obtained through some source or title, such as contract. Rights are qualitative and thus "inform" the person, whether human or corporate. Rights are also dichotomous: either a person has them or person has them or not. There are no degrees. In this sense, they cannot be measured in terms of more or less.

Justice has rights for its object: by respecting the rights of others, a person gives another what is her/his due. Indeed, the ancient Roman definition of justice states that each person is to give the other what is his/her due. From another perspective, a person, by respecting the rights of another, empowers the other. However, different theories of rights frequently provide various, and sometimes conflicting, sources or titles of rights. In a pluralistic society where many value systems exist in the same geographical and social context, a particular claim of one person or group might not be recognized or acknowledged by others. Thus arises conflicts of rights.

Power

The problem of conflict of rights creates one of the most perplexing problems in determining how transforming justice applies to concrete situations. Power is the capacity to bring about change in others according to the intent of the agent (powerholder). Like rights, power is relational; it always deals with another entity, human, corporate, or systemic. Power is quantitative; it can be measured, usually by its effect or impact. Furthermore, as quantitative, power can be added to or subtracted from, as every politician is aware on election day. Power can also be viewed as interacting. Political power can generate economic or social power; moral power can influence political power.

The source of power, unlike the title of rights, may be less certain. Depending upon the kind of power, it can be obtained through inheritance, contract, force, competition, manipulation, fraud or a combination of these. However, of itself, power is ethically neutral. The manner of obtaining power and its subsequent use determine whether it is an ethical good or an ethical evil.

Justice

Justice will be considered under the form of moral virtue. A moral virtue leads to action. Its value is in the behavior it elicits in the person who possesses it. Although a moral virtue, like every virtue, "perfects" the person who posesses it, it also leads the person to some form of controlled behavior. While the moral virtue of temperance perfects the person in the moderation in food and drink, the moral virtue of justice leads to behavior which refers to the rights or claims of some other person apart from the agent. Unlike temperance, justice is not subjectively determined by the peculiar limitations of the agent, but is objectively determined by the established rights of the other person. Unlike power, which can be added to or subtracted from, the moral virtue of justice "qualifies" the person in the sense that "value added" is understood in the process of production (*see* VIRTUE ETHICS).

As a general rule in transforming justice, rights must precede power in transforming justice. Or, to put the rule in a negative frame, ethically evil power must not be used to obtain a right: "might does not make right."

In transforming justice, the "value added" is the capacity to move the agent to respect the claims of others or have others respect the agent's claims. Thus, power becomes a means to the end of justice, which is equality, among other things. Rights become the grist for the mill of transforming justice. Transforming justice, however, uses power to make certain that these rights are respected both by the agent and by the receiver.

Finally, the traditional theories of justice, although they are directed towards others, have no way of "moving" the agent or the other person to respect rights. For example, racial and sexual discrimination still exist in spite of the civil-rights laws pertaining to women and minorities. This kind of social justice needs to be made operative. With power as an integral part of its concept, transforming justice can only exist in an operating form. Transforming justice is a moral virtue in the fullest sense; it can be that "value added" which modifies by qualifying humans and, consequently, their behavior to recognize or to receive rights. As a practice it leads to new approaches to such issues as racial and sexual discrimination, employee rights, company reorganization, terminations, and many other disturbing ethical issues which executives and managers have to face.

Bibliography

Berle, A. A. (1969). *Power*. New York: Harcourt, Brace & World.

Boatright, J. R. (1993). *Ethics and the Conduct of Business*. Englewood Cliffs, NJ: Prentice-Hall.

Gewirth, A. (1984). The epistemology of human rights. *Social Philosophy and Policy*, 1, 1–2.

Gewirth, A. (1992). Rights. In L. J. Becked (ed.), *Encyclopedia of Ethics*. New York: Garland.

McMahon, T. (1973). The moral aspects of power. Power and the word of God. In F. Bockle & J.-M. Pohier (eds), *Concilium: Religion in the Seventies*. New York: Herder and Herder.

Ozar, D. T. (1986). Rights: What they are and where they come from. Pp. 5-25. In P. H. Werhane, A. R. Gini, & D. T. Ozar (eds), *Philosophical Issues in Human Rights: Theories and Applications*. New York: Random House, 5–25.

Werhane, P. H. (1985). *Persons, Rights, & Corporations*. Englewood Cliffs, NJ: Prentice-Hall.

THOMAS F. MCMAHON

transnational corporations A single company operating in two or more nations, with one part exerting at least partial control over the others. Yet while the transnational is *transnational* by virtue of operating in many countries, and while in theory a transnational need not have a "home country" base (in contrast to a multinational corporation), it sometimes retains significant uni-nationality. Its upper. management is usually dominated by nationals of a single country, its stock is usually owned largely by residents of a single country, and its charter emanates from a single country (*see* MULTI-NATIONALS).

The meteoric rise of the transnational, which has occurred almost entirely since World War II, owes itself to a small set of key economic factors. These include a shortage of cheap labor in developed countries, increasing relevance of economies of scale, improved transportation, better communication, and increased worldwide consumer demand. These factors have proved especially potent set against a backdrop of the production life-cycle. A new piece of technology, such as the portable compact disk player, is usually the product of research and development in a highly industrialized economy. Later, domestic rivals enter the market, competing

with the original group of companies. At the same time, an export market develops in which competing producers are forced to seek other geographic areas in which profit margins are higher. Still later, as profit margins shrink, costs are reduced by tapping cheaper labor markets.

Three strategic and structural stances characterize transnationals (Doz, 1980). The first is a *Multidomestic* stance that utilizes domestic plants servicing their respective home markets. Taking such a stance, the home-country headquarters often serves as little more than a convenient umbrella under which largely autonomous domestic operations operate. Host-country management typically retains considerable managerial prerogatives, and products are tailored neatly to host-country tastes.

The second generic stance, is that of the *Global* transnational. In contrast to the Multidomestic stance, the Global stance unifies key elements of its global business, including manufacturing activities, managerial decision-making, and market strategy. Such a stance frequently employs standardization, economies of scale, and volume in order to enhance global competitiveness. Often subsidiaries in host countries will specialize in efficiently manufacturing a single component, with the result that a circle of subsidiaries cooperate to create the final product. Each subsidiary obtains from the others what it needs but does not produce. Corporate headquarters devotes considerable attention to arranging a minimizing of total expenses and a maximizing of revenues. In this way, centralized control is assumed.

The third and final stance allows a mixture of the first two. Called the *Administratively Controlled* stance, it operates without a formal integrative strategy, and permits economic variables to shape individual business decisions. While each major decision is either made by, or at least approved by, home-country corporate headquarters, individual decision contexts are evaluated on their own merits, without reference to a broader, integrative scheme.

All three types of stance operate against a backdrop of global profit-maximizing imperative. That is to say, the transnational operates in a transnational context for *the purpose* of earning more money than it would if remaining a domestic activity, with the consequence that factor prices can be minimized in sophisticated ways. If labor costs or taxes are too high in country X, the transnational can either move entirely to country Y or shift key components of its production process to country Y. Whereas domestic firms must pay for capital at the going rate, transnationals are free to choose among competing rates. And, if government officials fail to cooperate in country X, the transnational – far more so than its domestic counterpart – can force concessions by threatening to move or restructure.

Bibliography

Barnet, B. & Muller, R. (1974). *Global Reach: The Power of Multinational Corporations.* New York: Simon and Schuster.

Buckley, P. J. & Casson, M. C. (1976). *The Future of the Multinational Enterprise.* London: Holmes and Meir.

Caves, R. E. (1982). *Multinational Enterprise and Economic Analysis.* Cambridge: Cambridge University Press.

Chandler, A. (1986). The evolution of modern global competition. In M. E. Porter (Ed.), *Competition in Global Industries.* Boston: Harvard Business Review Press.

Doz, Y. L. (1980). Strategic management in multinational companies. *Sloan Management Review,* winter, 27–46.

Dunning, J. H. (1981). *International Production and the Multinational Enterprise.* London: Allen & Unwin.

Johnson, H. G. (1985). The multinational corporation as a development agent. *Columbia Journal of World Business,* **4**, 25–30.

Porter, M. E. (1990). *The Competitive Advantage of Nations.* New York: Free Press.

Vernon, R. (1966). International investment and international trade in the product cycle. *Quarterly Journal of Economics,* **80** (2), 190–207.

Zysman, J. & Tyson, L. (eds) (1983). *American Industry in International Competition, Government Policies and Corporate Strategies.* Ithaca: Cornell University Press.

THOMAS DONALDSON

trust   Trust is the expectation by one person, group, or firm, of ethically justifiable behavior – that is, morally correct decisions and actions based upon ethical principles of analysis – on the part of another person, group, or firm in a joint endeavor or economic exchange.

Trust is clearly essential in the conduct of human affairs. Most people would agree that neither stable social relationships nor efficient economic transactions are possible without a considerable degree of trust on all sides. Bok (1978) summarized the critical nature of this very basic concept when she stated, "When trust is destroyed, societies falter and collapse."

Yet trust has never been fully included in the behavioral and economic disciplines. It has often been acknowledged as important, but then neglected during analysis. This neglect may be due to the presence of an implied moral duty in the various definitions of trust. The trusted person clearly "owes" something to the trusting person in almost every discipline's view of the concept, but it is not obvious what that "something" is nor the precise extent of the duty. And, of course, moral duties are often viewed as somewhat of an anomaly in most of the behavioral and economic sciences.

Moral philosophy may be able to help provide a more exact definition of trust. "Duty" is certainly a moral concept, and almost all of the terms ordinarily associated with trust – honesty, integrity, reliability, and confidence – have a strong ethical base. This entry will look at the current definitions of trust in behavioral science, microeconomic theory, and normative philosophy, and show how they can be melded.

Trust in Behavioral Science

Trust in the behavioral sciences is thought to be the willingness of one person to increase his or her vulnerability to the actions of another person whose behavior he or she cannot control. If I trust you I let you manage my property, influence my career, and impact my life knowing full well that I cannot control your behavior. I also know full well that my loss, if the trust is broken, will be much greater than my gain if the trust is maintained. I further know that your loss – except in reputation – will be minimal under both circumstances, and that your gain can be immense if the trust is broken. Trust, in the behavioral sciences, is seen as a mixture of extreme vulnerability and absolute dependence.

Why would one person trust another, given this extreme vulnerability and absolute dependence? According to behavioral scientists there is the prospect for an ultimate joint gain through cooperation greater than either of us could achieve alone, and there is the expectation that you will put my interests at least on a par with if not slightly ahead of your own. Cooperative actions and disinterested decisions are both central to the definition of trust in organizational theory.

Trust in Economic Theory

Cooperative actions are also central to the concept of trust in economic theory, but there is no expectation of disinterested decisions here. Instead, there is an assumption that the people in any economic exchange will make decisions based upon self-interest. Consequently the concept of trust is usually viewed negatively in this discipline, as *dis*trust.

Principals (who can be individuals, groups, or firms) are said in microeconomic theory to employ agents (who also can be individuals, groups, or firms) to act in behalf of the principal, but there is always the danger that agents will accept the terms of the employment contract but still act in their own self-interests. This is the situation known as a "moral hazard" in economic thought. It is the result of opportunistic action on the part of the agent.

Principals, in order to avoid the possibility of moral hazards or opportunistic actions, install extensive controls on the behavior of their agents. These controls can be measures of performance or reviews of decisions. The problem is that performance in important tasks such as product design or strategic planning cannot really be measured, and decision reviews, while easily possible, add greatly to the cost. Further, there is always the question: "Who reviews the reviewer?" It is generally accepted in economic theory that controls and reviews are expensive substitutes for trust, and that it is necessary to rely upon a "good-faith effort" to adhere to contracts, and a "general willingness" not to take excessive advantage of the principal when an opportunity to renegotiate is available. Cooperative actions and disinterested decisions also seem to be required in the definition of trust within economic theory.

Trust in Normative Philosophy

Trust is much more an outcome of ethical decisions and actions than a component of those decisions and actions. Moral philosophy has traditionally been concerned with the factors that make a "right": act "right," not with the consequences of those "just" and "proper" and "fair" actions. It is possible, however, to view moral philosophy as a means of applying ethical principles to find the "right" degree of disinterestedness in any decision, or the "just" and "proper" and "fair" balance between self-interest and the interest of others. A decision cannot really look only at the interests of others, for that would be mere altruism which may or may not be desirable but is seldom achievable in any real-world situation. A decision that contains the "right" amount or the "just" and "proper" and "fair" balance of self-interest and other-interest would, in moral philosophy, be one based upon the ethical principles of analysis, and would, according to both behavioral science and economic theory, lead to greater trust on the part of all of those affected by the decision.

Bibliography

Baier, A. (1986). Trust and antitrust. *Ethics*, **96**, 231–60.

Barber, B. (1983). *The Logic and Limits of Trust*. New Brunswick, NJ: Rutgers University Press.

Bok, S. (1978). *Lying: Moral Choice in Public and Private Life*. New York: Pantheon Books.

Golembiewski, R. T. & McConkie, M. (1975). The centrality of interpersonal trust in group processes. In C. L. Cooper (Ed.), *Theories of Group Processes*. New York: Wiley.

Granovetter, M. (1985). Economic action and social structure: The problem of embeddedness. *American Journal of Sociology*, **91**, 481–510.

Hill, C. W. L. (1990). Cooperation, opportunism, and the invisible hand: Implications for transaction cost theory. *Academy of Management Review*, **15**, 500–13.

Ring, P. S. & Van de Ven, A. H. (1992). Structuring cooperative relationships between organizations. *Strategic Management Journal*, **13**, 438–98.

Zand, D. E. (1972). Trust and managerial problem solving. *Administrative Science Quarterly*, **17**, 229–39.

LARUE TONE HOSMER

truthtelling Truthtelling is not a matter of speaking the truth but is rather a matter of speaking what one *believes* to be the truth. So too liars do not necessarily say what is false; they say what they believe to be false. Further, one can mislead without lying. An executive answering in the affirmative the question whether some employees are in excessive danger on the job will mislead if he knows that in fact most employees are but does not say so. Yet he does not lie. Similarly there is no lie in an advertisement suggesting that those who use a certain product will win wealth and power. This article deals with the ethical and practical dimensions of truthtelling and lying only.

Sincerity is a virtue, and yet lies both great and trivial are sometimes in the best interest of the liar or even the party to whom they are addressed. While some, such as Augustine and Kant, have taken the view that lies are morally objectionable under any circumstances, others such as Grotius and Mill have thought there to be conditions under which lying is morally acceptable, and perhaps even obligatory. This latter position raises the question whether there are general principles in the light of which one may determine the moral status of a lie.

Our deeming sincerity a virtue may be due to the fact that each of us is better off in a society in which people are truthful most of the time than we would be in a society in which, say, people lie as often as they tell the truth. This fact may create a presumption against lying so that even those who are not deeply moved by the claims of morality will require special grounds for lying rather than being veracious. If so, then the general principles mentioned above could help to shed light on this presumption and the conditions under which it is reasonably overturned.

The Rationality of Truthtelling

That each of us is better off living in a society in which people are truthful most of the time than we would be in a society in which, say, people lie as often as they tell the truth, may be brought out with the following example. You and another person, X, are both people who act in their own best interest, and you have been placed in separate rooms. In each room there are two buttons, one red and the other green. If you both push the same button (no matter the color) then you each receive a large reward, say $1 million each. If you push different buttons then you each receive a small reward, say $1 each. You receive a slip of paper from X with the words, "I have just pushed the green button." Each of you knows that the other is self-

interested and each knows that the other is aware of the structure of the situation. Can you infer from these facts alone which button it would be rational to push?

It may seem obvious that the rational thing to do is to push the green button. But as Hodgson has pointed out, this inference presupposes that X, as a rational agent, is inclined to tell the truth. You have no reason to accept X's message as veracious unless you have reason to believe that veracity is in X's best interest. Perhaps X believes that the rational thing to do is to assert the opposite of what he believes to be the case. Unless this possibility can be ruled out it is difficult to see what ground you could have for pushing the green rather than the red button.

There is nothing intrinsically more rational about driving on the right side of the road than driving on the left. However, *given* that in a certain society the regularity is to drive on the right side of the road, sane drivers in this society have no incentive to deviate from this regularity. The regularity of driving on the right side of the road thus seems to be an *equilibrium*: an outcome that is a function of the choices of multiple agents, and such that no such agent has an incentive to deviate from this outcome. It has been suggested by Lewis that the practice of asserting only what you believe is another such equilibrium, in that given that speakers generally do so there is typically no reason to deviate from this regularity. This may be what Samuel Johnson has in mind in suggesting that even in Hell the devils tell one another the truth.

If we assume that X in the above scenario is from the same society as ours, we may be able to infer that X's message is sincere. On this basis we may then infer that the rational choice is to push the green button. This allows us to see the importance of conventions such as truthtelling in societies like ours: Were there no such convention we would be at a loss to know what to make of one another's utterance even if we knew what their words meant.

Each of us benefits from the practice of truthtelling. This suggests that in an individual case even the self-interested, amoral agent will presume against lying. What sorts of considerations can overturn this presumption?

Conditions that May Excuse Lying

It has been said that it is easy to tell one lie but hard to tell only one, since the covering up of a lie can involve one in further untruths or dissimulation. What is more, the liar runs the risk of being found out, with the consequent tarnishing of the liar's credibility. Nevertheless, it seems to be in one's best interest to lie to an enemy who, were they to have the truth, would do you harm. Further, there seem to be cases in which, not only is it in one's best interest to lie, one is right to do so. A farmer hiding Jews from Germans acts heroically in lying to Nazis who come to his door asking whether he is keeping any Jews in his house. Ethicists and theologians have dealt at length with the question of the conditions under which a lie is morally acceptable.

Augustine held all lies to be morally blameworthy, while conceding that some lies are more blameworthy than others. Following him, Thomas Aquinas held that only some lies constitute mortal sins. Kant held a more stern view, claiming that not only are lies wrong in all circumstances, but that the liar destroys his dignity as a person. Similarly we find in Dante's *Inferno* that liars are tormented in the eighth circle of Hell, and so are superior only to traitors.

Adopting a more temperate view, Grotius held that stating what one knows to be false is a lie only if it violates the right of liberty in judgment of the person to whom it is addressed. One with evil intentions gives up this right, and children have yet to acquire it, so lies to such people may be justified. However, an ailing person seems to have all his rights in place and yet a lie to such a person may well be justified.

Bok suggests four major conditions that can excuse lies: avoiding harm, producing benefits, fairness, and veracity itself. Concerning the first condition, some lies are done for the sake of preventing some evil greater than the evil of lying itself. The example of the farmer protecting the lives of the Jews he is harboring is a case in point. Similarly a lobbyist for a large firm may believe that preventing the layoffs that would result from her company's losing a large government contract justifies lying to public officials. Other untruths are calculated to produce benefits, as in the case of a lie told to a person on her deathbed to lift her spirits, or in the giving of a placebo.

Third, fairness is sometimes invoked as exculpating a lie. One form that this appeal takes is in the thought that the other party would have no qualms about deceiving the liar. Also, some might take their lie to be fair on the ground that it rectifies some earlier wrong done to them. Fourth, one might try to justify a lie on the ground that it is required to preserve one's reputation for veracity. One who has told a justified lie may need to tell other lies in order to protect her reputation for veracity. Bok argues forcefully that although each of these four conditions can legitimate a lie, we are all too prone to invoke them opportunistically in an effort to justify our deceits. One way to resist this tendency may be to highlight the respect in which the norm of truthfulness is one of many public commodities.

Liars as Free-Riders

Each of us benefits from an ability to presume that others are on the whole veracious. In light of this we see that the opportunistic liar is a "free-rider": such a person exploits a public commodity for her own purposes, such that were many others to do the same this commodity would cease to exist. The commodity that the practice of veracity creates is the ability to rely upon the word of others as in all likelihood sincere. Those interested in the preservation of diverse commodities for the future will scrutinize carefully any claim to justify a departure from the norm of truthfulness.

See also **advertising ethics; applied ethics; authenticity; bluffing and deception; conscience; consequentialism; decision theory; duty; ethical issues in information; ethics of marketing; golden rule, the; integrity; Kantian ethics; moral dilemmas; moral imperatives; promises, promising; rational choice theory; reflective equilibrium; self-deception; self-interest; social contract theory; trust; universalizability; utilitarianism**

Bibliography

Aquinas, T. (1922). *Summa Theologica*, trans. by the Fathers of the English Dominican Province. London: Burnes Oates & Washburn. (Distinguishes among the degree of turpitude of various kinds of lie).

Augustine (1952). "Lying" and "Against lying." In *Treatises on Various Subjects*, (Ed.), R. J. Deferrari. New York: Catholic University of America Press. (Early and highly influential prohibition against all forms of lying).

Bok, S. (1978). *Lying: Moral Choice in Public and Private Life*. New York: Pantheon. (A philosophical account with attention paid to practical issues).

Grotius, H. (1925). *On the Law of War and Peace*, trans. F. Kelsey. Indianapolis, Ind.: Bobbs-Merrill. (Defines lying in terms of the rights of those to which the lie is addressed).

Hodgson, D. H. (1967). *Consequences of Utilitarianism*. Oxford: Oxford University Press. (Questions the source of the norm of truthtelling on purely instrumental grounds).

Kant, I. (1949). On a supposed right to lie from benevolent motives. In *The Critique of Practical Reason and Other Writings in Moral Philosophy*. Chicago: University of Chicago Press. (Defends a view of lying as unjustified under all circumstances).

Lewis, D. (1969). *Convention: A Philosophical Study*. Cambridge, Mass.: Harvard University Press.

Lewis, D. (1972). Utilitarianism and truthfulness. *Australasian Journal of Philosophy*, **50**, 17–19. (Each of these two works defends a conception of a norm of truthfulness as an equilibrium).

MITCHELL S. GREEN

U

unconscionability The legal doctrine of unconscionability empowers courts to police contracts against unfairness by invalidating all or part of a contract that the court finds was "unconscionable" at the time it was made. The doctrine is embodied in Section 2-302 of the US Uniform Commercial Code. The Uniform Commercial Code is a lengthy statute governing eight distinct areas of commercial law. Article 2, where 2-302 appears, deals with the sale of goods. The Uniform Commercial Code was drafted in a collaborative effort by two groups of academics and practitioners, the National Conference of Commissioners on Uniform State Laws and the American Law Institute. It was then enacted, at different times and with minor variations, by the legislature of each state.

The Code states:

> (1) If the court as a matter of law finds the contract or any clause of the contract to have been unconscionable at the time it was made the court may refuse to enforce the contract, or it may enforce the remainder of the contract without the unconscionable clause, or it may so limit the application of any unconscionable clause as to avoid any unconscionable result.

Section 2-302 has been described as "enact[ing] the moral sense of the community into the law of commercial transactions" (*Jones* v. *Star Credit Corp.*, 59 Misc.2d 189, 191; 298 N.Y.S.2d 264, 266 (1969).)

Although Section 2-302 gives judges considerable power to police contracts, it offers little guidance as to how to do so. Official commentary to 2-302 states that the provision is designed to avoid "oppression" and "unfair surprise," and suggests that "one-sidedness" is a relevant factor. However, the Code nowhere defines "unconscionability." It leaves unanswered whether the evil aimed at in 2-302 is a defect in the process by which the parties reached their agreement, unfair terms, or some combination of the two. Courts and commentators use the terms "procedural unconscionability" (or "non-substantive unconscionability") and "substantive unconscionability" to distinguish between the doctrine's use in policing bargaining misconduct and its use in policing contractual terms (Leff, 1967; Schwartz, 1977).

The concept of "procedural unconscionability" is consistent with the traditional legal principle of protecting private agreements that are an expression of the free will of the parties. Contract law is essentially enabling law. It assists parties in regulating their own affairs by allowing them to design "law" specifically tailored to their transaction or relationship. Provided no third party is adversely affected, enforcement of such agreements tends to maximize welfare and foster individual autonomy. (Epstein, 1975, pp. 293–4; Wertheimer, 1992, p. 480). Because parties are assumed to know their own best interests, it is unnecessary for courts to examine the substance of contracts to determine whether a fair bargain has been made. These arguments for enforcing private agreements are undercut, however, when the agreement is not a product of free assent. For this reason, courts have traditionally refused to enforce promises procured by duress, fraud, mistake, or undue influence, and promises made by minors, the mentally ill, or others who lack the capacity to form binding agreements.

"Procedural unconscionability" is also aimed at defects in bargaining or assent. However, courts have applied the doctrine to reach a wider range of situations than is covered by the traditional contract defenses. For example, courts have found procedural unconscionability where one party lacks opportunity to dicker over the terms of the agreement, as in industry-wide form contracts; where contract terms are buried in fine print or couched in unintelligible language; where one party does not understand, or fails to appreciate, a risk assumed under the contract (such as a right to repossess or a waiver of warranty); where there is a gross disparity of bargaining power; or where one party is particularly susceptible or vulnerable. (See, e.g., *Henningsen v. Bloomfield Motors, Inc.*, 161 A.2d 69 (N.J. 1960); *Gianni Sport Ltd. v. Gantos, Inc.*, 391 N.W.2d 760 (Mich. App. 1976); *Williams v. Walker-Thomas Furniture*, 350 F.2d 445 (D.C. Cir. 1965); *Frostifresh v. Reynoso*, 54 Misc.2d 119, 381 N.Y.S.2d 964 (1967).) The doctrine of unconscionability has been applied most frequently to consumer sales contracts, but courts have also applied it outside the consumer context.

Courts do not refuse to enforce contracts on the basis of procedural unconscionability alone; the procedural defect must have resulted in an unfair term. Terms that courts have frequently found unfair include "add-on clauses" in consumer credit sales (*Williams*); clauses disclaiming warranties, limiting damages, or giving up procedural rights (*Henningsen*; *Allen v. Michigan Bell*, 549 P.2d 903 (Kan. 1976)); and price terms that are grossly disproportionate to the market value of the item sold (*Jones*; *Frostifresh*). The more controversial question is whether substantive unfairness, alone, can be the basis for refusing to enforce a contract. Most courts require both procedural and substantive defects for a finding of unconscionability. Nevertheless, substantive unfairness appears to be the driving force behind unconscionability doctrine. Once courts find unfair terms, they are willing to look hard for defects in bargaining and assent. In some cases, courts treat the presence of an unfair term as evidence of a procedural defect (e.g. *Jones*, which inferred procedural unfairness from an unfair price term). The effect of such holdings is to classify the agreement as unconscionable on the basis of substance alone.

Scholars and practitioners in business ethics should find the doctrine of unconscionability a profitable area of study. There is a rich case law

embodying judges' perceptions of the meaning of fairness and voluntariness in commercial transactions. The cases invite reflection about paternalism and the extent to which society should attempt to "enact the moral sense of the community" into commercial law. Each time a court refuses to enforce a contract, it becomes more difficult for a similarly situated person to make a credible commitment to perform a similar promise, even if the commitment might be advantageous. Yet the ability to make credible commitments – to form binding contracts – is a prerequisite to full participation in commercial markets. The doctrine of unconscionability pits the value of the right to contract against the values of fairness and protection from exploitation.

See also **fairness; paternalism**

Bibliography

Chirelstein, M. A. (1992). *Concepts and Case Analysis in the Law of Contracts*, 2nd edn. Westbury, NY: Foundation Press.

Dees, G. (1992). Unconscionability and fairness: Comments on Wertheimer. *Business Ethics Quarterly*, 2, 497–504.

Epstein, R. (1975). Unconscionability: A critical reappraisal. *Journal of Law and Economics*, 18, 293–315.

Farnsworth, A. (1990). *Contracts*. Boston: Little, Brown, 323–39.

Leff, A. (1967). Unconscionability and the Code – The emperor's new clause. *University of Pennsylvania Law Review*, 15, 485–559.

Schwartz, A. (1977). A reexamination of nonsubstantive unconscionability. *Virginia Law Review*, 63, 1053–83.

Wertheimer, A. (1992). Unconscionability and contracts. *Business Ethics Quarterly*, 2, 479–96.

JENNIFER M. MOORE

unions *see* LABOUR UNION

universalizability A thesis about moral statements, held by most, though not all, moral philosophers, namely that to make a moral judgment about one situation commits one to accepting a similar judgment about any situation having the same universal non-moral properties, no matter what individuals occupy what roles in the two situations. The thesis is associated above all with Kant, but is related to the views of earlier thinkers, and to the Christian (and pre-Christian) golden rule. "Individuals" is best taken (though Kant thought otherwise) to include all sentient beings, human or non-human (*see* KANTIAN ETHICS; GOLDEN RULE, THE).

The thesis is crucial for moral reasoning. The following confusions about it are common.

(1) Universalizability is not the same as generality or simplicity, although simple general rules do have a place at the intuitive level of moral thinking. The universal non-moral properties in question may be highly specific. Thus a believer in the universalizability of moral statements does not have to believe that they ought always to be made in accordance with very simple general rules. Specific (even very detailed) differences between situations may make a moral difference, provided that they can be expressed without reference to individual roles. Thus a lie told to someone in one situation could be wrong, but a lie told to someone in a subtly different situation not wrong, if the difference were morally relevant. Kant was unclear about this.

(2) References to individuals are not the same as specifications of relations in which the individuals stand. Thus, if Jane is John's mother, it is not a breach of the thesis to say that John has a certain duty to Jane in virtue of being her son. The universal principle here is that all sons owe this duty to their mothers – for example, to care for them in old age, or to do so in certain minutely specified circumstances. It is not relevant that a son can have only one (genetic) mother.

(3) It is likewise not relevant that no two actual people and no two actual situations are exactly similar. Hypothetical people and situations can be imagined that *are* exactly similar in their non-moral universal properties, and we can ask what should be done in these exactly similar situations if *we* occupied different roles in them (for example, that of the victim of a dirty trick that we are thinking of playing in our present actual role).

(4) The roles in the situations include the desires of the people in them; so I cannot argue,

"I wouldn't mind it being done to *me*," if my victim very much minds it being done to *him*.

The argument from universalizability thus goes as follows: we say to someone planning a wrong act, "Are you prepared to say that the same ought to be done to you, if just the same situation were to recur, but with you in your victim's place?" Most people, if they understand what "ought" means, will say that they are not.

R. M. HARE

utilitarianism A moral theory that regards welfare, or the good of individuals, as the ultimate value, and evaluates other things, such as acts, solely by their promotion of that value (*see* VALUES). Utilitarianism gives content to the idea that doing the right thing means doing good – making the world better than it otherwise would be. The theory has proved to be perennially attractive and resilient in the face of challenging objections.

Utilitarianism is a normative, not a descriptive theory (*see* NORMATIVE/DESCRIPTIVE). It does not assume that our actions or value judgments reflect an unqualified commitment to promoting welfare. Utilitarians assume a critical attitude towards conventional morality and existing institutions. The founders of modern utilitarianism, Jeremy Bentham (1748–1832) and John Stuart Mill (1806–73), were effective advocates of social reform (*see* BENTHAM, JEREMY; MILL, JOHN STUART).

Utilitarianism is regarded by many theorists as a species of CONSEQUENTIALISM, which asserts that "intrinsic" value (the most basic kind of value) should be brought into existence, and that acts, motives, and institutions should accordingly be judged by their "instrumental value" (their capacity to realize basic value). As a species of consequentialism, utilitarianism holds that the good of individuals is the only basic value and should accordingly be maximized. Non-utilitarian varieties of consequentialism regard some other things, such as beauty, knowledge, or justice, as intrinsically valuable.

Utilitarian theories incorporate various conceptions of welfare. Bentham embraced a "hedonistic" conception, in terms of "pleasure" and the absence of "pain." Mill believed that the pleasures which differentiate human beings from other animals are "higher" and more valuable than physical pleasures. He advanced a complex conception of human welfare, which emphasizes the exercise of distinctive human faculties.

Some objections to utilitarianism concern a particular conception of welfare, such as hedonism, and do not challenge the utilitarian idea that right conduct depends on the promotion of welfare. Other criticisms concern the theory's focus on welfare to the exclusion of other goods, and do not challenge the consequentialist idea that right conduct depends on the promotion of intrinsic value.

Utilitarianism (and more generally consequentialism) may be contrasted with theories claiming that some set of rights or duties (rather than a value such as welfare) is morally basic. John Locke (1632–1704) held, for example, that certain "natural" rights are morally basic. Immanuel Kant (1724–1804) developed a theory within which duties are morally basic (see RIGHTS; DUTY; LOCKE, JOHN; KANTIAN ETHICS).

More recently, W. D. Ross argued that morality imposes a diverse set of obligations, or "prima facie duties," including some that are essentially "backward-looking," such as honoring one's moral commitments and compensating others for wrongful injuries one has done them. Utilitarianism, by contrast, is essentially "forward-looking": moral requirements are held by it to be grounded on the difference conduct can make to the future history of the world. Commitments one has made, wrongs one has done to others, indeed past events generally are morally relevant, according to utilitarianism, only insofar as they affect the future consequences of conduct. Utilitarians accordingly recognize particular moral rights or duties when, but only when, they believe the recognition of those rights or duties would promote welfare. Critics see this facet of utilitarianism as evidence of a fundamentally misguided approach to moral responsibility.

Some utilitarians have argued that utilitarianism satisfactorily accommodates moral rights and obligations. To succeed, their arguments must overcome what may be called the trumping problem. It means little to embrace moral rights and obligations if they are not accorded special weight in practice. If I have promised to help you with a particular task, I am not morally free to decide what to do when the time comes by determining whether my helping you would maximize welfare. My obligation can be outweighed by important conflicting considerations, but it outweighs the utilitarian consideration that I might do a trifle more good by breaking my promise. Precisely because of his commitment to maximizing welfare, it would seem that a utilitarian should be guided by that utilitarian consideration. If so, the obligation is accorded no weight at all in practice, and the utilitarian's recognition of it would seem empty. Similar difficulties attach to the utilitarian recognition of moral rights. It is unclear whether utilitarianism (or any form of consequentialism) can solve this problem.

Utilitarianism differs from ethical egoism, a normative theory which holds that an individual may properly serve her own interests, however her self-serving conduct might affect others (see EGOISM, PSYCHOLOGICAL EGOISM AND ETHICAL EGOISM). Ethical egoism says that one should take others' welfare into account only insofar as helping, hurting, or ignoring others would have an impact on one's own welfare.

Utilitarianism regards the welfare of any single individual as no more or less important than the welfare of any other individual. At the level of principle, therefore, it rejects the conventional assumption that a political community may properly serve its own interests first and that its public officials are morally bound to give priority to those interests. Utilitarianism holds that a policy reflecting that conventional assumption might be justified, but only if and when such a division of labor would maximize welfare throughout the world. Utilitarianism requires that laws and public policy serve as far as possible the interests of all who may be affected. No individual's interests may be discounted or double-counted because of her location, citizenship, nationality, class, race, creed, or gender – indeed, for any reason whatsoever.

Although utilitarianism may be considered egalitarian because it requires that equal consideration be given to all, it does not assume that all individuals should be treated the same. It would endorse unequal treatment whenever the general welfare would be maximized by unequal treatment. Because different individuals have different NEEDS, differential treatment is in some respects unproblematic. Medicine, for example, should be allocated only to those who require it.

But utilitarianism also implies that one may properly favor one's family or friends only if and when such a policy would best serve the general welfare. Critics have regarded this as an implausible consequence of the theory. They believe that a conscious commitment to utilitarianism would undermine meaningful relationships with other persons, because close relations with others involve according their interests special weight.

Critics argue further that a distinctively human life involves commitment not only to some other persons but also to some personal projects. Given the vast array of unmet needs around the world – indeed, within our own communities – it would seem that a conscientious commitment to promoting welfare would place unrelenting demands on one's time, resources, and efforts. Critics believe that utilitarianism demands more sacrifice than it is reasonable for a morality to require. We draw a distinction between acting as morality requires and acting above and beyond the call of duty. Critics believe that utilitarianism's demands on the individual obliterates this distinction.

Some utilitarians believe that welfare is best served when economic resources are distributed equally. This notion is based on the phenomenon of "diminishing marginal utilities." A hundred dollars is more useful to an impoverished person than to someone who is affluent. The quality of life for a poor man can be improved more than the quality of life for a rich man would be decreased if a hundred dollars were transferred from the rich man to the poor man. In practice, however, such transfers have considerable costs, which constitute utilitarian obstacles to economic equalization. If justice requires equal distribution of resources, then utilitarianism will have difficulty accommodating its dictates (see JUSTICE, CIRCUMSTANCES OF).

Bentham came to believe that the interests of those who occupy high public office tend to conflict with the interests of their subjects. Because those who are ruled far outnumber those who rule, he held that welfare is best served when public policies are dedicated to promoting the "greatest happiness of the greater number." That famous slogan thus reflects an application of the utilitarian principle, not the principle itself.

As the foregoing suggests, it often seems that the interests of different individuals can come into conflict in the real world. Whenever that happens, utilitarianism does not care whose interests are served, so long as welfare in the aggregate is promoted as much as it is possible to do.

Critics of utilitarianism charge that, as a consequence, utilitarianism can have morally objectionable implications. It is imaginable, for example, that the aggregate welfare would best be served by exploiting some individuals for the benefit of others. Systems like that have existed in our world – serfdom and SLAVERY are uncontroversial examples – which some have defended as beneficial on the whole. For such a system to be condoned by utilitarianism, however, the total benefits generated must not merely exceed the total costs; the system must promote welfare to a greater degree than any alternative system that is available. Critics hold that, even if utilitarian support for such a system is in fact unlikely, utilitarians wrongly reject such systems by calculating benefits and costs rather than recognizing that exploitative social systems violate inviolable rights.

In practice, exploitative systems attack not only the living standard of those who are exploited but also their dignity and SELF-RESPECT. It is unclear whether utilitarianism can fully account for those terrible costs. The possibility that it can is suggested by the fact that one's quality of life is devastated by conditions that undermine dignity and self-respect.

As many of these examples imply, utilitarianism assumes that "interpersonal comparisons of utility" are possible. Consider first commonplace estimates of SELF-INTEREST. These require rankings of alternatives involving benefits and costs; they do not strictly require that we sum and therefore measure benefits and costs. Utilitarianism assumes that welfare gains and losses to a given person are measurable, and that the units of measurement for gains are equivalent to those for losses. It then adds a significant complication: it assumes, further, that units of measurement for gains and losses have interpersonal validity. It presupposes that there is some way of rigorously comparing the gains and losses of one person with the gains and losses for any other person. Utilitarianism makes no sense otherwise. But no one has ever adequately explained how such measurements can be made.

One should reject utilitarianism if one has good reason to believe that interpersonal comparisons of utility are not merely difficult but impossible. Believing this, some theorists have developed evaluative principles that do not require interpersonal comparisons, such as certain conceptions of ECONOMIC EFFICIENCY. Consider the concepts of "Pareto-superiority" and "Pareto-optimality": Allocation of resources B is Pareto-superior to allocation of resources A if, and only if, the move from A to B would result in someone gaining without anyone losing. And A is a Pareto-optimal allocation of resources if, and only if, it is impossible to reallocate resources from A so that some person gains without anyone losing. These concepts require that we determine whether anyone gains or loses, but they do not require that we compare one person's gain or loss with anyone else's gain or loss.

Although no one has yet proved that interpersonal comparisons of utility are in principle possible, commonplace reasoning frequently involves such comparisons. And the reasoning which has led theorists to reject interpersonal comparisons of utility may be questioned. It is based on the assumptions that welfare must be understood in terms of "pleasures" and "pains," and that these are "private," inaccessible to others, so that it makes no sense to think we might objectively measure the intensity of a pleasure or pain. But pleasure without pain is just one particular conception of welfare. It seems plausible to suppose that it is in a person's interest to have good health, ample resources, interesting opportunities, good companionship, and self-respect. In supposing this, one need not assume that such advantages can be analyzed exhaustively in terms of pleasure and the absence of pain. Whether welfare, properly understood, is susceptible to the necessary measurements remains to be seen.

Some utilitarians believe that right conduct is determined by actual consequences. Others believe it depends on the consequences that one can reasonably predict. Each alternative

offers difficulties. On the first view, if all the available evidence is misleading, utilitarianism can condemn one's conduct even if one has acted most conscientiously. On the second view, utilitarianism can imply that it is wrong to do what actually has the best consequences. Utilitarians address these difficulties in part by distinguishing between judgments of acts and judgments of persons.

As a moral theory, utilitarianism applies the welfare criterion in order to determine which acts are morally right and which are morally wrong. The simplest and most important form of the theory applies the welfare criterion directly to conduct. The result is "act-utilitarianism," which holds that each and every act should promote welfare as much as possible. Utilitarianism has recently been given different forms. One is "rule-utilitarianism," which applies the welfare criterion indirectly to acts and directly to social rules. Rule-utilitarianism says that conduct should conform to social rules which promote welfare as much as possible. Rule-utilitarianism can itself be developed in various ways.

Critics have advanced many objections to utilitarianism beyond those already mentioned. For example, we usually assume that competent adults should be left free to find their own ways, which includes making their own mistakes (so long as they exercise due care for others' welfare). Invasions of that freedom are condemned as paternalistic. It would seem that utilitarianism must sometimes approve or even require such interventions. Utilitarians have, however, disagreed. Because his conception of welfare places a premium on the individual's free exercise of her own judgment, developing her own goals, and working toward them, Mill (for example) believed that utilitarianism, properly understood, would not condone objectionable paternalism.

See also **altruism and benevolence; happiness; moral rules; paternalism; privacy; punishment; supererogation; welfare economics**

Bibliography

Bentham, J. (1789). *An Introduction to the Principles of Morals and Legislation*. (Many editions are currently available).

Glover, J. (Ed.), (1990). *Utilitarianism and Its Critics*. New York: Macmillan. (A useful collection of studies, with an extensive bibliography).

Mill, J. S. (1863). *Utilitarianism*. (Many editions are currently available).

Moore, G. E. (1912). *Ethics*. (A twentieth-century classic).

Scheffler, S. (Ed.), (1988). *Consequentialism and Its Critics*. New York: Oxford University Press. (A useful collection, with an extensive bibliography).

Sidgwick, H. (1874). *The Methods of Ethics*. (A highly esteemed classic of utilitarianism. A 7th edn was published in 1907).

Smart, J. J. C. & Williams, B. (1973). *Utilitarianism: For and Against*. Cambridge: Cambridge University Press.

DAVID LYONS

V

values The verb, "to value," like the nouns, "value" and "values," and the adjective "valuable," have a wide range of meanings in ordinary speech because they are used in many different contexts. But all of these meanings and all uses of these words build on one central idea: to value something is to consider it a candidate for action aimed at achieving it. We speak and think most clearly, in other words, if we consider the verb "to value" as the primary guide to the meanings of these words. Then the adjective, "valuable," tells us that someone values the thing so described; and the nouns, "value" and "values," pick out the characteristics that valuing focuses on, that is, the characteristics that make a thing a candidate for action aimed at achieving it. If we interpret these words in this way, then an uncommon but accurate synonym for "valuable" would be "choiceworthy" (a term borrowed here from Terrence Irwin's translation of Aristotle's *Nicomachean Ethics*). It is difficult to think of any exact synonym for the more abstract nouns, "value" and "values," although the word "goodness" sometimes means almost the same thing as "value." (*See* ARISTOTLE).

The activity of valuing involves a valuer and something valued. The valuer must be the kind of being that acts and is drawn to action by characteristics in things. Thus, there is a link between talk of values and people's *motivations* for acting (*see* MOTIVES). But valuing is not simply reactive; it involves judgment, and this is why a person can provide a satisfactory answer to the question, "Why did you do that?" by citing the value/values that the action is aimed at achieving. That is, values refer to people's *reasons* for acting and their judgments about such reasons. This is why ethics, as the study of people's judgments about what they ought to do, always has an important place for values,

i.e., for the characteristics that people value and so aim to achieve in their actions (*see* ETHICS).

In addition to a valuer, the activity of valuing also involves something valued. It is an intentional activity; that is, it is not wholly self-contained in the valuer, but links the valuer to something else, to the thing valued, via the characteristics (values) in it which prompt or explain action aimed at achieving it (*see* INTENTIONALITY). In this respect, statements about valuing are always, in part, descriptions of something, since they identify characteristics of things that the valuer takes to be real and worth acting for. But statements about valuing also serve as explanations of actions, as reasons offered to other persons to explain why a certain action was done in the past or is being done in the present or is being considered for the future. In this way statements about valuing always play a normative function as well, showing other persons who want to understand our actions why these actions are reasonable (*see* NORMATIVE/DESCRIPTIVE).

Things valued can be of many sorts. But the characteristics of things that valuing picks out are characteristics that make action worthwhile. So it is appropriate to ask if there is any class of characteristics that is fundamentally worthwhile to act for, or whether the valuableness of things – what is worth acting for – is completely variable. Answering this question requires a three-step sorting process.

First, some things are valued only "instrumentally," that is, as means to other things. For example, I value taking the subway in order to get to my destination. I value getting to my destination, let us say, in order to shop for something; and I value shopping in order, in one possible scenario, to give my friend a birthday gift; and so on. It seems obvious, however, that this chain of explanations cannot go on forever and still be an adequate explanation. Instead we expect to find, at the end of such a chain, something that is not valued for the sake of something else; that is, something (or things) valued "for its own sake," as we commonly express it. In philosophers' terminology, things valued for the sake of something else are called "instrumentally" valuable; and a thing valued "for its own sake" is said to be "intrinsically valuable."

Second, is there any common characteristic among the things that people consider intrinsically valuable? This is a disputed point. But a good case can be made that, for humans, only *experiences* are intrinsically valuable, and that all the non-human things that humans value, and all other characteristics of humans besides experiences that humans value, are all valued instrumentally and for the sake of certain kinds of experiences that these things are means to in various ways.

The third question is whether there is any pattern in the experiences that humans value intrinsically. Is there some fairly definite set of experiences that are intrinsically valued by humans generally and that are the only ones that humans generally value intrinsically? This is a highly disputed question that has been written about, pro and con, by philosophers, psychologists, and other theorists about the human condition, as well as by novelists, playwrights, and many others for centuries. There are some very plausible candidates for experiences that all people, at least all people of mature years and sound mind, intrinsically value. Among these are: pleasure (or certain kinds of pleasure); self-determination or autonomy; certain kinds of human relationships (e.g. just exchanges; fulfilling one's social role; friendship; love); and a sense of integrity or of the unity of the self. (*See* AUTONOMY; HAPPINESS; HARM; INTEGRITY; INTERESTS AND NEEDS; JUSTICE; ROLES AND ROLE MORALITY; TRUST.)

Those who argue that there is no such pattern can point to the wide range of things that people value in daily life. But much of this diversity of human aims disappears once these aims are sorted out specifically in terms of the experiences that people intrinsically value. A more serious objection for those who see a pattern in these intrinsic values concerns the qualifier: "at least all people of mature years and sound mind." Is this a legitimate qualifier or a way of avoiding evidence contrary to the proposed pattern?

The judgments people offer to explain their actions have been of interest to philosophers and other moral theorists for many centuries (*see* MORAL REASONING; PRACTICAL REASONING). One tradition of theorizing about these judgments has paid particular attention to value statements and to the characteristics of things they identify as choiceworthy. This approach to moral theory is commonly called "UTILITARIANISM" or "CONSEQUENTIALISM." But these theorists might very accurately be called "Value-Maximizers," because they hold that what a person morally ought to do in any situation in whichever course of action available to an actor will produce the maximum of intrinsic value, i.e., of experiences worth having for their own sake. These theorists describe human moral reflection at its best as a process of: 1) evaluating alternative courses of action to determine what instrumental and then what intrinsic values they would yield (and what disvalues and hindrances to values as well), and for whom; and then 2) comparing these evaluations to determine which course of action yields the greatest value. On the value-maximizers' account of morality, this course of action is the one that the actor ought to do.

There have been many varieties of value-maximizing moral theories. Some have held that each human ought to maximize values for self alone; others have seen morality as maximizing values for everyone affected by a course of action; and others have offered other, more complex answers to the "for whom?" question. They have also differed in their views about what sorts of experiences are intrinsically valuable. (*See* ARISTOTLE; BENTHAM, JEREMY; EGOISM, PSYCHOLOGICAL EGOISM AND ETHICAL EGOISM; MILL, JOHN STUART.)

The other traditions of moral theorizing, on the other hand, consider valuing to have, not a central but at best, a subordinate role within sound moral reflection. They have consequently paid much less attention to value statements and to the characteristics that humans value in things, and have explained moral reflection in a variety of other ways. (*See* DUTY; FAIRNESS;

FRIEDMAN, MILTON; JUSTICE; KANTIAN ETHICS; LIBERALISM; LIBERTARIANISM; MORAL RULES; NOZICK, ROBERT; RAWLS, JOHN; RIGHTS; SOCIAL CONTRACT THEORY; VIRTUE ETHICS.)

DAVID T. OZAR

virtue ethics

Overview

A virtue ethic, like any ethic, describes human character and action in an evaluative manner. Virtue ethicists, such as Plato and Aristotle, believe that all human beings aim at being happy. In the language of virtue ethics, happiness is the "end" of human action. Agents are happy when they are doing well or thriving. More specifically, human beings are happy when they are fulfilling their peculiarly human potentialities. While a cat will be satisfied leading an animal's life of sensation and appetite, a human being needs something more. A human's life will not be a full one unless that person is, in addition to sensing and desiring, also maximally exercising the specifically human capacity to choose and to reason.

For the virtue ethicist, the process by which an organism realizes its particular potential and grows into its peculiar being or actuality is natural. Indeed, the Greek word for nature – *physis* – simply means a growing characterized by a successive and progressive realization of a certain end state. Since this fulfilling growth only occurs under specific conditions, it is the task of the virtue ethicist to specify these conditions. By doing so, the virtue ethicist hopes to make his or her audience more aware of the conditions to which they must pay attention if they, too, want to realize their nature or, equivalently, to be happy.

What are these conditions? First and foremost, human happiness depends upon participation in community, be that the community of a household, a clan, a business, or the larger political community. A community is "natural" if human growth (i.e., actualization) depends upon it. The human family is natural because no child becomes an adult without parents who nurture the child and teach her skills for survival. Similarly, human beings are "by

nature" political beings because they cannot fully realize their peculiarly human rationality without participation in the larger political community. By providing and enforcing a rule of law, the political regime frees its citizens from having to constantly protect themselves from marauding thieves and murderers. In addition, the law makes for regular and predictable interactions among citizens. Such predictability, in turn, helps make deliberation possible. People can plan actions only when there is some stability in their environment (e.g., when banks do not arbitrarily choose not to open on some day; or when airlines do not willy-nilly refuse passengers because of their race or sex, etc.). Furthermore, by legislating public education, including the teaching of ethics, the political regime not only develops agents' ability to think and reason about the human condition and the surrounding world. It also aims at getting its citizens to see the necessary connections between their happiness and that of the community at large. Educated citizens will demonstrate the loyalty needed for the community to continue to be healthy and for subsequent generations to have a chance at actualizing their human potentiality.

Human happiness depends upon a second condition as well. To be happy, the agent must be virtuous. Virtue is not to be taken as some extraordinary or saintly goodness. Rather, a human virtue is a state or condition that serves to realize some dimension of human potential. Thus, while it would be better for soldiers to fight only in wars they know to be just, Aristotle treats even unthinking courage as virtuous. The soldier who acts to take a stand in the face of death thereby develops his or her ability to take risks and confront the consequences. Insofar as this ability is a critical life skill, this "false" courage is virtuous.

While "false" courage is a virtue, truly courageous persons do not fight to death simply because ordered to do so. Instead, they consider whether a given situation demands such a stance. Their thoughtfulness points to a third condition for human happiness. To fully (i.e., excellently) realize their human potentiality, persons must learn to deliberate well. Deliberation does not consist of merely identifying means to an end. Someone who deliberates re-thinks the end at the same time as she analyzes means to the end. Thus, the deliberative daughter who is considering how best to care for her elderly mother will try to identify various options for care. Some means might include placing the mother in a nursing home; getting a residential nurse; or having the mother stay with the daughter. If the daughter is on the road to becoming virtuous, she uses her thinking about these various alternatives to further clarify what will count as "caring" for her mother. If she thinks the mother would like an in-house nurse because that will preserve the mother's independence, then the deliberative daughter refines her end of caring for her mother. "Caring" now means not merely physically tending to her mother but also meeting her mother's need for independence. Deliberation, unlike means–end cunning, examines the end along with the means in figuring out how best to achieve a desired end.

The person who fails to deliberate and who relies instead on simple cunning is little more than a crafty animal. Animals, too, can identify means to an end. To the extent an agent is little more than an animal, that agent is neither a virtuous nor a happy *human being*. The virtuous person's happiness inheres in the active life of deliberating. By consistently trying to deliberate about how best to act, agents develop their deliberative skill. They thereby realize their specifically human capacity to deliberate instead of merely engaging in cunning calculations. They also come to grasp important connections between the ends and means, linkages not apparent to vicious persons who fail to deliberate. Consequently, they are less frustrated because the end their action brings about tends to be the end they foresaw and wanted to achieve. The virtuous person's reward is happiness understood as an entire life of satisfying actions, while the vicious person's punishment is a life of actions that produce both unexpected and unintended consequences for himself and others.

Relevance of Virtue Ethics to Business

While virtue ethicists care about issues such as workers' rights and consumer protection, they are also concerned to raise the larger question of the meaning and goodness of business. Business is a practice, akin to the other professions and arts. Like all other professionals, business-

persons either realize or fail to realize their happiness through their activity at work. Persons who view their jobs with "another day, another dollar" mentality are not likely to be happy. Such a mentality turns action into a means to make money. In terms of the above discussion, the agent with this mentality becomes little more than a cunning animal.

The virtuous businessperson, by contrast, always asks whether a proposed act will help to actualize his human being. If, for example, an act manifests contempt for his fellow citizens and for the law, the agent will refrain from it. For business, like the household, is a part of the larger political community. The virtuous person does not deliberately act in ways that destroy the laws that make his and others' happiness possible. Instead, the businessperson who desires to be happy will strive to make friends within the corporation, friends who can help the agent arrive at sound choices. The virtuous businessperson will also support his or her corporation's charity drives and other community projects. From the perspective of the virtuous agent, there can be no question as to whether business should be socially responsible (see SOCIAL RESPONSIBILITY). Insofar as business is a part of society, the acts of corporations and their employees will affect the society at large and, hence, the happiness of persons who are by nature political beings.

Distinctive Insights of the Virtue Ethics Approach

Virtue ethics has become increasingly popular among business ethicists who think this mode of analysis offers important and distinctive insights. According to virtue ethics, what makes an action good is not its conformity to some rule(s) but rather its tendency to fulfill human actuality. Virtue ethics resembles situation ethics inasmuch as both emphasize the need to evaluate particular, and possibly unique, features of a situation in arriving at a decision (see SITUATION ETHICS).

Unlike situation ethics, however, virtue ethics employs a non-relativistic standard for evaluating a course of action. Stated roughly, that principle is: What is humanly good and desirable is what actualizes human being. Not every decision made with respect to a situation is equally good. A sloppy, ill-considered decision or a choice that undermines the happiness of other members of the political community is not as fine and good as a carefully thought through choice consistent with (and preservative of) human virtue. Since what counts as being consistent with human virtue is itself often not immediately obvious in a particular situation, the agent who desires to be happy will investigate this question as well with her friends and colleagues.

One strength, then, of virtue ethics is its ability to provide non-relativistic, yet situation-sensitive, guidance to agents. Virtue ethics is also appealing because it brings to the fore features of action often overlooked by other modes of ethical analyses. Suppose, for example, that a businessman wonders whether he should bribe government officials in order to get a government contract. The Kantian ethicist will argue that the action will not be right if a description of the act's maxim involves the agent in a contradiction of will (see KANTIAN ETHICS). If we take the maxim in this case to be "Act to circumvent government rules and regulations in order to be able to do business with government," the maxim is clearly self-contradictory. Since all governments require rules in order to govern, the agent's envisioned act commits him to a practice that would destroy the very institution with whom he wants to do business. No rational agent therefore can will this act. Hence, it is immoral from the Kantian point of view.

While the virtue ethicist will acknowledge the force of the Kantian objection, it will not be decisive. She will urge the businessman to consider the consequences of this act for his character and long-term ability to lead a happy life. He should deliberate as to how the proposed means (bribing) may impact the end (doing business with the government). To successfully work with the government, the corporation's representatives will need to develop mutual trust. Doing so may be difficult if the relation begins in an underhanded fashion. Furthermore, if the businessman does win the business through a bribe, he cannot claim honestly that he succeeded because he had the superior product or because of his ability to help the customer see what service is best for the customer. The businessman is little more than a conduit for money in this case. He adds little to the transaction. Since his action does not

develop any of his particularly human capacities, the virtue ethicist will suggest that the businessman who relies upon bribery may wind up feeling dissatisfied and alienated from his work.

Virtue ethics may also be contrasted with UTILITARIANISM. The utilitarian will consider whether the act of bribing maximizes the happiness of the society as a whole. One could argue that the act would benefit the bribed official. In the short run, bribery might benefit the company and the businessman as well, assuming the company gets the contract and is not simply tricked by the government official into paying ever more in bribes. If these and other benefits outweigh the various costs of bribery (e.g., the company has to pay bribery fees it would not have to pay if the bidding system were not corrupt), then the utilitarian will judge the action a good one and will recommend its performance.

The virtue ethicist will listen to the utilitarian's analysis. But once again it will not be decisive. Unlike the utilitarian, the virtue ethicist does not assign equal weight to all benefits and costs. Virtue ethics weighs those consequences impacting human growth most heavily. The businessman who pays the bribe initially may be overjoyed at winning the contract. How, though, will he win the next contract? He has not developed his selling skills, and not all contracts can be procured through bribes. By taking the easy route of offering a bribe and by failing to take a stand against corruption, the businessman is choosing a path not likely to serve him well in the future. The virtue ethicist is more inclined than the utilitarian to evaluate each choice from the perspective of the whole of life. As Aristotle puts it, "one swallow does not a summer make" nor does a single act make for a happy life.

Weaknesses of Virtue Ethics Analysis

Critics of virtue ethics worry that the approach is too simplistic. The analysis posits a timeless, invariable human nature. Yet recent discoveries of anthropology show that humans have changed dramatically over time. If so, then it is questionable whether happiness can be said to be the human good. If human nature is indeed variable, happiness, too, must change over time.

In addition, since the virtue ethicist makes claims that are simultaneously descriptive and evaluative (e.g., "all men are by nature political"), some critics have alleged that this approach confuses descriptive with prescriptive claims. If "ought" cannot be derived from "is," then virtue ethics must be on shaky ground.

Of course, these criticisms are themselves controversial. Readers should consult materials listed below and judge the relative merits of virtue ethics for themselves.

Bibliography

Aristotle. (1975). *Nicomachean Ethics,* trans. H. Rackham. Cambridge, Mass.: Harvard University Press.

Broadie, S. (1991). *Ethics with Aristotle.* New York: Oxford University Press.

Donaldson, T. (1992). The language of international corporate ethics. *Business Ethics Quarterly,* **2**, (3), 271–82.

Hartman, E. M. (1996). *Organizational Ethics and the Good Life.* New York: Oxford University Press.

Plato. (1968). *Republic,* trans. A. Bloom. New York: Basic Books.

Rorty, A. (1980). *Essays on Aristotle's Ethics.* Berkeley: University of California Press.

Salkever, S. (1990). *Finding the Mean: Theory and Practice in Aristotelian Political Philosophy.* Princeton: Princeton University Press.

Sherman, N. (1989). *The Fabric of Character.* Oxford: Clarendon Press.

Solomon, R. C. (1993). *Ethics and Excellence.* New York: Oxford University Press.

DARYL KOEHN

W

welfare economics The study of decision-making with the aim of enhancing *social* welfare, in contrast to an *individual's* happiness or a *firm's* profit. It is therefore a subject which should be of value to government, since government is meant to be an agency for promoting social welfare. It should, however, also be of interest to an individual who is not committed solely to enhancing his or her own happiness, or even to the "enlightened" firm or business corporation that seeks not only to increase its profit but also has some commitment to the general well-being of society.

Suppose in choosing between two projects, A and B, all the relevant facts are known. It is known how much who will gain from each project, how much damage each project will do to the environment, and so on. This is in itself of course not enough to choose between the projects. The choice depends on *what* it is that one is seeking to achieve. If a certain firm is evaluating these projects in order to maximize its profits, the facts may point to the choice of A. If the aim is to maximize social welfare, then the same facts point to B. However, the second decision-problem is in some fundamental ways more complicated than the first one because unlike "profits," what constitutes "social welfare" may itself be controversial.

It follows that welfare economics has two main concerns. The first is the abstract problem of deciding what constitutes social welfare, given that individuals in a society have widely divergent and often conflicting objectives. The second concern is the more mundane one of deciding how to choose between projects, taxation schemes, industrial regulation, environmental policy and so on, given some agreed-upon notion of social welfare. The former concern relates welfare economics to moral philosophy and ethics, a boundary with considerable intellectual trespassing (Sen, 1987). The latter explains the overlap of welfare economics with issues of cost–benefit analysis and public policy (Atkinson, 1983; Ng, 1979).

Regarding the constitution of social welfare, one of the earliest and, in economics, arguably the most influential position has been a utilitarian one. With roots a respectable two centuries ago and in the works of Jeremy Bentham (1748–1832) and the two Mills (James, 1773-1836 and John Stuart, 1806–1873), UTILITARIANISM is an ethical doctrine that requires us to maximize the sum total of everybody's utility or happiness. Hence, a welfare economics wedded to utilitarianism would simply sum the total benefit that results from each project or action, giving equal weight to all human beings, and then recommend the project that yields the larger aggregate welfare.

Though the utilitarian method has been and still is widely used in assessing the goodness of alternative government policies or projects, like tax schemes or new airports, it came under severe attack in the first half of this century. One set of criticism pertained to the fact that utilitarianism requires us to *sum* everybody's utility. It is easier to agree that social welfare should *depend* on every individual's utility, but not necessarily be their sum. We may, for instance, argue that if a project impoverishes a rich man by two dollars (assuming for simplicity that dollars measure individual utility) and enriches a poor person by one dollar, this may be a desirable project even though the sum total of utility in society is lowered. The Bergson–Samuelson social welfare function (see Samuelson, 1947; Graaff, 1957) allows for such flexibility which is not there in the utilitarian system.

The second criticism of utilitarianism, and one that also applies to the Bergson–Samuelson method, is that it entails interpersonal comparisons between different people's utility. But can we really compare one person's happiness with another's? (See Basu, 1995, for discussion.) How do we know whether a dollar would make Guildenstern or Rosencrantz happier? So if we have only one dollar to give away and we want to maximize social welfare, whom do we give it to?

A method that tries to circumvent this problem and has been immensely influential in modern welfare economics is the method of Vilfredo Pareto (1848–1923). (See PARETO OPTIMALITY.) Welfare economics defines a *Pareto improvement* for a society as any change that leaves no one worse off and at least one person better off. A *Pareto optimal* state is then defined as a situation from where no further Pareto improvements are made.

One reason why the idea of Pareto optimality shot into prominence in economics was the discovery of a major theorem, the so-called Fundamental Theorem of Welfare Economics. The Fundamental Theorem is essentially a formalization of conjectures which date at least as far back as the writings of ADAM SMITH (1723–90). It states that, given some condition, perfect competition in an economy ensures that the economy will attain Pareto optimality. The importance of this theorem stems from the fact that it has been used – perhaps somewhat cavalierly – to justify a variety of government policy, for example, the enactment of antitrust legislation in order to encourage competition among firms, and, also, at times, to justify unbridled *laissez-faire*.

An advance which gave welfare economics a big boost was the discovery of a theorem of gigantic proportions – Kenneth Arrow's (1951) general impossibility theorem. An Arrovian social welfare function – "SWF" – is a rule by which individuals' rankings over a set of alternatives (e.g., candidates in an election) are converted into a social ranking. Instead of fixing a particular "SWF," Arrow developed some reasonable axioms that we would want any "SWF" to satisfy. The impossibility theorem demonstrates that no "SWF" can satisfy these axioms. The theorem was remarkable because it was so unexpected; its proof relied on no

standard mathematics but just careful chains of deduction. A large literature emerged to "solve" the problem (see Sen, 1970). The literature has grown so as to straddle the formal algebra of voting theory on the one hand and the conceptual world of moral philosophy on the other.

Instead of being a separate field of study, welfare economics is increasingly a method of analysis that underlies diverse branches of economics. With one foot in the groves of academe and the other in the practitioner's workplace, welfare economics is here to stay as an essential part of the economist's repertoire.

Bibliography

Arrow, K. J. (1951). *Social Choice and Individual Values*. New York: Wiley. (2nd and revised edition in 1963.)

Atkinson, A. B. (1983). *Social Justice and Public Policy*. Brighton: Wheatsheaf; and Cambridge, Mass: MIT Press.

Basu, K. (1995). On interpersonal comparison and the concept of equality. In W. Eichhorn (ed.), *Models and Measurement of Welfare and Inequality*. Berlin: Springer-Verlag, 491–510.

Graaff, J. de V. (1957). *Theoretical Welfare Economics*. Cambridge: Cambridge University Press.

Ng, Y.-K. (1979). *Welfare Economics*. London: Macmillan.

Samuelson, P. A. (1947). *Foundations of Economic Analysis*. Cambridge, Mass.: Harvard University Press.

Sen, A. K. (1970). *Collective Choice and Social Welfare*. San Francisco: Holden-Day.

Sen, A. K. (1987). *On Ethics and Economics*. Oxford: Blackwell.

KAUSHIK BASU

welfare rights   are rights to or concerning well-being. Primarily, welfare consists in the state or condition of doing or being well; good fortune, happiness, or well-being of a person, community, or thing. Hence, primary welfare rights are often called rights to well-being. It is useful to classify the various conceptions of rights to welfare roughly on the basis of three distinct concepts of welfare. In the relevant senses, the word "welfare" is used to refer to 1) the happiness or well-being of a person, 2) a source of happiness or personal well-being, or 3) the organized provision for the basic well-being of the needy members of a community.

Gregory Vlastos is the most influential advocate of the first conception. He argues that there is a fundamental human right to well-being. The content of this right is best described as the well-being or welfare of each individual person, that is, the enjoyment of value in all the forms in which it can be experienced by human beings. One person's right to well-being is equal to that of every other person simply because one person's well-being is as valuable as that of any other's. From this generic human right to well-being Vlastos derives more specific welfare rights, such as the moral rights to education, medical care, or work under decent conditions. At this point his reasoning moves to the second conception of welfare rights best illustrated by the writings of Martin Golding. He contrasts option rights, that involve a limited sovereignty over persons or things, with welfare rights, claims to the goods of life which are conferred by the social ideal of a community. The content of each welfare right is some element in or means to the right-holder's personal good or well-being. Examples of the former might be health or freedom from pain; instances of the latter would be food or education. The clearest version of the third sort of conception is Carl Wellman's definition of a primary welfare right as a right to some welfare benefit or benefits. A welfare benefit is any form of assistance – monetary payment, good or service – provided to an individual because of his or her need. Although the most obvious examples are public welfare benefits, such as (in the US context) social security payments or food stamps, there are also private welfare benefits, such as the disaster relief provided by the Red Cross or the food and shelter the Salvation Army offers to the homeless.

In order to understand fully the language of welfare rights, one must not only identify the relevant meaning of "welfare," but also the presupposed conception of a right. Most discussions of welfare rights interpret them according to Wesley Newcomb Hohfeld's conception of a claim. Thus, to assert that Jones has a right to adequate medical care is to say that Jones has a claim against some second party to be provided with medical care and that this

second party has a duty to Jones to provide such medical care to him or her.

This interpretation poses a conceptual problem when resources are so scarce that adequate medical care is unavailable. Since no individual or government can have any duty to do the impossible, there could be no universal human right to medical care. Joel Feinberg, who adopts a claim theory of rights, suggests that in such cases one is using "a right" in a manifesto sense asserting a potential claim-right that ought to determine present aspirations and guide present policies. H. J. McCloskey avoids this predicament by adopting an entitlement theory of rights. Rights are entitlements *to* do, have, enjoy or have done, not claims *against* others. Thus, although a welfare right involves an entitlement to the efforts of others or to make demands on others to aid and promote our seeking after or enjoying some good, the special circumstances will determine who, if anyone, has any implied duty.

Most libertarians conceive of rights negatively as claims that others *not* interfere with one's liberty of action or private property (*see* LIBERTARIANISM). Although most liberals accept such negative rights, they also assert various positive rights, claims against others to provide one with goods or services (*see* LIBERALISM). Because welfare rights seem to be positive rather than negative rights, welfare liberals can and usually do affirm their existence, while many libertarians conclude that there is a conceptual incoherence in any attempt to combine the negative concept of a right with the positive concept of an implied duty to provide welfare benefits. James Sterba suggests that there are negative as well as positive welfare rights. Those who lack the resources necessary to satisfy their basic needs have rights that others not interfere with their taking what they need from those who possess more than they basically need. Because welfare rights can be either negative liberty-rights or positive claim-rights, Sterba defines them as rights to acquire or to receive those goods and resources necessary for satisfying one's basic needs.

However one defines "welfare rights," it is essential to distinguish between the very different species of rights to which this expression can refer. The two most important genera are legal rights conferred by the rules or principles of some legal system and moral rights conferred by moral rules or reasons. Some legal welfare rights, such as the right to education, are in legal systems such as ours civil rights, rights possessed by every member of the society simply as a citizen. Others are special legal rights, rights one possesses by virtue of some more limited status, such as the right to Aid to Families of Dependent Children one possesses by virtue of one's status as an impoverished parent. The two most basic species of moral rights are human rights, rights one possesses simply as a human being, and civic rights, rights one possesses as a member of some society. Moral philosophers disagree about whether welfare rights, such as the right to social security or the right to an adequate standard of living, belong in the former or the latter category. The significance of this issue is in where the nature of implied duties lies. If these are civic rights, then it is one's society that has the obligation to provide for these rights; if they are human rights, then presumably other governments and even individual citizens of other nations also bear some responsibility for assisting those in need.

Another distinction that cuts across the previous classification is that between primary and secondary welfare rights. Carl Wellman distinguishes between primary welfare rights to welfare benefits and secondary welfare rights concerning, but not to, welfare benefits. This distinction can and should be generalized to cover all three conceptions of welfare. Examples of secondary welfare rights are the legal right of a recipient of some welfare benefit to a fair hearing before the termination of this benefit and the moral right of a worker that her employee provide equal pay for equal work.

Discussions of welfare rights are confusing, in part, because the expression "a welfare right" is used with such diverse meanings. Those who wish to think clearly about the political, legal, and moral issues concerning welfare ought not to try to identify the correct, or even the best, conception of welfare rights. Different conceptions are appropriate for different purposes. What is important is to recognize their differences in order to understand more fully the meaning of any given assertion or denial of a welfare right and to think and debate the relevant issues more accurately and fruitfully.

See also **rights; welfare economics**

Bibliography

Feinberg, J. (1980). *Rights, Justice, and the Bounds of Liberty*. Princeton: Princeton University Press.

Golding, M. (1968). Towards a theory of human rights. *The Monist*, 52, 521–49.

Hohfeld, W. N. (1919). *Fundamental Legal Conceptions*. New Haven: Yale University Press.

McCloskey, H. J. (1965). Rights. *Philosophical Quarterly*, 15, 115–27.

Sterba, J. P. (1981). The welfare rights of distant peoples and future generations. *Social Theory and Practice*, 7, 99–119.

Vlastos, G. (1962). Justice and equality. In R. Brandt (ed.), *Social Justice*. Englewood Cliffs, NJ: Prentice-Hall. 31–72.

Wellman, C. (1982). *Welfare Rights*. Totowa, NJ: Rowman & Allanheld.

Wellman, C. (1985). Welfare rights. In K. Kipnis & D. Meyers (eds), *Economic Justice*. Totowa, NJ: Rowman & Allanheld, 229–45.

CARL WELLMAN

whistleblowing A practice in which employees who know that their company is engaged in activities that (a) cause unnecessary harm, (b) are in violation of human rights, (c) are illegal, (d) run counter to the defined purpose of the institution, or (e) are otherwise immoral, inform the public or some governmental agency of those activities. The ethical problem is whether and under what conditions whistleblowing is acceptable behavior and/or morally required behavior. Whistleblowing, if required, would involve a conflict between the obligation of LOYALTY the individual is presumed to have to the company and the obligation to prevent harm the individual is presumed to have to the public. But the exact nature and demands of these conflicting obligations to the company and the public are disputed.

Most business ethicists claim that employees have some obligation to the company or employer, which is usually characterized as an obligation of loyalty. Whistleblowing violates that obligation. In that context the company is viewed as analogous to a sports team. In sports whistleblowing is the function of neutral, detached referees who are supposed to detect and penalize illicit behavior of opposing teams.

It is neither acceptable nor a responsibility of a player to call a foul on one's teammates. If the analogy holds, what is unacceptable in sports is also unacceptable in business. From this perspective whistleblowing is viewed as an act of disloyalty ("finking," "tattle tale") and there is a presumption against it. Consequently, a countervailing obligation to the public would be the only justification for overriding the obligation to the team or company. There is a wide range of views on the issue ranging from the position that whistleblowing as an act of disloyalty is never justified to the opposite position that employees owe no loyalty to a company and given their right to freedom of expression they can ethically disclose whatever they wish about a company, except where their work contract expressly or at least implicitly prohibits it.

Most business ethicists writing on whistleblowing maintain a fiduciary obligation of loyalty that whistleblowing violates, so the burden of proof or justification falls to the whistleblower. However, defenders of whistleblowing maintain that in conditions where companies violate ethical and/or legal constraints, whatever obligation of loyalty an employee has is abrogated, and whistleblowing is not only permissible but may also be morally required, on the grounds that individuals have a responsibility to the general public to prevent harm or illegal activity. Hence the conflict of obligations we mentioned. However, it is possible to argue that even if the illegal or immoral behavior of the company abrogates the responsibility of loyalty, there is no consequent good samaritan obligation to the general public to "blow the whistle."

So two arguments are needed. One to show whistleblowing is permissible, a second to show it is required. This latter argument is quite important, since blowing the whistle can lead to harm to the whistleblower. Under what conditions is one required to do what would likely harm oneself?

The argument for the permissibility of whistleblowing sets down a set of conditions to be met before a whistleblower can justifiably inform on her company.

1. The whistleblowing should be done for the purpose of exposing unnecessary harm, violation of human rights, illegal activity, or conduct counter to the defined purpose of the corporation, and should be done from the appropriate moral motive, that is, not from a desire to get ahead, or out of spite or some such motive. Nevertheless, whether the act of whistleblowing is called for is not determined by the motive of the whistleblower but by the company acting either immorally or illegally.

2. The whistleblower should make certain that his or her belief that inappropriate actions are ordered or have occurred is based on evidence that would persuade a reasonable person.

3. The whistleblower should have acted only after a careful analysis of the danger: (a) how serious is the moral violation? (minor moral matters need not be reported); (b) how immediate is the moral violation? (the greater time before the violation occurs the greater chances that internal mechanisms will prevent the anticipated violation); (c) is the moral violation one that can be specified? (general claims about a rapacious company, obscene profits, and actions contrary to public interest simply will not do).

4. Except in special circumstances, the whistleblower should have exhausted all internal channels for dissent before informing the public. The whistleblower's action should be commensurate with one's responsibility for avoiding and/or exposing moral violations. If there are personnel in the company whose obligation it is to monitor and respond to immoral and/or illegal activities, it would be their responsibility to address those issues. Thus, the first obligation of the would-be whistleblower, would be to report the unethical activities to those persons, and only if they do not act, to inform the general public.

5. The whistleblower should have some chance of success. Ought implies can, so if there is no hope in arousing societal or government pressure, then one needlessly exposes oneself and one's loved ones to hardship for no conceivable moral gain.

But these conditions speak mainly to the *permissibility* of blowing the whistle. A further, often overlooked question is under what conditions is it morally required (*obligatory*), if ever, for an employee to blow the whistle? The literature on this subject is sparse, except that there seems to be a good deal of tacit agreement that some sort of good samaritan principle is operative here. Hence if there is an obligation to prevent harm, under conditions where there is a need and the person is capable of preventing the harm without sacrificing something of comparable moral worth, and if the person is the last resort, then that obligation would operate in the case of whistleblowing. Conditions 4 and 5 may be read as assuming that there is a responsibility to blow the whistle. But to show that obligation requires showing there is an obligation to the general public to prevent harm (Simon et al., 1972).

In the corporate context, the company is seen as a team and expects loyalty. Forsaking the team to function as a detached referee to blow the whistle is seen as disloyal and cause for punitive action. In such a culture, to blow the whistle requires a certain moral heroism. Given the fact that society depends on whistleblowers to protect it from unscrupulous operators, justified whistleblowers need some protection. To assure the existence of necessary whistleblowers (somebody's got to do it), sound legislation is needed to protect the whistleblower.

Finally, whistleblowing is not restricted to the area of business. It occurs in all walks of life. Professionals may be held to the standards of their profession, that sometimes require blowing a whistle. For example, accountants and engineers have a dual obligation to their clients and to the public. Hence, they have a fiduciary responsibility to report certain illegal or potentially harmful activities if they encounter them in the course of their auditing or accounting or constructing. These obligations come from the professional status of the accountants and engineers, just as such obligations extend to all professionals, such as doctors and lawyers, who have obligations to their profession and the public to blow the whistle on colleagues who violate certain canons of appropriate behavior. But beyond the professions, whistleblowing is required in other walks of life: for example, the participants in an honor code have a responsibility to report violations. While such whistleblowing activity is viewed unfavorably, it is a necessary part of human activity.

Enlightened companies, aware that harmful, immoral, or illegal behavior that needs to be reported is likely to occur from time to time, have begun to make provisions for regularizing the monitoring of behavior, with ombudspersons or corporate responsibility officers. Such offices provide an outlet for those who feel obliged to report the unseemly behavior of their companies, without the need to go public. These provisions are desirable because they will alleviate the necessity of going public and blowing the whistle on harmful or illegal behavior.

Bibliography

Bok, S. (1980). Whistleblowing and professional responsibility. *New York University Professional Quarterly*, 11 (summer), 2–7.

De George, R. (1986). *Business Ethics*, 2nd edn. New York: Macmillan.

Duska, R. F. (1985). Whistleblowing and employee loyalty. In J. R. Desjardins & J. J. McCall, (eds), *Contemporary Issues in Business Ethics*. Belmont, Calif.: Wadsworth, 295–300.

Glazer, M. P. & Glazer, P. M. (1989). *The Whistleblowers: Exposing Corruption in Government and Industry*. New York: Basic Books.

Larmer, R. A. (1992). Whistleblowing and employee loyalty. *Journal of Business Ethics*, 11, 125–8.

Nader, R., Petkas, P., & Blackwell, K. (1972). *Whistleblowing*. New York: Bantam Books.

Simon, J. G., Powers, C., & Gunneman, J. P. (1972). *The Ethical Investor*. New Haven: Yale University Press.

Westin, A. F. (1981). *Whistle Blowing: Loyalty and Dissent in the Corporation*. New York: McGraw-Hill.

RONALD F. DUSKA

white knight A "friendly" buyer for a company in the context of an auction or an unwanted bid or hostile tender offer for the company. "Friendly" is usually defined from management's standpoint as a buyer which will retain management, not break up the target company, and/or not lay off employees. Typically the white knight purchases the shares at a premium to the raider's bid, and obtains or is given the support of the target's management and board of directors – indeed, this support may be manifested by a "lockup" agreement to sell certain key assets to the white knight. In short, the white knight is a form of anti-takeover defense. White knight defenses usually succeed in denying the target company to the raider.

The public image of the white knight is positive, as the name suggests. Yet the use of a white knight defense raises a number of ethical issues for the management and directors of both the target company and the white knight. The first issue is *wealth transfer*: Niden (1993) reports a loss in the white knight's market value of equity (over and above the general change in the market) of 3.8 percent, or a loss in value of $13.4 million upon the announcement of the white knight's bid. Banerjee and Owers (1992) find that the white knight's losses are accompanied by gains to the raider and target shareholders. These results are consistent with the hypothesis that white knights overpay – as in other auction settings, the *winner's curse* seems to operate in contests for corporate control.

A related ethical issue is *conflict of interest and managerial duty*. A potential conflict of interest exists between management's (and the board of directors) duty to maximize the value of the company for its owners, and to preserve their own executive and board positions. By encouraging white knight bids and agreeing to lock-up provisions is management maximizing value for its owners? Herzel and Shepro (1990) argue, however, that pre-empting an auction by selling the company to a favored buyer may not be improper. Auctions may not be appropriate if a suitable buyer is willing to pay a high price in a negotiated deal, but would otherwise avoid getting involved in an auction. And searching for other potential bidders may sour an advantageous deal (*see* CONFLICT OF INTEREST).

Bibliography

Bannerjee, A. & Owers, J. E. (1992). Wealth reduction in white knight bids. *Financial Management*, 21, 48–57.

Herzel, L. & Shepro, R. W. (1990). *Bidders and Targets*. Oxford: Blackwell.

Niden, C. M. (1993). An Empirical examination of white knight corporate takeovers: Synergy and overbidding. *Financial Management*, 22, 28–45.

ROBERT F. BRUNER

women at work   Most women have always been "at work," but traditionally, fewer women than men have engaged in paid work. In 1890, for example, women made up only 17 percent of the US labor force; by 1980, women were 44 percent of the US labor force. In 1985, 54.5 percent of the US women 16 years of age and older and 64.7 percent of the women between the ages of 25 and 64 were employed (*Statistical Abstract of the United States*, 1988, Table No. 627). In the Scandinavian countries, typically 75 percent or more of adult women are in the labor force. The same was true in many countries of the former Soviet Union, but unemployment among women has increased dramatically since the collapse of communism. Nevertheless, during the 1970s and 1980s, women increased their share of the labor force in most countries of the world (United Nations, 1991). Furthermore in all areas of the world today, women in the prime childbearing years (25–44) are more likely to be employed than either younger or older women (United Nations, 1991, Table 6.8). This represents a change in most of the industrialized countries where, in the past, women of prime childbearing years were less likely than either younger or older women to be employed.

The topic of "women at work" as a coherent subfield is less than 20 years old and it is interdisciplinary, involving researchers from management, psychology, sociology, economics, etc. It is worth noting that the research tends to focus disproportionately on women in non-traditional jobs (i.e., management and the male-dominated professions) and women at higher organizational ranks (managers and executives). Likewise, the research focuses disproportionately on women who are white and middle or upper class. These features characterize research on WORK in general, not just women at work.

In all of the research, gender figures prominently, and women and their experiences are either overtly or covertly compared with men. Sex differences is a common theme in the research and encompasses both differences between men and women and differences between the treatment of men and women. Women tend to work in "women's jobs," jobs defined in a particular time and place as appropriate for women. Although there are some consistencies across countries, cultures, and organizations (e.g., jobs involving children tend to be labeled women's jobs), examples of one job being a "man's job" in one country, culture, or organization, and a "woman's job" in another are common. This is true, for example, of medicine, sales, and clerical work.

Women's work is characterized by horizontal and vertical segregation. Horizontal segregation means that women and men work in different occupations. In 1970 in the US about 55 percent of women worked in the 20 most female-dominated occupations (Jacobs, 1989, Table 2.4). Sex segregation is most often measured by the index of segregation (also known as the index of dissimilarity, D) which tells the percentage of one sex who would have to change jobs so that they would be distributed across jobs the same as the other sex. In the US, sex segregation has declined from about 76 in 1910 to 62 in 1981 (Jacobs, 1989), and it has done so, not because more men are working in jobs traditionally held by women (they are not), but because women have moved into traditionally male jobs such as law, medicine, management, and the professorate.

Vertical segregation means that men and women are located at different places in the hierarchy in their work. Women tend to be located in lower-level positions in their occupations and in their organizations whereas men are found in jobs throughout the hierarchy. Women are said to face a GLASS CEILING in that they are rarely found above certain hierarchical levels. Like horizontal segregation, vertical segregation is also decreasing except at the top.

In general, the research on women at work fits into one of three categories: sex differences, problem focused, and changes initiated to alleviate problems (e.g., Firth-Cozens & West, 1991).

One type of research focuses on differences and similarities between the sexes. Among the topics covered are the following: differences in masculinity and femininity and their implications; differences or similarities in management style or leadership style; sex differences in career choices and career interests; and differences and similarities in achieving style. Early research focused on traits or characteristics believed to be associated with women more than men, such as fear of success. A few areas are notable for the lack of expected sex differences. For example, while there is an active debate about whether men and women exhibit different leadership styles, the extant research suggests that men and women in leadership positions exhibit few differences. And despite the fact that women's and men's job experiences tend to differ, they tend to report similar levels of job satisfaction, and in recent years, job commitment.

A large body of research on women at work focuses on problems faced by women. These topics include the following, listed with some researchers and theorists in each field: biases in selection, placement, performance appraisal, and promotion (Nieva & Gutek; Swim et al.); SEXUAL HARASSMENT (Fitzgerald; Gutek; Pryor; Terpstra & Baker; Powell); obstacles to achievement, advancement, and attainment of positions of LEADERSHIP (Larwood; Morrison); lack of MENTORING (Ragins; Fagensen); sex discrimination (Heilman; Crosby); the pay gap (England; Olson; Konrad; Langton); stereotyping (Fiske; Borgida); lack of job mobility (Brett); conflict between work and family responsibilities (Pleck; Brett; Davidson; Cooper). Other researchers have noted the problems faced by tokens (women who are numerically rare) (Kanter; Laws) and the problems faced by women when there are few women in top management positions in the organization (Ely).

A third type of research focuses on the success or failure of attempts to alleviate problems faced by working women (see for example, Sekaran, 1991), including the impacts of laws and other programs aimed at providing EQUAL OPPORTUNITY, addressing affirmative action, establishing the comparable worth of jobs, and eliminating sexual harassment. But laws are not the only approach to alleviating problems faced by working women. In general, the type of solution sought depends on the way the problem is defined. Nieva & Gutek (1981; see also Gutek, 1992) listed four models of problem definition and some problem-solving strategies that follow from them. They are: the individual-deficit model wherein the problem is defined as problem people; the structural model wherein organizational structures and policies hamper women (see Kanter, 1977); the sex-role model wherein social roles and role expectations and role stereotypes hamper women; and the intergroup model wherein men and women are viewed as opposing groups fighting over a limited amount of desirable jobs, POWER, and influence. They conclude that the most commonly proposed solutions fit the individual-deficit model. Women are given opportunities to overcome their "deficits" through training and self-help materials targeted at them. Examples include dressing for success, assertiveness training, how to write a business plan or obtain venture capital. Increasingly men too are targets of training aimed at sensitizing them to issues like sexual harassment and sex discrimination.

Overall, the topic of women-at-work has attracted a lot of research attention over the past 20 years or so. While the field is not bereft of theory, so far much of the research is descriptive, a necessary step because the topic is fraught with misperceptions and misinformation.

Bibliography

Betz, N. & Fitzgerald, L. (1987). *The Career Psychology of Women*. New York: Academic Press.

Firth-Cozens, J. & West, M. (eds). (1991). *Women at Work: Psychological and Organizational Perspectives.* Milton Keynes, England: Open University Press.

Gutek, B. A. (1993). Changing the status of women in management. *Applied Psychology*, **43** (4), 301–11.

Gutek, B. A. & Larwood, L. (eds). (1987). *Women's Career Development*. Newbury Park, Calif.: Sage Publishers.

Jacobs, J. (1989). *Revolving Doors: Sex Segregation and Women's Careers*. Stanford: Stanford University Press.

Kanter, R. M. *Men and Women of the Corporation*. New York: Basic Books.

Nieva, V. F. & Gutek, B. A. (1981). *Women and Work: A Psychological Perspective*. New York: Praeger Publishers.

Sekaran, U. (Ed.), (1991). *Womanpower*. Newbury Park, Calif.: Sage Publishers.

Statistical Abstract of the United States. (1988). Washington, DC: US Government Printing Office.

Swim, J., Borgida, E., Maruyama, G. & Meyers, D. G. (1989). Joan McKay versus John McKay: Do gender stereotypes bias evaluations? *Psychological Bulletin*, **105** (3), 409–29.

United Nations. (1991). *The World's Women: Trends and Statistics, 1970–1990*. Social Statistics and Indicators, Series K, no. 8, New York: The United Nations.

BARBARA A. GUTEK

women in leadership Women in leadership refers to the exercise of leadership by women. Equal Employment Opportunity legislation together with the press for equality in the workplace brought about by the Women's Movement have likely provided the impetus for this relatively new area of inquiry in the field of leadership. This work now constitutes one of the four main themes in contemporary leadership research (Calas & Smircich, 1988). It has centered primarily on questions about whether or not men's and women's leadership styles and, to a lesser extent, leadership effectiveness are different in ways that are consistent with cultural stereotypes.

Leadership Style

In their meta-analysis of the literature on gender and leadership style, Eagly & Johnson (1990) found evidence for both the presence and absence of leadership-style differences between the sexes. There was no support in organizational studies and minimal support in laboratory studies for the gender-stereotypic expectation that women lead in an interpersonally oriented style and men in a task-oriented style. Consistent with stereotypic expectations, however, this analysis revealed overall that women tended to adopt a more democratic or participative style than men did. Researchers have typically offered either person-centered explanations for sex-difference findings, such as socialized differences in female and male personality or skills (Hennig & Jardim, 1977), or situation-centered explanations, such as differences in the power and status of the organizational positions women and men hold (Kanter, 1977).

Although much of the sex-difference research in the leadership field has been motivated by feminist interests in promising gender equity, recent critics have argued that assumptions underlying this work have served to reinforce bias against women. For example, implicit in much of this research is the concern that sex differences reflect or have been used to legitimate the unequal treatment of men and women; therefore, an assumption underlying this work is that such differences should be repudiated and, in an ideal world, eradicated. Critics of this approach argue, however, that this assumption reinforces an asymmetric view of the role gender plays in leadership: it casts men's leadership as generic leadership uninfluenced by masculine gender and male experience; as such, men's leadership constitutes the presumed gender-neutral norm against which women's leadership is measured and evaluated. To the extent that women deviate from this norm their leadership is viewed as less effective or absent altogether. Hence, comparative studies of leadership have tended not only to devalue women but in so doing to narrow our understanding of what might constitute the full range of effective leader behavior.

This criticism has led some feminist scholars to reconceive the meaning of leadership to include the relational and emotional competencies women have developed as leaders in the domestic sphere of home and family, competencies, they argue, that men tend to lack (Helgesen, 1990). Hence, rather than seeking to overcome traditional feminine experience, these scholars exalt it, urging organizations to accommodate women in their feminized difference. In contrast to traditional research on women in leadership, much of this work rests on the assumption that neither organizations nor leadership are gender neutral; rather, gender bias permeates both organizations and organizational research in ways that devalue women and limit understanding. Evidence for the validity of this perspective has been largely descriptive, based on case studies of women's experiences in organizations and on reinterpretations of previous sex-difference findings (Helgesen, 1990; Rosener, 1990).

More recently, scholars whose work is grounded in post-structural feminism have offered yet another perspective on women and leadership style. This perspective represents a thoroughgoing break from the preoccupation with sex differences characteristic of previous research. Again, these scholars take issue with the unexamined assumptions underlying this work, arguing that the very focus on difference itself, regardless of whether and how it is recast and revalued, is both a source and a consequence of relations of domination. Juxtaposing the leadership literature with contemporaneous literature on sexuality and subjecting both to a cultural analysis called deconstruction, Calas & Smircich (1991) analyze leadership as a form of male homosocial seduction. As such, leadership promotes the values of masculinity in organizations, including masculine definitions of femininity. Hence, they argue, just as masculine identity and masculine experience have shaped the contours of discourse on leadership, so too

have they shaped the contours of what we have come to believe are women's essential qualities of nurturance and caretaking. According to a post-structural feminist perspective, theories of women's leadership that attribute these (or any other) qualities, whether repudiated or exalted, to all women, are further oppressive because they elide racial, ethnic, class, and sexual identity differences among women and obfuscate forms of sexism to which different women are differentially subjected. They recommend abandoning general theories of either women or leadership in favor of partial and highly contextualized narratives to explore new meanings and new possibilities for the exercise of leadership by both women and men.

Leadership Effectiveness

Research on women's leadership effectiveness has centered largely on the role of sex-bias in both real and perceived effectiveness. A meta-analysis of experimental research on sex-bias in leader evaluations showed a small overall tendency for people to evaluate women leaders less favorably than men (Eagly, Makhijani, & Klonsky, 1992). Researchers have typically attributed such findings to the cultural stereotypes people hold about men and women which put women at a relative disadvantage.

Research in organizational settings has tended to be more qualitative and theoretical, focusing primarily on strutural determinants of leader effectiveness (Kanter, 1977). This work has suggested that where women leaders are situated in the organization's power structure and the number of women who are in the organization's senior ranks are key to understanding both how they are perceived and how well they will do in leadership positions. Because women tend to be in low-power positions thay are both less desirable and less effective as leaders; at the same time, their token status in many organizations heightens their visibility and creates increased performance pressures, isolation, and stereotyped roles for women leaders. Finally, there is some literature from a psychodynamic perspective that explores the unique difficulties women face in leadership roles, difficulties that stem from unconscious fantasies and fears of women's power and the strongly held stereotype that women possess legitimate authority only to nurture (Bayes &

Newton, 1978; Dumas, 1980). According to this perspective, these dynamics make it difficult for women leaders to mobilize resources in effective ways. Research in either laboratory or organizational settings that measures and compares men and women leader's effectiveness along specific dimensions is scant and inclusive.

Bibliography

Bayes, M. & Newton, R. M. (1978). Women in authority: A sociopsychological analysis. *The Journal of Applied Behavioral Science*, **14**, 7–20.

Calas, M. B. & Smircich, L. (1988). Reading leadership as a form of cultural analysis. In J. G. Hunt, R. Baliga, P. Dachler, & C. Schreisheim (eds), *Emerging Leadership Vistas*. Lexington, Mass.: Lexington Books, 201–26.

Calas, M. B. & Smircich, L. (1991). Voicing seduction to silence leadership. *Organization Studies*, **12**, 567–601.

Dumas, R. G. (1980). Dilemmas of Black females in leadership. *Journal of Personality and Social Systems*, **2**, 3–14.

Eagly, A. H. & Johnson, B. T. (1990). Gender and leadership style: A meta-analysis. *Psychological Bulletin*, **108**, 233–56.

Eagly, A. H., Makhijani, M. G., & Klonsky, B. G. (1992). Gender and the evaluation of leaders: A meta-analysis. *Psychological Bulletin*, **111**, 3–22.

Helgesen, S. (1990). *The Female Advantage: Women's Ways of Leadership*. New York: Doubleday Currency.

Hennig, M. & Jardim, A. (1977). *The Mangerial Woman*. Garden City, NY: Anchor Press/Doubleday.

Kanter, R. M. (1977). *Men and Women of the Corporation*. New York: Basic Books.

Rosener, J. (1990). Ways women lead. *Harvard Business Review*, Nov./Dec., 119–25.

ROBIN ELY

work   any activity that produces services and products of value to others, is not synonymous with "occupation," a particular work activity and social role that one assumes on a regular basis; nor is all work paid, as, for example, home childcare. Yet "work" has come to mean "paid labor," and the terms "work," "occupation," and "employment" are almost interchangeable. Despite the obvious importance of work, leisure is traditionally valorized. The Ancient Greeks, for example, believed that labor brutalized the mind, making it unfit for contemplation. In *Genesis*, a lifetime of work is Adam's punishment. In the modern period, as ardent a defender of capitalism as ADAM SMITH commented that the worker, over a lifetime of labor, "becomes as stupid and ignorant as it is possible for a human creature to become" (Smith, 1936, II, p. 303).

The classical view of work (with roots in Smith and JOHN LOCKE (1632–1704)) implies a free market where rational, self-interested, autonomous individuals with different abilities, interests, and preferences meet and make mutually beneficial exchanges. Despite the potential for conflict, particularly in a context of scarcity, this view maintains that the system minimizes conflict. The right to property is the fundamental basis for the free market, and government exists to protect that right and to ensure that exchanges occur voluntarily. Employee rights are "special rights" which derive from binding contractual agreements with employers.

The classical view has recently faced serious challenges, in particular that it depends on a flawed assumption that all participants in the market have similar bargaining power. Though the classical view rightly maintains that one is free to reject some particular job, the worker is NOT free to reject ALL jobs. Further, critics see work not as a necessary evil, but rather as constitutive of our nature as human beings. More radical critics argue for the rejection of capitalism itself; moderates (Ewing, 1977) defend reforms like, for example, employee bills of rights.

Philosophical analyses of JUSTICE and resource allocation feature discussions of work and access to jobs as issues for distribution theories. (*See* RAWLS, JOHN; NOZICK, ROBERT.) Ethical analyses of work explore competing views of human nature implied in competing theories of management like theory x and theory y, where the former claims that workers would rather not work, are prone to laziness, and need almost constant supervision; and the latter that workers are motivated and productive if work is fulfilling. Business and professional ethics concerns include the "culture" of work and role responsibility; the place of morality in the decision-making process; and the role of worker participation.

The Right to Work

To have a right to X is to have a *prima facie* claim to X which generally overrides considerations of expediency. Analyses of rights also distinguish negative rights to non-interference from positive rights to certain social goods and services (strictly speaking, "positive" and "negative" refer to the obligations imposed on others). If one has a right to live and must work to live, does one have the right to work? The Universal Declaration of Human Rights (1981) states: "Everyone has the right to work, to free choice of employment, to just and favourable conditions of work and to protection against unemployment." Virtually everyone agrees that individuals should have the opportunity to pursue their desired employment without interference. Disagreement arises over whether this right is positive, since this notion conflicts with the competitive basis of the free market. Capitalists like MILTON FRIEDMAN and classical libertarians like Robert Nozick reject the notion of such a right for three reasons: 1) it cannot be universal, particularly given limited resources; 2) it violates the fundamental right to property, requiring state intervention; and 3) it destroys initiative and motivation in guaranteeing work. Defenders of a positive right to work maintain that this right is too inextricably connected to self-esteem and human dignity to make it dependent on the caprices of the market (Nickel, 1978). (*See* RIGHTS; RIGHT TO WORK; LIBERTARIANISM.)

The Right to Meaningful Work

Surveys repeatedly reveal that most people would continue to work, even with financial independence; yet, most people also report that they would change jobs if they could. This suggests that the interest, challenge, and autonomy which are thought to be essential to meaningful work are absent in most occupations. Harry Braverman emphasizes the fragmentation and dehumanization of work in modern "postcapitalism," that "technological complexity" has made work demeaning and routine. Others maintain that new technologies have made possible an improved standard of living, more leisure, and freedom for real creativity (*see* MEANINGFUL WORK).

KARL MARX argued that capitalism's demand for ever greater profit leads to the degradation of work and the alienation of the worker. For Marx, alienation results from the capitalist mode of production because the worker has no control over the production process, does not own the products of her labor, and is separated from other workers who are not allies but competitors. The worker "does not fulfill himself in his work" (1964, p.110), resulting in a "renunciation of life and of human needs" (1964, p.150). Some claim that the right to work is not enough if work is not meaningful. They defend greater worker participation in workplace decisions and the "democratization" of work (Schwartz, 1982).

Others maintain that the demand itself is unintelligible. Who defines "meaningful"? Who will do the "meaningless" jobs? How are such decisions made? If by the individual, unresolvable conflicts over scarce resources will occur; if by some centralized planning agency, violations of rights and economic inefficiency will result.

The Rights of Workers

No one questions whether workers have the right to life by virtue of being citizens. But do workers *as* workers possess rights? For some analysts, workers are virtually "rightless" when they arrive at work. Others have argued (often using a Kantian framework) that workers as workers have certain entitlements (*see* KANTIAN ETHICS). These may include:

The right to due process. The US Supreme Court has ruled that the due process clause of the 14th amendment does not extend to the private sector of the economy. Employers (in the absence of a specific contract) may hire, fire, or demote "employees at will" (roughly 60 million in the US), without notice and without reason. The notion of "employment at will" has been challenged in recent literature as violating the right to equal consideration, since EAW would allow for deserving and undeserving employees alike to be fired (Werhane, 1985) (*see* EMPLOYMENT AT WILL).

The right to privacy. Do employers have the right to use polygraphs to screen prospective employees or use surveillance to prevent employee theft? Some have argued that the right to privacy – the right to control how much and what sort of information others can know about one – requires that there be limits to what employers may do (*see* PRIVACY; ETHICAL ISSUES IN INFORMATION).

The right to blow the whistle. Some maintain that whistleblowers – those who make public immoral or illegal behavior by an employer or supervisor – are disloyal and deserve no protection; others that the right to free speech includes the right to blow the whistle and overrides loyalty when harm may come to innocent third parties; and still others that employees have no obligations of loyalty to employers because of the for-profit nature of their relationship (Westin, 1981) (*see* WHISTLE-BLOWING).

The right to workplace safety. Do employers have an obligation to inform employees of potential hazards on the job? To compensate employees for work-related injury? To what extent are employers responsible for unforeseeable damages? If one accepts the notion of an implied contract, what are its conditions? Can an employee, for example, refuse without fear of reprisal to work ("informed refusal") with certain dangerous substances? (*see* WORKER SAFETY; DISCRIMINATION IN EMPLOYMENT).

Gender and race discrepancies in wages still exist, even after controlling for qualifications and types of occupations. Further, women and people of color tend to be segregated in lower-paying, less prestigious occupations. Should we take active steps to try to remedy this inequality? If so, what steps? The classical view maintains that inequality *per se* is not unjust if it results from voluntary market transactions, and that rational employers seek the most qualified and therefore do not discriminate. Critics maintain that institutional racism and sexism coupled with socialization explain present inequities and that voluntary measures are inadequate. Instead, they argue that AFFIRMATIVE ACTION PROGRAMS are essential to redress the inequity. At times this policy is defended on grounds of compensatory justice. Others, however, maintain that past injustices are morally irrelevant and that preferential hiring policies are justified by society's goal of eliminating racial and sexual inequality.

Bibliography

An earlier version of this entry appeared in Becker, L.C. & Becker, C.B. (eds) (1992). *Encyclopedia of Ethics.* New York: Garland, 1336–40.

Braverman, H. (1974). *Labor and Monopoly Capital.* New York: Monthly Review Press.

Ewing, D. (1977). *Freedom Inside the Corporation.* New York: McGraw-Hill.

Fox, M. F. & Hesse-Biber, S. (1984). *Women at Work.* Palo Alto, Calif.: Mayfield Publishing.

Friedman, M. (1962). *Capitalism and Freedom.* Chicago: University of Chicago Press.

Gini, A. R. & Sullivan, T. J. (eds) (1989). *It Comes with the Territory: An Inquiry Concerning Work and the Person.* New York: Random House.

Marx, K. (1964). *The Economic and Philosophical Manuscripts of 1844,* trans. M. Milligan, (Ed.) D. Struik. New York: International Publishers.

Marx, K. (1906). *Capital,* trans. S. Moore & E. Aveling. Chicago: Charles H. Kerr and Co.

Nickel, J. W. (1978–9). Is there a human right to employment? *Philosophical Forum,* **10,** 149–70.

Nozick, R. (1974). *Anarchy, State and Utopia.* New York: Basic Books.

Rawls, J. (1971). *A Theory of Justice.* Cambridge, Mass.: Harvard University Press.

Schwartz, A. (1982). Meaningful work. *Ethics,* **92,** 634–46.

Smith, A. (1936 [1776]). *The Wealth of Nations,* (Ed.), E. Cannon. Chicago: University of Chicago Press.

Werhane, P. (1985). *Persons, Rights and Corporations.* New York: Prentice-Hall.

Westin, A. F. (1981). *Whistle Blowing.* New York: McGraw-Hill.

Westin, A. F. & Salisbury, S. (eds) (1980). *Individual Rights in the Corporation.* New York: Pantheon.

DIANE C. RAYMOND

work and family Programs, policies, and practices designed to help people manage the boundary between work or professional life and family or personal life.

Work–family programs include parental leave, child and elder-dependent care support (on-site day care, child, eldercare referral services, financial subsidies for dependent care), flexible work systems (part-time work, compressed work week, flextime), job sharing, work–family sensitivity training, and work from home (telecommuting, the virtual office). Some companies have now relabeled existing general employee benefits "work–family programs," e.g. employee assistance programs, disability insurance/income, tuition aid, etc. What these programs share is an intent to help employees manage the boundary between their personal (family, private) lives and their professional (public, work) lives. Considerable difference of opinion remains about which programs to implement; how much influence companies, individuals, and government will have in determining programs; and who will or who should pay for them.

Early discussions about work and family focused attention on programs and policies designed to limit, if not eliminate, the intrusion of dependent concerns on work productivity. More recently the discussion has begun to build on the need for programs of some type to assist dual career couples, working parents, and elders by focusing more attention on what is impeding the implementation of coherent, consistent, and fair work and family policies. Companies that have tried various work–family programs have found their implementation challenging. Work–family policies are often misaligned with or undermined by other corporate policies, social norms, and gender-role expectations. Barriers include widespread belief in the existence of, and necessity for, a boundary between work and family lives; what some executives see as unrealistic expectations that companies take care of dependents resulting from individuals' personal decisions; a gap between policy and everyday managerial practice when employees attempt to use work–family programs; employer liability; invasion of privacy; and unfairness or backlash from those who do not have dependents. Aligning programs, policies, and practice can grow into a major effort to change organizational culture.

Research, Areas of Inquiry

Programs. In addition to widespread research on the specific types of programs needed, much of the program-oriented research is designed to assess the potential benefits to companies with enlightened work–family programs and policies implemented by sensitive managers. Research asserts that work–family programs can decrease absenteeism, tardiness, turnover, and product waste while increasing employee commitment, morale, and empowerment.

Policies and Practices. Many companies attempt to mandate acceptance of work–family programs, adding them to a menu of other human-resource management strategies for the increasingly diverse workforce of the 1990s. This strategy of trying to implement work – family programs while keeping existing systems and cultural values in place has caused difficulties. Managers frequently (re)interpret work–family in fairly narrow terms (flextime for women parents only, for example). In most cases the onus is on employees to present some plan for maintaining productivity while using this program, or to accept some negative consequence (e.g. a mommy track or limited promotion opportunity). The negotiation between the manager and the employee often ends up with one (the manager) or both of them prioritizing work over family. If an employee has a risk-adverse manager it is possible that the request to use some work–family program will be denied. Work–family programs are still seen mostly as privileges from benevolent organizations implemented by sensitive managers. In short, in the US, managers in companies are making work–family policy. This is not necessarily the case in other countries, where government has more influence.

Theorizing

The work–family boundary: It is argued that the boundary between work and family, if it exists, is permeable, asymmetrical (i.e., work interferes more with family than family interferes with work (Frone et al., 1992)), or mythical. Moreover, insistence that work *should* be separate from family is dysfunctional for society, unrealistic given current workforce demography (working parents, more women as paid workers, greater numbers of dual career couples, aging population), gendered (has a more negative impact on women than on men), and unfair.

The dichotomy – work vs. family: Productivity and other business needs were often placed in contrast to or conflict with employee needs. This mirrors the public/private dichotomy. The boundary theories mentioned above challenge the assumed separateness of the two spheres. The dichotomy theories challenge the unequal valuation of the two spheres, and explore possibilities for integrated, blended lives at home and at work.

Definition of family: Most companies define family as the nuclear family. This narrow definition of family is being challenged on a number of fronts. Alternative definitions of family include extended family (by blood and marriage), friends, co-habitants, and emotional supporters. The definition of family becomes increasingly important for determining who is and who is not eligible for work – family benefits.

Re-thinking work assumptions: Many see work–family relationships as requiring changes in our assumptions about work. With changes in both technology and workforce demographics, it is becoming easier to work from a number of locations. But we have ingrained assumptions about the need to be seen by managers in order to be seen as committed. Many organizations also manage by crisis with the hero managing the crisis visibly being recognized and rewarded. For work–family to succeed, it is argued that "face time" (i.e., time spent in the office) must be decoupled from commitment, and task productivity rather than firefighting needs to become the corporate norm.

Connecting work–family to gender equity: Balancing work and family is a top priority for men and women that cuts across class and racial lines. Much of the earlier research and common discourse assumed work–family was a women's issue. This notion is being challenged. Men are becoming outspoken about their changing roles. This is particularly evident in dual-career couples. In one study, dual earners both restructured their work, although women restructured work more than men did. These researchers argue that the increase in women at work expanded women's roles rather than caused a redefinition of gender roles for both men and women (Karambaya & Reilly, 1992). Examining practices, assumptions, and policies that cause unequal opportunities and constraints (hence gender inequity) is a major new research stream.

The ideas for this entry come from my role as a researcher with the Ford Foundation Work–Family/Gender Equity Project. All collabora-

tors have published work and/or work in progress on this subject. Collaborators include Lotte Bailyn, Susan Eaton, Joyce Fletcher, Dana Friedman, Ellen Galinsky, Maureen Harvey, Deborah Kolb, James Levine, Barbara Miller, Joyce Ortega, Leslie Perlow, and Rhona Rapoport.

Bibliography

Frone, M. R., Russell, M., & Cooper, M. L. (1992). Prevalence of work–family conflict: Are work and family boundaries asymmetrically permeable? *Journal of Organizational Behavior*, 13, 723–9.

Hall, D. T. (1990). Promoting work–family balance: An organization-change approach. *Organizational Dynamics*, winter, pp. 5–18.

Hochschild, A. & Machung, A. (1989). *The Second Shift: Working Parents and the Revolution at Home.* New York: Viking.

Karambaya, R. & Reilly, A. H. (1992). Dual earner couples: Attitudes and actions in restructuring work and family. *Journal of Organizational Behavior*, 13, 585–601.

National Research Council. (1991). *Work and Family: Policies for a Changing Workforce. Panel Report on Employer Policies and Working Families, Committee on Women's Employment and Related Social Issues and Commission on Behavioral and Social Sciences and Education,* (eds) M. A. Ferber & B. O'Farrell, with L. Allen. Washington, DC: National Academy Press.

Schor, J. B. (1992). *The Overworked American: The Unexpected Decline of Leisure.* New York: Basic Books.

ROBIN D. JOHNSON

worker safety The development of the Industrial Revolution radically transformed the nature of human work and human relations. Every year in the US over 10,000 workers are killed on the job and about 2.8 million are injured. There are over 100,000 deaths from diseases due to exposure to physical and chemical hazards in the workplace. The medical and other costs of work-related deaths and injuries is estimated at over $8 billion yearly. Work safety issues include reducing workplace hazards and implementing safety standards without significant reductions in efficiency. It concerns such matters as the hazardous nature of some work, its organization (hours, speed), and the quality of the work environment. Although the safety of work continues to improve in the West due to labor unions, legislation, and enlightened entrepreneurs, attention is still focused on industries where exposure to such substances as textiles (brown lung disease), paint odors (emphysema), benzene (leukemia), lead (sterility), microwaves (cataracts, lower sperm count), petrochemicals (tumors, sterility), coal dust (black lung), asbestos (cancer, asbestosis), and excessive noise (hearing loss) still occurs.

Initially, concern for worker safety came in the form of compensation for injuries as it did in Germany in the late nineteenth century. In the US, legislation to compensate workers started as early as 1920 but it did not cover the reduction of workplace hazards. Conservative free-market defenders objected to government interference in the marketplace which they claimed raised prices and weakened the freedom of contract, a cornerstone of capitalism. Defenders of increased regulation argued that workers were often in a weak bargaining position and usually had to take any job available.

An important case involving worker safety concerned the Johns Manville (now Manville) corporation, a manufacturer of asbestos. Corporate documents show that the company knew as early as the 1930s that its workers were in danger of developing cancer from exposure to asbestos but did nothing to protect its workers. When this information became public in the 1980s, thousands of employees sued the company, leading Johns Manville to establish a fund to pay employees and to declare bankruptcy.

In 1970, Congress passed the Occupational Safety and Health Act (OSHA) requiring employers to maintain certain minimum conditions to protect its workers. The law mandated that a safe work environment be provided through appropriate supervision and training of workers. Penalties for violation range from monetary judgments to criminal prosecution of specific individuals responsible within the firm.

Today, worker safety continues to be important for employees and employers. Concerns for secondhand cigarette smoke has led employers either to ban smoking in the workplace or to provide special smoking areas. Injury due to repetitive hand motions by keyboard operators is another focus of regulators. Many employee-rights advocates believe that OSHA is under-staffed and too influenced by the private sector it seeks to regulate, while others debate the nature of acceptable risk. The global nature of the marketplace that allows firms to move to areas with minimal or no provision for safety of workers is also a concern. Some ethicists argue that the best way to reduce dangerous and unhealthy working conditions is to restructure the modern corporation towards greater democracy and to empower employees, for example, by giving workers a voice in plant safety, and/or by installing them on the boards of directors, thus enabling them to influence relevant safety policies directly.

Bibliography

De George, R. T. (1990). *Business Ethics.* New York: Macmillan.

Grcic, J. (1985). Democratic capitalism: Developing a conscience for the corporation. *Journal of Business Ethics,* 5, (2), 145–50.

Shaw, W. H. & Barry, V. (eds). (1995). *Moral Issues in Business,* 6th edn. Belmont, Calif.: Wadsworth.

Velasquez, M. G. (1982). *Business Ethics: Concepts and Cases.* Englewood Cliffs, NJ: Prentice-Hall.

Werhane, P. H. (1985). *Persons, Rights and Corporations.* Englewood Cliffs, NJ: Prentice-Hall.

JOSEPH GRCIC

INDEX

Compiled by Meg Davies (Registered Indexer)